# Contents

# Acknowledgements

The authors and publisher would like to thank the following for allowing use of copyright material:

Science Photo Library for Section 1 opener

Glyn Kirk/Action Plus for Figs C, D, 1.29b(ii), 2.21c(ii), 6.1a, 6.1b, 6.14, 7.15, 9.1, 9.20, 9.25, 9.27, 9.35, 10.8, 12.10, 12.14, 13.2a, 13.3, 15.21, 19.2, 19.4, 20.2, 20.3, 23.2, 23.4b, 23.7, 23.11, 24.7, 25.3, 25.12, 25.14, 27.10, 27.11, 28.5

Chris Barry/Action Plus for Fig. E

Neil Tingle/Action Plus for Figs 1.10, 1.29b(i), 1.29b(iii), 2.21b(ii), 4.7, 5.1, 5.15, 6.3, 6.12, 2.21a(ii), 8.3, 10.20, 12.9, 15.1, 18.1, 20.5, 21.9, 24.11, 24.12, 24.16, 24.17, 25.6, 25.7, 25.13, 26.3, 26.6, 26.9, 26.14

George Tiedeman/NewSport/Corbis for photograph in Fig. 1.11

Franck Faugere/DPPI/Action Plus for Fig. 7.1

Leif Saul for 'ATP - Like a rechargeable battery' Fig. 4.3

Photo News/DPPI/Action Plus for photograph in Fig. 3.9

DPPI/Action Plus for Fig. 4.10

Gary I Rothstein/Action Plus for Fig. 4.15

Mike King/Action Plus for Fig. 6.4

Shelly Gazin / The Image Works for Fig. 6.9

Sean Aidan; Eye Ubiquitous/Corbis for Fig. 6.15

Richard Francis/Action Plus for Figs 10.18, 18.2, 23.5 and 25.19

Chris Brown/Action Plus for Fig. 11.1

Icon/Action Plus for Figs 13.2b, 15.11, 15.13 and 24.13

Steve Bardens/Action Plus for Fig. 13.6

AKG/International Olympic Committee for Fig.14.2

AFP/Getty Images for Figs14.9a and 14.9b

Steve Grayson/Action Plus for Fig. 15.9

Kirk Sides/Action Plus for Fig. 15.10

Mary Evans Picture Library for Figs 16.3, 16.4, 16.5, 16.8, 16.10 and 16.13

Marylebone Cricket Club, London/ Bridgeman Art Library for Fig. 16.15

Wingfield Sporting Gallery, London/Bridgeman Art Library for Fig. 16.16

Private Collection/Bridgeman Art Library for Fig. 17.5

Getty Images for Figs 17.9, 17.10 and 17.12

Clive Brunskill/Getty Images for Fig. 25.24

Matthew Impey/Action Plus for Fig. 19.3

Matthew Clarke/Action Plus for Figs 21.4 and 24.20

Steve Bardens/Action Plus for Fig. 23.4a

Police Sunglasses/Advertising Archives for Fig. 24.10

Jeff Zelevansky/Action Plus for Fig. 24.14

Eric Bretagnon/DPPI/Action Plus for Fig. 24.19

Leo Mason/Action Plus for Fig. 25.4

Action Plus for Fig. 25.5

Christophe Simon/AFP/Getty Images for Fig. 26.5

Dave Rogers/Getty Images for Fig. 26.4

Michael Pissotte/Action Plus for Fig. 27.5

Tony Henshaw/Action Plus for Fig. 27.13

All figurative drawings are by David Graham. It has not always been possible to trace copyright holders; any omissions brought to our attention will be corrected in future printings.

## Exam Board Signposts

The signposts **A**, **E** and **O** stand for A = AQA, E = Edexcel and O = OCR and indicate when a section is relevant to a particular exam board. Where no signposts appear the section is relevant to all students.

For a detailed breakdown on the composition of your course see the 'Exam Board Tables' at the end of the book.

# ANATOMY, EXERCISE PHYSIOLOGY AND THE BIOMECHANICS OF HUMAN MOVEMENT

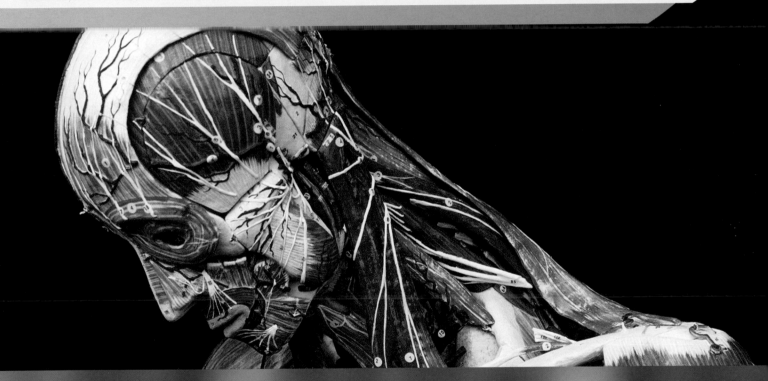

1

# INTRODUCTION

When examining the performer in action, an understanding of anatomical and physiological concepts within a sporting context is required. For example, a distance run involves the interaction and coordination of many of the body's systems to enable successful performance; the cardiovascular and respiratory systems work together as a delivery service, delivering oxygen and nutrients to fuel the working muscles, while simultaneously ridding the body of any undesired waste products of metabolism such as carbon dioxide. Meanwhile the skeletal and muscular systems are interacting; the bones acting as levers to provide movement, while the muscles (the engines of movement) provide the power to drive the levers. The nervous and hormonal systems direct and control the body's actions to enhance performance. The body is therefore a complex machine with the components or systems working together to enable effective participation in sport.

## What is exercise physiology?

Exercise or sports physiology (to ease confusion these terms have been used interchangeably in this book) is a branch of the much broader area of anatomy and physiology:

- Anatomy is the study of the body's **structure**
- Physiology seeks to discover how the body works and **functions**.

Sports physiology then puts these findings into a sporting context and specifically examines how the body adapts and develops in response to exercise.

Training has a significant part to play in the body's development and as such is vital to the study of sports physiology.

The terminology used when studying anatomy and physiology can sometimes be a little complex, particularly if you are new to the subject. The following section may ease your understanding, by explaining some of the terms that are regularly featured throughout the text.

## Terms of direction

When describing regions of the body, positions relative to the 'anatomical position' are used. The anatomical position refers to a person standing upright, facing forwards, with arms positioned downwards and the palms of the hand facing forwards.

The table overleaf provides a list of common terms of direction central to the study of anatomy and physiology. Relate these to the position of parts of your body.

You may have heard, for example, of the superior vena cava which refers to the vein that feeds blood

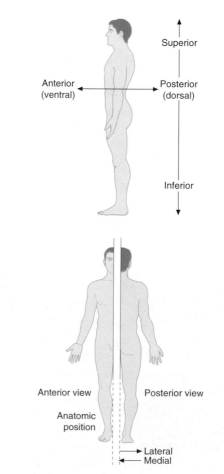

Fig A. Directional terms in the body

from the upper body into the right atrium of the heart, whereas the inferior vena cava supplies the heart from the lower body.

| Superior | A structure higher or closer to the head than another |
|---|---|
| Inferior | A structure lower or closer to the foot than another |
| Medial | Towards the midline of the body |
| Lateral | Away from the midline of the body |
| Anterior/ventral | Towards the front of the body |
| Posterior/dorsal | Towards the back of the body |
| Superficial | Towards the surface of the body |
| Deep | Internal or below the surface of the body |
| Proximal | A structure or body part closer to the point of attachment than another |
| Distal | A structure or body part further away from the point of attachment than another |
| Left | Towards the left side of the body |
| Right | Towards the right side of the body |

# Planes and axes of the body

In order to explain the body's movements, it is often useful to view the body as having a series of imaginary lines running through it. These are known as the **planes of movement** or the planes section. The imaginary lines divide the body up in three ways (see fig B). Firstly, the **median or sagittal plane** splits the body vertically into the left and right sides, **the horizontal or transverse plane** divides the body into superior and inferior sections and runs horizontally, while the **frontal or coronal plane** runs vertically and divides the body into anterior and posterior sections.

The body or body parts can move in these planes and a knowledge of them will certainly be of benefit to the coach and athlete. In gymnastics, for example, movement in all planes may occur in the performance of full twisting somersaults. What other sporting situations can you think of where a knowledge of planes of movement may be of use? In addition, the body (or body parts) can rotate around one of three axes in the body. When performing a front somersault, for example, the body rotates about the **horizontal axis**. A full twisting jump

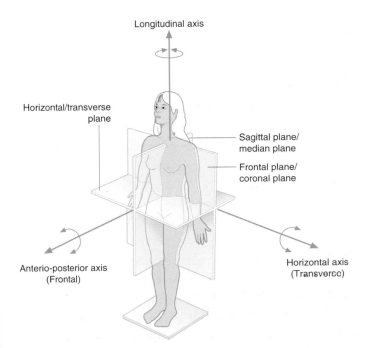

Fig B. Body planes and axes

Table A. Body planes and movement patterns possible in each

| Plane | Movement pattern |
|---|---|
| Frontal plane | Abduction<br>Adduction<br>Inversion<br>Eversion<br>Lateral flexion<br>Elevation<br>Depression<br>Protraction<br>Retraction |
| Sagittal/median plane | Flexion<br>Extension<br>Dorsiflexion<br>Plantarflexion |
| Horizontal plane | Medial rotation ⎫ rotation<br>Lateral rotation ⎭<br>Horizontal abduction<br>Horizontal adduction<br>Pronation<br>Supination |

Fig C. A gymnast performing a front somersault in the median plane about the horizontal axis

Fig D. A gymnast performing a cartwheel in the frontal plane about the anterio–posterior axis

involves the body rotating about the **longitudinal axis**. Finally, when performing a cartwheel the body rotates about the **anterior-posterior** or **frontal** axis. Table A summarises the movement patterns which occur in each of the body's planes.

For further investigation into this, and other factors concerning the body's movement, refer to chapters 1 and 9.

## Anatomical language

Sometimes it is possible to work out an anatomical term through basic understanding of more general terms. Words are often prefixed or suffixed to give greater meaning. For example, any word suffixed by '**itis**' means inflammation; any word prefixed by '**arthr**' relates to a joint. Therefore the condition '**arthritis**' is an inflammation of the joints. The table on p 5 gives common prefixes and suffixes together with their meanings.

Fig E. A trampolinist performing a full-twisting somersault jump in the horizontal plane about the longitudinal axis

ACTIVITY 2

Using the table below, define the following terms:

- bradycardia
- cardiac hypertrophy
- osteocyte
- periosteum
- pericardium
- myofilament
- glycolysis
- somatotype
- hepatitis
- cardiovascular

| prefix/suffix | definition | prefix/suffix | definition |
|---|---|---|---|
| a- | without | hyper- | excessive |
| ab- | away from | -itis | inflammation |
| ad- | towards | lip- | fat |
| -algia | pain | -lysis | breaking up |
| an- | without | macro- | large |
| arthr- | joint | mono- | one |
| brady- | slow | -morph | shape/form |
| brachi- | arm | myo- | muscle |
| cardio- | heart | neuro- | nerve |
| cerebro- | brain | osteo- | bone |
| chondr- | cartilage | peri- | surrounding |
| -cyte | cell | pneumo- | air/gas/lungs |
| derm- | skin | poly- | many |
| ergo- | work | somato- | body |
| femor- | leg | syn- | together |
| glyco- | sugar | tachy- | fast |
| haem- | blood | therm- | heat |
| hepato- | liver | -trophy | nourishment |
| hypo- | deficient | -vascular | blood vessel |

# 1. An Analysis of Human Movement

## Chapter introduction

In order for humans to move and perform sporting activity, the interaction of the skeletal and muscular systems is necessary.

Muscles contract moving bones, which pivot and rotate about the joints of the body. In doing so a series of lever systems operate that enable a force to be transferred through the body causing the body or indeed an object to move in a desired direction. There now follows a brief discussion on each of the following three components:

- bones
- joints
- muscles

In the first instance, we will consider each of the components individually and then collectively towards the end of the chapter where we will see how they interact to enable the body to perform such a wide range of movements.

## Part I   The skeleton

### The skeletal system

The 206 bones that make up the human skeleton are specifically designed to provide several basic functions, which are essential for participation in physical activity. In conjunction with other components of the skeletal system (including the periosteum, ligaments and joints), the skeleton can perform the following functions.

### Functions

#### Support

The skeleton provides a rigid framework to the body, giving it shape and providing suitable sites for attachment of skeletal muscle.

#### Protection

The skeleton provides protection for the internal organs. For example: the vertebral column protects the spinal cord; the cranium protects the brain; and the rib cage principally protects the heart and lungs.

#### Movement

The bones of the skeleton provide a large surface area for the attachment of muscles – the engines of movement. The long bones in particular provide a system of levers against which the muscles can pull.

#### Blood production

Within the bones, bone marrow produces both red and white blood cells. Red blood cells are generally produced at the ends of long bones such as the humerus (arm) and the femur (thigh), and in some flat bones such as the pelvis and sternum (breastbone). White blood cells are usually produced in the shafts of long bones.

#### Mineral storage

The bones of the skeleton have storage capabilities for vital minerals such as calcium and phosphorus,

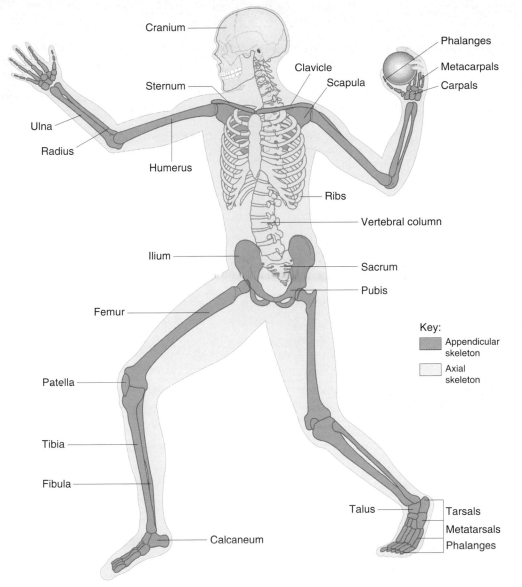

Fig 1.1. Bones of the axial and appendicular skeleton
*Source*: Davis, Kimmet and Auty (1986).

which can be distributed to other parts of the body when required.

## The structure of the skeleton

The bones of the skeleton can be divided into two distinct categories; the axial and the appendicular skeleton:

- the **axial** skeleton provides the main area of support for the body, and includes the cranium (skull), the vertebral column (spine) and the rib cage.

- the **appendicular** skeleton consists of the appendages or the bones of the limbs, together with the girdles that join onto the axial skeleton.

## The structure of the vertebral column

The vertebral column consists of 33 bones; 24 bones are individual and unfused, while the remaining nine are fused together. There are five principal areas of the vertebral column.

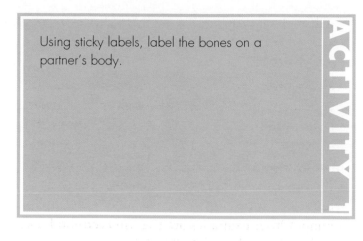

ACTIVITY 1

Using sticky labels, label the bones on a partner's body.

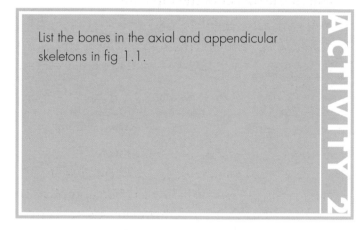

ACTIVITY 2

List the bones in the axial and appendicular skeletons in fig 1.1.

## The cervical vertebrae (7 unfused bones)

The cervical vertebrae are essentially the bones of the neck, and support the weight of the head by enabling muscle attachment through the transverse and spinous processes. The top two vertebrae, the atlas and the axis, enable the head to move up and down and side to side respectively.

## The thoracic vertebrae (12 unfused bones)

The 12 thoracic vertebrae allow the attachment of the ribs. These bones, together with the ribs, form the rib cage which protects the heart and lungs.

## The lumbar vertebrae (5 unfused bones)

The 5 lumbar vertebrae are the largest of all the individual vertebrae. Their large centrum or body offers a great deal of weight-bearing capacity, while their large processes secure the attachment of the muscles. This muscle attachment, together with the intervertebral discs of cartilage, forms cartilaginous

joints, which enable flexion and extension (forward and backward movement) and lateral flexion (side to side movement) of the trunk.

## The sacral vertebrae (5 fused bones)

The 5 fused sacral vertebrae form the sacrum which fuses to the pelvis at the sacroiliac joint. The sacrum and the pelvis bear and distribute the weight of the upper body.

## The coccyx (4 fused bones)

The coccyx forms the very base of the vertebral column, and acts as a process for muscle attachment.

Each vertebra consists of two parts:

- a vertebral body (centrum)
- a neural arch.

The size of each vertebral body increases from the cervical vertebrae to the lumbar vertebrae, in order to support the weight of the body. The neural arch enables muscles to attach via the transverse and the spinous processes, while the articular processes link to adjacent vertebrae.

In between each vertebra exists a disc of fibro-cartilage – a tough, resilient tissue which helps to absorb shock and allows a small amount of movement between the vertebral bodies.
The vertebral column also exhibits four curves as shown in fig 1.2. The cervical and lumbar curves

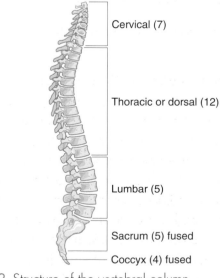

Cervical (7)

Thoracic or dorsal (12)

Lumbar (5)

Sacrum (5) fused

Coccyx (4) fused

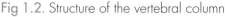

Fig 1.2. Structure of the vertebral column

are **convex** in shape; the thoracic and sacral curves are **concave**. These curves of the vertebral column increase the strength of the structure as well as absorbing shock from jumping or walking, and thus reduces the risk of injury.

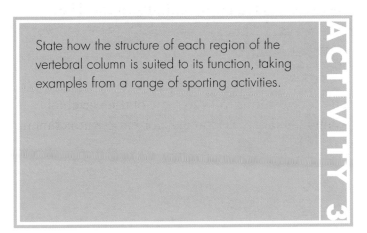

State how the structure of each region of the vertebral column is suited to its function, taking examples from a range of sporting activities.

ACTIVITY 3

# Skeletal tissues

The tissues making up the skeletal system consist of cartilage and bone.

## Cartilage

Cartilage is a soft, slightly elastic tissue. It is avascular, meaning that it does not possess a blood supply and receives nutrition via diffusion from the capillary network outside the tissue.

All bones start out as cartilage in the developing foetus, until it is gradually replaced by bone.

There are three basic types of cartilage found in the body:

1. **Hyaline or articular cartilage** is a fairly resilient tissue and is found on the articulating surfaces of bones that form joints. It is bluish in colour and is composed of a fine network of collagen fibres. The cartilage protects the bone tissue from wear and reduces friction between articulating bones. Joint movement improves the nutrition supplied to this tissue and can encourage growth. Hyaline cartilage therefore often thickens as a result of exercise which further protects the joints. During the exercise period, articular cartilage

will soak up synovial fluid released from the synovial membrane, thus improving mobility at the joint.

2. **White fibrocartilage** is a much denser tissue. It is tough, and its shock absorption properties mean that it is often found in areas of the body where high amounts of stress are imposed. For example, the semi-lunar cartilages of the knee joint resist the huge amount of stress often incurred as a result of performing activities such as the triple jump. Other examples are the intervertebral discs and in the socket of the hip joint.

3. **Yellow elastic cartilage** is a much more pliant and flexible tissue giving support and also flexibility. The external ear and the epiglottis are examples.

## Bone

Bone differs from cartilage in that it is a rigid, non-elastic tissue and is composed approximately of 65% mineral components (including calcium phosphate and magnesium salts) and 35% organic tissue such as collagen, a protein which gives the bone some resilience and prevents the bones from breaking on the slightest of impacts. Viewed under a microscope, it can be seen that mature bone consists of cells called **osteocytes** which are supported by thick collagen fibres which exist in a matrix composed of minerals.

Bone tissue can be categorised into either compact or cancellous, and is best illustrated by viewing a longitudinal cross-section of a long bone.

**Compact bone** or hard bone forms the surface layers of all bones and the whole of the cylindrical shaft of long bones. It goes some way towards protecting bones from external forces or impacts and has great weight-bearing properties. Surrounding the compact bone is the **periosteum**, which is a fibrous and extremely vascular tissue. In addition to its vital role in bone development, the periosteum enables tendons to attach to bones, which transmit the muscular 'pull', and therefore allows movement to take place.

**Long bones**

Long bones are cylindrical in shape and are found in the limbs of the body. Examples of long bones include:

• femur
• tibia
• humerus
• phalanges (although not great in length, these possess the cylindrical shape and so also fall into this category).

The primary function of long bones is to act as levers, and they are therefore essential in movement. When running for example, the psoas, iliacus, and rectus femoris muscles pull on the femur to cause flexion of the hip, effectively lifting the leg off the ground. The rest of the quadricep group (the vasti muscles as well as the rectus femoris) then pull on the tibia causing extension to take place at the knee joint, enabling the lower leg to 'snap' through. This is the first stage of a running action. Their other vital function is the production of blood cells which occurs deep inside the bone.

**Flat bones**

Flat bones offer protection to the internal organs of the body. Examples include:

• the sternum
• the bones of the cranium
• the bones of the pelvis
• upon close inspection, it can be seen that the ribs are also flat.

Flat bones also provide suitable sites for muscle attachment, with the origins of muscles often attaching to them. In this way the muscle contracting has a firm, immovable base against which to pull, and can therefore carry out its function effectively. For example, a major function of the quadricep muscle group is to pull on the tibia, causing extension at the knee. In order to raise the tibia, the muscle must have a stable base against which it can pull, in this case, the ilium. The bone can now act as a lever and cause movement to occur as outlined earlier. The pelvis, sternum and cranium also produce blood cells.

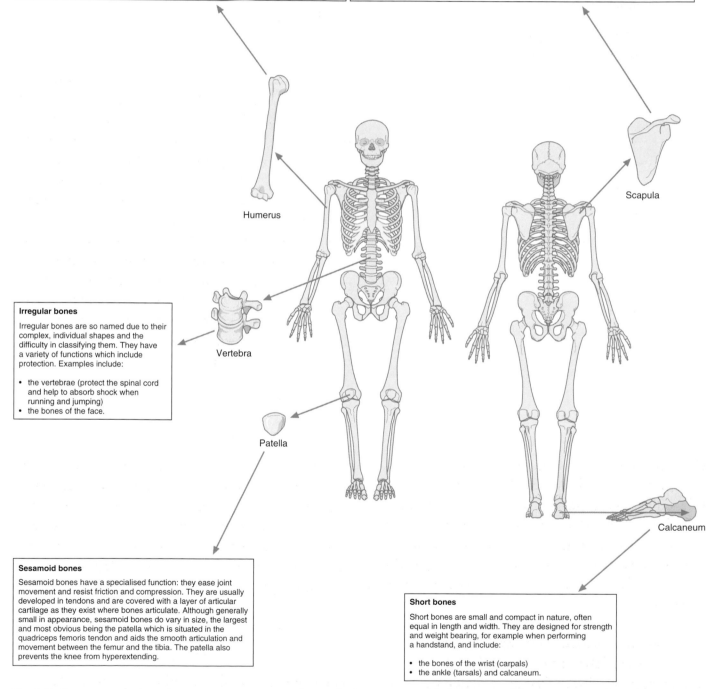

Humerus

Scapula

**Irregular bones**

Irregular bones are so named due to their complex, individual shapes and the difficulty in classifying them. They have a variety of functions which include protection. Examples include:

• the vertebrae (protect the spinal cord and help to absorb shock when running and jumping)
• the bones of the face.

Vertebra

Patella

Calcaneum

**Sesamoid bones**

Sesamoid bones have a specialised function: they ease joint movement and resist friction and compression. They are usually developed in tendons and are covered with a layer of articular cartilage as they exist where bones articulate. Although generally small in appearance, sesamoid bones do vary in size, the largest and most obvious being the patella which is situated in the quadriceps femoris tendon and aids the smooth articulation and movement between the femur and the tibia. The patella also prevents the knee from hyperextending.

**Short bones**

Short bones are small and compact in nature, often equal in length and width. They are designed for strength and weight bearing, for example when performing a handstand, and include:

• the bones of the wrist (carpals)
• the ankle (tarsals) and calcaneum.

Fig 1.3. Bones are designed to carry out a variety of specific functions, and fall into one of five categories, largely according to their shape

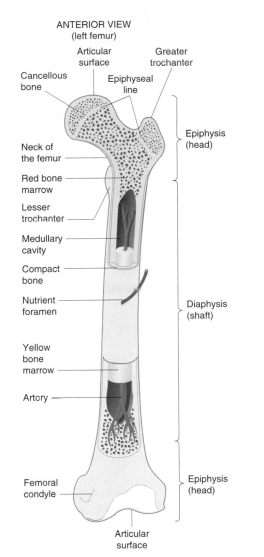

ANTERIOR VIEW
(left femur)

Articular surface — Greater trochanter

Cancellous bone — Epiphyseal line

Epiphysis (head)

Neck of the femur

Red bone marrow

Lesser trochanter

Medullary cavity

Compact bone

Nutrient foramen

Diaphysis (shaft)

Yellow bone marrow

Artery

Femoral condyle

Epiphysis (head)

Articular surface

Fig 1.4. Structure of a long bone viewed in cross section
*Source:* Kapit & Elson (1993).

**Cancellous** or spongy bone lies beneath and alongside compact bone, and has a honeycomb or **trabecular** appearance. This criss-cross matrix of bony plates is developed along lines of stress on the bones and is constantly reorganised in response to the altering orientation of stress. For example, the stress alters when an infant starts to walk as opposed to crawl.

The trabecular matrix has proved to be the most effective way of combining strength with the minimum of weight, so that bones can take much stress, yet are light and easily moved. In addition to this function, the spaces of the cancellate bone are filled with red bone marrow, since the bony plates offer some protection to the manufacture of red blood cells here.

With the important function of blood production, the bony tissue is extremely vascularised, enabling nutrients to reach the bone and blood produced within the bone to enter the body's circulatory system. Bone is formed through the process of **ossification**.

### Ligaments

Ligaments are a tough, fibrous connective tissue that is composed almost entirely of thick bundles of collagen fibres. Their main role is to attach one bone to another and therefore they typically occur at joints and are responsible for stabilising them to enable effective movement to take place. Take the knee joint, for instance. This joint needs to be very stable in order for us to move effectively and consequently is surrounded by an intricate network of ligaments, each responsible for limiting the movement in a given direction. The lateral and medial ligaments, for example, prevent any sideways movement, while the cruciate ligaments prevent anterio-posterior (backwards and forwards) movement of the tibia.

# Part II  Joints and articulations

So far we have seen that some bones of the skeleton act as levers, which move when muscles contract and pull on them. Where two or more bones meet, an articulation or joint exists. However, movement does not always occur at these sites, and joints are typically classified according to the degree of movement permitted.

## Classification of joints

### Fixed or fibrous joints

These are very stable and allow no observable movement. Bones are often joined by strong fibres called sutures; eg, the sutures of the cranium (skull).

## Cartilaginous or slightly movable joints

These are joined by a tough, fibrous cartilage which provides stability and possesses shock absorption properties. However, a small amount of movement usually exists: for example, between the lumbar bones intervertebral discs of cartilage occur, allowing some movement as shown in fig 1.6.

## Synovial or freely movable joints

These are the most common type of joint in the body, and the most important in terms of physical activity, since they allow a wide range of movement.

The joint is enclosed in a fibrous **joint capsule** which is lined with a synovial membrane. Lubrication is provided by **synovial fluid** which is secreted into the joint by the **synovial membrane**. In addition, where the bones come into contact with each other, they are lined with smooth yet hard wearing **hyaline or articular cartilage**.

Synovial joint stability is provided by the strength of the muscles crossing the joint, which are supported by **ligaments** that may be inside or outside the capsule. Ligaments are very elastic and lose effectiveness to some degree when torn or stretched.

Some synovial joints possess sacs of **synovial fluid** known as **bursae**, which are sited in areas of increased pressure or stress and help reduce friction as tissues and structures move past each other. **Pads of fat** help to absorb shock and improve the 'fit' of the articulating bones. This is particularly true in the knee joint to help the articulation of the femur and tibia.

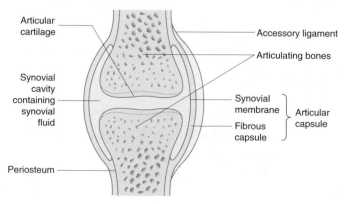

Fig 1.6. A cartilaginous joint

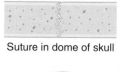

Suture in dome of skull

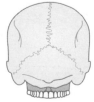

Fig 1.5. A fixed joint

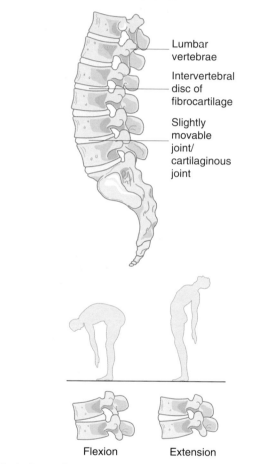

Fig 1.7. A typical synovial joint

# Common synovial joints

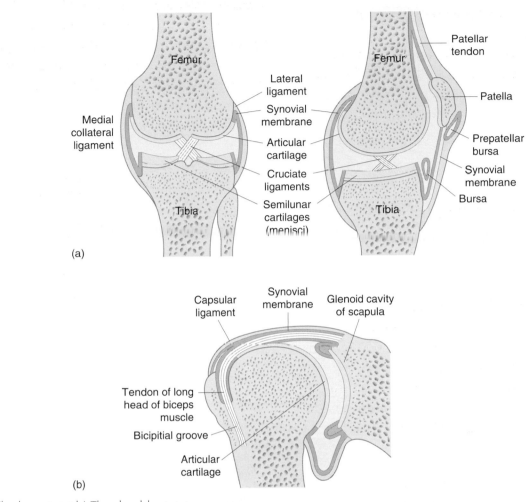

(a)

(b)

Fig 1.8. a) The knee joint b) The shoulder joint

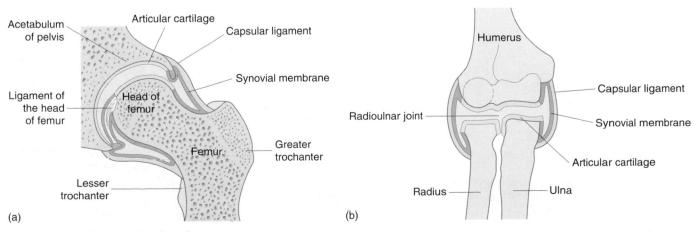

(a)

(b)

Fig 1.9. a) The hip joint b) The elbow joint

Explain how the knee joint is structured and how this suits its function in relation to sporting activity.

# Types of synovial joint

Synovial joints can be further subdivided into six basic types.

1. A **hinge joint** is a uniaxial joint which only allows movement in one plane. For example: the knee joint only allows movement back and forth. Strong ligaments exist in order to prevent any sideways movement.

Try to explain, where possible, how each type of synovial joint shown in fig 1.10 below has a role to play in sporting activity.

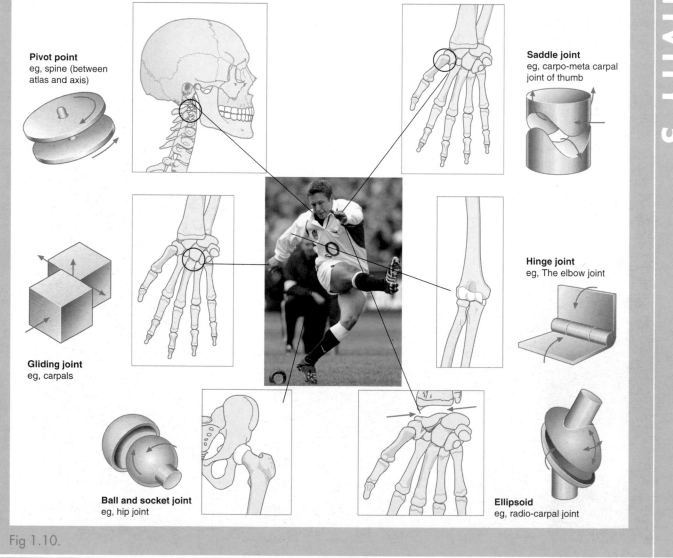

**Pivot point**
eg, spine (between atlas and axis)

**Saddle joint**
eg, carpo-meta carpal joint of thumb

**Gliding joint**
eg, carpals

**Hinge joint**
eg, The elbow joint

**Ball and socket joint**
eg, hip joint

**Ellipsoid**
eg, radio-carpal joint

Fig 1.10.

2. A **pivot joint** is also uniaxial, which allows rotation only. For example: the cervical vertebrae where the axis rotates on the atlas.

3. An **ellipsoid joint** is biaxial, allowing movement in two planes. For example: the radio-carpal joint of the wrist allows back and forth as well as side to side movement.

4. A **gliding joint** is formed where flat surfaces glide past one another. Although mainly biaxial they may permit movement in all directions. For example: in the wrist, where the small carpal bones move against each other.

5. A **saddle joint** is biaxial and generally occurs where concave and convex surfaces meet. For example: the carpo-metacarpal joint of the thumb.

6. The **ball and socket joint** allows the widest range of movement and occurs where a rounded head of a bone fits into a cup-shaped cavity. For example: in the hip and shoulder.

## Movement patterns occurring at synovial joints

The movements that occur at joints can be classified according to the action that is occurring between the articulating bones. These are called **movement patterns**. A movement of a limb or body part will always have a starting point (point A) and a finishing point (point B). Through analysing the position of the finishing point relative to the starting point, we can form a classification of movement. You may also recall the discussion in the introduction on body planes, this can also aid our understanding and classification of joint actions. Movement classifications will also come in pairs, since if we

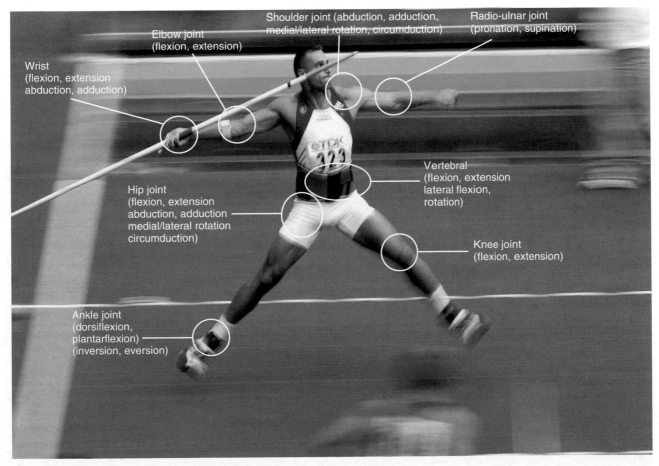

Fig 1.11. Joints and their associated movement patterns

can perform a movement in one direction we must be able to return the body part to its original starting position.

Major movement patterns that play a significant role in sporting activity are outlined in table 1.1.

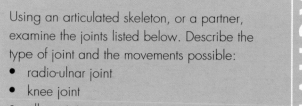

**ACTIVITY 6**

Using an articulated skeleton, or a partner, examine the joints listed below. Describe the type of joint and the movements possible:
- radio-ulnar joint
- knee joint
- elbow joint
- hip joint
- shoulder joint
- skull and cervical vertebrae
- ribs and thoracic vertebrae
- lumbar region.

**ACTIVITY 7**

What movement patterns occur at:
- the shoulder and elbow during the performance of a tennis serve?
- the hip and knee during a squat thrust?
- the hip, knee and ankle during the 'recovery' and 'kick' phase in the breaststroke?

Table 1.1. A table of movement patterns

| Joint action | Diagram |
|---|---|
| **Flexion**<br>Flexion occurs when the angle between the articulating bones is decreased. For example: by raising the lower arm up to touch the shoulder, the angle between the radius and the humerus at the elbow has decreased. Flexion of the elbow has thus occurred. Flexion occurs in the **median plane** about the **horizontal axis**. A muscle that causes flexion is known as a 'flexor'. In the instance at the elbow, the **bicep brachii** is the flexor muscle. | |
| **Extension**<br>Extension of a joint occurs when the angle of the articulating bones is increased. For example: when standing up from a seated position, the angle between the femur and tibia increases, thus causing extension at the knee joint. Extreme extension, usually at an angle of greater than 180° is known as **hyper extension**. Extension occurs in the **median plane** about **the horizontal axis**. A muscle that causes extension is known as an 'extensor'. In the example of the knee joint, **the quadricep femoris group** is the extensor. | |
| **Abduction**<br>This is movement of a body part away from the midline of the body or other body part. For example:<br>• if arms are placed by the sides of the body and then raised laterally, abduction has occurred at the shoulder joint<br>• if fingers are spread out, movement has occurred away from the midline of the hand, and abduction has occurred. | |

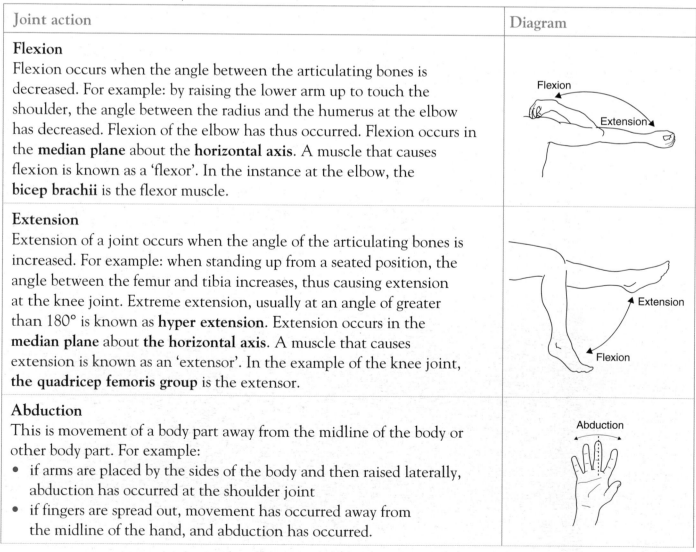

(Continued)

Table 1.1. (*Continued*)

| Joint action | Diagram |
|---|---|
| Abduction occurs in the **frontal plane** about an **anterio-posterior axis**. However, horizontal abduction takes place in the **horizontal or transverse plane**. | |
| **Adduction**<br>Adduction is the opposite of abduction and concerns movement towards the midline of the body or body part. For example, by lowering the arm back to the sides of the body, movement towards the midline has occurred and is termed adduction. Adduction occurs in the **frontal plane** about an **anterio-posterior axis**. However, horizontal adduction takes place in the **horizontal or transverse plane**. | Adduction |
| **Circumduction**<br>Circumduction occurs where a circle can be described by the body part and is simply a combination of flexion, extension, abduction and adduction. True circumduction can only really occur at ball and socket joints of the shoulder and hip.<br><br>As circumduction is a combination of flexion, extension, abduction and adduction it occurs in the **median and frontal planes**. | Circumduction of shoulder |
| **Pronation**<br>Pronation occurs at the elbow and involves internal rotation between the radius and humerus. It typically occurs where the palm of the hand is moved from facing upwards to facing downwards. Pronation occurs in the **horizontal plane** about a **longitudinal axis**.<br><br>**Supination**<br>Supination is the opposite of pronation and again takes place at the elbow. This time the movement is lateral rotation between the radius and humerus and generally occurs when the palm of the hand is turned so that it faces upwards. Supination occurs in the **horizontal plane** about a **longitudinal axis**. | Pronation<br><br>Supination of forearm |
| **Horizontal abduction/adduction**<br>Horizontal abduction involves movement of the arm across the body in the **horizontal plane**. To explain this further attempt the following exercise:<br><br>1. Stand with your arms by your side.<br>2. Raise your right arm up in front of you, until it reaches 'shoulder height'. | |

(*Continued*)

Table 1.1. (*Continued*)

| Joint action | Diagram |
|---|---|
| 3. Move your arm (from the shoulder) out to the right. This is horizontal abduction.<br><br>4. Now move your arm across your body towards your midline – this is horizontal adduction of the shoulder.<br><br>Sometimes horizontal abduction is known as **horizontal extension** and horizontal adduction is known as **horizontal flexion**. | 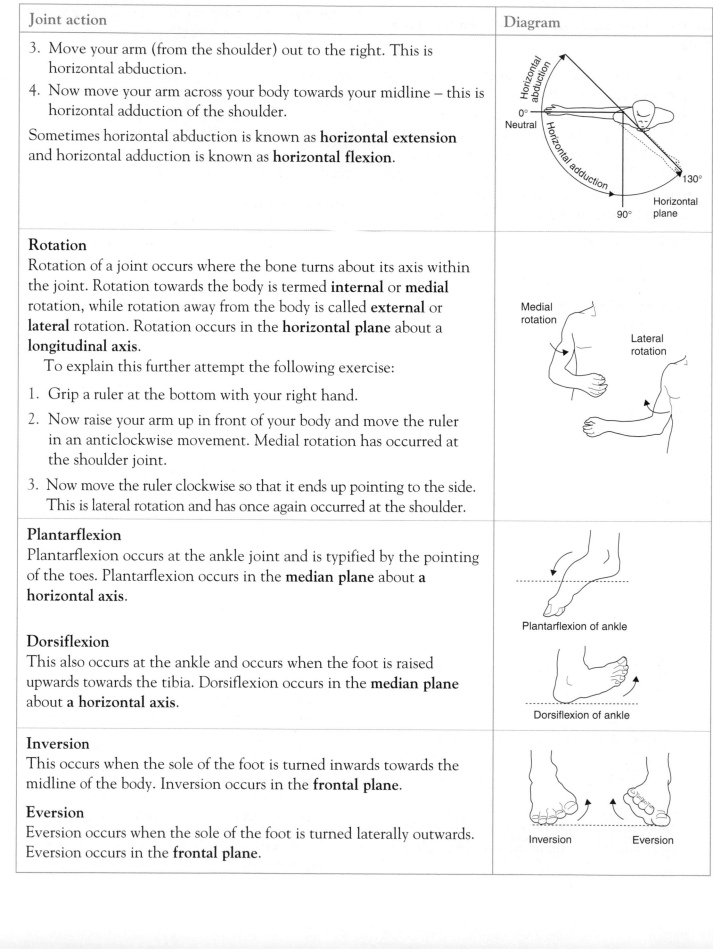 |
| **Rotation**<br>Rotation of a joint occurs where the bone turns about its axis within the joint. Rotation towards the body is termed **internal** or **medial** rotation, while rotation away from the body is called **external** or **lateral** rotation. Rotation occurs in the **horizontal plane** about a **longitudinal axis**.<br><br>To explain this further attempt the following exercise:<br><br>1. Grip a ruler at the bottom with your right hand.<br><br>2. Now raise your arm up in front of your body and move the ruler in an anticlockwise movement. Medial rotation has occurred at the shoulder joint.<br><br>3. Now move the ruler clockwise so that it ends up pointing to the side. This is lateral rotation and has once again occurred at the shoulder. | |
| **Plantarflexion**<br>Plantarflexion occurs at the ankle joint and is typified by the pointing of the toes. Plantarflexion occurs in the **median plane** about **a horizontal axis**.<br><br>**Dorsiflexion**<br>This also occurs at the ankle and occurs when the foot is raised upwards towards the tibia. Dorsiflexion occurs in the **median plane** about **a horizontal axis**. | |
| **Inversion**<br>This occurs when the sole of the foot is turned inwards towards the midline of the body. Inversion occurs in the **frontal plane**.<br><br>**Eversion**<br>Eversion occurs when the sole of the foot is turned laterally outwards. Eversion occurs in the **frontal plane**. | |

# Exercise and the skeletal system

Exercise has many beneficial effects for the skeletal system:

1. **Skeletal tissues become stronger** since exercise imposes stress upon the bones, which encourages the laying down of bony plates and the deposition of calcium salts along the lines of stress. This reinforces the criss-cross matrix and improves the tensile stress of the bone. Strength training will be particularly beneficial in developing the strength of skeletal tissues.

2. **Hyaline cartilage thickens** which aids the cushioning of the joint, and therefore protects the bones from wear and tear.

3. **Tendons thicken** and can withstand greater muscle force.

4. Flexibility and mobility training may enable ligaments to stretch slightly to enable **a greater range of movement at the joint**.

# Part III    The muscular system

No study of human movement or exercise is complete without a study of the muscular system. The muscles interact with the skeleton to provide movement.

This section highlights the structural and functional characteristics of **muscle tissue**, including types of muscle, properties of skeletal muscle (skeletal muscle is particularly relevant to the study of movement, so it will be examined in the greatest detail), the structure of skeletal muscle at molecular level, and the process and types of muscular contraction.

## What is a muscle?

Muscles comprise approximately 45% of the total body weight, and total in excess of 600.

There are three types of muscle tissue:

1. **Skeletal** muscle, which is external and used primarily for **movement** of the skeleton. These often occur in layers, with 'deep' muscles lying underneath 'superficial' muscles.

2. **Cardiac** muscle which is found only in the **heart** and used to force blood into the circulatory vessels.

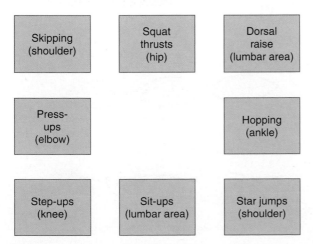

| Skipping (shoulder) | Squat thrusts (hip) | Dorsal raise (lumbar area) |
| Press-ups (elbow) | | Hopping (ankle) |
| Step-ups (knee) | Sit-ups (lumbar area) | Star jumps (shoulder) |

Fig 1.12.

Table 1.2. Comparing muscle types

| Skeletal | Cardiac |
| --- | --- |
| • Voluntary | • Involuntary |
| • Contract by impulse from the brain | • Generates own impulses (myogenic) |
| • Parallel fibres | • Interwoven, intercalating fibres |
| • Less/smaller mitochondria | • More/larger mitochondria |
| • Motor unit organisation | • Auto-ventricular network of fibres |

3. **Smooth** muscle which lies internally and has several functions including forcing food through the digestive system (peristalsis) and squeezing blood throughout the circulatory system via arteries and arterioles.

As skeletal muscle is responsible for the body's mechanical movement, and is central to our study of movement analysis, its properties and functions are now examined.

## Properties of skeletal muscle

Skeletal muscle possesses three essential properties:

1. **Extensibility**: this is the ability of muscle tissue to lengthen when contracting and provide the effort required to move the lever system (bones), producing coordinated movement.

2. **Elasticity**: this is the ability of muscle tissue to return to its normal resting length once it has been stretched. This can be compared to an elastic band that will always resume its resting shape even after stretching. This therefore enables the muscle to prepare for a series of repeated contractions which is normally required during the performance of exercise.

3. **Contractility**: this refers to the capacity of a muscle to contract or shorten forcibly when stimulated by nerves and hormones (excitability).

All these properties are essential for all body actions including locomotion, posture and facial expressions.

## Functions of skeletal muscle

Skeletal muscle has several important functions within the body:

1. **Movement**: skeletal muscles attach to bones, against which they pull to enable movement. For example, when running the hip flexor muscles pull on the femur to lift the leg off the ground, while the quadricep muscles contract to pull on the tibia to straighten the leg at the knee joint.

2. **Support and posture**: the muscles are seldom fully relaxed and are often in a constant state of slight contraction. In order to adopt an upright position many muscles within the legs and torso are contracting statically to ensure that the body is balanced. This is also known as **muscle tone**.

3. **Heat production**: the contraction of skeletal muscle involves the production of energy. In breaking down glycogen to provide this energy, heat is released. This accounts for why the body becomes hot when exercising. When the body is cold, the muscle often goes through a series of involuntary muscle contractions (commonly known as shivering) in order to release heat and keep the body warm.

## Skeletal muscle structure

When viewed under the microscope, skeletal muscle can be seen at molecular level.

The muscle belly is surrounded by a layer of **epimysium** (fig 1.15a), a thick connective tissue surrounding the entire surface of the muscle. This is continuous and eventually forms **tendons** which join

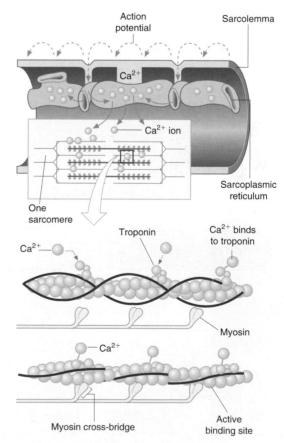

Fig 1.13. The structure of actin and myosin

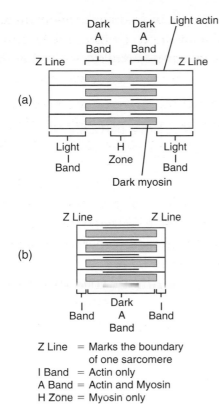

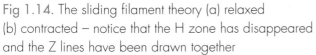

Z Line = Marks the boundary
of one sarcomere
I Band = Actin only
A Band = Actin and Myosin
H Zone = Myosin only

Fig 1.14. The sliding filament theory (a) relaxed
(b) contracted – notice that the H zone has disappeared
and the Z lines have been drawn together

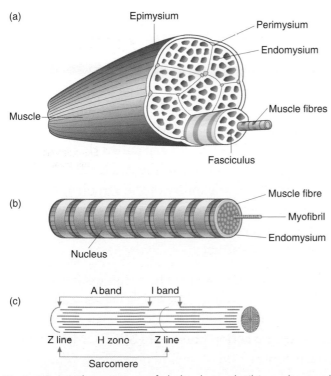

Fig 1.15. (a) The structure of skeletal muscle (b) single muscle
fibre, showing characteristic striations (c) myofibril, illustrating
a sarcomere

the muscle onto bones. The muscle belly is composed of many bundles of fibres known as **fasiculi** (fig 1.15a). Each fibre within a single fasciculus contains many smaller fibres called **myofibrils** (fig 1.15b) which provide the contractile unit of the muscle. These myofibrils have characteristic dark and light bands (striations) which represent a **sarcomere** (fig 1.15c). This pattern is repeated along the length of the myofibril.

Sarcomeres have a highly organised structure, and at the most fundamental level the sarcomere is composed of two protein-based **myofilaments**:

• a thick **myosin** filament, and

• a thinner **actin** filament.

The interaction and overlapping of these two myofilaments enables muscles to contract through the **sliding filament theory**.

## The sliding filament theory

Myosin filaments are composed of many myosin molecules, which are made up of two parts: a rod, and a head, which together form a golf-club shaped molecule. The heads of each molecule contain **ATPase**, an enzyme used to break down adenosine triphosphate (ATP), which, in doing so, releases energy for muscular contraction. This energy is used to bind the myosin cross-bridge onto the actin filament, thereby allowing muscular contraction.

The sliding of the filaments past each other takes the form of a **ratchet mechanism**, whereby the myosin cross-bridges continually attach, detach, reattach etc. It is the sweeping action or the 'power stroke' of the myosin head which causes the actin filaments to be pulled towards the centre and slide past the myosin filaments. It is the breakdown of ATP that releases the energy which enables the attachment and detachment of the myosin head.

The action of the sliding filaments during contraction causes shortening of all sarcomeres, and therefore all muscle fibres.

# Muscle relaxation

The relaxation of muscle is a passive process: the cross-bridges uncouple, causing the sarcomere to lengthen and return to its pre-contracted length.

# Muscle contraction

To understand how skeletal muscle contracts, a basic understanding of the nervous system is needed, as muscle contraction involves the interaction of the muscular system with the nervous system (neuromuscular interaction).

When a muscle is required to contract, an electrical impulse is emitted from the **central nervous system**. The electrical impulse begins at the brain and is transmitted to a muscle via the spinal cord and by nerve cells called **motor neurones**.

## A E  The motor unit

One motor neurone (nerve) cannot stimulate the whole muscle, but is only capable of stimulating a number of fibres within it. The motor neurone, and the fibres it stimulates, is called a **motor unit**, which is the functional unit of skeletal muscle.

The number of fibres innervated by a single motor unit varies, depending upon the precision of movement required. For example the eye, which requires a great deal of control and precision in order to focus, will possess between one and five

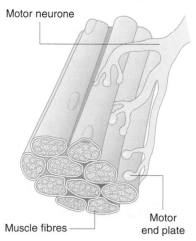

Motor neurone

Muscle fibres

Motor end plate

Fig 1.16. A motor unit

fibres per motor neurone, while the rectus femoris muscle of the quadricep group requires greater power to enable a basketball player to perform a jump shot, and therefore possess up to 2,000 fibres per motor neurone.

*Note:* the fibres within a particular motor unit will usually be of the same type, either *fast* twitch or *slow* twitch.

Motor units are therefore recruited depending upon the activity being undertaken, and the recruitment is based upon twitch response time or speed of contraction. A powerlifter therefore will only recruit motor units that are composed of fast twitch (type 2b) fibres, while a marathon runner will largely recruit motor units consisting of slow twitch or type 1 fibres. These motor units can resist fatigue and contract repeatedly due to their greater aerobic capacity and ability to store glycogen.

## Muscle fibre innervation

A muscle fibre is innervated when an impulse is of suitable strength. The point at which the motor nerve meets the muscle fibre is known as the **motor end plate**, and forms the **neuromuscular junction**.

When a nerve impulse arrives at the motor end plate, calcium ions enter the synaptic knob and a transmitter substance called **acetylcholine** is released; this aids the spread of the impulse to the muscle fibre across a small gap called the synaptic cleft. If sufficient acetylcholine is released, there is a change in the permeability of the sarcolemma to sodium and potassium ions; now the muscle fibre is said to have 'action potential' – which is the capability to contract.

An incoming response may be either excitatory or inhibitory. An excitatory response which causes muscle contraction will produce an **excitatory post-synaptic action potential (EPSP)**, which will cause a contraction of muscle fibres if a given threshold or intensity is reached or exceeded. If this threshold is not attained, then the sum of the individual effects of several impulses can be used until the threshold is exceeded. Once this point is reached, a depolarisation or decrease in the electrical potential across a membrane occurs, which triggers the release of calcium ions from the **sarcoplasmic reticulum**; this in turn removes the inhibitory effect of tropomyosin and enables the myosin cross-bridge to attach to the actin filament to cause muscle fibre contraction.

Following excitation, a chemical called **cholinesterase** is released which blocks the effect of acetylcholine and prepares the muscle fibre for the arrival of subsequent stimuli, so that the muscle fibres in a given motor unit can once again contract.

## The all or none law

Each fibre within a motor unit contracts according to the all or none law. This principle states that when a motor unit receives a stimulus of sufficient intensity to elicit a response, **all the muscle fibres within the unit will contract at the same time and to the maximum possible extent**. If, however, the stimulus is not of significant intensity, the muscle fibres will not respond and contraction will not take place.

The degree to which a muscle contracts is dependent upon several factors, including the number of motor units recruited by the brain. This will determine the force that can be generated within the muscle. The greater the strength required, **the greater the number of motor units** (and therefore the number of muscle fibres) **that contract**. For example, more motor units will be recruited in the biceps brachii when the body weight is being lifted in a chin-up, than when performing a bicep curl with a very light weight.

A second consideration is the frequency with which impulses arrive at the muscle fibres. The motor unit will respond to a stimulus by giving a 'twitch' – a brief period of contraction followed by relaxation. When a second impulse is applied to the motor unit before it completely relaxes from the previous stimulus, the sum of both stimuli occurs, increasing

the total contraction. This process is known as **multiple wave summation**. Furthermore, when rapid firing of stimuli occurs, giving muscles little or no time for relaxation, **tetanus or tetanic contraction** takes place, increasing the total contraction still further. This is illustrated in fig 1.19. This increase in total contraction can be explained by the augmented release of calcium ions which causes greater cross bridge attachment of myosin onto actin.

A sportsperson who requires a high degree of force to be generated over a relatively short period of time, such as a shot putter, can achieve this through **multiple wave summation**. However muscle fatigue will soon ensue. The athlete that requires to generate

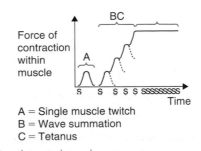

Fig 1.17. The all or none law

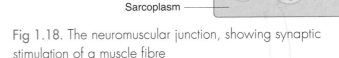

Fig 1.18. The neuromuscular junction, showing synaptic stimulation of a muscle fibre

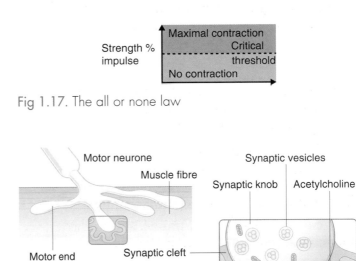

A = Single muscle twitch
B = Wave summation
C = Tetanus

Fig 1.19. Muscle twitch and contraction

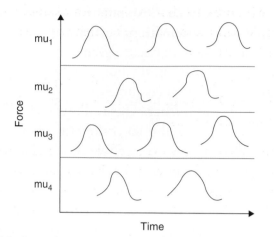

Fig 1.20. Spatial summation. Note that when some motor units contract, other are relaxing

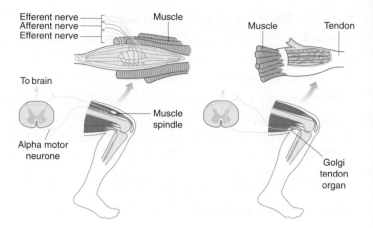

Fig 1.21. Muscle spindle apparatus

muscular forces over an extended period of time, such as a marathon runner, will recruit motor units slightly out of synchronisation, so that they do not all contract at the same time. This means that the whole of the muscle shares the workload, since when some motor units contract others will be recovering, thus spreading fatigue throughout the muscle. This phenomenon is known as **spatial summation** (see fig 1.20). You can see that motor unit 1 and motor unit 3 are contracting simultaneously while motor units 2 and 4 are recovering. Motor units 2 and 4 then contract while motor units 1 and 3 relax.

## A  Control of muscular contraction

In order for effective movement to be performed, muscle action should be controlled. The body possesses several internal regulatory mechanisms to ensure that smooth and safe movement prevails:

1. **Proprioceptors**: these are sense organs located in joints, tendons and muscles which provide kinaesthetic feedback concerning the body's movement. This informs the body of the extent of movement that has taken place.

2. **Muscle spindle apparatus**: are very sensitive receptors which exist between skeletal muscle fibres. They relay information via **afferent** or **sensory** neurones concerning the state of muscle contraction and the length or extension of the

muscle. When a muscle is stretched, the spindle is stretched and it sends an impulse to the spinal cord, indicating how much and how fast the muscle has stretched. If a muscle is stretched too far, the muscle spindle apparatus will alter tension within the muscle and cause a **stretch reflex**, whereby the muscle is automatically shortened. When performing **plyometrics**, for example, the quadriceps lengthen quickly upon landing. The muscle spindles detect the lengthening and send afferent impulses to the spinal cord, which then relay motor (efferent) neurones to the quadriceps initiating the stretch reflex. This causes a very powerful shortening of the muscle group and enables the athlete to bound upwards. This basic function of the muscle spindle helps to maintain muscle tone and protect the body from injury.

3. **Golgi tendon organs**: are thin capsules of connective tissue which exist where muscle fibre and tendon meet. They serve the same purpose as muscle spindle apparatus by triggering a reflex action when very high tensions are developed within the muscle and tendon. However they differ from the muscle spindle in that when activated they cause the muscle to relax.

## Muscle fibres

Muscles are composed of thousands and thousands of individual muscles fibres, which are held together by connective tissue. However, muscle fibres may differ in physiological make-up and it is the **type** of

Table 1.3. Basic characteristics of fast twitch and slow twitch

| Slow twitch (Type 1) | Fast twitch (Type 2) |
|---|---|
| Red | White |
| Contract slowly | Contract rapidly |
| Aerobic | Anaerobic |
| Endurance based | Speed/strength based |
| Can contract repeatedly | Easily exhausted |
| Exert less force | Exert great forces |

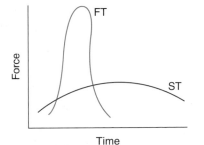

Fig 1.22. Muscle fibre twitch response. Fast twitch fibres generate higher forces for a shorter space of time when compared to slow twitch fibres

fibre which exists that explains, for example, the difference in performance between a sprinter and a marathon runner.

Skeletal muscle has two main fibre types: **slow twitch** and **fast twitch**; see table 1.3 and table 1.5 for their characteristics.

Fast twitch and slow twitch fibres vary in different muscles and in different individuals; these proportions tend to be inherited. Essentially a marathon runner may have almost 80% slow twitch fibres which are designed for long periods of low intensity work, while sprinters will have approximately the same percentage of fast twitch fibres, which can generate extremely high force but fatigue easily.

**Fast twitch** muscle fibres have recently been subdivided into **type 2a** and **type 2b**:

- **Type 2a**, also referred to as **fast oxidative glycolytic fibres (F.O.G.)** pick up certain type one characteristics through endurance training. They therefore tend to have a greater resistance to fatigue. Activities which are fairly high in intensity and of relatively short duration, such as a 200 m swim or an 800 m run may well rely on type 2a fibres.

Table 1.4. Slow twitch muscle fibre composition of various athletes

| Athletic group | Shoulder (deltoid) | Calf (gastrocnemius) | Thigh (vastus lateralis) |
|---|---|---|---|
| Long distance runners | | 79% (m) 69% (f) | |
| Canoeists | 71% (m) | | |
| Triathletes | 60% (m) | 59% (m) | 63% (m) |
| Swimmers | 67% (m) 69% (f) | | |
| Sprint runners | | 24% (m) 27% (f) | |
| Cyclists | | | 57% (m) 51% (f) |
| Weight lifters | 53% (m) | 44% (m) | |
| Shot putters | | 38% (m) | |
| Non-athletes | | | 47% (m) 46% (f) |

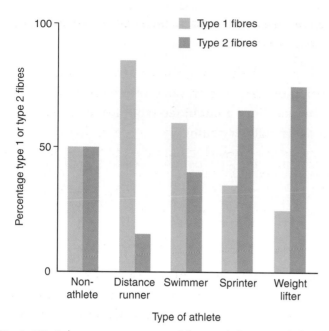

Fig 1.23. Relative percentages of fast and slow twitch fibres in a range of sporting activities

• **Type 2b**, pure fast twitch fibres called **fast twitch glycolytic (F.T.G.)** are used for activities of very high intensity and have a much stronger force of contraction. This is because the motor neuron that carries the impulse is much larger; there are generally more fibres within a fast twitch motor unit; and the muscle fibres themselves are larger and thicker. We would expect a power lifter or a sprinter to possess a large proportion of fast twitch fibres.

## Connective tissues

Connective tissue is responsible for holding all the individual muscle fibres together. It surrounds individual muscle fibres and encases the whole muscle, forming tendons, which attach the muscles to bones and transmit the 'pull' of the muscle to the bones, to cause movement and harness the power of muscle contractions. Tendons vary in length and are composed of parallel fibres of collagen. They attach directly to the periosteum of the bone via a tough tissue known as **Sharpey's fibres**.

The point of attachment for each muscle are termed the **origin** and the **insertion**:

• The **origin** is the end of the muscle attached to a stable bone against which the muscle can pull. *This is usually the nearest flat bone.*

• The **insertion** is the muscle attachment on the bone that the muscle puts into action.

---

Under the headings of slow twitch, fast oxidative glycolytic and fast twitch glycolytic, list as many sporting activities as you can which predominantly use that fibre type.

**ACTIVITY 9**

---

Construct a continuum with type I at one end and type 2b at the other. Collect pictures from as many different sports and activities as possible and stick them along the continuum, relating the position to the fibre type that the activity predominantly requires. Table 1.4 will help you get started.

**ACTIVITY 10**

---

Using table 1.4 account for the differences in fibre content between the different classes of athletes. Explain your answers.

**ACTIVITY 11**

For example, the bicep has its origin on the scapula. This gives a firm base against which the bicep can pull in order to raise the lower arm. (The bicep is a flexor muscle, and its job is to allow flexion at the elbow.) Since the bicep raises the lower arm, it must be attached to that body part via the insertion. In fact the bicep has its insertion on the radius.

The muscle belly is the thick portion of muscle tissue sited between the origin and insertion. It is not unusual for a muscle to have two or more origins, while maintaining a common insertion: the term 'bicep' can be broken down to mean two ('bi') heads ('ceps'). The bicep has two origins or heads which pull upon one insertion in the radius, and puts the lower arm into action.

## Antagonistic muscle action

Muscles never work alone. In order for a coordinated movement to be produced, the muscles must work as a group or team, with several muscles working at any one time. Taking the simple movement of flexion of the arm at the elbow, the muscle responsible for flexion (bending of the arm)

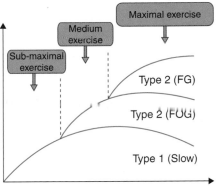

Fig 1.24. Motor unit recruitment and intensity of exercise

Table 1.5. Structural characteristics of muscle fibres

| Characteristics | Slow twitch (Type 1) | Fast oxidative glycolytic F.O.G. (Type 2a) | Fast twitch glycolytic F.T.G. (Type 2b) |
|---|---|---|---|
| Speed of contraction (ms) | Slow (110) | Fast (50) | Fast (50) |
| Force of contraction | Low | High | High |
| Size | Smaller | Large | Large |
| Mitochondrial density | High | Lower | Low |
| Myoglobin content | High | Lower | Low |
| Fatiguability | Fatigue resistant | Less resistant | Easily fatigued |
| Aerobic capacity | High | Medium | Low |
| Capillary density | High | High | Low |
| Anaerobic capacity | Low | Medium | High |
| Motor neuron size | Small | Large | Large |
| Fibres/motor neuron | 10–180 | 300–800 | 300–800 |
| Sarcoplasmic reticulum development | Low | High | High |

*Source*: (Adapted from Sharkey *'Physiology of Fitness'*, Human Kinetics 1990).

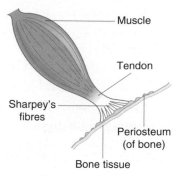

Fig 1.25. Sharpey's fibres

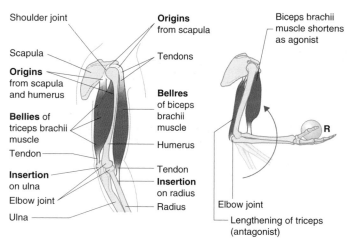

Fig 1.26. Diagram of antagonistic muscle action at the elbow joint

is the biceps brachii, and the muscle which produces the desired joint movement is called the **agonist** or **prime mover**. However, in order for the bicep muscle to shorten when contracting, the tricep muscle must lengthen. The tricep in this instance is known as the **antagonist**, since its action is opposite to that of the agonist. The two muscles however must work together to produce the required movement.

**Fixator** muscles or stabilisers also work in this movement. Their role is to stabilise the origin so that the agonist can achieve maximum and effective contraction. In this case the trapezius contracts to stabilise the scapula to create a rigid platform. **Neutralisers** or **synergist** muscles in this movement prevent any undesired movements which may occur, particularly at the shoulder where the bicep works over two joints.

It can thus be seen that for this apparently simple movement of elbow flexion, integrated and synergistic (harmonious) muscle actions are required to enable the necessary smooth movement.

Furthermore, the roles of each muscle are constantly changed for changing actions. For example, in the action of elbow extension, the roles of the bicep and tricep are reversed so that the tricep becomes the prime mover or agonist (since the tricep is an extensor and thus produces this movement pattern), while the bicep becomes the antagonist, to enable the smooth and effective contraction of the tricep.

Below is a list of commonly used **antagonistic pairings**:

- Pectorals/Latissimus dorsi
- Anterior deltoids/Posterior deltoids
- Trapezius/Deltoids
- Rectus abdominus/Erector spinalis
- Quadriceps group/Hamstring group
- Tibialis anterior/Gastrocnemius and soleus
- Biceps brachii/Triceps brachii
- Wrist flexors/Wrist extensors.

# Reciprocal inhibition

When the agonist contracts in order to perform the desired movement, it usually forces the antagonist to relax. This phenomenon is known as **reciprocal inhibition** (sometimes seen as reciprocal innervation) because the agonist inhibits the antagonist from contracting. Such inhibition does not always occur, however. In a very few cases coordination can actually occur. Take for instance a sit-up. When you perform a sit-up you would normally expect the abdominals to inhibit the contraction of the muscles in the lumbar region of the back. In this situation, however, the spinal erectors also contract – this is one reason why sit-ups are good for strengthening the back as well as the stomach.

Table 1.6. Types of muscle contraction

| | Isotonic | | Isometric |
|---|---|---|---|
| | Concentric | Eccentric | Static |
| **Muscle action** | Muscle shortens | Muscle lengthens while contracting | Muscle remains the same length while contracting |
| **Example** | Bicep: when raising a weight | Bicep: when lowering a weight | Bicep: holding a weight in a static position |

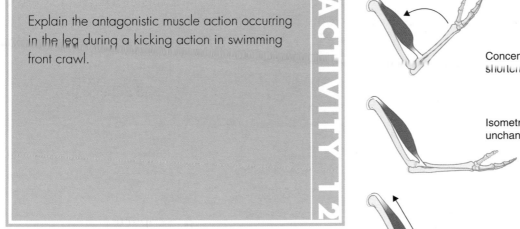

Explain the antagonistic muscle action occurring in the leg during a kicking action in swimming front crawl.

ACTIVITY 12

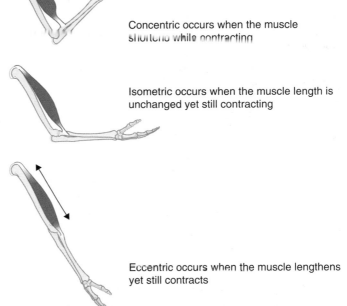

Concentric occurs when the muscle shortens while contracting

Isometric occurs when the muscle length is unchanged yet still contracting

Eccentric occurs when the muscle lengthens yet still contracts

Fig 1.27. Types of muscle contraction in the bicep brachii

# Types of muscular contraction

In order to produce the vast range of movements of which it is capable, the body's muscles either shorten, lengthen or remain the same length while contracting. Indeed, muscle contractions are classified depending upon the muscle action which predominates:

- **Isotonic** contractions refer to those instances when the muscle is moving while contracting. This can further be divided into **concentric and eccentric** muscle actions.
- **Concentric** contractions involve the muscle shortening while contracting as happens in the bicep brachii during the upward phase of a bicep curl or in the tricep during the upward phase of a push-up.
- **Eccentric** contractions on the other hand involve the muscle lengthening while contracting (remember that a muscle is not always relaxing while lengthening!). This can

be seen in the bicep during the downward phase of the bicep curl or in the tricep during the downward phase of the press-up. The eccentric contraction of the bicep during the downward phase is used to counteract the force of gravity. This is because gravity acts on the mass of the weight and forearm causing extension at the elbow. If the bicep does not contract to control the rate of motion caused by gravity, then the movement will be very quick resulting in injury.

**Plyometrics** is a type of strength training which is based on a muscle contracting eccentrically.

Sometimes, however, a muscle can contract without actively lengthening or shortening; in this instance the muscle is going through **isometric** contraction – the muscle remains the same length while contracting. In fact the majority of muscles will contract isometrically in order for us to maintain posture. These static contractions occur while holding a weight in a stationary position or when performing a handstand.

Normally when a muscle contracts the angular velocity of the muscle shortening or lengthening varies throughout the contraction. However, specialist hydraulic machines have been devised so that it is possible to keep the speed at which the muscle lengthens or shortens constant, but not necessarily the resistance applied. The speed of the movement cannot be increased. Any attempt to increase the velocity results in equal reaction force from the machine. In this way **isokinetic** exercise, as it is called, is excellent for strength training.

**ACTIVITY 13**

1. Using sticky labels, label the muscles on a partner's body. Try to label as many as you can without looking at your textbook.
2. Collect as many pictures of bodybuilders as you can and label/identify the defined muscles.

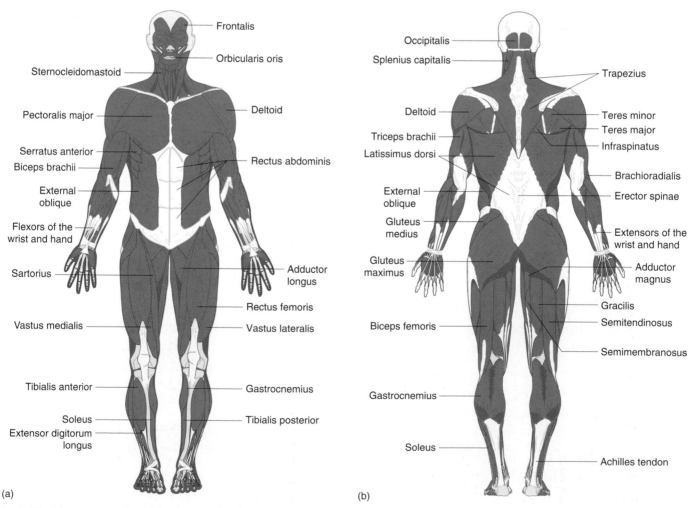

(a)                                                                     (b)

Fig 1.28. Skeletal muscles of the human body (a) anterior view; (b) posterior view

Table 1.7. Major muscles, their origins and insertions together with suggested strengthening exercises

| Major muscle/group | Origin | Insertion | Strengthening exercise |
|---|---|---|---|
| **Trapezius**<br><br>Acromion process<br><br>**Action**<br>**Upper:** adducts and rotates scapula, laterally flexes neck and head.<br><br>**Middle:** adducts and elevates scapula.<br><br>**Lower:** rotates scapula.<br><br>Spine of scapula | Base of the skull<br>Thoracic vertebrae | Acromion process<br>Clavicle<br>Scapula | Shoulder shrugs |
| **Pectoralis major**<br><br>Anterior view<br><br>**Action**<br>Medial rotation of the humerus. Flexes the shoulder and horizontally adducts humerus. | Sternum<br>Clavicle<br>Rib cartilage | Humerus | Barbell chest press |

(Continued)

Table 1.7. (Continued)

| Major muscle/group | Origin | Insertion | Strengthening exercise |
|---|---|---|---|
| **Deltoids**<br><br>Posterior deltoid — Humerus — Anterior deltoid — Middle deltoid<br>**Action** Anterior deltoids—flexion of shoulder / Middle deltoid—abduction of shoulder / Posterior deltoid—extension of shoulder | Clavicle<br>Scapula<br>Acromion process | Humerus | Deltoid 'fly'<br> |
| **Triceps brachii**<br>Posterior view<br><br>Clavicle — Humerus — Scapula — Ulna<br>**Action** Extends (straightens) forearm. | Humerus<br>Scapula | Ulna (olecranon process) | Triceps extension<br> |

(Continued)

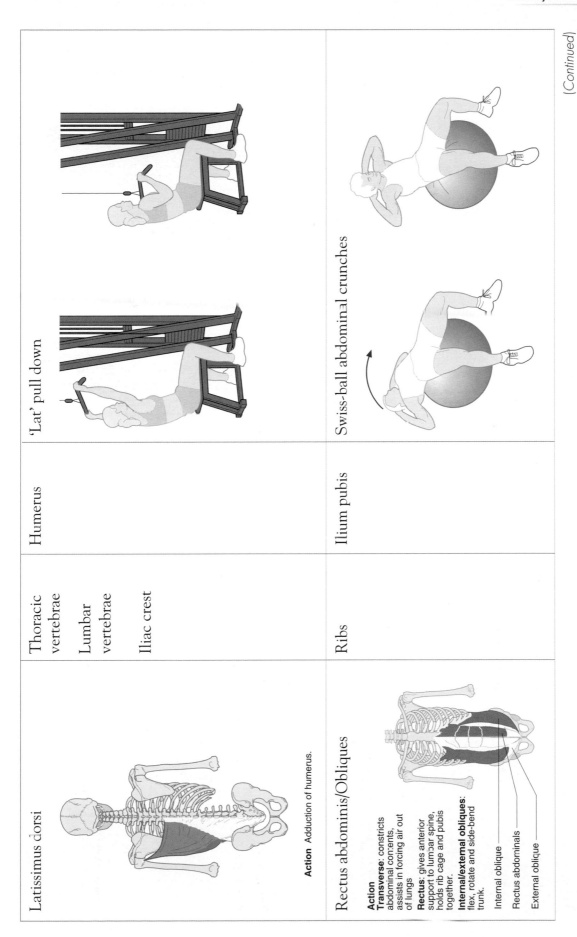

## Latissimus dorsi

| | | 'Lat' pull down |

Thoracic vertebrae
Lumbar vertebrae
Iliac crest

Humerus

**Action** Adduction of humerus.

## Rectus abdominis/Obliques

| | | Swiss-ball abdominal crunches |

Ribs

Ilium pubis

**Action**
**Transverse:** constricts abdominal contents, assists in forcing air out of lungs
**Rectus:** gives anterior support to lumbar spine, holds rib cage and pubis together.
**Internal/external obliques:** flex, rotate and side-bend trunk.

Internal oblique

Rectus abdominals

External oblique

Table 1.7. (Continued)

| Major muscle/group | Origin | Insertion | Strengthening exercise | |
|---|---|---|---|---|
| **Gluteus maximus**<br><br>Ilium<br>Femur<br>Sacrum<br>Posterior view<br>**Action** Extends hip, laterally rotates femur. | Ilium<br>Vertebrae<br>Femur | Femur | Hip extensor | |
| **Gluteus medius/minimus**<br>Posterior view<br>Gluteus medius<br>Gluteus minimus<br>*This lies under the gluteus medius*<br>**Action** Abduct femur, medial rotators. | Ilium | Femur | Hip abduction | |

(*Continued*)

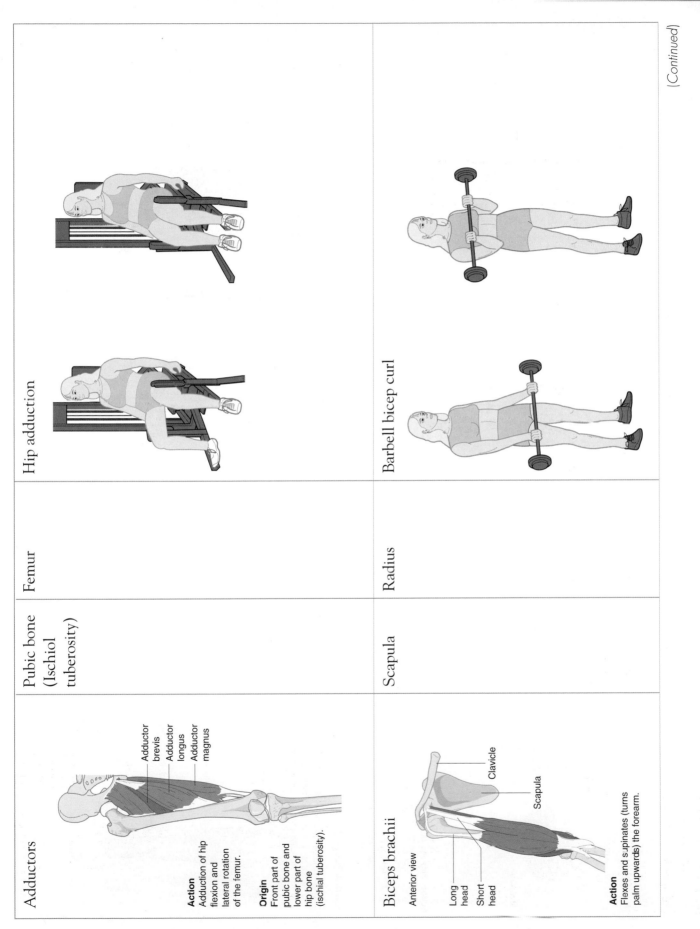

## Adductors

**Action**
Adduction of hip flexion and lateral rotation of the femur.

**Origin**
Front part of pubic bone and lower part of hip bone (ischial tuberosity).

- Adductor brevis
- Adductor longus
- Adductor magnus

Pubic bone (Ischiol tuberosity)

Femur

Hip adduction

## Biceps brachii

Anterior view

- Clavicle
- Scapula
- Long head
- Short head

**Action**
Flexes and supinates (turns palm upwards) the forearm.

Scapula

Radius

Barbell bicep curl

Table 1.7. (Continued)

| Major muscle/group | Origin | Insertion | Strengthening exercise |
|---|---|---|---|
| **Wrist flexors/extensors** <br><br> <br> **Action** **Flexors:** flex the wrist **Extensors:** extend the wrist | Humerus <br> Radius <br> Ulna | Carpals <br> Metacarpals <br> Phalanges | Wrist curls (flexors) <br> Reverse wrist curls (extensors) <br> |
| **Quadricep group** <br> *The quadriceps are made up of four muscles.* <br> *The rectus femoris acts on **both** the hip and knee joint.* <br> *The vasti muscles (medialis, intermedialis and lateralis) act on the knee joint only.* <br> <br> **Action** <br> Extends lower leg at the knee, flexes femur at the hip | Ilium <br> Femur | Tibia <br> (via patella tendon) | Leg extensions <br> |

(Continued)

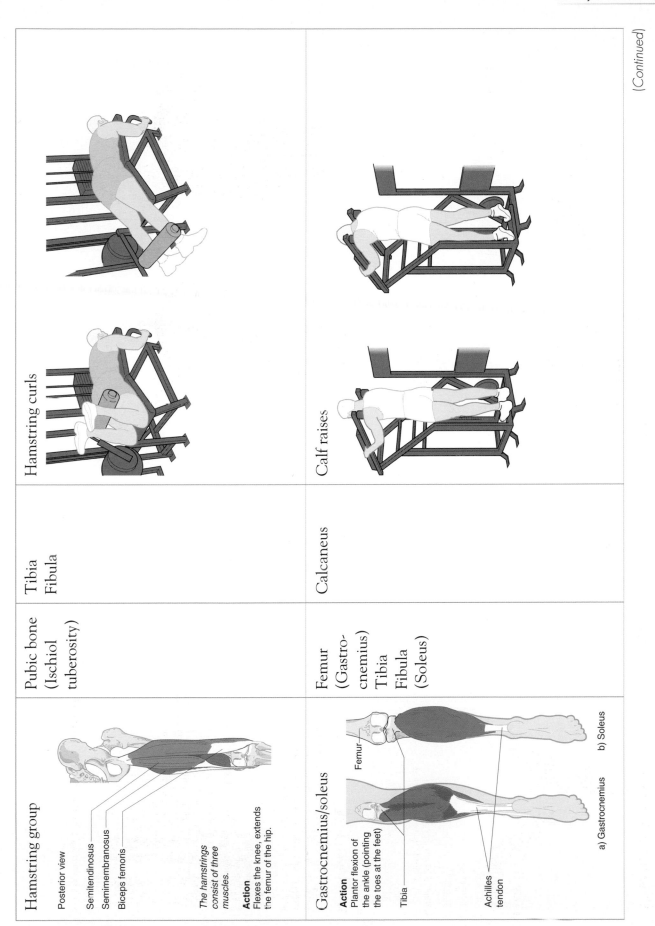

## Hamstring group

Posterior view

Semitendinosus
Semimembranosus
Biceps femoris

*The hamstrings consist of three muscles.*

**Action**
Flexes the knee, extends the femur of the hip.

| | |
|---|---|
| Pubic bone (Ischiol tuberosity) | Tibia Fibula |

Hamstring curls

## Gastrocnemius/soleus

**Action**
Plantar flexion of the ankle (pointing the toes at the feet)

Femur

Tibia

Achilles tendon

a) Gastrocnemius

b) Soleus

| | |
|---|---|
| Femur (Gastro-cnemius) Tibia Fibula (Soleus) | Calcaneus |

Calf raises

Table 1.7. (*Continued*)

| Major muscle/group | Origin | Insertion | Strengthening exercise |
|---|---|---|---|
| Tibialis anterior 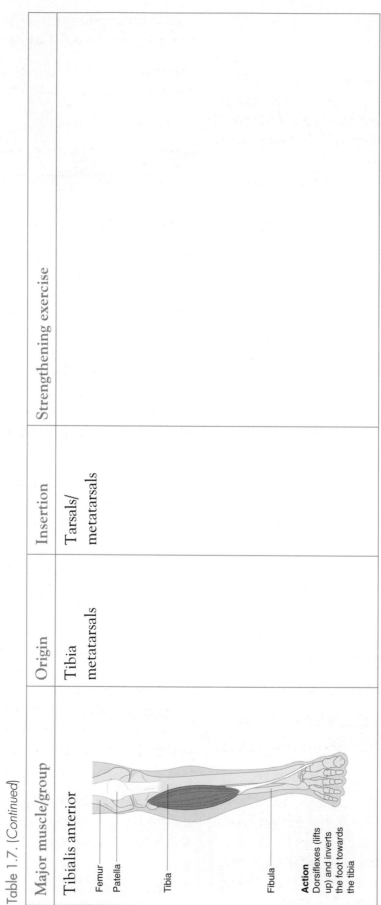 Femur<br>Patella<br>Tibia<br>Fibula<br>**Action**<br>Dorsiflexes (lifts up) and inverts the foot towards the tibia | Tibia metatarsals | Tarsals/ metatarsals | |

# Movement mechanics

## Levers

Efficient and effective movement is made possible by a system of **levers**. These are mechanical devices used to produce turning motions about a fixed point (called a **fulcrum**). In the human body, bones act as levers, joints act as the fulcrum and muscle contractions provide the force to move the lever about the fulcrum.

A basic understanding of lever systems can be used to explain rotational motion, and help athletes develop the most efficient technique for their sport.

There are three types of levers, and each is determined by the relationship of the **fulcrum (F)**, the point of application of force or effort (E) and the resistance (R) or load (L).

1.  **First** class lever: the **fulcrum** lies between the **effort** and the **resistive force** (load).
2.  **Second** class lever: the **resistance** lies between the **fulcrum** and the **effort**.
3.  **Third** class lever: the **effort** is between the **fulcrum** and the **load**.

A simple way of determining the class or order of the lever system operating during a specified movement is to remember the following rhyme,

'**For 1, 2, or 3** think **F, L, E**' to determine the middle component of the lever system, i.e.

- **For 1 or first class lever, F is in between L and E**
- **For 2 or second class lever, L is between F and E**
- **For 3 or third class lever, E is between F and L.**

But BEWARE there may be more than *one* lever system operating at a joint. For example, when flexing the elbow, as in a bicep curl, the effort comes from the point of insertion of the biceps brachii on the radius. This movement involves a 3rd class lever. However, when extending the elbow, as in throwing the javelin, the effort is generated by the triceps brachii via its point of insertion on the ulna. This movement involves a 1st class lever.

The majority of movements in the human body are governed by third class levers.

## Functions of levers

Levers have two main functions:

1.  increase the resistance that a given effort can move.
2.  increase the speed at which a body moves.

**First** class levers can increase both the effects of the effort and the speed of a body; **second** class levers tend only to increase the effect of the effort force; **third** class levers can be used to increase the speed of a body. An example of a third class lever in the body is the action of the hamstrings and quadriceps on the knee joint, which causes flexion and extension of the lower leg. The extent to which this can increase, depends upon the relative lengths of the **resistance arm** and the **effort arm**:

1.  **The resistance arm (RA) or weight arm (WA)** is the part of the lever between the fulcrum and the resistance. The longer the resistance arm, the greater speed can be generated.
2.  **The effort arm (EA)** is the distance between the fulcrum and the effort; the longer the effort arm, the less effort required to move a given resistance. In sport, implements are often used such as rackets or bats to increase the length of the effort arm which will increase the force that an object such as a ball is struck. However, the optimal length of an implement should be determined by the strength of the person handling it which is why, for example, junior tennis rackets have been designed.

The relative efficiency of the lever system is expressed as the **mechanical advantage** (MA) which can be determined as follows:

$$MA = \frac{\text{effort arm}}{\text{resistance arm}}$$

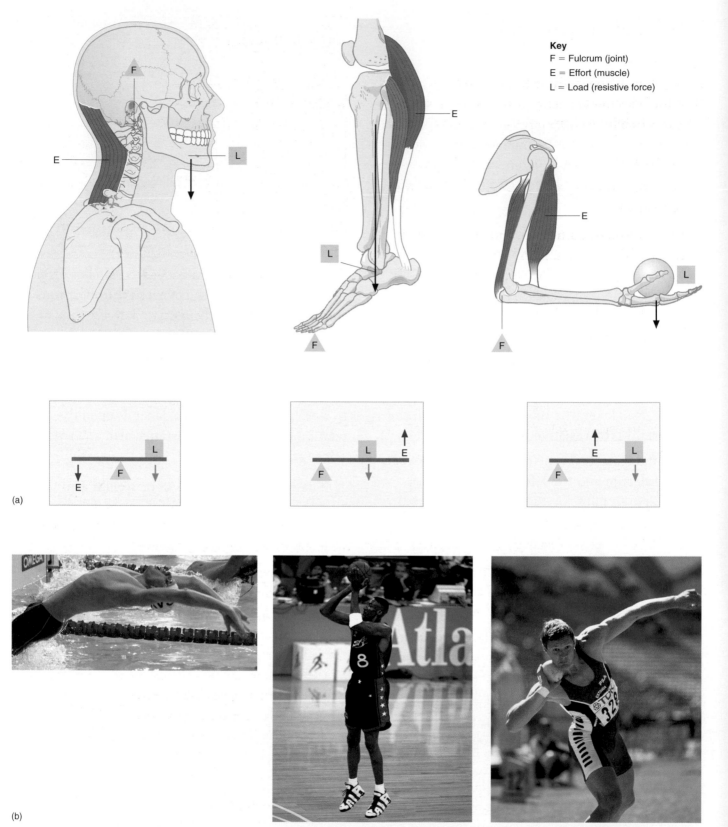

**Key**
F = Fulcrum (joint)
E = Effort (muscle)
L = Load (resistive force)

(a)

(b)

Fig 1.29. Lever systems and their application

# Putting it all together

## Movement analysis

Kinesiology is the study of body movement, and thus includes muscle action. When studying this unit it is helpful to consider the following:

- the function of the muscles contracting

- how the muscle is contracting (eg, concentric or eccentric)

- the movement patterns occurring at joints as a result of the movement

- the plane in which the movement occurs

- the axis about which the movement occurs

- the lever system in operation.

The following table summarises the key movement patterns and muscle action. With this information you should be able to apply your knowledge to a wide range of sporting activities.

Table 1.8. The musculo-skeletal system: movement analysis

| Joint | Action | Plane | Muscles used | Diagram | Example |
|---|---|---|---|---|---|
| **Hip** | Flexion | Median | Psoas<br>Iliacus<br>Rectus femoris | | eg, performing a 'tuck' jump in trampolining |
| | Extension | Median | Gluteus maximus<br>Biceps femoris<br>Semimembranosus<br>Semitendinosus<br>Gluteus medius (posterior) | Extension — Flexion | eg, preparation to kick a football |
| | Abduction | Frontal | Gluteus medius<br>Gluteus minimus<br>Tensor fasciae latae | | eg, performing a cartwheel |
| | Adduction | Frontal | Adductor magnus<br>Adductor brevis<br>Adductor longus<br>Pestineus<br>Gracilis | Abduction — Adduction | eg, the kick action in breaststroke |

*(Continued)*

Table 1.8. (Continued)

| Joint | Action | Plane | Muscles used | Diagram | Example |
|---|---|---|---|---|---|
| **Hip** | Medial rotation | Horizontal | Gluteus medius<br>Gluteus minimus<br>Tensor fasciae latae | | eg, rotational movement when throwing the discus |
| | Lateral rotation | Horizontal | Gluteus maximus<br>Adductors | | eg, a side foot pass in football |
| **Knee** | Flexion | Median | Semitendinosus<br>Semimembranosus<br>Biceps femoris<br>Popliteus<br>Gastrocnemius | | eg, preparing to kick a conversion in rugby |
| | Extension | Median | Rectus femoris<br>Vastus medialis<br>Vastus lateralis<br>Tensor fasciae latae | | eg, rebounding in basketball |
| | Medial rotation (when flexed) | Horizontal | Sartorius<br>Semitendinosus | | eg, breastroke 'kick' phase |
| | Lateral rotation (when flexed) | Horizontal | Tensor fasciae latae<br>Biceps femoris | | e.g. breastroke recovery |
| **Ankle** | Dorsi flexion | Median | Tibialis anterior<br>Extensor digitorum longus<br>Peroneus tertius | | eg, landing from a lay up in basketball |
| | Plantar flexion | Median | Gastrocnemius<br>Soleus<br>Peroneus longus<br>Peroneus brevis<br>Tibialis posterior<br>Flexor digitorum longus | | eg, pointing toes when performing a handstand |
| | Inversion | Frontal | Tibialis anterior<br>Tibialis posterior | | eg, line kicking in rugby |

Table 1.8. (*Continued*)

| Joint | Action | Plane | Muscles used | Diagram | Example |
|---|---|---|---|---|---|
| | | | Gastrocnemius Soleus | | (kicking a ball with outside of the foot) |
| | Eversion | Frontal | Peroneus longus Peroneus brevis | | eg, kick phase in breastroke |
| | Flexion | Median | Anterior deltoid Pectoralis major Coracobrachialis | | eg, blocking of the net in volleyball |
| | Extension | Median | Posterior deltoid Latissimus dorsi Teres major | | eg, butterfly arm pull |
| | Adduction | Frontal | Latissimus dorsi Pectoralis major Teres major Teres minor | | eg, landing phase of a straddle jump in trampolining |
| **Shoulder** | Abduction | Frontal | Medial deltoid Supraspinatus | | eg, straddle jump in trampolining |
| | Horizontal abduction | Horizontal | Posterior deltoid Trapezius Rhomboids Latissimus dorsi | | eg, preparing phase of throwing the discus |
| | Horizontal adduction | Horizontal | Pectoralis Major anterior deltoid | | eg, execution phase of throwing the javelin |
| | Medial rotation | Horizontal | Subscapularis | | eg, butterfly armpull |
| | Lateral rotation | Horizontal | Infraspinatus Teres minor | | eg, preparing for a forehand drive in tennis |
| **Elbow** | Flexion | Median | Biceps brachii Brachialis Brachioradialis | | eg, preparation for a set shot in basketball |
| | Extension | Median | Triceps | | eg, execution of a set shot in basketball |

Table 1.8. (*Continued*)

| Joint | Action | Plane | Muscles used | Diagram | Example |
|---|---|---|---|---|---|
| **Radio-ulnar** | Pronation | Horizontal | Pronator teres<br>Pronator quadratus<br>Brachioradialis | | eg, putting top spin on a tennis ball |
| | Supination | Horizontal | Biceps brachii<br>Supinator | Supination  Pronation | eg, recovery phase of the arms in breastroke |
| **Wrist** | Flexion | Median | Wrist flexors | Extension   Flexion | eg, wrist snap in basketball shot |
| | Extension | Median | Wrist extensors | | eg, initial grip of a shot against neck |
| **Movement of the trunk** | Flexion | Median | Rectus abdominus<br>Internal obliques<br>External obliques | Extension   Flexion | eg, crouching at start of a swimming dive |
| | Extension | Median | Erector spinae<br>Iliocostalis spinalis | | eg, a backflip in gymnastics |
| | Lateral flexion | Frontal | Internal oblique<br>Rectus abdominis<br>Erector spinae<br>Quadratus laborum | Lateral flexion | eg, a cartwheel |
| | Rotation | Horizontal | External oblique<br>Rectus abdominis<br>Erector spinae | | eg, follow through on a tennis serve |
| **Movement of the scapulae** | Elevation | Frontal | Levator sapulae<br>Trapezius<br>Rhomboids | | eg, recovery phase of butterfly armpull |
| | Depression | Frontal | Trapezius (lower)<br>Pectoralis minor<br>Serratus anterior (lower) | | eg, thrusting off a horse when performing a handspring |

Table 1.8. (*Continued*)

| Joint | Action | Plane | Muscles used | Diagram | Example |
|-------|--------|-------|--------------|---------|---------|
| **Move-ment of the scapulae** | Protraction | Frontal | Serratus anterior | | eg, recovery phase in breastroke |
| | Retraction | Frontal | Rhomboids Trapezius | | eg, pull phase in breastroke |
| | Upward rotation | Frontal | Trapezius (upper) Serratus anterior | | eg, recovery phase in front-crawl |
| | Downward rotation | Frontal | Rhomboids Levator scapulae | | eg, front-crawl arm pull |

**ACTIVITY 15**

Table 1.9 shows one joint movement used in basketball. Think of other sporting situations and complete the table accordingly. You will find it useful to study the various tables throughout the chapter.

**ACTIVITY 16**

For each of the following joints, state which muscles are used for the movement patterns shown in brackets:
- Knee (flexion and extension)
- Hip (flexion, extension, abduction, adduction)
- Shoulder (flexion, extension, abduction, adduction)
- Ankle (plantar flexion, dorsi flexion, inversion, eversion).

Table 1.9. Variety of joint movements

| Sport | Action | Movement pattern | Muscles working | Type of contraction | Plane system | Lever system |
|-------|--------|------------------|-----------------|---------------------|--------------|--------------|
| Basketball | Jump shot | Extension at knee | Quadricep group: rectus femoris vasti muscles | Concentric | Median | 3rd class |

For your course you need to be able to complete a full movement analysis for a range of skills. Over the following pages there are some skills from a variety of activities. In each case, study the movement that has occurred from phase 1 to phase 2 and complete a full movement analysis on the joints specified. Use the format of table 1.9 and don't forget to cover all aspects of the movement!

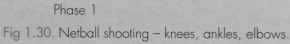

Phase 1

Phase 2

Fig 1.30. Netball shooting – knees, ankles, elbows.

Phase 1

Phase 2

Fig 1.31. Kicking – hip, knee, ankle

Phase 1

Phase 2

Fig 1.32. Throwing the javelin – shoulder, radio-ulnar, wrist

Phase 1

Phase 2

Fig 1.33. The sprint start – hips, knee, ankle

Phase 1

Phase 2

Fig 1.34. The tennis serve – shoulder, elbow, wrist

# Summary

- The skeleton has five basic functions: support, protection, movement, blood production, mineral storage.
- The axial skeleton consists of those bones that provide the greatest support and include the skull, vertebral column and the rib cage.
- The appendicular skeleton consists of the bones of the limbs and their respective girdles.
- The vertebral column is divided into five areas: cervical vertebrae, thoracic vertebrae, lumbar vertebrae, sacral vertebrae and coccygeal vertebrae.
- The rib cage is composed of twelve pairs of ribs which together provide protection for the vital organs and enables the process of inspiration.
- Bones can be categorised as either long, short, flat, irregular or sesamoid.
- There are three types of cartilage in the body: hyaline or articular cartilage, white fibrocartilage, and yellow elastic cartilage.

- Bone is a rigid non-elastic tissue composed of mineral and organic tissue. There are two types of bone: compact or hard bone and cancellous or spongy bone.

- Ossification is the process of bone formation. It can occur within the membranes (intramembranous) or through replacement of cartilage (endochondral).

- Joints are classified according to the degree of movement allowed. There are three basic types of joint; fixed or fibrous joints, and cartilaginous joints.

- Movement at synovial joints can be classified as flexion, extension, abduction, adduction, rotation, pronation, supination, circumduction, plantar flexion, dorsiflexion, inversion and eversion.

- The whole of the skeletal system can be strengthened through performing exercise.

- There are three types of muscle tissue: skeletal, smooth and cardiac.

- Skeletal muscle properties include extensibility, elasticity and contractility.

- Functions include movement, support and posture, and heat production.

- There are two basic types of muscle fibre: Slow twitch or type 1 and fast twitch or type 2 fibres. Fast twitch fibre can be further subdivided into fast oxidative glycolytic or type 2a and fast twitch glycolytic or type 2b.

- Muscles are attached to bones via tendons. The origin of a muscle is that attachment onto a stable bone, usually the nearest flat bone. The insertion is the muscle attachment onto the bone that the muscle puts into action.

- Muscles often work together in order to produce coordinated movements: antagonistic muscle action. A muscle directly responsible for the joint movement is the agonist. An antagonist often lengthens in order for the agonist to shorten.

- Muscles can contract in several ways: isotonic (shortening or lengthening), concentric (the muscle shortens), eccentric (the muscle lengthens). A muscle can also contract without any visible movement (isometric).

- Skeletal muscle fibres are composed of many smaller myofibrils. Each myofibril is characterised by dark and light bands which represent sarcomeres. Sarcomeres are composed of two proteins – actin and myosin. Interaction of the actin and myosin causes muscular contraction (the sliding filament theory).

- Muscular contraction: interaction of the muscular system and nervous system.

- A motor unit is the functional component of skeletal muscle and consists of a motor neurone and a number of muscle fibres that that motor neurone controls. A single muscle can possess thousands of motor units.

- Each fibre within a motor unit will contract maximally or not at all and depends upon the intensity of the stimulus. This is known as the all or none law.

- Strength of contraction can be determined by the number of motor units recruited by the brain to perform a specific task, or by considering the frequency that impulses arrive at muscle fibres.

- Muscle action is controlled by internal regulatory mechanisms which include proprioceptors, muscle spindle apparatus, and Golgi tendon organs.

- The analysis of muscle contraction and joint action is called kinesiology.

# Review Questions

1. Name the bones that articulate at the following joints:
   a) knee
   b) hip
   c) shoulder
   d) elbow

2. How is the knee joint structured for stability?

3. List the types of movement that occur in the medial plane.

4. Explain how it is possible for us to bend down and touch our toes. What movement patterns are brought about during this action?

5. What is the function of articular cartilage?

6. How is the shoulder structured to enable the different types of movement patterns of which it is capable?

7. List four types of movement that take place in the horizontal plane.

8. State the functions of the following:
   a) bursae
   b) cruciate ligaments
   c) patella
   d) carpals
   e) thoracic vertebrae
   f) collagen
   g) the atlas and axis.

9. Outline the benefits that training has on the skeletal tissues.

10. Analyse the action of a tennis serve. State the movement patterns and joint actions that occur at the shoulder and elbow. State the planes in which these movements take place and the axes about which they occur.

11. Explain how the properties of skeletal muscle enable it to perform its function when sprinting. Use the correct names of muscles, where appropriate.

12. Skeletal muscle is composed of different types of fibre. What are they? Explain how the structure of these fibres is suited to the requirements of performers in a variety of sports.

13. When performing a jump shot in basketball, many different muscles work in the lower body. Identify the muscles working on the hip, knee and ankle joints, and state the specific roles that each of these muscles have (ie, are they agonists, fixators, etc.).

14. What are the essential ingredients to successful analysis of movement? Use these to analyse an overhead clear in badminton, with particular reference to the shoulder, elbow and wrist actions.

15. Identify one stroke in swimming. State the muscles that are contracting in each phase of the stroke (e.g., either the 'kick' or 'recovery' phase in the leg action) and state the **type** of contraction taking place in each muscle.

16. Give definitions of the following terms: Epimysium, Fasciculi, Myofibrils, Sarcomere, Actin, Myosin, Tropomyosin, Troponin.

17. Outline the process of muscle fibre innervation. What is the function of 'acetylcholine'?

18. Why is an understanding of 'the all or none law' important to an athlete undertaking a weight training programme?

19. Explain the role of the muscle spindle apparatus when performing a triple jump.

20. What is the importance of calcium and ATP in muscle contraction?

## Further reading

Arnould-Taylor, *A Text Book of Anatomy and Physiology*, (Stanley Thornes Publishers Ltd, 1988)

Clegg, *Exercise Physiology* (Feltham Press, 1996)

Davis, Bull, Roscoe and Roscoe, *Physical Education and the Study of Sport* (Wolfe Medical Publishers, 1991)

Kapit and Elson, *The Anatomy Colouring Book* (Harpers Collins College Publishers, 1993)

Hay and Reid, *Anatomy, Mechanics and Human Motion* (Prentice Hall, 1988)

Seeley, Stephens and Tate, *Anatomy and Physiology* (Mosby Year Book Inc., 1992)

Sharkey, *Physiology of Fitness* (Human Kinetics, 1990)

Wilmore and Costill, *Physiology of Sport and Exercise* (Human Kinetics, 1994)

Wirhead, *Athletic Ability and the Anatomy of Motion* (Wolfe Medical Publishers, 1989)

# 2. The Cardiovascular System – The Maintenance of Blood Supply

## Chapter introduction

This chapter will examine the structure and function of the cardiovascular system, including the heart, the vascular system and the blood and its performance when performing physical activity.

The second part of the chapter will focus upon the response of the cardiovascular system to exercise, looking in particular at factors such as cardiac dynamics including changes in heart rate, stroke volume and blood pressure.

We will learn how the heart, blood vessels and blood adapt in response to the demands of exercise; links are made to chapter 7 on training and health-related implications.

## The cardiovascular system

The human body is an amazing machine, and at the centre of its operation is the heart. The heart is a muscular pump that beats continuously, over 100,000 times per day, which together with the blood vessels and the blood provides the tissues and cells with the essentials for life itself – oxygen and nutrients.

## The structure and function of the heart

The heart lies behind the sternum (breastbone) and ribs, which offer protection. In adults, it is about the size of a clenched fist – although trained athletes often experience cardiac hypertrophy, which is an enlargement of the heart.

In terms of structure, the heart is composed of four chambers:

- The two chambers at the top or superior part of the heart are called the **atria**.
- The two lower or inferior chambers are termed **ventricles**.

The ventricles are much more muscular than the atria since it is here that the pumping action of the heart which circulates the blood all over the body occurs.

As well as being divided transversely (into upper and lower portions), the heart can also be divided into left and right halves (sagitally) due to a muscular partition called the septum. Now study figs 2.1 and 2.2 and get to know the structure of the heart.

## The heart as a dual action pump

This separation into left and right is essential for the heart to carry out its function effectively, since each side has slightly different roles:

- The left side of the heart is responsible for circulating blood rich in oxygen throughout the entire body. This is known as **systemic circulation**.
- The right side is responsible for ensuring that oxygen-poor blood is pumped to the lungs where it can be reoxygenated. This is known as **pulmonary circulation**.

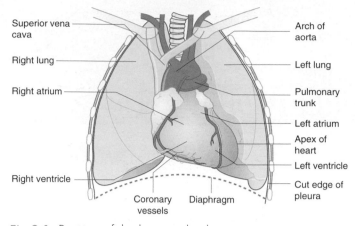

Fig 2.1. Position of the heart in the thoracic cavity

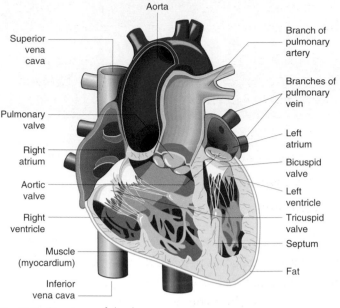

Fig 2.2. Structure of the heart

The major vessels act as entry and exit points for the blood to enter or leave the heart, and are all situated towards the top of the heart. To ensure a smooth passage of blood through the heart, a number of **valves** exist. These valves make sure that the blood only flows in one direction and are also responsible for the 'lub-dup' sounds of the heart. The 'lub' results from the closure of the **atrio-ventricular valves** (also known as the **bicuspid** and **tricuspid valves**), and the much sharper 'dup' sound occurs when the **semi-lunar valves** (**pulmonary** and **aortic valves**) snap shut. These valves also prevent back flow of blood, ensuring a uni-directional flow through the heart.

The thick muscular wall of the heart is called the **myocardium** and is composed of cardiac muscle fibres. It is situated between the **endocardium** on the inside, a thin layer of single cells which lines the chambers, and the **pericardium** on the outside (a visceral membrane forming the pericardial sac in which the heart sits) to protect it from the surrounding lungs.

Covering the exterior of the heart are **coronary arteries** which feed the heart muscle with blood; being a muscle, it still requires the fuel to keep the pump working continually. Blockages of these arteries are responsible for many problems of the heart, and in particular cardiovascular diseases such as hypertension, angina pectoris and myocardial infarctions (heart attacks).

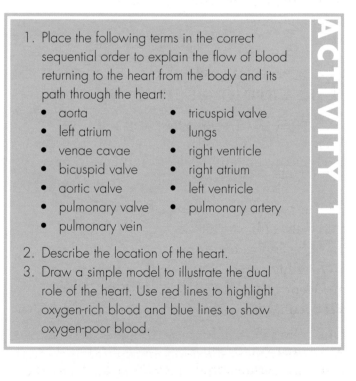

1.  Place the following terms in the correct sequential order to explain the flow of blood returning to the heart from the body and its path through the heart:
    - aorta
    - left atrium
    - venae cavae
    - bicuspid valve
    - aortic valve
    - pulmonary valve
    - pulmonary vein
    - tricuspid valve
    - lungs
    - right ventricle
    - right atrium
    - left ventricle
    - pulmonary artery

2.  Describe the location of the heart.
3.  Draw a simple model to illustrate the dual role of the heart. Use red lines to highlight oxygen-rich blood and blue lines to show oxygen-poor blood.

**ACTIVITY 1**

## The cardiac cycle

The cardiac cycle refers to the process of cardiac contraction and blood transportation through the heart. As mentioned above, the heart can be viewed as two separate pumps to serve its dual purpose, and the cardiac cycle explains the sequence of events that takes place **during one complete heartbeat.** This includes the filling of the heart with blood (or **diastole phase**) and the emptying of the blood into the arterial system (or **systole phase**).

Each cycle takes approximately 0.8 seconds and occurs on average 72 times per minute. There are four stages to each heartbeat:

1. atrial diastole
2. ventricular diastole
3. atrial systole
4. ventricular systole.

Each stage depends upon whether the chambers of the heart are *filling* with blood while the heart is relaxing (**diastole**) or whether they are *emptying*, which occurs when the heart contracts (**systole**) forcing blood from one part of the heart to another or into the arterial system, and subsequently to the lungs and the body.

The first stage of the cardiac cycle is **atrial diastole**. The upper chambers of the heart are filled with blood returning from:

* the body via the venae cavae to the right atrium; and
* the lungs via the pulmonary vein to the left atrium.

At this time the atrioventricular valves are shut but as the atria fill with blood, atrial pressure overcomes ventricular pressure. Since blood always moves from areas of high pressure to areas of low pressure, the atrioventricular valves are forced open, and **ventricular diastole** now takes place. During this stage the ventricles fill with blood and the semi-lunar valves remain closed. The atria now contract, causing **atrial systole** which ensures that all the blood is ejected into the ventricles. As the ventricles continue going through diastole, the pressure increases, which causes the atrioventricular valves to close. Ultimately, the ventricular pressure overcomes that in the aorta and the pulmonary artery. The semi-lunar valves open and the ventricles contract, forcing all the blood from the right ventricle into the pulmonary artery and the blood from the left ventricle into the aorta.

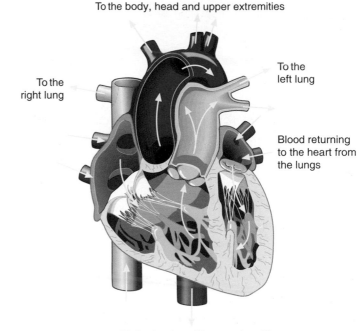

To the body, head and upper extremities

To the right lung

To the left lung

Blood returning to the heart from the lungs

To the trunk and lower extremities

Fig 2.3. The path of blood through the heart
*Source*: Tortora (1991).

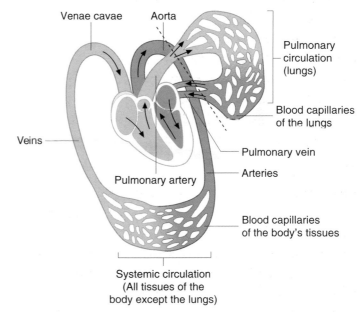

Venae cavae

Aorta

Pulmonary circulation (lungs)

Blood capillaries of the lungs

Pulmonary vein

Arteries

Blood capillaries of the body's tissues

Veins

Pulmonary artery

Systemic circulation (All tissues of the body except the lungs)

Fig 2.4. The heart as a dual action pump

This is **ventricular systole**, and once completed, the semi-lunar valves snap shut. The cycle is now complete and ready to be repeated.

Generally the complete diastolic phase takes approximately **0.5 seconds** and the complete systolic phase lasts **0.3 seconds**. However, it is

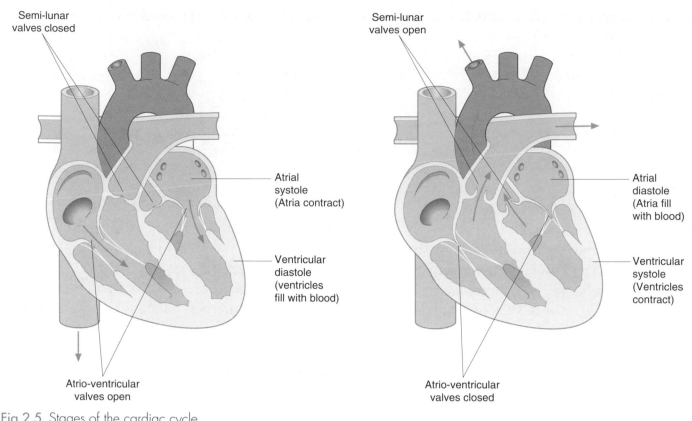

Fig 2.5. Stages of the cardiac cycle
*Source:* Tortora (1991).

interesting to note that trained athletes have been reported to have a longer diastolic phase of the cardiac cycle, enabling a more complete filling of the heart. In this way, the trained athlete can increase venous return and therefore stroke volume (refer to Starling's law of the heart) during resting periods, which accounts for the decreased resting heart rate (known as bradycardia) often experienced by trained atheletes.

# How the heart works

The heart works by producing impulses which spread and innervate the specialised muscle fibres. Unlike skeletal muscle, the heart produces its own impulses (ie, it is **myogenic**), and it is the conduction system of the heart which spreads the impulses throughout the heart and enables the heart to contract.

From fig 2.6 it can be seen that the electrical impulse begins at the pacemaker: a mass of cardiac muscle cells known as the **sino-atrial node (S.A. node)** located in the right atrial wall. It is the rate at

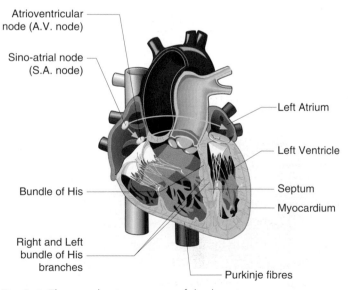

Fig 2.6. The conduction system of the heart

which the S.A. node emits impulses that determines heart rate. As the impulse is emitted, it spreads to the adjacent inter-connecting fibres of the atrium, which spreads the excitation extremely rapidly and causes the atria to contract. It then passes to another specialised mass of cells called the atrioventricular node (A.V. node). The A.V. node acts as a distributor and passes the action potential to the **Bundle of His**, which, together with the branching **Purkinje fibres**, spreads the excitation throughout the ventricles.

There is a delay of about 0.1 second from the time when the A.V. node receives stimulation to when it distributes the action potential throughout the ventricles. This is crucial to allow completion of atrial contraction, before ventricular systole begins so that as much blood as possible is passed from the atria to the ventricles. The relationship between the electrical activity of the heart and the cardiac cycle can be shown through an electrocardiogram trace (ECG). From fig 2.8, it can be seen that three clearly visible waves accompany each cycle. The first, the P wave, indicates the spread of an impulse throughout the atria (atrial depolarisation) which causes atrial systole. The second wave, the QRS complex, is a much larger wave and indicates the spread of the impulse throughout the ventricles (ventricular depolarisation). The T wave shows atrial repolarisation which occurs just before the ventricles can relax. The trace does not exhibit an atrial repolarisation since the large QRS wave masks it.

## Heart regulation and control

The heart is governed by the **autonomic nervous system (ANS)** which operates without us having to think about it. In respect to the heart, it is the ANS which determines the rate at which the pacemaker (S.A. node) sends out impulses. The **sympathetic** and **parasympathetic** nervous systems are the two subdivisions of the autonomic nervous system and control the cardiac regulatory centre in the medulla oblongata in the brain. They are fundamental to the

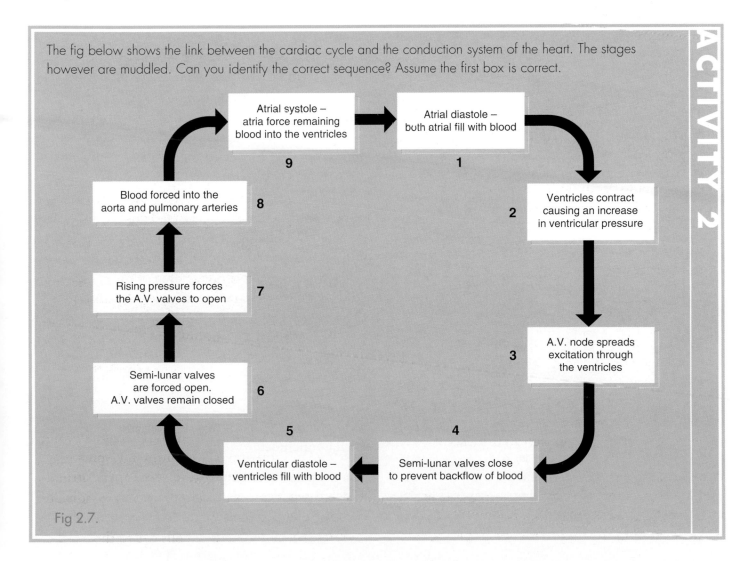

The fig below shows the link between the cardiac cycle and the conduction system of the heart. The stages however are muddled. Can you identify the correct sequence? Assume the first box is correct.

**ACTIVITY 2**

Atrial systole – atria force remaining blood into the ventricles — 9

Atrial diastole – both atrial fill with blood — 1

Blood forced into the aorta and pulmonary arteries — 8

Ventricles contract causing an increase in ventricular pressure — 2

Rising pressure forces the A.V. valves to open — 7

A.V. node spreads excitation through the ventricles — 3

Semi-lunar valves are forced open. A.V. valves remain closed — 6

Ventricular diastole – ventricles fill with blood — 5

Semi-lunar valves close to prevent backflow of blood — 4

Fig 2.7.

regulation of the heart and work antagonistically as follows:

1. The **sympathetic nervous system** increases heart rate by releasing **adrenaline** and **noradrenaline** from the adrenal medulla. Adrenaline increases the strength of ventricular contraction, and therefore stroke volume, while noradrenaline (a transmitter substance) aids the spread of the impulse throughout the heart, and therefore increases heart rate.

2. The **parasympathetic nervous system**, on the other hand, releases **acetylcholine**, which slows the spread of impulses and therefore reduces heart rate, returning it to the normal resting level.

Essentially there are three main factors that determine the action of the cardiac regulatory centre. They are as follows:

1. **Neural factors** – Once exercise begins proprioceptors within the muscles, tendons and joints relay messages to the cardiac centre informing it that the amount of movement has increased and therefore muscles will require a greater supply of blood.

   **Chemoreceptors** located in the aorta and carotid arteries inform the centre of changes to the chemical composition of the blood – in particular reacting to increased levels of carbon dioxide. The cardiac centre increases the heart rate in order to speed up carbon dioxide removal.

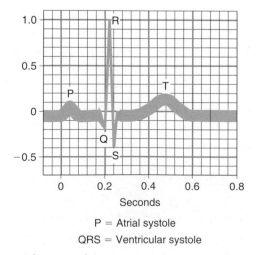

P = Atrial systole

QRS = Ventricular systole

Fig 2.8. An electrocardiogram trace

Meanwhile **baroreceptors** respond to changes in blood pressure as a result of increased activity.

2. **Hormonal factors** – Once stimulated the sympathetic nerves cause the release of adrenaline and noradrenaline which increases the strength of ventricular contractions of the heart and increases heart rate and together greatly increases cardiac output. In addition these hormones help control blood pressure and help in the redistribution of blood to the working muscles through **vasoconstriction** and **vasodilation** of arterioles.

3. **Intrinsic factors** – When exercise commences there is an increase in body temperature which helps increase the flow of blood around the body (as blood becomes less viscous) and helps increase heart rate through increasing the speed of nerve impulse transmission.

## Regulation during exercise

At rest, the parasympathetic system overrides the sympathetic system, and keeps heart rate down. However, once exercise begins, the sympathetic system increases its activity, the parasympathetic system decreases in activity, and so heart rate is allowed to rise. Increased metabolic activity causes an increased concentration of carbon dioxide and lactic acid content in the blood, which increases acidity and decreases blood pH. These changes are detected by **chemoreceptors** sited in the aortic arch and carotid arteries. They inform the sympathetic centre in the upper thoracic area of the spinal cord to increase heart rate in order to transport the carbon dioxide to the lungs where it can be expelled. Messages from the sympathetic centre are sent to the **S.A. node** via **accelerator nerves** which release adrenaline and noradrenaline upon stimulation.

Other factors which increase heart rate during exercise include:

- increased body temperature – and therefore decreased blood viscosity (the relative 'thickness' of the blood)

- increased venous return (a result of the increased action of the muscle pump).

Both of these factors will result in a greater **cardiac output**.

Once exercise ceases, sympathetic stimulation decreases and the parasympathetic system once again takes over. The parasympathetic system responds to information from **baroreceptors** – the body's

Table 2.1. The autonomic nervous system and cardiac function.

| The sympathetic function | The parasympathetic function |
|---|---|
| • Increased heart rate | • Decreased heart rate |
| • Increased strength of contraction | • Decreased strength of contraction |
| • Vasodilation of arteries supplying the muscles and the heart | • Vasoconstriction of arteries supplying the muscles and the heart |
| • Some vasoconstriction of arteries of the abdomen, kidneys and skin | • Vasodilation of arteries in abdomen, kidneys and skin |

in-built blood pressure recorders. When blood pressure is too high, messages are sent from the cardiac inhibitory centre to the S.A. node via the vagus nerve. The parasympathetic nerve then releases **acetylcholine**, which decreases the heart rate.

This continuous interaction of the sympathetic and parasympathetic system ensures that the heart works as efficiently as possible, and enables sufficient nutrients to reach the tissue cells to ensure effective muscle action.

Adrenaline and noradrenaline released from the adrenal medulla (situated at the top of the kidneys) generally have the same effect – increasing heart rate and increasing the strength of contraction. They also help to increase metabolic activity, convert glycogen into its usable form – glucose, make glucose and free fatty acids available to the muscle and help redistribute blood to the working muscles. The release of such hormones, controlled by the sympathetic system, results from many factors including exercise, emotions, excitement and stress.

Place the following stages in the control of the heart rate in the correct order:

1. Sympathetic nerves release adrenaline/ noradrenaline.
2. Parasympathetic nerves emit impulses and release acetylcholine.
3. Proprioceptors (e.g. muscle spindles) detect changes in motor activity.
4. Increases the activity of the S.A. node and causes an increase in heart rate.
5. Chemoreceptors detect changes in carbon dioxide and the pH of the blood.
6. Once exercise ceases baroreceptors detect elevated blood pressure in the aorta and carotid arteries.
7. Decreases the activity of the S.A. node and reduces heart rate slowly back to resting levels.

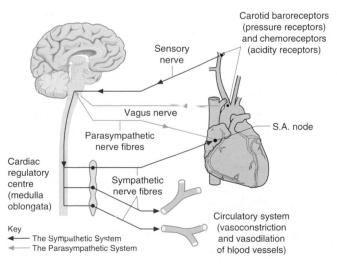

Fig 2.9. The regulation of heart rate

ACTIVITY 4

- Fill in the missing gaps:
  The ___ is a bundle of specialised cardiac muscle cells which generate action potentials and govern the heart rate. Impulses are spread across the atria and reach the ___ which delays the action potentials from spreading through the ventricles.
- Discuss the difference between cardiac and skeletal muscle in terms of structure and function.
- Describe the structure and function of the heart's conducting system.
- Explain the role of the autonomic nervous system before, during and after embarking upon a distance run.

# Cardiac dynamics

## Cardiac output

Cardiac output is the volume of blood that is pumped out of the heart from one ventricle per minute. Cardiac output is generally measured from the left ventricle, and is equal to the product of stroke volume and heart rate. The relationship between these variables is summarised below.

$$\text{Cardiac output} = \text{Stroke volume} \times \text{Heart rate}$$
$$Q = S.V. \times H.R.$$

- The stroke volume is the volume of blood ejected into the aorta in one beat.
- The heart rate reflects the number of times the heart beats per minute.

On average, the resting stroke volume is 75 ml per beat, and the resting heart rate for a person is 72 beats per minute. Therefore, cardiac output at rest is:

$$Q = S.V. \times H.R.$$
$$= 75\,\text{ml} \times 72\,\text{bpm}$$
$$= 5,400\,\text{ml/min} \ (5.4\,\text{L/min})$$

However, during exercise the cardiac output may rise to 30 L/min – a six-fold increase!

Training signals an improvement in cardiac output *during exercise*, brought about by an increase in stroke volume due to the larger volume of the left ventricle, and the **hypertrophy** (enlargement) of the heart (sometimes referred to as '**athletes' heart**'). At rest, **cardiac hypertrophy** plays an important role, since increased stroke volume (which accompanies hypertrophy) allows the resting heart rate to decrease. This is known as **bradycardia**. The increased size of the ventricular cavity in trained athletes allows a longer diastolic phase during which time the heart can fill up with more blood. This stretches cardiac fibres and increases the strength of contraction, with the resultant effect of increasing stroke volume. **Consequently, cardiac output does not change at rest following training**.

Bradycardia occurs as a result of an increase in parasympathetic activity and a decrease in cardiac sympathetic activity, often to the extent that resting heart rate decreases to 60 bpm and below. During exercise, the hormones have a great influence on stroke volume and cardiac output. Adrenaline and noradrenaline increase the force of cardiac contraction, by increasing the contractility of cardiac muscle fibres. Muscle fibres are elastic and can stretch during the diastolic phase of the cardiac cycle which allows a more complete filling of the heart and thus increases cardiac output. This relationship is known as **Starling's law** and there appears to be a linear relationship between cardiac output and exercise intensity (see fig 2.11c).

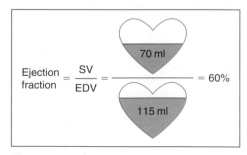

$$\text{Ejection fraction} = \frac{SV}{EDV} = \frac{70\,\text{ml}}{115\,\text{ml}} = 60\%$$

Fig 2.10. The ejection fraction

Using the text and fig 2.11, complete the table below: NB: Don't forget the units!

| Variable | Definition | Approximate resting value | Approximate exercise values |
|---|---|---|---|
| Heart rate | | | |
| Stroke volume | | | |
| Cardiac output | | | |

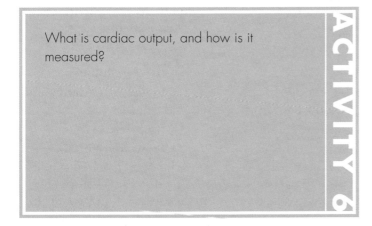

What is cardiac output, and how is it measured?

## The trained heart

We have examined how the heart responds and adjusts to exercise in the short time of an exercise session. Let us now turn our attention to the effects of long term training on the heart.

As mentioned above, the heart of an athlete is larger than that of a non-athlete and often displays greater vascularisation. **Cardiac hypertrophy** is characterised by a larger ventricular wall and a thicker myocardium. Endurance athletes tend to display larger ventricular cavities, while those following high resistance or strength training régimes display thicker ventricular walls.

Cardiac hypertrophy is accompanied by a decreased resting heart rate. This can easily be demonstrated by comparing the resting heart rates of trained and untrained people. When the heart rate falls below

60 bpm, **bradycardia** is said to have occurred, and is due to a slowing in the intrinsic rate of the atrial pacemaker (S.A. node) and an increase in the predominance of the parasympathetic system acting upon the pacemaker.

Some endurance athletes have recorded resting heart rates of below 30 bpm! Since the resting cardiac output for an athlete is approximately the same as that of a non-athlete, the athlete compensates for the lower resting heart rate by increasing stroke volume. This increased resting stroke volume is greatest among endurance athletes (as great as 200 ml/beat) due to the increased size of the ventricular cavity. The increase can also be as a result of improved contractility of the myocardium, which is highlighted by the increased **ejection fraction** reported by athletes. The ejection fraction represents the percentage of the blood entering the left ventricle which is actually pumped out per beat. It is calculated by dividing the stroke volume by the volume of blood in the ventricles at the end of the diastolic phase (EDV). On average this is approximately 60% but can reach 85% following training (see fig 2.10).

## The vascular system

Having examined how the heart works to pump the blood into the network of blood vessels, we will now take a closer look at how the blood supports the functioning of the body and how the blood vessels ensure that sufficient blood reaches the body's tissues.

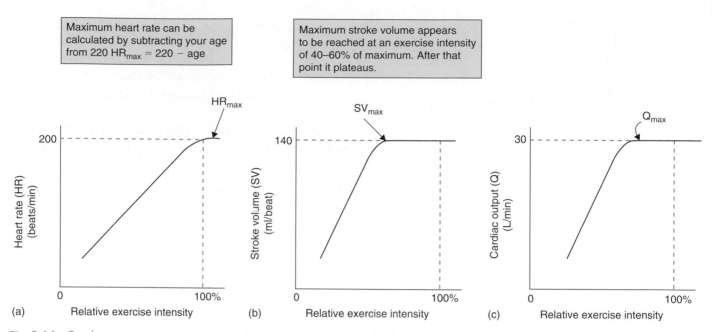

Maximum heart rate can be calculated by subtracting your age from 220 $HR_{max}$ = 220 − age

Maximum stroke volume appears to be reached at an exercise intensity of 40–60% of maximum. After that point it plateaus.

Fig 2.11. Cardiac responses to exercise (a) Heart rate response; (b) Stroke volume response; (c) Cardiac output response

# The blood

Blood consists of cells and cell fragments surrounded by a liquid known as **plasma**. The average male has a total blood volume of 5–6 L, and the average female blood volume is approximately 4–5 L.

## Functions of blood

The blood's functions are fundamental to life itself and include:

- transportation of nutrients such as glucose, and oxygen

- protection and fighting disease through the interaction with the lymphatic system

- the maintenance of homeostasis, including temperature regulation and maintenance of the acid–base (pH) balance.

The blood is responsible for transporting oxygen to the body's cells and removing metabolites such as carbon dioxide from the muscle to the lungs. The blood also transports glucose from the liver to the muscle, and lactic acid from the muscle to the liver where it can be converted back to glucose. Further functions include the transportation of enzymes,

hormones and other chemicals all of which have a vital role to play in the body, no more so than during exercise.

The blood protects the body by containing cells and chemicals which are central to the immune system. When damage to blood vessels occurs, the blood clots in order to prevent cell loss.

The blood is vital in maintaining the body's state of equilibrium; eg, through hormone and enzyme activity, and the buffering capacity of the blood, the blood's pH should remain relatively stable. In addition the blood is involved in temperature regulation and can transport heat to the surface of the body where it can be released. All these factors are particularly important during exercise to ensure optimal performance.

## Blood composition

- **Plasma** (55% of blood composition) – this is a pale yellow fluid composed of water (90%), proteins (8%) and salts (2%).

- **Erythrocytes** – these are red blood cells or corpuscles which contain **haemoglobin**, an iron-rich protein which is responsible for all the oxygen transport in the blood. The ability of the

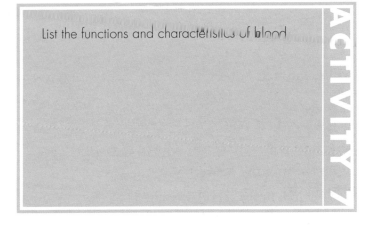

55% Plasma
(90% H₂O
7% plasma proteins
3% other)

45% Formed elements
(99% red blood cells
1% white blood cells +
Platelets)

Fig 2.12. The constituents of blood

blood to carry oxygen is determined by haemoglobin concentration, which may be increased through endurance training.

- **Leucocytes** – these are white blood cells, and are involved in combating infection. Although larger than red blood cells, white blood cells are fewer in number.

- **Thrombocytes** – thrombocytes or platelets are small bits of cytoplasm derived from the bone marrow, which play an important role in blood clotting, and so limit haemorrhaging.

## Blood viscosity

Viscosity refers to the thickness of the blood and its resistance to flow. The more viscous a fluid, the more resistant it is to flow. The greater the volume of red blood cells, the greater the capacity to transport oxygen. However, unless it is accompanied by an increase in plasma, viscosity may also increase, and restrict blood flow. Viscosity may also increase when plasma content decreases due to dehydration (which may accompany endurance-based exercise).

**Haematocrit** is the percentage of the total blood volume composed of red blood cells and typically varies between 40% and 45%.

- **Haemoconcentration** is an increase in the proportion of red blood cells in the blood, and is usually as a result of a decrease in blood plasma volume.

- **Haemodilution** is a decrease in red blood cell volume, due to an increase in plasma volume.

Training brings about an **increase in total blood volume**, and therefore an increase in the number of red blood cells. However, the plasma volume increases more than blood cell volume so the blood viscosity decreases. This facilitates blood flow through the blood vessels, and improves oxygen delivery to the working muscles.

List the functions and characteristics of blood

ACTIVITY

## Blood vessels

The vascular network through which blood flows to all parts of the body comprises arteries, arterioles, capillaries, veins and venules.

### Arteries and arterioles

Arteries are high pressure vessels which carry blood from the heart to the tissues. The largest artery in the body is the **aorta** which is the main artery leaving the heart. The aorta constantly subdivides and gets smaller. The constant subdivision decreases the diameter of the vessel arteries, which now become arterioles. As the network subdivides blood velocity decreases, which enables the efficient delivery and exchange of gases.

Arteries are composed of three layers of tissue:

1. an outer fibrous layer – the tunica adventitia or tunica externa

2. a thick middle layer – the tunica media

3. a thin lining of cells to the inside – the endothelium or tunica intima.

The tunica media comprises smooth muscle and elastic tissue, which enables the arteries and arterioles to alter their diameter. Arteries tend to have more elastic tissue, while arterioles have greater amounts of smooth muscle; this allows the vessels to increase the diameter through **vasodilation** or decrease the diameter through **vasoconstriction**. It is through vasoconstriction and vasodilation that the vessels can regulate blood pressure and ensure the tissues are receiving sufficient blood – particularly during exercise.

Arteries and arterioles have three basic functions:

- to act as conduits carrying and controlling blood flow to the tissues
- to cushion and smooth out the pulsatile flow of blood from the heart
- to help control blood pressure.

## Veins and venules

Veins are low pressure vessels which return blood to the heart. The structure is similar to arteries, although they possess less smooth muscle and elastic tissue. Venules are the smallest veins and transport blood away from the capillary bed into the veins. Veins gradually increase in thickness the nearer to the heart they get, until they reach the largest vein in the body, the **venae cavae**, which enters the right atrium of the heart.

The thinner walls of the veins often distend and allow blood to pool in them. This is also allowed to happen as the veins contain pocket valves which close intermittently to prevent back flow of blood. This explains why up to 70% of total blood volume is found in the venous system at any one time, at rest.

## Capillaries

Capillaries are the functional units or the vascular system. Composed of a single layer of endothelial

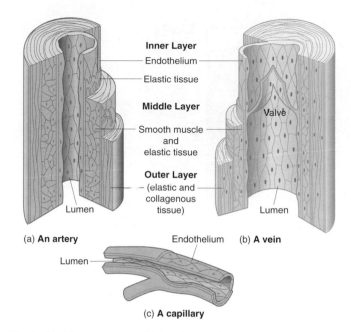

Fig 2.13. The structure of blood vessels
*Source:* Tortora (1991).

cells, they are just thin enough to allow red blood cells to squeeze through their wall. The capillary network is very well developed as they are so small; large quantities are able to cover the muscle, which ensures efficient exchange of gases. If the cross-sectional area of all the capillaries in the body were to be added together, the total area would be much greater than that of the aorta.

Distribution of blood through the capillary network is regulated by special structures known as **pre-capillary sphincters**, the structure of which will be dealt with later in this chapter.

# The circulatory system

The blood flows through a continuous network of blood vessels, which form a double circuit. This connects the heart to the lungs, and the heart to all other body tissues.

# The double circulatory system

**Pulmonary circulation** transports blood between the lungs and the heart. The pulmonary artery

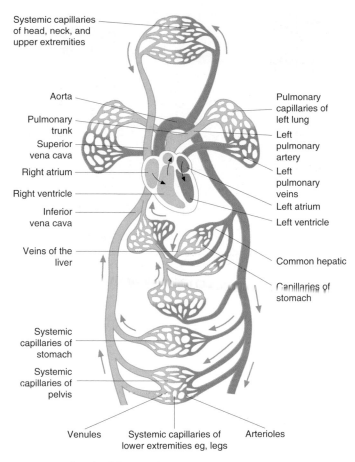

Systemic capillaries
of head, neck, and
upper extremities

Aorta

Pulmonary
trunk

Superior
vena cava

Right atrium

Right ventricle

Inferior
vena cava

Veins of the
liver

Systemic
capillaries of
stomach

Systemic
capillaries of
pelvis

Pulmonary
capillaries of
left lung

Left
pulmonary
artery

Left
pulmonary
veins

Left atrium

Left ventricle

Common hepatic

Capillaries of
stomach

Venules    Systemic capillaries of    Arterioles
lower extremities eg, legs

Fig 2.14. The double circulatory system

carries blood low in oxygen concentration from the right ventricle to the lung, where it becomes oxygen-rich and unloads carbon dioxide. The pulmonary vein then transports the freshly oxygenated blood back to the heart and into the left atrium.

The blood returning to the left atrium is pumped through the left side of the heart and into the aorta, where it is distributed to the whole of the body's tissues by a network of arteries. Veins then return the blood, which is now low in oxygen and high in carbon dioxide concentration, to the heart where it enters the right atrium via the venae cavae. This circuit is known as **systemic circulation**.

## The venous return mechanism

Venous return is the term used for the blood which returns to the right side of the heart via the veins. As mentioned earlier, up to 70% of the total volume of blood is contained in the veins at rest. This provides a large reservoir of blood which is returned rapidly to the heart when needed. The heart can only pump out as much blood as it receives, so cardiac output is dependent upon venous return. A rapid increase in venous return enables a significant increase in cardiac output due to Starling's law.

There are several mechanisms which aid the venous return process:

- **The muscle pump** – As exercise begins, muscular contractions impinge and compress upon the veins, squeezing blood towards the heart. Pocket valves inside the veins prevent any backflow of blood that might occur. This is illustrated in fig 2.15.

Copy out the table below and write a short explanation in each box.

| Vessel | Brief outline of vessel structure | Function of each vessel |
|---|---|---|
| Arteries/arterioles | | |
| Capillaries | | |
| Veins/venules | | |

ACTIVITY 8

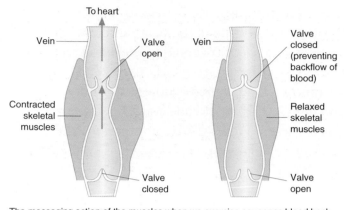

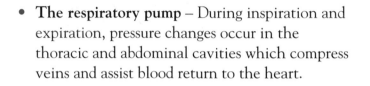

The massaging action of the muscles when we exercise squeezes blood back towards the heart increasing venous return and therefore cardiac output.

Fig 2.15. The muscle pump and venous return

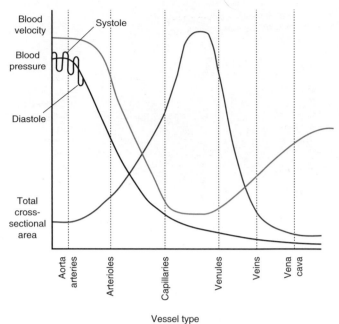

Fig 2.16. The relationship between blood vessel type, total cross-sectional area, blood velocity and blood pressure

- **The respiratory pump** – During inspiration and expiration, pressure changes occur in the thoracic and abdominal cavities which compress veins and assist blood return to the heart.

These two mechanisms are essential at the start of exercise. As exercise commences the muscles contracting squeeze the vast amount of blood within the veins back towards the heart to enable stroke volume to increase and optimal delivery of nutrients to the working muscles.

## A E Blood pressure

Blood pressure is the force exerted by the blood against the walls of the blood vessels. It is necessary to maintain blood flow through the circulatory system and is determined by two main factors:

1. Cardiac output – the volume of blood flowing into the system from the left ventricle.

2. Resistance to flow – the opposition offered by the blood vessels to the blood flow. This is dependent upon several factors including blood viscosity, blood vessel length and blood vessel radius.

**Blood pressure = Cardiac output × Resistance**

Therefore, blood pressure increases when either cardiac output or resistance increases.

Blood pressure in the arteries also increases and decreases in a pattern which corresponds to the cardiac cycle during ventricular systole. It is highest when blood is pumped into the aorta and lowest during ventricular diastole.

Blood pressure is usually measured at the brachial artery using a **sphygmomanometer**, and is recorded as millimetres of mercury (mmHg) of systolic pressure over diastolic pressure:

- **Systolic** pressure is experienced when the heart pumps blood into the system.
- **Diastolic** pressure is recorded when the heart is relaxing and filling with blood.

The typical reading for a male at rest is:

$$\frac{120 \text{ mmHg}}{80 \text{ mmHg}} = \frac{\text{Systolic}}{\text{Diastolic}}$$

During exercise, blood pressure changes and is dependent upon the type and intensity of the

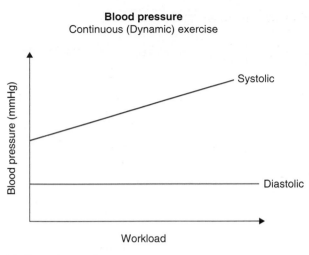

(a) Dynamic exercise

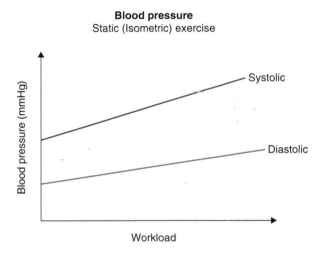

(b) Static (Isometric) exercise

Fig 2.17. The effects of exercise upon both systolic and diastolic blood pressure

exercise being performed. During steady aerobic exercise involving large muscle groups, the systolic pressure increases as a result of an increased cardiac output, while diastolic pressure remains constant, or in well trained athletes, may even drop as blood feeds into the working muscles due to increased arteriole dilation. The increased systolic pressure associated with exercise is largely the result of increased cardiac output associated with an increased intensity. This ensures that adequate blood is supplied to the working muscle quickly. During high intensity isometric and anaerobic exercise, both systolic and diastolic

pressure rise significantly due to increased resistance of the blood vessels. This is a result of muscles squeezing the veins, increasing peripheral resistance and an increase in intra-thoracic pressure due to the contraction of the abdominals. When weight lifting for example, competitors often hold their breath during exertion which causes a significant increase in both systolic and diastolic pressure.

It is essential that blood pressure is regulated and where possible at rest maintained within a normal range. High blood pressure can cause serious complications to the heart, brain and kidneys whereas low pressure can result in insufficient oxygen and other nutrients reaching the muscle cells.

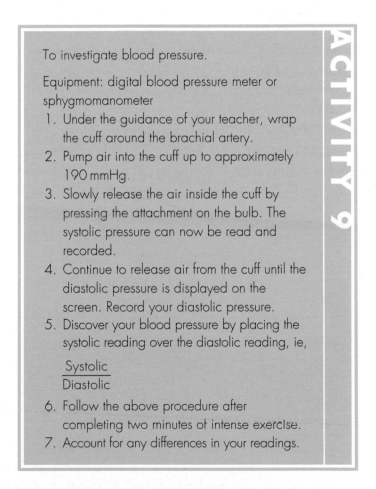

To investigate blood pressure.

Equipment: digital blood pressure meter or sphygmomanometer
1. Under the guidance of your teacher, wrap the cuff around the brachial artery.
2. Pump air into the cuff up to approximately 190 mmHg.
3. Slowly release the air inside the cuff by pressing the attachment on the bulb. The systolic pressure can now be read and recorded.
4. Continue to release air from the cuff until the diastolic pressure is displayed on the screen. Record your diastolic pressure.
5. Discover your blood pressure by placing the systolic reading over the diastolic reading, ie,

   Systolic
   _____
   Diastolic
6. Follow the above procedure after completing two minutes of intense exercise.
7. Account for any differences in your readings.

ACTIVITY 9

The vasomotor control centre outlined in the following section is responsible for regulating blood pressure.

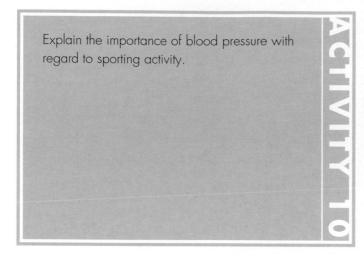

Explain the importance of blood pressure with regard to sporting activity.

*ACTIVITY 10*

If you have access to a programme such as Excel, using the data in Table 2.2, construct a pie chart to show the relative distribution of blood at rest and during maximal effort.
(If you do not have access to such a programme you could simply draw a pie chart.)

*ACTIVITY 11*

## Redistribution of blood during exercise

Blood flow changes dramatically once exercise commences. At rest, only 15–20% of cardiac output is directed to skeletal muscle; the majority goes to the liver (27%) and kidneys (22%). During exercise however, blood is redirected to areas where it is most needed. For example, during exhaustive exercise the working muscles may receive over 80% of cardiac output. This increased blood flow to the muscle results from a restriction of blood flow to the kidneys, liver and stomach. This process is known as **shunting** or **accommodation**.

## Vasomotor control

The redistribution of blood is controlled primarily by the **vasoconstriction** and **vasodilation** of arterioles. It reacts to chemical changes of the local tissues. For example, vasodilation will occur when arterioles sense a decrease in oxygen concentration or an increase in acidity due to higher $CO_2$ and lactic acid concentrations. When embarking upon a distance run, the increased metabolic activity increases the amount of carbon dioxide and lactic acid in the blood. This is detected by chemoreceptors and sympathetic nerves stimulate the blood vessel size to change

Table 2.2. Blood flow changes during exercise in $cm^3/min$

| Organ | At rest ($cm^3$) | % Blood flow | Maximum effort ($cm^3$) | % Blood flow |
|---|---|---|---|---|
| Skeletal muscle | 1,000 | 20 | 26,000 | 88 |
| Coronary vessels | 250 | 5 | 1,200 | 4 |
| Skin | 500 | 10 | 750 | 2.5 |
| Kidneys | 1,000 | 20 | 300 | 1 |
| Liver/gut | 1,250 | 25 | 375 | 1.25 |
| Brain | 750 | 15 | 750 | 2.5 |
| Whole body | 5,000 | 100 | 30,000 | 100 |

*Source*: Clegg, *Exercise Physiology*, Feltham Press 1995.

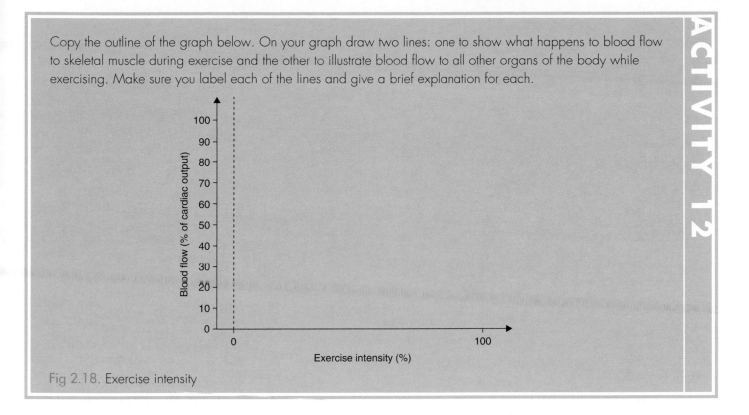

Copy the outline of the graph below. On your graph draw two lines: one to show what happens to blood flow to skeletal muscle during exercise and the other to illustrate blood flow to all other organs of the body while exercising. Make sure you label each of the lines and give a brief explanation for each.

Fig 2.18. Exercise intensity

shape. Vasodilation will then allow a greater blood flow, bringing the much needed oxygen and flushing away the harmful waste products of metabolism.

Sympathetic nerves also play a major role in redistributing blood from one area of the body to another. The smooth muscle layer (tunica media) of the blood vessels is controlled by the sympathetic nervous system, and remains in a state of slight contraction known as **vasomotor tone**. By increasing sympathetic stimulation, vasoconstriction occurs and blood flow is restricted and redistributed to areas of greater need. When stimulation by sympathetic nerves decreases, vasodilation is allowed which will increase blood flow to that body part.

Further structures which aid blood redistribution are **pre-capillary sphincters**. Pre-capillary sphincters are ring shaped muscles which lie at the opening of capillaries and control blood flow into the capillary bed. When the sphincter contracts, it restricts blood flow through the capillary, and deprives tissues of

oxygen; conversely when it relaxes, it increases blood flow to the capillary bed. These are illustrated in fig 2.20.

- Name the major blood vessels in the body, beginning with those affecting the heart. In each case, state how the structure is suited to their function.
- Explain how vasoconstriction and vasodilation function in the body and how they can affect the athlete while exercising.
- What are the major differences between the heart of a trained athlete and that of an untrained person?
- Discuss how the vasomotor centre operates.

## The pulse rate

The pulse is a pressure wave which is generated from the heart each time the left ventricle pumps blood into the aorta. The increased pressure causes

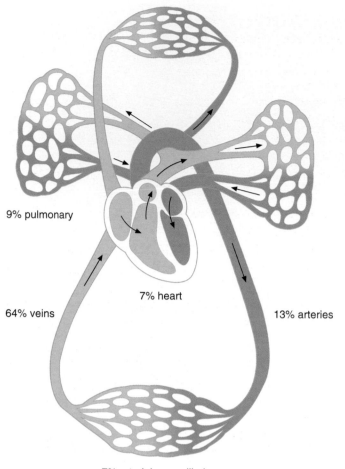

9% pulmonary

7% heart

64% veins

13% arteries

7% arterioles, capillaries

Fig 2.19. The distribution of blood in the body at rest

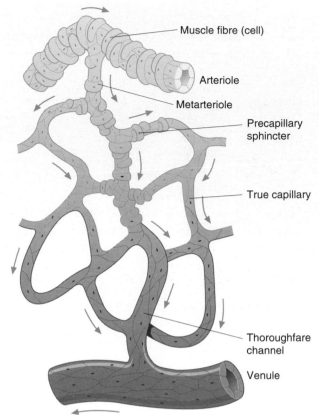

Muscle fibre (cell)

Arteriole

Metarteriole

Precapillary sphincter

True capillary

Thoroughfare channel

Venule

Fig 2.20. A precapillary sphincter

slight dilation of the arteries as the blood travels through them around the body and this can be felt at various sites on the body. The most common sites where the pulse can be palpated are:

- the radial artery
- the carotid artery
- the femoral artery
- the brachial artery
- the temporal artery.

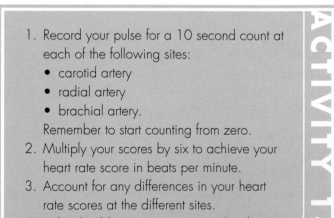

**ACTIVITY 14**

1. Record your pulse for a 10 second count at each of the following sites:
   - carotid artery
   - radial artery
   - brachial artery.
   Remember to start counting from zero.
2. Multiply your scores by six to achieve your heart rate score in beats per minute.
3. Account for any differences in your heart rate scores at the different sites.
4. Why should you never use your thumb to measure your pulse?

An investigation to examine heart rate response to varying intensities of exercise.

Equipment: stop watch, gymnastics bench, metronome

1. Record resting heart rate for a 10 second count at the beginning of the class.
2. Record heart rate for a 10 second count at the carotid artery immediately prior to exercise.
3. Start exercising by stepping onto and off the bench at a low intensity, keeping in time with the metronome.
4. Record your pulse after one, two and three minutes of exercise. After the third minute of exercise, stop the test. Continue to record your pulse each minute during recovery.
5. Once your heart rate has returned to its resting value (or within a few beats) repeat the test at a medium intensity. Record your results as before.
6. Repeat the exercise for a third time but at a very high intensity. Once again record your results.
7. Convert your heart rate scores into beats per minute by multiplying by six.
8. Now use your results to plot a graph for each of the three workloads. Plot each graph using the same axes, placing heart rate along the 'Y' axis and time along the bottom 'X' axis. Don't forget to show your resting heart rate values on the graph.
9. For each of your graphs explain the heart rate patterns prior to, during and following exercise.

| Time | Exercise intensity | | |
|---|---|---|---|
| | Low | Med | High |
| Resting HR | | | |
| HR prior to exercise | | | |
| Exercise 1 min | | | |
| Exercise 2 min | | | |
| Exercise 3 min | | | |
| Recovery 1 min | | | |
| Recovery 2 min | | | |
| Recovery 3 min | | | |
| Recovery 4 min | | | |
| Recovery 5 min | | | |
| Recovery 6 min | | | |
| Recovery 7 min | | | |

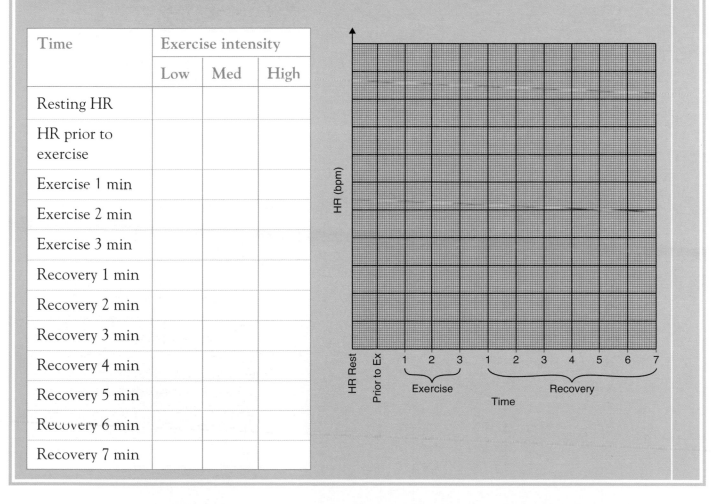

# ACTIVITY 16

Using fig 2.21 account for the different patterns in heart rate for sub-maximal and maximal exercise.

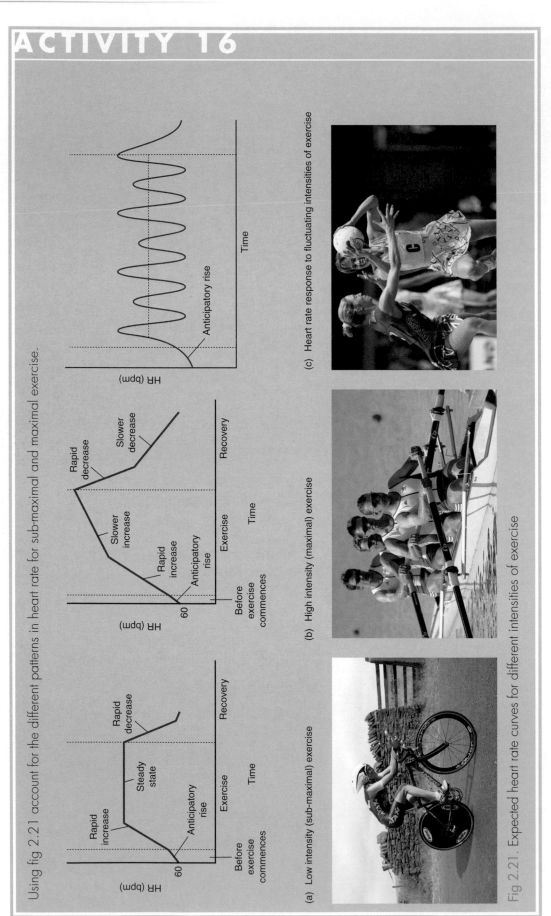

(a) Low intensity (sub-maximal) exercise

(b) High intensity (maximal) exercise

(c) Heart rate response to fluctuating intensities of exercise

Fig 2.21. Expected heart rate curves for different intensities of exercise

Wearing a heart rate monitor, participate in an invasion game of your choice for at least 15 minutes (eg, netball, football, basketball). Don't forget to record your resting heart rate – and your heart rate immediately prior to the start.

At a maximum of 3 minute intervals record your heart rate for the duration of the game.
NB: The longer you participate in the game the better!!

Copy out and complete the table and graph below.

| Time | Heart rate |
|------|-----------|
| Rest | |
| Prior to exercise | |
| 1 | |
| 2 | |
| 3 | |
| 4 | |
| 5 | |
| 6 | |
| 7 | |
| 8 | |
| 9 | |
| 10 | |
| 11 | |
| 12 | |
| 13 | |
| 14 | |
| 15 | |

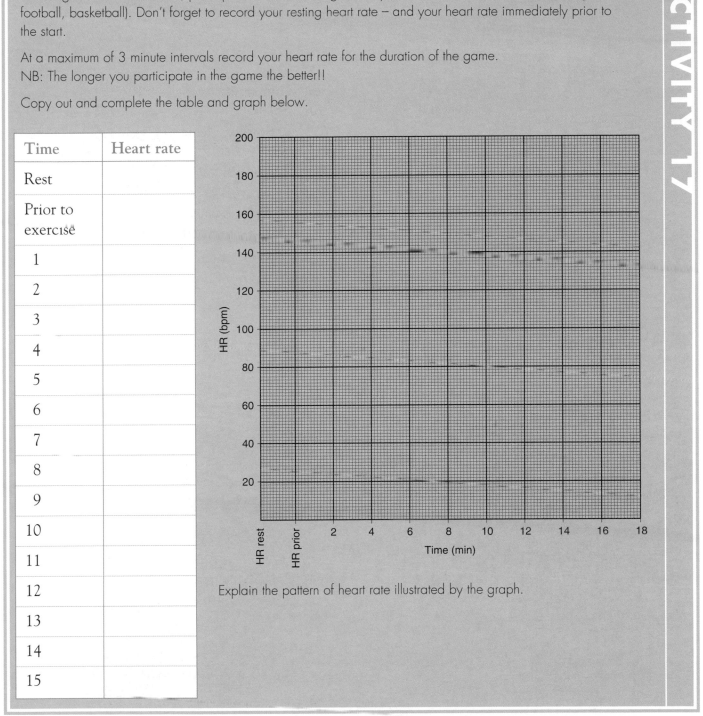

Explain the pattern of heart rate illustrated by the graph.

Complete the table below showing the responses of the cardiovascular system to exercise, giving a brief explanation for each. The heart rate response has been completed as an example.

| Factor | Increase/decrease | Explanation |
|---|---|---|
| Heart rate | ↑ increase | During sub-maximal exercise HR increases rapidly at first and then plateaus into steady state, where oxygen demand is being met by supply.<br>During maximal exercise HR increases proportionally with exercise intensity until a maximum level is reached. This will also be the point of $\bar{V}O_2$ max.<br>The release of hormones such as adrenaline and noradrenaline cause the increase in heart rate. |
| Stroke volume | | |
| Cardiac output | | |
| Blood pressure | | |
| Blood flow to working muscles | | |
| a-$\bar{V}O_2$ diff | | |
| Blood acidity | | |
| Parasympathetic activity | | |
| Sympathetic activity | | |

**ACTIVITY 18**

# Summary

- The structure of the heart is specially adapted to its function.
- Valves within the heart ensure a unidirectional flow of blood.
- The sounds of the heart are a result of these valves snapping shut. The lub sound results from the closing of the atrioventricular valves, while the dub results from the closure of the semi-lunar valves.

- Typically the heart is composed of three layers: an outer pericardium, a thick muscular layer called the myocardium, and a smooth inner endocardium.

- Coronary arteries ensure the heart receives an adequate supply of blood.

- The cardiac cycle explains the passage of blood through the heart. It consists of four stages: Atrial Diastole, Atrial Systole, Ventricular Diastole and Ventricular Systole.

- The heart is myogenic – it creates its own impulses.

- The impulse is emitted from the S.A. node, the surrounding fibres are innervated causing the atria to contract. The impulse eventually arrives at the A.V. node, where it is dispersed down the bundle of His and throughout the Purkinje fibres, causing the ventricles to contract.

- The heart rate is governed by the parasympathetic and sympathetic nervous systems. The sympathetic nervous system increases heart rate by releasing adrenaline and noradrenaline, while the parasympathetic nervous system slows the heart down through the action of another hormone, acetylcholine.

- Increases in heart rate during exercise are largely the result of increased metabolic activity increasing the concentration of carbon dioxide.

- Cardiac output is the volume of blood pumped out of one ventricle in one minute. Stroke volume is the volume of blood pumped out of one ventricle in one beat, and heart rate the number of times the heart beats per minute.

- Cardiac hypertrophy is the enlargement of the heart often resulting from endurance training.

- Bradycardia is the reduction in resting heart rate (usually below 60 bpm) which accompanies cardiac hypertrophy.

- The vascular system encompasses the blood and blood vessels.

- The blood's main functions are the transportation of oxygen and the maintenance of homeostasis.

- Typically blood is composed of plasma (water, proteins and salts) erythrocytes, leucocytes and thrombocytes.

- Major blood vessels consist of arteries, arterioles, capillaries, venules and veins.

- The continuous network of blood vessels in the body is known as the circulatory system, which is composed of the pulmonary and systemic circuits.

- Blood returning to the heart via the veins is known as venous return. It is aided by the muscle and respiratory pumps.

- Blood pressure is the force exerted by the blood on the inner walls of the blood vessels. It is a product of cardiac output and resistance of the vessel walls.

- Blood flow is controlled by the vasomotor centre which causes blood vessels to vasodilate and vasoconstrict and determines the degree of blood reaching various parts of the body.

# Review Questions

1. Describe the path that blood takes through the heart, from the point at which it enters via the venae cavae to where it exits via the aorta.

2. When using a stethoscope, is it possible to hear the heart beating? What creates the heartbeat and when do these sounds occur during the cardiac cycle?

3. Describe the action of the sympathetic and parasympathetic nervous system on the heart before, during and following exercise.

4. Outline the major functions of the blood. Explain the importance of blood when exercising.

5. Sketch and label a graph showing the heart rate pattern expected from an athlete completing a 400 m run in a personal best time of 45 seconds followed by a 15-minute recovery period. Account for these changes.

6. Outline the major factors which affect cardiac output during exercise.

7. During exercise the return of blood to the heart is paramount. Explain how the body achieves this and relate to Starling's law.

8. Explain what you would expect to happen to blood pressure in the following instances: (a) an athlete undertaking a steady swim (b) an athlete completing a 100 m sprint (c) a weight lifter performing a maximal lift (d) an athlete completing the cycling stage of a triathlon.

9. Endurance training results in significant benefits to the heart and vascular system. What are these benefits and how do they contribute to a 'healthier lifestyle'?

# 3. The Respiratory System – Oxygen Supply and Transport

## Chapter introduction

During exercise the body requires oxygen to produce energy to fuel muscular contraction. It is the role of the respiratory system to ensure that sufficient oxygen is taken into the body and transferred to the body's tissues to satisfy the demand. Likewise the respiratory system is responsible for ensuring adequate removal of waste products such as carbon dioxide and lactic acid.

This chapter examines the structure and function of the respiratory system, including detail on the lungs and the respiratory airways. It also looks at the mechanics of breathing, the process of inspiration and expiration and definitions of lung volumes and capacities. Simple investigations of measurement of these volumes are also included.

The chapter studies gaseous exchange, partial pressures and the transport of gases in the body; factors that may influence oxygen delivery and uptake; and oxygen consumption and the response of the respiratory system to training. Links can be made to other chapters of the book, particularly chapters 6 and 7, on fitness and training.

## External respiration

External respiration involves the movement of gases into and out of the lungs and the exchange of gases between the lungs and the blood is known as pulmonary diffusion.

On its journey to the lungs, air drawn into the body passes many structures as outlined below.

### Nasal passages

Air is drawn into the body via the nose. The nasal cavity is divided by a cartilaginous septum, forming the nasal passages. The interior structures of the nose help the respiratory process by performing the following important functions:

1. the mucous membranes and blood capillaries moisten and warm the inspired air

2. the ciliated epithelium filters and traps dust particles which are moved to the throat for elimination

3. the small bones known as chonchae increase the surface area of the cavity to make the process more efficient.

### The oral pharynx and larynx

The throat is shared by both the respiratory and alimentary tract. Air entering the larynx passes over the vocal chords and into the trachea. In swallowing, the larynx is drawn upwards and forwards against the base of the epiglottis, thus preventing entry of food.

### The trachea

The trachea or windpipe is approximately 10 cm in length and lies in front of the oesophagus. It is composed of 18 horseshoe-shaped rings of cartilage which are also lined by a mucous membrane and ciliated cells which provide the same protection against dust as the nasal passageways. The trachea extends from the larynx and directs air into the right and left primary bronchi.

### The bronchi and bronchioles

The trachea divides into the right and left bronchus which further subdivide into lobar bronchi (three feeding each lobe on the right, two feeding each

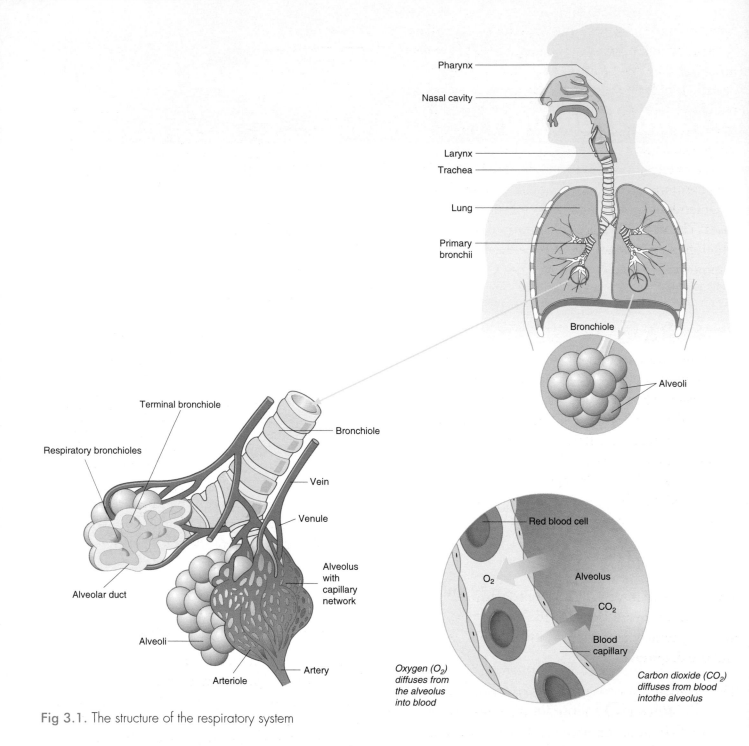

Fig 3.1. The structure of the respiratory system

lobe on the left). Further subdivision of these airways form bronchioles which in turn branch into the smaller terminal or respiratory bronchioles. The bronchioles enable the air to pass into the alveoli via the alveolar ducts, and it is here that pulmonary diffusion occurs.

## Alveoli

The alveoli are responsible for the exchange of gases between the lungs and the blood. The alveolar walls are extremely thin and are composed of epithelial cells which are lined by a thin film of water, essential for dissolving oxygen from the inspired air.

Surrounding each alveolus is an extensive capillary network which ensures a smooth passage of oxygen into the pulmonary capillaries. The tiny lumen of each capillary surrounding the alveoli ensure that red blood cells travel in single file, and that they are squeezed into a bi-concave shape increasing the surface area and enabling the greatest possible uptake of oxygen. It has been estimated that each lung contains up to 150 million alveoli, providing a tremendous surface area for the exchange of gases. The alveoli walls also contain elastic fibres which further increase the surface during inspiration

# Breathing mechanics

The lungs are surrounded by pleural sacs containing pleural fluid which reduces friction during respiration. These sacs are attached to both the lungs and the thoracic cage, which enables the lungs to inflate and deflate as the chest expands and flattens. The interrelationship between the lungs, pleural sacs and thoracic cage are central to the understanding of the respiratory processes of inspiration and expiration.

## Inspiration

The process of inspiration is an active one. It occurs as a result of the contraction of the respiratory muscles, namely the **external intercostal** muscles and the **diaphragm**.

The external intercostal muscles are attached to each rib. When they contract, they cause the rib cage to pivot about thoracic vertebral joints and move upwards and outwards, much like the handle of a bucket as it is lifted. The diaphragm, a dome-shaped muscle separating the abdominal and thoracic cavities, contracts downwards during inspiration, increasing the area of the thoracic cavity. As the chest expands through these muscular contractions, the surface tension created by the film of pleural fluid causes the lungs to be pulled outwards along with the chest walls. This

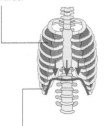

**a) Inspiration**

External intercostal muscles cause the rib cage to pivot on the thoracic vertebrae and move upwards and outwards.

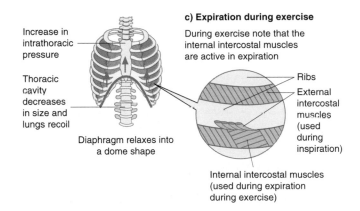

External intercostal muscles contract and swings ribs upwards

Sternum

Spine

Diaphragm contracts downwards, increasing the 'depth' of the thoracic cavity.

**b) Expiration at rest**

Relaxation of respiratory muscles cause the rib cage to move downwards and inwards.

Increase in intrathoracic pressure

Thoracic cavity decreases in size and lungs recoil

Diaphragm relaxes into a dome shape

**c) Expiration during exercise**

During exercise note that the internal intercostal muscles are active in expiration

Ribs

External intercostal muscles (used during inspiration)

Internal intercostal muscles (used during expiration during exercise)

Fig 3.2. Action of the rib cage during a) inspiration and b) expiration

action causes the space within the lungs to increase and the air molecules within to move further apart.

As pressure is determined by the rate at which molecules strike a surface in a given time, the pressure within the lungs (intrapulmonary pressure) decreases and becomes less than that outside the body. Gases always move from areas of higher pressure to areas of lower pressure, so that air from outside the body rushes into the lungs via the respiratory tract. This process is known as **inspiration**.

During exercise, greater volumes of air can fill the lungs since the **sternocleido-mastoid** and **scaleni** muscles can help increase the thoracic cavity still further.

## Expiration

The process of expiration is generally a passive process and occurs as a result of the relaxation of the respiratory muscles used in inspiration. As the external intercostal muscles relax, the rib cage is lowered into its resting position, and the diaphragm relaxes and domes up into the thoracic cavity. The area of the lungs is thus decreased and intrapulmonary pressure increases to an extent where it is greater than atmospheric pressure. Air inside the lungs is forced out to equate the pressure inside and outside the body.

During exercise, the process of expiration becomes more active as the **internal intercostal** muscles pull the ribs downwards to help increase the ventilation rate. These muscles are ably assisted by the **abdominals** and the **latissimus dorsi** muscles.

---

**ACTIVITY 1**

- Complete the table below naming the muscles responsible for inspiration and expiration at rest and during exercise.
- How might training affect these muscles?

|  | Rest | Exercise |
|---|---|---|
| Inspiration |  |  |
| Expiration |  |  |

---

# Pulmonary diffusion

Pulmonary diffusion is the term used to explain the process of gaseous exchange in the lungs. It has two major functions:

1. to replenish the blood with oxygen where it can then be transported to the tissues and muscles

2. to remove carbon dioxide from the blood which has resulted from metabolic processes in the tissues.

## Partial pressure of gases

Central to the understanding of gaseous exchange is the concept of partial pressure. The partial pressure of a gas is the **individual pressure that the gas exerts when it occurs in a mixture of gases**. The gas will exert a pressure proportional to its concentration within the whole gas. Thus the partial pressures of each individual gas within a mixture of gases should, when added together, be equal to the total pressure of the gas.

For example, the air we breathe is composed of three main gases: nitrogen (79%), oxygen (20.9%) and carbon dioxide (0.03%). The percentages show the relative concentrations of each gas in atmospheric air.

At sea level, total atmospheric pressure is 769 mmHg which reflects the pressure that atmospheric air exerts. For example:

- The concentration of $O_2$ (oxygen) in the atmosphere is approximately 21%

- The concentration of nitrogen in the air is approximately 79%

- Together they exert a pressure of 760 mmHg at sea level.

Therefore the $pO_2$ (partial pressure of oxygen) is calculated as:

$$pO_2 = \text{Barometric pressure} \times \text{fractional concentration}$$
$$= 760 \times 0.21$$
$$= 159.6 \text{ mmHg}$$

Partial pressure of gases explain the movement of gases within the body, and account for the processes of gas exchange between the alveoli and the blood, and between the blood and the muscle or tissue.

---

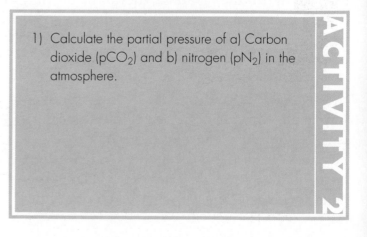

**ACTIVITY 2**

1) Calculate the partial pressure of a) Carbon dioxide ($pCO_2$) and b) nitrogen ($pN_2$) in the atmosphere.

# Gaseous exchange at the lungs

It is the imbalance between gases in the alveoli and the blood that causes a pressure gradient, which results in a movement of gases across the respiratory membrane (which facilitates this movement by being extremely thin, measuring only 0.5 mm). This movement is two-way, with oxygen moving from the alveoli into the blood and carbon dioxide diffusing from the blood into the alveoli. The partial pressure of oxygen ($pO_2$) in the atmosphere is approximately 159 mmHg ($0.21 \times 760$ mmHg), which drops to 105 mmHg in the alveoli since the air combines with water vapour and carbon dioxide which is already present in the alveoli.

## The diffusion gradient

Blood in the pulmonary capillaries which surround the alveoli has a $pO_2$ of 45 mmHg, since much of the oxygen has been already used by the working muscles. This results in a pressure gradient of approximately 60 mmHg which forces oxygen from the alveoli into the blood, until such a time that the pressure is equal on each side of the membrane.

In the same way, carbon dioxide moves along a pressure gradient from the pulmonary capillaries into the alveoli. With a $pCO_2$ of 45 mmHg in the blood returning to the lungs and a $pCO_2$ of 40 mmHg in the alveolar air, a small pressure gradient of 5 mmHg results. This causes $CO_2$ to move from the pulmonary blood into the alveoli, which is later expired. Although the pressure gradient is relatively small, the $CO_2$ can cross the respiratory membrane much more rapidly than oxygen, as its membrane solubility is 20 times greater.

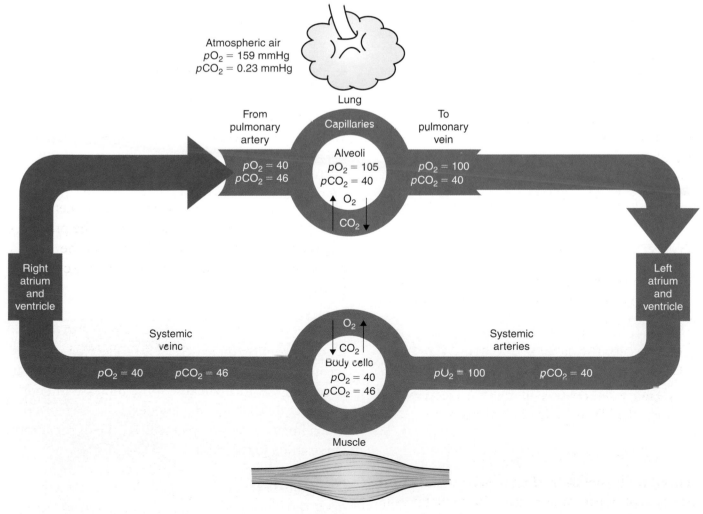

**Fig 3.3.** Partial pressures of oxygen and carbon dioxide at various sites in the body

Endurance athletes, with larger aerobic capacities, will have greater oxygen diffusion ability (the rate at which oxygen diffuses into the pulmonary blood from the alveoli) as a result of increased cardiac output, increased alveoli surface area, and reduced resistance to diffusion.

## E O The effect of altitude

With altitude there is a decrease in atmospheric pressure but the percentages of gases within the air remains identical to that at sea level (nitrogen 79%, oxygen 20.9%, carbon dioxide 0.03%). However, it is the partial pressure of the gases that changes in direct proportion to an increase in altitude.

For example: at rest the $pO_2$ of arterial blood is approximately 100 mmHg while that in resting muscles and tissues is 40 mmHg. The difference between the two indicates the pressure gradient and ensures an efficient movement of oxygen from the blood into the muscle. The $pO_2$ of arterial blood at an altitude of 8,000 ft drops significantly to approximately 60 mmHg while that in the muscles remains at 40 mmHg causing the pressure gradient to fall to 20 mmHg at altitude. This dramatic reduction in the pressure gradient reduces the movement of oxygen into the body's muscles and performance decreases.

Many endurance athletes often undertake a period of altitude training before major events. The reasons and benefits of such training are discussed later in chapter 6.

> • Explain what is meant by the partial pressure of a gas.
> • State how this affects gaseous exchange around the body.
> • What happens to the partial pressure of oxygen ($pO_2$) and carbon dioxide ($pCO_2$) in the muscle cell during exercise?
>
> ACTIVITY 3

# The transport of oxygen

The majority of oxygen is carried by the red blood cells combined with **haemoglobin**; this is an iron-based protein which chemically combines with oxygen to form **oxyhaemoglobin**.

$$\text{Haemoglobin} + \text{Oxygen} \rightarrow \text{Oxyhaemoglobin}$$
$$\text{Hb} + O_2 \rightarrow HbO_2$$

Each molecule of haemoglobin can combine with four molecules of oxygen, which amounts to approximately 1.34 ml. The concentration of haemoglobin in the blood is about 15 g per 100 ml, thus each 100 ml of blood can transport up to 20 ml of oxygen (1.34 × 15). However, the amount of oxygen that can combine with haemoglobin is determined by the partial pressure of oxygen ($pO_2$). A high $pO_2$ results in complete haemoglobin saturation, while at lower $pO_2$, haemoglobin saturation decreases.

Haemoglobin is almost 100% saturated with oxygen at a $pO_2$ of 100 mmHg (which is the $pO_2$ in the alveoli). Therefore, at the lungs, haemoglobin is totally saturated with oxygen, and even if more oxygen were available, it could not be transported. As the $pO_2$ is reduced, haemoglobin saturation decreases accordingly. This is largely due to the increased acidity of the blood (decrease in blood pH), caused by an increase in $CO_2$ content or lactic acid, and causes a shift in the haemoglobin saturation curve to the right. This is known as the **Bohr shift**, and explains how oxygen is dissociated from haemoglobin at lower pH values in order to feed the tissues.

During exercise, increased $CO_2$ production causes a greater dissociation of oxygen due to the decrease in muscle pH. A further cause is the increase in body temperature that accompanies exercise; as oxygen unloading becomes more effective, the dissociation curve shifts to the right.

To summarise, endurance performance is reliant upon the quick and effective dissociation of

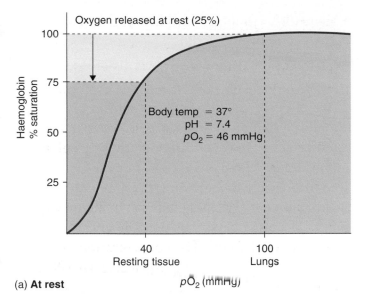

(a) **At rest**

At rest the $pO_2$ in the alveoli is approximately 100 mmHg. At this point the haemoglobin is almost 100% saturated with oxygen. In resting muscles and tissues the $pO_2$ is approximately 40 mmHg. At this point haemoglobin is only 75% saturated with oxygen. This means that 25% of the oxygen picked up at the lungs is released into the muscle to help in energy production

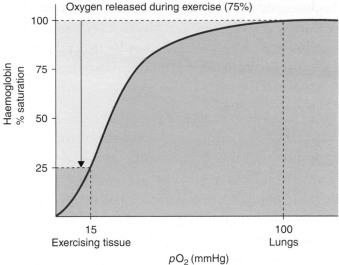

(b) **During exercise**

During exercise the $pO_2$ in the alveoli remains at approximately 100 mmHg with almost 100% haemoglobin saturation. In working muscles the $pO_2$ can be greatly reduced when compared to resting figures. The diagram shows a $pO_2$ in working muscles of 15 mmHg. This represents an oxy-haemoglobin saturation of 25% meaning that 75% of the oxygen picked up at the lungs is released into the muscle to help meet the extra energy demands.

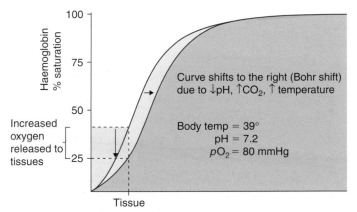

(c) **The Bohr shift**

During exercise there is an increase in the production of carbon dioxide in the muscle cell raising the $pCO_2$. As a result of this and increases in the concentration of lactic acid, blood acidity increases causing a fall in the pH. Energy produced in the muscle cell increases temperature. These factors cause a shift in the curve to the right (known as the Bohr shift) which results in an increased release of oxygen.

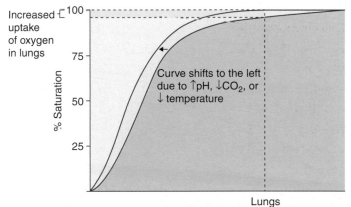

(d) **Following exercise**

Once exercise ceases we see an increase in blood pH, a decrease in $pCO_2$ and a decrease in temperature in the lungs. The curve shifts to the left returning to its resting position. It results in an increased ability of haemoglobin to pick up oxygen at the lungs.

Fig 3.4. The oxygen–haemoglobin dissociation curve

oxygen from haemoglobin which in turn is dependent upon four factors:

- A fall in the $pO_2$ within the muscle
- An increase in blood and muscle temperature
- An increase in the $pCO_2$ within the muscle
- A fall in pH due to the production of lactic acid.

The overall efficiency of oxygen transport is therefore dependent upon haemoglobin content, and many athletes have sought to increase haemoglobin content through the illegal practice of **blood doping**. By removing blood which is subsequently replaced by the body, the athlete reinfuses it, to increase blood volume and more importantly haemoglobin content. Results of research on the practice of blood doping are conflicting, and it should always be remembered that it is illegal under the current Olympic Committee doping rules.

More recently the preferred cheater's drug has been **EPO** – a synthetic version of **erythropoietin**, a glycoprotein that occurs naturally in the body and stimulates the production of red blood cells. The drug's advantages are that it can increase the oxygen carrying capacity of the blood and therefore improve endurance performance. But EPO has a potentially fatal side, as well as being illegal for competition, it is expensive and several top cyclists have died following misuse of the drug. Thankfully a new test has recently become available to detect use of this potentially fatal drug.

> ## ACTIVITY 4
>
> 1. During resting conditions approximately 5 ml of oxygen is transported to the tissues in each 100 ml of blood. We know from earlier discussions that cardiac output at rest is approximately 5000 ml/min. Calculate how much oxygen is delivered to the tissues each minute.
> 2. During exercise the oxygen transport can be increased by up to three times due to the greater release of oxygen from haemoglobin. In addition, the rate of oxygen transport can increase five-fold due to the increase in cardiac output while exercising. Calculate how much oxygen can now be delivered to the tissues when exercising.

# The transport of carbon dioxide

Carbon dioxide produced in the body's tissues is also transported in the blood in various ways:

- approximately 8% is dissolved in the blood plasma

- up to 20% combines with haemoglobin to form **carbaminohaemoglobin**
- up to 70% of carbon dioxide is dissolved in water as **carbonic acid**.

Initially carbon dioxide reacts with water to form carbonic acid. However carbon anhydrase, an enzyme found in red blood cells, quickly breaks down to free a hydrogen ion ($H^+$) and form a bicarbonate ion ($HCO_3^-$):

$$CO_2 + H_2O \rightarrow H_2CO_3 \rightarrow H^+ + HCO_3^-$$

The hydrogen ion ($H^+$) combines with haemoglobin to form haemoglobinic acid. This causes oxygen to disassociate from the haemoglobin, and shifts the oxygen disassociation curve to the right (the Bohr shift):

$$H^+ + HbO_2 \rightarrow HHb + O_2$$

In this way, the bicarbonate ion frees oxygen for tissue respiration and can aid in the removal of carbon dioxide and other metabolites such as lactic acid. As the blood returns to the lungs, the $pCO_2$ is low and the $H^+$ and bicarbonate ion reassociate to form carbonic acid once again. The instability of this acid causes it to split further into water and carbon dioxide, where particles can diffuse into the alveoli and be expired:

$$H^+ + HCO_3^- \rightarrow H_2CO_3 \rightarrow CO_2 + H_2O$$

This reduction in hydrogen ion concentration of the blood is central to the body's **buffering** system, a system which tries to negate the effects of lactic acid accumulation. When blood pH falls during high intensity exercise, the bicarbonate ion helps to resist the change in pH by absorbing damaging hydrogen ions which have been given up by acids such as lactic acid.

**ACTIVITY 5**

- Explain how the oxyhaemoglobin disassociation curve can aid our understanding of gaseous exchange. How might increases in blood acidity affect the curve?
- Outline how $CO_2$ is transported in the body. What is the role of the bicarbonate ion in this process?

# Gas exchange at the muscles and tissues

We have seen how oxygen is brought into the lungs and transported to the capillary beds on the muscles. We now need to turn our attention to how the oxygen can enter the muscle cell.

The process is similar to the exchange of gases at the lungs: the partial pressure of the gases in the blood and tissues determines the movement of oxygen and carbon dioxide into and out of the tissue cells. The high partial pressure of oxygen in the arterial blood and the relatively low $pO_2$ in the muscles causes a pressure gradient which enables oxygen to dissociate from haemoglobin and pass through the capillary wall and into the muscle cytoplasm. Conversely, the high $pCO_2$ in the tissues and low $pCO_2$ in the arterial blood cause a movement of carbon dioxide in the opposite direction. The production of carbon dioxide in fact stimulates the dissociation of oxygen from haemoglobin as we learned in the previous section, and this (together with greater tissue demand for oxygen) increases the pressure gradients during exercise.

Once oxygen has entered the muscle cell, it immediately attaches to a substance called **myoglobin**, which is not dissimilar to haemoglobin and transports the oxygen to the **mitochondria**, where **glycolysis** can take place. The concentration of myoglobin is much higher in the cells of slow twitch muscle fibres, as these are more suited to aerobic energy production. Myoglobin has a much

higher affinity for oxygen than haemoglobin and also acts as an oxygen reserve, so that when demand for oxygen is increased, as for example during exercise, there is a readily available supply.

The **arterial-venous oxygen difference (a-$\bar{V}O_2$ diff)** is the difference in oxygen content between the arterial blood and venous blood, and can measure how much oxygen is actually being consumed in the muscles and tissues. At rest only about 25% of oxygen is actually used; this however increases dramatically during intense exercise to up to 85%. Fig 3.5 illustrates the a-$\bar{V}O_2$ diff at rest and during intense exercise.

**ACTIVITY 6**

Draw diagrams to show how and why gases move between:
- the alveoli and the pulmonary capillaries
- the systemic capillaries and the muscle.

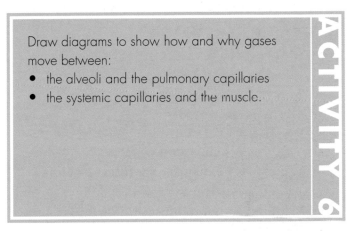

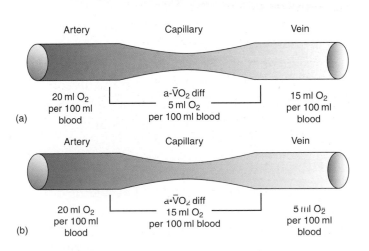

*Note*: During intense exercise (b) more oxygen has been extracted and used by the working muscles increasing the a-$\bar{V}O_2$ diff up to 15 ml $O_2$/100 ml blood

**Fig 3.5.** The arteriovenous oxygen difference (a) at rest and (b) intense exercise

# Lung volumes and capacities

## Lung volumes

During normal quiet breathing, we inspire approximately 500 ml of air; the same amount is exhaled during the process of expiration. This volume of air inspired or expired is known as **tidal volume**. Of this 500 ml, only about 350 ml makes its way to the alveoli. The other 150 ml remains in the passageways of the nose, throat and trachea and is known as **dead space**. The volume of air which is inspired or expired in one minute is called **minute ventilation** and is calculated by multiplying tidal volume by the number of breaths taken per minute. On average we breathe 12 to 15 times per minute, so our resting minute ventilation can be calculated as follows:

$$
\begin{aligned}
VE &= \text{T.V.} \times f \\
&= 500\,\text{ml} \times 15 \\
&= 7{,}500\,\text{ml/min} \ (7.5\,\text{L/min})
\end{aligned}
$$

However, at rest we can still inspire much more air than our normal tidal volume. This excess volume of air inspired is the **inspiratory reserve volume**. It can be defined as the maximum volume of air inspired following normal inspiration, and measures approximately 3,300 ml. Following normal expiration at rest we can also expire more air; this volume is known as the **expiratory reserve volume** and measures approximately 1,200 ml. The lungs can never completely expel all the air they contain. Approximately 1,200 ml remains in the alveoli to keep them slightly inflated and regulate pressure; this volume is called the **reserve volume**.

## Lung capacities

Lung capacities can be calculated by adding together different lung volumes. For example:

1. Inspiratory capacity is the sum of tidal volume and the inspiratory reserve volume, and amounts to 3,800 ml.
2. Functional residual capacity is the sum of expiratory reserve volume and residual volume, and accounts for approximately 2,400 ml.
3. Vital capacity is the amount of air that can be forcibly expired following maximal inspiration and is the sum of tidal volume, inspiratory reserve volume and expiratory reserve volume; this measures about 5,000 ml.
4. Total lung capacity is the sum of all volumes and on average is approximately 6,000 ml.

The **Forced Expiratory Volume (FEV1)** is the percentage of vital capacity that can be expired in one second. This is approximately 85% and gives an indication of the overall efficiency of the airways. A low reading may assume that the airways are resisting the passage of air during expiration and consequently the efficiency of the gaseous exchange process at the lungs may decrease. A summary of lung volumes and capacities, their values and the effect of exercise is outlined in table 3.2.

## E Respiratory complications

Many of us probably have or know someone who suffers from **asthma**. Asthma causes bronchial airways to constrict and inflammation of mucous membranes, which results in shortness of breath and restriction to ventilation. However, asthma should not prevent asthmatics from participating in an exercise programme. In fact many past Olympic athletes have asthma and have competed at the top level. What is important is that asthmatics follow a few simple rules before and during their exercise session. Medication is obviously vital. The purpose of asthma medicines is to control asthma so that individuals can fully undertake what they wish to do without allowing their asthma to get in the way, this includes exercising. There are two main types of asthma medicine – bronchodilators which relieve the symptoms of asthma and anti-inflammatories which help prevent asthma attacks, and assuming both are used correctly they should enable individuals to participate fully in exercise programmes.

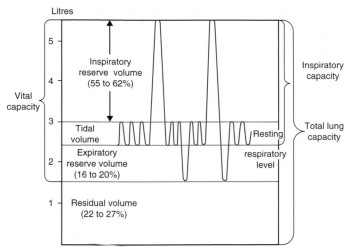

Fig 3.6. Lung volumes shown by a spirometer trace

ACTIVITY 7

An investigation to estimate total lung capacity. Equipment required – a hand-held spirometer.
1. Take a deep breath and exhale.
2. Take another deep breath until you cannot take in any more air.
3. Place your mouth tightly around the spirometer and expel all air possible. (If you bend forward slightly towards the end of exhalation you will be able to force all air out of the lower area of the lungs. This represents your vital capacity (VC).
4. Record your results.
5. Now calculate and record your residual volume:
   Males = Residual volume = 0.24 × VC
   Females = Residual volume = 0.27 × VC
6. Using fig 3.6 estimate your total lung capacity.

Tips for exercising with asthma:

- Do not start exercising if you have symptoms of your asthma.

- Follow appropriate warm-ups prior to and cooldowns following exercise.

- Stop if an asthma attack develops.

- In cold or damp conditions try to exercise indoors.

- Always train with a partner in case an attack develops.

If these tips are followed, asthmatics should fully benefit from their exercise programme and it may help to actually control their symptoms to boot!

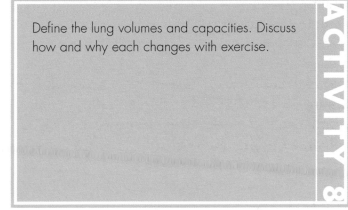

Define the lung volumes and capacities. Discuss how and why each changes with exercise.

ACTIVITY 8

# Ventilation during exercise

During exercise, both the depth and rate of breathing increases. The tidal volume increases by utilising both the inspiratory reserve volume and the expiratory reserve volume; consequently both these volumes decrease during exercise, while tidal volume may increase six-fold. Since both tidal volume and the frequency of breathing increase during exercise, minute ventilation increases dramatically – values up to 180 L/min have been recorded for trained endurance athletes.

Changes in ventilation occur before, during and after exercise as shown in fig 3.7. Before exercise starts there is a slight increase in ventilation; this is called the **anticipatory rise** and is the result of hormones, such as adrenaline, stimulating the respiratory centre. Once exercise begins there is a rapid rise in ventilation caused by nervous stimulation. During submaximal exercise this sudden increase in ventilation begins to slow down and may plateau into what is known as the **steady state**. This assumes that the energy demands of the muscles are being met by the oxygen made available, and that the body is expelling carbon dioxide effectively. During maximal exercise, however, this steady state does not occur, and

Table 3.1.

|  | Tidal volume (Tv) × Frequency = (Breaths/min) | | Minute ventilation |
|---|---|---|---|
| Rest | 500 ml (0.5 L) | × 15 | 7.5 L/min |
| Maximal work | 4000 ml (4.0 L) | × 50 | 200 L/min |

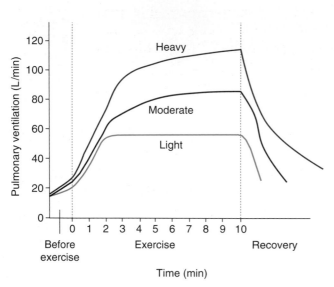

*Note*: The anticipatory rise prior to exercise and the continual increase in ventilation during intense exercise.

**Fig 3.7.** Respiratory response to varying intensity of exercise

ventilation continues to increase until the exercise is finished. This is thought to be due to the stimulation of the respiratory centre by carbon dioxide and lactic acid, and suggests that it is the body's need to expel these metabolites rather than its desire for oxygen which determines the pattern of breathing. If exercise intensity continues to increase to a point near the athlete's $\overline{V}O_2$ **max** (the **maximum** amount of oxygen that can be taken in, transported and utilised in one minute) then the amount of oxygen entering the body is not sufficient to meet the demands of the working muscles. Because the athlete is working at maximal levels they are unable to meet the body's requirements and the athlete may need to stop exercising, or at the very best, significantly reduce the intensity of the exercise. In this way oxygen supply can once again meet the demands imposed by the body.

During recovery from exercise, ventilation drops rapidly at first, followed by a slower decrease.

The more intense the preceding exercise, the longer the recovery period and the longer ventilation remains above the normal resting level. This is largely due to the removal of by-products of muscle metabolism such as lactic acid and will be discussed further in chapter 4.

# Respiratory regulation

Ventilation is controlled by the nervous system, and this enables us to alter breathing patterns without consciously thinking about it. The basic rhythm of respiration is governed and coordinated by the respiratory centre, situated in and around the medulla area of the brain. The **pneumotaxic area** is responsible for regulating the rate of breathing, while the **apneustic** area regulates the depth of breathing. During inspiration nerve impulses are generated and sent via the **phrenic and intercostal nerves** to the inspiratory muscles (external intercostals, and diaphragm) causing them to contract. This lasts for approximately two seconds after which the impulses cease and expiration occurs passively by elastic recoil of the lungs.

During exercise, however, when breathing rate is increased, the expiratory centre may send impulses to the expiratory muscles (internal intercostals) which speeds up the expiratory process.

It is however the chemical composition of the blood which largely influences respiration rates, particularly during exercise. The respiratory centre has a **chemosensitive area** which is sensitive to changes in the blood acidity. Chemoreceptors located in the aortic arch and carotid arteries assess the acidity of the blood and in particular the relative concentrations of $CO_2$ and $O_2$. If there is an increase in the concentration of $CO_2$ in the blood, the chemoreceptors detect this and the

Complete the table below showing the responses of the respiratory system to exercise. The first factor has been completed for your.

| Factor | Increase/decrease | Explanation |
|--------|-------------------|-------------|
| Respiratory rate | ↑ increase | The respiratory rate increases directly in proportion to exercise intensity. Initially there is a rapid rise in the rate of breathing. This is largely due to proprioceptive feedback from skeletal muscles. There then follows a more gradual increase or sometimes a plateau in respiratory rate depending upon exercise intensity. This is determined by increases in $CO_2$ and lactic acid content of arterial blood as well as an increase in body temperature. |
| Expiratory reserve volume | | |
| Oxygen content of arteries | | |
| Minute ventilation | | |
| Tidal volume | | |
| Oxygen consumption | | |
| Max. oxygen comsumption | | |
| a-$\overline{V}O_2$ diff | | |
| Action of respiratory muscles | | |
| Transport of carbon dioxide | | |

ACTIVITY 9

- Explain the process of increased breathing rates during exercise.
- Why do breathing rates remain high following exercise, even though exercise has ceased?

ACTIVITY 10

respiratory centre sends nerve impulses to the respiratory muscles which increase the rate of ventilation. This allows the body to expire the excess $CO_2$. Once blood acidity is lowered, fewer impulses are sent and respiration rates can once again decrease. This regulation of breathing is aided by a series of **stretch receptors** in the lungs and bronchioles, which prevent over-inflation of the lungs. If these are excessively stretched the expiratory centre sends impulses to induce expiration – this is known as the **Hering–Breur reflex**.

Table 3.2. Lung volumes and capacities defined; resting values and changes during exercise

| Lung volume or capacity | Definition | Approximate normal values (ml) | Changes during exercise |
|---|---|---|---|
| Tidal volume (TV) | Volume inspired *or* expired per breath | 500 | Increase up to 3–4 litres |
| Inspiratory reserve volume (IRV) | Maximal volume inspired from end-inspiration | 3,300 | Decrease |
| Expiratory reserve volume (ERV) | Maximal volume expired from end-expiration | 1,000–1,200 | Slight decrease |
| Residual volume (RV) | Volume remaining at end of maximal expiration | 1,200 | Slight increase |
| Total lung capacity (TLC) | Volume in lung at end of maximal inspiration | up to 8,000 | Slight decrease |
| Vital capacity (VC) | Maximal volume forcefully expired after maximal inspiration | 5,500 | Slight decrease |
| Inspiratory capacity (IC) | Maximal volume inspired from resting expiratory level | 3,800 | Increase |
| Functional residual capacity (FRC) | Volume in lungs at resting expiratory level | 2,400 | Slight increase |
| Dead space | Volume of air in the trachea/ bronchi etc. that does not take part in gaseous exchange | 150 | None |
| Minute ventilation | Volume of air inspired/expired per minute $VE = TV \times F = 500 \times 15 = 7,500\,ml$ | 7,500 | Large increase (200 L/min) in trained athletes |

With reference to fig 3.9 state what the effect of exercise is upon:
- Tidal volume
- Expiratory reserve volume
- Inspiratory reserve volume

ACTIVITY 1

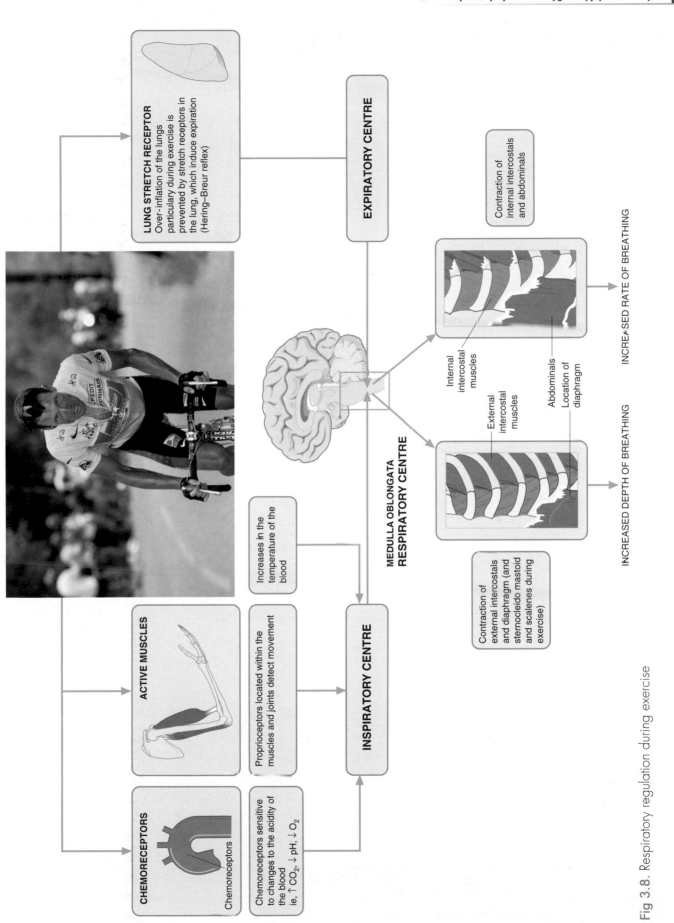

**CHEMORECEPTORS**

Chemoreceptors

Chemoreceptors sensitive to changes in the acidity of the blood ie, ↑ $CO_2$, ↓ pH, ↓ $O_2$

**ACTIVE MUSCLES**

Proprioceptors located within the muscles and joints detect movement

Increases in the temperature of the blood

**LUNG STRETCH RECEPTOR**
Over-inflation of the lungs particulary during exercise is prevented by stretch receptors in the lung, which induce expiration (Hering–Breur reflex)

**EXPIRATORY CENTRE**

**INSPIRATORY CENTRE**

**MEDULLA OBLONGATA RESPIRATORY CENTRE**

Contraction of external intercostals and diaphragm (and sternocleido mastoid and scalenes during exercise)

Contraction of internal intercostals and abdominals

External intercostal muscles

Internal intercostal muscles

Abdominals

Location of diaphragm

INCREASED DEPTH OF BREATHING

INCREASED RATE OF BREATHING

Fig 3.8. Respiratory regulation during exercise

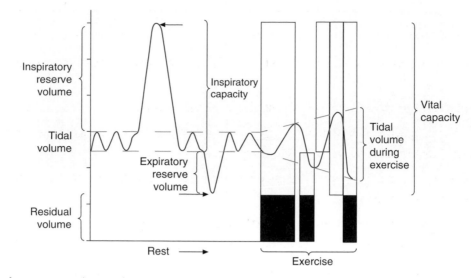

Fig 3.9. The effect of exercise on lung volumes

# Summary

- Respiration can be divided into external and internal respiration.

- External respiration is the process of getting air into and out of the lungs.

- Inspiration occurs when the respiratory muscles contract, lifting the ribcage upwards and outwards and lowering the diaphragm. The resultant pressure differential causes air to rush into the lungs.

- Expiration at rest is a passive process, simply a result of the intercostals and diaphragm relaxing. This once again causes a pressure differential and air is forced out of the lungs.

- Oxygen enters the blood stream at the alveoli through the process of diffusion.

- Gaseous exchange occurs as a result of differences in concentration of oxygen and carbon dioxide around the body.

- The partial pressure of a gas is the individual pressure the gas exerts when in a mixture of gases and explains the movement of gases in the body.

- Oxygen is transported around the body by combining with haemoglobin to form oxyhaemoglobin.

- Carbon dioxide is largely transported as a bicarbonate ion. Some however combine with haemoglobin to form carbominohaemoglobin and some dissolves in the blood's plasma.

- Respiration is governed by various levels within the brain. The main regulatory mechanism is performed by chemoreceptors within the aortic arch and carotid arteries. These assess the concentration of carbon dioxide within the blood.

# Review Questions

1. Trace the path of inspired air, outlining the structures it passes on its journey from the nasal cavity to the alveoli.

2. Identify the muscles used in respiration at rest and during exercise.

3. Sketch a graph to show what happens to oxygen consumption ($VO_2$) during an exercise session that gets progressively harder (eg, the multi-stage fitness test).

4. Identify and explain four factors that influence the efficiency of gaseous exchange between the lungs and the pulmonary capillaries.

5. Explain the importance of the partial pressure of gases in the respiratory process.

6. How are oxygen and carbon dioxide transported in the body?

7. Outline and explain the changes that occur to lung volumes and capacities during exercise.

8. What is asthma, and what precautions might an asthmatic need to take before participating in exercise?

9. What factors influence the respiratory system during exercise?

10. How does the body combat increases in blood acidity resulting from intense exercise?

# 4. Energy for Movement

## Chapter introduction

Where do muscles get the energy to provide movement? This chapter aims to answer this and other questions that may arise from the study of muscle physiology.

Energy is fundamental to the study of sport and as such, this chapter will examine the sources of energy for muscular contraction and in particular the role of adenosine triphosphate (ATP), carbohydrates and fats in energy provision.

We will see how the resynthesis of ATP occurs via the alactic, lactic and aerobic energy systems, and how training can enhance the energy output from the three energy pathways.

## O E Definitions of energy, work and power

Energy is the capacity of the body to perform work and can exist in many different forms including mechanical, chemical, heat and electrical. Under certain circumstances energy can be transferred from one form to another, and it is this that really interests us here. For example, chemical energy found in food is transformed into mechanical energy to enable us to move, or indeed can be transformed into potential energy and stored in the body for use at a later date. The units of energy measurement can be calories (more commonly kilocalories (kcal)) or joules (or kilojoules). One calorie is equal to 4.184 joules.

Work can be defined as the product of the force applied to an object and the distance through which the body moves in the direction of the force. More simply

$$\text{work} = \text{force (Kg)} \times \text{distance (m)}$$

Looking at the above equation the resulting product should be measured in Kgm, however, typically, work done is measured in joules. To convert Kgm into joules we need to take account of acceleration due to gravity on the mass of an object, so we need to multiply the mass by $10\,\text{m/s}^2$ (or $9.81\,\text{m/s}$ to be exact). In order to calculate the work done by a person weighing $80\,\text{kg}$ walking over $10\,\text{m}$ we would perform the following equation:

$$\begin{aligned}
\text{work} &= \text{force (Kg)} \times \text{distance (m)} \\
&= (\underset{\text{mass}}{80\,\text{Kg}} \times \underset{\substack{\text{acceleration} \\ \text{due to gravity}}}{10\,\text{m/s}^2}) \times 10\,\text{m} \\
&= 8000\ \text{joules}
\end{aligned}$$

Power is defined as the amount of work performed per unit of time. Power is measured in Watts.

$$\begin{aligned}
\text{power} &= \frac{\text{work (joules)}}{\text{time (seconds)}} \\
&= \text{Watts (joules/second)}
\end{aligned}$$

If the person in the above example took 10 seconds to walk the $10\,\text{m}$ then the amount of power produced can be calculated as follows:

$$\text{power} = \frac{\text{work}}{\text{time}} = \frac{8000\ \text{joules}}{10\ \text{seconds}} = 800\ \text{Watts}$$

# The body's energy sources

All movement requires a series of coordinated muscle contractions, which in turn requires a supply of energy. For movement to occur the body must transfer stored chemical energy to mechanical energy. The chemical energy requirement of a cell is supplied by the breakdown of **adenosine triphosphate** (ATP) – a high energy compound.

Molecules of ATP consist of atoms held together by a set of bonds which store energy. It is the breaking or splitting of the outermost bond that releases the energy used to fuel all the processes within the body, and in particular, the contraction of skeletal muscle which facilitates movement. It is the splitting of ATP, for example, that releases the energy to stimulate the myosin cross-bridge attachment to the active site on the actin filament during the sliding filament theory of muscular contraction, which has been detailed in chapter 1. You may remember that the stimulus for ATP splitting is the enzyme **ATPase** and that since energy is given off, some in

the form of heat, it is known as an **exothermic reaction** (this is shown in fig 4.2).

There is, however, only a limited amount of this high energy compound in the muscle cell, which is sufficient only to produce several 'powerful' contractions; or in a practical context, to run as fast as you can for a few seconds. ATP must therefore be constantly resynthesised in order to provide a continuous supply of energy.

ATP resynthesis at rest or during prolonged steady state exercise occurs via aerobic metabolism – the breakdown of carbohydrate and fat in the presence of oxygen. But, this process is rather slow, and cannot meet the demands of high intensity exercise, such as a 100 m sprint where the body requires energy very rapidly. The body has therefore adapted several ways in which to resynthesise ATP to ensure a continuous supply of energy.

There are three basic pathways or energy systems which govern the replenishment of ATP and therefore energy supply. Which system operates is largely dependent upon how immediate the energy is required, how intense the activity, and whether or not oxygen is present. The three energy systems are:

1. the alactic or ATP-PC system
2. the lactic acid system
3. the aerobic system.

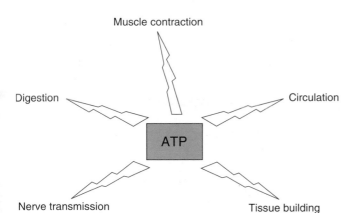

Fig 4.1. ATP provides the energy for all energy-requiring processes in the body

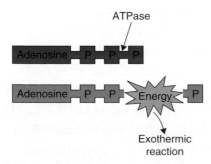

Fig 4.2. The splitting of ATP

Fig 4.3. ATP needs constant resynthesis

Table 4.1. The body's energy sources

| Energy source | Release of energy | Energy provided |
|---|---|---|
| ATP | Adenosine triphosphate, existing in muscle tissue is broken down by the enzyme ATPase into Adenosine Diphosphate, an inorganic phosphate and Energy | 7.6 Kcal/mole |
| Creatine phosphate | Creatine phosphate existing in muscle tissue is broken down by the enzyme creatine kinase into creatine and free phosphate. The energy released from this reaction is used to resynthesise ATP | 7.6 Kcal/mole |
| Carbohydrate (glycogen) | Carbohydrate is eaten and converted into glycogen where it is stored in the muscles and liver. When needed glycogen is converted to glucose and metabolised via the lactic acid pathway and aerobic system to release energy to resynthesise ATP | 4.1 Kcal/g |
| Fats (fatty acids) | Fats consumed are stored as adipose tissue and triglycerides. When needed triglyceride is broken down into glycerol and three fatty acid molecules. Free fatty acids undergo beta-oxidation and enter the aerobic system which releases energy to resynthesise ATP | 9 Kcal/g |
| Protein (amino acids) | Nitrogen is removed from the amino acids (deaminated) and the remainder is converted into glucose and enter the Krebs Cycle | 4.1 Kcal/g |

Quite simply, the more intense the activity (eg, the faster the athlete runs) the more s/he will rely on anaerobic energy production from the ATP-PC or lactic acid pathways. Conversely, the less intense and the longer the duration of the activity the more the athlete will rely on the aerobic system of energy production.

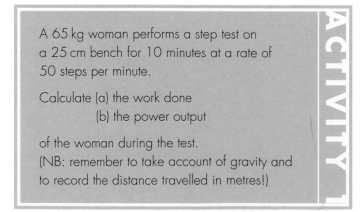

A 65 kg woman performs a step test on a 25 cm bench for 10 minutes at a rate of 50 steps per minute.

Calculate (a) the work done
(b) the power output

of the woman during the test.
(NB: remember to take account of gravity and to record the distance travelled in metres!)

ACTIVITY 1

# The alactic/ATP-PC system

This is the first of the anaerobic pathways, implying that oxygen is not directly used. This pathway involves the rapid regeneration of ATP through another energy rich compound existing in the muscles, named **creatine phosphate** (also known as phosphocreatine, PC). Creatine phosphate is broken down in the sarcoplasm of the muscle cell due to the action of the enzyme **creatine kinase**. Creatine kinase is stimulated by the increase in 'free' phosphates (Pi) resulting from the breakdown of ATP into ADP + Pi + energy. Unlike ATP, the energy derived from the breakdown of phosphocreatine is not directly used for muscle contraction, but instead rebuilds ATP so that it can once again be broken down to maintain a constant supply of energy. This is an **endothermic reaction** as energy is consumed by ADP + Pi to form ATP.

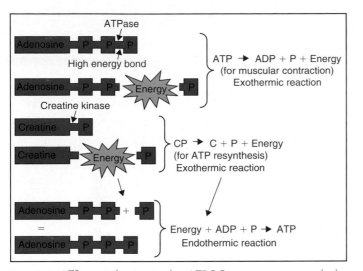

Fig 4.4. ATP resynthesis via the ATP-PC system – a coupled reaction

Once ATP has been broken down to give adenosine diphosphate, a 'free' phosphate and energy which is used for muscular work, it must be resynthesised for further use.

Since ATP resynthesis requires energy itself, phosphocreatine is broken down almost simultaneously to provide the energy for ATP resynthesis; ie, by using this energy to rejoin the free phosphate back on to ADP to once again form ATP. This is known as a **coupled reaction** (see fig 4.4).

## Features of the system

The most important feature of this system is the speed and immediacy that ATP can be resynthesised through PC since creatine phosphate exists alongside ATP in the sarcoplasm of the muscle cell. This system is therefore used during the initial stages of very intense muscular activity, such as sprinting, throwing, jumping, or indeed to provide the energy to start exercising after rest.

The main problem with this system, however, is that like ATP, PC is very limited within the muscle (although there is approximately four times the amount of PC than ATP), and its levels fall as it is used to replenish the depleted ATP. Fatigue occurs when phosphocreatine levels fall significantly and they can no longer sustain ATP resynthesis. This

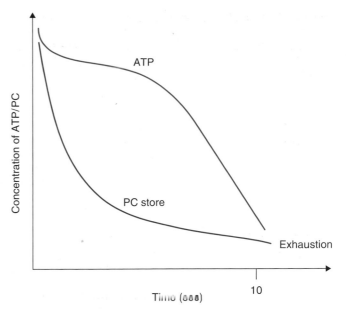

ATP levels remain high while phosphocreatine stores fall rapidly. This is because the energy from phosphocreatine is used to resynthesis ATP, preventing the levels of ATP from falling. After approximately 10 seconds phosphocreatine stores within the muscle are depleted and levels of ATP fall rapidly.

Fig 4.5. The effects of exercise upon muscle phosphogen stores

usually occurs after 8–10 seconds of maximum effort, such as that which occurs in a flat out 100 m sprint.

Since the resynthesis of phosphocreatine also requires energy (using energy from ATP again), it can only be replenished when there is sufficient energy available in the body; this is usually through the aerobic pathway when the intensity of exercise is low or during recovery once exercise has stopped.

If exercise continues after the 8–10 second threshold of the ATP-PC system, the muscles must rely on other sources of energy available for ATP resynthesis.

## The lactic acid pathway

Once phosphocreatine has been depleted within the muscle, ATP must be resynthesised from another substance – **glycogen**. Carbohydrate is eaten in the form of sugar or starch and is stored in the muscles and the liver as glycogen.

Before glycogen can be used to provide energy for ATP resynthesis, it must be converted to the

**ACTIVITY 2**

Data collection

The parameters of this task would be:

- Mark out a 100 m track.
- Position a student with a stopwatch at each 10 m interval.
- A starter will start the 100 m sprinter by waving his/her arm.
- At this point all the timers start their stopwatches.
- As the sprinter passes each 10 m interval, the timer should stop the stopwatches, keeping the time on the display until it has been written down and recorded.

**ACTIVITY 3**

We now have our primary data which can be used and recorded in table 4.2.

Graph of distance against time

- Plot a graph of distance (Y axis) against time (X axis) – second column of table 4.3.
- Mark on your graph any straight (or almost straight) portions – note that when drawing a line through your graph points *do not* connect up the points but draw a smooth curve or line which best fits the motion that is represented.
- Mark on your graph any obviously curved portions.
- Write a brief description of what you understand may be happening during the straight and curved bits of the graph.
- If you know how to, work out the slope (gradient) of the graph at 1.0 and 5.0 seconds after the start. What do these values tell you about the action of the runner?

**ACTIVITY 4**

Computation of speed of runner

- Using the information that speed

$$= \frac{\text{distance moved}}{\text{time taken}},$$

using a calculator calculate the speeds of the runner at successive 10 m intervals. Record this value in the second column of table 4.2. (Remember that the distance moved is always 10 m and the time taken is the time recorded in the third column of table 4.3.)

- Now work out the average time at which this speed was taken by, for example, for the 10–20 section of the table, working out a time half way between the 10 m time and the 20 m time. This then should be done for all sections of the run, and entered in column 3 of table 4.2.

**ACTIVITY 5**

Analysis of speed and energy production

- At what point did the athlete start to slow down?
- Account for this slowing down.
- Explain the process of energy production through the run.

compound **glucose-6-phosphate**; a process which in itself requires one molecule of ATP.

The degradation or breaking down of a glucose molecule to liberate energy is known as **glycolysis,** and since the initial stages of the process are performed in the absence of oxygen, it

has become technically known as **anaerobic glycolysis**.

Once glycogen has been converted to glucose-6-phosphate, glycolysis can begin. Glycolytic enzymes – **Phosphofructo kinase (PFK)** and **Glycogen phosphorylate (GP)** – work on breaking down the glucose molecule in a series of reactions (12 in total) in the **sarcoplasm** of the cell. Glucose-6-phosphate is downgraded to form **pyruvic acid,** which in the absence of oxygen is converted to **lactic acid,** by the enzyme **lactate dehydrogenase,**

Table 4.2. Speed against time for the runner

| Section of race (m) | Speed for the section ms$^{-1}$ | Time at the middle of the section/s |
|---|---|---|
| 0–10 | | |
| 10–20 | | |
| 20–30 | | |
| 30–40 | | |
| 40–50 | | |
| 50–60 | | |
| 60–70 | | |
| 70–80 | | |
| 80–90 | | |
| 90–100 | | |

Table 4.3. Times at 10 m intervals during the run

| Distance moved/m | Time at this points/s | Time for previous 10 m |
|---|---|---|
| 0 | 0.0 | |
| 10 | | |
| 20 | | |
| 30 | | |
| 40 | | |
| 50 | | |
| 60 | | |
| 70 | | |
| 80 | | |
| 90 | | |
| 100 | | |

LDH. This process frees sufficient energy to resynthesise three moles of ATP, but this process uses up energy, so a net gain of 2ATP results:

a) $C_6H_{12}O_6 \rightarrow 2C_3H_6O_3 + \text{Energy}$
b) $\text{Energy} + 2P + 2ADP \rightarrow 2ATP$

## Features of the system

The lactic acid system only frees a relatively small amount of energy from the glycogen molecule (approximately 5%), as the lactic acid produced inhibits further glycogen breakdown as it restricts glycolytic enzyme activity. Lactic acid levels may increase from 1 mmol/kg muscle at rest to 25 mmol/kg muscle during intense exercise.

This system does however release energy relatively quickly and is therefore responsible for supplying ATP in high intensity, short term exercise such as a 400 m run or a 100 m swim.

Although the lactic acid system is used between 10 seconds and three minutes, it peaks in those events **lasting about one minute**. It also comes into play at the end of aerobic events when the intensity increases, as it does during the sprint finish of a 5,000 m race.

To see how the remaining 95% of energy is released from the glucose molecule, we must look at the aerobic system.

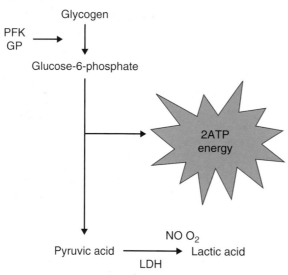

Fig 4.6. A summary of anaerobic glycolisis (the lactic acid system)

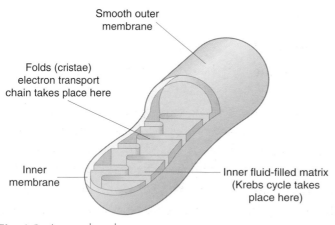

Fig 4.8. A mitochondrion

Fig 4.7. A 400 m hurdler will be working predominantly in the lactic acid system

# The aerobic system

As the name suggests, this energy system differs from the previous two, as it requires the presence of oxygen. Although it takes approximately three minutes to extract the remaining 95% of energy from the glucose molecule, the aerobic system has a tremendous energy yield (18 times greater than the anaerobic processes and is therefore worth waiting for!).

The initial stages of the aerobic process are similar to those of the lactic acid system, except that the fate of pyruvic acid changes when oxygen becomes available. Under anaerobic conditions pyruvic acid is converted to lactic acid which has a

**ACTIVITY 7**

Enzymes and energy production
State the enzymes involved at each stage of energy production.

| Stage of energy production | Enzymes responsible |
|---|---|
| ATP splitting | |
| Creatine phosphate splitting | |
| Glycogen → pyruvic acid | |
| Pyruvic acid → lactic acid | |
| The aerobic pathway | |

**ACTIVITY 8**

- State and explain the process of energy production during a 10,000 m run. Give precise details of energy systems used at various stages of the run.
- Construct a graph to illustrate the food fuels used against time in this event.

**ACTIVITY 9**

Complete table 4.4, giving the predominant energy system used for the following activities.
- A gymnast vault
- A 100 m butterfly swim
- Throwing a cricket ball
- A squash rally
- A steady 5 mile run
- Running a marathon

fatiguing effect upon the muscles. In the presence of oxygen during light or low intensity exercise, however, pyruvic acid is converted into a compound called **acetyl-coenzyme-A**, which is combined with **oxaloacetic acid** to form **citric acid** before it enters the **Krebs cycle** (fig 4.9).

Under these aerobic conditions, the glucose molecule is broken down further in special powerhouses or factories existing in the muscle cell, known as **mitochondria**. These lie adjacent to the myofibrils and exist throughout the sarcoplasm. Slow twitch fibres possess a greater number of mitochondria than fast twitch fibres, which enables them to provide a continuous supply of energy over a long period of time.

Using fig 4.9, it can be shown that the total downgrading of one molecule of glycogen can provide enough energy to resynthesise **38ATP**:

- 2 during anaerobic glycolysis
- 2 during the Krebs cycle
- 34 during the electron transport system.

Because of the vast energy supply gained through aerobic metabolism, this system is mainly used in the endurance based activities where energy is required over a long period, as well as supplying the energy required by the body at rest, or while it is recovering from any exercise – aerobic or anaerobic in nature.

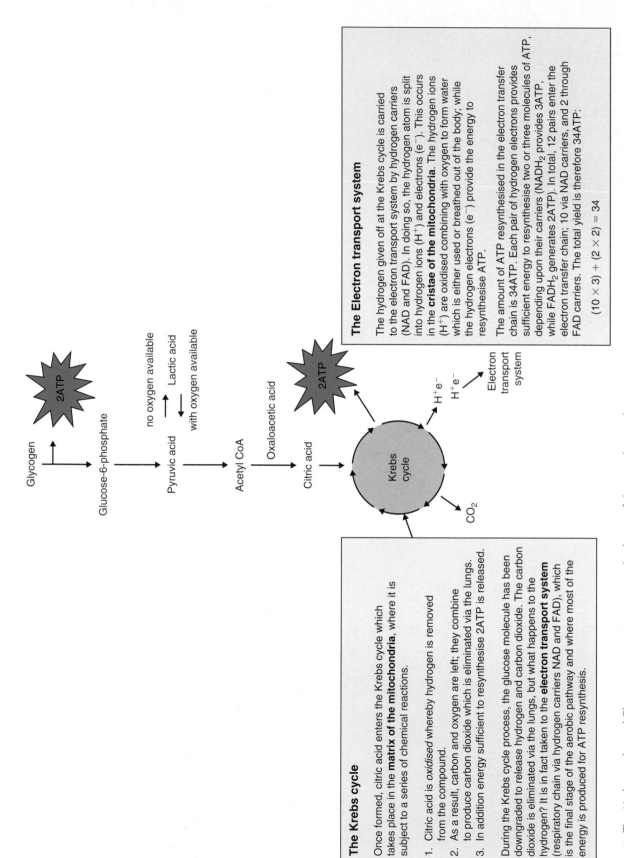

## The Krebs cycle

Once formed, citric acid enters the Krebs cycle which takes place in the **matrix of the mitochondria**, where it is subject to a series of chemical reactions.

1. Citric acid is *oxidised* whereby hydrogen is removed from the compound.
2. As a result, carbon and oxygen are left; they combine to produce carbon dioxide which is eliminated via the lungs.
3. In addition energy sufficient to resynthesise 2ATP is released.

During the Krebs cycle process, the glucose molecule has been downgraded to release hydrogen and carbon dioxide. The carbon dioxide is eliminated via the lungs, but what happens to the hydrogen? It is in fact taken to the **electron transport system** (respiratory chain via hydrogen carriers NAD and FAD), which is the final stage of the aerobic pathway and where most of the energy is produced for ATP resynthesis.

## The Electron transport system

The hydrogen given off at the Krebs cycle is carried to the electron transport system by hydrogen carriers (NAD and FAD). In doing so, the hydrogen atom is split into hydrogen ions ($H^+$) and electrons ($e^-$). This occurs in the **cristae of the mitochondria**. The hydrogen ions ($H^+$) are oxidised combining with oxygen to form water which is either used or breathed out of the body; while the hydrogen electrons ($e^-$) provide the energy to resynthesise ATP.

The amount of ATP resynthesised in the electron transfer chain is 34ATP. Each pair of hydrogen electrons provides sufficient energy to resynthesise two or three molecules of ATP, depending upon their carriers ($NADH_2$ provides 3ATP, while $FADH_2$ generates 2ATP). In total, 12 pairs enter the electron transfer chain; 10 via NAD carriers, and 2 through FAD carriers. The total yield is therefore 34ATP:

$$(10 \times 3) + (2 \times 2) = 34$$

Glycogen

2ATP

Glucose-6-phosphate

no oxygen available

Pyruvic acid ⇄ Lactic acid
with oxygen available

Acetyl CoA

Oxaloacetic acid

Citric acid

2ATP

Krebs cycle

$CO_2$

$H^+ e^-$
$H^+ e^-$

Electron transport system

**Fig 4.9.** The Krebs cycle and Electron transport system – the heart of the aerobic pathway!

Fig 4.10. A cyclist will work predominantly in the aerobic system

Table 4.4. Predominant energy systems

| Activity | Energy system used | Fuel | Approximate duration |
|---|---|---|---|
| A gymnastic vault | | | |
| A 100 m butterfly swim | | | |
| Throwing a cricket ball | | | |
| A squash rally | | | |
| A steady 5 mile run | | | |
| Running a marathon | | | |

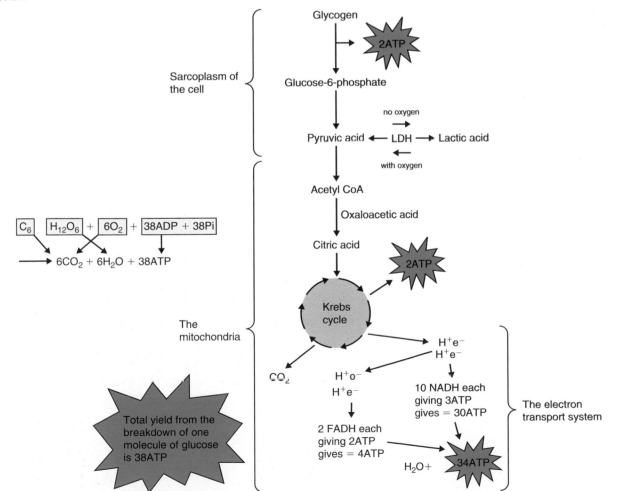

Fig 4.11. The complete breakdown of glycogen into carbon dioxide, water and energy

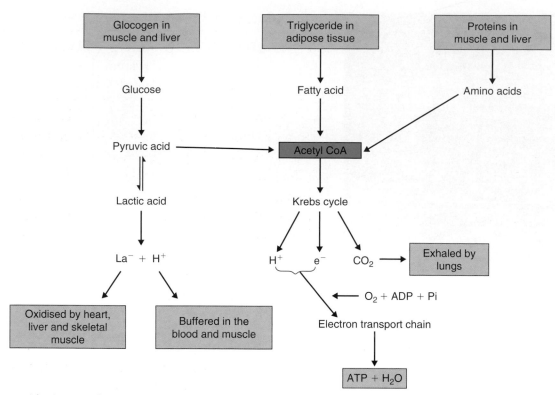

Fig 4.12. A simplified view of energy metabolism

Table 4.5. Energy systems and training

| Energy system used | Endurance | Time in use | Examples | Training aimed at | Examples of training |
|---|---|---|---|---|---|
| ATP | Max speed, strength and power | 0–3 sec | • Max lift<br>• Weight lifting<br>• Tennis serve | • Increasing stores of ATP<br>• Hypertrophy of fast twitch fibres | • Max lifts<br>• Sprint starts |
| ATP-PC | Speed and power | 3–8 sec | • 100 m sprint<br>• Badminton smash<br>• Fast sprints | • Increasing stores of ATP-PC<br>• Increasing size of specific muscles<br>• Hypertrophy of fast twitch fibres | • Repetition sprints<br>• Acceleration sprints<br>• Short sprint interval training<br>• Run in weighted belts<br>• Running up hills<br>• Running up stairs<br>• High weight/ few reps<br>• Plyometrics |

*(Continued)*

Table 4.5. (Continued)

| Energy system used | Endurance | Time in use | Examples | Training aimed at | Examples of training |
|---|---|---|---|---|---|
| Lactic acid | Local muscular endurance<br><br>Anaerobic capacity | 10 sec–3 min peaks at 1 min | • 400 m run<br>• 'kick' phase in 1,500 m<br>• Full court press in basketball<br>• Canoeing | • Overloading the system, causing: large amounts of lactic acid to be produced, increasing lactate tolerance, and increase rate of lactate removal | • Repeated bouts of intense exercise (eg, run, swim, etc)<br>• Short recovery<br>• Work relief<br>• Programmes should last several months<br>• Interval training |
| Aerobic | Aerobic endurance | Excess of 3 mins | • Long distance<br>• Running<br>• Team games<br>• 5,000 m<br>• Marathon | • Increasing aerobic energy stores of:<br>a) Muscle glycogen<br>b) Triglycerides<br>• Mitochondria<br>• Enzyme capacity<br>• Increasing myoglobin | • Long duration training – up to two hours<br>• Swimming<br>• Long distance running<br>• Cycling<br>• Little rest |

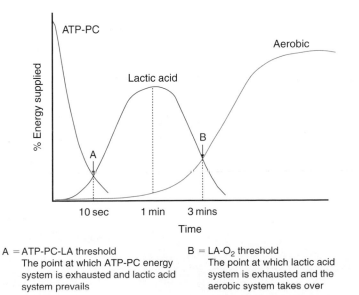

A = ATP-PC-LA threshold
The point at which ATP-PC energy system is exhausted and lactic acid system prevails

B = LA-O$_2$ threshold
The point at which lactic acid system is exhausted and the aerobic system takes over

Fig 4.13. Energy supplied against time

Table 4.6. Major characteristics of muscle energy systems

|  | ATP-PC | Lactic acid | Aerobic (carbohydrate) | Aerobic (fat) |
|---|---|---|---|---|
| Main energy source | ATP, PC | Muscle glycogen | Muscle glycogen | Muscle fats fatty acids |
| Exercise intensity | Highest | High | Lower | Lowest |
| Rate of ATP production | Highest | High | Lower | Lowest |
| Power production | Highest | High | Lower | Lowest |
| Capacity for total ATP production | Lowest | Low | High | Highest |
| Endurance capacity | Lowest | Low | High | Highest |
| Oxygen needed | No | No | Yes | Yes |
| Anaerobic/aerobic | Anaerobic | Anaerobic | Aerobic | Aerobic |
| Characteristic track event | 100 m sprint | 800 m run | 5–42 km run | Ultramarathon |
| Time factor at maximal use | 1 to 10 sec | 30 to 120 sec | More than 5 min | Hours |

(*Source: Williams, 1989*).

# The energy continuum

The energy systems do not simply turn themselves on and off when required. In fact all three systems are always in operation during exercise and even at rest. What does differ is the relative importance and contribution that each makes to the activity. In the example of a marathon run, in the first few minutes of a race the athlete will gain energy from the ATP-PC system and the lactic acid system, until the athlete reaches steady state and the aerobic system can meet the demands of the exercise. The lactic acid system may also operate when running up hills or increasing pace towards the end of the run. Each activity can be plotted along an energy continuum to determine the relative contribution of each energy pathway. For many activities it is possible to construct an **energy profile**. This is illustrated for a basketball player in fig 4.15 (page 107).

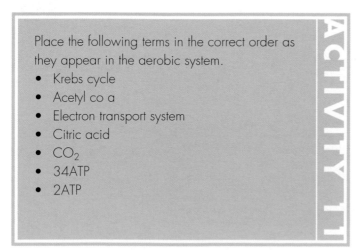

Place the following terms in the correct order as they appear in the aerobic system.
- Krebs cycle
- Acetyl co a
- Electron transport system
- Citric acid
- $CO_2$
- 34ATP
- 2ATP

ACTIVITY 11

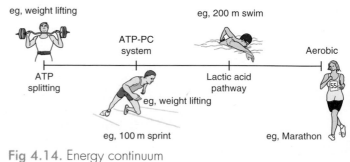

Fig 4.14. Energy continuum

Complete the table below marking correct statements with a tick in the appropriate box.

| Statement | ATP-PC system | Lactic acid system | Aerobic system |
|---|---|---|---|
| a Takes place in the presence of oxygen. | | | |
| b Uses glycogen and fatty acids to resynthesise ATP. | | | |
| c Predominates in activities lasting 1–2 mins. | | | |
| d This system can take place in the absence of oxygen. | | | |
| e This system produces a net gain of two ATP. | | | |
| f Phosphocreatine is the fuel used to resynthesise ATP in this system. | | | |
| g This system is used during sub-maximal exercise. | | | |
| h When I've been using this system it can take me up to 1 hr to recover. | | | |
| i This system relies solely on glycogen. | | | |
| j This system involves a coupled reaction. | | | |
| k This system is my immediate store of energy and is used in activities that are of short duration and high intensity. | | | |
| l This system is sometimes known as anaerobic glycolysis. | | | |
| m This system only takes 2–3 minutes to replenish. | | | |
| n The enzyme phosphofructokinase (PFK) is used in this system. | | | |
| o This system predominates in activities lasting over three minutes. | | | |

Complete the table below with the relevant information.

| Energy pathway | ATP Splitting | ATP-PC | Lactic acid | Aerobic |
|---|---|---|---|---|
| Duration | 0–3 secs | | | |
| Intensity | | | | Low |
| Site of reaction | | | Sarcoplasm | |
| Enzymes | ATPase | | | |
| Fuels used | | Creatine phosphate | | |
| Equation to summarise | | | | $C_6H_{12}O_6 + 6O_2 + 38ADP + 38Pi$ $\rightarrow$ $6CO_2 + 6H_2O + 38ATP$ |

*ACTIVITY 12*

*ACTIVITY 13*

On a large sheet of paper, draw an energy continuum which includes ATP splitting at one end and the aerobic system at the other, with the ATP-PC system and the lactic acid system in between. Now collect a wide range of action photographs covering a variety of sports from magazines or newspapers. If you have access to the internet you could download your pictures rather than using newspapers and magazines. Place each photo along the continuum illustrating the predominant energy system in operation during the action taken. Beside each photograph write a short commentary justifying the position you have chosen along the continuum.

# Food fuels used for ATP resynthesis

Food is the basic source of energy for cellular activity in the human body. It is ingested, digested, absorbed and stored in the form of various nutrients, which can then be used to resynthesise Adenosine Triphosphate.

The main energy providing nutrients include:

1. **Carbohydrates** which are stored in the body as glycogen.
2. **Fats** which are stored as triglycerides and are broken down to free fatty acids and provide energy.
3. **Proteins** or amino acids which can be utilised for energy once converted to glucose.

## Carbohydrates

As shown via the aerobic system, one molecule of glycogen can resynthesise up to 38 moles of ATP, given its complete downgrading.

Carbohydrate occurs in the body as glycogen or glucose. Some glucose is available in the blood, but this is rarely used for muscle contraction. It is more widely used to supply the brain and energy requirements of the nervous system.

Fig 4.15 shows a basketball player and the relative contribution of each energy system to the game. Using the internet or pictures from newspapers and magazines, complete similar energy profiles for a range of sporting activities.

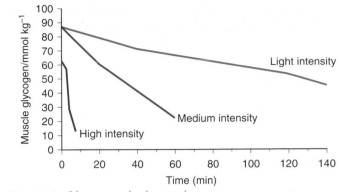

Fig 4.16. Glycogen depletion during intense exercise

Table 4.7. A recommended carbohydrate loading regimen *Source*: Williams, 1989.

| Day 1 | Moderately long exercise bout (should not be exhaustive) |
|---|---|
| Day 2 | Mixed diet; moderate carbohydrate intake; tapering exercise |
| Day 3 | Mixed diet; moderate carbohydrate intake; tapering exercise |
| Day 4 | Mixed diet; moderate carbohydrate intake; tapering exercise |
| Day 5 | High-carbohydrate diet; tapering exercise |
| Day 6 | High-carbohydrate diet; tapering exercise or rest |
| Day 7 | High-carbohydrate diet; tapering exercise or rest |
| Day 8 | Competition |

*Note*: The moderate carbohydrate intake should approximate 200 to 300 g of carbohydrate per day; the high carbohydrate intake should approximate 500 to 600 g of carbohydrate per day

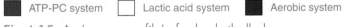

| 15% ATP-PC | 60% Lactic acid | 25% Aerobic |
|---|---|---|

■ ATP-PC system ☐ Lactic acid system ■ Aerobic system

Fig 4.15. An 'energy profile' of a basketball player

Energy for muscular contraction stems from the muscle and liver glycogen. However, these stores are limited – the human body can only store approximately 80 g of glycogen in the liver and approximately 15 g of glycogen per kilogram of muscle in the muscle tissue. This provides a substantial amount of energy, sufficient to fuel a 10 mile run. In order to maximise glycogen stores many athletes will undergo a regime of glycogen loading. This involves manipulating the amounts of glycogen consumed in the days leading up to the event, table 4.7 outlines one method of glycogen loading.

By far the most abundant source of energy in the body however is stored as fat.

## Fat

Fat is also a valuable source of energy and takes several forms in the body. The main energy source derived from fat is **triglycerides**. Before it can be used to liberate energy, however, stored triglyceride must be converted to **free fatty acids (FFA)**. The transport of free fatty acids to the muscle fibres is slow, and the break down requires a greater amount of oxygen than that required to break down glycogen. This puts added stress upon the oxygen transport and delivery system, hence glycogen is the preferred source, particularly when there is a lack of oxygen available.

During the complete breakdown of a fat molecule, the free fatty acids must go through a process of **Beta (β) oxidation** before it enters the Krebs cycle. It can now follow the same path as glycogen metabolism.

During endurance exercise, such as a marathon run, the body will have to use a mixture of carbohydrate and fats. At the beginning of the race the athlete will be predominantly using glycogen, but since free fatty acids constitute the preferred fuel under these conditions, the quicker the athlete can introduce fat as a source of fuel, the greater capacity of the body to conserve glycogen for later in the race when the intensity may increase. The body cannot use fat alone since the solubility of fat in the blood is poor and fatty acids cannot therefore be sufficiently transported to the muscle cell to supply the body with all its energy requirements. In this way fat is said to be **hydrophobic**. The athlete must therefore use glycogen sparingly throughout the race so that s/he avoids 'hitting the wall'. This is the stage where the body has depleted all glycogen reserves, and the body tries to use fat as a sole source of fuel.

Similarly, **hypoglycaemia** occurs when stored liver glycogen is depleted and is unable to sustain blood glucose levels. This is also more likely to occur in endurance based events such as the marathon or a cycling tour. This condition is more readily remedied by ingesting sugary drinks as soon as possible; these will rapidly increase blood sugar levels and energy supply to the brain. Indeed, recovery can be so quick that there has been occasion when athletes in high endurance events, such as the Tour de France, have been

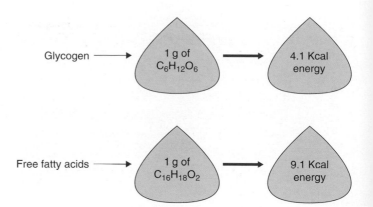

Fig 4.17. The energy yield from 1 g of glycogen and 1 g fat

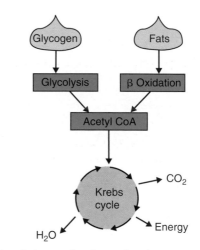

Fig 4.18. Breakdown of a fat molecule

hypoglaecemic one minute and after ingestion of a sugary drink have rejoined the race within minutes.

One of the major effects of training is an increased reliance on fatty acids for ATP production during prolonged exercise. This is largely due to an increase in the number of mitochondria (those factories for aerobic energy production).

## Protein

Protein is the third of the energy-providing nutrients. It is not as significant as the other two energy providers, supplying approximately 5–10% of total energy, and is mainly used when glycogen stores in the body are low.

Typically, protein provides the building blocks for muscle growth and repair, and this is its primary function. By using protein as an energy source, we may be detracting it from its main purpose and

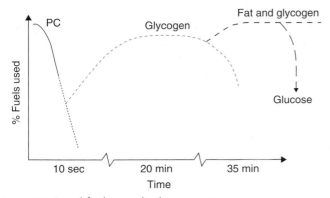

Fig 4.19. Food fuels supplied against time

## ACTIVITY 15

- Identify the principal food fuel energy sources for each of the following activities a) a triathlon, b) a maximum weight lift c) a 1000 m cycle sprint d) 10 Km run e) a 200 m swim
- Describe the pattern of fuel usage during an intermittent sport such as rugby or netball. Use specific examples from your chosen sport.
- What are the advantages *and* disadvantages of using fat as an energy source during exercise.

cause little muscle adaptation. It is much more advisable to keep glycogen stores replenished by following a high carbohydrate diet.

## Further reading

Clegg, *Exercise Physiology* (Feltham Press, 1996)

Davis, Bull, Roscoe and Roscoe, *Physical Education and the Study of Sport* (Wolfe Medical Publishers, 1991)

Fox, *Sports Physiology*

Katch and Mcardle, *Nutrition, Weight Control and Exercise* (Lea and Febiger, 1988)

Seeley, Stephens and Tate, *Anatomy and Physiology* (Mosby Year Book Inc., 1992)

Sharkey, *Physiology of Fitness* (Human Kinetics, 1990)

Wilmore and Costill, *Physiology of Sport and Exercise* (Human Kinetics, 1994)

# Summary

- Energy is the capacity to perform work.
- All energy required within the body is directly provided by a high energy compound called adenosine triphosphate (ATP), which is present in all muscle cells.
- The energy required to resynthesise ATP comes from the breakdown of food and other chemicals within the body.
- The ATP-PC or alactic system is the energy system used for extremely short bursts of high intensity exercise – up to 10 secs of activity. It is an anaerobic pathway.
- The lactic acid system is another anaerobic system. This system uses energy from the breakdown of glycogen to resynthesise 2ATP. This energy system is predominantly used for activities lasting 1–3 mins in duration.
- The aerobic system is the most efficient means of providing energy to resynthesise ATP. With oxygen the glucose molecule can produce a total gain of 38ATP. The Krebs cycle occurs in the matrix of the mitochondria and removes hydrogen and releases carbon dioxide. Sufficient energy to resynthesise 2ATP is also released at this stage. Further breakdown of the glucose molecule takes

place in the cristae of the mitochondria via the electron transport system, where sufficient energy to resynthesise 34ATP molecules is released.

- The mitochondrion is the powerhouse of the muscle cell and is where all energy is supplied aerobically within the body.
- The main energy providing nutrients are glycogen, fats and proteins. For endurance based events the body relies upon fats and glycogen, while for shorter activities the body will rely solely on glycogen.

# Review Questions

1. Explain the role played by the mitochondria in energy provision.

2. What factors might lead to a marathon runner 'hitting the wall'?

3. Construct an energy systems graph which depicts the energy system used against time during a 1500 m run.

4. Draw a diagram to illustrate how the alactic system can maintain levels of ATP within the muscle.

5. With reference to the **intensity** of exercise, explain why it is important to view the energy systems as existing as a continuum. Use examples from an activity to support your answer.

6. What is meant by the respiratory exchange ratio? What is its importance in participating in endurance-based activity?

7. We only have sufficient glycogen stored in the body to complete a 10 mile run. Where is glycogen stored in the body, how much can be stored, and explain why endurance athletes can obviously still function for longer than ten miles?

8. Define the terms 'Work' and 'Power'. State the units of measurement for each.

9. Draw an 'energy block profile' for an Olympic rower.

10. Outline some training methods that you would like to develop and improve your ATP-PC system.

# 5. Fatigue and Recovery

## Chapter introduction

This chapter is a natural successor from the energy systems. It examines:

- the causes of fatigue
- the relationships between metabolic by-products and fatigue (including a detailed study of the effects of lactic acid)
- how the athlete can recover from fatigue.

The concepts of oxygen deficit and debt will be studied, along with ways in which the coach and athlete can speed up the recovery process.

## A E Causes of fatigue

Fatigue is a rather generic term which we use to try to explain feelings of muscular tiredness or perhaps laboured breathing during exercise. However, the causes of fatigue are many, and may differ considerably depending upon the activity being undertaken. For example, the experience of fatigue when completing a 400 m run to exhaustion will be totally different to that experienced when performing a marathon run.

There now follows a brief discussion of some of the major causes of fatigue that might be experienced during exercise.

### a) Maintenance of ATP resynthesis

The previous chapter outlined the importance of ATP and its continual resynthesis in the supply of energy for all body processes, including muscular contraction. It therefore follows that if there is insufficient ATP available to sustain muscle contraction, performance will deteriorate.

Fig 5.1. There are many causes of fatigue experienced by sports performers

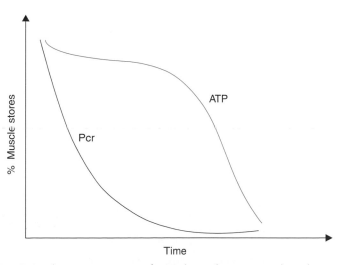

Fig 5.2. The maintenance of ATP through creatine phosphate

Knowledge of the appropriate usage of the energy systems together with a strategy to maximise their efficiency is essential if an athlete wishes to combat the effects of fatigue. This can be achieved through the implementation of a suitable training programme.

In the first instance it is perhaps the depletion of phosphocreatine that is significant, and numerous studies have shown that muscle fatigue during high intensity exercise such as a 100 m sprint coincides with the depletion of phosphocreatine.

## b) Hydrogen ion ($H^+$) accumulation

Following intense exercise, lactic acid will begin to accumulate in the muscles, which is often associated with the cause of fatigue. It is however the hydrogen ions which disassociate from lactic acid (leaving lactate) that are responsible for the feelings of pain and fatigue associated with activities such as the 400 m run which is of relatively short duration but of very high intensity. Essentially the excess hydrogen ions increase the acidity of the muscle (a decrease in pH) leading to acidosis. One reason why our legs turn to jelly having accumulated lactic acid is that the decreased pH inhibits the action of glycolytic enzymes such as phosphofructokinase (PFK) and therefore energy can no longer be released from our food fuel (glycogen). The body has some arsenal in resisting changes in pH, known as buffers. These try to reduce the effects of an increase in hydrogen ions and are dealt with later in this chapter.

## c) Glycogen depletion

Perhaps more relevant to endurance activity, glycogen depletion is another major contributor to muscle fatigue. If you remember from chapter 4 glycogen is a primary fuel source responsible for ATP resynthesis during both high and low intensity exercise. Once glycogen stores are completely depleted muscles are unable to sustain contraction, since the body is unable to use fat as a sole source of fuel – it can only be used in combination with glycogen. Furthermore, the rate at which glycogen is depleted is dependent upon the intensity of the activity being undertaken. A sprinter, for example, will use glycogen at a rate 20 to 30 times greater than that of a marathon runner. Bearing this in mind, the marathon runner must not be tempted to increase intensity early in the race since this may prematurely deplete his/her glycogen stores. Endurance training can 'switch on' fat metabolism earlier so that the rate at which glycogen depletes is decreased.

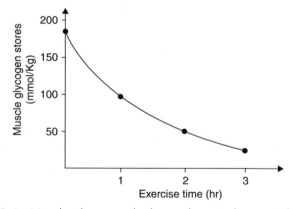

Fig 5.4. Muscle glycogen depletion during sub-maximal exercise

## d) Decreased availability of calcium ions

It is thought that depletion of phosphocreatine stores and a build-up of lactic acid causes calcium to accumulate in the sarcoplasmic reticulum and that calcium ions cease to be released for muscle contraction. With an absence of calcium the muscle fails to contract since the sliding filament theory of muscle contraction cannot take place. During contraction calcium ions bind to troponin, causing exposure of the cross-bridge, allowing myosin to attach and initiate muscular contraction.

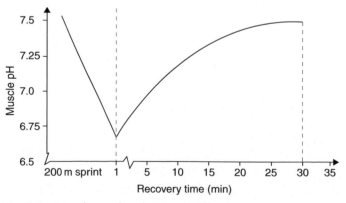

Fig 5.3. Muscle acidity during a 200 m sprint

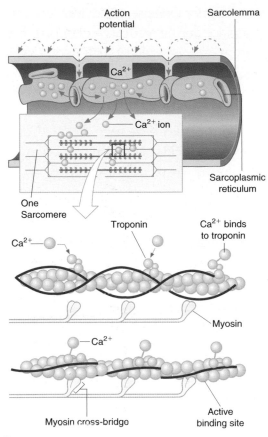

Fig 5.5.

### e) Failure of neural transmission

You will recall from chapter 1 that in order for a muscle to contract the nerve impulse must overcome the synaptic cleft (a gap which separates the nerve ending and the muscle fibre) in order to reach the muscle fibre. Some studies have shown that the transmission of the impulse becomes limited in fatigued muscles, due to a decreased

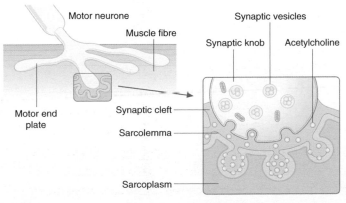

Fig 5.6.

availability of acetylcholine, the neuro-transmitter that relays the impulse across the synaptic cleft.

### f) Dehydration

Water loss through sweating is accelerated during prolonged exercise and in hot conditions, and it is essential that this fluid is replaced in order to maintain a good state of hydration. Dehydration of as little as 2% of body weight will have a detrimental effect on performance. Even small losses of water can impair performance and

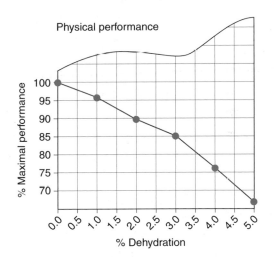

adversely affect work capacity in a number of ways. These include:

- reducing the efficiency of the circulatory functioning largely by a drop in blood pressure, which reduces blood flow to the active muscles

- inhibiting the thermoregulatory centre which can lead to problems such as heat stroke

- the loss of electrolytes such as sodium, chloride and calcium. Although it was once believed that this loss may induce muscle cramps, it is still an area of contention; many studies show that such losses may not have a direct effect on performance.

In order to maintain optimal performance, rehydration is essential. Drinks with a carbohydrate content of more than 6% can be consumed before and following exercise to top up the body's energy and fluid stores, while drinks with a carbohydrate content of less than 6% can be consumed during exercise to prevent dehydration. Sports drinks have been developed to cater for the needs of specific athletes. **Isotonic drinks**, such as Lucozade Sport, replace fluids and electrolytes lost through sweating and can boost glucose levels in the blood. **Hypertonic drinks** have a much greater concentration of carbohydrate and are normally used following exercise to increase glycogen stores.

**ACTIVITY 1**

To identify the causes of fatigue in a maximal press-up test.

Equipment: gym mat
　　　　　　stopwatch

On the command 'go' perform as many press-ups as you can (if you cannot perform full press-ups, box-press-ups will suffice). Your partner will count the number of press-ups and time the duration of the test. It is important to perform press-ups to exhaustion – until you can do no more.

Record your results.

* Number of press-ups completed
* Time to exhaustion

Now answer the following questions:

1. Did you pace yourself throughout the task or did you start off very fast and slow down towards the end of the task?
2. Which muscle groups felt most fatigue?
3. What 'sensations' or 'feelings' caused you to stop?
4. Based on the intensity and duration of the task discuss the pattern of phosphocreatine and glycogen depletion.
5. Discuss the role that the accumulation of hydrogen ions and lactic acid may have had on your performance.

# The recovery process following exercise

Why is it that a sprinter breathes and pants so deeply after a race, even though they may only have run 100 metres? Compare this to a 400 m runner or even a marathon runner. What conclusions can you draw about the pattern of recovery?

Whatever the prior exercise, rapid and deep breathing is commonplace during recovery. It happens because recovery from exercise is dependent upon **oxygen**, and the increased breathing rate helps to increase oxygen consumption. The oxygen utilised during this recovery period is used to rebuild muscular stores of **ATP** and **PC** that may have been depleted, and to **remove any lactic acid** that may have accumulated in the muscle during the preceding exercise.

Additionally, a marathon runner will have almost completely depleted his/her glycogen stores during the run and must eat in order to fully recover. The recovery process is therefore concerned with returning the body to its pre-exercise state.

# Excess post-exercise oxygen consumption (EPOC)

Excess post-exercise oxygen consumption represents the total volume of oxygen that is consumed

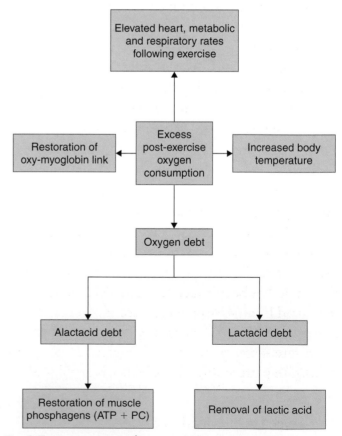

Fig 5.7. Components of excess post-exercise oxygen consumption (EPOC)

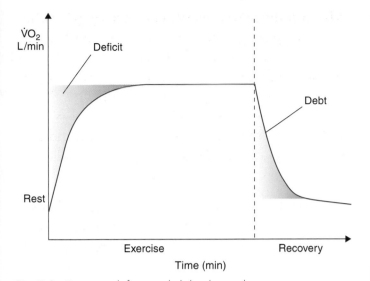

Fig 5.8. Oxygen deficit and debt during low intensity (sub-maximal) exercise

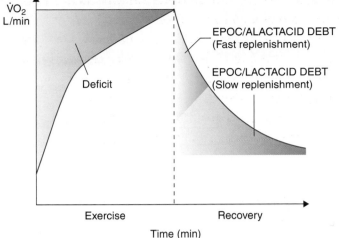

Fig 5.9. Oxygen deficit and debt during high intensity (maximal) exercise

following exercise which enables the body to fully recover, and return it to its pre-exercise state. Traditionally the term oxygen debt has been used to explain the restoration of muscle phosphagens (ATP and PC) and the removal of lactic acid. However, this does not take into account the extra oxygen that is required during the recovery process to keep respiratory rates and heart rates elevated or the repayment of oxygen effectively 'borrowed' from the myoglobin oxygen store. In this way EPOC is now the favoured term and the oxygen debt is viewed as forming a part of this process.

# The oxygen debt

An oxygen debt will accrue when the body has undertaken some form of exercise anaerobically. This will occur at quite intense levels of exercise, lasting up to three minutes or when the anaerobic threshold has been exceeded. The debt can be measured by analysing oxygen consumption pre- and post-exercise, or more simply by examining heart rate scores before and after exercise, since the heart rate pattern directly reflects oxygen delivery and usage.

The oxygen debt is used to compensate for the oxygen **deficit**. This deficit is the amount of extra oxygen required to complete the exercise if all the

energy could have been supplied aerobically. As oxygen is not available for approximately the first three minutes of exercise, a deficit will always accrue.

It does not necessarily follow that oxygen debt always equals oxygen deficit because during recovery the oxygen debt must also:

- supply oxygen to provide energy for restoration of the **oxymyoglobin link**
- supply energy for the **increased cardiac and respiratory rates** that remain elevated during the recovery phase.

Consequently the amount of oxygen consumed during the oxygen debt is greater than that which might have been consumed during the oxygen deficit.

Using fig 5.10
- Explain what is meant by the oxygen deficit.
- For what is the oxygen consumed during part 'A' used?
- Express EPOC using the letters from the key.

**ACTIVITY 2**

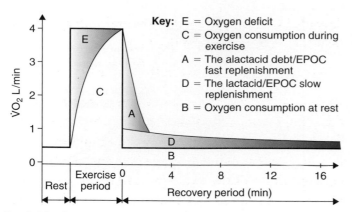

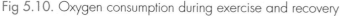

Fig 5.10. Oxygen consumption during exercise and recovery

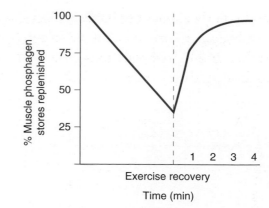

Fig 5.11. Muscle phosphagen replenishment following exercise

Typically the oxygen debt consists of two components:

1.  the **alactacid** debt or (**fast replenishment**)
2.  the **lactacid** debt or (**slow replenishment**)

# The alactacid debt (fast replenishment)

The alactacid debt is the first component of the oxygen debt that is replenished. As the name suggests, it is the volume of oxygen required to restore phosphagens used in the **alactic or ATP-PC energy system** – namely phosphocreatine. It takes a fairly short period of time to resynthesise phosphocreatine: approximately 2–3 minutes, in which time 2–3 litres of oxygen can be consumed over and above that which is normally consumed at rest and used to provide the energy for this resynthesis.

This assumes that following a bout of intense work, such as a maximum lift, where the predominant energy system used is the alactic energy system, the body should be recovered sufficiently after three minutes of rest to repeat the exercise. Within the fast component of EPOC, the very first amount of oxygen consumed is used to resaturate myoglobin with oxygen.

# The lactacid debt (slow replenishment)

The lactacid debt is the volume of oxygen consumed during recovery used to remove lactic acid from the muscles, which has accumulated

during anaerobic work. Most of the lactic acid is removed into the blood or oxidised in the mitochondria via the aerobic system with oxygen. to give **carbon dioxide and water**. Lactic acid is also converted into **muscle and liver glycogen**, **glucose** and **protein** and some excreted from the body as **sweat** or **urine** – see table 5.1.

The process of lactic acid removal takes approximately one hour, but this can be accelerated by undertaking a **cool down** or some form of exercise recovery, which ensures a rapid and continuous supply of oxygen to the muscles, which helps in the dispersion of lactic acid.

The oxygen consumed during this phase may also be used to *supply the respiratory muscles and the heart with energy to remain slightly elevated* during the recovery period.

## Removing lactic acid through buffering

Removal of lactic acid also relies upon the buffering capacity of the body, especially the blood, which weakens and neutralises the effect of lactic acid.

Table 5.1. The fate of lactic acid

| conversion into carbon dioxide and water | 65% |
| --- | --- |
| conversion into glycogen | 20% |
| conversion into protein | 10% |
| conversion into glucose | 5% |

The blood is fairly efficient at buffering lactic acid due to the hydrogen carbonate ion produced by the kidneys; this absorbs hydrogen ions from the lactic acid and forms carbonic acid, which is eventually degraded to form carbon dioxide and water, both of which are eliminated via the lungs.

$$H^+ + HCO_{3-} \rightarrow H_2CO_{3-} \rightarrow H_2O + CO_2$$

Indeed, some athletes seek to improve their buffering capacity by '**soda loading**' which involves drinking sodium bicarbonate several minutes before an event. The idea here is to increase the concentration of the hydrogen carbonate ion in the blood and therefore make the 'mopping up' of lactic acid more effective. Although evidence suggests that performance may be improved through this practice, side effects include vomiting and diarrhoea.

Training with small amounts of lactic acid in the system may also improve the resistance and buffering capacity of the body. By improving blood flow to the muscle, the body becomes more efficient at moving lactic acid from the muscle into the blood, which can degrade it and prevent the associated fatiguing effects.

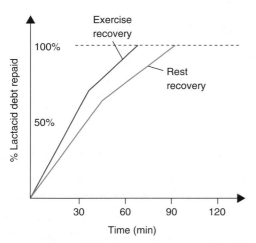

Fig 5.12. Repayment of the lactacid oxygen debt during rest recovery and exercise recovery
*Note*: Repayment of the lactacid debt can be accelerated by following a period of exercise recovery (cool down) following exercise

- Fig 5.13 shows the depletion of muscle phosphagen stores during a 100 m sprint. Copy out the graph onto graph paper and complete the recovery curve using information from table 5.2.
- If the performer was required to complete another 100 m sprint after 120 secs. what implications will this have for the performer? Draw this pattern of phosphagen depletion and a subsequent 60 secs recovery on your graph.
- Interval training (bouts of work followed by periods of rest) is central to sprint training. Draw a graph to show the pattern of phosphagen depletion and recovery during one set of 6 × 50 m sprints with a 60-second recovery between each work interval.
- What tactics might a basketball coach employ, having this knowledge of the recovery process?

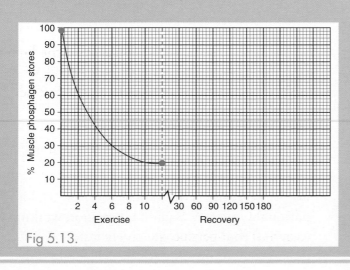

Fig 5.13.

Table 5.2.

| % Muscle PC restored | Time (secs) |
| --- | --- |
| 50 | 30 |
| 75 | 60 |
| 87 | 90 |
| 93 | 120 |
| 97 | 150 |
| 99 | 180 |

# The effect of lactic acid accumulation

Even though the blood will always contain a small amount of lactic acid even at rest (approximately 1–2 millimoles/litre of blood), during high intensity work (such as a 400 m run) this may increase 15-fold to 30 millimoles/litre of blood. The following discussion examines just what the effects of such an increase have on the performer.

During high intensity exercise, muscle fatigue occurs at a **pH of 6.4** and noticeably affects muscle function. Nobody knows exactly how such acidity causes fatigue, but it is thought that protons dissociate from lactic acid and associate with glycolytic enzymes, thus making them acidic. In this state, the enzymes lose their catalytic ability and energy production through glycolysis ceases. Muscle contraction may also be impaired, as high acidity may inhibit the transmission of neural impulses to the contractile elements of the muscle and obstruct the contraction process. This is particularly true of very high intensity exercise lasting between 30–120 seconds.

# Measurement of lactic acid

Lactic acid and lactate, usually used interchangeably, are not actually the same substance: Lactate is a *product* of lactic acid which splits to give lactate molecules and hydrogen ions.

Since blood lactate measurement is much easier than taking muscle biopsies, it is the most widely used method of assessing lactic acid accumulation.

## Reasons for measuring lactic acid

The measurement of lactic acid has several practical uses to the coach and athlete:

- It can determine and assess training intensities to ensure the athlete is working at suitable levels and is producing energy by the most effective energy system for their activity.
- The data provides information on the athlete's current work capacity and fitness levels.
- The data also assesses the effectiveness of the current training regime.
- The principal use of lactate measurements in the laboratory is to establish the anaerobic threshold or point of 'Onset Blood Lactate Accumulation', which gives an indication of endurance capacities (OBLA).

## Onset of Blood Lactate Accumulation (OBLA)

OBLA is the point at which lactate begins to **accumulate** in the blood, usually taken as when it reaches a figure of 4 mmol/litre of blood. It is often used to predict endurance capacities and potential, since the longer an athlete can delay the build-up of blood lactate the longer s/he can continue exercising. OBLA is usually measured by a test of increasing intensity and that gets progressively more difficult, such as a treadmill test. The concept of OBLA or anaerobic threshold can be explained by using the following example:

- If a person takes part in a task of progressively increasing intensity, such as the multistage fitness test, a point is reached where energy can no longer be sustained completely by aerobic means.
- If intensity increases further, the deficit of energy requirements must be met by anaerobic metabolism.
- By doing so, blood lactate concentration rises, until such a point is reached where lactate concentration is sufficiently high to cause complete muscle fatigue.
- The point at which lactic acid begins to accumulate in the muscles is the point of onset of blood lactate accumulation or anaerobic threshold, and is measured as a percentage of $\dot{V}O_2$ max reached before this rise in acidity (see chapter 7 for further discussion).

Fig 5.14 illustrates the OBLA test results of a national Under 19 Squash Champion working on a treadmill that gets progressively faster. We can see that at low running speeds blood lactate only

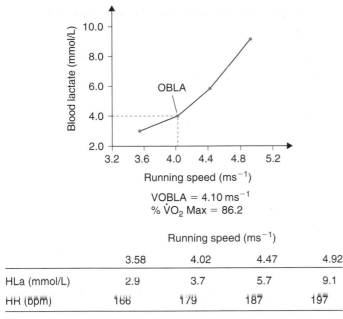

VOBLA = 4.10 ms$^{-1}$
% $\dot{V}O_2$ Max = 86.2

| | Running speed (ms$^{-1}$) | | | |
| --- | --- | --- | --- | --- |
| | 3.58 | 4.02 | 4.47 | 4.92 |
| HLa (mmol/L) | 2.9 | 3.7 | 5.7 | 9.1 |
| HH (bpm) | 166 | 179 | 187 | 197 |

The test shows that this squash player is using a large percentage of his $\dot{V}O_2$ max, resulting in a more successful endurance performance

Fig 5.14. The OBLA of a national U19 squash champion

increases relatively slowly. But as running speed increases above 4 ms$^{-1}$ blood lactate levels increase rapidly and a distinct change in gradient can be seen on the graph. Where the gradient of the graph increases reflects the point of OBLA.

# Delayed onset of muscle soreness (DOMS)

No discussion of fatigue would be complete without mentioning the **delayed onset of muscle soreness** or **DOMS**. DOMS is characterised by tender and painful muscles often experienced in the days (usually 48 hours) following heavy or unaccustomed exercise. The explanation of this soreness is relatively simple and results from the damage to muscle fibres and connective tissue surrounding the fibres, and the associated oedema (increased tissue fluid) within the muscle compartment. The soreness is usually temporary and goes within a couple of days as the muscle fibres repair themselves but in the meantime it can have a negative effect on the force generating capacity of the muscles affected. Studies have shown that DOMS is most likely to occur following **eccentric muscle contraction** and can result therefore from weight-training, plyometrics or even walking down steep hills.

To reduce the effects of DOMS it is advisable to complete a thorough warm-up prior to exercise and

Fig 5.15. An 800 m runner will accrue a large lactacid debt component

An investigation into muscle soreness.

To complete this investigation you will be required to perform a series of bicep curls in a weight training or fitness facility.

*   Perform a warm-up.
*   Find your 1 rep-max for the bicep curl (ie a weight that you can only perform one repetition – this may take several attempts to find – see chapter 7 for more detail of 1 rep-max.)
*   Now calculate 75% of your 1 rep-max.
*   Perform as many repetitions of the bicep curl at 75% 1RM. Repeat this three more times, allowing 3–4 minutes rest between each set.

Answer the following questions:

1.  Did you feel any muscle soreness *during* the activity? If so can you account for this soreness?
2.  Did you feel any muscle soreness 24–48 hours after this exercise? If so, what might have been the causes of this delayed onset?
3.  If you felt any delayed onset of muscle soreness, exactly where did you experience it (eg, in the centre of the muscle belly, towards the elbow, etc.)?
4.  Which part of the action of the bicep curl is most likely to have caused the muscle soreness?

a cool-down following exercise. If possible, in the early stages of a training programme try to reduce the eccentric aspect of the muscle action. A final factor is to ensure that during the training session you progress from low intensity work through to higher intensity bouts of work.

# Other factors affecting recovery

## Restoring the oxymyoglobin link

It was previously mentioned that some oxygen consumed during the oxygen debt may not be attributed to oxygen deficit which has accrued during exercise. One such factor is the restoration of the **oxymyoglobin link**, ie the saturation of myoglobin, so that oxygen can once again be transported to the mitochondria for energy provision.

Through exercise, oxygen is dissociated from myoglobin to enable aerobic glycolysis and therefore

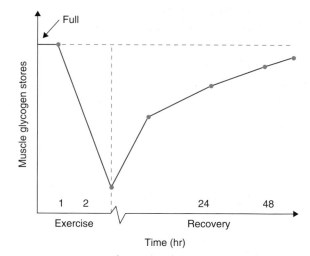

Fig 5.16. Restoration of muscle glycogen stores following a marathon. *Note:* Pre-exercise glycogen stores may not be gained since the marathon runner may have followed a programme of glycogen loading prior to the event

aerobic energy supply. During recovery the oxygen must be reassociated with myoglobin. To ensure a continuous supply of energy this replenishment occurs very rapidly, and is accomplished within the first minute of recovery, and therefore forms part of the alactacid debt or tart component of EPOC.

# Restoring muscle glycogen stores

During exercise glycogen may have been depleted in order to provide energy. The repletion of muscle glycogen is a long process and can take up to 48 hours, depending upon the duration and intensity of the preceding exercise.

It is now widely agreed that refuelling with a high carbohydrate diet within one hour of exercise will speed up the recovery process. The energy for glycogen replenishment is made available from the aerobic pathway.

**Investigation:** To determine the energy systems and the recovery process in operation during a simple shuttle run test.

Before task one, ensure that you warm up thoroughly. Following each task, get a partner to record how you are feeling. You may wish to refer to heart rate, respiratory rate, levels of fatigue in the muscles, etc.

**Task one**: Identify two baselines of a tennis court. Start at one end and on the command 'Go' sprint *as fast as you can* to the far baseline and back. Get a partner to record your time and write this in the table below.

**Task two**: Using the same baselines repeat task one, but this time sprint to the far end and back *five* times – a total of ten shuttles!

**Task three**: Once again repeat the above task but this time complete a steady forty-length shuttle run (there and back twenty times).

Now answer the following questions:

1. Which energy systems are dominant in each run?
2. In which of the tasks did you recover quickest? Give reasons for this.
3. With reference to task three, comment on how you felt at various stages of the run. Account for these feelings.
4. For each of the runs, state what fuels are in use and when.
5. How do you think you could improve your times for each of the tasks?
6. Specifically how will training improve the energy derived from each system?

**ACTIVITY 6**

Copy the following table and complete the recovery time for each factor.

| Recovery process | Recovery time |
|---|---|
| Restoration of oxymyoglobin link | |
| Restoration of muscle stores of ATP and PC | |
| Repayment of fast component of EPOC (Alactacid debt) | |
| Removal of lactic acid<br>a) with a cool-down<br>b) without a cool-down | |
| Repayment of slow component of EPOC (Lactacid debt) | |
| Restoration of muscle glycogen stores | |

**ACTIVITY 7**

# Summary

- The body requires oxygen to recover from exercise.
- An oxygen debt will accrue when some form of anaerobic exercise has taken place.
- Oxygen breathed in during the recovery period is known as the excess post-exercise oxygen consumption (EPOC).
- An oxygen debt can be defined as the amount of oxygen consumed during recovery above that which would normally have been consumed at rest during the same period of time.
- The oxygen deficit is the amount of oxygen that an anaerobic task would require if the task could be undertaken aerobically.
- An oxygen debt consists of two components, the alactacid debt and the lactacid debt.
- The alactacid debt is the oxygen consumed to resynthesise ATP and PC and takes approximately 2–3 minutes.
- The lactacid debt is the oxygen consumed to remove lactic acid from the muscles.
- Lactic acid can be broken down to form carbon dioxide and water, converted to muscle and liver glycogen, converted into protein, and converted into glucose.
- Effective removal of lactic acid relies upon the buffering capacity of the muscle and blood.
- Some oxygen consumed during the recovery period will be used to reinstate the oxymyoglobin link.
- Glycogen depletion through exercise may take up to 48 hours to restore.

## Review Questions

1. What may be responsible for the decreased effect of lactic acid accumulation during exercise, following a training régime?
2. Immediately following high intensity exercise what happens to the following:
   - Blood and muscle pH
   - Blood lactate levels
3. What is meant by 'buffering'? How can a knowledge of this help the performer and coach?
4. Outline the recovery patterns for:
   - a weight lifter who has just completed a maximum lift
   - a 400 m hurdler who has just achieved a personal best time
   - a cyclist completing a 50 km training ride.
5. An athlete is to compete in two events at an athletic meeting: an 800 m run, followed by 1500 m run about one hour later. What advice would you give concerning recovery?
6. Explain why the oxygen debt is often larger than the oxygen deficit.
7. What is meant by OBLA? Generally at what point is OBLA said to have occurred in the body?
8. Why does a coach often use heart rate as a means to gauge recovery of an athlete during a training session? Use your knowledge of the alactacid (fast) and lactacid (slow) recovery phases.

# 6. The Measurement of Fitness

## Chapter introduction

Sports physiology is the study of how the body's structures and functions adapt in response to exercise, and in particular how training can enhance the athlete's performance. Fundamental to sports physiology is a knowledge of fitness and training. This chapter explores the whole realm of fitness, and in particular, the complexities involved in defining fitness. A detailed investigation into the components of fitness and fitness testing is the main focus of this chapter, using information gathered from my own research and case studies from the fitness testing laboratory at Lilleshall National Sports Centre. This provides a complete guide to fitness measurement and assessment. A battery of tests has been included for you to perform. Make sure that these fitness tests are conducted in a safe environment and in an appropriate manner. Assessment of your fitness levels can be completed by evaluating your test scores and comparing them to the tables which you will find in Appendix 3.

This chapter will form an excellent introduction to chapter 7, Training for Successful Performance.

## Fitness considerations in physical activity

The term 'fitness' is difficult to define, since it means many different things to different people. For example one individual may see himself as being 'fit' if he can run for the bus without getting too out of breath, whereas a physically active person may see a quick heart rate recovery as a measure of fitness, following a distance run. However, in the search for an acceptable definition that encompasses most individuals, Dick (1989) has defined fitness as

*'... the successful adaptation to the stressors of one's lifestyle ...'*

This suggests therefore that all of us must look closely at the stressors of our everyday activities, and see how well we cope with those stressors if we are to gauge our fitness levels satisfactorily.

Another frequently quoted definition is

*'... the ability to undertake everyday activities without undue fatigue ...'*

This once again is a very generic definition which encompasses everybody; athletes and non-athletes alike. The everyday activities undertaken by an athlete in heavy training for a major competition are obviously going to be very different from those experienced by a non-athlete.

When considering physical activity, however, it would not be acceptable to rely solely upon this definition, since the fitness requirements of various activities differ dramatically from each other. We therefore need to be a little more specific in our definitions. For example, consider the different fitness requirements of a 100 m sprint and a marathon run:

- The sprint requires a tremendous amount of power, strength and speed in order to travel a relatively short distance in the quickest time possible. It also requires the muscles to work in the absence of oxygen and as such the composition of the muscle tissue will need to be specialised to accommodate this.

(a)      (b)

Fig 6.1. The fitness demands of a distance runner (a) are very different to those of a sprinter (b)

- The marathon run requires the body to work for an extended period of time, and therefore relies upon the endurance capabilities of the cardiovascular and muscular systems. Oxygen consumption is essential in this instance and similarly the body will have become adapted to take in, transport and utilise as much oxygen as possible during the run.

# The components of fitness

The components of fitness relate to the requirements of a given sporting activity, and can help to explain success or failure in sport.

A distinction can be made between components which are generally considered to be **health-related** (health benefits may be gained through improvements in these components), and those that are **skill-related**, although both will affect performance in sport.

**Health-related** factors are **physiologically based** and determine the ability of an individual to meet the physical demands of the activity; the **skill-related factors** are based upon the **neuromuscular system**

Table 6.1. Components of fitness

| Health-related factors | Skill-related factors |
| --- | --- |
| • strength | • agility |
| • speed | • balance |
| • cardio-respiratory endurance/aerobic capacity | • coordination |
| • muscular endurance | • reaction time |
| • flexibility | • power |
| • body composition | |

and determine how successfully a person can perform a specific skill. Both are required in all activities, but the relative importance of each dimension may differ. For example, a person may be physically suited to tennis, possessing the necessary speed, endurance and strength requirements, but may not possess the hand-eye coordination needed to strike the ball successfully. In this instance the individual may be best advised

Copy out table 6.2 and for each activity tick the *two* components of fitness that you think are the most important.

Table 6.2. Components of fitness for different activities

| Activity | Speed | Strength | Cardio-vascular endurance | Muscular endurance | Flexibility | Power | Reaction time | Agility | Balance | Coordination | Body composition |
|---|---|---|---|---|---|---|---|---|---|---|---|
| swimming | | | | | | | | | | | |
| squash | | | | | | | | | | | |
| marathon | | | | | | | | | | | |
| tennis | | | | | | | | | | | |
| cycling | | | | | | | | | | | |
| rugby | | | | | | | | | | | |
| sprinting | | | | | | | | | | | |
| x-country skiing | | | | | | | | | | | |
| aerobics | | | | | | | | | | | |
| basketball | | | | | | | | | | | |
| judo | | | | | | | | | | | |
| gymnastics vault | | | | | | | | | | | |
| badminton | | | | | | | | | | | |
| netball | | | | | | | | | | | |
| cricket | | | | | | | | | | | |

to switch to an activity that requires fewer skill-related components, such as distance running.

# Health-related components of fitness

## Strength

Strength relates to the ability of the body to apply a force. The recognised definition of strength is,

*the maximum force that can be developed in a muscle or group of muscles during a single maximal contraction*

However it is how we apply strength that is important when analysing sporting activity. Three classifications of strength have been identified:

- maximum strength
- elastic strength
- strength endurance.

An athlete who requires a very large force to overcome a resistance in a single contraction, such as we see in weight lifting, or performing a throw in judo, will require **maximum strength**. An athlete who requires to overcome a resistance rapidly yet prepare the muscle quickly for a sequential contraction of equal force will require **elastic strength**. This can be seen in explosive events such as sprinting, triple jumping or in a gymnast performing tumbles in a floor routine. Finally, an athlete who is required to undergo repeated contractions and withstand fatigue, such as a rower or swimmer, will view **strength endurance** as a vital determining factor to performance.

## Factors affecting strength

Strength is directly related to the **cross-sectional area of the muscle tissue** as well as the **type of**

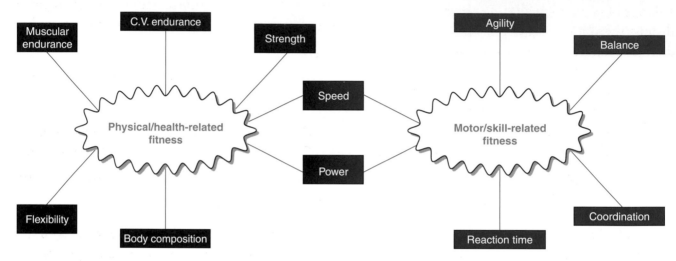

Fig 6.2.

Table 6.3. A summary of the main factors that determine

| Type of muscle fibre | Fast twitch fibres can produce high levels of force (strength) over a short period of time. Slow twitch fibres on the other hand can only produce lower levels of force but over a longer period of time. |
| --- | --- |
| Age | Although strength can be gained at any age, the rate of strength gain appears to be greatest from your teenage years to your early twenties. We are at our strongest at this point. |
| Gender | Although men's and women's muscle tissue are characteristically the same, men generally have more muscle tissue than women due to the effect of testosterone. So although gender does not affect the quality of the muscle it does the quantity! |
| Limb and muscle length | The length of limbs determine the body's leverage systems. People with shorter limbs tend to be able to lift heavier weights due to their more advantageous lever systems. In the same way people who have developed longer muscles will have a greater potential for developing size and therefore strength! |
| Other factors include … | Point of tendon insertion, lifting technique |

**muscle fibre** within the muscle. Fast twitch (white fibres) can generate greater forces than slow twitch (red fibres).

The optimum **age** to develop strength appears to be in the early to mid-twenties. As the body ages, less protein becomes available in the body for muscle growth, and the stress and anaerobic nature of strength training also makes it an inappropriate method of training during old age.

In this age of **gender** equality it is highly appropriate to dismiss the notion of a weaker sex. In fact, relative to cross-sectional area of pure muscle tissue, men and women are equal in terms of strength. It is the greater fat content of women and the higher testosterone levels in men that can create the difference in the cross-sectional area of muscles and therefore strength, to the advantage of males.

## Measuring strength

Strength can be measured with the use of dynamometers which give an objective measure of the force generated within various muscles or muscle groups. The easiest strength test to administer is using the **Handgrip Dynamometer** which measures grip strength generated by the muscles in the forearm.

Record the maximum reading from three attempts for both left and right hands.

**Advantages**

- a simple and objective measure

**Disadvantages**

- the validity of the handgrip test has been questioned, since it only indicates strength of muscles of the forearm.

Another common test of strength is the **one repetition maximum test** (1RM test). This assesses the maximal force a subject can lift in one repetition using free weights or other gym equipment.

**Advantages**

- weight training equipment is easily accessible.

**Disadvantages**

- when performing maximal lifts the threat of injury is more apparent and so safety is essential.
- it can be difficult to isolate individual muscles.

## Muscular (strength) endurance

*Muscular (strength) endurance is the ability of a muscle or group of muscles to sustain repeated contractions against a resistance for an extended period of time*.

Slow twitch muscle fibres will ensure they receive a rich supply of blood to enable the most efficient production of aerobic energy.

This enables the muscles to contract repeatedly without experiencing the fatigue due to the

Fig 6.3. A weight lifter – maximum strength is vital to successful performance

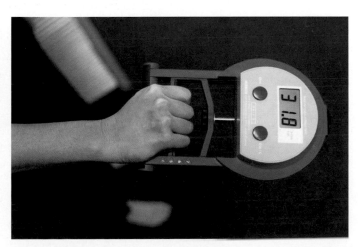

Fig 6.4. The handgrip dynamometer test

build-up of the lactic acid. Activities that require muscular endurance are numerous but can best be highlighted by using the example of rowing. Individual muscle groups are required to contract at high intensity for a period of approximately five minutes (or as long as it takes to complete the 2000 m course!). Muscular endurance relies upon the efficiency of the body to produce energy under both anaerobic and aerobic conditions, together with an ability of the body to deal with and '**buffer**' the lactic acid.

## Measuring muscular endurance

A test for muscular endurance will assess the ability of one muscle or a group of muscles to continue working repeatedly. A simple test to measure the endurance of the abdominal muscle group is the **NCF** Abdominal Conditioning Test. See Appendix 3 for test ratings.

### Equipment

- NCF abdominal conditioning tape
- Tape recorder
- Stopwatch
- Gym mat

Follow the instructions given on the tape. Subjects are required to perform as many sit-ups as possible, keeping in time to the bleeps emitted from the tape. Get a partner to count the number of sit-ups completed correctly, and time the duration of the work period. Subjects should withdraw from the test when they can no longer keep in time to the bleeps, or when technique deteriorates noticeably.

### Advantages

- easy to administer with little equipment
- large groups can participate in the test at once
- the abdominal muscles can be easily isolated.

### Disadvantages

- correct technique is essential for successful completion of the test

## Cardio-respiratory endurance or aerobic capacity

Cardio-respiratory endurance is dependent upon the ability of the cardiovascular system to transport and utilise oxygen during sustained exercise. It can be defined as:

*the ability to provide and sustain energy aerobically*.

Cardio-respiratory endurance is the component of fitness that underpins all aerobic activities which include long distance running, cycling or swimming, as well as being a contributory factor to many other sporting situations.

## Maximal oxygen uptake ($\dot{V}O_2$ max) and the anaerobic threshold (OBLA)

We are now going to look in detail at how maximal oxygen uptake can be specifically related to successful endurance performance. Maximal oxygen uptake can be defined as

*the maximal amount of oxygen that can be taken in, transported and consumed by the working muscles per minute.*

It is largely dependent upon the difference in oxygen content of inspired and expired air.

When exercise commences, the volume of oxygen increases sharply at first, and then levels out into a **steady state**. This steady state in oxygen consumption represents a balance between the energy demands of the muscle and the amount of oxygen supplied to the muscle to meet these demands. At this steady state, a cyclist (for instance) should be able to continue exercising for a long period of time, theoretically until his energy stores of glycogen and fat are depleted. If the cyclist then comes up against a hill, oxygen consumption must increase in order to meet the increased energy demands (assuming the cyclist remains at the same speed).

Steady state may once again occur when energy demands are met by oxygen supply. If the cyclist subsequently comes up against a steeper hill, oxygen consumption will again need to increase until steady state is reached once again. If exercise intensity continues to increase in this manner, oxygen consumption will continue to increase, until such a point is reached where the body cannot consume any more oxygen – this point is known as the **maximal oxygen uptake** or **$\dot{V}O_2$ max**.

Once this point has been reached, if there is a subsequent increase in intensity (such as cycling up a steeper slope or increasing speed), then the body must meet the extra energy requirements through anaerobic means. This causes severe problems to the cyclist or athlete since anaerobic respiration causes an onset of lactic acid and ultimately fatigue. The only way that this can be prevented is by reducing the intensity of the exercise so oxygen consumption can fall below the point of $\dot{V}O_2$ max. However, this may decrease all chance of a successful performance. Fig 6.6(b) illustrates this scenario.

The point at which lactic acid starts to accumulate in the body is known as the anaerobic threshold, or **onset of blood lactate accumulation (OBLA)**. It is measured as the percentage of $\dot{V}O_2$ max reached before lactic acid starts to accumulate.

$$\%\dot{V}O_2 \text{ max utilised}$$
$$= \frac{\dot{V}O_2 \text{ (amount of } O_2 \text{ used)}}{\dot{V}O_2 \text{ max (maximum potential)}}$$

*For example:*

$$\frac{\dot{V}O_2 \text{ used}}{\dot{V}O_2 \text{ max}} = \frac{30 \text{ ml/kg/min}}{60 \text{ ml/kg/min}} = \frac{30}{60}$$
$$= 50\% \text{ of } \dot{V}O_2 \text{ max used}$$

The athlete in this example is not utilising his aerobic capacity efficiently, which could be a result of poor training methods or a lack of training and results in OBLA being reached prematurely.

$\dot{V}O_2$ max can only increase by 10–20% however, through training, as it has a 93% genetic component. This assumes that an athlete with a $\dot{V}O_2$ max of 50 ml/kg/min may expect to increase this to 60 ml/kg/min through training. In order to assess our physiological potential in terms of endurance capacity it may well be necessary to take a look at our parents and grandparents!

However, the anaerobic threshold or OBLA is a **product** of training and can be heightened through following an appropriate training programme, so that aerobic efficiency is improved by utilising a greater percentage of $\dot{V}O_2$ max before the onset of lactic acid. The reasons for this are discussed in chapter 8.

### Factors affecting aerobic capacity

Physiological factors that determine aerobic performance include the possession of a large proportion of slow twitch muscle fibres, a proliferation of mitochondria and large myoglobin

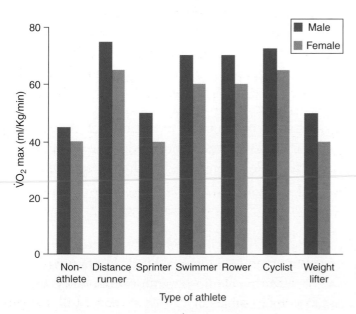

Fig 6.5. Approximated values of $\dot{V}O_2$ max for a range of sports

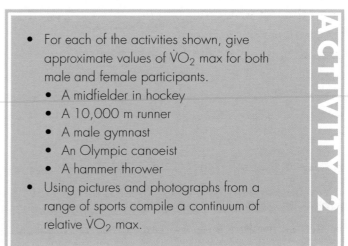

- For each of the activities shown, give approximate values of $\dot{V}O_2$ max for both male and female participants.
  - A midfielder in hockey
  - A 10,000 m runner
  - A male gymnast
  - An Olympic canoeist
  - A hammer thrower
- Using pictures and photographs from a range of sports compile a continuum of relative $\dot{V}O_2$ max.

ACTIVITY 2

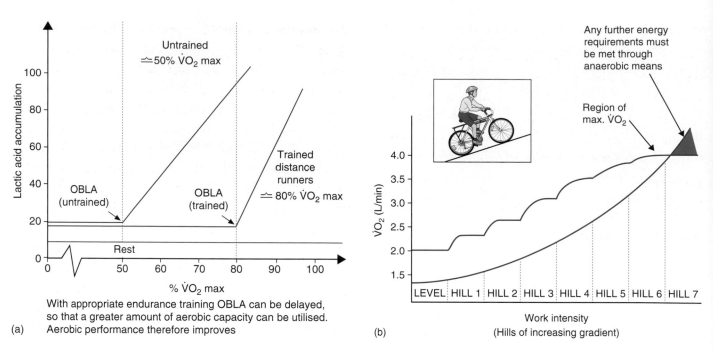

Fig 6.6. (a) A comparison of the OBLA between the trained and untrained. (b) Oxygen consumption during a cycle ride of progressive intensity

Table 6.4. A summary of the main factors that determine aerobic capacities

| | |
|---|---|
| Genetics | Although there is some contention as to exactly how much genetics affects VO2 max, there is no doubt that it is significant. Some studies have suggested as much as 93%! |
| Age | After the age 25 VO2 max is thought to decrease at about 1% per year. Regular physical activity however can off-set some of this decline. |
| Training | Undertaking the right training can improve VO2 max by between 10–20% |
| Gender | Women tend to have VO2 max scores that are about 15–30% lower than men of the same group. As a simple rule subtract 10 ml from the equivalent male score. |
| Body composition | Research suggests that VO2 max decreases as body fat percentage increases. This could contribute to some of the differences in VO2 max between males and females. |
| Lifestyle | Obviously a lifestyle that involves smoking and having a poor diet will have an adverse effect upon VO2 max. |
| Exercise mode when testing | Care should be taken to select the most appropriate mode of testing VO2 max for an athlete. A swimmer should have their VO2 max test conducted while swimming, a runner on a treadmill, and a cyclist on a cycle ergometer! Treadmill tests seem to produce the highest ratings |

stores. These help in the production of large amounts of energy via the aerobic pathway. Perhaps the major influencing factor of cardio-respiratory performance is the maximum volume of oxygen an individual can consume ($\dot{V}O_2$ max). This has a very large genetic component, and is influenced little by training. Factors affecting cardio-respiratory endurance are summarized in table 6.4.

## Measuring aerobic capacity

Aerobic capacity can be assessed by measuring a person's $\dot{V}O_2$ max: a simple prediction of $\dot{V}O_2$ max can be made through the **NCF multistage fitness test**. This is a progressive shuttle run test which means that it starts off easily and gets increasingly difficult. See Appendix 3 for test ratings.

## Equipment

- 20 m track (or flat non-slippery surface)
- NCF cassette tape
- Tape player
- Tape measure and marking cones

Follow the instructions given on the tape. Subjects are required to run the 20 m distance as many times as possible, keeping in time to the bleeps emitted from the tape. Each shuttle of 20 m should be run so that the individual reaches the end line as the bleep is emitted.

The difficulty increases with each level attained, and speed of running will need to be increased accordingly. Continue to run as long as possible until you can no longer keep up with the bleeps set by the tape. If you fail to complete the 20 m shuttle before the bleep is emitted you should withdraw from the test, ensuring that the level and shuttle number attained has been recorded.

## Advantages

- scores can be evaluated by referring to published tables
- large groups can participate in the test at once
- limited equipment required.

## Disadvantages

- the test is maximal and to exhaustion and therefore relies, to a certain extent, on subject's levels of motivation
- the test is only a **prediction** and not an absolute measure of $\dot{V}O_2$ max
- the test may favour subjects more used to running. Swimmers for example may not perform as well as they might in a swimming pool.

Another test of aerobic capacity is the **PWC170 Test**. PWC stands for 'Physical Work Capacity' and this is sub-maximal test. Subjects are required to perform three consecutive workloads on a cycle ergometer, while the heart rate is monitored. Initially a workload is set that increases the subject's heart rate to between 100 and 115 beats per minute. The heart rate is measured each minute until the subject reaches steady state. The test is repeated for a second and third workload which increases the heart rate to between 115 and 130, and 130 and 145 beats per minute respectively. Each steady state heart rate and respective workload is graphed and used to predict a workload that would elicit a heart rate response of 170 beats per minute. The score can then be compared to standard tables and a prediction of $\dot{V}O_2$ max given.

## Advantages

- cycle ergometers often contain a pulse monitor, and therefore the heart rate is easily monitored.
- this is a **sub-maximal** test.

## Disadvantages

- as the test is performed on a bicycle it may favour cyclists.
- this is only a **prediction** of $\dot{V}O_2$ max based on heart rate scores
- the test is **maximal** and therefore relies upon participant's motivation
- full sit-ups are not recommended to be undertaken on a regular basis, due to excessive strain being placed on the lower back region.

**ACTIVITY 3**

- How could a knowledge of maximal oxygen uptake ($\dot{V}O_2$ max) help the coach and athlete in the design of training programmes?
- Outline the $\dot{V}O_2$ max scores expected from a rugby player, a shot putter and a triathlete.
- Explain the concept of the anaerobic/lactate threshold (OBLA). How would a knowledge of this help to improve endurance performance?

## Flexibility

Flexibility can be defined as *the range of movement possible at a joint*.

Flexibility is determined by the elasticity of ligaments and tendons, the strength and opposition of surrounding muscles (including antagonists) and the shape of the articulating bones. Although flexibility is most commonly associated with activities such as trampolining and gymnastics, it is in fact a requirement in all sports since the development of flexibility can lead to both an increase in speed and power of muscle contraction.

### Factors affecting flexibility

Often the degree of movement is determined by the **type of joint**, since joints are designed either for stability or mobility. The knee joint for example is a hinge joint and has been designed with stability in mind. It is only truly capable of movement in one plane of direction (it is uniaxial), allowing flexion and extension of the lower leg. This is due to the intricate network of ligaments surrounding the joint, which restricts movement. The shoulder joint on the other hand is a ball and socket joint and allows movement in many planes (it is polyaxial) since few ligaments cross the joint. However, the free movement at the joint comes at a price, as the shoulder joint can easily become dislocated. Flexibility training is even more important for athletes, since there is a distinct reduction in mobility from the age of 8 years, and following

periods of inactivity. A summary of all the factors affecting flexibility can be seen in table 6.5.

### Measuring flexibility

The **Sit and Reach test** can be easily administered. It gives an indication of the flexibility of hamstrings and lower back. See Appendix x for test ratings.

### Equipment

- Sit and reach box

Sit down on the floor with your legs out straight and feet flat against the box. Without bending your knees, bend forwards with arms outstretched and push the cursor as far down as possible and hold for two seconds. Record your score.

### Advantages

- an easy test to administer
- there is plenty of data available for comparison.

### Disadvantages

- the test only measures flexibility in the region of the lower back and hamstrings, so it cannot give an overall score of flexibility
- the extent to which a subject has warmed up may well affect results, when comparing to norms.

Another test of flexibility involves the use of a **goniometer**, a piece of equipment used to measure the range of motion at a joint. The 'head' of the goniometer is placed at the axis of rotation of a joint while the arms are aligned longitudinally with

Table 6.5. A summary of the many factors that can affect flexibility

| Internal factors | External factors |
|---|---|
| The type of joint | The temperature of the local environment |
| Bony structures which limit movement (eg, a deep socket) | Age |
| The elasticity of the muscle tissue | Gender |
| The elasticity of the surrounding tendons and ligaments | Restrictions of clothing |
| The temperature of the joint and associated tissues | Injury |
| Strength of the opposing muscle group | Activity level |

the bone. A measurement in degrees can be taken which gives a very **objective** reading that can be used to assess improvement. One small disadvantage of this piece of equipment is that it is not always easy to identify the axis of rotation of a joint.

## **A E** Speed

*– the ability to put body parts into motion quickly, or the maximum rate that a person can move over a specific distance.*

Speed is a major factor in many high intensity, explosive activities such as sprinting, vaulting in gymnastics or fast bowling in cricket. However, speed is not simply concerned with the rate at which a person can move his/her body from point A to point B. Although this may be important during sprinting or when running down the wing in rugby, other sports require the athlete to put his/her limbs into action rapidly such as when throwing the javelin. Our definition of speed therefore encompasses both aspects of speed. A fast bowler in cricket for example does not necessarily need to run at maximum pace but must be able to put his arm into action rapidly to achieve an effective outcome. Speed tends to be **genetically determined** due to the physiological make-up of the muscle, and as such is least affected by training and can take some time to develop. Once again, **fast twitch (FTG)** muscle fibres tend to be beneficial in activities where speed is essential, since they can release energy for muscular contraction very rapidly. There are many physiological factors that help to determine speed, which include: the ability to select motor units accurately, the elasticity of muscle tissue, and the availability of energy supply (ie the ATP-PC system). However, the role of body mechanics and the efficiency of the body's lever systems are also integral in determining speed of the body or body part, and in this way developing appropriate technique is essential.

### Measuring speed

The simplest measure of speed is a **30 m sprint**. Mark out 30 m on a non-slip surface and sprint as hard as you can from a flying start over the course. Record the time taken. See Appendix 3 for 30 m sprint test ratings.

### Advantages
- equipment is readily available.

### Disadvantages
- timing can be affected by error.
- affects of weather and running surface may affect the results.
- this does not test the speed of individual body parts.

## **A E** Body composition

Body composition is concerned with the physiological make-up of the body with regard to the relative amounts and distribution of muscle and fat. Body composition is commonly defined as:

*the component parts of the body in terms of the relative amounts of body fat compared to lean body mass.*

For an average 18-year-old, men range from 14–17% fat, while women range from 24–29%. Body composition has an important role for élite athletes and more generally in health and well-being. Excessive body fat can lead to obesity and the associated complications such as cardiovascular diseases. For the athlete high body fat can result in a reduction in muscle efficiency and contributes to greater energy expenditure, since more weight requires more energy to move around and a

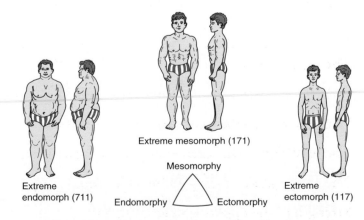

Extreme mesomorph (171)

Mesomorphy

Extreme endomorph (711)

Endomorphy    Ectomorphy

Extreme ectomorph (117)

Fig 6.7. Somatotyping: the three extremes of body type

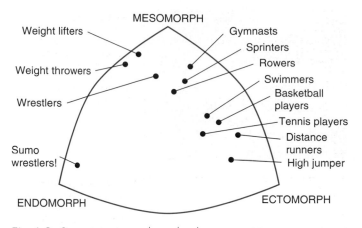

Fig 6.8. Somatotyping relates body composition to sporting activity

Fig 6.9. A body composition assessment through hydrostatic weighing

consequent increase in oxygen consumption. Body composition requirements vary with different sports but generally the less fat the better. Muscle mass is desirable for those activities or sports that require muscular strength, power and endurance.

The relative shape of the body or **somatotype** can also be mentioned at this point. Somatotyping is a method used to measure body shape. Three extremes exist:

1. **Endomorphy** – the relative fatness or pear-shapeness of the body.

2. **Mesomorphy** – the muscularity of the body.

3. **Ectomorphy** – the linearity or leanness of the body.

The characteristics of a performer's body can be categorised according to these somatotypes and plotted on the delta shaped graph.

It is very rare that an individual would be classed as an extreme endo, meso or ectomorph at the apex of the delta. More realistically they would possess characteristics of all three, but the relative contributions of each somatotype would differ depending upon the activity. For example, rowers tend to be very lean yet very muscular with little body fat, and are placed accordingly (see fig 6.8).

Measuring body fat

Body fat is measured in a variety of ways:

1. **Hydrostatic weighing** considers water displacement when the body is submerged in water, but requires a large hydrostatic weighing tank, and a knowledge of the subject's residual volume is required for the calculation.

2. **Bioelectrical impedance** is another popular objective measure whereby a small electrical current is passed through the body from wrist to ankle. As fat restricts the flow of the current, the greater the current needed, the greater the percentage of body fat. Although this test requires specialist equipment, it is becoming more accessible with the introduction of simple scales which transmit an electrical current.

3. The most common and simplest measure of body fat is made through the **Body Mass Index** (BMI). Through calculation of an individual's BMI, body fat can be predicted. The body mass index is calculated by measuring the body mass of the subject (weight in kg) divided by the height (in metres) of the individual squared.

ie:

$$BMI = \frac{\text{weight in kg}}{\text{height in m}^2}$$

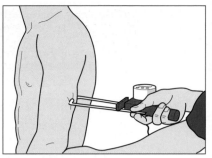

1. **Triceps brachii**
   With the pupil's arm hanging loosely, a vertical fold is raised at the back of the arm, midway along a line connecting the acromion (shoulder) and olecranon (elbow) processes.

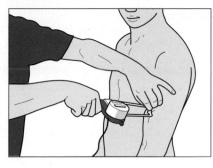

2. **Biceps brachii**
   A vertical fold is raised at the front of the arm, opposite to the triceps site. This should be directly above the centre of the cubital fossa (fold of the elbow).

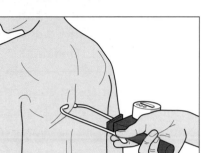

3. **Subscapular**
   A fold is raised just beneath the inferior angle of the scapula (bottom of the shoulder-blade). This fold should be at an angle of 45 degrees downwards and outwards.

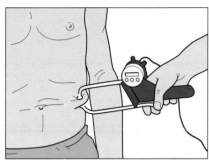

4. **Anterior suprailiac**
   A fold is raised 5–7 cm above the spinale (pelvis), at a point in line the anterior axillary border (armpit). The fold should be in line with the natural folds downward and inwards at up to 45 degrees.

Fig 6.10. Body fat measurement

The higher the score, the greater the levels of body fat.

| | |
|---|---|
| healthy | 20–25 |
| overweight | 25–30 |
| obese | >30 |

Although this test is very quick and a prediction can be made instantaneously, it can obviously be inaccurate since it does not make a difference between fat mass and muscle mass. So large, lean muscular athletes may well fall into the wrong category.

4. **Skinfold measures** using callipers: by far the simplest measure. On the left side of the body, take measures at the following sites:

   * biceps
   * triceps
   * subscapular
   * supra iliac

Add the totals together in millimetres and record your results.

At this stage, you may wish to make some other anthropometrical measures such as length of bones and overall height, muscle girths or circumferences, and condyle measures at the joints.

**Advantages**

* a simple test that is widely used
* scores can be used to identify changes in body fat over time.

**Disadvantages**

* the testing procedure can vary between tester. For example was the measurement taken in exactly the correct place.

# Skill-related components of fitness

**A** **E** Agility

Agility is defined as:

*the ability to move and change direction and position of the body quickly and effectively while under control*.

With reference to this definition we can see that many factors are involved in agility including balance, coordination, speed and flexibility. However, agility is required in a range of sporting activities from tumbling in gymnastics to retrieving balls in volleyball. Although activities can be undertaken to improve agility, development of this skill-related component is limited.

## Measuring agility

Agility is most commonly measured via the **Illinois agility run**. See Appendix x for test ratings.

### Equipment

- tape measure
- cones
- stopwatch

Set up the course as illustrated in fig 6.11. Lie flat on the floor at the start position. On the command 'go' get to your feet and complete the course in the quickest time possible. Ask your partner to time you and record your results.

### Advantages

- the testing procedure is simple to administer with little equipment required
- a widely used test with easily accessible rating.

### Disadvantages

- since agility is influenced by many other factors such as speed, balance and coordination, the validity of test scores could be questioned
- this test is not sport specific. The agility demanded for different sports is very specific. For example, in some games such as hockey the player must be agile while using a stick to control the ball. Where possible, agility tests should show relevance to the particular activity for which the athlete is being tested.

## A E Balance

Balance is defined as:

*the maintenance of the centre of mass over the base of support. This can be while the body is static or dynamic (moving).*

Balance is an integral component in the effective performance of most activities. In gymnastics, for example, it may be necessary to maintain a balanced position when performing a handstand. This is **static balance**. However, in games such as rugby, players must maintain balance while moving, for example when side-stepping or staying on their feet in the tackle in rugby, also requires balance – this is known as **dynamic balance**.

Again balance can be improved only slightly through training, but one effective method involves the maintaining of balance on a 'wobble' or balance board.

A simple assessment of balance can be gained by using a **balance board**.

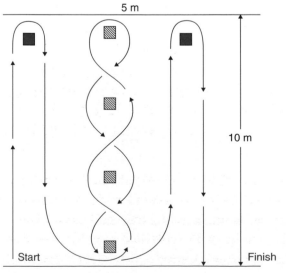

Fig 6.11. The Illinois agility run test

Fig 6.12. A gymnast on a beam requires both static and dynamic balance

## A E Coordination

Coordination is defined as:

**the interaction of the motor and nervous systems and is the ability to perform motor tasks accurately, and effectively**.

When serving in tennis for example, the tennis player must coordinate the toss of the ball with one hand with the striking of the ball with the racket head at the optimum position. This requires coordination. A swimmer performing breaststroke must coordinate the pull of the arms with the strong kick phase to ensure effective performance.

## A E Reaction time

Reaction time can be defined as:

**the time taken to initiate a response to a given stimulus**.

This stimulus may be visual, for example, in responding to a serve in tennis, or aural in responding to a gun in athletics or verbal guidance from players and coaches. Colin Jackson, one of the fastest starters in the world in the 1990s, explained his success by 'going on the "B" of the Bang'. Reaction time is dependent upon the ability of an individual to process information and initiate a response by the neuro-muscular system. Reaction time can be improved through training.

### Measuring reaction time

Although the most accurate measures of reaction time will involve the use of a computer program, a simple test is the stick drop test.

### Equipment

• A metre ruler

A partner holds a metre rule in front of you. Place your index finger and thumb either side of the 50 cm calibration without making contact with the ruler itself. Without warning the partner should release the ruler, and you must catch it with your finger and thumb as quickly as possible. Record the calibration at the point your index finger lies.

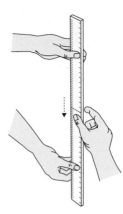

Fig 6.13. The stick-drop test of reaction time

### Advantages

• the testing procedure is simple and easy to administer with little equipment required.

### Disadvantages

• the relevance of a stick drop test to sporting activity is questionable. Where possible the testing environment should reflect the environment of the game or activity for which the athlete is being tested.

• the test only measures visual reaction time, but in many sporting situations, such as the 100 m sprint, reaction time to an audio cue is required.

## A E Power

**the amount of work done per unit of time; the product of strength and speed**.

Power can also be thought of as explosive strength where the ability to exert a large force over a short period of time is paramount. It relies on the

Measuring your fitness levels: complete the measuring tests outlined above and record your results. Make sure you warm up thoroughly and perform the tests under the guidance of your teacher.

ACTIVITY 4

interaction of the neuro-muscular system to recruit fast twitch fibres as rapidly as possible.

## Measuring power

Power can be measured with the help of a jump metre.

### Equipment

- jump metre

Standing with your legs straight on the mat of the jump metre, pull the string taut. In one smooth movement, bend the knees and explode upwards. Record the score. Repeat and take the highest score. If a jump metre is not available, the vertical jump test is similar.

# Issues of testing

## Why test?

In order to measure fitness levels, a battery of recognised tests has been developed, which are easily administered and evaluated. These tests are outlined below.

Through testing it is possible to:

- identify the strengths and weaknesses of the athlete
- provide baseline data for monitoring performance
- provide the basis for training prescriptions
- assess the value of different types of training and help to modify training programmes
- predict physiological and athletic potential
- provide comparisons with previous tests and other élite performers in the same group
- identify overtraining syndrome
- identify talent
- enhance motivation
- form part of the educational process.

## Validity and reliability of testing

**Validity** of testing is concerned with *whether the test measures exactly what it sets out to.* We have

discussed for example, that the sit and reach test is a valid test for the assessment of flexibility in the lower back and hamstrings but not at the shoulder. The validity of a test is further improved if the test is sport specific ie, the testing environment should resemble the activity being tested, so that specific muscle groups and fibres together with specific actions from the sport are actually being assessed. A further question of validity is – are the tests truly replicating the sporting environment accurately? We would have to question therefore the validity of the multi-stage fitness test to a swimmer. A much more appropriate test of $\dot{V}O_2$ max for a swimmer would be conducted in the confines of a swimming pool. **Reliability** on the other hand questions the accuracy of the test results. If a test is reliable *it should be possible to gain the same or similar result during a retest*, ie, the results should be consistent and reproducible. The testers should be experienced and equipment should be standardised. The sequencing of tests is also important since if more than one test is to be conducted during the same session the order of the tests could affect results. When any type of testing is undertaken, it must be remembered that many things contribute to performance, and fitness tests look solely at one aspect. Other factors to be considered when testing include **motivation** and the **testing environment** – is the athlete really pushing him/herself in the tests, particularly when some tests require the athlete to work to near exhaustion? *Submaximal tests are therefore often favoured over maximal tests* since they do not require the athlete to undergo the duress and strain of maximal tests and therefore increase the reliability of the results. Additionally, maximal tests could interfere with an athlete's training programme. In order to maximise the reliability of a specific test, it may be necessary to repeat the test several times in order to minimise the possibility of human error. Other factors to take into account when conducting tests are **safety**, the ability to interpret the results and ensuring that correct standardised testing procedures and protocols are used. All these factors should ensure that any tests conducted are valid and reliable.

# A E Individual differences in fitness measures

## Heredity and performance – the genetic debate

One of the most enduring discussion points in the sporting arena is the genetic debate nature versus nurture – *are successful performers born (nature) or made (nurture)*? Everybody differs in their physiological make up and consequently this may affect their level of success in a given sport. Numerous studies have been conducted in this area and have largely concluded that physiological and fitness constructs such as the relative proportions of muscle fibre types (ie: fast twitch v slow twitch), $VO_2$ max, anaerobic speed, and reaction time are largely genetically determined. That is not to say that such components of fitness cannot be improved through training; they can of course but only up to our pre-determined level set out by the genetic blueprint presented to us by our parents – this has been supported by studies on identical twins who appear to respond identically to identical training programmes.

## The battle of the sexes! Anatomical and physiological differences between males and females

We should all hopefully be aware that males and females differ in terms of anatomy and physiology! Females, for example, typically have a smaller skeletal frame, a smaller heart, smaller lungs and a higher percentage of body fat than their male counterparts. Muscle and bone mass tend to be similar in males and females up until the age of 13. During puberty, however, the influence of the hormone testosterone on males is such that it causes a greater increase in bone and particularly muscle mass.

But what effect do these differences have on the levels of fitness of females?

As we can see from table 6.6 the oxygen transport system of females is not as effective as that of males since the smaller lung capacity, smaller heart and lower level of haemoglobin in the blood reduces the $VO_2$ max of females significantly. However, it is interesting to note that when $VO_2$ max differences are considered in absolute terms (L/min) the difference in values can be as much as 40% but when body size is taken into account (ml/kg/min) this difference narrows to about 20%. Once again it is testosterone that appears to make all the difference. Testosterone actively promotes the production of haemoglobin and can increase the concentration of red blood cells so that each litre of male blood can carry up to 11% more oxygen than a litre of female blood.

When we consider anaerobic capacity and strength the lower scores in females can be largely attributed to a lower percentage of muscle mass. In general muscular strength of adult women is about two-thirds that of adult men – however when expressed relative to lean body mass or muscle cross-sectional area, strength is similar between males and females.

## Other issues in measuring fitness

When planning fitness tests it is important to follow a few simple guidelines:

- Ensure (where possible) that the variables tested are relevant to that sport

- Ensure that the tests selected are valid and reliable

- Ensure that the testing administration and protocol are strictly adhered to

- Ensure that all tests are carried out with due regard for health and safety

- Ensure that results are interpreted in the correct manner

- Ethical considerations such as human rights need to be taken into account.

Table 6.6. A summary of the anatomical and physiological differences between males and females

| Females compared to males | Effect upon exercise performance |
|---|---|
| • Smaller skeletal structure. Shorter limbs, narrower shoulders, broader pelvis | • Lower muscular strength and power |
| • Less muscle mass | • More weight to carry that is not metabolically active. Reduced strength and power |
| • More body fat | • Increase in non-functional weight using up oxygen during exercise |
| • Smaller heart | • Lower cardiac output and stroke volume. Reduced oxygen delivery to the muscle |
| • Lower blood haemoglobin level | • Reduced oxygen transport |
| • Smaller lung capacity | • Less oxygen entering the body |
| • Lower $VO_2$ max | • Lower aerobic capacity and reduced endurance performance |

| Variables with little or no differences between the sexes |
|---|
| • Distribution of muscle fibre types |
| • Lactate threshold when measured as a percentage of $VO_2$ max |
| • Metabolic capacity per gram of muscle |
| • Relative improvement in aerobic and anaerobic capacity and muscle strength following training |

# Testing the elite athlete

The above fitness measures are well recognised and simple to administer which makes them very appropriate for this level of study. However, elite athletes may require greater objectivity in their results if they are to compare themselves accurately with other elite performers in their group. Specialised laboratories have therefore been established which dedicate themselves to sports testing. One such laboratory is the Human Performance Centre at Lilleshall; another is the National Sports Medicine Institute at St Barts Hospital, and what follows is an example of some of the tests they now administer on the elite sports performer.

# The anaerobic capacity test (the Wingate cycle test)

This test is designed to assess each player's ability to exercise anaerobically without experiencing the effect of fatigue through lactic acid build-up. The longer an individual is able to work flat out at high intensity, the greater his/her anaerobic capacity.

Each subject is required to perform a maximal 30-second bout of exercise (sprint) on a bicycle ergometer which has been specially linked to a computer. During the bout of exercise the computer records the peak power reached, which relates to the body's explosive power ability, as well as the mean power. This is an indication of the body's

Fig 6.14. The anaerobic capacity test

ability to sustain high intensity effort. The percentage of fatigue sustained can also be recorded. Those subjects who are able to sustain and achieve high levels of power throughout the test are those with the greatest ability in anaerobic events.

# OBLA test (Onset of Blood Lactate Accumulation)

The lactate threshold, or point of onset of blood lactate accumulation, is the point at which the body appears to convert to anaerobic energy production and lactic acid starts to accumulate. Below the lactate threshold the body works aerobically and prolonged exercise can take place, with a blood lactate volume of 2–3 mmol per litre of blood. Exercise above the lactate threshold (which usually occurs at 4 mmol per litre of blood) can only usually be sustained for approximately one minute. (To highlight this, think of how your legs feel at the end of a flat out 400 m run!)

The test is performed in four stages where subjects are required to run at speeds of 8, 9, 10 and finally 11 miles per hour. At the end of each stage blood samples are taken by a small prick on the finger, and analysed for blood lactate. The point at which blood lactate rises significantly (usually 4 mmol/litre of blood) indicates the point of onset of blood lactate accumulation, and the running speed which corresponds to this is recorded. Improvements in endurance ability can be observed where lower lactate levels are recorded for the same intensity of exercise; this shows that the body has adapted to cope better with this intensity of exercise through buffering lactic acid.

**ACTIVITY 5**

See table 6.7 for each of the components of fitness; give a recognised test, a brief description of the test and how each test can be evaluated.

Table 6.7. Tests for components of fitness

| Fitness component | Recognised test | Description of test | Evaluation |
|---|---|---|---|
| aerobic fitness | | | |
| anaerobic fitness | | | |
| strength | | | |
| muscular endurance | | | |
| flexibility | | | |
| body composition | | | |
| speed | | | |

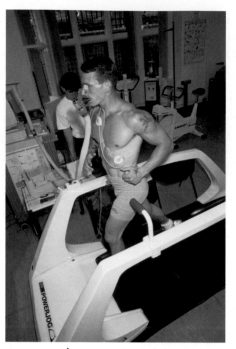

Fig 6.15. Measuring $\dot{V}O_2$ max through direct gas analysis

# Maximum oxygen uptake test ($\dot{V}O_2$ max test)

The multistage fitness test gives a reasonable prediction of $\dot{V}O_2$ max, but it is purely a prediction and not a truly objective measure of the volume of oxygen that the body can take in, transport and utilise.

There are a wealth of tests to achieve this objective measure, but the most accurate is **direct gas analysis**. Subjects are measured at progressively increasing intensities on one of many laboratory ergometers (treadmills, cycle or rowing machines tend to be the most popular), while breathing through respiratory apparatus which is linked to a computer. The computer analyses the relative concentrations of oxygen and carbon dioxide inspired and expired. Since the concentrations of these in the surrounding environment are known, it is fairly simple to calculate the amount of oxygen consumed and the amount of carbon dioxide produced over time.

The subject continues to work at increasingly higher work intensities, until such a time is reached when the body's oxygen consumption does not increase further with increasing workloads. At this point the subject's body is working at its aerobic

limit, and any further increments in workload must be met through anaerobic means. This is the point of maximal oxygen uptake, and the amount of oxygen being consumed can now be recorded. $\dot{V}O_2$ max can be measured in absolute terms: ie, 1/min for non-weight bearing activities such as swimming, cycling and rowing, or relative to body weight in $ml\,kg^{-1}\,min^{-1}$ (millimetres of oxygen per kilogram of bodyweight per minute). The higher the value of $\dot{V}O_2$ max, the more efficient the body is at exercising under aerobic conditions.

The results of the lactate threshold test and maximal oxygen uptake test can be used in conjunction to determine the percentage of maximum oxygen uptake the subject uses when exercising at the point of lactate threshold (an individual will rarely be able to exercise at 100% of $\dot{V}O_2$ max). The higher the value, the better the subject will be able to sustain exercise at fairly high intensities for long periods of time without getting fatigued, since they can delay the onset and effects of lactic acid which can inhibit muscle action (see fig 6.6a and 6.6b).

Discuss the merits of fitness testing. Outline some tests you may use to assess an athlete's level of fitness and how you would evaluate them.

**ACTIVITY 6**

# Haematology

Haematology is the study of blood and its component parts which can significantly affect our performance during exercise. The functions of blood are well documented in chapter 2.

The first part of this test considers haemoglobin content at rest. This component transports oxygen from the lungs to the muscle site and other organs. Low haemoglobin levels can lead to premature fatigue as there is a limit to the oxygen carrying capabilities of the body. Low levels can easily be rectified by increasing the amount of iron consumed in the diet. Recommended normal values for males are 14.0–18.0 grammes per decilitre of blood.

This test involves taking a sample of blood via a simple thumb prick which is then analysed.

## Haematocrit

Haematocrit measures the amount of fluid in the blood – ie, its current state of hydration, which concerns the proportion of solids (blood cells) to plasma in the blood. Normal haematocrit for males occur in the region of 42–45%. If blood haematocrit is too high, there may be too many red blood cells in the blood relative to plasma; as a result the blood viscosity increases which slows down the flow, and hinders oxygen transport to the muscles. This high value can also reflect that dehydration has occurred, which is obviously a problem in endurance events. Drinking plenty of fluids is essential to prevent performance from deteriorating and to keep the body in an adequate state of hydration.

## Muscle power and strength

Muscle force can be tested by an **isokinetic dynamometer** linked to a computer. It measures muscle strength at different angles and speeds of contraction and can be linked to the speeds most appropriate to the athlete's event. By exerting a force against the dynamometer, muscle strength and power can be assessed.

**ACTIVITY 7**

Compare and contrast the relative merits and limitations of the multi-stage fitness test and direct gas analysis in the assessment of aerobic capacity.

## Summary

- Fitness requirements differ tremendously between athletes and activities.
- Health-related components of fitness are largely physiologically based and include strength, speed, cardiorespiratory endurance, muscular endurance, flexibility and body composition.
- Skill-related components of fitness include agility, balance, coordination, reaction time and power and are dependent upon the interaction of the nervous system with the muscular system.
- Fitness testing is imperative for the elite athlete since it can identify weaknesses and assess the value of the training programme.
- Any fitness tests conducted should be repeated regularly to ensure reliability.
- Maximal Oxygen Uptake of $\dot{V}O_2$ max is the maximum amount of oxygen that can be taken in, transported and consumed by the working muscles per minute. It is the best predictor of aerobic capacity and can only increase through training by 10–20% since it has a 93% genetic component.
- The anaerobic threshold or onset of blood lactate accumulation (OBLA) is the point at which lactic acid starts to accumulate. It is measured as a percentage of $\dot{V}O_2$ max reached before lactic acid accumulation. OBLA is a product of training and therefore increases through endurance training.

# Review Questions

1. Identify two physical fitness components and two motor fitness components that will be required in **a)** sprint running and **b)** gymnastics. Give details of when each component will be needed within the activity.

2. Identify two tests to assess each of: **a)** muscular endurance **b)** aerobic capacity. State how each can be evaluated.

3. In any test, validity and reliability are important. How would you ensure that an investigation was valid and reliable?

4. Critically evaluate the validity and reliability of the multi-stage fitness test as a measure of aerobic capacity.

5. Explain the division of physical fitness into general fitness and specific fitness.

6. Using the example of basketball, suggest how you might adapt a test of agility to make it more specific.

7. What factors contribute to aerobic capacity of an individual?

8. Construct a somatotype delta graph and show where you would place **a)** a rock climber, **b)** a rugby prop forward, **c)** a tour cyclist and **d)** a heavyweight boxer.

9. The structure of the female cardio-respiratory system differs from that of the male. What effects does this have on the endurance performance of a female when compared to a male?

10. Outline the factors that determine the flexibility of an individual.

# 7. Training for Successful Performance

## Chapter introduction

Drawing upon knowledge gained from chapter 6, this chapter seeks specifically to investigate how training can improve and enhance fitness levels.

The chapter consists of two main sections. The first discusses the principles and types of training that can be employed in a training regime, culminating in considerations needed when designing long-term training programmes. Having acquired this knowledge it is hoped that the reader will be able to design such a programme for the athlete. Throughout this section, the benefits of training on the body systems are highlighted; the second part of this chapter synthesises this information, so that a complete picture is given of the adaptive responses of the body to exercise and explains just what happens to the body to account for improved performance.

## The principles of training

The principles of training are essentially the rules or laws that underpin a training programme. If these rules are not followed then any training undertaken will become obsolete and worthless. There are many principles of training that the coach and athlete must bear in mind in the design of an effective training regime.

## Specificity

The law of **specificity** suggests that any training undertaken should be relevant and appropriate to the sport for which the individual is training. For example, it would be highly inappropriate for a swimmer to carry out the majority of his/her training on the land. Although there are certainly benefits gained from land-based training, the majority of the training programme should involve pool-based work.

The specificity rule does not govern just the muscles, fibre type and actions used but also the energy systems which are predominantly stressed. The **energy system** used in training should replicate that predominantly used in the event. The energy systems should also be stressed in isolation of each other so that high intensity work (stressing the anaerobic systems) should be done in one session, whereas more aerobic and endurance based work should be completed in a separate session. When designing a weight training programme for a shot putter, for example, the coach will ensure specificity by using weights or exercises (such as an inclined bench press) *that replicate the action of shot putting.* He will ensure

Fig 7.1. A cyclist will follow the principle of specificity as most training undertaken will focus on the legs

that the exercises use the same **muscle group** and **muscle fibres** that the athlete recruits during the event and that the repetitions are undertaken explosively, using the alactic (ATP-PC system) energy pathway, which of course is the predominant energy system used during the shot putt.

# Progressive overload

This rule considers the intensity of the training session. For improvement and adaptation to occur, the training should be at an intensity where the individual feels some kind of stress and discomfort – this signifies overload and suggests that the old adage 'no pain, no gain' has some truth in it, especially for the elite athlete. **Overload** for the shot putter may therefore involve lifting very heavy weights, or indeed using a shot that is heavier than that used in competition. If exercise takes place on a regular basis the body's systems will adapt and start to cope with these stresses that have been imposed. In order for further improvement to occur, the intensity of training will need to be gradually increased – this is **progression** and can be done by running faster, lifting heavier weights, or training for longer.

# Reversibility

Also known as 'regression' or detraining, this explains why performance deteriorates when training ceases or the intensity of training decreases for extended periods of time. Quite simply, if you *don't use it you lose it!*

Seven weeks of inactivity has been shown to have the following physiological effects. Significant decreases in maximum oxygen uptake have been recorded – up to 27%, which reflects a fall in the efficiency of the cardiovascular system. In particular, stroke volume and cardiac output can decrease by up to 30%. During exercise, increases in both blood lactate and heart rate have been shown to increase for the same intensity of exercise. Muscle mass and therefore strength also deteriorate but at a less rapid rate. Now you may be able to understand why pre-season training feels so tough even after just 6–8 weeks of inactivity.

# Individual difference

This suggests that the benefits of training are optimised when programmes are set to meet the needs and abilities of an individual. What may help one athlete to improve may not be successful on another. The coach must therefore be very sympathetic to the needs of the individual athlete and adjust training programmes accordingly.

# Moderation

To prevent overtraining it is essential that the training programme is planned sufficiently well to include a variation in training intensities and to include regular rest days. By simply following a ratio of three hard sessions to one easy session overtraining should be avoided.

# Variance

Variety is the spice of life. So to prevent boredom, staleness and injury through training it is necessary to ensure that the training programme employs a range of training methods and loads so as not to impose too much psychological or physiological stress on the performer.

# The F.I.T.T. regime

The coach may also wish to consider the F.I.T.T. regime when designing the training programme. These letters stand for:

- F = frequency of training
- I = intensity of exercise
- T = time or duration of exercise
- T = type of training.

### 'F'

The **frequency of training**. The elite athlete will need to do some sort of training most days, depending upon the activity being undertaken. Endurance or aerobic type activities can be performed five or six times per week, but more intense or anaerobic activities such as strength or speed work should be performed three or four times per week, as sufficient rest days are required for the body tissues to repair themselves following this high intensity work.

## 'I'

The **intensity of the exercise**. This also depends upon the type of training occurring, and can be quite difficult to measure objectively. Some ways of gauging the intensity of exercise are outlined below:

- Calculating the **training zone**
- Calculating the performer's $\dot{V}O_2$ max and working at a percentage of it
- Calculating the **respiratory exchange ratio**
- Using lactate tests
- Also more basic tests such as the 'talk test'.

For aerobic work, exercise intensity can be measured by calculating an individual's 'training zone'; this is represented by the training heart rate and so involves observing heart rate values. This has become much easier with the advent of the heart rate monitor.

The most established method of calculating the training zone is known as the **Karvonen Principle**. Karvonen developed a formula to identify correct training intensities as a percentage of the sum of the maximum heart rate reserve and resting heart rate. Maximum heart rate reserve can be calculated by subtracting resting heart rate (HRrest) from an individual's maximum heart rate (HRmax):

$$\text{Maximal heart rate reserve} = \text{HRmax} - \text{HRrest}$$

Where an individual's maximal heart rate can be calculated by subtracting their age from 220:

$$\text{Maximal heart rate} = 220 - \text{age}$$

Karvonen suggests a training intensity of between 60–75% of maximal heart rate reserve for the average athlete, although this can obviously be adapted to account for individual differences.

$$\text{Training heart rate 60\%} = 0.60 \text{ (maxHR reserve)} + \text{HRrest}$$

Consider the following example to illustrate the value of this measure of intensity:

A 20-year-old rower, with a resting heart rate of 65 bpm is aiming to build up his endurance capacities for a forthcoming event. He is advised to train between 60–75% of his training heart rate reserve in the weeks prior to the event. To calculate his training zone, the rower used the Karvonen formula as follows:

$$
\begin{aligned}
\text{Training heart} \\
\text{rate 60\%}
\end{aligned}
\begin{aligned}
&= 0.60 \text{ (HRmax} - \text{HRrest)} \\
&\quad + \text{HRrest} \\
&= 0.60 \text{ (200} - 65) + 65 \\
&= 81 + 65 \\
&= \textbf{146 beats per minute}
\end{aligned}
$$

$$
\begin{aligned}
\text{Training heart} \\
\text{rate 75\%}
\end{aligned}
\begin{aligned}
&= 0.75 \text{ (HRmax} - \text{HRrest)} \\
&\quad + \text{HRrest} \\
&= 0.75 \text{ (200} - 65) + 65 \\
&= 101 + 65 \\
&= \textbf{166 beats per minute}
\end{aligned}
$$

Thus the rower now has some precise figures to use to ensure that he is training at the correct intensity. In order for some kind of aerobic adaptation to occur, the rower must be exercising within his **target zone**, between 146 and 166 beats per minute.

This is a valued measure of exercise intensity since it relates closely to both the stress being imposed on the heart and the vascular system and the per cent of $\dot{V}O_2$ max at which the athlete is working.

Another method of monitoring the intensity of training is through working the athlete at a **percentage of $\dot{V}O_2$ max**. For the elite endurance athlete, this should be no less than 70% of $\dot{V}O_2$ max, while those exercising for health-related reasons will see benefits from training at just 50% of their $\dot{V}O_2$ max. Fig 7.2 shows the linear relationship between heart rate and oxygen consumption ($\dot{V}O_2$). If the athlete's HRmax is known, then it is possible for the coach to extrapolate the $\dot{V}O_2$ max from the graph in fig 7.2.

A coach could also use **lactate tests** to ensure the athlete is working sufficiently hard and analyse oxygen consumption and carbon dioxide production to determine the **respiratory exchange ratio**. The Respiratory Exchange Ratio (RER) or Respiratory Quotient is a method of determining which energy providing nutrient is predominantly in use during exercise. It is represented as follows:

$$RER = \frac{\text{Volume of } CO_2 \text{ expired per minute}}{\text{Volume of } O_2 \text{ uptake per minute}}$$

The closer the value is to 1.0 the more likely it is the body is using glycogen as a fuel, whereas the expected value for fats is 0.7. Intermediate figures suggest that a mixture of fuels is being utilised which is obviously the expected norm. Obviously the harder the athlete is working the more he or she relies on using glycogen as a fuel.

'T'

The **time or duration that the exercise is in progress.** For aerobic type activities, the athlete should be

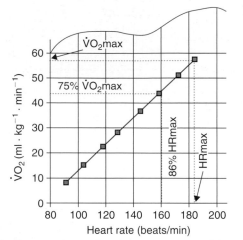

Fig 7.2. The linear relationship between HR and $\dot{V}O_2$

- Using table 7.1 and fig 7.3, calculate your training zone (between 60 and 75% of your maximum heart rate reserve).
- Now complete a 15-minute run, ensuring your heart rate lies at 70% of your MHR.
- Sketch the heart rate curve expected.

Table 7.1. The training zone

| AGE | | 20 | 25 | 30 | 35 | 40 | 45 | 50 | 55 | 60 | 65 | 70 | 75 | 80 |
|---|---|---|---|---|---|---|---|---|---|---|---|---|---|---|
| 55% | 19 | 18 | 18 | 17 | 17 | 17 | 16 | 16 | 15 | 15 | 14 | 14 | 13 | 13 |
| 60% | 21 | 20 | 19 | 19 | 19 | 18 | 18 | 17 | 17 | 16 | 16 | 15 | 15 | 14 |
| 70% | 24 | 23 | 23 | 22 | 22 | 21 | 20 | 20 | 19 | 19 | 18 | 18 | 17 | 16 |
| 80% | 27 | 27 | 26 | 25 | 25 | 24 | 23 | 23 | 22 | 21 | 21 | 20 | 19 | 19 |
| 90% | 29 | 28 | 28 | 27 | 26 | 26 | 25 | 24 | 23 | 23 | 22 | 21 | 21 | 20 |

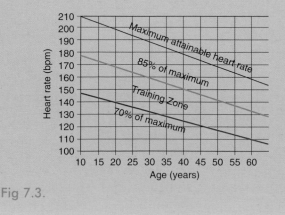

Fig 7.3.

Use table 7.1 as a calculator to work out your target training zone at various intensities. All scores reflect your heart rate for a 10 second count. Don't forget to start counting from zero! If you fall between age ranges take the next stage group up. For example, if you are 18 and wish to train at 70% of your maximum heart rate, find the age group 20 along the top of the table and move down until you come to 70% of MHR. Your target 10 s pulse rate should be 23 beats. You may wish to convert this to beats per minute, in which case multiply the figure in the box by six.

**An investigation into training intensities – the training zone!**
- Using the Karvonen Principle, calculate your training zone.
- Record your resting pulse rate
- In groups of three work on a given method of aerobic exercise (eg, running, step-ups, rowing, cycling). One person should be exercising at a steady pace, the second keeps an eye on heart rate and the third records the results.
- Record heart rate at the following times:
  - a) Immediately prior to exercise
  - b) 2 mins after exercise commences
  - c) 5 mins after exercise commences (ensure you are in the zone!)
  - d) 7 mins after exercise commences (still in the zone?)
  - e) 10 mins after exercise commences (stop exercise now!)
  - f) 1 min after exercise stops
  - g) 3 mins after exercise stops
  - h) 5 mins after exercise stops
- Copy out and record your results in the table below

| HRrest | Prior to Ex | 2 mins during | 5 mins during | 7 mins during | 10 mins during | 1 min after | 3 mins after | 5 mins after |
|--------|-------------|---------------|---------------|---------------|----------------|-------------|--------------|--------------|
|        |             |               |               |               |                |             |              |              |

- Construct a graph to illustrate your heart rate before, during and after exercise. Identify on your graph your training zone.

**ACTIVITY 2**

training within his/her training zone for a minimum of 20–30 mins. However, duration should not be considered in isolation since intensity of training often determines the duration of the training session.

## 'T'

The **type or mode of training that is undertaken**. This really relates to the principle of specificity as discussed earlier in this chapter.

# Warm-ups and cool-downs

## Warm-up

One might not immediately think of warm-ups and cool-downs as a principle of training, but as they should be undertaken prior to and following every training session and will improve the effectiveness of training, it seems highly appropriate to discuss them here.

Before embarking upon any type of exercise, it is imperative to perform a warm-up, as it is fundamental to safe practice.

A warm-up should prepare the body for exercise. It can prevent injury and muscle soreness, and has the following physiological benefits:

- The **release of adrenaline** will increase heart rate and dilate capillaries, which in turn enable greater amounts and increased speed of oxygen and blood delivery to the muscles.
- The speed of oxygen delivery is further improved as a result of the **decreased viscosity of the blood** which occurs as a consequence of the increase in muscle temperature.

- **Increased muscle temperatures** associated with exercise will **facilitate enzyme activity** as well as encourage the disassociation of oxygen from haemoglobin. This increases muscle metabolism and therefore ensures a readily available supply of energy through the breakdown of glycogen.

- Increased temperatures also lead to decreased viscosity within the muscle. This enables **greater extensibility and elasticity of muscle fibres** which ultimately leads to increased speed and force of contraction.

- Warm-ups also make us more alert, due to an **increase in the speed of nerve impulse conduction**.

- Increased production of synovial fluid ensures efficient movement at the joints.

- Certain **psychological benefits** can also occur through a warm-up, particularly if the individual has certain superstitions or rituals they follow. Think of the New Zealand All Blacks Rugby Team performing the Haka, prior to kick off.

Furthermore, it should not be forgotten that warm-ups should be *specific* to the activity that follows, and include exercises which prepare the muscles to be used and activate the energy systems required for that particular activity.

To ensure the athlete gains as much from the warm-up as possible, the following stages should be followed:

1. The first phase of a warm-up has the purpose of **raising the heart rate**, increasing the speed of oxygen delivery to the muscles, and of course raising the body temperature. This can be achieved by performing some kind of cardiovascular exercise such as jogging.

2. Now that muscle temperature has increased, the athlete can perform some mobility or stretching exercises. It is essential that both static stretches and some calisthenic type activities are performed where the muscle is working over its full range. Press-ups, squat thrusts and lunges are good for this.

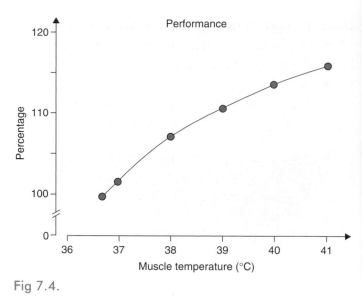

Fig 7.4.

3. The final stage of a warm-up should involve a **sport-specific or skill-related component** where the neuromuscular mechanisms related to the activity to follow are worked. For example, practising serving in tennis, tumble turns in swimming or shooting baskets in basketball.

## Cool-down

Following exercise, a similar process must be followed in order to prevent unnecessary discomfort; this is a cool-down. It involves performing some kind of light continuous exercise where heart rate remains elevated. The purpose is to keep metabolic activity high, and capillaries dilated, so that oxygen can be flushed through the muscle tissue, removing and oxidising any lactic acid that remains. This will therefore prevent blood pooling in the veins which can cause dizziness if exercise is stopped abruptly. A cool-down may also result in limiting the effects of **DOMS (Delayed Onset of Muscle Soreness)** which is characterised by tender and painful muscles often experienced in the days following heavy and unaccustomed exercise. The explanation of this soreness is quite simple and results from the damage to muscle fibres and connective tissue surrounding the fibres. The soreness is usually temporary and goes within a couple of days as the muscle fibres repair themselves. DOMS is most likely to occur following eccentric contraction and can result from weight training, plyometrics or even walking down steep hills. The final part of the cool-down period should involve a period of stretching activity, which should hopefully facilitate and improve flexibility as the muscles are very warm at this stage.

> **ACTIVITY 3**
>
> You are aiming to compete in a marathon. Outline some of the principles of training you would employ to ensure your training regime is successful.

> **ACTIVITY 4**
>
> Design a warm-up programme for a sport of your choice. What activities would you include in your programme, and why?

Now that we understand the basic laws which govern training, the next stage in our search for a beneficial training programme is to determine the method or type of training that is best employed.

# Training methods
## Continuous methods

Continuous methods of training work on developing endurance and therefore stress the **aerobic energy system**. Central to this method of training is the performance of rhythmic exercise at a steady rate or **low intensity** which use the large muscle groups of the body over a long period of time (between 30 mins and two hours). Good examples of such activities include jogging, swimming, cycling or aerobic dance. The intensity of such exercise should be at approximately 60% to 80% of HRmax, as outlined in the **Karvonen Principle** so the body is not experiencing too much discomfort while exercising.

The great advantage of this type of training, however, is that great distances can be covered without the lactate build-up associated with anaerobic training methods. Distance runners, for example, may total up to 140 miles per week, a distance equivalent of London to Lincoln.

With such high mileage comes the danger of injury, particularly to the muscles and joints, so any programme should be thoroughly scrutinised. Other disadvantages of this type of training are that it can be quite monotonous, and although good in developing an aerobic base for all activities, it is not necessarily sport specific when it comes to team games. The health-related benefits of continuous training have been well documented; jogging and aerobics are very popular, and as long as individuals are made aware of the injury risk factors, there is no reason why the majority cannot participate safely.

### Fartlek, or speedplay

This is a slightly different method of continuous training. It is a form of endurance conditioning, where the **aerobic energy system** is stressed due to the continuous nature of the exercise. The only difference, however, is that throughout the duration of the exercise, the speed or intensity of the activity is varied, so that both the **aerobic and anaerobic systems can be stressed**. Fartlek sessions are usually performed for a minimum of 45 minutes, with the intensity of the session varying from low intensity walking to high intensity sprinting. Traditionally Fartlek training has taken place in the countryside where there is varied terrain, but this alternating pace method could occur anywhere and you could use your local environment to help you; for example:

- Easy jog for three lamp posts
- Sprint for one lamp post

- Easy jog for three lamp posts
- Sprint for one lamp post
- Repeat three further times
- Walk for one minute
- Jog at 75% of MHR for five minutes
- Repeat four times.

Devised by a Swede, Gosta Holmer, many physiologists have adapted this method of training.

A few examples now follow:

**The Gerschler method** involves jogging for 10 minutes followed by 30 seconds of long, fast strides followed by 90 seconds jogging recovery. The jogging recovery decreases by 15 seconds after each 30 second stride-out. For example, the next bout of exercise would involve 30 seconds fast followed by 75 seconds jog recovery, the next 30 seconds of work is followed by 60 seconds of jog recovery and so on until the athlete only has 15 seconds of recovery. Having completed this one set of 30 second strides the athlete will repeat once more 30 seconds fast followed by 90 seconds jogging, etc.

**The Saltin method** involves a 10-minute warm-up jog followed by three minutes of sustained fast running with 60 seconds of jog recovery, repeated six times. This is useful for middle distance and cross country runners, and perhaps for boxers, who must sustain all-out effort over three-minute rounds.

This type of training can be very individual and the athlete can determine the speed or intensity at which he/she wishes to work. It can also be fun and offers variety to what some regard as the monotony of continuous jogging. Since both aerobic and anaerobic systems are stressed through this method of training, a wealth of sportspeople can benefit. It is particularly suited to those activities that involve a mixture of aerobic and anaerobic work; eg, field games such as rugby, hockey or soccer. However, to make the session more sport specific for games players

the direction of running should be altered to mimic the running pattern within a game – for example, side to side and backward running should be included as well as running forwards in a straight line.

# Intermittent training

Intermittent methods of training involve periods of work or exercise interspersed with **periods of recovery**. Athletes appear to be able to perform considerably more work when the session is broken down into short intense periods of effort and recovery breaks, and the physiological benefits are great.

## Interval training

This is probably the most popular type of training used in sport for training the elite athlete. It is very versatile and can be used in almost any activity, although it is most widely used in swimming, athletics and cycling. Interval training can improve both aerobic and anaerobic capacities and enables the athlete to exercise at the specific intensity necessary to *train the relevant energy system* for that activity.

In order for the correct system to be stressed, several variables have been identified which can be manipulated. These variables include:

1. Distance of the work interval (duration)
2. Intensity of the work interval (speed)
3. The number of repetitions within a session
4. The number of sets within a session
5. Duration of the rest interval
6. Activity during the rest interval.

In order to train the relevant energy system, the coach must ensure that the variables have been adjusted appropriately:

1. **For the ATP-PC** system, the duration of the work period should last for 3–10 seconds, or an equivalent distance that can be covered in that time at the highest intensity (depending upon the activity being performed).

## ATP-PC system development

eg, 3 ×10 × 30 m (wbr) 5 mins rest between sets

Where:
| | |
|---|---|
| 3 | = No sets |
| 10 | = No of repetitions |
| 30 m | = Distance of work interval |
| wbr | = Walk back recovery |

## Lactic acid development

eg, 8 × 300 m runs 3 mins work relief

Where:
| | |
|---|---|
| 8 | = No of repetitions |
| 300 m | = Distance of work interval |
| 3 mins | = Recovery period |

## Aerobic development

eg, 4–6 × 2–5 min runs – work:relief ratio = 1:1 (2–5 min)

Where:
| | |
|---|---|
| 4–6 | = No of repetitions |
| 2–5 mins | = Duration of work period |
| W:R | = 1:1 (2–5 mins) = Recovery period |

2. Intensity should be assessed by the athlete working at a percentage of their maximum effort or personal best time for the distance. For the ATP-PC system this should be 90–100%.

3. Generally, the number of repetitions depends upon the length of the work period. For the ATP-PC system, the work interval is relatively short and we can expect to perform up to 50 short intense bouts within a session.

4. These 50 repetitions may be divided up into a number of sets (a group of work and rest intervals), to ensure that the athlete does not get unduly fatigued; eg, 5 sets × 10 reps.

5. Between each repetition is a period of rest which can be determined by the time it takes for the heart rate to return to about 150 beats per minute. It can be compared to the work interval time, expressed as the **work:relief (rest) ratio**. For the ATP-PC system where the work interval is relatively short, the rest period may take three times that before the heart lowers to 150 bpm. This would be expressed as a work:relief ratio of 1:3.

6. The type of activity that takes place during these rest intervals differs, depending upon the energy system being trained. The ATP-PC system for example requires no activity apart from perhaps some light stretching during the recovery phase, while the lactic acid system will require active recovery involving light jogging or walking.

**For the lactic acid system**, an exercise period of between 15 seconds and 90 seconds should be performed at a moderate intensity. Up to twelve

repetitions may be completed over two or three sets with a work to relief ratio of 1:2. This should give time for some although not all lactic acid to be removed. Thus in successive work intervals, the body must work with some lactic acid already present within the system, which should improve the buffering capacity of the body. To speed up the removal of lactate during the relief period, some light exercise should be performed, such as rapid walking or jogging, this is known as **work relief**.

**To train the aerobic system**, the work interval should be much longer, perhaps up to seven or eight minutes in duration. The intensity should again be moderate (and certainly faster than any pace undertaken during continuous training) and measured as a percentage of personal best times for the distance. The longer exercise periods mean that fewer repetitions are needed, maybe only three or four in one session, which can be performed in one set. In order to put extra stress on the aerobic system the recovery time is usually much shorter in comparison to the work period. A work:relief ratio of 1:1/2 may be used where the athlete rests for half the time it took to complete the work period.

Table 7.2. Interval training prescriptions

| Major energy system | Training time (min:sec) | Repetitions per workout | Sets per workout | Repetitions per set | Work: relief ratio | Type of relief interval |
|---|---|---|---|---|---|---|
| ATP-PC | 0:10 | 50 | 5 | 10 | | rest-relief (eg, walking, flexing) |
| | 0:15 | 45 | 5 | 9 | | |
| | 0:20 | 40 | 4 | 10 | 1:3 | |
| | 0:25 | 32 | 4 | 8 | | |
| ATP-PC/LA | 0:30 | 25 | 5 | 5 | | work-relief (eg, light to mild exercise, jogging) |
| | 0:40–0:50 | 20 | 4 | 5 | 1:3 | |
| | 1:00–1:10 | 15 | 3 | 5 | | |
| | 1:20 | 10 | 2 | 5 | 1:2 | |
| LA/$O_2$ | 1:30–2:00 | 8 | 2 | 4 | 1:2 | work-relief |
| | 2:10–2:40 | 6 | 1 | 6 | | |
| | 2:50–3:00 | 4 | 1 | 4 | 1:1 | rest-relief |
| $O_2$ | 3:00–4:00 | 4 | 1 | 4 | 1:1 | rest-relief |
| | 4:00–5:00 | 3 | 1 | 3 | 1:½ | |
| Major energy system | Training distance (M) | | | | | |
| | Run Swim | | | | | |
| ATP-PC | 50 10 | 50 | 5 | 10 | 1:3 | rest-relief (eg, walking, flexing) |
| | 100 25 | 24 | 3 | 8 | | |
| ATP-PC/LA | 200 50 | 16 | 4 | 4 | 1:3 | work-relief (eg, light to mild exercise, jogging) |
| | 400 100 | 8 | 2 | 4 | 1:2 | |
| LA/$O_2$ | 600 150 | 5 | 1 | 5 | 1:2 | work-relief |
| | 800 200 | 4 | 2 | 2 | 1:1 | rest-relief |
| $O_2$ | 1,000 250 | 3 | 1 | 3 | 1:½ | rest-relief |
| | 1,200 300 | 3 | 1 | 3 | 1:½ | |

The requirements of an interval training session can be expressed as the **interval training prescription**. For example, a swimmer may have the following session prescribed:

$$2 \times 4 \times 200\,\text{m W:R 1:1/2}$$

where:    2 = number of sets
4 = number of repetitions
200 m = training distance
1:1/2 = work to relief ratio.

Some examples of interval training regimes are outlined in table 7.2.

**Sprint interval training sessions** are specifically designed to stress the ATP-PC system, improving its capacity and **increasing the muscle stores of ATP and PC**. This obviously has a direct effect upon sprinters or any activity where bursts of speed are required.

**Fast interval training sessions** develop anaerobic endurance and therefore stress the lactic acid system. The **buffering capacity of the body improves**, which delays the onset of fatigue and decreases the effect of lactic acid. This training is of particular importance to 400 m runners and sprint swimmers.

The aerobic system is stressed **by performing slower intervals** which improves the oxidative capacity of the body. Any endurance-based event such as distance running or swimming will benefit from this type of training, in addition to field games such as rugby and hockey.

Again, as with other training methods, it is important to ensure that where possible the session is adapted to suit the requirements of the game. For

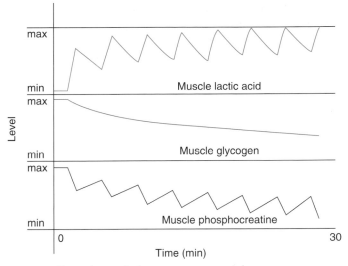

Fig 7.5. Physiological changes occurring during a training session

example, a squash player may adapt the work period to include running to one corner of the court and returning to the 'T' then running to the second corner and back to the 'T', running to the third, etc, until all four corners have been touched – this might represent on repetition of a work period which can then be followed by a period of rest.

## Circuit training

Circuit training involves performing a number of calisthenic exercises in succession, such as press-ups, abdominal curls, step-ups etc. Each exercise is usually performed for a set amount of time or a set number of repetitions, and the circuit can be adapted to meet the specific fitness requirements of a given sport or activity (see fig 7.6).

When planning a circuit there are several factors that need consideration. The first of these is the most fundamental – what exactly do you require the circuit for? Once you have answered this you can choose the exercises to include (see examples of exercises in table 7.3). You will also need to consider.

• the number of participants
• their level of fitness
• the amount of time, space and equipment that are available.

Having considered all these points you can now go ahead and plan the layout of your circuit.

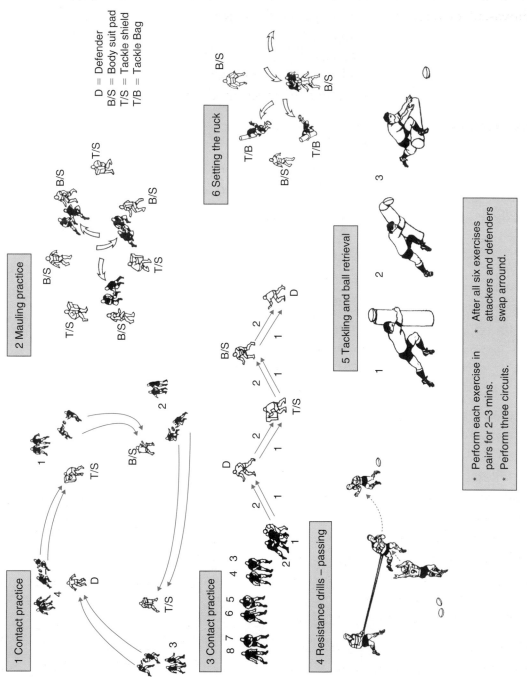

D = Defender
B/S = Body suit pad
T/S = Tackle shield
T/B = Tackle Bag

1 Contact practice

2 Mauling practice

3 Contact practice

4 Resistance drills – passing

5 Tackling and ball retrieval

6 Setting the ruck

* Perform each exercise in pairs for 2–3 mins.
* Perform three circuits.

* After all six exercises attackers and defenders swap arround.

Fig 7.6. Rugby contact circuit

**ACTIVITY 6**

Design a circuit training session for an activity of your choice. Give reasons for the exercises you have chosen and explain how the principle of progressive overload could be applied. Table 7.3 might help in the selection of some exercises.

Table 7.3. Exercises to include in a circuit

| Cardiovascular exercises | running around the gym<br>skipping<br>step-ups<br>cycling on an ergometer<br>bounding exercises on a mat |
| --- | --- |
| Trunk exercises | abdominal curls<br>crunchies<br>dorsal raises<br>trunk twists |
| Arm exercises | press-ups/box press<br>bicep curls<br>tricep dips<br>shoulder press<br>squat thrusts<br>chin-ups to beam |
| Leg exercises | single leg squats<br>any of the cardiovascular exercises<br>outlined above |

One golden rule when devising the layout of the circuit is that *the same body part should not be exercised consecutively*. Therefore the sequence of the exercises should be as follows: arms, trunk, cardiovascular, legs, arms, trunk, cardiovascular, etc. The exception is for experienced athletes performing an 'overload' circuit where the endurance of one muscle group is being trained.

The great benefit of circuit training is that it is extremely adaptable, since exercises can be included or omitted to suit almost all activities. It also enables large numbers of participants to train together at their own level. With regular testing, improvements in fitness are easily visible through circuit training as current work can be compared to previous test scores. Fig 7.7 illustrates a 3 in 1

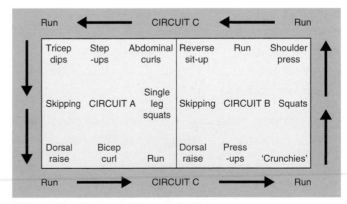

Each participant is to complete each circuit.
Circuit A = 8 exercises × 30 secs = 4 mins
Circuit B = 8 exercises × 30 secs = 4 mins
Circuit C = Run around outside = 4 mins
Repeat 2 or 3 times

Each participant is to complete circuit A, B and C with 60 secs walking recovery between circuit.

Fig 7.7. A general fitness circuit

circuit, whereby each participant completes circuits A, B and C. This circuit is particularly good for general conditioning and enables large numbers to participate.

# Strength training

Strength gains are sought by many athletes and usually occur either through **weight or resistance training methods,** or through a further type of training known as **plyometrics.**

With advances in technology and the improvement in the quality of weight machines, weight training has increased in popularity in both athletic and recreational training regimes. It can be used to develop several components of fitness, including strength, strength endurance and explosive power. Which of these are stressed at a particular time is determined by manipulating the weight or resistance, the number of repetitions and the number of sets. Central to the devising of an effective weight training programme is the principle of **one repetition maximum (1RM).** The 1RM is the maximum amount of weight the performer can lift with one repetition. Once this has been found for each exercise the coach can design a programme adjusting the resistance as a percentage of the athlete's maximum lift.

For activities where **maximum strength** is required, such as power lifting or throwing the hammer, training methods which increase muscle strength and size will be required. Essentially this will involve some form of **very high resistance, low repetition exercise.** For example:

• Performing 3 sets of 2–6 repetitions at 80–100% of maximum strength, with full recovery between sets.

Key points for power development are:

a) the movement and contraction period must be explosive to ensure the muscle works rapidly

b) use very high loads or resistance which will encourage the muscle to recruit all its motor units

c) ensure the muscle recovers fully between sets, enabling the relevant energy system to recover.

To train for activities which require **strength endurance,** such as swimming or rowing, a different approach to training will be required. In order to perform more repetitions, *a lighter load or resistance* is needed and the following programme might be prescribed:

• 3 sets of 20 repetitions at 50–60% of maximum strength with full recovery between sets.

One aspect of strength that is difficult to improve through regular resistance training is **core strength.** Core strength is the combined strength of all the muscles from your hips to your armpits – and is responsible for many things including posture. An increase in core strength can lead to increases in virtually all other types of strength and dramatically reduces the chance of injury during strength training. The best method of improving core strength and stability is with the use of a Swiss ball. Simply performing abdominal crunchies or leg raises on the Swiss ball will strengthen the abdominal and lower back muscles, the 'core' of the body's strength.

## Plyometrics

Power is the ability to produce maximal muscular forces very rapidly. It is determined by the force exerted by the muscle (strength) and the speed at which the muscle shortens:

$$\text{Power} = \text{Force} \times \text{Velocity}$$

It thus follows that by improving either strength or speed of shortening, power may be improved. One method of training which may improve the speed at which a muscle shortens is plyometrics.

It has long been established that muscles generate more force in contraction when they have been previously stretched. Plyometrics enables this to occur by taking the muscle through an **eccentric (lengthened) phase** before **a powerful concentric (shortening) phase.** This stimulates adaptation within the neuromuscular system whereby the muscle spindles within the muscle cause a **stretch reflex,** which prevents muscle damage and produces a more powerful concentric contraction of the muscle group. This has important consequences for sprinting,

Table 7.4. The development of different types of strength

| Objective | Intensity of training load | Repetitions in each set | Number of sets | Recovery between sets | Evaluation procedures | Training of value for |
|---|---|---|---|---|---|---|
| development of maximum strength | 85–95% | 1–5 | normal 2–4 advanced 5–8 | 4–5 mins | maximum lift dynamometer | weight lifting, shot, discus, hammer, javelin, jumping events, rugby and contact sports, men's gymnastics |
| development of elastic strength | 75–85% | 6–10 | (4–6) | 3–5 mins | standing, long and vertical jump capability | all sports requiring 'explosive' strength qualities – sprinting, jumping, throwing, striking |
| development of advanced level of strength endurance | 50–75% of maximum | 15–20 | (3–5) | 30–45 secs | maximum reps possible | rowing, wrestling, skiing, swimming, 400 m, steeplechase etc. |
| development of a basic level of strength endurance | 25–50% of maximum | 15–20 | (4–6) | 60 secs | maximum reps possible | generally required for all sports suitable for young and novice competitors and fitness participants |

*Source:* Leeds University, 1988.

Concentric contration taking place in the quadricep muscle group

Eccentric contraction taking place in the quadriceps muscle group

Fig 7.8. Examples of plyometric exercises

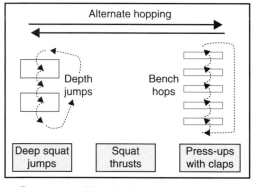

Alternate hopping

Depth jumps

Bench hops

Deep squat jumps

Squat thrusts

Press-ups with claps

Rotate around the circuit twice one minute on each exercise stretch off during rest intervals

Fig 7.9. A plyometrics circuit

jumping and throwing events in athletics, as well as in games such as rugby, volleyball and basketball where leg strength is central to performance.

Exercises that might form part of the plyometrics session include:

- bounding
- hopping
- leaping
- skipping
- depth jumps (jumping off and onto boxes)
- press-ups with claps
- throwing and catching a medicine ball.

Taking the example of **depth jumping** (fig 7.8), here the athlete drops down from a box or platform 50–80 cm high. On landing the quadricep muscle

group lengthens, pre-stretching the muscle. A stretch reflex causes the muscle to give a very forceful concentric contraction driving the athlete up onto a second platform. Furthermore the exercise becomes more effective if the athlete spends as little time as possible in contact with the ground when landing. This particular plyometric activity can also be made sport specific. For example, a basketball player could perform a rebound after dropping down from the box or a volleyball player perform a block, etc. Due to the high impact nature of the plyometrics individuals would need to be screened for injury and participants would need to undergo a thorough warm-up.

Key points to consider when undertaking plyometric training:

- warm up thoroughly;
- use a flat, non-slip landing surface that has good shock absorbing properties, such as a grass field;
- make sure any boxes or benches used are sturdy and safe;
- ensure you follow guidelines on technique of the exercises, ie, landing on the ball of your foot, then rocking back onto your heel and then taking off from the ball of the foot again. The sequence should therefore be 'ball-heel-ball';
- progression in exercise should be gradual to avoid soreness;
- if you experience joint or muscular pain stop immediately.

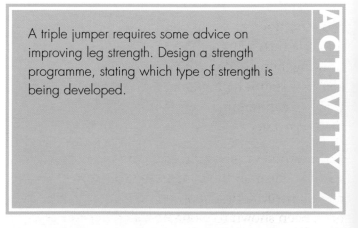

A triple jumper requires some advice on improving leg strength. Design a strength programme, stating which type of strength is being developed.

ACTIVITY 7

The strength gains and muscle hypertrophy associated with strength training may only start to

**Parachute running**

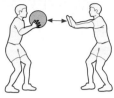

**Aim**
Enhance running strength and power and improve stride length

**Method**
• Athlete wears a belt with a small parachute attached by a cord which increases air resistance

**Bag jumps with 180-degree turn**

Start

**Aim**
Explosive lower body development

**Method**
• Start in a two-point stance (one foot in front of the other)
• Jump over the first bag, rotating 180 degrees while in the air
• Land between two bags and immediately jump over the second bag, rotating 180 degrees in the opposite direction
• Jump and rotate over 4 to 6 bags

**Medicine ball bull in a ring**

**Aim**
Improve quickness and elastic strength

**Method**
• Partners face each other and chest pass a medicine ball rapidly

**Fig 7.10.** From Brown/Femingo/Santana, *Training for Speed, Agility & Quickness*, Human Kinetics, 2000

become evident after about eight weeks of training, and are largely due to the increase in size and volume of the myofibrils.

# SAQ training

SAQ stands for **speed**, **agility** and **quickness**. It is a relatively new type of training that is used in many team games such as rugby and football and is designed to improve the speed, agility and quickness of a performer. Central to this activity are resistance drills, perhaps using bungy ropes, ladder drills to improve leg speed and jumping activities to improve leg speed and strength. Fig 7.10 gives some exercises used in SAQ training.

# Mobility training

Mobility training is the method employed to improve flexibility. It is often a neglected form of training, but should be incorporated into every athlete's training programme. Effective flexibility training can improve performance and help prevent the occurrence of injury.

The method of stretching used in mobility training should centre on the connective tissue and the muscle tissue acting upon the joint, as these tissues have been shown to elongate following a period of regular and repeated stretching. Two types of stretching have been identified and outlined below.

## Active stretching

The athlete performs voluntary muscular contractions, and holds the stretch for a period of 30–60 seconds. By consciously relaxing the target muscle at the limit of the range of motion, muscle elongation may occur following regular contraction.

## Passive stretching

This refers to the range of movement which can occur with the aid of external force. This is generally performed with the help of a partner who can offer some resistance, although gravity and body weight can also be used.

One method of flexibility training that has emerged from passive stretching is **proprioceptive neuromuscular facilitation (PNF)**. This seeks to decrease the reflex shortening of the muscle being stretched, which occurs when a muscle is stretched to its limit. A simple PNF technique is now outlined:

1. Move slowly to the limit of your range of motion with a partner aiding (passive stretch). Hold for a few seconds.

2. Just before the point of discomfort, isometrically contract the muscle being stretched for between 6 and 10 seconds.

3. After the hold, the muscle will release, having stimulated a Golgi tendon organ (GTO)

response which causes further **relaxation** of the muscle and enabling further stretching of the muscle with the aid of a partner.

PNF stretching relies on the fact that when a muscle contracts isometrically when stretched, the stretch reflex mechanism of the muscle spindles is switched off. The GTO causes relaxation of the muscle and therefore enables the muscle to stretch further than previously. A second PNF method is known as the CRAC method (Contract–Relax, Antagonist–Contract).

With continued practice of PNF, a new limit of the muscle stretch may occur, but, don't forget that pain is the body's signal that damage is occurring, and athletes should not stretch beyond the slight discomfort.

Furthermore, stretching and mobility training should only be performed after a thorough warm-up where an increase in body temperature has occurred. This is easily achieved by performing a period of light cardiovascular exercise, centring upon those muscle groups that are to be stretched. In addition, wear warm clothing while performing the stretches to maintain body temperature; if possible, perform in a warm environment.

Complete the table below comparing the different types of training outlined.

| Type of training | Predominant components of fitness trained | Energy system stressed | Example of a training session | Example when used |
|---|---|---|---|---|
| Continuous | | | | |
| Fartlek | | | | |
| Interval | | | | |
| Circuit | | | | |
| Strength/Weight | | | | |
| Strength (Plyometrics) | | | | |
| Mobility (Proprioceptive Neuromuscular Facilitation) | | | | |

**ACTIVITY 8**

# Altitude training

Altitude training is a method of training based on the principle that with an increase in altitude, the partial pressure of oxygen ($pO_2$) in the atmosphere decreases by about a half, causing the body to adapt by *increasing red blood cell mass and haemoglobin levels* to cope with a lower $pO_2$. It is widely used by endurance athletes to enhance their oxygen carrying capacity and when athletes return to sea level these increases remain, yet the $pO_2$ has increased which means that the body can transport and utilise more oxygen, giving improved endurance performance. However, there appears to be contradictory evidence concerning the benefits of altitude training and recent evidence suggests that living at altitude while training at sea level produces the greatest endurance performance and in doing so athletes can increase oxygen carrying capacity of the blood by up to 150%.

Indeed some athletes live in special cabins at sea level that mimic the conditions of altitude so that the athletes don't actually have to travel abroad.

Table 7.5. Types of training

| Type | Advantages | Disadvantages |
|------|-----------|---------------|
| Continuous | • time efficient<br>• trains cardiovascular and muscular endurance<br>• easy to follow routine programme<br>• can be sports-specific, eg, distance running<br>• less chance of injury because lower intensity | • athletes may need higher intensity can be monotonous<br>• may not be specific to some activities, eg, team sports |
| Fartlek | • adds variety of pace<br>• train at higher intensity than in continuous training | • may not be sports-specific<br>• higher intensity may increase risk of injury |
| Interval | • adds variety of pace and duration<br>• can be very sports-specific, eg, sprinting | • more time is needed<br>• increases risk of injury due to higher intensity |
| Circuit | • trains cardiovascular and muscular endurance as well as strength<br>• time efficient<br>• can be very sports-specific | • not maximal improvements in endurance and strength<br>• need access to equipment |
| Aerobic circuit | • time efficient<br>• can train at high intensity<br>• can be very sports-specific | • need access to equipment<br>• higher risk of injury |

From Abernethy *The Biophysical Foundations of Human Movement, Human Kinetics,* 1997

There are, however, some disadvantages associated with altitude training. As well as being expensive many athletes have found that training at altitude can cause altitude sickness and as a consequence they cannot train at the same intensity as they would at sea level and so actually suffer from detraining.

# Responses and adaptations to training

We have already mentioned that the reason behind training is to improve our components of fitness, the capacity of each energy system and overall performance. The body responds to the stresses that training imposes upon it and subsequently adapts and adjusts to meet the demands of the exercise that is occurring.

## Short-term responses

Short-term responses to exercise are the ways in which the body's systems adjust to cope with the exercise during a training session. They are the immediate responses of the body. At the end of the exercise period the body will return to its normal resting state.

## Cardiovascular responses to exercise

We have established in previous chapters that many adjustments are made by the cardiovascular system during exercise to ensure adequate delivery of oxygen and nutrients to the muscle and efficient removal of metabolites from the muscle. Such adjustments include an **increased heart rate** between 60–80 bpm at **rest** to between 160–180 bpm during exercise.

We also see a slight **increase in stroke volume** during exercise, with the elite athlete increasing stroke volume from 110 ml/beat to 170 ml/beat while exercising; this is due to **Starlings law**.

There is also an **increase in cardiac output** (cardiac output is a product of heart rate and stroke volume). Cardiac output may increase from 5–6 L at rest to 30 L during exercise.

More importantly, however, is the adjustment made in the **redistribution of blood** being pumped around the body. At rest, only about 20% of the cardiac output is distributed to the working muscles. During exercise, however, when there is greater demand for oxygen up to 85% of cardiac output may be distributed to the working skeletal muscles. This can occur through accommodation and **shunting** of blood from inactive tissues such as the stomach and kidneys to the working muscles. Adjustments in blood pressure are also seen during exercise due to the increased blood flow and vasoconstriction of blood vessels which ensure a rapid flow of blood to the working muscles.

# Respiratory responses to exercise

Respiratory responses occur largely because of the increase in muscle metabolism which takes place as a result of the increased activity. Increased muscle glycogen breakdown results in greater amounts of carbon dioxide production, which decreases blood pH and stimulates the respiratory centre to **increase ventilation**. With higher exercise intensity (usually exceeding 60% of $VO_2$ max), increased production of lactic acid may occur. This also increases acidity and again stimulates the respiratory centre to increase ventilation.

# Long-term adaptations

Long-term physiological adaptations are those changes that occur in the body as a result of following a long term training programme.

## Muscular adaptations

Depending upon the type of the prior training, different adaptations will occur in the muscle.

We are first going to look at the changes that occur following a period of aerobic training and then take a look at the anaerobic changes that may arise.

## Aerobic adaptations

These occur in the muscle as a result of following an endurance-based training programme. Examples of activities that can be performed include swimming or jogging, although any continuous type activity will lead to some adaptation.

Regular stimulation of the muscle through aerobic-based exercise will cause changes to occur within the muscle cell. In particular, the structure of the muscle fibres may alter. Since the performance of endurance exercise stresses the **slow twitch muscle** fibres, these respond by **enlarging** by up to 22%. This gives greater potential for aerobic energy production since larger fibres mean a greater area for **mitochondrial activity**.

Indeed, endurance training leads to an *increase in both size and number of mitochondria*. Some studies have reported mitochondria size to increase by up to 40% and the number by over 100%. Since the mitochondria are the factories that produce our aerobic energy, increases in size and number can be associated with the economies of scale achieved by large businesses and an increase in production of energy will result.

Endurance training may also *increase the activity of our oxidative enzymes* which work on breaking down our food fuel to release the energy stored within. As a result, there is more scope to use glycogen and fat as a fuel. The oxidation of both these fuels increases, providing greater amounts of energy. With hypertrophy of slow twitch muscle fibres there is a corresponding *increase in stores of glycogen and triglycerides* which ensures a continuous supply of energy, enabling exercise to be performed for a longer period of time.

A further benefit of aerobic training is the *increase of up to 80% in myoglobin* content within the muscle cell. Myoglobin is the substance within the muscle that carries oxygen to the mitochondria, and is similar in structure to haemoglobin. With greater amounts of myoglobin, more oxygen can be transported to the mitochondria which further improves the efficiency of aerobic energy production.

All of these aerobic adaptations associated with endurance training ensure that a higher percentage of $VO_2$ max (maximum oxygen uptake) can be attained before the onset of blood lactate accumulate (OBLA) is reached and thus the onset of fatigue can be delayed. Generally, $VO_2$ max is not a product of training as it is largely genetically determined but these metabolic adaptations within the muscle that occur as a result of training may slightly increase an individual's $VO_2$ max in the region of 10–20%.

### Anaerobic adaptations

The anaerobic or lactate threshold is a product of training, and improvements in this will certainly improve endurance performance.

While training at very high intensity, eg, sprint or strength training, **hypertrophy of fast twitch muscle fibres takes place. Increases in levels of ATP and PC** within the muscle occurs which increases the capacity of the ATP-PC or alactic energy system. The efficiency of this system is further improved through increased activity of the enzymes responsible for breaking down ATP and PC. These include **creatine phosphokinase** and **myokinase**.

Training at high intensities for up to 60 seconds has also been shown to increase the **glycolytic capacity** of the muscle, largely through increasing the activity of glycolytic enzymes. This improves the muscles' ability to break down glycogen in the absence of oxygen and means that the athlete can exercise for longer periods of time before feeling the effects of fatigue.

This is further aided by improvements in the **buffering capacity of the muscle**, which enables the muscles to tolerate lactic acid more effectively. When lactic acid accumulates in the muscle, hydrogen ions ($H^+$) are released, inhibiting glycolytic enzyme activity and interfering with the contractile elements of the muscle. Bicarbonate ions existing in the muscle and the blood mop up these hydrogen ions, reducing acidity. By following an anaerobic training programme, the buffering capacity of the body increases substantially, and enables the body to work for longer periods of time and at higher levels of acidity.

## Cardiovascular adaptations to training

Following endurance training, many cardiovascular adaptations arise. In the first instance, the actual size of the heart may increase – **cardiac hypertrophy**. This enables the heart to work more efficiently, particularly at rest. The increase in thickness of the myocardium (cardiac tissue) enables the left ventricle to fill more completely with blood during the diastole phase of the cardiac cycle. This allows the heart to pump more blood per beat since the thicker walls can contract more forcefully, pumping more blood into the systemic system and ultimately to the muscles.

Consequently, *stroke volume increases both at rest and during exercise*. With an increase in stroke volume at rest, the heart will no longer need to pump as many times per minute to achieve the same amount of blood flowing to the body's tissues.

Since the heart seeks to work as efficiently as possible resting heart rate decreases as a result of the endurance training that has taken place.

When resting heart rate falls to below 60 beats per minute, **bradycardia results**, which explains the very low resting heart rates often experienced by top endurance athletes; for example, Indurain, the many times Tour de France champion, is reported to have a resting heart rate of around 30 bpm!

As an athlete's stroke volume increases, the **maximum cardiac output** of the trained athlete also increases. Cardiac output may increase by up to 30–40 min in trained individuals. However, it is important to note that there is little or no change in the values of resting cardiac output, due to the decrease in resting heart rate that accompanies endurance training.

The adaptations mentioned above have centred on the structure and function of the heart. We now need to discuss those training-induced changes that occur in the vascular and circulatory systems:

- One reason that accounts for greater performances in aerobic events following training is the **increased capillarisation** of trained muscles. New capillaries may actually develop which enables more blood to flow to the muscles and enables more oxygen to reach the tissues. Furthermore, existing capillaries become more efficient and allow greater amounts of blood to reach the muscles, which also become more efficient at extracting the oxygen due to the muscular adaptations mentioned above.

- Improvements in the vasculature efficiency (especially the arteries) to **vasoconstrict** and **vasodilate, improve the redistribution of blood** by shunting the supply to the active muscles and tissues, so that there is a greater supply of oxygen for energy production in these working muscles.

- These efficiency gains also result in a **decreased resting blood pressure** following endurance training, although blood pressure during exercise of a submaximal or maximal nature remains unchanged.

- **Increases in blood volume** following training can be attributed to an increase in blood plasma (the water component of the blood). This has the important function of decreasing the blood viscosity and enabling the blood to flow around the body more easily, thus enhancing oxygen delivery to the muscles and tissues.

- An **increase in red blood cell volume** and **haemoglobin content** is also higher in the trained athlete which further facilitates the transport of oxygen around the body. However, although haemoglobin content increases, the increase in blood plasma is greater and consequently the blood haematocrit (the ratio of red blood cell volume to total blood volume) is reduced, which lowers the viscosity of the blood and facilitates its progress around the body.

## Respiratory adaptations to training

Endurance performance is dependent upon oxygen transportation and utilisation, but no matter how good the functioning of these are, improvements in performance will not happen unless we can get oxygen into the body. The respiratory system is responsible for receiving oxygen into the body and dealing with the waste products associated with muscle metabolism.

Respiratory functioning does not usually hinder aerobic performance, and the adaptations that take place merely aid the improved cardiovascular functioning.

Following training, there is a *reduction in both resting respiratory rate and the breathing rate during submaximal exercise*. This appears to be a function of the overall efficiency of the respiratory structures induced by training.

Surprisingly there are *only very small increases in lung volumes following training*. Vital capacity (the amount of air that can be forcibly expelled following maximum inspiration) increases slightly, as does tidal volume during maximal exercise. One factor to account for these increases is the *increased strength of the respiratory muscles* which may facilitate lung inflation.

Pulmonary diffusion (the exchange of gases at the alveoli) will become more efficient following training, especially when working at near maximal levels. The

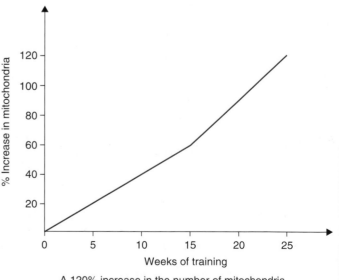

A 120% increase in the number of mitochondria following a 25-week endurance programme. Size of mitochondria may also increase by up to 40%

Fig 7.11. The increase in the size and number of mitochondria as a result of endurance training

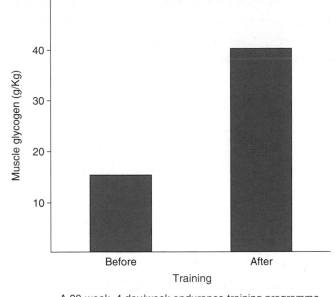

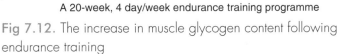

Fig 7.12. The increase in muscle glycogen content following endurance training

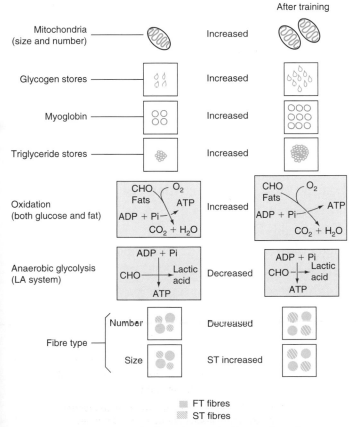

FT fibres
ST fibres

Fig 7.13. A summary of physiological effects of endurance training on the muscle
*Source*: Davis, Kimmet and Auty (1986).

increased surface area of the alveoli during exercise together with their *increased capillarisation*, ensures that there is ample opportunity for gaseous exchange to take place, and thus guarantees sufficient oxygen is entering the blood.

## **O E** Ergogenic aids

Sports culture is filled with pills, potions, powders, new training equipment and psychological techniques which all claim to give athletes the 'winning edge' and to increase the adaptive responses outlined above.

An ergogenic aid is *any substance or method used by an athlete with the sole aim of improving or enhancing performance.* Ergogenic aids are not a new phenomenon. Ancient Greek athletes, for example, ate mushrooms to improve their chances of winning the laurel wreath, and the Aztecs reportedly ate human hearts to gain advantage over their rivals.

There now follows a brief discussion which outlines the many different forms of ergogenic aid and considers the reasons why some athletes will resort to using illegal forms of aid.

There are five categories of ergogenic aids:

### Physiological aids

These aids are ones which seek to boost the physiological adaptive responses of the body such as improved oxygen transport. Some of these aids are perfectly legal such as altitude training but others such as **recombinant erythropoietin (RhEPO)** and blood doping are illegal.

Copy out and complete the table below which highlights a range of ergogenic aids. You may need to undertake some research on some of the ergogenic aids outlined. Some have been completed for you to get you started:

| Ergogenic aid | Definition and method of use | Category of ergogenic aid | Performance benefits | Side effects | Legal/ Illegal |
|---|---|---|---|---|---|
| Glycogen loading | | | | | |
| Creatine supplementation | | | | | |
| Recombinant erythropoetin (RhEPO) | A synthetic form of EPO that stimulates red blood cell production. It is artificially manufactured and injected into the body | Physiological | Can boost red blood cell production and therefore oxygen carrying capacity. It can improve maximal oxygen uptake ($\dot{V}O_2$ max) | Increased blood viscosity can slow the flow of blood down – particularly at rest. This increases the risk of blood clotting, and inhibits the body's production of 'natural' EPO. CAN BE FATAL | Illegal |
| Human growth hormone | A synthetic substance injected into the body to stimulate protein synthesis and ultimately increase muscle mass. | Hormonal/ pharmaco-logical | Increases muscle strength and can decrease the percentage of body fat that accompanies the increased metabolic activity. It can also increase bone density | Abnormal development of bone and muscle tissue. A broadening of the hands, face and feet can occur. Abnormal enlargement of vital organs such as the heart. CAN LEAD TO HEART FAILURE | Illegal |
| Parachutes | | | | | |
| Blood doping | | | | | |

**ACTIVITY 10**

| Ergogenic aid | Definition and method of use | Category of ergogenic aid | Performance benefits | Side effects | Legal/illegal |
|---|---|---|---|---|---|
| Anabolic steroids | | | | | |
| Nasal strips | | | | | |
| Colostrum | | | | | |
| Visualisation | | | | | |
| Bungy ropes | | | | | |
| Alcohol | | | | | |
| Amphetamines | | | | | |
| Caffeine | | | | | |

Read the section, 'Long-term adaptations' (pp 164–7). Then copy out the table given below and complete by extracting and summarising the relevant information.

| Musculo-skeletal adaptations | | Cardio-vascular adaptations | Respiratory adaptations |
|---|---|---|---|
| Anaerobic | Aerobic | | |
| Hypertrophy of fast twitch fibres | Hypertrophy of slow twitch fibres | Cardiac hypertrophy | Increased strength of respiratory muscles |

**ACTIVITY 11**

## Hormonal/pharmacological aids

The majority of pharmacological aids are illegal. They seek to enhance athletic performance by boosting the levels of hormones and neural transmitters which are naturally released by the bodies. Examples of illegal pharmacological aids include **anabolic steroids**, **amphetamines** and **human growth hormone (HGH)**.

## Nutritional aids

Nutritional aids largely include dietary supplements such as **vitamins**, **creatine** and **glutamine** and by and large are legal. However, it should be observed that excessive doses of these supplements can be illegal. For example, the International Olympic Committee (IOC) has banned caffeine above a urine level of 12 micrograms/ml. Other legal forms of nutritional aid include **glycogen loading** and **soda loading**.

## Mechanical aids

Mechanical ergogenic aids are specialised equipment or devices that enhance performance. Examples include more flexible poles for pole vaulting, **aerodynamic helmets in cycling**, low drag **lycra body suits** for sports such as speed skating and swimming. Mechanical aids by and large are legal, although there may be some restrictions upon equipment in competition.

## Psychological aids

This form of performance enhancement revolves mainly around mental training and conditioning techniques that are used to combat stress and anxiety associated with competition. Examples would include **self-hypnosis**, **visualisation**, **cue utilisation** and **goal setting**, all of which are perfectly legal.

# Designing a training programme or personal exercise programme

We have seen from this chapter that training will induce changes in the muscular, cardiovascular and respiratory systems which make their functioning more efficient and hopefully improve endurance performance. We now need to discuss how a coach or an athlete can design a training programme to guarantee and maximise the effects of these adaptations.

Training programmes do not come in a standard 'one-size fits all' package that suits everybody; they have to be made to measure and designed specifically for the individual. For example, Denise Lewis would need a very different programme to one designed for Paula Radcliffe.

The problem that a coach faces when designing a programme is that not only are all athletes different but each sport requires different components of fitness at varying levels of importance. A programme should therefore be balanced yet specific

enough to ensure that the demands of both the athlete and sport are being met.

When planning a training programme, the following factors should be considered to ensure a worthwhile experience for the athlete:

- the performer's needs
- the sport and related fitness components
- the principles of training
- the types of training that can be employed
- the training year
- the major competitions of the year, and when they occur.

We have discussed the first four considerations earlier in this chapter. There now follows a short explanation of how a training programme can be structured to ensure optimal performance of the athlete.

**ACTIVITY 12**

1) For your chosen activity prioritise the relevance of each of the fitness requirements.
2) Make a list of the key competitive periods of the training year. This might include major athletic meets or swimming galas or indeed league or cup games for game players. Having completed this task you will be better equipped to determine the requirements of your training programme and optimise the performances of yourself or others.

# Periodisation and the training year

It is important to structure the training programme so that the athlete can achieve the best possible improvements in performance, to reduce the likelihood of overtraining and ensure that peak performance occurs in the climax of the competitive season. To achieve this, the training programme should be viewed as a year-long process divided into specific periods designed to prepare the athlete for optimal performances. This is known as **periodisation**. The long-term training plan which is usually one year in length but can be longer, (perhaps for an athlete preparing for the Olympic Games or a Soccer player preparing for a World Cup competition) is known as a **macro-cycle**. This **macro-cycle** is subdivided into periods of 2–8 weeks which concentrates training on particular areas – these phases are known as **meso-cycles**. Meso-cycles are further divided into individual or weekly training sessions known as **micro-cycles** which again have specific aims and objectives. It is essential that the athlete incorporates sufficient rest within each micro- and meso-cycle in order to prevent overtraining. This sometimes happens in a **3:1 ratio** whereby in a micro-cycle (one week's worth of training) the performer may have three 'hard' sessions and one 'easy' session; or in a meso-cycle the athlete may undertake three 'hard' weeks of training and one 'easy' week.

Typically the periodised year has 4 periods.

| Phase 1 | Preparation 1 | High intensity loading Endurance base needed eg, Heavy weights, long runs |
|---------|---------------|---------------------------------------|
| Phase 2 | Preparation 2 | Competition specific intensity eg, Speed work, plyometrics, some technique work |
| Phase 3 | Competition | Develop and stabilise competition fitness. Taper for major competitions |
| Phase 4 | Transition | Active rest and recuperation |

Fig 7.14 outlines the periodised year for a rugby player. Phases 1 and 2 relate to the preparation period, phase 3 is the competition period – notice this is at the peak or apex of the triangle to mirror peak performance during the competitive phase, while phase 4 relates to the transition period.

## The preparation period

The preparation period includes the off-season and pre-season aspects of the periodised year.

During the off-season stage, general conditioning is required through a well-rounded programme of aerobic endurance training, mobility training and training to maintain strength to provide a base upon which to build.

During the pre-season stage there is a significant increase in the intensity of training. This is the time when much of the strength work should be undertaken, through lifting heavier weights or working against greater resistances, and working at higher speeds. Towards the end of this period the coach should employ some competition specific training; eg, working on sprint starts for the sprinter.

A 100 m sprinter will taper by reducing the total number of repetitions performed in training by 30–50% but still working at maximum effort.

Applying the preparation period to a 400 m runner – although success in the 400 m is largely down to anaerobic fitness, aerobic conditioning is essential. A good aerobic base will help boost anaerobic performance and enable higher intensity and volume of anaerobic training to be undertaken.

## The competition period

Training during the competition period should be aimed at maintaining levels of conditioning achieved during the pre-season phase. Maximum

A periodised overview of training for a netballer

| Oct | Nov | Dec | Jan | Feb | Mar | Apr | May | Jun | Jul | Aug | Sep |
|-----|-----|-----|-----|-----|-----|-----|-----|-----|-----|-----|-----|
| Competition | | | | | | Transition | | | Preparation | | |

The table below shows the periodised year of an international rugby player in a month-by-month format. Study the periodisation and answer the following questions:

| Peak months | July | Aug | Sept | Oct | Nov | Dec | Jan | Feb | Mar | Apr | May | June |
|---|---|---|---|---|---|---|---|---|---|---|---|---|
| Heavy weights | ✓ | ✓ | | | | ✓ | ✓ | | | | | |
| Speed endurance | ✓ | ✓ | ✓ | | | ✓ | ✓ | | | | | |
| Technique and match sharpness | | | ✓ | ✓ | ✓ | | | ✓ | ✓ | ✓ | ✓ | |

1) Why are heavy weights performed during the months specified?
2) Explain the timings of the technique and match sharpness sessions.
3) When is the transition period?
4) Why are Oct/Nov, Feb/March and April the 'peak months'?
5) Using the four phases of periodisation (preparation 1, preparation 2, competition and transition) complete the periodised year for a 100 m sprinter on the calendar below:

| Oct | Nov | Dec | Jan | Feb | Mar | Apr | May | June | July | Aug | Sept |
|---|---|---|---|---|---|---|---|---|---|---|---|
| | | | | | | | | | | | |

6) Some sportspeople require a double-periodised year. Explain this term and show how this might occur on the calendar below:

| Oct | Nov | Dec | Jan | Feb | Mar | Apr | May | June | July | Aug | Sept |
|---|---|---|---|---|---|---|---|---|---|---|---|
| | | | | | | | | | | | |

*ACTIVITY 13*

strength training is reduced and much of the training should be centred on competition specific aspects. For the endurance athlete, however, training at high intensity is still important in preparation for competition. In order to ensure that the athlete is perfectly prepared and can **peak** for competition a process known as **tapering** may be undertaken. Tapering involves manipulating the volume and intensity of training 2–3 weeks prior to competition to ensure that the athlete is fully recovered from any hard training undertaken, and that muscle glycogen stores can be fully replenished, without the effects of de-training occurring. The two key factors to successful tapering are to:

• maintain intensity of training

• decrease the volume of training by approximately one-third. For example, if I normally train at 80% HRmax for 45 mins, when tapering I should maintain the intensity, ie, continue to train 80%

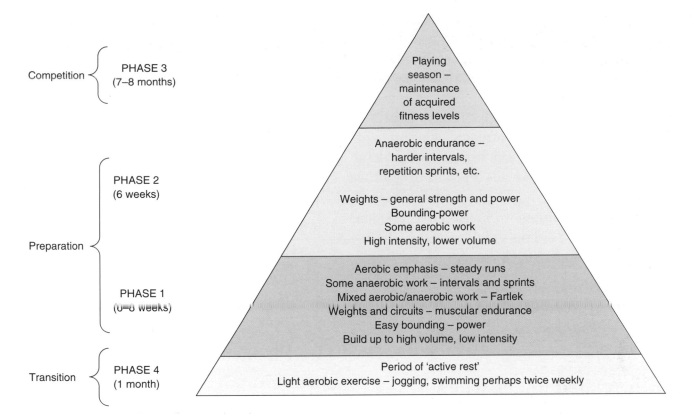

Competition { PHASE 3 (7–8 months)

Preparation { PHASE 2 (6 weeks)

PHASE 1 (0–8 weeks)

Transition { PHASE 4 (1 month)

Playing season – maintenance of acquired fitness levels

Anaerobic endurance – harder intervals, repetition sprints, etc.

Weights – general strength and power
Bounding-power
Some aerobic work
High intensity, lower volume

Aerobic emphasis – steady runs
Some anaerobic work – intervals and sprints
Mixed aerobic/anaerobic work – Fartlek
Weights and circuits – muscular endurance
Easy bounding – power
Build up to high volume, low intensity

Period of 'active rest'
Light aerobic exercise – jogging, swimming perhaps twice weekly

Fig 7.14. The periodised year for a rugby player

HRmax but reduce the volume of training to 30 mins. This should hopefully lead to optimal performance during competition.

# The transition period

Following a hard season of competition the body needs to recuperate, and the transition period bridges the gap between the season passed and the next training year. Essentially the transition period should be a period of **active rest** with some low intensity aerobic work such as swimming or cycling. The transition period is vital and should not be omitted; as well as giving the body a break from all the hard work in psychological terms, it can enhance motivation for training during the following periodised year.

# Overtraining

Overtraining is a common problem to elite athletes as they strive for greater improvement. It is caused by an imbalance between training and recovery, which usually occurs when insufficient time has

Fig 7.15. For major events, athletes will need to taper their training in order to peak

been left for the body to regenerate and cause adaptation before embarking upon the next training session. In their search for the best possible performance in competition, elite athletes are often tempted to increase training loads and frequency of training above optimal levels, which can lead to symptoms of overtraining. These symptoms include enduring fatigue, loss of appetite, muscle tenderness, sleep disturbances and head colds. The coach can identify overtraining syndrome by physiological testing, which may show the athlete having an increased oxygen consumption, heart rate and blood lactate levels at fixed workloads. In order to combat overtraining the coach should advise prolonged rest, and a reduction in training workloads for a period of weeks or even months. This should restore both performance and competitive desire.

Furthermore, by ensuring adequate rest days and following the **3:1 hard:easy ratio** the coach and athlete should avoid falling into the overtraining trap.

# Health-related issues when designing a training programme

## Training the young athlete

It has long been established that children differ physiologically, and that their reasons for participating in exercise may differ substantially from their adult counterparts. Coaches must therefore scrutinise every aspect of the training programme to tailor-make it for the child and not just replicate one that s/he has used previously with adults. Children are not miniature adults. However, having said that, recent research shows that children can benefit from regular exercise ranging from aerobic training to strength training. It appears, however, that children prefer interval type exercise specifically related to a sport, probably because they find continuous type training monotonous and it suits their shorter attention spans.

## Exercise and asthma

You will recall from chapter 3 some of the symptoms and causes of asthma. As asthma is prevalent in the young, here is a reminder of some of the considerations needed when prescribing an

exercise programme. Tips for exercising with asthma:

- Do not start exercising if you have symptoms of your asthma.
- Follow appropriate warms-ups prior to and cool-downs following exercise.
- Stop if an asthma attack develops.
- In cold or damp conditions try to exercise indoors.
- Always train with a partner in case an attack develops.

If these tips are followed, asthmatics should fully benefit from their exercise programme and it may actually help to control their symptoms.

# The Physical Activity Readiness Questionnaire (PAR-Q)

Before prescribing an exercise programme, participants should be screened and this is usually accomplished by the participant completing a Physical Activity Readiness Questionnaire (PAR-Q), an example of which is shown in fig 7.16. If there are any doubts concerning the individual's ability to participate then they should preferably have a medical examination by their doctor.

The intensity of exercise should be light at first, with a gradual introduction of increments. Ideally, all fitness elements should be included in the exercise programme, although it is advised to keep high intensity work to a minimum; anaerobic work should never be advised for those with cardiovascular defects since this puts tremendous strain upon the heart. Consequently, the aerobic system should be predominantly stressed, using the large muscle group rhythmically at fairly low intensity. Try to avoid high impact activities, as undue stress on the bones and joints could cause skeletal complications. Swimming and cycling are good forms of exercise for this, since they are non or partial weight-bearing activities, which obviously reduces the stresses and strains on the body. The American College of Sports Medicine gives the

# PAR-Q & YOU

(Physical Activity Readiness Questionnaire)
(for people aged 15 to 69)

Regular physical activity is fun and healthy. Though being more active is very safe for most people, the questions below are designed to assist individuals aged 15 to 69 in determining whether they should see their doctor before increasing physical activity or exercise. Individuals over 69 years of age who are not used to being active should check with their doctor.

Common sense is your best guide when you answer these questions. Read the questions carefully and answer each one honestly

| YES | NO | |
|-----|-----|---|
| | | Has your doctor ever said that you have a heart condition and that you should only do physical activity recommended by a doctor? |
| | | Do you feel pain in your chest when you do physical activity? |
| | | In the past month, have you had chest pain when you are not doing physical activity? |
| | | Do you lose your balance because of dizziness or do you ever lose consciousness? |
| | | Do you have a bone or joint problem that could be made worse by a change in your physical activity? |
| | | Is your doctor prescribing drugs for a heart condition or drugs that affect your blood pressure? |
| | | Do you know of any other reason why you should not increase your physical activity? |

| | |
|---|---|
| **IF YOU ANSWERED:** | Talk with your doctor by phone or in person BEFORE you start becoming more physically active or BEFORE you have a fitness appraisal. Tell your doctor about the PAR-Q and which questions you answered yes. |
| **YES TO ONE OR MORE QUESTIONS** | You may be able to do any activity you want as long as you start slowly and build up gradually or you may need to restrict your activities to those which are safe for you. Talk with your doctor about the kinds of activities you wish to participate in. |
| **NO TO ALL QUESTIONS** | If you answered NO honestly to all PAR-Q questions, you can be reasonably sure that you can start becoming much more physically active - begin slowly and build up gradually, this is the safest and easiest way to go. Take part in a fitness evaluation – this is an excellent way to determine your fitness level. |
| **DELAY BECOMING MUCH MORE ACTIVE:** | If you are not feeling well because of temporary illness such as a cold or a fever, wait until you feel better; or If you are or may be pregnant, talk to your doctor before you start becoming more active. |

I have read, understood and completed this questionnaire. Any questions I had were answered to my full satisfaction.

**Name:** _____ **DATE:** _____

**SIGNATURE:** _____ **WITNESS:** _____

**SIGNATURE OF PARENT**
**or GUARDIAN:** (for participants under the age of 18) _____
*Adapted from PAR-Q, Canadian Society for Exercise Physiology*

**Fig 7.16.** Physical Activity Readiness Questionnaire

following recommendations for health-related exercise programmes:

- The activity should use large muscle groups that can maintain exercise for a prolonged period of time.

- The intensity should be between 40–85% $\dot{V}O_2$ max or 55 to 90% of age-predicted HRmax.

- Duration of 15–60 minutes of continuous or interval training.

- A frequency of 3–5 times per week.

- Include moderate intensity strength training of major muscle groups twice per week.

It is necessary to monitor everyone for signs of distress during the exercise. Care should also be taken to ensure the environment is conducive to such exercise. Older individuals can overheat and dehydrate quickly in hot conditions, and a cold temperature can deprive the heart of oxygen since respiratory and vascular vessels may constrict.

**ACTIVITY 14**

Design a Physical Activity Readiness Questionnaire specifically related to an exercise session of your choice. Justify the questions you have included.

# Summary

- In order for a training programme to be successful the athlete must follow the laws or 'principles of training'. These include specificity, progressive overload, reversibility, individual differences, moderation frequency, intensity, time, type, warm-ups and cool-downs.

- There are a number of training methods that can be employed by an athlete. These include continuous methods such as Fartlek or intermittent training methods such as interval training, circuit training, weight training and plyometrics. Mobility training is often neglected and athletes should incorporate some form of stretching activity into every session.

- A well-planned training programme will cause the body to adapt positively. The adaptive responses can be categorised into the following categories: aerobic muscular changes, anaerobic muscular changes, cardiovascular adaptations and respiratory adaptations.

- When designing a training programme the coach must ensure that it is tailor-made for the athlete. The training year should be structured initially into three main phases: the preparation period, the competition period and the transition period. This is known as periodisation.

- The periodised year can be further sub-divided into training blocks known as macrocycles (usually a year long), mesocycles (2–8 weeks) and microcycles (weekly or individual trianing sessions).

- To prevent overtraining the coach and athlete should ensure that sufficient rest days are included in the training programme and follow the 3:1 ratio. (3 hard sessions/weeks to 1 easy session/weak)

- When designing a health-related exercise programme, participants should be screened and preferably given the all clear by their doctor. Exercise should be of light intensity and therefore aerobic in nature. High impact exercise should be kept to a minimum.

# *Review Questions*

1. What structural changes are brought about within a muscle as a result of:
   - a strength training programme using weights
   - an endurance training programme?

2. State the importance of flexibility to sporting activity. How might you begin to improve flexibility? Use sporting examples where necessary.

3. Discuss ways in which training intensity can be determined.

4. Design a circuit training programme for a specific group of people. State the exercises you would use and explain why. What other considerations might be necessary?

5. Outline some training regimes designed to improve
   - the aerobic system
   - the anaerobic systems (ATP-PC and Lactic Acid System)

6. Explain how the principle of specificity can be applied to the design of a training programme for a squash player.

7. Explain how the periodised year can lead to optimal performance in competition.

8. How might you construct a training programme to ensure that overtraining syndrome does not occur to athletes in your charge?

9. You are asked to prescribe a 10-week exercise programme for a group of middle-aged men who have been relatively inactive for some years. What factors do you need to consider in preparing the programme?

10. State the type of exercises you would include in this programme and give reasons for your choices.

11. What factors do you need to consider when training a young athlete?

12. Why might the BMI not be the most accurate measure of obesity?

# 8. Nutrition for Performance

## Chapter introduction

In addition to following a well-planned and organised training programme, it is now widely recognised that diet and nutrition is vital to successful performance. Many athletes now employ the services of nutritional experts in striving to be at the peak of their physical capacities.

Since the physical demands of training and competition on the athlete are high, much research has been undertaken concerning the extent to which diet can ease these demands. This chapter will explore the dietary requirements of the high level performer, and the use of diet as an ergogenic performance-enhancing aid (through supplementation and diet manipulation).

## Nutritional effects upon performance

Whatever the sport or activity, it has now become widely recognised that nutrition is of great importance. A well-balanced diet is essential for optimum performance in both training and during competition. Athletes place enormous demands on their bodies when competing at the highest level, and to enable the body to function at its peak during the daily training regimes, an adequate diet is needed. Not only should the athlete's diet be designed to provide the energy required during exercise, but it should also provide the necessary nutrients for tissue growth and repair and those needed to keep the human machine functioning at its optimal level.

Essentially there are seven groups of nutrients that should be included in the athlete's diet:

1. Carbohydrate
2. Fat
3. Protein
4. Vitamins
5. Minerals
6. Water
7. Dietary fibre.

## Carbohydrate

Carbohydrate comes in various forms, including:

- simple sugars (glucose, fructose)
- complex starches (rice, pasta, potatoes).

Carbohydrate is vital to the athlete since it is the primary energy fuel (particularly during high intensity exercise), it is essential for the nervous system to function properly and also determines fat metabolism in the body. Intake should comprise approximately 65% of the athlete's diet.

Carbohydrate is stored in the **muscles and liver as glycogen**, but the amount that can be stored here is limited and therefore regular refuelling is needed. Excellent sources of carbohydrate include cereals, fruit and vegetables and confectionery – the latter should only be included in the athlete's diet in moderation. Carbohydrates are absorbed by the body at different rates. The **glycaemic index** is an indication of the absorption rates of different foodstuffs. Foods with a high glycaemic index can

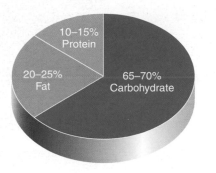

Fig 8.1.

be absorped rapidly by the body, while foods with a low glycaemic index are absorbed at a much slower rate. The glycaemic index is vital to the coach since it ensures that the athlete has consumed and stored adequate energy reserves.

## Fat

Fat is also a major source of energy in the body, particularly during low intensity exercise such as endurance activities. Up to 70% of our energy is derived from fat during our resting state.

Typically fat exists in the body as:

- triglycerides (the stored form of fat), or
- fatty acids (the usable form of fat for energy production).

When sufficient oxygen is available to the muscle cell, **fatty acids** constitute the favoured fuel for energy production, as the body tries to spare the limited stores of glycogen for higher intensity bouts of exercise and this can delay the effects of fatigue. This is known as **glycogen sparing**. Through training, the body adapts by increasing its ability to use fat as a fuel. The body, however, cannot use fat as its sole fuel source, due to its low solubility in the blood. This means that transportation of fat to the muscle cell is slow and so energy production in the muscle is usually fuelled by a combination of glycogen and fat. One explanation for marathon runners '**hitting the wall**' is that glycogen stores are completely depleted, and the body attempts to supply all the energy required by metabolising fat. The hydrophobic (low water solubility) quality of fat, however, inhibits this metabolism, energy

production is slow and the muscles fail to contract. Furthermore fat requires approximately 15% more oxygen to metabolise than carbohydrates.

Eating fat alone does not improve the muscle's ability to use it as a fuel source and the problems associated with excessive fat consumption are well documented.

It is recommended therefore that the athlete should keep the consumption of fatty foods low (at a maximum of 30% of total calories consumed) which will ensure adequate energy stores, good health and a greater proportion of calorie intake to be supplied by carbohydrate.

## Protein

Proteins are chemical compounds composed of chains of amino acids. They provide the building blocks for tissue growth and repair (including muscle tissue), produce enzymes, hormones and haemoglobin, and can provide energy when glycogen and fat stores are low.

Typically protein should constitute approximately 15% of total calorie intake or approximately 1.5 g protein/Kg of body weight per day should be sufficient for most sportspeople. Good sources include meat, fish, poultry, dairy products and beans and pulses.

The use and worth of protein supplementation as an ergogenic aid remains unclear, but it is generally thought that sufficient protein can be gained from the athlete's diet. Excessive protein consumption may in fact pose some health risks, as the kidneys may become overworked in excreting any unused amino acids.

## Vitamins

Vitamins are chemical compounds required only in small amounts by the body. However, they perform a vital role in energy production and metabolism.

Generally the body can gain the required amounts of vitamins through a well-balanced diet. Vitamins are largely found in fresh fruit and vegetables and wholegrain cereals, although some athletes believe that supplementation will enhance energy production and subsequently lead to improved athletic performance. Taking a multivitamin pill may prove useful as a precaution for some athletes, but megadoses of up to 100 times the recommended daily allowance (often expressed by athletes) are definitely not needed and may in fact cause some health problems.

## Minerals

These nutrients are also required in relatively small amounts by the body, but are vital for tissue functioning. Many of the minerals are dissolved by the body as ions and are called **electrolytes**. These have the important function of maintaining the permeability of the cell, and also aid the transmission of nerve impulses and enable effective muscle contraction.

Many minerals may be lost through sweating during exercise. These must be replaced quickly and there is now a vast array of fluid replacement products on the market designed for just that purpose.

## Water

Water is a nutrient whose importance is sometimes neglected. It is essential for the sportsperson, as it carries nutrients to and removes waste products from the body's cells, and helps to control body temperature. Water makes up about 50–60% of a young person's body weight, up to a third of which is contained in the blood plasma. (Plasma carries oxygen via the red blood cells to the working muscles, transports nutrients such as glucose and fatty acids, transports hormones vital to metabolism and removes waste products such as $CO_2$ and lactic acid.)

Water loss through sweating is accelerated during prolonged exercise and in hot conditions, and it is essential that this fluid is replaced in order to maintain a good state of hydration. Dehydration of as little as 2% of body weight will have a detrimental effect on performance. Even small losses of water can impair performance and adversely affect work capacity in a number of ways. These include:

- reducing the efficiency of the circulatory functioning largely by a drop in blood

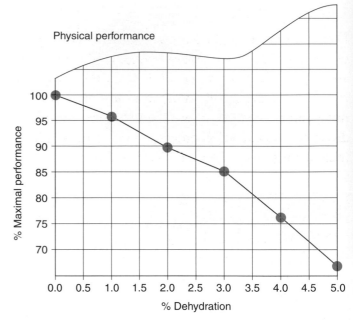

Fig 8.2. Dehydration index

pressure, which reduces blood flow to the active muscles

- inhibiting the thermoregulatory centre which can lead to problems such as heat stroke

- the loss of electrolytes such as sodium, chloride and calcium. Although it was once believed that this loss may induce muscle cramps, it is still an area of contention; many studies show that such losses may not have a direct effect on performance.

In order to maintain optimal performance, rehydration is essential. Drinks with a carbohydrate content of more than 6% can be consumed before and following exercise to top up the body's energy and fluid stores, while drinks with a carbohydrate content of less than 6% can be consumed during exercise to prevent dehydration. Sports drinks have been developed to cater for the needs of specific athletes. Isotonic drinks, such as Lucozade Sport, replace fluids and electrolytes lost through sweating and can boost glucose levels in the blood. Hypertonic drinks have a much greater concentration of carbohydrate and are normally used following exercise to increase glycogen stores.

# Dietary fibre

Dietary fibre, or roughage, should be an essential part of every athlete's diet. Fibre is found in all plant cells and is part of a plant that cannot be entirely digested. As such it causes a bulk in the intestine, absorbing many times its weight in water and helping the whole digestion and excretion process. Good sources of fibre include nuts, vegetables, beans and pulses.

# The athlete's diet

What you eat before, during and after exercise will have a direct effect on how you perform, either in training or in competition. Athletes undertaking daily training sessions need a high energy intake through eating carbohydrates, which should form up to 60% of total energy intake. Research points to the athlete having 4–6 small meals a day rather than 2–3 larger ones. This ensures that muscle and liver glycogen stores are kept topped up throughout the day. One big misconception by novice athletes is to consume sugary foods prior to training or competition in order to boost glucose, and therefore energy, levels. Glucose levels are increased through consumption of sugary foods, but high levels of blood glucose cause an increased release of insulin which eats away at the body's energy stores depleting them much more rapidly than if the sugary food had not been consumed.

On the day of competition or if there is going to be a particularly hard training session, the athlete should eat a meal high in carbohydrate 3–4 hours

Fig 8.3. Rehydration while performing

before competing to keep blood glucose levels high throughout the duration of the competition.

If you are involved in heats or bouts of work over the day, it will be necessary to top up glycogen stores by consuming small amounts of carbohydrate through snacks such as dried fruit or one of the many carbohydrate drinks on the market. Fluids such as water should also be taken during competition to prevent dehydration.

Following the competition or training, it is necessary to refuel the body as soon as possible in order to resynthesise muscle and liver glycogen stores. A high carbohydrate meal should be eaten within two hours of the cessation of the exercise to start this refuelling process. Water and isotonic supplements should also be taken to replenish those lost through sweating and aid in rehydration.

## Glycogen loading

Some athletes seek to manipulate dietary intake before competition in order to optimise performance. One method of doing this is by **glycogen loading** or **supercompensation**. This process involves depleting the glycogen levels seven days prior to the event by doing endurance-based training, and then starving the body of carbohydrate over the following three days by omitting such foods

Table 8.1. A recommended carbohydrate loading regimen
*Source*: Williams, 1989.

| day 1 | moderately long exercise bout (should not be exhaustive) |
|-------|----------------------------------------------------------|
| day 2 | mixed diet; moderate carbohydrate intake; tapering exercise |
| day 3 | mixed diet; moderate carbohydrate intake; tapering exercise |
| day 4 | mixed diet; moderate carbohydrate intake; tapering exercise |
| day 5 | high-carbohydrate diet; tapering exercise |
| day 6 | high-carbohydrate diet; tapering exercise or rest |
| day 7 | high-carbohydrate diet; tapering exercise or rest |
| day 8 | competition |

*Note*: the moderate carbohydrate intake should approximate 200 to 300 g of carbohydrate per day; the high carbohydrate intake should approximate 500 to 600 g of carbohydrate per day.

from the diet. For the remaining days leading up to competition the athlete will consume high carbohydrate meals to boost muscle glycogen stores up to twice that normally stored.

This method of manipulation is widely practised in endurance events and maximises energy production

Table 8.2. The advantages and disadvantages of glycogen loading

| Advantages | Disadvantages |
|------------|---------------|
| • Increased glycogen synthesis | • Water retention and bloating |
| • Increased muscle stores of glycogen | • Weight increase |
| • Increased endurance capacity | • Muscle stiffness, fatigue and tiredness |
| • Delays fatigue and enhances endurance performance | • Depression and irritability during the depletion phase |

via the aerobic pathway. Recent research has shown, however, that total depletion of glycogen may not be necessary for trained athletes. The three days of carbohydrate starvation will cause great fatigue, and lead to an increased risk of injury and possibly kidney problems. Simply resting for three days prior to competition and eating high carbohydrate meals may maximise glycogen stores. It is important to point out, however, that storage of glycogen requires a greater ingestion of water and water intake must increase accordingly. This will obviously be of use anyhow to the athlete, since it will help prevent dehydration during the endurance race.

# Summary

- A well-balanced diet is essential for successful performance in sport both while training and in preparation for competition.

- Seven groups of nutrients should be included in an athlete's diet. These are carbohydrate, fat, protein, vitamins, minerals, water and dietary fibre.

- Carbohydrate in the form of sugars and starches is the main energy provider for the high intensity athlete – it is stored in the muscles and the liver.

- Fat is the major source of energy in the body and is mainly used during low intensity endurance-based activities. Stored fat is broken down into free fatty acids – its usable form. The body cannot use fat alone but uses a combination of fat and glycogen.

- Proteins are composed of amino acids, the body's building blocks. They are also an energy provider, but are only used when glycogen stores are very low.

- Vitamins can aid in the production of energy. Given a well-balanced diet there should be no need for supplementation.

- Minerals are vital for tissue functioning, transmission of nerve impulses and enable effective muscle contraction.

- Water is an essential nutrient. Water loss during exercise can impair performance in a number of ways. It certainly contributes to heat stroke and can induce muscle cramps.

- Athletes should ensure they receive adequate energy supplies. A high carbohydrate diet of up to 60% of total energy intake is essential. Many small meals are better than 2 or 3 larger ones.

- Glycogen loading or supercompensation is a form of diet manipulation to ensure the energy stores of the body are at their greatest prior to a competition.

## Review Questions

1. What nutritional advice would you give to a triathlete both in training and preparing for competition?

2. Why might increased muscle glycogen stores increase performance? How would you increase the muscle glycogen stores of your athletes?

3. Explain how diet may be used as an ergogenic acid.

4. What are some of the effects on the body of dehydration? How does this affect performance in sport?

5. Why might consumption of sugary foods prior to competition lead to a decrease in performance?

6. What nutritional advice would you give to a hockey player, playing in a tournament that requires five or six games to be played in one day?

7. Outline the advantages and disadvantages of using fatty acids as a fuel during exercise.

8. With reference to exercise intensity explain the fuel usage of a performer during an activity of varying intensity.

# 9. Biomechanics – The Mechanics of Motion

## Chapter introduction

In order to fully understand human motion, a basic understanding of mechanics is required. The term 'biomechanics' literally means 'the mechanics of living beings' and biomechanists analyse human performance from a scientific standpoint with the aim of achieving optimal sporting techniques, improving the design of equipment and determining the stresses imposed on the body during performance in order to prevent injury. This chapter provides a comprehensive yet digestible guide to mechanical factors contributing to sports performance.

Central to the study of biomechanics are Newton's laws of motion, and this chapter will use these laws as the primary focus.

There follows an investigation of linear and angular motion through practical experimentation, enabling students to relate specifically to sporting situations.

## Force

Force is the 'push' or 'pull' exerted upon an object or body, which may either cause motion of a stationary body or a speeding up, slowing down or even a change of direction of a moving body. Forces can either be generated **internally** to the body via muscular contractions or **externally** through the action of gravity, friction and the forces of air and water. Without such forces, movement would not be possible, but optimal performance can take place when all forces are understood and adapted to the same aim. For example:

• Jonathan Edwards' world record triple jump at the 1995 World Championships: everything from the run up, the hop phase, the step phase, the angle of the jump and the landing were all at an optimal level, resulting in a gold medal and world record jump.

Central to this performance were internal and external forces exerted upon his body.

Force is a **vector quantity** – it has both magnitude and direction which, when considered with the point at which the force is applied, determines the resultant action or direction of the **resultant force** (see fig 9.3). Where forces act in different directions, the resultant can be found by

Fig 9.1. Jonathan Edwards' world record-breaking triple jump in the 1995 World Championships

constructing a **parallelogram** of forces, with the resultant force lying along the diagonal of the parallelogram.

All forces are measured in **Newtons**. One Newton represents the force required to give a 1 kg mass an acceleration of 1 m per second squared. To illustrate the forces acting on a body, see fig 9.2: a free body

diagram is drawn which also shows the magnitude of such forces (by length of the line drawn) and the point at which the force is applied (see fig 9.6).

Weight is a force and as such is characterised by magnitude (proportional to mass), direction (always downward) and the point of application will be at the centre of gravity of the body.

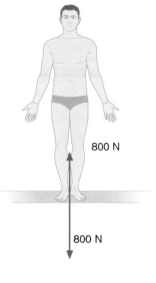

800 N

800 N

Fig 9.2.

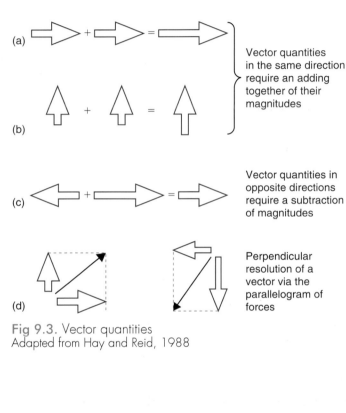

(a) Vector quantities in the same direction require an adding together of their magnitudes

(b)

(c) Vector quantities in opposite directions require a subtraction of magnitudes

(d) Perpendicular resolution of a vector via the parallelogram of forces

Fig 9.3. Vector quantities
Adapted from Hay and Reid, 1988

6 ms⁻¹

10 ms⁻¹ Resultant force

8 ms⁻¹

Fig 9.4. The parallelogram of forces. The resultant of two vectors is calculated via the parallelogram of forces

Fig 9.4 shows the resultant force of a rugby player travelling at 8 m/s when tackled by an opposition player who imparts a force of 6 m/s to the ball carrier. By constructing a parallelogram of forces and using Pythagoras' theorem, the resultant force can be calculated, ie:

$$\text{Resultant force} = \sqrt{8^2 + 6^2} = 10 \text{ m/s}$$

# Linear motion
## Velocity

With reference to sporting performance, we are always concerned with how fast a body or an object is travelling – ie, their speed. However, speed is a **scalar quantity** where direction is never really considered. When considering linear motion, biomechanists normally require a direction, and as velocity is a vector quantity and has both size and direction, this is the preferred term.

$$\text{Speed} = \frac{\text{distance travelled}}{\text{time taken}}$$

$$\text{Velocity} = \frac{\text{displacement}}{\text{time taken}}$$

Both quantities are generally measured in metres travelled per second.

## Acceleration

In many sporting situations, such as 100 m sprint, acceleration should also be considered in order to analyse an athlete's successful performance. Acceleration represents the *rate* of change of velocity; as such it is a vector quantity, possessing both magnitude and direction.

$$\text{Acceleration} = \frac{\text{change in velocity}}{\text{time taken}}$$

$$\text{or} \quad \frac{v - u}{t}$$

where, $v$ = final velocity
$u$ = initial velocity
$t$ = time.

# Newton's laws of motion

Newton's laws of motion explain the principles of acceleration and movement, and are explained below, using the example of a 100 m sprinter.

## Newton's first law – the law of inertia

At the beginning of the race, an athlete remains stationary in the blocks. According to **Newton's first law of motion**:

*Every body at rest, or moving with constant velocity in a straight line, will continue in that state unless compelled to change by an external force exerted upon it.*

This suggests that a body or an object has a tendency to resist any change in its state of motion – if a body is travelling in a straight line at constant speed, it will continue to do so unless acted upon by a force.

The same is true for the sprinter in the set position in the blocks. S/he will remain stationary unless a force is exerted upon the blocks. The force exerted must be great enough to overcome this inertia, and in doing so the sprinter will move forward out of the blocks. However, the inertia of an object is directly proportional to its mass, so a body with a greater mass will need a larger force to overcome its inertia than a body with less mass. Once out of the blocks, the athlete will quickly accelerate as there has been

**Fig 9.5.** A sprinter in the blocks will have to overcome their inertia in order to drive out of them

## a) Beginning

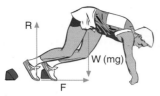

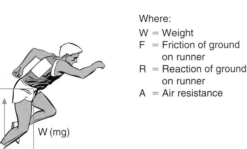

Where:
W = Weight
F = Friction of ground
on runner
R = Reaction of ground
on runner
A = Air resistance

## b) End

Fig 9.6. A free body diagram showing the forces acting on a sprinter at the beginning and end of a race

a change in velocity (which is zero when the sprinter is in the blocks).

# Newton's second law – the law of acceleration

In order to generate a greater acceleration, the athlete must generate a greater force. This is **Newton's second law of motion**, which states that:

*The acceleration of a body is **proportional** to the force causing it, and the acceleration takes place in the **direction** in which that force acts.*

This is sometimes expressed as **F = ma**:

- F = force generated
- m = mass of body or object
- a = acceleration

The acceleration of a body due to gravity is $-9.81$ m/s$^2$. The negative sign indicates that the acceleration caused by gravity is directed downward or towards the centre of the earth. The weight of a body is equal to its mass multiplied by the acceleration due to gravity (9.81 m/s$^2$). As the mass of a body increases, its weight increases proportionally.

If the mass and acceleration of the sprinter are known, it is simple to compute the force required to give that acceleration. For example:

mass of athlete = 74 Kg
acceleration = 4.6 m/s$^2$
F = ma
F = 74 Kg × 4.6 m/s$^2$
F = 340 Newtons

Remember, a Newton is the force which gives a mass of 1 Kg an acceleration of 1 m/s$^2$.

After about five seconds of a 100 m sprint we would expect the sprinter to have reached maximum velocity, and (according to Newton's first law) to remain at this constant velocity, so why does the athlete start to slow down? The explanation is relatively simple:

- physiological effect of the sprint – this is the main cause. The muscle stores of **ATP** and **PC** which provide the energy for muscular contraction are depleted.
- the effects of air resistance (although negligible).

This slowing down of the athlete represents a change in velocity and therefore is known as **deceleration**. In fact most sprinters will start to slow down after 80–90 m and the winner will often be the person who takes longer to slow down!

# Newton's third law – the action/reaction law

**Newton's third law of motion** states that:

*When one object exerts a force on a second object, there is a force **equal** in magnitude but **opposite** in direction exerted by the second object on the first.*

More simply, to every action there is an equal and opposite reaction. The sprinter on the blocks experienced a force propelling him/her forward. From Newton's third law we can deduce that as the athlete pushed backwards and downwards on the

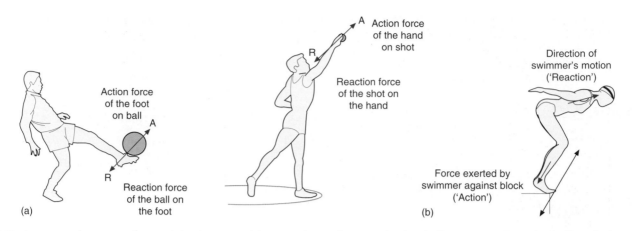

**Fig 9.7.** Action and reaction forces (a) when an athlete applies a force to the football or puts a shot, the ball and shot exert an equal force on the athlete's foot or hand; (b) action and reaction forces in a swimming start

blocks, the blocks pushed the athlete upwards and forwards out of the blocks.

Reaction forces can easily be seen in the field of sport:

- A footballer kicking a ball exerts a force upon it in order to set it in motion (N1); according to Newton's third law (N3), the ball will exert an equal and opposite force onto the kicking foot.

- The high jumper exerts a force upon the ground in order to gain height, by the ground exerting an upward force upon him/her.

For the high jumper to gain upward acceleration the Reaction force must be greater than the Weight force of the athlete.

The Reaction force
= Weight force + Internal muscular force

**ACTIVITY 1**

1. Collect pictures from newspapers or the internet of a range of sporting activities. Beside each picture draw a free-body diagram to show the application and forces acting upon the performer. Some examples of actions are given below:
   a) A high jumper at take-off
   b) A hockey player taking a penalty 'flick'
   c) A gymnast performing a handstand.

2. Apply Newton's three laws of motion to a swimmer diving from the blocks and completing a 100 m butterfly race.

**ACTIVITY 2**

An ice hockey puck gliding across the ice has a very low coefficient of friction.

a) Sketch a diagram to illustrate the forces acting on the puck in each of the following four situations: (assume air resistance and friction between the puck and the ice is negligible)
- The puck at rest prior to being struck by the stick
- While the stick is in contact with the puck
- While the puck is travelling across the ice
- While the puck strikes the back wall

b) In this situation, where a stationary puck is struck by a stick and travels across the ice until it strikes and rebounds from an end wall, there are several changes in horizontal linear velocity experienced by the puck.

Copy the graph below and draw a line representing the changes in horizontal linear velocity experienced by the puck. For each phase, A, B, C, D, E, explain your reasoning.

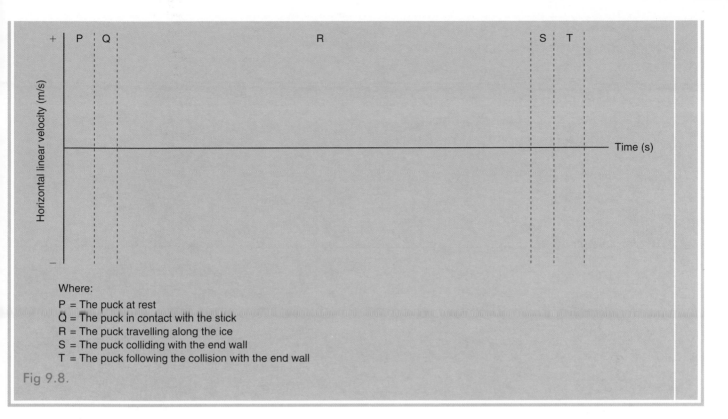

Where:
P = The puck at rest
Q = The puck in contact with the stick
R = The puck travelling along the ice
S = The puck colliding with the end wall
T = The puck following the collision with the end wall

Fig 9.8.

# Momentum, impact and impulse

## Momentum

Momentum is the amount of motion a moving object has and is the product of its mass and velocity:

Mo = m × v

- A sprinter with a mass of 75 Kg and a velocity of 10 m/s has a momentum of 750 Kg m/s.

From the above equation it can be seen that a body's momentum can be changed by altering either its mass or velocity. However, in sporting activity the mass of a body or object generally remains constant, so any change in momentum must be due to a change in velocity (acceleration). For example:

- a long jumper may increase velocity by changing their approach run, in order to increase their momentum before take off. Once in the air, the velocity and mass of the jumper remains constant, so momentum is said to be conserved.

This extends Newton's first law of motion:

*In any system of bodies that exert forces on each other, the total momentum in any direction remains constant unless some external force acts on the system in that direction.*

## Impact

Momentum becomes more important in sporting situations where collisions or impacts occur. The outcome of the collision depends largely upon the amount of momentum each of the bodies possessed before the collision took place. The body with greater momentum will be more difficult to stop. For example:

- if a prop forward weighing 90 kg and a scrum half weighing 60 kg were both travelling at the same velocity, the prop forward would have a greater momentum and would need to apply a larger force to stop his path to the try line.

- the speed at which the squash ball is struck is determined by the momentum of the racket head at the time of impact.

A change in momentum is synonymous with a change in acceleration and as such relates to Newton's second law of motion (p 187). This is expressed as:

$$F = ma$$

In order to work out the acceleration (a), the following equations must be used:

$$a = \frac{v - u}{t}$$

thus:

$$F = \frac{m(v - u)}{t}$$

$$F = \frac{mv - mu}{t}$$

$$Ft = mv - mu$$

$$Ft = \text{change in momentum}$$

## Impulse

This final equation suggests that any change in momentum is dependent upon the product of the force and the time that that force is applied to an object, known as **impulse**. It therefore follows that any increase in the force applied or the time over which the force is applied, the outgoing momentum of the object will increase. This has important implications for sporting situations where acceleration of a body or object is essential. For example:

- a follow through of a racket or hockey stick will ensure that the time over which the force has been applied is at its maximum; the change in momentum or acceleration of the ball will be greater than if a follow through had not been performed. This is illustrated in fig 9.9.

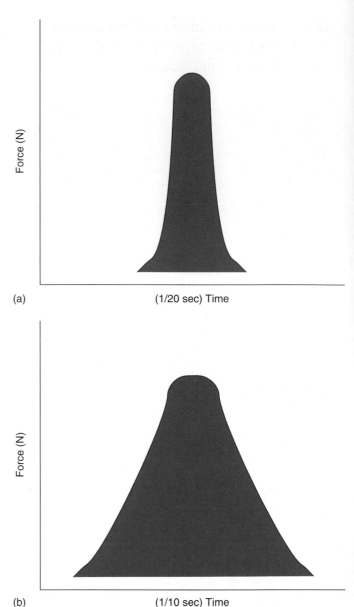

(a)　(1/20 sec) Time

(b)　(1/10 sec) Time

Fig 9.9. The effect of a follow through on the outgoing momentum of a hockey ball (a) force exerted without a follow through; (b) force exerted with a follow through

- the shot put: over time the technique of this event has been transformed. Originally a sideways stance was adopted before the put. However, the O'Brien technique (see fig 9.10) aims to apply a force over a longer period of time by incorporating a one and three-quarter turn and increasing the acceleration of the shot. Again by performing a follow through the athlete can ensure that the time of contact has been maximised. Of course in addition to developing this technique the athlete still requires the necessary physical attributes in order to apply a large force to the implement.

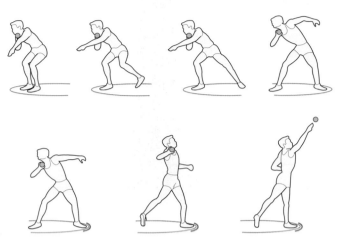

Fig 9.10. The O'Brien technique

- water polo: a player catching the ball with one hand will aim to decrease the velocity over a long period of time and so decrease the force exerted by the ball on the hands. S/he does this by meeting the ball early and withdrawing the catching hand in the direction of the ball's motion, thus cushioning the impact; this will prevent the ball hitting the hand and bouncing off uncontrollably.

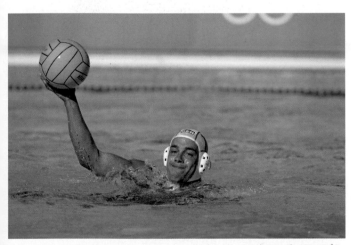

Fig 9.11. A water-polo player will decrease the velocity of an incoming ball by meeting the ball early and taking the catching arm back in the direction of the throw.

- cricket: when catching a fast moving cricket ball, the same principle applies, which can prevent injury to the hands.

Other examples include the use of crash mats in activities such as gymnastics and high jump.

Impulse is often illustrated through graphs. We can see from fig 9.12 that there are two elements to an impulse graph. The first area represents the impulse of a body landing on the ground (this is known as negative impulse), while the second area represents the impulse of the body due to the ground reaction force (positive impulse). In fig 9.12a there is a small negative impulse but a large positive impulse which indicates a body that is accelerating, its velocity is increasing. A high jumper, for example, imparts a large force over a very short period of time, which causes a large positive impulse that results in vertical acceleration. In fig 9.12b there is a large negative impulse that is followed by a small positive impulse. This represents a body that is decelerating. A volleyball player for example upon landing from a block absorbs a large force over a long period of time decreasing his vertical velocity. Fig 9.12c shows a body travelling at constant velocity where positive and negative impulses are equal, and the

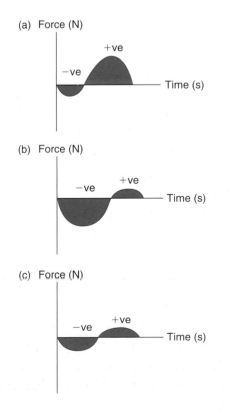

Fig 9.12.

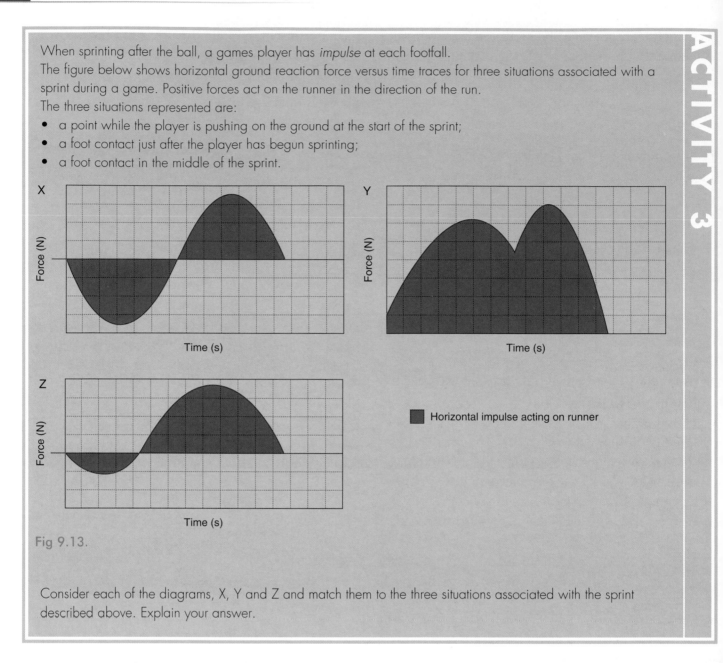

When sprinting after the ball, a games player has *impulse* at each footfall.

The figure below shows horizontal ground reaction force versus time traces for three situations associated with a sprint during a game. Positive forces act on the runner in the direction of the run.

The three situations represented are:

- a point while the player is pushing on the ground at the start of the sprint;
- a foot contact just after the player has begun sprinting;
- a foot contact in the middle of the sprint.

Fig 9.13.

Consider each of the diagrams, X, Y and Z and match them to the three situations associated with the sprint described above. Explain your answer.

net impulse is zero, for example, in the middle of a 100 m sprint.

## Frictional force

Friction is a force which acts on the interface of surfaces which are in contact, and acts in the *opposite direction to the direction of motion*. The magnitude or size of the frictional force will determine the relative ease or difficulty of movement for the objects in contact.

The *coefficient of friction* indicates the ease of movement and is determined by the amount of molecular interaction between the two surfaces in contact. For example:

- The coefficient of friction between a rugby boot and grass will be much larger than that between an ice skater's skate and an icy surface.

- In order to increase the coefficient of friction, a rugby player might remove mud and grass from his boots before packing down for a scrummage.

- The volleyball court is regularly swept to remove perspiration which will enable a firmer grip between shoe and court.

The coefficient may also be increased by maximising the force that presses the surfaces together:

- Mountain bikers often sit back over the driving wheel when riding up a muddy slope in order to gain a better grip of the tyre on the surface.

Friction forces can further be increased by increasing the surface area in contact with another:

- An athlete wears spikes when running on a tartan track.
- A racket player may wear a glove in order to maintain a firm grip.

# Fluid forces

We are now going to turn our attention to fluid forces such as those offered by air and water. When a body or object moves through air or water, it is affected by fluid friction which *acts in the opposite direction to the motion of the moving body.* The amount of air resistance or fluid friction experienced depends upon the *shape of the object and the speed at which the object is moving.*

# Air resistance

Air resistance is prevalent in most sporting activity, although its affects on performance can vary greatly. Consider the examples below. How might air-resistance affect each?

- the long jump
- projectiles such as balls, shuttlecocks and javelins
- cyclists
- sprinters.

## Air resistance and projectile motion

Air resistance offered to a projectile while in flight may change the **parabolic flight path**. Some examples of flight paths expected from a variety of projectiles are illustrated in fig 9.14.

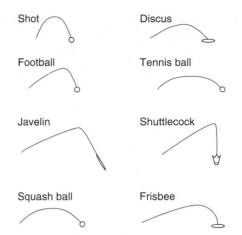

Fig 9.14. The expected flight paths of a variety of projectiles

Using fig 9.14, for each flight path illustrated, state if it is parabolic, nearly parabolic or asymmetric. In each case suggest reasons for the shape of the flight path.

Flight paths can be categorised as:

- parabolic (a uniform symmetrical shape)
- nearly parabolic
- asymmetric.

To discuss the effect of air resistance on flight paths, we will examine more closely the flight of a shot put and badminton shuttlecock.

## Shot put – a study of projectile motion

Fig 9.16 shows the parabolic flight path of a shot put.

Flight is governed by the ratio of weight to air resistance. Since air resistance is dependent upon the size, shape and speed of an object, all slow moving objects have little air resistance. The weight of the object will be the determining factor and will almost form a parabolic arc. This is illustrated in figs 9.15 and 9.16.

Faster moving objects have greater air resistance. This causes rapid deceleration and slowing down of the projectile until a point is reached where once again weight becomes the determining factor, leading to an asymmetric flight path. Observe the flight of a badminton shuttlecock from a high serve: it will decelerate rapidly and drop vertically – hopefully on the back baseline. Fig 9.15b illustrates the forces acting on a shuttle cock during flight.

# Fluid dynamics

When an object which is uniform in shape, such as a football, travels slowly through the air, the layers of air flow past the object in smooth symmetrical flow lines. This is known as **laminar flow**; see fig 9.17.

However, many objects in sport are fast moving and do not allow laminar flow. This is because as air

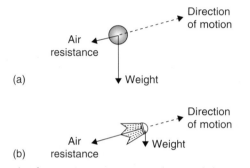

**Fig 9.15.** The forces acting on (a) a shot and (b) a shuttlecock in flight

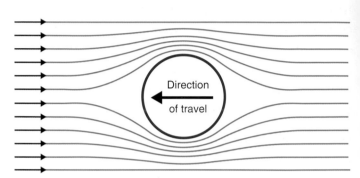

**Fig 9.17.** Laminar flow of air around a slow moving ball

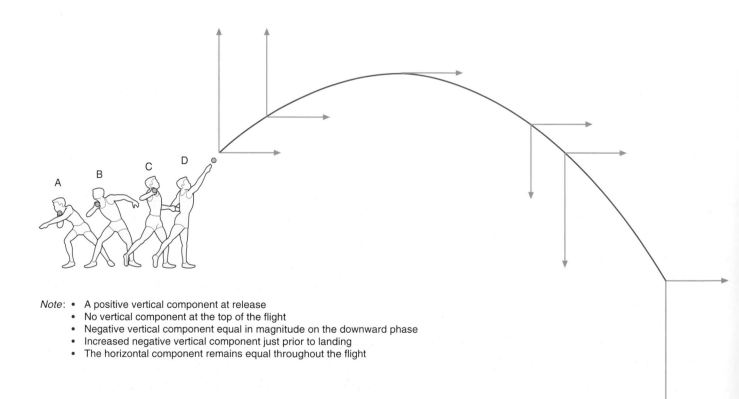

*Note:*
- A positive vertical component at release
- No vertical component at the top of the flight
- Negative vertical component equal in magnitude on the downward phase
- Increased negative vertical component just prior to landing
- The horizontal component remains equal throughout the flight

**Fig 9.16.** The parabolic flight path of a shot put showing the vertical and horizontal changes in velocity during the flight

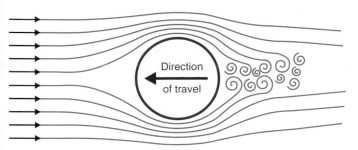

Fig 9.18. Turbulent flow of air around a fast moving ball, causing a drag force

Fig 9.19. Streamlining a cycle helmet can reduce drag, and promote laminar flow

travels around an object, the layer of air directly in contact with the object's surface is slowed down by surface friction. On a fast moving object, the air is unable to keep in contact with the surface and breaks away to form fast moving eddies of air. This is termed **turbulent flow**; see fig 9.18.

Because the air is fast moving at the back of the object, it has relatively lower pressure in comparison to that at the front. This causes a force pulling the ball back, since *objects will always move from areas of higher pressure to lower pressure*. This force is known as drag.

In activities where maximum speed is the aim, drag must be minimised and this is achieved through **streamlining**. The clearest example of this is cycling:

- A new cycle helmet was designed which aimed to encourage laminar flow around the head; see figs 9.19 and 9.20.

- The shape of the racing bike has changed dramatically to minimise the area of the cyclist in contact with the air. Lotus developed the bike on which Chris Boardman won the 1992 Olympic title – this had a lightweight carbon fibre frame and numerous aerodynamic design features.

- Graeme Obree, the 1995 world pursuit champion, adopted a position on the bike in order to improve streamline and reduce the drag force: his head was positioned far out in front of the handlebars, low over the front wheel, while his arms were tucked in under his chest.

## The Bernouilli effect

A series of experiments conducted by Bernouilli demonstrated that when flow lines get closer

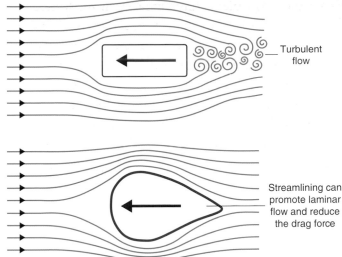

Fig 9.20. A cyclist tries to reduce the effects of drag by streamlining

together, velocity increases and there is a resulting drop in pressure. This had important implications for the design of objects in flight, perhaps the most important being the design of aeroplane wings.

Fig 9.21 shows that the flow lines on the upper surface of the wing have to travel further than the flow lines on the lower surface, and must therefore increase in velocity in order to reach the back at the same time as those on the bottom. As the velocity increases, pressure decreases. A pressure differential exists between the upper and lower surfaces, and a **lift force** results, keeping the plane in flight.

This principle has also been applied to Formula 1 racing, but the aerofoil is inverted, causing a

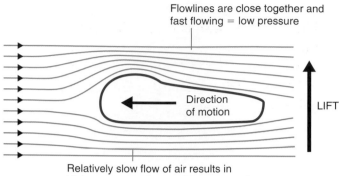

Fig 9.21. The Bernouilli effect explains how aeroplanes can stay in flight

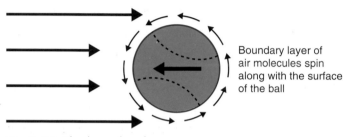

Fig 9.22. The boundary layer

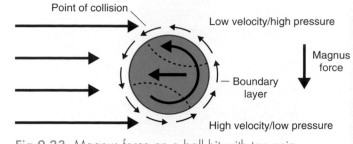

Fig 9.23. Magnus force on a ball hit with top spin

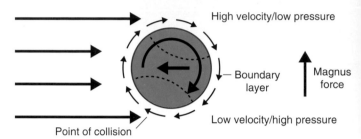

Fig 9.24. Magnus force on a ball hit with back spin

Fig 9.25. A soccer player can use the magnus effect by placing side spin on a football to cause the path of the ball to curve

downward force enabling the car to hold the bend much better.

The Bernouilli effect applied to spinning objects is known as the **magnus effect**. When an object in fluid (including air) spins, the air molecules in contact with the object *spin* with it, creating a **boundary layer**; see fig 9.22. When air molecules spin with the object, they eventually collide head on with the mainstream air flow on one side of the object only; see fig 9.22. This head-on collision causes a decrease in velocity and a higher pressure results.

This causes a pressure differential with the opposite side of the ball, since on this side the boundary layer flows in the same direction as the mainstream air flow. The pressure differential causes a **magnus force**, directed from the high pressure region to the area of low pressure; see figs 9.23 and 9.24.

- The magnus effect is heightened when new balls are used in tennis, since the nap or fuzz of the ball traps a much larger boundary layer of air and causes a greater pressure differential.

- Soccer players use the magnus effect from free kick situations or corners to curve the flight path of the ball. The kicker places a side spin on the ball, curving it around the wall of defensive players in front of goal; see fig 9.25.

# Fluid resistance

The effect of fluid resistance is most clearly illustrated by the forces that act upon the swimmer;

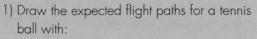

1) Draw the expected flight paths for a tennis ball with:
   • Top spin
   • Back spin

2) Draw the expected flight path (from above) of a golf ball hit with
   • Slice
   • Hook

ACTIVITY 5

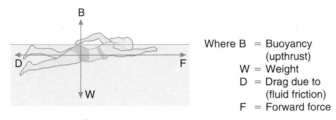

Where  B = Buoyancy (upthrust)
       W = Weight
       D = Drag due to (fluid friction)
       F = Forward force

Fig 9.26. The forces acting upon a swimmer

which is illustrated in fig 9.26. The drag force shown is dependent upon four main factors:

1. **The forward cross section of the swimmer**. To reduce drag, the swimmer should adopt as streamlined a position as possible: maintain a flat position close to the surface, without dropping the feet.

2. **The surface area in contact with the water**. This concerns the swimmer's body shape – elite swimmers tend to be very lean (verging on ectomorphic), which reduces the friction derived from body contact.

3. **Surface effects**. Swimmers attempt to minimalise turbulent flow by wearing shiny swimsuits, wearing swimming hats and 'shaving down' – the practice of removing body hair. These practices allow the water to flow past the body more smoothly and limit the drag force.

4. **Speed of the swimmer**. The relationship between speed and drag is positive – the faster you swim, the greater the drag. As in competitive

swimming, the aim is to swim as fast as possible. There is little swimmers can do to prevent this, but adopting an efficient technique that minimalises drag yet enables fast swimming should be a priority for all swimmers and coaches.

# Gravity

Gravity is an external force that naturally occurs and pulls a body or object towards the centre of the earth. Newton's law of gravitation states:

*All particles attract one another with a force proportional to the product of their masses, and inversely proportional to the square of the distance between them.*

Due to the immense difference between the mass of the earth and objects involved in sporting activity (including human bodies), the gravitational force of attraction between the two bodies is large, and has a significant effect upon performance.

# Centre of mass (C.O.M.)

An important feature of gravitational pull is that it always occurs through the centre of mass or weight of an object, which is *where the weight tends to be concentrated*. This point signifies that point about which the object or body is balanced in all directions. For spherical objects such as a shot the mass is distributed symmetrically around its centre, which therefore indicates its centre of mass. Due to irregular body shapes, however, the centre of mass is not so obvious for humans. For a person standing erect with hands by their sides, the point of centre of mass is approximately at navel height, but this point is constantly changing during movement. For example:

• if a person raises one arm above their head, the centre of mass will move further up the body

• if the person adducts their arm to the right of the body, the centre of mass will move slightly to the right.

Draw a line graph for parts (c), (d) and (e) to show the change in the centre of mass for each athlete stated.

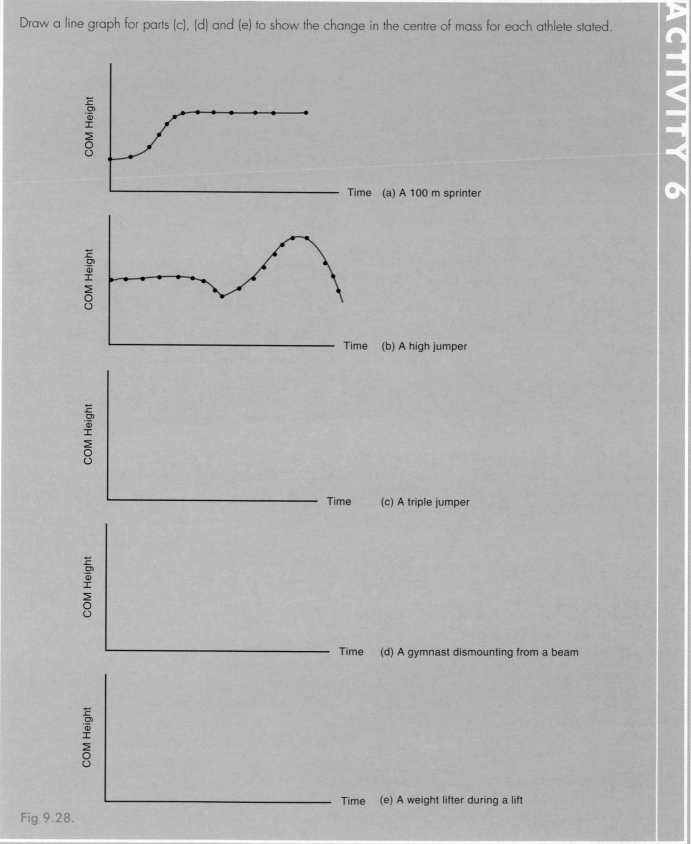

Fig 9.28.

Thus depending upon the shape of the body the centre of mass will vary.

Athletes and coaches can use their knowledge of this concept in order to improve performance. A perfect example is the high jump:

- The Fosbury flop was developed so that greater heights could be achieved. By arching the back, the centre of mass will move outside the body, and may pass underneath the bar while the jumper actually travels over the bar! The jumper using the Fosbury technique will therefore not need to raise their centre of mass as high as someone performing a western roll technique when clearing the same height.

The position of the centre of mass is also important for maintaining balance. An object or person will remain in balance as long as the centre of mass remains directly over its base of support (because the force of mass will always act directly down). As soon as the centre of mass moves away from the base of support, the object will become more unstable. For example:

- a gymnast on a balance beam: as soon as the centre of mass moves outside the beam, the gymnast will become unstable and fall.

Fig 9.27. The Fosbury flop can enable the high jumper centre of mass to actually travel *under* the bar!

If the centre of mass is lowered or the base of support is increased, the more stable the object or body:

- Rugby players forming a platform for a ruck take a large step and lower their hips. This ensures a stable platform and enables them to stay on their feet.
- A judo player has a wide stance, in order to resist attacks from their opponent.

# Levers, turning effects and angular motion

## Levers

Efficient and effective movement is made possible by a system of levers. These are mechanical devices used to produce turning motions about a fixed point (called a fulcrum). In the human body, bones act as levers, joints act as the fulcrum and muscle contractions provide the force to move the lever about the fulcrum.

A basic understanding of lever systems can be used to explain rotational motion, and help athletes develop the most efficient technique for their sport.

There are three types of levers, and each is determined by the relationship of the **fulcrum (F)**, the point of application of force or **effort (E)** and the **load (L)** or **resistance (R)**.

- First class lever: the fulcrum lies between the effort and the resistive force.
- Second class lever: the resistance lies between the fulcrum and the effort.
- Third class lever: the effort is between the fulcrum and the weight.

The majority of movements in the human body are governed by third class levers.

### Functions of levers

Levers have two main functions:

- increase the resistance that a given effort can move.
- increase the speed at which a body moves.

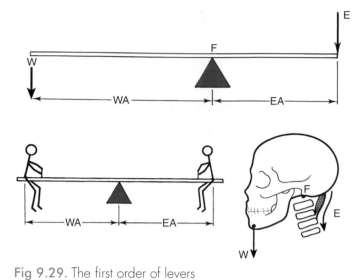

Fig 9.29. The first order of levers

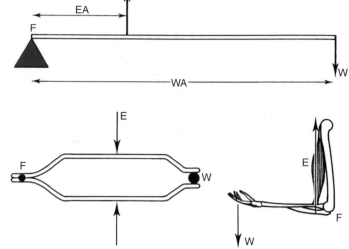

Fig 9.31. The third order of levers

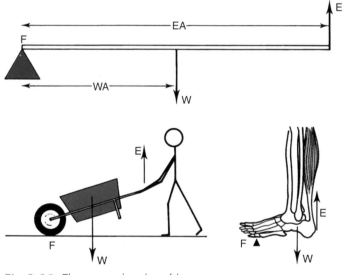

Fig 9.30. The second order of levers

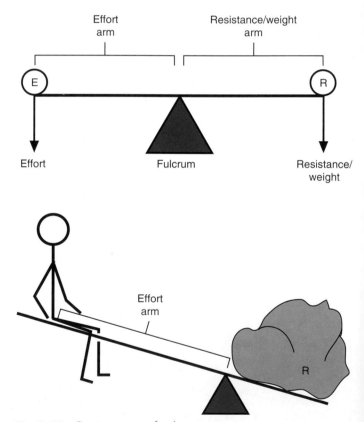

Fig 9.32. Components of a lever system

First class levers can increase both the effects of the effort and the speed of a body; second class levers tend only to increase the effect of the effort force; third class levers can be used to increase the speed of a body. An example of a third class lever in the body is the action of the hamstrings and quadriceps on the knee joint, which causes flexion and extension of the lower leg. The extent to which this can increase depends upon the relative lengths of the resistance arm and the effort arm:

- **The resistance arm** (RA) or **weight arm** (WA) is the part of the lever between the fulcrum and

the resistance: see fig 9.32. The longer the resistance arm, the greater speed can be generated.

- **The effort arm** (EA) is the distance between the fulcrum and the effort; the longer the effort arm, the less effort required to move a given resistance. In sport, implements are often used such as rackets or bats to increase the length of the effort arm which will increase the force that an object such as a ball is struck. However, the optimal length of an implement should be determined by the strength of the person handling it which is why, for example, junior tennis rackets have been designed.

The relative efficiency of the lever system is expressed as the **mechanical advantage** (MA) which can be determined as follows:

$$MA = \frac{\text{effort arm}}{\text{resistance arm}}$$

# Levers and turning effects

The levers of the human body are capable of rotational movement only, so the majority of movements in sporting activity are of an angular nature about a joint (fulcrum). The twisting or turning effect of an applied force is known as the **moment of force** or **torque**, and is directly related to the distance between the point of application of the force (muscle insertion) and the fulcrum (joint). This is the **moment arm** (MA) and can be applied either to the effort arm or the resistance arm.

The largest turning effect or rotation will occur where the moment arm is at its longest or the force applied is at its greatest. For example:

- when preparing to dive from a platform, by leaning out before the dive the moment arm is lengthened and the rotational effect is increased – see fig 9.33.

The moment of a force is equal to the product of the force applied multiplied by the length of the moment arm:

Moment of force = magnitude of force
× the perpendicular distance between the line of action of the force and the pivot

$$M = F \times MA$$

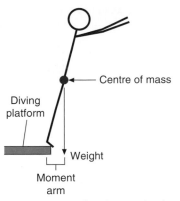

Fig 9.33. The moment arm of a diver – by leaning out in preparation for a dive, the moment arm is increased (lengthened), increasing the rotational effect

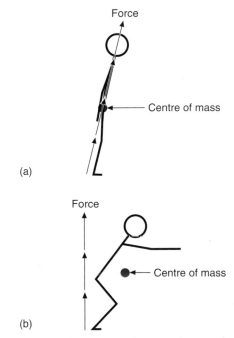

Fig 9.34. Eccentric forces (a) when applying a force through the centre of mass, the resulting motion will be linear (b) when applying a force which does not pass through the centre of mass, the resulting motion will be angular

## Eccentric force

The turning effect of the diver is produced by a force which is not passing through the centre of gravity. This off centre force is called the **eccentric force**, and is vital for rotation to occur. Look at fig 9.34. When the force is applied through the centre of mass as in fig (a), the resulting motion will be **linear**, but when the force is applied outside the

Fig 9.35. A diver will use the principle of eccentric force to generate rotation in the dive

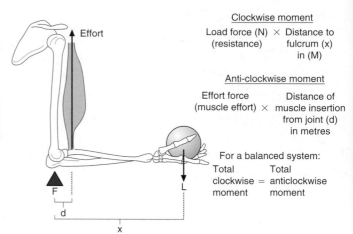

Fig 9.36. The principle of moments

centre of gravity as in fig (b), the resulting motion will be **angular**. By moving the centre of gravity, the diver can produce an eccentric force to perform either a clockwise rotation (front somersault) or an anticlockwise rotation (back somersault).

Now look at fig 9.36. When holding such a weight, there is a tendency for this moment to turn the lever clockwise. In order to balance the lever at the fulcrum and hold the weight in a static position, the bicep must produce a force equal to the clockwise moment.

Total clockwise moment = Total anticlockwise moment

Clockwise moment = force × distance of load to fulcrum

Anticlockwise moment = Effort (load) force (of muscle) × distance of muscle insertion from the joint

y (force of resistance) = z (force of muscle)

This is commonly known as the **principle of moments**, and explains how a system can be balanced about a fulcrum.

# Angular motion

Quantities used to explain linear motion also apply to angular motion: displacement, velocity and acceleration. However, in rotating bodies we consider these quantities in their angular forms, namely angular displacement, angular velocity and angular acceleration.

# Angular displacement

Just as the distance travelled by a body moving linearly can be measured, so can the distance of an object rotating around an axis. Angular displacement is usually measured in degrees; where there is one complete rotation, the body will have passed through 360°. If the direction of rotation is stated when describing angular distance, the term angular displacement is used.

# Angular velocity

The angular velocity of a body is the angle through which a body rotates about an axis in one second. It is calculated as the angle described in a given time divided by that time. For example: if a trampolinist performing a tucked back somersault, turns through 360° in 2 seconds, their resulting angular velocity will be 180° per second. However, the standard unit for angular motion is **radians per second** (rads/sec) and so we must convert degrees turned into radians.

2π radians = 360°

1 radian = 57.2958°

1 degree = 0.017453 radian

# Angular acceleration

This is the rate of change of angular velocity, and is measured in radians/sec$^2$.

# Moment of inertia

The moment of inertia of a body is its *resistance to rotational or angular motion*. When already rotating, the moment of inertia is the resistance of a body to a change in the state of rotation; this can be compared to its linear counterpart.

The moment of inertia of a body is determined by its **mass** and the *distribution of its mass around the axis of rotation*. The further its mass is away from the axis, the greater its moment of inertia and the more force is required to make it spin or stop it spinning if rotation is already occurring. Where the body's mass is concentrated about the axis, the lower the moment of inertia and the faster the rate of rotation.

In a sporting context this can be seen when comparing the rate of spin of a layout somersault and a tucked somersault:

- In a layout somersault the mass is distributed away from the axis of rotation. The gymnast will have a large moment of inertia and the rate of spin is slow.
- In the tucked position the gymnast's mass is concentrated around the axis of rotation, the moment of inertia is decreased and the rate of spin is increased.

Similarly, an ice skater will rotate much faster when the arms are pulled into the body, since the moment of inertia is decreased.

Fig 9.37. A slalom skier rounding a flag

The moment of inertia can be calculated as follows:

Moment of inertia = the sum of (mass of body part × distance from the axis of rotation, squared)

$$= \Sigma(m \times r^2)$$

- By decreasing the value of r, the moment of inertia is decreased and angular velocity increases.
- If r doubles, the moment of inertia increases by $2^2 = 4$.
- If r increases four-fold, the moment of inertia increases by $4^2 = 16$.

# Newton's first law of angular motion

*A rotating body will continue to turn about its axis of rotation with constant angular momentum unless an external couple or eccentric force is exerted upon it.*

This law is also known as the law of **conservation of angular momentum**.

**Angular momentum** is the product of the **moment of inertia (MI)** and **angular velocity (ω)**:

Angular momentum = MI × ω

This equation demonstrates the inverse relationship between the moment of inertia and rate of spin

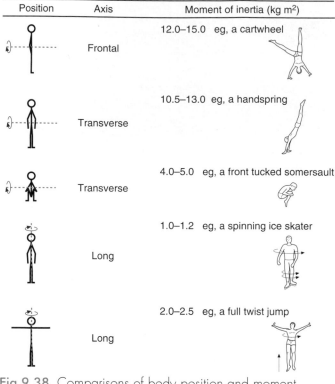

| Position | Axis | Moment of inertia (kg m²) |
|---|---|---|
| | Frontal | 12.0–15.0 eg, a cartwheel |
| | Transverse | 10.5–13.0 eg, a handspring |
| | Transverse | 4.0–5.0 eg, a front tucked somersault |
| | Long | 1.0–1.2 eg, a spinning ice skater |
| | Long | 2.0–2.5 eg, a full twist jump |

**Fig 9.38.** Comparisons of body position and moment of inertia
*Source*: Hay & Reid, 1988.

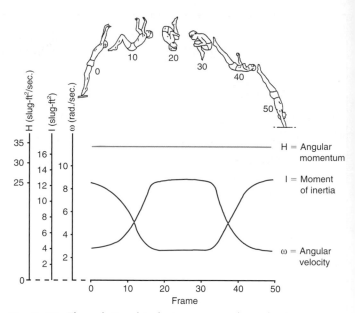

**Fig 9.39.** The relationship between angular velocity, moment of inertia, and angular momentum

(angular velocity); if one increases, the other decreases, and vice-versa. For example:

- during a tumble, the only external force acting on a gymnast is her weight which acts through her centre of gravity and cannot affect her angular momentum.

*Angular momentum is therefore conserved and remains the same.* In order to decrease the rate of spin, a gymnast must therefore redistribute her mass and increase the moment of inertia. This is done by extending out of the tuck position before landing.

The inverse relationship between angular velocity and moment of inertia and its effect upon angular momentum is illustrated in fig 9.39.

# Newton's second law of angular motion

*The angular acceleration of a body is proportional to the torque causing it and takes place in the direction in which the torque acts.*

By increasing a turning effect or torque, greater angular acceleration can be achieved.
For example:

- a gymnast increases angular momentum on a high bar when building up for a dismount that includes a number of somersaults.

# Newton's third law of angular motion

*For every torque that is exerted by one body on another, there is an equal and opposite torque exerted by the second body on the first.*

This is another action–reaction law and can easily be seen in sporting activity:

- In the long jump, as the legs are brought forward and upward to land, a reaction force causes the arms to be brought forward and downward.

- When a trampolinist performs a pike jump, the legs are brought up clockwise as the arms are brought down anticlockwise to meet them.

# Summary

## Newton's laws

### First law

*Every body continues in its state of rest, or of uniform motion in a straight line, except in so far as it may be compelled by impressed forces to change that state.*

### Second law

*The rate of change of momentum is proportional to the impressed force, and the actual change takes place in the direction in which the force acts.*

### Third law

*To every action, there is an equal and opposite reaction, or the mutual actions of the two bodies in contact are always equal and opposite …*

## Linear motion

$$\text{Speed} = \frac{\text{distance moved}}{\text{time taken}} \ (\text{ms}^{-1}) \qquad\qquad \text{Velocity} = \frac{\text{displacement}}{\text{time taken}} \ (\text{ms}^{-1})$$

Acceleration = change of speed per second $\qquad a = \dfrac{v - u}{t} \ (\text{ms}^{-2})$

$V^2 = U^2 + 2as$
$S = Ut + \frac{1}{2}at^2$

(where V = final velocity, U = initial velocity)

Force = mass × acceleration, F = ma (N)

Kinetic energy = ½ × mass × (velocity)$^2$

Weight = mass × gravity, W = mg

## Impulse + impact

Momentum = mass × velocity, momentum = mv (Kgms$^{-1}$)
Impulse = force × time, f × t
Impulse ∴ = change of momentum, Ft = mv − mu (Ns)

## Levers

Moment of force = force × distance to fulcrum (Nm)
(couple)
Total anticlockwise moment = total clockwise moment

Angular motion

1 radian = 57.2958 degrees
1 degree = 0.017453 radians

$$\text{Angular velocity} = \frac{\text{angle turned through in radians}}{\text{time taken}} \quad \text{(rads/sec)}$$

(angle turned per second)

Moment of inertia = the sum of [(mass of body part) × (distance from the axis of rotation)$^2$]
∴ MI = Σ(m × r$^2$)

Rotational energy = ½ × moment of inertia × (angular velocity)$^2$

Angular momentum = angular velocity × moment of inertia

# Review Questions

1. A weight lifter exerts an upward force of 2000N on a bar bell of 170 kg. What is the vertical acceleration?

2. Draw free body diagrams of the following, showing all the forces acting upon them:

   (a) A high jumper at take-off

   (b) A gymnast performing a handstand

   (c) A diver at take-off.

3. A knowledge of centre of mass can be of great benefit to the sportsperson. Using examples from sport show how the centre of mass and its adjustment can enhance performance.

4. Analyse the human lever system. Classify the type of lever in operation at as many joints as possible. Give sketch diagrams to show the lever system in action.

5. What factors affect the degree to which air resistance influences the flight path of projectiles?

6. Give at least three examples from sport where fluid friction affects:

   (a) an object

   (b) a sportsperson.

7. State the effects of this fluid friction in each case.

8. What do you understand by the term Magnus Effect? Explain how a knowledge of Magnus forces can assist a tennis player.

9. What do you understand by the term Moment of Inertia?

10. Using diagrams to support your answer, show how body shape and angular velocity are related in the performance of a trampolining routine.

11. Give examples from sporting situations where changes in the moment of inertia affects performance.

12. Sketch pin-men diagrams of body positions which generate high rates of spin and compare with those body positions which lead to low rates of spin.

13. Sketch a graph to show angular velocity against time as a trampolinist travels through a tucked front somersault. Add to your graph a corresponding line showing the moment of inertia.

14. How would the resultant force of a person performing a vertical jump differ from the high jumper performing the Fosbury flop technique?

15. Explain why the 'hitchkick' technique has developed in the long jump.

## Further reading

Davis et al., *Physical Education and the Study of Sport* (Wolfe Publishing Ltd, 1991)

Davis, Kimmet and Auty, *Physical Education: Theory and Practice* (MacMillan, 1986)

F W Dick, *Sports Training Principles*, 2nd edn (A & C Black, 1989)

G Dyson, *The Mechanics of Athletics* (University Press, Cambridge, 1977)

T Ecker, *Basic Track and Field Biomechanics* (Tafnews Press, 1985)

J Watkins, *An Introduction to the Mechanics of Human Movement* (MTP Press, 1986)

R Wirhed, *Athletic Ability and the Anatomy of Motion* (Wolfe Publishing Ltd, 1984)

# HISTORICAL, SOCIAL AND CULTURAL ASPECTS

# INTRODUCTION

Sport sociology is an approach which attempts to determine the place of physical activity in the cultural hierarchy. Society is a dynamic concept as it is constantly changing and adapting, sometimes gradually evolving over centuries, and in other instances revolutionary changes are experienced almost overnight. Sport will reflect and influence the society of which it forms an integral part.

Cultural research in this area has expanded to include other societies which are modelled on different plans and motivated by different ideals. Societies ranging from primitive to modern industrial are now studied: the organisation of physical activities and type of participation are viewed as an essential part of that society.

The following chapters will hopefully highlight to you the impact society has on sport and vice versa, how this process is ongoing, continuing to affect **your** personal experiences of participating in sporting activities. Imagine a situation where you have no facilities to train, no clubs to belong to, and where the system of coaching is so underdeveloped athletes cannot improve. Imagine living in Victorian times, how different our experiences in terms of leisure, recreation, sport and education would have been. In comparison to the Victorian era:

- there is now more equality of opportunity for different social classes, ethnic groups and women
- sport has enhanced international communication
- sport as big business has created questions about ethics and the politics of sport
- perhaps more importantly, experiencing the human emotions connected to participation in sporting activities is what makes it a valuable subject of study.

These are relevant issues and where necessary we will use the discipline of sociology to help us gain a wider understanding.

## Factors affecting sport in society

Several factors can influence and be influenced by the system of sport and they are outlined in the diagram below. The arrows suggest the symbiotic relationship.

## Task

Consider each factor and try and extend them into sub categories. For example, Education could include:

- state and private schools
- facilities
- government policies
- National Curriculum
- physical education and so on.

It is useful at this stage to choose one factor that interests you and research what influence it may have had on sport or vice versa in the past or present day.

This should have given you some understanding of the type of issues that will be covered in later chapters. We will study the:

- social and cultural make-up of the United Kingdom
- the conceptual understanding of Play, Leisure, Recreation, Physical Education and Outdoor Education/Recreation and Sport

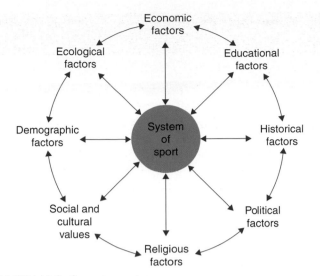

DIAGRAM 1. Sport in society

- the system of sport and physical education in the United Kingdom
- the historical development of physical activities, sports and physical education

First of all it is necessary to understand clearly what is meant by the terms Play, Leisure, Recreation, Physical Education, Outdoor Education, Recreation and Sport.

# 10. Concepts of Physical Activity

## Chapter Introduction

The aim of this chapter is to explore the various concepts of physical activity: play, leisure, physical education and sport. We have already used some of these terms, but it is necessary at this stage to explore each term in its own context; ie, what characterises each concept, its uniqueness and also its common elements. We will also follow the theory of each concept with a brief look at how the theory has affected the development of the activity in society.

For ease of study we will start from the least organised, play, and move on to the most highly organised, sport.

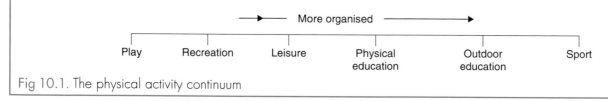

Fig 10.1. The physical activity continuum

Here is a list of terms to be covered in this chapter. It is important that you understand them and how they interrelate with each other.

- Play
- Recreation/physical recreation/active leisure
- Leisure/purposeful leisure
- Physical education/school sport
- National Curriculum
- Outdoor pursuits/outdoor education/outdoor recreation
- Risk/danger
- Sport
- Classification of sporting activities
- Analysis of activities

## A O Play

Play is something which children *and* adults do. It takes different forms and has different motives and benefits for each, but it can assume a great significance and importance to people's lives. A quick look in the dictionary to investigate what we mean by the word 'play', reveals that it conjures up many different meanings; eg, 'to occupy or amuse oneself in a sport; to fulfil a particular role – he played defence; a dramatic production; play fair'. It is very difficult to extract one meaning alone, but we must attempt to tease out the common characteristics which are relevant to our field of study and have been developed by psychologists such as Huizinga, Piaget, Callois and Ellis.

Play to the Ancient Greeks was associated with childhood. Play served to integrate children into Greek culture, acting as a form of social control, as well as developing the mental, physical and social well-being of the youngsters. The philosopher Aristotle believed children should have an early diet of games, tales and stories. These would better serve the developing child than formal lessons.

In the Middle Ages, the Church focused on the preparation of the soul for the after life. Play was therefore given a low status, being seen as a threat to the social order and a waste of time. Work for salvation attained high status and the two concepts were separated. This coincided with the harsh life many children experienced, which carried on into the nineteenth century where many were sent to work at a very early age. However, it was also at this time that French Philosopher Rousseau reinstated play as an important part of 'getting back to nature' in the text *Emile*. He claimed that simplicity and freedom should be an important part of a child's development into an adult, allowing spontaneity and self expression. However, it would be some time before most children experienced this concept.

# Classical theories of play

- Surplus energy
- Preparation
- Recapitulation
- Relaxation

These theories tend to concentrate on the instinctive nature of man and tend to reflect only certain aspects of play behaviour.

## J Huizinga

The contribution of Huizinga, a Dutch cultural historian, lies in the detailed way he describes play; he provides observations but does not attempt an explanation of play. His descriptions include the following:

- Play is creative; it is repeated, alternated, transmitted; it becomes tradition.
- Play is a stepping out of real life.
- Play is uncertain. The end result cannot be determined.
- All play has rules, and as soon as the rules are transgressed, the whole play world collapses.
- Play is social. A play community generally tends to become permanent, encouraging the

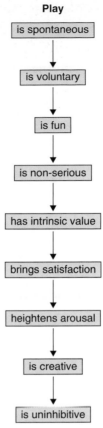

Fig 10.2. Values of play

feeling of being together in an exceptional situation, of mutually withdrawing from the rest of the world.

*'Play is a voluntary activity or occupation exercised within certain fixed rules of time and place, according to rules freely accepted but absolutely binding, having its aim in itself and accompanied by a feeling of tension, joy, and the consciousness that this is different from ordinary life'*

(Huizinga, 1964)

## Piaget

Piaget, a Swiss psychologist, claimed that play is:

- an end in itself
- distinguished by the spontaneity of play as opposed to the compulsion of work
- an activity for pleasure
- devoid of organised structure.

Piaget believed that play was the most effective aspect of early learning. Much educational thinking has been influenced by this thought. Play is crucial for development and intelligence: the child uses its intelligence in play and is manipulative; s/he adapts to the environment by modifying feelings and thoughts through:

- assimilation – child imposes own knowledge on reality, thus can change reality
- accommodation – child fits into environment.

## Callois

Callois, a French sociologist, developed a theory which suggested that play is a reflection of society. He used Greek terms to develop four forms of play:

- **Agon** (competition) – contest or struggle, eg, competitive games.
- **Alea** (chance) – the end is determined by chance or fate.
- **Mimicry** (role taking) – eg, children playing mummies and daddies.
- **Ilynx** (vertigo) – eg, fast-moving activities which induce giddiness.

These can all be distinguished from each other by two other aspects:

- **Paidia** – the pure ideal of children's play, where fun is the key element
- **Ludus** – when activities become more organised.

When we move from play to sport, the ludic element becomes more prominent.

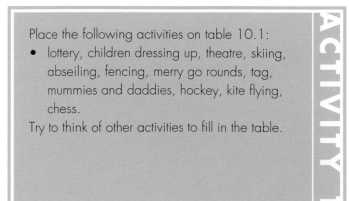

Place the following activities on table 10.1:
- lottery, children dressing up, theatre, skiing, abseiling, fencing, merry go rounds, tag, mummies and daddies, hockey, kite flying, chess.
Try to think of other activities to fill in the table.

ACTIVITY 1

Table 10.1. Categorising activities

|  | Agon | Alea | Mimicry | Ilynx |
|---|---|---|---|---|
| Paidia |  |  |  |  |
| Ludus |  |  |  |  |

## Ellis

Recent theories of play tend to be concerned with the 'individual' explanation of play. Ellis summarises five major theories:

1. **Generalisation** and **compensation** – people select activities which will either reflect or compensate for their world of work.
2. **Catharsis** – the purging and consequent release of strong emotions. It suggests that aggressive tendencies can be subdued, but research suggests that experiencing aggression, such as involvement in sport, can lead to more aggression.
3. **Psychoanalytic** – the Freudian idea that play is motivated by pleasure.
4. **Development** – Erikson's idea that children can learn through play, the ability to master reality.
5. Play is ritualised to provide social traditions.

# Modern theories

Play is regarded as stimulus-seeking behaviour. In his book, *Why people play*, Ellis developed the notion that play involves the integration of three theories:

- learning
- developmental
- arousal seeking behaviour (behaviour is motivated to maintain an optimal level of arousal).

He claims that:

*'When the primary drives are satisfied the animal continues to emit stimulus seeking behaviour.'*

However, when the situation is too complex it reduces arousal; at the opposite end, if the outcome is too predictable, the lack of uncertainty will also reduce arousal. Imagine a sporting contest where the opponents are not well matched. Both know the result is a foregone conclusion, so an intermediary level is sought. This theory has the advantage of incorporating work and play, rather than separating them.

The following definition is a useful amalgamation of the different theories of play.

*'Play is activity – mental, passive or active. Play is undertaken freely and is usually spontaneous. It is fun, purposeless, self initiated and often extremely serious. Play is indulged in for its own sake; it has intrinsic value; there is innate satisfaction in the doing. Play transports the player, as it were, to a world outside his or her normal world. It can heighten arousal. It can be vivid, colourful, creative and innovative. Because the player shrugs off inhibitions and is lost in the play, it seems to be much harder for adults, with social and personal inhibitions to really play.'*

(Adults play but children just play more
G. Torkildsen)

# Implications of play

## Education

The importance given to play in terms of children's ability to learn more effectively has been taken seriously by many educationalists. Certainly in the early years there is a focus on play activities through which children will learn.

Exploratory learning led to a more **heuristic** teaching style (a device or strategy that serves to stimulate investigation). The teacher's role changed from being purely instructional to one of initiating a guidance form of learning.

## KEY WORD

### Heuristic
Comes from the Greek word 'eurisko' meaning 'serves to discover or reaches understanding of'. Through heuristic play children are satisfying their natural need to explore, and are discovering for themselves the properties and behaviour of different objects and materials. The play eliminates any sense of failure as it has open-ended possibilities rather than pre-determined goals set by adults.

## Physical education lessons

There are aspects of physical education which do not match the concept of play. For example: it is compulsory; the content is chosen by the teacher; the teacher is in authority over the group; the group does not initiate the activity spontaneously.

## Recreation

Recreation managers should also take note of the positive experiences which play can generate in everyone's lives, not only children's.

## Central government

Children's play is in receipt of central government funding which highlights the importance placed upon it.

**ACTIVITY 2**

1. What strategies as a teacher could you use to help inject a more playful element in a PE lesson, while achieving your educational objectives? (The following section on physical education may give you some ideas).
2. What possible constraints can operate on the play world of children?
3. Taking a play activity of your choice, say how and why spontaneity can exist.

# Recreation/physical recreation/active leisure

The word 'recreation' originates from the Latin word 'recreatio', which means to restore health. Recreation has long been connected with relaxation and recuperation of the individual. It has been particularly valued during the nineteenth and twentieth centuries, with the emergence of an industrialised, machine controlled workforce. Recreation is thought to be useful in restoring people's energies for work. However, as with other concepts of physical activity, people participate for many different reasons. Many sections of the community are not in paid employment and yet participate in recreation. Physical recreation is where the activity requires the individual to expend a reasonable amount of energy. This is also known as 'active leisure'.

Other ideas focus on recreation as being: activity based; not an obligation; socially acceptable; morally sound; an emotional response; an attitude; a way of life.

# Theories of recreation

## Serving the needs of human beings

J. B. Nash evaluates recreation as creative social contribution and a way of satisfying human inner urges. He developed the participation model where the recreative lifestyle is 'active participation experience'. Nash regards play as the childhood preparation for recreation in adult life and as a practice for work.

## A leisure time activity

The most widely accepted view of recreation is simply activities in which people participate during their leisure time. One problem with this viewpoint is that many people are biased towards thinking that recreation can only be sport or physical activity.

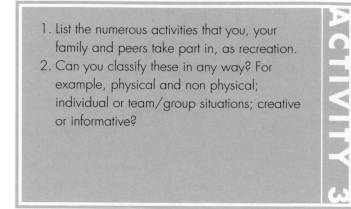

ACTIVITY 3

1. List the numerous activities that you, your family and peers take part in, as recreation.
2. Can you classify these in any way? For example, physical and non physical; individual or team/group situations; creative or informative?

M. Neumeyer describes recreation as any activity, either individual or collective, which is pursued during one's leisure time. Recreation has four elements:

- behavioural expression
- intrinsically valuable
- rewards found within the activity
- socioculturally conditioned.

## Valuable to individual and society

Many theorists (H. Meyer; C. Brightbill; G. Butler) espouse the idea that recreation must be of 'value', either to the individual or society. This is always a problem area, because whose values are more important? This is particularly significant when considering the provision for recreation by the public and voluntary agencies. What are the presumptions under which they organise their services?

## Recreation as re-creation

J. S. Shivers concentrates on the idea of recreation as an 'experience'. Recreation wholly absorbs the individual at any one moment and helps provide 'psychological homeostasis', ie, the satisfying of psychological needs, and the process of mental rebalancing. Recreation is the harmony and unity experienced between mind and body. This occurs at the *time* of the experience; the *value* is felt later.

The degree to which individuals feel this 'completeness' of recreation will vary, probably will

**Recreation**

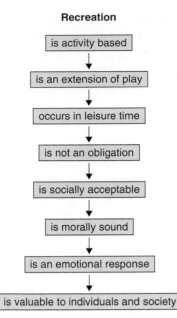

is activity based
↓
is an extension of play
↓
occurs in leisure time
↓
is not an obligation
↓
is socially acceptable
↓
is morally sound
↓
is an emotional response
↓
is valuable to individuals and society

Fig 10.3. Values of recreation

only occur in its purest sense on a few occasions. Those occasions would undoubtedly be extremely memorable and personally uplifting. Do you have any such experiences?

## A social process

J. Murphy believes recreation is a *process*, which requires exploration, investigation, manipulation and learning behaviour. This theory is similar to theories of play, examined earlier. He claims that the physical, psychological, social and educational processes are the outcome of recreation, and lead to self realisation.

## A social institution

R. Kraus takes a different slant:

- Voluntary activities must to some degree be determined by the choices made available. This involves the social institutions and agencies which have developed, eg, churches, schools, industries, voluntary agencies, government departments, etc.

- Skill levels associated with many activities take time to master.

- Motivation to participate is rarely completely intrinsic.

# Recreation planning

- Services should be developed so that people can find recreation and fulfil individual needs.

- Programmes should take a holistic approach, ie, concern for the whole person.

- Access should be available to all citizens

- Planning for recreation *activities* can be measurable and operable, but planning cannot guarantee a recreation *experience* (a particular incident or feeling).

Recreation planning certainly has its place within this modern and rapidly changing society, but for many people, true recreation is not about having their leisure time organised in the same way that the world of work is organised, as this brings its own constraints. Improvements can be made:

- Recreation managers need to create an environment where recreation is most likely to occur.

- Work conditions can be improved to give people greater chances of self expression, recreation activity and recuperation.

- Education can be extended to include leisure skills, helping people to realise and achieve their potential.

Discuss the following:
- Why is play a more important aspect of a child's life and recreation more significant for adults?
- What is the significance of the word 'process'?
- What are the suggested outcomes of participating in recreational activities for the individual and society?

ACTIVITY 4

## Summary of theories of recreation

*'Recreation consists of activities or experiences carried on within leisure, usually chosen*

*voluntarily by the participant – either because of satisfaction, pleasure or creative enrichment derived, or because he perceives certain personal or social gains to be gained from them. It may also be perceived as the process of participation, or as the emotional state derived from the involvement.'*

(R. Kraus, 1971)

Recreation can be viewed as:

- an extension of the 'play' experience
- a personal experience – the value to the individual
- the nature of an activity
- an institution and structural framework
- a process – what happens to an individual.

# A O Leisure

The Ancient Greeks regarded 'leisure' as important for the development of the 'whole' man, his mind and body. This, however, was a state reserved only for the wealthy members of society. The growth of Christianity had a negative effect on leisure time, believing it to have little value in the preparation of the soul for the later life. The Puritan work ethic is a concept developed in the sixteenth and seventeenth centuries which valued the benefits of labour as opposed to the temptations of idleness. It has had far-reaching effects on how we view leisure; even today, work is given a much higher status than leisure activities.

## Theories of leisure

There are four major approaches to looking at leisure.

### Leisure as time

This refers to surplus time; ie, time left over when practical necessities have been attended to. These necessities were referred to by the Countryside Recreation Research Advisory Group in 1970 as 'work, sleep, and other needs' (including family and social duties). C. Brightbill claims that

people need the time, opportunity and choice to enjoy true leisure. He contrasts true leisure with enforced leisure, such as illness, unemployment or forced retirement.

> **ACTIVITY 5**
>
> - Fill in a weekly timetable with all the 'necessities' mentioned above, including sleep, paid work, college/school work, domestic responsibilities, etc. Then try to approximate the amount of time you have left as leisure.
> - Fill in the activities you consider to be part of your leisure time.

### Leisure as activity

Leisure activities can be subdivided into different categories of interest: sport; home entertainment; hobbies and pastimes; reading; public entertainment; holiday activities such as sightseeing.

J. Nash believes that leisure activities occur on four levels:

1. creative involvement
2. active
3. emotional
4. passive

Each is attributed a value; those at the apex are considered more worthy as leisure than those at the base.

Other theories claim that it is the meaning the activities have for the individuals participating which is more important than the activities themselves.

J. Dumazadier believes that leisure must be freely chosen and should benefit the individual in terms of relaxation, diversion or broadening of horizons. He uses the term 'semi leisure' to include such activities as DIY which can be pleasurable as well as being functional.

Fig 10.4. Values of leisure

## Leisure as an end in itself

This contradicts the idea of free time being leisure. The state of mind with which a person approaches this free time is crucial. In its ideal state, leisure should be an opportunity for self expression (J. Pieper; C. Brightbill; S. de Grazia).

## The holistic approach

J. Dumazadier believes leisure has three main functions:

1. relaxation
2. entertainment
3. self fulfilment.

In other words, leisure holds a meaning for people and this is what is most important. It can relieve stress, be an antidote to boredom and allow freer movement than is allowed in many work places.

The concept of leisure is still undergoing changes. Many people are now motivated to work, not for the sake of work but to allow them the opportunity to enjoy their leisure status. Many feel their true identity is not that which occurs at work, but that which emerges during leisure.

## Leisure and work

- Leisure is generally something people do not have to do, whereas most people have to work to earn a living.

- Work and leisure can both create a sense of self worth, creativity and personal development within a person.
- The common belief that people have more free time for leisure in the modern world, can be challenged by the fact that economic circumstances can force people to take on extra work.

In modern industrial societies, work can determine:

- how much time a person has for leisure
- how much energy they can bring to their leisure
- whether leisure can be pursued through work.

## Purposeful leisure

'Purposeful leisure' is a term used by communist governments who, as they operate an authoritarian system, require as much control over their population in leisure as they do in other areas of social life. This is social control, extolling the belief that rebellious tendencies can be curbed and political messages can be equally learnt through the leisure situation.

## Growth and change in leisure time

There are many reasons for the growth and change in leisure time in the UK:

- working hours have been reduced by the application of technology
- labour-saving gadgets enable people to spend much less time on domestic chores in the home
- increase in life expectancy
- increase in disposable incomes
- decline in the role of traditional social structures like the church and family
- education for everyone
- mobility of a large section of the population
- public provision of leisure facilities including the ability to hire equipment which would otherwise be out of reach of the majority of the population

- early retirement
- high unemployment.

## Popular (low) culture

Individuals choose their own leisure within the context of their own culture, values and identity; the majority of the population will also be exposed to marketing forces of leisure. Popular culture is therefore defined by what is available and what represents social development.

Popular culture can also create change and trends, eg, skateboarding, public marathons. Different aspects are given prominence at different times but generally there is less of a tendency to maintain traditional established practices. The far-reaching effects of the mass media as it transmits Western popular culture across the world can, however, result in a uniformity of cultures, rather than the richness and variety of cultures which characterise different countries.

**ACTIVITY 6**

Consider the following factors and suggest how they can affect and be affected by leisure:
- occupation
- trends
- levels of participation
- leisure provision in society
- women's lives
- media.

## High culture

This traditionally refers to the cultural pursuits of the higher social classes and they usually reflect the privileged lifestyles of wealth, education and more free time. Activities pursued by this group of people are often not made easily accessible to the lower social classes, and there is a sense of cultural separation. These activities are often considered to operate on a more intellectual and refined manner to those of popular culture.

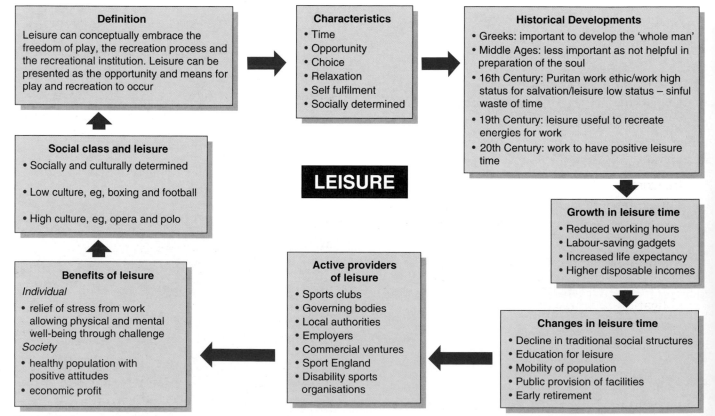

**Definition**
Leisure can conceptually embrace the freedom of play, the recreation process and the recreational institution. Leisure can be presented as the opportunity and means for play and recreation to occur

**Characteristics**
- Time
- Opportunity
- Choice
- Relaxation
- Self fulfilment
- Socially determined

**Historical Developments**
- Greeks: important to develop the 'whole man'
- Middle Ages: less important as not helpful in preparation of the soul
- 16th Century: Puritan work ethic/work high status for salvation/leisure low status – sinful waste of time
- 19th Century: leisure useful to recreate energies for work
- 20th Century: work to have positive leisure time

**LEISURE**

**Social class and leisure**
- Socially and culturally determined
- Low culture, eg, boxing and football
- High culture, eg, opera and polo

**Growth in leisure time**
- Reduced working hours
- Labour-saving gadgets
- Increased life expectancy
- Higher disposable incomes

**Benefits of leisure**
*Individual*
- relief of stress from work allowing physical and mental well-being through challenge
*Society*
- healthy population with positive attitudes
- economic profit

**Active providers of leisure**
- Sports clubs
- Governing bodies
- Local authorities
- Employers
- Commercial ventures
- Sport England
- Disability sports organisations

**Changes in leisure time**
- Decline in traditional social structures
- Education for leisure
- Mobility of population
- Public provision of facilities
- Early retirement

Fig 10.5. Summary of leisure

- Select activities which can be categorised as popular or high culture.
- Discuss the elements which make them different.
- Investigate the different approaches taken by the media towards activities from the two ends of the spectrum.

Summarise theories of leisure.

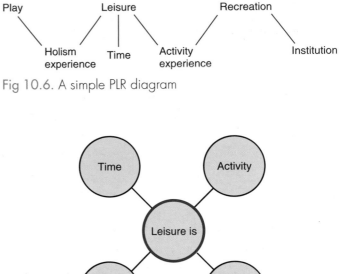

Fig 10.6. A simple PLR diagram

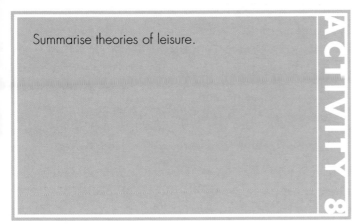

Fig 10.7. Multidimensional concept of leisure

# Integrating play, recreation and leisure

Each concept has its own distinct nature, but they also have similarities; they are multidimensional and link together.

## Similarities

- freedom
- self expression
- satisfaction
- quality
- self initiated
- no pressure or obligation to take part
- range of activities
- experiential

## Differences

- emphasis, eg, play has a strong emphasis on childlike spontaneity and unreality
- functions, eg, for learning, refreshing, recreating or just being!

## Interrelationships

Leisure can be the pivot upon which the other two concepts can be embraced.

*'leisure can conceptually embrace the freedom of play, the recreation process and the recreation institution. Leisure can be presented as the opportunity and the means for play and recreation to occur.'*

(*Torkildsen*)

A recreation programme combines planning, scheduling, time tabling and implementation, using resources, facilities (eg, swimming pools, parks, natural resources, etc) and staff to offer a wide range of services and activities. The activities will range from allowing spontaneity to being completely structured.

- What factors should recreation managers take into account when building and planning services?
- Explain the difference between the terms 'leisure' and 'recreation'.
- Name two home-based leisure activities and two non-home-based leisure activities.

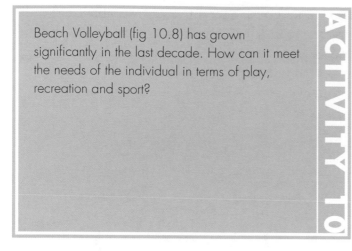

Beach Volleyball (fig 10.8) has grown significantly in the last decade. How can it meet the needs of the individual in terms of play, recreation and sport?

Fig 10.8. Play, recreation, leisure or sport?

# A O Physical education

## What is physical education?

Physical education is an academic discipline (an organised, formal body of knowledge), which has, as its primary focus, the study of human movement. It may be viewed as a field of knowledge, drawing on the physical and human sciences and philosophy, with its main emphasis on physical activity. As this field of knowledge has broadened, the subject specific areas have increased. Sub-disciplines have emerged which have diversified the subject and related it to career opportunities; examples are – sport sociology, biomechanics, sports medicine, exercise physiology, sport philosophy, history, psychology, sports management. You will probably recognise some of these from your own 'A' level physical education course.

Physical education at this level may seem a far cry from what you have experienced over the last twelve years at school. At this stage it is necessary to know what is meant by the term and to appreciate that a philosophy has developed over the last century, and will continue to do so, sometimes changing radically the practice of our subject.

Consider these philosophical viewpoints:

- All participants, regardless of athletic ability, should have equal amounts of playing time on the school curriculum.
- Physical educators should be role models and practise on the playing fields what they preach in the classroom.
- Physical education is only useful in that it provides a break from academic lessons.
- Physical education should be compulsory.

Physical education is an educational process which aims to enhance total human development and performance through movement and the experience of a range of physical activities within an educational setting. Total development means acquiring activity specific skills and knowledge, as well as fostering positive attitudes and values which will be useful in later life. Physical education can help us to achieve a quality of life and a vitality which can be lacking in sedentary lifestyles.

The key words are:

- Range of physical activities
- Movement
- Activity specific skills
- Knowledge
- Values
- Educational setting.

## Aims and objectives

Physical activity involves doing, thinking and feeling. Children need to know *how* to perform or express themselves, know *about* physical activities and also benefit from the enriching experience of knowing how it *feels* to perform.

Already we have given physical education some very difficult challenges. We are assuming that all the outcomes are positive, but this is clearly not the case. Among your peers are those who have enjoyed their physical education experiences but also those who definitely did not! Before we can hope to achieve the positive benefits, we must clarify the aims, objectives and desired outcomes from the physical education curriculum.

Table 10.2. What a child receives from quality physical education

| Physical skills | Physical fitness | Knowledge & understanding | Social skills | Attitudes & appreciations |
|---|---|---|---|---|
| ↓ | ↓ | ↓ | ↓ | ↓ |
| In: | such as: | ot: | such as: | such as: |
| Games<br>Gymnastics<br>Dance<br>Swimming<br>Track and<br> field<br>Outdoor and<br> adventurous<br> activities<br>Fitness<br> programme | Functional fitness<br> capacities<br> essential to health<br> and well-being<br>Cardiorespiratory<br> efficiency<br>Muscular strength<br>Muscular<br> endurance<br>Flexibility<br>Motor ability<br> capacities:<br>• speed<br>• balance<br>• agility<br>• coordination<br>• reaction time | Safety<br>Physical skills<br>Physical fitness<br>Body systems<br>Learning processes<br>Social skills<br>Scientific<br> principles<br> of movement<br>Environmental<br> concerns<br>Rules<br>Strategies<br>Community<br> recreational<br> opportunities | Fair play<br>Cooperation;<br> teamwork; sharing<br>Responsibility<br>Leadership and<br> citizenship<br>Competition<br>Communication;<br> listening; speaking;<br> performance;<br> demonstrating<br>Operating with rules<br>Self control:<br> work under pressure<br>Following directions<br>Resourcefulness<br>Self direction<br>Consideration of<br> others | Desire to participate<br> in physical activities<br>Desire to be<br> physically active<br>Interest in health<br> and responsibility for<br> personal care<br>Appreciation of fair<br> play operating within<br> the rules<br>Respect for team-mates,<br> opponents and officials<br>Appreciation of own<br> abilities and the<br> abilities of others<br>Appreciation of the<br> relationship between<br> exercise and health<br>Appreciation of<br> quality effort in the<br> work of others<br>Feelings of pride and<br> loyalty in the<br> accomplishments of<br> self, school and others<br>Interest in a positive<br> self concept |

*Source*: The British Journal of Teaching Physical Education Autumn 2002.

## Aims

Physical education aims to:

- develop a range of psycho-motor skills

- maintain and increase physical mobility and flexibility, stamina and strength

- develop understanding and appreciation for a range of physical activities

- develop positive values and attitudes like sportsmanship, competition, abiding by the rules

- help children acquire self esteem and confidence through the acquisition of skills, knowledge and values

- develop an understanding of the importance of exercise in maintaining a healthy lifestyle.

## Objectives

Physical education can affect different areas of development. For example:

- The children will be able to complete a 20-minute run – physical development.

Table 10.3. The structure and function of a practical session: definition of terms, relating to a practical session

| Term | Definition | Related to educational setting |
|---|---|---|
| structure | the way in which something is constructed or organised; the arrangement and interrelationship of parts | a lesson within a school timetable; compulsory; age, size, sex and ability of group; location; authority structure |
| function | the special activity or purpose of a thing or person | |
| objectives | something one is trying to achieve or reach | transmit knowledge and skills; safety; success for all abilities; enjoyment; fitness |
| strategies | the planning and directing of the whole operation of a curriculum or lesson; a plan to achieve something (such as the objectives) | effective grouping; personal knowledge; varied teaching styles (instruct, guide); discipline; differentiated tasks to cater for varying abilities; rewards systems |
| content | the substance of a thing or occasion | change kit; warm up; skills; small/conditioned game; full game |
| constraint | to confine, restrain, inhibit, restrict | duration of a lesson; ability of group; condition of facility or equipment |
| evaluation | to set the value of; to judge or assess the worth of something | to test (physical, verbal, written) at end of session or block; own feeling or judgement of lesson (should be ongoing) |
| authority | the power or right to control; a position that commands power | headteacher, teacher, prefect, captain |
| conflict | a state of opposition between ideas, which can lead to tension | relationships (teacher/child, child/child, teacher/teacher); ideas (compulsory, kit, showers) |
| dysfunction | any disturbance or abnormality in the function of a group | discipline problems |

- The children will execute the correct technique for a gymnastic vault – motor development.
- The children will be able to explain the scoring system in badminton – cognitive development.
- The children will display enthusiasm and enjoyment and participate in the extra-curricular activities – affective or emotional development.

> **ACTIVITY 11**
>
> Ask a group of your peers about their experiences of physical education (including the types of activities, what they enjoyed most or least). You can ask general or more specific questions.

> **ACTIVITY 12**
>
> Imagine you are taking a practical session with Year 9; a team game within the physical education timetable. Using table 10.3 as a guide, draw up a detailed plan of your lesson. (This could assist students following the CCPR Community Sports Leaders Award or on teaching practice, and can be used as a role play situation within your academic group.)

## A balanced physical education programme

A balanced programme should attempt to offer a variety of activities selected from each group in table 10.4 (p. 226), in order to maximise fully the opportunities to be gained from the different activities. There should be a balance of activities which are:

- team orientated
- individual

- competitive
- non-competitive movement based.

## Who chooses the physical education programme?

In the United Kingdom there is a decentralised system where the teacher and individual school have the power to produce their own programme, though they are increasingly bound by government guidelines. The National Curriculum now sets out which subjects are to be taught at each Key Stage of a pupil's schooling. Physical education is compulsory from Key Stage 1 (ages 5 to 7) through to Key Stage 4 (up to age 16).

At this point it will be useful to remind yourself about the meaning of the terms centralised and decentralised.

> ## KEY WORD
>
> **Centralised:** means to draw under central control – the central government directs policy across a country. State legislation coordinates and supports policies such as an education curriculum. France is an example of a centralised system whereby teachers are instructed what to teach, when to teach and sometimes how to teach. Although the United Kingdom is not completely centralised in this manner, the National Curriculum brought in after the Education Reform Act 1988 was a move in this direction.

Advantages of a centralised system:

- provides uniformity of experience
- is a coordinated system
- funded by the government.

Disadvantages of a centralised system:

- can be rigid and inflexible
- may not cater for different local needs

ACTIVITY 13

- Study the aims of physical education and see how you might link these to the activities shown in table 10.4.
- Tick the activities which you experienced during your secondary education. Do you think that you received a balanced physical education programme?
- Conduct a survey of approximately six schools in your local area. Try to find out what they offer their pupils. Can you find parallels or many variations? Does what is on offer reflect the different nature of the schools?

Table 10.4. A balanced physical education programme

| Games | | | | Movement |
|---|---|---|---|---|
| Invasion | Net | Striking/field | Rebounding | |
| football netball hockey rugby | tennis volleyball table tennis | cricket rounders softball | squash | gymnastics dance trampolining athletics swimming |

# KEY WORD

**Decentralised:** means dispersal away from the centre towards outlying areas. It is a system of government which is organised into smaller, more autonomous units. Examples are local authorities in the United Kingdom and the individual states in the United States of America. The government in power often gives guidelines, which can be interpreted at a local level.

What are the advantages and disadvantages of a decentralised education system?

ACTIVITY 14

- can be difficult to monitor the system effectively, particularly in large countries
- can reduce the initiatives of individuals such as good teachers.

# National Curriculum [www.dfes.gov.uk/nc]

The National Curriculum attempts to raise standards in education and make schools more accountable for what they teach. Physical education continues to be one of only five subjects which pupils of all abilities must pursue, from their entry to school at age 5 until the end of compulsory schooling at age 16.

Attainment targets and programmes of study have been written for physical education. Children are required to demonstrate the knowledge, skills and understanding involved in areas of various physical activities, including dance, athletics, gymnastics, outdoor and adventurous activities and swimming. There are four Key Stages.

In the document 'Sport: Raising the Game', the government went one step further, and produced a revised PE curriculum which took effect in August 1995.

This has been superseded by Curriculum 2000 changes, being brought more into line with other National Curriculum subjects. The programmes of Study and Attainment Targets are outlined below.

## The importance of physical education

Physical education develops pupils' physical competence and confidence, and their ability to use these to perform in a range of activities. It promotes

---

**Key Stage 1**

During key stage 1 pupils build on their natural enthusiasm for movement, using it to explore and learn about their world. They start to work and play with other pupils in pairs and small groups. By watching, listening and experimenting, they develop their skills in movement and coordination, and enjoy expressing and testing themselves in a variety of situations.

*Breadth of study*
During the key stage, pupils should be taught the knowledge, skills and understanding through dance activities, games activities and gymnastic activities.

---

Fig 10.9. Key Stage 1 – programme of study

---

**Key Stage 2**

During key stage 2 pupils enjoy being active and using their creativity and imagination in physical activity. They learn new skills, find out how to use them in different ways, and link them to make actions, phrases and sequences of movement. They enjoy communicating, collaborating and competing with each other. They develop an understanding of how to succeed in different activities and learn how to evaluate and recognise their own success.

*Breadth of study*
During the key stage, pupils should be taught the knowledge, skills and understanding through five areas of activity:

a) dance activities
b) games activities
c) gymnastic activities

and two activity areas from:

d) swimming activities and water safety
e) athletic activities
f) outdoor and adventurous activities.

---

Fig 10.10. Key Stage 2 – programme of study

---

**Key Stage 3**

During key stage 3 pupils become more expert in their skills and techniques, and how to apply them in different activities. They start to understand what makes a performance effective and how to apply these principles to their own and others' work. They learn to take the initiative and make decisions for themselves about what to do to improve performance. They start to identify the types of activity they prefer to be involved with, and to take a variety of roles such as leader and official.

*Breadth of study*
During the key stage, pupils should be taught the knowledge, skills and understanding through four areas of activity. These should include:

a) games activities

and three of the following, at least one of which must be dance or gymnastic activities:

b) dance activities
c) gymnastic activities
d) swimming activities and water safety
e) athletic activities
f) outdoor and adventurous activities.

---

Fig 10.11. Key Stage 3 – programme of study

---

**Key Stage 4**

During key stage 4 pupils tackle complex and demanding activities applying their knowledge of skills, techniques and effective performance. They decide whether to get involved in physical activity that is mainly focused on competing or performing, promoting health and well-being, or developing personal fitness. They also decide on roles that suit them best including performer, coach, choreographer, leader and official. The view they have of their skilfulness and physical competence gives them the confidence to get involved in exercise and activity out of school and in later life.

*Breadth of study*
During the key stage, pupils should be taught the knowledge, skills and understanding through two of the six activity areas.

---

Fig 10.12. Key Stage 4 – programme of study

## Attainment Targets

### Level 1

Pupils copy, repeat and explore simple skills and actions with basic control and coordination. They start to link these skills and actions in ways that suit the activities. They describe and comment on their own and others' actions. They talk about how to exercise safely, and how their bodies feel during an activity.

### Level 2

Pupils explore simple skills. They copy, remember, repeat and explore simple actions with control and coordination. They vary skills, actions and ideas and link these in ways that suit the activities. They begin to show some understanding of simple tactics and basic compositional ideas. They talk about differences between their own and others' performance and suggest improvements. They understand how to exercise safely, and describe how their bodies feel during different activities.

### Level 3

Pupils select and use skills, actions and ideas appropriately, applying them with coordination and control. They show that they understand tactics and composition by starting to vary how they respond. They can see how their work is similar to and different from others' work, and use this understanding to improve their own performance. They give reasons why warming up before an activity is important, and why physical activity is good for their health.

### Level 4

Pupils link skills, techniques and ideas and apply them accurately and appropriately. Their performance shows precision, control and fluency, and that they understand tactics and composition. They compare and comment on skills, techniques and ideas used in their own and others' work, and use this understanding to improve their performance. They explain and apply basic safety principles in preparing for exercise. They describe what effects exercise has on their bodies, and how it is valuable to their fitness and health.

### Level 5

Pupils select and combine their skills, techniques and ideas and apply them accurately and appropriately, consistently showing precision, control and fluency. When performing, they draw on what they know about strategy, tactics and composition. They analyse and comment on skills and techniques and how these are applied in their own and others' work. They modify and refine skills and techniques to improve their performance. They explain how the body reacts during different types of exercise, and warm-up and cool-down in ways that suit the activity. They explain why regular, safe exercise is good for their fitness and health.

### Level 6

Pupils select and combine skills, techniques and ideas. They apply them in ways that suit the activity, with consistent precision, control and fluency. When planning their own and others' work, and carrying out their own work, they draw on what they know about strategy, tactics and composition in response to changing circumstances, and what they know about their own and others' strengths and weaknesses. They analyse and comment on how skills, techniques and ideas have been used in their own and others' work, and on compositional and other aspects of performance, and suggest ways to improve. They explain how to prepare for, and recover from, the activities. They explain how different types of exercise contribute to their fitness and health and describe how they might get involved in other types of activities and exercise.

### Level 7

Pupils select and combine advanced skills, techniques and ideas, adapting them accurately and appropriately to the demands of the activities. They consistently show precision, control, fluency and originality. Drawing on what they know of the principles of advanced tactics and compositional ideas, they apply these in their own and others' work. They modify them in response to changing circumstances and other performers. They analyse and comment on their own and others' work as individuals and team members, showing that they understand how skills, tactics or composition and fitness relate to the quality of the performance. They plan ways to improve their own and others' performance. They explain the principles of practice and training, and apply them effectively. They explain the benefits of regular, planned activity on health and fitness and plan their own appropriate exercise and activity programme.

### Level 8

Pupils consistently distinguish and apply advanced skills, techniques and ideas, consistently showing high standards of precision, control, fluency and originality. Drawing on what they know of the principles of advanced tactics or composition, they apply these principles with proficiency and flair in their own and others' work. They adapt it appropriately in response to changing circumstances and other performers. They evaluate their own and others' work, showing that they understand the impact of skills, strategy and tactics or composition, and fitness on the quality and effectiveness of performance. They plan ways in which their own and others' performance could be improved. They create action plans and ways of monitoring improvement. They use their knowledge of health and fitness to plan and evaluate their own and others' exercise and activity programme.

### Exceptional performance

Pupils consistently use advanced skills, techniques and ideas with precision and fluency. Drawing on what they know of the principles of advanced strategies and tactics or composition, they consistently apply these principles with originality, proficiency and flair in their own and others' work. They evaluate their own and others' work, showing that they understand how skills, strategy and tactics or composition, and fitness relate to and affect the quality and originality of performance. They reach judgements independently about how their own and others' performance could be improved, prioritising aspects for further development. They consistently apply appropriate knowledge and understanding of health and fitness in all aspects of their work.

Fig 10.13. Attainment Targets – end of key stage descriptions

physical skilfulness, physical development and a knowledge of the body in action. Physical education provides opportunities for pupils to be creative, competitive and to face up to different challenges as individuals and in groups and teams. It promotes positive attitudes towards active and healthy lifestyles.

Pupils learn how to think in different ways to suit a wide variety of creative, competitive and challenging activities. They learn how to plan, perform and evaluate actions, ideas and performances to improve their quality and effectiveness. Through this process pupils discover their aptitudes, abilities and preferences, and make choices about how to get involved in lifelong physical activity.

This initially sounds encouraging and positive but fig 10.14 shows data published by the European Union of Physical Education Association. The survey shows the amount of time spent per week on physical education in schools in the USA and the UK. At the primary level the UK is ninth out of ten and at secondary level the UK is placed at the bottom of the table.

The DfES also conducted a survey in the 1990s, which showed that some schools are still not devoting two hours a week to physical education as recommended.

## Assessment in physical education

Aims and objectives will depend on how achievement is evaluated and how well the children have progressed is one element within the evaluation. Several types of assessment are used in physical education departments, such as longitudinal student profiles, purely quantitative data like fitness tests or generalised comments.

**ACTIVITY 15**

- Summarise the general requirements for each key stage of the National Curriculum.
- What factors may a teacher have to take into account when devising a syllabus?

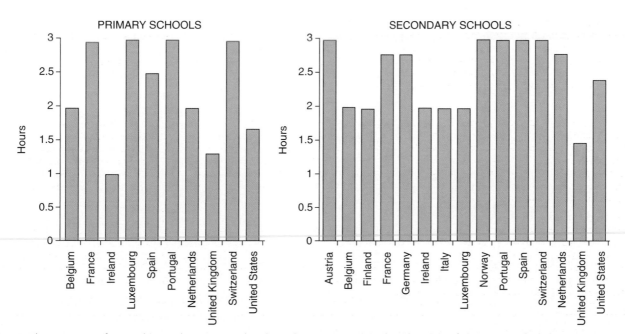

Fig 10.14. The amount of time devoted to PE in schools in the UK compared to the rest of Europe and USA
Source: European Union of PE Associations.

Children need to be able to show what they know, what they can do and what they understand. They can show this through written and verbal language, and in a performance situation.

Assessment should be made of the whole person, not just physical skills. Aspects of their personality such as their ability to work with groups or individually, and their ability to abide by rules should be assessed.

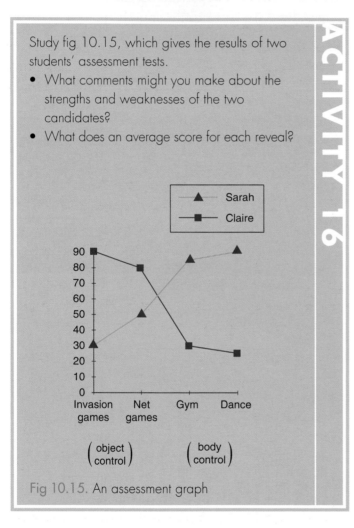

**ACTIVITY 16**

Study fig 10.15, which gives the results of two students' assessment tests.
- What comments might you make about the strengths and weaknesses of the two candidates?
- What does an average score for each reveal?

Fig 10.15. An assessment graph

# Administration of physical education in the UK

The UK has a system of private and state school education, and of comprehensive and grammar schools. The nature of schools can be as diversified as the people they house. Local authorities used to have a large influence on how education operates in their areas; they would be the middle man between the schools and the government. During the 1980s,

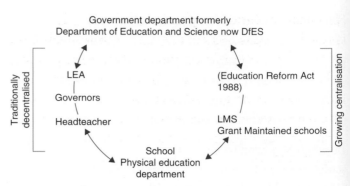

Fig 10.16. Changes in administration: the government can now deal directly with the school, rather than through the LEA

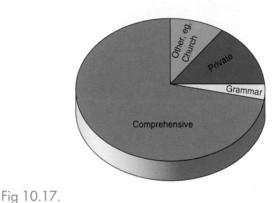

Fig 10.17.

the government implemented increasingly centralised policies, such as the National Curriculum, the Local Management of Schools (LMS) and the growing number of grant maintained schools (GMS), which resulted in them leaving local authority control. The government sought more direct control of education, and through the Education Reform Acts of 1986 and 1988, they have restricted the freedom of teachers, schools and local authorities to construct their own syllabus.

## Private schools

Education in this country began with private schooling for the social elite. Pupils enjoyed extensive facilities and focused on the 'character building' aims of education, as preparation for responsibilities in later life as employers, officers, members of the clergy and so on. Competitive team games developed to serve these aims. There was always a concentration on sport rather than a physical education emphasis and this is still prevalent today. As a result sport coaches still tend to be employed for their specialist sporting prowess. This is particularly evident for schools wishing to continue a sporting tradition. Competitive fixtures are a recognised feature and the prestige which arises from winning helps to distinguish it from other schools.

## State education – primary schools

State education began after the Forster Education Act 1870 which initiated compulsory schooling for all. Compulsory schooling begins at the age of five. As mentioned above, in the state system physical education is compulsory and is a core subject of the National Curriculum; students must spend at least two hours a week on this subject. The class teacher is usually in charge, though is not usually a specialist. Some schools may hire specialist help for certain activities, eg, swimming.

The content of the lessons is usually based on movement and ball skills. Learning by moving and doing is considered essential to the physical, emotional, intellectual and social education of young children. Children's own play is generally very physical and enjoys a lot of repetition, as this enables them to master skills which increases their sense of worth. The physical education programme can use this as a foundation. Variety is also important as their concentration span can be limited and they need to be stimulated by interesting situations.

In addition to the curriculum, many schools also offer club activities like gymnastics, netball, soccer, country dancing, etc. This tends to be at the discretion and goodwill of the teachers.

## Secondary education

As children approach the end of the compulsory years of schooling, it is necessary to foster in them an awareness of the opportunities available in the community. As a result of the philosophy of educating children for their leisure time, schools began to offer options programmes in the later years where a wider variety of activities, sometimes using community facilities, could be experienced. Smaller groups guided by additional non-specialist staff made this possible. Students should be informed about and put into contact with local clubs and sports centres. This is an area of weakness in the United Kingdom; there are traditionally poor links between schools and community sport, as a result of trying to keep a distance between sport and physical education. This will be discussed in more detail later.

Physical education as an examination subject has flourished. A rapidly growing number of students opt to take GCSE and 'A' level examinations, and some GNVQs offer sport and physical education as a focus.

# Developments in school sport

The term 'sport' refers to the 'physical activities with established rules engaged in by individuals attempting to outperform their competitors' (Wuest, Bucher, 1991). Its main focus is on improving performance standards rather than the educational process and mainly takes place outside the formal curriculum. It is usually viewed as an opportunity for children to extend their interest or ability in physical activities.

The changes in society and education in the last 20 years have affected school sport (ie, the extra-curricular opportunities), with a reduction in emphasis on the sporting elite, which sometimes required a disproportionate amount of resources for a few children. Extra-curricular clubs, open to all, became more acceptable. The situation did not change overnight, however; many teachers continued to focus on competitive sports, and extra-curricular activities were affected by these factors:

1. The teachers' strikes in the early 1980s – the contractual hours and lack of monetary incentives tended to diminish teachers' goodwill, and clubs were disbanded.

2. Financial cuts were felt in terms of transport.

3. The local management of schools allowed schools to supplement their funds by selling off school fields.

4. The increasing amount of leisure and employment opportunities for children meant they were less attracted to competing for their school team.

5. The anti-competitive lobby became more vocal: they espoused the theory that competition in sport was not good for children's development.

This all led to the claim that school sport was in decline, although the report produced in 1995 by the Office of Her Majesty's Chief Inspector of Schools, 'Physical Education and Sport in Schools – A Survey of Good Practice', concluded 'that there was little to support the notion of irrevocable decline'.

Fig 10.18. School sport encourages teamwork

Table 10.5. Advantages and disadvantages of competitive sport

| Advantages | Disadvantages |
| --- | --- |
| Children have natural competitive instinct, and as more motivated to practise, enjoyment of sport increases | Continued feelings of failure can cause stress and anxiety |
| Can raise self esteem and learn how to cope with failure and success | The need to win can encourage unsporting behaviour |

# A|O Government involvement

## 'Sport: Raising the Game'

The focus of the 1995 document is mainly on reinstating the status of school sport within school life. It formed part of the Conservative government's overall strategy to develop an effective sporting continuum.

The publication of this document showed a recognition that school sport had declined, and the government wanted to rectify the situation:

A high quality physical education for all children is central to the Government's new PE School Sport and Club Links Strategy (PESSCL).

### Physical education or sport?

This is an ongoing debate, which resurfaced in the 1995 document with the government's decision to give competitive sport a higher status. The terms 'physical education' and 'sport' are complex. There is an overlap between them but their central focuses are different. The aim of the former is to educate the person, while the latter has other purposes, eg, achieving excellence, fitness, earning an income, etc. A good physical education programme can be the foundation on which the extra-curricular opportunities can be extended and enhanced. However, physical education teachers should not necessarily feel pressured into allowing a 'sport' ethos to creep into the curriculum.

## Sport Education

Sport Education is a term used to describe a pupil-centered approach rather than teacher-centered. Children are encouraged to be continually involved in the learning process. This gives every child an opportunity to have some form of success within school physical education even if they are not particularly physically gifted. Children are given responsibility for organising aspects of lessons, for example, equipment management, practice drills, working constructively in teams to include each member and so on. Inclusion is therefore a key factor.

## The role of the physical education teacher and sport coach

A physical education teacher is qualified to teach or instruct children in a range of physical activities. The main focus of the physical education teacher is on the needs and all-round development of the child rather than aiming for sporting excellence. The UK has long had a tradition of keeping school physical education separate from sport coaching, hence the poorer school-club links that exist as a result.

## A O Outdoor pursuits

Outdoor pursuit activities take place in the natural environment including situations which are dangerous and challenging, suggesting conquest of natural obstacles or terrain. Examples of such activities would be rock climbing, skiing and sky diving. New activities continue to develop mostly as a result of technological advances, such as jet skiing and windsurfing.

Table 10.6. Differences between teaching and coaching

| Teaching | Coaching |
|---|---|
| Teach a range of activities | Tend to specialise in an activity |
| Activity is compulsory | Performers have chosen to participate |
| Teacher comes under government Department of Education and Skills (DfES) | Coach is under remit of governing bodies and SportCoach UK |
| Teaches a wide range of ability | Performers tend to be of similar ability |

These activities can be participated in through a recreational and/or educational approach.

- **Outdoor education:** participation in outdoor pursuit activities in the natural environment developing educational values. For example, a school may offer orienteering within the school grounds or arrange a visit to a National Park or other area where adventurous activities may be undertaken.

- **Outdoor recreation:** participation in outdoor pursuit activities within the natural environment in an individual's free time.

When individuals participate in a *recreational* capacity there are no rules as such, no winners or losers and therefore no officials. There is usually,

- List as many activities as you can which take place in the natural environments of water, mountains, air and countryside.
- Where people do not have easy access to these areas, how could you adapt the urban environment for them to learn the basic skills of some of these sports?

ACTIVITY 18

however, a code of etiquette concerning safety and conservation of the natural environment.

Recently many of these activities have become *sports*, involving scoring systems and officials, for example, white-water slalom races and speed climbing.

These activities can place the individual in situations which are dangerous and challenging, and which induce exhilaration, fear and excitement. They can be competitive, but more often against the elements or the human body, than against another person.

The personal qualities required for and enhanced by these activities include:

- self reliance
- decision making
- leadership
- the ability to trust others
- the ability to be trusted.

These activities are not usually done alone, and the ability to work with others to overcome obstacles and find solutions is important; so too is the need to conquer fear of danger and the unpredictable. They often create unique situations which cannot be found playing in sports such as netball or soccer.

## Risk – real and perceived

The main challenge for the participant occurs against the elements requiring them to differentiate between real and perceived risk.

## Growth of outdoor and adventurous activities

There has been a considerable growth both in the traditional (eg, canoeing, rock climbing, abseiling, climbing) and 'new' (eg, jet skiing, snow boarding, mountain biking) adventure sports. The reasons for this growth can be explained by:

- increasingly sedentary lives, which makes some people seek a more active and exciting leisure time
- increased leisure time and standards of living, which make these activities more accessible
- the development of new and exciting technology sports
- the appreciation of the natural environment particularly as a release from urban pressures.

According to Mortlock, there are four broad stages of adventure:

- **Play** – little challenge in developing skills/boredom could set in
- **Adventure** – more challenging environment/ skills developed under safe conditions
- **Frontier Adventure** – the individual is placed in more difficult terrain where well-learned skills can be put to the test/challenge/conquest
- **Misadventure** – where things go wrong either due to lack of preparation or due to more extreme terrain and climatic conditions.

### Danger

Danger is the state of being vulnerable to injury. In the sporting arena this risk is heightened in outdoor

---

# KEY WORDS

Risk is the possibility of incurring injury or loss; to expose to danger or a hazard. Outdoor and adventurous activities or outdoor pursuit activities pose situations of real and perceived risk.

- *Real risk*: risk from the natural environment such as a rock fall. Leaders need to be aware of the potential risks when planning routes and so on.

- *Perceived risk*: this is where the sense of adventure comes from and which leaders need to be aware of.

However, if the perceived risk is too great for the ability level of the performer then feelings of anxiety could become too much.

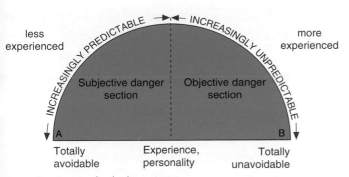

Fig 10.19. Mortlock diagram

*Source: The Adventure Alternative. C. Mortlock*
*Note*: Beginners will work at the left end of the base line AB.
Experienced climbers will work from the right end of the base line.

and adventurous activities. There are two types of danger outlined by Mortlock.

*Subjective danger* is that which is under the control of the individual such as choice of safe and appropriate equipment, and choice of route, however there is no such control over *objective danger* such as an avalanche.

**ACTIVITY 19**

- If you were a leader of a mixed ability group, which stages would you aim to achieve for your group and which factors would you aim to avoid?
- Plan an activity which could come under the outdoor education umbrella. Note the pitfalls which could arise.

## Are outdoor pursuit activities for everyone?

These activities should be available to everyone, regardless of wealth, race, sex or health. Many of these activities are being made more available to people with disabilities in the community, particularly through organisations such as the Calvert Trust; at their centres near Keswick, Exmoor and Kielder Water, the emphasis is on ability, achievement and enjoyment, and a range

of disabilities such as physical, mental and sensory disabilities, is catered for. The Commission concluded that more information about these activities should be directed towards people from ethnic minorities to increase their participation. 'A Countryside for Sport' (1993) sets out the Sports Council's policy on encouraging newcomers. Established in 1994, 'The Foundation for Outdoor Adventure' should assist in providing information to ethnic community leaders.

## Outdoor education and the school curriculum

There are strong reasons why outdoor education should be included in the school curriculum; namely, the benefit to the personal and social education of children, through experiential learning. The National Curriculum does not require that outdoor education is taught, though schools can arrange for it to be included. The skills which can be directly experienced and learned are an intrinsic element of Key Stages 3 and 4 of the adventurous activity option in physical education.

In an already constricted timetable, few schools have the commitment to the subject to support and sustain outdoor education:

- The Education Reform Act 1988 increased the problems schools experienced in offering these activities.

- The fundamental changes to the way in which schools are funded have also seriously affected the opportunities for teachers to gain valuable in-service training in order to achieve the appropriate qualifications.

- Local education authorities may no longer have access to sufficient funds to provide for this training.

- The law regarding charging pupils for out of school activities may cause schools to limit or abandon such activities, as voluntary contributions may not be sufficient. This could mean that only the wealthier schools are able to participate, so these activities would retain their elite image.

- The increasing concern over safety issues is another problem for schools.

## Risk assessment

Fears about liability are preventing people from teaching and learning about risk. Outdoor pursuit activities *are* dangerous. The freedom to face, assess and manage the risk is what attracts people to these sports. Society has become increasingly averse to facing risk and all efforts are made to protect children from any dangerous situations. Is this really a healthy attitude?

Risk assessment is becoming a familiar term to anyone involved in leading other people. There is a danger that precautions like this will actually prevent schools from offering experiences such as these. Sport is not above the law and it has had to reflect the changing attitudes of society.

## Cross-curricular issues

Other subjects could also utilise and benefit from outdoor education as it has useful cross-curricular implications; environmental issues which can be highlighted are inequalities in wealth distribution, land use, forestation and deforestation, energy sources and the problems caused by people and pollution. However, it must not lose its own unique contribution in its own right. The United Kingdom lags far behind many other countries in its provision, and many outdoor education residential centres have been threatened with closure.

## Tourism and environmental safeguards

Outdoor pursuit activities are growth sports, but there are also some problems which need to be addressed. The areas in which they often take place are country parks, nature reserves, green belt areas, areas of outstanding natural beauty and national parks. Conflicts can emerge between the sport participants, land owners and the environment. The

Fig 10.20. Outdoor activities should be available to everyone

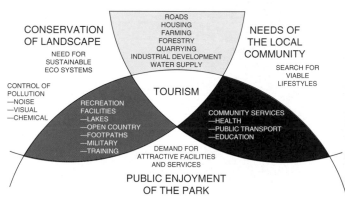

Fig 10.21. Causes of conflict in a national park

UK is a relatively small island with a high density population. Problems caused by the growth in tourism and outdoor activities will be more keenly felt than in much larger, low population density countries such as the USA and France.

Some of the problems caused are:

- erosion of land and river banks
- pollution caused by motor sports
- the increase in the number of vehicles disturbing wildlife and local residents.

The most radical solution would be to *ban* the activities, but it might be more viable to *plan* for these activities in order to minimise the damage done to the environment. The agencies concerned need to liaise to produce effective strategies. These would include the Sports Council, the CCPR, the governing bodies of the individual sports, the local authorities, the Countryside Commission and the National Parks Authorities.

## National parks

There are ten national parks in the United Kingdom: the Brecon Beacons, Dartmoor, Exmoor, the Lake District, Snowdonia, the Norfolk and Suffolk Broads, the North York Moors, Northumberland, the Peak District, the Pembrokeshire Coast and the Yorkshire Dales.

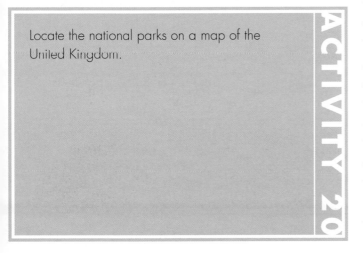

Locate the national parks on a map of the United Kingdom.

ACTIVITY 20

These areas are governed by the national park authorities, which are local government bodies. They have two statutory duties:

* to protect and enhance the character of the landscape
* to enable the public to enjoy the recreational opportunities of the area.

They also need to protect the social and economic well-being of the local community.

National parks cater for a wide range of interests: they provide walkers with pleasant open countryside for enjoyment, accommodation for tourists and a livelihood for farmers and foresters, quarrymen and gamekeepers, rangers. The movement to establish these parks came from two main sources:

* access to mountains and moorlands (ramblers in the North of England)
* landscape preservation (Southern England middle class amenity lobby).

Increasing industrialisation and urbanisation amidst the changing relationships between rural and urban areas were important factors in the formation of the parks.

## The Outward Bound Trust

The Outward Bound Trust began to pioneer outdoor activities in the 1940s. It has five centres in Britain, including Aberdovey in Wales, Ullswater in the Lake District and Loch Eil in Scotland. The organisation is now worldwide. Outward Bound works in partnership with the Duke of Edinburgh's Award Scheme. Its main aim is to promote personal development training for young people, placing them in challenging situations, such as physical expeditions, skill courses and the city challenge which is the urban equivalent. The challenging and often rugged activities include living in the wilderness, mountain climbing, canoeing, skiing and touring on bicycles. The first school was founded in Wales in 1941 by Kurt Hahn, an educator, to help young sailors who were 'outward bound' to sea.

## A|O Sport

What is sport? We know that Sport England refers to numerous activities as sport; we have sports clubs; hunting is called a sport; a person can be referred to as 'a good sport', and so on. In general we use the term loosely in normal conversation, but when we are relating important sociological concepts to sport (such as discrimination, concepts of femininity and its relationship to physical education), it is necessary to focus quite specifically on what we mean by the term. See chapter 16 for a comprehensive history of sport.

A definition of sport would be useful, to examine the key elements. Sport can be defined as:

*'institutionalised competitive activities that involve vigorous physical exertion or the use of relatively complex physical skills by individuals whose participation is motivated by a combination of intrinsic and extrinsic factors'*

(*Coakley, 1993*)

What do we mean by some of these terms?

### Institutionalised

- A standardised set of behaviour recurs in different situations.
- Rules are standardised.
- Officials regulate the activity.
- Rationalised activities involve strategies, training schedules and technological advances.
- Skills are formally learned.

### Physical activities

- skills, prowess, exertion
- balance, coordination
- accuracy
- strength, endurance

The extent of the physical nature of the activity can vary and can lead us to question whether an activity such as darts is a sport. Darts is referred to as a sport via the media, but the fact that it does not require much physical exertion can place it lower down on the sport continuum, even though it meets other criteria for inclusion as a sport. Any activity which does not meet all the criteria listed above would have less status as a sport.

| *Intrinsic* | *Extrinsic* |
|---|---|
| • self satisfaction | • money |
| • fun | • medals |
| • enjoyment | • fame |
| • own choice | • obligation |
| • 'play spirit'. | • praise. |

Most people will combine both of these motivations in the approaches they adopt towards sport participation. Colin Montgomerie says:

*'I used to get tense about the money angle of it, the financial situation you found yourself in when suddenly you had to putt for a prize the size of someone's salary. Now it's not the financial side, it's trying to beat my peers. I don't need to be paid. Don't tell the sponsors that. But when I finish a tournament and I've beaten my peers, I don't need to be paid. The feeling I have is terrific, of success and freedom, if you like. That's what I do it for.'*

(The Daily Telegraph *Sat. Oct. 16, 1999*)

Huizinga also identified characteristics of sport. These are:

- dexterity – involves an element of skill
- strategy – aspect of planning or tactic
- chance – sporting outcomes are usually unpredictable based on luck, injury, weather, etc.
- exultation – the 'feel good' factor/intrinsic elements of fun and enjoyment.

**ACTIVITY 21**

- Think of a couple of activities you regularly participate in but possibly at different levels with different attitudes. List the reasons why you may participate in both.

## Progression from play → recreation → sport

The following situation may help clarify this complex concept as we have developed the argument so far:

Two friends who kick a football in the street are involved in an informal, social occasion. Physical exertion is present and skills are developing, but the people are involved in recreation rather than sport. If they challenged two other friends to a competition, this has moved to a situation called a contest or match. It is competitive but still under informal conditions. Only when they follow formalised rules and confront each other under standardised conditions can their situation be called sport.

Merely playing a recognised physical activity is not enough to allow us to call it sport. The situation under which it is operating is also important and needs consideration.

# Amateurism and professionalism

There are two types of sports performers:

1. A person who competes as an **amateur** does so on the grounds that they will not receive monetary reward for their involvement in sport.

2. A **professional** sportsperson is one who earns an income from their sport.

These relate to the administration of their sport and not to the level of their performance. It is important to understand that amateur does not suggest a lower level than that of a professional.

# Benefits of sport

Sport can:

- act as an emotional release

- offer individuals an opportunity to express their own individuality

- help in the socialisation of people, ie, encourage a collective spirit and persuade people away from social unrest

- help people achieve success when other avenues of achievement are not available to them

- help highlight issues which can be changed

- help achieve health and fitness

- have economic benefits to individuals (income) and nations' economies

- create a challenge and provide enjoyment.

# Problematic areas

- Sport can help to retain and reinforce discrimination.

- Too much emphasis can be placed on winning, and financial rewards intensify this.

- Competition, if not handled well, can be damaging.

- Excessive behaviour can be encouraged through sport.

- Spectator sport can begin to outweigh active participation.

- Media coverage can dominate sports and their type of coverage can determine the wealth of a sport.

# AO Classification of sporting activities

When we examined the nature of physical education, in particular, the need for children to experience a balanced physical education programme, we referred to activities such as games and movement. These in turn could be classified into further categories: the Council of Europe and the Sports Council have identified four main categories of sporting activity:

1. Conditioning activities

2. Competitive games and sports

3. Outdoor adventure activities (covered on pp. 233–7)

4. Aesthetic movement or gymnastic movements.

# Conditioning activities

These are activities which are primarily designed to improve the physical and mental condition of the performer. Examples of such activities would be aerobics and also circuit and weight training. A programme of work is set and should be followed on a regular basis if it is to have the desired effect. They are easily adaptable for both the recreational and more serious performer. Some participants will participate purely for the general conditioning effect, while others will use it to achieve fitness for a particular sport. In some cases, they have developed into competition sports in their own right, for example, weight lifting and aerobics. They have competitions at all levels with rules, regulations and scoring systems.

# Competitive games and sports

The main aim of competitive participation is to find out who is the best given equal circumstances. For example, athletes are matched within categories of level of ability, such as club, county or national standard; by age, weight and often gender, to make the competition as fair as possible. They adhere to the same standardised rules, which makes the unpredictability of the outcome more exciting. Their skill level, physical and mental fitness will be the main criteria of winning.

As one unit wins, another must lose. However, during a game an individual can still make successful contributions like winning a contest within the game; eg, the defender who marks an opposing attacker out of the game. A player can enjoy the game even though they lost, simply because the effort, challenge and physical work was worthwhile.

## Athletics

This category includes races, field athletics and weight lifting. The athlete who wins the 100 m is the person who reaches the tape first. All race events, whatever the form of locomotion, are decided in this way: the high jumper clears the bar; the thrower achieves the furthest distance in the competition. The explosive or sustained power of the athlete is tested. In order to be fair to their opponents, athletes adhere to strict rules and also may take it in turns. This is called a quantitative, **objective** method of assessment, where scientific criteria is applied. The advances in the level of technology used have allowed extremely fine units of measurement to be used.

---

**ACTIVITY 23**

- List as many ways as you can of scientifically measuring the outcomes of athletic contests.
- Consider arguments for and against calling synchronised swimming a sport.

---

# Games

This category includes ball, fighting and target sports. Within a game situation, competitors interact with each other, and in the case of team games, with their own team mates. Interaction will take the form of verbal communication like calling out, coding messages and preparing strategies; non-verbal communication takes place through signals, signs and facial expressions. Players need the ability to process a lot of information which is constantly changing and this requires them to make decisions either quickly, or more slowly, as in a strategic approach to the activity. Players will bring to the game situation their own skill level, attitudes and previous experiences. They will have certain expectations also. They will want to play well and have their achievements recognised, will want to win and socialise with other players.

The wide variations of activities existing in this category enable us to subdivide them further.

## Invasion games

These are games where one team invades the territory of their opponents. Examples would be hockey, netball, basketball and football. Scoring is usually in the form of goals and points, and the winner is the team who achieves the most goals or points within the allocated time period. The contest can last for one match or extend over a longer period of time, as in a league.

Invasion games are about maintaining possession of the ball by passing effectively within your team or creating possession by tackling or intercepting. Some invasion games allow personal *contact*, while others have strict rules forbidding it. The principles of play are based mostly on attacking and defending, and numerous strategies will be worked on to achieve the advantage. A range of skills and techniques are developed. They are usually 'open' (flexible) skills, as the game situation is always changing and the player is usually reacting to another's move. However, in situations like a penalty stroke in hockey, the skill could be described as closed.

## Net games

This category includes tennis, volleyball and badminton, and constitutes a situation where opponents are separated by a net. These can be individual or team games. The winner is decided by who wins the most games, sets or rubbers. Domination in this instance is achieved by playing shots which the opponent is unable to return. The skills are again mainly 'open' except in the serve situation where the server has control; this is why so much importance is placed on the serve. All net games start with a serve, though they vary as to how points are scored in relation to the serve.

Rallies involve opponents hitting the object into each other's territory. The players must return the object immediately and on the rebound. Only in volleyball does a team have the option to move the ball around before returning it over the net.

A further category of net games are called 'rebounding' games, where the principles of play are the same but where a net is not used. Such activities include squash, fives, racquetball and rackets.

## Innings games

Games such as cricket, baseball, softball and rounders are included in this category. An innings is the opportunity a team has to score. The playing area is defined as infield and outfield. The infield gives the opportunity for striking the ball in order to score runs, while the outfield is used to field or defend the ball and cut down on the opportunities for the opposing side to score runs. The aim is to get the other team out. A contest will occur between the bowler and batter who are put in a one-on-one situation.

## Target games

The main characteristic of these games (archery, snooker, golf, darts, tenpin bowling) are that they require a high degree of accuracy when aiming at a target, which may be stationary or moving.

# Gymnastic movements

These activities rely on the repetition of a movement pattern. Technical expertise (technique) and artistic interpretation are the two main factors which are assessed. The body is used as an art form, with appearance and individuality forming an important element. The 'performance' is assessed.

In activities such as ice skating where the winners are chosen by judges, there can be more questionable outcomes than in competition sports. This type of assessment is called qualitative or **subjective** assessment.

- Rearrange the following activities listed below under these categories – Adventure, Conditioning Dance and Sport

| | | |
|---|---|---|
| Trampolining | White water rafting | Circuit Training |
| Hockey | Lacrosse | Skiing |
| Judo | Jet ski | Tap Dance |
| Aerobics | Rugby | Basketball |
| Swim Racing | Tai Chi | Rhythmic Gymnastics |
| Weight Training | Ballet | Netball |

- We have already shown how the Game category can be further subdivided. Give the following game activities a subclass and consider similar games that could be allocated to each subdivision.

Basketball        Golf        Boxing        Rounders        Tennis

## Analysis of activities

Beashel and Taylor (1996) analyse each sporting activity by breaking the activity down into component parts.

### Structural

- nature of sport problem
- scoring system
- rules
- behaviour of players
- roles of officials
- penalties for rule infringements

### Strategic

- planning and decision making
- directly related to sport problem, eg, moves or sequences in gymnastics, technical difficulty or tariff, artistic interpretation or, series of shots/rallies in net games, play a winner or force an error, pre-planned but subject to change

### Technical

- techniques – perfect movement and its outcome
- requires controlled movement of body to produce specified patterns and outcomes
- skills – performer's learned capacity to reproduce the technique, eg, types of skills, open/closed, etc.

### Physical

- body conditions required for success
- varies depending on the sport of performer's role within the sport, eg, types of fitness/cardiovascular/flexibility

### Psychological

- mental and psycho-social conditions required for successful sport performance
- mental battle involved in competitive sport
- controlled aggression/assertiveness
- pain involved
- concentration
- limelight role
- anticipation.

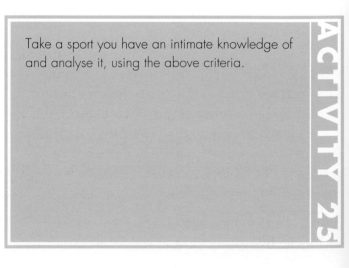

Take a sport you have an intimate knowledge of and analyse it, using the above criteria.

Using an A3 sheet of paper, list as many key words as you can under play, recreation, leisure, physical education, outdoor recreation and sport.

# Summary

- You should have a clearer picture of differences between the concepts of play, recreation, leisure, physical and outdoor recreation/education and sport; their unique features and also features which complement and relate to each other.

- People become involved in sport for various reasons and at various levels; each activity provides different challenges and experiences.

- Play is the least formal of the activities and sport is the most organised.

- Each of the concepts has implications for the individual and for society.

- For both leisure and Physical Education it is useful to understand how they have both developed over a period of time.

- Very often the physical activities used are the same – it is the attitude with which they are undertaken which makes the difference.

## Review Questions

1. Give five characteristics of the concept of Play.
2. What word does the term 'recreation' derive from and what does it mean?
3. What is the implication of the words 'activity' and 'experience' when applied to the term recreation?
4. How can work affect people's leisure time?
5. What factors have led to the growth in leisure time?
6. What do the terms 'high' and 'low' culture mean?
7. What are the key terms that characterise the term Physical Education?
8. Name five aims of Physical Education.

9. Describe the Sportsmark Award.

10. What is the main difference between Outdoor Education and Outdoor Recreation?

11. What constraints determine the level of Outdoor Education while at school in the United Kingdom?

12. Briefly describe the work of the Outward Bound Trust.

13. What are some of the benefits and problems associated with participating in sporting activities?

14. What are the four main classifications of sporting activities?

15. What do the terms 'structural', 'strategic', 'technical', 'physical' and 'psychological' mean when attempting to analyse sporting activities?

# 11. The Administration of Sport and Sporting Policies

## Chapter introduction

This chapter explores the role that sport and physical education assume in the political arena. It examines the organisation, administration and policy making process of sport which should help you to reflect on major issues such as policies for school physical education sport, policies for increasing sport participation by groups such as women, ethnic minorities, disabled, low socio-economic groups and such.

By the end of this chapter you should understand the role of leading sport organisations and their policies for participation and excellence.

### Sport organisations

Department of Culture Media and Sport (DCMS)
UK Sport
Sport England
National Governing Bodies
Central Council of Physical Recreation (CCPR)
Sport Leader UK (Formerly British Sports Trust)
Disability Sport England
Sport Coach UK
Local Authorities
British Olympic Association
International Olympic Committee
International Sport Federations

The importance with which the government in power views sport makes a huge difference to the opportunities available from the 'grass roots' of sport to sporting excellence.

The structure, function and financing of each organisation will be covered first and details of significant policies will be covered at the end of the chapter in alphabetical order.

## KEY WORDS

**Structure:** The way in which something is constructed or organised: the arrangement or interrelationship of parts. An example in a school would be Governors/ Headteacher/ Senior-Staff/Teaching Staff/Students.

**Function:** The special activity, purpose or role of an organisation or person. An example of the function of a school would be to educate young people.

**Funding:** Income that is generated, for example internally or externally, and expenditure incurred to meet the function of the organisation.

# The politics of sport

Before we explore the concept of how sport and politics interact, we may find it useful to begin with a definition of politics:

*'the science and art of government; dealing with the form, organisation and administration of a state or part of one, and of the regulation of its relations with other states … Political [means] belonging to or pertaining to the state, its government and policy'.*
(Oxford English Dictionary)

Let's take some of the key words and look at their possible meaning to sport.

## Administration

The administration of sport can be seen as developing from the community, eg, a local sports club forms the base of the pyramid, and is surmounted by its regional, national and international counterparts. The international governing bodies of sport (the International Olympic Committee, the Commonwealth Games Federation and the European Sports bodies) are political bodies. They are concerned with governing sport, making decisions, creating and distributing finances and resources, and often their dealings must reflect the political climate in which they operate.

## Relations with other states

The relationships between states with regard to sport began as soon as worldwide travel and unified rules of competition developed. Sport can provide international goodwill: it can promote cultural empathy and understanding between nations, and athletes are seen as ambassadors of their country. The Olympic Charter promotes the view that sport promotes world peace by improving international understanding and respect.

However, sport can also reinforce conflict: the sense of belonging to a country encourages a sense of patriotism and nationalism, and thus is all the more powerful when conflict is prevalent, be it war or sport. Sport represents and reinforces images and feelings of communal, regional and national identity. Powerful symbols are used, eg, national anthems, team colours, flags and ceremonies. Sporting conflict results in winners and losers. Winners can be viewed as superior and powerful, whereas losers are inferior and powerless. Sport is often portrayed as being more than just a contest between two opposing sides, and success is attributed to countries as much as to the athletes themselves. For example, the Scottish rugby ground at Murrayfield evokes vivid messages and images of Scottish identity and nationhood, and England is often portrayed as the 'old enemy'.

## Policy

Policy suggests decision making based on the ideology (set of ideas) or philosophy of those in power. This is relevant from local to international situations. Numerous indicators can be used to determine the importance a government places on sport:

- the expenditure for sport
- the position or status of sports ministers within a government
- the type and amount of sport legislation produced.

Politics reflects the power systems within a culture – who has the power and how do they use it? Sport and physical activities have sometimes been used by various governments, individuals and administrators for political reasons. The British government used to be in control of many of the world's sports organisations, but there has been a shift in power, and Britain is no longer so prominent.

The commercial world plays an extremely important role in sports decision making, at local, national and international level. The cost of staging sports events, particularly at international level, is extraordinarily high:

- The constructing of stadiums requires capital which often only governments can raise.
- The running of events increasingly involves those who pay international television fees.
- Revenue for major events requires huge commitment from governments.

Equally, sport is now a major market for governments, and the trend in the United Kingdom has been for the government to receive more money from sport than it contributes.

# Political uses of sport

## Social factors

Sport can be used to introduce or reinforce social harmony. Government inquiries into inner city riots usually include reference to the need to provide better sporting facilities. This can be taken to have various meanings:

- Boredom creates dysfunctional activity; by providing the highest standard of sporting facilities and by educating people to use them constructively in their leisure time, we can help to improve people's quality and enjoyment of life, giving them less reason to involve themselves in anti-social activities.

Fig 11.1. Does sport divert people's attention away from political and social problems?

- The 'bread and circuses' theory: this is more controversial, and claims that sport can be used to divert the attention and energy of the masses away from the problems of the political and social system in which they live.

## Sport as 'character-building'

Sport would also seem to have socialising qualities, which can be used as a political tool. In the nineteenth century, English public schools placed great importance on the values gained from the boys' involvement in team games, such as the ability to work in a team, cooperation, leadership and the response to leadership, obeying rules, respecting authority and so on.

## Propaganda

Sport can be used as political propaganda; eg, in the 1930s, the Nazi Youth groups aimed to indoctrinate young people in the values of Nazi Germany.

## Defence and work

Sport has also been used to raise the fitness level of populations in order to better prepare them for defending their country and to make them more productive in the workplace:

- Following heavy losses in the Boer War, attention was focused on the physical deterioration of the British troops in the nineteenth century.
- Physical fitness among the working classes became official policy in Britain by introducing compulsory fitness exercises in state schools in the early twentieth century.
- In the old Soviet Union, a national fitness campaign called 'Ready for Labour and Defence' was compulsory for its citizens and was still operational in the latter half of the twentieth century.

Thus, we can see there are various reasons why national governments become involved in sport. See fig 11.2 for a summary of these points.

Fig 11.2. National government involvement in sport

- Choose four functions of sport from fig 11.2. Explain in detail how each operates.
- Consider the stance of the Department for Culture, Media and Sport. Which of these functions is the British government most concerned with?

## State intervention

We have already established that it is extremely difficult to keep sport and politics separate. However, a crucial point can be the nature of the involvement and the *type* of political system which operates:

### Centralised political system

A centralised system at a simple level means to draw under central control – the central government directs policy across the country. An example of this is the former Soviet Union. The Soviet Union under Communist rule was not initiating a 'new' use of sport when it sought to make use of sport's ability to improve the health and hygiene of the population, boost morale,

production and military effectiveness, integrate a diverse nation of peoples with varying cultural backgrounds, and to provide an international image for their regime. What was new was the extent of the central control, with state legislation to coordinate and support policies. Sport and its usefulness was considered too important to be left to chance. Sport would have the same attention, assistance and planning as other social agencies, such as education.

### Decentralised political system

A decentralised system is one where the administration of government is reorganised into smaller, more autonomous units. Examples are local authorities in the United Kingdom; and the individual States of America, who control their own affairs while the federal government becomes involved in matters of national importance. The government in power can give guidelines, but would not normally enforce them. The local authority could then use the guidelines to suit their particular needs.

## Sport and politics in the United Kingdom

We have been suggesting that sport cannot be seen as an activity which only has relevance to those who practise it; it also serves various functions of a society.

In the United Kingdom, sport and politics have traditionally been kept separate. The reverse side of the coin is that many people genuinely defend the right of sport to be free from direct political control, seeing it as a danger to the autonomy of the traditional sporting governing bodies and not necessarily having the best interests of sport at heart. Many wish sport to be above the concerns of politics; they do not wish sporting heroes to be the object of sociological analysis, or for sport to be tarnished by political concerns – sport should be an escape from the everyday world.

Traditional social class barriers, the development of sport through the 'grass roots' and the dominant sporting ethos of amateurism, have had an important impact on the relationship between the political and sporting agencies in the UK. The amateur code was an important part of the nineteenth-century tradition of team games in public schools: sport was regarded as important for the individual benefits rather than for financial gain. However, it must not be forgotten that amateurism itself was a code based on a political model. It was the privilege of the gentry to be able to participate in sport for 'the love of it', while other social classes were excluded, lacking the time and money. The ideals of amateurism should be viewed in this light: we have clung on to this tradition in a modern and fast-changing society, and sportspeople are having to fight for their right to earn a living from sport. They are often in conflict with their own sports administration; eg, the lengthy negotiations in 1996 between the English Rugby Football Union and the English rugby clubs.

Today the issue of sport and politics is never far away. The number of politically motivated sports organisations in Britain is still increasing. The issue of the building of the new national stadium is one such case. UK Sport, Sport England, the British Olympic Association, UK Athletics, Wembley National Stadium Limited, the Department for Culture, Media and Sport (DCMS), and the Football Association all had their own interests and solutions with the resulting confusion over the choice of venue and design. Labour's manifesto at the 1997 general election promised that Britain would bid for the Olympics and other world class events.

In the current climate the government policies for participation and excellence in sport have become crucial to all the other sports organisations. It is therefore necessary at this stage to determine exactly why the national government would become more involved in sports policy when traditionally sport and politics were kept separate.

# Government policies

In recent years the British governments, both Conservative and Labour, have sought increasingly to assume more control over Physical Education and Sport. They represent a change in the development of DCMS policy and funding to promote Social Inclusion in the context of the National Strategy for Neighbourhood Renewal.

Policy Action Team 10 (PAT) has the job of maximising the impact on poor neighbourhoods of government spending and policies on arts, sport and leisure.

In conjunction with the Social Exclusion Unit (SEU) success is deemed to depend on community involvement rather than policies being imposed from above.

## Why should the government wish to spend money on sport and leisure?

The stance taken is that sport can make a valuable contribution to delivering the four key outcomes of:

- lower long-term unemployment
- less crime
- better health
- better qualifications.

It can also develop:

- individual pride
- community spirit to enable communities to run regeneration programmes themselves.

An integrated approach is envisaged in order to dovetail the monitoring and effectiveness of sport activities with other Action Teams, eg, the Department for the Environment, Transport and the Regions, Department for Education and Skills, Department of Health and so on. 'Joined up Government' is the key term.

---

**Executive summary**

**Findings**
Arts and sport, cultural and recreational activity, can contribute to neighbourhood renewal and make a real difference to health, crime, unemployment and education in deprived communities.

1. This is because they:
   a  appeal directly to individuals' interests and develop their potential and self-confidence
   b  relate to community identity and encourage collective effort
   c  help build positive links with the wider community
   d  are associated with rapidly growing industries.
2. Barriers to be overcome are:
   a  projects being tailored to programme/policy criteria, rather than to community needs
   b  short-term perspectives
   c  promoting arts/sport in communities being seen as peripheral, both to culture/leisure organisations and in regeneration programmes
   d  lack of hard information on the regeneration impact of arts/sport
   e  poor links between arts/sport bodies and major 'players', including schools.
3. Principles which help to exploit the potential of arts/sport in regenerating communities are:
   a  valuing diversity
   b  embedding local control
   c  supporting local commitment
   d  promoting equitable partnerships
   e  defining common objectives in relation to actual needs
   f  working flexibly with charge
   g  securing sustainability
   h  pursuing quality across the spectrum: and
   i  connecting with the mainstream of art and sport activities.
4. Social exclusion issues arise with various groups irrespective of their geographic location. This is particularly the case with ethnic minority groups an disabled people where special and systematic arrangements need to be made:
   a  to invest in people and capacity within these groups and to build an information base against which future progress can be measured
   b  to cater specifically for their needs in general regeneration programmes and culture/leisure policies
   c  to engage directly with people within these groups, and actively to value and recognise diversity
   d  to develop, monitor and deliver action plans to promote their access and involvement and to meet their needs.

Fig 11.3. Executive summary – policy action team 10
*Source*: Department for Culture, Media and Sport.

## Neighbourhood regeneration

Sport should be used to engage those who feel most excluded in society such as disaffected young people and people from ethnic minorities. Organisations that receive public funds should work actively to engage those who have been excluded in the past.

> 'Arts and sport are not just an "add-on" to regeneration work. They are fundamental to community involvement and ownership of any regeneration initiative when they offer means of positive engagement in tune with local interests'.
> (DCMS)

# The organisation of sport in the United Kingdom

The organisation of Sport and Physical Education is a dynamic aspect and therefore it is important and more interesting if you attempt to keep up to date with changes as they occur.

The web sites for some of the major organisations are given. These are correct at the time of writing.

# The role of central government
## Minister for Sport

In the 1960s, the creation of the post of Minister for Sport provided a focus for the coordination and formulation of policy.

The creation of the position had two main purposes:

1. to enable sport and recreation to perform a key role across a wide range of government policy: to improve the nation's health, to

Table 11.1. The benefits of sport

| Nature of benefit | Experienced by excluded | Strength of evidence | Nature of evidence | | | |
|---|---|---|---|---|---|---|
| | | | Lab/ experimental | National/ large | Case study survey | Meta analysis/ study review |
| National | | | | | | |
|   identity | − | + | | | * | * |
|   prestige | + + | + | | | * | |
|   reduced health | − − | + + | * | | * | * |
|     costs | | | | | | |
|   trade | | + + | * | | | |
| Communal | | | | | | |
|   community/ | − − | | | | * | * |
|     family | | | | | | |
|     coherence | | | | | | |
|   lower law and | − − − | + | | | * | * |
|     order costs | | | | | | |
|     (especially | | | | | | |
|     for youth | | | | | | |
|   job creation | + / − | + | | | * | * |
|   environmental | | | | | | |
|     (created/ | | | | | | |
|     renewed) | | | | | | |
| Personal | | | | | | |
|   physical health | | | | | | |
|     (heart, lungs, | | | | | | |
|     joints, bones, | | | | | | |
|     muscles) | | | | | | |
|   better mental | − − − | + + + + | * | * | * | * |
|     heath (coping, | | | | | | |
|     depression) | | | | | | |
|   better self | + / − | + + | * | | * | * |
|     esteem/image/ | | | | | | |
|     competence | | | | | | |
|   socialisation/ | + + + | + + + | * | | * | * |
|     integration/ | | | | | | |
|     tolerance | | | | | | |
|   general | + + | + + | * | | * | * |
|     quality of life | | | | | | |

The strength of positive and negative experience in col 2 and of evidence in col 3 is shown by the number of + and − ;
* show where the particular form of evidence is available.
*Source*: Department for Culture, Media and Sport.

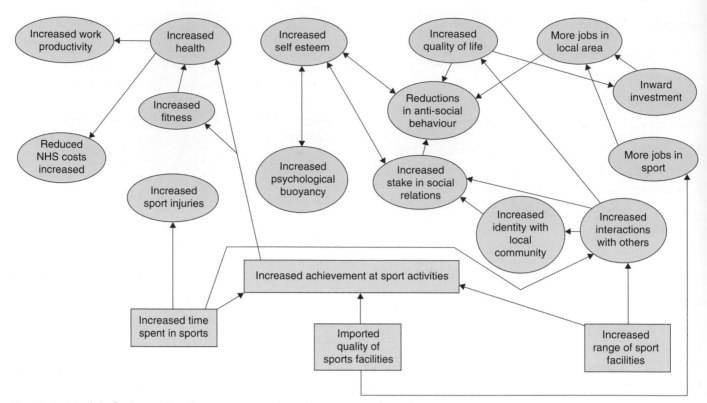

Fig 11.4. Model of relationships between sport & wider economic benefits
*Source*: Department for Culture, Media and Sport.

alleviate social deprivation, and to channel the energies of the young.

2. to enable governing body representatives and volunteers to serve sportsmen and women, providing a financial, advisory and legal framework.

The Department of National Heritage was founded in 1992, and the Minister for Sport moved to it from the Department of the Environment. There were two main advantages:

1. Sport was located firmly within a wider cultural and leisure brief.

2. Sport now had a voice at cabinet level.

However, the department also had responsibility for the arts, broadcasting, films, tourism and heritage. It was also responsible for the funding of national galleries and museums, and sport had to compete in this arena.

## Structure

The Minister for Sport has a Sport and Recreation Division (referred to from now on as SARD).

Coordination is mainly gained through informal contacts – but not many issues have affected all departments at the same time. SARD is administered by civil servants, and sport policy can sometimes be overshadowed by other issues, such as health, education and defence. This has led to an ad hoc approach, with SARD having little contact with the main providers of sports opportunities for the majority of the public, that is, the local authorities.

This fragmentation of responsibility and interest is apparent at all levels of sports policy. Certain limitations are apparent with the role of the Minister for Sport:

• The role of the Minister is to advise and consult, not to direct.

• S/he coordinates sport rather than controls it.

• S/he now comes under the DCMS, which also has competing responsibilities.

However, these limitations should not be overstated for the Minister can exert considerable influence on policy, when required. This would mainly depend on:

- the prominence of sporting issues to the government
- the quality, ambition and style of the Minister in office.

Make sure you know who the current Minister of Sport is and try to keep track of any initiatives, opinions or events with which s/he becomes involved.

# Department of Culture, Media and Sport [DCMS]
## www.culture.gov.uk

Following the restructuring of sport this department assumed control of sport, becoming the central government department responsible for government policy on the arts, sport and recreation, the National Lottery, libraries, museums and galleries, broadcasting, films, to mention a few. Sport therefore has to compete alongside these other areas.

It is headed by the Secretary of State and then there are the Parliamentary Under Secretaries of State, one of which represents sport.

In 1999 a radical new structure to strengthen the role of UK Sport was introduced. A 'Sports Cabinet' was set up under the chairmanship of the Secretary of State for Culture, Media and Sport to work alongside UK Sport and to bring together Ministers with responsibility for sport in the four Home countries.

The department promotes its policies for the range of sectors that can be broadly defined as 'culture'. It intends to take a cross-sectoral view where policy is concerned. The themes to this approach are:

- the promotion of access for the many not just the few
- the pursuit of excellence and innovation
- the nurturing of educational opportunity
- the fostering of the creative industries.

In relation to sport this can be translated as:

- Sport for All, aiming to widen access to sport and recreation to the masses.
- Achieving Excellence in national and international competition.
- The Youth Sports Unit promotes the importance of Physical Education and Sport for young people, in conjunction with the Department for Education and Skills (DFES) and also has responsibility for children's play, via education and training.
- Major international events are a high priority such as attracting the 2006 World Cup and the 2012 Olympic Games. The department will support the relevant organisations in terms of bidding for and staging the events.

Details of the recent major government policies involving sport will be covered now as the other

| Policies for participation | Policies for excellence |
|---|---|
| • Sport: Raising the Game (1995) | • Sport: Raising the Game |
| • A Sporting Future for All (2000) | • A Sporting Future for all |
| • 'Game Plan' (2002) | • 'Game Plan' |
| • Best Value through Sport | • Best Value through Sport |
| • Step Into Sport: Leadership and Volunteering | • Step into Sport: Leadership and Volunteering |
| | • PE School Sport and Club Links Strategy (PESSCL) |

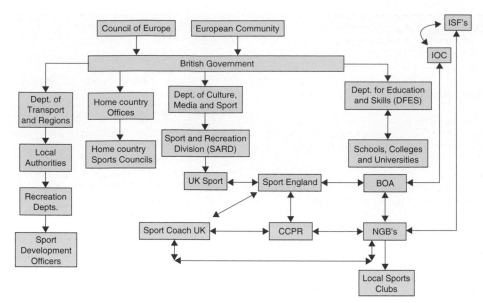

Fig 11.5. Organisation of sport in the UK

sports organisations have had to develop policies that meet the expectations of government.

# Sport: raising the game

In 1995 the Prime Minister, John Major, produced a statement laying out his aims for the development of Sport in the UK, entitled 'Raising the Game'. Figure 11.7 relates the most important sections.

---

**ACTIVITY 2**

- What values did John Major assign to participation in sporting activities?
- What four 'pillars' of education does he refer to?
- Give reasons why there may be a significant drop out rate in sport participation on leaving school.
- John Major refers to a continuum from the primary school to Olympic standard. What suggestions does he make to realise this transition?

---

After the publication of this report a more streamlined structure for the organisation of sport in the United Kingdom emerged:

- Under the revised system the Great Britain Sports Council disappeared and the newly

established English Sports Council (now Sport England) assumed responsibility for the development of sport in England.

- The Home Country Sports Councils (NI, Wales and Scotland) remained largely unchanged.

- A new organisation – UK Sport – took responsibility for issues that required a nationwide approach such as doping control and the siting of the national Sport Institute.

- Governing bodies drew up their plans to meet the requirements.

- School sport was given encouragement in the form of a variety of initiatives:
  Sportsmark and Sportsmark Gold Awards
  Sports college status
  Schools and sport clubs to form firmer links
  National Junior Sports Programme.

1. The **Sportsmark** scheme recognises the best schools with additional gold star awards for the most innovative. Teachers who make an extra commitment to school sport can, *at the governors' discretion*, receive additional salary points.

2. The weak links with community sport have already been highlighted. To attempt to overcome this the government welcomed the idea of improving links by accepting and

I set up the Department of National Heritage to protect, enhance and develop the arts, leisure and sport. That is why we are publishing ideas to rebuild the strength of every level of British sport.

These new plans are the most important set of proposals ever published for the encouragement and promotion of sport. I want us to bring about a seachange in the prospects of British sport – from the very first steps in primary school right through to the breaking of the tape in an Olympic final.

The existence of the National Lottery has transformed forever the prospects of British sport. Indeed, this was one of my principal aims when I decided to create the Lottery. It was a way to provide resources for sport – and other good causes – that would be unlikely ever to come directly from the taxpayer.

The £300 million a year that the Lottery in full flood will provide for sport will revolutionise it over the years ahead. It will make possible the creation of a new British Academy of Sport for the best of our young men and women. It will help generate the resources for some of our other targets – for example, to achieve the target I am setting today, to bring every child in every school within reach of adequate sports facilities by the year 2000.

In this initiative I put perhaps highest priority on plans to help all our schools improve their sport. Sport is open to all ages – but it is most open to those who learn to love it when they are young. Competitive sport teaches valuable lessons which last for life. Every game delivers both a winner and a loser. Sports men must learn to be both. Sport only thrives if both parties play by the rules, and accept the results with good grace. It is one of the best means of learning to live alongside others and make a contribution as part of a team. It improves health and opens the door to new friendships.

My ambition is simply stated. It is to put sport back at the heart of weekly life in every school. To re-establish sport as one of the great pillars of education alongside the academic, the vocational and the moral. It should never have been relegated to be just one part of one subject in the curriculum. For complete education we need all of those four pillars of school life to be strong.

Sports education is only the first step to a lifetime's enjoyment of sport. Sporting opportunities must continue after school. So we shall be looking to colleges and universities to do more to promote sport among their students. At present, too many teenagers find it difficult to transfer their sporting interests to the world outside school. So we will also aim to improve the sporting links between school and club sport. In that way we can improve access to high quality coaching and promote sensible arrangements to share facilities and equipment. There is much to gain in this, both for clubs and for schools.

Fig 11.6. Extracts from John Major's address, 12 July 1995

### ACTION
### Agenda

#### SPORTSMARK CRITERIA

To achieve a Sportsmark schools might expect to:
i.    Offer a minimum of two hours a week of formal PE lesson time;
ii.   Offer at least four hours each week of structured sport outside formal lessons: schools will be expected to provide all interested pupils with the opportunity to participate in sport at lunch-times, in the evenings and at weekends;
iii.  Devote at least half the time spent on PE both inside and outside formal lessons to sports which, if not the full game, should be played in a form judged appropriate for the year group by the relevant sports governing body;
iv.   Encourage teachers and others involved in extra-curricular sport to gain coaching qualifications or leadership awards enabling them to lead sports matches;
v.    Encourage teachers to improve their individual coaching skills by taking advantage of the different levels of awards/qualifications provided by the national governing bodies of sport;
vi.   Ensure in secondary schools that pupils of all ages have the opportunity to take part in competition if possible, and promote competition within their own school and against other schools;
vii.  Have established links with local sports clubs: schools will be expected to have developed links with a number of local sports clubs as a way of providing pupils with further sporting opportunities outside school hours. Sportsmark schools are likely to be among those successfully competing for the Sports Council's challenge fund for school–club links; and
viii. Encourage pupils to take part in sports governing bodies' award schemes.

Fig 11.7. Extracts from *Raising the Game*

encouraging the voluntary assistance offered by coaches. However, this is dependent on the initiative of the individual teachers and schools. Finance, needless to say, is also limited.

3. Schools must record in their annual prospectuses their sporting aims and their provision for sport.

Some people were concerned that the Conservative government's agenda appeared to be about the winning of major international and World Cup events. Is it the aim of schools to set the foundations for success at international level? If so, the professional coaches should perhaps have as much contact with school teams as the physical education teacher has.

The problem of liaison and contact with outside agencies appears to be more of a problem. Initiatives have begun and are being successful, such as TOP Play, BT TOP Sport, and Champion Coaching (which involves 145 local authorities). The aim is to guide the young person from school to community sport and provide coaching training and experience for teachers and coaches involved. This is a top priority for the Sports Council and National Coaching Foundation, and the traditional notion of keeping sport coaching out of schools is being challenged.

## Sports college status

The sports college initiative was launched in June 1996. It was part of a specialist schools programme, which includes centres for technology, arts and modern languages. It allows schools with particular strengths to build upon them, attracting pupils with those interests. It is hoped these schools will be more than just schools, rather a centre for sport and physical education encompassing all sectors of the community.

**Objectives:**

- Extend the range of opportunities available to children which best meet their needs and interests.
- Raise the standard of teaching and learning for PE and sport in schools.

- Develop characteristics which identify the schools to the local community and local schools.
- They should be of benefit to local schools, called the 'family of schools' network.
- Attract local sponsors who should take an active role in the school's development.
- A school that wishes to apply needs to raise £50,000 sponsorship for a capital project to improve existing sports facilities.
- The development plan drawn up by the school will show its vision.

**Organisations involved:**
The DfES lays down the guidelines. The Youth Sports Trust, a charitable organisation employed by the DfES, offers development and sponsorship guidance.

**Funding:**
Successful schools will receive:

- a one-off capital grant of £100,000
- recurrent funding for four years of £120 per pupil
- opportunity for a further three years of funding for schools who have met their targets.

## The National Council for School Sport

Membership is open to national sports organisations in England and Wales responsible for the development of their sport in schools. The aims of the Council are to:

- coordinate the work of the schools' national sports associations
- encourage the formation of new associations
- provide a forum for discussion
- encourage involvement in the International School Sport Federation.

The official journal is the *Sports Teacher* magazine.

## Smith and Hoey launch a Sporting Future for All (April 2000)

Chris Smith, the Secretary of State for Culture, Media and Sport and Kate Hoey, the Minister for Sport, launched the government's strategy for sport – 'A Sporting Future for All'. They promise a new deal with governing bodies in sport.

The strategy sets out the government's vision for sport in the twenty-first century and highlights the importance of coordinating sport between schools, local clubs and organisations.

The strategy includes:

- a new fund of £75 million from the government over two years with a target of matched funding from the lottery to add to it for primary schools to provide new, multi-purpose sports and arts facilities for pupils and the wider community
- devolved lottery funding to governing bodies in return for modernisation of their administration, increased involvement with schools through coaching and visits by elite performers, and a commitment to invest at least 5% of TV rights revenue in grassroots facilities and activities
- ring-fending of 20% of lottery sports awards for youth sports projects
- establishment of Sport Direct, a national telephone helpline to advise people how to get involved in sport in their local area
- establishment of a fast track system for elite performers to become coaches
- a comprehensive audit of sport facilities to be undertaken by local authorities and Sport England.

In April 2000 the following government policy was launched.

## Smith and Blunkett launch radical boost to School Sport

Chris Smith and David Blunkett, Education Minister, launched the five point plan to make schools the nurseries of sports stars of the future:

- a new fund of £75 million over two years from the government matched by the lottery for primary schools to provide 300 new, multi-purpose sports and art facilities for pupils and the wider community

- goal of having 110 specialist sports colleges in place by 2003 with close links to governing bodies of sport and help for talented young people to tie in with the UK Institute of Sport
- establishment of 600 school sport coordinators by Sport England, paid for with lottery money, to develop more inter-school competitive games
- developing after-school sport and physical education. The £240 million out-of-hours learning programme funded jointly by the New Opportunities Fund (£160 million) and the standards fund (£80 million) currently supports sport, art, homework and computer clubs outside normal school hours
- encourage World Class Performance athletes to visit a minimum number of schools each year.

In addition the DfES will set up an advisory panel on school playing fields underpinning the government's rules to prevent sales without rigorous consultation. Sales have been cut from 40 a month to three with proceeds ploughed back into schools and school sport.

A key policy that tries to integrate sport with various other policies is Best Value.

## Best value

### Local authorities should:

- take on board the principles of community development approach and should build on ways in which leisure strategies and services are developed and provided, creating targeted programmes linked to networked projects
- aim to improve the four key indicators of crime, health, education and employment
- assess provision according to the social, ethnic and professional background of users and potential users
- plan for culture/leisure-based community work rather than having isolated policies
- youth services should promote and enhance young people's talents

- seek value for money from their assets/facilities, ensuring the widest feasible use of them (eg, school facilities out of school hours).

## Lottery distributors should:

- fund community run multi-purpose community venues in areas with poor access to facilities, which can flexibly meet local needs rather than isolated use

- consider how to 'market' the lottery for groups who could be classed as socially excluded and to make use of the flexibility provided by the 1998 Lottery Act by matching funding when assessing applications from neighbourhoods which have regeneration initiatives.

Talented individuals with limited opportunities could benefit from an area bursary scheme designed to help them to develop employment potential. The National Endowment for Science, Technology and the Arts (NESTA), ACE (The Arts Council of England) and Sport England should also seek to involve commercial partners from the relevant industry.

## Department for Culture, Media and Sport (DCMS) should:

- ensure neighbourhood renewal is a high priority on the agenda with culture/leisure sector involved

- make effective use of regeneration funds

- involve all groups in society in the sport strategy

- monitor and follow through policies

- monitor impact of sponsored bodies' social inclusion policies through QUEST (Quality, Efficiency and Standards Team).

## Sport England should address its basic policy aims:

- to sustain cultural diversity
- to combat social exclusion
- to promote community development.

should consider joint policies with other agencies such as:

- partnerships managing New Deal for Communities

- pathfinders to spend on sport- related activities

- proposals regarding the allocation of Sportsmatch monies in areas of regeneration

- funding agreements with governing bodies

- ensuring the Voluntary Sector plays a part in community development

- proposals as to how it will tighten the social inclusion objectives and targets given in its funding agreement with DCMS.

# The Governments' Plan for Sport – game plan

## Game Plan: a strategy for delivering Government Sport and Physical Activity Objectives, December 2002

It provides a broad context and research evidence for sports policy. It covers broad issues:

- grass roots participation could be improved
- international success is better than perceived
- the hosting of mega events has not always been successful
- the problems of funding issues in sport
- the complexity of the structures responsible for delivering sport policy.

These three major government policies for sport in under a decade highlight the importance sport is beginning to have in the United Kingdom.

The following organisations must try to address many of these issues. In some cases they overlap.

# Sport England
## www.sportengland.org

Sport England began its role in January 1997 and is accountable to Parliament through the Secretary of State for Culture, Media and Sport who operates under the DCMS. Sport England also operates ten regional offices across England providing partnerships across public and private sectors.

## Objectives

The objectives of Sport England are to lead the development of sport in England by influencing and serving the public. Its aim is:

- start – get people to participate
- stay – retain people once they have started
- succeed – achieve higher levels of performance.

Members of the Council are appointed by the Secretary of State for Culture, Media and Sport. Their responsibilities include:

- approving all policy matters and operational and corporate plans for Sport England
- bringing independent judgement to issues such as strategy and resources
- ensuring all financial matters are regulated and operate efficiently.

A series of advisory panels guide Sport England in the following areas:

- Lottery
- Local authorities
- Women and sport
- Disability
- Racial equality
- Government body investment.

## Funding

The work of Sport England is jointly funded by:

- the Exchequer for maintaining England's sports infrastructure and

| Policies for participation | Policies for elite performance |
|---|---|
| • Active programme | • World class programme |
| • Sportsmark/Activemark Scheme | • Academies |
| • National Junior Sports Programme (TOP) | • Sportsearch |
| • Sport Action Zones | |
| • Step into Sport | |

- through the National Lottery via the Sport England Lottery Fund which is earmarked for the development of sport in England
- sport as part of the overall social inclusion policy and neighbourhood regeneration work.

Detail of policies can be found at the end of the chapter in alphabetical order.

# UK Sport www.uksport.gov.uk

Established in 1997 by Royal Charter as part of the restructuring programmes, UKS took responsibility for issues that need to be dealt with at UK level. UK Sport's mission is to help our athletes become world class performers. It is to take on a role above that of the Home Country Sport Councils on issues that require strategic planning, administration, coordination or representation for the benefit of the UK as a whole. It is funded through Exchequer and Lottery Funding. In 1999–2000 it received approximately £12 million and £20.5 million respectively to fund sporting projects of UK significance, which rose to £25 million of National Lottery money in 2003. It has a remit to:

- encourage and develop higher standards of sporting excellence in the UK
- identify sporting policies that should have a UK-wide application
- identify areas of unnecessary duplication to avoid administration waste

- develop and deliver appropriate grant programmes in conjunction with the governing bodies and home country sport councils

- oversee policy on sport science, sports medicine, drug control, coaching and other areas where there is a need for a consistent UK-wide policy

- coordinate policy for bringing major international events to the UK

- represent the UK internationally and increase the influence of the UK at an international level.

It performs these aims through four key directorates:

- **Performance Development** – provides advice to UK/Governing Bodies on their planning processes; allocates Exchequer funding; advises on applications for Awards from the Lottery Sports Fund.

- **UK Sports Institute** – Central Services is based in London with regional network centres. The Olympic sports are mainly catered for and it is primarily for potential and elite athletes, including athletes with disabilities. The main support services of Sport Science, Sports Medicine, Lifestyle Management Services, Information services and a range of facilities help to create an environment where world class athletes are more likely to develop.

- **International Relations and Major Events** – the globalisation of sport and the cultural, social and economic benefits accrued by events such as the Olympic Games and World Cup make it imperative for the UK to be in a strong position at the centre of international decision making. There is a need to promote and enhance the position and reputation of the UK sports system internationally. It links with organisations such as the European Union and British Council to develop initiatives in place like South Africa.

- **Ethics and Anti-doping** – the directorate is responsible for the coordination of an effective testing programme and a comprehensive education programme. Its quality work was recognised in 1997 by the awarding of certification of management, the first organisation in the world to receive one.

This trend towards coordinating policies for sporting excellence began in the 1980s and the formation of the National Coaching Foundation, now Sport Coach UK, was an integral part of this movement.

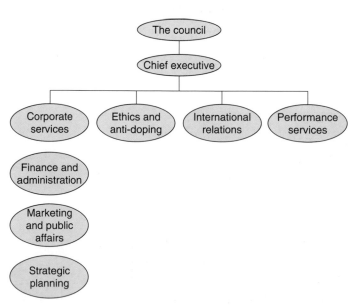

Fig 11.8. UK sport

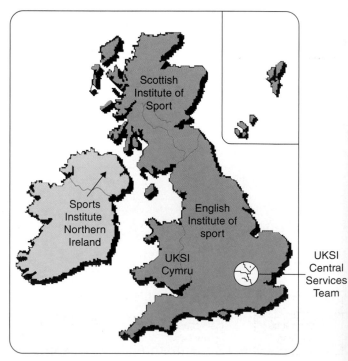

Fig 11.9.

## Sport Coach UK

This organisation provides a range of educational and advisory services for all coaches and complements the award schemes of the individual governing bodies. This has enjoyed increasing success. It oversees the running of the 16 National Coaching Centres which are primarily based in Institutions of Higher Education (see fig 11.10).

The aims of Sport Coach UK and the means by which they will deliver their intentions are:

- lead and develop the national standards of coaching and the various other qualifications

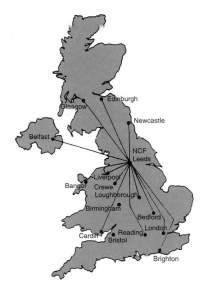

Fig 11.10. The location of National Coaching Centres in the UK

available. Examples are the Diploma in Professional Studies; the Coaching for Teachers courses; BSc (Hons) in Applied Sports Coaching.

- working with organisations such as the local authorities, governing bodies, the British Olympic Association and Higher Education to improve the standards and professional development of coaches

- provide high quality education programmes products and services, such as coaching literature, videos, seminars and workshops, factsheets and databases, that reflect the needs of coaches and are accessible to them. Most are available from 'Coachwise Limited', Sport Coach UK's wholly owned trading company.

High quality education programmes consist of:

- sport specific knowledge (techniques/tactics)
- performance-related knowledge (fitness/nutrition/mental preparation)
- ethics and philosophy (codes of practice)
- management/vocational skills (planning/time/money)
- teaching/coaching methodology (communication skills)
- practical coaching experience.

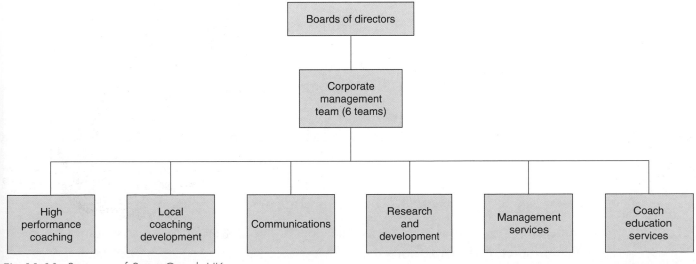

Fig 11.11. Structure of Sport Coach UK

Funding is provided by:

- the United Kingdom Sports Council (UKSC) and Sport England 66% grant aid
- 29% earned income (including 4% subscription)
- 5% other grant aid donations.

## What are National Standards?

Like performers, coaches develop depending on their interest, knowledge, commitment, skills and opportunities. One coach may aspire to work to become the National Coach, while others are keen to develop their skills to be the best coaches working with beginners. The National Coach will be the one that media attention focuses on. However, both coaches are fundamental to the sport. We recognise that different levels and types of performers require different levels and types of coaches.

Table 11.2 illustrates the *vertical* progression that a coach may take.

## A E The British Olympic Association (www.olympic.org.uk)

### Structure

The International Olympic Committee (IOC) requires that each country organise a National Olympic Committee (NOC). Each governing body of the competitive Olympic sports (recognised by the IOC) should be represented, alongside officers of the British Olympic Association (BOA) and the two IOC representatives.

### Function

Their function is to:

- encourage interest in the Olympic Games through undertakings such as liaison with schools
- foster the ideals of the Olympic movement
- organise and coordinate British participation; the BOA needs to organise the participation of

Table 11.2. Levels of coaching

| Level of coach | What should a coach be able to do? | How NGBs might describe a coach |
|---|---|---|
| Level 5 | Coaches having significant and repeated success at the highest level of the world stage. Competent to assume full responsibility for the organisation, management and delivery of all elements of a world class performer's (team's) preparation for competitive international success. | National Coach |
| Level 4 | Coaches with substantial and proven practical coaching experience at club and representative level. Competent to take full responsibility for the management of every aspect of a performer's (team's) preparation for competition at an international level. | Regional Coach Mentor Coach |
| Level 3 | Coaches competent to plan, coach and evaluate an annual coaching programme for committed club level and representative performers competing at county, regional and/or national levels. | Advanced Coach Club Coach Senior Coach |
| Level 2 | Coaches competent to plan, coach and evaluate a series of sessions for recreational participants and those competing in local leagues. | Coach Instructor Teacher |
| Level 1 | Competent to assist more experienced coaches and lead sections of safe, fun, recreational sessions. | Assistant Coach Leader |

500 athletes and officials including all travel arrangements or equipment and horses

- assist the governing bodies of sport in preparation of their competitions
- advise on public relations with the press (a relatively recent function)
- provide a forum for consultation among governing bodies
- organise an Olympic Day in the UK
- raise funds through the British Olympic Appeal, mainly from private sources, business sponsors and the general public.

You have probably already noted the absence of a government grant. This is the tradition of the BOA: to be independent of government. Preparations for the 2004 Olympic Games in Athens began early in order to raise the required £6 million.

The BOA has developed a new marketing strategy for its national sponsors through the creation of the British Olympic Gold Club.

This Club includes total exclusivity to use the BOA logo in a particular product category in the lead up to and during the Olympic Games. There is a variety of corporate hospitality opportunities, appearances by Olympic medallists, licensing opportunities and regular sponsor workshops.

Since 1988, the BOA has also had to adapt to changes as have other organisations already mentioned, and since 1992 have added the following to their list of duties:

- advice on training on nutrition and sports psychology for Olympic coaches
- medical and careers advice for athletes
- sponsoring medical research into fitness and athletic injuries.

The British Olympic Medical Centre at Northwick Park was restructured, and athletes now have access to all the medical support they require for an Olympic games. A sport-specific strategy was developed to help athletes cope with the problems of jet lag, acclimatisation and dehydration. The BOA are committed to giving Britain's sporting talent the best chance of achieving international success at the highest level as illustrated by the superb warm weather training facility that has been set up and run by the Orlando Regional Health system using the Disney Wide World of Sport facilities.

## Team GB

Team GB represents the whole of the Olympic team – past, present and future. This is to provide a more positive and familiar association for the public, as BOA is mainly an administrative body. The aim is to heighten awareness for all athletes and for the Olympic movement in the United Kingdom.

## Other interested organisations

Countryside Commission
Forestry Commission
National Playing Fields Association
National Rivers Authority
English Tourist Board

# Countryside commission

This is a public body with a wide range of responsibilities in England and Wales, and was formed under the National Parks and Access to the Countryside Act 1968. It has various functions, including:

- the selection and designation of National Parks, AONB (Areas of Outstanding Natural Beauty) and country parks
- the establishment of long distance footpaths and bridleways
- the provision of information services about the countryside
- advice on the use of the countryside for open air recreation balanced by a concern for conservation

- carrying out research and experimental projects
- giving grants and loans to non-public bodies.

## The Forestry Commission

This has two main organisations:

1. The Forestry Authority – the main advisory and grant aiding arm of the Commission.

2. Forest Enterprise – covers the forests and woodlands. Walking and sometimes cycling is encouraged. They encourage private landowners to allow public access through special grants.

## National Playing Fields Association

Founded in 1925, this body aims to ensure that there are opportunities for all to participate in their chosen activities, by stimulating the provision of playing fields and other facilities for indoor and outdoor recreation. It encourages the adoption of Play Leadership Schemes for children.

## National Rivers Authorities (NRA)

The NRA protects and improves inland and coastal waters of England and Wales. It has responsibility for pollution control and water-based recreation activities. An important initiative in this area is the river canoeist's guide to responsible enjoyment of rivers. British Waterways covers similar ground but mainly around the canal networks.

## English Tourist Board

Its primary aim is to encourage tourism; as interest increases in activity holidays, the tourist board are continually having to improve standards. The national governing bodies of the relevant sports are being asked to assist in the quality assurance initiative piloted in Wales.

# International organisations

It would be superficial to treat the organisation and administration of sport from a purely national level, therefore a brief view of the international links will be made.

International Olympic Committee (IOC) (www.olympic.org/ioc)
Council for Europe (www.coe.fr/eng/act)
International Sport Federations (ISF)
Commonwealth Games Federation (CGF) (www.commonwealthgames.org.uk)

## **A E** International Olympic Committee (www.olympic.org/ioc)

The IOC is the umbrella organisation of the Olympic Movement whose primary responsibility is the regular staging of the summer and winter Games.

The Executive Board is headed by the IOC President, then has four Vice Presidents and six additional members. All the members of the Executive Board are elected by the Session, by secret ballot, by a majority vote.

The role of the Executive Board is to:

- observe the Olympic charter
- administer the IOC
- attend to all internal affairs of the organisation
- manage the finances
- inform the session of any rule changes or bye-laws
- recommend suitable persons for election to the IOC
- establish agendas for the session
- appoint the Director General and Secretary General.

The Executive Board meets when convened by the President or at the request of members.

The session takes decisions on issues such as drug abuse, political boycotts, television contracts and world sport development.

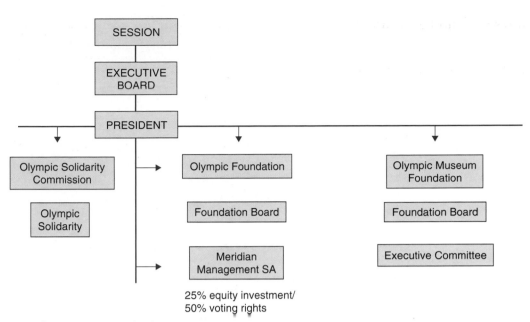

Fig 11.12. Structure of the International Olympic Committee

## The members

These are individuals who act as the IOC's representatives in their respective countries. They are not delegates of their country within the IOC. The IOC chooses its members from among persons who they consider suitably qualified.

## The National Olympic Committees (NOC)

These bodies (approximately 200) are responsible for the well-being of their athletes and for upholding the fundamental principles of Olympism at a national level. Each Committee provides training centres and funding to ensure their athletes are able to compete under conditions comparable to athletes from other nations. Only an NOC is able to select and send teams and competitors for participation at the Olympic Games. They also supervise the preliminary selection of potential city bids.

## Council of Europe
### www.coe.fr/eng/act

The Council of Europe is an international organisation based in Strasbourg. It was established in 1949 by 10 countries and now has 41 members.

This has reflected the increasing concern for stability in Europe and the return of previously authoritarian regimes to the European democratic fold. Under the general concern for democratic security the Council for Europe has laid down a series of common principles governing the protection of national minorities and has fixed new priorities for cooperative efforts such as social cohesion, human rights and major cultural and educational challenges.

The Council of Europe comprises:

- a decision-making body: the Committee of Ministers
- a deliberative body: the Parliamentary Assembly
- a voice for local democracy: the Congress of Local and Regional Authorities of Europe.

The Committee of Ministers draws up the activities programme and adopts its budget.

They have made recommendations on diverse subjects such as spectator violence at sport events, nature conservation, the media and protecting minorities. The European Cultural Convention is of particular significance to our field of study as it forms the basis for intergovernmental cooperation in the fields of education, culture, Europe's heritage, sport and youth activities.

## Areas of priority for cooperation

- Promoting Sport for All via the 'Sports for All Charter' (1975) updated via the European Sports Charter and backed by the Code of Sport Ethics and

- drawing up rigorous ethical principles.

Since 1992 the work of the Committee for the Development of Sport (CDDS) aims to make ethical, safe and healthy sport accessible to everybody through the widest possible cooperation and the appropriate distribution of responsibilities between governmental and non-governmental organisations.

The Council of Europe is active on two fronts to maintain the integrity and virtues of sport:

- promoting sport for all as a means of improving the quality of life

- facilitating social integration and contributing to social cohesion particularly among young people.

## A E International Sports Federations (ISF)

An International Sport Federation is the World governing body for that sport. An ISF's main responsibilities are:

- to organise events
- to arrange sponsorship and television contracts
- to formulate the rules which will be adhered to by the national governing bodies.

At the Olympics, they are responsible for the technical aspects of their sport and the officials. An example of an ISF is FIFA, the Fédération Internationale de Football Associations, founded in 1904 (www.fifa.com) and the International

Amateur Athletic Federation (www.iaaf.rog). They establish the playing and eligibility rules, set the schedules for events and select the referees, judges and other officials to 'run' their respective sports at international competitions.

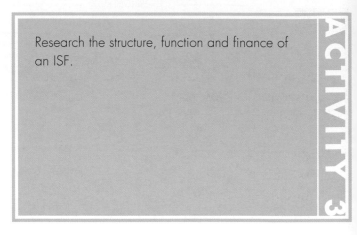

Research the structure, function and finance of an ISF.

ACTIVITY 3

## International Paralympic Committee

This body is the international representative organisation of elite sports for athletes with disabilities. It is an umbrella organisation representing all sports and disabilities. Its function is to:

- organise, supervise and coordinate the Paralympic and other multi-disciplinary competitions at the elite level.

It is a non-profit organisation formed and run by 160 National Paralympic Committees and five disability-specific international sports federations.

## Commonwealth Games Federation (CGF)

After the Olympic Games, the Commonwealth Games is the next most important multi-sport competition in the world, involving 65 countries with a range of 25 sports (no team sports). It maintains a strong British influence.

The role of the CGF is to promote and organise the four-yearly games, establish satisfactory conduct guidelines and encourage amateur sport. The Federation is not as wealthy as the IOC and depends heavily on voluntary help. Sports seeking acceptance to the Olympics often try to be accepted by the CGF first.

# A O Central Council of Physical Recreation www.ccpr.org.uk

This organisation was originally founded in 1935 to have responsibility for sport and recreation in the UK. It had three main objectives:

1. to encourage as many people as possible to participate in physical activity
2. to provide the governing bodies with a separate organisation to represent their collective interests to the Sports Council (now Sport England)
3. to increase public awareness and knowledge of the importance of sport.

They set up regional offices and the first national sport centres, and as such, the organisation was a precursor to the Sports Council. In 1972, the Sports Council took over the overall responsibility for sport, and the personnel of the CCPR were merely transferred from one to the other. It was inevitable perhaps that similar policies would be adopted, at least until each organisation defined its individual roles more clearly. Thus, the CCPR became the representative and consultative body to the Sports Council. It became the chief means of preserving the traditionally voluntary and independent nature of organised sport in the UK.

A useful way of simplifying one of its roles is to visualise it as the middle man between Sport England and the autonomous governing bodies whose interests it represents. The CCPR can liaise across a wide range of sporting activities and bring together specialist bodies.

The CCPR Executive Committee has divided sport and recreation into six divisions: see fig 11.13.

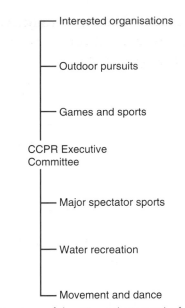

Fig 11.13. Structure of the Central Council of Physical Recreation

## CCPR policy towards current issues

It supports 'dual use' policy: this recommends increased access to sporting facilities but protests against Compulsory Competitive Tendering, viewing it as a threat to the British tradition of the provision of public sporting facilities. This emphasises the nature of the CCPR – an organisation which looks after the interests of sport for the people.

## Financing the CCPR

The CCPR is financed from five main sources:

1. subscriptions and donations from its members
2. support from industry and commerce
3. sponsorship by individuals or companies of particular events and projects under the CCPR
4. sales of its own publications and research findings
5. contractual support from the Sports Council.

## CCPR achievements

The CCPR is concerned about the sale of playing fields in schools and is firm in its campaign to stop this happening.

'A Sporting Chance' The CCPR National Conference of Sport and Recreation November 1999. The issues addressed are those of equity issues and explores sports role tackling Social Exclusion and providing Equality of Opportunity.

## **A** **E** Sports Leaders UK (formerly British Sports Trust)

Sports Leaders used to be the charitable arm of the Central Council of Physical Recreation. Now it has gained its independence. In 1998, 43,000 people were trained to become leaders of sport in their communities. Many of these people were aged between 14 and 25. This was achieved via the Sports Leader Awards which aim to achieve five core values:

- personal development
- a stepping stone to employment
- developing leadership
- volunteering in communities
- reaching youth crime.

| Policies for participation | Policies for excellence |
| --- | --- |
| Leadership Awards | |
| Step into Sport | |

## Youth Sports Trust (YST)

The YST is a registered charity set up in 1994 to improve sporting provision for young people in the United Kingdom. Its mission is to develop and implement a linked series of quality sports programmes, known under the umbrella term, the *National Junior Sports Programme*. The Trust also works alongside the DfES to support maintained secondary schools that are applying for 'Specialist Sports College' status. The organisation is becoming increasingly influential in the coordination and provision of sport both in schools and the local community.

| Policies for participation | Policies for excellence |
| --- | --- |
| National Junior Sports Programme | |
| Step into Sport | |
| School Sports Coordinators | |
| Sports Colleges | |

## **A** **O** Local authorities

We have already mentioned the burden on local authorities to provide leisure facilities in their area. This is decreed under mainly permissive legislation, such as the Physical Training and Recreation Act 1937 and the Local Government Miscellaneous Act 1976, which stated that a local authority 'may provide … such recreational facilities as it thinks fit'.

The following factors stimulated local government involvement:

- The creation of the Sports Council (1972), the Tourist Boards (1969) and the Countryside Commission (1968).
- The creation of new sporting and recreational facilities, in particular leisure centres and country parks.
- Increased leisure and a steady rise in the standard of living.
- Increase in the rate and frequency of sport and recreation participation.
- Creation of 'service' departments within local authorities following the restructuring of local government in 1974, eg, a leisure service department.

A two-tier structure emerged, of District and County Councils. Leisure provision assumed greater importance, but a lack of coordination halted its progress. Recreational planning was encouraged through government reports, particularly the 1975 White Paper 'Sport and Recreation'.

Leisure, by the 2000, is mainly the responsibility of one specialist department. Excluding educational provision, authorities' net expenditure on revenue support for sport exceeds £500 million a year in England and Wales.

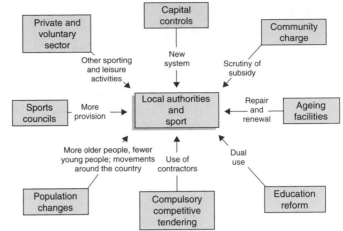

Fig 11.14. Pressures on local authority sports policy

As legislation is mainly permissive, it is not surprising that wide variations in provision and expenditure can be found between local authorities.

## Pressures on local authorities

Local authorities operate within certain restrictions:

1. The community charge and the capital control regimes affect the ability of local authorities to fund new developments and their attitudes to subsidies.

2. Increased competition from the private sector, partly due to the establishment of Compulsory Competitive Tendering and the effects on dual use policies following the Education Reform Act 1988 require improved management on behalf of local authorities.

3. Sport and physical recreation also has to compete with nine other departments: the arts and cultural provision, libraries, entertainment and catering services, museums, heritage and conservation, tourism, youth and community services, adult education and selective social services.

4. The term 'leisure' encompasses a wide range of activities, like sport and physical recreation, education, tourism, social and cultural. This is illustrated in table 11.3.

## Positive aspects

Positive features emerge, nonetheless:

- Financial expenditure has remained reasonably steady.

- Leisure is a popular demand by local residents.

- Leisure is increasingly valued for its own benefits and not just as a means of meeting other policy objectives like reducing vandalism or improving the nation's health.

- Leisure in the 1990s was also perceived to be of economic benefit to a local area, particularly in its ability to attract tourism.

Table 11.3. Various leisure activities

| Sport | Education | Tourism | Social | Cultural |
|-------|-----------|---------|--------|----------|
| Sports centres<br>Playing fields<br>Ski slopes | Libraries<br>Swimming pools | Museums<br>Conservation<br>Country parks | Youth clubs<br>Community<br>centres | Theatres<br>Art galleries |

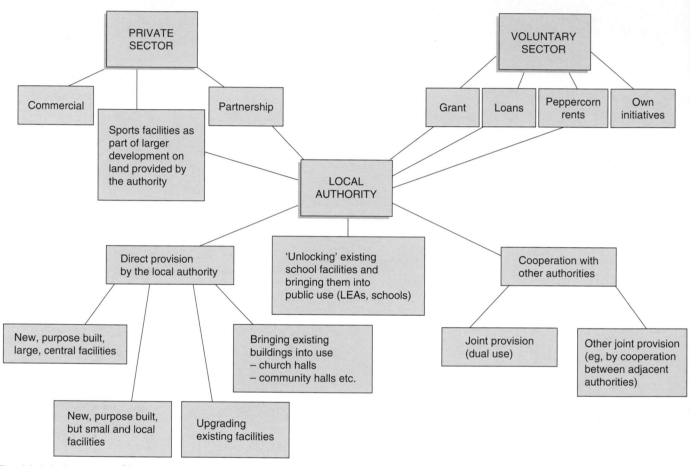

Fig 11.15. Provision of leisure services

# Dual Use

This was a policy in the 1970s which aimed to maximise use of local leisure facilities. The local authority and particularly the local education authority own much of the sporting facilities in any local area, yet at weekends and holidays these facilities are often unused.

Dual Use was a policy to enable community use of school sporting facilities.

One of the problems with Dual Use was the ad hoc administrative arrangements.

# Joint Provision

Joint Provision built on the Dual Use policy but often new facilities were built, with shared funding and a centre manager was usually in charge.

Can you think of any local examples of these two policies?

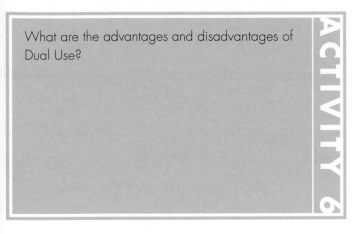

What are the advantages and disadvantages of Dual Use?

**ACTIVITY 6**

## Compulsory competitive tendering (CCT)

Following the Local Government Act 1988, a range of local authority services were tendered, including the management of local authority leisure services. The Conservative government wanted to ensure a more competitive market in order to reduce costs.

Compulsory Competitive Tendering is slightly different from privatisation of large companies. The local authority would still:

- own the facilities
- control the prices
- set quality standards
- influence programming
- retain the ability to decide policy.

Local authorities were to become 'enablers' rather than providers. An 'enabler' needs to plan, coordinate, and facilitate the provision of leisure services. To do this they must think strategically, to identify and make explicit their objectives when planning new capital projects. This is not to suggest they were not doing this before the legislation. Four main areas need to be considered: planning and research; development within the community, eg, Action Sport; management, eg, accessibility, price range and quality experience; marketing, eg, to ensure that target groups are identified on the basis of market research.

## Role of a sport development officer

- Research
- Marketing

Table 11.4. Advantages and disadvantages of CCT

| Advantages | Disadvantages |
|---|---|
| Reduce unit costs by 20% | Could result in worse pay and conditions for employees |
| Free local authorities from the day-to-day running problems | Sport no longer regarded as a social service |
| Help to review the use of manpower | CCPR felt it was a serious attack on traditional provision of sports facilities |

- Negotiating
- Planning
- Communication
- Organisation and evaluating

## Best value

Many local authorities place sport as a central feature in their work on:

- healthy living
- regeneration
- social inclusion and other key objectives.

Local government will work closely alongside Sport England in the changing landscape of cultural activity such as Best Value and Regional Cultural Strategies.

The document, 'The Value of Sport' responds to the challenge 'Why invest in sport?' and demonstrates that sport can make a difference to people's lives and to the communities in which they live. It emphasises that for every pound spent on sport there are multiple returns in improved health, reduced crime, economic regeneration and improved employment opportunities.

The document highlights how sport needs to justify continued investment:

- through seeking public support for local authority investment
- by making an impact locally within health improvement programmes
- by ensuring that it is part of the Government's 'Pathfinder Area' initiatives related to social exclusion and included within programmes in the 'New deal for Communities'.

These policies have been a result of the public sector being forced to account more for the use of local taxes in order to improve the efficiency of provision and use of resources.

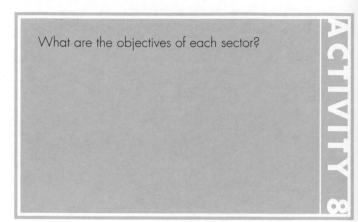

What are the objectives of each sector?

ACTIVITY 8

Research the document 'Best Value through Sport' produced by Sport England. As a group or class consider;

a) the social, economic and environment benefits that sport can bring to local communities

b) the liaison required between different organisations.

c) Search on the internet or try to obtain a copy of the 'Best Value' report for your local area and discuss its findings and recommendations.

ACTIVITY 7

# Local provision for leisure

Provision for physical recreation in any local area comes from three main sources:

- Private
- Public
- Voluntary

# Governing bodies of sport

## History

With the increasing popularity of sport during the late nineteenth century, it became necessary for individuals and clubs taking part to agree on a common set of rules or laws. In most areas this led directly to the formation within each sport of a governing body, with the task of agreeing rules for the sport so that all clubs and individuals could compete on equal terms.

The persons responsible for the establishment of the governing bodies were mainly the educated, middle and upper classes, and there is still a tendency for sport administration in the UK to be the domain of the middle classes.

## Structure

It is difficult to generalise across all the governing bodies, as some are extremely wealthy (eg, the Football Association), while others are still heavily reliant on grants. However, there are some common characteristics:

- executive boards and officers
- elected by clubs through local, regional and county representatives
- many have separate organisations in the four home nations (England, Scotland, Wales, Northern Ireland)
- many still have separate organisations for men and women.

Below is a list of the professional staff of the Badminton Association, as an example of a governing body. See fig 11.16 for the hierarchical structure.

| Private sector | Public sector | Voluntary sector |
|---|---|---|
| • Privately owned/registered companies<br>• Trading on normal profit and loss/self financed<br>• Membership entrance fees<br><br>• Managed by owners/their employees<br><br>• Must operate and survive in open market/make a profit/compete | • Business operations run by local authority departments<br>• Trading on set prices/charges etc<br>• According to a pre-set budget<br><br>• May involve subsidies as a matter of policy/Council tax or equivalent<br>• Managed by local authority employees | • Business operations owned by 'members'<br>• Possibly on trust/charity basis<br>• Trading on normal profit and loss/break even<br>• Managed through a members committee<br>• May employ staff<br>• Financed by membership fees/fund raising/sponsorship |

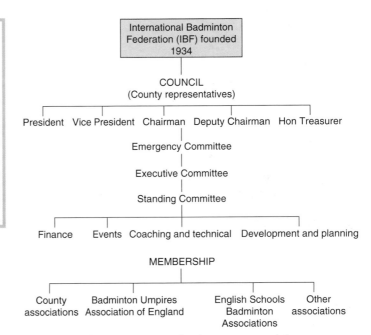

**ACTIVITY 9**

With reference to the financing and management of sports provision for the general public, briefly explain what is meant by:
- The private sector
- The public sector

Fig 11.16. Organisation and administration of the Badminton Association

- Chief Executive
- Accountant
- Director of Coaching and Development
- Coaching Manager
- Events Director
- Tournament and County Liaison Officer
- Press and Public Relations Manager
- P.A. to the Chief Executive
- Coaching Secretary
- Secretarial Staff

There are approximately 300 governing bodies in the UK. Many are unpaid volunteers, though this situation has improved somewhat by the appointment of paid administrators (largely dependent on the size and scale of the individual governing body).

These organisations proudly retain their autonomy from political control and each other. They become a more collective voice when represented to Sport England by the CCPR. Their main functions are to:

- establish rules and regulations (in accordance with the International Sports Federations, ISF)

- organise competitions

- develop coaching awards and leadership schemes

- select teams for country or UK at international events

- liaise with relevant organisations such as the CCPR, Sports Council, local clubs, British Olympic Association and the International Sports Federation.

## Recent changes for governing bodies

Examples of some changes are:

- growth of new sports, setting a challenge to the older traditional sports

- the decline in extra-curricular school sport and a dependence on the governing bodies to try to fill this gap

- the blurring in definition of amateur and professional sport

- the need to compete internationally with countries who have developed systematic forms of training have made the governing bodies develop the coaching and structuring of competitions and devote more money to the training of their elite sportspeople.

Governing bodies have a variety of finance sources: drawn from member clubs, associations and individual members, or receiving grant in aid from Sport England. The 1990s and 2000s have seen the dominance of television sports coverage and consequently sponsorship affects many sports. Governing bodies have had to meet this challenge and market themselves in the modern world if they wish to take advantage of these opportunities. Sports like snooker, badminton, squash and

**ACTIVITY 10**

Research in your class the development of a particular governing body. Choose from different categories, eg, traditional, professional, a new growth sport, or a sport which has recently experienced rapid change etc.

athletics have moved into the arena of big business. **Commercial sponsorship** is now a desirable form of income.

Most governing bodies, particularly if in receipt of lottery funding, are required to draw up policies for increasing participation in their sport and also to develop talent to the highest levels.

The example used here is taken from the Lawn Tennis Association (see p 275).

**ACTIVITY 11**

Research your local centre (eg, a sports centre, a country park, a water-based recreational facility etc).
Note carefully:
- its provision of a variety of activities
- its costing system
- access for people with disabilities
- opportunities for the Sports Council's target groups
- ease of access for the local catchment area
- opening hours
- social areas
- club use
- competition use of the centre, etc.

Be as thorough as you can.
Following your findings write a report which concentrates on the positive as well as the negative, with any recommendations.

LTA performance journey

| Policies for participation | Policies for sporting excellence |
|---|---|
| • Attracting kids | • The Performance Plan |
| • Mini tennis centres (over 500 centres/ 50,000 children involved/mini tennis Awards scheme/50 county coaches) | • LTA Tennis Academy Programme |
| • Junior tennis (JNT tennis programme) | • Futures Programme |
| • Schools tennis (3,000 attended teacher training programme/3,742 schools affiliated to BSTA/Nestle ladder) | • Performance Clubs |
| • Specialist sports colleges | • Intermediate Squads |
| • City Tennis Club Programme – very much aimed at improving equality of opportunity in inner cities (Tony Blair official ambassador) | • Senior Squads |
| • 20 clubs with purpose-built Kids Zones | • ProCoach System (allows instant capture and feedback to players via four cameras on court) |
| • 'Play Tennis' a national promotion to raise participation (10,000 clubs took part) | • Plans for a National Tennis Centre |

*Source*: LTA website.

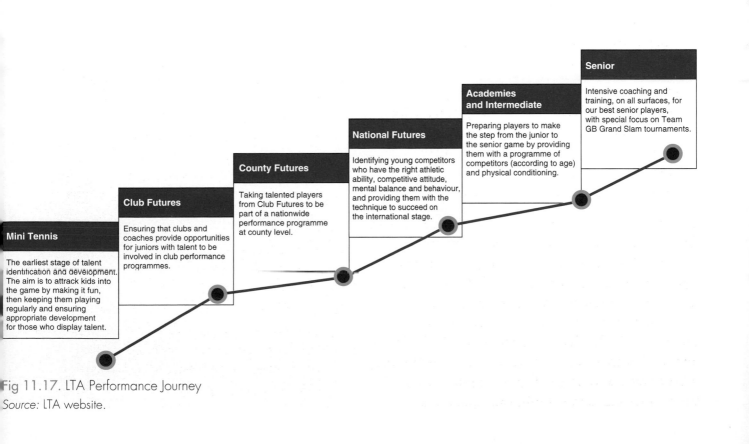

Fig 11.17. LTA Performance Journey
*Source*: LTA website.

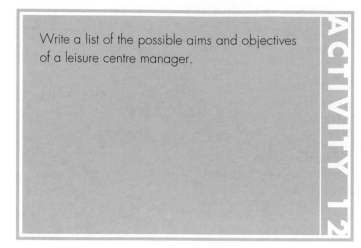

Write a list of the possible aims and objectives of a leisure centre manager.

**ACTIVITY 12**

## National sports centres

These are run by Sport England – See fig 11.19. It is recognised that only by providing appropriate training facilities will it be possible for the UK to compete effectively in international sport.

## Plas y Brenin

Based in Snowdonia, this is the national centre for mountain activities. It trains leaders and offers courses in the Alps, Scotland and in Snowdonia. They run award schemes and employ full-time instructors who work with the governing bodies.

# Local facilities

## Local voluntary sports clubs

These would normally be affiliated to the national governing body, eg, football, cricket, hockey. However, private clubs may be linked to business firms. Figure 11.18 and table 11.5 give examples of sports club administration and organisation.

## Holme Pierrepont

This centre offers an artificial canoe slalom course, a 200 metre regatta lake and an artificial ski tow, amongst its facilities. The key governing bodies (the British Canoe Union, the British Water Ski Federation and the National Federation of Anglers) make extensive use of this facility.

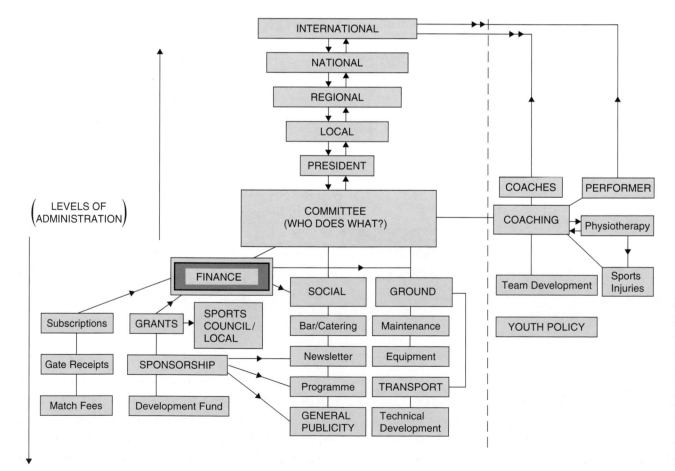

Fig 11.18. Administrational framework of a large athletic club

Table 11.5. Administration of a sports club

| Role of officers | Club meetings | Finance | Practical management | Club safety |
|---|---|---|---|---|
| Club president | Management | *Income* | Administration | Health & Safety |
| Vice president | committee | Subs | Staffing | at Work 1974 |
| Club chairman | Agenda | Match fees | Finance | Injuries (rel. to |
| Club secretary | Minimum | Sale of clothing | Bar | facilities) |
| Club treasurer | attendance | Bar | Management | Accidents |
| Fixtures secretary | Voting | Social events | Legal | Governing |
| Social secretary | procedures | Lotteries | Facility care | body regulations |
| Press officer | Minutes | | Insurance | Training awards |
| Club groundsman | Regularity of | *Capital costs* | | Insurance |
| Captains | meetings | Loans/grants | | |
| Bar manager | a.g.m. | Breweries | | |
| Membership secretary | | Banks | | |
| Training & coaching | | Local authority | | |
| Junior section | | Sports council | | |
| Senior members | | | | |

Fig 11.19. National Sports Centres in the UK

## Crystal Palace

Also a multi-purpose facility, it has a world famous stadium, swimming pool, and a variety of indoor facilities and artificial surfaces. A sports injury clinic provides for individual treatment.

## Bisham Abbey

The main activities include tennis, squash, hockey, weight lifting and golf. An Excellence partnership has been forged with the British Amateur Weightlifters Association. Elite squads account for approximately 70% of use.

## Lilleshall Hall

This is a multi-purpose centre with a particular specialism in gymnastics and football. Governing bodies account for 75% of use. The human performance fitness testing centre is open to all and signifies the attempt to coordinate the fields of sports medicine, physiotherapy and rehabilitation.

## Manchester

It contains the velodrome for cycling, and has been accredited an Olympic training centre by the BOA. This is in recognition of the fact that it provides the very best training opportunities and services for British cyclists. It is managed by the British Cycling Federation on behalf of the Sports Council.

# National Cities of Sport

Sport England is developing a more coordinated approach toward a coherent sports facilities plan, and as such, designated Birmingham, Sheffield and Glasgow as the first National Cities of Sport. The Cities of Sport Programme aims to create a network of cities with the vision, commitment and resources to bid for and stage major sporting events. It hopes to bid by using a planned, coordinated approach supported by an infrastructure at both local and national level, and management expertise; it is very important to develop partnerships among councils, universities, media and business community as well as sports organisations.

# New national stadium

Creating a new national stadium at Wembley is a decision of national importance. Millions of pounds of National Lottery money will be spent with the intention of providing a stadium which will cope with modern-day seating capacities (80,000) and spectators' expectations (easily accessible, safe and comfortable), and with the capability of attracting European and world single or multi-sports events.

# Finance

Government funding
National Lottery funding
(www.english.sports.gov.uk/lottery)
Voluntary sector
Governing Bodies
SportAid (previously Sport Aid Foundation)
(www.sportsaid.org.uk)
Football Trust
Gambling
Foundation for Sport and the Arts
Sponsorship
Tax
Funding for sport in the United Kingdom is a mixture of government, private and commercial incentives.

# Central government

The Exchequer funds sport, via the DCMS. Funds are allocated to Sport England and UK Sport for fostering, supporting and encouraging the development of sport and physical recreation. They in turn provide grants to governing bodies in sport.

The DCMS is developing new Funding Agreements such as:

- UK Sport is the proposed distributor of the Lottery funding ensuring equal treatment of all UK athletes. Sport England is responsible for the distribution in England of sport's share of the Lottery funding.
- In 1999/2000 Sport England received £4.5 m and UK Sport received £12.6 m in Exchequer funding from the DCMS to assist their work.
- Children's Play received central funding.
- The Football Licensing Authority has been reconstituted as a Sports Ground Safety authority.

# Local government

Local authorities spend nearly £900 m per annum on sport and active recreation in England. It is a heavy burden for an already over-stretched budget.

# The voluntary sector

This is the area in which most sporting activity occurs. Individuals come together to form clubs and associations which are run to benefit the participants. They are generally self financing; annual subscriptions and match fees provide the bulk of the revenue and indicate the 'grass roots' development of sport in the UK.

# Governing bodies

Governing bodies receive their income from grants from the Home Country Sport Councils, sponsorship, affiliation fees, donations, insurance, commission and royalties, marketing, interest receivable and profit on sale of investments.

Expenditure goes on elite squads, matches, publications, salaries and personal expenses, international affiliation fees, promotions, press and publicity, development officers and so on.

| | Funding (in £ millions) allocations | | | |
|---|---|---|---|---|
| | 1998–1999 | 1999–2000 | 2000–2001 | 2001–2002 |
| ESC (of which Sportsmatch) | 36.5<br>3.2 | 37.9<br>3.4 | 38.0<br>3.4 | <br>3.4 |
| UKSC | 11.6 | 12.6 | 12.6 | 12.6 |
| Children's Play | 0.4 | 0.5 | 0.5 | 0.5 |
| FLA | 0.9 | 0.9 | 0.9 | 0.9 |

Fig 11.20a. Funding allocations 1999–2002

| | 1997–1998 | 1998–1999 | 1999–2000 |
|---|---|---|---|
| Sports | 50,144 | 49,434 | 51,923 |
| of which: | out tum | provision | plans |
| English Sports Council of which: Sportsmatch | 36,925<br>3,200 | 36,489<br>3,200 | 37,873<br>3,373 |
| United Kingdom Sports Council | 11,824 | 11,600 | 12,600 |
| Children's play | 400 | 400 | 500 |
| Football Licensing Authority | 896 | 896 | 900 |
| British Chess Federation | 49 | 49 | 50 |
| Other sports support | 50 | | |

Fig 11.20b.

Wide variations exist depending on the size and type of governing body. For example, is it a female club in which case sponsorship will be harder to find? Is it a professional organisation where commercial markets are readily available?

**ACTIVITY 13**

Why should a Local Authority spend large sums of money on sport when it is a permissive duty rather than a mandatory one?

## AO Sports Aid

The Sports Aid Foundation, now SportsAid was set up in 1976, to enable top amateur athletes (at both junior and senior level) to train with similar privileges enjoyed by state sponsored athletes abroad. It is another self-financing organisation which draws funds from commercial, industrial and private sponsors and fund-raising projects. Outstanding competitors generally receive the money. They receive grants according to their personal needs, cost of their preparation, training and competition and are usually recommended by their governing body. Since 1976, over £5 million has been given to over 5,000 competitors. Grants are awarded through its charitable trust to talented athletes who are in education, on low income or have disabilities.

SportsAid has three main objectives:

- to further the education of young people through the medium of sport
- to encourage those with social or physical disadvantages to improve their lives through sport
- to enable those living in poverty to take advantage of the opportunities offered by sport.

A typical national grant is £500 per year. A regional grant is usually £150–£250 per year. To qualify for a national SportsAid grant you must be:

- aged between 12–18 years (special cases may be made)
- in genuine financial need and therefore not in receipt of a National Lottery World Class Performance grant
- a member of a national squad.

In December 1999 SportsAid was asked to play a vital role in the development of young British sport talent by partnering Sport England in the 'World Class Start Programme'. The costs were met by a combination of lottery money and funds raised by SportsAid's ten new regional charities. Governing bodies received the Lottery's contribution – approximately £10 million so that they could employ coaches, stage training camps and provide essential support for potential world class performers. The contribution of SportsAid was to offer direct financial assistance to the athletes and their families.

## Gambling in sport

Commercial betting and gaming is allowed under strict licensing regulations. This includes card games and casinos, but the bulk comes from greyhound and horse racing, and football matches.

## Football Trust

With the aim of putting money back into sport, the Football Trust has been set up to supervise the levying of money from football pools and 'Spot the ball' competitions. Its income is over £32 million

a year. Much of this money will be used to improve facilities for both performers and spectators (in line with the Taylor Report recommendations).

The Trust has announced plans to establish a nationwide Grass Roots Facilities Scheme. Over £1 million has been allocated and will be available for pitch and changing facilities for local authority owned, non league clubs, schools, voluntary bodies and other organisations.

The Football Trust has received over £150 million since 1990 for safety work at League football clubs, financed from a 3% Pool Betting duty concession extended in the 1999 Budget.

## The National Lottery

In 1994 the Sport England Lottery Fund was launched with a broad policy strategy. It achieved many successes including the Priority Areas Initiative; funding for 1000 community projects in the first year; promise of funding for the new national stadium and funding for talented young stars. Problems occurring at this time were: the system was too slow, too bureaucratic and too centralised. The government has acted to address some of these issues.

The Lottery Sports fund has earmarked £20.5 million a year for UK Sport to administer to our top UK medal hopes through the World Class Performance Programme and to help attract and stage major sporting events in the UK. Sport now benefits by around £300 million per year from the Lottery.

- World Class Events Programme:

Aim: stage major international events such as the Olympics, Paralympics, World,

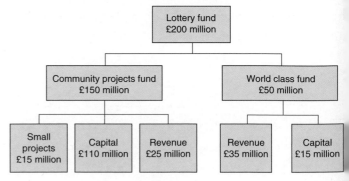

Fig 11.21a. Distribution of lottery funds

| Award details | |
| --- | --- |
| Months and awards | 53 |
| Projects founded to date | 2,936 |
| Total awarded to date | £934,179,807 |
| Total project cost to date | £1,634,854,001 |
| Average projects funded per month | 55 |
| Average amount awarded per month | £30,846,302 |
| Number of countries covered | All |
| Number of sports covered | 61 |

| Application details | |
| --- | --- |
| Total applications to date | 7,073 |
| Total amount requested to date | £3,603,486,322 |
| Total project cost to date | £5,555,048,103 |
| Average applications per month | 133 |
| Average amount requested per month | £67,990,308 |
| Number of countries covered | All |
| Number of sports covered | 78 |

Fig 11.21b.

European and Commonwealth in the United Kingdom
Funds: £3 million p.a. providing 35% of the cost of bidding and staging events

• World Class Start Programme:

Aim: help governing bodies identify and develop young talent by providing qualified support staff
Funds: £10 million p.a.

• World Class Potential Programme:

Aim: help governing bodies develop potential medal winners by setting up training and competition programmes
Funds: £15 million p.a.

• World Class Performance Programme

Aim: support our elite athletes
Fund: Since 1997 grants totalling over £64.6 m have been committed to over 30 sports in the Programme and 2100 athletes have received support

## SCSI School Community Sports Initiative

This has been established to help schools apply for increased levels of funding from the National Lottery Sports Fund, to develop good school/community sports facilities.

> **ACTIVITY 14**
>
> The National Lottery has had a considerable moral, economic and social impact. What do you consider to be the advantages and disadvantages of the good causes scheme and what suggestions for change would you make?
>
> What opportunities exist for the funding of amateur athletes?

## Foundation for Sport and the Arts

This organisation was set up by the pools promoters in 1991 to channel funds into sport and the arts. It has contributed more than £400 million towards sport projects and is financed from 3% Pool Betting Duty concession extended in the Budget. The pools provide approximately £43.5 million p.a. which can be used for the benefit of sport. It works closely with the Sport England and administers grants. Its main aims are to

• support the improvement of existing facilities

• assist the construction of new sports venues

• help with appropriate sports projects (schools, disabled, Olympic and Paralympic teams).

The sums involved are quite substantial, eg, £1 million to Northern Ireland's Sports Training Centre, £100,000 to Widnes Rugby League FC to assist with the upgrading of the facilities following the Taylor recommendations, £200,000 to Yorkshire & Cleveland Riding for the Disabled.

## Sponsorship

The private sector contributes approximately £400 million a year to sport, involving more than 2,000 British companies assisting schemes from national excellence programmes to local grass roots schemes.

## The Institute of Sports Sponsorship (ISS)

This is one of the main national organisations concerned with sports sponsorship. It was set up in association with the CCPR Sports Sponsorship Advisory Service, and acts as a grouping of commercial companies and public bodies with an interest in sport.

## Tax

The introduction of the Uniform Business Rate in 1990 meant that rates for some sports clubs tripled. This is generally considered as unfair, as they are non-profit making and in addition provide a social service. The British Olympic Association, which receives no government assistance, has to pay approximately £750,000 on £5 million raised. Britain is the only country to tax its Olympic fund raisers.

## Sporting Policies for Participation and Excellence

### Activemark

Activemark is an award scheme for primary schools that recognises good practice within the physical

|  | Charitable Status | Inland Revenue Scheme |
|---|---|---|
| Direct taxes | Primary purpose trading income exempt from tax | Gross income from fundraising and trading exempt from tax where turnover is less than £15,000 (all such income is taxable if the threshold is exceeded) |
|  | All rental income exempt | Gross income from property exempt from tax where less than £10,000 (**all** such income is taxable if the threshold is exceeded) |
|  | 80% mandatory relief from uniform business rates | Under separate legislation that took effect in 2004, mandatory rates relief at 50% for clubs with a rateable value of less than £3,000 reducing to no relief for rateable values more than £8,000 |
| Incentives to give | Gift Aid on individual and company donations | Gift Aid on individual donations only |
|  | Payroll giving | No payroll giving |
|  | Income tax relief on gifts of shares | No income tax relief on gifts of shares |
|  | Inheritance tax relief on gifts | Inheritance tax relief on gifts |
|  | Gifts of assets on no-gain no-loss basis for capital gains | Gifts of assets on no-gain no-loss basis for capital gains |

*(Continued)*

(*Continued*)

| | Charitable Status | Inland Revenue Scheme |
|---|---|---|
| Fundraising | Business: relief on gifts or trading stock<br><br>Grants available from other charities, eg, community foundations, and other bodies supporting charities | Business: relief on gifts or trading stock<br><br>Will not attract charitable sources of funding |
| Regulation | Charity Commission regulation and audit<br>Public recognition of and trust in charity and Gift Aid concepts<br>Charity Commission definition based on health benefits of physical recreation<br>Sports must be capable of improving **physical** health and fitness<br>Significant social activity to be kept separate from charitable activities | Inland Revenue regulation and audit<br><br>Public awareness of CASC brand to be developed<br><br>Inland Revenue definition based on the value of sport as a factor in community cohesion<br><br>Uses Sports Council's list of recognised sports<br><br>Social membership permitted |

*Source*: Sport England website.

education provision. The higher gold level can also be achieved. The 'Activemark' and Activemark Gold awards schemes recognises and rewards primary, middle and special schools that provide young children with the opportunity of receiving the benefits of physical activity. It has been developed in partnership with the British Heart Foundation (BHF) and has the theme: 'Get Active, Stay Active'. To achieve an award the school needs to:

- offer a broad and balanced physical education programme
- provide an environment that encourages physical activities
- teach children the importance of staying active for life
- provide enhanced curricular provision through some additional opportunities for physical activity

- have an effective inclusion policy for pupils with disabilities

Activemark Gold recognises all the above plus:

- realistic in-depth physical education and physical activity development plans
- a commitment to providing a range of additional, high quality opportunities for physical activity.

A team of assessors appointed by Sport England reviews the schools against these rigorous criteria.

## Active Sports Programme

This scheme, coordinated by Sport England, is based on four policy headings:

- active schools – forms the foundation
- active communities – looks at breaking down the barriers to participation and considers equity issues

- active sports – links participation to excellence such as participation in the Millennium Youth Games
- World Class England – operates four programmes of 'World Class Start', 'World Class Potential', 'World Class Performance' and 'World Class Events'.

They are meant to act as building blocks and are not necessarily linear. They also complement the Sports Councils participation pyramid of foundation, participation, performance and excellence. The majority of the funding will come from the National Lottery and there will be a strengthening of the regional set up via local authorities. There will be a framework around all experiences available to potential participants such as the National Junior Sports Programme, Sportsmark, and Coaching for Teachers.

## A Sports Leaders UK Leadership Awards

There are four different awards catering for different age groups and needs.

**JSLA:** The Junior Sports Leader Award is for 14–16 year olds and is taught mainly in schools within the National Curriculum for Physical Education. The Award develops a young person's skills in organising activities, planning, communicating and motivating.

**CSLA:** For those over 16 years old, this popular award is taught is schools, colleges, youth clubs, prisons, and sports and leisure nationwide.

**HSLA:** This Award builds on the skills gained through the Community Sports Leader Award to equip people to lead specific community groups such as older people, people with disabilities and primary school children. The award includes units in event management, first aid, sports development and obtaining a coaching award.

**BELA:** This award is for those interested in the outdoors and builds the ability to organise safe expeditions and overnight camps.

## Sport Action Zones

Sport Action Zones (SAZs) are a response by Sport England to address the issue of sporting deprivation in the most socially and economically deprived areas of the country. Participation levels in these areas is considerably below the national average.

Sport is believed to be valuable in contributing to the lives of people in these areas as well as helping in the regeneration of the communities. Sport is acting in association with many other agencies such as health, education, lifelong learning initiatives and so on. At the time of writing twelve such zones have been created, evenly spread around the country including inner cities and rural areas. Sport England in association with other partners helps fund the zones for an initial five-year period.

Examples of the kind of work the zones are carrying out include:

- Working with young people involved in anti-social behaviour
- Working with community health services to support people in poor health
- Providing education, training and support for community sport workers in other sectors who might use sport to meet their objectives
- Setting up local clubs where none exist
- Making local sport centres more accessible
- Engaging with local community groups, especially ethnic minority groups.

# Sportsmark

A scheme introduced in the government report, 'Sport: Raising the Game' in 1995, that recognises and rewards the schools that provide the best physical education and sports provision to their pupils and the local community. The additional Gold Award is presented to those offering exceptional provision. To obtain the award various criteria have to be achieved.

# ACE UK (Athlete Career & Education Programme)

This programme is modelled on the Australian Institute of Sport (AIS). It provides a tailored service that encourages athletes to take control of all aspects of their lives. ACE UK enables them to identify their personal strengths and weaknesses and supports them to integrate career, education and sporting demands in order to ensure all-round success in their lives. Sports performers who are part of the World Class Programme, BOA Gold Passport holders or have left these schemes during the past 12 months are eligible to benefit from the programme.

Once athletes have expressed an interest in the programme they will have an Individual Athlete Assessment with their local advisor. The focus of this support includes:

- Integration planning – helping athletes to combine the demands of sport with other personal matters
- Educational guidance – providing advice for those athletes who wish to continue with their studies
- Career planning – helps athletes discover their own strengths and interests and match possible career opportunities
- Transitional support – for those athletes who are injured, relocating or nearing the end of their programmes, offering guidance on future options
- OPEN – access to the Olympic and Paralympic Employment Network

- Training and development programmes – a wide range of subjects is offered from financial planning to communication skills.

# Sporting Ambassadors programme

This programme gives sports heroes and heroines (approximately 200 at present in a wide range of sports) the chance to motivate and inspire young people to participate in sport. They communicate through the primary, secondary and special schools, youth and sport clubs emphasising the benefits of physical activity and a healthy lifestyle.

The ambassadors:

- visit the different venues
- present cups, certificates and badges as well as show their own achievements
- speak at school assemblies and small groups about their experiences as elite performers
- coach groups of young people.

# Sports colleges

Sports colleges are part of the specialist schools programme run by the DfES.

As of September 2003, there are 228 designated sports colleges with a government target of at least 400 by the end of 2005.

They will have an important role in helping to deliver the government's Plan for Sport:

> 'They will become important hub sites for school and community sport providing high quality opportunities for all young people in their neighbourhood.'
>
> Richard Caborn, Minister for Sport

# School sport coordinators

By 2006, there will be 3,200 school sport coordinators working across families of schools with 18,000 Primary Link Teachers.

The partnership around a sports college starts with an average of four schools, ultimately growing to eight schools. Each partnership receives a grant of up to £270,000 a year. This pays for the full time Partnership Development Manager.

The Primary Link Teacher (PLT) is located within each of the primary/specialist schools within the partnership with a remit to improve PE and school sport within the primary school. They have 12 days a year to become link teachers.

The School Sport Coordinator (SSCo) is a partnership based around families of schools with a team made up of a Partnership Development Manager (PDM), SSCo and PLT. Their role is to enhance opportunities for young people to experience different sports, access high quality coaching and engage in competition. They are released two days a week.

The Partnership Development Manager (PDM) is usually located within a sports college and manages the development of the partnership and the links with other PE and sport organisations.

The overall aim of the partnership is to ensure children spend a minimum of two hours a week on high quality PE and school sport. Six strategic objectives have been set:

- strategic planning – develop and implement a PE/sport strategy
- primary liaison – develop links particularly between Key Stages 2 and 3
- out of school hours – provide enhanced opportunities for all pupils
- school to community – increase participation in community sport
- coaching and leadership – provide opportunities in leadership, coaching and officiating for senior pupils, teachers and other adults
- raising standards – raise standards of pupil achievement.

## Academies

Academies are a new type of school. The school leadership need to draw on the skills of sponsors and other supporters in order to develop educational strategies to raise standards and contribute to diversity in areas of disadvantage.

They are all ability schools established by sponsors from business, faith or voluntary groups working in innovative partnerships with government and education. Running costs are met in full by the DfES. Local education authorities are expected to consider the scope for such establishments in areas of disadvantage. They offer a broad and balanced education specialising in one or more subject areas.

## Sports schools

There is a small selection of specialist sports schools in the UK, but again there is no centralised approach. Some examples are Millfield, Kelly College, Reeds School and Lilleshall. The advantages of such institutions are the combination of top quality coaching, education, accommodation, medical science, a pool of similar talent, an organised competition structure and links with professional clubs. However, there are some disadvantages also. They form a private network of schools which results in an exclusive system drawing inevitably from a limited pool of talent; young people may have to experience residential, institutionalised life away from home, and the physical and psychological demands are high.

A project called 'The Training of Young Athletes' (TOYA) was established in 1987 by the Institute of Child Health. Its remit was to 'examine the effects, both positive and negative, which prolonged training and competition can have on the development of youngsters'. Some of the positive aspects highlighted were a high level of fitness and self esteem, but negative aspects included injuries and 'burn out'.

This research was further developed in 1996 with the commissioning by the then English Sports Council of the 'Development of Sporting Talent Study' (1997). The research tried to gain a better understanding of the social, environmental and institutional factors that influence the chances of individuals developing their sporting excellence and careers in sport.

# PE School Sport and Club Links Strategy (PESSCL)

A high quality Physical Education for all children is at the heart of the government's new strategy and brings together a number of existing programmes. PESSCL is to be delivered by the DfES and the DCMS through various programmes (see below). Linked delivery on coaching will also support delivery and local authorities need to come together to ensure the effective delivery of these programmes. Over the next few years the government is investing £459 million to transform PE and school sport.

## Gifted and talented

It is part of the government's wider strategy to improve gifted and talented education. It aims to improve the range and quality of teaching, coaching and learning for talented sportspeople in order to raise their aspirations and improve their performance, motivation and self esteem. It also aims to encourage young talent to join sports clubs and strengthen the relationship between schools and national governing bodies (NGB). Up to 10% of pupils in primary and secondary schools will be supported. It will include the introduction of 'talent development camps' for pupils in years 6 and 7. Nationally, the programme will include:

- a web-based resource for teachers, coaches and parents
- a national support network for talented young athletes with disabilities
- NGB-organised national performance camps for elite young athletes
- a national faculty of gifted and talented trainers to provide continuing professional development
- extra curriculum provision for academically able 11–16 year olds in PE and Sports Studies
- a school-based profiling and tracking system.

## Step Into Sport

Sport relies on 1.5 million volunteer officials, coaches, administrators and managers. Step Into Sport is aiming to build on this trend and extend the 'grass roots' interest in this area into a more coordinated strategic approach by NGBs, county sports partnerships and clubs. It should ensure that clubs are ready to receive, develop and deploy a steady supply of volunteers.

Between 2002 and 2004 it was delivered in almost 200 School Sport Coordinator partnerships across all 45 county sport partnership areas by a consortium of the Youth Sports Trust (via the Top Link Programme – see National Junior Sports Programme), the British Sports Trust (via Sports Leader Awards) and Sport England, each with their own responsibilities.

This is a new initiative funded by the DCMS and the Home Office Active Communities Unit, which brings together the BST and Sport England to encourage young people to become more involved with sport in their local communities. The aim is to provide a structured pathway to attract over 48,000 young people aged 14–19 into voluntary sports coaching over the next two years. The network of partnerships will be mainly focused around the government's Sport and Education Action Zones.

## National Junior Sport Programme

The National Junior Sports Programme was launched in February 1996 by the Sports Council, working alongside the Youth Sports Trust. Its aim is to encourage young children from the age of four to become involved in sport. It will provide kit, coaching and places to play, and the more talented performers can be identified from a wider base. It will be a rolling programme and many teachers will be trained. The advantage is that it can fit neatly into the current physical education system. There are four main elements:

- Top Play (4–9-year-olds)
- Top Sport (7–11-year-olds)
- Champion Coach
- Top Club (11 years+)
- Top Link

| Option | What happens | Opportunities for volunteers |
|---|---|---|
| 1 YST: | All secondary schools within the partnership areas are provided with resources to introduce Sport Education as a support to their PE provision | Young people participate in Sport Education within PE lessons, giving them the opportunity to plan, organise and evaluate their PE experience |
| 2 BST: | Secondary school teachers, youth workers and other organisations are provided with support and training to run Junior Sports Leader Award (JSLA) courses | Young people move on to a JSLA |
| 3 YST: | Students use the Top Link programme to plan and stage a festival of sport for their local primary schools | Volunteers use the skills learned within the JSLA to stage their own event |
| 4 BST: | Each school, youth group or other organisation is supported in running CSLA, HSLA or BELA and other sports specific leadership training | Volunteers progress onto CSLA, HSLA or BELA or develop their leadership skills in a specific sport through NGB links |
| 5 YST: | Students are encouraged to participate in active volunteering in their local community and sports clubs | Young people, supported by mentors, undertake volunteering in their local community and gain recognition of this through Step into Sport awards |
| 6 BST: | Each partnership is supported to develop training and volunteering opportunities for parents and other adults | Adults are provided with opportunities to undertake leadership training through the CSLA course |
| 7 SPORT ENG: | County Sports partnerships are supported to develop volunteer support programmes to create volunteering opportunities for young people | Young people and adults are directed towards local volunteering opportunities |
| 8 SPORT ENG: | NGBs are supported by Sport England to develop volunteer strategies | Support structures are available within NGBs to help volunteers |
| 9 SPORT ENG: | Resource training and support is provided to develop locally based volunteer coordinators | Young people and adults have the support of local volunteer coordinators |

Due to a change of sponsor, Ecclesiastical Insurance, the Youth Sport Trust has expanded its TOP family to include the latest addition – Ecclesiastical Insurance TOP Link which will encourage secondary school pupils to develop sport festival days for their primary feeder schools. The main aim of this initiative is to develop vital links between primary and secondary schools.

Funding will come from the National Lottery, Sport England, Youth Sports Trust and business sponsorship (£14 million in total).

More recent initiatives have come from the Health Education Authority (1998) which targets girls aged 12–18 years, youth of low economic status and adolescents aged 16–18 including those from ethnic minorities, with disabilities, or clinical conditions like obesity, diabetes or depression.

Champion Coaching, initiated by the National Coaching Foundation, now Sports Coach UK, in association with governing bodies, developed programmes of taster courses for 11–14 year olds but although it has seen success the youngsters appear to emerge from the more privileged socio-economic groups.

Active Schools and Active Communities, the latest programmes of Sport England, require local authorities, schools and clubs to plan and work together.

- **active schools:**     forms the foundation
- **active communities:**  looks at breaking down the barriers to participation and considers equity issues
- **active sports:**     links participation to excellence eg, millennium youth games
- **World Class England:**  operates start, potential, performance, events.

They are intended to act as building blocks and are not necessarily linear. They complement the concept of the participation pyramid of foundation, participation, performance and excellence.

There have been growing calls for more 'inclusive' physical education programmes. These programmes need to cater for the diversity of students, their needs and the schools they attend. It is possible that the government focus on competitive team sports, since the publication of 'Sport: Raising the Game' may not be successful as studies suggest these are not the sporting activities which attract this age group (Coalter 1999). Sustaining the broader choice at school is likely to support lifelong participation.

In the New Opportunities Fund, lottery fund money will be available for schemes that encourage the value of sport as character building and diversion such as summer play schemes, after school clubs and so on.

The National Junior Sport Programme is intended to support the National Curriculum as an additional resource for teachers.

Coaching for Teachers is a joint initiative funded by Sport England and coordinated by the National Coaching Foundation with support from BAALPE and PEA (Physical Education Association) to involve teachers in extra-curricular activities.

## School Club Links

The overall aim is to increase the proportion of children guided into clubs from SSCo partnerships. Primarily, seven major sports will be focussed on (tennis, cricket, rugby union, football, athletics, gymnastics and swimming). The reasons for *their* selection included:

- the capacity of the NGB
- they are central to the National Curriculum
- their ability to help lead other sports

The FA School to Club Links Programme

| Opportunities | Description |
|---|---|
| FA Charter Standard Schools Programme | Involves primary, middle, secondary and special schools, independent and state. Requires as part of the criteria for all schools to form a partnership with a local charter standard club for boys and girls |
| FA Charter Standard Development Club | Requires clubs who have met the development criteria (minimum of 5 teams) to create a partnership with a local school or schools as part of their football development plan |
| FA Charter Standard Community Clubs | Requires clubs (minimum 10 teams male and female) to form schools to club links and appoint a voluntary schools liaison officer |
| FA TOP Sport Football Community Programme | Targets young people aged 7–11 who are less likely to be participating in football for their school due to more limited opportunities and help them move onto Charter Standard Club |
| Active Sports Girls Football Programme | The Active Sports Programme is a fundamental part of the FA's strategy for the development of girls' football. The framework includes a school to club link scheme for 10–16 year olds called 'Kick Start' |
| FA Soccability Community Programme | This is an educational programme designed as part of the FA TOP Sport Football Programme to assist young people with disabilities to participate in football |

- popular with both sexes
- multi skills
- mix of individual and team sports
- focus of government initiatives and investment.

The key organisations working together are DCMS, Sport England, the Youth Sports Trust and the relevant governing bodies.

Let's take a glance at how one governing body, the Football Association, is meeting the aims of the School to Club Links Programme

## Sportsearch programme

Sportsearch is an interactive, computer-based programme that was piloted in the UK in 2000. It enabled secondary school students in the country to find a sport that matches their physical attributes and interests. It was part of the Active Schools Programme and it will be implemented via the government's National Grid for Learning (NGfL).

## Sport medicine

Modern sports medicine has been defined and developed by the organisation of clinical services to serve all people who become involved in vigorous physical exercise and those who assist, advise or care for them. This includes physicians and paramedical specialists as well as educators, coaches, exercise scientists, psychologists and sociologists.

The IOC have advanced this area due to their responsibility for establishing effective standards for athletic qualification. The 1928 Games was the first time the term sports medicine was used. Testing women for gender was used

Sportsearch programme

| How it works | Benefits |
|---|---|
| complete 10 physical tests and a number of fitness tests | help young people to discover what sports they are good at |
| results entered into a PC | links them to local sports clubs |
| young person answers series of questions about preferences | creates a database of clubs, and links to other sport agencies |
| programme provides a ranked selection of sports | coordinates the technology and investments of NGfL |
| programme gives appropriate contacts to pursue the sport | forges cross-curricular links with numeracy, literacy and IT |
| system advises young people on fitness, allows them to access a national database, take part in surveys, competitions and past research projects | develops research projects with and for young people |

| | |
|---|---|
| World Class Start | Potential for future success |
| World Class Potential | Medal within 8 years |
| World Class Performance | Medal within 3 years |
| World Class Events | |
| World Class Coaching Programme | |

following the Berlin Games and for banned substances in 1968.

The major issues in sports medicine today are the artificial aids to sports performance, the causes of sudden death in young, apparently healthy athletes and the age at which young athletes should enter competitive sport activities.

# World Class Programme

- the World Class Programme provides funding for training, coaching and so on
- performers are selected and recommended by their governing bodies

- the governing bodies are required to draw up development plans and need to meet the targets they set if they are to maintain the same level of funding
- for the performer to receive a 'personal award' they must meet rigorous requirements of training, competing and upholding the ethical standards outlined by the NGB
- the money comes from the lottery and the Exchequer.

The examples given below relate to a World Class Potential performer in Badminton (2002).

| | Weekly training commitment | Structured cell training |
|---|---|---|
| Level 1 | 4–6 hours | 2 hours weekly |
| Level 2 | 9–12 hours | 4 hours weekly |
| Level 3 | 11–14 hours | 4 hours weekly |
| Level 4 | 12–20 hours | Up to 20 hours weekly JPC/HPC |
| Level 5 | 18–24 hours | Central training/up to 20 hours weekly |

## The World Class Programme

This was established to help national governing bodies develop a comprehensive system through which talented individuals can be identified to achieve success consistently in important international competitions such as the Olympics and Paralympics.

## World Class Start

This programme will help identify and nurture a specific number of potential performers with the necessary characteristics to achieve future World-Class success. Consortia of local authorities and other providers will be helped to put in place coaching schemes and support programmes to give children the best possible sporting start.

## World Class Potential

This programme will assist the development of talented performers to win medals in future (10 years) international competitions.

## World Class Performance

This programme supports the training programmes of elite performers who can win medals in the next six years.

Partnership funding is expected to cover 10% of costs.

Funding: Overall – £50 million p.a.

- World Class Start – £10 million p.a. Sport England Lottery Fund
- World Class Potential – £15 million p.a. Sport England Lottery Fund
- World Class Performance – £25 million p.a. UK & Sport England Lottery Fund

It is also hoped that £1 million p.a. will be raised by SportsAid for individuals in the World Class Programme.

## World Class Coaching Programme aims to deliver five key services

- *Profiling* – each coach is profiled and agrees to become involved in one of the following areas: scholarships, mentoring and/or expert solutions.
- *Scholarships* – opportunity for coaches to become involved with international/national experts and develop experience in a world class environment.
- *Mentoring* – provides the coach with one-to-one platform to exchange experiences and knowledge. They are able to choose from observational mentoring, skill development mentoring and professional development mentoring.
- *Expert solutions* – provides the solutions to sport specific issues which will benefit the athlete within the current Olympic cycle.
- *World Class Coaching Conference* – cross sport programme for coaches in the UK, this attracts national and international speakers to discuss relevant issues.

**ACTIVITY 15**

1. Which benefits of sport are highlighted in these case studies?

CASE STUDY: Community Games

The Community Games (Ireland) is an independent voluntary organisation operating through the local community. It provides opportunities for children and young people to experience a wide range of sporting and cultural activities. Community Games is sponsored and supported by the government, national sponsors and local authorities.

The Games is a country wide movement – non-political and non-sectarian – which operates at

area, county, provincial and national levels. Membership is open to anyone who wishes to participate. Some of its aims and objectives include: encouraging community spirit and a love of sport and culture amongst members of the community and promoting a better understanding between people of different cultures and environments. It also encourages community members to work with children, and many adults have found the Community Games an ideal way of meeting and making new friends.

Liverpool's Community Games (first held in 1998) are based on the same principle, with the main purpose of fostering community development and identity through sporting and cultural endeavour. Piloting initially on a small scale, this is extending to some other parts of Liverpool in 1999 and it is intended that the games will run throughout the city and then eventually throughout the country. It is distinctive to other

'Games' in that it stresses the merits of participation rather than winning competitions. Recognising that all children are not physically or temperamentally suited to sport, Community Games will aim to provide a balance of other games and cultural activities.

CASE STUDY: Ivybridge Estate, Hounslow

Hounslow Borough Community Recreation Outreach Team, together with Housing Management and Youth Service, devised a programme of activities to benefit all youngsters on the Ivybridge estate. After consulting the youngsters on the estate, it was clear that football coaching sessions would be popular with both boys and girls. An unexpected bonus of the sessions, held in a multi-sport area on the estate, has been the high level of ability and skill shown by the youngsters.

This has resulted in many of the boys being referred to Brentford FC School of Excellence. Two girls have also gone on to join women's football teams and other young people have become involved in coaching and refereeing. As a result of the youngsters asking for refreshments a youth café was established in the estate's community centre, organised and run by the young people during the sessions. Another benefit was that the young people felt included in life on the estate. They have since participated in the Tenants' Association and have been involved in planning a new community centre for the estate.

Source: Department of Culture, Media and Sport

2 What strategies were employed to achieve a measure of success?

# Summary

- Sports policy is characterised by a high degree of fragmentation between central government departments. There is heavy reliance on local government to provide facilities and opportunities for sport and recreation.

- In local authorities, there is a decentralised approach towards the organisation of sport and recreation, reflecting the political system in the UK. There is a slender thread of cohesion through the organisations, but there are also areas of overlap and conflict.

- As with much of the administration of sport in the UK it is a mixture of tradition and compromise.

- There has been a steady expansion in the internationalisation of sport and it has brought challenges for the National Governing Bodies to adjust their rules and take note of the international sporting calendar.

- The pattern of funding for sport in the UK will be dominated by sponsorship. Government grants (local and central) and funds from the governing bodies and private individuals make the next share. Relatively small but important market niches are funded by the SAF (Sports Aid) and the BOA.

- British sports bodies must cast off their traditional amateur, elitist approach to join the modern, professional sports world, if this country is to allow its athletes the same opportunities as those from rival countries.

- The type of political and economic system is crucial in determining the nature of state intervention; centralised or decentralised, capitalism or communist.

# Review Questions

1. Describe the function of the following organisations:
   - Department for Culture, Media and Sport
   - Sport England
   - Sport Coach UK
   - Disability Sport England
   - Central Council of Physical Recreation
   - Sports Leaders UK

2. What is the role of the Sports Minister and who is the current sports minister in the United Kingdom?

3. Why were governing bodies for sport initially established? What are the main functions of governing bodies?

4. What changes have governing bodies had to undertake in more modern times?

5. What does the term 'permissive' mean in relation to the provision of leisure by local authorities?

6. Name six forms of finance for sport in the United Kingdom.

7. What do the terms private, voluntary and public mean in relation to provision for leisure?

8. Outline the main idea of 'Best Value' as a policy for recreation and sport.

9. What was the effect of the government report 'Sport: Raising the Game'?

10. Describe the five levels of coaching as defined by SportCoach UK.

11. What are the nine reasons given for explaining National Government Involvement in sport? Choose two and explain in more detail.

12. What advantages are there to sport being free from political control?

13. Briefly explain what Compulsory Competitive Tendering means and give an example of how it can affect sport.

14. Name four ways in which sport and politics have become entwined in the United Kingdom.

15. What does centralised and decentralised mean?

16. How can sport policies help the government's overall aim of Neighbourhood Regeneration?

17. Outline the main features of the policy 'A Sporting Future for All'.

18. What is meant by the term policy?

19. List 10 wider economic benefits which can result from sport.

20. Copy and fill in the table below.

| Organisation | Major Sport Policy | Characteristics of Policy |
|---|---|---|
| DCMS | | |
| Sport England | | |
| UK Sport | | |
| NGB | | |
| Sportscoach UK | | |
| YST | | |
| BOA | | |
| CCPR | | |
| IOC | | |
| ISF | | |

# 12. Levels of Performance – Participation to Excellence

## Chapter introduction

This chapter investigates the various levels of participation in sporting activities. This will range from the broad base of the pyramid where the main emphasis is on participation, to the apex of the pyramid where the focus is on the standard of performance. For ease of study, society will be categorised into distinct groups based on age, disability, gender, socio-economics, culture and race, and each will be studied in relation to their sporting participation.

We will concentrate on various social groups and the policies developed to increase their levels of physical activity, and try to establish some of the reasons for low participation.

Many of the qualities assigned to sport are well recognised – opportunity for self knowledge, personal achievement, good health, enjoyment, skill acquisition, social interaction, responsibility, development of confidence and so on. We should therefore be concerned that certain sections of the population are missing the chance to benefit from such an enriching experience.

By the end of this chapter you should understand the following terms:

- Participation
- Sports equity
- Exclusion/inclusion
- Racism
- Sexism
- Disability sport
- Excellence
- Talent Identification

You should also understand the role of the following organisations and policies:

- Commission for Racial Equality and 'Kick it Out'
- Women's Sport Foundation and Brighton Declaration/Windhoek Call for Action
- Disability Sport England and functional classification systems

## The issue of participation – 'Participation Pyramid'

The need for a more coordinated and fair approach to the provision of sporting activities addresses two main areas:

1. sports development: enabling people to learn basic sports skills with the possibility of reaching a standard of sporting excellence.

2. sports equity: redressing the balance of inequalities in sport ie, equality of access for everyone, regardless of race, age, gender or level of ability.

Sport England has a sport development continuum:

- Foundation: learning basic movement skills, knowledge and understanding; developing a positive attitude to physical activity.

- Participation: exercising one's leisure option for a variety of reasons – health, fitness, social.

- Performance: improving standards through coaching, competition and training.

- Excellence: reaching national and publicly recognised standards of performance.

Before we study levels of participation let us first examine a summary of participation trends outlined by the DCMS. This should highlight to you the reason for this chapter.

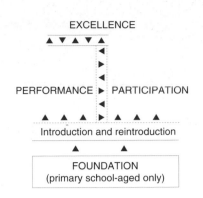

Fig 12.1. Sports development continuum model

## Summary of participation trends

- The quality and quantity of participation in sport and physical activity in the UK is lower than it could be, and levels have not changed significantly over recent years:

- for sport: only 46% of the population participate in sport more than 12 times a year, compared to 70% in Sweden and almost 80% in Finland;

- for physical activity: only 32% of adults in England take 30 minutes of moderate exercise five times a week, compared to 57% of Australians and 70% of Finns.

- Young white males are most likely to take part in sport and physical activity, and the most disadvantaged groups least likely. Participation falls dramatically after leaving school, and continues to drop with age. But the more active in sport and physical activity you are at a young age the more likely you are to continue to participate throughout your life.

- The UK's performance in international sport is better than we often think. UK Sport's index of success places us third in the world. However, we are not as successful in the sports we care most about.

- The UK successfully hosts major sporting events each year (such as Wimbledon or the London Marathon), with little government involvement. Problems have arisen with the so called 'mega events' (Olympics, FIFA World Cup, UEFA

European Championships, World Athletics Championships and the Commonwealth Games) requiring significant infrastructure investment. Historically, there has been poor investment appraisal, management and coordination for some of these events.

- Total government and lottery expenditure on sport and physical activity in England is estimated to be roughly £2.2 bn a year. A significant proportion of this is distributed via local authorities. The funding of sport and physical activity is fragmented and some strands of funding may not be sustainable as money from the National Lottery and TV rights is decreasing and local government budgets are being squeezed. In contrast, there is major public investment planned for school sports facilities.

- Broadly speaking, sport and physical activity is delivered through four sectors: local government, education (schools, FE and HE), the voluntary (clubs and national governing bodies of sport) and the private sectors. The role of the health sector in physical activity is also important. However, government's interaction with these sectors is through a complex set of organisations with overlapping responsibilities and unclear accountability. The situation is further complicated at the international level because some sports compete as UK/GB, some as Home Countries, and some as both.

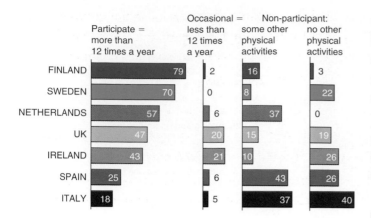

| | Participate = more than 12 times a year | Occasional = less than 12 times a year | Non-participant: some other physical activities | no other physical activities |
|---|---|---|---|---|
| FINLAND | 79 | 2 | 16 | 3 |
| SWEDEN | 70 | 0 | 8 | 22 |
| NETHERLANDS | 57 | 6 | 37 | 0 |
| UK | 47 | 20 | 15 | 19 |
| IRELAND | 43 | 21 | 10 | 26 |
| SPAIN | 25 | 6 | 43 | 26 |
| ITALY | 18 | 5 | 37 | 40 |

A number of comparative studies show that participation in physical activity in the UK is higher than that of some European countries. However, compared to Scandinavian countries, participation in sports and physical activity is low. The picture is that of a north/south divide with those countries most similar to Britain in terms of culture and weather achieving greater levels of participation.

Fig 12.2. Comparison of participation in sport
*Source*: Compass 1999.

It is important to understand the sociological basis for inequality in sport. It is not intended to be a thorough sociological review – merely a tool to help us achieve a greater understanding of the issue.

## All men are equal?

In the descriptive sense this is patently untrue: human beings do not possess the same amount of physical, mental or moral qualities. In the prescriptive sense, however, people ought to treat one another with equal respect, dignity and consideration.

## Stratification of society

Society can be divided into layers, as are rocks (ie, rock strata). The divisions are based on biological, economic and social criteria, eg, age, gender, race and social class. The dominant group in society, which controls the major social institutions like the media, law, education and politics, can exercise control over the more subordinate groups. This need not be the majority – take the case of previous minority white rule in South Africa. Using this classification, the dominant group in the UK could be described as white, male and middle class; the subordinate groups would be women, ethnic minorities, people with disabilities and belonging to the working class.

Discrimination can occur when opportunities available to the dominant group are not available to all social groups.

---

**KEY WORD**

**Discrimination** means 'to make a distinction: to give unfair treatment especially because of prejudice', and it occurs when a prejudicial attitude is acted upon. Discrimination can be overt, eg, laws which form part of the structure of a society, such as the former political system of apartheid, or a membership clause for a private sports club. This can be officially wiped out by changing the law, but covert discrimination (hidden or less obvious), eg, people's attitudes and beliefs, can be very hard to dislodge.

---

When subordinate groups in society are discriminated against, their opportunities are limited, including opportunities of social mobility (the pattern of movement from one social class to a higher or lower one). This can also be affected by whether the social system is closed (an extreme example is the Hindi caste system in India), or open (a true egalitarian democracy).

## Sport and stratification

Sport is often described by sociologists as a microcosm of society: it reflects in miniature all facets of society. This includes the institutionalised divisions and inequalities which characterise our society. Sporting institutions are equally controlled by the dominant group in society, and stratification in sport is inevitable when winning is highly valued.

It is highlighted even more when monetary rewards are on offer.

Sport is often cited as an avenue for social mobility:

- physical skills and abilities – professional sports requires little formal education
- sport may create progression through the education system eg, athletic scholarships
- occupational sponsorship may lead to future jobs
- sport can encourage values such as leadership and teamwork skills, which may help in the wider world of employment.

Although sport for all campaigns are no longer a direct function of Sport England these target groups are still under-represented in sport participation. More recently they are being dealt with at governmental level, under the DCMS, using the term 'Social Exclusion Groups'.

## Social exclusion

*Aspects of exclusion*

- Ethnicity
- Gender
- Disability
- Youth
- Age
- Sexuality
- Poverty
- Exclusion in rural areas/cities.

## Defining exclusion

The term can be attributed to Rene Lenoir, Secretary of State for Social Action for the Chirac Government (1974).

In the most intensive study of exclusion Europe wide, it is seen as a consequence of unemployment and low income (Roch and Annesley, 1998) leading to exclusion from a fair share of social goods and capital in the form of recognition, income and work. Three main causes of changes in social welfare were identified:

- mass unemployment and insecure employment
- family restructuring with a rapid growth of one-parent families and workless households
- growing inequality with a group of really poor separated from the rest – an economic underclass.

The UK is considered a liberal welfare regime. Sport was seen by the British Labour Government of the 1970s as 'part of the fabric of the social services' (Sport and Recreation White Paper 1975). Various concepts emerged during the last two decades of the twentieth century regarding the relationship between recreation, welfare, the individual and the community. This culminated in Ravenscroft (1993) using the term 'inclusive citizenship', arguing that access to leisure and recreation should be seen as part of the concept. The Social Exclusion Unit's (SEW) definition of social exclusion is 'a shorthand label for what can happen when individuals or areas suffer a combination of linked problems such as unemployment, poor skills, low incomes, poor housing, high crime environments, bad health and family breakdown'.

*So what about the role sport can play in this situation?*

Many studies have been carried out and moves are underway for improving the perception of recreation from a purely utilitarian one to the earlier nineteenth century one which focused more on the wider benefits to society on which the parks and recreation movement began. The following organisations are beginning to take a similar stance:

- The Institute of Leisure and Amenity Management
- Sport England
- New Zealand Hillary Commission for Sport
- Council of Europe.

When considering this area you will need to address the following terms:

- Descriptive: explain and give examples of how discrimination occurs for the identified groups in society.

- Reformative: suggest solutions to the identified problems.

Table 12.1 shows a summary of the nature and strengths of the benefits of sport and also the

Study table 12.1. Which groups suffer the worst levels of constraint?
What are the major factors restricting:
- female participation
- older people
- ethnic minorities.

ACTIVITY 1

Table 12.1. Constraints and exclusion in sport and leisure DCMS

| Group excluded / Constraint/exclusion factor | Youth | | | Poor/un-employed | Women | Older people | Ethnic minority | People with dis-abilities/ learn dif-ficulties |
| --- | --- | --- | --- | --- | --- | --- | --- | --- |
| | Child | Young people | Young delinq. | | | | | |
| Structural factors | | | | | | | | |
| Poor physical/social environment | + | + | + + | + + | + | + | + + | + |
| Poor facilities/ community capacity | + | + | + + | + + | + | + | + | + + |
| Poor support network | + | + | + + | + + | + | + | + | + + |
| Poor transport | + + | + + | + + | + + | + + | + + | + | + + |
| Managers' policies and attitudes | + | + | + + | + + | + | + | + + | + + |
| Labelling by society | + | + | + + + | + | + | + | + + | + + |
| Lack of time structure | + | + | + + | + + | | + | | + |
| Lack of income | + | + | + + | + + + | + | + + | + | + + |
| Lack of skills/personal and social capital | + | + | + + + | + + + | + | + | + + | + + |
| Fears of safety | + + | + + | + + | + + | + + + | + + + + | + + | + + |
| Powerlessness | + + | + + | + + + | + + | + + | + + | + + + + | + + |
| Poor self/body image | + | + | + + | + + | + | + | + + | + + |

The number of + signs shows the severity of particular constraints for particular groups.

experiences of the excluded groups without direct action by the state or voluntary organisations.

# Constraints and exclusion in sport

These can be broken down into three main categories:

- Environmental/structural (economic, physical and social factors)
- Personal constraints (internal and psychological)
- Attitudes of society and provider systems (policies and managers' practices can act as barriers or enablers).

The evidence suggests that:

- large numbers of people are affected
- policies such as discount schemes/adaptations for disability sport will have little impact if managers do not actively promote their facilities and services. The target population (women, ethnic, poor, aged and disabled) must be made to feel secure in attending these venues.

## Main constraint factors

- Poverty is constantly being highlighted as the factor that contributes to 'locking people in', accentuating their feelings of isolation and powerlessness.
- Time (quoted by many groups, rich, poor and retired).
- Chronic unemployed (greatest problems of structuring time).

Combinations of aspects of exclusion can be said to lead to double deprivation, for example, being

Table 12.2. Agencies involved in sports development

| |
|---|
| • Governing bodies of sport |
| • Local authorities |
| • National sports councils |
| • Voluntary sector sports clubs |
| • Schools/education sector |

*Source*: Higher Sports Leader Award.

Table 12.3. Barriers to participation

| Attitudes | Access | Programme |
|---|---|---|
| Stereotyping | Facilities | Range of activities |
| Lack of confidence | Transport | Inappropriate for ability |
| Lack of self motivation | Timing of openings | Inappropriate delivery style |
| Image of sport | Lack of information | Quality of provision |
| Family/personal relationships | Official procedures | Too competitive |
| Cultural norms | Fees | Not enough fun |
| Lack of interest | Childcare | |
| Too competitive | Lifestyle | |
| | Health | |
| | Education | |
| | Socio-economic status | |
| | Other activities | |

*Source*: Higher Sports Leader Award.

elderly and from an ethnic minority. If exclusion is prolonged in youth it can have lasting effects in terms of playing recreationally, socialising and competing to achieve.

A recent survey by the previous English Sports Council (ESC) (1998) showed that 38% of elite performers from 14 sports were from the professional and managerial social groups compared to 19% of the population. Only 10% were from the semi and unskilled compared to a quarter of the population. The conclusions drawn by the ESC was 'that the opportunity to realise sporting potential is significantly influenced by an individual's social background. So, for example, a precociously talented youngster born in an affluent family with sport loving parents, one of whom has achieved high levels of sporting success, and attending an independent private school, has a 'first class' ticket to the sporting podium'.

# Better partnerships and joined up thinking

There has been enough evidence to highlight the problems encountered by certain groups and many schemes to counteract them. Pressures to account publicly on schemes have tended to concentrate on short-term outputs rather than long-term ones.

Using the formula of dividing outputs by inputs gives a value for money measure. This is only possible where both have been recorded and many schemes do not do this.

Inputs are financial, human or material resources, including time and whether paid or not. Outputs are short-term products, for example, the number of participants in different groups in an event or programme. A specific example would be the number of new clubs or junior or veterans' sections formed.

Outcomes result in:

- sustained changes in provision and its use
- attitudes, for example, accessibility to facilities

- behaviour, for example, increase in participation
- relationships between individuals and organisations, for example, school–community partnerships to the use of school facilities by the community.

# Evaluation of public sector programmes

The following suggestions were put forward by Thomas and Palfrey (1996) as being useful markers for evaluating public sector programmes:

- effectiveness
- efficiency
- equity
- acceptability (equal to customer satisfaction)
- accessibility (information, resources etc)
- appropriateness (relevance to need)
- accountability (to public and investors)
- ethical considerations (values and how conflicts will be resolved)
- responsiveness (speed, accuracy, empathy)
- choice.

Problems with earlier government programmes were outlined in 'Bringing Britain together: a national strategy for neighbourhood renewal' (1998):

- mainstream services not joined up
- initiative-itis – too many programmes to respond to

**ACTIVITY 2**

Select a group affected by exclusion and devise a specific programme to cater for their needs. What recommendations would you make for any new national or local programmes that were to be initiated?

- too many rules to be met
- lack of cooperation
- too little investment in people
- patchwork policies displace problems to new areas
- poor links beyond the neighbourhood
- not harnessing community commitment
- neglecting what works.

## Sports equity

| Overcoming discrimination: | Can be achieved through: |
|---|---|
| • Recognising your own prejudice | • Sharing common values |
| • Understanding the difficulty | • Promoting equality through sport |
| • Talking to people | • Working in partnership |
| • Support from others | • Endorsing the law |
| • Thinking of alternatives | • Challenging discrimination |
| • Go on a training course | |
| • Using a policy/ guidelines | |

# Race

Race is the physical characteristic of an individual, while ethnicity is the belonging to a particular group, eg, religious, lifestyle. Racism is a set of beliefs or ideas based on the assumption that races have distinctive cultural characteristics determined by hereditary factors, and that this endows some races with an intrinsic superiority. The media promotes the popular idea of sport enabling many individuals to 'climb out of the ghetto' as well as lack of equal opportunities and racism in sport. Sport England and governing bodies have sought to encourage non-discriminatory attitudes to combat racism and to open up organisations to equal opportunities.

# Examples of racism in sport

In sport, racism can be seen in a system called 'stacking'. This refers to the disproportionate concentration of ethnic minorities in certain positions in a sports team, which tends to be based on the stereotype that they are more valuable for their physical skills than for their decision making and communication qualities. In American football there has been a tendency to place ethnic players in running back and wide receiver positions. In baseball, until fairly recently, they have tended to be in outfield positions. According to Grusky's theory of centrality (1963), this restricts them from more central positions which are based on coordinative tasks and require a greater deal of interaction and decision making. Significantly, coaches who make these decisions are generally white. Sociological studies have revealed the self-perpetuating coaching subculture which exists in American sport (J Coakley, 1994). When existing coaches need to sponsor a new coach, they are likely to select one with similar ideas.

# Attempts to overcome racism in sport

## 'Let's stamp racism out of football'

This was a large scale, national campaign begun in 1993–1994, intended to cut racial harassment out of football. It was supported by CRE/PFA (Commission for Racial Equality and Professional Footballers Association) and supporters' groups, the FA, the Football Trust, the Premier and Endsleigh Leagues. In 1994–1995, over 10% of clubs took specific action. It is now simply called 'Kick it Out' and has received support from subsequent Sports Ministers. The anti-racism campaigns were initiated by fans themselves culminating in the national campaign. The focus has now shifted to study to what extent racism exists at the 'institutional' level.

It is a recognition that clubs who reap financial benefits of fielding players from ethnic minorities

| | 1985/1986 | | 1989/1990 | | 1995/1996 | |
|---|---|---|---|---|---|---|
| | **Nos** | **%** | **Nos** | **%** | **Nos** | **%** |
| White | 1,332 | 92.3 | 1,302 | 89.5 | 1,732 | 88.3 |
| Black | 111 | 7.7 | 152 | 11.5 | 231 | 11.7 |

Fig 12.3. The proportion of black players at football league clubs
*Source:* Singer & Friedlander's review 1998/1999 season.

| | 1985/1986 | 1989/1990 | 1995/1996 |
|---|---|---|---|
| | % | % | % |
| Goalkeeper | 0.9 | 0 | 1.8 |
| Fullback | 19.8 | 15.8 | |
| Centreback | 12.6 | 15.2 | 28.7 |
| Midfield | 15.3 | 12.5 | 21.5 |
| Forward | 51.3 | 56.5 | 47.9 |

Fig 12.4. Positional breakdown of black players
*Source:* Singer & Friedlander's review 1998/1999 season.

| | White | Black | Difference± |
|---|---|---|---|
| Premiership | 1,377.1 | 2,317.2 | +940.1 |
| Division 1 | 306.6 | 571.9 | +265.3 |
| Division 2 | 67.6 | 106.3 | +38.7 |
| Division 3 | 22.8 | 28.3 | +5.5 |
| All Divisions | 475.9 | 919.5 | +443.6 |

Fig 12.5. Average transfer costs of players during 1995/1996 season (£000s)

should also show a greater responsibility and consideration for all its customers or members. It was highlighted in the media as a serious issue requiring action, with particular regard to Paul Ince, Mark Stein and Andy Cole. Concern is also felt that ethnic minority players should experience equal opportunities in reaching the administerial levels of the game.

A recent study by Malcolm and Last at the Centre for Research into Sport and Society at the University of Leicester their findings suggested that

at first it would appear at the elite level there are few barriers for players to overcome.

Compared to the number who claim to be of Afro-Caribbean origin on the General Household survey (1%) they would appear to be well represented and particularly at the Premiership level (17.5% in 1995/1996).

## Positional play

Over a ten-year period 50% of black players played in forward positions. This can mean occupying glamorous positions, high goal scoring and higher transfer fees. Average black players in the Premier League commanded transfer fees £1 million more than white players.

However, the main difference occurs in the different career paths taken by black footballers. Few break their way into management positions, for example as directors, as FA committee members and so on. Also, few Asian players have broken through into the professional ranks.

## Race and education

There has been a tendency for teachers to act upon a stereotype labelling children from ethnic minority groups and developing certain expectations of them. This can be self-perpetuating, as children can internalise these misconceptions and regard the sport side of educational life as the only successful route for them.

## Studies of ethnic minority participation in sport

In 1991, the Greater Manchester Conurbation was selected as a region to try to identify the relationship between ethnicity, culture and participation in sport. African, Bangladeshi, Caribbean, Chinese, East African, Asian, Indian, Pakistani and a comparable British white group were studied. The striking results were the gender differences:

- To be female and a Muslim, Hindu or Sikh is likely to result in a lower participation rate. The higher the importance placed on religion, the more this trend increased, as a strong patriarchal structure operates (Carroll and Hollinshead, 1992–1993).

- Women in these research studies did express a wish to increase their participation and this should have implications for sport policies.

Respect for cultures must also be considered:

- Asian groups do not rate sport and PE as highly as some of the other groups, and there is a lack of role models.

- Some cultural traditions can conflict with active sport participation habits, such as showing parts of the body, sharing changing facilities, attending co-educational classes.

The biggest provider of facilities for all groups was the local authority. Problems the ethnic groups encountered were 'feeling an outsider', racism, and lack of single-sex provision.

To summarise the results of the study:

- Sport is generally popular with ethnic groups – the Asian Games attract thousands of people.

- Special assistance is needed.

- Clubs should be supported but integration not forced.

- Information should be available about sport provision.

- Ease of access is important.

- Group leaders who may persuade other members to participate should be encouraged to train.

- Sport development officers from ethnic minorities should be appointed.

- Greater media coverage, such as Channel 4's Kabbaddi, have helped to raise the awareness of the general population.

In sport, Verma and Derby (1994) have given a useful overview of participation in sport by ethnic minorities who are educated alongside their white counterparts. They have the same interests in sport but with more limited opportunities of women and girls, particularly acute in Islamic cultures with traditions against body exposure and participation in mixed groups.

Provision of segregated transport and sessions have been successful in supporting short-term participation, eg, Asian women's swimming, fitness and sport schemes.

Football in the Community Scheme involves them as participants as well as coaches and leaders.

## Ethnicity and Sporting Participation 2000

### Sports Participation and Ethnicity in England 1999/2000

The survey was part of Sport England's commitment to better understand the extent and causes of inequity in sporting opportunities for certain groups in the population and ways to overcome them. The findings have particular relevance to the 'Active Communities' programme, which aims to extend sporting opportunities for all.

The findings:

- For ethnic minority groups the overall participation rate in sport is 40% compared to 46% national average.

- Only the Black Other group (60%) has participation rates higher than the population as a whole. Black Caribbean, Chinese, Pakistani and Bangladeshi were lower than the national average. These figures were similar for women from the same groups. However, the gap between men's and women's participation is greater amongst ethnic minority groups than it is in the population as a whole.

Reasons given for constraining factors in participation are similar to the population as a whole, for example, 'work/study demands, home and family responsibilities, lack of money, laziness' and so on but some also quoted negative experiences in sport due to ethnicity. These instances were higher for the Black Other men and less relevant for the Chinese section of the population.

Defining ethnicity is fraught with problems as it is almost impossible to identify a whole group and presume they will have similar experiences. This is particularly so where religion, culture, values, language, generation, age, gender, length of residency in a country and nationality all play a part in creating considerable diversity of experiences, expectations, way of life and behaviours. However, for the purposes of a national quantitative survey it is required that people be classified into 'broad ethnic groups'. The groups people could choose from were:

- White
- Black Caribbean
- Black African
- Black Other
- Indian
- Pakistani
- Bangladeshi
- Chinese
- None of these (17%) became 'Other'

Participation was defined as 'having taken part in sport or physical activities on at least one occasion in the previous four weeks, excluding walking'. It does not include referring or coaching.

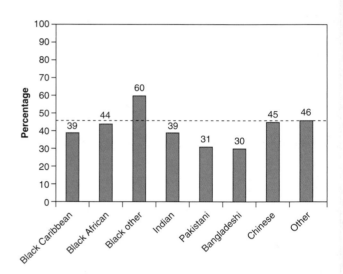

Fig 12.6. Participation in at least one activity (excluding walking) over the last four weeks (all respondents)

Table 12.4. Negative experience in sport due to ethnicity (% saying 'yes')

|  | Black Caribbean | Black African | Black (other) | Indian | Pakistani | Bangladeshi | Chinese | Other |
|---|---|---|---|---|---|---|---|---|
| Men | 11 | 6 | 21 | 8 | 7 | 10 | 2 | 7 |
| Women | 6 | 2 | 14 | 1 | 3 | 9 | 0 | 3 |
| Total | 8 | 4 | 17 | 5 | 5 | 9 | 1 | 4 |
| *Base (men)* | 207 | 104 | 61 | 435 | 245 | 60 | 54 | 220 |
| *Base (women)* | 269 | 148 | 86 | 447 | 262 | 81 | 61 | 295 |

**Table 12.5.** Factors related to ethnicity that deterred participation in sport while at school (in school lessons)

| | Black Caribbean | Black African | Black (other) | Indian | Pakistani | Bangladeshi | Chinese | Other |
|---|---|---|---|---|---|---|---|---|
| Nothing – enjoyed sport at school | 74 | 71 | 72 | 68 | 60 | 74 | 54 | 64 |
| PE teachers insensitive to cultural needs | 0 | 0 | 0 | 0 | 1 | 2 | 0 | 1 |
| Unfair treatment from teachers due to ethnicity | 1 | 0 | 1 | 1 | 0 | 1 | 0 | 0 |
| Unfair treatment from pupils due to ethnicity | 1 | 0 | 1 | 0 | 2 | 1 | 0 | 1 |
| PE teachers didn't give me attention due to my ethnicity | 0 | 1 | 4 | 0 | 0 | 1 | 0 | 0 |
| Other related to ethnicity | 1 | 1 | 0 | 1 | 1 | 1 | 0 | 2 |
| *Base (all ethnic minorities)* | *471* | *247* | *147* | *875* | *497* | *141* | *112* | *517* |

Table 12.6. Participation rates in the 4 weeks before the interview – Top ten sports ranked by GHS (all respondents)

| Active sports, games and physical activities[1] | Black Caribbean | | Black African | | Black (Other) | | Indian | | Pakistani | | Bangladeshi | | Chinese | | Other | | GHS 1996 % |
|---|---|---|---|---|---|---|---|---|---|---|---|---|---|---|---|---|---|
| | rank | % | rank | % | rank | % | rank | % | rank | % | rank | % | rank | % | rank | % | % |
| Walking | 1 | 34 | 1 | 37 | 1 | 36 | 1 | 31 | 1 | 24 | 1 | 19 | 1 | 28 | 1 | 42 | 44 |
| Any swimming | 7 | 6 | 6 | 7 | 6 | 12 | 3 | 11 | 4 | 8 | 3 | 8 | 4 | 8 | 2 | 15 | 15 |
| Keep fit/yoga | 2 | 19 | 2 | 17 | 2 | 24 | 2 | 13 | 2 | 9 | 5 | 7 | 2 | 16 | 2 | 15 | 12 |
| Snooker/pool/billiards | 3 | 9 | 5 | 8 | 3 | 16 | 4 | 10 | 5 | 6 | 2 | 10 | 6 | 5 | 4 | 10 | 11 |
| Cycling | 5 | 8 | 8 | 4 | 4 | 14 | 7 | 4 | 8 | 3 | | 1 | 4 | 8 | 5 | 6 | 11 |
| Weight training | 3 | 9 | 6 | 7 | 6 | 12 | 6 | 5 | 7 | 4 | 6 | 6 | 9 | 3 | 5 | 6 | 6 |
| Any soccer | 5 | 8 | 4 | 11 | 4 | 14 | 5 | 7 | 2 | 9 | 3 | 8 | 6 | 5 | 5 | 6 | 5 |
| Golf | | 0 | | 0 | | 2 | | 1 | | 0 | | 0 | 9 | 3 | | 1 | 5 |
| Running (jogging etc.) | 8 | 4 | 3 | 13 | 8 | 8 | 7 | 4 | 8 | 3 | | 1 | | 1 | 5 | 6 | 4 |
| Tenpin bowls/skittles | 10 | 3 | | 1 | 10 | 3 | | 2 | | 0 | | 0 | 6 | 5 | 9 | 5 | 3 |
| Badminton | | 2 | | 2 | 10 | 3 | 7 | 4 | 8 | 3 | 7 | 3 | 3 | 10 | 10 | 3 | 2 |
| Tennis | | 2 | 8 | 4 | | 2 | | 2 | | 2 | | 1 | | 1 | | 2 | 2 |
| Table tennis | | 1 | 10 | 3 | 10 | 3 | | 1 | | 1 | | 1 | | 2 | | 1 | 2 |
| Cricket | | 0 | | 0 | 10 | 3 | 10 | 3 | 5 | 6 | 8 | 2 | | 0 | | 1 | 1 |
| Self defence/martial arts | 10 | 3 | | 2 | 9 | 5 | | 2 | | 1 | | 0 | 9 | 3 | | 2 | 1 |
| Basketball | 8 | 4 | | 2 | | 0 | | 1 | | 1 | | 1 | | 2 | | 2 | 1 |
| Carram-board | | 0 | | 0 | | 0 | | 1 | | 0 | 8 | 2 | | 0 | | 0 | – |
| Base (=100%) | | 478 | | 253 | | 147 | | 890 | | 514 | | 155 | | 116 | | 528 | 15,696 |

[1] Participation on at least one occasion in the previous four weeks.
1 ranking of individual sports within each ethnic group.

## Conclusions

An important result of the survey is the complexity of the whole issue. There is considerable variation in the levels of participation between different ethnic groups, between men and women and between different sports. The results also challenge the stereotypical view which suggests that low levels of participation in sport by certain groups are more a reflection of culture and choice rather than other constraints such as provision, affordability and access.

The issue of racial discrimination was touched on and although variable at its highest as many as one in five said that they had had a negative experience in sport related to their ethnicity. This should be a concern of policy makers.

> **ACTIVITY 4**
>
> State what factors may be responsible for the lower levels of participation rates by ethnic minority groups and suggest strategies in overcoming these inequalities.

# Gender

Gender means the biological aspect of a person, either male or female; gender roles refer to what different societies and cultures attribute as appropriate behaviour for that sex. These can vary from culture to culture and also change historically within a culture. We learn our expected role through a process called **socialisation**, which simply means the learning of cultural values and is equally applicable to table manners! We learn firstly through primary socialisation (mainly from our close family group at an early age), and then through secondary socialisation from the wider world of institutions. What emerges are the terms masculinity and femininity, in relation to gender roles.

Gender role models are first asserted in children's play and early in primary schools there are clear differences in the preferences of girls for less structured activities.

> **ACTIVITY 5**
>
> 1. Write a list of what you consider to be the dominant characteristics of these two gender roles, masculinity and femininity.
> 2. Write a list of the qualities necessary to succeed in sport at a high level.
> 3. Which gender role best fits the sport role model?

Matters of self image and body image – 'sports women being portrayed by the media as either muscle-bound superwomen or sleek and fit beyond the reach of normal women'.

Historical factors regarding the role of women cannot be discounted.

- Sport was always seen as a male preserve. Males developed and controlled most of the modern-day sports.
- Men, as the dominant group in society, denied or limited opportunities for women in the types of sports they could participate in.
- The role of women was stereotypically seen as being the housewife or mother.
- The types of activities women were encouraged to participate in were those considered appropriate to their role and therefore, socially acceptable.
- Middle and upper class ladies in the nineteenth century began to play sports such as golf, tennis, horse riding, archery and so on. These

Table 12.7. Women in the twentieth century: unequal sporting opportunity

| Reasons | Evidence | Action required |
|---|---|---|
| • Domestic role<br>• Social stereotyping<br>• Femininity<br>• Sport's association with male characteristics<br>• Sport's association with muscularity<br>• Blurred leisure time<br>• Male traditionally more money, power, transport, leisure<br>• Fewer role models<br>• Less media coverage | • Inequalities in PE and Sport<br>• Unequal provision of facilities<br>• Lack of variety of activities<br>• Few female coaches/administrators<br>• Restricted club access<br>• Lack of crèche facilities<br>• Unequal financial provision<br>• Less participation than men | • Equal provision in school Sport and PE<br>• More facilities for women<br>• Women-only sessions/target group<br>• Better links between schools and clubs<br>• Balance of recreational and competitive sport<br>• Widen women's horizons<br>• Media/advertise/publicise<br>• Create positive role models<br>• Promote health-related activities<br>• Positive discrimination of female coaches and administrators |

activities were not particularly physically demanding and did not involve physical contact or aggression.

- Activities that females could play socially with males were also highly valued, for example croquet followed by lawn tennis.

- Working class women had the least leisure opportunities of all.

In the present day, opportunities for women have increased in terms of greater independence via more disposable income and transport; availability of more sports, clubs and competitions, more media coverage and women in positions of responsibility in sports organisations. The overriding feature has been the increasing emphasis placed on health, fitness and the stereotypical feminine figure.

This has led major organisations like Sport England and the previous Sports Councils to target women as being under-represented in sport participation. They have actively pursued policies to promote sport/physical activity to this group.

## The body as a social construct

The notion that the body might be of sociological interest has become popular since the 1980s. This can relate to the 'ideal' shape of women and men.

There are four main perspectives of interpreting the body: medical, social construct, feminist and phenomenological.

- **Medical model:** The body is viewed as a machine that can break down and need repair. This is the dominant model for health and fitness.

- **Social construct model:** This belief holds the view that the way people view themselves and others is not shaped by biology but rather the sort of society in which they live and the sorts of ideas that are popular at any given moment. In a society like ours a thin body shape is likely to offer high status and be sought after. Douglas' work in 1966 showed that where women lived in societies where they were expected to do hard physical labour, larger body sizes for females are preferred and produced, as women seek to match up to these societal expectations.

- **Feminism:** Gendered expectations exist for both males and females though more negative connotations have become synonymous with the female body mainly due to natural bodily functions such as menstruation and shape. This can involve individuals having extreme responses to dieting and exercise.

  These factors lead people to shape their own self identity and self image. This can be called a phenomenological approach.

- **Phenomenological:** This approach is interested in how self image and identity are affected and how they shape notions of the 'normal' body shape. Body shape can be changed by radical dieting, exercise programmes and cosmetic surgery. Individuals often express how different they feel as people when they undergo changes to their body shape that they consider being more acceptable. This approach concentrates on the perception of the individual rather than on the social or collective ideas about the body and body shape.

## Sexism in sport

Sexism is the belief that one sex is inferior to the other, and is most often directed towards women. It is sometimes based on the idea that women are not best suited to roles which carry prestige and influence. Traditionally women have been denied the same legal, political, economic and social rights enjoyed by men.

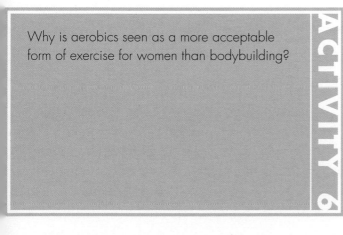

Why is aerobics seen as a more acceptable form of exercise for women than bodybuilding?

**ACTIVITY 6**

Don't underestimate the long-lasting effect of attitudes which are handed down through the generations. Sexism against women operates in sport in numerous ways:

### The Barr sex test

This requires a sample of cells to be scraped from the inside of a woman's cheek to determine the amount of 'Barr Bodies' present (chromatins). If the count drops below a minimum percentage, the athlete is disqualified. Princess Anne was the only female Olympic athlete who was not required to take this test.

## The Sex Discrimination Act (SDA) 1975

This act made sex discrimination unlawful in employment, training, education and the provision of goods, facilities and services; ie, a female should be treated in the same way as a male in similar circumstances.

- Competitive sport is excluded by section 44 of the Act. Separate competitions for men and women are allowed where 'the physical strength, stamina or physique puts her at a disadvantage to the average man'. Problems have occurred where female referees and PE teachers have been denied promotion on the grounds of being a woman, and some successful appeals have been made.

- Private sports clubs can legally operate discriminatory policies, under Sections 29 and 34. After an appeal in 1987, the EC recommended that all clubs which are not genuinely private must remove any barriers which discriminate against men or women.

## Women and professional sport

Professional sport still tends to favour men, even in activities such as pool, where physical strength differences could be questioned.

Only women who are very dedicated and committed move through from participation to performance sports. Myths and negative stereotypes still abound, and the media give much less coverage to women's sport:

- Surveys have shown that national newspapers give less than 6% of total sport space to women's sport.
- The Women's Sport Foundation found in a four-week period in 1991, a 90% male bias in photographs and articles in newspapers.
- Television rarely covers women's team games which the majority of school girls play, even though the national teams are internationally quite successful.
- There are more sport competitions for men.
- Financial constraints affect women more than men, as they attract less sponsorship to help with training, equipment, travelling and general fees.

Female power in sports organisations and levels of administration have not matched the rise in female sport participation.

- Few women reach the top levels of coaching: in 1992 there were only eight female coaches at the Olympics, compared with 92 male coaches.
- Mixed governing bodies, such as swimming, badminton, tennis, riding and cycling all show a poor ratio of female decision makers in proportion to the amount of female participants.

The problem has increased with a more professional and bureaucratic environment, and perhaps reflects the inappropriateness of the male model of sport, women's lack of access to political systems and the poor recruitment mechanisms operating in these institutions.

However, improvements are occurring slowly. The first woman Vice President of the IOC was appointed in 1997.

Female football in the United Kingdom is now professional. The Football Association set up a full-time professional league of women's teams in 2000. Millions of pounds was spent and women

players can train full time. Women's football is confirmed as the UK's fastest growing sport.

- 1993 – 500 clubs
- 2005 – 6,200 clubs

England ladies have a full-time coach and 1,000 players attend 30 regional centres of excellence.

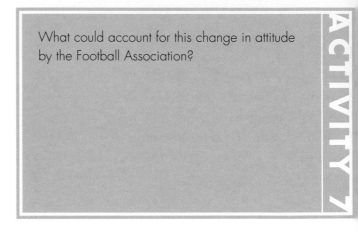

ACTIVITY 7

What could account for this change in attitude by the Football Association?

An interesting competition took place in 2003 when Annika Sorenstam became the first female golfer to take on the men in professional competition in 58 years: 'I'm not putting the guys to the test here, or men against women. I would like to emphasise that. I don't want to get into any political things. I don't have anything to do with that. It's not any goal. I don't want to put the guys on the defensive'. Although it caused a storm of protest from certain quarters the event went ahead. Annika did not make the cut but she was certainly not outplayed and has caused us all some pause for thought.

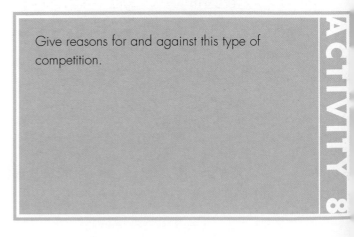

ACTIVITY 8

Give reasons for and against this type of competition.

## The Womens Sports Foundation (WSF)

This is a voluntary organisation promoting the interests of women and girls in sport and recreation. There is a network of regional groups and a wide range of activities and events are organised. Their regular publication is *Women in Sport Magazine*.

## Female participation in recent years

In 1996 The General Household Survey (GHS) reported that men were more likely to participate in a sport or physical activity than women. 87% of men compared with 77% of women had taken part in at least one activity during the previous 12 months.

## The state of play

- Six out of ten women (58%) compared with seven out of ten men (71%) participate in either outdoor or indoor sport.

- For both genders, walking was the most popular activity with 73% of men and 64% of women having walked at least two miles in the previous year.

- Women are more likely than men to have received tuition (27% compared with 19% of regular participants).

- Over three times as many males as females participated competitively in the previous 12 months (32% of regular male participants in comparison to 10% of regular female participants).

- Men are more likely to be a member of a sports club.

- The greatest differences in participation between men and women are to be found in:
  - Cue sports (7.9% of women and 32.6% of men)
  - Soccer (1% of women and 24.3% of men)
  - Cycling (16% of women and 27% of men)
  - Weight training (6.1% of women and 27% of men)
  - Golf (4.4% of women and 18.8% of men)
  - Darts (3.9% of women and 14.2% of men)
  - Fishing (1.1% of women and 10.3% of men)

- Participation rates for women are higher than men in:
  - Indoor swimming (37% of women and 32.5% of men)

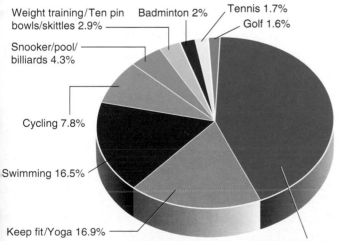

Fig 12.7. Women's top 10 sports in GB in 1996 (GHS) participation on one or more occasions in the previous four weeks

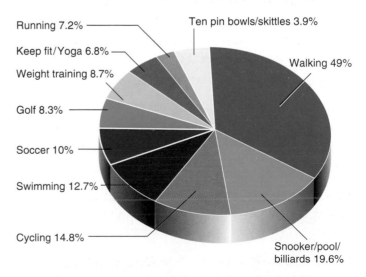

Fig 12.8. Men's top 10 sports in GB in 1996 (GHS) participation on one or more occasions in the previous four weeks

– Keep Fit/Yoga (29.4% of women and 10.4% of men)

– Horse riding (4.1% of women and 1.8% of men)

The General Household Survey indicates general trends within those sports with the largest participation rates, it fails however to identify significant growth patterns within sports starting from a relatively small participation base.

The following participation figures have been supplied by the respective national governing bodies. They reveal substantial growth in sports which have traditionally been viewed as 'male sports'.

Table 12.8. Cricket participation rates in England, October 1997–September 1998

|  | Girls | Boys |
|---|---|---|
| Primary Schools | 354,040 | 625,350 |
| Secondary Schools | 138,908 | 649,067 |
|  | Women | Men |
| Total No. Club | 187 | 6,697 |
| Participants | 4,267 | 220,784 |

Football is the number one sport for girls and women. There are now 61,000 women competing in clubs affiliated to the Football Association and there is also a similar increase in the number of girls' football teams which are developing within schools. There are 40,000 more under-14 girls playing at school than ten years ago.

Table 12.9. Football female participation rates in England, October 1989–September 1998

| Seniors | 1989 | 1993 | 1997 | 1999 |
|---|---|---|---|---|
| Teams | 263 | 400 | 600 | 700 |
| Players | 7,000 | 10,000 | 14,000 | 17,500 |
| Juniors |  |  |  |  |
| Teams | – | 80 | – | 1,000 |
| Players | – | 2,000 | – | 25,000 |

**ACTIVITY 9**

Why has there been an increase in female football participation in the UK?

One problem holding back the amount of girls taking up the sport, however, is the lack of career prospects. There are still only approximately 19 England-based professional players.

The FA has put in place a series of initiatives to increase opportunities:

- In 1997 it launched its Talent Development Plan for Women's Football
- Establishment of 42 Centres of Excellence – to develop 10–16 year olds
- 19 Women's Football Academies – 16 years plus
- In 2001 the National Women's Player Development Centre was launched in Loughborough University – for the most promising.

See pp 412–3 for a comparison of the USA approach towards female soccer.

Kay (1994) confirmed that women are constrained in their leisure time by the needs of housekeeping and caring for dependants and by lower car ownership than men. These effects are stronger for women in the lower socio-economic groups. Women's participation in indoor sport has grown, mainly due to the fitness boom and aerobic classes but is still in decline in terms of outdoor sports. Fears of attack in urban parks and the countryside have been cited as additional problems faced by women in addition to time and transport constraints.

Table 12.11 gives some of the reasons why women have less time for sport than men.

Table 12.10. Growth in women's Rugby Union

|  | 1988 | 1992 | 1996 | 1999 |
|---|---|---|---|---|
| Total no. of clubs* | 263 | 400 | 600 | 700 |
| No. of youth clubs U16's | 7,000 | 10,000 | 14,000 | 17,500 |
| No. of senior registered players | – | 80 | – | 1,000 |
| Other players including students & merit table players | – | 2,000 | – | 25,000 |

* Many clubs have more than one team.

Table 12.11. How the hours of the week are spent for the average male and female

|  | Full-time working male | Full-time working female |
|---|---|---|
| Work and travel to work | 47.2 | 42.3 |
| Household chores, essential cooking and shopping | 12.0 | 24.5 |
| Other non-discretionary activities (other shopping, caring for children, personal hygiene) | 13.9 | 18.6 |
| Free time | 45.9 | 33.6 |

*Note*: this table assumes 7 hours sleep per night.
*Source*: the Henley Centre, 1991.

## Girls and physical education policies

Physical Education policies, through the government initiatives in the National Curriculum, can still appear to show preferences for the competitive team games, sex-differentiated programmes and traditional teaching methods that may alienate many girls.

NIKE and the Youth Sport Trust are cooperating in a scheme that aims to support the delivery of Physical Education and sport to girls, 11–14 years of age, in secondary schools.

### ACTIVITY 10

Women continue to face social, political and prejudicial barriers to sport. Identify as many examples of inequalities as you can under these three categories.

## The Brighton Declaration on Women and Sport 1994

In Brighton on 5–8 May 1994, sport policy and decision makers at both national and international level met. It was organised by the British Sports Council and supported by the British Olympic Committee; 82 countries took part. There was a wish to increase the momentum that had already begun to narrow the gap between male and female sport participation across many continents.

The following points were developed:

1. Equal opportunity should be available through all social structures, and anti-discrimination legislation should be implemented.

2. Facilities should take into account the needs of women, particularly in the provision of childcare and safety.

3. Physical education in particular should take into account the differing approaches and aspirations of girls to active sport involvement, compared with those of boys.

4. Women involved in high performance sport should be supported in terms of competition opportunities, rewards, incentives and recognition.

5. Sporting organisations should develop policies and programmes to increase the number of women coaches, advisers, decision makers, officials, administrators and sports personnel at all levels. Particular attention needs to be directed at recruitment, development and retention.

6. Research and information in sport should equally reflect women's involvement.

7. Action for change must be coordinated. Women themselves can do much to improve the situation but this can only really be effective if they are helped through the social structures operating.

# Windhoek Call for Action 1998

By 1998 over 200 organisations worldwide had adopted the Brighton Declaration. In 1998 the second World Conference was held in Windhoek, Namibia, resulting in the Windhoek Call for Action.

From Brighton to Windhoek 'Facing the Challenge' – this is a document produced by the UK Sports Council and the International Working Group on Women and Sport.

The publication charts the progress made from 1994–1998 in developing a sporting culture that

**Fig 12.9.** Women can be just as aggressive as men

enables and values the full involvement of women in every aspect of sport. It provides an international overview of strategies and action plans adopted by women and sports in various countries. It considers the challenge that lies ahead and the implementation of the Windhoek Call for Action.

## What women can do:

- Develop a positive attitude to a healthy lifestyle; find out what is available locally and encourage a friend to go with them; be determined!

- Having developed an interest, join a club to gain access to coaching and facilities; lobby a governing body, local authority and the media to increase availability and opportunity of coaching, facilities, competition and coverage.

- Attend courses to improve career prospects; apply for senior positions; become a coach or administrator; gain relevant qualifications.

- Be aware that family responsibilities can coexist with other aspirations.

## What organisations can do:

- Ensure equality of opportunity to acquire sports skills.

- Adopt policies on child care, transport, access, pricing, and programming of facilities.

- Recognise that women do not form an homogeneous group. Women who have disabilities, are members of an ethnic minority, have heavy domestic responsibilities, have busy working lives, or are school leavers, will all require some specific action directed at them.

- Positive images of women should be widely seen in a variety of sport promotional material and not only the traditionally female sports. This will help provide much-needed role models for young girls.

- Redress inequalities in competition, coaching, financial assistance and improve the talent identification process.

- Review recruitment practices and establish appropriate training and allow flexible working hours.

- Publicise the achievements of women's contributions to sport.

Sport England investigated the specific needs and preferences of women and they came up with five principles called the '5c's':

- promote **confidence**
- a **comfortable** atmosphere
- **choice** of activity
- **convenience** of programmes
- **consultation**.

## The International Working Group on Women and Sport (IWG)

This is an informal coordinating body consisting of governmental and non-governmental organisations which was established as an outcome to the Brighton conference with the aim of promoting the development of opportunities for girls and women in sport and physical activity.

# Sport and people with disabilities

According to the Labour Force Survey 2004 there are 6.5 million adults with disabilities in Britain; 11.1% of the population. Approximately 5 million have a disability severe enough to limit everyday activities and 1 million have a learning disability;

What do the four levels of foundation, participation, performance and excellence mean? Discuss the main issues which affect women's involvement in sport.

ACTIVITY 11

69% are over the age of 60 and only 5% are under 30 years of age.

Many people experience discrimination which effectively excludes them from active social participation. Yet sport can help to integrate them into the rest of society and add to their quality of life. De Pauw and Gavron (1995) described the barriers as similar to those for women – lack of organised programmes and informal early experiences, role models, access, and of economic, physiological and social factors. In the UK the special needs of athletes with disabilities are catered for by six national disability sports organisations:

1. The British Amputee Sports Association
2. The UK Sports Association for People with Mental Handicap
3. Cerebral Palsy Sport
4. The British Les Autres Sports Association
5. Disability Sport England, formerly the British Sports Association for the Disabled, probably the most important organisation in the UK for people with disabilities
6. The British Paralympic Association.

A new organisation, the English Federation of Disability Sport (EFDS), acts as the main supporting and coordinating body for the development of sport for all people with disabilities. This is part of a recently restructured disability sport network. In turn the EFDS has the support and direct involvement of all the major disability sport organisations and will promote a corporate approach at national and regional level to determine priorities and the implementation of programmes.

A growing number of opportunities exist; the National Federation of Gateway Clubs has over 660 affiliated clubs, giving 40,000 people with disabilities an opportunity to take part in leisure activities.

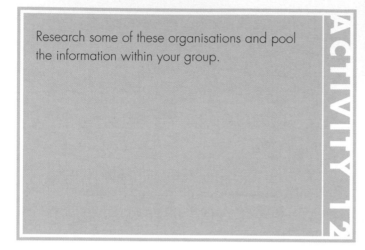

Research some of these organisations and pool the information within your group.

ACTIVITY 12

Fig 12.10. Wheelchair tennis

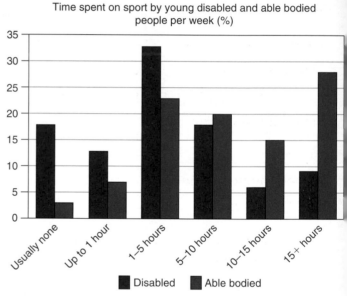

Fig 12.11. Young people with disabilities have a low rate of participation

*Source: Sport England's Disability Survey 2000 – Young People with a Disability and Sport.*

# Disability sport

A term used to suggest a more positive approach towards the participation in sport of people with disabilities. It covers people with a physical, sensory or mental impairment. The term disability is used when impairment adversely affects performance. Other terms used are handicapped sports; sports for the disabled; adapted sport; wheelchair sport and deaf sport.

Competitive sports have either been designed specifically for people with disabilities, such as goalball, boccia and polybat for the visually impaired or have been modified, such as volleyball and wheelchair basketball/tennis.

Current trends tend to focus on the sport rather than on the disability, to allow closer involvement with mainstream sport which previously has not catered for the needs of athletes with disabilities. The increasing numbers of participation should provide role models for people with disabilities. It is very important that all these organisations, both mainstream and special needs, cooperate and pool their resources in joint programmes of work; the creation of one federated organisation might help the situation.

Integration into mainstream sport does not have to mean participating at the same time as everyone else. It is more significant that facilities, competitions, training and coaching should be equally available to people with disabilities as to able-bodied people.

# Inclusiveness

Developing an inclusive approach to all aspects of school life, including physical activity, can act as a route into inclusion in the wider community.

## Goalball

- A 3-a-side game.

- Aim is to score a goal by rolling the ball along the floor into your opponent's goal.

- Developed for visually impaired people.

- Features which enable visually impaired people to play:
  - The ball has a bell inside
  - The playing court has tactile markings
  - All players wear eyeshades to ensure that everyone is equal when it comes to visual perception.

- Goalball is currently played in 87 countries.

- It is a paralympic sport, and has European and World Championships.

- British Blind Sport (BBS) is the organisation responsible for the sport in the UK.

- Approximately 15 clubs and school teams in the UK.

- The BBS organises 10 one-day tournaments a year, termly national schools competition, national championships and the British Goalball Cup.

- There are at present no award schemes or coaching courses for Goalball.

## Polybat

- A one-to-one hitting game played on a modified table tennis table.

- The table has no net and has panels on the two long sides of the table.

- Aim is to hit the ball past your opponent and off the end of the table or to cause your opponent to lift the ball off the table.

- The name Polybat came from Nottingham Polytechnic who invented the game, and the hitting bat.

- Developed as a result of an increased level of young people who had severe impairments entering the special school system in the 1980s.

- In 1990 the game was introduced into the Disability Sport England National Mini Games and is now played at numerous junior regional events.

- A fast growing sport currently played in Brazil, Canada, New Zealand, Spain and the USA.

## Boccia

- Boccia pronounced 'botcha'.

- Similar to bowls.

- Target game.

- Aim is to get your Boccia balls closer to the jack than your opponents.

- Played individually (IvI), in pairs or in teams of three.

- Originally designed for people with a severe impairment and in particular for people with cerebral palsy.

*(Continued)*

*(Continued)*

- All participants must play from a seated position.

- Played locally in schools and clubs, at regional and national competitions and internationally at the Paralympics and World Games.

- Internationally it is played in over 30 countries.

- An estimated 5,000 people play Boccia in UK.

- Coordinating body is The British Boccia Federation.

*Source:* Tutor File Higher Sports Leaders Award British Sports Trust.

The main barrier to the participation of people with disabilities in the activities of their choice is as much a matter of social attitudes and environmental barriers as their medical condition.

The Inclusion Spectrum, designed by Ken Black, the Inclusive Sport Officer for the Youth Sport Trust, identifies five different approaches:

- **Inclusive**: activities where everyone is included without adaptations or modification

- **Modified activities:** changes to rules, area or equipment are made in order to include people with disabilities

- **Parallel activities:** participants do the same activity but approach the task according to disability

- **Included activity:** 'reverse integration' where people with disabilities participate in games adapted specifically with disability in mind such as boccia and goalball

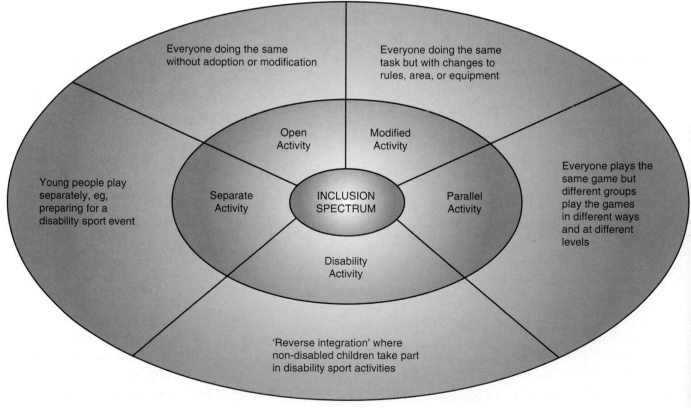

Fig 12.12. The inclusion spectrum

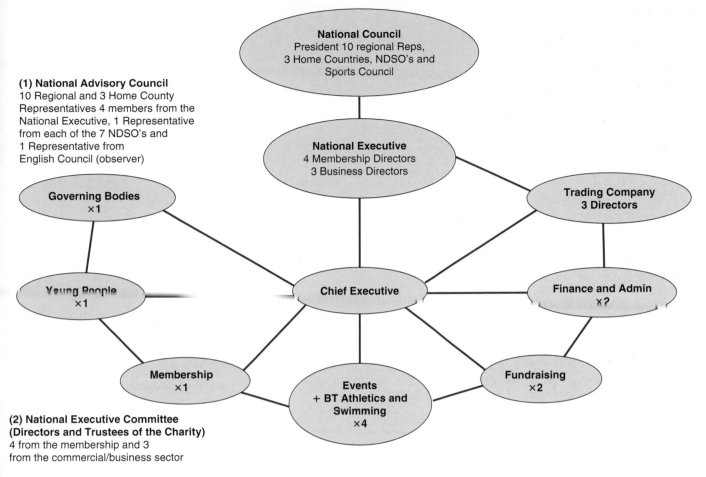

**(1) National Advisory Council**
10 Regional and 3 Home County
Representatives 4 members from the
National Executive, 1 Representative
from each of the 7 NDSO's and
1 Representative from
English Council (observer)

**(2) National Executive Committee
(Directors and Trustees of the Charity)**
4 from the membership and 3
from the commercial/business sector

**Fig 12.13.** Disability Sport England – organisation

- **Separate activities:** where people with disabilities practise an activity on their own or with disabled peers, eg preparing for a disabled sports event.

## Improving opportunities

### Disability Sport England www. euroyellowpages.com/dse/dispeng.htm

This organisation was formally known as the British Sports Association for the Disabled which was founded in 1961 by Sir Ludwig Guttman, a neuro-surgeon who worked from Stoke Mandeville hospital.

Disability Sport England is about:

- promoting the benefits of sport and making it accessible to everyone regardless of ability.
- helping talented athletes reach the highest levels such as the Paralympic Games.

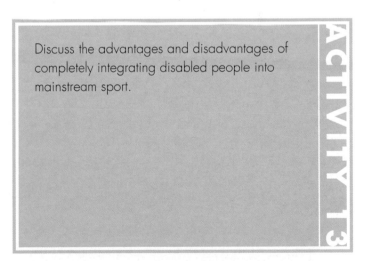

Discuss the advantages and disadvantages of completely integrating disabled people into mainstream sport.

ACTIVITY 13

Liaison with the Sports Councils will mean a more coordinated approach towards setting foundations in developing young people; talent development; coaching; national governing bodies; local authorities; membership services and management administration.

## The aims

- To **provide** opportunities for people with disabilities to participate in sport.
- To **promote** the benefits of sport and physical recreation by people with disabilities.
- To **support** organisations in providing sporting opportunities for people with disabilities.
- To **educate** and make people aware of the sporting abilities of people with disabilities.
- To **enhance** the image, awareness and understanding of disability sport.
- To **encourage** people with disabilities to play an active role in the development of their sport.

## Sport England

Sport England has supported the development of national bodies for disability sport and the appointment of specialised regional and local Development Officers.

The previous Sports Council, Yorkshire and Humberside (1995), showed good practice in governing body schemes in table tennis, canoeing and gymnastics.

Sport England has implemented various projects aimed at improving sporting opportunities for people with disabilities.

1. The campaign 'Every Body Active' was set up following research which highlighted several major problems encountered by people with disabilities; in particular a lack of awareness amongst mainstream leisure providers and PE teachers as to the special needs of this group of people.

2. The 'Pro-motion' campaign established in 1990 is now a national programme intending to raise awareness, training, liaison and resources.

Much of Sport England's work is regionally developed and coordination is therefore difficult to achieve. However, several common features emerge:

- promotion and development of training programmes

- inclusion of information about disabled sport in publications
- liaison with relevant organisations
- encouragement of local authorities and governing bodies to consider the needs of people with disabilities
- development of coaching opportunities
- appointment of sport development officers with special interest in this area.

The Sports Council's policy document 'Sport and People with Disabilities' was published in 1993, and is a national statement of intent for which it will be accountable.

The former Conservative government carried out research and published a report, 'Building on Ability'. As a result, the following initiatives were set up:

- the development of a national disability equality training course
- the identification of examples of good practice involving the participation at a local level of young people with disabilities
- a national governing bodies liaison project, involving 40 schemes and promoting integration with 23 governing bodies

**Fig 12.14.** There are many sports which can be adapted for people with disabilities

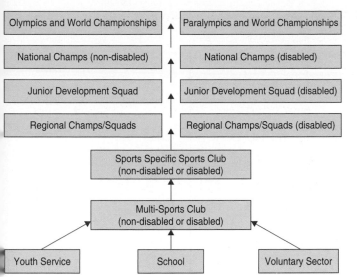

| Olympics and World Championships | Paralympics and World Championships |
|---|---|
| National Champs (non-disabled) | National Champs (disabled) |
| Junior Development Squad | Junior Development Squad (disabled) |
| Regional Champs/Squads | Regional Champs/Squads (disabled) |

Sports Specific Sports Club
(non-disabled or disabled)

Multi-Sports Club
(non-disabled or disabled)

| Youth Service | School | Voluntary Sector |
|---|---|---|

**Fig 12.15.** Pathways in sport for people with disabilities

- support the Pro-motion programme which seeks to develop sport and recreational opportunities for those with a multiple disability.

## Local authorities

Local authorities play a crucial role at local level, because of their leisure departments. The planning and architects departments are also important when trying to build functional and imaginative facilities. When facility tenders are reviewed and renewed under the compulsory competitive tendering regulations, the needs of people with disabilities must be considered.

## Excellence

Excellence in sport performance has grown substantially, both in the number of competitions and variety of activities. The Paralympics (so called because it runs parallel to the Olympics) and the World Championships are the notable examples.

As knowledge about training, coaching and the input of sport science increases, the performance levels of athletes with disabilities will undoubtedly improve.

## Classification

This is an attempt to group sport competitors to enable fair competition. It was initially used for sport by gender, where separate competitions developed for men and women, and by weight in sports such as boxing. It is now used to include individuals with disabilities.

Two types of classification are used:

- **Medical classification:** this developed in the 1940s and was dominant into the 1990s. It was based on the level of spinal cord lesion. It was designed to enable individuals with similar severity of impairment to compete against one another. It was used for wheelchair athletes and amputees. Many other disability sport federations adopted this system, resulting in a multiple classification system.

- **Functional classification:** an integrated classification system that places emphasis on sport performance by disability groupings rather than by specific disability. This has enabled disability sport to move on from its original rehabilitation base to elite competitive sport. Wheelchair basketball was the first Paralympic sport to experiment with this system. This system demands that athletes be evaluated on what they can and cannot do in a particular sport.

## Facilities

Facilities are gradually improving for users with disabilities, partly under the Safety at Sports Grounds Act 1975, and also through a growing desire to provide access. The programming of activities and the attitude of staff are also important considerations.

Outdoor facilities are increasing provision, for example, those run by the Calvert Trust and Scope. Several important sports centres exist, such as the Ludwig Guttman Sports Centre at Stoke Mandeville and the Midland Sports Centre for the Disabled in Coventry.

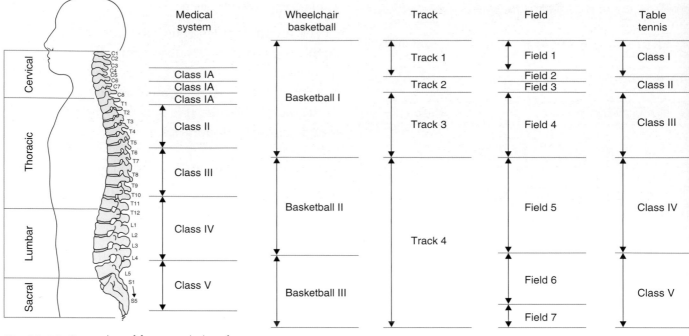

**Fig 12.16.** Examples of functional classification systems
*Source*: Disability and Sport.

**Table 12.12.** Cerebral palsy athletes (USCPAA and CPN-ISRA) functional profiles

| Class | Functional profiles |
|---|---|
| Class 1 | Moderate to severe spasticity – severe involvement of all four limbs. Poor trunk control. Poor functional strength in upper extremities. |
| Class 2 | Moderate to severe spasticity – severe to moderate involvement of upper extremities and trunk. Poor functional strength and control of upper extremities. Propels wheelchair with legs. |
| Class 3 | Fair functional strength and moderate control in upper extremities. Almost full functional strength in dominant upper extremity. Propels wheelchair with one or both arms slowly. |
| Class 4 | Moderate to severe involvement of lower limbs. Functional strength and minimal control problems in upper extremities. Uses wheelchair for daily activities and sports. |
| Class 5 | Good functional strength; minimal control problems in upper extremities. Ambulates on two legs for competition. |
| Class 6 | Moderate to severe involvement of all four extremities and trunk; walks without aids. May use assistive devices for track events. |
| Class 7 | Moderate to minimal hemiplegia. Good functional ability is non-affected side. Walks without aids. |
| Class 8 | Minimally affected hemiplegic or monoplegic. Minimal coordination problems. Good balance and is able to run and jump freely. |

*Note*: 1–4 wheelchair for competition, 5–8 ambulatory for competition.
*Source*: Disability and Sport.

ACTIVITY 14

- Make a checklist to see how a local leisure facility is designed to cater for the needs of people with disabilities in your area.
- Once you have agreed a comprehensive list, visit a variety of facilities (ie, indoor, countryside, water) and review their effectiveness.
- Suggest effective modifications which could be made.

# Future trends: (adapted from de Pauw)

| Sport for all | Elite level |
|---|---|
| • Increasing numbers of individuals with disabilities will participate at all levels in the sport pyramid.<br><br>• Equity issues will continue to be addressed for groups who suffer the lowest levels of participation, particularly females and low income groups.<br><br>• Public awareness and acceptance of disability sport will increase. | • Structured competitive programmes will operate from local, regional, national and international levels.<br><br>• Coordination between sport organisations concerned with disability sport with those that are more sport specific.<br><br>• Athletes with disabilities will continue to specialise in sport events, with classification and competitions becoming sport specific. This will result in improved standards of performance.<br><br>• People with disabilities will participate more as coaches and officials especially as current athletes retire from competition. |

# Summary

- Societal attitudes are changing towards wider participation and competition by athletes.
- The original rehabilitation purpose through sport has given way to sport for sports sake.
- The Olympic sport movement will continue to shape the future direction of disability sport.
- Classification, drug testing, advances in technology, improved training and coaching, techniques and sports medicine will further influence disability sport.

# Sport for people aged 50 and over

This age group is increasingly affluent as personal pensions improved during the twentieth century and people may have more disposable income. They are also generally more active and healthy than ever before, and an increase in physical activity can help to prevent the inevitable onset of ageing. Approximately three slightly strenuous sessions per week of 20 minutes duration are advised. Medical advice may need to be sought, particularly if the person has not participated in physical activity for some time. The important checks are cardiovascular, respiratory and orthopaedic.

## Ageing by numbers

*   89,000 men in their nineties in 2001
*   324,000 women in their nineties in 2001.

## Barriers to physical activity for older people

*   Perception of self (How we see ourselves)
*   I'm too fat
*   My health is not good enough
*   I'm too old
*   I'm not the sporty type
*   I'm too shy or embarrassed
*   Time barriers (or excuses?)
*   I'm too busy with work
*   I have grandchildren to look after
*   I have an elderly relative to look after

Social benefits of sport are also stressed, because this can be a time of dramatic change for many people. Some may become widowed; some may retire or be made redundant, and family obligations may change. Active lifestyles can help people overcome great social change. Thus, this group of people comprises a potentially rich market for sport.

**ACTIVITY 15**

In 1990 Allied Dunbar produced a survey on the physical capabilities of over 2,000 men and women; it was published in 1992. Research some of the findings. (This could link in with your Exercise Physiology unit.)

Since the Sports Council's campaign, '50+ All to Play For' in 1983, more activities have been promoted for this age group. Here are some of the most popular ones:

*   Indoors – keep fit; aerobics; dance; carpet and short mat bowls; table tennis.
*   Outdoors – walking/rambling; cycling; jogging; archery; canoeing; golf; tennis; swimming; cricket; hockey; bowls.

Many other more adventurous activities are also enjoyed.

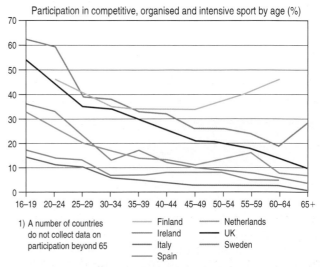

**Fig 12.17.** Participation in competitive and organised sport declines with age in most EU countries
*Source:* Compass 1999.

**ACTIVITY 16**

Select some of the activities mentioned and suggest why they are particularly suited to people over 50. Think about the physiological and social aspects of the activity.

Competitive days need not be over; many sports have veteran and 50+ sections. Other ways of getting involved are as sports leaders, such as coach, referee, club officials. Organisations which should be involved in developing this kind of activity are: local authority departments responsible for sport and recreation; sports centres and swimming pools; adult education classes; the national and regional sports councils; the governing bodies of sport.

# Benefits of physical activity for older people

## Social benefits

Promotion of a more positive and active image of older people by:

- Increased contribution to society by older people
- Enhanced social integration, formation of new friendships and the widening of social networks
- Role maintenance and new role acquisition
- Maintenance of caring skills.

## Health benefits

- Prevention and management of chronic heart disease and stroke
- Prevention and management of type II diabetes
- Management of weight and obesity
- Prevention of osteoporosis

- Reduction of accidental falls
- Prevention of (colon) cancer
- Improvement in length and depth of sleep
- Even when taken up in later life.

## Psychological benefits

- Reduction in stress and anxiety and improvement in overall psychological well-being
- Reduction in depression
- Improvements in cognitive function, self-esteem and self worth
- Improvements in perception of health
- A reduction of loneliness and isolation
- Enhanced feeling of worth to society.

# Sport for young people

First of all we must recognise that not all young people share common lifestyles; they may have different socio-economic backgrounds, parental attitudes, social experiences and so on. Youth is often seen as a transition from school and childhood to work and adulthood. Individuals who struggle with this transition often become isolated from the main community and 'drop out', become deviant and when considered in larger numbers can form an underclass. This group will experience exclusion from society. Sport participation is mostly a result of early positive experiences in physical education curricula and recreational activities.

As early as 1960 the Wolfenden Report was concerned that the lack of provision for sport in the United Kingdom was poorer than in other European states and this led to the **'post school gap'** which results in a drop in participation on leaving school.

Some constraining factors are:

- the concentration in clubs on the talented youngsters
- the tradition of single sport clubs in the United Kingdom as opposed to more multi-sport clubs in Europe.

**ACTIVITY 17**

List other possible reasons why young people may 'drop out' of sport on leaving school and suggest ways in which to combat this.

Physical activities are promoted by a wide range of individuals and agencies, such as:

- the education system, in particular the physical education programme
- sports clubs and governing bodies
- play workers
- the youth service
- local authorities.

It is necessary for these agencies to coordinate their efforts. For example, national governing bodies and schools associations need to jointly plan programmes which will support a common youth sport policy.

In previous years, the Sports Council targeted the age band 13–24 years. However, recent research (General Household Survey) suggested that low participation was not the problem, but that young people do not play as many sports as children.

**ACTIVITY 18**

Consider the following groups of young people and suggest some of the *advantages* and *disadvantages* they face in terms of sports participation:
- full-time education
- full-time employment
- unemployed
- young women
- young mothers
- young people in rural areas.

However, young females still participate less than their male counterparts. On leaving school, more casual sports are enjoyed, alongside adventure sports and health-related activities.

## Obesity and young children

The British Heart Foundation report 'Couch Kids – the growing epidemic' published in 2000 says, 'Tackling overweight and obesity must start in childhood for two reasons:

because it is much easier to prevent becoming overweight than to correct it,

because it is easier to adopt healthy eating patterns when children are young.

The report contains some alarming statistics:

- Nearly 70% of 2–12 year olds eat biscuits, sweets or chocolate at least once a day, while less than 20% eat fruit and vegetables more than once a day.

- More than a third of children are not meeting the recommended activity guidelines – generally agreed to be at least one hour's moderate intensity activity each day.

- The time traditionally spent on active play is being used up on sedentary activities like watching television or playing computer games. More than a quarter of 11–16 year olds watch TV for more than four hours each day.

- Active transport to and from school has decreased. Car journeys to school have doubled in the last 20 years. Just one per cent of children cycle to school.

Sport England launched its Sportsmark Award and Activemark to encourage schools to help children adopt more positive attitudes towards physical activity.

## Youth and delinquency

A large body of literature has developed worldwide on this issue suggesting increasing concern at governmental levels. The general consensus appears to be that sport:

- increases self esteem, mood and perception of competence and mastery, especially through outdoor recreation
- reduces self-destructive behaviour (smoking, drug use, substance abuse, suicidal tendencies)
- improves socialisation both with peer group and adults
- improves scholastic attendance and performance.

### Schemes

Several schemes run to help this particular group but usually are not long enough and are participated in voluntarily suggesting those more hardened offenders will not benefit. An experience of a few days to a few weeks may in the short term be of benefit but if the individuals return to the same physical and social complex or deprivation the old values and behaviour patterns will re-emerge.

Sport therefore may not be the whole solution but may form part of it.

# Socio-economic groups

The term 'social class' can refer to a person's income, status in society, family background and educational experiences. The development of sport in the nineteenth century was initially in the powerful and influential hands of the upper and middle classes. The working class male stamped his presence on the new mass spectator sports of football, boxing and horse racing, but administrative control was still in the hands of the middle classes. The working classes had to wait for the provision of recreational rights and public facilities.

Much research has concluded that lower socio-economic backgrounds do lead to a lower participation rate in sporting activities. This can be attributed to a variety of reasons:

- the cost of facilities
- the dominant middle class culture which operates in sport centres
- the lack of leadership roles

- a general lack of health
- the lower self esteem of low income groups (in particular the unemployed) which can encourage feelings of helplessness, inferiority, and isolation from major social institutions.

Table 12.13. Participation in sport by socio-economic group (GHS, 1998)

| Socio-economic group | Percentage participating in at least one sport in last four weeks | | | |
|---|---|---|---|---|
| | 1987 | 1990 | 1993 | 1996 |
| Professional | 65 | 65 | 64 | 63 |
| Manager | 52 | 53 | 53 | 52 |
| Junior non-manual | 45 | 49 | 49 | 47 |
| Skilled manual | 48 | 49 | 46 | 45 |
| Semi-skilled | 34 | 38 | 36 | 37 |
| Unskilled | 26 | 28 | 31 | 23 |
| **Total** | **45** | **48** | **47** | **46** |
| Difference between professional and unskilled | 39 | 37 | 33 | 40 |

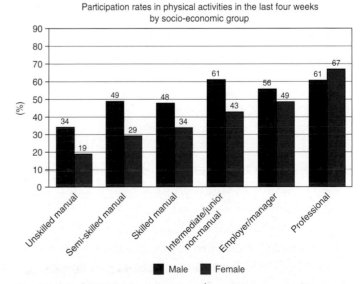

Fig 12.18. Participation varies with socio-economic group
*Source:* Centre for Leisure Research, GHS.

A working class 'sub culture' can operate where norms and values are different from the dominant group, and are passed down from one generation to the next. This has been termed the 'cycle of poverty', where one form of deprivation tends to reinforce another. It is a very complex area which the sport initiatives need to address if they are to be successful in mobilising this section of the community.

Social exclusion does not just affect recreational participation: its effect is also felt at the elite level and its costly preparation training.

We have looked at categories of people within society and particularly at the participation base of the sports pyramid. Now it is time to discover how some people manage to extend beyond the recreational and performance end of the sports continuum, and onwards to sporting excellence.

---

- Summarise the main factors which result in the socially excluded groups having fewer opportunities to participate in physical recreation and sporting activities.
- What 'action plans' could governing bodies and other relevant organisations put in place to improve this situation?

ACTIVITY 19

---

# Excellence
## What does 'excellence' mean?

Excellence can be defined as a 'special ability beyond the norm, to which many aspire but few go on to achieve'. There are some problems with using words like this. For example, we often talk about personal excellence, but this may not mean according to national or international standards. The athletes who broke records half a century ago were still excellent for their era, even though today their times or distances would not measure up. A performer could have excellent technique but not achieve the highest scores in top competition. For our purposes, excellence means the superior, elite athletes at both amateur and professional level, able bodied as well as disabled, who reach the pinnacle of performance in their chosen sport.

The 'sport for all' base, ie, the provision of sport for the masses and the elite, is a compatible system; the wider the base of the pyramid, the greater the apex. This was very much the philosophy of the former USSR, which promoted sport with a compulsory national fitness campaign, which was a coherent talent identification system followed by a rigorous training and coaching schedule. They believed that success at the highest levels could help reinforce the policies, lifestyles and attitudes of the political state and were prepared to fund a centralised approach to the achievement of a sports excellence programme, which would draw from the widest base of participants as possible.

Excellence usually suggests a specialism of one activity, and is judged by international and world standards.

The providers of excellence in sport are mainly: the DCMS, UK Sport, Sport England, British Olympic Association, Disability Sport England and the British Paralympic Association, SportsAid; the centres of excellence; sports schools; local authorities; sports clubs; school sport associations; schools.

Numerous strategies have been developed for various sections of the community, not only to encourage participation but also to enable talented and committed people to strive for excellence. Historically, the UK has not had a nationally organised plan for identifying talent, and it has mostly been an ad hoc approach with luck playing a large part. The support system for the development of excellence is mainly located outside schools.

# Why pursue excellence in sport?

- Sport represents a challenge in people's lifestyles which have become increasingly sedentary and controlled.

- Many people are also curious about their own and the human species' potential; sport is sometimes called the last frontier, as our limitations are still not yet known.

- Sport can provide an alternative employment path with the added attraction of high social status if high level success is achieved.

- It gives individuals a high self esteem, a feeling of worth and quality in their lives.

---

## KEY WORD

**Esteem:** to have great respect or high regard for. Talented athletes who reach the pinnacle of their sport are awarded honour and prestige that raises their social status. Sociologically this can give a finer analysis than a purely social class differentiation. Such athletes may become role models to younger children. Athlete's own self esteem is also raised by a sense of achievement.

---

## Social advantages of pursuing excellence

Sporting success can boost national pride and morale (governments are usually keen to be connected with this); a reduction in anti-social behaviour; the role models of sport attract a large spectator audience; economic benefits; the excellence end of the continuum feeds the base of sport for all.

## Disadvantages of excellence

- It is elitist – it can only serve the interests of a few.
- Costly resources are required for a minority of sports participants.
- Over-specialisation and obsession with a physical activity can occur, which may have damaging physiological and psychological effects.

- The moral value of sport can be lost due to the 'win at all costs' attitude, which is made worse when the stakes become higher.

During the last 20 years there has been increasing pressure from all sections of British sport for the administrators to concentrate more resources into the pursuit of excellence. A national strategy for achieving excellence has begun to take root (see fig 12.19). The key to achieving a nationally coherent programme lies in linking together all the complex jigsaw pieces which currently operate in isolation. The support services of sport science, sports medicine, lifestyle counselling and information technology must also be integrated to produce an effective multi-disciplinary approach. The days of the coach being the sole provider of support to the athlete are almost gone – particularly at the highest levels of performance. The coach–athlete relationship is still a crucial element,

Fig 12.19. National strategy for achieving excellence

but other people who hold specialist knowledge also play their part in the development of the athlete. Consistency from all the support team is paramount. The value of sport science is unquestioned but it must work alongside coaching expertise.

## Talent identification

Talent identification can be defined as the process by which children are encouraged to participate in the sports at which they are most likely to succeed, based on testing certain parameters as the first step in progressing from beginner to international athlete. Talent identification follows this as the next phase in the achievement of sporting success.

The United Kingdom has tended to rely on a number of uncoordinated factors such as being spotted by a sport scout or having the opportunity to belong to a club that specialises in a particular sport or coming from a supportive and higher economic social background.

Other countries such as the former USSR and East Germany had a much more proactive approach even early in the twentieth century. Today Australia is leading the way (see chapter 15).

The DCMS proposed in its Game Plan for Sport (2002) that they would encourage the delivery of future talent development programmes according to the Long Term Athlete Development Model (LTAD) developed by Balyi (1998). The model is based on five main principles:

- train and perform well long-term rather than winning
- train rather than over-compete
- broad generic skills before specialisation
- flexible talent development model to account for variation between sports
- athlete centred and involvement of parents – better integration of key partners

## Conclusion

Talent identification and consequent development of athletes to the elite stage requires a complexity of factors to come together.

The athletes themselves require certain physical, psychological and social advantages.

| Physical | Superior health and fitness; body composition for particular sport; trained energy systems; high pain threshold, etc. |
|---|---|
| Psychological | High competitiveness; high urge to achieve; persistence; dedication; mental toughness. |
| Social | Access to high quality facilities and coaching; reliable and sufficient funding; family support; coordinated sport policies; appropriate levels of local, regional and national competition. |

- Write an account of your own experiences in sport, from the early days to the time when you began to take a more serious interest.
- Make a note of your role models, family background, sex, race, schooling, sports club, peer group, and relate how each might have contributed positively or negatively towards your involvement in sport.

ACTIVITY 21

# Summary

- The broader the base of sport participation, the greater the talent pool from which to draw in order to increase the chances of sporting excellence.
- Unequal access to the 'sport for all' ideal will negatively affect the sports pyramid.
- Sport initiatives must take careful note of the complex nature of the various groups they seek to help.
- A nationally coordinated approach towards excellence needs to be further developed if Britain is to compete on equal terms with other nations.

## Review Questions

1. Draw the Sport Participation Pyramid or sport development continuum and briefly explain each stage.
2. What is meant by the term 'the dominant group' in society and how can this group affect sporting opportunities?
3. How can sport be an avenue of social mobility?
4. What does the term 'stacking' refer to in sporting situations?
5. Suggest four strategies organisations can implement in order to improve the participation of women in sporting and recreational activities.
6. Why is the 50+ age group a suitable target for sports organisations to target in order to increase their levels of participation in sporting and recreational activities?
7. What does the term 'Social Exclusion' mean and what measures can be taken to address the issues?
8. What is the significance of the emergence of the term 'Disability sport'?
9. What is the significance of the term 'Inclusiveness' when referring to disability and sporting participation?
10. What factors have led to a lower participation rate amongst the lower socio-economic groups?
11. What needs to be considered when using the term 'excellence in sport'?
12. Which organisations in particular are concerned with developing excellence in the United Kingdom? (see previous chapter.)
13. What advantages and disadvantages are there in the pursuit of excellence?
14. What is 'Talent identification' and what strategies are in place to develop it in the United Kingdom at present?
15. What physical, psychological and social factors are required for the development of an elite athlete?
16. How can the elite athletes be used to inspire and motivate young people to participate and continue in sport?
17. What is meant by Sports Science and what contributions can it make to the development of excellence in sport?
18. What do the terms commitment, resources and expertise in relation to excellence in sport mean?

# 13. Issues in the Modern Day Sports World

This chapter covers areas and issues in the sports world which cause concern and media interest. In order to gain a deeper insight into these issues, you will need to draw upon information and knowledge gained from other chapters

By the end of this chapter you should understand the following terms:

- Globalisation
- Commercialisation
- Sponsorship
- Media and its effects on sport
- Deviance
- Aggression
- Hooliganism
- Doping/drugs
- Sport and the law

A detailed analysis of how these issues affect and are in turn affected by the following international competitions will be made in chapter 14:

- Olympic Games
- World Cup

A brief outline of the Commonwealth, Paralympic and Asian Games is also included in chapter 14.

## KEY WORD

**Globalisation** is the process whereby different nations are more closely interrelated; this has its advantages for sport, but there is a danger of different cultures losing their true identity as the Western values of sport become increasingly dominant across the world. The influx of international players into home teams is also a reflection of globalisation.

## The commercialism of sport

Historically, sport has been used as a way of entertaining the public. As it developed the qualities to attract large crowds, the term 'spectator sports' emerged. Initially, sports would generate money on a more personal level. The participants could receive some monetary reward and the spectators would wager on the event, partly to increase the excitement of the event but also to have the opportunity to win more money than they could from their everyday occupation. When these entertainments became more regular, certain individuals recognised the opportunity to make more money using an organised approach. Promoters and patrons started to accrue more profit than the participants, and even the wagering became more structured.

Today this has evolved into a situation where sport is heavily commercialised, packaged and presented to worldwide audiences. Countries with a market economy have been most open to this kind of development; capitalism encourages its population to work in competitive conditions to create profitable enterprises. The availability of widespread television coverage has attracted large scale businesses who can use sport to promote their products, and the development of technology has meant that sports which had once been national pastimes, eg, basketball in the USA, are now able to look further afield and seek global audiences.

The potential for profit in the television age was realised in the 1980s, with the emergence of entrepreneurs like Robert Maxwell, Bernard Tapie, Kerry Packer and Rupert Murdoch. They recognised the loyal fans as captive customers and clubs as unexploited assets. More importantly they realised that gate receipts were no longer the key to profits. Media rights, sponsorship deals and merchandising were to become the future potential.

# The development of commercialisation

The large audiences needed to give support in the form of live spectators for gate receipts and possessing television sets to view the sports at home, tend to be found predominantly in advanced technological societies who possess enough free time, disposable income, and the means to travel easily to different sporting venues. It is no coincidence, therefore, that commercial sports originally began in the nineteenth century in Britain – the country to first develop industrialisation and communication networks.

Professional sport grew steadily and included activities such as cricket, ball games, prize fighting and pedestrianism. Competitors could be paid for their efforts and coaching and training methods developed alongside; more detail can be found in chapter 16.

It is interesting to see this development in Britain, which had, as its ruling class, the elite upper class who developed the 'amateur' concept which was aimed at keeping monetary values out of sport. The business side of sport was delayed in Britain in comparison to the USA, who had no compunction about putting sport and money together. By the 1990s, even in Britain, sport had become big business.

## Sporting goods

The manufacture of sports goods, once a specialist market producing equipment and clothing for the participants, has now become a sports industry providing mainstream fashion items for people who may never get out of breath! The development of trainers as a status symbol for young people is the result of a very successful advertising campaign.

The sports clothing and equipment industries form another important part of the global sports complex. Companies such as Nike, Reebok, Adidas and Slazenger have global businesses and employ thousands of people, many of them in less developed countries. Sales of sports clothing, equipment and shoes exceed $30 billion in the USA alone. Product endorsement by leading sports stars has a huge impact on global sales. Companies in sectors as diverse as whiskey and financial services regularly use sports sponsorship as a way to promote global brands.

## Changing the rules

Some sports have changed as a result of commercial interest. For example, rules to speed up the action to prevent spectator boredom, changes in scoring to create more excitement, evenly balancing competitors to achieve uncertain outcomes (as this has been proved to increase spectator interest) and providing breaks in play so sponsors can advertise their products. Reassuringly, however, the basic structure of most sports (ie, the format and goals) has remained the same.

## Changing organisations

The organisations in charge of individual sports have found that their remit has changed over the years. This again can be highlighted in Britain where the governing bodies were originally based on the principle of amateurism. They have had to adapt to commercial pressures, if they have wanted their sport to maintain its status. Amateur sport receives its main funding from sponsorship and individual donations. Some sports are wealthier than others, but they all need to pay for athletes' training, operating expenses and the staging of events. Staff with expertise in financial management and publicity are hired rather than those purely with an interest in the sport itself, and decisions related to revenue are not necessarily made with the good of the athletes at heart. This has led to some athletes seeking more control, 'taking on' the organisations concerned, and setting up their own players' association in order to project a collective voice; eg, the PGA (Professional Golf Association) the ATP (Association of Tennis Professionals). Athletes' protests include rule changes, the competitive season being extended or the need to create more revenue for themselves.

## Revenue for athletes

The public image is that athletes are grossly overpaid. However, this is only the case for a minority of athletes. In the USA, the courts decided that professional athletes who were likely to have short careers were not really overpaid. Athletes have also traditionally not enjoyed many rights within their employment contracts. This was legally challenged by the athletes in the 1970s, when it was found that the majority of athletes did not earn as much as television entertainers. To attract endorsements, athletes need a strong public image so that people will recognise and identify with

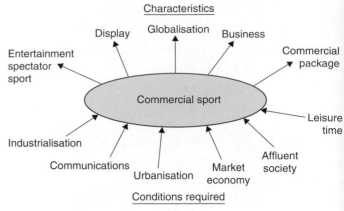

Fig 13.1. What is commercial sport?

them. Women and black sportspersons may be the victims of prejudice against them.

### Michael Jordan and Tiger Woods

These are the highest paid sportsmen in the modern era.

The total economic impact of Michael Johnson (through gate receipts, TV rights, sponsorships, sales of sports goods, etc.) was estimated at over $10 billion.

Nike also sponsors the world's most best golfer, Tiger Woods. By the time he was 24 he had earned tournament winnings of $17 million. Endorsement contracts added a further $60 million. The significance of golf as a sport is that it is a long-term career compared to many other sports. As such Tiger could be predicted to earn as much as $6 billion during his career.

- Research the changes in rugby union and rugby league since 1994. (The CD Roms of *The Guardian* and *The Times* newspapers are useful sources of information.)
- How has the mass media made sport part of the entertainment industry? In your discussion/response cover the following areas:
  a) the performer
  b) the format and organisation of sport and competitions.

ACTIVITY 1

**Fig 13.2a.** Tiger Woods earned $80.3 m in 2004, of which $70 m was for endorsing products (*Source: Forbes*)

**Fig 13.2b.** Despite being retired Michael Jordan still earned $35 m in 2004 (*Source: Forbes*)

# Summary

- Commercial sports have developed under certain social and economic conditions – urbanisation, industrialisation, effective communications, surplus disposable income and a large population with high living standards and sufficient leisure time.
- The basic structure of sports have remained the same but commercialisation has been influential.
- Mass audiences sometimes demand drama and excitement rather than aesthetic appreciation.
- Control of sport needs to be balanced between the owners and athletes.
- Amateur sports are becoming pressurised by the need to generate more money.

# KEY WORD

**Sponsorship** is the provision of funds or other form of support to an individual or event in return for a commercial return. It is of mutual benefit to both parties.

# Sponsorship

Sponsorship is now an intrinsic aspect of sports funding. Through the medium of television, business sponsors of sport can create the images they want, allow identification with the sports stars and introduce the 'new' populations into the game to their product.

## The Olympic Games

The International Olympic Committee (IOC) has expanded its investments to include 200 nations, and has made the Olympic Games one of the biggest media events in the world. Sponsorship for the Games is set up on a global basis. The Olympic Programme (TOP) involves approximately

Fig 13.3. Sports teams often advertise a sponsoring company on their kit

44 companies, including Coca-Cola, Adidas and Kodak (Adidas actually brought the idea to the IOC). Sponsorship is necessary, as the staging of the event is enormously expensive, well recognised after the 1976 Games in Montreal almost went bankrupt. Tax payers were unwilling to shoulder the burden of cost, while television companies were willing to pay large sums to transmit. Without international coverage (167 countries) the sponsors would not be willing to invest so much, and events might not be able to take place.

## Aspects of sponsorship

A **sponsorship agency** is an agency which specialises in advising on or organising sponsored events and programmes, and which may be employed either by a sponsor or a sports body. It acts as a broker, bringing together the sponsor and the sports body to create or organise an event or programme which is mutually beneficial to both parties (The Howell Report, p 341); eg, West Nally and Mark McCormack International Management Organisation.

An individual athlete may also have an agent who promotes the competitor to gain financial benefits for each of them. The marketing of athletes or events is an integrated and professionally planned promotion.

**Trust Funds** are a means for an amateur athlete to receive money from their sport. They are managed by the governing body and accept money from subventions, for advertising services or as participation money. It will be held until retirement from the sport, but funds for athletic expenses can be withdrawn before retirement.

Athletes will often display companies names on their equipment, clothing and vehicles. This is known as **endorsing** a product. The performers are contracted to declare publicly their approval of a product or service. When Eric Cantona was at Manchester United Football Club, he endorsed Nike products, but his team mate Ryan Giggs endorsed Reebok goods. Sports stars have emerged as 'personality advertising', and are used as a big sell. Gary Lineker and Paul Gascoigne teamed up to a partnership of a different kind – an advert for Walkers crisps. It has been suggested that sports performers are beginning to resemble 'human billboards'.

**Perimeter advertising** is where advertising boards surround pitches and are sold off in metres to commercial organisations, providing a stationary form of advertising.

**Ambush or guerrilla marketing** is a term used when one brand pays to become an official sponsor of an event and another competing brand attempts to connect itself with the event without paying the sponsorship fee and more importantly without breaking any laws. They attract consumers at the expense of competitors, undermining the event's integrity and its ability to attract sponsors in the future. The cases that attract most press coverage are the 'big' players with plenty of resources such as Nike, Reebok and Coca-Cola. So what about some recent examples? Nike's ambush of the 1996 Atlanta Olympics is still seen as the ambush of all ambushes. Saving the US$50 million that an official sponsorship would have cost, Nike plastered the city in billboards, handed out 'swoosh' banners to wave at the competitions and erected an enormous Nike centre overlooking the stadium. These tactics resulted in major organisations like FIFA to counteract more aggressively ambushing strategies.

To become sponsor of the 2002 Winter Olympics in Salt Lake City, Anheuser-Busch paid more than US$50 million. It paid for the right to use the word 'Olympic' and the five rings logo. Schirf Brewery, a local and very small company, came up with the clever and legal idea of marketing its delivery trucks with 'Wasutch Beers. The Unofficial Beer. 2002 Winter Games'. Without using the magic word Olympic or using the logo of the five rings it had successfully connected itself to the Games.

The danger to major events like the Olympics and World Cup is that they rely heavily on corporate sponsorship. These partners need to be assured of sole rights otherwise they will withdraw revenue if they feel it is money not well spent. Events can ill afford to lose this income.

---

Betting on sport has traditionally involved horse racing, boxing and football. In the UK horse racing accounts for 70% of revenue for the top three bookmakers, yet less than a tenth of the UK population are regular race followers.

New technology could transform the gambling industry in future years, broadening the range of sports betting. In the UK 70% of the population play the National Lottery but only 6% use betting shops.

What impact could discreet, user-friendly betting via the internet, mobile phone or interactive TV have as mass market appeal?

---

## Advantages and disadvantages

Sponsorship and advertising have been key factors in the redevelopment of many sports. They provide capital to sport, while at the same time:

- securing an appropriate image for the sponsor. For example: Gillette used to sponsor cricket, creating an 'English' image for their product; Coca-Cola sponsor the Olympics and school sport, conveying fun and liveliness.

- achieving specific marketing objectives.

There are some disadvantages, though. There has been uneven development across sports. Sponsors tend to come forward where there are already large audiences; a diversion of sponsor money away from the minority sports can cause a decline in those sports. For example, in 1978 the World Squash Championships were cancelled due to a lack of sponsor and no guaranteed television coverage; in the case of football, increased television coverage helped to cause a reduction in live attendances. Elite sport can be promoted at the expense of the grass roots due to its ability to attract media coverage.

There can be sensitivity about political advertising which can cause problems; Thames Television blocked out coverage of the 1985 Edinburgh Games when the organisers, Edinburgh Council, refused to move an anti-apartheid banner. Some sports have been adapted to suit TV coverage. In cricket, the one day game has developed to increase the pace, which has placed priority on certain skills. The tobacco company, Rothmans, encouraged attacking and batting skills and defensive bowling, and paid more in sponsorship when the ball was driven to the boundary – so that their adverts appeared more frequently!

Sponsors sometimes withdraw when their objectives are not achieved or where there is no perceived gain. There can be contradictory messages when a product being advertised is considered dangerous to people's health. Tobacco companies were banned from general advertising on British television in 1965. Sport, which achieved a significant percentage of a network's output, was therefore a good advertising proposition for the tobacco companies. The main sport beneficiaries of tobacco sponsorship have been motor racing, tennis, cricket, golf, show jumping and snooker. However, the Sports Council did not accept tobacco sponsorship and did not make its Sport Sponsorship Advisory Service available to it. Tobacco has in the past contributed 10% of total sponsorship, and the government could not compensate for this amount, should tobacco advertising be banned from sport. This poses the question: is tobacco bad for health but good for sport?

# TOBACCO COMPANY SPONSORSHIP IN FORMULA ONE

## WHAT THEY GET

During a typical Grand Prix – which is watched by more than 340 million TV viewers – images or mentions of tobacco or brand names and logos are broadcast some 6,000 times, making an F1 car the world's most powerful advertising medium. Each year tobacco companies spend an estimated £125–£200 million sponsoring Formula One.

## COST

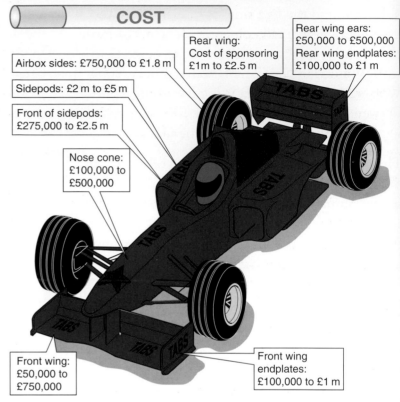

Airbox sides: £750,000 to £1.8 m

Sidepods: £2 m to £5 m

Front of sidepods: £275,000 to £2.5 m

Nose cone: £100,000 to £500,000

Rear wing: Cost of sponsoring £1m to £2.5 m

Rear wing ears: £50,000 to £500,000
Rear wing endplates: £100,000 to £1 m

Front wing: £50,000 to £750,000

Front wing endplates: £100,000 to £1 m

Fig 13.4. Tobacco company sponsorship in Formula One

# Bernie Ecclestone's Empire

This one individual shows how power in sport can be concentrated. In June 2000 the Fédération Internationale de l'Automobile (FIA), the sport's governing body, sold FI's commercial rights to Ecclestone for a 110-year period! For $360 million Ecclestone was awarded sole rights to negotiate fees from promoters of Grand Prix races and 'sole authority' to sell television rights worldwide for a sport whose 17 races each year pull in an aggregate TV audience of around 5 billion.

## An example of sponsorship – Coca-Cola

Coca-Cola has made a heavy impact on the sports sponsorship scene. The company views sport sponsorship as a way of gaining access to their customers.

**ACTIVITY 2**

List the positive and negative effects of tobacco sponsorship and account for the factors you mention.

Coca-Cola provides the customer with things in which they can participate, eg, signed footballs, days out at training grounds, good seats at prestigious sports events. This is the world of corporate hospitality.

- Coca-Cola prefer to be synonymous with a sport, rather than a team. They had a five-year contrac at Wimbledon tennis championships, which started in 1997. They occupied the suite next to the Committee suite to entertain their major customers, VIPs, editors of key opinion-forming journals and so on. In addition they secured the advertising and 'pouring rights', which meant that any drinks used by players or officials was contained in a Coke receptacle, whether or not it was a drink of Coke. In other words, they were involved in 'presence marketing' which is a term used to mean the saturation of a venue with their product.

- The slogan 'Eat Sleep Drink Football' created by Ivan Pollard is now being reworked as an advert to appeal to the Brazilian market.

- Within a country, the company selects the most popular sport and chooses sport personalities with clean cut, wholesome images, like Glen Hoddle, Les Ferdinand and Alan Shearer. Ryan Giggs and singer Peter Andre have been sponsored as a route into the fashion world.

- They also provide benefits to an area hosting an event. The Olympic Stadium at Atlanta (which interestingly is 'the home of Coke') was almost rebuilt by Coca-Cola – including the roads, hotels, athletes' accommodation and Centennial Park.

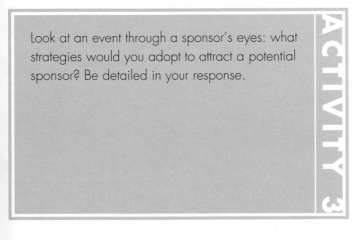

Look at an event through a sponsor's eyes: what strategies would you adopt to attract a potential sponsor? Be detailed in your response.

**ACTIVITY 3**

## The Howell Report (1983)

We have already addressed some of the problems sponsorship can create for sport. The Howell Report sought to make recommendations. Here are some examples:

- The Sports Council, CCPR and individual governing bodies should seek control and accept responsibility for the application, provision and practice of sponsorship in sport.

- Governing bodies should establish sponsorship committees to help regulate sponsorship, and these should include competitor representatives. Governing bodies should not rely too much on business sponsorship, and should diversify approaches if the sponsors pull out.

- Proper ethical standards and policies to protect sports performers from exploitation should be ensured.

- Sponsors should aim to support sport both at the grass roots and at the elite level. They can gain experience at local and regional levels, while also providing a social service. They should aim to give prior notice of their intention to withdraw their support.

- Trust funds should be monitored carefully by the governing bodies.

- The Sports Aid Foundation should market itself more efficiently to achieve its targets.

- High ethical standards should be everyone's main concern: influential sponsorship deals should be compatible with the interests of sport; full knowledge of all arrangements should be made available.

Though sponsorship has provided much needed capital for sport, the bedrock of funding in the UK is still a combination of public funding and the massive voluntary and unpaid commitment of sports enthusiasts.

## The media

The media includes newspapers, radio and television broadcasting, and the Internet, by which information is conveyed to the general public.

# Newspapers

The early types of sports news-sheets, notably *Bell's Life* (1822) and *Sporting Life* (1865), provided short, detailed sports reports. General newspapers gradually began to include sport sections, bringing sport to those people who may have had little contact with sport but who now were able to recognise sports performers. By the 1920s, the mass audience for sport had emerged. Sports reports in newspapers could summarise events and appeal to a wide range of audiences at different times (unlike television coverage). Today there are two major types of newspapers:

1. The tabloids, such as the *Sun* or the *Mirror*, tend to have a large section devoted to sport, but focus on particular types of sport – mainly those with broad appeal and male dominated.

2. The broadsheets such as the *Guardian* or *The Times* tend to cover and analyse sport in more depth; they offer slightly more variety of sport, but there is still a predominance on male sport.

> Take a selection of newspapers. Estimate the ratio given over to sport and the ratio of different types of sport. Can you come to any conclusions? Is there a difference in emphasis between the tabloids and broadsheets as suggested here?
>
> **ACTIVITY 4**

# Radio

Radio started to report live events in the 1920s, which gave the broadcast an immediacy; this was strengthened by the advent of television broadcasting. The BBC traditionally has shown sports events without the advertisers' influence whereas in the USA they scheduled events to maximise advertisers' demands.

# Television

Television has the advantage of being able to broadcast instantaneous sporting action to a large audience, relatively cheaply. Because the relatively low cost of sports broadcasting compared favourably with drama and light entertainment, and the high ratings gained, it is not surprising that sport features so heavily on television schedules, particularly at weekends.

> The relationship between sports and media has become symbiotic. Media commentators claimed that BSkyB (part of News International) would lose 60% of its subscribers if its Premier League rights were to be lost. A bidding war saw Premier League rights for 2001–04 sold for over $500 m a year, with BSkyB yet again outbidding its rivals.

Television has helped to bring lesser known or rarely watched sports to the foreground; it has helped participants to reach superstar status, and consequently raised the performers' earnings. This has sometimes put athletes under great pressure to make more performance appearances than is good for them, physically or mentally.

However, television reporting can also over-dramatise problems within the sports world. Also, deals made between sporting bodies and the media can favour certain sports, such as the alliance between Adidas and FIFA.

## The effect on sport

Some sports have changed to make them more amenable to media coverage. Television coverage can also influence positively or negatively the participation rates in a sport. Over the last 50 years, terrestrial television in the UK has expanded from one channel to five. The new channels need to seek out new markets, and when the new Channel 4 arrived, it boosted the viewing and participating figures for volleyball and table tennis, and gave significant coverage of the ethnic game kabbadi.

> Rights to Soccer's World Cup (2002–06) were sold for $2 billion, shared between Kirch/ Taurus and Sporis/ISL.

- Volleyball became a regular sports feature between 1980 and 1984 – the number of affiliated players rose by 70%.

- Conversely, when table tennis no longer received television coverage, its membership of participating players dropped by a third. The governing bodies in both cases were convinced that the changed rates of participation were not coincidences. If women's sports received more coverage, would we see the rise in female participants that so many organisations are trying hard to achieve?

The increasing concentration of power and money in a limited number of giant conglomerates, especially when combined with club ownership and merchandising interests, has led to a number of instances where unease has crept in. A notable case was when in 1998 BSkyB tried to buy control of Manchester United, but the UK Monopolies and Mergers Commission blocked the bid. The argument made was that it would further divide the clubs on a financial basis.

## ACTIVITY 5

### Ring fencing

Certain prestigious sports events, particularly international events, should be available to the 'ordinary' viewer on terrestrial TV rather than the more exclusive satellite or cable subscription channels.

Discuss the validity of this statement.

## Sports commentators

The media reports on what actually happens and as such is objective; yet as readers, viewers or listeners, we must take into account the values and beliefs of those who commentate on the events. The commentators are the mediators who describe and analyse the action for the viewer at home. They can become celebrities in their own right and are sometimes associated with just one sport; eg, Murray Walker (motor racing), John Motson (football), the late Dan Maskell (tennis at Wimbledon), Harry Carpenter (boxing). The style of presentation has become closely related to the culture of the mass audience. Events are hyped up, where the commentators discuss the likely outcome of an event for hours before, advising viewers on how to interpret the situation.

## Influence of technology

The increase in technology has enabled an effective combination of detailed coverage with fast action tension. The use of zoom lenses has meant less reliance on fixed angle lenses, and makes possible close-ups of players, catching facial and verbal expressions which spectators at live events could not hope to capture; it is possible to fit cameras in a racing car, under water, and in a goal, which give the viewer at home a privileged viewing position. Action replays and freeze frames enable a detailed analysis to take place. Interactive technology enables viewers at home to make individual choices such as following their favourite performer.

Communication satellites enable live transmission around the world. This has had a growing impact on viewing audiences. Television rights can be granted to companies who do not transmit to many homes. The Broadcasting Act 1990 in the UK declared that all rights to broadcast sport can be sold to the highest bidder.

## Media coverage and social values

- Television coverage concentrates on the conduct of the participants and spectators, and is generally sympathetic to officials. Different sports receive different emphasis of coverage; eg, tennis players who behave badly are often described as 'brats' which has a very middle class tone, whereas in soccer, the language used might be 'thugs', possibly showing more intolerance of working class behaviour.

- Gender inequalities in sport can be reflected by the media. Men figure more as participants and media sport professionals, whereas women tend to comment on women's sports, if at all. There have been recent challenges to this position, eg, Sue Barker for the BBC. Non-contact sports for women are given more positive media coverage, such as tennis, gymnastics and track athletes. The massive inequality in coverage tends to reaffirm the stereotype that sport is for men, and women have little to comment on.

- The media can help generate a sense of nationalism, particularly since the development of international coverage of events where the symbols of nationalism are displayed for all to see – rituals, flags, ceremonies, parades, uniforms and anthems – making them highly emotive events.

- In the UK, sportspeople from ethnic minorities can become potent role models for young people, and their representation can promote equality of opportunity. However, the media can also promote the stereotype that black people can excel in sport and physical activity but not in other areas of life. Similarly to women, people from ethnic minorities are not prominent in the controlling positions of power in the media, like commentators and directors, writers, producers, photographers, etc.

## Who controls sport?

Traditionally this was undeniably the gentlemanly elders of Western society, as a result of personal contacts rather than competence or democracy. They were not prepared for the predatory world of commercial exploitation that was to emerge in the twentieth century.

In the modern era the power over the organisation of sport and its revenue lies in only a few hands, via a monopolistic ruling body or a small group of individuals or companies. Although some sports stars can wield some leverage due to their high wages and crowd-pulling potential, the majority of professionals have to do what they are told. They are bought, sold and transferred as commodities.

Ruling bodies in sport have all lost out to businesses such as Rupert Murdoch's News International, Mark McCormack's International Marketing Group, Ted Turner's Time Warner (owner of Home Box Office), Nike and the Kirch Group.

Fox, Sky and Star TV networks give Rupert Murdoch unique power in broadcasting. Contracts include NFL and Major League baseball in the USA, Premier League soccer in the UK, and the Cricket World Cup. Murdoch companies have been extending sports coverage via the Internet – predicted to be the key medium for future sports fans.

Golf and tennis are among the few major sports which have a relatively democratic form of government – in that the players decide very much how things should be run and make their own decisions over where and when they will play and which sponsorship deals to take.

ACTIVITY 6

Watch a sport event on television and record it. Then analyse in detail for a particular aspect; eg, comments made by the commentators, the language used, reference to certain players. This will be time-consuming, but if done as a class activity you could each report on a different event and compile some interesting information.

# Fair play, sportsmanship and gamesmanship

## Contract to compete

Whenever we walk onto a football pitch, netball court, participate in a swimming competition or any other type of competitive sport we have entered into an unwritten mutual agreement with our opponents.

What is the nature of such a contract?

- Keep to the rules/not cheating but being committed to the sport
- To play as well as we can/showing commitment to others
- To allow others to demonstrate their skill and effort
- Understanding for the need of codes of fair play/sportsmanship/etiquette and so on

In different areas of this book we mention terms such as Olympism, Athleticism and Amateurism.

Together they have formed the bedrock of British sporting traditions.

It may be useful at this stage to look up these terms and then consider these common characteristics:

- Physical and moral qualities are emphasised
- Enjoyment in effort, regardless of outcome
- Learning to win and lose with honour
- Enhancing quality of life
- End result not as important as the process

If we contrast these principles with the dominant sport ethic in the USA, the Lombardian ethic, there are very clear differences. The popular image of the ethic is taken from the saying of the coach, Vince Lombardi, 'Winning isn't the most important thing, it's the only thing'. This emphasises the competitive, achievement-orientated, reward-based type of sport behaviour: the end justifies the means: Nice Guys Finish Last.

Are the principles on which British sport is based still relevant today?

# Deviance

Behaviour which goes against the society's general norms and values is called 'deviant' behaviour. This can include behaviour which is against the law and therefore criminally deviant, eg, burglary, or against the moral values of the society but which is not criminally deviant, eg, promiscuity.

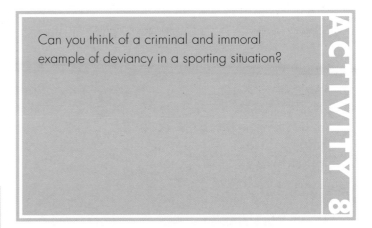

Can you think of a criminal and immoral example of deviancy in a sporting situation?

**ACTIVITY 8**

Consider what constitutes the breaking of this contract. Give specific instances related to sport.

**ACTIVITY 7**

# Approaches to deviancy

## Relative deviancy

Deviant behaviour can reflect the balance of power in a society. Who decides what is lawful and what is morally right? Usually those with the most control, ie, the dominant culture. Right and wrong can mean different things to different people and is sometimes

| Relevant | Not relevant |
|---|---|
| • These principles are still encouraged in everyday life, <br> eg, respect for rules, others <br> • Physical Education still encourages the moral qualities as much as the physical development <br> • In the UK we still separate Physical Education from Sport <br> • Fair Play Awards are still given significance in major competitions <br> • Athletes are still considered positive role models for children <br> • If not evident sport could be dysfunctional | • Can hinder hunger for success; many believe these codes have let the UK slip behind in an area they once dominated <br> • We compete against countries like the USA and Eastern Europe who are motivated by very different ideals/philosophies <br> • They belong to a past culture of 'gentlemanly sport' that highlighted the values of the upper social classes |

dependent on culture, gender and social class. Those who do not conform to the rules and identify as a group with similar interests, acting in a manner which is not conventional in the dominant culture, can be classed as members of a subculture. Examples are the special group of athletes bonded by a sense of commitment; football hooligans; rugby clubs. This view suggests that deviance can be relative, and that deviants are victims of a power system which makes the rules.

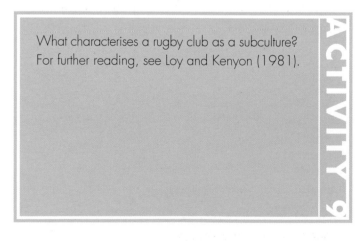

What characterises a rugby club as a subculture? For further reading, see Loy and Kenyon (1981).

ACTIVITY 9

## Absolute deviancy

Another view of deviancy takes an absolute view of right and wrong, and regards deviant behaviour as morally bankrupt. The solution is to establish more

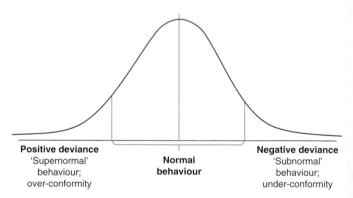

**Positive deviance** — 'Supernormal' behaviour; over-conformity   **Normal behaviour**   **Negative deviance** — 'Subnormal' behaviour; under-conformity

Fig 13.5. A normal distribution approach to understanding deviance
*Source*: Coakley (1993).

control by creating more rules and punishing the perpetrators more successfully and publicly.

## Normal distribution approach

An alternative to the absolute and relative approach is proposed by Coakley (1993). He suggests there is a 'normal distribution' of behaviour which falls into a range of acceptances. Deviance occurs when behaviour falls outside this range, *on either side*; ie, there can be under- and over-conformity.

# Deviance in sport

Athletes are encouraged to behave in ways that would not be allowed in other areas of life. This can pose special problems for sport. 'On the field' deviance includes 'violations of norms that occur while preparing or participating in sports events' (Coakley, 1993). It can be caused by the pressure of media coverage or commercialism, or the pressure to win. Similar behaviour outside of the sport situation could result in arrests and prosecutions.

## Under-conformity and negative deviancy

This is a situation where an athlete reject rules; at the extreme extent, this could be anarchic. Negative deviancy involves cheating and deliberately harming another player, and should be easy to control because a rule violation can be punished appropriately.

## Over-conformity and positive deviancy

This is a situation where an athlete goes too far in conforming with the rules. Examples are, where training becomes obsessive; where performance-enhancing drugs are taken; when normal life suffers or where athletes participate in sport despite injury, and are praised by the organisers and media. The athlete takes risks, makes sacrifices and pays the price, in order to conform to the norms of the group. This form of deviance can be harder to control and would benefit from a reassessment of the sport ethic and the meaning given to sport by those in control – the organisers, sponsors and media.

According to Coakley (1993), the sport ethic has four core elements:

- athletes make sacrifices for the game
- athletes strive for distinction
- athletes accept risks and play through pain
- athletes accept no limits in the pursuit of possibilities.

We will now look specifically at the following issues:

- Aggression in sport by athletes
- Spectator violence, in particular football hooliganism

**ACTIVITY 10**

Have you ever been in a situation where you were expected to adopt 'positive' forms of deviance? What was the outcome? How did you feel?

- Drug taking by athletes
- Sport and the law.

# Aggression in sport

The various theories of aggression are covered in greater detail in the psychology section of this book. Aggression includes any behaviour which *intends* physical or psychological harm to another person. This distinguishes it from other terms used in sport situations, such as assertive, rough, competitive. Intimidation is the threatened intent to harm, using verbal or physical means. Sports vary in their nature, and so the extent through which aggression can be expressed also varies. Activities involving physical contact are more easily open to shows of aggression than activities where players are separated from each other. However, a game like netball which according to the rules, is a non contact game, can often involve aggression.

Theories that sport helps to cause aggression are based on the following:

- participating in or spectating sport leads to frustration, which leads to violence
- sportspeople learn to associate violence as a means to achieve success
- the dominance of 'male' behaviour in sport leads people to believe that men are naturally superior to women because they have greater strength and more violent tendencies.

People care about the result of sporting action, and victory can be used to reflect superiority in other aspects of life. Frustration can lead to the emotional response of anger which can, in the sporting arena, be expressed as a violent response. The cause of frustration could be an official's decision during a game or environmental conditions. Frustration can be stimulated when athletes use equipment which are associated with violence.

Which sports do you think would be most likely to lead to aggression in sport?

ACTIVITY 11

Aggression is likely to be prevalent when spectators identify strongly with one particular side and are likely to feel anger quite easily, where similar opportunities for aggression and frustration are present. Contact sports are therefore most likely to lead to violence on the pitch, and this is compounded when large rewards are available for winning and when expectations of coaches and fans are high. Tolerance of rule violations seem to increase as the level of competition increases.

An extreme case is ice hockey, where 'enforcers' are employed to act as hit-men. Yet these are players who do not necessarily feel anger or frustration associated with the game. They intimidate and carry out violent acts because that is their primary task in the game.

As female participation in contact sports has increased, it has become apparent that they also use violence as a strategy, but research (though limited as yet) generally concludes that they are not as violent as men. Sport has long been a male

preserve, and mistakes made during a game often result in sexist comments such as 'playing like a girl'. Thus, some sportsmen feel the need to prove their masculinity beyond doubt, by using violent means; this implies that aggressive behaviour can be the result of social conditioning, and is not merely a natural masculine trait.

# Spectator violence

A number of general approaches to deviance can be applied to the specific form of deviant behaviour which is termed 'football hooliganism'. Football hooligans have been defined by the Sports Council as 'those people who were dealt with by the police for offences occurring in connection with attendance at football matches'. A dictionary definition of a hooligan is a 'disorderly and noisy young person who behaves in a violent and destructive way'. A distinction needs to be made between supporters, fans and hooligans. Supporters and fans manage their emotions effectively; Guttman (1986) concluded that spectating at sports events did not result in an increase in violent behaviour. Hooligans on the other hand go to matches to engage in aggressive and violent behaviour before, during or after the game. Considering the amount of sports events and the number of people spectating on a regular basis, it is clear we are dealing with a minority of people, albeit a media-attracting minority.

## Sociological approaches to hooliganism

Early theories of hooliganism concentrated on social class, and tried to explain the behaviour of hooligans in terms of their social status. However, it is no longer a useful way of describing people, as class distinctions are not clear-cut in modern society. Furthermore, whereas early theories were based on the premise that most football hooligans were uneducated, less well off members of society, recent studies have discovered that a large number of people who cause trouble at football matches are highly educated professional people, who often need to keep their identities as football supporters separate from their working lives. It is in fact difficult to find any one single factor to explain deviancy as it applies to football hooliganism; a synthesis of approaches is required.

Hooliganism at football matches has been exaggerated and distorted, and should be seen in a wider socio-economic and historical context. The media has a tendency to sensationalise the news and to amplify the problem being reported.

Football has had a long, fluctuating history of crowd disorders, and Pearson (1983) suggests that such problems date back to the seventeenth and eighteenth centuries.

Marsh (1978) argued that aggravation at football matches is effectively a 'highly distinctive, and often ceremonial system for resolving conflict'; behaviour at football matches is a ritual action. Behaviour is structured and ordered rather than chaotic; the fighting itself has rules, and much of it is not serious.

Taylor (1971) argues that football is now a passive spectator sport rather than a participatory one. The increasing professionalism, control by wealthy directors and change from grounds to stadiums, have taken away any sense of control or participation from the spectators, and football hooliganism could be a response to resist these changes.

Arousal seeking and risk taking appear to be compensatory acts. This idea links with Elias and Dunning's theory (1970), who suggested in their title, *The quest for excitement in unexciting societies*, that in industrialised societies there are fewer opportunities for people to express themselves freely.

Brown (1991) believes that some hooligans become addicted to the activity just as gamblers and alcoholics do. Increasing stimulation is needed to generate high arousal because of psychological deprivation. People who have not had enough opportunity to experience a wide range of rewarding experiences can be forced to use narrower strategies to deal with life's problems.

## Practical factors which contribute to hooliganism

There are a number of important factors which can contribute to the *level* of violence at sports events:

- Violence shown by the players seems to transmit itself to the spectators.

- Pre-event hype can also increase the level of violence, so the media and organisers should take some responsibility for the way they promote the event.

- Controversial officials' decisions can sometimes cause an increase in violence, particularly if the situation is at a crucial stage. The need for competent officials is essential.

- The supporter group dynamics, ie, the size and structure of the group, their social and cultural backgrounds, the importance associated with the event and the historical relationships of those attending.

- The authorities' strategies for controlling the event.

- The amount of alcohol consumed before the event.

In Britain, the short distance between sporting locations has enabled the establishment of a tradition of away fans travelling to every game. The two sets of fans openly display their allegiance

Fig 13.6. Spectator violence

through the symbols of colours, flags, scarves, songs and so on. This is not possible in larger countries where supporters have further distances to travel.

ACTIVITY 12

Taking all the factors mentioned above, discuss comprehensive measures which could be employed to control the level of violence amongst participants and spectators.

## Dealing with hooliganism

Hooliganism initially took place in football grounds. These were easily accessible, spectators were not segregated and matches occurred at regular intervals. Trouble generally erupted when goals were scored. However, when the authorities began to use strategies like fenced pens with close police scrutiny, the violent activity began to move away from the grounds.

The Taylor Report following the Hillsborough disaster led to measures such as abolishing the soccer terraces. By 1994–5 season all Premier League and First Division clubs had to upgrade their stadiums to be all seater facilities. This has led many people to complain of the lack of atmosphere, as they feel that the excitement generated by large crowds is being eradicated.

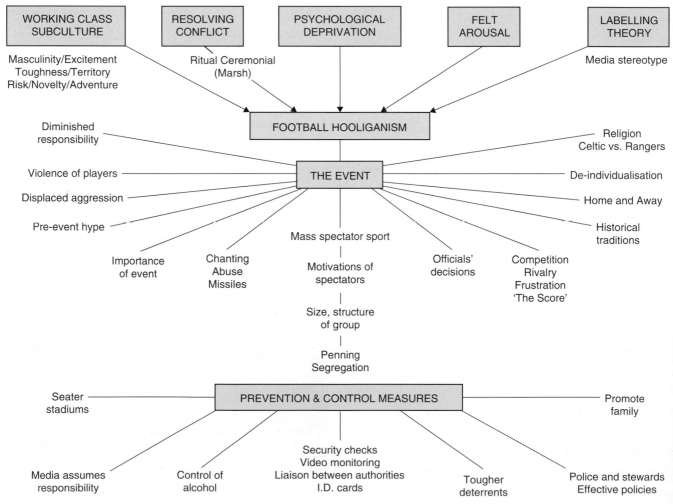

Fig 13.7. Points to remember about hooliganism

Video monitoring has been installed at most grounds so that police can closely monitor crowd movement. Freeze frames can highlight particular trouble makers. Information is stored on computer in the National Criminal Intelligence Service and allows police liaison in England and Europe.

Perimeter fencing was not successful in preventing violence, and neither was the identity card scheme. However, the level of hooliganism has decreased in the last few years. Some have complained that the police measures reduced much of the fun element and increased the risk element too much.

## Summary

The relationship between sport and aggression has been covered in some detail. It is a complex social phenomenon which requires a synthesis of perspectives.

Putting time between the player and the frustration seems to be a more substantial argument than sport either increasing or decreasing the level of 'natural' violence found in humans.

- Frustration combined with anger, opportunities and stimulus cues lead to aggression.

# Drugs in sport

The history of drug abuse is as old as sport. Athletes in Greece and Rome took substances to improve their athletic performance. However, drug use in modern sport has become regular and systematised. Research shows that it is more than a peripheral problem, and operates at both amateur and professional levels, among male and female athletes and across a wide variety of sports. Factors which led to an increase in the use of drugs include:

- advances in biology and medicine
- the use of drugs in World War II
- the development and availability of testosterone, steroids and growth hormones in the 1950s.

Weight trainers in particular demonstrated the possible results of using these drugs, other athletes who recognised their potential capitalised on this. Drugs allow athletes to control their bodies; they can alter their bodily functions, though this will result in a *loss* of power if used unwisely. The 'substance availability hypothesis' ties in closely with the type of positive deviance mentioned earlier, where an athlete is over-committed to the sport ethic and is willing to risk all for the opportunity to perform at their highest level.

In the last 20 years, drug taking has become a very common part of top class sport. This in spite of the efforts of various national and international doping committees, and the establishment of the

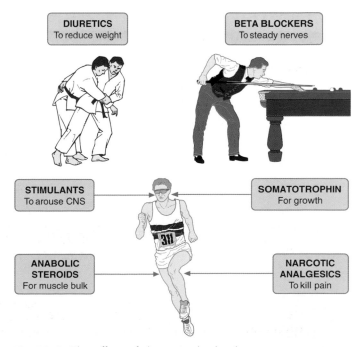

Fig 13.8. The effect of drugs on the body

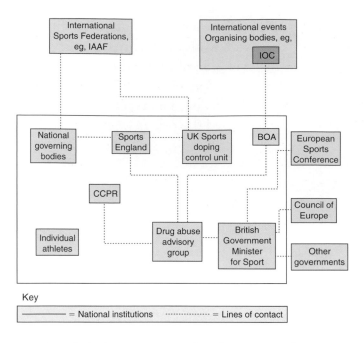

Key

—— = National institutions  ............ = Lines of contact

**Fig 13.9.** Links between national and international organisations
*Note*: The Institutional context of anti-doping policy

International Olympic Committee Medical Commission in 1967. It appears that the chemists supplying sportspeople with drugs, are trying to keep one step ahead of the chemists working to keep sport free from the effects of drugs. One of the problematic areas is defining an illegal drug, and the effects they have on the performer and performance; what is artificial, natural, foreign, fair or abnormal?

The organisations responsible for their sport generally have to take control of the testing for drugs in their sport. This will take place at both the national and international levels. Figure 13.9 is an example of the action taken over a period of time and the links between the domestic and international organisations.

## Which drugs are used?

The International Amateur Federation Rule 144 on doping states:

• doping is forbidden

• doping is the use by or distribution to an athlete of certain substances which could have the effect of improving artificially the athlete's physical and/or mental condition and so augmenting his athletic performance.

It lists a total of over 80 individual drugs classified under stimulants, narcotic analgesics and anabolic steroids, and states that chemically or pharmacologically related drugs are also forbidden.

'Ergogenic aids' refer to any substance that improves performance.

1. A survey (*Time* 1998) of 100 top runners in the USA found that 50 of them said they would take a certain drug knowing that although it could make them Olympic champions, it could kill them in a year. Discuss the issues involved in this situation.
2. Group discussions:
   a) It has been suggested that the media, sponsors and lawyers now control sport. Discuss the implications of this with reference to drug taking and enforcement of testing procedures.
   b) Should we be able to see the best performance possible despite the consequences?
   c) It has been suggested that governing bodies 'turn a blind eye' to some drug takers. Discuss the reasons why this may be the case and what are the implications for the sport?

1. Find out information about a well-documented case of an athlete charged with taking drugs; eg, Ben Johnson, Diane Modahl.
2. What are the problems of defining a drug for normal purposes and those for sport?
3. How would you persuade an up-and-coming young athlete not to take drugs?

Table 13.1. Effects of various drugs

| Types of drugs used | Reasons for use | Side effects | Which sports? |
|---|---|---|---|
| Anabolic steroids – 'artificially produced male hormones' eg, nandrolone testosterone | Promote muscle growth Increase lean body weight Ability to train harder with less fatigue Repair body after stress Increased aggression | Liver damage Heart disease Acne Excessive aggression Females: male features irregular periods | Power and explosive events eg, weight lifting athletics swimming |
| Narcotic analgesics – 'pain killers' eg, morphine methadone | Reduce amount of pain Mask injury Increase pain limit | Highly addictive Increase initial injury Breathing problems Nausea and vomiting | All sports |
| Stimulants – 'stimulate body mentally and physically' eg, amphetamine ephedrine | Reduce tiredness Increase alertness Increase competitiveness Increase aggression | Rise in blood pressure Rise in body temperature Increased heart beat Loss of appetite Addiction Death | Cycling Boxing |
| Beta blockers – can be used medically eg, antenolol propranolol | Steady nerves Stop trembling | Low blood pressure Slow heart rate Tiredness | Shooting Archery Snooker Diving |
| Diuretics – 'remove fluid from body' eg, triameterine bendrofluazide | Lose weight quickly Increase rate of passing urine | Dehydration Faintness Dizziness Muscle cramps | Jockeys Boxers |
| Peptide hormones – 'naturally occurring' eg, erythropoietin/HCG analogues 'synthetic' eg, EPO | Stimulate growth of naturally occurring steroids Build muscle Mend tissue Increase oxygen transport | Muscle wasting Abnormal growth of hands and feet EPO – increases red cells in blood Clotting Stroke | Similar to steroids |
| Blood doping – injection of blood to increase number of blood cells | Body more energy to work | Allergic reactions Hepatitis or AIDS Overload circulatory system Blood clots | Running Cycling Marathons Skiing |

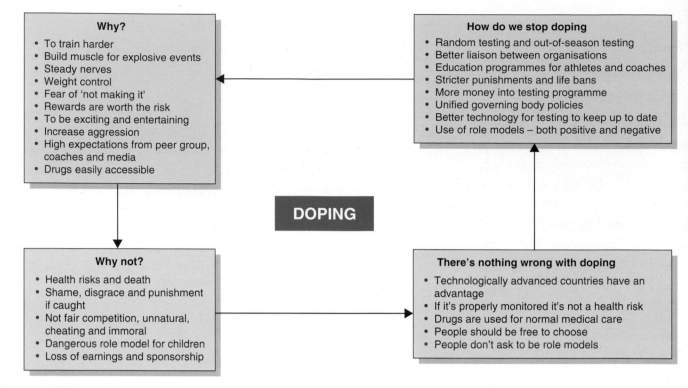

Fig 13.10. Doping

# Sport and the law

Generally in most countries sports law does not exist. More often established legal principles are applied to new problems generated by sport, such as performance enhancing drugs and legal requirements imposed by sport organisations.

# Players

There has been an increase in sports legislation and legal challenges to the administrators of sport. Sport has traditionally been perceived as being outside and almost above the law, and as such has retained autonomy for a greater length of time than most other social agencies. But the number of prosecutions of sports players for assaults which occurred within the confines of the game, has increased. Should assaults be viewed separately to a similar occurrence outside a sports setting? On the one hand, players have understood the activity they are taking part in, and by participating they have accepted that the rules of the game control the extent of physical contact which is allowed. On the

other hand, a foul could be considered outside the rules and, therefore, no contract was entered into.

The results of this type of judicial reasoning have led to convictions of assault. Yet many people would also accept that the rules are not taken literally and terms such as the 'professional foul' are a part of the game. Rugby referees have been prosecuted for allowing a situation to develop which caused harm to a player. Whatever the rights or wrongs of these cases, they evidently have far-reaching consequences for the world of sport.

# Drug misuse

Virtually no sport is without the problem of having to tackle the misuse of drugs. The Diane Modahl case illustrated how entwined sport and the law can become. The Portuguese Athletics Federation in June 1994 tested and found the sample positive with an incredibly high reading of 42:1. The British Athletics Federation (BAF) banned the athlete for four years. Modahl appealed and the focus was on the testing procedure and degradation over time which could cause an increase in testosterone.

The result was the first time the BAF sport administrators had been sued for alleged defective procedures. Modahl resumed her athletic career.

## Violence

Injury is a part of sport though deliberate intent is not normal. Boxing however intends to inflict harm but is accepted so long as it abides by a proper system of rules. Changes to boxing-related law would require an Act of Parliament, which at the moment seems unlikely. Martial arts have to be recognised by Sport England and so far include karate, tae kwon do and jujitsu. Some kick boxing and Thai boxing groups are not recognised. Soccer and rugby have witnessed criminal proceedings from incidents directly related to the sport. An example occurred in 1995 when Duncan Ferguson was convicted, following a head butt against an opponent. He was the first professional soccer player to be imprisoned for an on-the-field assault. Another notable case was Elliot vs Saunders (1994) following a tackle which ended the career of Elliot. Although the case was not won by Elliot, Liverpool FC accepted liability for its employee's wrongdoing.

## Players' rights

Jean Marc Bosman, a Belgian footballer, forced the authorities to address the issue of players' rights to play the game. The European Court of Justice recognised in this case that there was no reason why professional sports players should not enjoy the benefits of the single market and in particular the free movement of workers. This has resulted in national competitions being open to players throughout Europe and has revitalised major European leagues. The new legislation also abolished transfer fees if a player was out of contract.

## Influence of television

Television is mostly responsible for the financial boom in football but the reliability of the income is not guaranteed as is demonstrated in the restrictive practices court case against the Premier League, BSkyB and the BBC. The case is about the League's right to negotiate a television deal on behalf of all the clubs; it is claimed individual clubs should have the right to negotiate their own television contracts. If the case goes against the Premier League and in favour of the clubs the bigger clubs will be able to negotiate very lucrative contracts, making even more money available to players.

## Players vs Officials

This is a very controversial issue. In the case of Smolden vs. Whitworth and A.N. Other (1996) the court held a referee liable for crippling injuries suffered by Smolden in a colts rugby union game. At the same time Whitworth was cleared of any liability. The laws of the game were changed to allow fewer than eight players in a scrum and to ban contest scrimmaging. The implications for referees, many of whom are voluntary and amateur, are considerable. Are referees to owe a duty of care to clubs in their application of the laws of the game?

## Supporters

The attitude and behaviour of supporters has also been controversial in the eyes of the law. The growth of hooliganism in the 1970s and 1980s brought into question the ability of the football clubs to regulate the behaviour of their supporters.

A definition of sport and the law could be 'the application of legal principles to all levels of amateur and professional sport'.

Table of examples: try to find examples of particular incidents that have happened recently or in the past. Consider relevant organisations that may have influence in these cases. The first one is given as an example.

| Incident | Organisation | Example |
|---|---|---|
| Use of drugs | Governing bodies (national and international) | D. Modahl 1994 |
| Sexism | | |
| Assault (on and off the pitch) | | |
| Spectator problems, eg, hooliganism | | |
| Match fixing and corruption | | |
| Child protection (help public, private and voluntary sector identify unsuitable people to work with children) | | |
| Liability/accident/personal injury law (prove negligence – equipment/product/security/ safety procedures/staff experience – know Risk Management) | | |
| Commercial law (licensing team logos and clothing) | | |
| Contractual aspects/commercial/ employers/employees | | |
| Anti trust (forbids an organisation to create a monopoly) | | |
| Countryside and Rights of Way Act 2000 (remove occupiers and owners' liability for anyone injured as a consequence of natural accidents on their land, eg, landslides) | | |

ACTIVITY 15

# Summary

- Sport, sponsorship and the media are all interdependent on each other for their success and popularity.
- The media can transform sport into a crucial part of people's lives. Without coverage, sport would have a much lower profile.
- The concept of masculinity tied up with sport success, achieved through violent means, could have consequences outside of the sport setting.
- Violence amongst spectators can be determined by the event, the crowd dynamics and other social factors.
- Drug-taking conforms with the positive deviance model and can be the result of the over commitment to the sport ethic rather than a reflection of declining moral standards. Athletes mostly make their own decisions and cannot be seen wholly as victims of a power system.
- The *greater use* of drugs is due more to the wider availability of drugs.
- Testing has not developed sufficiently to counteract the use of drugs.
- New norms need to be created for sport and athletes should have some participation in this process.

## Review Questions

1. What is meant by the term 'globalisation' and give an example of how this has affected any area of sport.
2. What conditions are required for commercial sport to develop?
3. Give five examples of how commercialisation has affected sport.
4. Give a definition of sponsorship.
5. What is a trust fund and what are the advantages of an athlete having access to one?
6. In table form give the advantages and disadvantages of sponsorship to sports and their performers.
7. Describe four ethical considerations mentioned in the Howell Report in order to control the possible negative effects of sponsorship issues.
8. How has the media helped to retain discrimination in sport?
9. What is the difference between positive and negative deviancy? Give examples of how each may operate in the sport situation.
10. How can sporting situations encourage aggression?
11. What elements within a football match can lead to spectator violence?
12. What are anabolic steroids and how can they help sport performance?
13. What social issues can encourage a performer to take drugs?
14. What are the problems associated with a performer taking drugs?
15. What strategies can be implemented in order to prevent athletes taking drugs?

# 14. International Sporting Competitions

## Chapter introduction

Now we will look at some of the issues raised in chapter 13 in the context of major international competitions. We will look in detail at the:

- Olympic Games
- World Cup

By the end of this chapter you should be able to understand the terms:

- Olympic Games – ancient and modern
- Politics and the Olympics
- City bids
- Olympic marketing
- Role of women in the Olympics
- Presidents of the International Olympic Committee

- World Cup
- Paralympic Games
- Commonwealth Games
- Asian Games

We will also consider the position of the Paralympic, Commonwealth and Asian Games.

## Politics and international sporting events

Across the different countries of the world, sport commands a similar passion and interest. It may take a different form in some areas but its make up is quite similar. Travel and mixing of cultures has led to this situation. In the UK, we are becoming more exposed to sport from other countries, and their sports are being transplanted into our own culture; for example showing American Football on British television has led to a massive increase in participation.

Incidents involving sport and international politics are well known. We will mention a few briefly, but it would be useful for you to research these in more detail.

## South Africa and apartheid

In 1956 the South African government made sport a formal part of its apartheid policy: non-whites were excluded at all levels. They did not only enforce this policy at home. They also rejected the New Zealand cricket side which was to field Maoris in 1960. The New Zealanders agreed not to send any Maoris within their touring side, but this continuing contact with South Africa led to their own isolation, culminating in a boycott of the 1976 Montreal Olympics, after New Zealand were admitted.

A world ban on South African sport was declared in 1964, and was considered by some to be an effective punishment. South African teams were denied the opportunity to display their sporting excellence, something which was extremely important to them. However, they went to great lengths to attract world class competition: in 1969–70, the English Rugby Union entertained a Springbok touring team but suffered from widespread public demonstrations against their decision.

In 1992 black and white athletes marched together as members of the South African team.

However, in 1999 the South African government ruled out race quotas for national teams despite the paucity of blacks representing their country five years after the end of apartheid. The sports minister said, 'Players who have got into national teams should always feel they have got there because they have earned it'.

## ACTIVITY 1

There have been many instances of pressure being exerted by those in political power over sportspeople. Choose any two from the list below and find out as much detail as you can:
- Gleaneagles Agreement 1977
- 1980 Moscow Olympics
- 1984 Los Angeles Olympics
- Apartheid
- Blood sports
- Football hooliganism.

## ACTIVITY 2

Read this extract from George Orwell's 'The Sporting Spirit' taken from *Shooting an Elephant*, which gives a personal account of what he considers to be the link between sport and politics.
*'I am always amazed when I hear people saying that sport creates goodwill between the nations and that if only the common peoples of the world could meet one another at football or cricket, they would have no inclination to meet on the battlefield.*
*Nearly all the sports practised nowadays are competitive. You play to win and the game has little meaning unless you do your utmost to win. On the village green, where you pick up sides and no feeling of local patriotism is involved, it is possible to play simply for the fun and exercise, but as soon as the question of prestige arises, as soon as you feel that you or some larger unit will be disgraced if you lose, the more savage instincts are aroused. Anyone who has played even in a school football match knows this. At the international level, sport is quite frankly mimic warfare. But the significant thing is not the behaviour of the players but the attitude of the spectators, of the nations who work themselves into furies over these absurd contests and seriously believe at any rate for short periods – that running, jumping and kicking a ball are tests of national virtue.*
*As soon as strong feelings of rivalry are aroused, the notion of playing the game according to the rules always vanishes. People want to see one side on top and the other side humiliated, and they forget that victory gained through cheating or through the intervention of the crowd is meaningless. Even when the spectators don't intervene physically, they try to influence the game by cheering their own side and rattling opposing players with boos and insults. Serious sport has nothing to do with fair play. It is bound up with hatred, jealousy, beastfulness, disregard of all the rules and sadistic pleasure in witnessing violence; in other words it is war minus the shooting.'*

## ACTIVITY 3

Consider the following questions:
- What is the author's opinion of competition?
- How does the author make a distinction between two types of physical activity?
- What elements of conflict, cohesion and expectancy are given in the passage?
- What vocabulary does the author use to reinforce the view that modern sport is merely 'mimic warfare'?

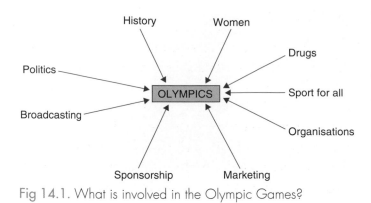

Fig 14.1. What is involved in the Olympic Games?

# Olympic Games

The modern Olympic Games are among the world's greatest sporting events but they have their origins in Ancient Greece.

## Ancient Olympic Games

The ancient Games had been a religious festival, held every four years in honour of Zeus (the Greeks' chief god) and they lasted over 1000 years. The first recorded games are believed to have started in 776 BC and were to last until AD 395. Rituals and wreaths of olive leaves as prizes ensured a fair and honourable competition. The independent city states, which constituted Greece prior to unification in 338 BC, gathered together at Olympia in the sacred grove at Altis to honour the gods, enjoyed the highest levels of competition, and shared their common Greek culture. Less importance was placed on spectators though they came in their thousands, later being drawn from Spain and Africa as the competitions intensified.

A sacred truce was proclaimed for a stated period. It did not attempt to prevent wars but stated that wars should not interrupt or interfere with the Games. Safe passage for the thousands who made their way to Olympia was guaranteed.

Early Olympic programme over five days:

**Day 1:** oath ceremony; boys' events; prayers and sacrifices

**Day 2:** procession of competitors and contests in equestrian events and pentathlon

**Day 3:** procession of ambassadors, judges, athletes, the sacrifice of 100 oxen to Zeus; footraces and a public feast

**Day 4:** combat events and the race in armour

**Day 5:** procession and crowning of victors; feasting and celebrations.

## The athletes

The competitors had to be:

- free (non slaves)
- male Greeks (women were barred on pain of death)
- free from religious or Olympic sanctions
- prepared to swear a solemn oath that they would abide by the rules
- trained to a high standard.

Competitors had to compete nude, to prevent women from taking part.

Victory and success were highly valued and so specialised training, coaching, excesses and profit making came early. Material rewards were mostly given on the athletes' homecoming and by the 6th century this included cash prizes. Athletes themselves became cult figures. Professionalism in sport was perfectly acceptable to the ancient Greeks and their later Roman counterparts.

## Women at the Ancient Games

Women were excluded from the Olympics, so they held their own Games at Heraia with only one event, the foot-race, which was divided into different age groups.

**776 BC** the women-only Games of Heraia followed the same four-yearly pattern as the 'men-only' Olympic Games. There were three other similar festivals at Delphi, Isthmia and Corinth.

**440 BC** Kallipateira, on pain of death if discovered, sneaked into the Olympic Games to see her son's victory.

**396 BC** Kyniska, the Spartan princess, became the first female Olympic champion as owner of the winning horse in the chariot race.

## Sponsorship

Sponsorship was well known in the sport of chariot racing, not just by individuals but by states wishing for publicity.

## Demise of the Games

The threat to the Games came from Rome incorporating mainland Greece into her empire and with it much of Greek culture. The Christian emperor Theodosius 1 banned all pagan rituals including the Olympic Games in AD 391.

## Olympic terms

- **Olympiad** – the interval elapsed between the close of one games and the start of another
- **Panhellenic** – all Greek
- **Pankration** – all-powerful combat involving boxing and wrestling
- **Pentathlon** – combination of events for the all-round athlete (jumping, discus, javelin, 200 m run, wrestling)
- **Stadion** – stadium built with a rectangular track
- **Palaistra** – a place where training in combat and jumping events took place
- **Gymnasium** – athletes could practise on the indoor running track and throwing areas
- **Hippodrome** – horse track on an open stretch of level ground
- **Hellanodikai** – Greek judges, chosen by lot to preside over different events. They wore purple robes and were renowned for impartiality. They meted out punishment to offending athletes
- **Polis** – city state.

What differentiated the Greeks and their sports from other cultures during the same era was the institutionalisation and regularity of festivals.

What differentiated the ancient Olympics from our modern day festival was the merging of physical contests with divinity rather than our more secular approach.

## Modern Olympic Games

Baron Pierre de Coubertin established the modern Olympic Games in 1896 following a visit to England in the nineteenth century where he was impressed with the amateur code of public school team games and code of athleticism. He also became aware in 1890 of the Much Wenlock Olympic Games held in Shropshire. He was worried about the poor physical health of his own people and their lack of national pride. He revived the ancient Olympic Games of Greece based on these ideals, hoping to regenerate a sense of French nationalism as well as a romantic view of furthering international understanding.

He convened a conference in Paris in 1894 to determine the nature of the competition he envisaged:

- eligibility standards of participation
- an administrative body, the International Olympic Committee, to oversee the running of the event
- the first Games to be awarded to Athens for 1896.

Subsequent Games are shown in Table 14.2.

## Symbols of the Olympic Games

### Flag

By 1914 the symbol of the IOC had emerged – the famous five interconnecting rings, all in different colours, displayed on a white background. The rings

Table 14.1. Games comparison 1896/1996

|                   | Athens | Atlanta    |
|-------------------|--------|------------|
| Days              | 5      | 17         |
| Sports            | 9      | 26         |
| Events            | 32     | 271        |
| Countries         | 13     | 200        |
| Athletes          | 311    | 10,500     |
| Tickets available | 60,000 | 11 million |

Table 14.2. Modern Olympic Games

| Summer Olympic Games | Winter Olympic Games |
| --- | --- |
| 1896 Athens (Greece) | |
| 1900 Paris (France) | |
| 1904 St Louis (USA) | |
| 1908 London (Great Britain) | |
| 1912 Stockholm (Sweden) | |
| 1916 Berlin (not celebrated) | |
| 1920 Antwerp (Belgium) | |
| 1924 Paris (France) | 1924 Chamonix (France) |
| 1928 Amsterdam (Holland) | 1928 St Moritz (Switzerland) |
| 1932 Los Angeles (USA) | 1932 Lake Placid (USA) |
| 1936 Berlin (Germany) | 1936 Garmisch-Partenkirchen (Germany) |
| 1940 Tokyo/Helsinki (not celebrated) | 1940 |
| 1944 London (not celebrated) | 1944 |
| 1948 London (Great Britain) | 1948 St Moritz (Switzerland) |
| 1952 Helsinki (Finland) | 1952 Oslo (Norway) |
| 1956 Melbourne (Australia) | 1956 Cortina D'Ampezzo (Italy) |
| 1960 Rome (Italy) | 1960 Squaw Valley (USA) |
| 1964 Tokyo (Japan) | 1964 Innsbruck (Austria) |
| 1968 Mexico City (Mexico) | 1968 Grenoble (France) |
| 1972 Munich (Germany) | 1972 Sapporo (Japan) |
| 1976 Montreal (Canada) | 1976 Innsbruck (Austria) |
| 1980 Moscow (Soviet Union) | 1980 Lake Placid (USA) |
| 1984 Los Angeles (USA) | 1984 Sarajevo (Yugoslavia) |
| 1988 Seoul (Korea) | 1988 Calgary (Canada) |
| 1992 Barcelona (Spain) | 1992 Albertville (France) |
| 1996 Atlanta (USA) | 1994 Lillehammer (Norway) |
| 2000 Sydney (Australia) | 1998 Nagano (Japan) |
| 2004 Athens (Greece) | 2002 Salt Lake City (USA) |
| 2008 Beijing (China) | 2006 Turin (Italy) |

ig 14.2. Collection of early Olympic programmes, 1912–1964

epresent the five continents involved in the Olympic Games – Europe, Asia, Oceania, Africa nd the Americas.

## Motto

The Olympic motto is 'Citius, Altius, Fortius' which means 'swifter, higher, stronger'.

The following message also appears on the scoreboard at every Olympic Games:

*'The most important thing in the Olympic Games is not to win but to take part, just as the most important thing in life is not the triumph but the struggle. The essential thing is not to have conquered but to have fought well.'*

## Goals

The six goals of the Olympic movement are based on Coubertin's original motivations that the Games were to enhance human development. These ideals can be called 'Olympism'.

*Olympism – 'a philosophy of life, exalting and combining in a balanced whole the quality of body, will and mind. Blending sport, culture and education, Olympism seeks to create a way of life based on the joy found in effort, the educational value of good example and respect for the universal fundamental ethical principles'.*

The six goals can thus be summarised:

* personal excellence
* sport as education
* cultural exchange
* mass participation
* fair play
* international understanding.

## Olympic flame

This has its traditions in the ancient Games lit at the altar of Zeus. In Berlin the tradition of the torch relay from Olympia to the host city began.

## Olympic oath

The competitors vow:

*'In the name of all the competitors I promise that we shall take part in these Olympic Games respecting and abiding by the rules which govern them in the true spirit of sportsmanship.'*

## Peace

Pigeons or doves were first used as a symbol of peace in 1896.

# Olympic Charter

This charter contains the principles, rules and byelaws adopted by the IOC. It governs the organisation and operation of the Olympic movement and lays down the conditions to be observed during the Games. The main purpose is to:

* contribute to building a peaceful and better world
* educate youth through sport
* enter into sport without discrimination
* observe the Olympic spirit of friendship, solidarity and fair play.

# Political pressures

The Games have been affected by wider political situations and are often remembered as much for the political events surrounding them as the athletic feats. One of the key reasons is that the Games have provided a focus for the country hosting the event. Their political systems are given prominent media coverage and instances have occurred where governments have used this to promote their political message.

The **1936 Olympics** were held in Berlin, and Adolf Hitler used this opportunity to promote the values of the Third Reich on the world stage. The authorities supported the athletes considerably, as they were to show the superiority of the Aryan race. Jesse Owens, a black American, was to upset this plan when he won four gold medals which were to be withheld from him by Hitler. Almost as a direct consequence of the huge propaganda exercise, the Games would not be held again until 1948.

The **1956 Olympics** were held in Melbourne but saw the withdrawal of China due to the entry of Taiwan, enemies of communism. It was not until 1984 that both countries competed at the same time.

The **1968 Mexico Games** witnessed two black Americans being sent home as a result of their 'black power' salute. The reason behind this protest was the discrimination still in existence in the United States. Tommie Smith said.

Table 14.3. Olympics and politics

| Year | Venue | Political activity and affected countries |
|------|-------|-------------------------------------------|
| 1936 | Berlin | Germany used Games for Nazi propaganda<br>Hitler's Aryan race theory discredited – Jesse Owen, a black athlete, won four gold medals |
| 1956 | Melbourne | Soviet Union invaded Hungary. Spain and Holland withdrew in protest<br>China withdrew because of Taiwan's inclusion<br>Egypt and Lebanon did not compete because they were fighting for the Suez Canal |
| 1964 | Tokyo | South Africa's invitation cancelled in 1963<br>Indonesia and North Korea not allowed to compete because they had taken part in an international tournament considered unsatisfactory by the IOC |
| 1968 | Mexico City | South Africa's invitation withdrawn because of threatened boycott by other countries, over apartheid<br>2001 Mexicans killed and many more injured by army during demonstration against use of government money for the Games – widespread poverty in the country<br>Black American athletes gave clenched fist salute – against treatment of Black Americans |
| 1972 | Munich | Rhodesia's invitation withdrawn because of apartheid – other countries threatened to boycott if they competed<br>Israeli athletes and officials assassinated by Palestinian terrorists |
| 1976 | Montreal | 30 nations in total did not attend<br>African nations boycotted Games because New Zealand rugby team had toured South Africa<br>French Canadians were angered that the Queen was to perform the opening ceremony<br>Taiwan withdrew<br>Several competitors banned for using anabolic steroids<br>Two Romanians and one Soviet athlete asked for political asylum in Canada |
| 1980 | Moscow | Soviet Union had invaded Afghanistan and because of the Soviets' record on Human Rights and their refusal to withdraw troops, 52 nations boycotted the games led by the USA |
| 1984 | Los Angeles | Soviet Union withdrew, along with many Eastern European countries, Cuba and others<br>Some felt that it was in retaliation, but official reason given was over 'concern for the safety of their teams'<br>It was felt that the organisers had violated the Olympic charter |
| 1992 | Barcelona | South Africa returned to Olympic competition after abolition of apartheid<br>Germany competed as one nation<br>Soviet Union had ceased to exist and the individual countries competed in their own right |
| 2000 | Sydney | Controversy over IOC bribery and corruption led to changes in the bidding procedure |

'If I win I am an American not a Black American. But if I did something bad they would say "Negro"'.

Equally, when opponents to the government wish to make a political protest they also have a prime opportunity when the eyes of the world are watching. The result is often a boycott of countries from the Games. A boycott is the refusal of a faction to participate in a sporting event in order to deliver a political message, and is usually a rejection of a political regime.

The Soviet Union boycott of the **Los Angeles Games in 1984** had a large effect on the event. The reasons for the boycott were complex but involved.

- a reaction to the American boycott of the Moscow Olympics in 1980
- fear of defection of their own athletes to the West
- the ability of the men's track and field team
- the ideological problem of being a part of successful capitalist games.

> Table 14.3 charts some of the political situations that have surrounded some of the Olympic Games. Select one of those listed and find out information in greater detail.
>
> ACTIVITY 4

## Commercial pressures

Today sport organisations allied with national governments mount elaborate plans to win the approval of the IOC to host the Olympic Games. They do this for a variety of reasons:

- civic and national pride
- political gain
- economic benefits.

## City bids

The selection of the host city is vitally important as the success of the Games can often be dependent on the site chosen. Each candidate city must demonstrate to the IOC that its bid to stage the greatest multi-disciplinary event in the world has the support of its people and its political authorities.

Many factors may play their part, not necessarily purely financial or technical.

A manual for bidding cities was available for the 2000 bid. It contains evaluation criteria which the candidate cities have to fulfil. The Evaluation Commission is responsible for preparing a complete evaluation report after visiting each city. The procedure now has two phases owing to the large number of bids:

- Phase I – Selection of the finalists on the basis of the Evaluation Commission report
- Phase II – Members of the IOC given the opportunity to visit the finalist cities before voting.

Voting takes place by secret ballot. Each member is only allowed to vote for one city. After each round if no one city has an absolute majority the city with the fewest votes is eliminated. Successive rounds are held until one city achieves a majority.

Following allegations of misconduct during the Salt Lake City bid for the Winter Olympics in 2002, suggestions for a selection college were put in place for Turin 2006. This selection college would select two finalist cities from among the six finalists. The selection of the host city took place immediately after one another on the same day. The IOC president was unable to vote for the host city on this occasion.

London's bid for the 2012 Olympic Games has been in full swing recently. The decision to bid commits the government, London and the British Olympic Association to a £17 million process which will end in 2005 when the International Olympic Committee announces its choice. If successful

**City details – Manchester**

**General comments**

The Bid Committee enjoys strong relations with the National Olympic Committee. The bid is supported by the private sector and local and national government, including all major political parties. All capital costs will be covered by the private sector, underlining commitment to long-term investments for the city, and underwritten by the government, which has also confirmed its total support of the bid.

The Commission's visit was well organised and reflected a professional bid team with good experience and thorough planning. The City is experienced in organizing large, high-security events. The Bid Committee carefully studied the Barcelona Games, sending experts to cover various fields of activity including security.

The Bid Committee has paid attention to involving the community in its plans and has developed a project to promote Olympism in local schools.

The venue strategy is a highlight, comprising a compact concept of an innercity games with a well-planned legacy and after-use of all facilities. The Olympic Ring, of which the radius is a 20-minute drive from the Olympic Village, contains 21 of the 25 sports and all facilities for the Olympic Family. Ten sports are within walking distance of the Olympic Village.

**City details – Sydney**

**General comments**

The Commission's visit was well organised, reflecting a professional team with much experience and well thought-out planning. The Bid Committee enjoys excellent relations with the National Olympic Committee. Sydney thoroughly analysed the Barcelona Games, sending experts in various fields to study conditions during the Games, particularly as regards security and accreditation. The bid offers conditions over and above what is required by the IOC.

Sydney offers a solid bid and a safe environment for the Olympic Games. The Commission met with Prime Minister Paul Keating, who confirmed the Australian government's support of the bid. The Commission also received reports confirming the support of all political parties, the trades' unions and environmentalists, notably Greenpeace, for the bid. Support was noted across the board, including the Federal and State Governments, the city, the business community and the local population.

The compact nature of the bid is a great asset with the majority of competitors being able to walk to their competition venues. The Commission felt that the concept of the Games was based on priority to the athletes. One Olympic Village, enabling all participating athletes to fully enjoy the Olympic experience, is a positive factor.

With 140 ethnic groups living in Sydney, language should not cause any problem. The Bid Committee has paid great attention to involving the local population in the bid. Forty thousand volunteers have already committed themselves to work for the Games, with 100,000 expected by September 1993. A regional school project promoting Olympism is in place.

An agreement exists whereby the Sydney organising committee would be largely composed of members of the Bidding Committee.

Fig 14.3. Extracts from the evaluation commission report on 2000 Olympics bid

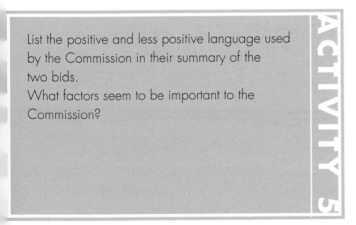

**ACTIVITY 5**

List the positive and less positive language used by the Commission in their summary of the two bids.

What factors seem to be important to the Commission?

London will then face a bill of more than £4 billion to provide the facilities and infrastructure required.

## London Olympic Games 2012 – the key benefits

### Winnability for 2012

In the UK only London has the size and status to be selected by the IOC when put up against other world cities. Paris and New York are the main threats from a number of contenders, although Vancouver winning the 2010 Winter Games will weaken any North American bid for 2012. Given that IOC President Jacques Rogge said that any bid from London would be 'formidable', London would have a good chance of success in a run-off with Paris.

### British sport

There is a tremendous feel-good factor associated with the staging of an Olympics. Both Spain and Australia achieved their highest medal tally on home soil. The inspiration will drive many of our youngsters to take part in sport and pursue dreams of becoming an Olympian.

### Health, crime and education

Increased participation in sport will in turn lead to a healthier society. Anecdotally, participation in sport has led to downturns in youth crime and is a stimulus for education.

## Social inclusion

The Olympics would be a driving force for breaking down divisions whether they be age, gender, race or religion. This diversity would be celebrated through the staging of the Olympic and Paralympic Games. The Games would be the catalyst for the drive towards a more sustainable society.

## Regeneration and new housing

Improved infrastructure including the provision of 4,000 new and much-needed homes in East London will be delivered. It will stimulate and bring forward the comprehensive upgrade of the East End environment by developing contaminated and under-used land.

## Employment

Staging a Games in London would create around 9,000 new full-time jobs, of which 3,000 would be in the local East End economy. Businesses would be encouraged to relocate to the area through improved technological and transport links.

## Legacy

Provision of facilities for both elite and grass root sports with defined legacies. Up to 100 training venues will be required in the form of refurbished school and community facilities.

## Tourism

An independent study has shown that there was over £2 billion in inbound tourism spending in Australia attributable to the staging of the Olympics in 2000. The Games give a country a unique opportunity to showcase itself to a huge global audience.

## UK investment

Inward and outward UK investment, expertise and the raised profile of staging the Games would have a beneficial impact on UK exports. Staging the Sydney Games has allowed Australian companies to win 10% of the capital projects in Beijing, bringing in £1.1 billion.

## Convention industry

Staging the Games would provide a significant boost to the convention industry. The Premier of New South Wales reported that the Sydney Games created bookings for £223 million worth of international business conferences. Such opportunities will not be limited to London alone.

## British cities

It is not only London that can gain, other British cities and regions would gain through the preparation and training camps for overseas teams and through the staging of the football and sailing.

# London's Olympic bid: a timeline

**January 2003**
London's bid is debated in Parliament.

**February 2003**
The Cabinet defers its decision on whether to back the bid due to the looming war in Iraq.

**April 2003**
Tony Blair is reported to have decided to back the bid but the government makes no official comment.

**May 2003**
Cabinet Minister Tessa Jowell announces the government will 'back London to the hilt' and will set aside £2.375 billion to pay for the staging of the Games.

**11 July 2003**
The British Olympic Association officially notifies the International Olympic Committee that London will bid.

**15 July 2003**
The deadline for cities to inform the IOC passes, leaving London, New York, Paris, Madrid, Moscow, Leipzig, Istanbul, Rio de Janeiro and Havana to do battle for 2012.

**15 January 2004**

BOA must hand the IOC further details of its plans for venues, transport and security.

**May 2004**

IOC rejects least attractive bids.

**15 November 2004**

Formal bid must be handed in to IOC.

**February and March 2005**

Each bidding city spends a week hosting the IOC's evaluation commission, which consists of 10–15 IOC members.

**May 2005**

Commission reports its findings.

**July 2005**

The IOC's 128 members meet in Singapore to choose the host city for the 2012 Games.

*Source:* BBC Sport

# Olympic marketing

'Marketing has become an increasingly important issue for all of us within the Olympic Movement. The revenues derived from television, sponsorship and general fundraising help to provide the movement with its financial independence. However, in developing these programmes we must always remember that it is sport that must control its destiny not commercial interests. Every act of support for the Olympic Movement promotes peace, friendship and solidarity throughout the world.'

*Juan Antonio Samaranch*

It has always been up to the Games Organising Committee to raise the necessary funds. In 1896 this occurred via ticket sales, commemorative medals, programme advertising and private donations. Today this is done mainly through the sale of TV rights, sponsorship, licensing, ticket sales, coins and stamps. It is estimated to have generated US$3.5 billion for the Olympic quadrennium 1997–2000.

The IOC retains 7–10% of the revenues with the remainder going to the Organising Committees, the International Sport Federations (ISF) and National Olympic Committees (NOC). Included in these are the International Paralympic Committee and Paralympic Organising Committee.

## Objectives of Olympic marketing

Under the presidency of Samaranch the IOC has established the following objectives via a strategic marketing plan carried out by the IOC Marketing Department. These are:

- to ensure the financial stability of the Games
- to promote continuity of marketing across each Olympic Games
- to provide equity of revenue distribution between the OCOGs, the NOCs, the International Federations and provide support for the emerging nations
- to provide free air transmission across the whole world
- to protect the Olympic ideals by safeguarding against unnecessary commercialisation
- to attract the support of marketing partners to promote Olympism and Olympic ideals.

# Sponsorship

The International Olympic Committee has expanded its investments to include 200 nations and has made the Olympic Games one of the biggest media events in the world. Sponsorship for the Games is set up on a global basis as the IOC recognised it possessed a valuable marketing tool for companies beginning to realise the potential of the global marketplace. The Olympic Programme (TOP) established in 1985 is now in its fourth cycle. For TOP IV there are eleven world-wide sponsors each of whom enjoys total exclusivity in their respective business areas. When the programme was launched fewer than 10 NOCs had

Olympic marketing revenues 2001–2004

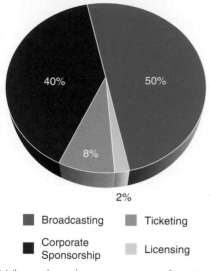

Fig 14.4a. Where does the money come from?

Olympic marketing revenue distribution 2001–2004

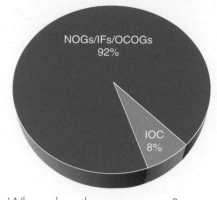

Fig 14.4b. Where does the money go to?
*Source*: International Olympic Committee.

any form of marketing revenue. Now all 200 NOCs receive funding via this programme. They also provide services such as equipment, cameras, software and so on.

Sponsorship is necessary, as the staging of the event is enormously expensive, well recognised after the 1976 Montreal Games that almost bankrupted the city. Taxpayers were unwilling to shoulder the costs, while television companies were willing to pay large sums to transmit. Without international coverage (167 countries) the sponsors would not be willing to invest so much. The Los Angeles Games marked a turning point whereby the IOC began to modernise its marketing policies through TOP. However, some problems were apparent. The revenue gained from the 1984 Games came almost exclusively from television rights to the United States, which could cause the IOC to be vulnerable. Also sponsors who sold the world-wide rights found that some individual NOCs required them to be bought separately. This led to Levi handing back the rights.

Samaranch wished to:

- find alternative sources of funding
- have more authority in television negotiations.

TOP allowed exclusive rights to a few selected international companies, paying more than the

| Coco-Cola | John Hancock | Kodak | McDonald's | Panasonic |
| SAMSUNG | Schlumberger | Sports Illustrated | Swatch | VISA | Xerox |

Fig 14.5. Top partners: The following companies are Top Partners for the Athens 2004 Olympic games

previous 300 companies had done. They in turn benefited from linking their product with the Olympic themes of excellence, participation and fair play. It was to prove a valuable symbiotic relationship.

**TOP I** (1985–1988)
**TOP II** (1989–1992)
**TOP III** (1993–1996)
**TOP IV** (1997–2000)
**TOP V** (2001–2004)

Olympic revenue increased dramatically, while dependence on US television rights reduced.

The Olympic Games remain, with Wimbledon Tennis Championships, the only major sporting events that do not have stadium advertising. Many would feel this justifies the claim that commercialism is being controlled. However, it is clearly a marketing judgement also because should stadium advertising be permitted there would be a drop in revenue from both television and sponsors as there would be a loss of exclusivity.

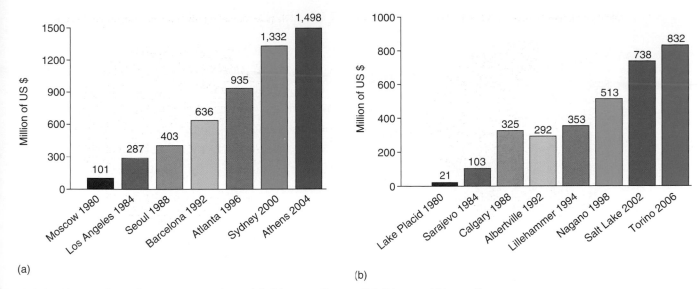

Fig 14.6. Olympic broadcast revenue charts (a) Olympic Games (b) Olympic Winter Games

## What does it cost a company?

**1984**   Coca-Cola $30 million
Visa International and Mars $22 million each
Eastman Kodak $21 million

These sums only buy the right to use the Olympic rings in advertising and promotion outside the arena.

## What do companies have to do?

It costs the company two or three times as much again for the company to promote through advertising, staff incentive schemes, hospitality programmes, etc. However, many feel they cannot afford to be seen not to be involved with the most prestigious sporting event in the world. Market research has also shown that consumers show a decided preference for products displaying the Olympic symbol. It is held in equal esteem with such humanitarian brands as the Red Cross and UNICEF.

The ethics of commercialism are always being addressed but it is doubtful if ethics would override serious marketing objectives. The one benefit of commercialisation is the opportunity for the Solidarity fund to assist under-funded NOCs.

Licensing existed in the time of the 1896 Games. This means the rights to sell memorabilia. After a few years of 'trash and trinkets' the Lillehammer Winter Games developed a more quality-controlled product.

## Broadcasting

The influence of television developed as the twentieth century advanced. Major sporting events could not exist in their current format without it. It was in Tokyo that the first satellite relay of the Games took place incorporating stereo sound from all venues. It was the inability of the IOC to attract enough advertising for both the Summer and Winter Games that resulted in the decision in 1986 to hold the two Games alternately every two years. The hope was to improve marketing prospects.

The fundamental IOC policy is outlined in the Olympic Charter, to ensure maximum presentation of the Games to the widest possible global audience free of charge. TV rights are therefore sold only to companies who can broadcast coverage throughout their respective countries or territories. This policy is set for the 2008 Games. TV rights continue to account for just less than 45% of Olympic revenue.

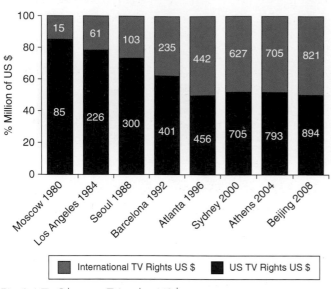

Fig 14.7. Olympic TV rights US$

## Olympic Solidarity est. 1961

Olympic Solidarity is the body responsible for managing and administering the share of the television rights of the Olympic Games that is allocated to the NOCs. This was made possible following the Los Angeles Games when the Olympic Solidarity budgets were established on a quadrennial plan allowing fixed annual assistance to the NOCs. Since the first quadrennial cycle there has been an increase of 430%.

The basic ideas upon which it is based are those of generosity, understanding and international cooperation, cultural exchanges, the development of sport and its educational aspects, and the promotion of a society concerned with human dignity and peace. Specific programmes exist for the most disadvantaged NOCs.

Its specific objectives are 'The aim of the Olympic Solidarity is to organise aid to NOCs recognised by the IOC, in particular those which have the greatest need of it. This aid takes the form of programmes elaborated jointly by the IOC and the NOCs, with the technical assistance of the IFs if necessary'.

# Women and Olympism

Women have overcome bigotry and apathy towards their participation in sport and particularly the Olympic Games. However, the number of events and athletes and members of the IOC have increased and look set to continue if better media coverage and more female representation in the decision-making corridors are encouraged.

**1894:** Baron Pierre de Coubertin did not invite women to the Olympic congress. They were also excluded from participating in the Olympic Games. A Greek woman ran the marathon unofficially. De Coubertin's view of women was that their only role should be to 'bestow garlands upon the athletes'.

**1900:** two events for women introduced at the Paris Games, where the organisers of the Universal Exhibition allowed tennis and golf. Charlotte Cooper of England became the first woman to win a gold medal.

**1904:** the Games at St Louis were part of the Louisiana Purchase Exhibition which allowed archery for women and some boxing! These events were not recognised by the International Olympic Committee.

**1908:** the suffragette movement threatened the London Games if women were excluded. Forty-three women from four countries competed in figure skating, tennis and archery. A woman was a member of the winning crew in the 7-metre yacht race.

**1912:** fifty-five women from ten countries were to participate in swimming and tennis. However, due to the refusal of the United States to allow women swimmers due to improper dress, the tennis players walked out in sympathy.

**1919:** the First World War deprived de Coubertin of the opportunity to ban female competition as the role of women had changed in society along with attitudes.

**1920:** one hundred and thirty six women from twenty countries participated in tennis, swimming, archery, figure skating and yachting.

**1922:** the first female organised (International Women's Sports Federation – IWSF) Olympic Games took place in Paris as a protest at the exclusion of women by the Amateur Athletics Federation. Athletes from eight countries competed in eleven athletic events before crowds of 30,000.

**1924:** the first Winter Olympics. Women were always to participate following the IOC vote to allow greater participation.

**1928:** Amsterdam saw women participate in the 800 metres. Five out of the eight competitors collapsed, resulting in the event being banned for 36 years.

**1930:** the third 'Women's World Games' in Prague was a success. A Czech, later admitted by the authorities to being a man, won the 800 metres. This saw the beginnings of 'femininity testing'.

**1935:** 135 nations now affiliated to the IWSF which espoused the idea of women organising their own Games entirely and leaving the Olympics to the men. The International Amateur Athletics Federation decided to recognise women's athletics in 1936 resulting in the demise of the women's organisation and opportunity of self-government.

**1948:** the 'Flying Dutchwoman' (and mother of two) Fanny Blankers-Koen, won four gold medals.

**1952:** the first mixed event saw the female Lis Hartel taking silver medal in the equestrian event.

**1956:** the Winter Games in Italy saw the first female to take the Olympic oath for all competitors.

**1960:** Rome saw an increase in female competitors five times that of men. There were now 30 women's events with 537 competitors.

**1964:** two sisters were suspected of drug taking while a speed skater made Olympic Winter Games history by winning her sixth gold medal.

**1968:** at Mexico City Enriquetta Basilio becomes the first woman to carry the Olympic flame into the stadium. Sex tests for women introduced.

**1972:** a female, Olga Connelly, elected captain and flag bearer of the United States team. This is not mentioned in their Olympic Yearbook.

**1973:** 10th Olympic congress in Bulgaria. Only three women out of 102 National Olympic committees represented.

**1976:** East German women dominated the track and swimming events. First female to be disqualified for drug taking.

**1980:** mother-daughter success. The daughter of the 1952 discus silver medallist won gold in the relay in Moscow.

**1981:** 11th Olympic congress now had six women delegates from 149 NOCs. First women appointed to the International Olympic committee. Princess Anne was to become one of Britain's members.

**1984:** Joan Benoit won the first women's Olympic marathon in Los Angeles. Evelyn Ashford set a new Olympic record in the women's 100 metres at 10.97 seconds. Women's 400 m and heptathlon had their Olympic debut.

**1988:** in Seoul Jackie Joyner-Kersee improved her own heptathlon record by 79 points to secure gold. Rosa Mota dominated the marathon. Tennis returned but with the proviso that fewer women than men be allowed to compete.

**1992:** at Barcelona Gail Devers overcame serious illness to win the 100 m. Judo became an Olympic sport.

**1996:** at Atlanta Women's football introduced as a new Olympic discipline.

**2000:** Sydney four new sports and 24 new events for women. They also competed for the first time in the same number of team sports as men.

**2004:** Kelly Holmes wins gold in 800 m and 1500 m for Great Britain.

Efforts are being made to have more women as instructors and participants in Olympic solidarity programmes, in particular with scholarships for athletes and coaches. This will help promote them in the decision-making structures of sports organisations. Despite some progress their level of participation in these areas is very low. In a training programme for sports leaders enabling members to become directors of national courses which ran between 1986 and 1993, only 33 out of 292 members were women.

The NOCs and the International Federations were to have as a goal that at least 10% of all officers in their decision-making structures should be women. Since the reign of Samaranch a woman has been co-opted as a member of the IOC for the first time. The IOC currently has 105 active members.

# Sport for all

Sport for all is a movement promoting the Olympic ideal that sport is a human right for everyone regardless of race, social class and sex.

The IOC set up a Sport for All Working Group in 1983 to establish how the Movement could help promote activities that increased health and fitness.

In 1987 the Commission launched the Olympic Day run which takes place every year on June 23rd, celebrating the IOC foundation day in 1894. The run is arranged by 170 NOCs all over the world and is open to men, women and children of all ages. A substantial number of people with disabilities have started to take part. In 1999 approximately 766, 765 participants were recorded. Olympic Solidarity provides revenue and Coca-Cola has been heavily involved since 1989.

# Drugs

The IOC has taken a stance on drugs in sport:

- coordination against drug taking
- sponsor conferences
- accredit laboratories

- establish a list of banned substances.
- **1962** following the death of the Danish cyclist in 1960 the IOC made a resolution against doping
- **1961** IOC Medical Commission set up
- **1968** drug testing in the Winter Olympics (mainly amphetamines)
- **1975** anabolic steroids were banned
- **1976** testing for anabolic steroids at Montreal Games
- **1981** creation of the 'Doping and Biochemistry of Sport' sub-commission within the IOC Medical Commission. This committee produces the list of banned substances which is recognised by the whole of the sports world
- **1988** the International Olympic Charter Against Doping in Sport was adopted. This was replaced in 1995 by the IOC Medical code
- **1997** international experts brought together to discuss research on the three substances testosterone, EPO and human growth hormone
- **1999** after the shocking events in the world of cycling the IOC convened a World Conference on Doping.

# The IOC Medical Commission

This organisation has three main responsibilities:

- gives guidance and approval to the host country of an Olympic Games on medical and paramedical equipment and facilities at the Olympic village
- responsible for doping control at the Olympic Games, for classifying the pharmacological substances and methods and for proposing sanctions to the IOC Executive Board when doping rules have been contravened
- the Commission is also responsible for femininity control for women's sporting events at the Games and issues certificates of femininity to those who have passed this control.

Table 14.4. Faster, higher, further

| Women and Men at each Olympiad | | | | | | | |
|---|---|---|---|---|---|---|---|
| Summer | | Place | Date | Nations | Women | Men | Total |
| I | 1896 | Athens, Greece | 6–15 April | 13 | – | 311 | 311 |
| II | 1900 | Paris, France | 20 May–28 October | 22 | 12 | 1318 | 1330 |
| III | 1904 | St Louis, USA | 1 July–23 November | 13 | 8 | 617 | 625 |
| * | 1906 | Athens, Greece | 22 April–2 May | 20 | 7 | 877 | 884 |
| IV | 1908 | London, England | 27 April–31 October | 22 | 36 | 2020 | 2056 |
| V | 1912 | Stockholm, Sweden | 5 May–22 July | 28 | 55 | 2491 | 2546 |
| VI | 1916 | Berlin, Germany | Not held due to war | – | – | – | – |
| VII | 1920 | Antwerp, Belgium | 20 April–12 September | 29 | 64 | 2628 | 2692 |
| VIII | 1924 | Paris, France | 4 May–27 July | 44 | 136 | 2956 | 3092 |
| IX | 1928 | Amsterdam, Netherlands | 17 May–12 August | 46 | 290 | 2724 | 3014 |
| X | 1932 | Los Angeles, USA | 30 July–14 August | 37 | 127 | 1281 | 1408 |
| XI | 1936 | Berlin, Germany | 1–16 August | 49 | 328 | 3738 | 4066 |
| XII | 1940 | Tokyo, then Helsinki | Not held due to war | – | – | – | – |
| XIII | 1944 | London, England | Not held due to war | – | – | – | – |
| XIV | 1948 | London, England | 29 July–14 August | 59 | 385 | 3714 | 4099 |
| XV | 1952 | Helsinki, Finland | 19 July–3 August | 69 | 518 | 4407 | 4925 |
| XVI | 1956 | Melbourne, Australia† | 22 November–8 December | 67 | 371 | 2813 | 3184 |
| XVII | 1960 | Rome, Italy | 25 August–11 September | 83 | 610 | 4736 | 5346 |
| XVIII | 1964 | Tokyo, Japan | 10–24 October | 93 | 683 | 4457 | 5140 |
| XIX | 1968 | Mexico City, Mexico | 12–27 October | 112 | 781 | 4749 | 5530 |
| XX | 1972 | Munich, FRG | 26 August–10 September | 122 | 1070 | 6068 | 7156 |
| XXI | 1976 | Montreal, Canada | 17 July–1 August | 92 | 1251 | 4834 | 6085 |
| XXII | 1980 | Moscow, Soviet Union | 19 July–3 August | 81 | 1088 | 4238 | 5326 |

*(Continued)*

Table 14.4. (Continued)

| Summer | | Place | Date | Nations | Women | Men | Total |
|---|---|---|---|---|---|---|---|
| XXIII | 1984 | Los Angeles, USA | 28 July–12 August | 140 | 1620 | 5458 | 7078 |
| XXIV | 1988 | Seoul, South Korea | 17 September–2 October | 159 | 2194 | 6197 | 8391 |
| XXV | 1992 | Barcelona, Spain | 25 July–9 August | 169 | 2704 | 6652 | 9356 |
| XXVI | 1996 | Atlanta, USA | 19 July–4 August | 197 | 3512 | 6806 | 10,318 |
| XXVII | 2000 | Sydney, Australia | 15 September–1 October | 199 | 4069 | 6582 | 10,651 |
| XXVIII | 2004 | Athens, Greece | 13–29 August | 201 | – | – | 10,500 |
| Winter | | Place | Date | Nations | Women | Men | Total |
| I | 1924 | Chamonix, France | 25 January–4 February | 16 | 13 | 281 | 294 |
| II | 1928 | St Moritz, Switzerland | 11–19 February | 25 | 27 | 468 | 495 |
| III | 1932 | Lake Placid, USA | 4–15 February | 17 | 32 | 274 | 306 |
| IV | 1936 | Germisch-Partenkirchen, Germany | 6–16 February | 28 | 80 | 675 | 755 |
| – | 1940 | Sapporo, then St Moritz, then Garmisch-Partenkirchen | Not held due to war | – | – | – | – |
| – | 1944 | Cortina d'Ampezzo, Italy | Not held due to war | – | – | – | – |
| V | 1948 | St Moritz, Switzerland | 30 January–8 February | 28 | 77 | 636 | 713 |
| VI | 1952 | Oslo, Norway | 14–25 February | 30 | 109 | 623 | 732 |
| VII | 1956 | Cortina d'Ampezzo, Italy | 26 January–5 February | 32 | 132 | 687 | 819 |
| VIII | 1960 | Squaw Valley, USA | 18–28 February | 30 | 144 | 521 | 665 |
| IX | 1964 | Innsbruck, Austria | 29 January–9 February | 36 | 200 | 986 | 1186 |
| X | 1968 | Grenoble, France | 6–18 February | 37 | 212 | 1081 | 1293 |
| XI | 1972 | Sapporo, Japan | 3–13 February | 35 | 217 | 1015 | 1232 |
| XII | 1976 | Innsbruck, Austria | 4–15 February | 37 | 228 | 900 | 1128 |
| XIII | 1980 | Lake Placid, USA | 13–24 February | 37 | 234 | 833 | 1067 |

(Continued)

Table 14.4. (*Continued*)

| Winter | | Place | Date | Nations | Women | Men | Total |
|--------|------|-------|------|---------|-------|------|-------|
| XIV | 1984 | Sarajevo, Yugoslavia | 8–19 February | 49 | 276 | 1002 | 1278 |
| XV | 1988 | Calgary, Canada | 13–28 February | 57 | 317 | 1128 | 1445 |
| XVI | 1992 | Albertville, France | 8–23 February | 64 | 488 | 1313 | 1801 |
| XVII | 1994 | Lillehammer, Norway | 12–27 February | 67 | 522 | 1215 | 1737 |
| XVIII | 1998 | Nagano, Japan | 7–22 February | 72 | 787 | 1389 | 2176 |
| XIX | 2002 | Salt Lake City, USA | 8–24 February | 77 | 886 | 1513 | 2399 |

\* Tenth anniversary Games, official but not numbered.
† This total includes the 13 women and 146 men who took part in the equestrian events, which were held in Stockholm.
*Source:* Adrienne Blue/www.olympic.org/uk

The IOC signed agreements with the NOCs and the International Federations in 1994.

'*Doping contravenes the ethics of both sport and medical science*'.

The IOC Medical Commission bans:

- the administration of substances belonging to the selected classes of pharmacological agents: stimulants, narcotics, anabolic agents, diuretics, peptide hormones and analogues
- the various doping methods: blood doping, pharmacological, chemical and physical manipulations.

IOC Recommended Sanctions for positive cases in doping control:

1. Androgenic anabolic steroids, amphetamine related and other stimulants, caffeine, diuretics, beta-blockers, narcotic analgesics and designer drugs:
   - Two years for the first offence
   - Life ban for the second offence.

2. Ephedrine, phenylpropanolamine (when administered orally as a cough suppressant or painkiller)
   - A maximum of three months for first offence

Table 14.5. Number of IOC accredited laboratories

| | |
|------|----|
| 1986 | 18 |
| 1987 | 21 |
| 1988 | 20 |
| 1989 | 20 |
| 1990 | 21 |
| 1991 | 21 |
| 1992 | 23 |
| 1993 | 23 |
| 1994 | 24 |
| 1995 | 24 |
| 1996 | 25 |

- Two years for second offence
- Life ban for third offence.

A fair hearing will be granted to an athlete with the presence of the head of the IOC accredited laboratory that reported the result.

## Accredited laboratories

The IOC accredits laboratories that meet the required standards and operate according to appropriate procedures. This process is reviewed annually. Accreditation guarantees that samples are analysed in accordance with recognised procedures maintaining high standards.

The growth in the number of laboratories is shown in table 14.5.

At present there are 27 accredited laboratories across the five continents. The number of samples analysed in 1997 was 106,561.

# World Anti-Doping Agency

This was established in 1999 in Lausanne to promote and coordinate the fight against doping in sport at the international level. Members will be drawn from a balance between the public bodies and the Olympic movement and the framework was developed among international sporting and intergovernmental organisations. Athletes will also be represented. High ethical principles are to be followed and the main focus will be on unifying the approach towards the problem of doping. Its activities will include research, education and prevention.

# Presidents of the International Olympic Committee

## Avery Brundage 1952–1972

The impact of Brundage on the Olympic movement was enormous. He had to see the Games through many turbulent years including the controversies over the state sponsored amateurs of the Soviet Union; the expulsion of South Africa in 1972; the IOC's recognition of Taiwan and China's isolation until 1984.

He tried to steer sport clear of politics and his philosophy was:

- the Olympic Games should remain amateur
- the Olympic movement should not embrace commercialism
- women's role in the Olympics should be reduced
- the Olympic Games should not seek a global impact
- South Africa should not be excluded.

However, on one point he did accede to the need for television to boost the coffers by advertising the Olympic movement. The rule 49 came into being: televising of the Olympic Games of more than three minute news briefs aired three times a day would have to be bought.

He was therefore much more popular with conservatives than with those who had more liberal viewpoints.

# Juan Antonio Samaranch

Some achievements:

- loosening of the eligibility code, rule 26 of the Olympic Charter. Professionals were now admitted. One effect of this was to outweigh the unbalanced nature of the superiority of the state sponsored amateurs (stamateurs). However, it also created the travesty of the stars of the National Basketball Association of the USA competing against Angola, Lithuania and Croatia in Barcelona 1992.

- increasing the commercialisation and marketing of the Games in order that they could continue on a more secure basis

- IOC membership to include athletes, more members of the International Federations and NOCs and women!

- stabilising east-west, communist-capitalist relations in the run up to Seoul

- acceptance in 1992 of a team from the newly independent states from Russia

- Drug Programme improvements

- acceptance of South Africa back into the Olympic Movement

- personal knowledge of most of the 172 member NOCs

- creation of an Olympic museum in Lausanne.

# Jacque Rogge

The current Olympic President is Jacque Rogge whose influence has not as yet been fully realised.

# Future of the Olympic Games

Balance is needed to ensure the future of the Olympic movement. Commerce must be balanced by philanthropy, there must be pageantry to help uphold the traditions and every effort made to get most of the world's great male and female athletes to the Olympic stadiums:

- the size of the Games needs to be controlled
- the wealth they generate needs to be distributed back into the Games and towards worthy initiatives
- cultural differences must be recognised

- emphasise the belief in the philosophy of 'Olympism' – that there is joy, educational and ethical value in sporting effort.

# A World Cup

The first World Cup was held in Uruguay in 1930. The cup got its name from Jules Rimet who is considered to be the founding father of the World Cup. FIFA decided to hold the competition every four years. It was contested three times before the Second World War interrupted the competition. When it resumed it was to become the one of the greatest single sports events of the modern world.

Table 14.6. World Cup 1930–2002

| Year | Host | Champion | Runner-up | Third | Fourth |
|------|------|----------|-----------|-------|--------|
| 1930 | Uruguay | Uruguay | Argentina | USA/Yugoslavia | – |
| 1934 | Italy | Italy | Czechoslovakia | Germany | Austria |
| 1938 | France | Italy | Hungary | Brazil | Sweden |
| 1950 | Brazil | Uruguay | Brazil | Sweden | Spain |
| 1954 | Switzerland | West Germany | Hungary | Austria | Uruguay |
| 1958 | Sweden | Brazil | Sweden | France | West Germany |
| 1962 | Chile | Brazil | Czechoslovakia | Chile | Yugoslavia |
| 1966 | England | England | West Germany | Portugal | USSR |
| 1970 | Mexico | Brazil | Italy | West Germany | Uruguay |
| 1974 | West Germany | West Germany | Netherlands | Poland | Brazil |
| 1978 | Argentina | Argentina | Netherlands | Brazil | Italy |
| 1982 | Spain | Italy | West Germany | Poland | France |
| 1986 | Mexico | Argentina | West Germany | France | Belgium |
| 1990 | Italy | West Germany | Argentina | Italy | England |
| 1994 | USA | Brazil | Italy | Sweden | Bulgaria |
| 1998 | France | France | Brazil | Croatia | Netherlands |
| 2002 | South Korea/Japan | Brazil | Germany | Turkey | South Korea |

Some dramatic episodes have been notable such as the United States defeat of England in 1950; North Korea's defeat of Italy in 1966; Cameroon's emergence in the 1980s and their opening match defeat of Argentina in 1990.

Today it has an accumulated audience of over 29 billion people (South Korea/Japan 2002).

The format of football lends itself to the television screen very comfortably and technical advances have made it even more appealing. Television has given FIFA the chance to project the game globally and television rights represent a major source of revenue.

FIFA initiated an innovative marketing policy in the 1970s strengthening during the 1980s and 1990s. FIFA's partner in this venture has been ISL Worldwide. ISL is responsible for coordinating and composing the group of prominent multinationals who lend their financial and logistical support to the World Cup and other events. FIFA has tried to ensure that the influence of the sponsors does not encroach on the integrity of the sport.

## Women

The Women's World Cup has reflected the improving standards of play, the high profile of the top women players, particularly evident in the United States of America, the emergence of the professional leagues and the increasing number of participants and spectators who are attracted to female football.

## Fair Play

International Fair Play campaigns are one of the means by which FIFA tries to uphold the traditional values of sport. All players playing in the World

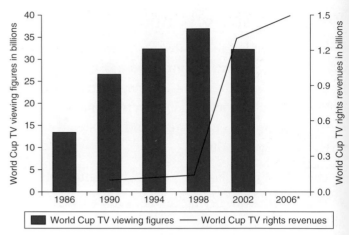

Fig 14.8. World Cup TV viewers and rights revenues

Cup finals and other events are obliged to sign a Fair Play declaration.

## Youth

The World Youth Championship was first held in 1981 though a similar tournament had been initiated by FIFA in Tunisia in 1977. This competition is for Under 20s and there is also one for Under 17s. The developing countries are more likely to excel and smaller national football associations can host the competition at this level.

## The Olympic Football Tournament

This tournament acted as the world's football championship until the 1930s saw the advent of the World Cup. Nowadays the competition is open to Under 23s as a compromise between the IOC and FIFA allowing FIFA to uphold its principle of a pyramid of age groups for male players from Under 17 level through to the World Cup.

The Women's Olympic Football tournament was introduced in 1996.

Table 14.7. World Cup attendance 1930–2002

| | Number of matches | Complete attendance | Attendance pr. game |
|---|---|---|---|
| Uruguay 1930 | 18 | 434,500 | 24,139 |
| Italy 1934 | 17 | 395,000 | 23,235 |
| France 1938 | 18 | 438,000 | 26,833 |
| Brazil 1950 | 22 | 1,337,000 | 60,773 |
| Switzerland 1954 | 26 | 943,000 | 36,269 |
| Sweden 1958 | 35 | 868,000 | 24,800 |
| Chile 1962 | 32 | 776,000 | 24,250 |
| England 1966 | 32 | 1,614,677 | 50,458 |
| Mexico 1970 | 32 | 1,673,975 | 52,317 |
| West Germany 1974 | 38 | 1,774,022 | 46,685 |
| Argentina 1978 | 38 | 1,610,215 | 42,374 |
| Spain 1982 | 52 | 1,856,277 | 35,698 |
| Mexico 1986 | 52 | 2,441,731 | 46,956 |
| Italy 1990 | 52 | 2,514,443 | 48,355 |
| USA 1994 | 52 | 3,567,415 | 68,604 |
| France 1998 | 64 | 2,775,000 | 43,359 |
| South Korea/Japan 2002 | 64 | 2,722,390 | 42,537 |

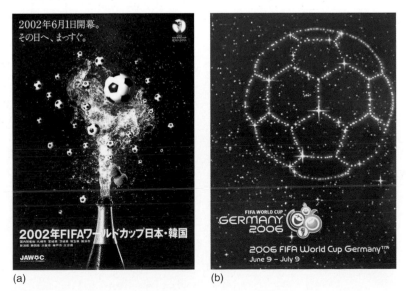

(a)    (b)

Fig 14.9. World Cup posters

# A E Paralympic Games

Originally an annual sports meeting for semi-paralysed competitors – it is properly called the International Stoke Mandeville Games after the founding hospital in Buckinghamshire, England, and was originally known as the Paraplegic Games. The idea of such athletic activity as recommended treatment for patients whose lower limbs and trunk were paralysed was conceived during the Second World War and developed into regular competition. The international aspect of the Games was strengthened in 1960 when they were held in the Olympic City of Rome.

The Paralympics are for athletes with physical and sensorial disabilities. Paralympic means parallel to the Olympic Games – not paraplegic. The Paralympic Games are about ability, athletic endeavour and elite performance.

The Special Olympics serve mentally retarded youth and adults. They were established to provide year round sports training and athletic competition in approximately 23 Olympic-type sports for ages 8 years and up.

## Elite training

Many countries have national research and training centres to provide the optimal environment, facilities and equipment for athletes with disabilities to train for their specific sports.

In 1984 Claudine Sherrill wrote 'The ultimate athlete can be anyone, disabled or able-bodied, who demonstrates the capacity to dream, the unwavering intent to be the best, and the willingness to pay the price of long, hard, strenuous training.'

In the 1984 Los Angeles Games two wheelchair races were included as demonstration events. The aim of this was to:

- integrate sports for athletes with disabilities into the international sports movement while preserving the identity of sport for disabled athletes.

Australia's Olympics in 2000 was a 60-day sport festival with two components: the Olympic and Paralympic Games. The Sydney Games hosted over 4,000 athletes, 2,000 coaches and many other supporting officials. The Paralympic athletes

Table 14.8. The Paralympics

| Date | Venue | General information |
|------|-------|---------------------|
| 1988 | Seoul, Korea | 60 countries/4,000 athletes<br>370 world records set<br>600 Paralympic records<br>Paralympic athletes selected for drug testing |
| 1992 | Barcelona | 'sports without limits'<br>60,000 spectators<br>use by athletes of Olympic village<br>United States won, Germany second, Great Britain third |
| 1996 | Atlanta | Media attention, awareness, sponsorship<br>4,000 athletes<br>from 100 nations<br>19 sports (14 Olympic) |

competed in 18 sports, 14 of which are on the Olympic Sport Programme. The athletes stayed in the Olympic village and competed in the Olympic stadium. An advantage of this set-up is that the resources are already in place and it would be an impossible task to host them at the same time as the Olympics!

**Paralympic Symbol:** consists of three Taeguks symbolising the most significant components of the human being: Mind, Body, Spirit.

**Paralympic Motto:** Mind, Body, Spirit.

**Organisers:** International Paralympic Committee, founded 1998.

# Commonwealth Games

Originally called the British Empire Games, inaugurated in 1930 in Canada, they are run by the Commonwealth Games Federation. The name of the Games has changed over the years reflecting

Table 14.9. The Commonwealth Games

| Date | Venue | General information |
|------|-------|---------------------|
| 1930 | Hamilton, Canada | |
| 1934 | London | 16 nations |
| 1938 | Sydney, Australia | Happy contrast to Berlin Olympics |
| | | WORLD WAR II |
| 1950 | New Zealand | |
| 1954 | Vancouver, Canada | 'mile of the century' Bannister-Landy |
| 1958 | Cardiff, Wales | 35 nations protests over South Africa 'selection by colour' policy; South Africa banned |
| 1962 | Perth, Australia | 35 nations |
| 1966 | Kingston, Jamaica | |
| 1970 | Edinburgh, Scotland | Queen attended for the first time |
| 1974 | New Zealand | 1977 Gleneagles Agreement to be upheld by Commonwealth Games |
| 1978 | Edmonton, Alberta | |
| 1982 | Brisbane, Australia | |
| 1986 | Edinburgh, Scotland | Boycotts of African nations against British government not administering sanctions vs. South Africa |
| 1990 | Auckland, New Zealand | |
| 1994 | Victoria, Australia | South Africa return 63 out of 67 nations competed |
| 1998 | Kuala Lumpur, Malaysia | |
| 2002 | Manchester, England | |

changing political and cultural status of the differing countries and their relationship to Britain.

| 1930–1950 | British Empire Games |
| | British Empire and Commonwealth Games |
| | British Commonwealth Games |
| 1978+ | Commonwealth Games |

The Olympic Games were already well established in the earlier half of the twentieth century but the domination of athletes from the United States, unsporting behaviour and the loss of power and control being felt by the Empire internationally led to a need for something smaller and more private. Re-establishing prestige was also a strong motivation.

The XVII Games came to Manchester in 2002, the first Games of the new millennium. They ran for 10 days with more than 5,000 athletes from 72 countries attending. A global audience of over 1 billion enjoyed what was termed the 'Friendly Games'.

## E Asian Games

Area championship contested by males and females from all Asian countries originally affiliated to the IAAF but since 1982 to the OCA (Olympic Council of Asia). The Games were established in New Delhi, India, in 1951, but have been plagued by political controversy. Pakistan initially refused to enter due to its location and China because of the participation by Formosa. In 1962 Formosa and Israel were excluded. There was an Arab boycott of the 1966 Games in Bangkok due to the inclusion of Israel.

(Principal communist countries of Asia including Cambodia, China, Indonesia, North Korea and

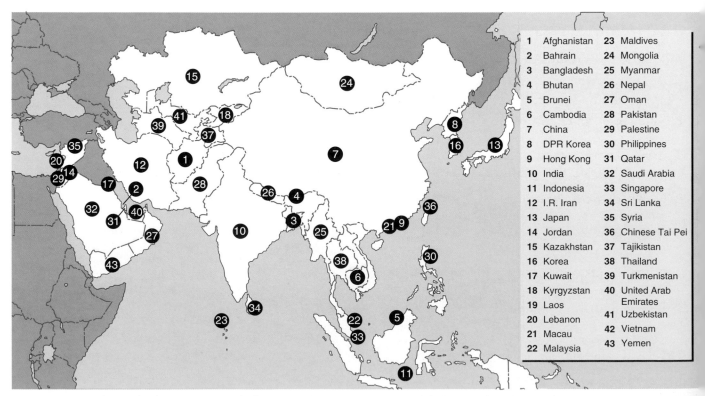

Fig 14.10. Members of Olympics Council of Asia

| 1 | Afghanistan | 23 | Maldives |
| 2 | Bahrain | 24 | Mongolia |
| 3 | Bangladesh | 25 | Myanmar |
| 4 | Bhutan | 26 | Nepal |
| 5 | Brunei | 27 | Oman |
| 6 | Cambodia | 28 | Pakistan |
| 7 | China | 29 | Palestine |
| 8 | DPR Korea | 30 | Philippines |
| 9 | Hong Kong | 31 | Qatar |
| 10 | India | 32 | Saudi Arabia |
| 11 | Indonesia | 33 | Singapore |
| 12 | I.R. Iran | 34 | Sri Lanka |
| 13 | Japan | 35 | Syria |
| 14 | Jordan | 36 | Chinese Tai Pei |
| 15 | Kazakhstan | 37 | Tajikistan |
| 16 | Korea | 38 | Thailand |
| 17 | Kuwait | 39 | Turkmenistan |
| 18 | Kyrgyzstan | 40 | United Arab Emirates |
| 19 | Laos | 41 | Uzbekistan |
| 20 | Lebanon | 42 | Vietnam |
| 21 | Macau | 43 | Yemen |
| 22 | Malaysia | | |

Table 14.9. Host cities of the Asian Games

| Date | Venue | Information |
|---|---|---|
| 1951 | New Delhi, India | Slogan 'Ever Onward Asians' |
| 1954 | Manila, Philippines | |
| 1958 | Tokyo, Japan | Defeated nation of war; Korea sends a large team |
| 1962 | Jakarta, Indonesia | Indonesia rejects Israeli and Taiwanese teams |
| 1966 | Bangkok, Thailand | Korea wins second place |
| 1970 | Bangkok, Thailand | Korea gives up right to host the games |
| 1974 | Tehran, Iran | Socialist countries take place for the first time<br>China joins the Games |
| 1978 | Bangkok, Thailand | Arab oil dollars help Thailand to host the Games<br>Pakistan unable to host the Games |
| 1982 | New Delhi, India | China defeats Japan as the continent's leading sports nation<br>OCA takes over from AGF |
| 1986 | Seoul, Korea | 'Seoul to the world, world to Seoul'<br>China triumph again |
| 1990 | Beijing, China | China wins 60% gold medals |
| 1994 | Hiroshima, Japan | First provincial city (non-capital) to host Games<br>'Asian Harmony' |
| 1998 | Bangkok, Thailand | |
| 2002 | Pusan, Korea | |

north Vietnam had created GANEFO – the Games of the New Emerging Forces, in 1963.)

The Asian Games became quadrennial from 1954 but are held in between the Olympic Games quadrennial. A full Olympic programme of track and field events is held but the general performance standards have been poor with Japan dominating the Games.

The Asian Games are held for the purpose of developing intercultural knowledge and friendship in Asia.

The 43 member countries and regions affiliated to the OCA are all eligible to compete in this multi-sports event. As well as being a sports event it also includes exhibitions of architecture, painting and sculpture as well as performances of music and traditional Japanese arts.

The OCA was established in 1982 as a successor to the Asian Games Federation and is the body coordinating the Asian Games.

## Significance of Hiroshima

This was the first city to experience the devastating effects of atomic bombing and has striven to become recognised as an International City of Peace and Culture, contributing to the realisation of lasting world peace. The mascot for these Games was a pair of doves called PoPPo (male) and CuCCu (female) with the slogan 'Asian Harmony'.

Table 14.10. Sports events in Pusan Games 2002

| Athletics | Swimming | Archery | Badminton | Basketball |
|-----------|----------|---------|-----------|------------|
| Bowling | Boxing | Canoeing | Cycling | Equestrian |
| Fencing | Football | Golf | Gymnastics | Handball |
| Hockey | Judo | Kabbadi | Karate-do | Modern Pentathlon |
| Rowing | Spak Takaw | Shooting | Softball | Soft Tennis |
| Table Tennis | Volleyball | Weightlifting | Wrestling | Wushu |
| Yachting | Body Building | Tae Kwon do | Tennis | * |

* and 10 international cultural events.

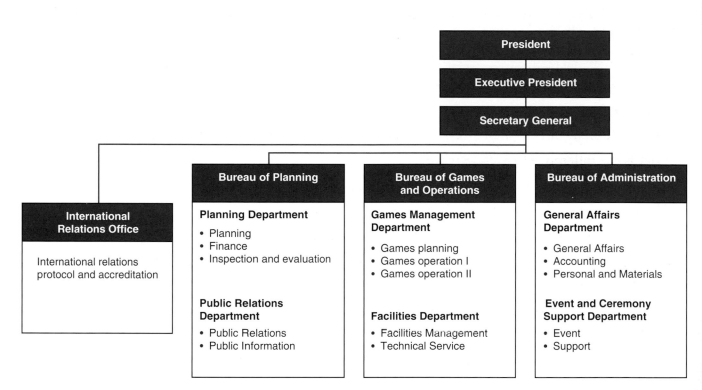

Fig 14.11. Organisation of Pusan Games

## The 2002 Pusan Asian Games

Games objectives:

- To promote solidarity, harmony and peace among Asians
- To develop Pusan as an international centre.

Games information

Venue – city of Pusan
29th September–14th October 2002
16 days duration
Organiser: Pusan Asian Games Organising Committee
Participation: athletes and officials from 43 member nations (approx. 15,000)

# Review Questions

1. Which city hosted the first modern Olympic Games? Can you give a reason for this?
2. What similarities and differences are there between the ancient Games and their modern counterpart?
3. What reasons did Coubertin have for reinventing the modern Olympic Games?
4. Describe four symbols of the Olympic Games.
5. When were women first allowed to participate at the modern Olympic Games? What was the name of the 'women only' ancient Olympic festival?
6. What were the reasons for the political upheavals at the 1936, 1956, 1968, 1972 and 1980 Olympic Games?
7. What similarities are there between the Olympic Games and the World Cup?
8. What are the achievements of Samaranch as President of the IOC but what organisational problems have been highlighted during his reign?
9. What benefits do sponsors of the Olympic Games achieve?
10. Why is football such a popular media game?
11. What does the term Paralympic mean?
12. What are the benefits of the Paralympics being held immediately after the Olympic Games?
13. What is the difference between the Special Olympics and the Paralympics?
14. What factors played their part in the realisation of the Paralympic Games?
15. Which countries take part in the Commonwealth Games?
16. Why are the Commonwealth Games still popular today?
17. What effects has the South African apartheid policy had on the Commonwealth Games over a number of years?
18. What are the objectives of the Asian Games?
19. What political controversies surrounding the Asian Games have occurred?
20. What was the significance of the Hiroshima hosting the Asian Games?

# 15. Cultural and Comparative Studies

## Chapter introduction

This chapter will explore the effect of different cultures on the development of sport and physical activities. Physical activity or games are cultural institutions determined by the culture in operation, but may also influence how a culture operates. Discovering the meanings and significance of games in various cultures and their function with regard to cultural values and related social structures is an interesting project.

Culture denotes the way of life of a society, encompassing the language, customs, dress, as well as the symbols and artefacts which people develop. These are passed down through generations with whatever modifications any single generation wishes to make. Some cultures gradually evolve while others can be revolutionary and change almost overnight. Individuals are socialised into learning the cultural values of their society and institutions and social structures are founded to achieve specific aims for that culture. Examples of different cultures are:

- Primitive (Samoa, Maori, Eskimo)
- Emergent (Kenya, Argentina)
- Ancient (Greece, Rome)
- Modern Western and Eastern (USA, France and Australia).

We will study these cultures in this order.

## Does sport reflect culture?

When we take part in a game or sport, we subject ourselves to special rules and behaviour, which may reflect opinions and values held in other areas of life. Two key values which operate in society and also in games, are competition and cooperation. The former can be described as trying to achieve what another person is trying to achieve at the same time; the latter can be defined as working with others to achieve the same end. Four main factors can determine which is dominant within the culture:

1. the natural environment which 'houses' the culture
2. the level of technology
3. the dynamics of the social structures
4. the education system.

Using this level of categorisation, a social system which is dependent on the initiative of the individual, where property is valued for individual ends, where there is a single scale of success and where a strong development of the ego is in operation, would be conducive to competitive behaviour.

Conversely, a social system which does not depend on the initiative of the individual, or on exercise of power over people, has a fairly rigid social hierarchy and a weak emphasis on status, will be conducive to cooperative behaviour. Various cultures such as the Samoans could be regarded in this light.

## O E Primitive cultures

### Samoa

The Samoan culture has been described as cooperative by Mead (1976). An attempt was made to study this society before the culture was exposed to outside influences and began to change.

The Samoan economy depended primarily on agriculture, with land held by the household groups. Each individual within this group contributed to the total result, which was then shared by all. Property was valued for groups, not individuals. The individual was only important in terms of the position which he or she occupied in the overall scheme. The individual also held multiple roles and therefore did not develop a fixed response to himself or others. Casting lots was used to help selection for various tasks. Matters were decided by 'wheeling round the coconut'.

Rivalry between districts acted as a cohesive force within the group. This unity increased the communities' strength which enabled them to succeed in warfare. Tribal war was quite frequent, so strength and endurance were valued qualities.

Children were viewed as aggressive, violent and destructive, and in need of discipline which they gained from nurses, themselves also children. Conforming to the society was an integral part of learning, and failure to do so could mean expulsion from the group.

Competitive games gave people an outlet for their intense spirit of rivalry, but individual prowess did not determine the successful outcome. Success would be decided by the result of a large number of simultaneous contests, and the victory of the community would be sought to the extent that particularly talented individuals would be kept apart so as to prevent a decisive contest. Contests would be used to gain as many victories as possible against inferior opponents. Prizes were not given though success was highly valued.

Games involving teamwork did not appear in Samoan life until contact with Britain, America, Germany and New Zealand; cricket then became the sport for the Samoans. It was initially adapted to reflect their own values – there could be 200 on a side, and the game could last from four to twelve days in order to let everyone have a bat. Rugby and baseball were also modified to make them more compatible to the Samoan way of life.

## The Maori culture

Before New Zealand was colonised by Britain, the native Maori people were an integrated, cooperative political society. Their cooperative nature was dictated by their system of having a fixed status from birth. This rank in the society could not be changed, thus preventing the necessity for competition. This is an example of a 'closed' social structure, similar to the Indian caste system, which keeps the individual in his/her place in society.

The most valuable personality traits were generosity, individual achievement and resourcefulness, innate abilities and talents. The individual identified with his tribe; the means of production were collectively owned and the returns of the labour belong to the group. This fostered cooperative attitudes through work.

Recreation was an important element in Maori life. Many games and amusements developed from tribal myths, and the people relied heavily on games, pastimes and vocal music to conserve the ancient folklore. Any social occasion was a signal for children and youths to have scheduled contests. Many of the games involved manual dexterity like knucklebones, where throwing and catching was important, or distance throwing.

Fig 15.1. The Haka is performed by the New Zealand rugby team at all international fixtures; it is a Maori war chant

In Maori culture, games seemed to serve various functions:

- training for war
- acquiring grace and skill
- contributing to economic efficiency
- recreation
- promoting tribal loyalty
- an outlet for healthy competition in an otherwise cooperative social structure.

The tribal society can be said to have three dominant characteristics:

- **natural**    unsophisticated lifestyle
  natural environment
  sports or physical activities reflect
    man's adaptation
  running, canoeing, equestrian skills
  functional

- **ritual**    customs and traditions
  religious significance for most
    activities, eg, appeasing the gods
  showing appreciation
  relationships within and between
    tribes established
  ceremonies and dancing
  festivals, etc.

- **survival**    defence of territory
  military preparedness
  skill in combat
  Examples of activities: mock battles;
    bow and arrows.

How was the life of the American Red Indian or Native Americans ritualised, natural and concerned with survival?

ACTIVITY

# Eskimos

The Eskimos on Nelson Island live in one of the last areas to be exposed to the outside world. They derive most of their subsistence from the ocean and the economic pursuits for the most part are individual, where survival depends on personal skills, self-reliance and independence, and hunting skills and achievement are highly valued. Games of physical skill are overwhelmingly preferred to other types, especially those which require dexterity, strength and endurance. Individual self-testing games are by far the most popular with the Eskimos. The games foster a spirit of competition but the social morality of the group places a high value on non-aggressive behaviour. This insures against disruptive aspects. There is little emphasis on equipment, which displaces possessiveness. They play marbles but they do not win someone else's marbles. They know the winning game but they choose to ignore it, leaving with the marbles they arrived with. Rewards in the form of prizes are given but not immediately. Materially the winner is the winner of the last game. They play very few formal games, which may be a reflection of the value of equality in their society.

> '*Eskimo culture is noted for its lack of rigid, formal, hierarchically ordered social relationships which is consistent with their emphasis on essentially equal standards of living for everyone and lack of formal authority in leaders. This preference for the unstructured and the permissive may help to explain the children's preference for informal play*'.
>
> The Reflection of Cultural Values in Eskimo Children's Games: *Lynn Price Age*

It seems that cooperative societies do develop competitive games, but the way in which the results are treated distinguishes them from modern day competitive societies.

How do such societies compare with a modern society?

# Modern societies

At this stage it would be useful to gain a general understanding of how modern societies can vary simply from their economic systems. Very often the economic system operating tells us a lot about the values of a society.

## Economic systems

A term that stems from the control of material resources and is often dependent on political ideologies. There are several forms, including:

- **Market economy** – which allows market forces to determine the allocation of resources. Factors of production are determined by supply and demand. This type of system allows freedom of choice and can efficiently allocate resources leading to economic growth. However, it leads to inequality of income and those with most money usually hold the most power. It is also open to monopolies, which can lead to exploitation, for example the United States of America.

- **Socialism** – a system that involves collective ownership of the means of production and a major role for the state in the provision of services. In its extreme form of *communism* it dominated the centrally planned economies of Eastern Europe until 1989. China, North Korea and Cuba are still mainly governed in this way.

- **Mixed economy** – one that combines a market economy with some centrally planned or state run enterprises. It is a way for governments to regulate the workings of the market through legislation, eg, the United Kingdom.

- **Transitional economy** – occurs in countries which have previously had centrally planned economies and are now allowing market forces to operate at least in some parts of the economy. Many East European countries are in transition.

Some would argue that the focus on maximising profits has led to the development of the 'good life', while others would claim that the single scale of success, namely monetary values, can alienate many within a population.

## United States of America

The USA is the strongest power in the American continent and is a pluralist and egalitarian society; the former means that all the different ethnic groups are autonomous but interdependent and have equal power; the latter is a belief that mankind should have the opportunity for equality – politically, socially and economically.

The dominant sporting ethos in the USA is that of professional sport, reflecting the capitalist drive of American society. Competition became accepted as early as the 1870s as a basic principle in sound economics and therefore part of the great American enterprise. Competition has become a prime value in education, politics and the military. The traditional pioneering background of America has led to a favouring of physical strength and ability to 'play the game'. Americans also value cooperation which is reflected in their desire to form voluntary associations. Many of the pioneers sought companionship in collective effort, and it is through team sports that Americans combined their desire for individualism within a collective endeavour.

The term 'antagonistic cooperation' describes a situation where two units are in conflict but within a wider system of cooperation (Sumner 1940). Huizinga describes it as 'two groups standing in competition but bound by a spirit of hostility and friendship combined'. Sutton Smith believes that competitive games can only take place when opponents respect and have confidence in each other: in anatomical terms, muscle movement is dependent on two antagonistic muscle groups in balance.

An interesting point to note is that during the nineteenth century, America inherited many team games from the UK, yet their team games developed along different lines. The Americans rationalised and systemised sports, when the British were trying to resist this trend (for more information on the USA see later in this chapter).

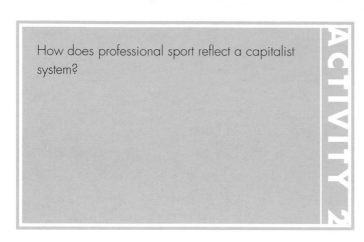

ACTIVITY 2

How does professional sport reflect a capitalist system?

## Summary of differences between cooperation and competition

In many cooperative cultures:

- competition played an essential part in the enjoyment of games, but there was little emphasis on the part played by the individual

- the games reflected the culture and in the case of Samoa, exposure to modern games led to an early adaptation and modification of games, to integrate with Samoan culture

- there was a lack of specialisation and hierarchy in their games, which perhaps reflected their simplified social structures.

In modern competitive societies:

- games were valued for the character traits they were thought to foster

- cooperation was valued but individual achievements highly rewarded

- there was a sharp division of labour and intense specialisation.

## Sport as religion

In many of the early cultures physical and sporting activities could not be seen as separate from religion. Gradually over the centuries sport became more secular as society increasingly lost its older form of worship.

Today many people argue that modern day sport acts as a new form of religion or 'quasi-religion'. (See table 15.1.)

## The former USSR

The former Soviet Union was governed according to a communist philosophy. The class divisions were supposedly broken down, private ownership was abolished, and equality for all was a high priority. However, their system of sport appeared to contradict their general political theories. The regime which gained power in 1917 after the overthrow of the Russian monarchy, viewed sport as a vehicle to promote a new, world-wide identity for the country, and targeted success at the Olympic Games as its primary aim. A massive sporting programme was set up which required huge resources, in a country which lacked some of the most basic amenities. The government was willing to pour resources into elite sport, which ultimately meant vast funding for a few, and *not* equality for all. Elite athletes were given special privileges, and although competition was not generally encouraged in society, it was justified in sport as success enhanced the value of communism to other world powers.

Sport in this instance is *not* seen to reflect the culture; it was directly used to serve a particular political purpose.

## KEY WORD

**Communism:** is an *economic system* based on the abolition of private ownership with an emphasis on state control and collective responsibility.

Table 15.1. Sport as religion

| Sport as religion | Difference between Religion (a) and Sport (b) | Sport and religion as cultural practices |
|---|---|---|
| Both have buildings for communal gatherings: (stadiums/churches) | a) Sacred and supernatural<br>b) Profane and material | Created by people as a means to live amongst others. Both are 'social constructs' |
| Both have procedures and dramas for improvement:<br>• sport skills/time outs<br>• religion prayer books/retreats | a) Transcend material life to spiritual level<br>b) Focus on material issues in pursuit of pleasure, fame, etc. | To make life satisfying and meaningful |
| Both have organisations and hierarchies:<br>• IOC/athletic directors/coaches<br>• CofE/bishops and priests | a) Grounded in faith<br>b) Grounded in rules/relationships | Both have males in controlling and powerful positions |
| Both have festivals and special values as a result of cultural occasions<br>• Easter Sunday/SuperBowl | a) Non competitive<br>b) Competitive | |
| Both have ritual events before, during and after major events:<br>• initiations/baptisms<br>• anthems/hymns<br>• half time talks/sermons | a) Spirit of service and love for others<br>b) Spirit of self achievement and advancement at expense of others<br><br>a) Rituals are expressive and process orientated<br>b) Rituals are instrumental and goal orientated | Both are open to change. An example would be the acceptance of both: women priests and women footballers |
| Both have heroes and legends<br>• halls of fame/saints | a) Mystical and pure<br>b) Clear-cut and crude | |
| Both used to enhance other values in society | | |
| Both evoke strong emotions and are meaningful in people's lives | | |
| Both emphasise asceticism – discipline; self denial; repetition; development of character; 'no pain no gain' | | Both have separate sections and cults which may have evolved by being marginalised by the main cultural ideology |

Table adapted from Coakley 1998

How does the financial reward and support given to top performers differ in capitalist and socialist states?

ACTIVITY 3

| Latin America | Colonised by Spain and Portugal<br>Catholic<br>Some Marxist Revolutions/ wealth in a few hands |
|---|---|
| Asia/SE Asia:<br>China, India<br>S Korea, Japan, Malaysia<br>Cambodia, Vietnam | Highly populated<br>Wealthy<br><br>Poor |

## O E Emergent or developing countries

According to Coghlan (1992) developing countries can be defined as:

> 'A range of sovereign states that are to a lesser extent in a process of social and economic change needing cooperation and assistance from others that are better placed.'

Some countries in Africa, Latin America and South East Asia can be referred to as developing countries, or more recently, as less economically developed countries (LEDC); these countries were previously referred to as the Third World. Developing countries can be post industrial such as South Korea or non industrial, eg, Bangladesh/Mozambique. Some are wealthier while others have already begun in the development of sport and physical education. An example of the latter is India, which by 1985 had a National Institute of Sport with a Sports Science faculty, 600 trained coaches and higher degrees in sports research.

There is a wide diversity across these countries:

| Africa | Black/brown/white<br>Christian/Muslim<br>Marxist/Capitalist<br>various languages –<br>English/French/Portuguese/ Arabic/native |
|---|---|

It is difficult to address 'sport for all' in such diverse settings.

Jurgen Palm in his book *Sport for All – Approaches from Utopia to Reality* (published by I.C.S.S.P.E. 1990) wrote:

> 'Sport for All owes its characteristics to the international transfer of ideas, methods and programmes… There can be no doubt any more that in spite of different socio-cultural, economic and even climatic conditions throughout the world, there is a universal acceptance of the Sport for All movement. This calls for a structure of international cooperation and a system of aid from the developed to the developing countries.'

All developing countries need to address the following issues:

- economic and social growth – the priority
- poverty, disease, undernourishment – widespread
- education, health, communications – high priority
- schools, hospitals, factories, roads, infrastructure – will come before sport and physical education.

Why should sport and physical education be a priority given these circumstances? It cannot be a main priority in Sierra Leone with a four-year civil war: 10,000 people killed; children on the front line. It could be argued that they would:

- give a concentration on health
- contribute to quality of life

broad range of participation can lead to the development of elite sports people.

They do not necessarily come under either the communist or capitalist system and may operate a disassociation strategy. In other words Model 1 and Model 2 may not necessarily be their development objective.

| Model 1 | Model 2 |
|---|---|
| Democratic industrial consumer<br>Economic growth<br>Free enterprise<br>Competitive production | Socialist sport and physical culture (eg, old Soviet approach) |
| Sport – industrial and social education<br>Profitable market | |

But they were all colonised by wealthier countries in the West. As a result, the culture of the colonising nation was imposed on these countries. Their games and rituals were considered inferior to games such as cricket, soccer and netball, and youths were encouraged to discard their cultural heritage. These countries faced common social and sporting problems:

- Their economies were land-based, yet they were experiencing a shift towards an industrial economy.
- An increase in urban populations led to a less active society.
- Their sport infrastructure could not initially match the West in terms of organisation and facilities.
- Western sport tends to be more specialised, requiring more resources.
- Discrimination under colonial rule usually excluded native participation in sport at a high level. Independence helped to produce a

democratisation of sport, where the masses can experience activities previously enjoyed by the governing elite.

New, independent governments faced a difficult decision in relation to sport: should they:

1. provide scarce resources for the mass of the population, or
2. fund an elite group of athletes in order to compete on the world stage?

The greater status given to Western sport tended to demote the rural areas in terms of financial resources, and the towns and cities would be given consideration first.

The prestige, international standing and potential financial gain, achieved through a successful elitist sport programme, has proved hard for governments to ignore. If they follow this route, they are well advised to select carefully the sporting activities which will help them realise their aims, basing their selection on their scarce resources and the experience of the population.

A key factor is the Gross Domestic Product (GDP), that is, the amount of money per head of population generated by one country. Without this wealth external help may be required to provide sport and physical education services.

## External help

- Bilateral aid between – services and resources
  countries          training courses
           university places
- Solidarity fund – used by the IOC from TV revenue of Olympic Games to develop sport in developing countries
- International Sport Federations like FIFA and IAAF use TV fees for training coaches, athletes, officials/administrators
- UNESCO – policy to support International Charter for Sport and PE (weak results so far)
- In the United Kingdom courses sponsored by the British Council in conjunction with the Sport

England's finances, visits by experts to developing countries – to advise and stimulate sport

- VSO (Voluntary Service Overseas) employs young people to assist in sport programmes.

## KEY WORD

**Bilateral aid** – bilateral aid between countries has been increasing whereby a developed country assists materially with services and resources one not so fortunate

The developed world could:

- ensure that IOC takes on a coordinating role
- share expensively acquired research, for example that done already by Germany, Australia, the USA and the UK
- develop links between Institutes of Higher Education in developed and developing countries
- encourage bilateralism through the Council of European Sports conferences
- allocate higher resources to developing their sport in these countries through the ISF
- make use of continental regional sports bodies who have local knowledge, for example the Supreme Council for Sport in South Africa.

Developing countries need to have:

- a clear statement of policy
- priorities indicated/'shopping list' of needs
- Sport for All as well as elite sport
- commitment to long-term programmes
- former Soviet bloc – new democratic governments need help in a different way as the promotion of sport and elitism is no longer a central policy and the structure of their society has changed fundamentally, philosophically, economically and socially.

Changes in current world:

- New Latin American perspectives at the end of authoritarian eras

- Transformations in the Arab world
- Globalisation in all sectors of human action
- Appearance of economic power blocs and networks, for example, the European Union and Commonwealth
- End of the Cold War
- Changes in Central and Eastern Europe.

This should allow for the possibility of more integration.

*Anomalies:*

- A country could be developed industrially and technologically but may be in the development stage of a particular sport and may equally require assistance in that area. An example would be the 1996 Cricket World Cup – Holland had little success against the 'developing' countries of India, Pakistan and the West Indies.
- Brazil is a developing country that could help another country to develop football.
- Some developing countries have excellent sport facilities, for example, India hosted the 1996 Cricket World Cup, but most do not have good or even fair facilities across a range of international sports.

## Elite sport

There is a need for a balance between the development of elite athletes in international sports and participation in indigenous activities. The danger is that Western sport symbolises civilisation and progress. However, there is an increasing willing participation of developing countries in Olympic Games, Soccer and Cricket World Cups and IAAF World Championships.

Success at international level appears to be affected:

- 1992 Barcelona Olympic Games – 815 medals – 82.6% developed countries; 17.4% developing countries.

The gap between the 'haves' and 'have nots' is widening due to:

- commerce, industry and TV
- loosening of amateur regulations.

Table 15.2 shows how the medals were shared at the Commonwealth Games in Victoria, Canada, in 1994.

There is a fairly obvious line to be drawn above Nigeria. Medals are not a 100% sign of success of a country's sport policies, but they can be an indicator. Sport should be about equal competition, the so-called 'level playing field'. Although international sport can do little to assist a country to raise its GNP, which in turn could provide more revenue for sport, it could do more than it does. It is a situation international sport organisations need to address more acutely.

## Opportunities for girls and women

Patriarchal power has often prevented women from taking an active role in many societies. Socialisation and schooling is sexist.

Table 15.2. 1994 Commonwealth games medal table

| Australia | 182 |
| --- | --- |
| Canada | 128 |
| England | 125 |
| New Zealand | 41 |
| Nigeria | 37 |
| India | 24 |
| Kenya | 19 |
| Zimbabwe | 6 |
| Zambia | 4 |
| Pakistan | 3 |
| Ghana | 1 |

patriarchal power – men control women's reproductive capacity control of family sexual control women at home – male leisure outside home

Nigeria – cultural patterns and social expectations sports gear perceived as unfeminine young girls encouraged to bond with mother fear of developing muscular bodies

However, Nigerian women have made a breakthrough in sport participation.

Muslims – In Algeria and Afghanistan girls do not show face, arms or legs. Islamic fatalism and Hindu mysticism have controlled access of sport to women.

Muslim women have experienced some changes:

- Women's Liberation Movement
- education
- increased participation in the labour force
- greater role in social and economic arenas.

In 1992 the 1500 m gold medallist Algerian Hassiba Boulmerka was banned from praying in the nation's mosques, as Islamic fundamentalists believed she had sinned for running 'half naked'. She was forced to train in Italy as she was prevented from training in an Algerian stadium.

| Africa – | little emphasis on sport for women |
|---|---|
| South America – | isolated but growing links with the USA and Europe. Brazilian women excel at basketball and volleyball. |
| Asia – | women mainly hampered by social and religious conditions. |

Perhaps these countries need an organisation similar to the UK's Women's Sports Foundation whose sole task is to promote female sport.

# Kenya

Organised national athletics dates from 1951 when the Kenya Amateur Athletic Association (KAAA) was first formed and later affiliated to the International Amateur Athletic Federation. Athletics and meetings gained a new status graduating from the status of school and village meetings to serious competition. In 1952 there was the first meeting with Uganda and in 1955

Fig 15.2. Kenyan athletes have dominated middle- and long-distance running events for almost 20 years

Tanzania (then Tanganyika) joined in. An East African Amateur Athletic Board was formed and other neighbouring countries were included.

The far-sighted KAAA provided international competition and training believing their athletes could be of world class standard. The Community Development Officers organised meetings at locational, divisional and district level.

Kenya's athletes soon began to make their presence felt at international level. In 1958 they began to collect medals at the Commonwealth Games. In 1967 the National Secondary School Championships were initiated and have become a productive nursery of international talent. In 1964 Kenya gained its first Olympic bronze medal; in 1968 they took eight medals.

Kenya now has two stadiums of world international standard – the Moi-International Sports Centre and the Nyayo National Stadium.

Kenya hosted the 4th All Africa Games in 1987 and won the gold medal in all long-distance running events at the 1988 Seoul Olympics.

The Kenyans have also developed world class performances in team games such as hockey, boxing, volleyball, karate and soccer.

The success of these athletes has served to inspire the younger generation. The government has posted Sports Officers to all provinces and districts to develop Sports Programmes with the result that new talent are springing up from rural areas.

At the national level is the Kenya National Sports Council supervising more than 30 individual sporting associations such as Golf, Rugby, Tennis, Judo, Polo, Chess, Netball, Squash, Cricket, Shooting, Badminton, Bridge, Bowls and Swimming.

Basketball is the fastest growing sport in Kenya. The country has a national League featuring Division 1 and 2 format. The league runs year long with national tournaments throughout the year. Kenya's national women's team made history by featuring in the World Championships in Australia. The men's national team is currently ranked fourth out of all the countries in Africa.

Kenyan players have become a commercial commodity to the United States market with a number of players currently on basketball scholarships in top American institutions.

The Harambee Stars, Kenya's national football team, qualified for the second round qualifiers for the 1998 World Cup. Kenya also hosts the Safari Rally, which along with the Paris-Dakar is one of the most exciting events on the continent.

# Argentina

Argentina is the second largest country in area in South America. It covers nearly 2,800,000 square km or 29% of the area of Europe. There are four main physical areas: the Andes, the North, the Pampas and Patagonia. Tourist areas are concentrated mainly on Buenos Aires and the Atlantic coast. It is bounded by Uruguay, Paraguay and Bolivia to the north, and Chile to the west beyond the Andes.

Much of Argentina is low lying and flat though the Andes rise to a height of 6,959 m. The climate ranges from subtropical in the north-east to temperate in the central region to arid and semi-arid and cold in the south and along the mountains.

Unlike the population in other areas of Hispanic America 85% of Argentines are of European origin. The remainder can be classified as Mestizo, Native American (Indian) or other groups. Immigrants arrived in large numbers between 1850 and 1940 (45% from Italy, 32% from Spain). Despite the mix of ancestry and languages the Argentines are fiercely nationalistic.

Argentines place a high value on individuality. A symbol of the past that is supposed to represent this aspect of their character is called *Gaucho* – a near mythical figure who is independent, brave, athletic, a bold warrior, loyal and generous.

The opportunities for sporting activities are numerous: rafting, gliding, trekking, fishing, skiing, safaris, tracking wildlife in the Andes mountains and so on.

## Politics

The country was under Fascist rule in the 1920s and 1930s but Juan Peron (1946–1955) created a middle way between capitalism and communism calling it national socialism. By the late twentieth century fascism has given way to a philosophy of cooperation between people of various civilisations and ideologies.

## Sport

Football is the national sport. Basketball, rugby, tennis and volleyball are also important. The English introduced football and polo in the nineteenth century; there are high quality fishing areas in the Lake District of the Patagonian Andes and skiing in the Andean resorts. In the summer months resorts such as Mar del Plata are popular.

## Education

Argentina has one of the better educated populations in Latin America which is reflected in its large number of schools and high literacy rate. Primary education is free and compulsory. Secondary education is offered in private and state institutions. Higher education suffered constraints while the military governments were in power (1976–1983) but has increased since the civilian government took over. Major universities are The National University of Cordoba, the University of Buenos Aires, Mendoza, La Plata, Rosario and Tucuman.

## Health

National, provincial and local authorities run the hospitals and clinics as well as private organisations. Developed areas experience high levels of sanitation and health but these rapidly deteriorate in more rural areas.

The social welfare system was set up under Peron as well as a social security system to be of benefit to all workers. Economic depression sees the movement of large numbers of people from rural to urban areas. This can cause housing problems.

## Mass media

The media are well advanced in the Latin American nations. All of the largest newspapers are published in Buenos Aires. In the capital various foreign language papers serve the ethnic groups. The majority of the radio and television stations are privately operated and have periodically become agents of state propaganda.

# Relationship between soccer, politics, culture and social change in Latin American societies

It can be argued that football in Latin America has tended to reinforce nationalistic, authoritarian, class-based and gender-specific notions of identity and culture. In Europe there has been a stronger politicisation of football directed at social change by both professional clubs and supporters. Professionalism and materialism have replaced the 'ludic' or play element of football. Football could be said to be a political tool of mass manipulation and social control. Its original function has become a type of secular religion.

The Latin American experience of football is quite different to that of the United States of America which tried to maintain its national heritage of American football, though it succumbed to the commercial allure of soccer by successfully hosting the World Cup in 1996. Latin America adopted the game for its more ludic properties: the quest for excitement, the triumphs and joy associated with the game. Latin America has produced the most scintillating players, for example Pele, currently Brazil's Minister of Sport and once graced with the title 'Safo' (essentially the man inspired by divine spark). Spurred by massive and passionate crowds Argentina, Brazil and Uruguay have a long history of regional and international football success. Football is the national sport in most of the Latin American countries.

## Nationalism

After having largely broken from colonial rule the idea of nationhood has been consolidated. The idea of 'nation' is 'imagined, created and constructed', by Latin American political and cultural elite in speeches, literature, various art forms and various organisations. Football has become entwined with this concept especially as it is a mass appeal sport without the class distinctions of other sports. Thus it could unify all social groups. This is important in multi-ethnic nations like Brazil and Peru.

Women experience different opportunities. There has been a proliferation of women's clubs in Argentina and Brazil; Guatemalan women have broken through powerful, traditional, social barriers with the introduction of league and cup competitions. However, as late as 1979 the women of Paraguay were banned from playing football in the belief it was contrary to their femininity.

Despite this, football is a great social equaliser offering popular expressions of celebration and pride for national victories, or emotions of gloom following defeats.

## Authoritarian regimes

Like Cuba, the military regimes of Latin America have traditionally used football to strengthen nationalist loyalties. Football stadiums have had dual purposes – to play football and as detainee areas or assassination venues (El Salvador).

The Brazilian military government of the 1960s used the game to make the vast terrain more familiar by implementing the 1969 Sports Lottery. Its aim was to raise national consciousness, raise funds for social projects and include football results from distant provinces (Lever 1988). In 1978 the Argentinian military junta staged and won the World Cup. This resulted in large investments obscuring the more negative aspects of the regime's human rights record.

Many Ecuadorians connected the early successes of the nation's qualifying World Cup triumphs to President Abdula 'El Loco' Bucaram's passion for football and the state's funnelling of additional incentive funds to the national programme and players. They attributed the losses to his exit from the post for apparent 'mental incompetence'.

## Class warfare

Football in Latin America always had the support of the social elite as it had originally been imported from Britain by the upper and middle classes. Current club names reflect the past associations with Britain. Examples are Liverpool of Uruguay and Wanderers of Chile.

Street football developed amongst the dispossessed social classes such as the workers, black slave descendants, rural migrants to the cities and the vast number of 'mestizos' (mixed race) against the more institutionalised white elite sides.

It is this dual mix that is the flavour of Latin American football. The encouragement of football by the higher classes towards the working classes is very similar in its development to Britain in the nineteenth century.

Similarly, the rise of professional football created opportunities for upward mobility often denied to these lower socio-economic groups. Thus more inclusive forms of nationhood were developed.

The future may be determined by the military régimes either in power or threatening on the sidelines; American interference in places such as Nicaragua; the largely foreign economic dominance; the increasingly global trend towards neo-liberal, Western market solutions.

# Summary

To summarise – the priorities that developing countries assign to sport may be interpreted as follows, but not necessarily in this order:

- nation building
- integration
- defence
- hygiene and health
- social functions
- international recognition.

# Classical civilisations

## Ancient Greece

Much of the character of modern day sport originated in Greece, about 1000 BC. The Ancient Greeks institutionalised the need of humans to compete and be the best, to discover the limits of man's powers. The athletes of Greek society were revered as earthly gods: they received monetary rewards, could be appointed military generals, and their names were recorded for posterity. The word 'athlete' comes from the Greek word 'athlos' which means prize: the result of contests involving hard physical endeavour and suffering. Athletes were supposed to train seriously for their event which included following a strict diet.

The Greeks held a national event, the Panhellenic games, every four years. The oldest recorded was in Olympia, 776 BC. However, they were religious festivals and the athletic enclosure would be surrounded by shrines. Military contests would be postponed in order for the games to be held.

By the sixth century BC specialisation had begun to take place, with intensive training for a specific event. The trainer had also assumed a place in this process. The professionalisation of sport was also underway. Athletes competed *for* money rather than being rewarded for a successful games. Corruption and bribery soon followed.

# Ancient Rome

The vast colosseums served the same function for the Romans as the Panhellenic games. In AD 1, there were 76 religious festival days celebrated by 'ludi', comprising shows, plays (mimicry) and games (agon). The spectators enjoyed real conflict, finding athletics dull in comparison. Their most exciting sport was the 'naumachia' where criminals would re-enact naval battles until they killed each other, and the winners could be given their freedom. Animals in direct contest with gladiators were prestigious occasions. Gladiators were highly trained, but would often have to fight to the death. Men were also killed for entertainment purposes.

Sport was a way of keeping the masses of people occupied and therefore gave them less reason or chance to rebel. The wealthy competed in their donations to their society and sponsorship to sport. This culture used sport as a spectacle; play had moved on to become display, and a patriotic sense was aroused when watching a difficult contest where the ultimate price of life would be paid. This was an era coming to an end.

## Summary of different cultures and sport

Examining different cultures and their relation to sport shows that games have been developed to perform various functions, including:

- bonding community groups

- providing socially approved outlets of aggression and opportunities to compete

- acknowledging important human events such as birth, marriage and death

- communicating with the gods (Ancient Greece)

- preparing children for later adult roles, and developing skills which would become economically important for the society

- training people for war and the workplace.

ACTIVITY 4

Match the dominant functions of sport to the different cultures:

| Functions of Sport | Cultures |
|---|---|
| Functional | |
| Religious | |
| Ritual | |
| Survival | |
| Recreational | |
| Integration | |
| Commercialism | |
| Nationalism | |
| Political indoctrination | |
| Natural excellence | |
| CULTURES<br>Primitive<br>Emergent<br>Western Democracy<br>Ancient | |

# Summary

- The type of political and economic system is crucial in determining the nature of state intervention; centralised or decentralised, capitalism or communist.

- A range of cultures was studied, highlighting the two key values of competition and cooperation. A common factor emerged between different cultures: human beings naturally take the utilitarian aspect of physical activity and transform it into a social experience.

- You should appreciate the complexity of games, recreations and sports to a variety of societies and not presume them to be a coincidental or superficial aspect of human life.

## Review Questions

1. What is a capitalist economy and how does this reflect professional sport?

2. The Eastern bloc, based on a communist philosophy, established a sport system to gain world standing in the arena of sport. How can these two approaches contradict each other?

3. Name four different types of cultures.

4. What characterises a primitive culture and how is this reflected in physical activity?

5. What are the common problems faced by developing countries such as Africa and Latin America in their approach to developing sport and what aid can developed countries give to the developing countries to improve their sporting experiences?

# Modern, Western and Eastern Cultures

Before we study the United Kingdom and its approach towards sport and physical education within the context of the overall culture in chapters 16 and 17, we will now undertake a similar study looking at the United States of America, France and Australia. A comparative approach is widely used in many other academic disciplines and is an attempt to describe, analyse and explain factors occurring within society. A reformative approach occurs when different cultures borrow and adopt ideas which may prove of benefit to their society.

Problems with initial attempts at comparative research lay in isolating a topic of study and not viewing it in the context of the whole system. It was recognised by the turn of the twentieth century that the individual aspect being studied needed to be seen as an integral part of that society. Only then can the value orientations which surround the particular parts of a culture be fully understood. Thus, a multi-disciplinary approach emerged involving economics, history, philosophy, sociology, psychology, anthropology, social science and science. This was pioneered by George Bereday and he presented four main stages:

- **description** – the systematic collection of data

- **interpretation** – analysis in terms of social sciences

- **juxtaposition** – a review of similar systems to determine the framework to be used to compare

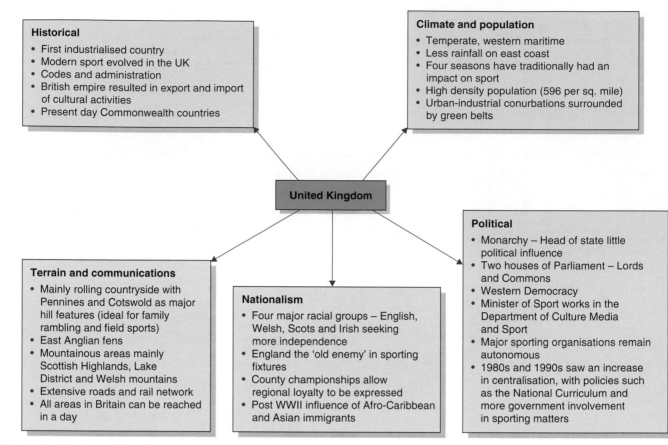

Fig 15.3. The United Kingdom

- **comparison** – first of select problems and then the relevance to the various cultures.

Comparative physical education and sport is still a fairly recent field of study; the International Society on Comparative Physical Education and Sport (ISCPES) was formed in 1980. Their publications can be useful sources of information.

# United States of America

At the end of this section you should have an understanding of the following key terms and how they reflect the system of sport and physical education in the USA.

## USA key terms

- Federal government and state autonomy

- Concepts of American sport: in particular Lombardian ethic; counter culture; radical ethic

- Ethnicity: in particular Native Americans; pluralist society; stacking and centrality

- Professional sport; draft system; 'big time' programmes

- Collegiate sport; Title IX; NCAA; adaptive P.E. intra and inter mural sports

- Outdoor recreation; summer camps; frontier spirit; National Parks.

**Terrain and resources**
- World's fourth largest country
- 52 autonomous states
- Three main geographical areas: east highlands, middle plains, west mountains
- Very rich mineral sources
- Fertile soil, productive for crops
- Plenty of fresh water

**Communication**
- Network of interstate buses. Airline travel heavily used
- Long distances between states mean that travelling to 'away' fixtures is difficult
- Radio and television companies almost entirely owned by private companies

**United States of America**

**Climate**
- Varied: very cold in Alaska, semi-tropical in Florida
- Rainy coasts of Oregon, dry lands of Mojave Desert

**Population**
- 75% of people live in cities
- Standard of living among highest in the world; more time for recreation than any other country
- Egalitarian, pluralistic and multicultural society

**History**
- Modern society grew from string of British colonies on East Coast
- Pioneering spirit of migration west during nineteenth century is important part of national character

Fig 15.4.

Fig 15.5. The United States of America

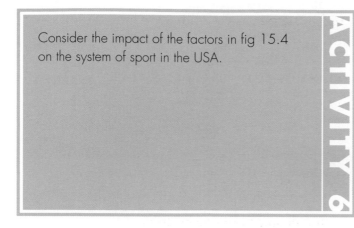

Consider the impact of the factors in fig 15.4 on the system of sport in the USA.

ACTIVITY 6

Imagine the trek west to settle in uninhabited wilderness areas, with a hostile indigenous population to overcome.
• What personal qualities would be most likely to prove successful?
• Can you relate any of these qualities to success in sport?

ACTIVITY 7

## Development and structure of government

Following the War of Independence in 1776, the colonies achieved their objective of freedom from Britain in 1781. They wished to detach themselves from the British elitist, closed social class system, which excluded the majority of people from opportunities of self improvement, on the grounds that they did not possess the preferred social status.

A new government with a federal constitution was founded, effectively creating a republic. A federal constitution is where the powers of government are divided between the national and the state or provincial governments. This was an important concept: the people had just broken away from a distant system of power over which they had little control, and did not want to replace it with another, so they sought to restrict the powers of the new national government via the constitution of the United States which serves as the Supreme Law of the Land. This isolation of the USA was to extend itself to sport as well as politics. The Bill of Rights guaranteed the basic rights of American citizens. The constitution establishes federalism with three separate branches:

• legislative (responsible for creating laws)
• executive (power to enforce laws)
• judicial (power to operate laws).

The government operates on three different levels – national, state and local:

• national government – with delegated powers
• state government – residual powers (where they work together, it is called concurrent power).

It is a

• **democracy** with a representative government which means the people elect leaders who will represent them.
• **republic**, which is where the chief of state is also elected by the people, unlike a monarch who inherits the title.
• **constitutional** government operating under a set of laws and principles outlined in the constitution.
• **federal** system with a sharing of power between the national, state and municipal governments.

The spread of white American culture was not without a price. The indigenous population of Indians were defeated and resettled, losing many of their ancient pastimes.

In the mid 1800s, the plantations in the South produced huge cotton crops, and black slaves were relied upon to do the manual labour. The different

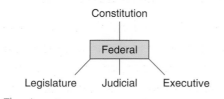

Fig 15.6. The American government

# KEY TERM

**American Dream:** The new competitive capitalist economy aimed to provide people with determination, talent and drive the opportunity to be successful. In theory people can experience upward social mobility regardless of social class. This is popularly called 'rags to riches' in the 'land of opportunity'. In sport this can be achieved from Little League to Professional and Olympic sport. Sporting terms reflect this need to achieve:

- Win at all costs
- Nice guys finish last
- Lombardian ethic.

# KEY WORDS

**Isolation:**

- New World trying to produce a new identity/escape from older culture
- Variety of emigrants in a pluralist culture no longer dominated by Britain
- Attempt to be separate and different
- Professional sport rather than nineteenth-century class based amateurism
- Win at all costs rather than process important
- Reflect technological changes of the new era.

**Pluralism:** A theory of society as several autonomous but interdependent groups having equal power. This theory does not accept that an elite purely makes decisions but that the state considers the opinions of many different interest groups and then acts in the best interests of everyone.

alues held in the North finally led to the Civil Var in 1861; Abraham Lincoln issued the mancipation Proclamation in 1863, pronouncing ll slaves in the confederacy to be free. However,

the Southern states continued to limit the rights of black people, and the experiences of black people are still not equal to those of white people, even in the early twenty-first century; legal rights do not always mean equal opportunity.

## Sport in the United States

As with Britain, in the nineteenth century there was an increasing rationalisation of sport:

- club membership was exclusive
- spectator sports were developing
- social class distinctions were introduced and reinforced through the amateur/professional divide
- organised sport carried the burden of achieving social and economic objectives and became serious in its orientation
- positive male character traits were closely allied to those needed to be successful in sport, as well as being useful in serving God and country.

By the 1920s these cultural links had become clearly defined, with the growth of spectator sports cleverly marketed in order to raise money and create profits. This occurred at both professional and intercollegiate level and national organisations were being established to control the rapid growth, eg, the National Collegiate Athletic Association (NCAA).

The powers of the federal government have expanded since the constitution was first designed. By 1983, the American government had involved itself in matters concerning sport in 11 areas – antitrust, criminal activities, restructuring sport, discrimination, capital support, tax/duty exemption, social work projects, sponsored publicity, health/fitness promotion, boycott and international athletic tours. Some of these areas are outlined below:

- **Antitrust** – this is where the US government regulates or opposes trusts, monopolies, cartels or similar organisations in an attempt to prevent unfair competition. Some incidences have involved the NCAA.

- **Criminal activities** – this involves organised crime in horse racing and betting. The 'fixing' of events was made a criminal offence in 1963.

- **Restructuring sport** – numerous attempts have been made to curb the violence in boxing, but efforts have failed as Congress is unwilling to impose sanctions on what is effectively a privately owned sport business. However, in 1978 the Amateur Sports Act was passed as an attempt to solve problems between the NCAA and the (Amateur Athletic Union) AAU. They had been unable to agree and this led to the establishing of the United States Olympic Committee. It effectively streamlined the amateur sports scene and allowed federal intervention.

- **Discrimination** – Title IX or the Education Amendment of 1972. In 1975, the Education for All Handicapped Children Act was passed which ensured the inclusion of children with special educational needs to regular physical education programmes.

- **Capital funding** – generally, Congress does not directly support sporting events, though this has become more prevalent, particularly for the Olympic Games and other prestigious events.

- **Tax exemptions** – these have also been granted in the area of sport. About three-quarters of the stadiums and arenas have been funded from federal sources. Few managers own the facilities, because if they are owned by the federal government the owners are exempt from taxes, maintenance and insurance costs – this is picked up by the tax payer.

- **Promoting health and fitness** – with escalating health costs, the government has turned its attention to preventative medicine and established the Office of Health Information, Health Promotion and Physical Fitness, and Sports Medicine. Its role is to coordinate all matters relating to education for health.

- **Boycott** – the most famous boycott was the one ordered by President Carter in 1980, to pressurise the National Olympic Committee to boycott the Moscow Games. It was successful in its campaign.

Overall, the government will act in sports matters but generally prefers to maintain a low profile; it intervenes only when deemed necessary.

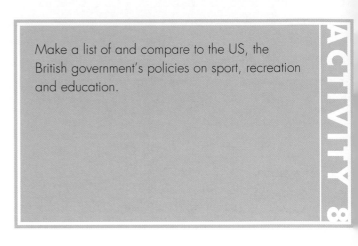

Make a list of and compare to the US, the British government's policies on sport, recreation and education.

ACTIVITY 8

## Concepts of American sport

There are three main sporting concepts operating in the United States.

1. The dominant concept is the **Lombardian** ethic which is based on the Protestant work ethic of self-discipline, clean living and mental alertness. The popular image of this ethic is taken from the saying of the coach, Vince Lombardi, 'Winning isn't the most important thing, it's the only thing'. This emphasises the competitive, achievement-orientated, reward-based type of sport behaviour.

2. The **Counter culture** is an attempt by some sections of American society to change the emphasis in sport to one where the process is the important thing and the outcome is unimportant. It comes from Grantland Rice's slogan, 'It's not whether you won or lost but how you played the game'. This tends to take an anti-competitive viewpoint and Eco Sport has evolved from it – cooperative rather than competitive games. The New Games Foundation aims to change the way people play by reducing the amount of equipment and skill and replacing them with informal situations, emphasising group effort rather than group reward.

Fig 15.7. Concepts of American sport

3. The middle line is the **Radical** ethic and is perhaps the nearest to the British stance, where the outcome is important but so too is the process. The quest for excellence can be strived for and achieved, but not at the expense of other values.

## Physical education

The American system houses a private and a public sector, with the former being self-financing and often associated with Church groups. A decentralised system operates, which means each state is in charge of its own education, administration and jurisdiction. This has the advantage of being more likely to meet the needs of each state, as considerations of wealth and climate can be catered for. The state is responsible for providing a free education, teaching programmes, certification of teachers, building standards and financial support.

Children begin nursery (kindergarten) aged four to five years, which aims to prepare them for their elementary education to educate them from the age of 6–12 years. Advancement to each grade is based on achieving specialised skills in a number of subjects. The secondary schools allow much choice in the upper grades, as subjects are career-based. The final aim is to pass the high school diploma.

In one sense, the system is similar to the UK, where local authorities have some input. However, the teacher in the USA does not have the same amount of freedom as the British teacher in choosing their teaching programme, as the superintendent of the local school board draws up a programme which the teachers implement. Thus at local level the system is more centralised.

- State level – Decentralised
- Local level – More centralised by local School Board

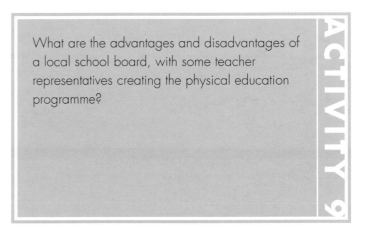

What are the advantages and disadvantages of a local school board, with some teacher representatives creating the physical education programme?

ACTIVITY 9

Physical education is an essential and basic part of the total educational programme from kindergarten to age 12. Physical activities are valued for their ability to enhance the unique characteristics of students on a physical, mental, emotional and social level. Children are encouraged to develop motor skills, knowledge and attitudes necessary to help them function within their society. You may well recognise some similarities to the British philosophy. Physical education is an integral part of most of the curriculum's content, and is seen as part of the whole sporting continuum.

Table 15.3. The American education system

| Ages | 4–5 | 6–12 | 12–17 | 17–19 | 17–22 |
|------|-----|------|-------|-------|-------|
| | Kindergarten | Elementary Grades 1–6 | High School Junior Senior Grades 7–12 | College Junior Technical | University |

Table 15.4.

| Age | England + Wales | Scotland | USA |
|-----|-----------------|----------|-----|
| 4/5 | Reception | Reception | Kindergarten |
| 5/6 | Year 1 | 1 | 1st Grade |
| 6/7 | Year 2 (KS1) | 2 | 2nd Grade |
| 7/8 | Year 3 | 3 | 3rd Grade |
| 8/9 | Year 4 | 4 | 4th Grade |
| 9/10 | Year 5 | 5 | 5th Grade |
| 10/11 | Year 6 (KS2) | 6 | 6th Grade |
| 11/12 | Year 7 | 7 | 7 (Junior High) |
| 12/13 | Year 8 | 8 | 8th Grade |
| 13/14 | Year 9 (KS3) | 9 | 9 (High School) |
| 14/15 | Year 10 | 10 | 10 (Sophomore) |
| 15/16 | Year 11 (KS4, GCSE) | Standard Grade | 11 (Junior) |
| 16/17 | Lower 6th | Highers | 12 (Senior) |
| 17/18 | Upper 6th (A-level) | (6th Year Studies) | (Junior College) |

As many sites are US-based, there is frequent reference to school years as 'K to 12'. This translation is given in the table.
Source: http://www.pearson.co.uk/education/

There are similarities in primary education with the UK, where the movement approach towards physical education is adopted with a more heuristic teaching style and is taken by the classroom teacher who is usually a non-specialist. This is not common in the secondary sector in the USA as a fitness testing approach takes over, whereas teachers in the UK tend to take the child-centred approach for a greater length of time. Fitness testing tends to suit a culture which is based on objectivity, accountability, quantification and the determination to produce the best they can.

The Physical Fitness Movement was influential in introducing fitness tests.

The physical education teacher in the USA is separate to the sports coach and generally has a lower status. Teachers in the USA are experiencing similar moves to improve the physical education experience as in Britain, and the thrust of America 2000 is TQM: total quality management where evaluating and respecting the needs of the learners is essential. It is a long-term plan to help all schools achieve the National Education Goals adopted in 1991. Other initiatives include OBE, outcome based education, and the Neighborhood Schools Improvement Act which will also involve a shift from traditional values.

There are various organisations which have responsibility for sport in schools. The State Athletic Association coordinates and regulates inter-scholastic athletic competition; the National Federation of State High School Associations (NFSHSA) established uniform rules for competition and gives guidelines and advice.

## Title IX

Women in the USA have historically experienced similar gender inequality as their British counterparts. Sport evolved along the male and masculinity concepts of competition, achievement, aggression and dominance which led to poorer opportunities for women and resulted in lower participation rates. Their positive female sporting images have tended to be similar to other western cultures: activities which require grace, and have little physical contact and so a lower level of aggression, and those in the supporting or cheerleading role which has its own high status, based on a glamorous, entertainment approach to women in the sporting arena.

The female participation rate did not radically change until the 1970s when a sudden rise in female participation in sports occurred and was visible at all levels from the youth sports to intercollegiate to amateur and professional. This can be attributed to several factors:

- the women's movement
- federal legislation
- the fitness movement
- an increased public awareness of women athletes helped by increased media coverage of female sport.

Federal legislation in the guise of Title IX, the Education Amendment of 1972, was one of the most influential factors as it made compulsory the equal treatment of men and women in education programmes which were in receipt of federal funding. It was enacted in 1972 by the Department of Health Education and Welfare and released in 1975. Women could take a case as far as the Supreme Court, and since then, numerous cases and judgements have been made. It stated that no discrimination should occur at either the programmes offered, the quality of teaching and availability of facilities, medical services, travel allowances and so on. All efforts should be made to teach co-educationally, though for heavy contact sports separation could occur. The equality should be proportional to the number of men and women participating.

Colleges and universities are required to disclose funding and participation rates broken down by gender.

Since 1990 hundreds of lawsuits and Civil Rights complaints have been filed under Title IX and State Equal Rights Amendments charging gender discrimination in sports in high school and college. Most of these have been resolved in favour of women, resulting in women's teams being reinstated when they were due to be cut, women's club sports being upgraded to varsity status and women coaches receiving equal pay.

In 1993 the Howard University head women's basketball coach sued Howard for sex discrimination under Title IX and the DC Human Rights Act saying she was paid much less than the men's head basketball coach. Breaking new ground with the first monetary award given by a jury in a Title IX case Tyler was awarded $2.4 million (later reduced to $1.1 million) in damages.

The California Chapter of the National Organisation for Women (NOW) filed suit against all twenty University campuses. In an out of court settlement, CSU officials agreed to provide equal opportunities and funding for women's and men's athletics on all campuses by the 1998–1999 school year.

Women athletes at Brown University have also used Title IX. Following a decision to cut two men's and two women's sports from their varsity roster the women gymnasts took Brown to court, claiming that the combined cut of $62,000 from the women's sport budget was more than the two men's teams budgets of $16,000. The judge also ruled that the University's ration of athletes did not mirror its ration of students.

### Female soccer

Since the American female soccer team won the 1999 World Cup the national interest in soccer has grown enormously. This event was all but ignored by Britain. The members of the team have become household names and believe it also sends out a message that they have won a victory in the battle for sexual equality.

The final was played before a Rosebowl crowd of more than 90,000, the largest audience for women's sporting event anywhere. The tournament opener pulled in 80,000. The soccer stars were on the front pages of the newspapers as they beat Germany, Brazil and China. Big League sponsors contributed and Nike, Adidas and traditionally male products like Chevrolet cars and Budweiser beer ran adverts showing off the team. A new product 'Soccer Barbie' is due to be launched. They were hailed as the 'Girls of Summer'.

What could have triggered this national interest when there is next to no soccer culture?

- America likes winners (they didn't lose a game).
- America likes glamour (photogenic stars, eg, Mia Hamm, Briana Scurry, Brandi Chastain).
- It doesn't have to compete with the men's game, as is the case in Britain. It has been reinvented as a woman's game in America.
- There was no governing body resistance as with the British Football Association.
- Females do not traditionally play American football.

- Soccer is less aggressive and violent than the American 'gridiron' counterpart.
- The women like the teamwork aspect in contrast to the pressure of individual performances in the more traditional tennis and gymnastics.
- Title IX has enabled the game to be nurtured financially as well as through co-educational PE classes.

At an administrative level, the previous governing of women's sports was the preserve of the Association of Intercollegiate Athletics for Women (AIAW), and they had the usual responsibilities of establishing policies and procedures governing competition and championships. In 1982 the

---

**ACTIVITY 10**

Compare the movements of the British Football Association as it aims to cast off its traditionally discriminatory stance towards female soccer.

---

**ACTIVITY 11**

Consider the comment by Sepp Blatter, president of FIFA – 'the future of football is feminine'.

NCAA and National Association of Intercollegiate Athletics (NAIA) took over.

**ACTIVITY 12**

- If there is a scholarship fund of $200,000 with 70 men and 30 women athletes, how much would the male and female athletes be entitled to?
- What problems do you think Title IX has caused within the educational institutions? Refer to both teaching staff, students and administrative details.
- What are the arguments for and against the UK adopting a similar policy to Title IX?

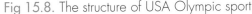

Fig 15.8. The structure of USA Olympic sport

## Adaptive sporting programmes

Adapted physical education is an umbrella term used to encompass areas such as dance, sport, fitness and rehabilitation for individuals with impairment across the lifespan. It has evolved from two major areas – the medical and educational perspectives – and was integrated in the 1950s. It recognised that teaching styles, facilities and equipment should be adapted to meet the individual needs of both regular and special students. The USA has again led the way in terms of legislation – federal legislation in 1975 required that there should be more inclusion in regular classes; in other words the mainstreaming of children with special educational needs – a movement from a medical to educational emphasis, with specialist training for teachers to help them deal more effectively with these children, and consultant monitoring. The Joseph F. Kennedy Jr. Foundation has been active in this area. The Sport for All and the Paralympics movement continue to exert pressure for change, in the way that people view disability and the possibilities for physical education and sport programmes.

## Intra-mural activities

These include highly structured competitive sports and games played to a high level, as well as sports participation of a recreational nature, where the

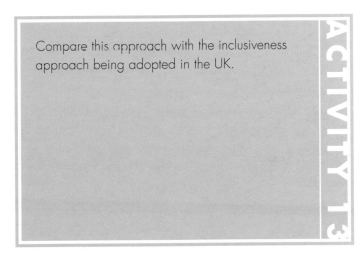

**ACTIVITY 13**

Compare this approach with the inclusiveness approach being adopted in the UK.

emphasis is more on the social experience. They occur outside regular school classes or hours with teams organised on the basis of grade, class, house, etc.

## Extra-mural activities

These generally refer to inter-school competitions, which again can be informal or highly organised and serious. The students go through a more selective process, the activities are widely reported by the press and considerable interest is taken by the local community.

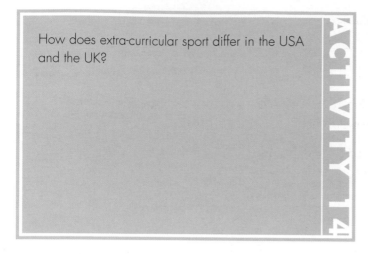

How does extra-curricular sport differ in the USA and the UK?

ACTIVITY 14

## Inter-scholastic sports

Schools belong to the State High School Athletic Associations, which in turn belong to the National Federation of State High School Associations. This organisation coordinates and regulates contests in sport, as well as other activities.

Inter-scholastic competition achieves its greatest emphasis in grades 10 to 12. Those who are carefully selected practise a few hours each day. Rivalry in the local school leagues is intense, and competitions from local, district and regional levels occur which culminate in the championship of the state. State tournaments exist but the size of the country inhibits national school tournaments. (It is worth nothing here that the size of each state is comparable to a European country.) Schools can be classified into divisions, depending on the size of enrolment. The coach is a member of the high school faculty, and money comes from donations from local booster clubs and local taxes.

Table 15.5. Comparison between physical education in the USA and the UK

| United Kingdom | United States |
|---|---|
| Traditionally decentralised<br>National Curriculum = more centralised<br>Key stages 1–4 | Decentralised at state level<br>Centralised at local level (school board) |
| Primary/heuristic/movement approach/non specialist teacher | Primary/heuristic/movement approach/non-specialist and specialist teachers |
| Secondary/skills focus/qualified teacher | Secondary/skills/fitness testing/measuring/qualified teacher |
| PE programme guided by National Curriculum but teacher choice included | Programme drawn up by local school board/less flexibility |
| PE compulsory<br>Exams voluntary GCSE/A Level | PE compulsory/low status compared to sport programme |
| Extra-curricular = voluntary/low status/poor school and club links/teacher responsibility based on goodwill | Extra curricular = high profile/sports coaches/funding |
| Government initiatives<br>'Raising the Game'<br>Sportsmark<br>'A Sporting Future for All 2000'<br>Active Schools | Government involvement<br>Title IX<br>Adaptive PE |

Table 15.6. The advantages and disadvantages of inter-scholastic sport

| Advantages | Disadvantages |
| --- | --- |
| Encourages pride and loyalty to school | Too much emphasis on competition and winning |
| Improves fitness levels | Most students are spectators, while players are often seriously injured during play |
| Develops teamwork skills, valuable for later life | Takes too many resources away from other educational programs |
| Strengthens links between school and community | Can assume too much importance, academic studies could suffer |
| Encourages students to become involved in school activities | Encourages outdated 'macho' involved in ideals |

These programmes are an accepted and high status part of the school and college system, and are thought to deliver positive educational goals. There are however critics who believe that their effects are more negative than positive. Table 15.6 offers both arguments.

### Inter-collegiate sport

America based its colleges and sporting activities on the nineteenth-century English universities and public schools. Harvard and Yale reflected the developing traditions of their British counterparts, Oxford and Cambridge. Professionalism hit inter-collegiate sport very soon and possessed the following characteristics:

- competition for non-cash prizes or for money prizes
- competition against professionals
- money was charged at the gates
- the costs of a training table (food costs) was not borne by the athlete
- athletes were recruited and paid, and professional coaches employed.

American students soon abandoned the British ideal of amateurism. There was a feeling that the college students were being distracted from the primary aims of a college education, and the management of college athletics was becoming too large for the students to handle. By 1900 nearly every college had an athletic committee, with control of athletics shared between the students and alumni, or the sole prerogative of the institution. Then with further development and expansion, inter-college regulation was needed. The National Collegiate Association was established in 1906 to control and create order in collegiate athletics; the NAIA in 1952; and the Association of Intercollegiate Athletics for Women in 1972.

Inter-collegiate athletics is based on two foundations:

1. The NCAA Division III for small institutions where sport and physical education are an integral part of students' lives.
2. Division I, where sport is run as an entertainment business and a training ground for professional and high level amateur sport, namely the Olympic Games.

Division II is a transition ground between the two. The lack of an effective club structure in the USA has made this an inevitable route for athletes wishing to pursue a career in sport.

### Olympic reserve

The Olympic reserve in the United States is drawn from the education sector via scholarships and collegiate sport programmes. The college tradition acts as a nursery for professional and Olympic performers.

### 'Big time' programmes

Generally it would be the responsibility of the principal to ensure that educational objectives are adhered to and that winning does not become over-stated. The problems become more obvious at the inter-collegiate 'big time' programmes where incentives can distract athletes from academic work and are characterised by commercialism, poor rights of athletes and distorted views of gender and race; in such instances these are more negative in their outcomes. Criticisms have been made about the lip service paid by some athletes and college administrators to the academic courses being undertaken by the high level college athlete. A difference needs to be made between the 'big time' collegiate sports and the lower profile levels which do not have scholarships and do not have the entertainment label tagged on; research has shown that academic studies do not suffer at this level.

## What is the NCAA?

The National Collegiate Athletic Association is a voluntary association of about 1,200 colleges and universities, athletic conferences and sports organisations which administers inter-collegiate athletics.

> What is the benefit of a system which develops such interest in college sport? Consider the value placed on the British colleges sport scene.
>
> ACTIVITY 15

### Sport and entertainment

There are four major popular sports in the USA – football, baseball, basketball and ice hockey. Sport in this instance has become a business and athletes are marketed as assets who are well known and who can help generate funds and advertise products with their skill, showmanship and positive health images. The sports are packaged and presented to the public, and sports tend to be loud, brash, energetic and involve huge productions – a show rather than a game, display rather than play?

### Baseball

In comparison to football, basketball and ice hockey, baseball is not a territorial game and is not governed by time. Its roots are rural, it has a slower pace and more of an individual focus. It is thought to have evolved from the game of rounders, though it has left this game far behind in the modern day sports world. It began as a more working class sport and developed in inner cities; as such it has similar social parallels to soccer in England, with more aggressive supporters than are found in American football.

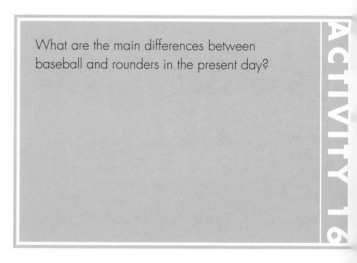

> What are the main differences between baseball and rounders in the present day?
>
> ACTIVITY 16

### American football

American football sums up the country's character – technological, territorial, physically violent and intimidating, a team effort and the epitome of specialisation. It originated from the game of rugby in Britain, but developed along different

Fig 15.9. Does American football epitomise the US character?

ines within its new culture. It developed further n the elite colleges and universities and was herefore a more middle class game. Its levelopment reflected America's attempts to create a new identity, separate from Europe, and the game was influenced by many other different cultures. It was not constrained by the amateur traditions and he 'win' ethic emerged alongside professionalism.

## Basketball

Basketball has more potential for improvisation than either baseball or American football due to the fluidity of play. The players are free to execute their own individuality and can perform cunningly deceptive moves. It was deliberately created rather

Fig 15.10. Basketball allows players to be creative and instinctive

than gradually evolving, as did baseball from rounders and football from rugby. The game was created by James Naismith to channel young men's energies and develop their moral character, and yet the game manipulates the rules by balancing the risk of penalty against the advantages to be gained. Basketball has become a symbol of black identity and black social power.

## Ice hockey

Ice hockey is the most violent of team games – fighting is part of the action, and is expected. The physical speed of the game and the implement used have made this game fast, brutal and violent. The players are dressed for protection but carry injury with pride and are willing to play on when injured. Team members play in a confined area with close and vocal supporters to whom winning has an intense emphasis. In contrast to basketball, ice hockey is predominantly a white game and this is probably due to its origins in sub-arctic Canada.

Though these dominant sports possess their own characteristics, they also contain common elements

Fig 15.11. Ice hockey is fast, brutal and frequently violent

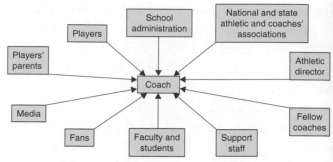

Fig 15.12. Role strain for the college coach

such as high scoring and fast play, requiring skill and power:

- They create entertainment through the media and sponsors, and tend to attract families rather than have single sex traditions.

- The facilities are extensive and of a high standard, both in terms of players and spectators.

- They operate as businesses controlled by owners, and are heavily marketed with their accompanying merchandise.

- They can carry racial identity and preferences.

- The games are very competitive and draws do not feature.

- The professional ethos of the Lombardian ethic with material rewards for success reflects the capitalist system.

Because of the size of the USA, there is not the tradition of home and away fans as in Britain, and the crowds are therefore less partisan.

## Coaching

Sports coaching emerged as a specialised profession in the 1870s and coincided with the growth of competitive sport. Similarly to Britain at the same time, the elite institutions had a vested interest in achieving team records and individual achievements. A split occurred between sports coaching and physical education. The former concentrated on competitive success, rewards for success, culminating in an intense pressure to win, particularly at inter-collegiate and professional levels. The latter, on the other hand, stressed the health, enjoyment and personal development as its major goals.

The role of the coach will often determine the type of behaviour which will most successfully achieve the desired outcome. Coaches are generally assertive, tough and focused on high achievement. As athletes progress up the sporting ladder, from high school to the youth leagues, to inter-collegiate and professional ranks, these aspects of a coach's behaviour would be expected to increase. As coaches are held accountable for the results and

- Compare the role of the sports coach with that of the physical education teacher in the USA.
- How would you change this situation in order to attract minority groups into coaching for a long term effect?

ACTIVITY 18

the results are scrutinised and publicly reported, they have a lot of pressure to succeed. This can lead to 'role strain' and ultimately to role conflict (Coakley, 1993). The coach has to interact with many different people, each with different expectations, and can find it difficult to meet everyone's needs. In America, young coaches need a mentor and they usually rely on the sponsorship of established coaches. This has tended to reinforce the perpetuation of values and can exclude women and ethnic groups.

## Ethnicity and sport

A 'race logic' was developed by the early colonialists in America, that black people were physically superior but mentally inferior to white people. Historically, the sports associated with black people during the slavery era were boxing and horse racing.

- In boxing, the white owners would train up a black boxer, and use the fight as a way of entertainment and opportunity for wagering. The boxer would have gained considerably less from the situation, and parallels can be drawn to the gladiatorial concept.

- In horse racing, white owners were involved in the training and planning but the jockeys were usually black, fulfilling a role which required a more mechanical and physical input.

These racial prejudices have been difficult to overthrow, and are still common within the social institution of sport. The tennis player Arthur Ashe was not allowed to play in certain parts of America, as tennis was at that time still a white, middle class sport. A similar situation was highlighted in 1997 with the emergence of Tiger Woods in the golfing arena, who has also experienced prejudice and discrimination.

## Stacking

Racial stacking in sports teams is a well reported issue, where players from a certain racial group are either over- or under-represented in certain positions in a sports team. Black players traditionally have not occupied positions which require decision making but have been placed in positions which rely on the physical attributes of speed, reflexes and strength. In football there have been few black quarterbacks, though in recent times when the role of quarterback has become more physical, there has been a corresponding increase in black quarterbacks. It does not necessarily mean that there has been an improvement in equal opportunities within the sport.

In baseball, black people have tended to occupy the outfield positions, despite the fact that there used to be a highly successful black baseball league when they would have fulfilled all those roles themselves! It was only when the white owners moved in that their status within the game began to change. There is a parallel with cricket in the nineteenth century, when the lower classes would occupy more physical positions, leaving the central positions requiring thinking, strategy and closer social interaction to the upper classes. This is also closely tied to Grusky's theory of centrality. A vicious circle is created and these beliefs perpetuated, as few black people become coaches or sports administrators.

The lower sport participation rates and ethnic sport preferences have also been determined by these ideological factors. The dominant group determines the access and opportunities available, and it is not easy for minority groups to challenge those social determinants, despite the exception who manages to create the American dream. They can become role models for their ethnic groups, but this can reinforce the stereotypes that only a particular type of sport is suitable for black people, and that sport rather than education is the most suitable avenue for social mobility.

## Native Americans

The original inhabitants of North America are the American Indians. There are nearly two million Native Americans in the United States made up from over 200 cultural groups, though Anglos have tended to stereotype them into one group and generally refer to them as Indians.

Sport amongst these groups has traditionally been associated with ritual and ceremony, though little research is available as Indian culture has undergone many changes following the colonisation of the United States. In modern sport, only when success and achievement have been notable in American football and baseball has any media attention been focused on them. Native American participation in sport has generally been limited, due to:

- poverty and poor health
- lack of equipment and programmes
- prejudice
- cultural isolation.

In 1983 the Iroquois National Lacrosse Team was established reflecting the origins of the game.

Lacrosse is America's oldest sport. The earliest documented reference to lacrosse dates back from the mid 1600s, but it has its roots in the ancient religion of the Huron, Iroquois, Chippewa and Sac. It was used to train warriors and resolve tribal conflicts. Legends describe contests between 1,000 males lasting for three days. Its original name was *baggataway*, meaning 'little brother of war'. The name lacrosse originated in 1636 when a Jesuit missionary named Jean de Brebeuf, while watching a Huron Indian contest, identified the similarities between the stick with a bishop's crozier. By the 1790s the sporting elements had overcome the war theme. It quickly became the national sport of Canada though it struggled for acceptance in the school system where it had to compete with the traditions of British public school sports of rugby and cricket. However, in the United States it developed in the colleges and universities. The game travelled to England where it became adopted as a girls' public school game.

> **ACTIVITY 20**
>
> What characteristics of the game of lacrosse may have helped it to survive while many other traditional Native American cultural pursuits ceased to exist?

## Other minority groups

The term 'Hispanic' is a generic term used to describe people whose origins can be traced to Spanish-speaking countries (approximately 22 million) and whose cultures are related by language, colonial history or Catholicism. Examples would be Chicanos and Puerto Ricans.

There are approximately 6.7 million Asian Americans in the United States. Very little sociological research has been done on any of these groups in relation to sport participation. Generally they are discriminated against in terms

Fig 15.13. Little League Baseball

tournaments is highly valued. Following local and regional playoffs, an annual world series is held where foreign teams can also enter.

The league is based on adult leagues, with some modifications: the diamond is two thirds the size and the games are limited to six innings. The season lasts 15 games, with no more than two games a week being permitted.

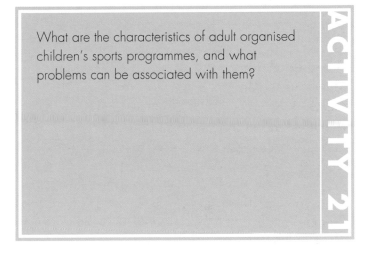

What are the characteristics of adult organised children's sports programmes, and what problems can be associated with them?

ACTIVITY 21

of racial stereotypes which make belonging to sports groups difficult and also their traditions may not always coincide with the true American sports.

## Children's organised sports programmes

If sporting activities carry socially desirable values, it is not surprising that a culture will try to develop such qualities in its young. An example of a well organised sports programme for children is Little League Baseball, which was established in 1939 and is now a business organisation employing full-time professional employees and volunteers. It was initially set up by parents who wanted a well-structured sporting programme. The league caters for 8–18 year olds and is the largest of its kind in the world attracting media coverage. A senior division for youngsters aged 13–15 and a big league for the 16–18 year old is also part of the programme.

Children are selected by competitive trials for their specified age range, and the winning of leagues and

## Senior programmes

At the other end of the age spectrum, is the US National Senior Sports Classic VI, the Senior Olympics. The US National Senior Sports Organisation promotes the image of healthy old age, aiming to establish positive role models for health and physical fitness. The opening ceremonies usually attract 10,000 athletes.

## Outdoor education and recreation

The importance attached to the 'great outdoors' in American society is evident in its literature and films. The links go back to the days of the pioneers and their efforts to overcome numerous obstacles in their attempts to push back the geographical frontiers. The scale and size of the country, with its varied land relief and climates, make for rich and exciting experiences. The character-building qualities which emerge from

Table 15.7. Principles of play, adult sporting programmes and Little League

| Pure characteristics of play | Adult-organised sports programmes | Description of Little League |
|---|---|---|
| Spontaneous | Organised | Established in 1930s |
| Creative | Serious | Business organisation |
| Developmental | Institutionalised | Full-time professionals and volunteers involved |
| Experimental | Rationalised | World's largest sports league for children |
| Enjoyable | Socialisation | Television coverage |
| Use initiative | Bureaucracy | Specified age groups |
| Rule making and enforcing | Competitive | Highly competitive |
| Develop moral judgements | Success valued highly | High degree of commitment required |

such experiences are still considered as important to America's future.

The National Parks are administered by the Bureau of Outdoor Education, which has developed a coherent structured approach. The land is classified according to its level of isolation; Class I would be close to towns and would be widely used, while Class V would be classed as wilderness areas where it is possible to wander undisturbed for days. There is nothing comparable to this latter section in Britain.

There has been an increase in the participation of high risk sports in the USA since the 1970s. These sports can be classed as a counter culture, because they oppose the social values of competition and chance, favouring stimulation and vertigo. The rise in popularity of such sports can be attributed to several factors.

Concerns over safety have led to action to regulate these sports in the form of The Federal Aviation Administration, and the National Park Service of the Department of the Interior which controls rock climbing and mountaineering. However, isn't this sort of regulation exactly what people may be trying to get away from?

## KEY WORD

**Frontier:** The limit of knowledge of a particular field. Sport is often called 'the last frontier' as we still do not know the limitations of human achievement in sport. It is an emotive term for Americans as it also links to the history of the settlement of their country as each frontier was moved from East to West. Qualities required to push back any frontier, be it geographical or of a sporting nature, are bravery, courage, strength and determination.

### Outdoor education camps

The camping movement did not gain acceptance until 1900. The first 100 camps were initiated by teachers and were supplemented by the YMCA, the Boy and Girl Scouts, Campfire Girls, etc. The American Camping Association was formed, and camping programmes gradually gained educational acceptance and helped to raise the status of welfare and general camps.

# Wilderness areas

Class I – Areas intensively developed near towns and designed for intensive use

Class II – Areas with substantial development for a variety of recreational use

Class III – Areas which are suitable for recreational use in the natural environment but within easy reach of habitation

Class IV – Areas of outstanding scenic beauty some distance from civilisation

Class V – Undisturbed roadless areas/natural wild conditions 'wilderness'

Class VI – Historic and cultural sites

# A typical day at camp

| | |
|---|---|
| 07.15 | Reveille. Short optional dip or jog. |
| 07.45 | Flag raising and personal inspection. |
| 08.00 | Breakfast, followed by clean-up of the cabin or tent. |
| 09.30 | 1st activity period. |
| 10.30 | 2nd activity period. |
| 11.45 | Optional general swim. |
| 12.30 | Lunch. |
| 13.30 | Rest hour supervision. |
| 14.30 | 1st afternoon activity period. |
| 15.30 | 2nd afternoon activity period. |
| 16.30 | Free time supervision. |
| 18.00 | Dinner. |
| 19.00 | Flag lowering – followed by special evening events. |
| 21.00 | First Bell – lights out for younger children. |
| 22.00 | Lights out for the seniors. |

*'While some routine is essential there is always something different planned to bring new experience into a busy, happy, healthy existence'*

There are several thousand summer camps for children throughout the USA and Canada, mostly permanent camps where children can reside for one to eight weeks. The camps take children from 6–16 years, and are responsible for their welfare 24 hours a day. 'Going to camp' for an extended period of time is a well-established tradition in the USA. There has been a tradition of sending urban children to the natural environment, and in a country where the summer holidays last three months, it is accepted that children spend time away from their parents.

There are different types of camps:

- **Private residential** – these are privately owned and cater for the high/middle income families. They run on a profit-making basis, providing permanent residential facilities, and operate all over the country. They have a range of facilities for various sports and crafts.

- **Day camps** – these can also be privately owned or run by organisations such as the YMCA or local towns.

- **Organisational camps** – these are run by Christian-based organisations like the Girl and Boy Scouts and the YMCA, though the emphasis on religion can vary.

- **Camps for underprivileged children** – these are operated by various social, philanthropic or religious agencies like the Salvation Army, and aim to give inner-city children a break from the urban environment. They are very heavily subsidised, with families paying little or nothing at all towards the cost. The facilities are more basic and the emphasis is on the recreational experience and appreciating the environment.

- **Special needs camps** – these are for people with physical or mental disabilities (adults as well as children), diabetics, people who are overweight (often termed Fat Camps), or who have special learning or behavioural problems.

Table 15.8. Comparison between outdoor education camps in UK and USA

| United Kingdom | United States of America |
|---|---|
| Less varied topography/climate | Wide variety topography/climate |
| High density population/small country | Moderate density population |
| Easy access to all areas<br>Erosion/pollution damage to natural environment | Large country (state cf. to European country) |
| Outdoor Education not compulsory<br>Depends on initiative of schools | Part of school curriculum |
| Local education authority residential centres under threat | |
| Outward Bound<br>Duke of Edinburgh Award Scouts/Guides | Outward Bound |
| Tradition of naturalism/escape | Traditions of pioneer/frontier spirit |
| 10 National Parks | National Parks classification areas<br>'Wilderness areas'<br>Federal control/safety measures |
| Some commercial companies, eg, PGL | Variety of Camp schools |

# Summary

- There is a decentralised system – each state operates its own administration.

- There are exclusive, private clubs, but which are different from British sports clubs.

- Careers in sport tend to take the route of collegiate sport as a feeder for the professional leagues as well as maintaining amateur eligibility.

- Inter-scholastic and collegiate sport is run on business and commercial lines, with control exerted by cartels.

- There is still discrimination in sport for female and black athletes, though legislation has laid the foundations for change.

- The dominant sports reflect the capitalist culture from which they evolved.

- The government tries not to become too involved in sport, but has produced much legislation in particular areas. Where business interests occur, the government tends to favour the sports bodies which will bring revenue and civic prestige.

- Children's sports programmes stress the dominant sporting values of adults and there is a tendency for an over-emphasis on winning.

# Review Questions

1. What does the term federal mean?
2. What was the fate of the Native American Indians following the spread of white culture?
3. What are the three concepts of American sports? Briefly outline what is meant by each.
4. Why does the physical education teacher in the USA not have the same amount of freedom in designing a curriculum as their British counterpart?
5. Why does fitness testing suit the American culture?
6. What is Title IX and what have been its effects in the American sport system?
7. What is meant by the term adaptive physical education?
8. What are the advantages and disadvantages of the inter-scholastic sport in the American education system?
9. What are the common characteristics of the dominant American sports of football, basketball, ice hockey and baseball?
10. What is the difference in the role of the sports coach and a physical education teacher in America?
11. What does 'stacking' mean and how can this be reflected in a sporting situation?
12. How does Little League reflect the culture of the United States?
13. What are wilderness areas and what type of recreational pursuits can be undertaken there?
14. What are the different types of summer camps in the United States of America?
15. How does capitalism and professional sport complement each other?

# European sport

In this section we will concentrate on recreation, sport and physical education in the French system. However, this country should not be seen in isolation from the rest of Europe.

Europe is the second smallest continent forming the western peninsula of the landmass of Eurasia; the border with Asia runs from the Urals to the Caspian and the Black Sea. Scandinavia, Italy and Iberia form particularly indented peninsulas and Britain and Iceland form the major offshore islands.

## Brief history of European sport

The roots of European sport began in pre-industrial Europe before competitive sport was organised.

Many countries enjoyed a wide variety of simpler forms of physical activity though similar characteristics could be seen:

**Ball Games** – played on foot for example, various forms of football (mob; hurling; Gaelic) by hand (fives; jeu de paume)

**Bowl Games** – played with a solid spherical object that is rolled or thrown at a target (flat green bowls; jeu de boules)

**Pin Games** – targets are knocked down (ten pin bowling has several historical variants)

**Throwing Games** – throwing a stick or stone for distance or to hit a target is a basic human movement pattern (hammer throwing; tossing the caber; barra in northern Spain – a type of javelin throwing)

**Shooting Games** – these have evolved in all cultures and still flourish in the modern hi-tech sports (popinjay in Flanders; Italian balestrieri or crossbow)

**Fighting Games** – wrestling is probably the oldest and the most universal traditional sport of mankind (Greco-Roman; Cumberland; French boxing or savate, uses both fists and feet; judo; swordplay; tug of war)

**Animal Games** – blood sports (bull and bear baiting; cock fighting; bull running; some have survived the civilising process – others have not)

**Locomotion Games** – traditional hill races in the Scottish Highland Games; the Dutch Fierljeppen, involves jumping for distance with a fen pole; palio of Siens annual horse race; old style regattas

**Acrobatics** – coded sets of physical exercise. They are used to keep the human body in good shape and stretch the limitations of the human neuro-muscular system. Professional acrobats have existed for many generations and gymnastic forms such as those developed by Ling and Jahn evolved systems of exercises even further.

Records exist in the form of literary sources such as Strutt's 'The Sports and Pastimes of the People of England' and visual paintings by Peter Bruegel of children's games in the 1560s. The old ways of playing were largely lost as the forces of modernisation broke up the old communities. Though some activities such as Asian martial arts have become popular in the modern age and in different cultures, those adopting cultures can sometimes change the original cultural associations that the game once had, particularly religious ones. Also, whereas children's games had traditionally been passed down through the generations their play has become increasingly home and technology bound.

Europe has now become part of the globalisation process and many institutions have developed to attempt to bring some kind of cohesion to this continent and in the process the domain of European rule appears to be growing.

At this stage it would be useful to remind yourself of the information covered in chapter 11 about the Council of Europe and the European Charter on Sport for All.

A summary is given here.

### European sport

In 1988 the European Commission identified sport as performing five functions within society:

- educational
- social
- cultural
- recreational
- public health.

The Commission's main role is to consult with sports organisations across Europe to plan for sport development and identify potential problems. Europe can be seen as having two distinct identities – Eastern Europe and Western Europe. In the former sport was used for political gains and was state run and funded. In the latter sport developed along a mixture of government and non-governmental line, both private and public provision.

### Features of sport in Europe

- *Grass Roots* approach, which is different to the more professional/business base approach in the United States of America.

- *National Identity* – the Amsterdam Declaration states 'Sport represents and strengthens national or regional identity by giving people a sense of belonging to a group, uniting players and spectators'. International competition remains an important element in countries demonstrating their culture and nationhood. This is again different to the United States where there is less need for inter-state competitions.

- Traditionally modern sport was born in Europe, which saw the birth of industrialisation and has a set place within our societies.

- Member states of the European Union have hosted a large percentage of world sport events; 54% summer Olympics; 50% football World Cups.

- European Union Regulations can be applied to sporting matters such as the Bosman ruling and the decision to phase out from 2001 all forms of tobacco sponsorship and advertising, except on premises where cigarettes are sold.

## Bosman Case

Case brought about by the Belgian footballer, Jean Marc Bosman. The 'Court of Justice' recognised in this case that there was no reason why professional sportspeople should not enjoy the benefits of the single market and in particular the free movement of workers. This has resulted in national competitions being open to players throughout Europe and has revitalised major European leagues. The new legislation also abolished transfer fees if a player was out of contract.

The structure of European sport tends to follow the pattern outlined in table 15.9. Each level is interdependent – both administratively and competitively.

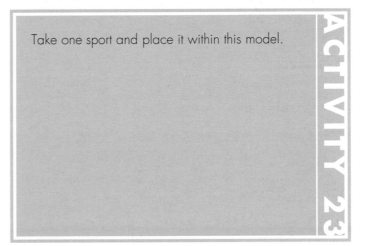

ACTIVITY 22

Research some information on a European sport competition.

Can you explain why Europe should have had such a major impact on world sporting events?

ACTIVITY 23

Take one sport and place it within this model.

Table 15.9. Structure of European sport

| European Federations | One national federation from each country<br>Organise European championships, administer rules<br>Form link to international federation |
|---|---|
| National Federations | Member regional associations<br>Regulate the sport nationally<br>Represent the sport in European and international level<br>Administer rules and disciplinary procedures |
| Regional Federations | Member clubs<br>Organise regional championships |
| Sports clubs | Basic unit<br>Mainly amateur |

*Council of Europe*: established in 1949 and focuses on cultural, sporting, educational and environmental issue; for example, the use of drugs in sport, the economic effects on sports investments, football hooliganism and developing support for the Paralympics. For the first 40 years it remained a Western European institution but since the countries of central and Eastern Europe opted for a democratic form of government its membership has grown.

*European Charter on Sport for All*: legislation requiring governments to promote sport as an important factor in human development. They should enable every individual to participate in sport, notably:

- all young people – who should receive physical education and acquire basic sport skills

- participation should take place in a safe and healthy environment.

In cooperation with the appropriate sporting organisations they should:

- ensure that everyone with ability and interest should be able to reach their own levels of personal achievement or publicly recognised levels of *excellence*

- protect and develop the ethical and moral basis of sport, protecting sports and sports people from exploitation for political, commercial and financial gain, including *drug* abuse.

## Promoting tolerant, fair and democratic sport open to everybody

### Some policies

In 1996 the Committee for the Development of Sport or Comité Directeur pour le Development du Sport (CDDS) together with the Dutch authorities established National Ambassadors by member states; Ruud Gullit was nominated European Ambassador. Their role is to encourage fair play in sport in their home countries and to set up programmes to teach and encourage tolerance in sport.

The CDDS has set up a mutual assistance programme known as SPRINT (Sports Reform Innovation and Training) to help new members reform their social structures. The programme covers legislation, funding, sports management training and the promotion of voluntary activities.

### Anti-Doping Convention

This opened for signature in 1989. As it is an open convention Australia and Canada are amongst its State Parties. It aims to:

- study the technical, legal, educational and scientific aspects of the doping problem

- cooperate with the International Olympic Committee and other sports bodies.

### Spectator behaviour and safety

The convention monitors the implementation of measures on:

- safety in sports stadia, international police cooperation, ticket sales, alcohol sales crowd control and preventative measures at high risk matches.

It cooperates with:

- UEFA and FIFA, the European and international governing bodies for Association Football.

## Democracy and sport

The intention of this policy is to follow up the European Sports Charter and the Code of Sport Ethics and promote the widespread enjoyment of safe and ethical physical activities, supported by public authorities and the voluntary sports movement.

Two areas have been given priority:

- Sport and the law: legal questions are assuming an increasing importance and policies need to be addressed systematically.

- Sport as a democratic movement: increase more generalised sport participation and sports involvement amongst all groups and ages (women, people with disabilities, prisoners, migrants, unemployed and the elderly for social and health benefits).

# France

Key terms you should understand at the end of this section:

- Baron de Coubertin
- Secretary of State for Youth and Sport
- Official Instructions
- Le Tiers Temps Pedagogique
- Le plein air
- Transplant classes (les classes transplantées)
- Colonie de vacances centre de vacances
- Baccalaureat
- Union Nationale du Sport de Scolaire (UNSS)
- License system
- Sport pours Tous
- INSEP
- Section Sport Étude (Sport Study Sections)

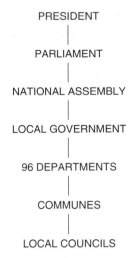

PRESIDENT
|
PARLIAMENT
|
NATIONAL ASSEMBLY
|
LOCAL GOVERNMENT
|
96 DEPARTMENTS
|
COMMUNES
|
LOCAL COUNCILS

Fig 15.14. French government

577 deputies, and is also elected. It is a democratic system in which numerous parties have an opportunity to gain seats. The President appoints the Prime Minister who deals with the day-to-day running of the country's affairs.

Local government is divided into 96 departments which in turn are divided into communes (towns and villages), governed by elected mayors and councils. The departments are grouped into 22 regions. France used to be highly centralised with the national government wielding power in the regions, through the prefects, who controlled police and law and order. However, since 1982, locally elected bodies such as town and regional councils have had more power, and the prefects' influence has started to decline. This was a result of the socialist policies of President Mitterand (1981–1995) who advocated the decentralisation of government. He was ousted from power by the Conservative Jacques Chirac.

## Physical education

Children are taught in primary schools from 6–10 years, then in a secondary school from 11–18 years. Schools and universities are state controlled and the traditional links between them make them interdependent.

Physical education comes under the control of the Secretary of State for Youth and Sport. The central

**ACTIVITY 24**

Consider the impact of the factors in fig 15.16 on the system of sport in France.

## Politics

Political power is shared between the President and Parliament. The former is elected by the people, and is head of state and the chief executive; the latter consists of the National Assembly comprising

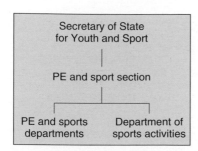

Fig 15.15. Department structure

administration comprises four sections, one of which is the Physical Education and Sports section. This section deals with two branches – the Physical Education and Sports Department and the Department of Sport Activities. There is a clear hierarchical system of role responsibility which can ease the planning and implementation of policy.

The Department of Sports Activities oversees and funds:

- the national sport federations (coordinate at local, regional and national level)
- Olympic preparation.

The Physical Education and Sports Department has responsibility for:

- research, documentation, training of PE teachers and sports coaches.

There are two kinds of federation – the single and multi sport. The local clubs, however, still form the basis of French sport, similar to the UK.

The French have strong traditions for intellectual rigour. The state lycées offer free tuition to all, but some are more exclusive. The state secondary school or colleges are similar to British comprehensive schools. The Baccalaureat is taken at 18 years and is a rigorous exam, essential for higher education (note the possibility that the British government may move towards a Baccalaureat system). There are also technical lycées for the more middle ability range. There are a mixture of state and private schools which are Catholic. The education system is centralised – decisions made by the government are transmitted

across the country. However, in reality, the further from Paris, the less adherence is made to governmental decisions.

## Primary education

*Tiers temps – one third teaching time for PE*
Primary school focuses on the child's physical and psychological development. The 1969 decree instituted the 'one third teaching time' system, or 'Le Tiers Temps Pedagogique', which is a fixed weekly quota of 27 hours to be spent at school. Of these 27 hours, six are devoted to PE and sport. This was believed to be the most flexible way of arranging sessions to meet the needs of individual schools and to break down the subject barriers.

The children are put in an exploratory situation which will help them discover things for themselves. High priority is placed on the fundamental motor skills of swimming and athletics. However, the reality does not always reflect the ideal. The primary school teacher, though given access to specialist help, is often not specialist trained, and facilities vary enormously. It is only in a few schools that the suggested time is given to PE and sport.

The institutionalised implementation of this system has allowed for the development of experimental classes in winter, by the sea and in the country; these are known as 'half time teaching classes'. The children spend two to three weeks in the natural environment while continuing their education. The classes are literally transplanted to a special centre, and have two main objectives:

1. to give the children an opportunity to get away from urban pollution
2. to discover and appreciate the natural environment.

They allow the children a wider appreciation of the variations within their own country. The class teacher is fundamental to the success of this system as they must plan and prepare according to the needs of their children.

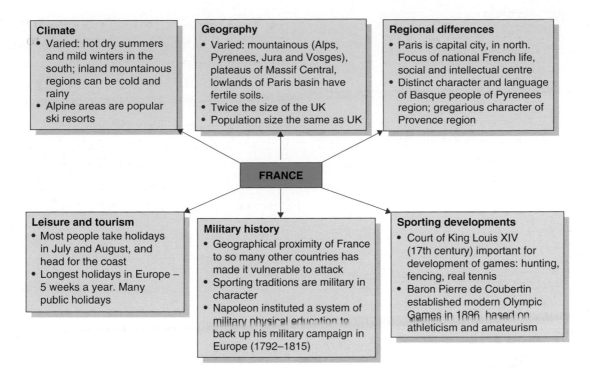

**Climate**
- Varied: hot dry summers and mild winters in the south; inland mountainous regions can be cold and rainy
- Alpine areas are popular ski resorts

**Geography**
- Varied: mountainous (Alps, Pyrenees, Jura and Vosges), plateaus of Massif Central, lowlands of Paris basin have fertile soils.
- Twice the size of the UK
- Population size the same as UK

**Regional differences**
- Paris is capital city, in north. Focus of national French life, social and intellectual centre
- Distinct character and language of Basque people of Pyrenees region; gregarious character of Provence region

**FRANCE**

**Leisure and tourism**
- Most people take holidays in July and August, and head for the coast
- Longest holidays in Europe – 5 weeks a year. Many public holidays

**Military history**
- Geographical proximity of France to so many other countries has made it vulnerable to attack
- Sporting traditions are military in character
- Napoleon instituted a system of military physical education to back up his military campaign in Europe (1792–1815)

**Sporting developments**
- Court of King Louis XIV (17th century) important for development of games: hunting, fencing, real tennis
- Baron Pierre de Coubertin established modern Olympic Games in 1896, based on athleticism and amateurism

ig 15.16.

Table 15.10. The structure of the education system

| Age | Education | Establishment |
|---|---|---|
| 2–5 | Pre-School (non compulsory) | Nursery School |
| 6–10 | Primary | Primary School |
| 11–14 | Secondary – 1st stage | College |
| 15–17 | Secondary – 2nd stage | Lycée |
| 18 | Higher | University, Grandes Ecoles |

Table 15.11. The weekly hours of PE and sport in schools

| Primary | | Secondary | |
|---|---|---|---|
| | | Stage 1 | Stage 2 |
| PE and Sport (Compulsory) | 1/3 teaching time 6 hrs | PE & Sport 3 hrs | PE & Sport 2 hrs |
| | | Sport (CAS) 2 hrs | Sport (CAS) 3 hrs |
| Sport (Optional) USEP half day | | UNSS half day School Sports Association | |

Optional = the pupil may select a sport of his/her choice. Takes place either in school, in CAS (sports centre), or in a club authorised by the Regional Directorate for Youth and Sport.

### Secondary education

*Centralised approach to the PE syllabus*
The Official Instructions of 1967 came from the Ministry for Teachers of PE and Sport. They consist of four main parts:

1. the place of PE and sport in education as a whole
2. a categorising of activities and their intended benefits to the children
3. the role of the teacher
4. the practical organisation of teaching PE.

These documents were intended as a guide to help the teacher plan the syllabus, while respecting the spirit of the instructions. Each school was expected to produce a programme of work which should include: floor or apparatus gymnastics, athletics, ball skills, combat sports, team sports.

*National Plan – government plans for provision of sporting facilities*
In addition to the compulsory PE and sports sessions on the timetable, a pupil must practise a sport either within a school sports association, or at a sports centre (Centre d'animation sportive, CAS), under the direction of the Department for Youth and Sport, or in a municipal or private club. The aim is to spend approximately five hours a week on physical activity and sport. The optional sport programme is very different from the class situation, and creates affinity groups.

The generally poor sports facilities at secondary schools hinder the implementation of an effective programme, and the choice of activities is much narrower than in Britain. From 1954, all schools were to be built with a gymnasium or sports field, but funds for this ambitious plan soon dried up. The government has encouraged the use of council facilities; but these are heavily used by many school groups, and the logistics of planning the time and transport creates problems for the teachers. Another inhibiting factor is the need for pupils to practise the restricted number of activities which will form part of their leaving certificate, taken at 15 at the end of the first phase of secondary schooling and

the Baccalaureat at 18. The school sport system is perceived as more important than the physical education by parents and pupils. They view PE more as a way of passing the exam. The club allows them the access to develop greater skill and prowess, more so than in Britain.

In this respect France is quite different from Britain. In France, there is a definite trend towards prioritising sport rather than PE, creating strong links between schools and clubs. This is similar to the USA. Recent British government policies suggest a shift in emphasis from physical education to sport.

Sports afternoons are supposed to be an official part of the school curriculum but the ongoing problems of administrators not having sufficient interest in physical education limits their effectiveness. The policy of sports afternoons is centrally controlled by a State Federation through to a Regional and Local Federation. The pupils must have a license (membership card), so statistical evidence of sport participation is available. Team games like soccer and rugby and individual sports like tennis, skiing and mountaineering are among the most popular sports according to the membership numbers. These statistics provide evidence of trends and projections which can be used for policy making, a medical reference point and can help to monitor standards for selection purposes.

Historically, school and university sport have been closely allied in France. The Association of School and University Sport (ASSU) was formed in 1963. They then separated in 1975, with the creation of the UNSS, Union Nationale du Sport Scolaire for school sport, USEP (Primary School Sports Union) for primary schools and the FNSU for university sport.

## Organisations for school sport

**Role of UNSS**
National Union of School Sport
Coordinates Wednesday afternoon activities
A multi-sport federation
Direct government control and funding from
    Secretary of State for Youth and Sport

Compulsory for all schools to join
Centralised policy.

*Advantages*:
Takes organisational and financial control away
from individual schools
Ensures a pyramid structure for promoting talented
performers
Fundamental unit which gives access to a maximum
number of children to sport.

USEP has a similar role to UNSS.

Schools formed sport associations whereby children
could practise, on a voluntary basis, the sport of
their choice at the times allocated on the timetable.
The school sports associations are therefore the
fundamental unit which gives access to a maximum
number of young people. The association aimed to
provide competitive educational events for both
junior and senior high schools. The PE teachers are
directly involved in the sport process as well as their
main priority of PE, which provides a natural
continuity. One conflict, which can arise, is when
talented youngsters go to play for a club.

The creation of 'mass formulae' are a proper
introduction to competitive sport. They are a system
of multi-sport competitions played over a period of
eight half days, the class as a social unit. The license
allows pupils to register for all sports. Competitions
are based on a pyramid structure with losers offered
further competitions adapted to their level. This
provides good preparation for helping students join
the federal or civil clubs, but there can be conflict
between the clubs and schools as they compete for the
most talented children. Teachers can also sometimes
feel that sport poses a threat to physical education.

## 'Sport pour Tous'

In 1972, the French National Olympic and Sports
Committee was given responsibility for a campaign
to promote sport for all, following France's
participation in the proceedings held by the
Council of Europe. The State Department for Youth
and Sport supplied a teacher of physical education
and sport to advise the Committee. The campaign

**ACTIVITY 25**

1. What parallels can you draw between physical education and school sport in the UK and France?
2. What has influenced the teaching of physical education in France? Consider the content and style of teaching in your answer.

was intended to convince the public of the necessity
for a minimal participation in physical pursuits
and sport, and to enable their access irrespective of
their social status. It was specifically aimed at non-
participating adults, and there were three levels at
which intervention could occur:

1. Leisure time: adults were encouraged to practise a
sport.

2. Place of work: it was stressed that workers needed
to be in better physical condition for their own
safety.

3. Place of residence: the development of sport has
greater potential where facilities are organised
close to places of residence. Making amenities
more accessible was therefore a prime aim.

The administration of sport, in both the UK and
France, is split between national, regional and local
levels. Both countries operate 'sport for all'
campaigns. However, France is more bureaucratic
at the sporting level, and financial aid is more
substantial. The state finances sport to a greater
degree than in the UK and yet the British are
experts in financing their own sport; and as such,
are perhaps more enthusiastic about sport, than a
people who rely on state aid for their recreation.

The slogans of French 'Sport for All' are:

• Within Everyone's Reach – the concept of equal
opportunities for people to participate should
they wish to.

Table 15.12. Comparison between French Physical Education system and the United Kingdom system

| United Kingdom | France |
|---|---|
| Traditionally decentralised | Centralised/Paris |
| National Curriculum = more centralised | Official Instructions/La Gym |
| Key states 1–4 | |
| Primary/heuristic/movement approach/ non-specialist teacher | Tiers Temps Non-specialist but access to a specialist |
| Secondary/skills focus/qualified teacher | La Gym = gymnastic emphasis |
| PE programme guided by National Curriculum but teacher choice included | Official Instructions Less teacher choice |
| PE compulsory | PE and Sport compulsory |
| Voluntary PE exams GCSE/A Level | PE formally assessed Brevet des Colleges Brevet d'Enseignement Professional Baccalauréat |
| Extra-curricular = voluntary/low status/ poor school and club links/teacher responsibility based on goodwill | Official school/club links USEP – primary UNSS – secondary Teacher for PE also coach for Wednesday afternoons License system |
| Outdoor Education not compulsory | Les Classes Transplantées (de mer, de vert, de neige) |
| Plas y Brenin | Le Centre National des Sports de Plein Air Les Sections Sports Etudes |
| Government initiatives: 'Raising the Game' Sportsmark 'A Sporting Future for All 2000' Active Schools | |

- Need to be Physically Active – the industrialised world suffers from the same problems of sedentary lifestyles, the over-consumption of food and passive hobbies. Being physically active should help alleviate many of today's health problems.

- A Noble Lifestyle – there tends to be a notion in both countries that sport is for the young and that there is little dignity in maintaining a sporting lifestyle as you get older. More emphasis needs to be given to the lifetime sports like golf.

- Mass Participation in a Wide Range of Activities – many of the French clubs are multi-sport and children are encouraged from an early age into developing a range of sport skills. In Britain we need to join separate clubs to participate in different activities.

- Socialisation of the Family and Continuity through sport – the tendency to segregate sport on the basis of gender, age and social class has perhaps tended to reduce the social aspect of physical activity. The French have a traditional tendency to have more mixing within sport and are less elitist than we are in Britain.

- Instil a Love of the Open Air – Le Plein Air is an important concept to the French. Much of France is rural and there is also the escape for the urban worker to more rural countryside.

- Spontaneity – the need to convert passive sport fans into active beings.

## Excellence in French sport

Excellence in sport is often taken up by national governments in its attempts to gain international prestige, and the realisation that sport has its place within international politics in the twenty-first century. Sport was initially a preparation for the military and subsequently a substitute for military conflict.

France concentrated on elitism more perhaps than any other European nation. France has a long history of physical excellence – its elite academies in the Renaissance era promoted the cultural development of aristocrats. Military defeats in the nineteenth century led to a reassessment of physical preparation in military and civic terms. As we have mentioned, Baron Pierre de Coubertin set out to revitalise the French nation in its approach towards physical activity.

This type of philosophy was taken up by de Gaulle, post World War II, as part of his nationalist policies in which he wanted political, economic and sporting success. Following the poor French results

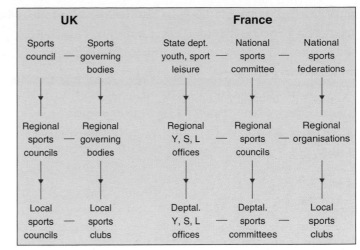

Fig 15.17. Comparison of French and British sports administration

## Comparison between British and French Tennis

- France: 7 men in world's top 60
          5 women in world's top 15
- Result of strength of French club structure
- 10,000 clubs in France (compared to 2,600 in Britain)
- 70–80% of these have junior sections (less than 10% of British clubs run junior sections)
- Adult club membership involves 20–25% of the fee going to develop the junior game
- Junior competitions begin early.
- Many clubs have a 'Kids Zone', which is dedicated to players of the future
- Mini tennis and transition tennis occur in these zones/fun areas away from adults
- Tennis is affordable in France (mostly private, costly and limited organisation in the UK)
- The LTA Performance Director (2000) is French and is trying to establish a comparable system in Britain via The National Performance Plan 2000.

in the Rome Olympics 1960 which dented national pride and prestige, he was reported as saying 'if we want medals we must pay for them. We (the state) must take up the organisation and financing of sport'. In 1966 he awarded the Legion of Honour to six champions. State aid was granted to improve facilities and administration support as part of a centralised approach. Ministerial decrees and instructions were supported by regional and departmental offices to coordinate the national policy.

## KEY WORD

**Nationalism:** a sentiment based on common cultural characteristics that binds a population and often produces a policy of national independence or separatism. It is also a very strong sense of loyalty or patriotism to one's country and often sport can help to develop this feeling. For example, during a major championship the progress of the team is followed and can intensify as the later stages are reached.

### INSEP

In the 1970s INSEP, the National Sports Institute, was created from the merging of the National Sports Institute (INS) and the teacher training establishment (ENSEPS), which aimed to produce the adult elite performer. It is a centre of excellence:

- It undertakes scientific research.

- It produces highly qualified teachers, coaches and administrators.

- Selection is undertaken by the federations (governing bodies) and there is constant feedback of the medical screening to coaches.

- It provides a venue for national team training in their quest for excellence.

- There is a permanent sport study section for over 100 children which caters specifically for swimming, gymnastics and tennis.

### Talent identification

The process of talent identification begins with the Brevet d'Aptitude Physique for 8–12 year olds. Another initiative is 'Aménagement du Rhythme de Vie de l'Enfant' (ARVE), which targets young people primarily to participate in sporting activity. At club level, the Carnet de Valeur Physique tests more specific skills for 10–18 year olds. The Regional Sports Study Sections involve 11–29 year olds in further laboratory screening, culminating at INSEP where medical, psychological, sociological, biomechanics measurements, physiology and physical training tests, take place.

### Sport study sections

Allied with this are the sport study sections. They provide special classes for talented children and certain schools offer certain sports. These have the usual advantages of sports schools – excellent facilities, coaching, medical and physiological tests, structured competition – while normal schooling continues. The pupils would still work towards the

## Categories of schools

- national category – international participants
- inter-regional category – national competitions
- promotional category – aims to find and nurture talent

What are the problems associated with such institutions?

ACTIVITY 26

Baccalauréat ABCD or G and reach a certain level in their chosen sport. One was established at Lycée Font Romeu, high up in the Pyrenees, for high altitude training.

The boarding school concept was favoured by the French and easily administered due to the national philosophy, direction and coordination by the Ministry of Sport and the centrally directed and uniform system of education. They have generally achieved moderate sporting success with good academic success.

Sport study sections are a part of the normal school system with specialised groups working in certain sports. High quality teaching and coaching is drafted in and movement on to specific centres is possible for specific sports excellence. By 1975 there were over 106 sport study sections catering for 2,000 pupils in 23 sports. In 1980 there were 145 catering for 3,400. There is heavy competition for places, and they are popular with parents and pupils.

## Outdoor education and recreation

The varied climate and land forms offer excellent choices in outdoor pursuit activities both within and outside of the school system. As in the USA, French people place a strong emphasis on getting children away from the cities to appreciate country life. There is a similar tradition in France as in the USA of parents taking separate holidays to their children, and the camp experience is a high priority.

### KEY WORD

**le plein air:** love of the fresh air. This is a popular concept in France and underpins the policy of developing an appreciation of the natural environment through physical activity. Their varied climate and terrain provide plenty of opportunities.

### Transplant classes

This priority begins at school as part of the curriculum with the transplant classes where children are taken into the country to appreciate the variety of regions in France as well as developing the outdoor pursuit skills of skiing, sailing, climbing and so on. The teacher accompanies the class, to combine normal teaching in the morning with an outdoor activity in the afternoon. They can cater for over a million children every year.

These classes focus on three different environments:

- classes de mer
- classes de vert
- classes de neige.

The 'colonies de vacances' are mainly aimed at low income, disadvantaged groups and the costs are subsidised. There are also camps for the wealthier sections of society, and they are very similar to the USA camp schools.

The Union Nationale des Centres de Plein Air (UCPA) is a world leading organisation for training in outdoor pursuits. It runs 51 centres, which can accommodate 60,000 per year and has extensive facilities, equipment and instruction. They concentrate on eight sports – skiing, climbing, underwater swimming, riding, sailing, coastal cruising and canoe-kayak. They also specialise in more

### KEY WORD

**Colonies de vacances:** outdoor summer camps in France. They were set up as part of a structured programme in order to take children away from the inner cities. It was intended that the children learn to appreciate the natural environment as part of the concept, 'le plein air'. They are aimed at low income, disadvantaged groups and the costs are subsidised by the state. They have permanent facilities set in attractive areas with professional and temporary staff.

general open-air activities such as Safari Photo which is like orienteering with a camera, and 'discovery of the mountains' in the Alps and Pyrenees.

British–French sport exchanges are popular as France offers a wider variety of terrain, climate and sports facilities than the UK. Governing bodies, the Sports Council and LEAs have long established links.

## Sport and ethnicity

Ethnic communities in France have generally maintained their own cultures and pastimes, which

> **ACTIVITY 27**
>
> Consider the place of outdoor education on the National Curriculum, the mainly fee-paying outdoor pursuit holidays which are available in the UK and British specialist Outdoor Pursuit Centres, in order to better understand the differences between France and Britain.

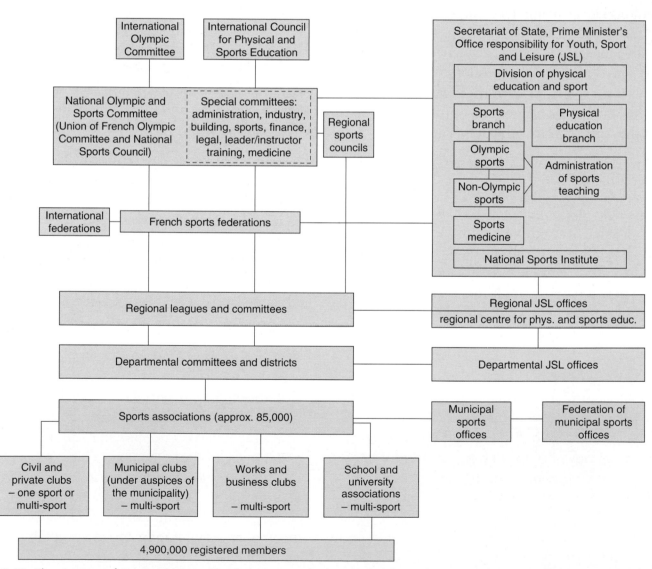

Fig 15.18. The structure of sport in France. The federation is the basic unit of French sport and is similar to the UK sport club. There are two types: single sport federations – cover one sport, e.g. cycling, and are responsible for selecting representatives for the national team; multi-sport federations – comprises clubs and associations where several sports are available

include pelota, bull fighting and boules or pétanque. Cultural traditions which have survived the rapid changes in the modern world tend to have common factors:

- They tend to be in isolated geographical areas which are less prone to outside influences and where changes take much longer to occur.

- They tend to be rural and agriculturally based, reflected in the strength-based activities, and activities which may once have had an initial utilitarian purpose.

- The connection to a particular area also gives it a cultural identity and local pride.

- Local competitions began as communities gathered together for recreation purposes.

- They often require simple, unsophisticated facilities and equipment.

- They were allowed to co-exist as an expression of democracy in pluralist society.

---

**ACTIVITY 28**

Compare the Highland Games to the French ethnic festivals.

---

## KEY WORD

**Pluralism/Plural societies:** the existence in society of different ethnic groups having distinctive ethnic origins, cultural forms, religions and so on. This is usually as a result of a policy of accommodation. Examples of such countries would be Western democratic cultures, such as France, the United Kingdom and USA.

---

**ACTIVITY 29**

Research some information on the Tour de France.

---

# Summary

- There is a centralised political approach to education and sport.

- The Federation (akin to British governing bodies) is the fulcrum of French sport, and is answerable to the Minister for Sport.

- There is a tradition of multi-sport federations like the UNSS, unlike the British tradition of single-sex clubs.

- Elite sport was encouraged by the policies of Charles de Gaulle, and has received state aid and support with the development of elite centres like INSEP.

- There are strong links between schools and civil clubs.

- The facilities in schools are generally poor and have led to more use of municipal facilities.

- Physical education is an examination subject on a compulsory basis and a rigid programme is followed.

- A programme of 'Sport pour Tous', similar to our Sport for All campaign, is aimed at improving the health of the nation.

## Review Questions

1. France has a centralised system of education. What does this mean and what effects can it have?
2. What is meant by '*tiers temps pédagogique*'?
3. In what way do the French distinguish between the two concepts of physical education and sport within the school system?
4. What is the *license* system and what are the advantages of such a system?
5. What are the seven slogans of French 'Sport for All'?
6. Which types of schools do the following two organisations, USEP and UNSS, cover?
7. What is the role of UNSS?
8. At how many levels is PE formally assessed in French schools?
9. What is meant by '*le plein air*' and how is this encouraged in the education system?
10. Where would a '*Classe de neige*' be held?
11. What are the Sport Study Sections and how do they operate?
12. As a Centre of Excellence INSEP performs various functions. Name five of them.
13. What is the main age range of top sports students attending INSEP?
14. How can you account for the survival of various ethnic sports in France?
15. What is the '*colonie de vacances*'?
16. What is the role of the PE and Sports Department and the Department of Sport Activities?
17. What does the term multi-sport federation mean? How does this differ from the UK system?
18. Where does the Olympic reserve develop from in the French system?
19. What influence was Baron Pierre de Coubertin to have on world sport?
20. What is meant by 'mass formulae' and how does this system operate?

# O E Australia

ACTIVITY 30

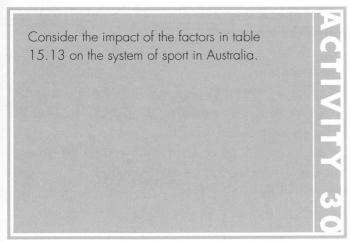

Consider the impact of the factors in table 15.13 on the system of sport in Australia.

- Active Australia
- Australian Sports Commission (ASC)
- Institutes of sport
- Indigenous Australian sports and colonial influence
- White Australia policy
- Aboriginal culture.

The term Oceania usually refers to the Pacific Basin, Melanesia, Polynesia and Australia. The peoples and their cultures are as varied as the land they inhabit.

Key terms you should understand at the end of this section are:

- Relationship between State and Federal government
- ACPHER
- PASE

## Politics

Australia is a member of the Commonwealth of Nations. The federal government is located in Canberra and conducts the national affairs. Similar to the United States, the Australian states have their own parliament and governor. It is a society based on democracy, with each citizen entitled to vote once they reach the age of 18.

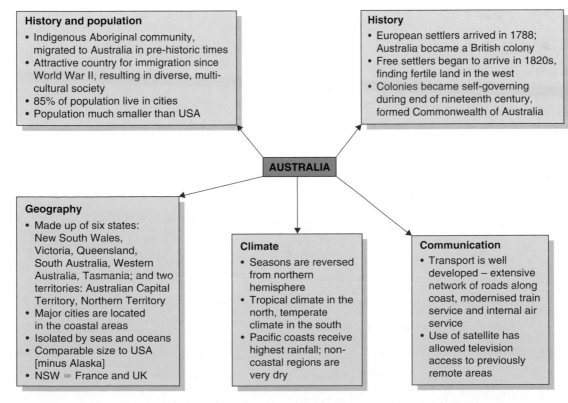

**History and population**
- Indigenous Aboriginal community, migrated to Australia in pre-historic times
- Attractive country for immigration since World War II, resulting in diverse, multi-cultural society
- 85% of population live in cities
- Population much smaller than USA

**History**
- European settlers arrived in 1788; Australia became a British colony
- Free settlers began to arrive in 1820s, finding fertile land in the west
- Colonies became self-governing during end of nineteenth century, formed Commonwealth of Australia

**AUSTRALIA**

**Geography**
- Made up of six states: New South Wales, Victoria, Queensland, South Australia, Western Australia, Tasmania; and two territories: Australian Capital Territory, Northern Territory
- Major cities are located in the coastal areas
- Isolated by seas and oceans
- Comparable size to USA [minus Alaska]
- NSW = France and UK

**Climate**
- Seasons are reversed from northern hemisphere
- Tropical climate in the north, temperate climate in the south
- Pacific coasts receive highest rainfall; non-coastal regions are very dry

**Communication**
- Transport is well developed – extensive network of roads along coast, modernised train service and internal air service
- Use of satellite has allowed television access to previously remote areas

Fig 15.19.

Legislative authority is held by the Federal Parliament, and political power rests with the Prime Minister who heads the government.

Australia has a multi-tiered system of government: a Commonwealth government, eight State and Territory governments and a large number of local or municipal governments. The Queen through her representative, the Governor-General, is still head of state. The political system follows the British Westminster system of by-cameral parliamentary democracy.

## Education

Education is compulsory for all Australian children between the ages of 6 and 15. Infant classes however, are available from age five. A free education is provided by the government in schools in all populated areas of the country. Similar to most other countries, fee-paying schools also operate and are often associated with religious denominations. Similar to the USA, the individual states have overriding responsibility for education, therefore generalisations are dangerous, although a centralised system does operate. Some funds are allocated by federal government from levied taxes, but the government does not have control over the states' spending. New policies show some similarities to the British model of Local Management of Schools where responsibility for salaries and maintenance, among other issues, has passed from the central administration to the individual schools.

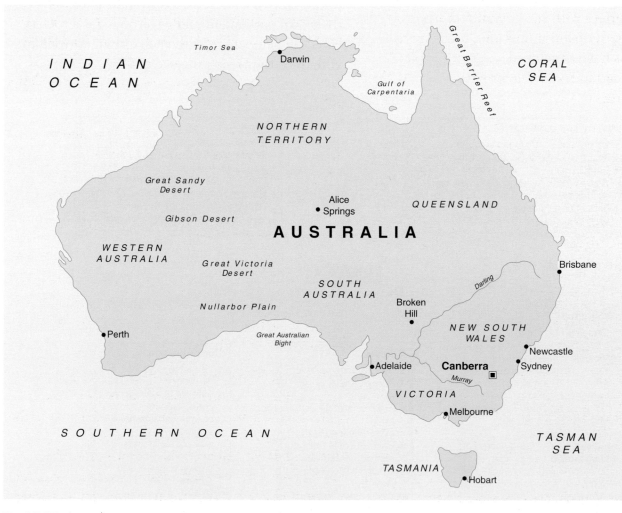

Fig 15.20. Australia

The State Department of Education lays down the educational content of syllabuses, trains the teachers and acts as a final authority.

Children who live in the outback are too far away from official schools, so they receive instruction over the air waves and send work to be graded. This operates under a programme called School of the Air. They can also attend a school which travels to them by railroad.

There are approximately 20 universities and a number of colleges that offer courses leading to undergraduate and advanced degrees.

## Physical education

Each state develops its own physical education. In some states, a considerable integration of school and council personnel and facilities has been realised. Local committees with sub committees made up of voluntary youth organisations and junior sport organisations have developed a number of play centres, recreation leadership programmes and coaching clinics.

Fig 15.21. Steve Waugh, one of Australia's highest scoring batsmen

Teachers are trained at colleges in two- or three-year diploma courses. Degree programmes have taken longer to establish. The teacher training programmes require the students to enter into a contract to complete the course and to serve as teachers for a certain period of time.

Outdoor activities are the norm in this favourable climate. Schools generally have good playing field facilities, swimming pools and outdoor gymnasia. In elementary schools, the emphasis tends to be on posture, gymnastics games and movement activities. At secondary level, conditioning or fitness activities, gymnastics, track and field games and swimming are integral parts of the programme. Girls participate more positively than their American counterparts.

Similarly to France, the sports afternoon, morning coaching session or sports day supplement physical education lessons. All pupils and teachers are expected to participate, with the more specialised teachers taking inter-scholastic teams. In reality, however, there is a high absentee rate from students who are not interested.

Competitive sports are controlled by amateur athletic associations and annual state championships are held in separate sports. In 1975 the National School Sports Council was established, which signalled the growing formalisation of school sport.

## Outdoor education

There is strong interest in the international Outward Bound Movement and the Duke of Edinburgh Award Scheme.

However, the level of Outdoor Education is not comparable to that found in France or the USA. It is lacking in organisation and funding and similar to the UK it relies on local government support and staff initiative. It was only in 1980 that the Australian Curriculum Development Centre developed aims for Outdoor Education and began a campaign for taking people to the natural environment.

Australia has four levels of Residential Centres:

- Outdoor Schools – extension of classrooms but they get first hand experience of natural environment

- Environmental Centres – focus on environmental studies

- Outdoor Pursuit Centres – largest group of field centres

- Outdoor Leisure & Environmental Centre – combined outdoor pursuits & environmental focus

## Outdoor recreation

Though it has topography and climate similar to the USA the population is much smaller and therefore there are large areas that are unpopulated. They do not grade areas as in the USA but they do have National Parks, which are run by individual States rather than by the Federal Government. Australians are becoming more aware of the natural environment but traditionally they have led more affluent/urban lifestyles.

- National Parks
- State Parks
- Regional Parks (5 mile radius of cities)

Mountain areas which have the benefit of snow are popular venues for weekenders and holiday enthusiasts. Swimming is the most popular sport – heavy emphasis is placed on this within the school curriculum, and it is the most popular participant sport.

The government commissioned a state-wide physical education and sport survey which was completed in 1993 but data and findings have been slow to emerge. The Federal response to the Report has been disappointing.

Important bodies such as the Australian Council for Health, Physical Education and Recreation (ACPHER) have agreed that all government schools should have weekly timetabled physical education lessons. However, constraints limited the schools' implementation of the recommended compulsory 60 minutes of physical education every day.

ACPHER has also proposed that all primary schools should have access to trained physical education specialists whether it be a permanent or peripatetic resource.

## Darwin region

| City limits | Open picnic sites |
|---|---|
| 30 miles | Nature parks (rambling/mountain biking etc.) |
| 50 miles | Katherine Gorge National Park<br>Kakadu National Park |

## Physical education in Victoria

It is useful to study a particular state as this can give more specific information about physical education as well as allowing a more general understanding of sport in Australia to take place. There has generally, across Australia, been a lack of political will to put in place coordinated and well-funded sports policies. However, there are exceptions and the state of Victoria is one of them.

With a new government, physical education has been viewed as a priority area by the Ministers of Education and Sport and Recreation as well as the Chief Executive of Education.

The Review of Physical and Sport Education in Victorian Schools was begun in 1993 by the Minister for Education in an attempt to develop a coordinated approach towards improving children's experiences and participation in physical and sport education. This resulted in the implementation of the Physical and Sport Education in Schools Policy in 1995, and has proved to be a watershed for Australian policy. Victoria received $2 million for the professional development and additional staffing for 'model' schools. Other schools were to share $1 million, to support efforts for improvements in facilities and participation.

The main recommendations were as follows:

1. PE and sport to be a high priority in the school charter and to receive accreditation for courses.

2. The training of non-specialist teachers to be upgraded. Already, approximately 8,000 teachers have attended new PASE courses.

The DSE also produced 'Health and Physical Education – Curriculum Standards Framework' in 1995. However, the level of bureaucracy may well cause some problems, especially for the non-specialist teachers. Tests have begun in mathematics and English, and physical education should be tested in the near future. As in France, the problems which can occur from schools teaching 'for the tests' have caused concern.

- The Victorian Primary and Secondary School Sports Associations organise inter-school sports throughout the state, benefiting from federal government grants.

- The Directorate of School Education supports staff development, and helps with the promotion of sport through these associations.

- School Sports Awards recognise excellence in major school sports and can be given to individuals, teams and coaches, and those who help the school in its attempts to improve the standards of school sport. You may recognise a

Table 15.13. Comparison between Physical Education in Australia and the UK

| United Kingdom | Australia |
|---|---|
| Traditionally decentralised<br>National Curriculum = more centralised<br>Key stages 1–4 | Decentralised – States<br>State Department of Education/lays down educational content and trains teachers/similar to USA |
| Primary/heuristic/movement approach/non-specialist teacher | Primary/movement based/should have access to trained staff (ACPHER) |
| Secondary/skills focus/qualified teacher | Secondary/skills/qualified teacher<br>PASE upgrade teacher qualifications |
| PE compulsory | PE compulsory |
| Voluntary PE exams GCSE/A Level | VCE – similar to A-Level PE<br>Testing similar to France |
| Extra curricular = voluntary/low status/poor school and club links/teacher responsibility based on goodwill | Sports afternoons supplement PE lessons<br>1975 National School Sports Council = formalising of school sport |
| Outdoor Education not compulsory | Not on level found in France & USA<br>1980 Australian curriculum Dev. Centre (dev. aims for O.Ed.)<br>Wide interest in Duke of Edinburgh Award and Outward Bound |
| Government initiatives<br>'Raising the Game'<br>Sportsmark<br>'A Sporting Future for All 2000'<br>Active Schools | Physical and Sport Education in Schools<br>Policy 1995 |

similarity here between the Sportsmark Awards the Conservative government promised to those schools who meet the criteria laid out in the document 'Sport: Raising the Game', in 1995.

- Similarly to the United States, the national television networks are becoming involved to show features on school sport, from school initiatives to information on individual students and sports events. This can encourage a community interest in school sport.

- Victoria has its own state 'Aussie Sport' programme (see below).
  - 'Be Your Best' Aussie Sport aims to help students and teachers learn the modified sports with the help of a Sport Development Officer.
  - 'Be Your Best' School Club Activity Days encourage links between schools and clubs.
  - 'Be Your Best' Allsports programme is an after school/weekend programme involving local sporting clubs and youth coaches.

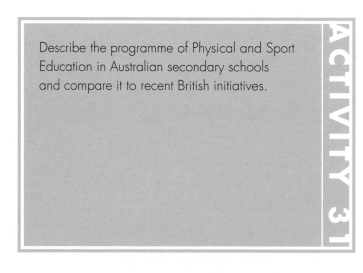

Describe the programme of Physical and Sport Education in Australian secondary schools and compare it to recent British initiatives.

ACTIVITY 31

## 'Aussie Sport'

'Aussie Sport' was a national sporting initiative committed to the development of young people through sport. The Australian Sports Commission (ASC) and the state departments of sport and education work closely together in order to foster positive community relationships, to ensure a coordinated approach to junior sport in their area.

'Aussie Sport' is about:

- supporting quality teaching and coaching
- promoting and developing quality sport for young people
- making sport more accessible, easier to play and enjoyable
- developing essential sporting skills in young people
- fostering greater community involvement in junior sport
- introduction of modified versions of major games, for example, Kanga Cricket for kids developed by the Australian Cricket Board
- using the skills of coaches as well as teachers.

Various programmes are tailored to suit different needs:

### Sportstart

This is aimed at working with young children through very informal play activities, such as simple games and activities, and playshop courses to help parents understand their children's play habits.

### 'Sportit!'

This is designed for primary school children to learn the basic motor skills used in the major sports. Packages have been designed to help teachers promote this area within the timetable allocation. The Modified Sport Programme is a way of reducing or putting in miniature, adult sport programmes. Examples are Netta Netball, Minkey and RooBall. Over 40 national sporting organisations have developed modified versions of their sport.

### 'Sport – Everyone's Game'

This aims to reach all groups within society and particularly those with lower active participation ratios. Examples include 'The Active Girls Campaign' and 'Willing and Able' (for people with disabilities). A computer program to help children select activities appropriate to them is available through 'Sport Search'. They can identify their own

Table 15.14. Aussie Sport codes of behaviour

| Players | Parents | Teachers |
|---|---|---|
| • Play by the rules<br>• Never argue with an official<br>• Control your temper<br>• Work hard for yourself and for your team<br>• Applaud good play from the opposition<br>• Treat all players with respect<br>• Cooperate with your coach and team-mates<br>• Play for fun, not just to please parents and coaches | • Remember that children play sport for their enjoyment<br>• Encourage children to participate<br>• Focus on the child's effort rather than winning or losing<br>• Never ridicule a child for losing<br>• Applaud good play by the opposition<br>• Support efforts to remove verbal and physical abuse from sport<br>• Respect official's decisions<br>• Support volunteer coaches, officials and administrators | • Encourage children to explore different kinds of sport<br>• Teach appropriate sports behaviour as well as skills<br>• Give priority for primary school children to free play activities, rather than highly structured games<br>• Keep up to date with the latest coaching practices<br>• Help children understand that playing by the rules is their responsibility<br>• Give children equal opportunities to participate |

characteristics and gain information about sports and the associated organisations.

Aussie Sport also runs leadership programmes for secondary school children, which can be compared to the British CCPR Community Sports Leaders Award.

### CAPS'

Challenge, Achievement and Pathways in Sport (CAPS) is a community club-based scheme for 14–20 year olds and enables them to acquire skills in the associated fields of coaching, management, officiating and so on.

### Sport for All

This concept is now an international movement and many countries are adapting policies to suit their cultural situations. Some concerns over the 'win ethic' promoted by 'Aussie Sport' led the Australians to develop the following programme.

***Active Australia***: a national programme run by the ASC where the focus is on participation and 'sport for all'. This programme integrated other programmes such as 'Aussie Sport' (est. 1986) and 'Aussie Able' into getting Australians 'up and active' at the foundation level of sport. This requires the adoption of a cohesive framework and corporate plan by Local State Sport Recreation Departments. A pack (provider model) is supplied to help clubs and organisations.

Active Australia identifies three main aims:

- to increase and enhance lifelong participation
- to realise the social, health and economic benefits of participation
- to develop a quality infrastructure with opportunities and services to support participation.

Its focus is entirely on sport for all rather than excellence.

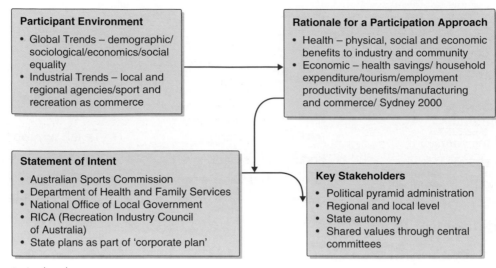

Fig 15.22. Active Australia diagram

The principles of Active Australia are:

- ensure access and equity
- lifelong involvement
- enjoyment in activity
- diversity and choice
- encourage improvement and quality of experience.

Its strategic directions are:

- policy and planning
- monitoring and evaluation
- training
- education advocacy
- industry

1. Make a list of Sport England's strategies for the future and compare them to this model.
2. Suggest reasons why 'Aussie Sport' was replaced by the more general heading 'Active Australia'.

ACTIVITY 32

- organisation and facility development
- promotion
- consultation and coordination.

## Talent identification

Attempts to screen for talented sports people has tended to focus on athletes who are already in the system and who have already shown a commitment to their particular activity. The Australians have recently tried to take this one step further by looking for potential talent in those not currently participating.

Sport specific profiles have been instigated, ie, the requirements from both a physiological and psychological viewpoint for a particular sport. Testing has then moved on to the schools to try to match the child to the sport they have been deemed most suited for. The teachers within the school environment carry out the initial tests on 14–16 year olds covering physical measurements and psychological assessments. The top 10% then progress to Phase 2 where more sport specific testing would take place in laboratories.

These children (approximately 10%) become part of a squad within the talent development programme. The state and the individual sporting associations are then responsible for the funding, and variations occur depending on the resources of facilities and coaching. Children who do not make the grade are encouraged to join local clubs to develop their talents.

In order to reduce the duplication of testing for a variety of different sports, each with their own interests at heart, the federal government has released funds for the development of elite athletes, under the Olympic Athlete Programme. The talent search is carried out by a national coordinator and eight state coordinators. These then liaise with the sport specific agencies, academies and school/recreation departments. Perhaps it was no coincidence that this followed the awarding of Sydney for the Olympic Games, in 2000. The sports most suited to this type of testing and most likely to achieve 'quick' results are reflected in those chosen for the search. These are athletics, canoeing, cycling, rowing, swimming, triathlon, water polo and weightlifting.

## ACTIVITY 33

1. What do you think makes these particular sports suitable for the talent identification programme?
2. Compare the testing for potential talent in Australia with the new SportSearch programme to be developed in the UK.

The response has been very encouraging. In 1995, 40% of all schools eligible to take part did so. At Phase 1 100,000 children took part; Phase 2 10,000; Phase 3 1,000. The aim of the programme was to improve the international standards of performance but there were positive developments for individuals who were tested and introduced to the sports they were best suited to, and encouraged a national interest for the Olympics in 2000.

## Types of sport

The English influence is evident in the sporting traditions of the Australians, both in the type of game such as cricket and rugby, but also in the attitudes of how you play the game, dress codes, etc. There is a strong middle class influence on and participation in sport. The working class element is not as traditional as in the UK.

- One of the first recorded cricket games was between two teams of the HMS Calcutta in 1803, and today Australian cricket attracts thousands of spectators. Competition against England (the Ashes) incites nationalist fervour.

- The Australian tennis teams are renowned and have won several Davis Cup competitions.

- Horse racing is an Australian passion (eg, Melbourne Cup).

- Swimming is popular, perhaps inevitably as a result of the climate and extensive coasts. The 'Australian crawl' was introduced at the turn of the twentieth century.

It is also interesting to note the recent tendency for Britain to emulate the Australian system for sport, eg, basing the UK Sport Institute (UKSI) on the Australian model.

### Australian football

This game dates back to 1858 when two men, Harrison and Wills, decided to design a purely Australian game. The game which emerged showed signs of influences from cricket (oval pitch), Gaelic football (being played by Irish troops) and the English game of rugby. The cricket pitches were used and were controlled by the cricket clubs. The Melbourne club is the oldest, founded in 1858. This game also helped to keep cricketers fit in the winter months. The size of the playing area even today is not a set distance but has minimum and maximum dimensions. The reason for this game not being successful internationally is the size of the pitch. It is difficult for already established pitches to be converted. The areas in Australia where the game flourishes are reported as having extensive facilities.

## Aussie Rules and Rugby league

- Premier matches form a series.

- Professionals play for their state rather than the home state of their club.
  *Advantage:* poorer states can use players who have moved to bigger clubs.
  *Disadvantage:* calculated at player's residence since age 15 rather than birth.

- Aussie Rules has a draft system similar to the USA.

> 1. Compare the structural variations in the game of Aussie Rules Football and professional soccer in the UK.
> 2. Consider the key elements of set pieces; restarts; tackles; violence and punishment; nature of the sport such as scoring, pitch and so on.
> Give cultural reasons for the differences you have mentioned.
>
> **ACTIVITY 34**

## Government involvement in sport

The Report of the Australian Sports Institute Study Group 1975 concluded that Australians 'spend an enormous amount of time and money on sport – thinking, talking, reading and writing about it, saving and spending for it and above all, loving it'.

Some facts: (source: ASC)

- Commonwealth, state and local governments expenditure $2.4 billion on sport and recreation (1995–1996).

- Employment figures for full-time jobs in sport-related areas was 218,000.

- 1997 one-third of adults participated in some form of physical activity.

- For the year 1996–1997 61% of 5–14 year olds participated outside of school sport.

- 1993–1994 $5.9 billion spent by consumers on recreation and sport.

- For the year 1994–1995 830,000 volunteers contributed 105 million hours to sport and recreation.

- For the year 1995 44.3% of Australians aged 15 years plus attended sport events as spectators.

> Explain the social and cultural influences that have resulted in sport having such a high profile in Australian society.
>
> **ACTIVITY 35**

## Organisation of Australian sport

The Australian system evolved from a community-based club structure catering mainly for mass participation in sport.

> *Advantage:* participate to individual's level of ability.
>
> *Disadvantage:* concentration on amateurism and volunteers. (Australia even slower to accept professionalism in participation and sport management than the UK from where it had inherited the amateur ethos.)
>
> *Result:* increased government involvement and funding in the 1980s recognised the need for a more professional approach.

A controversial but successful catalyst occurred with the attempts of media giant Kerry Packer. He started to commercialise and professionalise cricket in 1977 by establishing a professional World Series of Cricket.

Up to the 1980s the focus for youth sport tended to be on developing elite performance.

*Disadvantage*: high drop out rate of adolescents.

*Result*: more programmes in the 1980s and 1990s to stimulate 'sport for all' policies.

Up to the 1980s clubs and associations were uncoordinated and fragmented.

*Disadvantage*: catered for individual needs rather than promoting an integrated approach for federal funding.

## Current organisation

Figure 15.23 represents the current state of the organisation of sport. From the top to the bottom one can see that the government gives elite and funding support in general. The Australian Institute of Sport (AIS) and the Australian Sports Commission (ASC) supply the national sporting organisations with funds and services. Similar state organisations fulfil a similar role at state level. Local government is mostly involved in supporting the regional and local sport organisations with services and facilities in which to participate.

Government involvement therefore occurs at three levels:

- local
- state
- national.

## Federal

From 1972–1991 the federal government increased its spending on sport by 1400%. This only included ASC spending!

The government department responsible for sport is the Department of the Environment, Sport and Territories (DEST). The sport programme is divided into two sections.

- policy
- programme support and facilities.

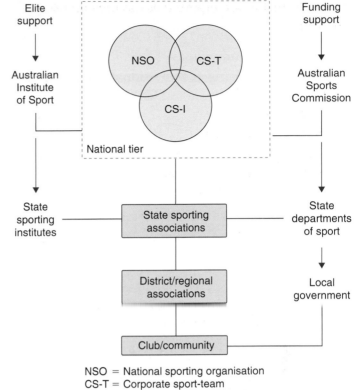

NSO = National sporting organisation
CS-T = Corporate sport-team
CS-I = Corporate sport-individual

Fig 15.23. The Australian Sport System (*Source:* Westerbeck 1995).

The overall objective of the sport programme was outlined in 1994:

'To contribute to the quality of life of all Australians by promoting and facilitating opportunities for participation in sport and recreation activities, encouraging sporting excellence, reducing harm associated with the use of drugs in sport and examining the economic and social impact of the sport and recreation industry.'

Separate federal agencies have been created for the Australian Sports Drug Agency and the Australian Sports Commission. The latter is by far the most important government agency.

## The Australian Sports Commission (ASC)

- statutory authority founded by Act of Parliament
- responsible for delivery of services to sport in Australia

- funded by DEST (1993–1994 $63.4 million)

- controlled by a Board of 12 Commissioners (high-profile individuals chosen for their corporate, sporting or professional leadership qualities) accountable to DEST

- financial and support services it provides range from identifying talent to promoting increased opportunities for participation (dual role similar to Sport England)

- in 1989 amalgamated with the Australian Institute of Sport (AIS)

- the AIS now a major division of the ASC and is involved with the national development of elite athletes

- a second major development, Sports Management, was established in 1993–1994.

| AIS | |
|---|---|
| Sports Development | 33.9% |
| Sports Management | 14.4% |
| Sport Science | 22.7% |
| Information Services | 6.1% |
| Marketing and Communication | 2.2% |
| Corporate Management | 1.6% |

To achieve its objectives the ASC will:
(*Source*: ASC)

- utilise as a catalyst the staging of the Sydney Olympics to encourage and to take advantage of a wide range of sport and sport-related opportunities for participation and enjoyment

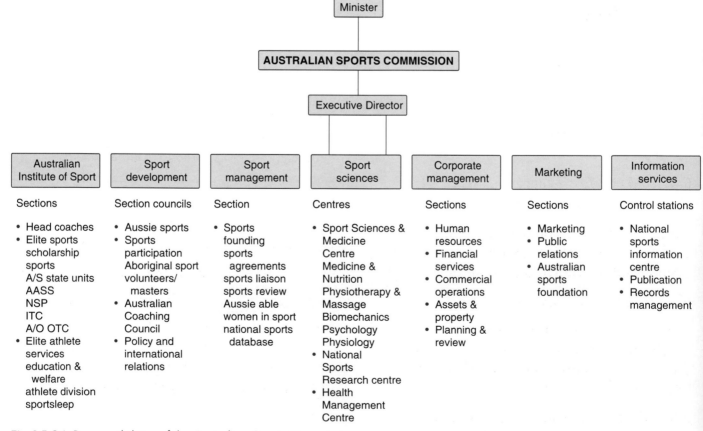

Fig 15.24. Responsibilities of the Australian Sports Commission

Sports Camps and Reservations (SCR) is a newly developed arm of the Australian Sports Commission. It coordinates five distinct areas:

- The National Sports Program (works with NSOs in providing specialised training camps at the AIS incorporating sports science, sports medicine, Olympic standard facilities and village residential accommodation)
- AIS Thredbo Alpine training centre (unique training facility)
- Commercial camps, conferences and commercial and major events
- AIS facilities
- International 2000 (project 2000; led up to Sydney Olympics; Canberra's taskforce identifying opportunities and partnerships for Canberra's future economic growth and community development)

SCR also offers all Australians the opportunity to experience the lifestyle of an elite athlete through commercial and conference packages at the AIS. Also major events from school-based tournaments through to international competitions

AIS Sports Science Sports Medicine personnel are considered to be leaders in the national and international arena.

The Australian Coaching Council (ACC) comes under the Sports Development section and is similar to the UK National Coaching Foundation (NCF). It is funded from the federal sport budget and undertakes a sports education function. It has a centralised organisation with the headquarters in Canberra supported by regional centres around Australia. Its main job is to develop the national coaching Accreditation scheme, which aims to get all coaches qualified.

- develop and implement policies, programmes and practices aimed at improving access and equity in all aspects of sport

- foster and encourage education and training in all elements of sports development

- encourage the provision of integrated, coordinated and quality support programmes for athletes and sporting organisations

- promote ethics and safety in sport

- maximise the availability of resources for the development of Australian sport, particularly through opportunities generated by the Sydney Olympics

- utilise the focus provided by the Sydney Olympics, raise the profile and increase the awareness of the benefits of sport and the ASC's programmes

- undertake and participate in international activities for the benefit of Australian sport

National Sporting Organisations (NSO)

- national representatives of their sport

- organises most of the amateur sport

- participation and elite leagues

- similar to UK governing bodies.

Confederation of Australian Sport (CAS)

- representative voice of NSOs (similar to UK CCPR)

- resource for services to sport

| Corporate organisation | National sporting organisation |
|---|---|
| NBL | Basketball Australia |
| Organises and manages professional basketball competition | Builds and organises amateur competition |
| Provide top quality entertainment | Promotes the support |
| 'Sell' the sport, hopefully to increase youth interest and participation | Helps supply new talent for NBL from amateur leagues |

- member organisations are autonomous
- 1992–1993 95 NSOs were members of CAS
- caters for needs of amateur sporting organisations.

## Corporate sport

As more and more sports turned professional or semi-professional new organisations were needed to cater for this section. They could only exist with corporate interest and support. There are five professional leagues:

Australian Football League (AFL)
New South Wales Rugby League (NSWRL)
National Basketball League (NBL)
National Soccer League (NSL)
Australian Baseball League (NBL)
The NSOs still administer responsibility in relation to rules and international competition.

Example: Basketball

## Private Sport Management Companies (eg, IMG International Management Group)

Private sport management companies emerged to:

- secure sponsorships
- advise in marketing strategies
- manage sport teams/personalities
- negotiate television rights and endorsement contracts.

Their influence has grown, very evident in golf with the Australian Open, the Australian Masters and the Greg Norman Classic.

> *Advantage*: ensured ongoing professionalism
> *Disadvantage*: blamed for focusing on commercial rather than sporting interests.

## Australian Olympic Committee (AOC)

- a National Olympic Committee (NOC)
- represents Australia in the Olympic movement
- prepares athletes and teams for winter and summer Olympic events
- provides a representative voice for them
- promotes and protects the interests of the IOC
- affiliated Olympic sports have a strong voice on the Executive of the AOC
- commission structure makes it more flexible (Planning and Review; Constitution; Marketing; Finance; National Fund Raising; Athletes; Medical; Doping; Education and Apparel)
- representatives of the commission can influence and implement policy.

Every state has a State Olympic Council:

- serves needs of state-based Olympic athletes
- two representatives per state nominated to represent the states at the AOC.

All efforts for the 1990s were geared up towards the Sydney 2000 Olympics.

*Academies of Sport*: training centres for the development of elite athletes usually with the aim of raising the profile of sport within a country, forming part of a national strategy in sport policy. Consequently, National Governments are usually heavily involved in the philosophy and funding of these centres as they can help create an important national identity. They have an emphasis on:

- top class coaching
- world class facilities
- scientific support.

Academies and Institutes of Sport can be either centralised or decentralised, targeting specific sports, which may be traditional or new to the country. They often concentrate on national sports or on those with an ethnic identity, often utilising higher education or local authority facilities. These centres can either be isolated from the ethos of mass participation or allow mass sport to run parallel to it, forming the structure beneath the pinnacle.

## Australian Institute of Sport (AIS)

The AIS was established in 1981 as a result of decline in world standing, lack of medals at world sporting events and lack of a formal structure to develop elite athletes. Its aim was 'to contribute to the development of elite sport in Australia through residential training programmes, camps and scholarship assistance'.

- Initially centralised in Canberra
- 1985 began to decentralise due to social problems encountered by young athletes (hockey to Perth; diving to Brisbane; volleyball to Sydney)
- states established their own Institutes (South Australia 1982; Western Australia 1984; Tasmania 1986; Victoria 1990)

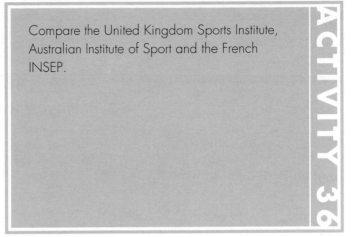

Compare the United Kingdom Sports Institute, Australian Institute of Sport and the French INSEP.

ACTIVITY 36

- funded 95% by federal government; 5% from commercial sponsorship, eg, Kellogg's
- 1989 merged with ASC
- provides training in 20 sports across Australia
- organises training camps for national teams
- provides grants to elite athletes and coaches
- delivers athlete advisory and employment services.

Achieves its objectives through a variety of programmes as shown in the table below:

| Programme | Explanation |
| --- | --- |
| Sport Talent Encouragement Plan (STEP) | Provide direct financial assistance to high performance athletes |
| Elite Coaching Scheme | Raise standard of coaching for high performance athletes |
| National Sports Plan/Sports Assistance Scheme (SAS) | Assistance to NSOs for training camps and technical seminars for athletes, coaches and officials |
| Intensive Training Centres (ITC) | Full-time Commonwealth funded coaches appointed to work with national and state-based coaches |
| Lifeskills for Elite Athletes Programme (SportsLEAP) | Reduce burden on athletes; short-term financial management of daily existence and career planning following retirement from performance |
| Scholarship Sports Programme | Main programme of AIS. Scholarship provides access to coaching, training facilities, sports science and medicine |

(*Continued*)

| | |
|---|---|
| | services; assistance with education and welfare; athletes receive full room and board (approx. $11 million per annum on around 500 scholarships) |
| Australian Athlete Scholarship Scheme | Similar to the SportAid in the United Kingdom, but it receives federal money and has a larger budget. The primary aim is to give direct financial aid to elite athletes who will have been nominated by their National Sporting Bodies |
| Olympic Athlete Programme (OAP) | Six-year $135 million programme following successful Olympic bid |

## State departments of sport

- Government involvement in sport at state level began in the early 1970s
- Each State or Territory has its own government department with responsibility for sport and recreation (for example Sport and Recreation Victoria)
- Promote mass participation as well as housing State Academies
- State Academies are centralised to some extent through the meeting of each executive officers at the National Elite Sports Council (NESC).

## Local government

- provision of parks, recreation centres, swimming pools etc.
- local government contributes approximately 73% of total government expenditure
- concentrates on recreation needs rather than sport needs
- local government councils decide on division of available funds

## AIS facilities

- Synthetic athletics track
- Indoor swimming centre
- AIS Arena – catering for all indoor court sports
- Ansett Sports visitor centre
- Gymnastic hall
- Soccer and hockey synthetic pitches
- Outdoor tennis courts
- Sports training facility
- National Sports Information Centre
- AIS residences
- Sport Sciences

- a trend towards competitive tendering is occurring to minimise debts and maximise control.

| Pyramid A | Government involvement | Four pyramids show the peak agency/ organisation at the apex of each |
|---|---|---|
| Pyramid B | Traditional sport system | Vertical channel of communication |
| Pyramid C | Sports development | Increasing width at lower level represents larger number of organisations and increased number of participants |
| Pyramid D | Corporate sport | Concentric circles show pattern and level of communication between organisations in each sector (only recently becoming more successful) |

# Conclusion

Fig 15.25 summarises the Australian sports organisations and their major responsibilities.

## Sydney Olympics 2000

(For general information on the Olympic movement see chapter 14.)

The Sydney 2000 Olympic Games: September/October 2000

10,200 athletes from 200 countries competed in 28 sports in 300 events over 16 days of competition. There were 5,100 officials and 15,000 media providing coverage for a world-wide audience of 3.5 billion. The successful Games bid ensured subsidised travel for athletes and officials. The staging of the Games was the responsibility of the Sydney Organising Committee for the Olympic Games (SOCOG).

The New South Wales government underwrote the Games and was responsible for providing venues and facilities, which were sensitive to the environment.

International sponsorship partnerships were crucial to the staging of the Games.

*Aboriginal and Torres Strait Islander participation*

The Sydney Organising Committee for the Olympic Games (SOCOG) tried to reflect the rich culture of these indigenous peoples.

It appointed a National Indigenous Advisory Committee, which made recommendations to

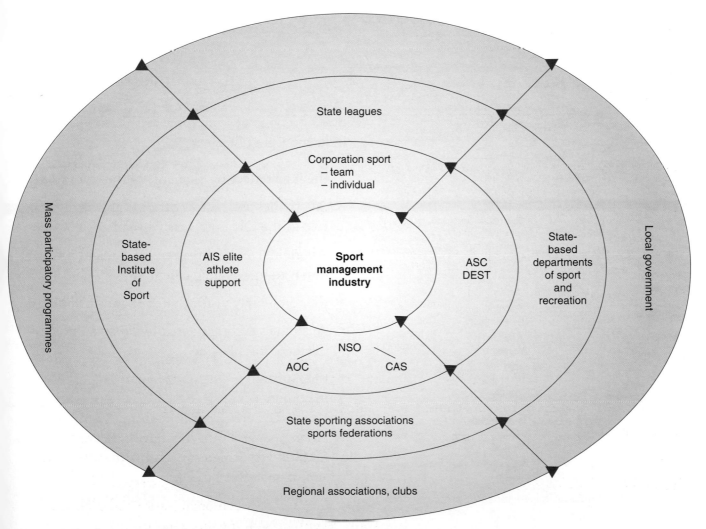

Fig 15.25. The four pyramids of Australian Sport

| The Budget was the result of eight months of detailed operational planning and review, and was approved the IOC in Monte Carlo on 21 May 1997 | |
|---|---|
| Games budget | A ($m) |
| **Revenues** | |
| Sponsorship | 828.8 |
| Consumer products | 61.1 |
| Ticket sales | 487.0 |
| Television rights | 954.6 |
| Total revenues | 2,331.5 |
| **Expenditures** | |
| Accommodation, Olympic family and medical | 82.9 |
| Ceremonies | 37.3 |
| Consumer products and creative services | 25.7 |
| Executive office and legal | 60.7 |
| Financial, risk and project management | 50.5 |
| Human resources, communications and community relations | 53.5 |
| Logistics | 43.9 |
| Media: Press and broadcasting | 184.2 |
| Sponsorship and general marketing | 135.4 |
| Sport | 78.2 |
| Technology, premises and administration | 363.7 |
| Ticketing | 42.5 |
| Torch relay, events and Olympic arts festivals | 38.4 |
| Transport and accreditation | 52.7 |
| Venue management and security | 363.6 |
| Venue and environment | 284.1 |
| Villages | 197.6 |
| Volunteers and uniforms | 30.9 |

Fig 15.26. Budget for Sydney 2000

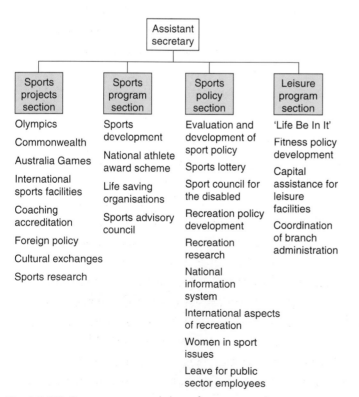

Fig 15.27. Section responsibilities for sport and recreation branch within the Ministry of Home Affairs

SOCOG on issues and projects that should include indigenous involvement, such as:

- the logo reflecting elements of the old cultures

- Aborigines and Torres Strait Islanders playing a role in the Olympic Arts Festival

- Aboriginal and Torres Strait Islander protocol observed in Olympic ceremonies

- the torch relay visiting sites of ancient interest

- Australia's Aboriginal Cathy Freeman was the Olympic torchbearer

- the Australian Olympic Committee (AOC) in conjunction with SOCOG and the ASC established an Olympic Training Centre for Aboriginal and Torres Strait Islander (OTCATS) athletes in Canberra. There were approximately 24 indigenous athletes on such scholarships in the lead up to the Sydney Games.

## The Victorian Institute of Sport (VIS)

The VIS is synonymous with Achievement, Success and Excellence in sport. It is a trustee company limited by guarantee receiving support from both government and corporate sectors. Central administration is located in South Melbourne.

> Currently more than 430 Victorian athletes are involved in programmes. Eight of the twelve programmes are Olympic sports: Athletics, Cycling, Gymnastics, Hockey, Rowing, Soccer, Swimming and Tennis and four non-Olympic sports: Cricket, Golf, Netball and Squash.

Each state has its own Institute of Sport, intended to promote excellence in sport. The VIS was established in 1990. It is supported financially by the government and private sectors, and a Board of interested and influential sportspeople establishes its philosophies. For example, individual sports federations can apply for admission, and acceptance will be based on whether they have the required number of registered athletes, how high their athletes are ranked, the selection procedures they operate from local to state level and their potential for attracting sponsorship which will partly be determined by the media profile they have developed. They can be included in the major VIS programmes or one-year courses.

Athletes have access to

- advanced coaching – fitness, skill, tactical and psychological aspects of their chosen sport
- competitive opportunities – national and international events
- career development – personal skills, education, future employment prospects.

Other initiatives include the National Coaching Accreditation Scheme and the International Standard Sports Facilities Programme.

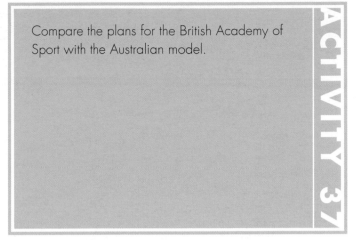

Compare the plans for the British Academy of Sport with the Australian model.

**ACTIVITY 37**

### Mass participation

The Australian 'Life Be In It' campaign used the media heavily to promote mass participation. The model starts at the person and aims to assist them in the learning process of making them aware of the need for physical activity, helping them to participate in physical activities and evaluating the participation to assess behavioural changes.

The national sport federations supported by the government carry much of the responsibility for organising mass activities. In contrast, the participant in America has to bear the main cost of participating.

## The Aborigines

Aborigines were the first original inhabitants of Australia. They lived in nomadic tribes and over the centuries they spread out across the continent, creating and maintaining their own territory in which they had freedom to hunt and fish, though they established only temporary accommodation. They lived in clans and several clans made up an extended family. The spiritual world was an integral part of the philosophy of the Aborigines. Boomerangs were used for hunting (non-returning) and sport (the returning boomerang). The Aborigine population has been decimated by military action, disease and exile into remote areas. Colonisation led to disease and death through military action and the loss of land rights has only

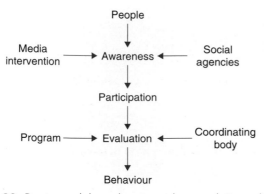

Fig 15.28. Basic model used in Australian and Canadian programs

recently being recognised and compensated for in the 'Native Title Act' (1994). This is an example of an ethnic people who were affected by the White Policy and whose fate was similar to that of the American Indians. They now form less than two per cent of the population. Traditional physical activities would have a functional base, for example, hunting and games as preparation for battles; they would also have had a strong religious and ritual meaning. The National Aboriginal Sport Foundation is part of the ASC and has founded the 'Aboriginal Sport and Recreation Programme'. Aboriginal culture has seen a revival within a more liberal society, though they still suffer severe discrimination.

National competitions exclusive to Aborigines have been organised, examples are:

- National Aboriginal Australian Rules Carnival
- Interstate Aborigine Rugby League Carnivals
- Special Aborigine Sports Days.

Colonisation has resulted in the anglicisation of Aboriginal culture. In the schools, reserves and missions the main games are now cricket, rugby and netball.

### Traditional sports

Many of their sports were linked to their subsistence lifestyle. With the exception of inter-tribal tournaments rules were few, easy to understand and often temporary; officials were not needed; winners

were rarely honoured as this was not the main purpose of participation.

- Through play and friendly contests males maintained fitness and military prowess.
- Tournaments were inter-tribal, called 'pruns' in Central Queensland. They followed rules of fair play and were used to settle personal scores or tribal disagreements.
- Used to strengthen internal relationships, promote goodwill and social intercourse.

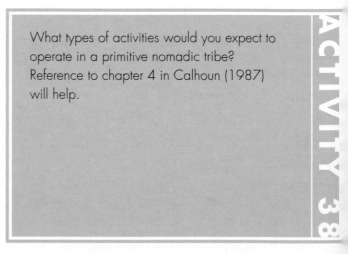

What types of activities would you expect to operate in a primitive nomadic tribe? Reference to chapter 4 in Calhoun (1987) will help.

ACTIVITY 38

### Sport and people with disabilities

The first opportunities for athletes with disabilities in Australia occurred in 1954 under the Australian Deaf Sports Federation; wheelchair sports began in 1972. The Australian Confederation of Sports

# Australian Aboriginals

Although the indigenous peoples of Australia lived by hunting and gathering, they also engaged in sports, many of which were tied to their subsistence skills. The major ones were:

1. Tree climbing.
2. Spear the Disc.
3. Pit Throwing: a heavy stick or bone attached to a piece of twine was thrown over an emu net into a hole dug specifically for the game.
4. Returning boomerang throwing.
5. Target and Distance Throwing: competitions involving the throwing of sticks, boomerangs, spears, or any other object at a specific target.
6. Kangaroo Rat, or Weet Weet: in this group game, the kangaroo 'rat', which was made out of a single piece of wood, was thrown so that it slid or bounced along the ground; the main aim was to achieve the furthest distance and/or the greatest number of hops.
7. Wrestling.
8. Mungan-Mungan: in the centre of the designated playing areas a *wormar* (a white painted stick representing a young girl) was placed, and the object of the game was for the young boys to keep the *wormar* away from the older men. Passing and tackling were essential features of the game, which continued until one team was too exhausted to play.
9. Catchball: catchball was the favourite and most widespread ball game and was played by both sexes. The game involved players tossing the ball back and forth while other players attempted to intercept it in the air.
10. Football: the most common mode of play was to kick the ball high into the air, higher and farther than anyone else.
11. Hockey: a ball-and-stick game resembling the European game of shinny was played by both sexes.

*Source*: Encyclopaedia of World Sport, Levinson

for the Disabled speaks on behalf of all handicapped sport groups to the government. Associations represented include paraplegic and quadriplegic people, deaf people, those suffering with cerebral palsy, amputees and so on. They generally have national governing bodies, with state associations.

Sport for people with learning difficulties follows a different route. Sport depends on access, awareness, attitudes, acceptance, ability (Little, 1987). There are segregated and integrated programmes depending on these factors, and can be unique to the sport, the club and the individual.

# Summary

- Geographically, Australia is similar to the USA, and a variety of scenery and climate allows for wide variations in sports, though with fewer opportunities for winter sports.

- Australia has felt the influence of the British sports scene and has maintained links with the old country for a longer period of time.

- Australia has similar government administrations to the USA and France.
- Mass participation and the pursuit of excellence are important objectives, though the latter has recently attracted more world attention.
- The original characteristics of sports have been adapted within the more isolated continent and now have their own unique character.
- Sport and physical education are given time on the timetable and outside sports coaches are used within the school setting.

## Review Questions

1. What does ACPHER stand for and what is its role?
2. Name three elements on the 'Active sport' programme and describe the aim of such a programme.
3. Talent identification is an important part of the Australian sport system. Describe how the Australians have implemented such an approach.
4. Each state has its own Sport Institute. What are the characteristics of these organisations?
5. What is the aim of the Capital Assistance Programme?
6. What are the European influences evident in the game of Aussie Rules football?
7. List three suggestions made under the 'Aussie Sport' code of behaviour for players, parents and teachers.
8. What do the Australians have in their education system, which is similar to the British Sportsmark Award?
9. What does PASE stand for?
10. What have been the similarities between the experiences of the Aborigine and American Indian populations?
11. What are the aims of the AIS and how does it attempt to achieve these aims?
12. What are the aims of the ASC and how does it attempt to achieve these aims?
13. Explain the terms decentralised and centralised and suggest how the Australian sport system operates in relation to these terms.
14. Compare the role of Sport England and the ASC.
15. Why has the Australian government placed so much emphasis on achieving excellence in sport?

## Comparative examination techniques

### The preparation of physical education teachers

Having studied each country within its own context, you will need to find a method of directly comparing aspects of sport and physical education across all four countries. A useful method would be to take a topic such as 'the preparation of physical education teachers'. You need to pull aspects of the topic together and then draw up a table and place key words under each country. This can be an effective way of revising.

Having considered how the subject of physical education is taught, we can assess how the teachers are prepared for their future role.

It is important that when you are asked to compare or contrast between different countries, that you clearly state each, rather than assuming that by mentioning one, the examiner will know that you understand the other. The examiner must be able to see a direct comparison in order to link the two together.

## Example 1

### Question:

What are the different values inherent in school sport in the UK and the USA?

### Answer:

| USA | UK |
|---|---|
| • success in victory | • value from playing/ intrinsic |
| • male games playing elite/female cheerleader | • equality between girls and boys |
| • elite sportspersons separate to main stream | • less status for games elite |
| • heavily financed | • no cheerleaders in UK |
| • professional/deviance orientation | • no financial privileges |
| | • amateur/PE 'value' system |

## Example 2

A response to a question about teaching and extra curriculum responsibilities in the UK and the USA could be shown as:

| UK | USA |
|---|---|
| teacher responsible | • coach responsible |
| goodwill/no extra pay | • coach highly paid |
| job security | • hire and fire |
| low community profile | • high media/community profile |
| range of activities | • specialist |

A descriptive account will usually gain minimum marks. You will need to show a deeper understanding by applying knowledge gained from each country and showing what effects this will

have had on physical education and sport. Thus, political and sociological analysis is required. Terms which you should incorporate in your responses are:

- decentralised/centralised
- democracy/egalitarian
- pluralist/assimilation/ethnic groups
- dominant culture/subculture
- legislative
- nationalism
- functional/utilitarian/recreational
- autonomous/state-controlled
- capitalist/socialist
- republic/federal

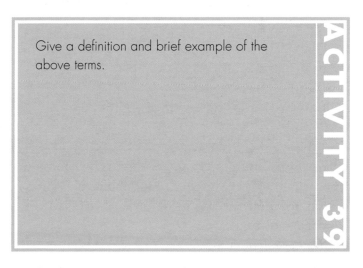

Give a definition and brief example of the above terms.

ACTIVITY 39

# Conclusion

## Issues

### Globalisation

It is important to recognise the globalisation of sport due to the technological developments of transport and the media. Countries learn from each other and the issues of human rights are slowly being addressed. Sports like baseball and American football are gaining acceptance outside of the USA.

### A 'core' programme

Despite the many differences existing across the countries we have looked at, there are also many similarities, such as mass participation, elite sport programmes, compulsory physical education and the development of sports for people with disabilities. A wider variety of sports has taken over from the traditional sports of gymnastics, football and track and field.

## Commercial sport

Sport is big business and forms a significant income for governments. The development of the consumer market for sports goods, as well as sports events given extensive coverage by the media, contribute to this.

## National government involvement in sport

This was summarised by Semoutiak as being for:

- political indoctrination
- labour and military efficiency
- national prestige
- international goodwill
- individualising and socialising function
- economic and legislative functions.

The reasons for different governments becoming involved in sport can reveal a lot about the values of that government and its opinion of physical education and sport.

## Values

- The old concept of amateurism has undergone many changes, and abuse is prevalent in many systems, where eligibility for the prestigious Olympic Games is at stake. Situations like trust funds have changed the nature of amateur athletics and the full-time training of student athletes for the inter-collegiate competitions are examples of double standards operating. This begs the question – is there a place for amateurism in the twenty-first century?
- Physical education or sport? This is a question of educational philosophy – if the achievement of sporting excellence is the primary aim, the sport ethic can become too dominant and

consequently damaging to children's personal development.

- The preparation of the sports professionals is consequently highlighted. Can the physical education teacher, with their primary concern being the individual development of each child through a variety of physical activities, really take on board the win ethic associated with sport and the increasing specialisation required for each individual sport? Consider the priority given to sport in the 1995 publication, 'Sport: Raising the Game'. Do they need to separate and remain with different aims? Does a system where there is a strong link developed between the school and community sport associations, such as in France, show an effective balance?

- Activity versus study? In an era when the industrialised countries of the world are concerned for the increasingly sedentary lifestyles of its citizens, physical education is showing a greater tendency to be examined on a theoretical level, possibly reducing the amount of physical energy expended.

- Nationalist tendencies can be reinforced through sport and can move from a unifying constructive factor to one which incites hatred, exploitation of athletes, unequal distribution of resources.

- The Olympic Games have moved from the original Coubertin aims of reviving French nationalism based on the English tradition of athleticism, to one of providing a world stage for governments to raise their prestige and for political power groups to vent their tensions.

- Is the sports business world beginning to edge out the ordinary supporter, with the increased admission prices? The characteristics of these sports may well continue to change.

- The deviant acts of aggression, drug abuse and lack of respect for sports officials is becoming all too prevalent as the win ethic assumes greater prominence.

Let's hope that in the future we can learn the best practices from each other and keep the positive nature of physical education and sport high on the agenda, for the development of future generations.

## Further reading

L Allison (ed), *The Politics of Sport* (Manchester University Press, 1986)

D Anthony, *A Strategy for British Sport* (C Hurst & Co, 1980)

T Arlott, *Oxford Dictionary of Sport* (Oxford University Press, 1975)

P Bailey, *Leisure and Class in Victorian England* (Cambridge University Press, 1981)

P Beashel, J Taylor, *Advanced Studies in Physical Education* (Nelson, 1995)

B Bennet, Howell & Simri, *Comparative Physical Education and Sport* (Lea & Febiger, 1983)

D Birley, *Sport and the Making of Britain* (Manchester University Press, 1993)

B Buford, *Among the Thugs* (Mandarin, 1992)

C Brightbill, *The Challenge of Leisure* (Prentice Hall, 1963)

C Bucher, D Wuest, *Foundations in Physical Education and Sport* (Mosby, 1991)

G Butler, *Introduction to Community Recreation* (McGraw-Hill, 1968)

D W Calhoun, *Sport, Culture and Personality* (Human Kinetics, 1987)

R Callois, *Man Play and Games* (Free Press of Glencoe, 1961)

E Cashmore, *Making Sense of Sport* (Routledge, 1991)

J Coakley, *Sport in Society: Issues and Controversies* (Mosby, 1993)

F Coghlan, *Sport and British Politics* (J Roscoe Publications, 1990)

Cohen, *Folk Devils and Moral Panics* (Blackwell, 1972)

F W Cozens, *Sports on American Life* (University of Chicago Press, 1953)

V Dalen, B Bennet, *A World History of Physical Education* (Prentice Hall, 1971)

Dumazadier, *Toward a Society of Leisure* (WW Norton, 1967)

E Dunning, *Quest for Excitement: Sport and Leisure in the Civilising Process* (Blackwell, 1986)

M Ellis, *Why People Play* (Prentice Hall, 1973)

J Ford, *This Sporting Land* (New English Library, 1977)

Gardiner, *Greek Athletic Sports and Festivals* (Brown, 1970)

S de Grazia, *Of Time, Work and Leisure* (Doubleday, 1962)

R Holt, *Sport and the British* (Oxford University Press, 1990)

B Houlihan, *The Government and Politics of Sport* (Routledge, 1991)

J Huizinga, *Homo Ludens* (Beacon Press, 1955)

—*The Play Element in Contemporary Sport* (Frank Cass, 1971)

J H Kerr, *Understanding Soccer Hooliganism* (Open University Press, 1994)

R Krause, *Recreation and Leisure in Modern Society*, 2nd ed. (Goodyear Santa Monica, 1978)

A Langley, *World Issues: Sports and Politics* (Wayland, 1989)

J Lieberman, *Playfulness, its Relationship to Imagination and Creativity* (Academic Press, 1977)

Loy, Kenyon, *Sport, Culture and Society* (Lea & Febiger, 1981)

J A Lucas, *The Future of the Olympic Games* (Human Kinetics, 1992)

T Marsh, *The Illusion of Violence* (Dent, 1978)

T Mason, *Sport in Britain* (Faber & Faber, 1988)

—*Only a Game* (Cambridge University Press, 1993)

N McFarlane, *Sport and Politics – A World Divided* (Willow Books, 1986)

P McIntosh, *Physical Education in England Since 1800* (Bell & Hyman, 1952/78)

M Mead, *Cooperation and Competition Among Primitive Peoples* (Gloucester Mass Peter Smith, 1976)

H Meyer, *Community Recreation* (Prentice Hall, 1964)

C Mortlock, *The Alternative Adventure* (Cicerone Press, 1984)

J Murphy, *Recreation and Leisure Service* (William C Brown, 1975)

J Murphy, *Williams and Dunning, Football on Trial* (Routledge, 1990)

J Nash, *Philosophy of Recreation and Leisure* (C V Mosby, 1960)

M Neumeyer, *Leisure and Recreation* (Ronald Press, 1958)

Pearson, *A History of Respectable Fears* (Macmillan, 1983)

J Piaget, *Play, Dreams and Imitation in Childhood* (Norton, 1962)

J Pieper, *Leisure, the Basis of Culture* (New American Library, 1952)

G Redmond (ed), *Sports and Politics; the 1984 Olympic Scientific Congress Proceedings, vol 7* (Human Kinetics, 1984)

G Sage, *Power and Ideology in American Sport* (Human Kinetics, 1993)

J Shivers, *Principles and Practices of Recreational Service* (Macmillan, 1967)

W Sumner, *A Study of the Sociological Importance of Usages, Manners, Customs, Mores and Morals* (Boston Ginn, 1940)

G Torkildsen, *Leisure and Recreation Management* (Spon, 1991)

Taylor, *Soccer Consciousness and Soccer Hooliganism*

M Tozer, *Physical Education at Thring's Uppingham* (University of Leicester, 1974)

*British Journal of Physical Education*

Central Office of Information, *Aspects of Britain 'Sport and Leisure'* (1994)

Audit Commission, *Sport for Whom?* (1989)

*The Hillsborough Stadium Disaster Final Report* (HMSO, 1990)

Sports Council publications:
*Fifty Plus and All to Play For* (1994)
*People with Disabilities and Sport* (1993)
*Sport in the Nineties – New Horizons* (Willow, 1986)
*Sport – Raising the Game* (1995)
*What is the Sports Council? Fact Sheet* (1994)
*Women and Sport* (1995)

CCPR publications
*The Organisation of Sport and Recreation in Britain*
*The Howell Report* (1993)

# 16. The Social History of Sport in the United Kingdom

So far we have examined the present day situation regarding sport and physical education. We have occasionally referred to how the past has influenced the present. Now it needs a more in-depth analysis. In other words, how and why have we arrived at the present day situation?

We will:

- chart some social changes which have been influential to our everyday lives and see how recreational activities have been affected

- apply knowledge gained in order to analyse a variety of physical recreational and sporting activities.

Whatever we discover about sport must not be seen in isolation. The system of sport influences and is in turn influenced by the social system – economic, geographical, educational, social and political factors.

By the end of this chapter you should understand the link of sport to:

- historical eras relevant to the specification you are following (Medieval England, Tudors and Stuarts, Hanoverian era, Victorian, twentieth century)

- popular to rational recreation

- social class

- religion and youth movements

- employment patterns

- influence of transport and technology

- the British Empire

- amateurism and professionalism

- World Wars

- changing role of women

At the end of this chapter we will also take a closer look at the development of particular activities.

You will need to have a basic grasp of British history. It is not useful to refer to Regency or Victorian times if you have no idea of where they fall in the overall scheme. English Heritage has produced a useful ruler charting the different eras in chronological order – see fig 16.1. Looking at the origins of sports and pastimes, it is clear that they were initially *functional*, eg, for military and hunting purposes. When societies depended less on survival, many activities took on a recreational dimension, such as children's play and the feasts and festivals which often had religious associations, either pagan or Christian (see fig 16.2). Our main focus is from the Victorian era to the present day, though it is useful to have an understanding of previous eras.

# O E Medieval England

The years between 1066 and 1485 are generally known as the Middle Ages. This period saw a change in fortunes for most people in England. The first half was prosperous allowing for the development of churches and universities. The bulk of the population were peasants in rural areas but there was an increase in the townsmen who were mainly merchants, lawyers and doctors. Their wealth increased as trade was made possible, due to fewer private wars between the different lords. The townsmen were above the serfs because they were free but below that of the lords, so they formed the beginnings of the middle class, who were to later grow even more powerful. They formed guilds which were special organisations to safeguard the rights of craftsmen and merchants to practise their trade within the town walls. As the middle class grew richer the kings began to choose them as their lawyers and officials. Their sons would then study in order to be able to make their way in the world. The Church was responsible for the basic education available. Boys were taught to read and write in Latin. Bishops established cathedral schools. Much of this was to change after the Reformation.

Festivals and feasts played an important part of life in the Middle Ages. Many recreational pastimes took place at this time. The horse was a significant feature for the nobility, who used them for hunting and the tournaments. Military activities were favoured over purely recreational ones and archery became a compulsory aspect of young men's lives. Some sports and games were banned as they were becoming so popular that it was feared they would interfere with men's archery practice, essential for the defence of the realm.

Festivals were held in honour of events that were important to people's daily lives; eg, the change of seasons, harvest, and the summer and winter solstices. As the pagan customs were taken over

| | |
|---|---|
| 43–450AD | Roman Britain |
| 450–613 | Anglo Saxon invasion |
| 613–1017 | Division into Kingdoms |
| 1017–1066 | Danish Rule |
| 1066 | William I |
| 1087 | William II |
| 1100 | Henry I |
| 1135 | Stephen |
| 1154 | Henry II |
| 1189 | Richard I |
| 1199 | John |
| 1216 | Henry III |
| 1272 | Edward I |
| 1307 | Edward II |
| 1327 | Edward III |
| 1377 | Richard II |
| 1399 | Henry IV |
| 1413 | Henry V |
| 1422 | Henry VI |
| 1461 | Edward IV |
| 1483 | Edward V |
| 1483 | Richard III |
| 1485 | Henry VII |
| 1509 | Henry VIII |
| 1547 | Edward VI |
| 1553 | Mary I |
| 1558 | Elizabeth I |
| 1603 | James I |
| 1625 | Charles I |
| 1649 | Commonwealth |
| 1660 | Charles II |
| 1685 | James II |
| 1689 | William III & Mary |
| 1702 | Anne |
| 1714 | George I |
| 1727 | George II |
| 1760 | George III |
| 1820 | George IV |
| 1830 | William IV |
| 1837 | Victoria |
| 1901 | Edward VII |
| 1910 | George V |
| 1936 | Edward VIII |
| 1936 | George VI |
| 1952 | Elizabeth II |

Fig 16.1. Dates of the coronations of England and (from 1603) Great Britain's monarchs

Fig 16.2. Functional and recreational origins of sport

by the Church they were given new religious meanings. 'Holy days' were put aside for feasting, which is how the word 'holiday' originated. In many countries towns and villages had their own special

A Falconer. 1575.
(From Turbervile's Booke of Falconrie
Hawking '—)

Fig 16.3. Frontispiece to the *Book of Falconrie*, 1498

festivals and saints' days which celebrated the death of a saint.

Easter is the most important feast of the Christian Church, and its date fixed the dates of the holy days connected to it – Lent, Shrove Tuesday, Ash Wednesday. Shrove Tuesday is the last day before the fasting of Lent, and was a time for feasting and fun. Recreations took place within a wide social pattern, and activities included mob football, wrestling, animal baiting, skittles and bowls. The minstrels provided entertainment, and were dancers, acrobats, composers and performers of music.

# Summary

Activities were:

- occasional, due to limited time and energy
- simple in nature and orally passed down through the generations
- affected by prohibitions if considered unnecessary to the society by the ruling class
- functional first, particularly for hunting and defence
- participated in during feasts and festivals as outlets for leisure pursuits
- mainly local in nature due to lack of mobility and frequent wars.

## O E The Tudor and Stuart Era (1485–1714)

### The Tudors

England changed rapidly under the Tudors. Religious disputes developed as people could not agree on how the Church should be run. Some wanted services similar to the old Catholic ways, while others wanted a 'purer' type of service. These people became known as Puritans; see below.

Under Henry VIII's rule, there was greater prosperity and more time for cultural pursuits like music, literature and the theatre. Henry was a great sports lover, and created one of the liveliest courts in Europe. He participated in all-day hunts and wrestling, and ordered his own real tennis court to be built at Hampton Court (it is still well worth a visit). Access to education, equipment and facilities enabled the upper classes the privilege of exclusive recreational activities.

Under Elizabeth, England was growing richer. Games and sports flourished at this time. This was the age of the Renaissance gentleman, who was knowledgeable, partook in the appropriate physical activities, and was appreciative of all art forms.

The mass of the population also enjoyed their traditional pastimes. Activities like mob football continued to develop, allowing for conjugal and

Fig 16.4. Staghunting was a popular pastime during the sixteenth and seventeenth centuries

territorial conflicts to be sorted out in an enjoyable manner. They were often disorderly and violent, allowing energies to be vented. Many activities were still regional, were played with a few simple rules (or none at all) and were passed down to future generations by word of mouth.

The baiting and killing of animals was also a great treat. People lived in harsh conditions, and held different attitudes about the treatment of animals compared with modern values. Activities like cock fighting, bull baiting, bull running were all popular. They originated in rural areas but were also enjoyed in the towns; there is an account of bull running in London as late as 1816. Again however, there were distinct social class divisions in physical activities.

## The Stuarts

After the death of Elizabeth I, James VI of Scotland (the son of Mary Queen of Scots) became James I of England. He had been brought up a Protestant, and

in 1617, issued a declaration known as the 'Book of Sports' which encouraged the notion of traditional pastimes, so long as they did not interfere with church attendance.

Following the civil war and execution of Charles I (James I's son) in 1646, Oliver Cromwell was made protector of Britain. He was intent on establishing Parliamentary rule allied with a Puritan lifestyle. Puritanism particularly objected to:

- practising sport on a Sunday
- inflicting cruelty on animals
- the idleness, drinking and profanity generally associated with sport and the public houses.

The effect of the Puritans on the development of sport was to be significant. They believed that people should concentrate on working hard and praying for salvation, and were opposed to recreational activities which they considered as sinful and a waste of time. As many of the traditional activities took place after church service on a Sunday, and many derived from pagan traditions, they came under fierce attack from the Puritans.

Cromwell failed to unite all the different factions, and Charles II returned as monarch in 1660. This period was known as the Restoration. Charles II was in favour of many sports. His Court enjoyed a lifestyle of ease, affluence and leisure; they occupied themselves lavishly on sporting pursuits, and there was an immediate revival of the 'courtly mould'. The Restoration helped to restore many of the previously banned popular activities, but never again to their past glories. The Cotswold Olympian games were revived by Robert Dover, who was both a supporter of the athleticism of the gentry but also longed for a return to 'merrie England', where all social classes had enjoyed recreations together. This was an annual sports event which was held with activities for the gentry and the peasantry. However, the influence of Puritan rule continued to be felt, and many recreational pursuits were slow to revive.

# Summary

- Traditional sports and pastimes experienced confusing and changing conditions.
- Tudor times allowed all classes to enjoy their recreation.
- Puritanism greatly curtailed many activities, establishing a new moral tone to society.
- There was some regaining of pastimes but never again was the 'merrie England' concept to emerge.

## **O E** The Hanoverian era (1714–1790)

The Industrial Revolution began in England in the middle of the 1700s and developed over a hundred years. It signified a dramatic movement of people from rural areas to the towns. Farming had become less important as small farms had been taken over by large landowners as a result of the enclosure system. The efficiency of the urban factories also put many people employed in the cottage industry out of work. Factory work required unskilled workers, who worked long hours in cramped, dirty conditions six days a week; young children were often employed in difficult and dangerous conditions.

Moving from rural areas to the new towns and cities had an enormous impact on people's lifestyles, not least on their recreational pursuits.

- Their previous games were increasingly difficult to accommodate, for example, mob football.
- Space was at a premium and so were facilities, so there was to be a shift in emphasis from a participation base to a more spectator based type of leisure pursuits.
- The economic conditions of people had changed, and their long working hours also curbed their opportunities for recreation.

Some activities such as cricket, racing, rowing and pugilism (forerunner to boxing) had already begun their first phases of organisation. Rules developed in activities which began to occur more frequently, where the upper classes had control and when the moral climate within society began to change. Sports clubs and governing bodies developed to meet the recreation needs of 'Old Boys' who had left their public school and university and wanted to continue participating in sport. Evidence for this:

- the publication of the Racing Calendar from 1727
- the formation of the Jockey Club in 1752
- the rules for cricket, which were first drawn up in 1727.

In the eighteenth century, the Methodists continued the Puritan work ethic; they strengthened the attack on popular sports, believing that sport and drinking on a Sunday would lead to an after-life in hell. The violence associated with many of the pastimes, like wrestling, football and animal sports was believed to be the cause of social unrest; employees would use them as an excuse to miss work, at a time when eighteenth-century employers required a more disciplined workforce in the mills.

# Victorian Britain

Victoria became Queen in 1837. Her reign was a period of dramatic social change, which is reflected in the development of games and sport during the nineteenth century.

## The working class

Under Queen Victoria's reign, social reformers campaigned for improvements in the physical and mental health of workers in society.

Parliament passed many laws and reforms to address the problems of women and children being employed in factories under terrible conditions and for long working hours, eg, the Reform and Factory Act 1832, the Ten Hours Act 1847 and the Factory Act 1878. The custom of a half-day Saturday began early in her reign, followed by the movement for early closing for shop workers on Wednesdays.

Factory owners created factory sports facilities and sponsored work teams. The development of the railways enabled them to send their workers on recreational trips, such as to the seaside. Employers hoped to gain the goodwill of their workers, increase morale and encourage the moral benefits of participating in team games.

From the 1870s onwards, there was a move to encourage a healthy, moral and orderly workforce, illustrated by the provision of parks, museums, libraries and public baths. Sport developed into an important part of working life. The Municipal Reform Act 1835 led to the building of parks in the towns and cities; the general public were encouraged to use these parks for recreational use after 1870. The reasons for providing parks were:

- to improve the health of the population
- to discourage crime on the streets
- as part of the Temperance movement, to wean people away from the evils of alcohol and gambling
- to instil morality in workers by following the rules of rational, organised sport
- to demonstrate a sense of social justice.

The skilled workforce gradually shifted their attentions and interests away from the traditional popular sports, taking up pastimes such as reading and quieter exercise in the park:

*The decline of traditional sports, especially those which involved fighting, was not simply a question of pressure from well-organised groups of evangelicals and businessmen; in addition to the agitation from abolitionists there was evidence of a gradual shift in public taste, especially amongst the literate and more highly skilled elite of working people themselves.*

R. Holt

By 1900, working people were heavily involved in sporting activity. There was a continuity between the traditional and modern sports; bowls, darts, billiards, fishing, pigeon racing and dog racing provided sporting entertainment.

## Sport for the upper classes

The upper classes were wealthy and powerful, possessed vast tracts of property and dominated Parliament well into the nineteenth century. They enjoyed a life of leisure, and were waited on by an army of servants. The aristocracy took part in local sports and affairs, usually in the form of patronage of prize fights (forerunner to boxing) and pedestrianism (road walking).

Wealthy aristocrats who wanted to be associated with new styles and trends, would sometimes spend large amounts of money on sporting events and particular athletes. It was an age where some aristocrats could lead and others would follow, examples are:

- the Duke of Cumberland's association with racing and prize fighting
- Lord Orford and coursing
- the Earl of Derby and cock fighting, and the hunt.

## KEY WORD

A **patron** is a person who sponsors any kind of artist or athlete from their own private funds. Patronage tends to occur amongst a privileged class within a hierarchical society.

A group of patrons would join together and form an association, eg, the Pugilistic Club, which would then organise the sport. When patrons withdrew their funds, preferring to sponsor different, perhaps

Fig 16.5. Prize fighting, c. 1840

more elite, sports, the effect was similar to modern day commercial sponsors pulling out of sports events; it usually led to a decline in the activity. With regard to animal sports, on the one hand they supported the ban on cock fighting, while maintaining their own passion for fox hunting; another example of the powerful safeguarding their own interests?

The French Revolution had shown the possible results of a breakdown in relations between the aristocracy and the ordinary people. The English gentry were not now so confident of the complete acceptance of the respect shown them by the lower classes.

The new rich (or nouveau riche) who emerged from the Industrial Revolution, became a strong 'middle class' section of society. They wished to emulate the upper classes by buying old estates, educating their children in the established public schools, and establishing their own recreations which would separate them from the working classes. They also brought Christian morality to their recreation.

## Inns and pubs

The inn had always been a social rural meeting place, and was used as a stopping place for the gentry on long journeys. A tradition of games developed, which was encouraged by the inn-keepers to increase their business; examples are fives, rackets, boxing, coursing, quoits. Many of the new sports clubs met in pubs, and they formed mutually beneficial partnerships:

- The village cricket teams would often use the field next to the pub.
- The hunt would have their stirrup cup at the pub followed by dinner.
- Liquor tents would be provided by publicans at sporting events.
- Bowling greens and boxing rings were built on to pubs, and pubs often organised a football team.

Those associated with sports were often regulars at the inns, so it was in the interests of the publican to encourage sport.

The English alehouse had to adapt to the new urban recreational needs. The pub became a focal point for workers trying to maintain a sense of identity, which was being eradicated in the new urban culture. As early as 1879, there were strings of clubs in Blackburn which were the culmination of the formalising of street corner teams. Boxing took over from the previous animal baiting sports of cock fighting and ratting.

## Religion

The Victorian era was a climate of suppressing vice and encouraging religion and virtue. Non-conformism and the Protestant ethic became more firmly entrenched. Sports became less brutal, gambling was driven underground and there was a decline in blood sports.

Some religious sects had a restraining influence on working class leisure, namely the Puritans, the Protestants, Sabbatarianism, Evangelists and Methodists.

### Puritans

The more extreme Protestants in the sixteenth and seventeenth centuries, who wished to purify the Church of England of most of its ceremony and other aspects which it associated with Catholicism. They were a growing body of influential townspeople with a strict, moral outlook to life shunning the more pleasurable activities. Play was considered to be idleness and a sinful waste of time. By the early seventeenth century the argument between the pleasure-seeking cavaliers and the Puritans had escalated.

## Protestant work ethic

The belief of the Protestant religion associated with the Calvinists and Lutherans of the seventeenth century. The emphasis is on worldly work that should be treated as a duty and as a means of earning salvation from God. Worldly success was seen as a sign that you were one of the 'chosen' to be saved, though reckless spending and enjoyment was not encouraged, rather a thrifty outlook towards life. Leisure time and recreational activities therefore were given very low status. This was to be a particular constraint for the working class who had no private means for recreation and were subjected to the values of the moral middle classes.

## Evangelism

The practice of spreading the Christian gospel. They emphasise personal conversion and faith for salvation. In the nineteenth century the Evangelists restricted the recreations of the working classes, believing their popular recreations to be sinful and associated with gambling and alcohol.

## Methodists

A system of faith developed by John Wesley and a non-conformist denomination. In the nineteenth century they believed popular recreations to be sinful, being associated with drinking and gambling. The Methodists were among the strongest opponents of animal sport in the eighteenth and nineteenth centuries and were to have a detrimental effect on recreation pastimes for the lower classes. They tried to provide alternative religious activities combining the vigour of the wake with a spiritual cause.

## Sabbatarianism

A religious sect following a strict observance of Sunday as the Sabbath. This had the effect of restricting the leisure activities of the working classes in the nineteenth century.

However, during the nineteenth century there was a distinct change in attitude of the church towards recreational activities. This was due to a variety of reasons, such as rational recreation had begun to take shape, and this acceptance of recreation was useful in promoting the Church as a more attractive place to be, as church attendance was declining.

The Muscular Christians, the YMCA and the youth movements like the Boys Brigade and Scouts were examples of the new approach.

## Muscular Christianity

Muscular Christianity was an evangelical movement, and Charles Kingsley was one of its most influential exponents. Kingsley helped to combine the Christian and the chivalric ideal of manliness. It was the return of the Platonic concept the 'whole man'. It improved one's ability to be gentle and courteous, brave and enterprising, reverent and truthful, selfless and devoted.

Kingsley believed healthy bodies were needed alongside healthy minds. Neglect of health was as lazy as a neglected mind. He also led the hygienic movement which was to have a deep effect on the working conditions of the poor.

There was little or no support for sport for its own sake at this time; sport should increase physical health and military valour, and create Christian soldiers. It was a fusion of physical with moral training.

Evangelical developments were directly linked with two philosophies – the muscular Christians were promoting what the nonconformists were sceptical of:

- Muscular Christians regarded cricket, boating and football as positive recreation.
- The Church was attempting to attract workers from the pubs by forming alternative social clubs such as Hand in Hand clubs.

Eventually there was a strong link with the club development of working class sport, particularly football, eg,

- Barnsley: 1887, Rev Preedy appointed.
- QPR: 1881, Rev Young appointed.
- Aston Villa: 1874, a Wesleyan Chapel built.

In Birmingham approximately a quarter of football clubs were explicitly connected to religious organisations between 1870 and 1885.

## The YMCA

The YMCA is a non-sectarian, non-political Christian lay movement. Its aims are to develop high standards of Christian character through group activities; improve the spiritual, social, recreational and physical life of young people. It began in London in 1844, led by George William, and initially concentrated on young men in the drapery and other trades. On the construction of the YMCA Gym at Liverpool in 1887, William claimed:

> 'The aim of the founders was not to furnish the public of Liverpool with increased facilities for athletic exercise, or intellectual development, important as these may be in themselves; but to multiply the number of Christ's true followers among the young men of our city, and to aid in strengthening their Christian character.'

## No sport on Sunday'

The proclamationists and muscular Christians were united by their desire to observe Sunday as a day of complete rest, without physical activity. This signified a slow development of working class sports, as workers were prevented from joining the elite sports, and parks were closed on Sundays. Wealthy people, who usually had private facilities, seemed to escape from the Sunday ban on sport, golf, tennis and croquet were regularly played on Sundays.

Alternative Sunday pastimes were encouraged by the muscular Christians, such as cycling, rambling and boating. The bicycle had revolutionised the English Sunday, and the clergy might with

advantage arrange short services for cyclists passing through their parishes.

**ACTIVITY 1**

What constituted the basis of Sabbatarianism, Evangelism and Protestantism and what influence did they have on working class leisure?

# Youth and religion

Major British youth movements admitted unlimited numbers of children, adolescents and young adults with the aim of promoting some sort of moral code of living. They also allowed for competitive activities and achieving awards and badges. The invention of adolescence as an age-defined social cohort segregated the young from adult status and created a social problem whose solution became the provision of adult supervised leisure pursuits. The middle classes were to use the combination of Evangelical Christianity, public school manliness, militarism and imperialism to instill normative values in the working classes.

The last decades of the nineteenth and beginning of the twentieth century saw the arrival of all the major British youth movements. This time was characterised by increasing economic and social unrest.

At home:

- Expanding influence of socialism
- Growing organisation of labour and the Labour Party
- Growing middle class fears of internal social change

Abroad:

- German naval developments
- Industrial competition from America and Germany

This led to a renewed cultural and social emphasis being placed by the ruling elite on the question of national unity. The gradual loss of control by the established Church led to the middle classes organising the leisure of working class adolescents. Youth movements were seen as a way to curb increasing juvenile restlessness.

We will look at the Boys' Brigade, the Scout Movement and Girl Guides.

## The Boys' Brigade

This movement successfully demonstrated that voluntary youth movements could reinforce the discipline of the schoolroom and work place. The movement began in Glasgow in 1883 founded by William Alexander Smith. It became a national organisation after 1885. His influences had been:

- involvement in the College free church
- the 1st Lanarkshire Rifle Volunteers and
- a need to discipline the rowdy working class boys attending his Sunday mission school.

It must also be stressed that the cultural superstructure provided by the Bible Classes and YMCA helped to make this movement possible.

One of the original members of Smith's first Glasgow company wrote:

*'when we reached thirteen most of us felt we were too big for the Sunday School and there was a gap of a few years until we were able to join the YMCA at seventeen. To fill this gap Captain Smith formed the Boys' Brigade. During that gap period many working class boys ran wild, became hooligans and street corner loafers'.*

Smith also felt that uniformed organisation would appeal to a sense of patriotism and martial spirit as well as being used primarily for a religious end. Boys were only admitted if they attended Sabbath School and punctuality and regular attendance were vital. Table 16.1 highlights the membership composition of the early movement. They were drawn mainly from the respectable working class section of Glasgow.

A weekly routine of drill, Bible classes and Club Room prevailed with an annual camp or the occasional field day to raise company funds. These activities would have been exciting for young adolescents confined to urban monotony.

### Other influences

The Scout Movement set up by Baden-Powell in 1907–1908 and the attempts of the War Office to incorporate the Brigade into a national cadet force and Smith's death in 1914 all had to be countered.

The public mood of anti-militarism ensured support for Smith in his determination to steer the Brigade away from the Army Council's influence.

Table 16.1. 1st Glasgow enrolment Figures, 1890–1895 (parental occupation)

|  | 1890–1891 | 1891–1892 | 1892–1893 | 1893–1894 | 1894–1895 | Total | % |
|---|---|---|---|---|---|---|---|
| Skilled manual* | 17 | 2 | 5 | 6 | 6 | 36 | 72 |
| Lower-middle+ | 4 | 2 | 6 | 2 | – | 14 | 27 |
| Unskilled† | 2 | – | – | 1 | – | 3 | 1 |
| Total | 23 | 4 | 11 | 9 | 6 | 53 | 100 |

\* = joiners, cabinet-makers, engine-fitters, shoemakers, masons, etc.
+ = salesmen, clerks, travellers, insurances, insurance agents, drapers, grocers, etc.
† = labourers, commissionaries.
*Source*: Youth, Empire and Society.

The success of the Boys' Brigade as a youth movement led other churches to consider imitating Smith's idea, recreating a similar blend of recreation and military training with the intention of binding the adolescent closer to religious influences.

Church Lads' Brigade     1891
Jewish Lads' Brigade     1895
Catholic Boys' Brigade     1896

They were all called upon to solve differing problems of social adjustment or racial accommodation in late Victorian England.

## The Church Lads' Brigade

This proved to be the most successful of all the rivals. The main founder was Walter Mallock Gee. He was particularly influential in combining it with the Temperance movement among the young, through the Church of England Temperance Society. It was consolidated as a military organisation in 1892 when the Governing Brigade Council was established. It was similar in that it drew its recruits from the artisans', or 'skilled workers', children. A deterrent to the lower sections of the working classes may have been the financial commitment required for membership.

1908          67 regiments
              118 battalions
              1300 companies
              70,000 boys enrolled

Values likely to appeal to the upwardly aspiring – sobriety, thrift, self-help, punctuality, obedience – were positively stressed in the Brigade handbook. They were unashamedly middle class values intended to counter the more working class street culture. It was almost the working class equivalent of public school *esprit de corps* and the norms of militarism and Christian manliness ethic.

They were more militaristic than the Scottish Boys' Brigade evidenced by their acceptance in 1911 of

the Army Council's recommendation to apply for local Territorial recognition as official cadets. Their initial religious objectives were weakened and they were to remain by far the largest national cadet force for 25 years. This militaristic approach, however, was to see a decline in numbers during the inter-war years due to the antimilitary view held by the public. By 1936 an attempt to demilitarise came too late and thus they could not rival the Boys' Brigade.

## The Scout movement

Baden-Powell, the founder of the Scout movement, was born in 1857. The major influences in his early life became evident in the movement he was to establish:

* family competitiveness amongst his brothers
* Charterhouse public school (school clubs and societies, particularly the rifle corps)
* British Army (particularly military experiences in Africa and India)
* intellectual thinking (Social Darwinism; social imperialism; social reform).

The public school code of Charterhouse was to find its expression in Scout Law – honour, loyalty and duty. The public school ethos of 'muscular Christianity' and athleticism was inherited by the Boy Scouts as a pastoral 'myth' of open air woodcraft, with the belief that Nature symbolised purity and encouraged class harmony. This was the opposite of the current trend towards capitalist, urban-industrial values.

The army life was to have an effect but Baden-Powell was not a supporter of unimaginative drill and instructed Scoutmasters not to pursue this type of activity. He also disliked bureaucracy. He was to achieve notoriety and become a national hero with the successful defence at the Siege of Mafeking. It came at a time when the British were suffering humiliating defeats in the Boer War and the public was ready to embrace news of a British success. This war revealed the military weakness of the British Empire and numerous Inquiries also pointed to the physical deterioration of the working classes and this was to become interchangeable with degeneracy and decadence.

Baden-Powell wanted to toughen up the next generation, creating a self-reliant, energetic manhood. Scouting was a response to the demand for organising British youth as efficiently as possible and he used the loss of the Roman Empire as an analogy to warn of the dangers of not holding on to the British colonies. He suggested inferior races were now in contention to win back their lands.

Social imperialism was a combination of patriotism and social reform that came above class distinctions. Raising an imperial race was seen as a necessity if the interests of the British Empire were to be realised.

Baden-Powell viewed scouting primarily as a form of physical and moral training to prevent national decadence. He sought the advice of William Smith, the founder of the Boys' Brigade, to help convert his 'Aids to Scouting' to a format suitable for boys. The already established YMCA also provided a ready-made platform to circulate his ideas.

The first Boy Scout camp took place in the summer of 1907. He used the publicity campaign experience of Arthur Pearson, a publisher who sponsored the movement by publishing 'The Scout', a weekly penny magazine.

The book 'Scouting for Boys' came out in six fortnightly parts before being issued in hard covers. Its contents included ten chapters covering topics such as: camp fire yarns on scout craft, campaigning,

camp life, tracking woodcraft, chivalry, life-saving and patriotism.

The result was the establishing of Scout troops by boys themselves. The training of leaders became urgent and local advisory committees, followed by County Scout Councils, were set up. Scouting was run on what appeared to be democratic lines with a chain of command reaching down from the Chief Scout to the Governing Council's Executive Committee, from the County Scout Councils to local District Scout councils and to local committees with some representation of the ordinary Scoutmaster. However, none of the top positions was open to election so the rank and file could not openly influence policy or change of leadership. It was a patriarchal form of government, a compromise between democracy and bureaucracy with some autocracy.

The outbreak of the First World War allowed the Scout movement to show its contribution. They gave air raid warnings, helped with the flax harvest, acted as messengers, guarded reservoirs, and ran mobile canteens in munitions factories and performed numerous other duties on the Home Front.

A lesser-known contribution of Scouting to national defence was the formation of the Scouts Defence Corps. Its object was to 'form a trained force of young men who would be immediately available for the defence of the

Fig 16.6. Modern day cubscouts

country should their services be required during the war'.

Throughout the 1920s Scouting retained its overwhelming position as a mass youth movement; increasing its total numbers in Britain alone from 232,000 in 1920 to 422,000 in 1930.

During the 1930s there was a decline, also felt by other youth movements. This can be accounted for by the economic depression, Baden-Powell's failing health and the proliferation of new leisure activities, particularly hiking and the Youth Hostel Association.

## Girls in uniform

These movements were derived from the boys' movements.

The first to become established was the Girls' Guildry, forerunner of the Girls' Brigade, at the turn of the twentieth century. Its birthplace was also in Glasgow. It was a combination of a senior Sunday school class, friendly club and a female equivalent of the Boys' Brigade. It even adopted the marching and drill popular at the time of the Boer War. The aim of the Girls' Guildry was to develop 'girls' capacities of 'womanly helpfulness' given full rein during the First World War in their work for the Red Cross.

By 1939 it had a total membership of 24,000. It arrived at a time when women were beginning to play a more conspicuous role in society but it was also considered an affront to those who felt the female sex should not be encouraged in unladylike behaviour. In the mid 1960s the various Girl Youth movements combined to form the Girls' Brigade, bringing membership to 100,000.

Britain's largest youth association is the Girl Guide movement comprising Brownies, Guides and Rangers. They owe their origin to a group of 'Girl Scouts' who in 1909 demanded an inspection by Baden-Powell. He had not intended his movement to include girls but gave way to social pressure and wrote, 'Girl Guides: a suggestion for character training for girls,' followed in 1918 by 'Girl Guiding'. He was later to become Chairman of the Guides.

Comment on the similarities and differences between the Boys' Brigade and the Scout Movement.
What social conditions contributed to the growth in youth movements at the turn of the twentieth century?

ACTIVITY 2

# Summary

Youth movements helped to:

- smooth the way for upper working class and lower middle classes into the urban industrial order of British society
- instil religious, moral and militaristic values
- provide an opportunity for the working classes to experience something of the elite public school education and values
- provide a mass leisure outlet for working class adolescents controlled by middle class adults
- provide opportunities for outdoor activity
- acceptance by young of the social order.

# The Romantic movement

The work of Romantic poets such as Wordsworth and Coleridge had a considerable influence on recreation in the countryside; their poems made the countryside attractive to town and city folk. The excursions began as exclusive pastimes, as time and money were required. Rambling was regarded as recreational, while mountaineering was taken more seriously, with the Alps being a favourite location. Ramblers tended to be drawn from the liberal, educated professions, who approached the activity with educational aims: an appreciation of the topography and local knowledge, and an aesthetic appreciation of natural beauty. Excursion tickets on the rail networks later helped the lower social classes participate.

# The transport revolution

The roads and canal systems in Britain were vastly improved during the eighteenth and nineteenth centuries. People, ideas, services and goods were mobile and could be transported around the country. Areas which had hardly been influenced by the outside world were now open to change. In terms of sport, inter-town fixtures could be held and spectators could travel to watch the spectacles. This tendency was to be transformed in the nineteenth century with the advent of the railways.

- Increased wealth and mobility enabled the sports of hare, stag and fox hunting to be more easily accessible to the middle classes. Animals could be transported with relative ease and comfort, and competitions changed from being on a local club level to national competitions between England, Ireland and Scotland.

- Ramblers, cyclists and mountaineers could access the countryside and more isolated areas.

- Fishing was revolutionised. In 1867 a book titled *The Rail and the Rod* was published; a guide to angling spots which could be reached within a 30-mile radius of London.

The major spectator sports of racing, cricket and football became national sports. Special excursion trains would carry spectators. William Clarke of Nottingham formed the first All England Cricket XI and transported them about the country, playing games against a variety of sides. The railways enabled them to play 30 or more matches a season, and allowed a high level of cricket to be enjoyed by those who would otherwise have been unable to experience such an event.

The game of soccer flourished, particularly in the newly industrial counties of Lancashire and Yorkshire. The teams and supporters travelled by rail. A team started by the Lancashire and Yorkshire Railway became Manchester United Football Club.

National sporting events then developed into international events, and foreign competition improved standards further. The rebirth of the Olympic Games in 1896 was only made possible by rail travel.

**ACTIVITY 3**

Using a variety of sports, explain how the communications by water, road and rail influenced the development of different sports.
- Consider the importance of rivers for sports and development of towns.
- Consider the development of roads to the present day.
- Consider the railway for transport of animals, and for bridging the link between rural and urban areas.

# The British Empire

In the nineteenth century, British imperialists believed they had a duty to spread their forms of government, religion and culture to those nations they considered less advanced or civilised. Some of the British colonies benefited by the growth of an infrastructure of roads, schools and hospitals, but the imposition of colonial rule permanently altered the cultures and traditions of the colonised countries.

The influence of the British Empire was felt across the world. Western culture (including sport and recreation) was spread via numerous groups of people – soldiers, administrators, missionaries, young men on the Grand Tour, engineers and businessmen. The public school ethos which viewed sport as a character-building vehicle was imposed on the colonies. British subjects imported and exported sports, usually modifying them to suit their own needs:

- Croquet came to England from Ireland, and was successfully transported to India.

- Polo was enjoyed by British soldiers in India, with the first polo match being played in England in 1871.

- Shooting was an experience in which most of the gentry participated, and their interest was fired up with the prospect of big game shooting in Africa, where they could collect and transport home their enormous trophies.

- Thoroughbred horses were exported to most of Britain's colonies, and with them the English style of racing.

- Football did not spread so easily within the Empire, perhaps because the colonial administrative staff preferred other activities.

## Professionalism and amateurism

The concept of amateurism was thought to reflect the Ancient Olympian spirit, placing the ideals of fair play and team spirit high above any material objectives. In the 1850s Dr Penny Brookes founded the Much Wenlock Olympic Games and formed a National Olympic Association. He had a pure sense of amateurism, and encouraged the citizens of Much Wenlock to delight in the challenge of sport with no thought for a reward. The first Games were held in 1850, and included events such as football, cricket, quoits, a blindfold wheelbarrow race, and chasing a pig through the town. It had all the trappings of a rustic festival, and perhaps reinvented the Cotswold Games first started in 1612 in Chipping Camden. By 1870 the events included track and field athletics, such as the pentathlon and tilting at the ring (a version of the jousting tournament).

The public school influence established its own definition of amateurism, which superseded the Much Wenlock version. Much of the public school version of athleticism was Olympian in outlook: combining physical endeavour with moral integrity, where the struggle was fought for the honour of the house or school. Baron Pierre de Coubertin visited both Much Wenlock and Rugby School in 1890, in the years preceding the foundation of the modern Olympic Games. He looked forward to a time when anyone would be able to participate, regardless of social standing or race.

In England there were two distinct phases of amateurism:

1. Originally, amateurs were gentlemen of the middle and upper classes who played sports in the spirit of fair competition.

2. There was a shift in definition of an amateur, from a straightforward social distinction, to a monetary one. Originally there had been no problems perceived by earning money from amateur sport.

Fair play was the bedrock upon which amateurism was based. It was important to adhere to the rules of the game, but it was expected that a player would discipline himself rather than wait for a referee's decision. A situation was recorded that the Corinthian Casuals, founded in 1882, would withdraw their goalkeeper on the awarding of a penalty to the opposing side, on the principle that they should accept the consequences of a foul.

There were advantages and disadvantages to the amateur code. It promoted restraint in victory and graciousness in defeat; the acceptance of rules and consequent respect for decisions. However, it excluded the working classes which was a moral argument for its abolition. In 1894 the Rugby Football Union and the Northern Union split due to the refusal of the authorities to allow northern players to have enough leisure time to compete on the same basis as players in the south. Employers could not accept 'broken time payments' (compensation for loss of wages), and by so doing, excluded manual workers who needed time to train and travel for sport. Similar conflicts were felt in rowing and cricket.

The following table is an attempt to organise the developments of these two concepts with the effect they have had on certain sports.

| Amateurism | Professionalism |
|---|---|
| • Evolved in nineteenth-century England.<br>• Code brought in by upper class.<br><br>*It is an ideal based upon participating in sport for the love of it rather than for monetary gain and the participation was deemed more important than the winning.*<br><br>• The gentleman amateur was a social class distinction of the amateur code.<br><br>*The gentleman amateur was drawn only from the upper classes and was regarded as having qualities of refinement associated with a good family; a man who is courteous, cultured and well educated. Although they may have participated in some activities with their lower class professional counterparts there was no shame should they lose, as they were not being paid neither were they involved in serious training.*<br><br>• Amateurism encompassed the belief in fair play and abiding by the spirit as well as the rules of the game.<br><br>• It originally had a monetary as well as a social class distinction in its efforts to exclude the lower class.<br><br>• The *Corinthians* were the epitome of amateurism.<br><br>*The Corinthians were consistent with St. Paul's letter to the Corinthians that 'not everyone can win but those that do should do so according to the rules and spirit of the time'. The Corinthians were drawn* | • Earning money from sport is a very old concept – it goes back to ancient civilisations such as Rome.<br>• Professional sport is an avenue of upward and downward social mobility.<br><br>*professionalism: engaging in a sporting activity for financial gain or as a means of livelihood means training is synonymous with improving standards and specialising in an activity.*<br><br>• The Gladiator was an early form of a professional sportsman.<br><br>*Gladiator: trained to fight in arenas to provide entertainment. This began as a concept in Ancient Greece/Rome but is now used to denote professional sport. The similarities between a gladiator and a professional footballer would be that both athletes:*<br><br>• *are involved in a physical contact sport relying on physical strength and speed*<br>• *have a strong likelihood of injury resulting in an early end to a career*<br>• *are treated as expendable; the 'hire and fire' policy*<br>• *athletes are bought and sold through transfer deals and treated as a commodity*<br>• *are paid by results*<br>• *have little control as they are 'owned' by a coach/manager*<br>• *have high media status and are treated as heroes*<br><br>Certain social factors are necessary for professional sport to flourish. The suggestion would be that ancient Rome and industrial |

(Continued

| Amateurism | Professionalism |
|---|---|
| *from the elite of Victorian society and followed this code during games.* | England in the nineteenth century would share some similarities: |
| • These meanings are arbitrary and socially determined hence they change over a period of time. | • *mass of a population living in close proximity* |
| • Sports have undergone major changes in their amateur/professional status. | • *large section of population with disposable income and leisure time* |
| | • *need for excitement* |
| | • *commercialism.* |

**Amateurism**

*from the elite of Victorian society and followed this code during games.*

- These meanings are arbitrary and socially determined hence they change over a period of time.

- Sports have undergone major changes in their amateur/professional status.

**Rowing** was originally open to amateurs and professionals but the gentleman amateurs disliked being beaten by their social inferiors. This resulted in a strict amateur definition instigated by the 'Amateur Rowing Association' called the 'manual labour clause':

*The formal exclusion of manual workers by the*

*'Amateur Rowing Association' in 1882. It excluded anyone who was by trade 'a mechanic, artisan or labourer' but was abolished in 1890. It was a device to retain a social distinction in sport as the gentry amateurs did not wish to be beaten by lower class professionals nor could they socialise with them after the sporting event.*

**Rugby football** developed in the nineteenth-century English public schools based on amateurism. The working class in the northern industrial towns adopted the game but needed to be paid to play or at least to receive compensation for loss of earnings while playing.

**broken time payments**: *payments made to compensate working class players for loss of earnings while playing sports such as soccer and rugby football. This tended to lead to professionalism in some sports and was looked down upon by the gentleman amateurs.*

In Rugby this was to lead to the North South split in 1896 – southern amateurs/northern professional. By 1996 even the Union game moved over to professionalism as a result of player pressure.

**Professionalism**

England in the nineteenth century would share some similarities:

- *mass of a population living in close proximity*
- *large section of population with disposable income and leisure time*
- *need for excitement*
- *commercialism.*

### Bread and circuses theory

*A theory which suggests the mass of a population can be kept relatively content and a cynical viewpoint may suggest that sporting activities can be used by governments to alleviate social problems by channelling people's energies in a socially acceptable form.*

- Professionalism was evident in a variety of sports in the nineteenth century:

- **pedestrianism**: *an early form of race walking. In the eighteenth and nineteenth centuries, with only horse racing and boxing as rivals, pedestrianism was very popular with much gambling involving men against time, distance and other walkers. Captain Barclay was a famous walker who in 1809 walked 1000 miles in 1000 consecutive hours. A pedestrian was also a group of lower class individuals who earned part of their money by competing in sporting activities for money, particularly rowing, footraces and cricket. It was the forerunner to the term professional.*

- **prizefighting**: *individuals were taught to defend themselves in gladiatorial schools in 'sword and buckle' contests. It was patronised by the wealthy and powerful, who wagered huge sums on the outcome of contests though would never have been combatants themselves. The activity employed virtually a professional core of men fighting in regular circuits, mostly concentrated around London. Rules were fairly loosely enforced and death was not uncommon.*

*(Continued)*

(*Continued*)

| Amateurism | Professionalism |
|---|---|
| In **cricket** the amateurs and professionals could play together under the auspices 'gentlemen vs players'. The gentlemen were the amateurs and the players were the professionals. | *When the sport was outlawed contests were organised on private land away from magistrates. Notable figures were Broughton, Mendoza and Tom Cribb.* |
| • The revival of the modern Olympic Games in 1896 was based on the amateur code as Coubertin had been impressed with the values associated with athleticism in the nineteenth-century public schools. | • *athletics developed under amateur rules in the public schools but in society a professional circuit was very popular. As with many professional sports in the nineteenth century they encountered problems with bribery, corruption and fixing of events.*<br>• *public schools employed professional watermen to coach the **rowing** teams when the prestige of winning became ever more important.* |
| During the twentieth century other terms emerged to describe performers that receive some form of payment, including: | In professional sport in the nineteenth century in England the role of the different social classes would be: |
| • Shamateurism – describes amateurs who receive 'under the table' payments. Trust funds were set up to try to combat this problem.<br><br>• Stamateur – describes state-sponsored amateurs and was common in Eastern bloc countries. | Lower class – performer<br>Middle class – agents, promoters, managers<br>Upper class – patrons |
| Amateurs can now officially receive financial aid from sponsorship, trust funds and organisations such as Sport Aid and the National Lottery. | • The inclusion of sports such as tennis and basketball in the Olympic Games in the twentieth century highlight the problems encountered by the modern day sports world in trying to adhere to the pure ideal of amateurism. |

## ACTIVITY 4

1. How has the concept of amateur changed for the top performer over the last few years?
2. The role and status of amateurs and professionals within sport have changed a great deal during the nineteenth and twentieth centuries.
   (i) In the late nineteenth century the 'gentleman amateur' was highly regarded. Describe the characteristics of the gentleman amateur.
   (ii) From 1850–1900 the status of amateurs and professionals varied between sports. Comment upon this statement in relation to:
      • cricket
      • rowing
      • rugby football.

# Rational recreation

Concern over the amusements of the lower classes became a more pressing concern in the nineteenth century.

Sports, museums, libraries and baths were to play a large part in the way in which the ruling classes and new middle class reformers saw the development of the lower classes into a more orderly, disciplined and moral workforce.

The urban developments had left the Established Church with little influence – a religious census in 1851 revealed very little attendance at any sort of Church by a large section of the population.

Large groups of youth were regarded as potential social problems.

The Boys' Brigade founded 1883, the Church Lads' Brigade and the Young Men's Christian Association were all used to improve the appeal of organised religion by recruiting and also as a form of social discipline.

Aston Vlla, Everton, Fulham and Bolton were all church-based football clubs.

Street football was banned and Military Drill in the Elementary Schools was tedious so adult workers usually had poor experiences of physical activity.

## Industrial influences

Industrial recreation programmes were not very widespread, although several individual projects were almost revolutionary in their social thinking.

West Ham Football Club developed from the philanthropic industrial policy of A.F. Hills, an old Harrovian. A range of activities was introduced as well as profit-sharing schemes. A sports stadium was built to cater for a variety of sports clubs.

The Cadbury family were Quakers who founded the model industrial community at Bournville, Birmingham. George Cadbury required women workers to learn to swim (for cleanliness) and men with heavy jobs to do weight lifting to protect themselves from industrial injury. Good sports facilities were provided as part of a company policy which 'rested on the importance of quick, well-executed work. Athletics and swimming, medical and dental care, proper breaks for meals and rest – all that helps to develop manual dexterity and visual awareness which are the commercial object'. The company was the first company in England to implement the half-day Saturday.

> ## KEY WORDS
>
> **Philanthropy** The practice of performing charitable or benevolent actions.
>
> **Quakers** Members of a Society of Friends; reject formal ministry; hold meetings where anyone can speak; promoted many causes for social reform.

# Summary of the Victorian era

- The gentry detached themselves from the people as a result of social change and pressures.
- New wealth and ambitions from the urban areas were beginning to be felt in the country lifestyle.
- Despite legislation some activities persisted – traditional activities do not simply die out overnight.
- Reformers and abolitionists tried to discipline the industrialised workforce.
- The upper classes tried to remove themselves from the middle classes who in turn tried to disassociate themselves from the working classes.

## Agenda for the century

The Empire was at its height, famous for the phrase, the sun shall never set on the British Empire'. However, Queen Victoria died and dramatic social changes that would change the face of the world began.

The industrial urban working classes emerged as a significant numerical body and were starting to understand the power they could yield as a united force. The Labour Party with its trade union connections was to put this power into effect.

Transport was increasingly affordable, particularly the railways.

Sport became part of the fabric of working class culture and was budgeted for. International sport competitions were to become more organised, evident by the London Games 1908; World Series baseball was conceived in America; the first Grand Prix was held at Le Mans in 1906; the Tour de France was staged in 1903.

Spectator problems occurred, for example when a wooden stand collapsed at Ibrox in 1902 and in 1909 people were injured at a riot at Hampden.

Traditions started early in the century took hold so fast they can still be recognised today, particularly in football, cricket and rugby.

## First World War 1914–1918

This war was fought mainly in Europe and the Middle East, in which the allies (France, Russia, Britain, Italy and the United States after 1917) defeated the central powers (Germany, Austria, Hungary and Turkey). Millions were to die in static trench warfare. It also became known as the Great War.

Nationalism revealed itself in war and it was glorified like a football match and the football match between British and German troops at Christmas 1914 set the tone for how sport was to be used during war time. Football grounds were used extensively for recruiting though eventually the Football League bowed to pressure to stop fixtures for the duration of the war. Following the war there were hopes for a more equal society though this was not immediately realised.

## Inter-War years (1919–1939)

There were two social moods following the First World War:

- to build a 'new' country with values learned from the conflict
- to regain some sense of fun and frivolity.

The initial burst of lavish living by the upper classes was not to last. The General Strike of 1926 culminated in the economic depression, high unemployment and the rise of Hitler in the 1930s.

The upper classes had wild parties, attended their tennis, golf and cricket clubs and took holidays abroad.

The working classes participated in some sort of leisure activity mainly on a Saturday afternoon. Football

saw enormous crowds; dog racing was first held on a track in 1926 at Belle Vue, Manchester. Bowls and darts were still popular pub games. It was still the exception to go on holiday apart from day trips or the Wakes Weeks when the mills and factories closed down. Only the wealthy went abroad at this stage and the middle classes tended to rely on the transport provided by the railways to go further afield.

However, the 1920s and 1930s were also characterised by the strikes and the Great Depression that saw unemployment levels and social discontent rise to an unprecedented level.

For the first time the government began to realise the importance of providing leisure and recreational opportunities for a mass of people. This was 'social control' where a mass of the population could be controlled by using their leisure time positively. The Central Council of Physical Recreation was formed in 1935, preceding the Physical Training and Recreation Act 1937.

Sport club membership provided problems as growing numbers applied for acceptance but their social standing left a little to be desired.

New interest in activities such as walking, bicycling and rambling was made possible by the growth in youth hostels.

County cricket was seeing a decline though club cricket was stronger than ever with southern businesses releasing players mid-week.

## Bodyline tour

The defeat of England in 1930 by Australia, particularly as a result of Bradman's batting, led the English to decide to use intimidatory bowling in the next series. Larwood and Jardine claimed it was a fair tactic and this is what caused the controversy. Bradman's batting slumped and England regained the Ashes. In the Third Test, injuries resulted from Larwood's bowling and the Australian Cricket Board sent a telegram to MCC saying in their opinion it was 'unsportsmanlike'. This was undermining the ability of the English to play in good faith. Politicians in Whitehall and the Australian Prime Minister applied pressure to have the matter settled. However, the MCC stuck by the team for the duration of the Series but Larwood's and Jardine's careers were over.

## International sport

The Test Series between England, Australia and South Africa was extended to include New Zealand, the West Indies and India. The Bodyline controversy occurred in the 1932–3 series. The Olympic Games began again and regular competitions took place between nations in golf, tennis and motor racing.

The newspapers were reporting sport events on special pages and the BBC reported eyewitness accounts on the late evening news. The wireless (TV started in 1938) helped to capture people's imaginations and the cinema became a universal attraction. Consequently sportsmen became national heroes.

The women were keen to demonstrate the new freedom the war had given them and team games were a popular pastime – in particular cricket, tennis, hockey and lacrosse.

## World War II 1939–1945

The war (1939–1945) in which the Allies, Britain and France, declared war on Germany as a result of the German invasion of Poland. After the war there was an extensive rebuilding programme following the German bombing raids, and facilities were more sophisticated than ever before. The therapeutic effect of recreational activities was highlighted for the physical, mental and emotional benefits. The commando training during the war had developed the use of obstacle training and this was how the first apparatus began to appear in schools combining the movement approach and problem solving learning techniques. It was adopted in physical education lessons with the Butler Education Act (1944) reforming education in Britain.

## Post-Second World War

Changes that occurred in recreational and sporting terms were dramatic:

- no distinction now between gentleman and players
- team games were giving way to more individual pursuits
- travel was now available to all classes, particularly hiking across different countries by the young
- the motor car enabled mobility for even the working classes
- air travel had become commonplace for sport teams which also resulted in an increase in competitions, particularly football on the continent
- stimulation and excitement took over from the pursuit of peace and quiet of the Romantic era
- entertainment outside the home became increasingly important
- television was to have a major impact on sports, creating interest in new heroes in sports otherwise unknown to millions. Also fees for professional sportspeople increased as well as the growth in spectating rather than participating.
- national and international standards rose at the expense of school performances
- local authorities were supplying more recreational facilities such as swimming baths, adventure playgrounds and so on
- the development of the National Parks opened up the countryside and encouraged outdoor activities
- recreation had come into its own for most of the population and had lost the 'should' or 'ought' philosophy. People were more free to choose their leisure pursuits than ever before.

# The changing role of women

The role of women in society has undergone some radical changes. However, it is important to distinguish between the:

- upper class
- middle class
- working class.

The involvement of women in football, since the late nineteenth century, highlights quite clearly that public interest in their competitive participation was high, until the Football Association banned them from playing on Football League grounds in 1921. Since then, the female game has made a slow recovery and is now beginning to attract media coverage at the higher levels. The USA female soccer team are household names and the Football Association and FIFA are taking positive steps to encourage the game.

| Women through the centuries | | | | | |
|---|---|---|---|---|---|
| Culture collision | | | | | |
| Victorian female stereotype | Health | Medical | Exercise | Emotional | Fair play |
| Social limitations | Games ethic. | | | | |

- Led to social sports – croquet; Tennis; Golf
  School sports – Lacrosse; Hockey; Netball.
- Headmistresses had autonomy/games played in peace and privacy/balance between emancipation and social respectability.
- Distinctions made between the characteristics and capabilities of men and women/ladies did not have to compromise status as ladies' fashion signalled changes and used to maintain status quo.

| Upper class | Middle class | Lower class |
|---|---|---|
| **Eighteenth Century**<br>- Cricket; croquet; riding<br><br>**Nineteenth Century**<br>- Pretentious education/ social/leisure/time/money/ femininity/fashion<br>- Rational sport<br>- Copy boys' education<br>- Athleticism modelled for women<br>- Victoria – sport and refinement<br>- Limited on medical grounds<br>- Social mixing<br>- Development of ladies' universities (Girton Hockey team 1890) | - Aspire to upper class lifestyle<br>- Proprietary colleges<br>- Own activities – lawn tennis/cycling<br>- Time and money not social breeding = restrictions<br>- Professions e.g. teaching<br>- Garden suburbs – golf/ tennis<br>- Sports clubs administrators<br>- Cheltenham ladies' college/ Roedean 1885 Miss Lawrence 1884 First ladies' singles Wimbledon | **Pre-nineteenth Century**<br>- Popular recreations/ occasional/festivals/rural<br><br>**Post-nineteenth Century**<br>- Working/urban/industrial<br>- Little time or money<br>- Few sport opportunities<br>- Education from 1870/drill/ femininity/sport male domain<br>- Improved work conditions/ gradual work outings/half-day Saturday/Bank holidays<br>- Women's factory football teams 1921 FA Ban women |

# Review Questions

1. What do the terms functional, recreational and religious mean in relation to the influence physical activities have within a particular culture? Give specific examples.

2. Write down in table form the summaries for the Medieval era and the Victorian era.

3. What was the significance of Shrove Tuesday in the recreational lives of people?

4. How did the constraints on free time and wages influence working class sport and how were conditions improved towards the end of the nineteenth century?

5. The Municipal Reform Act of 1835 led to the provision of public parks. What were the motives behind this provision?

6. What were the attitudes of the Protestant, Evangelist and Sabbatarian religions towards working class leisure?

7. Describe other factors which played their part in decreasing the leisure opportunities for the industrial working classes as they moved to the towns.

8. Explain the influence of a shorter working week on working class sport for men and women.

9. Why did some industrialists encourage young working class men to participate in sport and exercise?

10. What effect did the emergence of the middle classes have on recreational pursuits in Britain in the nineteenth century?

11. How did the inns and public houses cater for recreation?

12. Give some specific examples of how the railways affected recreation in the nineteenth century.

13. Why were youth movements considered a necessity in the nineteenth and early twentieth centuries?

14. What were the effects of the First World War on recreation in Britain?

15. What were the effects of the Second World War on recreation?

# Historical development of physical activities

The development of various physical activities within their overall social context should now make more sense. Always try to see the historical, political, economic, geographical, educational, and social and cultural aspects – as they will affect the pastimes and sports that we will study.

As well as learning about the history of specific sports it is also important that you can apply that knowledge and link it to present day developments. Other chapters will help you link the past to the present. Certain activities will be given where this ability can be tested. The activities will be:

- Lawn tennis
- Cricket

It would be useful if you could apply similar logic to other activities.

Figure 16.7 shows the generally accepted characteristics of popular and rational recreation. However, as with any other generalisation, there are occasions when the general does not hold true. In this case there would have been occasional discrepancies evidenced by the following:

- Some athletes would have travelled to some festivals, games and race meetings.

| Popular | Rational |
|---|---|
| • Occasional | • Regular |
| • Few, simple rules | • Complex, written rules |
| • Limited structure and organisation | • Highly structured |
| • Participation sport | • Spectator sport |
| • Physical force | • Refined skills |
| • Lower class development | • Upper class development |
| • Local | • Regional/national |
| • Limited equipment and facilities | • Sophisticated equipment and facilities |
| ↓ | ↓ |
| eg, MOB FOOTBAL | eg, REAL TENNIS |

Fig 16.7. Definition of popular and rational sports

- In the transition phase larger towns retained the rural pursuits such as mob games and bull baiting.

- Rules did not occur in all activities at the same time. Games such as cricket had early forms of rules and even mob games played to similar but limited rules year after year.

- There were approximately 46 holy days in the year allowing for animal sports, archery and so on.

- Not all activities were violent; for example, archery, bathing.

- Festival occasions could also be smaller occasions.

- Many activities were lower class in their association but the gentry often had some control either in the form of land ownership or prize giving.

- Many activities were male based but women ran the smock race, and played cricket early on.

We will now look in more detail at the following activities:

- Rural pastimes and festivals (Cornish hurling, Lakeland Sports, Highland Games)

- Blood sports (bull and bear baiting, cock fighting)

- Aquatic activities (spa towns, rowing, seaside, swimming)

- Racket sports (real tennis, rackets, fives, lawn tennis)

- Cycling

- Football

- Cricket

- Athletics

- Golf

# Rural pastimes and festivals
## Cornish hurling

A traditional game of football played in Cornwall. In Richard Carew's 'Survey of Cornwall' 1603 he gives a detailed description of a game of football or hurling as it was called in Cornwall, which reveals complex rules and strategies (for the time) for deceiving the opposition. In the east of Cornwall 'hurling to goales' involved teams of 15, 20 or 30 in which each player paired himself with another from the opposing team and attempted to block his advance, as in American football today.

*'The hurlers are bound to the observation of many lawes as that they must hurle man to man, and not two*

*set upon one manta once; the Hurler against the ball must not butt, nor handfast under the girdle; that he who hath the ball, must butt only in the other brest'.*

There was even an offside rule 'that he must deal no foreball, viz he may not throw it to any of his mates, standinge nearer the goale than himself'.

## Highland Games

These traditional festivals emerged from the struggles and developments peculiar to Scottish society. The activities were originally functional to the survival of the society. Types of activities were hill racing, throwing of the strength stones/tossing the caber, work and recreational pastimes of labourers and woodmen. Well-known venues are Braemar, Lonach, Aboyne, Glenislaand so on.

Images:

- Kilted athletes
- Attracks émigrés from all over the world
- Subcultures of the 'heavies'
- Bagpipes
- Sponsorship of Scottish whiskey
- Clan chiefs

The Highland Games have been a symbol of nationalism following the destruction of Scottish culture by the British administration, for example the Battle of Culloden. As an athletic festival they also provide employment for a band of semi-professional athletes who toured the basic circuit that developed in the north and the borders.

## Lakeland Sports

A traditional sporting festival based in the Lake District.

*1787 'Upon Stone Carr there have been held, time out of mind, races and other sports, such as wrestling, leaping (high jump) tracing with dogs (hound trailing)'.*

The English Lake District can draw a parallel between the sheep-based economy and many of the sporting occasions during the early nineteenth century tending to have social significance. Shepherds travel to buy and sell sheep. A show would be born – families would treat the occasion as a 'day out'. Following the showing and selling of sheep there would be sports and dance. They were based on a seasonal economy:

| Spring | Lambing | no time for sport |
|---|---|---|
| **Whitsuntide** | Lambing over | Hiring fairs (hiring of labour – also social occasion) |
| **Autumn** | Sheep fairs | 'wrestling or hurdle race for a fleece' |

# Blood sports

Blood sports as entertainment were a part of British life up to the end of the nineteenth century. In a violent society where minor offences were punishable by hanging, little moral consideration was given for the suffering animals.

Characteristics of blood sports: physical violence; gambling was usually involved; vicarious interest in the infliction of pain; popular in rural and urban areas; involved all social classes.

Reasons for popularity of blood sports: excitement; limited entertainment available; to win money by gambling; accessible, easy to stage; ancient notion that animals exist merely as a resource for humans; to strengthen the mentality of soldiers before entering warfare.

In the nineteenth century, blood sports were banned because:

- of a new era of evangelical and humanitarian concern
- of increase in concern over correct ways of behaviour; blood sports were not considered to be suitable in a civilised society

- the urban revolution stimulated new concepts of recreation

- of complaints of breaches of the peace occasioned by the assembly of large, rowdy crowds

- employers discriminated against employees likely to suffer injuries due to violent pursuits.

Legislation included:

- 1822 to prevent ill treatment of horses and cattle (not including the bull)

- 1824 Royal Society for the Prevention of Cruelty to Animals established

- 1835 baiting sports banned, including the bull

- 1840 Cruelty to Animals Act (cockfighting now illegal).

Here are some examples of blood sports:

# Bull and bear baiting

This sport was first recorded in the reign of Henry II. A bull or bear would be tied up and terriers would set at it, with the aim of hanging on without being dislodged; the dogs would fail if tossed away by the bull or bear. The dogs would eventually win, but betting took place on the performance of individual dogs. The bulldog was so-called because of its talent at this sport: with its thick set body, short legs and powerful jaws, it would cling to the bull and tear off chunks of flesh. It became a national symbol for British strength and determination.

Bear gardens were popular in the sixteenth century under the Tudors; there was one behind the Globe Theatre (where Shakespeare's plays were performed), and another in the Royal Palace. Four or five dogs would be let loose at the bear at the same time, and the fight ended when the supply of dogs ran out or the bear was too badly injured to carry on. Parliament tried to ban the practice in 1802, and was finally successful in 1835.

'Bull running' was a sport in which a bull was let loose in the streets of a town, and would be goaded by spectators with sticks; eg, at Tutbury and Stamford. The run usually ended on a bridge, and the bull would be spared if the crowd failed to toss it into the water. In rural areas, this sport was restricted to special festivals, but was more common in urban areas.

# Cock fighting

This was the most popular blood sport which set animal against animal; it was thought that cocks' natural aggression made for a fair fight, and each had an equal chance of victory if well matched. Cocks were bred and trained to fight, and metal spurs were added to their feet during the seventeenth century. Breeds included Piles, Blackreds, Pollcats, Pirchin, Ducks, Gingers and Shropshire Reds.

This was a sport popular across all social classes in urban and rural areas, for its entertainment value and gambling potential. Large towns had cockpits where regular contests took place; in 1800, there were seven cockpits in Newcastle. Failure to pay bets could result in the offender being hauled up in a basket above the pit (as in the Royal Cockpit at Bird Cage Walk).

'Throwing at cocks' was a favourite sport for Shrove Tuesday. Birds would be tethered, and people paid to throw stones or sticks at them. The birds' legs would usually break, and they would be killed.

# Aquatic activities

## Spa towns

Britain's inland spa resorts became fashionable in the nineteenth century when it became popular for the upper classes to 'take the waters', and railways helped their mobility. Spa towns have their origin in Roman times where they developed from mineral springs or holy wells. The Tudors established taking the waters as a standard medical practice, which was a tradition continued by the Georgians towards the end of the eighteenth century.

They also offered rest and relaxation away from the growing industrial towns. Some of the notable towns are Bath with its Roman remains and impressive Georgian architecture, Buxton with thermal springs high up in Derbyshire, and Harrogate.

# Rowing

The art of propelling a boat is practised as a sport in most countries, but it began as a utilitarian activity when it provided power for war ships and transport in industrial towns.

The River Thames formed one of the main highways in medieval times; wealthy people had their own state barges and the professional watermen plied for trade. Watermanship refers to the skill of handling a boat. By the beginning of the eighteenth century, there were more than 40,000 licensed watermen. There were frequent contests between the watermen, and betting on the barges was common.

The earliest account of a regatta on the River Thames was in 1775. This occasion was derived from the Italian 'regata', originally boat races on the Grand Canal in Venice.

The standard of rowing increased in the nineteenth century due to an increasing professionalism. Rowing races attracted an enormous following and were widely reported in the press. Many rowers became coaches of amateur crews and eventually, due to the rapid and powerful rise of amateurism and the First World War, professional contests gradually died out.

In 1715 Dogget instituted what is now the oldest sculling race in the world. Crews race for an orange livery with a silver badge, hence the title 'Dogget's Coat and Badge'. (Broughton the prize fighter was an early winner.) Rowing clubs which emerged were mostly amateur; one of the most famous was Leander in 1818.

Bumping races were a traditional form of racing, especially in narrow stretches. Crews would attempt to touch or bump the crew in front and crews would change place according to the number of bumps scored. The crew finishing first would take the title 'Head of the River'. The public schools took to rowing, as it met their values of athleticism.

The need to win these fixtures led to the hiring of professional watermen, but due to the amateur ethos

Leander Club is the oldest amateur rowing club in the world, believed to have been founded in 1818. Membership is a mark of distinction in the rowing world and a large proportion are former Oxford and Cambridge oarsmen. Leander's golden era came in the years between 1891 and 1914, during which they recorded 30 Henley wins (including 13 in the Grand Challenge Cup) and also won the Olympic eights in 1908 and 1912, and the Olympic pairs in 1908.

Fig 16.8. Swimming and rowing on the River Thames

What qualities of athleticism would be evident in a rowing fixture?

**ACTIVITY 6**

they reported that they were hired merely to provide competition! Rowing became competitive at Oxford and Cambridge Universities in the early years of the nineteenth century. The first University Boat Race took place at Henley in 1829; the Henley Regatta was established ten years later.

## Henley Regatta

In 1839 James Nash established this event initially to drum up trade for tradespeople and hoteliers of the town.

This soon became a great traditional event, reflecting the Victorian love of combining sporting events with a grand social occasion.

- Initially, only amateurs could compete.
- Non-British competitors were briefly banned in 1908.
- The Manual Labour clause excluded anyone 'who by trade or employment is a mechanic, artisan or labourer'.

However, it became less exclusive; the Manual Labour clause was abolished in 1890, and the Leander Club began to compete against teams such as the Thames Tradesmen and the Metropolitan Police. The Amateur Rowing Association was formed in 1882, followed by the National Amateur Rowing Association in 1890. The NARA was formed to counter the unfair manual labour clause. Exclusion was to be a monetary distinction rather than a social one.

Today Henley reflects the complex social class system. There are:

- Committee Lawn for Stewards and Guests
- Stewards Enclosure for Members and Guests
- Business and Club class
- Economy Class
- Public Banks.

*Changes:*

- 1946 women admitted to spectate but not to row
- training has become more scientific in terms of competitors' diet and technical developments in craft and coaching
- the event raises approximately £330,000 annual profit.

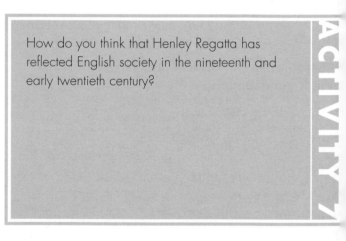

How do you think that Henley Regatta has reflected English society in the nineteenth and early twentieth century?

**ACTIVITY 7**

## The seaside

The fashion for sea bathing began in the eighteenth century when it was regarded as serving medical purposes, rather than for fun. The seaside resort took over in popularity from the spa towns. Bathing became popular in the 1720s and the first bathing machines made their appearance in Scarborough in 1753. Bathing nude was not uncommon at this time and the bathing machine afforded some privacy when costumes were heavy and uncomfortable. These would be pulled by men or horses to the seaside. They would later be replaced by bathing tents at the turn of the twentieth century. Men and women would have separate bathing areas. Mixed bathing and the wearing of costumes came in the nineteenth century.

During the Victorian era, the railways and steamers with their cheap excursion fares made the seaside resorts accessible to large numbers of people. Thomas Cook established his travel company in 1841 and laid on excursion trains. This resulted in the exodus of the upper classes to more isolated areas like the west country resorts. The creation of Bank Holidays in 1871 resulted in even more people visiting the seaside, sometimes as day trippers.

## Swimming

Swimming for recreation developed in the eighteenth century when rowing and yachting became popular:

- In 1734, the first open air swimming pool was built in London.
- Captain Webb swam the English Channel in 1875.
- Swimming was initially undertaken in Britain in natural facilities such as rivers and canals for recreation, hygiene and safety. The lower classes in particular used these facilities which made the middle and upper classes less ready to use them.
- Developments in swimming technique came particularly from the overseas influence, for example the front crawl came from the Indians and John Trudgeon learnt his stroke from the Bantu tribe in South Africa (which brought both arms over the water). He introduced this to England in 1873.
- The first modern Olympics in 1896 at Athens included the 100, 500 and 1200 metres freestyle.
- An increase in public baths following the Public Baths and Washhouses Act in 1840.
- The success in swimming races in Britain from the mid-nineteenth century led to a proportional increase in prizes which were usually won by 'professional swimmers' who were swimming teachers involved in giving lessons in return for money.

- The Amateur Swimming Association was formed in 1886 followed by FINA, Fédération Internationale de Natation Amateur.
- Teachers of swimming in Great Britain were excluded from racing.
- Women's swimming was introduced at the 1912 Olympic Games in Stockholm.
- The nature of the sport places it in the category of an athletic activity. The keeping of records by 'racing against the clock' is an important element. Other factors have also played a part – social acceptability and regulation governed both the style and materials worn by male and female swimmers.

> List some of the modern changes that have occurred in swimming. Consider types of swimming, facilities, access to participation and so on.
>
> **ACTIVITY 8**

## Racket sports
### Real tennis

This game originated in France, as suggested by the terminology: 'dedans', 'tambour', 'grille'. It was an activity of the French Royal court, and was made popular in England by the Tudors. One of the most famous courts is still in use at Hampton Court. This was the sport of the noblemen and royalty and in 1536 there were restrictive acts which forbade servants and labourers to play. This helped to retain the privileged status of the elite. The game was originally played with the hand, 'le jeu de paume', until the sixteenth century when rackets were used.

This was a very sophisticated, exclusive game requiring expensive facilities, equipment and an

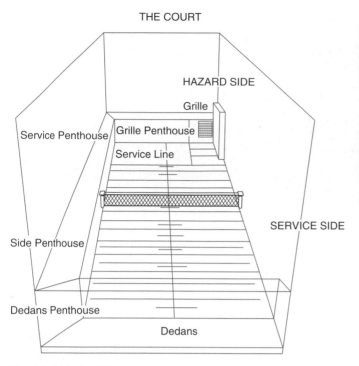

Fig 16.9. A Real Tennis court

Fig 16.10. An early version of tennis, taken from *Orbis Sensualium Pictus* by John Comenius, 1659

understanding of the complex rules and social etiquette of the game. The emphasis was on the individual's skill and tactical and strategic awareness; as ever, wagering was evident. It was the epitome of rational sport.

# Rackets

This game began in fairly humble circumstances in England. Open courts existed in the back yards of taverns and inns, and in many towns. They were social meeting places and there was always a wall to be used. Equipment could also be hired from publicans wishing to make the most of their business opportunities. They had all the requirements – willing opponents, alcohol and wagering.

The game was a test of strength and accuracy. In a four-handed match the players took alternate 'out' and 'in' games, which would lead to exciting rallies.

Rackets was taken up by the public schools for its simple qualities and the possibilities of using architectural features within the school

grounds. It was a game which suited the cult of athleticism, containing rules, etiquette and sportsmanship.

# Fives

Fives was played with the palm of the hand, wearing a glove, and the ball was hit against the wall. It was played in inns and other public places, and was a much more individual game than rackets. In the public schools it tended to be played more in the boys' recreation time and consequently did not establish well-known formal rules. As the game was not taken up at the universities, individual schools' variations continued. These qualities tended to make it a less favourable game than rackets as far as the staff were concerned.

# Lawn tennis

Real or Royal tennis was an aristocratic pastime and was not conducive to the lives of the middle and lower classes. However, in the nineteenth century the middle classes with their increasing wealth and leisure time wanted to establish their own form of recreation which would set them apart from the lower classes. The game became enormously popular midway through Queen Victoria's reign.

Fig 16.11. Lawn tennis was one of the few recreational activities that men and women could enjoy together in Victorian England

Major Wingfield took most of the credit for the game's popularity. His invention, which he called Sphairistike, had an hour-glass shaped court. He provided a commercial product which could be bought in kit form, making it attractive to the middle classes whose wealth was often determined by trade. The Marylebone Cricket Club (MCC) then took it one stage further, calling it lawn tennis and adopting an oblong shaped court.

It ousted croquet from the lawns of the middle classes, and proved to be an ideal game for large suburban gardens to be played by both social classes, in their increasingly leisured society. There were few recreational activities at this time that both sexes could enjoy together. The ladies were able to play privately away from the public gaze, and it was a game which helped to remove some of the stereotypes. They could run around becoming increasingly energetic and clothing began to be slightly less restrictive. Their schools also accepted the game as it was non-contact, had rules and was acceptable to the parents.

The middle classes also ensured its club development and the administrative structures. The lower classes had to wait until there was public provision, so their participation was delayed.

1. Who invented the game which he called Sphairistike and what is the game called today?
2. How did the structure of Real Tennis differ from mob football and how did this reflect the class of people who played them?
3. It has been suggested that Lawn Tennis is the only game that was invented by the urban middle class.
   a) Discuss this view and explain why there was a delay in working class participation
   b) Why was Lawn Tennis suitable for professional class ladies to play?
4. Tennis has been a part of the school physical education curriculum for the latter half of the twentieth century though the skills of tennis are challenging for young children to master.
   a) What strategies could you use to help children learn to adapt to the full game?
   b) How could a physical education teacher keep some elements of play while maintaining the educational aims of the lesson?
5. The democratisation of tennis has become an important issue in the late twentieth century.
   a) How has this been reflected in the approach of the Lawn Tennis Association towards the game?
   b) Discuss the view that tennis has changed from a Victorian garden party game to a highly commercial enterprise.

# Cycling

This was an activity which reflected the technological advances and social changes in the nineteenth century.

- The Hobby Horse (1818) was the forerunner to the bicycle. It was propelled by the rider who sat astride and pushed alternate feet on the ground.
- The Boneshaker (1868) was invented by the Michaux brothers in Paris.

- The Penny Farthing (1870–1890) – The large front wheel was developed to obtain more speed for every turn of the pedals, so that the wheel covered more ground.

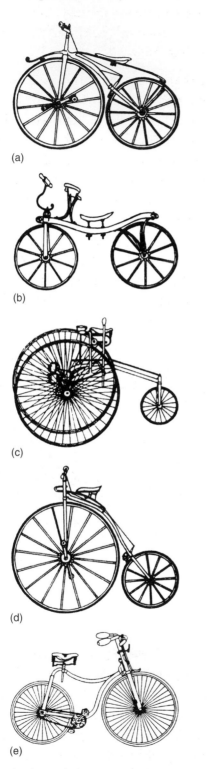

(a)

(b)

(c)

(d)

(e)

Fig 16.12. (a) The boneshaker, 1868; (b) The hobby horse, 1818; (c) The national royal tricycle, 1884; (d) The penny farthing, 1870; (e) The rover safety, 1885

- The National Royal Tricycle (1884) was developed from the Penny Farthing to make a safer ride.
- The Rover Safety (1885) was the machine that set the fashion and was built with the first Diamond frame.

The bicycle was developing during the machine age and could be produced in large numbers. It was an alternative mode of transport to the horse and cart, and consequently more appealing to the middle classes. The gentry initially retained their preference for the horse and were disdainful of 'new fangled' machines. The roads initially were poor, but improvements were gradually made.

The gentry ladies, however, were keen to take on this new form of transport which gave them a sense of freedom from their claustrophobic lives which required that they were chaperoned everywhere and were expected to fulfil rigid social roles. Further encouragement was given by the Royal daughters' use of the bicycle.

The growing interest in the countryside also made the bicycle useful, as a route out to the country lanes. The railways offered Rover tickets which would take the cycle and the cyclists further afield. Club developments became hugely popular, particularly the touring branch. Bicycles were expensive, however, and the majority of people had to wait for the secondhand trade to develop.

# Football

Football began as a mob game. It lacked the organisational features of the modern game and was characterised by large numbers of players, exclusively male and from the lower classes, involved in a territorial struggle. The game tended to be played occasionally on annual holidays like the Wakes as the people had limited free time, and would cover distances between villages. Due to only being played a few times a year there were limited rules, and hence violence, injury and sometimes death, were common as the game was determined by force rather than skill. There was no division of labour; players

Fig 16.13. England v Scotland at the Oval, 6 March 1875

had no particular roles, and there was a loose distinction between participating and spectating. This was originally a rural activity and reflected the harsh way of life lived by uneducated, rural people.

What changed the game out of all proportion to its original character? The gentry sons in the public schools began to play the game regularly on the school grounds. Though they started with variations in rules from school to school, they gradually began to develop them in the form of shape of goals, boundaries, limits on the size of the team and so on. A competitive structure emerged with inter-house and inter-school matches. Some variations remained and were distinctive to individual schools; the unique facility features like the Close at Rugby with soft turf and the Quad at Charterhouse, where the dribbling game emerged. There is also the Eton Wall game which still exists today.

University graduates further codified the game and established associations; the Football Association was established in 1863. When university graduates became employers they encouraged the game among the workers, partly to boost morale and loyalty, and also to instil middle class values and discipline. They also established their middle class sports clubs based on amateurism.

The roads and pavements were the playgrounds of working class children and they devised numerous types of street games. Football was one of them and most streets had a football team associated with a strong community feeling. The cramped living conditions and shortage of facilities led to a more spectator-based interest in the game. Developments in transport opened up the rest of the country for fixtures further afield.

There was therefore a curious development across the different social classes. The game began as a mob game by and for the lower classes. The public schools made it popular with the gentry in the south of England, who also incorporated middle class values within the game as it developed along strictly amateur lines – the southern amateurs. However, in the north of England it developed in the industrial towns, and professionalism soon crept in with clubs like Sheffield Wednesday being established, when Wednesday became early closing day. The Football League was established in 1885. When the two sides met there was a culture shock!

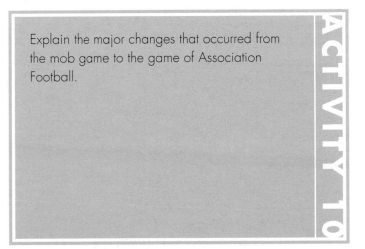

Explain the major changes that occurred from the mob game to the game of Association Football.

ACTIVITY 10

# Cricket

Cricket is one of the oldest established games and was played from the outset by both social classes; the aristocrats and the commoners played together. There were not many activities which both social classes played together, though they had particular roles within the game to signify their status. The game reflected the feudal structure of the village. The early clubs emerged from the rural village sides, with the gentry acting as patron.

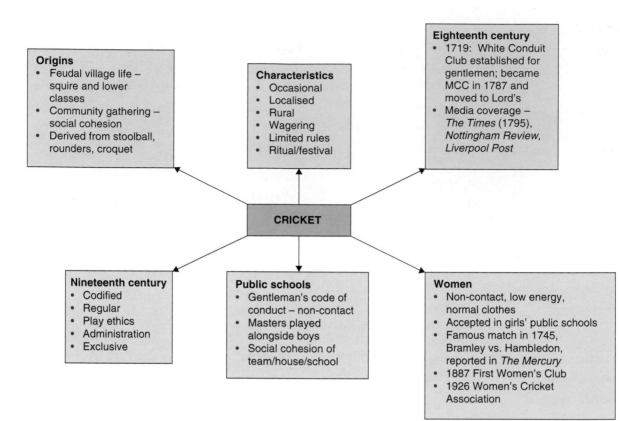

**Origins**
- Feudal village life – squire and lower classes
- Community gathering – social cohesion
- Derived from stoolball, rounders, croquet

**Characteristics**
- Occasional
- Localised
- Rural
- Wagering
- Limited rules
- Ritual/festival

**Eighteenth century**
- 1719: White Conduit Club established for gentlemen; became MCC in 1787 and moved to Lord's
- Media coverage – *The Times* (1795), *Nottingham Review, Liverpool Post*

**CRICKET**

**Nineteenth century**
- Codified
- Regular
- Play ethics
- Administration
- Exclusive

**Public schools**
- Gentleman's code of conduct – non-contact
- Masters played alongside boys
- Social cohesion of team/house/school

**Women**
- Non-contact, low energy, normal clothes
- Accepted in girls' public schools
- Famous match in 1745, Bramley vs. Hambledon, reported in *The Mercury*
- 1887 First Women's Club
- 1926 Women's Cricket Association

Fig 16.14. The development of cricket

Fig 16.15. 'Rural Sports' by Rowlandsen, c. 1811

There were a variety of reasons for this: the game took place in the summer season when light was at its best allowing the workers time to participate, and because of its non-violent nature, there were no threats to the gentry in playing with the peasants. The early rules and gentlemanly behaviour ensured a level of respectful behaviour.

Games would attract spectators in their thousands. The first written rules were drawn up by the Duke of Richmond in 1727 to help control country house games where sometimes large sums of money would hinge on the outcome. The MCC emerged as an organisational feature comparatively early in the game's development. The terms 'gentlemen' and 'players' emerged to distinguish the amateurs from the professionals.

Though it was a game to appeal to all social classes, county cricket remained quite exclusive, holding matches mid-week. The suburban middle classes began to take out county membership and the large grounds began to take over from the smaller, more portable fixtures. This would detach it even more from the working classes. The Lancashire League was established similarly to the Football League, to cater for the needs of the working classes.

Cricket was immediately acceptable in the public schools as it matched all the criteria for social control for the masters and athleticism for the boys. The rules meant a code of behaviour by the boys who would be expected to behave within the spirit of the game. The fags, or younger boys, would help the older boys in practice and the assistant masters would also play. When fixtures became prestigious and important to win, professionals were employed to raise the standards of play amongst the team.

The first official women's cricket match is recorded as having taken place in 1745, between Bromley and Hambleden. It grew in popularity during the nineteenth century, as women's clothing began to adapt to sporting conditions. The Women's Cricket Association was formed in 1926.

1. The acceptability of cricket as a respectable game was such that nineteenth-century public schools adopted it as a vehicle for the development of Christian gentlemen. The engraving by Rowlandsen called 'Rural Sports' captures the mood of a three-day county match between Hampshire and Surrey (see fig 16.16).
   a) What technical features point to this being an eighteenth-century match?
   b) The term 'Rural sports' was usually associated with popular recreation. What were the characteristics of this form of recreation, some of which may be evident in this engraving?
   c) What do you understand by the term 'gentlemen' and 'players' in relation to cricket?

2. Cricket was a popular game for both sexes from the seventeenth century onwards, though women's cricket saw a decline in the early nineteenth century.
   a) What aspects of nineteenth-century cricket made it such an attractive activity in boys' public schools?
   b) Why was cricket an acceptable game for women to play by the end of the nineteenth century?

3. The emergence of the West Indies in world standard Cricket was no coincidence. What may have motivated an emerging country to specialise in such an activity?

4. Games can be classified into certain categories – Invasion, Net and Innings. What are the characteristics of innings games?

5. Cricket is still as popular in these modern times but some elements of the game have changed. Suggest what some of these changes have been and account for them.

# Athletics

Many athletic activities developed from functional activities like the throwing events, while others from agricultural pursuits like hunting and clearing obstacles. Pedestrianism was similar to race walking, and developed in Stuart and Georgian Society where young men were sent ahead of a coach to warn the inn keeper of their imminent arrival. Wagers were placed and the gentry acted as patrons. It developed into an endurance event covering long distances against the opponent or the clock. Can you see the similarities between the sculling races like the Doggett Coat and Badge and the Prize Ring? It involved a working class performer and a gentry patron, but it was often a corrupt activity. Pedestrianism was a commercial attraction, with notable characters like Deerfoot the American earning large sums of money.

Hurdling is said to have evolved from the boys at public schools improvising in their leisure time and re-enacting events they saw at home like the association between hunting and hare and hounds and hurdling with horse racing. Other events were included like high and standing broad jumps, and athletics meetings began. They developed athletics clubs, eg, the London Athletic Club.

In 1896 the revival of the modern Olympic Games heralded an international appeal for athletics. Specialisation was taking over from the traditional all-round English amateur sportsman; play had moved on to competition and winning.

# Golf

The origins of golf are thought to derive from ancient activities played by the Patagonian Indians, from a game called *jeu de mal* in France and *het kolven* in Holland. However, the Scots claim that they were the first responsible for the game developing to its present form. It was banned in 1457 as it was feared that it interfered with people's archery practice.

The Stuarts made golf a Royal pursuit and Mary Queen of Scots was frowned upon for playing the game following her husband's death. The French Royal connection also brought the term

Fig 16.16. George Glennie putting at Blackheath, by Hardy Bridgeman, 1881

'caddy' which derived from the word cadets – the younger sons of the French aristocrats who came over to England as her pages. The Scots adopted this to mean loafers and scroungers! Many monarchs to follow were interested in the game.

The competition for the Silver Golf Club in 1744 was the first ever held in golf, and a Code of Rules was agreed.

However, golf originally seems to have been for the ordinary people, eg, the fishwives of Musselborough. From the seventeenth century onwards, equipment changes meant increased prices which effectively priced the fishermen and labourers out of golf. The first balls were made of turned boxwood followed by a feathery ball. Rubber balls wrapped in gutta-percha, in the nineteenth century, were much more expensive. The shafts were made from hickory which had to be imported from the USA. This led to the situation where the gentry played and the commoners carried the clubs as caddies. With the enclosure of land and the cost of laying out courses on expensive land near suburban areas, it soon became the exclusive preserve of a wealthy minority.

The proliferation of clubs meant an equal proliferation of local rules. By 1919 the matter of rules was passed to the Royal and Ancient Society. The clubs were governed by the upper and middle classes, and women were admitted on the understanding that a level of internal segregation was accepted. They could not vote or be shareholders.

Golf helped to foster a community life in the suburbs. Women from all social classes had played the game from its early days, and by 1898 there were 220 ladies' clubs. However, as the Victorian stereotype of female behaviour took hold of society, they met with problems.

They were considered physically inferior to men, which led to a miniature version of the course or from the forward tee on men's courses. They were advised to attempt no more than 70 yards for a drive.

ACTIVITY 12

In order to carry out research on activities and games, referring to a checklist can help to organise the information in a manageable format. Table 16.2 shows the checklist applied to badminton; research some details about the development of hockey using this approach.

Table 16.2. Gathering information about badminton

| Principle | Information | Reason |
|---|---|---|
| Origin | Evolved about 1870 from ancient children's game of Battledore and Shuttlecock<br>Army officers exported/imported – India | British Empire |
| Social event | Derives its name from the seat (estate) of the Duke of Beaufort at Badminton, Gloucestershire<br>Played in Victorian salons by men and women | Leisure activity, ie, upper class |
| Social class | Upper class | • Leisure time<br>• Space and equipment |
| Influences | • Duke of Beaufort<br>• Army | Played game on estate imported/exported games |
| Early game | • Hour glass shaped court<br>• Doubles popular but 3, 4 and 5 a side usual | To accommodate doors of Victorian salon<br>Singles considered selfish |
| Later game | 1870 Poona 1st laws<br>1893 Badminton Association<br>1899 All England Championships<br>1901 court made rectangular | Regulate court size and rules for competitions |

| Principle | Information | Reason |
|---|---|---|
| Sporting atmosphere | Equipment (net, rackets, shuttle); court (boundaries); spectators; recreation in leisure time | |
| Education | Not initially popular in either public or state schools | • No team game values<br>• Lack of facilities |
| Clothing | Men – informal day wear<br>Women – formal restrictive long dresses | Modesty |
| Amateurism professionalism | Originally amateur | Developed by Victorians – amateur code |
| Clubs | 250 clubs were members of the Badminton Association by 1914 | Victorians developed the club ethos; made competitions possible |
| Other | 1934 International Badminton Federation | |

# Summary

- From this selection of activities, you can see how sport within society is a dynamic experience, constantly changing to adapt to new pressures and sometimes exerting its own influence on society.

- From brutal and blood sports to a system where legislation curtailed activities or caused modifications.

- The change in emphasis from rural to urban sport with a philosophy of participation was hindered by lack of facilities and space.

- From watching in small local groups to mass spectatorism; business enterprise; improved communications and a national interest in sport.

- From local rules to fully codified rules formulating governing bodies.

- Control passed from the aristocracy to the middle classes.

- Bribery, corruption and vice largely eliminated, and with it the old concept of professionalism.

- Recreation was no longer the privilege of the nobility. By the end of the nineteenth century, the working class had won the same right to recreation.

- With the spatial restrictions of urbanisation came the desire to escape to the country. The weekend exodus became a national characteristic.

# Review Questions

1. List four characteristics of popular and rational recreation.

2. What caused the rise and decline of fencing and boxing?

3. How did fox hunting reflect the social status of the social classes in the nineteenth century?

4. What were the two types of angling that developed?

5. Why were blood sports popular in the eighteenth and nineteenth centuries and why were they later banned?

6. What were the first professional rowers called?

7. What was the 'manual labour' clause and which sport did it affect in particular?

8. Explain why Real Tennis was for the upper classes while Lawn Tennis developed for the middle classes.

9. Why did rackets meet the concept of athleticism while fives did not?

10. What factors made cycling a popular activity?

11. Explain the influence of the various social classes on the development of football.

12. In what way was the development of cricket different to that of football?

13. What is the link between hurdling as an athletic activity and the development of the public school's hare and hounds?

14. How and why did golf shift from being accessible to all social classes to being an exclusive activity of the middle and upper classes?

15. From Table 16.2 suggest some of the major influences on the development of the game of badminton.

# 17. Historical Development of Physical Education

We have studied the current situation concerning physical education mentioning briefly some historical events.

We are now going to look in more detail at how we came to the present position. We will cover:

- Public schools in the nineteenth century
- State school education from 1870, linking up to the present day.

By the end of this chapter you should understand the following terms:

- Public schools
- Technical development of activities
- Clarendon Commission
- Athleticism
- Muscular Christianity
- Notable headmasters, eg, Thomas Arnold of Rugby School
- Female education
- State schooling from 1870
- Swedish gymnastics
- Military drill and the model course
- Influence of the two World Wars on education
- Syllabuses of physical training
- Moving and Growing and Planning the Programme
- Educational gymnastics

It is very important that at the end of this chapter you are able to understand the link to the present-day education system, outlined in chapter 12.

Although for ease of study we will deal with the State and private sector separately, it is important to remember that the private or public schools which operated for the gentry or upper classes were already well established by the nineteenth century.

The State schools followed much later following the Forster Education Act 1870.

## The public schools

The sons of the gentry were educated at large, prestigious, fee-paying boarding schools. Separate schools for daughters were founded much later, and catered for very different needs; boys' schools were academic while girls' schools concentrated on social

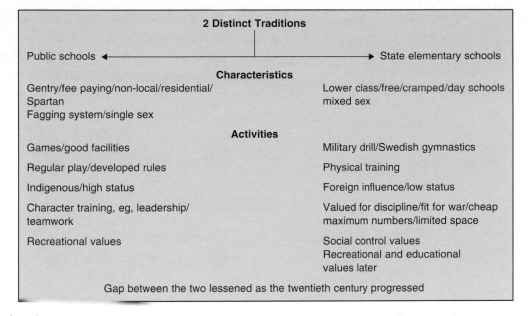

Fig 17.1. School traditions

accomplishments like sewing and managing a household.

There were originally nine elite institutions, which were called 'Barbarian' schools as they maintained the gentry tradition: Eton, Harrow, Rugby, Shrewsbury, Charterhouse, Westminster, Winchester, St Paul's and Merchant Taylor's.

The emergence of the middle classes has already been mentioned as a major change in the social structure of nineteenth-century Britain. When they acquired the necessary funds for their sons to attend these prestigious schools, they were unfairly rejected as the schools wished to remain exclusive, and so the middle classes began to build their own proprietary colleges which were based on the elite schools. Examples of these 'Philistine' schools are Cheltenham College, Marlborough and Clifton.

## Technical/formal development of activities

The development of sport in the public schools radically changed previous concepts of sport. The boys brought to their schools their experiences of games like cricket and mob football and country pursuits such as fishing and coursing. Before the formalisation of team games, the boys would leave the school grounds, and participate in rowdy behaviour; this often involved poaching, fighting and trespassing, drinking alcohol and generally bringing the school's reputation into disrepute, causing conflict with local landowners and gamekeepers.

However, during this stage, they had began the process of organising their own activities and devising new ways of playing; these were often associated with individual architectural features of the different schools, eg, cloisters for fives, and the Eton wall game. This is an old form of football, and survives to this day. It developed from the unique architectural feature of a long red brick wall which separates the school playing fields from the Slough road. Ten players per side work the small ball along a narrow strip, 4–5 yards wide and 118 yards long. The players are assigned their playing position and specialised role according to their physique. The wall was built in 1717, but the game became popular in the nineteenth century.

Thomas Arnold, the head of Rugby School, encouraged the boys to develop activities which

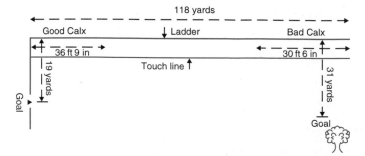

Fig 17.2. The Eton wall game

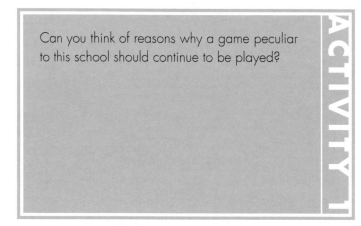

Can you think of reasons why a game peculiar to this school should continue to be played?

ACTIVITY 1

could be played on the school grounds and which would also highlight the more moral features of teamwork, such as self discipline, loyalty, courage; character-building qualities suitable for the prospective leaders of society.

The government was forced to intervene in public school education in 1861, when the Clarendon Commission was set up to 'inquire into the revenues and management of certain colleges and schools and the studies pursued and the instruction given there'. When the Clarendon Report was published in 1864, it strengthened the position of the headmasters by stressing the positive, educational features of team games as agents of training character. It did not place too much emphasis on skilled performance, but stressed moral qualities such as group loyalty. It also highlighted sports which were less useful, including hare and hounds, and gymnastics – both activities which focused on individual qualities. However, the report also revealed the extent to which games were becoming central to the school lives of the boys.

The Taunton Commission published in 1868 which examined other schools, also regarded gymnastics as inferior and less lively than the indigenous English games, which they recognised as having educational value. The headmasters rallied together at a conference in 1869 under the leadership of Edward Thring, and agreed that sport should encourage conformity in the boys' lives.

The Victorian public schools can be described as total institutions:

- The schools had institutional frameworks.
- The boys took part in regulated activities.
- The boys behaved in a way that was different to their role outside the school; eg, the fagging system placed younger boys in a subservient role to older boys. These were the sons of the gentry and would not normally be subservient to anyone.
- The boys were admitted and released on a termly basis.
- They had to assimilate the institutionalised values and rules in order to conform.

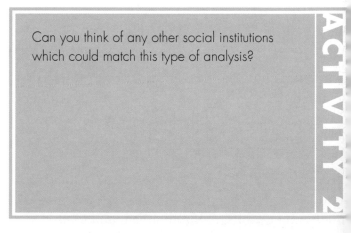

Can you think of any other social institutions which could match this type of analysis?

ACTIVITY 2

Cricket was already a fairly well-established game in society and as such was considered suitable for the boys; mob football, on the other hand, was played by the lower classes in society and was not so acceptable, until the boys devised a more organised format. The game of rugby supposedly began at Rugby School, when William Webb Ellis picked up the ball during a game of football and ran with it.

| Cricket | Football |
| --- | --- |
| • Earliest established game in English society accepted by boys' families | • Still a 'mob' game in the nineteenth century |
| • Differing positional roles made it acceptable for both social classes to play | • Played by lower classes in society |
| • Reflected the ideals of athleticism: teamwork/honour/ etiquette; team before individual | • Not popular with gentry until boys devised rules within the schools |
| | • 'Contact' nature of the game meant that the social classes would play separately for a long time |

The boys were in charge of organising the games, and senior bands of boys (normally called prefects) would be in control, reflecting the fagging system. Games committees were formed, eg, the Harrow Philathletic Club. The masters actively discouraged some activities (poaching and gambling) while others were allowed to exist on an informal recreational basis among the boys (fives and fighting). They actively encouraged the boys to organise team games.

Initially, inter-school fixtures were not feasible as no two schools had the same rules. However, by the mid-nineteenth century, the headmaster and staff started to organise sports. Games were seen as a medium for achieving educational aims with a moral social sense; they could also help combat idleness and as such were a form of social control. Boys who excelled in games were admired by the other pupils.

**Technical development of games:**

• boys brought local variations to the schools from their villages

• played regularly in free time

• developed individual school rules/skills/boundaries, etc.

• played competitively, ie, house matches

• self government meant boys organised activities initially

• later codified rules allowed inter-school fixtures

• development of games elite.

## Athleticism

*Physical endeavour with moral integrity*

The cult of athleticism stressed the physical and social benefits of sports:

• The physical benefits were seen to counteract the effects of sedentary lifestyles, and sport was viewed as therapeutic, invigorating and cathartic. It was also seen as a break from work.

• Sport would take place within a competitive situation which would help the boys learn how to cope with winning and losing all in a dignified manner. It helped to develop leadership qualities, and being captain was a high status office to hold.

The House system was instrumental to the competitive sport events, in which the manner of the performance was considered more important than the result.

Athleticism also met middle class values of respectability and order, for example, values such as sportsmanship, leadership and abiding by rules. The middle classes were to become the organisers and administrators of society, particularly highlighted in their role within governing bodies of sports clubs.

There were also opponents of this emphasis on athleticism, with many people believing it was becoming more important than the boys' studies,

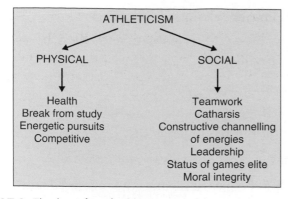

Fig 17.3. The benefits of athleticism

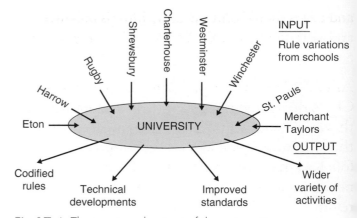

Fig 17.4. The input and output of the universities

Consider the following areas and compare the situation in a state school today with a public school in the nineteenth century:

- Physical education curriculum and the latest government proposals
- Physical education exams
- Student lifestyles (part time work, increase in leisure activities, etc).

and could lead to a regimentation of boys' thoughts and behaviour with a destruction of individuality. Old boys who returned as teachers after university were often employed for their games prowess as much as for their intellectual teaching contribution. They brought to the schools the new sports they had learnt at university, the fully codified versions of the games and also the philosophy to excel at their sport.

'The public schools were the first centres of excellence for sport and resembled modern day sports schools.' Discuss.

Fig 17.5. The early days of rugby, 'Will he do it?' by George Elgar Hicks

The public schools instituted the idea of the Sports Day, which operated as a public relations exercise to the old boys, parents and governors of the school. The funds of the school could benefit from generous donations and valuable publicity could be gained.

# Liberal headmasters

## Thomas Arnold

Thomas Arnold became headmaster of Rugby School in 1828 where he directed a crusade against personal sin, eg, bullying, lying, swearing, cheating, running wild. Pupils were to remain on the school grounds, he forbade shooting and beagling as these activities encouraged poaching, and fights should only occur within his presence and be supervised by the prefects who enforced his authority.

Arnold is known for his contribution to muscular Christianity, but he valued games only for what they could contribute towards the social control of the boys. The development of athleticism followed the cooperation of the boys in maintaining discipline and achieving Arnold's reforms.

*Tom Brown's Schooldays* by Thomas Hughes was published in 1860 and highlighted the Victorian ideal towards the physical side of the Christian gentleman. Hughes expanded the manliness ideals of Charles Kingsley – moral manliness became extrovert masculinity.

## Edward Thring of Uppingham

Uppingham rose from being an obscure grammar school to a famous public school in the nineteenth

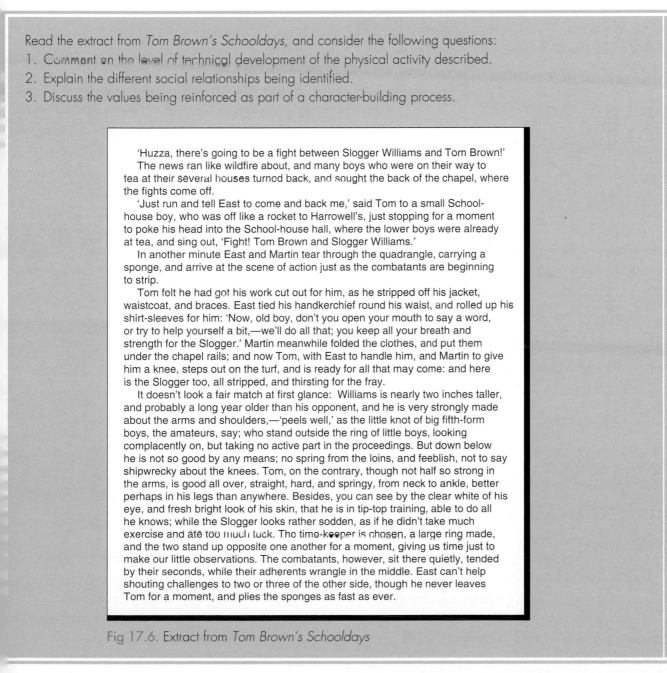

**ACTIVITY 5**

Read the extract from *Tom Brown's Schooldays*, and consider the following questions:

1. Comment on the level of technical development of the physical activity described.
2. Explain the different social relationships being identified.
3. Discuss the values being reinforced as part of a character-building process.

'Huzza, there's going to be a fight between Slogger Williams and Tom Brown!'

The news ran like wildfire about, and many boys who were on their way to tea at their several houses turned back, and sought the back of the chapel, where the fights come off.

'Just run and tell East to come and back me,' said Tom to a small School-house boy, who was off like a rocket to Harrowell's, just stopping for a moment to poke his head into the School-house hall, where the lower boys were already at tea, and sing out, 'Fight! Tom Brown and Slogger Williams.'

In another minute East and Martin tear through the quadrangle, carrying a sponge, and arrive at the scene of action just as the combatants are beginning to strip.

Tom felt he had got his work cut out for him, as he stripped off his jacket, waistcoat, and braces. East tied his handkerchief round his waist, and rolled up his shirt-sleeves for him: 'Now, old boy, don't you open your mouth to say a word, or try to help yourself a bit,—we'll do all that; you keep all your breath and strength for the Slogger.' Martin meanwhile folded the clothes, and put them under the chapel rails; and now Tom, with East to handle him, and Martin to give him a knee, steps out on the turf, and is ready for all that may come: and here is the Slogger too, all stripped, and thirsting for the fray.

It doesn't look a fair match at first glance: Williams is nearly two inches taller, and probably a long year older than his opponent, and he is very strongly made about the arms and shoulders,—'peels well,' as the little knot of big fifth-form boys, the amateurs, say; who stand outside the ring of little boys, looking complacently on, but taking no active part in the proceedings. But down below he is not so good by any means; no spring from the loins, and feeblish, not to say shipwrecky about the knees. Tom, on the contrary, though not half so strong in the arms, is good all over, straight, hard, and springy, from neck to ankle, better perhaps in his legs than anywhere. Besides, you can see by the clear white of his eye, and fresh bright look of his skin, that he is in tip-top training, able to do all he knows; while the Slogger looks rather sodden, as if he didn't take much exercise and ate too much tuck. The time-keeper is chosen, a large ring made, and the two stand up opposite one another for a moment, giving us time just to make our little observations. The combatants, however, sit there quietly, tended by their seconds, while their adherents wrangle in the middle. East can't help shouting challenges to two or three of the other side, though he never leaves Tom for a moment, and plies the sponges as fast as ever.

*Fig 17.6. Extract from* Tom Brown's Schooldays

century under its headmaster, Edward Thring. From the start he encouraged the playing of games:

- He played fives and football with the boys.
- The school day began early and finished at midday to accommodate games.
- He was the first to open a gymnasium in 1859 and incorporated swimming and athletics as part of the physical education programme.

Other public schools tended to ignore Thring's innovations and continued with their diet of games. Thring did not place so much importance on the games elite, and believed that non-athletic boys could enjoy games. Thring had attended Eton as a boy which is where he developed his love of physical activity; he truly promoted sports for the love of it.

## Spread of athleticism nationally and world-wide

- Old Boys'/Girls' network
- Universities codified rules, developed activities technically, improved and devised new ways of playing
- Sports clubs and governing bodies became significant administrative features
- Officers in army and navy influential on troops
- Clergy influenced parishioners
- Teachers went back into schools
- Employers encouraged games in their workforce
- The Empire enabled these developments to be spread world-wide.

## Female education

In the late 1800s the education of girls was very poor. It was pretentious and costly, with an emphasis on accomplishments for society rather than for the intellectual development of the girls. Music and dancing counted as the highest priorities, with writing and arithmetic being the lowest. 'Medical' reasons to limit women's sports

participation were legitimised; it was believed that women who participated in strenuous physical activity would become muscle bound, which would be detrimental to childbearing. As physical activity and educational examinations incorporated a degree of competitiveness, this was not conducive to the social image of how women should behave.

In the Victorian era, constructive education for women was regarded as a threat to the norms for behaviour for that society. As the struggle for women's rights developed, their increased wealth in the nineteenth century enabled women even greater leisure time. The pioneers of female education had to overcome mountains of prejudice. These were hard-headed, common sense groups of middle class women, stirred by a sense of women's duties rather than their rights. Two of these pioneers were Frances Mary Buss and Dorothea Beale. The former founded the North London Collegiate School and Camden School for Girls, while the latter transformed the derelict Cheltenham Ladies College and turned it into a serious educational establishment for the upper and middle classes. They started the process of changing the Victorian ideals, and public day schools for girls were modelled on these schools.

Miss Beale wanted to teach the rudiments of science but had to call it 'physical geography' to escape condemnation. The introduction of physical education caused the most controversy. At this time girls were not supposed to exercise at all. Allowing girls to run and jump, and the removing of corsets

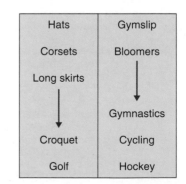

Fig 17.7. As sport for women developed, so did their clothing

was as culturally radical as the unbinding of Japanese women's feet.

The Schools Inquiry Commission 1868 was important for women's education, suggesting that girls' foundation schools would soon become a reality. By 1881, the universities recognised that girls had fulfilled the degree requirements of boys. By 1898, following the Endowed Schools Act, there were 80 endowed girls schools and by 1900 there were 36 girls' public day trust schools. The 1918 Act gave girls the same educational advantages as boys.

The improvement in general education was paralleled by the development of physical education for girls. There was a need for specialist physical education teacher training colleges; the first was established by Miss Bergman in 1885 at Broadhurst Gardens, using the Hampstead Gymnasium. She later moved to Dartford Heath in 1895, where physical education on a full-time specialist basis began. The object of the College was to teach gymnastics and swimming in girls' schools, to conduct outdoor games and to spread the knowledge of physiology and hygiene. Other training colleges soon followed:

- Anstey College, 1899.
- Chelsea College, 1898.
- I.M. Marsh College, 1899.

Miss Bergman was appointed Lady Superintendent of Physical Education in 1881 on the London School Board. The main emphasis came from

**Name. A.B.**
**Entered school, January, 1897.**

| | | DATE | DATE |
|---|---|---|---|
| | | January, 1897. | July, 1897. |
| Age - | | 14 | 14 ¾ |
| Height - | | 4 ft 9.5 in | 4 ft 9 ¾ in |
| Weight - | | 6 st 4.5 lbs | 6 st 7 ¾ lbs |
| Sight - | Right | Very good | Normal |
| | Left | Very good | Normal |
| | Colours | – | – |
| | Glasses | – | – |
| Hearing - | Right | Normal | Normal |
| | Left | Normal | Normal |
| Throat & c - | - | Normal | Normal |
| Breathing - | - | Normal | Normal |
| Lungs - | - | Normal | Normal |
| Heart - | - | Normal | Normal |
| Chest measure - | | 27 ½ | 28 ½ |
| Waist measure - | | 23 | 23 ½ |
| Chest formation - | | Good | Good |
| Spine - | - | Left curve (single) hollow back | Can stand perfectly straight |
| Muscles - | - | Good | Good and equal |
| Arch in foot - | | Normal, slightly flat | Still slightly flat |
| Development - | | Limbs short and broadly built | Does not stand as straight as she can, is lazy. Walks badly. |
| Remarks - | - | Rational corsets two inches too tight. Has never had backache. | |
| Advise - | - | If possible, special private gymnastics for three months. To see me in three months. | No more treatment at present: possibly next year |

**Name. D.D.**
**Entered school, September, 1897.**

| | | | October 1, 1896 | Nov 30, 1896 | Sept 16, 1897 |
|---|---|---|---|---|---|
| Age - | - | | 10 | - | - |
| Height - | - | | 4 ft 7 ½ in | - | - |
| Weight - | - | | 4 st 9 lbs | - | - |
| Sight - | Right | | Normal | - | - |
| | Left | | Normal | - | - |
| | Colours | | Normal | - | - |
| | Glasses | | - | - | - |
| Hearing - | Right | | Normal | - | - |
| | Left | | Deaf from wax | - | - |
| Throat & c - | - | | Tonsils enormous | Tonsils have been | - |
| Breathing - | - | | Nasal, fairly free | cut. R. still large | - |
| Lungs - | - | | Normal | - | - |
| Heart - | - | | Normal | - | - |
| Chest measure - | | | 22 ½ | 23 - | 24 - |
| Waist measure | (over stays) | | 21 | 21 | 21.1 ½ |

ig 17.8. Sheffield High School: physical education record

Swedish gymnastics with its focus on health rather than educational values. Miss Bergman modelled female education on that of the boys and was keen to implement some of the games available in schools. She wrote in the 'Teacher's Encyclopaedia' that the principal games represented in the English girls schools were hockey, cricket, basketball and lacrosse. She also saw the benefit of tennis but felt her students were already reasonably proficient from their social backgrounds.

The Board of Education Syllabuses however paid scant attention to games, and of 11 publications issued between 1919 and 1927, only one was devoted to non-gymnastic activities. The games which were advocated were those where speed of eye, foot and hand combined with team play and cooperation.

Despite these restrictions, women athletes began to emerge in the last quarter of the nineteenth century, such as Lottie Dodd, Mary Outerbridge and Constance Applebee. They tended to shine in sports where they did not have to overcome heavy objects and where spatial barriers and rules prevent bodily contact with the opponent.

Thus, physical activities for girls developed much later than those for boys, and the gradual development was linked to sociological factors and the development of female education in general. When prejudicial attitudes began to change, girls began to participate in activities such as tennis, hockey, gymnastics and cricket. They then developed their activities along similar lines to the boys; they established clubs and entered competitions. There was a concentration on female sports developing separately to boys, partly due to the single sex developments in schools, but social games like tennis allowed a mixing of the sexes.

**ACTIVITY 6**

What characterised those activities deemed suitable for middle class females in their private schools?

# Summary

Nineteenth-century public schools:

- provided an education for the social elite
- developed many traditional activities and games
- gave rise to the cult of athleticism parallel with the muscular Christian movement
- allowed games associated with character-building qualities, for example, courage and loyalty
- female education developed later but was to be based on the boys' system
- female education helped in the growing liberation of women at the end and beginning of the twentieth century
- influenced the development of sport nationally and world-wide through their positions of leadership in society.

# State education

Prior to 1870, the education of the masses had been the responsibility of the parish, and was very inconsistent. The Forster Education Act 1870 was a great milestone in social welfare, as it created a state system of education. There was a developing initiative to build more schools and the Act was the result of some radical changes in social thinking by philanthropists and social reformers.

Ever since the first Board Schools were built in 1870, teachers in the poorest districts were faced with the extreme poverty of many of its pupils. As many as three to four million children were living below the poverty line.

There were two main principles of state education:

1. There should be efficient schools everywhere throughout the United Kingdom.
2. There would be compulsory provision of such schools if and where needed, but not unless proved to be needed.

The existing British schools, foreign schools, under the Foreign Schools Society 1808, and national schools, under the National Schools Society 1811, would continue to provide the bulk of the nation's education, provided they were good enough. The main points of the Education Act were as follows:

- England and Wales divided into 2,500 school districts.
- The Churches were to decide if they needed to build new schools.

- Failing this, a School Board had to be elected by local people, to finance schools from the rates.
- The children would pay a small fee, with an increase in government grants. The very poor could receive free education.
- The school age was not less than five years but no more than 13 years. In London they were exempt at age ten if they passed grade V and were needed to work for the family income.

Mundella's Education Act of 1880 made education compulsory for all children between the ages of five and ten, without exception. In 1893 the compulsory school leaving age was raised to 11 and in 1899 to 12 years.

**ACTIVITY 7**

1. What faults could you find with the Education Act 1870?
2. What effect do you think the Education Acts had on poor children, teachers and parents?
3. Explain why there would have been a problem of non-payment of school fees.

## Overview of the development of state school physical education

The following table outlines the key dates and developments from drill to physical training to physical education within state schools.

Table 17.1.

| Date | Type of activity | Characteristics | Reasons | Problems |
|------|------------------|-----------------|---------|----------|
| 1870 Forster Education Act Terms: State schools/ Elementary schools | Military Drill | • War office exercises<br>• Regimented/straight lines<br>• NCO and teachers command – obey<br>• Dummy weapons<br>• Static/free standing<br>• Boys first – girls later<br>• No age distinctions<br>• Compulsory/centralised<br>• Working class children not required to think/class response no interaction | To train working classes for:<br>• military preparation<br>• work preparation<br>• discipline/obedience<br>• fitness<br>Useful for:<br>• accept place in society<br>• cheap/little space needed | • No education content<br>• Adult exercises for children<br>• Low status NCO |
| 1890 | Swedish drill included gymnastics | • Led by teachers<br>• Free standing<br>• Still instruction-based<br>• Based on scientific principles of the day (knowledge of body) P.H Ling 'father of gymnastics' | Suitable for state schools:<br>• Free standing/cheap/ little space needed<br>• Promote health and fitness<br>• Military preparation<br>• Discipline/social control | • Blamed for lack of fitness of troops in Boer War (1899–1902)<br>• Replaced by Model course |
| 1902–1904 | Model Course devised by Colonel Fox of War Office | As for military drill | Due to poor showing in Boer War | • No educational focus<br>• Adult exercises for children<br>• Did not cater for children's needs<br>• Replaced by gymnastics focus and syllabuses of PT |

| | | | | |
|---|---|---|---|---|
| 1904–1919 | Reinstatement of Swedish gymnastics First Syllabus of P.T. Board of Education | • Therapeutic approach<br>• Recognised different ages/sexes<br>• Improve health<br>• Physical development<br>• Medical basis<br>• Development of games (playground)<br>• Compulsory/centralised based | • Non-trained teachers<br>• Rehabilitation of soldiers<br>• Value of recreation for morale increase, fun/enjoyment<br>• Allow scope for teachers to use some initiative<br>• Still mainly instruction | • Centralised<br>• Little flexibility in content and style of teaching |
| 1914–1918 World War I | | Great War:<br>• Static trench warfare<br>• War glorified<br>• Millions died/followed by flu epidemic<br>1920s General Strike<br>1930s Economic depression/social unrest/unemployment/need for some government recreation provision/social control | | |
| 1933 | Last of the syllabuses of P.T. | • More free movement<br>• More creativity<br>• Group work<br>• More interaction between pupils/teachers<br>• Beginning of decentralisation | • Influence of Laban training of specialist teachers being felt<br>• Women's training influential | |

*(Continued)*

Table 17.1. (*Continued*)

| Date | Type of activity | Characteristics | Reasons | Problems |
|---|---|---|---|---|
| 1939–1945 World War II | | • Mobile fighting – different training of troops led to obstacle/problem solving/ assault courses led to apparatus in primary schools<br>• Bombing = destruction of facilities/re-building programme<br>• Men enlisted/women took over men's jobs<br>• 1944 LEA to provide sport/ recreation facilities in schools | | |
| 1952–1953 | Moving and Growing, Planning the Programme | • For primary schools<br>• Obstacle training from army/ apparatus<br>• Movement training from Centres of Dance<br>   • exploratory<br>   • creative<br>   • individual<br>   • fun<br>• Major games<br>• Skills/dance/movement/ swimming/national dances | • Result in changes in educational thinking<br>• Child-centered approach<br>• Teacher autonomy/ initiative<br>• Decentralised approach<br>• Properly trained teachers | |

| 1950s–1988 | | • Decentralised<br>• Total teacher autonomy/<br>  choice of activities<br>• Rise in use of educational<br>  gymnastics<br>• Heuristic/guidance style of<br>  teaching<br>• Children given a stimulus,<br>  children respond through<br>  movement<br>• Within their capabilities<br>• Imagination/creativity<br>• School recreation facilities<br>  improved since 1944<br>  Education Act | • Society less formal<br>• Fully trained teachers<br>• Educational rather than<br>  physical training<br>• Term 'Physical<br>  Education' now in use | • Government<br>  wanting more<br>  control<br>• Need for more<br>  teacher<br>  accountability<br>• Replaced by<br>  National<br>  Curriculum |
| 1988 | National Curriculum | (*see chapter 10*) | | |

# Characteristics of state schools

Experiences of children at state schools were very different from those of their gentry counterparts. Small buildings with little space and no recreational facilities allied with a philosophy which denied any recreational rights to the working class, and placed its own constraints on the physical activities available to the state school system.

Gymnastics formed the bedrock of early state school physical exercise. Foreign influences, in the form of Swedish and German gymnastics, combined with the English style under Archibald Maclaren. Guts Muths from Germany wrote the first text which gained significant recognition, called *Gymnastik für*

Fig 17.9. Massed drill in the yard of an Elementary School, 1906

Fig 17.10. Drill in a classroom of Townsend Road School, 1905

*die Jugend* in 1793. This was to influence Per Henrik Ling in Sweden and together they can be called the 'fathers of modern gymnastics'. The Schools Boards tended to favour the Swedish system for its free flowing, free standing exercises possibly due to the employment of Swedish inspectors; while the strength-based German gymnastics which utilised apparatus developed within the club structure.

## Swedish gymnastics

Suitable for state schools as it aimed to:

- suit the diverse objectives of physical exercise for the working classes
- promote health and fitness based on scientific principles gaining approval with the School Board
- encourage military preparedness
- improve industrial efficiency/work productivity
- foster social order/social control/discipline of large numbers of children
- promote the harmonious development of the whole body
- be safe and cheap
- be easy to learn and instruct.

The lack of fitness and discipline and the poor general health of the working classes had been noted in the Boer War (1899–1902) and blamed for the heavy loss of life suffered. Swedish gymnastics also came under threat as not being effective enough in improving the fitness of the working classes sufficiently for the hardships of war.

## The model course

### Military drill

A policy of drill and physical training was initiated but had little recreational value. In 1902 the model course was instituted by Colonel Fox of the War Office. The main aim of the course was to:

- improve the fitness of the working classes for military preparation
- increase their familiarity with combat and weapon

• improve discipline and obedience amongst the working classes.

Drill was characterised by commands issued by the teacher or NCOs (non-commissioned officers) to the children who would be standing in uniform military style rows and obeying the commands in unison. Large numbers could be catered for in a small space, and as the movements were free standing and required no apparatus, they were cheap. After 1873 boys and girls received drill.

The problems with this approach were that they were essentially adult exercises for children. They did not take children's needs and physical and mental development into account. There was no educative content and individualism was submerged within a group response. The use of NCOs also reduced the status of the subject as it did not use qualified teachers.

Owing to the problems and concerns over the model course, the Board of Education established a syllabus of physical training in 1904, 1909, 1919, 1927 and 1933. They stressed the physical and educative effect of sport:

• The physical content would have been very much influenced by their primary concern for the medical and physiological base from which they approached the subject. As such the therapeutic effect, the correction of posture faults, and exercises to improve the circulatory systems would have been foremost in their aims.

• The educational aims would try to develop alertness and decision making.

The 1919 Syllabus took into consideration the loss of life of the First World War, and the flu epidemic which hit the country shortly afterwards. Sir George Newman had recognised the beneficial effects of recreational activities in helping to rehabilitate injured soldiers. By 1933 there was more freedom of movement and a more decentralised lesson. This was a recognition of the increasing rights of the working classes and the educational value of group work.

## First World War

The First World War, also known as the Great War, was fought from 1914 to 1918, mainly in Europe and the Middle East in which the allies (France, Russia, Britain, Italy and the United States after 1917) defeated the central powers (Germany, Austria, Hungary and Turkey). Millions were to die in static trench warfare.

Nationalism revealed itself in war. Public schoolmen with their ideals of service were enthusiastic about the coming conflict. It was glorified like a football match and the football match between British and German soldiers at Christmas 1914 set the tone for how sport was to be used during war time. Football grounds were used extensively for recruiting and eventually the Football League bowed to moral pressure to stop fixtures for the duration of the war. Following the war there were hopes of a more equal society due to the massive loss of life sustained from all echelons of society.

# Post-Second World War developments

The Butler Education Act 1944 planned to reform education in Britain. It was a major social reform; it aimed to remove special privileges and ensure equality of opportunity for all. Its main provisions were as follows:

- There were to be 146 local education authorities to replace the previous 300. They were required to provide recreational facilities to specific sizes.

- The school leaving age was to be raised to 15 from 1947.

- All education in state maintained grammar schools was to be free. To attend grammar schools children now needed to pass the eleven plus exam, rather than pay.

- All children would leave the elementary school at 11 and move to a secondary school – either grammar or secondary modern. This was a complete separation of the primary from secondary education, and meant that new schools had to be built.

- More mature forms of physical education were required to suit the higher ages of the children. The HMI (His Majesty's Inspectorate) for PE now reported to the Chief Inspector, not the Chief Medical Officer.

- The 1944 McNair Report gave PE teachers the same status as other teachers.

| I | PLAY RUNNING OR MARCHING | Play or running about. The children should, for a minute or two, be allowed to move about as they please. |
|---|---|---|
| II | PRELIMINARY POSITIONS AND MOVEMENTS | Attention. Standing at ease. Hips firm. Feet close. Neck rest. Feet astride. Foot outward place. Foot forward place. Stepping sideways. Heels raising. Right turn and right half turn. Left turn and left half turn. |
| III | ARM FLEXIONS AND EXTENSIONS | Arms downward stretching. Arms forward stretching. Arms sideways stretching. Arms upward stretching. |
| IV | BALANCE EXERCISES | Heels raising. Knees bending and stretching. Preparation for jumping. Heels raising (neck rest). Heels raising (astride, hips firm). Heels raising (astride, neck rest). Head turning in knees bend position. Knees bending and stretching (astride). Leg sideways raising with arms sideways raising. Knee raising. |
| V | SHOULDER EXERCISES AND LUNGES | Arms forward raising. Arms sideways raising. Hands turning. Arms flinging. Arms forward and upward raising. Arms sideways and upward raising. |
| VI | TRUNK FORWARD AND BACKWARD BENDING | Head backward bending. Trunk forward bending. Trunk backward bending. Trunk forward bending (astride). Trunk backward bending (astride). |
| VII | TRUNK TURNING AND SIDEWAYS BENDING | Head turning. Trunk turning. Trunk turning (astride, neck rest). Trunk turning (feet close, neck rest). Trunk sideways bending. Trunk sideways bending (feet close, hips firm). Trunk sideways bending (feet close, neck rest). |
| VIII | MARCHING | Marking time (from the halt). Turnings while marking time. Quick march. Marking time (from the march). Changing direction. |
| IX | JUMPING | Preparation for jumping. *Note:* Work from this Column should be omitted until above exercise has been taught under IV. |
| X | BREATHING EXERCISES | Breathing exercises without arm movements. With deep breathing, arms sideways raising. |

*Note:* Exercises bracketed should be taken in succession.

Fig 17.11a. 1904 syllabus for physical education

PART ONE

**1**

**Introductory Activity**
1. Free running, at signal, children run to 'homes' in teams. (Four or more marked homes in corners of playground.) All race round, passing outside all the homes, back to places and skip in team rings.
2. Free running, at signal all jump as high as possible and continue running. Brisk walking, finishing in open files, marking time with high knee raising.
3. Aeroplanes. (Following the leaders in teams.)

**Rhythmic Jump**
1. Skip jump on the spot, three low, three high (continuously) (*Low, 2, 3, high, 2, 3, etc.*)
2. Astride jump. *Astride jumping – begin! 1., 2., 1., 2., etc. stop!*
3. Skip jump, four on the spot, four turning round about (8 counts) and repeat turning the opposite way (8 counts).

**2**

1. (Astride [Long sitting]) Trunk bending downward to grasp ankles. Unroll. (*With a jump, feet astride – place! [with straight legs – sit.!] Grasp the ankles – down! With unrolling, trunk upward – stretch! With a jump, feet together – place!*)
2. (Astride [Astride long sitting]) Trunk bending downward to touch one foot with opposite hand.
3. (Feet close [Cross-legged sitting].) Head dropping forward and stretching upward. (*Feet – close!) Head forward – drop! Head upward – stretch! (Crouch) Knee stretching and bending. ('Angry Cats') (Crouch position – down!) Knees – stretch! bend! up! down! etc. stand – up!*

**3**

1. As small as possible, as tall as possible. [(Crook sitting, Back to wall) Single arm swinging forward-upward to touch wall.] [(Crook sitting) Drumming with the feet, loud and soft.]
2. Single arm circling at a wall. (Run and stand with side to wall, nearest hand supported against wall about shoulder height, Circling with free arm. Turn about and repeat.)

**4**

1. Free running like a wooden man. Finish in open files in chain grasp. (One foot forward, heel level with the other toe). Knee full bending and stretching with knees forward. (Several times. Move the back foot forward and repeat.) (Lean standing) Hug the knee. [(Crook lying) Hug the knees. (Lower the feet quietly.)]
2. Running in twos, change to skipping, finish in a double ring facing partner holding hands. Knees full bend. Knee springing. Hands on ground and jump up. *Knees full bend! Knee springing – begin! 1, 2, 1, 2, etc. Stop! Placing the bands on the ground, with a jump stand – up!*
3. Form a ring. Gallop step left and right, at signal, run and stand with side to wall, nearest hand supported against wall (the other arm sideways). Kick the hand. (Turn about, or run to opposite wall and repeat several times with each leg.)

**5**

1. Brisk walking anywhere, change to walking on heels or toes, at signal run to open files facing partners. (Feet-close, Arms forward, Fists touching.) Trunk turning with single elbow bending. (Elbow raised and pulled back. 'Drawing the bow.') (Feet – close! With fists touching, arms forward – raise!) With the right arm, draw the bow – pull! Let go! With the left arm – pull! Let go! etc. Arms – lower!
2. Race to a wall and back to centre line and join right hand across with partner. Tug of war with one hand.
3. (Informal lunge with hand support.) Head and trunk turning with arm raising to point upward. (*Left (right) foot forward with knee bent and left (right) hand on knee (informal lunge) – ready!) With arm raising to point upward, head and trunk to the right, (left) – turn! With arm lowering, forward – turn. (Repeat several times.) With a jump, feet change!*

**6**

**Class Activity**
1. Running, jumping over a series of low ropes. (In ranks of six or eight in stream.)
2. Frog jump anywhere.
3. Free running or skipping, tossing up a ball and catching it. (A ball each. Who can make the greatest number of catches without missing.)

**Group Practices**
1. Running or galloping with a skipping rope. (A rope each.)
2. Running Circle Catch, with a player in the centre, throwing, or bouncing and catching a ball.
3. Sideways jumping over a low rope, partner helping. (Partner astride rope, performer holding partner's hands does several preparatory skip jumps on the spot and then a high jump over the rope landing with knees bent and standing up again.)
4. In two's, crawling or crouch jump through a hoop, held by partner.

**Game**
Odd Man.
Free Touch with 6 or 7 'He's.' ('He's' carry a coloured braid or bean bag as distinguishing mark.).
Tom Tiddler.

**7**

Free walking, practising good position, lead into school.

ig 17.11b. 1933 syllabus for physical education – excerpt

## Effects of Second World War

- destruction of schools/deterioration of equipment
- evacuation of children to rural areas
- male physical education teachers enlisted
- work taken over by older men and women
- more mobile style of fighting
- apparatus for schools from commando training
- movement away from therapeutic and medical value of physical education
- more emphasis on heuristic/guidance style of teaching.

After the war there was an extensive rebuilding programme and facilities were more sophisticated than before. The therapeutic effect of recreational activities was again valued. The commando training during the war had developed the use of obstacle training, and this was how the first apparatus began to appear in schools – scramble nets, rope ladders, mats and frames, hoops, wooden tables and benches.

The 'movement' approach began in physical education lessons; children were required to use their initiative and learn by discovery. This also demanded new teaching methods and there was the development of a more heuristic style which placed the teacher in the role of guiding the children rather than being purely instructional.

The influence of Isadora Duncan and Laban with their form of dance using the body as an expressive medium, was taken up by women teachers. Modern Educational Dance 1948 gave 16 basic movement themes and rudiments of free dance technique and space orientation. The word 'movement' came to reflect the 1940s and 1950s as 'posture' had reflected the 1930s.

## Moving and Growing, and Planning the Programme

These two publications were issued by the Ministry of Education in 1952 and 1953 respectively. They replaced the old syllabuses and were to be implemented in primary schools. They combined the two influences of:

- obstacle training from the army
- movement training from centres of dance.

Running parallel to these changes were:

- Circuit training (devised by G T Adamson and R E Morgan at the University of Leeds)
- Weight training – progressive resistance exercises
- Outward Bound Schools promoting adventurous activities to develop the personality within the natural environment in challenging conditions.

These publications developed as a result of changes in educational thinking which was to make learning stem from a more child-centred approach. The physical education teacher was now more autonomous with personal control over the physical education syllabus. The activities included agility, playground and more major game skills, dance and movement to music, national dances and swimming. The key words which separate them from earlier forms of physical activity in state schools are:

- exploratory
- creative
- individual
- fun.

## Educational gymnastics

During the 1950s to the 1970s, there was a significant rise in the uses of modern educational gymnastics. In this type of activity children were encouraged to respond with movement to a stimulus, or movement problem. For example, a teacher may set a task of finding as many different ways to travel across, along or over a bench. The child would be required to use a certain

Fig 17.12. Physical education in the 1950s

| 1870 | Drill | centralised |
|------|-------|-------------|
| 1904–1933 | Syllabuses of Physical Training | centralised |
| 1933–1988 | Physical Education teachers devise syllabus | decentralised |
| 1988+ | National Curriculum | more centralised |

Fig 17.13. Syllabus development of Physical Education in the United Kingdom

**ACTIVITY 10**

Trace the involvement of government in education from 1870 to the present day. Concentrate on political aspects like centralisation policies, the intended aims of education and the use made of physical activities. Consider also the social factors operating at each stage.

amount of imagination and creativity to answer the task.

However, there would be no right or wrong solution. The child was not forced to perform cartwheels but they could answer the task by responding with movements within their capabilities and therefore would develop confidence as they achieved a level of success.

This way very much a heuristic style of teaching as opposed to the more didactic and prescribed approach of the early twentieth century.

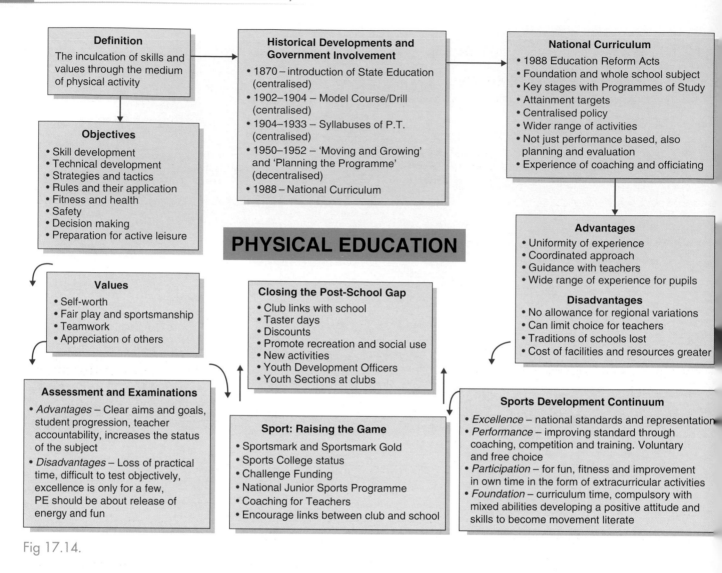

**Definition**
The inculcation of skills and values through the medium of physical activity

**Objectives**
- Skill development
- Technical development
- Strategies and tactics
- Rules and their application
- Fitness and health
- Safety
- Decision making
- Preparation for active leisure

**Values**
- Self-worth
- Fair play and sportsmanship
- Teamwork
- Appreciation of others

**Historical Developments and Government Involvement**
- 1870 – introduction of State Education (centralised)
- 1902–1904 – Model Course/Drill (centralised)
- 1904–1933 – Syllabuses of P.T. (centralised)
- 1950–1952 – 'Moving and Growing' and 'Planning the Programme' (decentralised)
- 1988 – National Curriculum

**PHYSICAL EDUCATION**

**Closing the Post-School Gap**
- Club links with school
- Taster days
- Discounts
- Promote recreation and social use
- New activities
- Youth Development Officers
- Youth Sections at clubs

**National Curriculum**
- 1988 Education Reform Acts
- Foundation and whole school subject
- Key stages with Programmes of Study
- Attainment targets
- Centralised policy
- Wider range of activities
- Not just performance based, also planning and evaluation
- Experience of coaching and officiating

**Advantages**
- Uniformity of experience
- Coordinated approach
- Guidance with teachers
- Wide range of experience for pupils

**Disadvantages**
- No allowance for regional variations
- Can limit choice for teachers
- Traditions of schools lost
- Cost of facilities and resources greater

**Assessment and Examinations**
- *Advantages* – Clear aims and goals, student progression, teacher accountability, increases the status of the subject
- *Disadvantages* – Loss of practical time, difficult to test objectively, excellence is only for a few, PE should be about release of energy and fun

**Sport: Raising the Game**
- Sportsmark and Sportsmark Gold
- Sports College status
- Challenge Funding
- National Junior Sports Programme
- Coaching for Teachers
- Encourage links between club and school

**Sports Development Continuum**
- *Excellence* – national standards and representation
- *Performance* – improving standard through coaching, competition and training. Voluntary and free choice
- *Participation* – for fun, fitness and improvement in own time in the form of extracurricular activities
- *Foundation* – curriculum time, compulsory with mixed abilities developing a positive attitude and skills to become movement literate

Fig 17.14.

# Summary

- Physical activity in state schools at the end of the nineteenth century concentrated on Military Drill and Swedish gymnastics.

- Emphasis was placed on activities suitable for the poor conditions in state schools and discipline of the working classes.

Disenchantment with these systems led to:

- the Board of Education producing syllabuses in the first three decades of the twentieth century which schools were required to follow.

- the syllabuses laid out the content and style of teaching as a guideline for teachers to follow

- strong emphasis was placed on teacher authority.

- there was still very limited major games teaching.

Syllabuses became defunct with the improvements in teacher training.

- The publications of Planning the Programme and Moving and Growing reflected the change in emphasis from purely physical and organic developments to a focus on the development of the 'whole' child through the Movement approach.

- The use of different terms over the years (drill, physical training and then physical education) reflect the gradual development of certain ideas. Changes occurred in content as well as the relationship between the teacher and the class.

# Review Questions

## History of Physical Education

1. What were the characteristics of the nineteenth-century public schools and the state schools?

2. Name the nine Barbarian schools.

3. What is the significance of the terms 'Barbarian' and 'Philistine' in relation to the nineteenth-century public schools?

4. Describe the process in the technical development of activities in the public schools.

5. Define the term 'athleticism' and discuss its influence on society.

6. What influence did the universities bring to bear in the development of sports?

7. Why was athleticism acceptable to the middle classes?

8. What is meant by the term 'self-government' in relation to the organisation of games in the nineteenth-century public schools? Give examples of how this system operated.

9. What influence did Miss Buss, Miss Beale and Madame Bergman Osterberg have on female education?

0. In what way was gymnastics used in state schools?

# PSYCHOLOGICAL ASPECTS
# OF SPORT AND PE

# 3

# INTRODUCTION

Since the second half of the twentieth century the status of sport and physical education within society has increased tremendously. This has been linked, in the main, to developing media, commercial and political interest and has resulted in increased pressure and demands being placed on sports performers. While this in turn has led to major improvements in both technological and physiological preparation it has also meant that more recognition has been given to the need to prepare performers psychologically.

It has long been recognised that even if a performer is physically trained to near perfection and supported by the best equipment and technology available this does not guarantee an excellent performance or victory. Research has been carried out by sports psychologists since the early 1960s in order to help us to:

- **understand** – learning/behaviour/performance and situations in sport

- **explain** – learning/behaviour/performance or factors that influence performance/events in a systematic manner

- **predict** – potential learning/behaviour/events or outcomes/performance

- **influence/control** – potential learning/behaviour/performance or events.

When observing sport, commentators and the media often use simplistic terms to explain why certain things happen. Phrases like 'there has been a psychological shift in the game', a performer is 'coping with pressure', a performer has been 'psyched out of the game', a performer has the 'wrong temperament', are all used, along with many others, to explain variations in performance.

Although such phrases are used often without a real understanding of what they mean, they do at least indicate the importance and influence of psychological factors within the context of sport and physical education. As you read through the next ten chapters you will gain a greater insight into the underlying theories and concepts which underpin the behaviour of both individuals and groups at all levels of sport. You will also gain a clearer understanding of the various strategies which sports psychologists have used to help develop and prepare performers individually or in groups (teams) to cope with the increased pressures of modern sport. It is generally recognised that the traditional approach to sport psychology (the pre-competition 'rousing pep-talk', the 'up and at them' approach) is of very little 'real' long-term value and in some cases could even be considered 'counterproductive', perhaps leading to poor performance in the short term.

In the same way that an athlete's physical and skills preparation cannot be developed overnight, psychological preparation needs to be developed over a prolonged period of time in order to be effective and retain long-term value. Developing your knowledge of sports psychology should give you a better understanding of the 'causes' and 'effects' of various psychological phenomena which underpin learning and performance in sport.

After reading this whole section on sport psychology you will gain a better understanding of:

1. The variety of factors, principles and theories that can affect the learning process during skill development.

2. Individuals' differences and the resulting influence on sports performance.

3. Social influences and their specific and general effect on both individual, group performers and participants.

4. Management of psychological effects in order to optimise performance.

# 18. The Nature of Skilled Performance

**Chapter introduction**

This chapter will give you a basic understanding of the terminology that is used by those involved in physical education and sport in relation to skill development and learning. You should be able to:

- understand the terminology of skill development and learning
- use it in the correct context
- relate it to practical examples.

Here is a list of the key terms to be covered in this chapter. It is important that you understand them and begin to use these in both your observation/analysis as well as your classroom discussions.

- Motor skill
- Perceptual skill
- Cognitive skill
- Simple skill
- Complex skill
- Ability

- Psychomotor ability
- Gross motor ability
- Perceptual ability
- Continuum
- Gross and fine skills
- Discrete, continuous, serial skills

- Self paced/externally paced skills
- Open/closed skills
- High/low cognitive skills
- Feedback

Once you have read this chapter you should gain a working understanding of:

- the phrase **skilled performance**
- the phrase **acquisition of skill**
- the terms **skill** and **ability**.

## What is skilled performance?

### ACTIVITY 1

In most occupations, sports, daily activities and in the development stages of young children the results of skill learning are evident.
- Discuss with your fellow students what you think makes a human activity a skilled performance.
- Try to come up with a short list of examples from various walks of life.

In discussion with your fellow students you will all have been able to suggest various examples of skilled performances, recognising perhaps that a:

- concert pianist may be said to be performing skilfully
- ballet dancer's coordination and timing are skilful
- perfect pass by a quarterback in American football is skilful
- long range three point score in basketball is skilful

- well-executed off drive in cricket is skilful
- gymnast performing a vault in the Olympic Games is skilful
- pole vaulter completing a vault is skilful
- potter using a potting wheel is skilful.

In other words we can all recognise the outcome or the end product of a skilful performance. However, as students of physical education and sport you need to know:

- how does this end product come about?

What process underlies the acquisition of skill and control of movement? How is skill acquired? What factors influence its attainment and how is it retained? The following chapters will help you develop a better understanding of the underlying processes involved in acquiring skill.

As a student of physical education and sport you should then be able to:

1. Analyse movement situations.
2. Recognise good practice and performance.
3. Recognise any faults or problems.
4. Solve any problems of how to improve skill levels and overall performance.

As you read through these chapters you will realise that the study of the acquisition of skill is not an exact science. There are no 100% 'correct' or right ways of acquiring skill. Having been made aware of the various related theories, concepts, principles and methods you should be able to:

- use this information to support your understanding
- develop your own ideas
- think about the implications for teaching and coaching.

# Using the term 'skill'

You may have noticed in the list of examples given or in your own discussions that the word 'skill' can be used in two slightly different ways. We can use the word to relate to skill as an act or task or use it as an indicator of quality of performance.

## Skill as an act or task

The word in this context is used to denote an act or a task that has a specific aim or goal to achieve, for instance a gymnast performing a vault. Further examples are:

- taking a penalty flick in hockey
- shooting a free shot after a foul in basketball
- serving in tennis.

If we observed players carrying out any of the examples given above on a regular basis and they were achieving a high percentage success rate then we would consider them as being skilful players. The use of the word in this context refers to a physical movement, action or task, involving some or all of the body, that a person is trying to carry out in a technically correct manner. Thus skill can be seen as goal directed behaviour.

## Skill as an indicator of quality of performance

The word in this context is probably a little more ambiguous than skill as an act or task. The word 'well' added to the description of the skill infers a qualitative judgement of the skill being made by you as the observer, for instance you may remark on a well-executed off drive during a cricket match. Very often we make judgements between players comparing performances, looking at players' achievements in the context of the class or school team or against set criteria. Thus we measure or assess in either relative or absolute terms. What you have to understand however, is: What makes it a 'well' performed skill? After reading through the rest of this chapter you should be able to understand, explain and apply the main criteria that are used to judge whether a performer is skilful or not.

## Defining different types of skill

Psychologists have considered different types of skill, trying to differentiate for instance between

Fig 18.1. A gymnastic performance is measured against set criteria (absolute)

Fig 18.2. Performance in a race is measured in relative terms

Fig 18.3. National league basketball player dribbling

motor skills and verbal skills. Examples of three different types of skill are:

1. **Intellectual skills or cognitive skills**
   Skills which involve the use of a person's mental powers, eg, problem solving, verbal reasoning (verbal skill).

2. **Perceptive skills**
   Interpreting and making sense of information coming in via the senses.

3. **Motor skills**
   Smoothly executing physical movements and responses.

When National league basketball players are performing a 'skilful' dribble and 'driving' the basket they are not only showing technically good movements (ie, showing motor skill) but in carrying out the action the player has had to make many decisions including:

- whether to dribble or pass
- how to dribble
- position of opposition
- position of own team mates
- context of game
- situation in game – winning or losing?
- time in game (how long to go?)
- do we need to score or keep the ball?
- what are the odds of making the dribble, drive and possible shot?

ACTIVITY 2

Consider two other activities in addition to fig 18.3. For each activity, make a list of the things the performer is having to consider and take into account.

This obviously involves a whole host of both cognitive skills and perceptual skills, as only after having taken into account all the various information (cues, signals, stimuli) being received from around them can a basketball player then carry out the necessary motor skill to any degree of proficiency. Therefore, as we can see, although many psychologists have tried to define the ways in which motor, cognitive and perceptual skills are independent of one another, from a physical educational and sporting point of view when we talk of skill we usually mean a combination of all three areas. Skill is therefore more than just technical excellence. In your further reading around this topic you will come across the phrase 'perceptual motor skills' or very often just 'motor skills' – the perceptual or cognitive involvement is usually implied.

## Complex skills and simple skills

In your consideration and discussions for activity 2 you will have concluded that in carrying out movement we are rarely just 'doing'. Some level of thought and decision making has usually taken place. However, as you develop your understanding in this area you will come to realise that certain sporting activities and physical movements require *more* thought, conscious control and decision making than others. These are known as complex skills whereas those activities and movements requiring very little conscious thought or decision making and only basic movement patterns are called simple skills (refer to information processing).

## Acquisition of skill

In the phrase 'acquisition of skill' the word 'acquisition' infers that skill is something that you can gain as opposed to something that you already have.

*'Skill is said to be gained through learning. Skill is said to be learned behaviour!'*

(B. Knapp)

# Definitions of skill

You will have a better understanding of the nature of skill if you consider a variety of definitions and see how those definitions have developed. The definitions given below emphasise the following aspects of skill:

## Definition 1

Skill involves:

- excellent performance (high quality)
- bringing together various abilities to a lesser or greater degree (dependent on which task) for a specific movement to be carried out.

## Definition 2

Skill involves:

- the intention to do it, it is not just luck; there must be a conscious decision and effort.

## Definition 3

Skill involves:

- learned ability – learning through practice and experience to use the appropriate innate abilities (See Abilities)
- pre-determined results – you have an aim to achieve
- maximum certainty – you are consistent in your achievement of success

In your group either individually or in twos and threes select one of the following definitions and consider what it is trying to imply or say and then feed back your understanding of the definition to the rest of the class.

- Professor G.P. Meredith, *Information and Skill*
  'Excellence of performance – the successful integration of a hierarchy of abilities (all the abilities we have) appropriate to a given task under given conditions.'

- Oldfield, *The Analysis of Human Skill* – New Biology
  'The behaviour which tends to eliminate the discrepancy between intention and performance.'

- Guthrie, from *Skills in Sport:* modified by B. Knapp
  'The learned ability to bring about pre-determined results with maximum certainty often with the minimum outlay of time, energy or both.'

- Argyle and Kendon, *The Experimental Analysis of Social Performance*
  'An organised, coordinated activity in relation to an object or a situation which involves a whole chain of sensory, central and motor mechanisms.'

- M. Robb, *The Dynamics of Skill Acquisition*
  'While the task can be physical or mental, one generally thinks of a skill as some type of manipulative efficiency. A skilled movement is one in which a predetermined objective is accomplished with maximum efficiency and with a minimum outlay of energy. A skilful movement does not just happen. There must be a conscious effort on the part of the performer in order to execute a skill.'

- R. Magill, *Motor Learning: Concepts and Applications*
  'An act or a task that has a goal to achieve and that requires voluntary body or limb movements to be properly performed.'

- minimum outlay of time and energy – you are performing the actions efficiently, you are not wasting time or energy.

## Definition 4

Skill involves:

- sensory-mechanisms – taking in information via the various receptor systems, eg, senses.

- central-mechanisms – brain (interpretations and decision making).

- motor-mechanisms – nerves and muscles system being used to create movement – but basically suggests that skills involve the use of the senses to detect and take in information, the brain to interpret the information and make decisions according to what you know about the situation, and the nervous system together with muscles to work the various parts of the body in order to carry out the action.

## Definition 5

This definition basically combines several main aspects of the others.

# Skill is a learned behaviour

From your discussions and feedback sessions relating to activity 3 you will have realised that the term 'skill' is a complex term to define. Any definition should, however, involve several important points. The better-known definitions which tend to be referred to are the ones by B. Knapp (after Guthrie), R. Magill, and M. Robb.

Overall you can see that, according to these various definitions, skill involves learning via practice and experience. A skilled performer learns to be effective and efficient in:

- achieving a well-defined objective (goal directed)

- maximising – being consistently successful (can be repeated)

- minimising – maintaining the physical and mental energy demands of performance at an

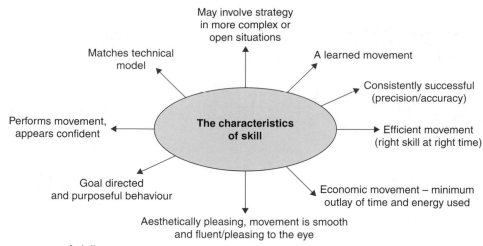

Fig 18.4. The characteristics of skill

optimum level (aesthetically pleasing, coordinated, precise, decisions)

- minimising – taking only the minimum time required (well timed).

Thus a skilful performer has gone through some form of '**learning process**'. There is intention in their performance ie, it is not just luck. It is not enough just to say they are accurate and have good technique, the key word is that they are '**consistent**'. The performance is also carried out '**efficiently**', ie, not wasting time or energy.

## Using the term 'ability'

It is important at this stage to consider another term which is very often synonymous with the word skill

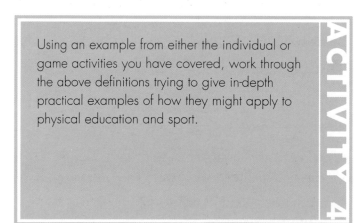

Using an example from either the individual or game activities you have covered, work through the above definitions trying to give in-depth practical examples of how they might apply to physical education and sport.

ACTIVITY 4

and is often used in definitions of skilled behaviour. The term is ability.

In your discussions of what constitutes skill, the term ability has probably often been used in the wrong context. Often in a variety of sports, players from abroad are referred to as having higher levels of ability than our 'home' developed players, when what we mean is that their skills in terms of technique are of a higher quality. It is the word 'ability' which is being used in the wrong context. We often talk of players as having 'lots of ability' when what we mean is they have developed high levels of skill.

## Definitions and characteristics of ability

It is important that you understand the differences between skill and abilities. The study of abilities comes under the umbrella of 'differential psychology'

*'Motor abilities are relatively enduring traits which are generally stable qualities or factors that help a person carry out a particular act.'*

(E. Fleishman)

*'Motor abilities are innate inherited traits that determine an individual's coordination, balance, agility and speed of reactions.'*

(R. Arnot and C. Gaines)

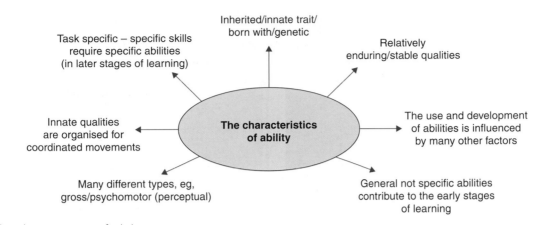

**Fig 18.5.** The characteristics of ability

It is sufficient at this stage for you to realise that abilities are said to be stable and enduring capacities or qualities and characteristics that a person has within themselves. A person is therefore born with these qualities. Abilities are said to be innate, inherited traits, factors that help, for instance, a person's agility, coordination, balance and speed of reactions.

A person trying to carry out a sporting activity will learn to use these underlying innate qualities or characteristics in an organised way in order to carry out coordinated movement.

## Taxonomy of human perceptual motor abilities – Fleishman, 1972

The work of Fleishman (1972), which is one of the better-known pieces of research, developed a taxonomy of human perceptual motor abilities. He carried out extensive testing of over 200 tasks, the results of which led him to propose that there seemed to be 11 identifiable and measurable perceptual motor abilities. In addition he identified nine physical proficiency abilities. These differed from perceptual motor abilities in that they are more generally related to gross physical performance.

1. **Limb coordination** – the ability to coordinate the movement of a number of limbs simultaneously.

2. **Control precision** – the ability to make highly controlled and precise muscular adjustments where large muscle groups are involved.

3. **Response orientation** – the ability to select rapidly where a response should be made, as in a choice reaction time situation.

4. **Reaction time** – the ability to respond rapidly to a stimulus when it appears.

5. **Speed of arm movement** – the ability to make a gross, rapid arm movement.

6. **Rate control** – the ability to change speed and direction of response with precise timing, as in following a continuously moving target.

7. **Manual dexterity** – the ability to make skilful, well-directed arm hand movements, when manipulating objects under speed conditions.

8. **Finger dexterity** – the ability to perform skilful controlled manipulations of tiny objects involving primarily the fingers.

9. **Arm hand steadiness** – the ability to make precise arm, hand positioning movements where strength and speed are minimally involved.

10. **Wrist finger speed** – the ability to move the wrist and fingers rapidly, as in a tapping task.

11. **Aiming** – the ability to aim precisely at a small object in space.

# Fleishman's proficiency abilities

Typically these more general athletic abilities could be considered physical fitness abilities.

1. **Static strength** – maximum force exerted against an external object.

2. **Dynamic strength** – muscular endurance in exerting force repeatedly, eg, pull ups.

3. **Explosive strength** – the ability to mobilise energy effectively for bursts of muscular effort, eg, high jump.

4. **Trunk strength** – strength of the trunk muscles.

5. **Extent flexibility** – the ability to flex or stretch the trunk and back muscles.

6. **Dynamic flexibility** – the ability to make repeated, rapid trunk flexing movements as in a series of stand and touch toes stretch and touch toes.

7. **Gross body coordination** – the ability to coordinate the action of several parts of the body while the body is in motion.

8. **Gross body equilibrium** – the ability to maintain balance without visual cues.

9. **Stamina** – the capacity to sustain maximum effort requiring cardiovascular effort, eg, a long distance run.

The above lists by Fleishman are not all embracing but are the result of his work in trying to identify and reduce to manageable and reasonable proportions the extensive list of abilities that have been identified by various research. Guildford's earlier work in 1958, for instance, identified abilities such as:

- impulsion
- speed
- static precision
- coordination
- flexibility.

Additional further abilities which have not been included by Fleishman are such things as:

- **Static balance** – the ability to balance on a stable surface when no locomotor movement is required.

- **Dynamic balance** – the ability to balance on a moving surface or to balance while involved in locomotion.

- **Visual activity** – the ability to see clearly and precisely.

- **Visual tracking** – the ability visually to follow a moving object.

- **Eye–hand coordination** – the ability to perform skills requiring vision.

- **Eye–foot coordination** and the precise use of hands or feet.

These and others are, however, equally acceptable abilities as they are measurable and quantifiable. In your additional background reading and task analysis you will probably come across many more. It is important to understand that all individuals possess all the above abilities identified, however we do not all possess them at equal or similar levels. If a person has not got the appropriate levels of specific abilities needed for a specific sport then the odds against them making it to the top in that sport may be high. But this does not mean that such a person has to give up all together. Practically no one is born with a package of superior abilities large enough to make for an overall athletic ability. Although researchers have tried to identify the possibilities of an 'all round general athletic ability' results have actually tended to support the view that specific skills require specific abilities.

However, while we are born with certain levels of abilities they can be trained and improved in specific situations.

# Ability is task specific

Certain skills may use different sets of abilities or they may use the same abilities put together in a different order. Also abilities are not necessarily linked or related; for example a person having high levels of trunk strength may not necessarily have high levels of explosive strength. If a person is good at throwing a cricket ball there is no guarantee that they will be good at throwing a basketball or a javelin. In other words the fact that a person does not have the level of abilities necessary to succeed at one activity does not mean that they do not have the potential to succeed in another activity requiring slightly different abilities or levels.

Performers learn to combine and use abilities in specific situations and for carrying out specific skills.

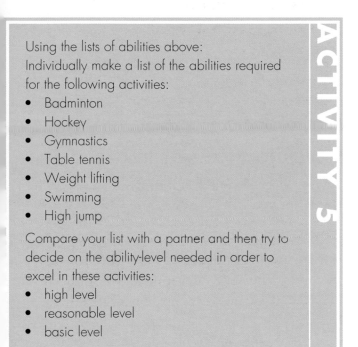

Using the lists of abilities above:
Individually make a list of the abilities required for the following activities:
- Badminton
- Hockey
- Gymnastics
- Table tennis
- Weight lifting
- Swimming
- High jump

Compare your list with a partner and then try to decide on the ability-level needed in order to excel in these activities:
- high level
- reasonable level
- basic level

For example, high jumpers need high levels of explosive strength.

In your discussions you will have found that while there is a certain degree of overlap between the requirements of activities, eg, strength, coordination and speed, when you came to analyse the level and type of abilities required they became much more specific to the sport being considered, eg, different types of strength. Dynamic strength is used in weight lifting but explosive strength in the high jump.

# The implications for teaching and coaching

1. What we have to ensure that we do not assume from this is that two people cannot achieve similar standards of performance in a physical activity because of different levels of genetically determined abilities. If one person, possibly with lower levels of specific abilities, is given the opportunity at an early age to use their abilities (eg, parents take them to the local sports club) and they are prepared to work hard learning to use their abilities in an appropriate manner then they could achieve a level of proficiency similar to a person who has not had the opportunity or is unwilling to develop higher levels of innate abilities.

2. By analysing the types of abilities needed for specific sports teachers and coaches could ensure that their students experienced the appropriate types of practice necessary for these abilities to be developed more fully. Since balance is an essential ability, required for the successful completion of a wide variety of complex or difficult skills, it would appear relevant for a PE programme in infant and junior schools to provide the opportunity for children to develop their balance ability in a variety of situations.

3. Teachers and coaches should ensure that children who show a high inherited potential for sports are not disadvantaged from an early age as a possible result of their personality and social environment. Some young children appear to display natural athletic tendencies often as a result of being initially bigger and stronger. This can result in early success, greater motivation, higher teacher expectations and further development. However, without early success even children with higher levels of innate ability will avoid continued participation in sport, thus building up what has been termed a skill deficit. This has obvious sociocultural implications for a child's future interest in sport.

4. The role of ability identification as predictors of potential achievements in learners has to be considered carefully. Consider the implications, both good and bad, if we were able to measure a beginner's abilities and then 'channel' them into the appropriate sport. Prediction studies have shown, however, that abilities which are

important at the early stages of learning (cognitive phase) are not necessarily the same as those which are important at the more advanced stages of learning (autonomous phase). For example, Fleishman's and Rich's 1963 work suggest that:

- a greater number of abilities (more general to the task) contribute to learning a task in the early stages than do so later on

- different and fewer abilities (more specific to the task) contribute more and more to success with practice.

5. The ability to take in information and make sense of it, in other words 'perceptual ability' involving cue selection, concentration, attention along with vision spatial orientation, are more important at the early stages of learning than later when learning is replaced more by kinaesthesis.

Verbal comprehension is also very important at the early stages of learning as a person is precluded if they cannot understand instructions or what is being asked of them.

It is therefore generally understood that while testing a person's abilities to assess future potential can be useful, testing of this kind is not accurate and should not be used in isolation.

There are many other factors psychological, physiological as well as sociocultural that can influence future performance levels. For example:

- motivation levels – attitude
- opportunity for early success
- amount of previous encouragement given
- coach/staff/parental expectations/demands/interest
- opportunity for practice
- availability of facilities/coaching/finance
- maturational age
- personality
- previous experience
- sociocultural background.

**ACTIVITY 6**

Consider the following situation and answer the question.

A coach has a large class for basketball. In order to achieve what they feel might be more effective teaching, they decide to divide the class up into smaller groups. The whole class is first asked to carry out various related tasks, eg, bouncing, catching, dribbling, shooting. As a result of observing the way people carried out these tasks the coach splits the class into groups according to each person's initial performance levels.

What are the possible implications of this approach for the whole class's future success at basketball?

## Classification of skills

Having worked your way through the chapter to this point you will be aware of:

- what constitutes a skill
- how specific skills are underpinned by the appropriate abilities.

This gives you a better understanding of the implications for teaching and coaching the acquisition of skills in the widest sense. You will have realised that different skills require different kinds and amounts of abilities and also possibly different patterns. In the same way in which we analyse skills to assess which different abilities are needed we can also analyse skills in relation to things they have in common. Looking at skills in terms of the characteristics that they have in common is called classification of skill and is part of the overall process of task analysis. By classifying skills that are involved in sporting activities:

- a teacher or coach is enabled to generalise across groups of skills and apply major concepts, theories and principles of learning to types of skills

- a teacher or coach will not necessarily have to consider each specific skill in a unique way

- a teacher or coach will be able to select the appropriate starting point for a learner

- the identification of the appropriate types of practice conditions required will be made easier, eg, whole, part, whole, massed or distributed (see Types of practice). Similar methods can be applied to skill within the same groupings

- the timing and types of instruction to be given is clarified, eg, verbal feedback, ongoing or terminal

- the detection and solving of any problems the learner may be facing is made easier

- a teacher or coach would probably not use the various classifications in isolation but move from one to another, or combine aspects of all of them at the appropriate time.

# Classification systems

Several different ways of classifying or grouping skills have been developed in order to try to help our understanding of motor skills. In order to solve the problem of listing skills under certain headings which could lead to confusion over where to list skills made up of several different aspects, the use of a **continuum** was devised. A continuum is an imaginary line between two extremes. This enables you to analyse skills and place them between two given extremities according to how they match the analysis criteria being applied.

Criteria                Criteria
   A                      B

## Gross and Fine classification

If you used the Gross–Fine classification given in Table 18.1 in terms purely of headings for lists of skills the criteria for analysing the skills would derive from the 'degree of bodily involvement' or the precision of movement.

As you can see from table 18.1, some skills do not fall easily into specific categories nor can they be listed exclusively under exact headings.

Darts, spin bowling and serving in a game of badminton all involve wrist finger speed and dexterity along with aiming accuracy which would suggest they should be taught as a fine skill. In addition however, in order for these small movements to be made, larger movements – particularly in spin bowling – have also had to be made which would suggest they

Table 18.1. Gross–fine skill classification

| Gross skills | Fine skills |
|---|---|
| • Involve large muscle movements | • Involve small muscle movements |
| • Major bodily movements skills associated with:<br>strength<br>endurance<br>power | • Small bodily movements skills associated with:<br>speed<br>accuracy<br>efficiency |
| • For instance<br>walking<br>running<br>jumping<br>kicking a football | • Associated more with industrial motor skills:<br>writing<br>painting<br>sewing |
| ?←Darts→? ||
| ?←Spin Bowling→? ||
| ?←Badminton→? ||

should be taught as a gross skill. Therefore the use of exact lists is not always possible when analysing what a skill is made up of. Hence the use of a continuum where the complex nature of motor skills can be taken into consideration; they can be placed on the continuum somewhere between the two extremes according to the degree of similarity they have to the various criteria being applied.

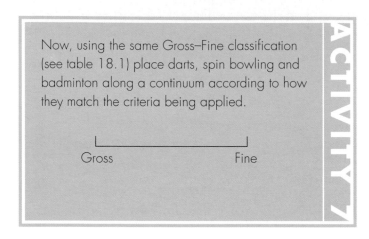

Now, using the same Gross–Fine classification (see table 18.1) place darts, spin bowling and badminton along a continuum according to how they match the criteria being applied.

Gross                          Fine

### The discrete serial, continuous continuum

This classification is made on the basis of how clearly defined the beginning and end of the skill is.

The use of this type of continuum has been popularised by researchers viewing performance from a human engineering perspective.

*Continuous skills:*

- should be practised as a whole (see section on Practice)
- are difficult to break into subroutines
- may lose the flow of the movement if broken down
- need kinaesthetic awareness (see information processing).

Kinaesthetic awareness is linked to the 'feel' or level of intrinsic feedback (internal) provided as a result of movements being correct or incorrect. This is provided via proprioceptors.

### The pacing continuum

This classification is based on the degree of control that the performer has over the movement or skill being carried out, ie, not governed by the actions of others. This classification is synonymous with the next classification, open and closed.

Table 18.2. The discrete, serial, continuous continuum

| DISCRETE | SERIAL | CONTINUOUS |
|---|---|---|
| skills | skills | skills |
| Criteria | Criteria | Criteria |
| • Well-defined beginning and end<br>• Usually brief in nature a single specific skill<br>• If skill is repeated have to start at beginning eg,<br> – a basketball free throw<br> – kicking a ball<br> – hitting, catching<br> – diving<br> – vaulting | • A number of discrete skills put together to make a sequence or series<br>• The order the distinct elements are put together is very important<br>• Each movement is both a stimulus and response eg,<br> – gymnastic routine<br> – triple jump<br> – high jump | • Poorly defined beginning and end<br>• Activity continues for an unspecified time – (ongoing)<br>• The end of one movement is the beginning of the next repetition eg,<br> – swimming<br> – running<br> – cycling |

Using the information in table 18.2 decide where the following activities fit on the continuum. Make sure you can justify your decision.

| DISCRETE | SERIAL | CONTINUOUS |
|---|---|---|
| • Hockey pass | • Serve in tennis | • Throw in at football |
| • Long jump | • Throwing a javelin | • Penalty flick in hockey |
| • Dance routine | • Skiing | • Aerobics |
| • 1500 m run | • Trampoline routine | • Penalty corner routine in hockey |

## The open/closed continuum

This is one of the better-known classifications and is based on the stability of the environment or situation in which the skill is being performed. More recently, with the emphasis moving towards information processing modules, classifications have been suggested that consider the degree of cognitive/perceptual involvement. Do skills have higher or lower levels?

Examples of high cognitive skills are:

• chess

• batting in cricket

• strategies/tactics.

Table 18.3. The pacing continuum

| Self paced/ Internal paced skills | Externally paced skills |
|---|---|
| • Performer controls the rate at which the activity is carried out | • Action is determined by external sources |
| • Performer decides when to initiate movement | • Involves the performer in reaction |
| • Involves pro-action | • More open skill eg, <br> – white water canocing <br> – receiving a serve in tennis |
| • More closed skill eg, <br> – shot put <br> – forward roll | |

## Decision making is critical

Examples of low cognitive/motor skills are:

• walking

• power lifting.

Table 18.4. The open/closed continuum

| Closed skills | Open skills |
|---|---|
| • Not affected by the environment | • Very much affected by the unstable changing environment |
| • Stable fixed environment (space/ time) predictable | • Externally paced environment |
| • Internally/self paced predominantly habitual stereotyped movements eg, <br> – headstand in gymnastics <br> – weight lifting | • Predominantly perceptual movement patterns require adjustment (adaptation) |
| | • Very often rapid adjustments, variations of skill needed eg, <br> – passing/receiving in netball or basketball <br> – tackling rugby |

# Key words

## Open/externally paced skills

'At every instant the motor activity must be regulated by and appropriate to the external situation.' (B. Knapp, 1972)

## Closed/skills

'Conformity to a prescribed standard sequence of motor acts is all important.' (H. Whiting, 1969)

---

**ACTIVITY 9**

Draw an open–closed continuum and place the following skills on it:

Free shot in basketball; serve in tennis; serve in badminton; dribbling within a game of football; rugby tackle; running 1500 m race; sailing; backhand defensive shot in table tennis; judo.

---

Primary determinant of success is the quality of movement.

Other researchers have considered the types and timing of feedback availability, for instance:

- intrinsic feedback (high or low levels available)
- ongoing/concurrent
- terminal
- delayed/immediate.

For example

No                       Yes

Intrinsic FB

Other research has considered the 'coherence' of a skill. This looks at whether a skill can be broken

---

down into parts (sub-routines) or whether it has to be taught as a whole. For example,

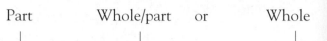

Part         Whole/part   or       Whole

Coherence

---

**ACTIVITY 10**

Select an open skill from one of the major game activities, for instance:

- tackling in hockey or rugby
- fielding in cricket
- passing in netball

Try to explain in detail all the aspects of the skill and situation that would have to be considered when carrying out the skill. Do not forget to apply all the criteria, showing why it would be classified as an open skill.

---

## The implications for teaching and coaching – skills classification

Knowledge of skills classification could help in identifying the appropriate teaching and coaching strategies. The use of the Fine–Gross classification would have a practical use in rehabilitation and training programmes within special education and would also be useful in infant and primary education. In addition it would help in identifying the levels and types of fitness and preparation needed for certain skills and activities.

It has also been suggested that it is often easier to teach more open or complex activities, eg, netball or basketball to beginners, by breaking the whole game down into a series of more closed skills where the beginner is not having to make lots of decisions (perceptual requirements) and adapt their skills before they have learnt the basics.

However, if for instance a skill is classified as an open skill it would be a very short-sighted teacher or coach who always demanded practice of the skill in isolation. Practice in a variety of realistic situations would be essential once the basic

Using the skills/techniques listed in Activities 9 and 10 build up a classification profile for each by placing them on the continuum below and justify your placements.

| Gross | | Fine |
|---|---|---|

| Discrete | Serial | Continuous |
|---|---|---|

| Externally paced | | Internally paced |
|---|---|---|

| Open | | Closed |
|---|---|---|

techniques had been learnt in isolation (see the sections on Schema and Types of practice).

## A E  Task analysis

Task analysis is the organised and systematic evaluation of an activity/task/game in order to find out the:

- constituent parts
- organisation
- relevant cues
- objectives/purpose.

It is important that the teacher or coach is aware of all the various demands being placed on a learner at any one time within either simple or complex skills.

It has been suggested that the major factors contributing to task difficulty are:

- the degree of perception necessary
- the degree of decision making involved

- the nature of the act itself (movement patterns)
- the feedback availability.

(J. Billing)

The effect of the above factors will depend on the relative level of the performer (see phases of learning and information processing). Therefore you can see that just labelling a task as difficult or easy is not enough. It is necessary to specify the degree and nature of the difficulty if appropriate and effective instructions and strategies are to be developed.

Figure 18.6 shows a task analysis for the tennis serve (executive programme) indicating the appropriate components (sub-routines) and identifying some of the underlying perceptual motor abilities necessary for the plan of action to be completed.

Figure 18.7 shows how motor skills can be analysed according to the complexity of each subcomponent.

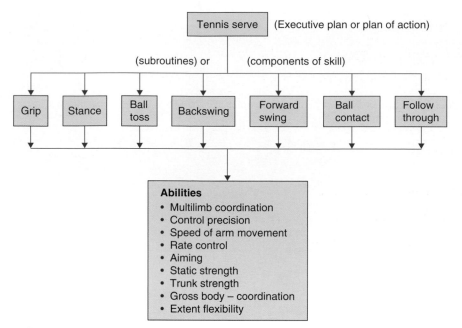

Fig 18.6. A task analysis for the tennis serve

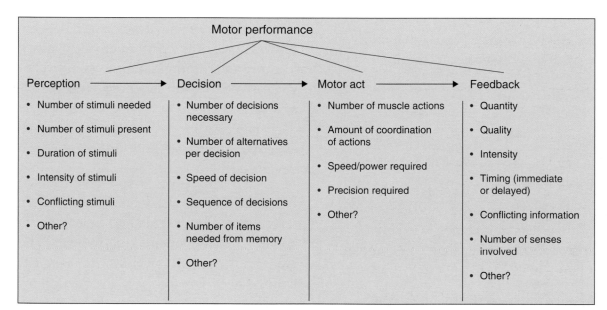

Fig 18.7. Analysing motor skills
*Source:* Adapted from J Billing, 1980.

# Summary

## Skills

1. Skill can be an act or task.

2. Skill can be used to indicate quality of performance.

3. Motor skills are essentially a combination of cognitive/perceptual and motor skills put together.

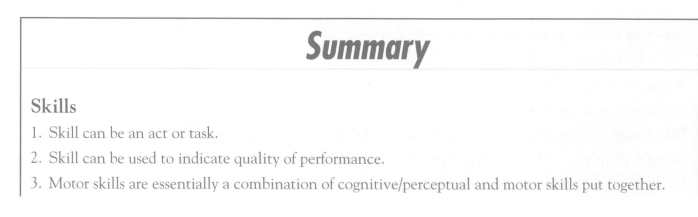

4. Skill is learned behaviour.

5. Skills have predetermined objectives to achieve.

6. Skill involves being able to carry out the action consistently.

7. Skills are performed with an efficient use of time and energy.

8. Skills involve 'internal processing' in addition to physical actions.

## Abilities

1. Abilities are innate enduring qualities or capacities.

2. Abilities are task specific. Specific skills need different abilities.

3. Abilities underpin skill development.

4. The idea of one overall 'athletic ability' is largely a myth.

5. Many other factors contribute to all-round athletic development.

## Classifying skills

1. It is important to consider all aspects of the skill/task being taught.

2. Classification considers the common characteristics of skills.

3. A continuum is a more effective tool in classifying skills.

4. Teaching strategies are linked to the in-depth analysis of skills.

## Review Questions

1. What is a motor skill and a perceptual skill?

2. What are cognitive skills?

3. What are complex skills and simple skills?

4. What is an ability? What is a psychomotor ability? What is gross motor ability?

5. What is meant by classification of skills?

6. Why do we classify skills?

7. What is a continuum and why is it used?

8. Differentiate between gross and fine skills. Give examples.

9. What are discrete, continuum, serial skills? Give examples.

10. What are self paced and externally paced skills? Give examples.

11. What are high and low cognitive skills? Give examples.

12. What are open/closed skills? Give examples.

13. What is the relationship between classification of skill and methods of practice?

14. What is the purpose of a coach/teacher carrying out a task analysis?

15. Select a specific skill/technique and try to carry out an in-depth task analysis.

# 19. The Principles of Learning

Learning plays a central role in most of psychology and as such it is one of the most expansively researched and discussed areas in the whole of psychology. Learning is said to be a hypothetical construct, in that it can only be inferred from either:

- observing behaviour; or
- testing, measuring and evaluating performance.

All human beings have tremendous capabilities for learning. As a student of physical education and sport it is not enough just to recognise that learning has or has not taken place (the end result or outcome); you should have a more in-depth understanding of the theories and principles associated with the underlying learning process and be able to apply this understanding to the practical learning situation.

Here is a list of the terms to be covered in this chapter. It is important that you understand them.

- Learning definition
- Inference
- Practice observation
- Retention tests
- Transfer test
- Cognitive learning

- Affective learning
- Effective learning
- Cognitive phase
- Associative phase
- Autonomous phase
- Performance curves

- Linear
- Negative
- Positive
- Plateaus
- Learning variables

It would be very convenient to have a list of absolute truths about the learning and teaching of specific motor skills related to every possible sports performance. However, your own individual experiences should help you realise that there are no conclusive statements and guarantees cannot be given. This is because:

- learning is a complex process during which many physical and psychological changes are taking place
- there are many variables to be considered
- it is very difficult to consider the many variables and parts of the learning process in total isolation
- most of what we know about how and why people learn is based on the practical application of theories alongside educated reasoning (behavioural evidence).

Once you have read this chapter you should gain an understanding of:

- definitions of learning
- different types of learning

- stages/phases of learning
- performance/learning curves
- major factors that can affect learning
- key issues surrounding how people learn.

# Definitions of learning

As we have discussed in the previous chapter, implicit in the understanding of the term skill is the notion that learning has taken place, that skill is learned behaviour. To become skilful involves a person's performance changing in line with certain criteria and characteristics associated with skill.

It is generally accepted that for learning to have taken place there has to be a recognisable change in behaviour and that this change in behaviour has to be permanent. Thus, the performance improves over time as a result of practice and/or experience becoming more consistent in terms of its:

- accuracy
- efficiency
- adaptability.

Learning has been defined as:

*'the more or less permanent change in behaviour that is reflected in a change in performance.'*

(B. Knapp)

*'a change in the capability of the individual to perform a skill that must be inferred from a relatively permanent improvement in performance as a result of practice or experience.'*

(R. Magill)

*'a relatively permanent change in behaviour due to past experience.'*

(D. Coon)

*'a set of processes associated with practice or experience leading to relatively permanent changes in the capability of skilled performance.'*

(R. Schmidt)

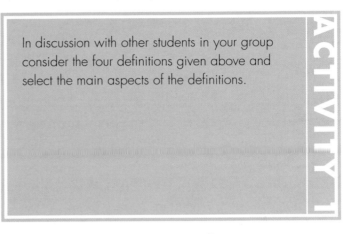

In discussion with other students in your group consider the four definitions given above and select the main aspects of the definitions.

In your discussion of the four definitions you should have concluded, and psychologists generally agree, that:

- learning is not a 'one-off' lucky effort/performance
- learning is *relatively* permanent

  (This does not mean, however, that the skill is performed 100% correctly each time. It does mean that a learner's capability to perform a particular skill consistently has increased.)

- learning is due to past experience and or practice.

## How do we judge if a skill has been learned?

There are various methods of assessing a performance in order that more accurate inferences can be made about learning. The general methodology would be to:

- **observe** – behaviour/performance
- **measure/test** – behaviour/performance
- **evaluate** – behaviour/performance

- **translate** – the information gained into meaningful conclusion
- **infer** – that learning has or has not taken place.

Three common methods of measuring and testing which have been used to enable teachers and coaches to make more accurate inferences with regard to learning have been:

- practice observations
- retention tests
- transfer tests.

**Measures** are actual values indicating skill levels. **Tests** are the procedures used to obtain the scores.

## Practice observation

This is when a teacher or coach records a learner's performance over a period of time in an accurate way in order to provide a quantitative means for evaluating progress: eg, results showing more accuracy or consistency in relation to time spent practising (see later section on performance curves).

## Retention tests

This is when a teacher or coach tests a student's performance after practice and then re-tests again after a few days and then again in order to check whether the initial levels of performance have been maintained, persisted or improved after a period of little or no practice.

## Transfer tests

This is when a teacher or coach determines how well a particular skill has been learned by seeing how well it can be performed in a different situation to that experienced by the student during practice: is the accuracy and consistency maintained from practice to game situation? (see also Transfer in Theories of Learning.)

Each of the above methods and many more can be used in various ways and at different times according to the needs of the teacher, learner or situation. A teacher/coach who is interested in

helping a learner/performer to improve should be able to evaluate whether improvement has been relatively permanent and not just a temporary change due to maturational or fitness changes for example. It is important that you understand that these are various measures or tests of **performance** and that it is from these that teachers or coaches make **inferences** with regard to motor learning. Having considered what is meant by the term learning and relating it to motor performance, it is important that you understand at this stage that while there is a general consensus as to how learning and, more specifically, motor learning can be defined, there are actually different **types** of learning that can be experienced. In addition, there are also different **phases** or stages within the learning process.

Practical examples of tests

| Observation | Retention | Transfer |
|---|---|---|
| How many successful shots on target per session | A performer has learned the overhead clear. Seven out of ten reached the back tramlines. A week later when the same test was completed the performer scored eight. | A performer has learned to pass a ball accurately through two cones in a drill situation. The same skill is now used in a full game situation. |

## Reasons for evaluation

- To give the learner/performer accurate/meaningful feedback.
- To assess whether goals/targets have been achieved.
- To assess the effectiveness of teaching/coaching strategies.

- To record progress/achievement over time.
- To assess performance potential.
- To carry out match/performance statistical analysis (eg, accuracy, technique, timing, errors, amount, frequency).

Evaluations can be:

- formative (ongoing – helps to provide feedback)
- summative (provides a summary over time).

Tests must be:

- valid – does it measure what it sets out to measure? (Sports skills tests usually lack validity.)
- reliable – is the measurement consistent?
- objective – can the same test be applied by different testers to gain the same measurement?

Measurements can be:

- qualitative – direct observation, usually of a subjective nature
- quantitative – precise/accurate monitoring of movement specifics, usually using technical equipment.

Learners and performers can be evaluated as follows:

- self-referencing – with reference to themselves
- norm-referencing – with reference to other people
- criterion referencing – with reference to external criteria.

# A E Types of learning

As you will have realised in your earlier discussions with regard to types of skill, in order to carry out motor skills at the highest levels more than just pure physical movement is involved. There is usually some cognitive and perceptual involvement to various degrees depending on the skill being carried out. In the same way therefore that motor skills involve more than purely the physical movement of muscles, limbs, etc, then learning can occur in more than just a physical way. There have

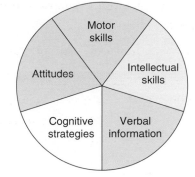

Fig 19.1. The categories of learning

been many different approaches to the analysis of what form learning can take in relation to the types of skills or situations being experienced.

Robert Gagné (1977) suggested that there are five main categories of human performance that may be developed by learning and that any learned capability whatever it is called, History, Geography, Physics, Football, Swimming, etc, has characteristics from one or other of these categories.

1. **Intellectual skills**
   Dealing with the environment in a symbolic way, eg, reading, writing mathematical symbols, etc.

2. **Verbal information**
   Learning to state or tell ideas or information by using oral, written or body language, ie, communication.

3. **Cognitive strategies**
   Learning to manage one's own learning, ie, use of memory, thinking, problem solving and analysis.

4. **Attitudes**
   Acquiring mental states which influence choices of personal actions, eg, choosing badminton rather than hockey as a preferred recreation.

5. **Motor skills**
   Learning to execute movement in a number of organised ways, either as single skills or actions, eg, catching a ball, or more comprehensive activities, eg, playing netball or basketball.

In carrying out activity 2 you will probably have come up with examples of learning under each heading.

1. Individually select a game activity, eg, netball, hockey, badminton, tennis, football, etc.
2. Using Gagné's categories as a guide, write a list of all the aspects of the activity that you may learn about when being introduced to the game.
3. Feed back your list to your member of staff along with everyone else in the group.

For example:

1. Developing particular motor skills, eg, catching, throwing, kicking, hitting/striking, etc, depending on the game.
2. Developing tactical awareness, defensive strategies and attacking strategies.
3. Learning the rules and regulations.
4. Learning the ethics/morals of the game, eg, sportsmanship.
5. Developing positive attitudes towards the game and sport in general.
6. Understanding training principles.
7. Learning how the body works and how to make it work more efficiently.
8. Learning how to analyse movement in order to recognise strengths and weaknesses in your own and others' game.
9. Communication skills, both verbal and non-verbal.
10. Learning to interpret information.

All these and probably many more examples will be on your lists. While we are primarily concerned with learning associated with motor skills, it is obvious that in order to learn motor skills we also experience learning in many other ways. Although experimental psychologists have tried, it is difficult to separate learning in its widest sense from motor performance, since all contribute to the level of motor skill achieved.

Table 19.1. The three types of learning

| Cognitive | Affective | Effective |
|---|---|---|
| to know | to feel | to do |
| • mental processes eg, <br> a) tactical awareness <br> b) strategies <br> c) problem solving <br> (inclusive of Gagné's categories 1, 2, 3) | • attitudes and values eg, <br> a) ethics <br> b) sportsmanship <br><br> (Gagné's category 4) | • motor learning eg, <br> a) physical <br> b) catching <br> c) passing <br><br> (Gagné's category 5) |

A more simplistic view of learning experienced within physical education and sport is seen in table 19.1. When asked to comment on the types of learning experienced within Sport & PE, you would need to refer to **Cognitive**, **Affective** and **Effective**.

In dealing with motor learning, it is often difficult to separate the various aspects as all will contribute in some way at some time to the level of skill. It is therefore necessary to develop all areas in order to make the learning process more meaningful, eg, a sensitive teacher or coach may find that in order to develop a student's high-jumping technique (effective learning) they may have to help the student understand the basic biomechanics of the movement and link this to their ability to analyse their own movement (cognitive learning). In addition positive attitudes may be needed with regard to specific physical training and psychological aspects, eg, confidence and focusing and holding the moral belief that the use of drugs is cheating (affective learning).

# Phases of motor skill learning

As there are different types of learning associated with the learning of motor skills there are also different stages or phases of the learning process.

In order to gain a clearer understanding of the learning process there have been many attempts to identify the various phases, or stages, that students go through when learning motor skills. It has been agreed that whatever the number and name of phases identified the phases are not separate or distinct, but that they gradually merge into each other as a person moves from being a novice to being proficient.

Having a better understanding of what is happening and what the learner is experiencing during each phase should help you in developing appropriate teaching and coaching strategies to ensure that the learning process is efficient and successful.

NB: Be careful not to confuse the three *types* of learning with the three *stages* of learning discussed previously!

# Three stage model

Paul Fitts and Michael Posner (1967) identified one of the better-known models which in its turn has been expanded upon by others.

The three phases identified are:

1. Cognitive.

2. Associative.

3. Autonomous.

While each of these phases has certain characteristics associated with it, movement from one phase to the other is seen as developmental and gradual along a continuum. The rate at which a performer progresses through the phases is different for each individual.

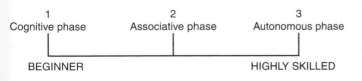

## Cognitive phase

This is the initial phase in the learning process when, as a beginner faced with a new skill or set of skills to learn, you want to be told what you need to know, for example:

- what is required of you?
- what task is to be performed?
- what are the basic rules?
- how do I hold the stick?

The beginner is trying to 'get to grips' with the basics while dealing with lots of visual, verbal and kinaesthetic information in the form of:

- demonstrations from the teacher or fellow students (visual guidance/mental picture)
- instructions and explanations (verbal guidance to help sequencing)
- initial trials/practice in the form of basic trial/error (kinaesthetic picture).

The emphasis in this phase is very much on early understanding or cognitive involvement (internalising information) in order that initial plans of action can be formulated. Beginners are directed towards important aspects of the new skill by paying attention to verbal cues. These cues may be highlighted or intensified in order to help concentration, eg, bigger or brighter bats and balls are often used, and any initial success is enthusiastically reinforced. The length of this phase varies according to the beginner and the strategies being used but it is generally a relatively short phase.

## Problems linked to cognitive phase

- Beginner has difficulty deciding what to pay attention to (see selective attention).
- Beginner has difficulty processing information (potential overload).
- Gross errors made (often uncoordinated movements).

Children do not always understand adult words and descriptions. Explanations are not always comprehended by the learner. Teaching/guidance needs to be **simple**, **clear** and **concise**.

Fig 19.2. In the cognitive phase it is important to keep information clear and simple

Demonstrations (visual guidance) are generally seen as being more effective than lots of verbal input at this stage.

As the learner has little idea of what constitutes correct performance the teacher may have to use physical guidance and actually physically manipulate the learner's limbs into the correct position.

## The associative phase

This intermediate or practice phase in the learning process is generally significantly longer than the cognitive phase, with the learner taking part in many hours of practice. The characteristics of this phase are that the fundamental basics of the skill required have generally been mastered and are becoming more consistent.

- the mental or early cognitive images of the skill have been associated with the relevant movements enabling the coordination of the various parts of the skill (subroutine) to become smoother and more in line with expectations
- motor programmes are being developed
- gross error detection and correction is practised
- the skills are practised and refined under a wide variety of conditions
- a gradual change to more subtle and detailed cue utilisation

- more detailed feedback is given and used
- greater use of internal/kinaesthetic feedback (comparison to ideal by performer).

While the skills are not yet automatic or consistently correct there is an obvious change in the performance characteristics.

## The autonomous phase

After much practice and variety of experience the learner moves into what is considered the final phase in the learning process, the autonomous phase. The characteristics of this phase are that:

- the performance of the skill has become almost **automatic**
- the skill is performed relatively easily and **without stress**
- the skill is performed effectively with little if any conscious control: it is **habitual**
- the performance is **consistent** with highly skilled movement characteristics
- skills can be **adapted** to meet a variety of situations.

The performer is able to:

- process information easily, helping decision making
- concentrate on the relevant cues and signals from the environment
- concentrate on additional higher level strategies, tactics, and options available
- detect and correct errors without help.

Once a player has reached this phase of learning it does not mean that learning is over. Although the performer is very capable, small improvements can still be made in terms of style and form, and to the many other factors associated with psychological aspects of performance which can help develop learning even further, eg:

- self evaluation of performance
- mental practice

Fig 19.4. In the autonomous phase skilled soccer players can dribble the ball habitually, enabling their attentional capacities to consider other aspects of the game at the same time, eg, movements of other players and options available

Fig 19.3. To remain in the autonomous phase regular reference back to the associative phase is essential, even for highly skilled professionals, in order to reinforce motor programmes

- stress management
- personal motivation.

# The relationship between learning and performance

As we have already stated, occasional good or 'one-off' performances are not a true indication of learning having taken place. There has to be a relatively permanent change in performance over time as a result of practice and or experience. One of the more traditional ways of gathering evidence in order to discover if learning has or has not taken place has been by comparing practice/performance observations. Performance levels over a certain length of time are recorded and the results are plotted on a graph, producing performance curves. Very often these curves of performance are inaccurately referred to as learning curves. This has been based on the assumption that changing levels of skill closely parallel performance scores. However, it is performance not learning that is being measured. By keeping records of skill performance over a period of time (eg, a lesson, one hour, a term, a season) an individual's, but more often a group's, progress can be plotted. This will provide a graphical representation of the specific aspect of performance being tested. Thus a picture of the relationship between practice and performance is presented from which inferences can be made. It has been suggested that the validity of performance curves as true representations of learning is problematical due to the many variables that may have an effect. However, as long as they are not used in total isolation, such curves do act as useful indicators of general trends in learning. Although they may be used to show changes in an

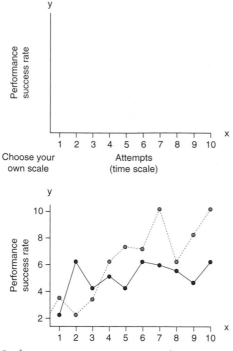

Fig 19.5. Performance success rate graphs

individual's performance of a particular motor skill or skills, performance curves tend to be more widely used to represent composite or group performance.

A performance curve consists of three areas:

- The vertical y-axis of the graph showing the level of performance being measured.

- The horizontal x-axis of the graph indicating the amount of time over which the performance has been measured.

- The shape of the curve from which **inferences** can be made between the amount of learning taking place.

## Types of performance curves

When analysing performance curves it has been found that graphs are made up of several different shapes within the overall context of the general

---

You are going to undertake a learning experiment in one-handed ball juggling. No practice is allowed beforehand or in between attempts.

1. Divide yourselves into pairs.
2. Have two tennis balls per pair and a piece of graph paper.
3. Have ten consecutive goes each at one-handed juggling.
4. Count the number of successive throw-ups each person can manage in each of their ten goes.
5. Log the results on a table as below.

| Attempts | 1 | 2 | 3 | 4 | 5 | 6 | 7 | 8 | 9 | 10 |
|----------|---|---|---|---|---|---|---|---|---|----|
| Success  |   |   |   |   |   |   |   |   |   |    |

6. Plot the performance of both yourself and your partner on a piece of graph paper and compare the graphs.
7. Average out your two scores and draw another graph.
8. Average out all the scores of the members of your group and draw a composite graph for the whole group.
9. What inferences can be drawn from this final graph?
10. What variables may have affected the individual and group performances? How could you make this experiment scientifically more valid?
11. What did you notice with regard to the shape of the curves as you average out more by adding more results?
12. A further way to develop your performance curves would be to treat the ten attempts as a block of trials and average this out. Then, over a period of time, repeat the block of ten attempts on a regular basis. This could be done with various skills, eg, basketball free throws, serving in tennis, target shooting in hockey or football, shooting in netball, etc.

**ACTIVITY 4**

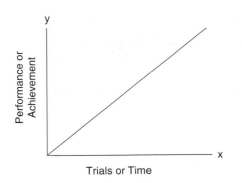

Fig 19.6. Linear curve of performance

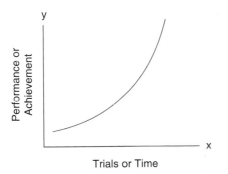

Fig 19.7. Negatively accelerated curve of performance

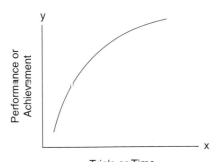

Fig 19.8. Positively accelerated curve of performance

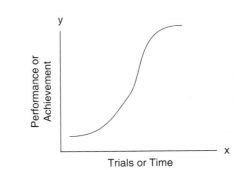

Fig 19.9. Ogive or S-shaped curve of performance

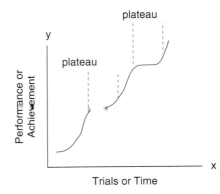

Fig 19.10. Plateau in performance

indicates small performance gains early on in practice followed by a substantial increase later in practice. Figure 19.9 is a combination of the previous types of curve. The plateaus in fig 19.10 indicate that during certain periods of practice or from one particular trial to another there was no significant improvement in performance.

## Plateaus

The levelling off in performance preceded and followed by performance gains has been called a plateau. Plateaus in performance and possibly learning have been the subject of considerable research. One of the earliest pieces of research to suggest that plateaus existed was by Bryan and Hunter (1897) when studying the performance of trainee telegraphers learning the morse code. Think of experiences you have had when trying to learn particular skills; there must have been times when initial success was followed by a period of time when, however hard you tried, no apparent improvement was achieved. Then, all of a sudden everything 'clicked' together and you cannot now remember what the problem was. Although such an

performance curve. The curves shown in figs 19.6–19.10 are termed smooth curves. However, as you will have noticed from your own individual graphs and further reading, curves found in research studies are usually erratic in nature.

Fig 19.6 indicates that performance improves directly in proportion to the amount of time or number of trials. In fig 19.7, the curve of decreasing gain indicates that a large amount of improvement occurred early on in practice and then although improvement usually continues, it is very slight in relation to the continued amount of time or trials. The inverse curve of increasing gain in fig 19.8

experience is often described by individual learners and by performers at the highest level, performance curves generally relate to group or class results and therefore experimental evidence to support the existence of plateaus related to individual learning is hard to come by. While we may experience plateaus in practice and performance it has been argued (F.S. Keller, 1958) that learning continues or at the very least plateaus do not necessarily mean that learning has also plateaued. In terms of learning development it is generally agreed that if plateaus do exist they are something that should be avoided as they can lead to a stagnation in performance and a possible loss of overall interest.

## Possible causes of plateaus

It has been suggested that the following factors have to be considered as possible causes of plateaus.

1. Movement from learning lower order or simple skills to higher order or more complex skills may create a situation in which the learner needs to take time to assimilate more involved information and attend to correct cues and signals (transitional period).
2. Goals or targets are set too high or too low.
3. Fatigue/lack of physical preparation.
4. Lack of variety in practice.
5. Lack of motivation/interest due to problems associated with the above.
6. Lack of understanding of plateaus.
7. Physical unreadiness for new skill or next stage.
8. Low level of aspiration.
9. Lack of ability to adapt skills.
10. Bad technique.

## Combating the performance plateau effect

A coach/teacher may have to consider the following strategies to reduce the effect of plateaus:

- ensure that the performer/learner is *capable* of performing the skill (see Thorndikes laws of learning)

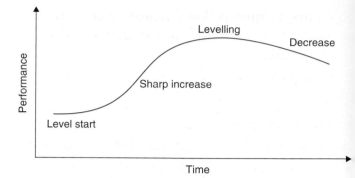

Fig 19.11. Example of a beginner completing a massed practice of given simple, closed sports skills

- Individually, consider the possible causes of plateaus given above and try to make some practical suggestions as to how a teacher or a coach might try to ensure that learners do not experience plateaus in their skill development.
- Present your suggestions to the class and compile a full list of suggestions and strategies.

ACTIVITY 5

- breaking the practice into shorter/distributed periods
- re-setting goals with agreement of performer
- offering extrinsic rewards/encouragement
- using mental rehearsal in practice
- using appropriate feedback
- arranging relevant competition against realistic opposition
- breaking serial skills into parts, eg, whole–part–whole practice (see section on practice)
- ensuring performer pays attention to appropriate cues (selective attention)
- emphasising role in team – enjoyment
- changing role/position/responsibility.

Fig 19.11 demonstrates the performance curve of a beginner.

- The graph starts at a low level because the beginner has a low skill level.

- At first progress is slow (shallow slope). The learner is still working out the requirements of the task.
- Early practice produces a sharp increase in performance level.
- The upper level is achieved due to either optimum performance or decrease in motivation.
- Levelling out can also be caused by poor coaching/lack of information on how to improve skill level or fatigue.
- The fall in performance is due to lack of motivation/boredom/fatigue/distraction/faulty technique.
- There is a build-up of reaction inhibition.

As you can see from your earlier experiment, discussions and reading there is no one curve of performance. The appearance of these curves is the function of a combination of variable factors. It is important that when you interpret the curves and make certain inferences you are aware of the many factors that can influence learning; if any of these are seen to be problems in the learning process, then the reasons or causes can be recognised, isolated and dealt with in the appropriate manner.

More recently research has been conducted using applied behavioural analysis in order to produce graphical evidence similar to performance curves. If gathered from correctly conducted experiments using control groups this evidence can help in determining, for instance, which instructional methods, types of motivation or reinforcement strategies are effective with certain groups or types of activities.

# Considerations in motor learning

There are many different factors called **learning variables** that you have to be aware of, understand and consider; these can influence the effectiveness of the learning process.

There are four main categories of learning variables. In considering these categories you may come across unfamiliar terms, which are explained in later sections.

## Category 1: *variables associated with the learning process*

The basic process that learners go through when faced with a new situation to which they have to respond is usually similar for all.

The learner will:

- observe the situation
- interpret the situation
- make decisions as to what they have to do
- decide on plans of action
- generate movement plans
- take in further information (feedback) as the result of actions becomes available in one form or another.

The learner can experience success or difficulty in any part of this process. Understanding it helps a teacher in the task of presenting useful information to the learner.

For a more detailed coverage of the information processing approach to learning see chapter 21.

## Category 2: *variables associated with individual differences*

A sensitive teacher or coach would try to develop a good knowledge of the individual differences listed below, and consider how they might affect the learner, in order to help the learning process.

- ability
- age (chronological and maturational)
- gender
- physiological characteristics, eg, physique (size, shape, weight linked to maturity, fitness)
- psychological, eg, motivation, attitudes, personality (see chapters 24–25)
- previous experience
- sociological aspects.

## Category 3: *variables associated with the task*

A teacher would need to consider:

- the complexity of the task, eg, simple or complex?
- the organisation of the task, eg, high or low?
- the classification of the task, eg, open/closed? fine/gross?
- the transfer possibilities.

An understanding of task analysis is essential (see the sections on task analysis) in order that the appropriate teaching strategies can be developed.

## Category 4: *variables associated with the instructional conditions*

Teachers and coaches can manipulate the learning environment in a variety of ways:

- through styles of teaching
- through mode of presentation
- by using different forms of guidance
- by choosing appropriate types of practice.

All the above approaches will have a considerable affect on the learning experience of the individual or group.

# Summary

- Learning is relatively permanent.
- Learning is due to practice or experience.
- Learning is inferred.
- There are different types of learning (cognitive, affective, effective).
- There are different phases of learning (cognitive, associative, autonomous).
- Learning develops along a continuum.
- There are different types of performance curves.
- Plateaus are to be avoided.
- Learning is affected by many variables.

# Review Questions

1. Explain the difference between performance and learning.
2. Why can we only infer learning has or hasn't taken place?
3. What are the characteristics associated with the three stages of Fitts and Posner's model of learning?
4. In what ways does a performer in the autonomous phase differ from a performer in the cognitive phase
5. How is the notion of a continuum related to learning development?

6. Why is the term performance curve used rather than learning curve?

7. What is a plateau in a performance curve? What do you think it would feel like to experience it?

8. Should we infer that plateaus in performance mean learning is not taking place?

9. How might you learn from performing wrongly?

10. What factors may cause plateaus in performance?

11. Consider an ogive-shaped curve of performance for a beginner and explain the reasons behind the shape.

# 20. Theories of Learning

## Chapter introduction

We have already seen that learning is a relatively permanent change in behaviour. In order to help your understanding of how this relatively permanent change in behaviour comes about it is necessary to consider some of the more important theories and models of learning that have been proposed since the turn of the last century. Having an understanding of major theories, together with an historical perspective of their development, should enable you to see the relevance and practical application of teaching and instructional conditions associated with the methods and strategies which are prevalent in physical education and sport today.

Here is a list of the terms to be covered in this chapter. It is important that you understand them.

### Theories of learning

- Stimulus
- Response
- Bonding
- Classical conditioning
- Operant conditioning
- Behaviour operants
- Law of readiness

- Law of exercise
- Law of effect
- Trial and error learning
- Reinforcement – positive and negative
- Punishment – tangible and intangible
- Drives
- Drive reduction

- Cognitive theory
- Gestaltism
- Insight learning
- Socialisation
- Social learning
- Observational learning

## Conditioning theories

In the early twentieth century **behaviourism** was thought to provide a scientific base for the explanation of human behaviour. This approach placed the emphasis on the learning environment where behaviour in response to specific stimuli could be observed and used to make predictions about future behaviour in relation to similar situations or stimuli. The early behaviouristic approach was based on what became known as **stimulus-response** theories or **theories of association** where the 'outcome' or 'product' was more important than understanding the process. It has been referred to as a very mechanistic and generalised approach implying that all learners can have their behaviour shaped or conditioned throug regular association (ie, practice) and manipulation of the learning practice environment by the teache or coach. The performer learns to associate certain behaviour (response) with certain stimuli from within the environment. Once this connection or bonding together of a particular stimulus and response occurs then the performer's behaviour becomes habitual, enabling predictions to be made about that person's future responses to the same or similar stimuli. Although dating from before the las century **Stimulus (S)** and **Response (R)** theories a: we know them owe much to the work carried out b

Pavlov, Thorndike and Skinner. Although both Pavlov (classical or respondent conditioning) and Skinner (operant conditioning) both represent the behaviouristic S–R approach to learning there are some important distinctions that need to be considered.

# Classical conditioning (Pavlov 1849–1936)

During his experiments Pavlov noticed that the dogs being used would salivate (unconditioned response) very often before their actual food (unconditional stimulus) would arrive in response to the noise of food being prepared, clanking of buckets, sight of the food, etc. Thus the dogs were learning to associate these other stimuli within their environment with the taste of the food. Pavlov conducted various experiments to see if he could produce the same behaviour but with alternative stimuli, eg, light, pictures, shapes.

In his later experiments Pavlov found that by pairing specific stimuli, ie, a bell, lights, shapes (conditioned stimulus) with the food (unconditioned stimulus) over a period of time he could produce the same salivation (unconditional response).

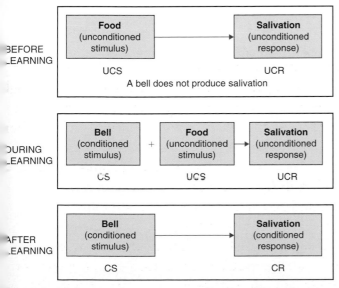

Fig 20.1. Pavlov's experiment to produce conditional response with conditioned stimulus

He found that although ringing a bell (stimulus) would not normally produce the salivation, by this continual pairing or association of food and bell he could eventually produce the salivation in the dogs by merely ringing the bell independently, thus creating a conditional response (CR) to a conditioned stimulus (CS).

You may ask what an experiment involving dogs and food has got to do with learning in sport and physical education. It is the principles associated with the theory that are important: Pavlov showed that a certain conditioned response and behaviour could be developed by association with a certain conditioned stimulus. This behaviour or response would eventually become automatic. If applied into a learning environment within physical education the teacher or coach can, through repetitive practice, get a beginner to associate a particular type of action or movement with a particular stimulus. It was felt that this approach could be generalised across all learners, with all students being treated the same, experiencing the same repetitive practice and being expected to behave in the same way. The traditional 'drill' technique, whereby all students in a class respond to the same stimulus or cue (almost reflex behaviour) with the students having no real choice, has developed from these basic S–R principles. Think of your time back in junior school. What happened when 'playtime' was over? Generally a teacher would come out into the playground and ring a bell or blow a whistle and all pupils would line up before being given permission to return to their classrooms. This is pure behaviourism, stimulus and response theory.

This approach relies very much on the teacher manipulating situations within the learning environment (gymnasium, hockey pitch, etc.) in order to create habitual responses. A criticism of classical conditioning is that although behaviour or response may be triggered automatically and may be correct, it is not necessarily linked to understanding – which may be needed if further or more complex skills and strategies are to be developed.

It also does not really explain what happens when teaching a novel skill, ie: what would be the unconditional stimulus?

This theory is concerned with the following:

- learning is dictated mainly by specific stimuli from the learner's situation/environment

- existing SR (stimulus–response) connections are replaced with new bonds

- the response remains the same but the stimulus changes

- classical conditioning techniques can be used by sports psychologists to help performers control anxiety, eg, relaxation or meditation techniques can rely on controlled breathing exercises using repetition of a calming phrase or repetition in drill training.

The use of well-timed commands (stimuli) to stimulate action is a very effective technique that is still used today. It can be applied to many sports.

Fig 20.2. A defender pressurised by an attacker (stimulus) kicks the ball off the pitch (response). Reinforcement will come from his manager or continual practice repetition

# Operant conditioning (Skinner 1904–1990)

In his later work on instrumental or operant conditioning, Skinner drew heavily on Thorndike's (1874–1949) three laws of learning. He did not totally reject the work done on classical conditioning by Pavlov but suggested that this view of how behaviour could be created was too simplistic. He saw the learner as being more involved in the learning process. Behaviour was not seen as being reflex or inevitable with the learner having no choice or alternative, as in classical conditioning. For Skinner, the learner's behaviour in the present situation was very much as a result of consequences of their previous actions. The learner associates the consequences of their previous actions with the current situation (stimulus) and responds accordingly taking into account whether those previous consequences were satisfactory, pleasing and successful or unsatisfactory, unpleasant and unsuccessful. These consequences would either serve to strengthen the bond between certain stimulus and response or weaken it. Skinner suggested also that these bonds could be further strengthened or weakened by the use of appropriate reinforcement, thus increasing or decreasing the probability of that behaviour happening again in the future. Both **positive** and **negative reinforcement** could be used to increase the probability of a certain behaviour happening again and punishment could serve to weaken the bond and thus reduce the probability of certain unwanted behaviour or performance happening again.

# Thorndike's laws of learning

Skinner's studies in operant conditioning developed out of considerable early research by Thorndike who, in developing his own research on 'trial and error learning' linked to S–R bond theory, proposed many laws of learning, the most famous of which are as follows.

## Law of readiness

In order for learning to be really effective the performer has to be in the right frame of mind psychologically as well as being physically prepared and capable of completing the task, ie, appropriate maturational development, motivation and prerequisite learning.

## Law of exercise

In order for the bond between the stimulus and response to be strengthened it is necessary for regular practice to take place under favourable conditions. Repetition of the correct technique is important, sometimes referred to as 'the law of use'. However, he suggests that failure to practise on a regular basis could also result in 'the law of disuse' when the bond is weakened. Appropriate or favourable conditions could be created by the use of reinforcement.

## Law of effect

The law of effect is central to understanding the essential differences between classical and operant conditioning. In his experiments to support this law Thorndike placed a hungry cat in a 'puzzle box' from which it could escape to be fed by 'operating' the correct mechanism. Initially the cat, although highly motivated, struggled to get out, reacting in a very random way.

Eventually through a process of 'trial and error' when repeatedly placed back in the box, the cat reduced its time in the box down from five minutes to five seconds and got fed (pleasurable experience). Thorndike concluded that:

- What happens as a result of behaviour will influence that behaviour in the future
- Responses that bring satisfaction or pleasure are likely to be repeated again
- Responses that bring discomfort are not likely to be repeated again.

This is not the same as classical conditioning where the stimulus always produces the same response whether it is good or bad. However, his basic premise was that:

- behaviour is **shaped** and **maintained** by its consequences.

**Shaping** is the gradual procedure/process for developing difficult/complex behaviour patterns in small stages.

For example, if a badminton player receives a return which is only half court and not too high he will 'smash'. If this proves to be successful and therefore pleasurable it will serve to strengthen the connection between the stimulus (half court return) and the response (smash) and thus make it more likely that this behaviour will be repeated the next time the same situation occurs. However, a problem sometimes associated with trial and error learning is that a beginner may learn a poor or wrong technique (R) which may be effective in a limited way. This may result in having to re-learn at a later date in order to weaken the S–R bond which they have developed.

Skinner went on to suggest that certain additional **reinforcement** or motivational techniques such as praise or rewards could serve to support even further his view of the law of effect.

The consequences of operants or behaviour, ie, performance can be:

1. positive reinforcement
2. negative reinforcement } strengthen behaviour

or

3. punishment – weaken behaviour.

The above reinforcements or punishments can come in various guises.

## Definition of reinforcement

Any event or action or phenomenon that by strengthening the S–R bond increases the probability of a response occurring again. In other words it is the system or process that is used to shape behaviour in the future.

**Positive reinforcement** usually follows *after* a learner has demonstrated a desirable performance, eg, the basketball player has developed the correct 'set shot' technique and receives praise from the coach. This will hopefully motivate and encourage the performer to repeat the correct 'set shot' technique and try to improve.

In discussion with a partner try to think of other types of positive reinforcements that may increase the probability of a response being repeated.

ACTIVITY 1

Fig 20.3. Punishment is used to eliminate undesirable behaviour. It tells us what not to do, not what to do!

**Negative reinforcement** again serves to increase the probability of a certain desirable behaviour happening again but it is by the withdrawing of a possible aversive stimulus, eg, a teacher or coach constantly shouting at their team from the sideline suddenly stops shouting. The team or players would assume that they were now behaving or performing in the correct way and thus try to repeat the same actions or skills again.

You must ensure that you do not confuse negative reinforcement with negative feedback or punishment.

## Definition of punishment

An event or action, usually an aversive stimulus, to try to reduce or eliminate undesirable behaviour, eg, a penalty is given in football for a foul within the penalty area or a red card is given to a player who repeatedly infringes the laws of the game. Punishment can be effective but may result in

frustration and bitterness and is seen by many as a negative approach.

## When and how to use reinforcers

In using reinforcement techniques a teacher or coach needs to be aware of the effect that different reinforcers may have and how and when to use them effectively to ensure the appropriate learning and performance of motor skills. Within operant conditioning once the teacher or coach has decided what the desired level of performance or skill level is they will use reinforcers knowledgeably to condition the learner's behaviour in the appropriate way. It may be that the teacher plans the lessons in order that success is gained quite easily in the first part of the session. Success itself can act as the reinforcer. As the skills become more demanding praise for achieving aspects of the desired response may be given. The teacher or coach must ensure that the praise is given soon after the correct behaviour is performed in order that the beginner can link it to their actions (temporal association) and has no doubt what it is for (see the section on feedback). In using reinforcers a teacher or coach needs to consider the following.

1. How often to use them (too much or too little, partial or complete)

2. Ratio of positive to negative

3. How soon after response

4. What type to use

5. Size and/or value of reinforcer.

All the above will be affected by the teacher's and beginner's interpretation and perception of the reinforcers used.

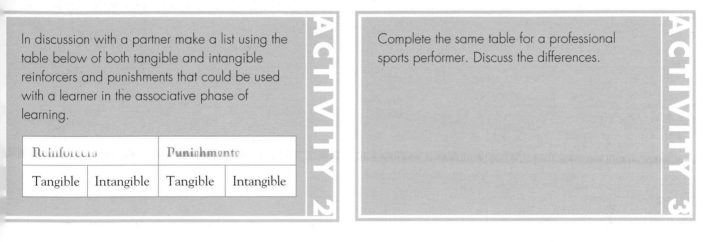

ACTIVITY 2

In discussion with a partner make a list using the table below of both tangible and intangible reinforcers and punishments that could be used with a learner in the associative phase of learning.

| Reinforcers | | Punishments | |
|---|---|---|---|
| Tangible | Intangible | Tangible | Intangible |

ACTIVITY 3

Complete the same table for a professional sports performer. Discuss the differences.

# Summary

## Practical application of operant conditioning

- Concerned with responses rather than stimuli.
- Not concerned with associations between stimuli and responses but with the association between responses and consequences
- Reinforcement is a key factor of this conditioning
- Reinforcement increases the probability of a behaviour occurring, eg, give praise when a successful performance occurs.

Skills can be taught using the operant method by:

- simplifying complex actions
- using a target area on wall/floor
- demonstration of correct style
- use of trial and error learning (have a go).

When the skill/performance (response) achieved relates closely to the desired action (response) the teacher can:

- give knowledge of results
- give praise/positive feedback/positive reinforcement.

This will strengthen the S–R bond and promote success.

- Shaping performance over time.

If the required skill/performance is not produced the teacher can weaken the bond between the stimulus and the inappropriate response (S–R) by:

- giving negative feedback
- using punishment.

In order to be more positive, and to decrease the probability of the poor performance re-occurring, the coach could teach other strategies to promote success as opposed to failure.

# Drive reduction theory (C.L. Hull, 1943)

While drive reduction theory is primarily linked to motivation it has strong links to learning and our understanding of S–R bonding; (see Arousal). Hull's theory suggested that continual repetition on its own may not serve to increase the strength of the S–R bond and thus shape the required performance. The strength of the S–R bond (learned behaviour) is affected by the:

- level of motivation or drive (desire to complete the task)
- intensity of the stimulus/problem
- level of incentive or reward
- amount of practice/reinforcements.

Hull believed that learning could only take place if drive reduction (acting as reinforcement) occurred, ie, the performer achieved the task that they were driven to attempt and that all behaviour (learned performance) derived from a performer's need to satisfy their drives.

There have been many criticisms of Hull's work but in relating it to physical education and sport we can see that once the S–R bond is strengthened and performance of the task has become a habit the performer is no longer driven to keep working (drive reduction). In order to develop skills learning or performance levels further and prevent 'inhibition' or lack of drive a teacher or coach must

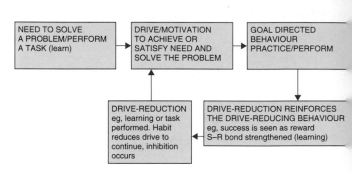

Fig 20.4. Hull's drive reduction theory

set further goals or more complex tasks to ensure that drive is maintained. Practices must be organised (see distributed practice) in order that the learner is constantly motivated, preventing 'inhibition' occurring.

It is also important that the teacher or coach ensure that only correct technique or good performance leads to the drive reduction as it is *this* S–R bond that will be reinforced. Bad technique or habits must not be allowed to achieve drive reduction.

## Simplistic summary of drive theory

- We are all motivated or have desires to achieve or solve problems – these are known as **drives**.
- When faced with learning a new skill we generally have a drive to achieve competent performance.
- Once we have practised and achieved this skill our drive naturally reduces as we have accomplished what we wanted to do.

- This reduction in our drive acts as a form of reinforcement and strengthens the S–R bond.

- If we continue to just do the same thing 'inhibition' occurs.

- At this point more/new goals need to be set.

# Cognitive theories

As research of human behaviour and performance developed further, many psychologists began to move away from the traditional behaviouristic approaches. Cognitive theorists saw the individual as being central to the process of learning, not merely reacting in a reflex manner (response) to outside influences (stimulus). Understanding of the total relationship between the many stimuli within the environment at any one time, and indeed their link to previous and future stimuli, was an essential part of cognitive theory.

Relationships between stimuli and certain responses were not learned in isolation but were part of the learner's awareness of a 'whole' variety of inter-related variables and experiences. It was argued that this would involve a whole host of cognitive processes such as use of senses, perception/interpretation, problem solving and being able to relate the present situation to previous similar experiences, thus involving memory.

The main early supporters of this approach, whose views have become synonymous with the cognitive approach, were known as 'gestaltists'. They believed that 'the whole is greater than the sum of its parts'. Gestaltists such as M. Wertheimer (1880–1943), K. Koffka (1886–1941) and W. Köhler (1887–1967) argued that in the learning situation a beginner will continually organise and reorganise mentally in relation to previous experiences the various aspects that they are faced with in order to solve a problem in the present situation ie, they would 'figure it out'. The time scale involved together with the strategies and methods used was seen as being different for each individual.

This view of learning is known as '**insight learning**': a learner suddenly discovers the relationship between the many stimuli they have been faced with and 'it all comes together!' (for instance a learner suddenly gets the timing of a serve correct). Insight learning often results in the performer progressing very quickly after periods of apparently little progress. It is then important that further questions, problems or goals are set in order to motivate the learner to develop their performance further. The association of S–R by 'trial and error learning' (or chance which is then reinforced when correct thus gradually strengthening the bond) has no role to play in the cognitive perspective. Learning is not seen as a random process. What is learned within insight learning is therefore not a set of specific conditioned associations but a real understanding (cognitive) of the relationship between the process and means of achieving the end result. For instance, a defending hockey player who has the reasons explained to them why, when they are the last person in defence, they should not commit themselves, but 'jockey' their opponent, keeping goal-side, as this will enable other players to get back to help or put pressure on the attacker possibly forcing a mistake, is more likely to understand when and why to carry out the coach's instructions in future situations and also see the relevance of their role.

This, it is argued, is better in the long run than simply being told what to do or possibly punished if they do 'dive in' and commit without thinking. In practice, following the cognitive approach it would be important that the teacher or coach had an in-depth understanding and knowledge of both the individual learner and the various coaching strategies relevant to the skills being taught. It seems that a variety of experiences is essential for learners to develop their 'insight' of the present task or problem using knowledge gained from previous situations. There is evidence to suggest that **insight** in the learner can be further developed by the teacher giving helpful hints or cues. This is particularly useful when considering transfers from previous learned activities or skills (see transfer of learning). Gestaltists would suggest that a learner experiences the 'whole' skill or activity, learning individually to develop his/her own map of understanding rather than 'part' or part- 'whole', step to step, association.

*'The whole is greater than the sum of its parts.'*

This whole learning approach allows learners to develop their own strategies and routes of understanding alongside general principles thus enabling the quicker learners to progress at their own rate: this has obvious links to the promoting of motivation and the developing of an individual's full potential.

# Socialisation

In global terms socialisation is seen as the life-long process of transmitting a culture by teaching and learning behaviours appropriate to the accepted norms, values and expectations of a society.

Socialisation, particularly within a sporting setting, is a dynamic process linked to the way in which people are influenced to conform to expected appropriate behaviour. Socialisation plays an important role in social integration.

General socialisation is heavily influenced by **prime socialising agents**. These are seen as:

- parents/family
- teacher/school
- peers/friendships
- coach/club
- media
- role models.

Although the parents and family are seen as the most important agents of socialisation all the others can exert a great influence in helping to create role models, real or imagined, that can be imitated. While socialisation can be considered in the global or national context of learning the norms, values

and expectations of society, it can also be viewed in the more specific context of how:

- sport can act as an agent of socialisation for society in general
- performers are socialised into specific sports/teams or groups norms, values and expectations.

## KEY WORDS

**Norms** are patterns of accepted behaviour within a particular society or sports group.

**Expectations** are commonly accepted positions and roles within a particular society or sports group which are actively promoted.

**Status** is the position in societies' or sports groups' social structure.

**Role** is the expected behaviour of a person related to their status within a particular society or sports group.

## Sport as an agent of socialisation

Sport in its widest sense is seen by many as an important aspect of life in most societies, and therefore a fundamental component of the socialisation process experienced by the vast majority of young people. Research in this area, although often criticised, argues that performers, particularly young children, who take part in sport are being taught skills both physical (motor) and cognitive that will enable them to participate fully and effectively within society as a whole (social learning).

The focus of this research has been on personality, moral behaviour, leadership roles, character building, cooperation, social roles and so on. It has been claimed that games teach young performers to develop appropriate attitudes and values by providing specific learning experiences. It has been shown, however, that not all learning in these situations is positive. The specific type of experience is important and has to be taken into account. The increasing 'professionalisation' of sport can serve to promote the 'win at all costs' attitude, thus leading young performers possibly to imitate deviant behaviour, eg, cheating and aggression. It has also been suggested that the traditional values and roles portrayed by sport and performers have heavily influenced gender stereotyping both in sport (eg, female activities, weaker, less suited to sport) and outside sport. This influence is coming under increasing criticism from within society at present. It is felt that sport and physical education should be doing much more to influence the image of women positively, together with that of other equally under-represented groups in both sport and society in general.

behaviour. In introducing certain cognitive factors which can only be implied from a person's social behaviour, social learning theorists, and Bandura in particular, emphasise the notion of learning through observation.

In the previous section we discussed the concept of socialisation through sport; the social learning perspective has been the traditional theme behind this notion. Learning is seen as taking place within a social setting in the presence of others with the learner and the socialising agent being involved in a two-way (reciprocal) interaction. A person, therefore, observes other people's behaviour in various ways not necessarily through direct interaction. The behaviour is taken in, the consequences assimilated and then copied in the appropriate situation at the appropriate time.

## KEY TERM

Socialisation into sport
- A process which results in adoption of the sport culture/norms/values
- Occurs with reference to player/coach/referee/spectator roles.
- Adopting sport behaviour appropriate to acceptable sport role models
- Agents eg, parents/peers/school/coaches/clubs/ families/media play a large role.

## KEY TERM

Socialisation through sport
- Values learnt through involvement with sport eg, unselfishness/loyalty/cooperation/ fairplay etc.
- Negative values may also be socialised eg, foul-play/racism/gender/stereo-typing/win at all costs attitude.
- Values influenced by agencies within sport eg, coach/captain/teacher/Governing Bodies.

## Social learning

Social learning theory came about as an important alternative explanation to conditioning. It was Bandura who, in the 1960s and 1970s, carried out more extensive research in this area. Although he viewed learning and behaviour as being linked to reinforcements (as had conditioning theories), he viewed the reinforcements as being more related to **vicarious reinforcement**. He saw this vicarious reinforcement as being the result of two elements, **observation** and **imitation**, particularly when related to the acquisition of social and moral

## Observational learning

In identifying observational learning, social learning theorists have emphasised a type of learning distinct from conditioning. New behaviour and attitudes are acquired by a performer in a sporting situation through watching and imitating the behaviour of others. The person who is being observed is referred to as the model and '**modelling**' is a term used synonomously with observational learning. Within physical education and sport, demonstrations are often used by teachers and coaches to give beginners a good technical model to work to. Very often this also serves to help a learner's specific confidence (see self efficacy). The degree of this effect will be enhanced if the person doing the demonstration is of similar ability (team mate) (similarity) and/or is of a high status (professional performer). In addition to showing a current technical model, observational learning or 'modelling' can also influence a performer's attitudes and moral behaviour by inhibiting or encouraging certain behaviour/performance (see persuasive communication/attitudes and aggression in 24).

Teachers and coaches often hope that the consequences of disciplining a certain team member for unacceptable behaviour, eg, substituting a player for fighting or arguing, will not only have an effect on the specific player substituted but will also affect the behaviour of other team members who are watching. The other players will internalise the consequences of the team mate's behaviour and are thus warned against copying it.

Modelling is not always carried out either by the observer or the model at a conscious or intentional level. Very often the model does not intend their behaviour to be copied and is usually unaware that

Fig 20.5. Is David Beckham a positive role model for beginners?

their behaviour is acting as a model for others. The behaviour of top professional sports performers can therefore, have either positive or negative repercussions for the behaviour of beginners.

Although role models are an important factor within observational learning they do not always have to be real or in direct contact. Remote sports stars, cartoon characters or fictional media-related models can prove equally influential. By identifying with the model the performer will not only replicate existing behaviour but may also reproduce certain behaviour in novel situations.

People of influence in physical education and sport have to be aware that unacceptable models of behaviour or attitudes are often being presented and possibly influencing the behaviour of others, eg, gender stereotyping and aggression.

Although for most learners and beginners the model is known directly by the observer and is usually a significant other, eg, parent, teacher, coach, team mate or professional sportsperson, the degree of the effect or endurance of observational behaviour will depend on several factors (see social learning and aggression).

Bandura's often quoted 'Bobo doll' experiments in relation to children learning aggressive behaviour through the observation of others, led him to suggest that imitation is more than just copying a model's behaviour and depends very much on how **appropriate**, **relevant**, **similar**, **nurturant**, **reinforced**, **powerful** and **consistent** the behaviour is. Further research has also shown that the learner not only has to imitate the behaviour but also identify with the role model.

# Important characteristics of models

## Appropriateness

If the behaviour of the model being observed is perceived by the observer as being appropriate in relation to accepted norms and values then it will increase the probability of it being imitated. For instance in our society male aggressive behaviour appears more acceptable than female aggressive behaviour (accepted norm) and therefore young beginners/learners are more likely to copy male aggressive behaviour than female. This has obvious repercussions for male/female stereotyping in western culture.

## Relevance

Again, in relation to the young performer's perceptions of the model is how relevant is the behaviour? Young males are more likely to imitate male models of aggression than are girls as they have in general been socialised into seeing this as part of the accepted male role in society. The behaviour should also be realistic ie, a live performance is more likely to have an effect than a video.

## Similarity

By as young as three years of age youngsters are beginning to identify with their 'gender roles' and will identify more readily with similar models.

## Nurturant

Whether the model is warm and friendly will have an effect on the likelihood of their behaviour, attitudes and morals being imitated. A teacher presenting an activity in a friendly unthreatening way is more likely to be taken notice of and is thus nurturing the appropriate behaviour (see styles of leadership).

## Reinforced

If a model's behaviour is reinforced or rewarded in any way then it is more likely to be imitated. Again this has repercussions for the media who very often directly or indirectly draw attention to certain behaviour thus reinforcing it in the eyes of the beginner. The imitation of gender appropriate behaviour is often reinforced by parents (significant others).

## Powerful

The more powerful model is seen to have a more significant effect than a less powerful one ie, more likely to be copied if highly skilled.

## Consistency

The more consistent the model's behaviour is, the more likely it is to be imitated. Research has shown, however, that sometimes a role model's inconsistent behaviour can inadvertently have an effect on young performers' behaviour.

A performer will take into account the above factors and evaluate them in relation to the consequences of the behaviour. These consequences can be viewed in two ways, the second more crucial than the first.

1. What were the consequences of the model's behaviour?
2. What are the perceived consequences of modelling the same behaviour for the observer (learner/beginner)?

The consequences may either be immediate or appear at a later stage.

If observers can imitate a certain behaviour at a later appropriate stage, then they are said to have socially learned it. In physical education and sport more long-term learning can also occur when young performers begin to 'think', 'feel' and 'act' as if they were the role model rather than consciously copying technical motor skills. Over a longer period young performers can assimilate the attitudes, values, views, philosophy and levels of motivation demonstrated by significant others (teacher or coach) to ensure that they become a 'model' professional themselves.

# Bandura's four stage process model of observational learning

While social learning theory (and others) takes into account the effect of reinforcement, Bandura's original model referred to learning without any direct rewards or reinforcement. He argued that beginners/performers learn and behave by observing other performers or events (vicarious experience), not merely from the direct consequences of their own behaviour.

The practical application of Bandura's research into observational learning can be related to the four stages of the modelling process identified in fig 20.6. This will help teachers and coaches to ensure that learners are focused and maintain their attention in order to produce a learned competent performance.

## Stage 1 – Attention

In order to ensure that a performer learns through observing it is very important that they give careful and specific attention to the model. The level of attention paid to a model will depend on the level of respect that the learner has for the perceived status and attractiveness of the model. A beginner, for instance, is much more likely to take notice of and try to emulate a highly skilled professional or a coach who has significant knowledge of the activity.

Attention is gained by models that are:

- attractive

- successful

- powerful

or those whose behaviour is

- functional.

Teachers and coaches must also be aware of the beginners/learners stage of learner in order to ensure that they don't overload them with too much information. A good coach will ensure that a beginner focuses on the main points and that their attention is not distracted in any way from the task. It is important that the demonstration:

- can be seen and heard

- is accurate

- focuses attention on specific details and cues

- maintains the level of motivation.

## Stage 2 – Retention

In order that modelling is effective the beginner must be able to retain the skill in their memory and

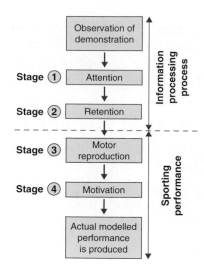

Fig 20.6. Adapted model of Bandura's observational learning process

recall it when appropriate. One way of achieving this is to use mental rehearsal. Another way is to ensure that the demonstration/practice is meaningful, relevant or realistic. By using symbolic coding in some form a coach can help the performer retain the mental image of the skill. Thus retention often involves cognitive skills.

## Stage 3 – Motor production

While a performer can pay attention and retain a clear picture of what is required of them they will in general need time to practise the modelled technique if they are to be able to carry out the skill themselves. It is important therefore, that the 'model' is appropriate to the capability level of the learner/observer: the observer must be able to act out the task. Therefore if complex tasks are being developed then the methodology of teaching and practice must allow for general progression and provide opportunity for staged success.

## Stage 4 – Motivation

If performance of the model is successful then this will provide the motivation for the learner to try to reproduce it again at the appropriate time.

Without motivation a learner will not carry out the previous three stages, i.e. pay attention, remember and practise the task.

According to Bandura, the level of motivation is dependent on:

- the level of external reinforcement (praise, appropriate feedback)
- the level of vicarious reinforcement
- the level of self reinforcement (sense of pride or achievement)
- the perceived status of the model
- the perceived importance of the task.

## Practical application of Bandura's model

In order to make demonstrations more effective a teacher or coach should:

- make sure the learner is aware of the importance and relevance of the skill to the final performance
- refer to a high status model
- get someone of similar ability to demonstrate to help self efficacy
- make sure the performer can see and hear well
- show complex skills from various angles and at different speeds
- highlight the main aspects of technique
- focus attention on a few points particularly for beginners and children
- not have too long a delay between instruction and demonstration
- allow time for mental rehearsal
- not allow too long a delay between demonstration and mental rehearsal
- repeat the demonstration if necessary
- reinforce successful performance.

# Summary

## Learning theories

- The key components of the behaviouristic perspective are stimulus (S) and response (R). The S–R theory is based on the concept that learning involves the development of connections or bonds between specific stimuli and responses.
- In classical conditioning, drill and habit are very important elements of every lesson.
- In operant conditioning, reinforcement is central to shaping behaviour.
- The teacher or coach must try to produce feelings of satisfaction to give strong reinforcements (law of effect).
- Hull's drive theory links motivation to the strengthening of the S–R bond.
- Cognitive theories suggest that performers must be able to understand events. The concept of 'insight' is a major aspect of cognitive theories.

## Socialisation

- Most behaviour in sport takes place within a social setting.
- Socialisation is the general continuous process of transmitting a culture to people and teaching them behaviour appropriate to the accepted norms, values and expectations of society.
- As a member of a sports group/team a performer can be socialised into the 'modelled' norms of that subculture. These can be carried over and influence behaviour outside the sporting situation.

- The family is the most important 'prime' socialising agent. However, teachers, coaches and high status models and peers can also heavily influence a performer's behaviour.

## Social learning and observational learning

- Social learning theory advocates that we learn and acquire new behaviours and attitudes, both acceptable and unacceptable, as a result of vicarious reinforcement through observation and imitation.
- The person being observed is the model.
- The effect of observational learning is dependent upon the model having certain characteristics.
- Observational learning can take place without intention.
- The effect and level of social learning through observation is increased if the model is of a high status and their behaviour is reinforced.
- Demonstrations are an important aspect of observational learning.
- The process of observational learning involves four stages: attention, retention, motor production and motivation.

# Review Questions

1. What is a theory of association?
2. Explain the S–R bond.
3. What is a major criticism of classical conditioning?
4. In what ways does operant conditioning differ from classical conditioning?
5. What does reinforcement mean?
6. How does positive and negative reinforcement affect the probability of behaviour happening?
7. How does punishment affect behaviour?
8. What is the law of effect?
9. Give a practical example to show your understanding of how behaviour is shaped and maintained by its consequences.
10. How does a teacher or coach prevent 'inhibition' developing?
11. What does 'insight learning' mean?
12. Why is the cognitive approach to learning thought to be more effective?
13. What do social psychologists mean by socialisation?
14. What part can sport play in this process?
15. What are socialising agents?
16. Why is observational learning important to social learning theory?
17. According to Bandura what are the main characteristics of a model that influence the likelihood of imitation taking place?
18. Explain Bandura's four stages of observational learning.

# 21. Information Processing

Information processing is a key topic and is central to your understanding of many other areas within this book. A sports performer uses information from the current situation, previous experience and their memory systems in order to reduce uncertainty and help them to decide how to act. Information processing is an approach which sees the development of human motor behaviour (motor learning) as a *process* rather than a specific stimulus and response relationship. It has developed under the umbrella of cognitive psychology.

Here is a list of terms to be covered in this chapter. It is important that you understand them and can apply the principles involved to practical situations within Sport and Physical Education:

## Information processing

- Display
- Cues/signals/stimulus
- Proprioceptors
- Exteroceptors
- Introceptors
- Kinaesthesis
- Selective attention

- Short-term sensory store
- Short-term memory
- Long-term memory
- Reaction time
- Hicks Law
- Psychological refractory period
- Channel capacity

- Feedback
- Knowledge of results (KR)
- Knowledge of performance (KP)
- Intrinsic feedback
- Extrinsic feedback

## What is information?

### Information:

- reduces uncertainty
- allows players to make decisions on actions
- comes from previous relevant experience
- comes from current experience/game/ situation.

## Information processing

Much of the terminology used in the various models is reflective of the post-war computer age in which it developed. The models appear to make comparisons between the ways in which machines function and process information and the ways in which humans 'achieve, retain and transform knowledge' (Bruner, 1972). Although research and the many models produced tend to suggest that the process learners go through is basically the same the information processing approach recognises the individuality of the learner. Individuals are studied as active beings using knowledge in ways personal to themselves. This involves a whole host of processes. In breaking down what is seen as a very complicated process into manageable proportions individuals will be involved in:

- information reception
- information translation
- information transmission
- information reduction
- information collation
- information storage
- information retrieval.

The information processing approach has been traditionally based on two assumptions.

1. That the processing of information can be broken down into various sub-processes or components/stages.
2. That each of these components has limitations in terms of capacity or duration which affect the amount of information that can be processed.

Information processing emphasises that:

- perception
- attention
- memory
- decision making and
- feedback

play an important part in the overall learning process.

# Information processing models

Various psychologists have put forward graphical representations (models) of how they see the various parts of the cognitive process relating together. These models are intended to aid understanding by helping teachers/coaches in their task analysis. The learning process is, however, a

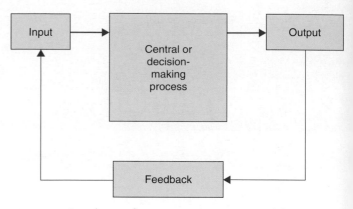

Fig 21.1. Simplistic information processing model

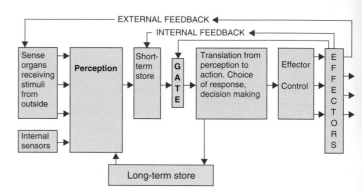

Fig 21.2. Welford's information processing model. (Adapted from A.T. Welford, 1976.)

changing, complex, multi-dimensional process and such models must be seen as hypothetical and flexible. Two of the better-known models which are generally referred to are Welford's (1976) and Whiting's (1970), in figs 21.2 and 21.3.

Both models reflect basically the same process:

- stimulus identification stage/input stage
- response identification/selection stage/central stage
- response programming stage/the output stage

although they use slightly different terminology.

## Stimulus identification stage (Input)

This stage is mainly a sensory stage where the stimulus (eg, a ball) is detected along with speed, size, colour, direction of movement, etc., from the display.

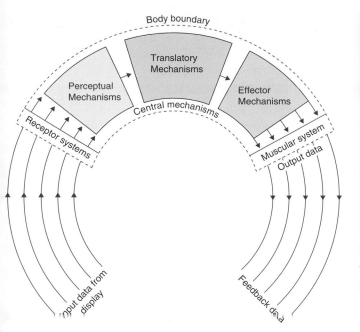

Fig 21.3. Whiting's model (1969) is a well-known illustration of the information processing theory. (Adapted from H.T.A. Whiting, 1970.)

## The display

This is the physical environment in which the learner is performing. The display for the player shown in fig 21.4 would be her own team mates, opposition, the pitch, ball, goal posts, the crowd and whatever else is going on in the vicinity of the game, whether important or not.

## Stimuli and cues

These are specific aspects of the display that are being registered by the learner's sense organs (eg, a ball being passed to them, or players calling for the ball).

## Sense organs, sensory systems and receptors

These are the receptors which take in the sensory information. There are three types or categories of receptors:

1. **Exteroceptors** – receive **extrinsic** information from outside the body (from the display):
   - visual
   - audition
   - touch
   - smell
   - taste.

Fig 21.4. The stimulus identification stage. A player hears her team mates call, sees the ball, feels her grip on the stick and braces her legs in ready position to receive the ball

2. **Proprioceptors** – nerve receptors within the body in muscles, joints, etc. providing **intrinsic** information regarding what class of movement is occurring. Kinaesthetic information is also provided about the feel or sense of movement. The inner ear also provides proprioceptive information eg, are you balanced?

3. **Introceptors** – information from the internal organs of the body, heart, lungs, digestive system, etc. This information is passed to the central mechanism of the brain via the body's sensory nervous system, eg, how fast the heart is beating, register fatigue, etc.

## Perception

This process involves the interpretation of the sensory input, along with discrimination, selection and coding of important information that may be relevant to the decision-making process. The process of selective attention and use of memory are important at this stage.

---

### KEY WORD

**Perception**: 'the process of assembling sensations into usable representations of the world.' (D. Coon, 1983)

---

## Response selection stage (central stage)

Having identified information from the display, this stage involves deciding on the necessary movement in the context of the present situation, eg, does the hockey player receive the ball and pass, change direction and dribble, or hold the ball?

### Translatory/decision-making mechanism

This involves an individual having to use the coded information received to recognise what is happening around them in order to decide on and select the appropriate motor programme to deal with the situation. Perception, selective attention short-term memory and long-term memory are all involved.

## Response programming stage (output)

In this final stage the motor systems are organised in order to deliver the chosen plan of action.

### Effector mechanisms/effector control

Motor programmes or schemas (plans of action – see Chapter 22) are selected and developed involving short-term and long-term memory. These plans, in the form of coded impulses, are sent via the body's *effector* or motor nerves to the appropriate muscles telling them what action to carry out.

### Muscular system/effectors

The muscles receive the relevant 'motor programme' or plan of action in the form of coded impulses, initiate the movement and the action is performed.

### Feedback

As a result of whatever action has been carried out the receptor systems receive information in various forms. There are many different types of feedback but it can be either extrinsic (from outside the body) or intrinsic (from within the body).

It can be seen that the body's control system (brain) through a series of receptors and effectors, controls our physical movements by evaluating the need for action and then executing it when and where it deems necessary. How effective this processing of

information is depends on many variable factors which will be discussed over the following pages.

# Memory

The memory is seen as a critical part of the overall learning process. It is central to our ability to receive the relevant information, interpret it, use it to make decisions and then pass out the appropriate information via the body's effector systems.

There has been much debate about the structure, organisation and capacity of the memory process with many modifications being suggested to the basic 'two-dimensional process' or 'multi-store' model of memory as described by Atkinson and Shiffrin (1968). It is generally suggested, however, that there are two main aspects of memory: short-term memory (**STM**) and long-term memory (**LTM**). These two parts of memory are in some way preceded by a third area known as the sensory system or short-term sensory store (**STSS**) which involves a selection and attention process.

The STSS receives all sensory information provided by sensory receptors. It can hold large amounts of information (it is virtually limitless). Information usually lasts in the STSS for a fraction of a second (maximum 1 second). Unless it is reinforced it will be lost – scanning is a way of reinforcing information.

## Selective attention

Owing to the apparent limited neurological capacity of the short-term memory suggested by many single channel models (eg, Broadbent 1958, Norman 1969, 1976) it is acknowledged that there is some form of selection system in order to prioritise information, although there are disagreements about the positioning of this filtering system (see Welford's model fig 21.2, the gating process).

The process of selective attention is responsible for selecting relevant from irrelevant information from the display. This allows the tennis player, for example, to focus on the specific cues being presented by their opponent when receiving serve

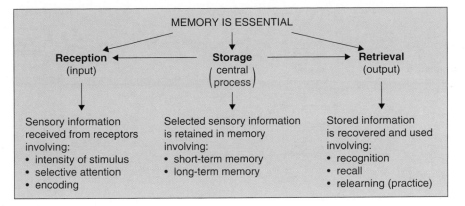

**Fig 21.5.** Memory is essential

(the grip, throw up of the ball, angle of racket, position in relation to service court, etc.) and ignore other aspects of the environment (display) which may distract them (eg, crowd, noise from the next court, ball boys, etc.) thus helping to prevent potential information overload. As well as increasing the time that a stimulus can remain in the STM, effective selective attention can help to reduce reaction time.

The efficiency of the short-term sensory store and the selective attention process is influenced by several factors.

- **experience** – know what to look for – an experienced tennis player will know what to look for when facing an opponent

- **arousal** – the more alert you are the more likely you are to choose the appropriate cues. In cricket, a batsman who is alert is able to pick up on spin, speed and direction of the ball

- **quality of instruction** – as a beginner you don't always know what to respond to. The coach or teacher can direct your attention verbally, visually, mechanically

- **intensity of stimulus** – the effectiveness of the senses (eg, short sighted, poor hearing) when detecting, eg, speed, noise, size/shape and colour.

Selective attention can be improved by:

- lots of relevant practice

- increasing intensity of the stimulus

- use of language associated with or appropriate to the performer in order to motivate and arouse

- use of past experience/transfer to help explanations

- direct attention.

## Short-term memory

Because the short-term memory appears to function between the STSS and the long-term memory receiving and integrating relevant coded information from both areas and passing on decisions via the body's effector systems (processing and storing information) it is often referred to as the 'working memory' or 'work space' (Atkinson and Shilfrin, 1971). The information in our STM at any one time is said to be our 'consciousness'.

### Capacity of STM

Compared with the two other aspects of memory the STM has very limited capacity hence the need for the process of selective attention (when only relevant information is encoded and passed to STM). Seven plus or minus two items ($7 \pm 2$) appears to be the maximum amount of information 'chunks' that any one person can hold. It has been suggested, however (Miller, 1956) that by practising a process called 'chunking' or grouping together of many items of information, a person can remember several 'chunks' of information rather than just seven individual items. Thus a games player with practice will possibly be able to remember at least seven different tactical moves or options happening around them rather than the seven aspects of a

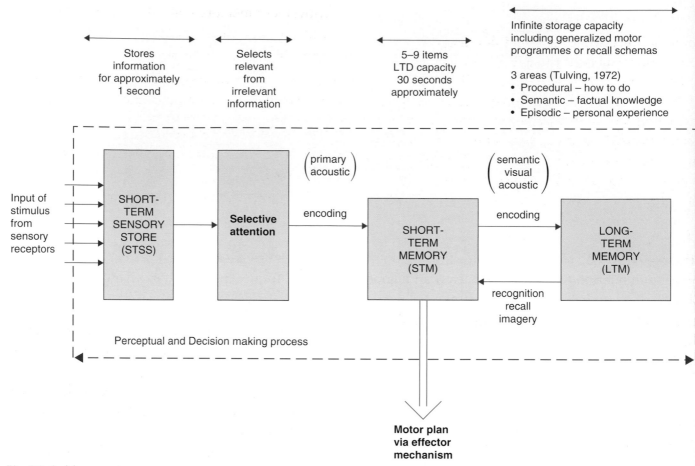

Fig 21.6. Memory stores

specific skill or strategy. In addition, a performer, by linking various aspects of a particular skill together, eg, a tennis serve, will see it as a whole, once learned, rather than as all the various parts of sub-routines of the service, grip, stance, throw up, preparation of racket, point of contact, follow through and recovery.

## Duration of STM

It is generally accepted that unless the $7 \pm 2$ item of information within the STM are reinforced in some way by practice, repetition or rehearsal then they will only remain in the short-term memory for a relatively short period of time: approximately 30 seconds. If 'attention' is directed away from the information being held in the short-term memory then it tends to be forgotten. In order to keep information 'circulating' within the STM, research has suggested that it is more effective for a person to repeat it verbally. Visual imagery, although slower,

can also be used. Important areas of information are passed on to the long-term memory for retrieval and use at a later date.

## Long-term memory

The long-term memory is what is generally thought of as someone's 'memory'. Information about past experiences is stored, including learned knowledge, perceptual skills, motor skills, etc. In short, all classes of information associated with learning and experience are retained in the LTM.

## Capacity of LTM

The long-term memory is thought to have unlimited capacity. It enables a performer to deal with present situations or tasks by using information that has been specifically learned (either behavioural or factual) or information gained from general past experiences.

## Duration of LTM

Information, once learned and stored in the long-term memory, is thought to be there indefinitely, perhaps permanently. The main problem with information stored in the long-term memory is one of retrieval. Once information has been rehearsed, reinforced and linked together in the appropriate manner within the STM (coding) it is passed to the LTM for storage. It is generally thought that once learned and stored in the LTM motor skills in particular are protected from loss. There is evidence to suggest that retrieval is more effective with skills that have been 'overlearned' (practised continually) and become autonomous. Skills that are linked or associated together in a more continuous way (cycling, swimming) rather than individual discrete skills (handstand, headstand) can also be retrieved more effectively.

## Retrieval of information

Retrieval of information that has been stored in the LTM for future use can take several different forms. The more common forms are recognition, recall, relearning.

- **Recognition:** when a tennis player sees something familiar with regard to a style of serve by their opponent or a defender in soccer sees several things happening in front of them and they have to make their mind up which one is the most dangerous and adapt their own movement to it having 'recognised' certain cues or signals (retrieval cues).

- **Recall:** when a performer has to actively search their memory stores for certain previously learned skills or information that may help solve a problem in the present.

- **Relearning:** if something has previously been learned but then forgotten it will possibly be easier to learn a second time round.

- **Imagery:** when a performer is able to 'hook' their present cognitive or motor situation onto some form of visual image of previously well-performed situation, skill or strategy (see mental rehearsal).

Movement memory is aided by verbal labels which can produce a mental image of the correct movement.

To ensure important information stays in the long-term memory a teacher/coach/performer will need to:

- rehearse/reinforce/repeat
- link or associate information with familiar information
- make information meaningful/relevant
- make stimuli more recognisable/intense
- group or 'chunk' information together
- use imagery.

## Decision making

In adopting an information processing approach to analysing how a performer uses present information in the form of cues and signals from the environment (display), in conjunction with previously learned or experienced information or movement skills in order to carry out some form of response (decision making), you should now have realised that this process takes time. Being able to select the correct plan of action (make a decision) quickly, is obviously critical in many sports, particularly those classified as using open skills, where adapting to continually changing situations is important, eg, tennis, basketball, hockey. It therefore follows that the quicker a performer can go through the whole process the greater advantage this should have for the motor action being carried out: anticipation becomes possible.

## Reaction time

Reaction time is seen as an important performance measure helping researchers to find out exactly what happens prior to a response being made (response preparation time) and what factors can affect the speed and effectiveness of the response.

- **Reaction time** is defined as:

    *'the time between the onset of a signal to respond (stimulus) and the initiation of that response.'*

    *(R.A. Magill)*

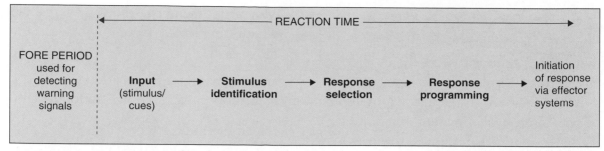

Fig 21.7. Reaction time

This is different to two other time zones very often associated and sometimes confused with reaction time, namely 'movement time' and 'response time'.

- **Movement time** is defined as 'the time from the initiation of the first movement to the completion of that movement'.
- **Response time** is defined as the time from the onset of a signal to respond (stimulus) to the final completion of the response or action, ie, reaction time + movement time.

Individuals differ considerably in their speed of reactions (reaction time – RT) or what has been termed 'response preparation time'. There are many important factors that can affect a performer's reaction time, usually associated with either the

- stimulus (type or amount)
- individual performer
- requirements of the task.

Response preparation time (decision making) can be affected by various factors associated with the amount of information and the number of decisions that have to be made.

## Simple reaction time

This is a specific reaction to a specific stimulus (one stimulus – one response), eg, reacting to a starter at the beginning of a race.

## Choice reaction time

This is when there are a number of alternatives: either a performer has to respond correctly when

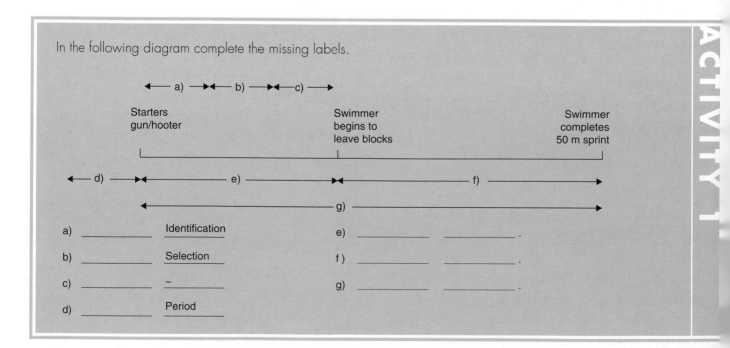

**Fig 21.8.** Matthew Hoggard. Not the quickest in the world but successfully employs lots of variation in his bowling

faced with several stimuli all requiring a different response or a performer has to respond correctly to a specific stimulus from a choice of several stimuli. Generally, the more choices a performer has to face with regard to either number of stimuli to deal with, or, more importantly, the number of optional responses, the more information they have to process and the longer or slower the reaction time is. This general 'rule of thumb' is based on Hick's Law (1952).

Hick's Law states that: 'Reaction time will increase logarithmically as the number of stimulus response choices increase.'

The linear relationship implies that reaction time increases at a constant rate every time the number of response choices is doubled. This has obvious implications for a performer when trying to outwit an opponent. A bowler in cricket is better placed to dismiss a batsman if they have more types of delivery at their disposal and can use them at various times to create a feeling of uncertainty in the batsman's mind – RT can be increased by over 50%.

## Stimulus–response compatibility

The compatibility of a stimulus and response (S–R) is related to how 'naturally' connected the two are. If a certain stimulus happens, what usual response does it cause? The more 'natural' or usual the response the quicker the reaction time.

The converse obviously applies, eg, in hockey, a player's natural response to a ball played down their left-hand side is to reach over with the stick in the left hand and lay the stick down taking the ball on the reverse (stimulus–response compatibility). However, if the coach wants a player to move across and take the ball on the open stick in order to be 'strong on the ball' after receiving, this, for most beginners, is S–R incompatibility (unnatural), therefore RT would be increased considerably.

Experienced sailors can reduce their reaction time to almost zero as they move the tiller of the boat in relation to wind changes (S–R compatibility). It appears almost natural.

## Predictability of stimulus occurring

The more predictable a stimulus is the more effective the response can be in terms of time and accuracy. If a performer can predict in advance what is going to happen by being able to pick up on various cues and signals or advanced information, then RT can be reduced dramatically. This pre-cueing technique, as it is sometimes called, has the similar but reverse relationship caused by Hick's Law regarding choice reactions.

In discussion with a partner, consider a badminton or tennis situation. What pre-cueing information might you be looking for when facing a serve? What might this enable you to do?

ACTIVITY 2

A player's reaction time, however, can only be reduced if they pick up on the correct cues and predict the correct stimulus.

## Previous experience/practice

The more experienced a performer is and the more practice they have had of making choices, and relating the compatibility and probability of certain responses to certain stimuli, then the more likely it is that their RT will be faster. The effect is obviously greater where choice RT rather than simple RT is involved. Hence the experienced badminton player, when placing the shuttle in various parts of the court, knows, through a good deal of appropriate practice, that only certain types of shot can be played by their opponent from this position. This will allow them almost to pre-select plans of action (see motor programmes, chapter 22), ie, anticipate, thus reducing their reaction times and response times to what appears to be almost instant processing.

## Anticipation

Anticipation is linked very closely to experience. Anticipation, where a performer is able to initiate

Fig 21.9. Experienced defenders can pick up on the appropriate cues/signals and anticipate attackers' movements/actions

movement programmes or actions with 'perfect timing' relies very much on a performer using signals and cues and recognising certain stimuli early, thus predicting what is going to happen. The defender in hockey or football who always appears in the right place at the right time to make the tackle or intercept the attacking pass is using their previous experience.

An experienced tennis player receiving a second serve would have picked up on their opponent's angle of racket and subtle positioning of feet, etc., to recognise that a top-spin serve, causing the ball to 'kick' up high and wide to the forehand, was probably coming over the net. He or she then prepares accordingly, thus processing has begun earlier. An inexperienced beginner on the other hand would not understand what a top spin serve can do to the ball or be able to recognise the warning signals/cues (selective attention). Thus they would be totally unprepared for the high bouncing ball when it arrived. Beginners need more processing time in order to organise, prepare and initiate a response.

### Types of anticipation

Two types of anticipation have been recognised: **spatial anticipation** and **temporal anticipation.**

- Spatial or event anticipation is when a performer can judge or predict what is actually going to happen and therefore prepares his/her appropriate actions accordingly, enabling the response to be initiated almost immediately the actual shot occurs, eg, blocking in volleyball.

- Temporal anticipation is when a performer knows what is going to happen but is unsure of when it will happen.

While temporal anticipation is useful, having *both* temporal and spatial anticipation is much more effective. The fact that many sports performers, particularly in 'open type' activities involving rapid changes in actions, rely heavily on anticipation means that as well as using anticipation to their own advantage they can also use the principles behind it to disadvantage opponents (see PRP below).

Factors affecting anticipation are:

- predictability of stimulus
- speed of stimulus
- time stimulus is in view
- complexity of response
- practice
- age.

# Psychological refractory period (PRP)

A performer using previous experience in order to help them anticipate certain moves or actions depends heavily on making the correct predictions in order to reduce the time needed to prepare a response. One way a performer can try to increase the RT of their opponent is by presenting certain false information, a certain stance or movement of the racket in tennis or stick in hockey which implies to the opponent that a certain shot or movement will occur (predicting). The opponent then processes this information in order to prepare and initiate a response. As the opponent's response to the first 'dummy' or fake action is initiated, the player changes the move or shot causing the opponent to re-evaluate the situation and react to the second set of stimuli. The processing of the new information, for

instance a drop shot in badminton rather than the anticipated overhead clear, takes time, creating a slight time delay. This delay in being able to respond to the second of two closely spaced stimuli is termed the **psychological refractory period** (PRP). In practice, if timed correctly, the opponent in tennis or badminton or defenders in hockey or basketball, are made to look foolish as, by the time they have reorganised their movement to deal with the second stimulus, the point has been won or they have been beaten by the attack.

Theoretically the delay is created by the increased processing time caused by a hold-up or 'bottleneck effect' within the response programming stage. Within this stage it is suggested that the brain can only deal with the initiation of one action or response when presented with two closely following stimuli. This is known as the single-channel hypothesis. A PRP will only occur, however, if the 'fake' or 'dummy' move or action is significant enough to cause the opponent to think it is actually going to happen.

There must also be no lengthy delay in carrying out the second stimulus or 'real' action as this may negate the whole significance of the PRP.

## How to make use of 'deception' in sport

- Deception makes use of the psychological refractory period.
- The response to one stimulus must be completed before the response to a second stimulus can begin.

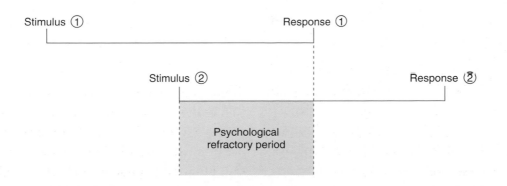

Fig 21.10.

- Therefore by introducing a second stimulus before the response to the first stimulus is completed the performer playing the dummy gains time.

- For example when setting a dummy in team ball games the ball player pretends to pass/run one way/direction then when the opponent responds to that movement the ball player changes direction/passes the other way.

- More time is gained because the opponent must finish the first movement before reacting and re-adjusting to the second stimulus.

- Deception creates uncertainty/insecurity.

## Strategies to deceive opponents

- Delay movements as long as possible.

- Disguise relevant cues.

- Emphasise non-important cues.

- Present false information, eg, fast early action then soft contact – 'selling a dummy' → This will create uncertainty → the opponent will slow down if alternatives are presented → should s/he tackle/try to intercept a pass etc → attention of opponent will be distracted by the uncertainty → reactions of opponent will be delayed by the second movements.

# Intensity of stimulus

There is evidence to support the view that as intensity of stimulus increases reaction time decreases, eg, larger, brighter implements (rackets or balls) for beginners in particular. (Links to cognitive phase of learning)

# Age

It is generally accepted while being relatively limited in early childhood RT improves rapidly through the developing years up until the optimum level which is thought to be the late teens/early twenties. After this it levels off only to slow down considerably as old age approaches. Lack of experience on which to base quick and effective decisions has been suggested to explain children's limited RT. Practice and experience will delay the effect of age.

# Gender

Research has tended to support the view that males have shorter reaction times although female reaction times deteriorate less with age. The factors already discussed, however, have much more of an influence than gender.

# Strategies to improve response/ reaction time

- Mental rehearsal – going over responses in your mind.

- Concentration/ignoring irrelevant signals.

- Practise reacting to specific stimuli/signals/cues (groove the response).

- Improve physical fitness.

- Anticipate.

- Concentrate on warning signals and early movements.

# Arousal, attention and alertness

Here are the three As of information processing.

## Arousal

The level of arousal of a performer is seen as a significant influencing factor upon their ability to make decisions quickly (response preparation time). We will consider various arousal theories and their links to motivation and performance in much greater detail within the psychology of sport section. As an introduction to the concept, arousal can be viewed as the energy or excitement levels of the individual generated at the time the performance is taking place. These levels can vary from extremely high, almost agitated behaviour to the lowest level, sleep. Both these extreme states are not recommended for the performer in sport as they do not create the 'optimum' state of mental readiness for effective decisions to be made.

## Attention

Over-arousal creates 'states of anxiety', causing lack of concentration and lack of attention to important coaching points (see anxiety).

Performing under high arousal conditions has been shown to reduce a performer's ability to pay attention to all the important and relevant aspects from the displays, possibly creating an inadequate response particularly if something unexpected happens. This phenomenon is known as **perceptual** or **attentional narrowing** (see arousal).

## Alertness

Linked to the concept of optimum arousal and levels of attention is the term alertness. Being continually prepared (alert) to pick up on specific changing cues/signals and thus make correct decisions has been, in the main, linked to the performer's ability to maintain arousal levels or state of readiness. For instance, when a goalkeeper in hockey or football is seen 'prowling' the 'D' or penalty area watching the game, keeping on their toes, they are working on maintaining 'alertness'. While it is relatively easy to maintain optimum levels of arousal and thus attention for very short periods, particularly if you are involved in the game continually, it is sometimes difficult to maintain alertness over longer periods, such as in a dull game situation or in repetitive practice situations.

# Feedback

The final part in the information processing system is feedback (FB). Strictly speaking feedback is a processing term referring to information coming from within the system rather than information coming from the outside world. Feedback is now generally referred to as all the information in its various forms that a performer receives as a result of movement (response produced information). When a performer is taking part in physical activity in any shape or form information is fed back into the system either during the activity or after the activity. This information can come from within the performer or from outside relating to the adequacy of their performance. This information is used to either detect and correct errors during the activity or to make changes/improvements the next time the skill is performed. As well as changing performance, feedback can also be used to reinforce learning and motivate the performer. It has been argued that without FB learning cannot occur. Evidence to support this view is provided by research conducted by Bilodeau and Bilodeau (1959, 1961) and G. Stelmach (1970). The nature of the feedback will alter depending on the performers' stage of learning, but it is vital that all information is accurate, limited to key points and relevant. Feedback in the early stages should be as frequent as possible – reducing as learning progresses in order to reduce the possibility of feedback dependency.

---

In discussion with a partner and using practical examples, try to create a list of as many different kinds of feedback that a performer may receive when taking part in sporting activities.

| Activity | Type of feedback | Example from sport |
| --- | --- | --- |

Try to think of possible methods or classifications that you might use to group together the different types of feedback you have thought of.

ACTIVITY 3

# Types and forms of feedback (FB)

## Intrinsic feedback

Sometimes referred to as internal or inherent feedback, this type of FB comes from within the performer from the propriceptors. When a golfer swings at the ball they can feel the timing of the arm movement and the hip movement in conjunction with a perfect strike of the ball. This is also referred to as **kinaesthetic FB**. The golfer can see and hear their club swing, and hear the ball being struck, which serves to back up the proprioceptive information being received. All this information is inherent to the task. The more experienced and skilled a performer is, the more effective their use of intrinsic FB will be.

## Extrinsic feedback

Sometimes referred to as external or augmented FB, this type of FB is information received from outside the performer about the performance and is given and used to enhance (augment) the already received intrinsic FB. This is the type of FB that is generally referred to in teaching and coaching. It can, however, be received from team mates within the context of a game. Performers usually receive this type of FB by visual or auditory means; for instance the coach or teacher tells or shows a performer the reasons why success or failure has occurred.

This form of information is used extensively during the cognitive and associate phases of learning. A less experienced performer will rely on guidance from the coach/teacher concerning their performance, as they have not yet developed their kinaesthetic awareness fully and cannot yet interpret feedback arising intrinsically.

Extrinsic FB can obviously be made up of a mixture of several different types and forms:

- Continuous
- Knowledge of results (KR)
- Positive
- Terminal
- Knowledge of performance (KP)
- Negative

## Continuous feedback

Sometimes referred to as ongoing or concurrent FB, this type of FB is being received *during* the activity. It is most frequently received as proprioceptive or kinaesthetic information, eg, a tennis player can 'feel' the ball hitting the 'sweet spot' of the racket when playing strokes during a rally.

## Terminal feedback

This is FB received by the performer *after* they have completed the skill or task. It can either be given immediately after the relevant performance or be delayed and given some time later.

## Positive feedback

This type of feedback occurs when the performance of a task was correct or successful. It can be used to reinforce learning, increasing the probability of the successful performance being repeated, eg, a coach or teacher praising a beginner when they catch a ball successfully.

Although positive FB is thought to facilitate perceived competence and help intrinsic motivation, it is important that a teacher doesn't give too much positive FB thereby distorting a performer's perceptions of their own performance and possibly affecting motivation.

## Negative feedback

This type of FB occurs when the performance of a task was incorrect, eg, a basketball player will receive negative FB in various forms if they miss a set shot: they see the ball has missed, friends comment, they realise they did not put enough power behind the ball and the teacher or coach ma indicate faults and suggest correction. All this should help to ensure that further shots are more successful.

# Knowledge of results and knowledge of performance

Knowledge of results (KR) is an essential feature of skill learning. Without knowing what the results of our actions have been we will be unable to modify them in order to produce the precise movements needed for the correct performance of a skill. One of the more important roles of a teacher or coach is to provide this type of information. Knowledge of results is usually given verbally, eg, a netball coach saying 'You missed the net by 10 cm' or an athletics coach shouting out lap times during training. This type of FB about goal or task achievement is thought to be very useful in the early phases of learning when beginners like to have some measure of their successful performance. An eight-year-old child will see her performance in terms of 'I scored a goal today' or 'Our team won all the games', not in terms of the quality of her own performance.

Once KR has been given it is then usually necessary for the teacher or coach to give information as to why or how the result came about. A hockey coach, when trying to develop passing, may give KR as in 'Your pass was far too wide'. They may support this by adding 'The reason it was so wide was because your left shoulder was not pointing towards your partner, your feet were not in the right position and your stick did not follow through in the direction the ball was meant to go'. This gives the performer additional (augmented) extrinsic information in order to help them know not only the result of the action (KR) but also know why the result was incorrect and how to correct the performance. This type of FB about the actual movement pattern is more like the FB given by a teacher and is known as 'knowledge of performance' (KP). Although most of the traditional research has been carried out with regard to KR, due to its ease of measurement, there has been a definite shift in emphasis towards researching KP particularly with the increased availability of more modern computer and video technology allowing greater mechanical analysis of technique and performance.

Knowledge of results (KR) as used in most psychology or coaching texts is referred to as:

*'Information provided to an individual after the completion of a response that is related to either the outcome of the response or the performance characteristics that produced that outcome.'*

(R. Magill)

## The use of feedback

Feedback can be used to help with:

- the correction of errors
- reinforcement
- motivation.

There are numerous studies to support the importance of feedback (KR) in the learning process. In referring back to Fitts' and Posner's phases of learning, feedback can be used to move the performer through the three phases of the learning process.

Once in the autonomous phase the performer should be less reliant on KR and should, through their knowledge and understanding of the activity, be able to detect their own errors and, in conjunction with kinaesthetic FB, be able to make corrections to their own performance.

Although skills can be learned without FB it is generally accepted that FB makes the learning

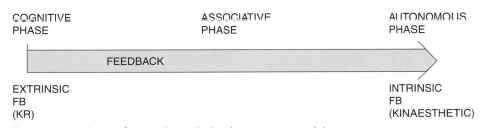

| COGNITIVE PHASE | ASSOCIATIVE PHASE | AUTONOMOUS PHASE |
|---|---|---|

FEEDBACK

| EXTRINSIC FB (KR) | | INTRINSIC FB (KINAESTHETIC) |

ig 21.11. How feedback moves the performer through the three stage model

process more efficient by improving error correction and developing better performance. Relating this to the section on motor programmes (chapter 22), we can see that if a performer receives additional information the quality of his or her generalised patterns of movement (schemas which help initiate and control movement) can be effectively enhanced, particularly in the early phases of learning. When considering the use of FB the teacher or coach needs to be aware of the following:

- current skill levels of the performer (phase of learning)

- nature of the skill (complexity/organisation/classification) and its transferability.

In relation to the above points, the coach or teacher has to decide on the following aspects of FB:

- general or specific

- amount (too much or too little)

- how to present it (visual/verbal)

- frequency, eg, after every attempt, or summary after several attempts (performer must not become dependent on extrinsic FB)

- time available for practice/processing.

Although the quantity, distribution and whether it is positive or negative are important considerations, the most crucial aspects of feedback are *quality* and *appropriateness*.

KR must not provide too much information otherwise the performer will not know what to pay attention to or how to use the FB to help future attempts. Attention must be directed to specific or major errors particularly with beginners. If major errors are left then this could lead to the performer assuming them to be correct, strengthening the incorrect S–R bond and making it much more difficult to deal with later. As well as telling the beginner what the problem is a teacher or coach must provide information on how the performer can correct the error.

Feedback (KR) must be meaningful and relevant to the phase of learning. Beginners might need general information whereas experienced performers may need more specific information. Sometimes, however, beginners may need much more specific information: a more experienced badminton player would understand 'Your positioning is not right' and probably rectify the fault immediately. The same statement made to a beginner would be of little value as they need much more specific FB with regard to the position of feet, angle of upper body or preparation of racket prior to the shot, etc. in order for them to make the necessary corrections. It is important that the FB given is useful to the performer and not just repetition of what is already obvious to them. Such repetition is called **redundant FB**.

Researchers have found that time intervals after the performance have a bearing on how KR should be used. A teacher needs to be aware that once KR has been given the performer has to have time to assimilate the information and put the KR into action. However, too long a delay could allow the performer to forget what has happened or to lose understanding of the relevance of the KR being given.

Feedback can also be used as reinforcement. Reinforcement, as you already know, increases the probability of certain behaviour being repeated. Using FB to strengthen the bond between stimulus and response is useful.

Positive FB has a great role to play in reinforcement. Both KR or KP can be useful in motivating a performer, maintaining interest and effort (direction and intensity). Seeing performance improve, eg, an athlete improving their personal best or a tennis player increasing the accuracy and percentage of successful first serves, should ensure that performers keep on practising. It is very helpful if this is carried out in a formal way with statistical evidence being logged by the teacher or coach. This information can be used both for the evaluation of current performance (error detection) and for future target setting. In this way, feedback can be used as an incentive. Using feedback in conjunction with goal setting has been recognised as being very effective in the learning process.

Consider the three stages of learning. For each stage make a list of the most appropriate and effective types of feedback (with examples) that a coach should use.

ACTIVITY 4

# Summary

- The human motor system can be viewed as a processor of information with sensory information passing through various stages.

- The performer is involved in gathering data, processing the relevant stimuli to form a decision, which is then executed by the muscular system.

- The process consists of three basic stages:
  - Stimulus identification (input)
  - Response selection (decision making)
  - Response programming (output).

- The effectiveness with which a performer processes various forms of sensory information often affects overall performance.

- Reaction time is an important measure of information processing speed, and is affected by many factors.

- In order to assess the effectiveness of the decision and completed actions, feedback is obtained from a variety of sources either internally or externally.

- Feedback provides information about errors to help make corrections and improve performance. It can act as reinforcement for correct actions and help to develop motivation.

- The quality of feedback information is important to ensure learning is effective.

- Performers at different stages of learning will use various forms of FB in different ways.

# Review Questions

1. What is meant by information processing?

2. (a) Draw a simple model of information processing.

   (b) Give practical examples from tennis or badminton for each of the parts of your simple model.

3. What are receptors? Explain the different types.

4. What happens within the three stages of stimulus identification, response selection and response programming?

5. Draw and label Whiting's model of information processing and explain the terms.

6. What are various parts of the memory process?

7. Draw a simple model to show your understanding of how the parts of memory link together.

8. What is the process of selective attention?

9. What is response preparation time better known as?

10. How does 'Hicks Law' relate to this response preparation time?

11. What other factors affect a performer's speed of reactions?

12. What is anticipation?

13. What are the possible good and bad effects of anticipating?

14. What does PRP stand for? Explain a situation in a game where it could be used to benefit performance

15. What are KR and KP?

16. When using feedback what does a teacher or coach need to be aware of?

17. In what ways can extrinsic feedback be used to modify performance?

# 22. Control of Movement, Motor Programmes and Schemas

## Chapter introduction

During discussions of information processing models as a way of explaining how the sports performer uses information to carry out certain actions in order to solve problems, we have often mentioned the notion of 'plans of action' or 'motor programmes' being selected from the long-term memory. These coded motor programmes are said to pass out by the short-term memory via the body's effector systems. The view that motor programmes exist is not a new one; it has been around since the turn of the twentieth century. After many years of research and argument the concept of motor programmes now appears to be generally accepted. However, the question of what a motor programme is exactly, and how it works to control movement, is still under discussion.

Here is a list of terms to be covered in this chapter. It is important that you understand them and can apply them to help you appreciate how human beings initiate, control, adapt and develop movement patterns within sporting situations.

- motor programmes
- executive programme
- sub-routines
- open loop control
- closed loop control

- memory trace
- perception trace
- schema
- recall schema
- recognition schema

## Motor programmes and control of movement

The traditional view of a motor programme was that it was a centrally organised pre-planned set of very specific muscle commands that, when initiated, allowed the entire sequence of movement to be carried out without reference to additional feedback. This view helped to explain how performers sometimes appear able to carry out very fast actions that have been well learned (particularly closed skills) without really thinking about the action, almost like a computer. In other words, they use very little conscious control. This has obvious links to Fitts' and Posner's autonomous stages of learning which was covered in an earlier chapter.

In relating this notion of automatic movement to information processing you can appreciate that the limited capacities of the memory process would easily be overloaded, and take considerable time, if every part of every action had to pass via the STM. The notion of a motor programme being decided upon and initiated from the short-term memory appears to solve the overload problem where, in relatively stable situations, movement can be carried out without the need for modification. This type of control of movement is called 'open loop control', without feedback. Two areas of research which support this view are:

1. Reaction time has been found to be longer in actions which involve more complex

movements. A tennis serve, for example, has many component parts. This suggests that the action is carried out following a pre-planned organisation.

2. In animal experiments involving **deafferention** where the afferent nerve bundles are severed near the spinal cord, it has been shown that even though the brain cannot receive sensory information via the central nervous system (no feedback) the animals are still capable of carrying out movement. This suggests that movement is centrally organised and that feedback is not critical in certain movements.

## Open loop control

Motor programmes or pre-learned mastered movements initiated on command are thought to be developed through practice. A series of movements is built up, starting with very simple movements, until certain actions are stored as complete movements. These complete movements or motor programmes can be stored in the long-term memory and retrieved at will; the whole movement to be carried out can then be initiated by one complete command. It is suggested that such skills are built up in a hierarchical or schematic way. See task analysis and sub-routines.

## Closed loop control

Within the closed loop model the loop is completed by information from the various sensory receptors feeding back information to the central mechanism or executive.

While it is accepted that there are many types of feedback, in this view of feedback control the feedback is internal (kinaesthetic) allowing the performer to compare what is actually happening during the movement with the point of reference, namely the correct or currently learned and stored motor performance. This evaluation of the movement currently being undertaken means errors, if any, can be detected and acted upon. All feedback goes back through the processing system, which means that the process of detecting and correcting errors is relatively slow.

Research has shown that the closed loop system of movement control generally works more effectively

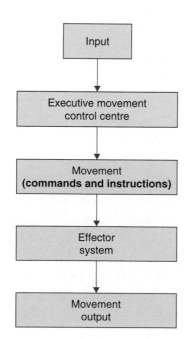

Fig 22.1. Simplified model of open loop control

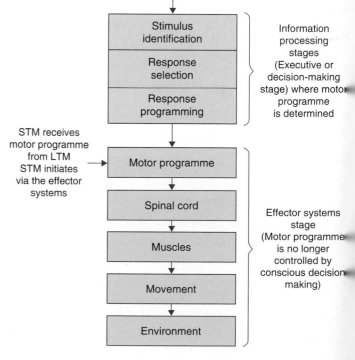

Fig 22.2. Expanded model of open loop control

with movements taking place over longer periods of time (continuous skills, eg, running) or with skills requiring slower limb movements (headstand or handstand). Closed loop models are not thought to be effective for controlling quick discrete-type movements; in this case open-loop control of movement appears to be a better explanation for what happens.

In practice, while in certain actions one specific mode of control may dominate, the fact is that most sporting activities involve both fast, slow, simple and complex movements in a whole variety of coordinated ways. This suggests that performers are continually moving between open loop and closed loop control, with all systems of control being involved in controlling the performers' actions.

## Schema theory

It was stated earlier that motor programmes were traditionally considered to be a specific set of pre-organised muscle commands that control the full movement. This suggests that specific motor programmes for all possible types of action are stored in the long-term memory awaiting selection and initiation. If we accept that motor programmes operate via continuously changing closed and open loop control (with or without the use of feedback), it is the stored motor programme which either directs all movements or is used as the point of reference for a movement to be compared against.

Although the question of how these motor programmes are structured and stored has been considered since the nineteenth century, it was not really until Jack Adams presented his closed loop theory specifically related to motor skills in 1971 that more up-to-date research began in earnest.

For Adams the motor programme was made up of two areas of stored information.

1. **The memory trace** – used for selecting and initiating movement, operating as an open loop system of control prior to the perceptual trace. It does not control movement.

2. **The perceptual trace** – used as the point of reference (memory of past movements) and also

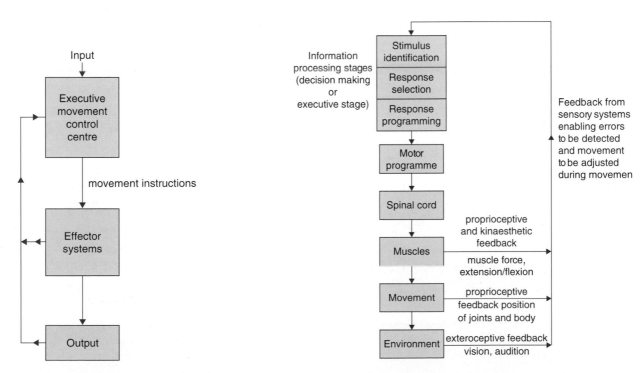

Fig 22.3. Simplified model of closed loop control

Fig 22.4. Expanded model of closed loop control

to determine the extent of movement in progress. Thus the perceptual trace is operating as a closed loop system of control making the ongoing necessary adjustment where/when needed.

The quality or strength of all these traces is built up and developed through practice with the performer using both intrinsic and extrinsic feedback, particularly knowledge of results (KR), which in the early cognitive stages is very often provided by the teacher or coach. Once the perceptual trace in particular is strong and well developed the performer is able to carry out his/her own error detection and correction. (Performer moves from associative phase to autonomous phase and learning).

Schmidt presented his well-known **schema theory** as a way of dealing with the limitations, as he saw them, of Adams' closed loop theory. Schmidt proposed that schemas, rather than the memory and perceptual traces suggested by Adams, explained recall of movement patterns. Instead of there being very specific traces for all learned or experienced movement, schemas as Schmidt saw them were *'a rule or set of rules that serve to provide the basis for a decision'*.

These generalised patterns or rules of movement solved the following dilemma:

- how do we store possibly thousands, if not millions, of specific programmes of movement?
- how do we initiate and control fast and more complex movements?

In addition, if we can only initiate movement via memory traces, developed through practice:

- how do we initiate movement in totally new situations that we have never faced before and have no memory trace of, or programme of movement for?

Schmidt suggested that we learn and control movements by developing generalised patterns of movement around certain types of movement experience, eg, catching, throwing. A performer does not store all the many specific but different types of catching and throwing; rather they collate various items of information every time they experience either catching or throwing. This helps in building up their knowledge of catching or throwing in general. Performers thus construct schemas which enable them at some future time to successfully carry out a variety of movements.

A schema for throwing can be adapted:

- returning a cricket ball to wicket keeper
- a long pass in basketball/netball
- a goalkeeper in football setting up an attack
- throwing a javelin
- playing darts.

By collating as much movement information as possible with regard to throwing we can adapt to new situations because we know the general rules associated with throwing long, short, high, low, etc. *Variety of practice* is essential. In order for schemas to be constructed and developed, the performer has to collate information from four areas of the movement: see table 22.1.

Whenever a performer takes part in an activity he or she will collate these four areas of information to form schemas of movement and store them in the long-term memory. The fact that these are abstract rules of response will enable the performer to cope in unfamiliar surroundings. In order to increase the possibility of the performer making the correct decision and being able to carry it out effectively, variety of practice is essential! It is important that the teacher or coach not only ensures repetition, but that practice is organised in order to take into account the various demands that the skill places on the performer in the 'real life' situation.

## Strategies/methods to enable schema to develop

- varied practice conditions
- avoid blocked or massed practice

Table 22.1. Recall and recognition schemas

| Recall schemas<br>Information is stored about determining and producing the desired movement (similar to memory trace) | 1. initial conditions (where we are) | • knowledge of environment<br>• position of body<br>• position of limbs |
|---|---|---|
| | 2. response specification (what we have to do) | • specific demands of the situation<br>• direction<br>• speed<br>• force |
| Recognition schema<br>information is stored enabling evaluation of movement | 3. sensory consequences (what movement feels like) | • information based on sensory feedback<br>• during and after movement<br>• involves all sensory systems |
| | 4. response outcomes (what has happened) | comparisons are made between<br>• actual outcome<br>• intended outcome<br>• KR is important |

- practice relevant to the game, eg, opposition
- include plenty of feedback – continuous and terminal
- realistic practice

- tasks should be challenging/gradually more difficult
- slow motion practice
- include transferable elements.

# Summary

- Motor programmes are pre-planned sets of muscular movements, stored in the memory, which can be used without feedback.
- Organised in a hierarchical structure with sub-routines making up executive programmes.
- Sub-routines, eg,

- Sub-routines are short fixed sequences which when fully learned, can be run off automatically without conscious control.
- 'Open loop' explains how we perform fast movements without having to think about them (subconsciously).

- Pre-learned mastery of motor programmes is essential for open loop control, feedback is not integral in motor control.
- Feedback and kinaesthesis are imperative in closed loop control.
- Schema are seen as generalised sets of movement patterns stored in the long-term memory, allowing performers to tailor movements to the specific demands of the situation they are faced with.
- Schema are built up through practice and experience.
- Schema theory works on the basis that there are four sources of information that are used and stored in order to modify the programme of movement.
- Variability of practice helps to develop schemas by the performers experiencing different situations.
- Schema theory suggests that every variation of a particular task/skill does not require the learning of a new motor programme.
- The principle of 'transfer' between tasks/skills is supported by schema theory. (See transfer of learning.)

## Review Questions

1. What are motor programmes?
2. What are the sub-routines of a tennis serve?
3. Explain open loop and closed loop control of movement.
4. What are the two types of schema? Explain their function.
5. What four sources of information are used to modify schemas?
6. Why is variability of practice important for the development of schemas?
7. What are the main strategies a coach can adopt in order to develop quality schemas?

# 23. *Turning Theory into Practice*

## *Chapter introduction*

In previous chapters, we have considered the nature of skilled performance, principles of learning and theories associated with learning. In general it is accepted that having a better understanding of the principles and theories associated with perceptual motor skill learning helps a teacher or coach prepare and deliver more effective teaching and coaching strategies. In order to create an effective learning environment a teacher or coach needs to consider many variables which can be categorised into several main areas. Here is a list of the terms to be covered in this chapter. It is important that you understand them.

- Complex skills
- Simple skills
- Organised skills
- High/low skills
- Sub-routines
- Interrelated skills
- Independent skills
- Transfer
- Positive transfer
- Negative transfer
- Retro-active transfer
- Pro-active transfer
- Bi-lateral transfer
- Near/far transfer
- Inter-task
- Intra-task
- Zero transfer
- Identical elements
- Similarity

- Transfer appropriate processing
- Visual guidance
- Verbal guidance
- Manual/mechanical guidance
- Forced response
- Physical restriction
- Massed practice
- Distributed practice
- Mental practice
- Whole method
- Part method
- Progressive part method
- Variations in teaching styles
- Command style
- Reciprocal style
- Discovery
- Guided discovery
- Problem solving

Once you have read this chapter you should gain an understanding of the considerations related to:

- the learning and performance process
- the learner/individual differences
- the task
- the instructional/practice conditions.

# Considerations linked to the learning and performance process

In considering the learning and performance process we have already stated that there is no definitive approach guaranteed to succeed. A teacher or coach needs to be aware of the positive and negative aspects of the many theories and models associated with effective learning. They then need to be able to use and adapt them where appropriate according to the individual needs of the learner and the demands of the situation.

# Considerations linked to learner/individual differences

Considerations related to the individual can be identified and researched in isolation but usually they are variables that are interlinked and difficult to separate in real life situations. They include:

- age – chronological age; maturational age (physical and mental)
- gender
- any personal limitations – sensory, physical, learning problems
- future expectations of performer/learner.

It is essential that a teacher/coach is aware that the above differences exist and is also aware of their possible effects on the learning process.

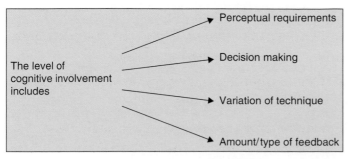

Fig 23.1. Coping with information – cognitive involvement

# Considerations linked to the task

When considering the task a teacher or coach would carry out a task analysis and would ask themselves:

- is it a simple or complex task?
- is it an organised or unorganised task?
- what is the classification?
- is transfer possible?

A knowledge of task complexity and task organisation will help the teacher to decide if a skill is best taught in the 'whole' or 'part' method.

# Complex or simple tasks

When deciding on the degree of complexity of a skill/task a teacher or coach will consider the difficulties it could present to the beginner. These difficulties are generally associated with the amount of information that the performer has to cope with when trying to complete the skill/task (cognitive involvement).

Complex tasks have a high degree of cognitive involvement and require a great deal of 'attention' to the skill. Simple tasks have a low level of cognitive involvement and require a lower level of attention. By being aware of the information processing and memory demands placed on a learner a teacher or coach can try to structure practices in order to reduce the complexity of skills.

One way of achieving this is for the teacher or coach to break down the main skill/task into various parts thus reducing the amount of information (cognitive involvement) the performer is having to cope with (see presentation and organisation practice). As the performer moves through the various stages of learning (see chapter 19) the amount of information they have to deal with can be increased.

# Organisation of a skill/task

Having suggested that complex skills can be broken down into their constituent parts to simplify them, some skills/tasks by their very nature are very difficult to break down into sub-routines and therefore have to be taught as a 'whole' movement. Skills or tasks that are difficult to break down are said to be **highly organised**: there is a very strong relationship between the components of the skill.

If a skill/task is said to be **low in organisation** this means that it can be broken down easily into sub-routines. These sub-routines can be practised in isolation, as they are relatively independent of each other, and then joined together in various ways to make the 'whole' skill again.

Fig 23.2. A handstand is highly organised: the components are interrelated

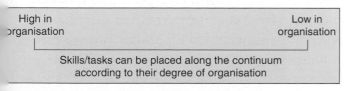

Fig 23.3. High to low organisation continuum

Some skills can be high in complexity and low in organisation, eg, gym/trampoline sequence.

Some skills can be low in complexity and high in organisation, eg, simple jumping, throwing, batting or hitting.

# Transfer

Having considered the complexity, organisation and classification of a skill/task a teacher needs to consider structuring the learning environment in order to take into account the concept of **transfer**. The instructional approaches used to introduce and teach skills/tasks to performers very often depend on the relationship between various skills that have either been taught previously or are going to be taught in the future. The transfer of performance and learning from one situation to another has been an essential element of organisational and instructional approaches for many years.

> ## KEY TERM
>
> Transfer of learning, the influence or effect of performing or practising one skill/task on the learning of another skill/task.

There is evidence to support the following general points.

1. That different types of transfer possibilities exist.

2. That certain practice conditions can either help or hinder the actual effect or degree of transfer.

3. That the amount and direction of transfer can be affected by many factors.

4. That teachers need to be aware of the principles associated with transfer.

5. That teachers need to be able to apply these principles in order to structure effective teaching or coaching situations.

## Types of transfer

The following are types of transfer:

- pro-active
- retro-active
- positive
- negative
- bi-lateral
- near
- far
- inter-task
- intra-task

## Pro-active transfer

When a skill/task presently being learned has an effect on future skills/tasks this effect is said to be pro-active. A teacher ultimately aiming to teach basketball may start off by introducing beginners to throwing, catching, passing, moving, dribbling, thus building up skills to be transferred into the future game situation. Simplified forms of more complex activities are introduced.

## Retro-active

When a skill/task presently being learned has an effect on previously learned skills/tasks this effect is said to be retro-active. This transfer is seen as working backwards in time.

## Positive transfer

Positive transfer, as the term suggests, is when skills/tasks that have been learned/experienced help or **facilitate** the learning of other skills. This can be positive retro-active or positive pro-active. **Similarities** in both skill components and information processing characteristics will help increase the possibilities of positive transfer. If these similarities are pointed out, particularly to beginners in the associative phase of learning, the effect of transfer can be enhanced further.

Important early work in this area was carried out by E.L. Thorndike who developed his identical elements theory in 1914. In this work he suggested that transfer possibilities are greater between tasks that have common elements. If the S–R bond expected in one task were the same as earlier learned S–R bonds then the effect of transfer would be greater. Thorndike's work was based on mental processes, but a practical application example related to motor skill learning is as follows.

(a)        (b)

Fig 23.4. The higher the degree of similarity between the tasks the greater the chance of positive transfer between the skills

A diver wishing to improve his coordination of turning and twisting may take part in trampolining practice in order to develop more control and possibly understanding of rotation and twisting. The components in the practice situation (trampolining) are very similar, and realistic to the main task, thus improving the likelihood of positive transfer occurring.

It is important, therefore, if we accept this basic principle, that a teacher or coach must ensure that practice situations are as realistic as possible. Research on similarities between the stimulus and response has shown that maximum positive transfer can be produced when the stimulus and response characteristics of the new skill are identical to those of the old skill. Other theories have supported the idea that it is general principles of understanding and movement that are transferred as well as the specific elements of a skill. Thus it is when the information processing requirements (cognitive components) are similar that the effect of transfer is greater.

A player involved in team games, such as either football or hockey, would be able to transfer their spatial awareness, tactical understanding of passing, moving and tackling from one game to another. Having learned to throw a cricket ball the basic principles of the movement can be transferred to throwing a javelin (see the schema theory). This view of positive transfer being more likely between activities having similar cognitive elements (information processing conditions) has been termed **transfer appropriate processing**.

## Negative transfer

When one skill/task hinders or inhibits the learning or performance of another skill/task this is known as negative transfer. Sports performers and coaches tend to believe that this happens on a regular basis. Thankfully the effects of negative transfer are thought to be limited and certainly temporary; it is thought to happen when a performer is required to produce a new response in a well-known situation (familiar stimulus). Stimuli are identical or similar but the response requirements are different. Initial confusion is thought to be created more as a result of the performer having to readjust their cognitive processes rather than problems associated with the motor control of the movement. The familiar example of tennis having a negative effect on badminton is often quoted, but although the two games have similar aspects, tactics, use of space, court, net, racket, hand-eye coordination, etc., the wrist and arm action are very different.

When a basketball or hockey coach changes tactics at set plays any initial negative transfer is thought to be as a result of the players having to readjust cognitive processes rather than inability to complete the movement task being asked of them. For example, a rugby player has always been taught to fall to the ground when tackled in order to set up a ruck for his team mates. If the coach changes tactics and decides to develop a mauling game it will be difficult for the player to stay on his feet in the tackle in order to set up a maul. In order to overcome or limit the effects of negative transfer

teachers and coaches should be aware of areas that may cause initial confusion. Practices need to be planned accordingly, ensuring that the players are aware (direct attention) of possible difficulties they may experience. At the same time the teacher or coach needs to be aware of possible positive effects and try to ensure that these outweigh the negative possibilities. In addition the psychological habits of positive attitude, sustained motivation and a conscientious approach to training and practice can also be transferred positively in order to limit any negative effect, as can an understanding of how to deal with new problems.

## Bi-lateral transfer

In the earlier discussion of transfer we considered transfer from one skill/task to another. Bi-lateral transfer, however, occurs when learning is transferred from limb to limb, ie, from the right leg to the left leg, etc. When a basketball coach tries to develop their player's weaker dribbling hand by relating it to earlier learned skills with the strong hand they are involved in bi-lateral transfer. This involves the player in transferring both motor proficiency and levels of cognitive involvement. The performer is thought to adjust and transfer the parameters of stored motor programmes linked to one limb action to the other (schema theory). Thus, with the appropriate practice, the levels of learning developed with the performer's stronger or 'preferred' hand or side can be transferred to the weaker hand or side.

> Consider why it is important for a learner to have reached a sound level of performance in one skill before trying to learn a new skill involving some aspects of the old skill/technique.

ACTIVITY 1

## Zero transfer

When one skill/task has no effect on the performance of another skill, eg, swimming on horse riding, zero transfer is said to occur.

# Research into transfer

## Inter-task

The effect of a skill/task on a different or new skill/task is called **inter-task transfer**. Typical experiments would relate to the amount of time saved in learning, for instance, the lay up shot in the game by using a particular type of drill in basketball practice.

## Intra-task

Intra-task transfer occurs when the relationship between two different types of practice or conditions of practice are considered. Comparisons can be made to show how different types of practice conditions might influence the learning of a specific skill/task.

## Near transfer

When a coach develops specific practices/skills which are very realistic and relevant to the 'real game' situation in order to try to help players in future games, this is referred to as **near transfer**.

## Far transfer

**Far transfer** is when a teacher or coach tries to develop general skills and understanding which may be used in the future to transfer to more specific games or activities. A teacher working with primary children on developing their coordination, spatial awareness or general throwing and catching skills for future use in basketball or netball is working on far transfer.

## Strategies a coach/teacher could employ to promote positive transfer

- Ensure that the movement and cognitive requirements of the skills are similar.
- Ensure that the performer understands the principles of transfer.
- Ensure that the performer is involved in the analysis of the skills.
- Ensure that the original skill is well learned before starting the new skill.
- Ensure that the performer practices in a closed situation before trying it in a game.
- Ensure that practice is realistic.
- Ensure variety of practice once the basics are mastered.
- Ensure principles of games are understood eg, width in attack, depth in defence.

## Links to complexity and organisation

- If a task is **complex** but **low** in organisation, transfer is promoted by practising an easy version of the task first before moving on to a more difficult version.
- If a task is **simple** but **high** in organisation more difficult practices can be introduced.

# Considerations linked with instructional/practice conditions

Finally, a teacher or coach has to consider possible variables associated with themselves and the situation when deciding on curriculum methods and strategies. These considerations can again be categorised into several main areas. When a teacher or coach is aware of all the previously discussed considerations to do with the learning process, the learner and the task, they can then ask themselves, in order to be effective:

1. What types of guidance shall I use?
2. What types of practice/presentation shall I use?
3. What style of teaching shall I use?

## Types of guidance

Guidance is information given to the learner or performer in order to help them limit possible mistakes (incorrect movement) thus ensuring that the correct movement patterns are carried out more effectively. While guidance or instructions are usually given to beginners when skills/tasks are unfamiliar, it is obviously used continually in various forms at all stages of learning and performance (see feedback and knowledge of results). The form of guidance given, together with its effectiveness, will depend on several aspects:

- the learner – motivation; stage of performer's experience/learning linked to their information processing capacities and capabilities
- the type/nature of the skill/task
- the environment or situation.

In order to facilitate the acquisition of skill formal guidance can take several forms:

- visual guidance
- verbal guidance
- manual/mechanical guidance.

If formal guidance does not serve to improve performance through the long-term retention of learning then it cannot be called guidance.

## Visual guidance

Visual guidance can be given in many different ways in order to facilitate the acquisition of skill:

- demonstration
- video/film/TV/slow motion
- posters/charts
- OHTs/slides
- modify the display.

Visual modes of receiving information are valuable at all levels. Visual guidance is, however, particularly useful in the early stages of learning (cognitive phase) by helping the learner establish an overall image or framework of what has to be performed. This modelling of the elements involved in skills is an important aspect of skill acquisition, however (see observational learning).

When presenting the learner, particularly beginners, with effective visual guidance it is important that:

- accurate/correct models of demonstration are used/given (usually provided by the teacher or an experienced performer)
- attention be directed in order that major aspects of the skill are emphasised/reinforced (refer to selective attention)
- demonstrations/models should not be too complex/lengthy (usually whole skill first then parts later)
- demonstrations/models should be realistic/appropriate
- demonstrations must be repeated or referred back to
- demonstrations can be combined with verbal guidance to highlight key points.

There are considerable differences of opinion with regard to the long-term effectiveness of visual guidance. However, for the more advanced performer, specific and complex information can generally be provided more readily by modern technology.

Visual guidance can also be used to highlight certain cues or signals from the display helping the selective attention processes of beginners in particular. Equipment in infant and junior schools is often brighter or bigger in order to help performers 'see things' more clearly.

The teacher or coach can modify the display more specifically by highlighting areas of the court or pitch that shots should be played into or by making target areas bigger. Routes of movement can also be indicated by markers, etc.

It is very difficult in reality to consider visual guidance in isolation as verbal explanations very often have to accompany the demonstration or visual image being presented.

## Verbal guidance

Verbal guidance is again a common form of guidance used by teachers or coaches and can be either very general or specific. A teacher may talk through a particular strategy in team games in order to give players a general picture of what is required before putting the move into practice. This **priming** helps to reduce the stimulus uncertainty (see decision making and reaction times). It is also useful to draw learners' attention to specific details of certain movements by giving verbal cues alongside visual demonstrations. Verbal labelling of specific aspects of a movement by a performer is also thought to facilitate learning. A teacher may help the beginner link their visual image of the task to certain verbal cues.

It is important that the learner does not become too heavily reliant on verbal guidance thus reducing their own ability to pay attention to aspects of performance, process information, make decisions and solve their own problems when guidance is removed. Verbal guidance is thought to be more effective with advanced performers who, because of increased experience and wider movement vocabulary, are able to transfer or transpose verbal comments into visual images more readily. Teachers or coaches may therefore find difficulty in simply describing certain movements to beginners particularly those involving more complex or highly organised skills. They will have to use a combination of both visual and verbal guidance in order to help the learner to internalise the information being presented.

In discussion with a partner try to think of ways you could verbally guide a performer through the pole vault.

**ACTIVITY 2**

When considering verbal guidance, it is important that it is: **clear/precise, relatively short** (not too lengthy), **appropriate** to the level of the learner, and **not overdone**.

Do not overload. Only a few important points will be taken in during the first few attempts. Children have very short attention spans (see information processing).

It is also useful to note that when giving verbal guidance:

- everybody should be able to hear
- the pitch and tone of the voice should be varied in order to encourage or emphasise a specific point
- a sense of humour is a great help.

## Manual/mechanical guidance

This type of guidance involves trying to reduce errors by in some way physically moving (called forced response) or restricting/supporting (called physical restriction) a performer's movements. This form of guidance is particularly useful in potentially dangerous situations. A performer may initially need physical or mechanical support in order to develop the confidence to 'have a go' themselves. In trampolining a coach may stand on the bed and physically support the beginner through the stages of a somersault (manual/physical guidance). With more advanced performers they may also use a twisting belt which would provide mechanical guidance by physically restricting the performer. A performer may have their response or actions **forced** by the coach or teacher. In taking a performer through an action they will very often take hold of the racket arm in tennis forcing the performer to carry out certain movements, eg, a backswing for early preparation.

While in the initial stages of learning, the use of mechanical aids, such as floats and armbands in swimming, serve a very useful purpose, it is important that beginners do not become over reliant on them and lose their own 'kinaesthetic

Fig 23.5. Manual guidance is important for beginners to boost their confidence

'feel' for the movement. There has to come a time, in gymnastics for example, where support for the learner has to be gradually removed once the teacher or coach is sure that the performer is 'safe'.

By producing his or her own movements and not relying on what has been termed 'a crutch' the performer can develop their own kinaesthetic awareness. This will help in reducing possible bad habits (negative transfer) and by increasing confidence should serve to develop the performer's motivation (refer to self efficacy).

## Disadvantages of verbal visual and manual guidance

### Visual guidance

- depends on coach's ability to demonstrate the correct model
- can be dependent on expensive equipment, eg video
- limited value to group coaching situation regarding technical skill

- dependent on coach's ability to demonstrate problems within skills
- some skills may be too complex to be absorbed by the performer
- some information presented may not be relevant
- some images may be rather 'static' and therefore give little information about movement patterns
- difficult to use in isolation.

### Verbal guidance

- heavily dependent on the coach's ability to express the necessary information
- less effective in early stages of learning
- dependent on the performer's ability to relate the verbal instruction/information to the skill under practice
- some techniques are very difficult to describe verbally
- verbal guidance can become boring if too lengthy.

### Mechanical guidance

- limited use in group situations
- limited use in fast/complex movement
- the 'feel' of the movement is not experienced by the performer to the same extent as an unaided movement
- kinaesthetic awareness can be limited
- performer may become reliant on the 'support'
- possible implied sexual misconduct.

ACTIVITY 3

Choose one type of guidance and in relation to a particular activity, discuss how you might adapt the guidance given when it is offered to a beginner (cognitive phase) and someone more experienced (associative/autonomous phase)

# Types, structure and presentation of practice

What types of practice shall I use? In deciding how to use their allotted time to benefit learners effectively, teachers or coaches need to make decisions about when to practise, and how often. In making these decisions they should consider whether practice is better all at once (**massed**), or whether breaks are required (**distributed**). Within these blocks of practice they will consider whether the skill should be taught as a whole, in parts or various combinations. The question of mental practice or rehearsal also needs to be considered.

As ever, there are no easy answers. Decisions made regarding questions or which type of practice would be more effective will depend on the:

- individual's stage of learning
- nature of the task
- nature of specific situation
- time available.

## Massed and distributed practice

For the purposes of this text, **massed practice** is seen as being almost continuous practice with very little or no rest at all between attempts or blocks of trials.

**Distributed practice** is seen as practice with relatively long breaks or rest periods between each attempt or block of attempts.

### Practice and the learner

Although massed practice may appear to save time as the teacher or coach does not have to spend time after long breaks either re-introducing the performer to the task or reducing psychological barriers (fear, anxiety, etc.), this may be a short-sighted policy as distributed practice for beginners is seen as being a more effective learning process. The length of the practice session should be appropriate to both the physical and

Table 23.1. Practice and the individual

| Massed practice | Distributed practice |
|---|---|
| **Better when the individual is:**<br>• experienced<br>• older<br>• fitter<br>• more motivated | **Better when the individual is:**<br>• beginner<br>• less experienced<br>• limited preparation (physical/mental)<br>• less motivated |

psychological maturity (state of readiness) of the performer. Beginners are more likely to be affected by lack of attention/concentration and lack of appropriate physical and mental fitness to sustain long periods of practice. Distributed practice with beginners, allowing for greater variation of practice, is seen as essential as it not only allows for better schema developments and transfer possibilities but also helps maintain motivation. Random practice is seen as being more effective than ordered.

Interestingly, research suggests that the learners and performers themselves are not always the best judges of structure and time allocation, generally preferring to rush through things superficially. There is evidence to support the view that for the more experienced/older/ fitter performer massed practice is more effective.

### Practice and the task

Practice sessions need to be long enough to allow for improvement but should not be overly long. While the effect of fatigue in relatively dangerous situations (gymnastics, outdoor pursuits) could be potentially serious, the effect of fatigue in massed practice can hinder performance in the short term although not necessarily skill learning in the long term. Alternatively, distributed practice for discrete skills may lead to lack of motivation due to the performer's frustration at having delays between attempts. Group or team activities can be practised for longer than individual tasks as players can have

Table 23.2. Practice and the task

| Massed practice | Distributed practice |
|---|---|
| **Better when the task is:**<br>• Discrete, brief in nature e.g., hitting a golf ball, shooting baskets<br>• Simple | **Better when the task is:**<br>• Continuous, requiring repetition of **gross skills** eg, swimming, cycling, running<br>• Complex – precision orientated<br>• Dangerous |

| Variable practice |
|---|
| • skills practised in new/different situations |
| • useful for open skills |
| • helps development of schema |
| • helps performer successfully adapt to meet the demands of the situation |
| • practice should be similar to 'real game' situation |
| • practice should be meaningful |
| • variety of massed and distributed practice |
| • will maintain motivation |

rests in between thus lessening fatigue and frustration. At the same time groups should not be so big that rest intervals or waiting times become over long thus demotivating learners or allowing opportunities for ill-discipline.

The use of rest periods or intervals needs to be considered within distributed practice. They can be used for the following:

• to reduce fatigue

• to reduce short-term inhibition

• to give feedback (KR and KP)

• to offer an alternative activity/novelty game (must ensure no negative transfer)

• to develop positive transfer

• to re-motivate

• to offer mental practice/rehearsal (see section below).

## Variability of practice

Repetition of skills is important in order to reinforce the correct movement patterns particularly at the early stages of learning and with closed skill ie, fixed practice. However, as already discussed in the sections on 'open skills' and 'schema' development variability of practice is also essential.

## Mental practice

The definition of mental practice is: **the mental or cognitive rehearsal of a skill without actual physical movement**.

When looking at the various types of practice available for a teacher or coach to use mental practice or mental rehearsal is an area often overlooked. We have mentioned above that time intervals or rest periods between practice can be used for mental practice.

Mental practice or rehearsal is seen as being very beneficial. In the early stages of learning (cognitive phase) mental rehearsal is initially seen as the learner going through a skill/task and building up a mental picture of the expected performance in their mind (a cognitive process). This may involve a performer in deciding how to hold a hockey stick or a gymnast going over the sequence of a simple vault in their mind. More advanced performers can use mental practice to rehearse possible alternative strategies or complex actions/sequences, thus almost pre-programming their effector systems and possibly helping with response preparation, reactions and anticipation. Mental practice can be a powerful tool in the preparation of the highly skilled performer. Top class skiers regularly use it to rehearse turns, imagine the approach to gates and certain aspects of the terrain. A traditionally held view has been that through mental practice a performer could slightly stimulate (below optimum threshold) the neuromuscular systems involved in activities and thus simulate (practise) the movement. In addition, mental practice is used regularly by more experienced performers in learning to control their emotional states. Optimum levels of arousal can be reached and maintained for effective performance. Wider developments in sports psychology have meant that mental rehearsal is being increasingly used to reduce anxiety and increase confidence, by getting the performer to focus their attention on winning, or performing successfully.

Although mental rehearsal is now seen as an important element of practice (better than no practice at all) (see fig 23.6) it is not seen as a substitute to be used exclusively; rather it is much more effective when used in conjunction with physical practice. In being aware of the effects of mental rehearsal it is important that teachers or coaches not only plan their sessions to allow time for it to take place but also that they teach performers how and when to use it effectively. Practice is essential.

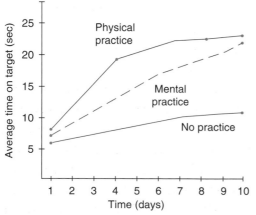

Fig 23.6. Comparison of effects of mental and physical practice on performance

*Source*: Rawlings, Rawlings and Chew Yilk (1972) *Psychonomic Science* 26 page 71. Copyright 1972 by Psychonomic Society Inc.

## The use of mental practice prior to performance

The performer needs to be advised to seek out a relatively quiet situation where they can focus mentally on the task. This will probably involve moving away from the competitive or performance situation.

The learner or performer needs to:

- go somewhere quiet
- focus on the task
- build a clear picture in their mind
- sequence the action
- imagine success
- avoid images of failure
- practise regularly.

## The use of mental practice between practices

When used in between physical practice a performer must try to re-create the kinaesthetic feeling and mental image they recently successfully experienced (remembering what was good). Equally so when a performer makes a mistake, stopping for a few seconds to reason why and then rehearse a good performance may have a positive effect on future performances.

This reviewing mentally of good and bad practice both during and after performance will help in building up good positive images. A golfer, when playing a practice swing, is very often mentally rehearsing the positive feel for the shot, imaging distance, angles of trajectory and power needed.

As already mentioned, more experienced performers can plan ahead, particularly in situations requiring adaptation or performance strategies. Where? What ifs? can be considered, determined and possibly pre-prepared for.

Mental practice within the associative phase (motor stage) can enhance learning, helping the performer develop the decision making and conceptual aspects of the skill which link to the specific skills being taught. Tactics and strategies can be brought together with the sequencing or skills. It can also be used to help create effective random practice.

## The uses of mental rehearsal in sport and physical education

- Mental rehearsal creates a mental picture of what needs to be done.
- Mental rehearsal evaluates possible movements and can mentally experience their outcomes (success/failure).
- Mental rehearsal can build self-confidence.
- Mental rehearsal can be used as a mechanism to focus attention.
- It has been proved that mental rehearsal actually produces small muscle contractions simulating actual practice.
- Performers at the cognitive stage of learning can use mental rehearsal to focus on the *basics* of a skill/the whole movement.
- Performers in the autonomous stage of learning can use mental rehearsal to control arousal level/to focus attention to immediate goals.

Mental rehearsal provides mental warm-up.

Mental rehearsal must be regularly practised if it is to be useful.

Mental rehearsal can be used before competition and in rest periods during competition.

Mental rehearsal must be as realistic as possible to be effective.

The performer can use all the different senses during mental rehearsal.

The performer can use mental rehearsal to envisage images of both success and failure.

May be used in rest periods during distributed practice.

May prevent physical 'wear and tear', eg, triple jumpers use mental rehearsal to save joints.

## Whole or part method of practice

Performers differ in their response to whole or part practice. The **whole method** of learning is when the activity or skill is presented in total and practised as a full/entire skilled movement or activity. The **part method** of learning is when the activity or skill is broken down into its various components or sub-routines and each sub-routine is practised individually.

Additional variations have been developed whereby whole-part, part-whole or progressive part methods have been used.

Whether it is effective to teach a skill as a whole or whether it is more effective to break it down into its various sub-routines depends very much on the answers to several questions.

1. Can the skill/task be broken down into its sub-routines without destroying or changing it beyond all recognition? (see complexity and organisation)
2. What is the degree of transfer from practising the parts (sub-routines) back to the main skill or activity (see transfer)?
3. What is the performer's level of experience (stage of learning)?

### Whole approach

It is argued that if a whole approach is used then a learner is able to develop their kinaesthetic awareness or total feel for the activity. The learner is usually given a demonstration or explanation of what is required, builds up a cognitive picture and then becomes acquainted through practice with the total skill; they are then able to positively transfer the actions/skills more readily to the competitive or 'real' situation. By being able to link together the essential spatial and temporal elements of the skill the activity/skill quickly becomes meaningful to the performer. This approach is seen as a more effective use of time and should be used whenever possible particularly when skills have low levels of complexity and high levels of organisation, eg, a bench press in weight training. Skills which are very rapid (discrete or ballistic in nature) are also usually better practised as a whole. Although they could possibly be broken down, the parts are usually very much interrelated and therefore if broken down the skill would be changed out of all recognition – with possible negative effects on transfer, eg, hitting a softball.

When a skill is complex, highly organised and thus difficult to break down, very often an easier way to present it to beginners has to be found. Simplifying the activity/task enables the performer to experience the whole activity but with less information and decision making to deal with. Equipment is very often made lighter or bigger/smaller and less technical rules are imposed, or fewer physical demands and dangers, eg, uni hoc, mini hockey, short tennis. In general experienced performers will benefit more from the whole approach as they are better prepared to deal with skills that cannot be broken down or are very complex.

## Part approach

Skills which are very complex but low in organisation lend themselves to being practised and learned more effectively by the parts method. An additional consideration is again how interrelated or independent the various sub-routines are. Just because sub-routines are easily separated does not mean, however, that they have to be practised by themselves. The part method, while allowing teachers and coaches to work on areas of the skill that a beginner finds difficult, also tends to be more time consuming.

Activities such as front crawl in swimming which are not too complex but low in organisation lend themselves to being taught by the part method. The arm action, leg action, breathing pattern and body position can all be analysed and taught individually. While each can be and usually are practised independently, allowing the performer to experience success and thus gain confidence, it is important that the performer is able to practise synchronising the various

sub-routines together. If the beginner does not experience the whole stroke there is a possibility that the kinaesthetic feel for the whole action could be lost, eg, the timing of breathing in coordination with the arm action. In breaststroke, where the kick, glide and pull have to be exactly synchronised, this is even more important. When teaching the skills of passing in major team games, eg, soccer, rugby, hockey, it is essential that they are not taught in isolation. The beginner needs time for the interrelated units or sub-routines to be practised together in order that they can make the natural link between the parts. This, therefore, becomes a more progressive part method with combinations of the whole.

## The progressive part method

The progressive part method or gradual metamorphosis is where earlier independent actions change their form to become something totally different. A learner being taught complex skills by the progressive part method benefits from the positive aspects of both part and whole

Fig 23.7. Serial skills such as the long jump, where the skills are sequentially ordered, lend themselves more to a part method of learning

methods. A gymnastic coach trying to develop a gymnast's routine would often follow this progressive part method. All the relatively complex but independent parts of the routine, eg, handstand, cartwheel, handspring, somersault, etc., are learned and practised in isolation, but then linked together into small units in order that the gymnast can experience and learn how to fluently link (sequence) the individual skills together. These units or blocks of skills are then linked again until eventually all the various parts of the action have been built up (the chain is completed) into the whole routine. These methods often rely on the operant method of learning discussed earlier. The teacher or coach endeavours to shape the complex performance by reinforcing good aspects of technique. The performer is rewarded in some way for successful achievement and gradually develops their movement repertoire along with their understanding of how the various aspects of the skill are interrelated.

# Whole-part-whole-method

A variation on the 'whole' or 'part' method that is often used with performers in the Cognitive/Associative stages is the 'whole-part-whole practice'. The teacher/coach introduces the complete skill, highlighting the important elements. The performer then attempts to carry out the skill. As a result of any problems or faults observed the teacher then breaks the whole skill down into various sub-routines in order to allow the learner to practise appropriate areas of difficulty. The isolation of the difficult elements may differ for

Table 23.3. Summary of methods of practice

| Whole method | Part method | Progressive part method |
|---|---|---|
| • Low level of complexity/ simple task<br>• High levels of organisation<br>• Interrelated sub-routines<br>• Discrete skills<br>• Short duration/ rapid ballistic<br>• Lacks meaning in parts<br>• Allows coordination of important spatial/temporal components | • High levels of complexity<br>• Low levels of organisation<br>• Independent sub-routines<br>• Serial tasks<br>• Slow tasks<br>• Lengthy or long duration<br>• Dangerous skills | • Complex task<br>• Helps 'chaining' of complex skills learned independently<br>• Allows for attention demands to be limited<br>• Allows for coordination of spatial/temporal components to be experienced<br>• Helps with transfer to whole |
| **Performer is:**<br>• experienced<br>• someone with high levels of attention<br>• in the later stages of learning<br>• older<br>• highly motivated<br>• using distributed practice | **Performer is:**<br>• a beginner<br>• someone with a limited attention span<br>• in the early stages of learning<br>• having problems with a specific aspect of skill<br>• someone with limited motivation<br>• using massed practice | |

individuals. Once the teacher is satisfied that the problem areas have been mastered the parts are then integrated back into the whole skill.

> Consider a golf stroke being carried out and decide how you would teach it taking into account not only its moderate levels of both complexity and organisation, but also the fact that it is a discrete skill. Should you use the whole, part, or progressive part method of practice?

ACTIVITY 4

Teaching by any specific method is not guaranteed to work and the better teachers and coaches are generally flexible, using various combinations of the three basic methods discussed at different times.

Many teachers begin an activity by allowing the beginner to experience the sequencing of the whole movement. They will then analyse strengths and weaknesses enabling them to develop a part method to deal with any problem areas. Then a progressive part process may develop where chunks or units of actions are practised together in a simplified task or small sided games. The performer is then allowed to return to the whole movement again. Small problem areas may continue to be practised in isolation in order to refine technique. Complete adherence to one or other method is not advisable or useful.

# Teaching styles

What style of teaching should you use? It is important that you are aware that the style of teaching adopted by a teacher or coach can considerably affect the learning environment. In planning strategies using the various methods

Table 23.4. Advantages of whole and part method

| Whole method | Part method |
| --- | --- |
| • Wastes no time in assembling parts<br>• Useful for quick discrete skills where a single complete action is required<br>• Better for time-synchronised tasks if the learner can cope with the level of the skill, eg, swimming stroke<br>• The learner can appreciate the end product<br>• The movement retains a feeling of flow/ kinaesthetic sense<br>• The movement can be more easily understood/the relationship between sub-routines<br>• The learner can develop their own schema/motor programme through trial and error learning<br>• Transfer to **real** situations from practice is likely to be positive | • Allows serial tasks to be broken down and learned in components, eg, gymnastic movement<br>• This reduces the demand on the learner when attempting complex skills<br>• Allows confidence and understanding to grow quickly or be gradually built up with more complex skills<br>• Helps to provide motivation to continue if progress can be seen to be being made<br>• This is especially important with skills which can be seen as being potentially dangerous, eg, some gymnastic skills<br>• Can reduce fatigue in physically demanding skills<br>• Allows the teacher to focus on a particular element and remedy any specific problems<br>• Provides stages of success<br>• Good for low organisational tasks which can be easily broken down |

Table 23.5. Disadvantages of whole and part method

| Whole method | Part method |
|---|---|
| • Ineffective with complex tasks<br>• Not appropriate in tasks with an element of danger<br>• Not always appropriate if group/performer of very low experience<br>• May overwhelm a performer and produce little success at first<br>• Could lead to learner losing confidence | • Transfer from part to whole may be ineffective<br>• Highly organised skills are difficult to break down in parts<br>• Loss of awareness of end product<br>• Loss of continuity/feel of flow<br>• Loss of kinaesthetic sense<br>• Can have a demotivating effect when not doing full movement<br>• Can be time consuming |

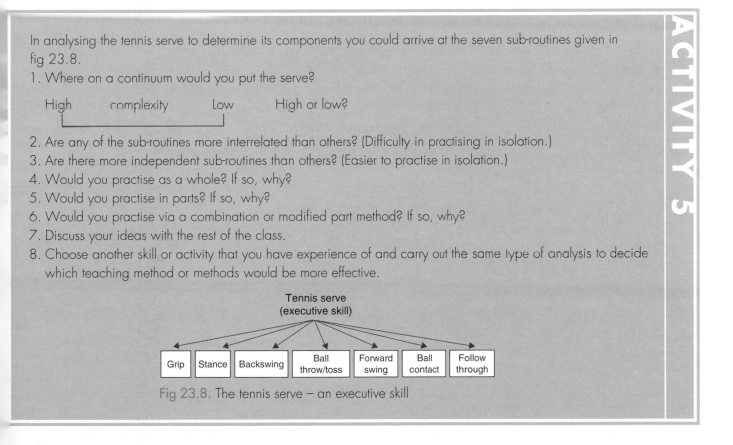

In analysing the tennis serve to determine its components you could arrive at the seven sub-routines given in fig 23.8.

1. Where on a continuum would you put the serve?

   High    complexity    Low    High or low?

2. Are any of the sub-routines more interrelated than others? (Difficulty in practising in isolation.)
3. Are there more independent sub-routines than others? (Easier to practise in isolation.)
4. Would you practise as a whole? If so, why?
5. Would you practise in parts? If so, why?
6. Would you practise via a combination or modified part method? If so, why?
7. Discuss your ideas with the rest of the class.
8. Choose another skill or activity that you have experience of and carry out the same type of analysis to decide which teaching method or methods would be more effective.

**ACTIVITY 5**

Tennis serve
(executive skill)

| Grip | Stance | Backswing | Ball throw/toss | Forward swing | Ball contact | Follow through |

Fig 23.8. The tennis serve – an executive skill

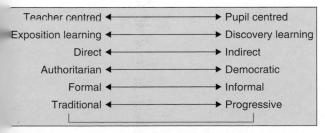

| Teacher centred | ←→ | Pupil centred |
| Exposition learning | ←→ | Discovery learning |
| Direct | ←→ | Indirect |
| Authoritarian | ←→ | Democratic |
| Formal | ←→ | Informal |
| Traditional | ←→ | Progressive |

Fig 23.9. Continuum of styles

already discussed a teacher or coach is trying to create a favourable learning environment. An effective style of teaching aims to present information and thus develop effective learning by promoting achievement, satisfaction and motivation. Teachers invariably adopt different styles in various situations. A teacher's or coach's

Table 23.6. Factors affecting teaching style

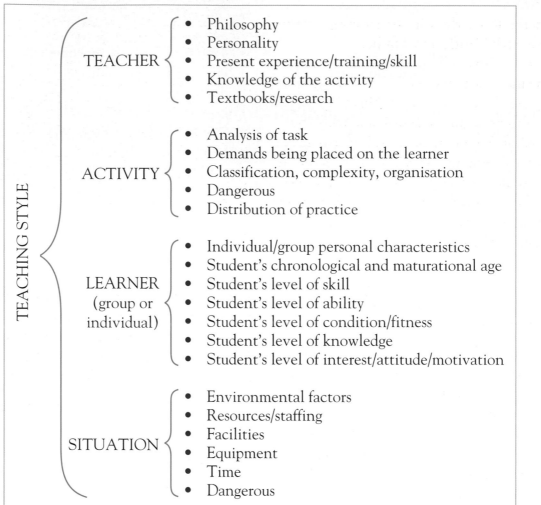

style of teaching is developed as a result of many factors. These are shown in table 23.6.

## Mosston and Ashworth's spectrum

In looking at the decisions to be made over what, when and how to teach and learn, Mosston and Ashworth (1986) developed their spectrum of teaching styles.

The more teacher orientated position, 'A', is referred to as the **command style**. The other end of the spectrum, where the learner makes more of the decisions, is referred to as **discovery learning**. There are obviously variations between the two extremes. For example:

- practice
- reciprocal

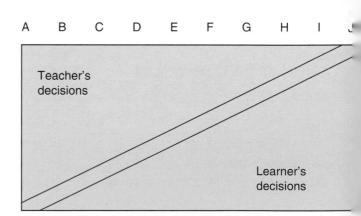

Fig 23.10. Spectrum of teaching styles
*Source:* Mosston and Ashworth (1986)

- self-check
- inclusion
- guided discovery
- problem solving
- discovery.

# Command style (A)

This style tends to see the teacher adopting a very authoritarian style! Within this rather behaviouristic approach there is little consideration given to the individual with all learners being treated in generally the same way. This style is thought to inhibit cognitive learning as thinking and questioning are not encouraged by the teacher. The teacher makes all the decisions. The learner is not allowed to develop responsibility for their own learning and is in danger of becoming a clone of the teacher by following movements, decisions and strategies dictated by the teacher. It can also lead to poor self discipline. This type of learning has limitations for developing open skills as these require the performer to be able to adapt and make their own decisions.

In addition, due to the formality of the situation there is little opportunity for any social interaction. This traditional approach helps to establish: pupil control, clear objectives/models for pupils, routine/organisation/rules, and safety procedures. It is useful when working with beginners, large groups and in dangerous and limited time situations. It is often adopted in the early stages of learning as a starting point from which other styles develop.

# Reciprocal style (C/D)

Developing further along the spectrum than command style this approach is based more on cognitive theories. Although what is to be taught or covered is still decided by the teacher, it allows learners to take slightly more responsibility and become more involved in the decision-making process. The sessions are structured in order that the objectives are clearly stated to the learners. The learners work in pairs taking alternative goes at being observer and performer. Although there is regular general and specific input from the teacher, the situation lends itself to more social interaction than the command style. Learners are encouraged to give feedback as a result of their own analysis and evaluation of the performer's progress. In analysing and evaluating their partner's performance the

Fig 23.11. Many aerobic classes are taught by a command style of teaching

learner is developing a greater understanding of the movement and passing this on to the partner. They should also be able to transfer this to their own performance when their partner has to reciprocate, giving additional individual feedback.

This style of teaching is useful in developing a learner's:

- self image
- confidence
- communication skills (encourage interaction)
- cognitive strategies (encourage decision making).

The teacher does, however, need to monitor the process carefully and interject regularly to ensure that incorrect techniques are not being developed and reinforced. It is also important that the learners are at the appropriate maturational level of development and can cope with both giving and receiving constructive criticism from their peers and not merely focus on the negative or destructive aspects.

# Guided discovery

This much more individualistic style of teaching is rather time consuming as the teacher sets a problem and leads the learner to the correct answer. In guided discovery the teacher generally has to lead the performer by providing the appropriate information, cues and questions in order to get the

Table 23.7. Advantages and disadvantages of the problem-solving approach

| Advantages | Disadvantages |
|---|---|
| • Gives a sense of responsibility for one's own learning<br>• Improves self-confidence<br>• Encourages creativity<br>• Aids self-fulfilment/self actualisation<br>• Allows for group interaction and therefore promotes cohesiveness (if in a group)<br>• Allows future strategies to be developed through a trial and error process<br>• Good for high level performer | • Not as good for early stage of learning as performers do not have enough knowledge to work with<br>• May not arrive at what teacher thinks is the correct solution |

learner to 'discover' effective and correct movement skills or the understanding associated with certain techniques. The teacher needs to have an in-depth knowledge of each pupil and be constantly evaluating progress. Due to inevitable time limitation, learning will not be uniform for all. Students will progress at different rates, creating extra demands on the teacher.

By using progressive question and answer techniques in association with reinforcement, teachers can guide a learner's greater understanding. In developing greater understanding in one area the performer will also learn to adapt decision making and reasoning processes from previous or correct skills (pro-active positive transfer) to future learning situations. In being more involved with their own learning the learner is thought to gain greater personal satisfaction together with a more positive self image which in turn will help to develop even greater motivation.

## Problem-solving approach

Very often associated with the guided discovery method discussed above, the problem-solving approach encourages students to be creative and develop their individual cognitive and performance processes. According to their different sizes, shapes, abilities and capabilities learners can approach

problems set by the teacher individually. For example:

• Find a way to dribble past your opponent in 1v1 situation.

• How could you gain the attack from this situation?

These more 'cognitive perspective' approaches are believed to have long-term benefits as learners are encouraged to think about, understand and adapt performance according to a variety of situations. Variety of practice is therefore important, particularly if the effects of positive transfer are to be developed. The development of *schemas* relies heavily on variety of practice and are a more cognitive explanation of how learners deal with new or novel situations.

Consider the styles discussed above and decide which style of teaching would be best suited to the following situations:
• abseiling on an adventure trip
• a group of well-motivated students with sound technical knowledge of the skills
• a teacher coaching four students per session
• a teacher of dance developing creativity.

ACTIVITY 7

# Summary

- Teachers must be able to adopt and adapt many theories associated with teaching and learning in order to develop a learning environment appropriate to the needs of the learner.
- Transfer refers to the influence of one activity/skill upon another. There are a variety of types of transfer and transfer can be effective forwards or backwards in time.
- Transfer between tasks that are very similar is greater than transfer between dissimilar skills.
- The relationships between skills/concepts and cognitive processes need to be pointed out and explained to learners in order to increase the probability of positive transfer taking place.
- Teachers should try to minimise the possibility of negative transfer occurring.
- When deciding on whole or part practice the complexity and organisation of a skill/task needs to be analysed in relation to the individual needs of the learner and the situation.
- Practice over an extended period with short practice periods and limited rest periods is generally found to be more effective.
- Teachers or coaches can adapt a variety of guidance techniques appropriate to the individual needs of the learner. Visual, verbal, mechanical/physical are the main types of guidance.
- The effectiveness of massed or distributed practice depends on the type of task, level of the learner and the situation.
- Sticking rigidly to one method of either whole or part practice is not generally advised. A combination is often more effective.
- Research studies have shown that learners can benefit greatly from mental practice. The effectiveness of mental practice is increased considerably if used in conjunction with, rather than instead of, physical practice.
- It is important that learners are taught how to use mental practice effectively.
- There are a variety of teaching styles that can be adopted and it is important that teachers are flexible in their approach to teaching and coaching styles.

# Review Questions

1. What are the four categories of variable factors that need to be considered by a teacher before they can develop an effective learning environment?
2. What are the main variables associated with the individual learner?
3. Using examples, explain complex and simple tasks.
4. What is meant by the organisation of a skill/task?
5. What type of task can be broken down into sub-routines?
6. What is meant when sub-routines are said to be interrelated?
7. What is meant by transfer of learning?

8. What are the main types of transfer?

9. In what ways can a teacher structure practices towards helping positive transfer?

10. Why is variety of practice important for a learner?

11. What use might simulators, eg, tennis ball machines, be in the learning of skills?

12. What might be the positive and negative effects of using a 'softball' for developing shot put?

13. In what ways can a teacher try to reduce the effect of negative transfer?

14. Give two practical examples of negative transfer.

15. What are the various types of guidance a teacher can give to a learner?

16. What are the advantages and disadvantages of using visual aids?

17. What problems may be caused by a lengthy set of instructions prior to practice?

18. When a demonstration is given, what important factors must a teacher consider?

19. Why is distributed practice more appropriate for a beginner?

20. What type of practice might suit a more advanced performer and why?

21. Choose two specific skills from an individual and a game activity and explain why you might use whole or part practice.

22. Is it possible to learn a skill by mental practice? Support your answer.

23. In what ways can a teacher help a learner use mental practice more effectively?

24. How and why would an experienced performer possibly use mental practice?

25. Why is it better for a teacher or coach to be flexible in their structuring of practice sessions?

26. What are the main reasons for a teacher adopting teaching style 'A' on Mosston's and Ashworth's spectrum of teaching styles?

27. What are the advantages of adopting a more discovery-learning or problem-solving style of teaching?

# 24. Individual Differences

Similarities and differences between individuals involved in sport are often obvious, eg, size, shape and gender to mention but a few. Similarities and differences in terms of a performer's physiological behaviour can also be easy to recognise, but the reason why a person *behaves* in a certain way is often not so easy to define. Research into the personal and individual factors that can influence sporting behaviour has been widespread. Trying to gain a better understanding of the psychological make-up of performers in a sporting setting, ie, 'what makes them tick?', has traditionally involved research into personality.

Here is a table listing the terms to be covered in this chapter. It is important that you understand them.

| SECTION 1<br>Personality | SECTION 2<br>Attitudes | SECTION 3<br>Aggression |
|---|---|---|
| • Credulous<br>• Sceptical<br>• Traits<br>• Social learning theory<br>• Interactionist<br>• Reliability<br>• Validity<br>• Iceberg profile<br>• Mood states | • Attitudes<br>• Values<br>• Three components of attitudes<br>• Attitude scales<br>• Socialisation<br>• Social norms<br>• Persuasive communication<br>• Cognitions<br>• Cognitive dissonance<br>• Dissonance<br>• Prejudice<br>• Stereotyping<br>• Self-fulfilling prophecy | • Aggression<br>• Assertion<br>• Instinct theory<br>• Frustration–aggression hypothesis<br>• Social learning theory |

# Section 1 – Personality

The proliferation of research in this area supports the view held by many that personality is a major factor in creating sporting behaviour. The research has traditionally been directed towards the relationship between individual performance and personality variables. Among the questions raised are the following:

- do the personalities of top class performers, moderate performers and non participants differ?
- can sporting success be predicted as a result of a performer's personality type?
- are the personalities of performers in various sports different or similar?

The early research of the 1960s and 1970s failed to produce many useful conclusions with regard to the relationship between personality and performance in sport. This was mainly as a result of problems with validity and research methodology.

The fact, however, that people began to predict how their captain, team mate, friend or even opponent was going to behave on the basis of what they believed them to be like (ie, stereotyping), means that personality is a concept that has real meaning in the context of sporting inter-personal behaviour. In presenting this 'credulous' viewpoint (Morgan, 1980) where personality is seen as a significant causal factor of behaviour we must, however, be aware that it is questioned by the 'sceptical' viewpoint, which argues that sporting success is not related to personality. What we must therefore do is take an overview and accept that we need to be aware of all the major theories of personality and how they relate to performance in sport. The word personality is a term which everybody uses to describe different things. However, psychologists have given a special, precise meaning to it. Personality is seen as a hypothetical construct in that it cannot be directly observed but only inferred from behaviour. It makes no sense therefore, to talk in general terms suggesting that someone has 'lots of personality' which will help them play sport. It is suggested that personality in the context of sport is not a thing that someone has or has not, but is more to do with how a person relates to another while taking part in physical activity and how they deal with the demands of a situation.

Consider, for example, the behaviour of people you know well, the captain of your sports team or your closest friend. It would appear that, in the main, their behaviour is hardly ever random or unpredictable. Usually they are consistent in the way they react or approach certain situations, eg, always aggressive and argumentative or stable and reliable. In addition, there are also consistent differences between people we know. Some people are outgoing, easy going, while others are quiet, withdrawn and lacking confidence. It is these factors that contribute to both the **behavioural**

**differences** between people and the **behavioural consistency** within people that are referred to as their personality.

---

### ACTIVITY 1

1. Individually within the class consider your own behaviour characteristics. Write down six characteristics which you think describe your personality (try to be honest).
2. The brave ones among you can have these listed on the board. As you go around the class, log the number of times 'common' descriptions come up. Discuss the results. Are you the same or different to others in your class?

---

### ACTIVITY 2

Consider some of the more well-known sports performers who are currently or have recently been involved in sport, eg, Jonathan Edwards, Roy Keane, Peter Ebdon, Paula Radcliffe.

Individually write down any words that you associate with these performers. Feed back your answers to the rest of the class and discuss the characteristics identified in terms of any similarities or differences.

---

## Approaches to the study of personality

There are many different definitions and explanations of personality in line with the many different theoretical approaches. Personality has been researched and studied via:

- an **idiographic** approach, based on the intense study of the individual – it emphasises the uniqueness of a person
- a **nomothetic** approach, which attempts to summarise differences between people through generalisation using statistical techniques to accumulate large amounts of data. Individuals ar studied by comparing them with each other in order to arrive at laws of behaviour that hold for all individuals across the population as a whole.

Table 24.1. Summary of the various approaches that have been taken in the study of personality

| Approaches | Most noted supporters/ initiators of research | Evaluation |
|---|---|---|
| **A** Psychoanalytical (ideographic approach) | Freud, Jung, Adler, Horney, Fromm, Aptizsch | Personality is a dynamic set of processes, constantly changing and often in conflict. Little impact on Sport Psychology. Individual behaviour differences are often expressed as a result of unconscious motives linked to conflict in early years. |
| **B** The trait and type approach (nomothetic/ ideographic) | Allport, Cattell, Eysenck | Individual causes of behaviour come from within, as a result of internal traits which are enduring and consistent across different situations. Seen as an oversimplified view of a complex concept. Fails to consider the influence of specific situations on behaviour. |
| **C** Humanistic/individual (ideographic) | Maslow, Rogers, Kelly | Views personality as a 'whole' experience, not to be divided into separate parts. Emphasis on the person. Personality is shaped by positive self growth. |
| **D** Cognitive/social learning approach | Bandura, Kelly | Focus is on the process of interpreting and evaluating the environment and experiences due to an individual's beliefs, thoughts and expectations. Behaviour influenced by observational learning and social reinforcement. |
| **E** Situational approach | Mischell | Draws from Social Learning theory. Environmental influences and reinforcements shape a person's behaviour in different situations. |
| **F** Interactional approach | Bowers | Personality is seen as a unique mixture of variables associated with both the person's psychological traits and the situation. |

# KEY WORDS

**Ideographic approach** Personality has been researched and developed based around an intense study of the individual. It emphasises the uniqueness of a person.

**Nomothetic approach** This is an attempt to summarise differences between people through generalisations using statistical techniques to accumulate large amounts of data. Individuals are studied by comparing them with each other in order to arrive at laws of behaviour that hold for all individuals and are generalised across the population as a whole.

# Definitions of personality

## Nature or nurture?

Due to the many different approaches and theories with regard to personality it is almost impossible to present a definition acceptable to all. However, in 1992 Richard Gross put forward a common sense definition which enables us to leave the starting blocks:

> *'Those relatively stable and enduring aspects of individuals which distinguish them from other people, making them unique but at the same time permit a comparison between individuals.'*

> (R. Gross)

Lazarus and Mowat (1979) gave an earlier definition:

> *'Personality is the underlying relatively stable psychological structures and processes that organise human experience and shape a person's actions and reactions to the environment.'*

> (Lazarus and Mowat)

Both definitions highlight certain questions that are central to the study of personality and sport.

1. Is personality made up of certain permanent or enduring characteristics?
2. Do these enduring characteristics affect how a person perceives a situation and therefore how they behave towards it?
3. If they are enduring characteristics, can they be identified?
4. Can they be measured?
5. Are they innate? (Nature)
6. Can these characteristics be influenced or changed? (Nurture)

# The psychoanalytical approach

Only relatively recently has sport psychology research begun to refocus attention towards this approach. Consideration has been given to how sports performers develop unconscious defence mechanisms for coping with stressful or anxiety-inducing situations (see chapter on optimising

Table 24.2. Personality is seen as having three aspects

| The **id** | These are unconscious determinants of behaviour, known as 'instinctive drives'; eg, aggression, which can affect us instantaneously |
|---|---|
| The **ego** | This is made up of the conscious part of personality which develops as a person tries to cope with the very often socially unacceptable demands of the id in relation to the superego |
| The **superego** | This acts as the person's moral conscience, ie, knowing which values or behaviour are wrong (see socialisation). These are developed throughout childhood by identification with parents of the same sex. |

performance). If inappropriate 'ego' defence mechanisms are used performers can 'freeze' or possibly deny the problem, potentially affecting performance and satisfaction.

Unconscious ego defence mechanisms can lead to amongst other things:

- **sublimation**: channelling possibly socially unacceptable drives into acceptable activities, for example, playing highly competitive physical contact sports such as rugby as a way of channelling aggression.

- **displacement**: transferring unacceptable feelings about someone or something towards someone or something which is fairly harmless or powerless and will not retaliate (see displacement aggression).

One of the most positive outcomes of this revised focus is the recognition that not all the behaviour of performers is always under conscious control; unconscious factors may well be the problem or cause of certain behaviours.

Historically the psychoanalytical approach has tended to be more associated with 'clinical' rather than 'sports' psychology. However, more open-minded and up-to-date research (E. Apitzsch, 1995, Giges, 1998, Conroy and Benjamin, 2001) has argued that this more in-depth clinical approach can help the sports performer where traditional cognitive behavioural strategies have failed.

*Limitations of the psychoanalytical approach*

- Difficulty of testing procedures
- Focuses mainly on internal causes of behaviour
- Little attention paid to the effect of the social environment
- Most sports psychologists are not trained/qualified to use it
- Only relatively recently has sports psychology research begun to refocus attention on this approach.

The psychoanalytical approach was first put forward in the early twentieth century by Sigmund Freud and further developed by the likes of C. Jung and E. Erickson. It is a very complex approach requiring human behaviour to be studied as a 'whole' dynamic process rather than trying to split personality up into smaller groups of traits and predictable behaviour patterns (predispositions).

Adult personality is seen as being shaped through the continuously changing (dynamic) conflict between unconscious instinctive drives (the id) and the more conscious 'ego' and 'superego'.

## The trait approach (Nature)

The trait or dispositional approach dominated the early study of personality but has been criticised for not taking into account how a particular situation might also influence an individual's behaviour in different environments. Thus it emphasises the person as opposed to the situation. Traits can be seen as being **relatively stable** and **enduring** characteristics which predispose a performer to act in a certain way, regardless of the situation or circumstances. These stable and enduring predispositions could be used to predict an individual's likely behaviour in a variety of situations.

Trait theorists believed that these personal characteristics or traits could be identified, were consistent and could be generalised across the population as a whole. Thus an extreme trait approach would suggest that if a person was assessed as being aggressive and as competitive then these characteristics would be displayed in all aspects of the person's behaviour (stable) at all times (enduring) and therefore it would be possible to predict this behaviour in all future situations. Two of the better-documented trait/type theories have been associated with Eysenck and Catell. Although both theories have distinct similarities in that they both propose neurological models, their structures of personality were derived quite differently.

## Eysenck's type theory (Nature)

Eysenck regarded personality as largely resulting from inherited (innate) tendencies. He attempted

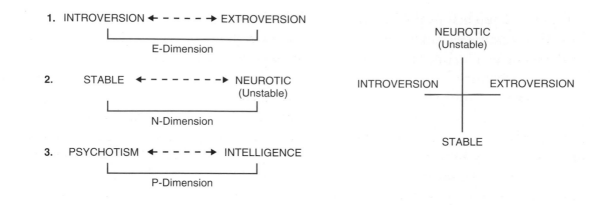

A third dimension of psychotism intelligence relating to how far a person was prepared to conform to society's rules and conventions was added later, in 1976

Fig 24.1. Major personality dimensions viewed on a continuum

to measure these inherited characteristics through a Personality Inventory (EPI, 1964) and Personality Questionnaire (1975). Those tested were expected to give a yes or no answer to a variety of test questions. Using a statistical technique known as factor analysis to identify general trends in his research evidence Eysenck identified two major personality dimensions which can be viewed more readily as a continuum (see fig 24.1):

The better-known extroversion/introversion dimension linked to a person's Reticular Activating System (RAS) related to how social or unsocial people appeared to be. The stable neurotic dimension linked to a person's autonomic nervous system referred to the levels of nervousness and anxiety that a person was susceptible to.

The RAS, which Eysenck argued affected the levels of introversion/extroversion, is part of the central cortex of the brain. It acts to either inhibit or excite brain activity in order to maintain optimum levels of alertness or arousal. He suggested that extroverts had an RAS which was biased towards inhibiting or reducing the affects of incoming sensory information therefore creating a severe state of under-arousal. According to Eysenck, extroverts therefore need increased levels of stimulation to maintain optimum levels of attention and brain functioning. They could become bored very easily and would tend to seek out and be happier in new and challenging situations, particularly those

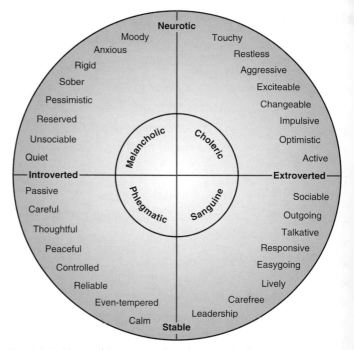

Fig 24.2. Eysenck's personality dimensions linked to personality characteristics (traits) generally displayed. Most people are not found at the extremes of the two dimensions but tend to come somewhere in the middle

involving other people, thus creating higher levels of stimulation to balance their naturally low levels of arousal. Extroverts, for example, were said to achieve optimum performance at higher levels of arousal preferably in team-orientated activities or those involving gross motor skills. Activities of a more continuous nature (cross-country and marathon running) could be demotivating to such personalities.

Introverts on the other hand had high levels of excitation naturally occurring within them (highly over-aroused). They therefore tended not to need external or additional stimulation or excitement in order to function at an optimum level. Introverts, for example, were said to achieve optimum performance at lower levels of arousal preferably in individual activities requiring more precision (shooting, archery, etc.). Many spurious claims have been made with regard to extroverts and introverts and tenuous links have been made with sporting performance (see the Evaluation of Trait theory, below). It was claimed that extroverts were more likely to take part in sport and be more successful, that they prefer team games and that;

- extroverts cope better in competitive and highly charged stressful situations
- extroverts cope better in the presence of distracting stimuli (eg, audience/noise)
- extroverts can cope with pain more easily than introverts.

The second stable-neurotic dimension (N) is related to emotionality and is based on the autonomic nervous system (ANS). The ANS enables us to react to stressful situations or experiences. A person who tended to display more stable characteristics would have an ANS which was fairly slow to respond to stressful situations. The ANS of a neurotic person would respond more rapidly and strongly to being in a stressful environment, predisposing them to becoming restless, excitable and anxious, none of which would bode well for an elite performer.

Both of these dimensions are independent of each other, therefore performers could be stable extroverts or stable introverts. Most people would score in the middle of the E and N dimensions but score low on the P.

## Cattell's theory (1965)

Cattell also adopted a trait approach to personality, but argued that more than just two or three dimensions were needed in order to create a full picture of a person's personality. He proposed that personality could be reduced to and measured in terms of 16 personality factors, hence his 16 PF Questionnaire. He argued that measuring these factors via his test would give an appropriate personality profile. In identifying certain common traits (possessed by all) and unique traits (possessed by some) he recognised that personality was more dynamic than Eysenck suggested and could fluctuate according to the situation.

By defining a wider personality profile Cattell's model was seen as providing a more accurate description of personality than Eysenck's. He did not claim that individuals would show similar scores each time they completed his questionnaire thus enabling deviations from the norm to be more easily observed and assessed.

He acknowledged that influences such as mood, motivation and situational factors would affect a person's responses and thus their overall profile.

**ACTIVITY 3**

- Complete Cattell's 16 Point Personality Factor Questionnaire (table 24.3) and produce an individual profile. Score yourself on a scale of 1 to 10 for each of the 16 personality factors.
- Compare yourself to the average and to the percentages underneath.
- Discuss your findings and consider what you think the profiles of more famous sports performers might be.

## Evaluation of trait theory

These two traditional theories received wide criticism and as a result of further research both Eysenck and Cattell continued to update their questionnaires. There has been much discussion as to the validity of the dispositional trait approach but it certainly provided a framework from

Table 24.3. Cattell's 16 point Personality Factors Questionnaire

| Factor | Low score description | Standard ten score (STEN) →average (%)← | | | | | | | | | | | High score description |
|---|---|---|---|---|---|---|---|---|---|---|---|---|---|
| | | 1 | 2 | 3 | 4 | 5 | | 6 | 7 | 8 | 9 | 10 | |
| A | RESERVED, DETACHED, CRITICAL, ALOOF (sizothymia) | ● | ● | ● | ● | ● | A | ● | ● | | ● | ● | OUTGOING, WARMHEARTED, EASY-GOING, PARTICIPATING (affectothymia, formerly cyclothymia) |
| B | LESS INTELLIGENT, CONCRETE-THINKING (lower scholastic mental capacity) | ● | ● | | ● | ● | B | | ● | ● | ● | ● | MORE INTELLIGENT, ABSTRACT-THINKING, BRIGHT (higher scholastic mental capacity) |
| C | AFFECTED BY FEELINGS, EMOTIONALLY LESS STABLE, EASILY UPSET (lower ego strength) | ● | ● | ● | | ● | C | | ● | ● | ● | ● | EMOTIONALLY STABLE, FACES REALITY, CALM, MATURE (higher ego strength) |
| E | HUMBLE, MILD, ACCOMMODATING CONFORMING (submissiveness) | ● | ● | ● | | ● | E | | | ● | ● | ● | ASSERTIVE, AGGRESSIVE, STUBBORN, COMPETITIVE (dominance) |
| F | SOBER, PRUDENT, SERIOUS, TACITURN (desurgency) | ● | ● | ● | ● | | F | ● | ● | | ● | ● | HAPPY-GO-LUCKY, IMPULSIVELY LIVELY, GAY, ENTHUSIASTIC (surgency) |
| G | EXPEDIENT, DISREGARDS RULES FEELS FEW OBLIGATIONS (weaker superego strength) | ● | ● | ● | ● | ● | G | | ● | | ● | ● | CONSCIENTIOUS, PERSEVERING, STAID, MORALISTIC (stronger superego strength) |
| H | SHY, RESTRAINED, TIMID, THREAT-SENSITIVE (threctia) | ● | ● | | | ● | H | ● | ● | ● | ● | ● | VENTURESOME, SOCIALLY BOLD, UNINHIBITED, SPONTANEOUS (parmia) |

*(Continued)*

Table 24.3. (Continued)

| Factor | Low score description | Standard ten score (STEN) →average (%)← | | | | | | | | | | High score description |
|---|---|---|---|---|---|---|---|---|---|---|---|---|
| | | 1 | 2 | 3 | 4 | 5 | 6 | 7 | 8 | 9 | 10 | |
| I | TOUGH-MINDED, SELF-RELIANT, REALISTIC, NO-NONSENSE (harria) | • | • | • | • | • | • | • | | | • | TENDER-MINDED, CLINGING, OVER-PROTECTED, SENSITIVE (premsia) |
| L | TRUSTING, ADAPTABLE, FREE OF JEALOUSY, EASY TO GET ALONG WITH (alaxia) | • | • | • | • | • | • | • | • | | • | SUSPICIOUS, SELF-OPINIONATED, HARD TO FOOL (protension) |
| M | PRACTICAL, CAREFUL, CONVENTIONAL, REGULATED BY EXTERNAL REALITIES, PROPER (praxemia) | • | • | • | • | • | | • | | • | • | IMAGINATIVE, WRAPPED UP IN INNER URGENCIES, CARELESS OF PRACTICAL MATTERS, BOHEMIAN (autia) |
| N | FORTHRIGHT, NATURAL, ARTLESS, UNPRETENTIOUS (artlessness) | • | • | • | • | • | • | | | • | • | SHREWD, CALCULATING, WORLDLY, PENETRATING (shrewdness) |
| O | SELF-ASSURED, CONFIDENT, SERENE (untroubled adequacy) | • | • | • | | | | • | • | • | • | APPREHENSIVE, SELF-REPROACHING, WORRYING, TROUBLED (guilt proneness) |
| Q₁ | CONSERVATIVE, RESPECTING ESTABLISHED IDEAS, TOLERANT OF TRADITIONAL DIFFICULTIES (conservatism) | • | • | • | | | • | • | • | • | • | EXPERIMENTING, LIBERAL, ANALYTICAL, FREE-THINKING (radicalism) |
| Q₂ | GROUP-DEPENDENT, A 'JOINER' AND RESOURCEFUL SOUND FOLLOWER (group adherence) | • | • | • | • | • | • | | | • | • | SELF-SUFFICIENT, PREFERS OWN DECISIONS (self-sufficiency) |

(Continued)

Table 24.3. (*continued*)

| Factor | Low score description | Standard ten score (STEN) →average (%)← | | | | | | | | | | High score description |
|---|---|---|---|---|---|---|---|---|---|---|---|---|
| | | 1 | 2 | 3 | 4 | 5 | 6 | 7 | 8 | 9 | 10 | |
| $Q_3$ | UNDISCIPLINED SELF-CONFLICT, FOLLOWS OWN URGES, CARELESS OF PROTOCOL (low integration) | • | • | • | • | • $Q_3$ | | • | • | • | • | CONTROLLED, SOCIALLY PRECISE, FOLLOWING SELF-IMAGE (high self-concept control) |
| $Q_4$ | RELAXED, TRANQUIL, UNFRUSTRATED (low ergic tension) | • | • | • | | • $Q_4$ | | • | • | • | • | TENSE, FRUSTRATED, DRIVEN, OVERWROUGHT (high ergic tension) |
| | a score of | 1 | 2 | 3 | 4 | 5 | 6 | 7 | 8 | 9 | 10 | is obtained of adults |
| | by about | 2.3 | 4.4 | 9.2 | 15.0 | 19.1 | 19.1 | 15.0 | 9.2 | 4.4 | 2.3 | |

which future personality research could develop. The trait approach:

- was seen as a rather simplistic or limited view of personality
- failed, according to cognitive theorists, to recognise that individuals are actively involved in subjectively constructing their own personalities
- failed, according to situational theorists, to recognise the specific effects of different environmental situations.
- failed to recognise that individuals do change.

Traits are seen as poor predictors of behaviour or at best predict a limited proportion of behaviour. The view of personality traits as rigid and enduring characteristics is questioned in terms of the validity and long-term reliability of the scales used. It is argued that although people may have certain core tendencies, or are disposed to act in certain ways, these behaviours are not general but specific to certain situations. Simply knowing a performer's personality traits does not always help us predict

how they will behave in specific circumstances. For example, certain performers, like Lee Bowyer, appear to get angry very easily during highly competitive situations whereas others, like Michael Owen, seldom get angry. However, this does not necessarily mean that Bowyer will be angry in all situations. The predisposition towards anger does not tell us what specific situations will provoke outbursts of unacceptable forms of behaviour. Thus a more interactionist perspective is suggested. The generalisation of specific traits across the population as a whole in order to predict behaviour is also questioned.

*The self report tests themselves have been widely criticised in terms of:*

- accuracy
- a participant's honesty
- a participant's desire to create a favourable impression
- a participant's possible lack of objectivity
- the fact that neurotics were seen as possibly over-emphasising certain traits
- inappropriate or ambiguous questions.

Answers could also be influenced by:

- the personality of the tester
- time of day
- a participant's previous experience of tests
- a participant's mood swings.

Finally, the concept of personality is seen as far too complex to be measured by a mere yes or no answer.

## The humanistic approach

The humanistic perspective approaches the concept of personality by focusing on the individual's perception of their own experiences within various environmental situations.

Personality is seen as developing as a result of what is meaningful to the individual. Humanists argue that the behaviour of all individuals is influenced by the human desire for self actualisation, which is the desire to explore and understand our world in order to achieve personal growth and fulfil our potential as human beings (see Maslow's hierarchy of needs in the chapter on motivation).

Other humanists (Rogers 1961) have focused on the actual process of achieving our potential and concentrated on the concepts of 'self'.

- Ideal self: the kind of person we would like to be (Olympic or World Champion)
- Actual self: our perceptions of what we actually are (County Number One)
- Self esteem: feeling good or bad about ourselves. Our level of self esteem, positive or negative, depends on how near our 'actual self' is to our 'ideal self'.

According to Rogers, basically all human beings need to feel good about themselves – **positive self regard**. For example, an athlete gaining a personal best at the national championships (brings them nearer their ideal self).

In addition, all human beings need to feel that others, particularly significant others (see socialisation) approve of them. In order to achieve this they would then behave in certain ways to earn approval – **conditional positive regard**. For example, a young athlete may continue to train and work hard at their event even though they might not be enjoying it at that particular time if they feel that it is valued by their parents and brings coach/club approval. Hence characteristics of determination, being well organised and self disciplined begin to be applied to their behaviour patterns.

## Situational perspective of personality (Nurture)

The situational perspective is based around theories of social learning (see social learning and Bandura). Social learning theory proposes that behaviour is determined more by the individual's situation than by 'unconscious drives' or 'biological predispositions'. Behaviour and personality are said to develop through a process of observational learning (modelling) and social reinforcement (see observational learning, Bandura and aggression – social learning). The situational approach suggests that personality is constructed and shaped as a result of strong environmental influences and indirect reinforcement factors which can override the individual's personality traits. For example, if a high-profile England rugby player is punched, trait theorists would argue a person with high levels of trait aggression would always punch back. Social learning/situational theorists would argue that the response would depend on the situation he was in, ie,

- how hard he was hit
- by whom
- in what context of the game (winning or losing)
- previous linked situations
- choices he had in terms of what he had to lose, ie, being sent off, fined, dropped, coach's attitude, his previous record, etc.

Personality tests are just one example of psychometric testing: a good test should have the following features.

**Discriminating power**

To be useful a wide distribution of scores should be produced. The 'ceiling' and 'floor' effects should be avoided.

**Standardisation**

Either norm referencing (Eysenck's EPQ/EPI and Cattell's 16 PF are both examples of normative tests) or criterion referencing can be used. Comparisons using mean/standard deviations are needed and standardised instructions are necessary to avoid possible bias on the part of the tester.

**Reliability**

All tests should be consistent and be capable of reproduction both **internally** and **externally**: that is, all test items should test the same thing and the test should produce the same results when repeated.

**Validity**

The test should measure what it claims to measure; in other words, it should have **internal validity**. This is ensured by asking:

- are the questions appropriate?
- does the test content cover the representative sample of behaviour it is intended to cover?

It should also have **external validity**. Is there a high correlation between test scores and the independent variable and can these scores be generalised to the population as a whole? Personality tests therefore, while being useful tools to generate impressions of performers, should not be used in isolation or as a means of selecting or assessing performers for teams or events. Care should also be taken in attaching labels to certain individuals or groups (see stereotyping).

Fig 24.3. The features of an effective personality test

- Personality traits
- Cognitive variables
- Physiological variables
- Psychological variables
- Sociological variables

Fig 24.4. The variables considered by sports psychologists

A person learns to behave in specific situations due to what has been observed and reinforced socially. A performer may appear confident in a specific situation, eg, on the pitch or within the context of a game where assertive behaviour is demanded by the coach and the situation. Outside or away from the situation the same assertive performer may behave in a very quiet, unassuming manner. Thus personality is seen as being relatively enduring but only in learned specific situations. While many such as Mischel (1968) supported this perspective, many psychologists viewed the approach with a degree of scepticism. It was felt that in trying to solve the limitations associated with the trait approach the situational perspective had taken up rather too extreme a stance. It was seen as being insufficient to predict behaviour accurately.

## Interactionist approach to personality (Nature and Nurture)

In deciding between the relative strengths of the person versus situation debate, many psychologists recognised that each, although being limited, represented a degree of 'truth' in explaining the nature of personality. Performers were seen as having certain core elements of personality which pre-disposed them to behave in certain ways, but at the same time were capable of being strongly influenced by changing environmental considerations. This compromise position is one which is taken at present by the great majority of sports psychologists: behaviour is explained as the result of a reciprocal interaction between both the individual's consistent psychological traits (core) and the situational factors present. This is of particular interest to sports psychologists due to the extreme situations in which sports performers can find themselves. They may, for instance, experience very high levels of stress in competitive situations, boredom in training, disappointments from losing or dependence on others in team games. When situational factors are strong, they are more likely to affect behaviour than personality factors. However, when situational factors are not strong then personality is more likely to affect behaviour.

This **interactionist approach** suggests therefore that if we wish to try to understand and predict an individual performer's behaviour we need to consider in depth both the individual person and the specific situation. In doing so, a much more complete picture and explanation of a person's behaviour can be developed. An early equation formula suggested by Lewin represents this relationship very simply. B = f(P.E.) where:

- **B** = behaviour (personality)
- **f** = function
- **P** = personality traits
- **E** = environment (eg, situation or context of game)

This is seen as a much more individualistic approach as it recognises that performers in similar sports do not necessarily exhibit the same behaviour. Just because some top class marathon runners appear more introverted in their behaviour does not mean that you have to be the same to get to the top. All rugby players are not extroverts all the time: it is not a prerequisite for success.

Coaches have to develop an in-depth knowledge of each 'unique' performer. This therefore becomes a much more dynamic approach. In addition to being aware of their physical, physiological,

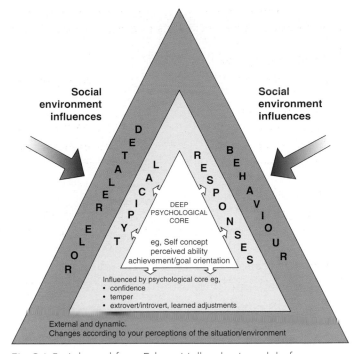

Fig 24.5. Adapted from Edwin Hollanders' model of Personality 1967 (Principles & Methods of Social Psychology, Oxford University Press)

intellectual and learning capabilities a coach needs to know about a performer's arousal and anxiety levels, confidence, levels of attention, attributions, achievement motivation, attitudes, etc. All these need to be considered in relation to the specific situations performers find themselves in. In addition what has been shown to influence behaviour further is the performer's perception (interpretation) of the situation.

This need has led to increased research to provide coaches with more information on such areas.

In trying to increase our understanding modern sport psychologists such as Martens (1975) and R.S. Weinberg (1995) see Hollanders' (1967) model of personality as providing a more systematic and comprehensive framework for understanding the concept of personality (fig 24.5).

This model in encompassing both a trait and social environment perspective encourages a multi-method approach to the study of personality.

Personality is viewed as being in three different levels or layers with the outer layers being more changeable or readily influenced by situation demands and environmental factors.

## Personality structure

- **Psychological core**: this is the most basic level of a performer's personality. It includes your attitudes and values (see attitudes), motives and perceptions/beliefs about your *self*. These deep-seated components represent the 'real you' and are the most stable and constant.

- **Typical response**: these tend to be the ways in which we learn to adjust and adapt to what is happening in the world around us. Usually typical responses lie somewhere between the core and role related behaviour due to the interaction of the two.

- **Role related behaviour**: this is based upon how we perceive our social situation. This is the most changeable and easily influenced aspect of our behaviour in day-to-day life. This continually changing/dynamic part of our personality allows us to experience and learn, which in turn influences our typical responses over time. Roles can change throughout time. Within one day a performer may experience training for oneself, being focused, etc. They may later be coaching a youth team or performers, ie, acting as a leader, and then go home to be a son/daughter or themselves be parents. This can lead to 'role conflict' (see roles and group behaviour).

## Type A and Type B personalities

In reviewing the effects of taking part in sport and fitness programmes on personality researchers have considered two personality dispositions, Type A and Type B personality (Girdano D.A. et al., 1990).

In looking at very specific areas of personality and its effect on coping with stress, a narrow band theory of personality associated with how people deal with stress was developed by Friedman and Rosenman (1959).

## Type A personalities

These people tend to:

- have a very strong competitive drive/need to succeed
- exhibit high levels of agitation/alertness and a tendency to be easily aroused
- generally work at a fast pace, are hasty or have strong sense of urgency
- find it hard to delegate, are intolerant or easily become hostile/angry
- need to be in control of the situation
- experience high levels of stress.

## Type B personalities

These people tend to:

- be more relaxed
- delegate easily
- be less competitive
- be less concerned to get everything done immediately
- be tolerant and methodical and are calm in dealing with problems
- experience low levels of stress.

Although both types were seen as being equally productive, their differences were defined as to do with cognitive emotional aspects linked to the concept of self. The tendency (disposition) towards anger/hostility is thought to increase the likelihood of stress-related disease. The development of these specific tendencies has been related not to specific recent situations (now) but to earlier sociocultural effects usually in terms of high expectations of performance due to early pressures. Fitness and exercise programmes have been shown to have a positive effect on the reduction of Type A behaviour, patterns which could lead to reducing the risk of cardiovascular disease.

The many types of research carried out have revealed a great deal of information on which to draw when trying to understand someone's behaviour.

1) Participants should know the purpose and use of the test.
2) Tests should only be carried out and interpreted by qualified/experienced people.
3) Personality test results should not be used in isolation to predict behaviour.
4) Other information taken should include a person's life history, interview, observations, performance assessments.
5) Sport specific tests should be used.
6) Both trait and state measures should be used.
7) Feedback should be given to participants.
8) Personality tests should not be used for selection purposes and/or to discriminate for places on teams.

Fig 24.6. Guidelines for personality testing – as suggested by the American Psychological Association 1974 in order to ensure tests used are appropriate and ethical

## Further problems associated with assessment and research into personality

As we have already seen, early research such as Eysenck's EPQ and EPI and Cattell's 16 PF have been criticised for their lack of sophistication and have problems of validity, methodology and interpretation of statistical data. Much of the more up-to-date research has been dogged by similar problems. The ethics of using personality tests has also been raised. Criticism of such tests as the Athletic Motivation Inventory (AMI) devised by Ogilvie and Tutko (1966) seemed to heighten sensitivity over the use and application of such research.

Most sports psychologists, however, still rely heavily on such sport specific objective inventory tests due to their ease of application and analysis. The Sport Competition Anxiety Test (SCAT) (Martens, 1990) is a popular example. Guidelines for the use of such tests have been drawn up to ensure both the validity and the ethical nature of testing (see fig 24.6).

## Personality and sporting performance

Returning to the questions posed earlier, research attempting to clarify these has been found to be very contradictory. However, the general findings of more up-to-date research indicate that:

. No obvious sporting personality-type distinguishes those involved in sport and non participants.

. No obvious consistent personality characteristics have been found to distinguish between different

Fig 24.7. Mood states can change dramatically!

types of sports performers – for instance performers participating in both team or individual sports are not disposed to certain specific types of personality behaviour.

3. Few personality differences have been found between male and female sports performers, particularly at the elite level. There is some evidence to suggest that there is a more marked difference between successful and unsuccessful female performers than in men. However, it has been suggested that this is linked more to socio-cultural effects.

4. To be successful in sport a person needs to demonstrate: positive mental health (iceberg profile fig 24.8; positive self perceptions (self confidence); positive/productive cognitive

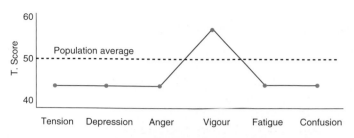

On Profile of Mood States (POMS) scores successful athletes were above the **waterline** (population norm) on vigour, but below the surface on the more negative moods, thus creating the profile of an iceberg.

Fig 24.8. The iceberg profile.

*Source:* Morgan, W.P. et al., 1987, Psychological monitoring of overtraining and staleness, British Journal of Sports Medicine.

strategies. The Iceberg Profile (Morgan, 1978) has been related to characteristics associated with elite sports performers; they tend to be more **vigorous** and have low levels of tension, depression, anger, confusion and fatigue.

5. Sport and Exercise Science research using mood states as a measure was originally carried out to examine people's attitudes towards exercise, related to their positive mental health. It recognised that people's attitudes and thus behaviour (see three components of attitudes) often *changed* according to their '*mood state*'. **Mood** states are seen as being temporary, as opposed to personality traits which are, as we know, seen as being relatively permanent. Morgan's (1975) work compared successful and unsuccessful athletes. Mood states have been found to differ in successful and less successful performers. Successful performers generally display more positive mood profiles. Whether this more positive profile of mood state (POMS) helps to create better performance or whether it is itself caused by the success in sport is inconclusive. D. Gill argues that less than desirable mood profiles are negatively associated with success in most achievement situations.

6. Successful performers have been found to be able to internalise – that is use cognitive (mental) strategies such as mental rehearsal, imagery or positive self talk for coping with anxiety more effectively than unsuccessful performers (see strategies for dealing with stress). However, these cognitive strategies have not been found to change personality traits.

7. The claim that sport can influence or develop certain positive or socially desirable characteristics or attributes has not been supported by research evidence. The philosophical statements often made by physical educationalists and activity centres that certain sports can develop character and socially desirable types of behaviour are therefore quite considerably undermined. There is even some evidence to suggest that taking part in competitive sport can actually have a detrimental effect on social life, by increasing anti-social behaviour and rivalry (see socioculture section).

8. The effect of taking part in sport and fitness work has been shown to have an immediate effect on mood states in the specific situation, and also help with a performer's concept of 'self'. The long-term or global influence on our individual personality traits is seen, however, to be of little effect.

# Summary

- Personality is the combination of those characteristics which make a person unique.

- Personality refers to those relatively stable and enduring aspects of an individual's behaviour.

- There are several theoretical perspectives.

- The study of personality has tended to consider is it as a result of 'nature' or 'nurture'.

- *Trait theories* see personality as being innate and stable predispositions, enabling behaviour patterns to be predicted in all situations.

- *Social learning theories* see personality being formed as a result of the environment influencing individual learning experiences. Thus it can change in different situations.

- *Interactionist theories* see personality as being a combination between traits and the environment. B = f(PE)

- A variety of methods can be used to test personality, the most common being questionnaires, observation and interviews.

- Personality tests should not be used in isolation as there are question marks over their validity.

- No definite findings concerning the different personalities of successful to unsuccessful performers. Team to individual performers. Male to female performers.

- The closest we can get to predicting the behaviour of an individual is through 'mood states' which link to the suggested 'iceberg' profile.

- For success in sport each individual must be viewed differently by the coach according to the three levels of personality. Made up of psychological core, typical response and role related behaviour.

## Review Questions

1. What do we mean by personality?
2. Explain the credulous and sceptical viewpoints of personality research?
3. What is the trait perspective view of personality?
4. What is the RAS? How did Eysenck relate this to personality characteristics?
5. How many personality characteristics did Cattell identify? How did these help?
6. What are the limitations of the trait perspective?
7. What are the main criticisms of personality tests?
8. Why is it important that research is valid and reliable?
9. What is the situational perspective of personality?
0. How does the interactionist approach differ from the trait approach?
1. Explain the equation B = f(PE)
2. What is meant by a personality core? Give an example.
3. What is meant by role related behaviour?
4. What is the iceberg profile? How does it relate to sports performers' 'mood states'?
5. How do type A and type B profiles differ?

# Section 2 – Attitudes

According to some psychologists attitudes are a major foundation stone of social psychology. A great deal of research has been undertaken into people's attitudes; however much of it has been of a descriptive nature and therefore open to similar criticisms to those levelled at personality research. Within the field of physical/health education and sport one of the often stated philosophical objectives is to promote positive attitudes and values, not only in competitive sports performers but also in the population as a whole. It is therefore important to know how to promote and maintain positive attitudes towards sport, exercise and health in general. Attitudes are very often linked to the concept of motivation (see motivation).
A performer who is highly motivated usually has a desire to achieve (see achievement motivation) and thus a positive attitude. They do not look to blame others for any problems associated with performance (see attributions).

The terms 'attitude' and 'values' are often used synonymously. Both refer to hypothetical constructs similar to personality in that, although they are seen as relatively stable dispositions, they cannot be measured directly, only inferred from behaviour that can be observed and tested, usually via questionnaires.

Although there has been much debate concerning the definition of attitudes, one of the most frequently used is that by Triandis (1971).

> 'ideas charged with emotion (positive or negative) which pre-disposes a class of actions to a particular social situation.'
>
> (Triandis)

## Attitudes and behaviour

As attitudes are one of the key determinants of our behaviour they can heavily influence the way in which we behave towards different types of 'attitude objects':

- people
- objects
- events
- ideas.

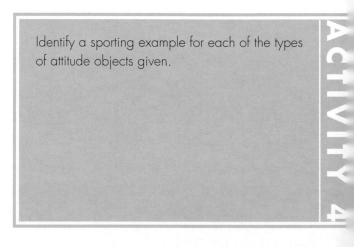

Identify a sporting example for each of the types of attitude objects given.

ACTIVITY 4

In her book *Psychological Dynamics of Sport* Diane Gill argues that our attitudes towards these attitude objects are not necessarily all embracing (global): just because a sportsperson has a negative attitude towards rugby it does not necessarily mean they have a negative attitude towards all sport, or just because they 'love' netball does not always mean that they will turn up and train hard at each session

# KEY WORDS

### Definitions

**Beliefs** represent the knowledge or information we have about the world.

**Values** are deep seated feelings or thoughts (emotions) which form the basis for evaluating if something is worthwhile. They are thought to be culturally determined.

**Attitudes** are therefore a blend of beliefs and values. They are learned via our interaction with the social environment (experience) and provide us with a means to express our values in either a positive or negative way.

When trying to measure attitudes it is therefore important to be specific.

In order to provide us with a better understanding of attitudes Secord and Backman (1964) proposed a structural approach to analysing the components of attitudes.

## Three components of attitudes

1. **Cognitive component**: what a person believes about the attitude object, eg, I believe that jogging is good for me and helps me to keep fit.

2. **Affective component**: what a person feels about the attitude object. This is usually linked to some form of evaluation related to a performer's values and past experience, eg, I enjoy keeping fit and healthy, it is important to maintain my lifestyle.

3. **Behavioural component**: reflects how a person actually responds or intends to act towards the attitude object as a result of 1 and 2, eg, I go jogging regularly four times per week and encourage others to go jogging. I watch athletics on TV and purchase fitness and health magazines to supplement my knowledge of jogging and fitness.

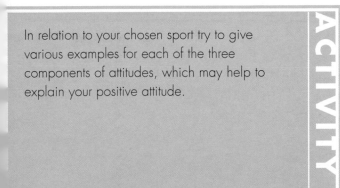

In relation to your chosen sport try to give various examples for each of the three components of attitudes, which may help to explain your positive attitude.

**ACTIVITY 5**

This is a simplistic analysis of attitudes, yet it provides a basis from which attitudes can be studied. Although most social psychologists would adhere to the three component analysis of attitudes they would suggest that a flexible approach must be maintained with regard to its application. There is evidence that it is not always possible to accurately predict a person's behaviour so simply. This is due to the fact that a performer's behaviour does not always reflect the inferred correlation to beliefs (cognitive) and feelings (affective). The classic study by La Piere (1934), although criticised by some, is traditionally used to illustrate the inconsistency between stated or observed attitudes and actual behaviour. In travelling over 10,000 miles around the USA with a Chinese couple he visited 251 hotels and restaurants. This period in American history was characterised by racial prejudice and stereotyping; however, they only experienced one example of discrimination. When he wrote to the various establishments, six months later, enquiring as to whether they would indeed accept Chinese people as guests 92% of the returns stated no! They would not serve Chinese. Further research in this area to support our earlier view from D. Gill begins to suggest that attitudes can only be used to predict behaviour when we measure and assess attitudes to *specific* aspects of our lives and whether or not there is a *stated intention* of behaving in a particular way. A child or performer is more likely to take part in a specific activity, eg, swimming, if they have stated a 'behavioural intention' to do so: 'I will take part in the swimming gala.' General or apparent positive attitudes towards sport will not be a true determinant of actual sporting behaviour. For example, just because a student appears to enjoy swimming and is reasonably good at it does not guarantee that they can be counted on to take part in the gala if they have not specifically said they would.

Research by **Fishbein** and **Ajzen** (1975) supports this view that a high degree of specificity between attitudes and behaviour is the key to predicting accurately.

Fishbein's model proposes:

1. Specific attitudes towards the sporting act must be considered in order to predict behaviour.

2. Attitudes towards the sporting behaviour along with accepted beliefs (normative) help to predict behavioural intentions more accurately.

3. Behavioural intentions related to sporting activity predict actual behaviour quite well.

The correlation between behavioural intention and actual behaviour is very high. Thus in sport we need to ensure that performers, beginners or experienced:

- see the relevance of specific fitness and practice programmes to specific activities

- gain direct experience of the fitness/practice programme thus providing more information about the attitude object

and that any negative attitudes are dealt with immediately.

# Attitude formation

In considering the earlier definition of attitudes you have become aware that attitudes are largely developed through *experiences*. Attitudes are developed by the following:

## Learning

Attitudes are almost entirely *learned*, although there is evidence to suggest certain aspects may possibly be genetically instinctive or inherently determined.

## Familiarity/availability

If a pupil encounters certain activities or sports on a regular basis they will generally develop a positive attitude towards that activity especially if they have ease of access. Think of the child who is regularly taken by its parents to watch and play a particular sport at the local club. A positive attitude will probably develop and if the child is encouraged to use good facilities they will probably end up (certainly during their early years) playing for the same team or club. Zajonc (1968) supported this notion of frequency helping to develop positive attitudes.

## Classical conditioning

Through the association of a certain activity or sport (conditioned stimulus) with a pleasant or unpleasant feeling (unconditioned response) a certain attitude may be formed.

## Operant conditioning

Positive reinforcement and rewards have been shown to help positive attitudes or at least strengthen already formed attitudes, eg, enjoyment of PE lessons, achieving personal goals/success, appreciating the need for a healthy lifestyle.

## Socialisation

This is seen as a major influencing factor in the formation of attitudes. Attitudes are learned from significant others either explicitly through instruction (see chapters on learning and guidance) from teachers, parents or coach or they may develop through social learning via observation, imitation and modelling. We cannot therefore underestimate the power of the media and high profile sports stars particularly in influencing the attitudes of young people. Stereotyping is a major problem created

---

- Disapproval of peers/family
- Socialisation against the activity eg, rugby league not for females, race/ age/gender constraints
- Negative role models
- Low status/unpopularity of the activity
- High motives to avoid failure
- Previous criticism of ability
- Use of attribution theory – previous failure attributed to internal stable attributions
- Performance goals rather than learning goals

- Negative self concept
- Perceived low ability
- Fear of failure
- Personality of the performer
- Previous poor performance – learned helplessness
- Perceived high task difficulty
- Fear of the danger of the activity
- Previous unenjoyable experience of the activity
- Personal constraints – age/gender/ race/size

Fig 24.9. Factors which contribute to a negative attitude to sport

through socialisation, particularly attitudes to issues of gender and different ethnic cultures (see prejudice/stereotyping).

## Peer groups and social groupings

Peer groups have also been found to exert a strong influence on people's attitudes. Inter-group attitudes are often formed as a way of defining, maintaining and possibly protecting the group.

# Measuring attitudes

There are several ways in which attitudes can be measured.

- questionnaires/rating scales
- physiological observation, eg, galvanic skin responses (GSR), pupil responses
- observed behaviour – inferences can be made from observing the degree of eye contact, body language or facial responses. Based on the critical assumption that behaviour and attitudes are consistent (not totally reliable)
- opinion polls
- sociometry
- structured interviews.

The reliability, validity and results of these forms of measurement have again been brought into question. Generally the three main scales used for measuring attitudes have been developed for questionnaires by Thurston, Likert and Osgood.

These attitude scales make certain basic assumptions:

- that attitudes can be expressed by verbal statements
- that statements have the same meaning for all participants
- that attitudes when expressed as verbal statements can be measured and quantified.

## Thurston scale (1931)

This is more a method of constructing an attitude scale. A list of statements representing a wide range of views in relation to a specific attitude object is prepared. In order to check any ambiguity and to evaluate the statements in terms of how favourable or not they are towards the attitude object they are given to a group of judges. The judges rate the statements on an 11-point scale (positive to negative). Any statements which produce substantial disagreement are thrown out until a list of 20 statements are left. As a result of the judges' 'mean' evaluation each statement is then allocated a rating value. The self report questionnaire is then tested with subjects being asked to state which of the statements they agree with and a mean attitude score is calculated from the value of the selected statements.

## Likert scale (1932)

This is the most commonly used form of attitude scale. It generally comprises a balanced number of statements with regard to a specific attitude object. The subject is asked to indicate how they rate each statement, usually on a 5-point scale: 1 strongly agree; 2 agree; 3 undecided; 4 disagree; 5 strongly disagree. The subject's attitude is measured by totalling the scores for each statement, usually showing a correlation. For example:

Aerobics is an excellent activity for keeping fit:

| | | |
|---|---|---|
| strongly agree | ☐ | +2 |
| agree | ☐ | +1 |
| undecided | ☐ | 0 |
| disagree | ☐ | −1 |
| strongly disagree | ☐ | −2 |

Likert scales have the advantage in that they do not expect a basic yes/no answer but rather they allow for degrees of opinion.

## Semantic differential scales (Osgood, Suci and Tannenbaum, 1957)

Usually subjects are asked to rate on a 7-point scale between two bi-polar adjectives which describe best their feelings towards a particular attitude object, eg, aerobics. For example:

Rate how you feel about aerobics for exercise.

good       +3 +2 +1  0  −1 −2 −3 bad
valuable   +3 +2 +1  0  −1 −2 −3 worthless
beneficial +3 +2 +1  0  −1 −2 −3 harmful

The questionnaires would have at least two bi-polar scales constructed around the three main factors associated with the meaning of words or attitude objects. For example:

- evaluative factor (good/bad)
- potency factor (strong/weak)
- activity factor (active/passive)

## The problems associated with attitude measurement are:

- inappropriate/ambiguous questions
- response bias
- people trying to present socially acceptable viewpoints
- people attempting to deliberately distort the results

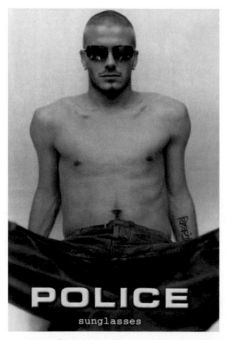

Fig 24.10. High profile sport stars are continually being used to promote campaigns and create positive images

- people tending always to answer yes or no or preferring certain points on the scale (people tend to agree rather than disagree)
- the way in which the questions are asked can also influence the answer.

# Changing attitudes

Up until now we have mainly concentrated on positive attitudes. What happens, however, if a person has a poor or very negative attitude? (see fig 24.9.) How easy or difficult is it to change a sportsperson's attitude? Attitude change has been the subject of much research. As we have already explained, the relationship between attitudes and general behaviour does not always appear very strong. Therefore attempting to change attitudes can be problematic. However, as stated, if the attitude is very *specific* it is possible.

Although attitudes are thought to be 'deep seated' and therefore resistant to change it is felt that attitudes can be influenced or gradually changed through learning (see chapter on learning), formal or informal social influences or persuasion.

Two of the main ways through which, psychologists have suggested, attitudes may be changed are:

- persuasive communication
- cognitive dissonance theory.

*Note*: In order to assess any attitude change, a person's or group's attitudes need to be measured prior to the attempt to change and then again afterwards.

## Persuasive communication

In their research into how easy it was to persuade a person to adopt a different attitude, Hovland, Janis and Kelly (1953) identified four basic factors (variables) that can affect all persuasion situations:

- who is trying to persuade?
- what is the message?
- whom is the message trying to reach?
- what is the situation context?

If we are trying to persuade specific groups of the population that participation in sport is good for them, what factors affect the level of success of such a campaign?

- is the fitness/health argument used?
- is the social argument used?
- is a trend/role model argument used?
- is the lifestyle argument used?
- who is going to front the campaign?
- what are the counter arguments?
- who is the target group?

In a sporting context, if we are trying to persuade individuals or groups to change their attitudes towards a particular policy, activity, etc. (attitude object), it is important that the person, teacher or coach presenting the persuasion is an expert and thus perceived as having high status or credibility.

Olympic or professional performers are often used to focus attention on campaigns to promote sport. The high profile and clean image of such sporting role models as Gary Lineker, Kris Akabusi, Sally Gunnell and Sharron Davis mean they are much in demand; all are now respected media personalities.

Table 24.4. Summary of variables affecting success rate of persuasion

| PEOPLE'S PERCEPTIONS OF | | | |
| --- | --- | --- | --- |
| Source | Message | Receiver/or audience | Context |
| (who) | (what) | (to whom) | (where) |
| **INDEPENDENT VARIABLE** | | | |
| • Status | • Accurate (easily understood/makes sense/unambiguous) | • Level of education, must be able to understand message | • Formal/informal or sporting/non sporting |
| • Credibility | • Order of argument gender, intelligence, personality, self esteem | • Individual differences, commitment | • Level of |
| • Expertise | • Presentation: confident/believable | • Function of original attitude (why they hold present attitude) | • Real life or experiment |
| • Likeability, attractiveness, trustworthiness | • One-sided message or two sides | • Persuadability (are they resistant to change) | • Availability of facilities/resources to support message or change |
| • Intention/motives | • Level of emotional appeal. Appeals to fear/failure | | |
| • Cultural background | • Be careful of hardsell (boomerang effect) | | |

Teachers and coaches have a vital role to play, using their expertise, likeability and trustworthiness to provide leadership in order to communicate positive attitudes to young people.

You should note that it is important that the person whose attitudes are being influenced does not feel threatened or they may become more defensive (resistant to change).

Try to set up a campaign, real or bogus, in your school or college, with the aim of persuading the students and staff to take a positive attitude towards health and fitness. Taking into account the information given in table 24.4 discuss in your group how you will present your campaign. This could also be done in conjunction with attitude measurement. Attitudes could be measured via a group-designed test/scale prior to the campaign and then re-assessed afterwards to judge the level of success.

ACTIVITY 6

## Cognitive dissonance theory (Festinger, 1957)

There have been several suggested theories associated with the notion of cognitive consistency (Heider, 1958; Osgood and Tannenbaum, 1955). However, based on the human need for cognitive consistency, Festinger's has been the most influential, generating an enormous amount of both research and theorising in relation to attitude change.

According to Festinger an individual knows certain things (cognitions) about their own attitudes, beliefs and thoughts in relation to their own behaviour and surroundings. These cognitions that people know or think about themselves can either be consistent with each other creating a good feeling (feeling of consonance) or they can be inconsistent creating a state of dissonance.

Festinger suggests that if a person experiences feelings of dissonance then they are generally motivated to change their beliefs, attitudes or

thoughts in order to return to a feeling of consonance (psychological harmony).

How often have you started a fitness programme, knowing that it is important to keep fit and that at least three sessions per week is desirable, only to lapse after a few sessions or weeks. Not being able to maintain a commitment known to be valuable can create Festinger's feeling of 'psychological discomfort', dissonance. Because of the human need for consonance, you are generally motivated to erase this feeling of dissonance (tension) ie, do something to reduce the imbalance between what we believe and how we are behaving.

In order to rationalise our knowledge, beliefs or thoughts we can reduce dissonance in various ways:

- **change one of the cognitions**, eg, training three times per week is only necessary if you don't work and have the time
- **reduce the importance of the cognitions you hold**, eg, I'm young, healthy and already reasonably fit therefore it is not as essential for me to train three times per week, as it is for someone who is unfit. You could also begin to

## KEY WORDS

**Consonance** is where the cognitions held have a high level of correlation, (eg, I am being assessed in gymnastics for my A level assessment. I need to train/practise to develop my skills and therefore I train twice a week outside the class.)

**Dissonance** is known as a 'negative-drive state' where the cognitions are at odds or in direct conflict with each other creating a feeling of psychological discomfort or tension, (eg, I am being assessed in gymnastics for my A level assessment. I need to train/practise to develop my skills. I don't train/practise outside class at all.)

associate with other like-minded non-fitness fanatics

- **suggest more consistent cognitions**, eg, either belittle the evidence that fitness is good for you or look for evidence that suggests too much exercise is actually harmful/can cause long-term damage through injuries.

In applying this theory within a sporting context it is suggested that teachers and coaches can try to change beginners' or elite performers' attitudes by highlighting certain cognitions that may create states of dissonance within the performer's mind. Convincing people to change their attitude is not a simple short term process, however, as individuals/teams are generally resistant to change. They tend to distort the truth or evidence that may prove their thoughts and beliefs wrong in order to maintain their perceptions of the status quo. Think of football supporters who regularly see their team lose. In order to justify their commitment to the team, comments may be made, such as 'well, our team always try to play football', 'we don't try to kick our way out of a game', etc.

There is much anecdotal or 'folk tale' evidence from social psychology with regard to the apparently broad application of dissonance theory to both PE and sport. It is, however, seen as a rather simplistic notion. Counter arguments have suggested that:

- dissonance cannot be measured
- it is difficult to identify states of dissonance
- what creates or is dissonance is not the same for all people
- individuals differ in strategies used to reduce dissonance
- people who experience high levels of anxiety tend to experience greater feelings of dissonance
- issues of no importance do not arouse dissonance
- many alternative experimental explanations have been given for attitude change, eg,

Incentive/Reinforcement theory (Janis et al., 1965); Impression Management hypothesis (Tedeschi et al., 1971); Self perception theory (D. J. Bem, 1965).

## Strategies to improve a performer's attitude

- Reward the success elements of performance.
- Reward the success elements of squad involvement.
- Agree targets/goals with the performer.
- Give the performer an appropriate role/responsibility.
- Use positive role models (significant others, eg, parents/coach) to demonstrate positive attitude.
- Give positive reinforcement of correct behaviour/attitude.
- Coach/teacher/significant others/media/government body give negative feedback/criticism/punishment of unacceptable behaviour/attitudes.
- Pressure to conform applied by peer group/team.
- Attribute earlier failure to unstable/changeable factors.
- Stress benefits, ie, health, financial, success.
- Ensure training/practice is variable/enjoyable to maintain motivation/interest.
- Stress performance/process goals rather than just outcome goals.

## Prejudice and stereotyping related to expected behaviour

Prejudice is an extreme or strongly held attitude (resistant to change) held prior to direct experience. Situations or people are pre-judged. In pre-judging a situation or a person we are expecting to see or experience certain types of behaviour in certain situations.

Although as already stated, we cannot accurately predict behaviour as a result of attitudes they can certainly have a considerable influence on it. Here is an analysis of prejudice via a triadic model:

- **cognitive component** of prejudice = stereotyping
- **affective component** is the strong feelings of hostility or liking towards the attitude object
- **behavioural** can be split into five stages according to Allport.

The behavioural component of prejudice can manifest itself in various ways:

- Anti-location = hostile talk – insult, racial jokes, etc.
- Avoidance = keeping a distance/but no harm.
- Discrimination = exclusion from civil rights/team, etc.
- Physical attack = violence against person/property.
- Extermination = indiscriminate violence against a certain group.

In relation to people, prejudice (extreme attitudes) serves to develop a certain expectancy of behaviour leading to stereotyping.

## KEY WORD

**Prejudice:** *'An antipathy either felt or expressed based on faulty or inflexible generalisations directed towards a certain group or an individual who is part of a group.'* (G. W. Allport, 1954)

## Stereotyping

This term, first suggested by Lippman (1922), relates to a person having a mental picture (cognitive schema) associating certain behaviour traits with a particular group or type of individual.

Research has tended to focus on the negative aspects of stereotyping in relation to such issues as gender and race. Extremely held attitudes (prejudice) can cause people to expect certain types of behaviour resulting in stereotyping. This can then affect *our* behaviour towards certain individuals or groups of people, eg, if a teacher or coach, as a result of stereotyping, sees boys as having more potential in some sports than girls, this

Fig 24.11. It has taken a long time for black golfers to be accepted in American golfing society

could in turn lead them to having certain expectations of boys and girls. These expectations can influence their behaviour towards both gender groups. They may be more demanding of the boys, perhaps spending more time with them. The boys' skills will probably improve considerably more than those of the girls as a result of this more positive attitude and behaviour thus supporting the teacher's or coach's earlier expectations (a self-fulfilling prophecy).

Although stereotypes are rarely accurate they are generally extremely resistant to change. Many are derived from indirect contact. The influence of the media has been responsible for portraying many poor images of certain categories of people.

Preconceived views can lead to common held stereotypical views. For example:

- girls are better than boys at aesthetic-type activities
- boys are more competitive than girls
- people with disabilities cannot play sport
- people with disabilities do not enjoy competitive sport
- black people are not very good at swimming
- certain sports are better suited to black people than white.

It has been shown that a person's perceptions of self can be affected by exposure to continuous

## KEY WORD

**Stereotyping:** *'The general inclination to place a person in categories according to some easily and quickly identifiable characteristics such as age, gender, ethnic group, nationality or occupation and then to attribute certain qualities believed to be typical to members of that category.'*

*(R. Tagiuri, 1969)*

**ACTIVITY 8**

In discussion of the following 'types' of people, think of the behaviour traits you generally associate with or expect from these people in certain situations:

- male rugby players in your school/college
- sports performers with disabilities
- female artists
- female athletes
- male/female hockey players
- working class/middle class football/rugby supporters
- doctors
- politicians
- different nationalities: Americans, French, German, Spanish, etc.

Consider where these perceptions come from. Are they true?

**ACTIVITY 9**

Can you think of a situation when behaviour expectancy affected by stereotyping can be of a positive benefit? Discuss the following:

- joining a new sports club
- going for a job interview.

Fig 24.12. Attitudes to athletes with disabilities have changed considerably over the past few years due to their success at international level

stereotypical attitudes and certain types of behaviour expectancies. This can influence and lead to differences in sporting achievement. Attitudes towards athletes with disabilities have changed considerably over the past few years due to their success at international level. There is still room for greater improvement!

Social and cultural norms in relation to PE and sport have changed considerably over the last 20 years. In order that they continue to change for the potential good of all in society it is important that teachers and coaches in influential positions (significant others) are very careful not to perpetuate unacceptable/negative stereotypes particularly at the very early stages of development. They must be prepared to challenge any areas of existing or future prejudice in relation to gender, racial or sociocultural issues.

# Summary

- Attitudes are specific and individual not global.

- Attitudes can considerably influence behaviour in sport.

- There is a need for more specific research in this area.

- Stereotyping is not 'bad' in itself, but it is important for teachers and coaches to be aware of inaccurate stereotypes and challenge them.

- Once formed, attitudes are very resistant to change and can lead to prejudice.

# Review Questions

1. Do attitudes really help us to predict behaviour?
2. What are the three ways we can analyse attitudes?
3. By giving examples from sport, try to show how attitudes can be formed.
4. What factors are important when trying to persuade someone to change their attitudes? Illustrate your answer with examples from sport.
5. What are the main problems associated with measuring attitudes?
6. What is dissonance?
7. Why are prejudices potentially dangerous?

# Section 3
# Aggression and its relationship to sport

In considering modern sport certain types of behaviour within sport are seen as acceptable and certain types of behaviour are unacceptable. So-called aggressive or unacceptable behaviour is witnessed on a regular basis within many sporting situations. It has been argued that the increase in aggressive and unacceptable behaviour on the pitch or court, etc, is merely a reflection of general behaviour within society as a whole.

The context in which the term aggression is used sometimes causes confusion. It can be applied in several different ways. Very often coaches demand more aggression from their players to 'win the ball', 'fight for the ball'. Aggressive tactics are often praised, eg, serve/volley in tennis, a full court press in basketball, harder tackling in rugby. These are all examples of where the word aggression is used as an adjective to infer that a performer is being energetic or persistent in their actions.

At the same time, however, many actions or types of behaviour are thought of as being unacceptable forms of aggression, eg, a rugby player stamping on a player in a ruck, brawls amongst players on a pitch, verbal abuse of officials, headbutting of opposition players, etc. None of these can be condoned in any shape or form: the word aggression used in such

situations denotes anti-social behaviour intended to harm another.

Opinions of whether an action is acceptable or unacceptable are going to be different for various people, as responses are heavily influenced by value judgements. Two people watching a particular hard tackle in rugby or hockey will very often disagree as to its level of acceptability and level of good or bad aggression. It is important, therefore, to note that within sport it is not easy to hang a particular label on actions in order to identify what is meant by aggression.

## Finding a definition of aggression

It can be seen from the above discussion that finding an acceptable definition of aggression is no simple matter. It is important, however, that we do

Fig 24.13. Aggression has an ambiguous role in sport

try as problems of misinterpretation by players, administrators and officials could have serious consequences.

Baron's (1977) definition of aggression appears to be a compromise/compilation between the various suggestions given below.

*'Aggression is any form of behaviour toward the goal of harming or injuring another living being who is motivated to avoid such treatment.'*

(R.A. Baron, 1977)

In relation to sport this definition stresses the idea that aggression is behaviour which is *intentional* and *deliberate* and involves injury to another person. From this, it can be inferred that aggression:

- is a first act of hostility, harm or injury
- involves physical or verbal action/behaviour (thinking is not being aggressive unless it leads to action)
- involves an implied intention (this can be difficult to interpret)
- is ultimately damaging, physically or mentally
- is outside the rules of the game (added later by sports psychologists).

A point worth noting is that anger is not seen as aggression but a state of emotional and physiological arousal – aggression is usually seen as the destructive behavioural expression of anger. The infliction of accidental harm is *not* seen as aggression.

In trying to clarify more clearly what is acceptable and what is not, Buss (1961), Feshback (1964) and Moyer (1976) made the distinction between two types of aggression:

1. **Hostile aggression** – aimed at solely hurting someone, the primary reinforcement is seeing pain or injury inflicted on another person. Moyer also termed this **reactive aggression**.

2. **Instrumental aggression** – is a means to an end, aggression to achieve a non-aggressive goal. The primary reinforcement being tangible reward (eg, praise–money–victory).

Although instrumental (also known as channelled) aggression appears initially more acceptable and covers most examples within sport, both types

## Definitions of aggression

Maslow (1968) distinguished between what he called natural/positive aggression (eg, self defence) and pathological aggression or violence.

Brown (1985) makes a distinction between aggression which does not always involve injury and violence which usually does.

Moyer (1984) introduces the idea of aggression being also verbal or symbolic, whereas violence manifests itself in physical damage to person or property.

Gross (1991) defined aggression as the intentional infliction of some form of harm to others.

Fig 24.14. Whether behaviour is acceptable/good aggressive or unacceptable/bad aggressive appears to be a question of interpretation

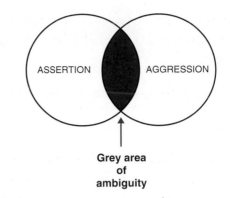

Fig 24.15. Assertion or aggression – the grey area of ambiguity

involve the *intention* to inflict injury or pain and it is debatable whether either should be encouraged in sport, as they fall outside the accepted rules of most sporting activities.

In trying to end the confusing use of the word aggression to explain acceptable sporting behaviour the term 'assertive behaviour' was suggested by Husman and Silva (1984).

## Assertive behaviour

Assertive behaviour is seen as acceptable but forceful behaviour. It is also:

- goal directed behaviour
- the use of legitimate verbal or physical force (involving energy and effort which, outside sport, could be interpreted as aggression)
- behaviour which has no *intention* to harm or injure
- behaviour which does not violate the agreed rules/laws/structures of the sport, eg, strong tackling in hockey, rugby, football; blocking in basketball; smashing in tennis/badminton, etc.

While most sports have specific rule structures to control the degree of assertive behaviour allowed, there are still problems associated with subjective interpretations, both general and specific. When, for instance, does a tackle in rugby become high? What in hockey constitutes a deliberate foul in the D'? When should a red card be given in soccer?

You should note that an action is described as aggression when the intention is clearly to harm or injure someone *outside* the laws of the game or activity.

Many sports, by their very nature, involve a high degree of physical contact which can lead either to its misuse or to misinterpretation of actions by an official. Officials often take into account the context of the assertive action, eg, what has gone on prior to the action, state of the game, where the incident happened on the court or pitch. Thus a member of a team winning 1–0 in an important match, who, as the last defender 'takes out' an attacker in the last few minutes, is generally deemed to have committed a conscious aggressive, not assertive, act (intention to harm or injure).

In discriminating between assertion and aggression sports psychologists accept that there are ambiguities when interpretations are made regarding the 'intention' or degree of force used. Obviously sports such as rugby, hockey, ice hockey or wrestling have a larger grey area than non-contact sports.

## ACTIVITY 12

Discuss the implications of such activities as boxing.

Now use what you know of definitions of aggression and compare assertive behaviour with aggressive behaviour in relation to the following scenarios. Tick the appropriate box to show whether you feel they are acts of aggression or assertion.

| Assertion | Aggression | |
|---|---|---|
| ☐ | ☐ | 1. In trying to head a football a player clashes heads with another player causing a serious injury. |
| ☐ | ☐ | 2. A boxer traps his opponent against the ropes and leads with his head into the chin of the opponent. |
| ☐ | ☐ | 3. A rugby player studs a player at the bottom of a ruck. |
| ☐ | ☐ | 4. Having been tackled hard earlier in the game as the attacking hockey player approaches the 'D' she lifts her stick to catch the defender's hands and head. |
| ☐ | ☐ | 5. Having been forced off the track the rally car driver runs over to the other driver who caused the crash and punches him in the face. |
| ☐ | ☐ | 6. The bowler in cricket beats the batsman with a fast ball and hits him on the thigh. |
| ☐ | ☐ | 7. A basketball player verbally abuses the referee for giving a personal foul against her. |
| ☐ | ☐ | 8. A basketball coach smashes a chair in protest at a referee's decision. |
| ☐ | ☐ | 9. A racing car driver slows down and cuts across the path of a faster driver coming up behind and stops him getting past. |
| ☐ | ☐ | 10. A bowler in cricket bowls a third successive bouncer in one over, hitting the batsman on the head. |

**ACTIVITY 13**

# Theories of aggression

Is it nature or nurture? In looking at possible causes of aggression psychologists have considered the following issues:

- why are some sports performers more aggressive than others?
- why do some performers find it hard to control aggression?
- are aggressive individuals born with certain innate characteristics
- are they a product of their learning and environmental influences?

The main theories associated with these questions are:

- instinct theory
- drive theory/frustration aggression hypothesis
- social learning theory.

## Instinct theory

Instinct theories view aggression as instinctive within human beings and developed as a result of evolution. In our fight for survival, aggression is seen as inevitable as with any other species. There are, however, two distinct perspectives on this theory: the psychoanalytical approach and the ethological approach.

## Psychoanalytical approach

Freud is the name usually associated with this approach to the instinct theory of aggression; aggression being viewed as a destructive drive. Freudian theory argues that our innate aggressive tendencies are expressed in the self destructive or **death instinct** called thanatos. This self directed, inner drive towards self aggression is balanced by our **life instincts** called eros. Freud and Lorenze (see below) saw aggression as building up within a person with eros helping to direct it away from self and into some other form of aggressive behaviour. This could be either acceptable behaviour – sport, expeditions, exploration, etc, or unacceptable behaviour – crime, brutality or eventually back inside a person's mind, leading ultimately to suicide.

Freud also maintained that when we want to behave in a way which we know is unacceptable, we cope by using 'ego defence' mechanisms, such as **displacement** (see personality). For example, if you have had a bad day at the office, rather than hitting your boss when he made you angry you behave aggressively in your match later that evening, which is more acceptable. Thus you redirect your emotional responses from a dangerous target to a more harmless one who will hopefully not retaliate.

ig 24.16. Lorenze argued that 'the greatest value of ompetitive sport is that it provides an outlet for aggressive nergies, providing a safety valve'

## Ethological approach

One of the more famous psychologists in this area is Konrad Lorenze who based his views on anthropological studies comparing human behaviour with the 'natural' ritualistic aggressive behaviour of animals. The example of human attempts at territorial control (invasions, etc) is often cited as justifying the comparison. This perspective sees aggression as building up within humans to create a drive which, if not released in some constructive way achieving catharsis (see below), will inevitably lead to some form of spontaneous destructive or aggressive behaviour. Like Freud, Lorenze argued that in acknowledging our natural aggressive instinct we should be able to control it through socially acceptable competitive sport (eg, invasion games where destructive aggression is controlled by rules and the referee).

## Catharsis

For instinct theorists the view that sport and exercise can be used to 'channel' aggressive urges into more socially desirable behaviour (either as a performer or spectator) is very important. This view of purifying the body and reducing drive (catharsis) is not, however, supported by creditable research particularly in sport. Evidence to show psychological differences before and after aggression has proved equivocal. It has even been suggested that rather than having a cathartic effect (drive reducing), watching aggressive behaviour may be drive enhancing, eg, the spectator who, having seen a particularly vicious boxing match, may be driven to reproduce aggressive behaviour (see social learning).

## Criticisms of instinct theory

In evaluating instinct theory psychologists feel that the parallels drawn between humans and animals are over simplified. Social learning processes are seen as being much more prevalent in human behaviour and need to be included in any explanation. Furthermore:

- no biological innate aggressive drive has ever been identified

Fig 24.17. According to instinct theory, taking part in sport should help to reduce aggression

- the measuring of any cathartic effect of aggression has proved difficult

- early human beings were not warriors but 'hunter gatherers,' eg, like modern day Inuit

- cross-cultural studies (Sian, 1985) do not support the view that all human beings are naturally aggressive

- cultural influences are seen as being more important determinants of human aggression than biological factors

- human aggression is not seen as being always spontaneous

- human aggression is seen as reactive and modifiable

- Lorenze does not take into account learning and socialising influences which are seen as overriding possible innate aggression

- aggression is seen more as a learned response linked to the human ability to reason.

# The frustration–aggression hypothesis

Published as a result of research carried out by Dollard, Doob, Miller, Mowrer and Sears (Dollard et al., 1939) the frustration–aggression hypothesis tried to deal with some of the limitations of instinct theory. Linked to drive theory it *proposes that*

*frustration always leads to aggression and aggression is always as a result of frustration.*

Players in a major final (eg, rugby) are trying to achieve (drive) a good performance and success (goal orientated behaviour). A player is continually tackled and sees the opposition constantly blocking the ball or encroaching (blocking of goal orientated behaviour), and becomes frustrated. They are then driven to do something about it (increase drive), possibly playing or working harder. If the frustration continues, this drive may become an aggressive drive and result in transgression of the rules or aggressive behaviour. When held, this player will retaliate with a punch; such aggressive behaviour will reduce frustration, which in turn will have a cathartic effect in the short term. However, in the long term, it may have a negative effect on the game and possibly result in further frustration.

## KEY WORD

**Frustration** Blocking of goal orientated behaviour.

## Criticism of early frustration–aggression hypothesis

This original model (fig 24.18), while initially finding support, has been found to have little credence in sport due, in the main, to its insistence that frustration always leads to aggression. Critics point out that:

- not all frustration leads to aggression in sport – people have been increasingly shown to be able

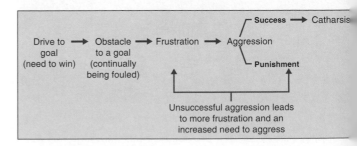

Fig 24.18. The frustration–aggression model is cyclic

to deal with frustration in alternative ways, ie, learned helplessness

- aggression can be a learned response and does not always happen as a result of frustration
- individual and situational differences are not taken into account
- the cathartic effect of aggression in sport is not upheld
- some aggressive participants have been shown to become more aggressive through participation in sport.

## Berkowitz's cue arousal (or aggressive cue) theory

As a result of further research several modifications to the original hypothesis have been suggested. Some of Dollard's (et al.) original theory has been combined with a more social learning approach; Berkowitz (1994) followed up on earlier work from Miller (1941) in concluding that although frustration may make aggression more likely other factors also needed to be understood. Frustration is not seen as being sufficient cause by itself. Berkowitz suggests that frustration creates a 'readiness' for aggression (anger creates psychological or physical pain).

Frustration leads to a pre-disposition to behave aggressively by increasing anger and arousal. This increased arousal and anger will only lead to aggression if certain socially learned cues or environmental stimuli are present. See table 24.5 (Berkowitz, 1993).

A defender in football who is easily beaten by an attacker who could go on to score, may lash out or kick the opponent particularly if the coach or manager has previously accepted such behaviour.

More anger is generated if the frustration is unexpected or seen as unfair. In most cases performers are able to use their developed mental processes of reasoning and thinking and not always respond to frustration with aggression. Performers may do so however if for some reason they cannot think logically at that precise moment.

## Social learning theory of aggression

Social learning theorists see aggression as being influenced by learning. Bandura (1973) states that aggression is not instinctive but a learned response. In his research Bandura has shown that a performer can learn to be aggressive by either having aggression reinforced (by it being successful or gaining coach approval) or by observation of aggressive behaviour (see social influences for a more detailed discussion of this topic). Bandura's (1965) well-known research demonstrated that

Table 24.5. Revised model of frustration–aggression hypothesis

| Frustration | $\implies$ | Increased arousal | $\implies$ | Socially learned cues/signals environmental stimuli | $\implies$ | Aggression |
|---|---|---|---|---|---|---|
| • Failure<br><br>• Unsuccessful<br><br>• Goals blocked<br>• Lose game or play badly | | eg, pain/anger approval by coach<br>• Creates a readiness to act | | eg, overt or covert | | |

children copy adults behaving aggressively in his 'Bobo doll experiment'. Children would often imitate the aggressive behaviour of the adults towards the large inflatable dolls. When the child was rewarded or witnessed the adult being rewarded for beating the doll, the level of aggression increased.

The application of this theory to sport is obvious. If sports performers, particularly high status players, are seen to behave aggressively, 'getting away with it' and achieving success, then a young player will be more likely to imitate those actions. This learning through observation of the behaviour of successful 'significant others' is referred to as vicarious learning; this is frequently seen in young players who model their behaviour on the actions of others.

A young player can receive reinforcement of sporting aggression in many ways. Although teachers, coaches, parents, managers, team mates and professional performers will rarely condone blatant aggression these significant others may well

inadvertently or covertly support or sanction aggressive behaviour. Young players are often encouraged to 'get their retaliation in first', 'make the opposition know you are there'. Gamesmanship and 'psyching out' the opposition are all condoned. Performers very often verbally abuse the opposition (aggression) in order to goad them into a retaliation which may just be enough to put them off their game or sufficient to warrant their being sent off.

Young basketball players quickly learn which aggressive (not assertive) actions are tolerated. Being aggressive on court can quickly gain them personal recognition.

Vicarious or observational learning of aggression usually happens very early in a performer's development: a performer will quickly learn what behaviour is acceptable or unacceptable in various specific situations (see observational learning). Through observation and experience a performer will evaluate the consequences of certain aggressive actions, either in terms of punishment or expected reward. When expected rewards (eg, prestige, tactical/psychological advantage or victory) are seen to outweigh the value of the punishment (eg, a foul given away, booking or possible sin-bin) a player will be prepared to transgress the rules.

The situational expectancies of success can be seen as high or low. Social learning theorists believe that reinforcement values/punishment values are major factors in influencing sports performers in the selection of aggressive behaviour (Silva, 1979). Thus performers are being socialised towards deviance. The social learning perspective, however, also sees the process as having possible positive effects. This more optimistic view suggests that if performers can learn aggressive sporting behaviour then they can also learn to be non-aggressive.

## Controlling and reducing aggression

When trying to manage or reduce aggression we first need to be aware of which situations are more likely to cause aggression to occur.

Fig 24.19. In classic cases of violence by top sports performers they were all subjected to extreme frustration, all became angry and lost control

## Situations that cause aggression

Although activities that have high levels of physical contact are thought to increase the probability of aggression this only happens if aggression increases the team's chances of winning (performance outcome) or the players interpret the contact as deliberate or intending to inflict harm. Specific cues such as a player's reputation, body language and possible verbal follow up lead to specific interpretation (see attributions).

Causes specific to individual aggression are:

- facing defeat (particularly when success has a high intrinsic or extrinsic value) (see motivation)
- when officiating is perceived as unfair
- embarrassment
- physical pain
- playing below expectations.

General causes of aggression are:

- that the effects or demands of the professional game encourage aggressive behaviour
- competition
- media intervention and comment
- belief that it facilitates performance outcome

- belief that it is OK to be more aggressive in sport than in other life contexts (bracketed morality)
- over arousal (excitation transfer)
- over emphasis on winning or the achievement of goals
- crowd reaction (displaced aggression)
- increased rewards
- linked to situational expectations.
- coaches and parents
- reinforcement/observation/vicarious processes.

## Strategies for controlling aggression

In being aware of what can create or predispose a performer towards aggressive behaviour we can propose the following strategies for trying to limit or control aggression amongst sports performers.

1. If a player is observed as displaying signs which may well lead to possible aggressive behaviour, eg, continual questioning of official's decisions or committing fouls, then a player should be removed from the game or situation in order to 'cool off' (continuous/rolling substitutions in basketball, hockey, allow for this).

2. Stress management techniques such as those discussed later can be used to teach sports performers to control their emotions and reactions to frustration. Relaxation prior to the game and mental practice focus efforts more effectively on fulfilling their role in the game.

3. Reduce the emphasis on winning (not so easy in professional sport) – aggression should not be the result of losing. Efforts should be made by the teacher or coach (significant other) to minimise any aggression experienced from losing.

4. Increase rewards for sporting or non-aggressive behaviour.

5. Reinforce assertive behaviour not aggressive behaviour.

6. Increase the profile of positive role models.

7. Emphasise the result of unacceptable behaviour by role models, eg, bad publicity; getting sent off.

Fig 24.20. The more frequently teams play against each other the more likely they are to be aggressive

8. Ensure that players are aware of the 'wider role' they play in society and the possible damaging effects of their behaviour.

9. Make sure that aggression does not pay dividends – check that rules associated with activities deter acts of aggression (increase numbers of red cards). The rules of many sports still present loop holes in control which encourage deviant behaviour.

10. Increase punishments for aggressive behaviour to reduce legitimacy of the action.

11. Players and coaches need to be more sensitive to the differences between assertive and aggressive behaviour in order to reduce the possibilities of retaliation.

12. Educate players and coaches on the appropriateness of certain types of behaviour (ethical/moral development). Emphasise their positive role in the team and discuss how aggressive behaviour may 'let down' their team mates.

13. Contain possible frustration by:
    - increasing performers' levels of fitness in order that they can compete continually throughout a match
    - ensuring that players have alternative game plans/strategies to deal with situations where original plans are being frustrated
    - adapting goals/targets
    - maintaining performers' attentional control, eg, desensitisation to noise/crowd/distractions/intimidation.

## Strategies for controlling spectator aggression

Again, observation of aggressive behaviour has been shown to increase violence off the pitch, but only if certain situational factors are also part of the equation, eg, crowd situations and/or large numbers of young males under the influence of alcohol. Controlling strategies include:

- limiting alcohol or banning it altogether
- reducing levels of rivalry
- removing spectators if they display aggressive tendencies
- increasing effectiveness of game officials thus reducing aggressive behaviour within the game
- reducing crowded situations (strict seating control)
- telling coaches that aggressive behaviour or inciting aggressive behaviour by themselves or their teams will not be tolerated
- getting the media to support these views by not positively emphasising aggressive behaviour
- make sporting situations more family orientated
- increase stewarding.

## Methods by which referees/officials can control aggression in sporting competitions:

- Officials can only operate within the rules/sanctions allowed within the game.
- Apply the rules correctly.
- Punish aggressive behaviour immediately (don't allow situations to escalate).
- Officials should be consistent in both judgement perceptions/interpretation and sanctions awarded.
- Officials must apply firmness/consistency/control from the start of the competition.

# Summary

### Aggression

- Aggression is intentional behaviour outside the rules directed towards the goal of harming or injuring another living being, when they are motivated to avoid such treatment.

- The main theories associated with the study of aggression are: instinct theory (ethological and psychoanalytical); drive theory; frustration–aggression hypothesis; social learning theory.

- More up-to-date research has ensured that instinct theory has little support in relation to sport. There is, however, some recognition of limited innate aggressive tendencies.

- There is little evidence to support the notion of catharsis.

- The revised frustration theory of aggression is seen as having some credibility, particularly when it is linked to social learning theory.

### Social learning

- Social learning theory advocates that reinforcement and modelling either of or by significant others are the main influential determinants of aggressive behaviour in sport.

- Social learning can also be seen as an optimistic approach.

- Having an understanding of what can cause aggressive behaviour allows teachers, coaches and performers to be more effective in controlling aggressive behaviour.

# Review Questions

1. Give a definition of aggression. How does this differ from assertive behaviour? Give examples.
2. Explain what is meant by a) hostile aggression, b) instrumental aggression, c) reactive aggression.
3. Why is instinct theory thought to be a too simplistic approach?
4. What is meant by the term catharsis?
5. By using examples from sport show what you understand by the frustration-aggression hypothesis.
6. Explain how aggression can be socially learned.
7. Why are significant others so important in relation to aggression?
8. Briefly explain the experiment by Bandura which supports a theory explaining aggression.
9. How do situational expectancies affect aggressive behaviour?
10. In what ways can we try to limit or control aggression both on and off the field?

# 25. Motivation in Physical Education and Sport

## Chapter introduction

Motivation is a key area of sport psychology. It is recognised as an essential feature in both the learning of skills and the development of performance. In addition it plays an important role in a learner's preference for and selection of activities. Psychologists all accept that motivation is necessary for the effective learning and performance of skills; however, the enormous amount of motivation-related research has been very diverse with psychologists posing many questions including:

- what motivates a learner/performer?
- what motivational factors can influence learning achievement and overall quality of performance?
- is motivation the same for all people in all activities?
- how can we maintain motivation?
- why do people take part in certain activities and not others?
- why do people stop participating in sport?

In evaluating the research we find that unfortunately there are, once again, no simple answers. What becomes obvious is that in order to gain an understanding of this complex and multi-functional concept we need to consider a wide variety of research. By taking an integrated approach to analysing motivation we will try to bring together the main aspects of various psychological perspectives. Motivation is the global term for a very complex process. Within this chapter we will introduce you to the following questions:

- what do sports psychologists mean by motivation?
- what are the different types of motivation?
- what are the effects of these different types on learning and performance?
- what are the main theories associated with motivation and achievement motivation?
- what different motivational techniques can be used in order to facilitate achievement motivation?
- what are the related and interdependent factors that can influence motivational behaviour?

In considering these areas you should develop a clearer understanding of the underlying processes involved in how and why motivation can differ from person to person.

Here is a list of the terms to be covered in this chapter. It is important that you understand them.

- Motivation
- Intrinsic motivation
- Extrinsic motivation
- Arousal
- Drive theory
- The inverted 'U' hypothesis
- Catastrophe theory
- Reticular activating system
- Optimum arousal
- Perceptual narrowing

- Cue utilisation
- Achievement motivation
- n. Ach
- n. Af
- Causal attributions
- Attribution process
- Attribution retraining
- Learned helplessness
- Self efficacy
- Vicarious experience

# Defining motivation

Answering the question 'What do we mean by motivation?' has been one of the fundamental difficulties faced by psychologists and explanations differ according to the psychological perspective adopted. The term 'motivate' comes from the Latin for move and motives are seen as a special kind of cause of behaviour that **energise**, **direct** and **sustain** a person's behaviour (Ruben and McNeil, 1983).

It has been suggested that human beings have both primary motives (survival and function, etc.) and secondary motives which are acquired or learned such as the **need for achievement** and self actualisation which are complex, higher order cognitive behaviours.

Motivation was historically linked with the concept of homeostasis, ie, maintaining the body's physiological balance. In order for a person's body to function correctly it requires certain essential elements: food, water, heat and rest (primary needs). If these basic elements are not available or lacking in any way the body needs to obtain them. Maslow highlighted the basic needs of a person as being a mixture of the physiological and psychological. If the body has developed a need then it will eventually strive to meet the need – the body will be driven psychologically to meet its needs. As well as being psychological, the desire to overcome physiological deprivation implies a motivational state.

- Physiological needs result in psychological drives.
- Drives are described as a tendency to fulfil a need.
- Drives result in *behaviour*.
- Maslow (1954) produced a psycho-social model referring to a human being's hierarchy of needs (see fig 25.1).
- This is a humanistic viewpoint.
- The **primary** or basic needs at the bottom of the triangle's hierarchy must be satisfied first. The needs at the top of the hierarchical structure are

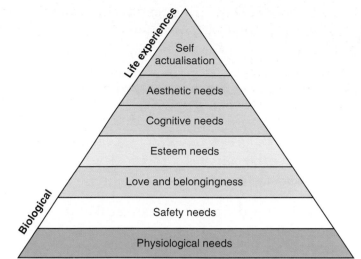

Fig 25.1. Maslow's 1954 hierarchy of needs

more difficult to achieve. Food and drink (basic) → acceptance → understanding → self actualisation

- **Individualistic** needs. Each person will achieve self actualisation in ways individual to themselves.
- The strength of various drives varies occasionally according to the person and the situation. Personal and social needs have been shown to take over from the physiological and safety needs.
- The pursuit of needs/goals that are in the future is one of the unique features of human behaviour. Individuals differ in their ability to set and realise such goals! See intrinsic motivation and Czikszentmitialy (1975) in particular.

Motivation is: *'the internal mechanisms and external stimuli which arouse and direct our behaviour'*.
(*G.H. Sage, 1974*)

*'The direction and intensity of one's effort.'*
(*Sage, 1977*)

*'A drive to fulfil a need.'*
(*D. Gill, 1986*)

Defining motivation in this generalised way can have certain disadvantages. Learners and performers may misunderstand the term when advised to '*be more motivated*', inferring certain character problems associated with themselves. It can also cause potential problems when motivational strategies are employed.

Seeing motivation as the *direction* and *intensity* of one's effort is regarded by more recent psychologists as too simplistic (M. Weiss, 1992) (Weinberg, 1995). However, for the purposes of this book we will accept Sage's definition as a useful starting point.

In analysing the definition we can see that it involves four main aspects:

1. **Internal mechanisms** – motivation is linked to and affected by a person's inner drives.

2. **External mechanisms**: motivation is linked to and affected by external factors that we can experience within our learning/performing situations.

3. **Arouse behaviour:** motivation is linked to a person's state of arousal that energises and drives our behaviour. The strength of the energised state will determine the degree of intensity of effort used to achieve the goal related behaviour.

4. **Direct behaviour:** motivation in its various forms can affect our goals or selection of activities as well as our maintenance of behaviour in activities (Richard Gross sees motivation as 'goal directed purposeful behaviour').

Motivation refers therefore to a general energised state which prepares a person to act or behave in some way. Motives relate to the direction that the behaviour will take or the goal which is set.

## Interactional view of motivation

In recognising that motivation (the intensity and direction of behaviour) is formed as a result of both 'internal and external mechanisms' we are said to be taking an **interactionist perspective** on motivation.

To develop optimum motivation a teacher or coach must not only analyse and respond individually to each of the aspects listed in fig 25.2 but also to how the factors interact together. Very rarely can blame

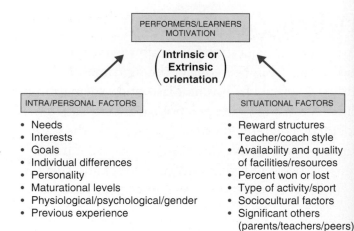

Fig 25.2. The interactionist view of motivation

for poor motivation be placed on any one factor alone.

## Why do performers take part in physical activities?

- The wish/desire/drive to participate in/perform well at a sport.

- Goal directed behaviour.

- Desire is associated with the expectation that the outcomes will be positive.

- The drive to achieve/will to win.

## Types of motivation

A person's behaviour is affected by many different kinds of motives coming from both internal and external mechanisms.

### Intrinsic motivation

The study of intrinsic motivation has been linked to cognitive theories. Intrinsic motivation is used to explain how learners/performers strive inwardly, being self determined in trying to develop competence or excellence of performance. They are said to have mastery orientation. A person who is intrinsically motivated will want to take part in the activity for its *own sake*, for *pure love of the sport*. The will focus on the enjoyment and fun of competition try to develop their skills to the highest possible level (*pursuit of excellence*) and enjoy the action and excitement of seeking out new challenges and affiliations in doing so. A performer pushing themselves hard in difficult circumstances and feeling a sense of control and pride at achieving a high level of personal skill is said to be intrinsically motivated. Intrinsic motivation is greatest when learners/performers feel competent and self determining in dealing with their environment.

## The 'FLOW experience'

Sports performers sometimes experience a situation when the timing of movements and actions appears perfect. They seem unable to do wrong. Everything they try works! It's one of those perfect days. They are said to be experiencing the ultimate intrinsic experience. Csikszentmihalyi (1975) describes this as the '*flow experience*'; in his research he identified the common characteristics of it as:

- a feeling that the performer has the necessary skills to meet the challenge
- complete absorption in the activity
- clear goals
- action and awareness are merged
- total concentration on task
- apparent loss of consciousness
- an almost subconscious feeling of self control
- no extrinsic motivation (goals, rewards, etc.)

**ig 25.3.** A highly skilled performer competing against an qually highly skilled opponent can achieve 'flow'

- time transformation (appears to speed up)
- effortless movement.

Many researchers in this area have tended to concentrate on analysing the factors which have a negative impact on intrinsic motivation whereas Csikszentmihalyi (1990, 1999) has focused on what makes a task intrinsically motivating. Such a peak experience, during which performers are able to lose themselves in the highly skilled performance of their sport, has been likened to Maslow's 'self actualisation' commented upon earlier in this chapter. Although it cannot be consciously planned for, the development of 'flow' has been linked to the following factors:

- positive mental attitude (confidence, positive thinking)
- being relaxed, controlling anxiety, and enjoying optimum arousal
- focusing on appropriate specific aspects of the current performance
- physical readiness (training and preparation at the highest level)
- optimum environment and situational conditions (good atmosphere)
- a shared sense of purpose (team games), good interaction.
- balanced emotional state, 'feeling good' and in control of ones body.

By focusing on aspects of their preparation which can help the development of the above factors, elite performers can increase the probability that the 'flow experience' can occur. Psychological preparation is just as important as physiological performance (Jackson et al. 2001).

Obviously limitations in any of the above factors can result in 'disrupted flow'. For example:

- injury
- fatigue
- crowd hostility

- uncontrollable events
- worrying
- distractions
- lack of challenge
- non optimal arousal
- Limited cohesion
- negative self talk
- poor officials
- poor preparation
- poor performance.

# Extrinsic motivation

Extrinsic motivation is related to Sage's external mechanisms.

If used appropriately extrinsic types of motivation (contingencies) can serve a very useful purpose in effectively developing certain required behaviours (learning) or levels of sporting performance. The behaviouristic view of learning discussed in earlier chapters is founded on the principles of reinforcement (rewards for success) and punishment. The systematic use of rewards, or 'Effective Contingency Management' as it is often referred to, is recognised as playing an important role in modifying and shaping learning and performance (see operant conditioning). Rewards can expedite learning and achievement, serve to ensure that a good performance is repeated or form an attraction to persuade a person to take part in certain activities (incentive).

While extrinsic motivation is most obviously seen in terms of tangible or materialistic rewards, it can also be intangible.

When using extrinsic rewards and reinforcements to enhance motivation a teacher or coach needs to be aware of how often they are used (frequency). Should reward or reinforcement be used at every good or successful attempt or every so many times (ratio)? How quickly after the event should reinforcement be used (interval)? What is the most

effective type of reinforcement to use? (see table 25.1). The value or quantity of the reward is also important (magnitude). In being aware of the above factors a teacher or coach clearly needs an in-depth knowledge of the likes and dislikes of the people being taught. The use of rewards is therefore closely linked to our earlier discussion in the chapter on reinforcement of learning.

Research into the use of reinforcement principles has produced the following recommendations when considering extrinsic motivation:

- positive reinforcement is 80 to 90 per cent more effective
- avoid the use of punishment apart from when behaviour is intolerable or unwanted
- in order to be effective, extrinsic feedback and reinforcement must meet the needs of the recipient (they must be important to or desired by the individual)
- continuous reinforcement is desirable in the early stages of learning
- intermittent reinforcement is more effective with more advanced performers
- immediate reinforcement is generally more effective, particularly with beginners

Table 25.1. Tangible and intangible extrinsic motivation

| Tangible | Intangible |
|---|---|
| • Trophies | • Social reinforcers |
| • Medals | • Praise from teacher/coach/peers |
| • Badges | • Smile |
| • Certificates | • Pat on the back |
| • Money | • Publicity/national recognition |
| | • Winning/glory |
| | • Social status |
| | • Approval |

Fig 25.4. Top level athletes may perform for a mixture of extrinsic and intrinsic reasons

- reward appropriate behaviour (cannot reward all behaviour)
  - (i) reward successful approximations, particularly by beginners (shaping) – performance will not always be perfect (trial and error)
  - (ii) reward performance – do not just focus on the outcome, ie, winning
  - (iii) reward effort
  - (iv) reward emotional and social skills

- provide knowledge of results (information regarding accuracy and success of movement – see feedback)

- the use of punishment should be restricted or avoided as although it can be effective in eliminating undesirable behaviour it can also lead to bitterness, resentment, frustration and hostility. It can arouse a performer's fear of failure and thus hinder the learning of skills.

Fig 25.5. By signing very lucrative contracts, top class players may feel that they have to perform not because they want to (intrinsic) but because of the extrinsic reward

## Combining intrinsic and extrinsic rewards

Consider top level sports performers such as Johnny Wilkinson and Venus Williams.
In discussion with a partner, try to suggest what motivates them to carry on once they have reached the top.

ACTIVITY 2

Look at the list of strategies for the use of extrinsic rewards. Try to give practical examples of how a teacher or coach might implement them in real life.

ACTIVITY 1

Both intrinsic and extrinsic motivation obviously play important roles in the development of skilled performance and behavioural change (learning). Extrinsic rewards are used extensively in sporting situations. Most major sports have achievement performance incentives linked to some form of tangible reward system. At first glance it would appear that the 'additive effect' of extrinsic rewards – money, cups and medals – and the high level of

Fig 25.6. Young sports participants very often feel the need to excel and win at all costs in order to satisfy their parents' ambitions

intrinsic motivation should result in performers showing a much greater level of overall motivation.

Although early research in this area supported this additive viewpoint, later research, for example by Deci (1971, 1972) and Lepper and Green (1975) began to suggest that under certain conditions (when intrinsic motivation is already high (Orlick and Mosher, 1978)) extrinsic motivation may actually decrease intrinsic motivation. This led to many practitioners discouraging the use of extrinsic rewards in an educational setting. Further research with regard to the reduction in intrinsic motivation linked this effect more to the person's perception of the original extrinsic reward. To further explain this potential positive or negative effect of extrinsic rewards Deci (1985) developed his cognitive evaluation theory.

> What happens when there are no further badges or trophies to obtain? How might a coach try to ensure levels of motivation are maintained?
>
> ACTIVITY 3

Intrinsic motivation can be affected by extrinsic rewards in two ways. The performer may perceive the reward as an attempt to **control** or manipulate their behaviour (the fun aspect becomes work). The performer may also perceive the reward as providing information about their level of performance. A reward could be perceived by a performer as increasing the individual importance of a particular achievement. In receiving the reward that certain level of achievement is perceived as high. If they do achieve and gain the reward (positive information) then this sign of high ability can help intrinsic motivation. If, however, they fail to achieve the reward (negative information) then they may perceive this as being a sign of incompetence or low ability, thus lowering future intrinsic motivation.

If a person perceives extrinsic rewards as controlling their behaviour or providing information that they are competent then intrinsic motivation will be reduced. To increase intrinsic motivation the reward should provide information and positive feedback with regard to the performer's level of competence in performance.

Teachers and coaches should therefore try to involve the performer in decision making and planning with regard to their training programmes and performance goals. By becoming involved the performer will feel a shared responsibility for any success or achievement thus increasing their intrinsic motivation because they feel in control and competent. The now obvious link between competitive success and increased intrinsic motivation was shown by Weinberg (1978).

As success and failure in competitive situations provide high levels of information with regard to a person's level of competence or incompetence it is important that a teacher or coach ensures that intrinsic motivation is not lost by a person who experiences defeat. This is done by emphasising performance or task goals and concentrating on more subjective outcomes, eg, an action performed well. For instance: although you lost the tennis match it was to a better player; your number of successful serves increased and your tactical use of certain ground strokes also improved. By focusing on the subjective evaluation of success or performance outcomes (winning is not everything) teachers, coaches and parents can improve the performer's positive perceptions of themselves (self image, self confidence) and thus dramatically increase intrinsic motivation.

In conclusion then, intrinsic motivation is highly satisfying because it gives the performer a sense of personal control over the situation in which they are performing. Being intrinsically motivated will ensure that an individual will train and practice enthusiastically thus hopefully developing their acquisition of skill (learning) and overall performance.

Extrinsic rewards, however, do not inherently undermine intrinsic motivation. It is essential that physical education teachers and coaches use them in addition to other strategies effectively. They must increase a learner's/performer's perceptions of success in order to develop intrinsic motivation within the overall educational and performance environment.

Successful strategies for the use of rewards to help develop intrinsic motivation should include:

1. Manipulation of the environment to provide for successful experience.
2. Ensuring that rewards are contingent on performance.
3. Emphasising praise (verbal – non verbal).
4. Providing variety in learning and practice situations.
5. Allowing learners to participate in decision making.
6. Setting realistic performance goals based on the learner's ability and present skill levels.

**ACTIVITY 4**

Look at the list of reward strategies in table 25.1. How many more can you think of? Now think of a sport or physical activity that you have taken part in or are still taking part in. Make a list of all the reasons or factors that influenced you to take part in that activity. Consider the following questions:

- why did you start?
- why did you stop?
- why are you still taking part?
- are the reasons and motives that prompt you to continue taking part the same as the reasons and motives that originally prompted you to start?
- was your motivation more to do with intrinsic or extrinsic factors?
- did situational factors have an influence on your level of motivation?

Compare and discuss your findings with the rest of the group.

# Arousal

Any discussion of motivation is closely linked to theories of arousal. In the everyday use of the terms it is not always easy to distinguish between motivation and arousal. They are also closely related to the notion of stress and anxiety (see chapter on optimising performance). In our earlier consideration of Sage's definition of motivation it was stated that motivation was affected by both intrinsic and extrinsic factors that served to energise and direct behaviour. Arousal is linked therefore to the 'energised' state that drives a person to learn or perform and is therefore associated with the intensity dimension of motivation. Evidence suggests, however, that arousal is not just an internal state. Arousal is therefore a topic which not only influences elite performance, but it can have considerable effect on a learner at the early stages of development. It is therefore a topic which is relevant to most aspects of sports psychology.

Fig 25.7. Arousal is a physiological state of alertness and anticipation which prepares the body for action

# Definition of arousal

Arousal can be defined as being a *general mixture of both the physiological and psychological levels of activity that a performer experiences; these levels vary on a continuum from deep sleep to intense excitement.*

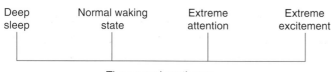

The arousal continuum

Highly energised states can be caused by an individual or team competing in an important competition. Arousal is not to be seen as good or bad, positive or negative, as it appears to represent the level of energy or effort that a learner/performer develops and applies to any sporting or learning situation. A sports performer can be highly aroused as a result of both winning and losing a competition or even looking forward to a competition (apprehension or excitement).

Placing the body under any form of physical (physiological) or mental (psychological) stress produces levels of arousal which can affect both information processing and final performance. If activities require a great deal of decision making

to be done quickly and accurately then the effects of arousal are even more marked. Traditionally arousal has been linked to and measured by its physiological effects.

# Arousal theories

Arousal theories suggest that our bodies need to be in a state of homeostasis (physiological and psychological balance). If the body is deprived or affected (put under stress – perceived or actual) in any way physiologically or mentally then arousal levels in the body are increased and we are motivated to behave in such a way as to reduce these levels back to the optimum level of arousal. Typical physiological reactions that are associated with increased arousal levels can be measured by heart rate, blood pressure, electronical activity, electromyograph, galvanic skin responses and biomechanical indicators such as adrenaline and epinephrine.

If an athlete is preparing for a big race (highly active) they need to be in a highly alert state (arousal). The body needs to ensure that it can meet all the physiological demands that may be placed on it. Muscles need to be supplied with blood sugars and oxygen, etc. The sympathetic system of the **autonomous nervous system** (ANS), ie, the glands hormonal and endocrine systems also help to maintain and prepare the body for action. The **parasympathetic system** of the ANS, on the other hand, will work to restore the body's resources for future use.

## Reticular activating system

The **reticular activating system** (RAS), which is part of the ascending structure of the spinal cord's link to the fore brain, is responsible for maintaining the general level of arousal or alertness within the body. It plays a part in our selective attention processes and serves either to inhibit or excite incoming sensory information to help our attention processes (see chapter 24 for a discussion of Eysenck's work on personality and arousal levels linked to the effect of the RAS). The psychologists' interest in arousal has tended to focus on the links between the physiological aroused state and the experience of associated emotions. Just as periods of high intense exercise (eg, playing football or netball) are associated with all the symptoms of a highly aroused state, eg, high levels of adrenaline, increased HR, breathing rates, etc, aroused states can be equally associated with the emotional states of fear, anger, apprehension, tension, worry and anxiety. Some evidence suggests that these emotional states are reciprocal with one affecting the other and vice versa. They are closely linked to the physiological state (see chapter 27). Within this chapter we are mainly interested in the psychological effects of arousal.

The various emotional states mentioned above are easily developed and often experienced particularly when exploring the unfamiliar (meeting something new or being asked to do something important or perform at a new high level of competition) and in the learning or acquiring of motor skills as well as the ultimate performance. Research has shown that levels of arousal can affect levels of perception, attention and movement control, all of which are obviously important in the learning and performance of motor skills.

As a learner's/performer's levels of arousal are important it must be equally important that they have the **appropriate** levels of arousal in order to promote effective concentration, attention and decision-making levels to produce optimum performance. Teachers and coaches have been aware for a long time of the need for performers to be mentally prepared and alert; this is commonly referred to as a sports performer being 'psyched up' (readiness to respond). The intensity of arousal levels is often a crucial factor in both competitive sport and learning situations. If arousal gets too high a learner/performer can become anxious and equally if it is too low then they may become bored and demotivated, both states resulting in a negative effect on learning and performance.

## Drive theory

Early research carried out by Hull in 1943 and later modified by J Spence and K Spence in 1966

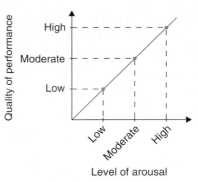

Fig 25.8. Original drive theories' view of the arousal/performance relationship

suggests that the relationship between arousal and performance is a linear one. All performance was originally thought to improve directly in proportion to increases in arousal (see fig 25.8).

In other words, the more a sports performer was aroused the better they would perform. Further research by Spence and Spence adapted this view slightly. This relationship has been expressed in the equation

**P = H × D**
Performance = habit strength × drive

Hull saw drive as being synonymous with arousal. Habit strength was seen as the learned response or performance behaviour; essentially, it is a theory related to learning – Hull saw the likelihood of learned behaviour (dominant response) occurring as being greater as drive (arousal) levels increased. This theory has very close links with Zajonc's theory of social facilitation (chapter 26). However, learned habitual behaviour may not always be the correct behaviour. The theory goes on to suggest that if the performer is a beginner trying to carry out newly acquired skills then increased drive (arousal) for whatever reason may cause the performer to rely on previously learned skills, thus the dominant response may be an incorrect response, so as arousal increases performance for the beginner will tend to deteriorate. A good example would be a beginner learning to serve in tennis. They have just been taught correctly how to serve, practised several times, appear to understand and carry out a reasonable serve. However, in a following competitive match their first serve hits the net and because of the increased pressure (drive/arousal) to get the second serve in they subconsciously revert back to their previously error-ridden learned serve, a little tap over the net in order to get the ball in play. Thus in the early stages of learning the effects of increased arousal on skill acquisition could lead to the dominant response being an incorrect one. In the latter stages of learning (autonomous) increased drive (arousal) levels would have a positive effect, as the dominant response would be the well learnt (habitual) and generally correct one. This is often called a 'grooved skill'. The many criticisms of this theory as a result of further research, together with observations of 'real life' situations in which even top class performers with highly developed habitual skill levels have been seen to fail in high arousal situations, has meant that this approach has generally lost credibility.

## The inverted 'U' hypothesis

This explanation of the relationship between arousal and performance originated as a result of work carried out as early as 1908 when the Yerkes and Dodson Law first suggested that complex tasks are performed better when one's level of drive (arousal) is low, while simple tasks are performed better when drive/arousal is high. It recognises that there are different degrees of arousal, over or under arousal, and that different people can be affected in different ways depending on the type of tasks they are faced with. Most sports performers and coaches can relate to the principles of the inverted 'U' hypothesis as most of them have experienced performances when both under and over arousal have inhibited their performance. They have also experienced times when their preparation has been exactly right, decisions have been made correctly and effectively and an excellent performance has resulted. This view contends that the relationship between arousal and performance is curvilinear, hence the inverted 'U' shape of the graph (see fig 25.9). Performance is said to improve up to a certain point of arousal; if arousal continues to increase beyond the optimal state then the performance will begin to decline.

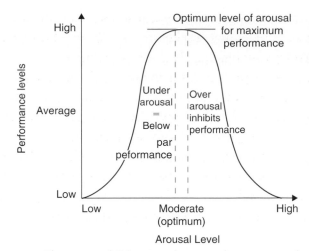

**Fig 25.9.** The inverted 'U' principle states that increased arousal improves performance only to a certain point after which further increased levels of arousal will have an adverse effect

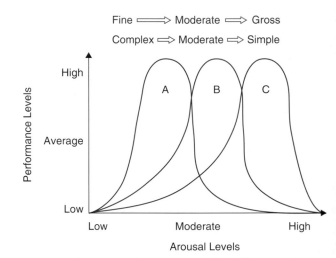

**Fig 25.10.** The inverted 'U' principle for different tasks: optimum arousal is higher for more simple tasks with more gross-motor control

It has been argued, however, that as a general principle, optimum levels of arousal are not the same for all activities or for all performers. The idea that optimum levels of arousal are variable according to the type and complexity of the task in relation to the individual performer has meant that the basic principles can be generalised and used by teachers and coaches to explain and predict behaviour in a whole host of situations. Teachers and coaches began to realise that the usual all-rousing pre-event pep talk was not necessarily the answer for all performers.

It has been found that motor skills generally need an above average level of arousal. If the skills or activity involve mainly gross movements and relatively simple skills using strength, endurance and speed, requiring little decision making, then higher levels of arousal will be found more effective. Activities involving very fine, accurate muscle actions or complex tasks requiring higher levels of perception, decision making, concentration and attention will be carried out more effectively if the point of optimum arousal is slightly lower.

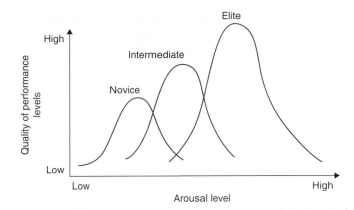

**Fig 25.11.** The relationship between arousal and the level of expertise or phase of learning

It is therefore very important that a teacher or coach assesses the appropriate levels of arousal for each task in order to ensure that the optimum level is achieved. Even within teams the different requirements of each particular role or position may require different levels of arousal at various times, eg, batting and bowling in cricket, where loss of concentration and coordination could be disastrous, require different levels of arousal to those of a general fielder. Adjusting arousal levels to suit both task and situation could involve the coach in trying to increase or decrease a performer's arousal levels. Levels of excitement and anxiety caused by high arousal may need to be controlled by various stress management techniques (see chapter on optimising performance). As you can appreciate, many sports or tasks involve combinations of both fine and gross skills along with varying levels of information processing linked to complexity. Even within the context of a game different players will need different levels of arousal and at different times. Past experience, amount of practice and stage of learning will also have an effect on the choice of appropriate level of arousal.

Beginners need different levels of arousal to those of a professional sportsperson. In addition the level of complexity is relative to the stage of learning and/or experience. What for an experienced performer is a relatively easy task may be very difficult and involve a great deal of information processing for a beginner. Even at moderate levels of arousal

Fig 25.12. Archery requires fine muscular control and high levels of concentration and as such optimum levels of arousal would be lower than those of, for example, a power lifter

Fig 25.13. Even within the context of a game/competition different players will need different levels of arousal and at different times

task (cue-utilisation). They focus their attention (perceptual narrowing). However, a performer's ability to focus their attention is severely hampered if arousal levels continue to increase. Perceptual narrowing continues which may cause a performer to miss important cues and signals (ineffective cue-utilisation) which could have a detrimental effect on performance.

This effect is even more noticeable if the cues and signals are not what was expected. Extreme levels of arousal can cause such acute levels of perceptual narrowing that a person is not able to concentrate or make decisions effectively, and can even hinder the smooth control of physical movements. This state of 'hyper vigilance' is commonly known as 'blind panic'. Perceptual narrowing is therefore an important aspect of both learning and performance where, in a state of high arousal, reactions to expected stimuli can be enhanced and reactions to inappropriate or unexpected cues and signals can be inhibited.

> **ACTIVITY 7**
>
> In discussion with your group try to recount a specific situation in which you have experienced 'panic' and been unable to concentrate on making the correct decisions. What sort of things 'triggered' these feelings? How did perceptual narrowing affect your cue-utilisation?

a beginner may 'go to pieces' and be unable to cope with what is required of them; an even lower level of arousal may be more appropriate.

The inability of a performer, particularly a beginner, to process the relevant information effectively has been linked to what has been called **perceptual narrowing** and **cue-utilisation theory**. These concepts help us to understand that as arousal levels increase a performer tries to pay more attention to those stimuli, cues and signals that are more likely and relevant in order to help them carry out the

It would be more appropriate, therefore, when dealing with inexperienced performers or beginners in a learning situation to ensure that levels of arousal are initially very low. Audiences, evaluation and competitive situations are best avoided.

Teachers and coaches need to get to know the learner/performer and be aware of the effects that the situation can have on them, ie, interactional perspective.

## Catastrophe theory

Several modifications to the inverted 'U' hypothesis have been put forward. One of the more interesting is that suggested by Hardy and Frazey (1987). The catastrophe theory is similar to the inverted 'U' hypothesis in that both argue that if arousal increases it will have a positive effect on performance up to a certain optimal level. Hardy and Frazey suggest, however, that any further increase in arousal will not result in a gradual fall-off in performance as seen in the symmetrical shape of the inverted 'U' graph; this shape can be altered by a slight reduction in arousal. Slight reductions of arousal return the performer to the previous optimum level and effective performance, eg, in a game of squash/tennis a player becomes argumentative and angry over a call causing his/her game to deteriorate, but calming words from the coach restore a balanced performance. Hardy and Frazey then argue that in highly competitive and important matches, where both high physiological arousal combines with high cognitive anxiety, if a squash player for example becomes upset enough (over aroused) for it to have a detrimental effect on his/her game, the deterioration is much more extreme and cannot be arrested merely by calming the player down a little. 'Going over the top' in this situation will have a dramatic effect on the ability to concentrate, make decisions and play shots effectively. In other words a catastrophe. Recovery from this catastrophe can be very difficult; extreme 'mental toughness' will be required if they are to work their way gradually back to optimum arousal and peak performance.

Figs 25.15 and 25.16 illustrates the different shape and effect (catastrophe predictions) of arousal on performance:

- at point A cognitive anxiety (worrying) and physiological arousal (somatic) are high – reaching this threshold creates a catastrophic effect

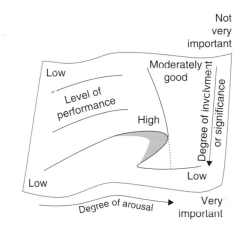

Fig 25.15. A three-dimensional 'catastrophe model' of arousal and performance in sport

Fig 25.14. The idea of catastrophe theory may explain why sometimes even extremely talented and highly motivated performers may not be able to get back to peak performance levels once they have become over aroused

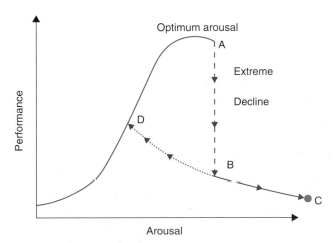

Fig 25.16. Catastrophe theory

*Source*: adapted from 'A catastrophe for sport psychology', by L. Hardy and J. Frazey, in Bass Monograph No. 1 (p 21), (British Association of Sports Science N.C.F., Leeds, 1988).

- at point B the performer either continues with their extreme over arousal causing performance to decline further to C or

- they get to grips with their problem, taking serious steps to calm down and refocus – performance will gradually improve to point D when arousal levels can return to the optimum levels: performance may once again reach the maximum effective level.

# Achievement motivation

Achievement motivation is related to the often-asked questions:

- why is it that some learners/performers achieve and some don't?

- why is it that certain performers are driven to be more competitive than others?

*'The need to achieve is a relatively stable disposition to strive for success.'*

(A.A.H.P.H.E.R.D. 1981)

The term achievement motivation was first put forward by Murray (1938) who, in describing 20 different human motives or needs, identified a human being's need for achievement as being linked to the personality of the performer. Competition is described as an 'achievement situation' whereby performance is compared to a relative or absolute standard. Achievement can, however, take place in non-competitive situations. Whether it is in competition or not, the fact that certain types of people are prepared (more motivated) to place themselves regularly in situations where their achievement is being compared or evaluated in some way generally labels them as being more competitive or 'achievement orientated' than others.

Gill (1986) gives the following definition:

*'A person who has high levels of achievement motivation would have a tendency to strive for success, persist in the face of failure and experience pride in accomplishments.'*

(D. Gill)

The level of a person's need to achieve (drive for success) is seen as a relatively stable disposition. A person who has a high need to achieve has a tendency to display a positive approach in relation to their achievement orientation as well as a positive success tendency. They will strive to achieve a high level of performance (mastery accomplishment). Thus having high levels of achievement motivation can make all the difference to how successful a performer is in both learning and high level performance situations.

Most of the research associated with achievement motivation in sport has revolved around the early classical theories put forward by Atkinson (1964 and 1974) and McCelland (1961). Although current research has tended to move on in terms of its interpretations of the cognitive processes affecting achievement motivation, the performance and preference predictions it enables us to make with regard to high and low achievers are still generally accepted. In trying to explain how a person's need to achieve (n. Ach) developed, thus enabling predictions of their future behaviour to be made, Atkinson took an interactionist stance, proposing that both **personality** factors and **situational** factors have to be considered. He recognised that knowledge of a performer's personality traits alone was not enough to give a clear indication of a person's future behaviour.

# Atkinson's personality components of achievement motivation

Atkinson suggested that all a performer's behaviour is greatly affected (eg, achievement motivation, competitiveness) by their ability to balance two underlying motives that we all possess within ourselves:

- **the need to achieve success (n. Ach)** – a person is motivated to achieve success for the feelings of pride and satisfaction they will experience

- **the need to avoid failure (n. Af)** – a person is motivated to avoid failure in order not to experience the feelings of shame or humiliation that will result if failure occurs.

You can probably appreciate from your own experience that sporting situations provide us with regular opportunities to experience success or failure. All sports performers are motivated by a combination of both, a need to be successful and the good positive feelings that are associated with winning, together with a wish to avoid the feelings of shame, embarrassment and possible humiliation associated with losing.

Atkinson's research suggested that high achievers in sport tended to have high levels of n. Ach and low levels of n. Af whereas low achievers in sport tended to have low n. Ach levels and high n. Af levels. Low achievers do not fear failure but they fear the negative evaluation associated with failure.

## The situational component of achievement motivation

Atkinson supports his predictions of behaviour and performance by cross referencing a performer's personality factors with situational factors. He claims that a performer will assess the situation they are faced with and evaluate:

- the probability of success along with
- the incentive value of that success.

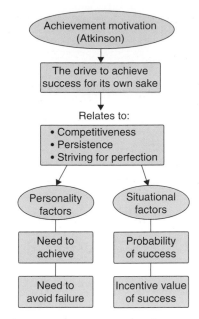

Fig 25.17. Atkinson's component of achievement motivation

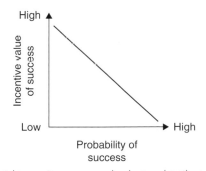

Fig 25.18. Atkinson's suggested relationship between the probability of success and the incentive value

The probability of success will obviously depend on whom you are competing against and/or the difficulty of the task. Thus if you are an average club golfer playing against a top professional, the probability of success is not very high. Your chances would be higher against a complete novice. The incentive value, however, of playing against a top professional and the satisfaction gained if you beat him, would be far greater. The satisfaction gained from you beating the novice would not be as high, as you would have expected to win (high probability).

Thus Atkinson's view of what factors contribute to levels of achievement motivation in people can be expressed by the following equation:

$$\begin{array}{c}
\text{Tendency of a person's achievement motivation or competitiveness} = (\mathbf{Ms} - \mathbf{Maf}) \times (\mathbf{Ps} \times [\mathbf{I} - \mathbf{Ps}])
\end{array}$$

Tendency of a person's achievement motivation or competitiveness $= (\mathbf{Ms} - \mathbf{Maf}) \times (\mathbf{Ps} \times [\mathbf{I} - \mathbf{Ps}])$

where:
- $\mathbf{Ms}$ = motive to succeed
- $\mathbf{Maf}$ = motive to avoid failure
- $\mathbf{Ps}$ = probability of success
- incentive value of success

# Current research and thinking on achievement motivation

Although Atkinson's work has been used as a platform, more up-to-date research in this area of motivation has tended to take a wider perspective. Achievement motivation is considered not merely as a single construct but from a more multi-dimensional perspective. Research has focused on a number of important areas:

- the performer's perception of achievement goals
- the performer's perceptions of 'success' in relation to the goals set
- the performer's perceptions of failure in relation to the goals set
- the performer's perceptions of their own abilities
- the performer's perceptions of the task or situation in relation to their own abilities
- the social and environmental factors.

In addition to the above, sport psychologists have also argued that achievement motivation should not be seen as a 'global' concept. A more sport specific form of achievement motivation has been termed **competitiveness** (Gill 1986).

## Achievement goal theory

It has been argued by Maehr and Nicholls (1980) and Dweck that levels of achievement motivation, and more specifically, competitiveness, will vary between performers according to both the reasons they are taking part in the activity (achievement goals) and the different meanings that success or failure has for the performer. Achievement goal

theories suggest that a performer's different 'achievement goals' can be either:

- outcome orientated or
- task orientated.

## Outcome goal orientation

A performer who is motivated by winning and beating the opposition because they enjoy the feelings they get from competing and comparing themselves with others is said to be 'outcome orientated', also known as competitive goal orientation. When this type of performer wins they are said to have high perceived ability. Their 'ego' is boosted as they see their success as a result of their own ability and develop high expectations of future success. When they lose, however, the opposite occurs. They see failure or lack of success as a result of their own limited ability (perceived low competence). This perceived low ability serves to increase their feelings of shame and humiliation as their 'ego' is deflated. It will probably have a negative effect on future expectations of success and thus achievement motivation. These feelings will be heightened if they have been unsuccessful in what they perceive as relatively easy tasks. They will tend to avoid challenging situations; reduce effort and possibly select activities or tasks that are either easy or ridiculously difficult.

## Task goal orientation

Performers who are task orientated also want to win but are not so interested in demonstrating their own ability in comparison to others. They are motivated by developing their own technical standards or personal performance levels in relation to their own previous levels of success. This more intrinsic type of motivation where performers are trying to master the inherent demands of the task are said to be more effective in the long run hence it is also sometimes referred to as mastery goal orientation. Because task orientated performers judge their success against their own standards they generally have high levels of perceived competence. They do not fear failure. It is not an affront to their own perceived ability nor is it internalised as a permanent personal characteristic. They see it as part of the challenge to improve. A performer will persist, effort will be increased or strategies changed in order to accomplish new goals or targets; very often this leads to improvements in their personal performance. This alternative task orientated view means that a performer focusing more on effort and personal standards will generally be protected from the feelings of frustration and disappointment associated with losing and be able to maintain motivation for longer. In reality most performers are motivated by both outcome and task mastery of performance goals. It is important, however, to know whether a performer is more task or outcome orientated. Teachers and coaches should try to stress task or mastery goals rather than outcome goals (see intrinsic motivation).

## Stages of achievement motivation and competitiveness

Achievement motivation is thought to develop through three sequential stages (Veroff, 1969) beginning in early childhood and continuing into adulthood. Being aware of these stages will help you understand why certain types of people are always competitive, develop rivalries and try to win everything in order to boost their own egos.

Sporting situations provide a great deal of opportunity for learners/performers to evaluate their own performance and compare ability and effort in relation to how difficult a task is.

## Veroff's three sequential stages of achievement motivation

A child must achieve success in each stage before they move on to the next stage. Many people may never reach the final stage in the sequence.

1. **Autonomous competence stage** – very early stage in a child's development, usually the first three to four years of life. Children focus on mastering skills in the environment and testing themselves. Autonomous evaluation builds up perceptions of personal competence.

2. **Social comparison stage** – at approximately the age of five years, children begin to compare themselves with others, focusing on competition. They want to be seen as being better than others within their peer groups. Some people are continually making normative comparisons (focusing on winning), whereas others focus on the informative value of comparisons (evaluating their own mastery of skills).

3. **Integrated stage** – there is no particular age level for entering this most desirable stage of achievement motivation. This involves a person in both autonomous competence and social comparison stages. A person who has reached this stage is able to mix and move from one stage to the other depending on the appropriateness of the situation.

**Fig 25.19.** It is important that children are taught when it is appropriate or inappropriate to compete and compare themselves socially and deal with the emotions of both

It is important that children are taught when it is appropriate or inappropriate to compete and compare themselves socially.

# Developing achievement motivation and competitiveness

It is not easy in today's society to downplay or easily avoid outcome goals. It is important therefore that teachers and coaches are careful in the way they emphasise certain kinds of behaviour and goals. They can greatly influence a performer's perceptions of success or failure, and thus future motivation, by attributing certain causes or reasons for success or failure.

While an integrated achievement orientation is said to be the ideal, several factors are thought to influence achievement motivation orientation:

- childhood experiences
- social environment (social learning)
- cultural differences
- significant others
- emphasis (direct or indirect) on task or outcome goals
- expectations
- attributions – those conveyed by the teacher or coach and those expressed by the performer.

Table 25.2. Comparison of n.Ach. and n.Af. performer characteristics

| Characteristics of a performer motivated to achieve | Characteristics of a person motivated to avoid failure |
|---|---|
| • Looks for challenges<br>  • seeks extremely hard task | • Avoids challenging tasks<br>  • seeks easy option |
| • Standards are important | • Dislikes 50:50 situations |
| • Persists for longer | • Gives up easily |
| • Values feedback | • Does not like feedback |
| • Enjoys evaluation situations | • Dislikes evaluation situations (possible shame)<br>• Performs worse in evaluation situations |
| • Not afraid of failure<br>• Takes responsibility for own actions<br>• Attributes performance to internal factors/controllable factors, eg,<br>    Success = Effort<br>    Failure = Lack of concentration | • Avoids personal responsibility<br>• Attributes failure to external factors, eg, luck, factors out of their control |
| • Optimistic | • Pessimistic |
| • Confident (high self-efficacy) | • Low in confidence |
| • Looks to complete the task quickly and effectively | • Takes a long time over task |
| • Task goal orientated | • Outcome goal orientated |

# Attribution theory
## Definition of attribution

Attribution theory has developed as a way of explaining how individuals and teams evaluate their levels of success and failure in performance situations. In addition it seeks to show how the reasons given by an individual or team for their success or failure may affect future achievement motivation in similar situations.

Achievement situations are assessed by both individuals and teams and reasons are given for how well they have performed. Inferences and assumptions are often made about other people's levels of behaviour which can directly affect a performer's attitude to and behaviour towards them (see stereotyping).

Attributions are seen as being what an individual or team interprets or perceives as being the causes of theirs or others' particular behaviour, particular outcomes or events. The reasons/causes or attributions that an individual or team gives for their success or failure can affect:

- immediate emotional reactions
- actual behaviour.

In addition it can have serious effects on a performer's aspirations, expectations, achievement/ motivation and future participation.

1. Imagine a winning team and a losing team. Discuss what reasons the different performers may give to explain their success or defeat.
2. Will they be the same reasons?
3. How do you think the reasons they give will affect future efforts and possible participation?
4. Attributions that we give for other people's behaviour can also affect our future attitudes towards them. What reasons do you think the coaches of the different performers might give for success or failure?
5. Do you think these might have any effect on their future relationships with the performers?

Now think of the last time you personally were successful in a physical activity and compare it to a time when you have been unsuccessful.

1. What reasons did *you* give for both performances?
2. Can you suggest reasons why you may have attributed the reasons you did?
3. Was it possibly to make you feel better about winning or losing?

In your discussions you will probably have come to realise that the different 'attributions' a person gives to explain success or failure are important. In referring back to our earlier discussion of what motivation is, attributions can affect the *intensity* and *direction* of our behaviour. If a performer taking part in a new activity, eg, basketball, is not getting on very well the reasons they perceive as being the cause for their apparent lack of success can have quite serious consequences for their future behaviour on court.

## Weiner's model of attribution

Since Fritz Heider first carried out his classic study on attributions in 1958 there have been several theories and models of attribution put forward. Although Weiner's model is not sport specific, it serves as a useful starting point in helping us understand the attribution process and its effects. In his research Weiner suggested that all the many thousands of reasons and explanations we might give for what has caused our success or failure can be grouped into certain common categories. These categories could then be related, compared and initially placed across two dimensions. After further research he later added a third dimension.

The four categories of **causal attributions** given by people for their level of success or failure were:

- ability
- effort

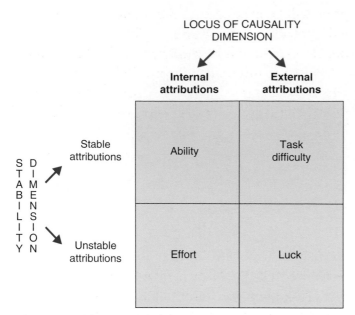

Fig 25.20a. Weiner's model

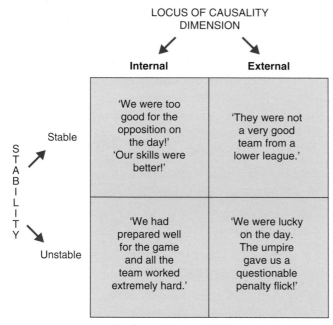

Fig 25.20b. Example of Weiner's model — attributions included: reasons why we won the hockey game!

- task difficulty
- luck.

In fig 25.20 you can see how Weiner placed these on his model.

The stability dimension is referring to whether the reasons/causes were relatively permanent (stable) or

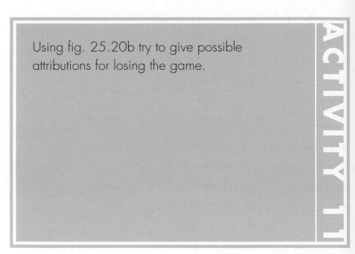

ACTIVITY 11

Using fig. 25.20b try to give possible attributions for losing the game.

ACTIVITY 12

Using Weiner's two dimensional model of attribution, place the following attributions for success or failure into the model, taking care to consider the various categories.

- 'I'm not very good at badminton'
- 'our swimming team is the best in the region'
- 'our team is not really good enough to win the cup'
- 'the referee was biased'
- 'the coach made us play to an unusual pattern'
- 'I couldn't be bothered to try'
- 'the opposition employed better strategies and tactics than us'
- 'they were better organised'
- 'the goalkeeper dropping the ball enabled Shearer to score'
- 'everybody tried their best'
- 'the rain caused the match to be abandoned and saved us'

changeable (unstable) in relation to time. **Ability** and **task** difficulty are seen as being stable factors in relation to time. **Effort** and **luck** are factors that can change from time to time. The stability dimension is related to our expectancies of future outcomes, for instance if you attribute success to your ability then as this is a relatively stable factor (at the time of the activity) you will probably expect to gain success at similar activities or tasks in the future. For example, if we have lost to this team in the past six games it affects expectations about the future: we will probably lose this match too. If we have stable attributions we hold the same expectations. The opposite effect will occur if you attribute failure to the stable factor of ability.

The locus of causality dimension is mainly linked to whether the attributions are internal (within performers) or external factors to the performer, eg, environmental. Ability and effort are therefore internal or personal to the performer. Task difficulty and luck are seen as being external to the performer.

Following criticisms of his work and further additional research (1985) Weiner reformulated his model, adding a further causal dimension, that of locus of control. This helped to explain the effective consequences of attributions that appear to be in or out of a person's control. The **locus of control** dimension has been shown to relate to the intensity of a performer's personal feelings of pride and satisfaction, shame and guilt. If a performer relates their success to internal causes and factors within their control, eg, ability (I was better) and effort (I tried hard) rather than external and uncontrollable factors, eg, I was lucky, and the task

was simple, then feelings of self satisfaction and pride will be maximised. As a result motivation will probably continue and possibly increase. The opposite effect will generally occur if failure is also attributed to internal and controllable factors. The emotional effect will be one of increased shame and dissatisfaction leading to possible decreased levels of motivation.

# The application of attribution theory in sport
## Self-serving bias

When making attributions performers very often have biases in common, tending to take credit for success and disassociating themselves from failures, blaming external factors. The traditional saying 'a bad workman always blames his tools' reflects this view. Researchers have tried to look at the correlation between the type of attributions given by successful performers and those given by poor performers (ie, winners and losers). The traditional Weinerian view was that winners attribute success to internal factors and losers to external factors in order to reduce feelings of shame and protect their egos. It has been shown that successful performers

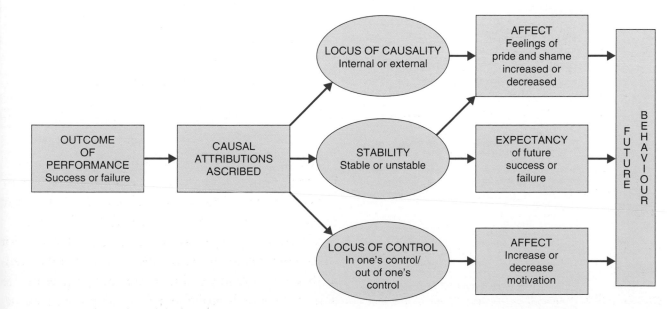

ig 25.21. An adapted model of attribution

do tend to attribute their success to internal factors (ability/effort) (**a self-serving bias**) to make them feel better about themselves, their group or team (self esteem is protected or enhanced). More up-to-date research, however, has suggested that contrary to original research and popular belief (see your answers to activities nine and ten) unsuccessful performers (losers), particularly individuals, do not try to protect their self esteem by *always* attributing failure to external factors (task difficulty or luck) in order to reduce feelings of shame. The performer's *perception* of the causes in relation to perceived success/failure are seen as being more important.

This has obvious links back to achievement motivation with regard to outcome goals and task goals. Weiner's original view was that high and low achievers differed in the types of attributions given and that these would affect future behaviour. High achievers were seen as attributing success to internal factors, eg, personal dispositions and high ability, thus they were experiencing more pride. Failure, however, was attributed by high achievers to unstable factors, eg, effort. They would therefore be more motivated to seek out and expect to do well in achievement situations.

Alternatively, low achievers tend to attribute success to external factors, eg, easy task, luck, generally uncontrollable factors. Failure is attributed to stable factors, eg, 'I am too small' or 'I am not good enough' ie, lack of ability. They therefore find achievement situations less satisfying and will be generally less motivated to continue the activity.

A performer's attributions will of course be affected by whether they view success or failure in terms of winning or losing (outcome goals) or whether they view it in terms of individual 'task' or 'mastery goals'. If a performer who has lost a tennis match judges their performance against previously set personal performance targets (mastery goals), eg, they achieved more first serves and their consistency of ground strokes improved, then their feelings of pride/shame will be different to those of the performer who judges themselves on outcome goals alone (I lost).

## Learned helplessness

It was Carol Dweck who first categorised performers as 'helpless' or 'mastery orientated'. Helpless performers attribute failure to themselves and see

| | High achiever | Low achiever |
|---|---|---|
| Motivational orientation | • High motivation to achieve success<br>• Low motivation to achieve failure<br>• Focuses on the pride of success | • Low motivation to achieve success<br>• High motivation to achieve failure<br>• Focuses on shame and worry that may result from failure |
| Attributions | • Ascribes success to stable factors and internal factors in one's control<br>• Ascribes failure to unstable factors and external factors out of one's control | • Ascribes success to unstable factors and external factors out of one's control<br>• Ascribes failure to stable factors and internal factors in one's control |
| Goals adopted | • Usually adopts task goals | • Usually adopts outcome goals |
| Task choice | • Seeks out challenges and able competitors/tasks | • Avoids challenges; seeks out very difficult or very easy tasks/competitors |
| Performance | • Performs well in evaluative conditions | • Performs poorly in evaluative conditions |

**Fig 25.22.** Summary of behaviour associated with achievement motivation

the task (stable factor) as insurmountable. 'Learned helplessness' **is an acquired state or condition related to the performer's perceptions that they do not have any control over the situational demands being placed on them and that failure is therefore inevitable (ie, they are 'doomed to failure').** After experiencing initial failure as a result of their perceived lack of ability (internal factor) in relation to the very hard task (stable external factor) they inevitably give up trying.

## Characteristics of self helplessness

- it can be **specific** to one activity or **general** to all sports
- performer is outcome orientated
- it usually results from previous bad experiences
- attributions to uncontrollable stable factors
- perceptions of low ability (feels incompetent)
- rarely tries new skills
- experiencing initial failure in new skills supports perceptions of limited ability

Fig 25.23. A performer learns by their repeated inability to change that failure is inevitable. Eventually they become passive and lose the motivation to act

- feelings of embarrassment
- future effort is limited (why bother? I'm no good).

Interestingly it has been noted that often both teacher or coach and performer attribute success or failure to different reasons. Research has shown that when attributing reasons for our own behaviour we tend to relate it to external factors and when attributing reasons for others' behaviour we tend to relate it to internal factors, such as lack of effort or poor ability. These differences in the application of attributions between an observer and performer are known as fundamental attribution errors. It is important that teachers and coaches are aware that attribution conflict can happen.

The teacher or coach has a very important role to play in preventing the formation of, or changing, inappropriate attributions in order to develop achievement motivation. It is important that when giving feedback to performers the teacher or coach does not negatively influence the performer's interpretation of success or failure by emphasising their lack of ability in relation to the task. If the teacher or coach implies that whatever the performer does they will never achieve the task then this could lead to the performer experiencing even greater levels of 'learned helplessness'.

A performer's lack of success should be attributed to problems with lack of consistency in technique, limited understanding, bad tactical decisions, lack of experience or insufficient effort. By attributing failure to things that are within their control, ie, things they can do something about, motivation can be maintained through the development and setting of realistic mastery goals in relation to the task. The performer will not become frustrated, behave badly or aggressively and become demotivated.

Getting performers to realise that failure is not inevitable and teaching them how to make appropriate attributions with regard to their performance, especially when they are possibly already experiencing 'learned self helplessness' is called 'attribution retraining' and is an important responsibility of the teacher or coach. In her research Dweck reported that 'attribution retraining' was even more effective than initial performance success in ensuring that performers deal more effectively with failure.

## Strategies for attribution retraining

- individual attention

- emphasise task goals

- monitor performer's attributions

- ensure teacher or coach's attributions do not make negative inferences.

One interesting factor to emerge from Dweck's work (and also emphasised by Gill) is that in heavily influencing the appropriateness of attributions for success or failure in children teachers and coaches have to be careful not to subconsciously infer gender inequalities;

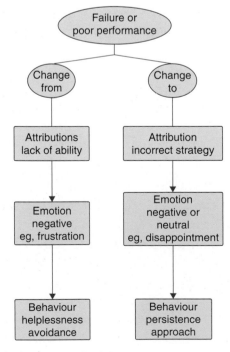

Fig 25.24. Attribution retraining process

via their expectations of success teachers can considerably influence young children's perceptions of their ability to achieve in and deal with situations.

It is also important that teachers and coaches are relatively honest in their approach to performers. There is no point in being unrealistic in the attributions given for success or failure. Young children in particular are relatively astute in perceiving their own levels of competence in relation to what is being asked of them. They need to know that they have the necessary skills to achieve the task even if their initial failure is attributed to a lack of effort. They must be confident in their own ability. If failure is as a result of a performer's limited ability then it is important that the teacher or coach redefines the goals/targets in relation to personal achievement, fitness, etc, rather than set goals which rely on comparisons (performance goals).

## Self efficacy

It was Albert Bandura (1977) who put forward the concept of self efficacy claiming the concept to be one of the more important explanations of success or failure. In his research he considered how a performer's self confidence can affect their motivation and ultimate performance. It has formed the theoretical basis adopted for most performance orientated research in self confidence and sport. Bandura stated that while self confidence can be viewed as a global disposition it is not always general but often specific to certain situations. Self efficacy is seen as the belief in one's ability in relation to a specific task in a specific situation. In its simplest form *self efficacy=situation specific confidence.*

Picture the team captain who is very confident during the match, coping with every demand. Yet the same person is lacking confidence and feels intimidated when asked to speak to TV reporters after the game or speak at the after-match dinner.

Generally in this context 'self efficacy' relates to the number of similar activities in which the performer feels efficacious.

Imagine again a young swimmer. She may have high levels of self efficacy when swimming in the shallow end of the pool, when she knows she can touch the bottom if needed. She may not experience high levels of self efficacy when she first performs in the deep end. It is therefore important that when we try to assess a person's levels of self efficacy we are aware that, although a performer may feel confident in some aspects of a skill, they may not feel confident in others due to the variations in perceived demand and perceived ability. A gymnast may feel confident at floor work but experience low levels of self efficacy when faced with the vault.

Bandura suggests that a performer makes judgements with regard to their capabilities to perform a specific task or deal with a certain situation. A performer's perceptions of the situation related to their expected level of self efficacy will affect their:

- choice of activity (direct)
- degree of effort (energise)
- level of persistence (sustain).

In other words, expectations of efficacy explain motivation. A performer therefore experiences high or low levels of self efficacy in a variety of situations. Although Bandura's earlier research provided a clear conceptual model of self efficacy, claiming it to be the critical variable, later research has shown that high self efficacy alone is not enough. A performer must also want to succeed and have the capability (ie, necessary skill levels/techniques) to succeed. In addition the other cognitive processes underpinning causal attributions will also affect the performer. To account for this additional research Bandura (1997) redefined the term self efficacy, employing the term **self-regulatory efficacy**.

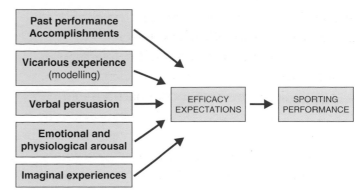

Fig 25.25. Adapted model showing information that affects self efficacy

According to Bandura the expected levels of self efficacy experienced by our example swimmer would have been developed from mainly four but potentially six sources of information. These are shown in fig 25.25. These sources are not mutually exclusive in terms of the information they provide, however some are more influential than others.

## Past performance accomplishments

Previous successful experience or mastery of specific or similar skills involved in the particular task faced is seen as the major and most reliable predictor of self efficacy. If you have practised hockey penalty flicks or basketball free throws regularly and have taken them at critical points

Fig 25.26. It has been suggested that teams exhibit group or collective self efficacy. They have a group belief that they can win and perform well in the face of adversity

in previous matches then you will feel confident of scoring if a similar situation arises again. The effect would be enhanced further if your previous success was attributed to controllable factors. Practising a specific skill successfully has more effect than being told you will be able to do it by the teacher or coach. This has obvious repercussions for teaching and coaching methodologies where building up a skill and gaining early success, eg, lowering the net in netball or making games simpler, eg, short tennis, have a much greater effect on a beginner's future specific confidence and thus effort and participation levels than just telling them they can do it in the main sport. Obviously previous failure could result in low levels of expected self efficacy.

## Vicarious experience

Sometimes referred to as modelling (refer to observational learning – Bandura), vicarious experiences although less effective than previous success has been found to be a reliable source of self efficacy. When a performer observes a successful demonstration, particularly by someone of similar ability, they are more likely to feel confident that they too can accomplish the same task. They are less anxious and are encouraged to 'have a go' themselves.

## Verbal persuasion

Teachers and coaches often try to persuade performers that they are capable of carrying out certain tasks. I have spent a considerable amount of time in gymnastics lessons encouraging students to attempt a certain vault, explaining that it will be perfectly safe, etc, in order to try to boost their confidence. In the majority of situations this type of social persuasion (see social learning theory) can work, although its effectiveness very much depends on who is doing the persuading (see attitudes).

Occasionally teachers or coaches may distort results or levels of truth (KR) in order to persuade performers that they are better than they are. They must be careful not to undermine their credibility. The learner/performer must have trust in them (significant other) and value their opinion.

## Emotional and physiological arousal

Very often performers perceive their 'natural' physiological arousal effects as being something negative. 'Why am I sweating?' 'Why is my heart beating faster?' 'Why am I breathing quickly?' Rather than interpreting these naturally occurring effects as signs of being ready and prepared physiologically for the activity performers often view these as being signs of physiological stress. They think they are not prepared. Bandura saw this as having a negative effect on their self efficacy. They feel ill-equipped to carry out the activity. Although further studies have questioned this effect certain research has suggested that very positive psychological preparation via goal setting, and various relaxation/stress management techniques, can help to change a performer's perceptions of arousal effects, ie, viewing them as signs that they are ready to compete, and help develop positive self efficacy. In addition to physiological cues, emotional moods can be influential in developing self efficacy. Positive emotional states, eg, happiness, exhilaration, and tranquillity, etc, can help a performer feel energised and therefore experience heightened self efficacy, whereas negative feelings of anxiety, depression and sadness can have the opposite effect (Maddox and Meier 1995).

## Imagined experiences

Research by Moritz et al. (1996) has supported the view that if performers imagine themselves or others carrying out skills or a match successfully then this can help to boost their self belief and ultimately generate positive notions of self efficacy. Imagining non-mastery of the said skills can obviously have the opposite effect.

ACTIVITY 13

Think of an activity/game that you or your group/team have taken part in and consider all the things that caused you initially to lack confidence. It may be that you still do. Make a list of all the causes of your lack of confidence. Now, for a different activity, make a list of why you felt very confident when taking part. Then, in relation to Bandura's model, try to suggest as many methods as possible by which your low self efficacy could have been increased.

ACTIVITY 14

Consider the statement below in relation to elite sports performers such as the various national teams in the 2003 Rugby World Cup.
'Teams exhibit group or collective self efficacy. They have a group belief that they can win and perform well in the face of adversity.'

# Summary

## Motivation

- Motivation is seen as energised, goal-directed purposeful behaviour.
- Motivation is closely linked to inner drives and arousal.
- Motivation can affect the direction and intensity of behaviour.
- Motivation can be intrinsic or extrinsic.
- Extrinsic motivation is behaviour motivated by external rewards, tangible and intangible, or punishment.
- Intrinsic motivation develops as a result of internal drives to achieve feelings of personal satisfaction and fulfilment (the flow experience).
- Rewards should be monitored carefully and linked to giving information regarding a performer's level of competence.
- Cognitive evaluation theory (Deci 1975) proposed that it is the performer's interpretation of the reward, not the reward itself, which can affect intrinsic motivation.
- Performers and coaches should have a shared responsibility in the planning and setting of achievable targets.
- Current thinking supports the interactionist view.

## Arousal

- Arousal is a physiological state of alertness and anticipation which prepares the body for action.
- The reticular activating system (RAS) is responsible for maintaining the general level of arousal within the body.
- The concept of arousal is very closely linked to motivation.

- Drive theory states that there is a linear relationship between arousal and performance (the more the better!).

- Inverted 'U' hypothesis suggests that the relationship is curvilinear. Increased arousal improves performance up to a certain point. Increases in arousal beyond this optimum level will have a detrimental effect on performance.

- Levels of optimum arousal will be different according to the complexity and nature of the specific task in relation to the individual's characteristics and the specific situation.

- Over arousal can create perceptual narrowing.

- Catastrophe theory suggests that in highly competitive situations the deterioration in performance caused by over arousal is much more extreme than the inverted 'U' theory maintains.

## Achievement motivation

- Achievement motivation is a predisposition to strive for success, to persist and to experience pride in one's success.

- Two types of motives which are likely to exist in evaluative situations have been identified: need to achieve (n. Ach); need to avoid failure (n. Af).

- Whether a person is a high achiever or low achiever has been found to affect task selection, effort and persistence.

- Competitiveness is sport specific achievement motivation.

- Goal setting is seen as an important tool in developing achievement motivation.

- The adoption of task orientated goals (mastery goals) which emphasise comparisons with one's own performance rather than outcome or ego orientated goals has been found to be more effective in developing achievement motivation.

## Attributions

- The reasons performers give to explain success or failure (causal attributions) have been found to be very influential on their expectations of future success or failure, level of emotional reactions (feelings of pride or shame) and thus future achievement motivation (high or low).

- Weiner's attribution model originally identified two dimensions: locus of causality (internal or external factors); stability (stable or unstable). A third dimension of locus of control was added later. This related to whether attributions given were under the performer's control or not.

- High and low achievers have been found to differ in the attributions they give (self-serving bias).

## Learned helplessness

- A performer who continually focuses on outcome goals and attributes failure to perceived low ability (internal stable factor), or success to external unstable factors (luck), all of which are out of their control, is likely to experience learned helplessness.

- Attribution retraining, if used effectively, can help performers reduce feelings of being inevitably 'doomed to failure'.

## Self efficacy

- Self efficacy theory has provided a model for social psychologists to study the effects of self confidence on behaviour.
- Self confidence in specific situations (self efficacy) has been closely linked to motivation and can affect choice, effort and persistence.
- Self efficacy is seen as an important factor only when a performer has the necessary skills, abilities and motivation to attempt a task.
- Performance success is seen as the most important factor in developing a performer's expectations of self efficacy.

# Revision Questions

1. What is meant by the term motivation?
2. How is arousal linked to motivation?
3. Outline the differences between drive theory and the inverted 'U' hypothesis in relation to arousal and performance.
4. What does a curvilinear shaped graph infer?
5. How does catastrophe theory differ from inverted 'U' theory?
6. In what ways can arousal levels affect learning and performance?
7. Explain the factors that can affect the level of 'optimum' arousal.
8. Explain the different types of extrinsic and intrinsic motivation and give examples.
9. Why is intrinsic motivation thought to be more effective than extrinsic?
10. What factors should a teacher or coach be aware of when using extrinsic rewards?
11. Identify three disadvantages of extrinsic motivation.
12. If a performer is intrinsically motivated will the introduction of extrinsic reward enhance motivation? Discuss whether you agree or disagree.
13. Explain three ways to develop intrinsic motivation.
14. What is meant by an interactionist view of motivation?
15. Give a definition of achievement motivation.
16. Explain the differences between a performer who has a high need to achieve and one who has a low need to achieve.
17. What did Atkinson mean by his formula:

    n. Ach
    motivation = (Ms = Maf) $\times$ (Ps 3 [I − Ps])?

18. What is the difference between achievement motivation and competitiveness?

19. How does achievement motivation affect sports behaviour?

20. What is meant by mastery/task goals and outcome goals?

21. What are the effects of emphasising one or the other on achievement motivation?

22. What are the three suggested stages of achievement motivation? Why are they important?

23. What is meant by the term causal attributions?

24. Why do sport psychologists think that attribution theory is important?

25. Explain the three dimensions identified in Weiner's model of attributions.

26. Using an example from sport explain how attributions can affect a performer's future behaviour.

27. What type of attributions might a high achiever give for their success or failure? Give examples.

28. What is meant by learned helplessness? And why is it important?

29. How can teachers or coaches try to alleviate the problem of learned helplessness?

30. How does self efficacy affect a performer's behaviour? Give specific sporting examples.

31. According to Bandura, what are the sources of self efficacy? Explain their effectiveness using examples.

# 26. Social Influences and Performance

In the previous chapters relating to the psychology of sport we have been mainly concerned with the relationship between the individual performer and various psychological variables resulting in the creation of certain types of behaviour or 'performance'. We have concluded that a performer's behaviour in relation to certain situations is as a result of many variables.

In accepting this interactionist viewpoint you should have become aware that a performer's behaviour is rarely as a result of individual factors, but usually as a result of many interrelated factors.

Every teacher or coach knows that they are not dealing with 'cocooned individuals': most sporting situations involve some form of social interaction. They have to be aware not only of the previous influences (sporting and non-sporting) of groups and teams on performance, but also that present performance is being either directly or indirectly linked to or influenced by the behaviour of others (reciprocal interaction).

This does not mean to say that we ignore all the individual factors discussed earlier in the book; rather the whole situation becomes more complicated. All the variable factors are impinging on the individual and each individual is affecting the others (Referback to social learning/socialisation in chapter 20).

Psychologists have carried out a great deal of research into the many different ways in which sports performers interact with one another and how other people's behaviour, or the social situation in which the performance is taking place, can influence performance.

Within this chapter we will explore these direct or indirect effects and you will become aware of what is meant by the following terms and how they can influence sporting performance:

- social facilitation
- group dynamics/cohesion
- leadership.

Here is a list of the terms to be covered in this chapter. It is important that you understand them.

- Social facilitation
- Coactors
- Evaluation apprehension
- Group dynamics
- The six Is
- Group structure
- Ringlemann effect

- Social loafing
- Cohesion
- The 'Great man' theory
- Nature/nurture
- Emergent leader
- Prescribed leader
- Task orientated

- Person/relationship oriented
- Situation favourableness
- Democratic
- Autocratic
- Contingency

## Social facilitation

As already stated in the introduction to this chapter, sporting performance is rarely carried out in total isolation. Usually our presence has an effect on another's sporting performance and the presence of others is seen as having an influence on our own behaviour and performance. Very often we are entirely unaware of these effects – thus the behaviour of a person either taking part in a physical education learning environment or performing at the very highest level is said to be influenced socially either directly or indirectly. The study of this effect is the study of **social facilitation**. In a sporting context the presence of others is usually thought of as the 'audience'; however, in social psychology 'presence of others' takes several different forms. The 'audience' can be primary spectators: those present at the event; or secondary spectators: those watching at home on TV or possibly reading about the event in the media. The audience can be also passive or supportive.

In addition to those watching, 'others present' can be fellow competitors, both opposition and team mates, teacher or coach. They could also be other people performing the same task or skill but not in direct competition, called **coactors**. When you practice at a golf driving range, for instance, although you are not in direct competition you are made aware of the presence and calibre of other players by your observation of the direction and length of their shots. This may influence your own efforts as though you were in competition. It has even been suggested that a performer actually training alone may have thoughts that will be enough to influence behaviour at the present time, eg, spur them on to greater effort as they imagine someone, somewhere, checking training schedules or observing the results of training made evident in a future performance. In other words, they are performing for a hidden audience.

Although the great majority of research in this area relates to work carried out by Zajonc, the earliest recorded research was by Norman Triplett in 1898. He established that the motor performance of cyclists differed according to whether they rode alone, in pairs or groups. To further his understanding of the effect of competition on performance he supported his earlier findings by conducting laboratory testing of children performing a fishing reel winding experiment. Triplett originally interpreted his findings in relation to the competitive element involved. The children were seen as unconsciously competing with one another showing a competitive 'instinct' or 'drive' which served to increase performance speed.

However, later research, eg, Allport (1924), Dashiells (1930) suggested that it was actually the 'mere presence' of others working alongside a person performing (coaction) that was the important factor, not necessarily the competition. Allport suggested that 'coaction' may increase quantity at the expense of quality. Inconsistencies within this early research were evident with both positive and negative effects being found.

## KEY WORDS

**Coaction** is the presence of other people currently performing the same task but not directly in competition.

**Audience** means the other people present but not competing or doing what the performer is doing.

## Zajonc and social facilitation

In his later work (1965), Zajonc tried to clear up the inconsistency found in earlier research. Patterns of behaviour and certain relationships were recognised.

Zajonc proposed that whether social facilitation occurred, and the level to which it occurred, depended very much on the nature of the activity or task being carried out. His theory was based around the notion of drive theory. He contended that the presence of an audience in any shape or form raised a performer's level of arousal. This level of arousal would increase a performer's drive. From your understanding of 'drive theory' you will remember that increased drive increased the probability of the dominant response occurring. Thus the presence of others can serve to enhance the performance of well-learned or simple tasks (eg, sit up), but have

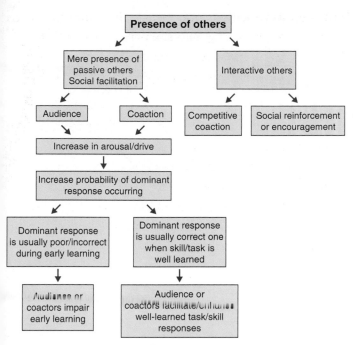

Fig 26.1. Zajonc's view of the relationship between drive theory and social facilitation

a negative effect on poorly-learned skills, or reduce the accuracy when complex skills are involved.

A high drive state caused by the presence of an audience is likely to increase the number of mistakes made, particularly by the inexperienced or beginners, thus increasing anxiety and further increasing arousal. This will have a 'snowball' effect further increasing the chances that irrelevant or incorrect motor performance will be carried out.

## Cottrells' evaluation apprehension theory

In linking social facilitation to arousal Zajonc's research presented a systematic attempt to identify the psychological processes underlying the effects of others on performance.

There are, however, several other views on the origins and effects of social facilitation. Cottrell (1968) argued that it wasn't just the mere presence of others that created higher arousal; there were different types of presence and each could have different effects on arousal (increasing or decreasing). Cottrell went on to suggest that it was more to do with a person's perceptions that they

were being 'evaluated' or assessed in some way by the 'others' present that created the higher arousal.

Thus the effects of social facilitation are enhanced by a performer's feelings of **evaluation apprehension**. The more expert an audience was perceived to be, the more the performance was potentially impaired.

## Home/away (advantage or disadvantage)

Other psychologists have questioned Zajonc's model which views the audience in a passive role, arguing that there is no such thing as a passive audience (Gahagan, 1975). Research has looked at the effect of 'home' and 'away' venues and supporters on performance. While we may intuitively imagine home advantage as a bonus it has in fact been shown to have possible negative effects with players feeling increasingly under pressure due to the greater expectations of the home crowd. The effect has also been shown to vary in relation to different sports.

## Home or away (supporting research)

- Most of the research has focused on home advantage.
- For major sports, teams tend to win more home matches than away.
- Home advantage was mainly due to audience support.
- The proximity of crowds to the playing area and resulting noise increase has been seen as a factor.
- Home advantage was more noticeable in the early rounds of competitions.
- Olympic hosts tend to win more medals than in games before or after.
- Home teams tend to play in a more attacking style within the rules (functionally aggressive behaviour).
- Away teams tend to contravene rules more and commit more fouls (dysfunctional aggressive behaviour).

- The more important the game the greater the negative effect on the home team.

- Supportive spectators can create expectations of success.

- Potential increases in home players' self-consciousness.

- Higher personal expectations cause home players to think too much rather than just playing automatically, causing 'championship choke'.

- Coaches are now much more aware of these problems and try not to create too much pressure.

In relating the effects of social facilitation to cognitive factors, Baron (1986, **Distraction conflict theory**) suggested that audience effects occur because the performer is distracted from the task. This distraction creates tension and conflict within their mind which increases arousal, leading to a greater number of errors.

In his '**self presentation theory**' Bond (1982) has suggested that a performer's main aim when performing in the presence of others is to present and maintain a favourable image to the audience. With easy tasks this is not a problem, but as tasks get progressively difficult they have two problems to face. One is the complexity of the task and the other their awareness that errors made are being seen by the audience. They then become embarrassed, increasingly self conscious and possibly over anxious as a defence against social ridicule; thus concentration and attention to the task is again divided and in general even more errors occur. This effect has also been linked to the 'home and away' phenomenon mentioned earlier. Although in physical education and sport we tend to draw intuitive conclusions regarding social facilitation, several researchers have in fact advised that the effects of social facilitation are so small that this possibly negates the drive effect of arousal. The inverted 'U' hypothesis has also resulted in many studies related to the causes and effects of arousal.

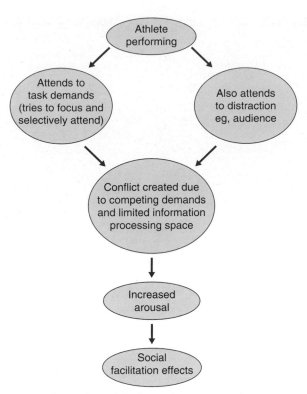

Fig 26.2. Adapted model of Baron's (1986) distraction-conflict theory

*Note*: The effect is even greater on more complex skills where increased levels of attention are required

Due to the inconclusive and equivocal nature of past and current research the main conclusions that can be drawn are that well-learned skills are generally affected in a positive way by the presence of an audience. However, performance can also be inhibited. If we could make more specific predictions then we would be able to explain why even highly experienced and very often 'extrovert' players who are supposed to be able to deal with audience expectations, pressure and evaluation sometimes 'choke' in the final rounds of an important competition.

Note: for further discussion of the effects and management of stress, arousal and anxiety see chapter on Optimising Performance.

# Group dynamics related to sport performance

Within physical education and sport the study of groups comes under the umbrella of 'social

Fig 26.3. Although previous experience of audiences and 'coping strategies' can help reduce the effects, highly skilled performers are occasionally seriously inhibited by an audience

psychology'. Research has generally shown that people tend to behave differently within the context of a group than they do as individuals. As most physical education and sporting situations, including most individual activities, tend to involve the interaction of performers the study of group dynamics is seen as an important topic. Research into small group processes in sport has generally revolved around the idea of 'teams' and how teachers and coaches can encourage them to work together to produce effective performance. It has also been related to such specific areas as group cohesion, leadership, structure, size, motivation, conformity and so on.

# What is a group?

What do we mean by the term group?

At first glance it may appear relatively simple: several people who come together? A meeting of more than one person? However, does that include people waiting at a bus stop? Or all the people actually swimming at the local pool?

The main feature that helps to define a group is that the members of the group must be **interacting** in some way over a period of time.

This interrelationship within 'the group' will involve mutual interdependence, communication and conformity to the same shared goals, norms and values. The members of the 'group' need to perceive the group's existence, be aware of its effect and that they are all members. They will, therefore, have a group identity which differentiates them from other groups.

> *'Groups are those social aggregates that involve mutual awareness and potential interaction.'*
>
> (J.E. MacGrath, 1984)

> *A group is '… two or more people who are interacting with one another in such a manner that each person influences and is influenced by each other person.'*
>
> (M.E. Shaw, 1976)

## The six Is

Groups are seen as continually changing and developing units of people; hence the term **group dynamics**, but however they are changing dynamically groups will exhibit and can be identified by the six Is. *When you think of groups think of the six Is.*

Groups have:

- Interaction (communication over a period of time)
- Interdependence (person and task to achieve common goals)
- Interpersonal relationships (mutual attraction)
- Identical goals/norms/values
- Identity (perception of groups' existence)
- Independence.

## How groups become teams

A group of individuals is not necessarily a team although all teams by definition are groups. In essence a *team* is any group of people who have in-depth interaction with each other in order to achieve shared objectives.

Although we have stated that groups in sporting terms would generally develop and exhibit the six

Is, this process is not a short one. A coach bringing together several individuals would have to work extremely hard over a considerable period of time to develop the six Is in order to maximise performance. Throughout this evolutionary process teams are constantly developing. A team therefore would normally be considered a very *strong* group.

Psychologists have produced several models of group formation. One of the better-known linear models is that developed by Tuckman. In order for groups of individuals to become a 'real team' Tuckman (1965) suggested that although the time scale may differ from situation to situation they all go through four key progressive stages of development: **forming**, **storming**, **norming** and **performing**.

## Stage 1 – Forming

The individuals come together and try to find out about each other (familiarisation). They try to get to know and understand what theirs and others' roles are within the group (assess strengths and weaknesses – social comparisons). Do they belong? Can they identify with or accept the expected and perceived roles, more formal structures and relationships within the group?

## Stage 2 – Storming

In this stage individual members or cliques within the group may begin openly to question certain formal group power structures and very often also challenge the status of the leader. Open hostility and stress may result as the members compete for power. The coach/teacher/leader has to work hard to reduce the effects of this situation by communicating with the group openly and objectively.

## Stage 3 – Norming

The group instability begins to disappear. The members begin to work together, displaying group cohesion. The members recognise the need for common goals and gain personal satisfaction from achieving tasks collectively and effectively; mutual respect for each member's contribution increases.

## Stage 4 – Performing

The members of the group now primarily identify with the team. They all have and are aware of their and others' roles within the team structure. All feel that they contribute individually and collectively to the productivity and success of the team. Each individual is said to experience psychological security within the context of the team. Energies are channelled to achieve group success.

> Imagine you are a coach of a newly formed team. What strategies might you employ to try to reduce the effects encountered in the storming stage? Discuss with the rest of the group. (You may find it useful to return to this activity after you have read the section on leadership.)
>
> **ACTIVITY 1**

# Structures and roles within groups and teams

All aspects of group structure are important to the effectiveness of the group or team. The structure will develop as a result of group interaction. During the 'forming stage' the group's structure will begin to develop; because of their perceptions of their own and others' expectations the individuals within the group will begin to adopt certain roles, both formally and informally. A role is the specific behaviour expected of a person occupying a certain position in the group's structure.

1. **Formal roles** – teacher; coach; team captain.
2. **Formal task or performance roles** – striker in football/hockey; goalkeeper football/netball/hockey, etc; penalty taker (hockey/football); goal kicker (rugby); goal shooter (netball).
3. **Informal roles** – team diplomat/social roles; team comedian/joker; team 'hardman' or 'stopper'.

Roles within a team or group structure:

- only have meaning within the context of the group/team
- can be expected, perceived and acted out
- are assessed or evaluated against expected behaviour (normative)
- have a certain level of status attached to them
- can lead to 'role conflict' (a person having more than one role).

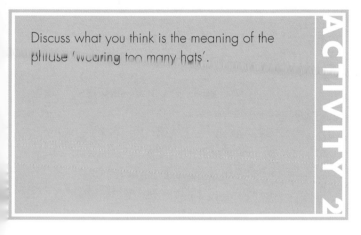

Discuss what you think is the meaning of the phrase 'wearing too many hats'.

**ACTIVITY 2**

Fig 26.4. In order to minimise the status differences coaches must ensure that substitutes are perceived by both players and themselves as an important and integral part of the team structure

It is important that players within a team or members of a group are aware of their role (**role clarity**) and are prepared to accept it and function in that role (**role acceptability**).

The effectiveness of the team can be seriously affected if a player is unaware of, doesn't understand or is unwilling to fulfil the role expected of them by the rest of the team. This area has obvious links to intrinsic motivation and the setting of clear and specific goals by the teacher, coach or leader (see goal setting and leadership).

In addition to accepting and taking on certain specific roles within the group/team, members will also adopt certain general and specific patterns of behaviour or beliefs. These are known as the **group norms**. All groups/teams will develop established norms of behaviour and performance, eg, degrees of effort in training, codes of dress, ways of celebrating or certain aggressive styles of play. Performers and coaches will have different ways of ensuring that team members conform to these norms. These could

involve either formal sanctions, eg, fines for being late, substitutions or suspensions, or informal sanctions, eg, the social pressure of being made fun of, etc. It is very important, therefore, that the teacher or coach establishes clear expectations of behaviour (norms) in order to ensure the highest standards of performance possible within a positive and supportive climate. It is, however, the team members' perceptions of these norms and roles which will be the main influence on whether a positive team climate is established.

Having looked at how groups are formed discuss in your groups the types of problems, both positive and negative, that managers or coaches may encounter by bringing into their teams big 'named stars' from different teams.

**ACTIVITY 3**

Adherence to specific group roles and norms in relation to the task can have a possible negative effect by inhibiting individual flair and development. Groups can also begin to be over comfortable with the situation and limit their effort.

## Establishing effective group performance

In modern day performance-orientated sport it is essential that the teacher or coach can develop the highest standards of performance possible. The process of bringing together talented individuals

We often hear generalised statements from coaches and the media, such as:

- 'They are a team of individuals!'
- 'They were all playing for themselves.'
- 'They were the most talented team on paper.'
- 'The best individuals don't always make the best team and win leagues.'

Look at the above quotes and discuss what you think they mean. What are the implications for the potential success levels of the teams involved?

ACTIVITY 4

Fig 26.5. The 'Los Galácticos' Real Madrid team had many of the best players in the world but won nothing in 2004 and 2005. It isn't necessarily the talent of a team that makes it great but how that talent is blended

who interact effectively to produce successful teams is central to the role of a teacher or coach.

Although most sports coaches would support the notion that bringing together the most talented players or performers would increase their chances of team success, they are also aware that this does not guarantee success. Following your discussions in the activities above, you will appreciate some of the pitfalls involved. In trying to account for this problem theoretically, Ivan Steiner (1972) suggested the following theory and model of group productivity.

## Steiner's model of group productivity

As a result of his research Steiner suggested that a successful team is often more than the sum of its parts (individual talents). Equally so an unsuccessful team is often less than the sum of its parts. The team's actual productivity (best level of performance) is equal to its potential productivity minus process losses due to poor team coordination, use of resources (talent) or limited motivation.

**Actual productivity = potential productivity – losses due to faulty group processes**

**Potential productivity = quantity and quality of the group's resources relevant to the task**

Resources relevant to the task include:

- an individual player's motor, physical and perceptual abilities
- an individual player's skills level
- group skill levels
- individual/group knowledge/experience
- individual/group physical/psychological resources – size, weight, fitness
- individual/group mental (cognitive) resources.

Socially identified resources relevant to the task include:

- age
- education

- religion
- occupation
- race
- gender
- socialisation.

In assessing a group's potential a coach can either average out or total up the attributes of the individuals concerned. However, the notion that the team possessing 'more' will perform better (while being a 'gut reaction' and one that usually rings true) is not always correct. According to Steiner's model, individual ability and skill level is probably the major influence on potential success thus the team with the best individuals has the greater **potential** for success. This very much depends however, on the type of activity, specific skill and the level of expected play (recreational/fun) or performance. The coach's job is, therefore, to ensure that the talent resource available is used effectively and that potential process losses are minimised. Only when this happens will

**actual productivity = potential productivity**

## Problems with the group process

Very often the underdogs can outshine the top team due to problems with coordination of the relevant resources available (process faults).

Process faults can be of two types, either:

1. **Coordination losses**: team work/strategies break down or are not understood or are ineffective. Coaches of very complex team games, eg, basketball or netball, very often blame a team's inability to maintain their 'shape' as a reason for losing a game.

2. **Motivational losses**: individual or group loss of confidence, perhaps all team members may not be giving 100% effort or individuals are relying on other 'star' players.

**ACTIVITY 5**

Different sports require different resources and levels of interaction. Consider the following sports and answer the questions.

rugby    bowls    synchronised swimming
cricket    athletics    volleyball    tennis (doubles)

(a) What do you think would be the valuable physical and mental resources needed to help develop potential success?

(b) What would be the potential problems (process faults) that a coach may have to deal with?

## Group coordination and cooperation

When working together as a pair (eg, a tennis double) or as a group, research has shown that the most effective teams include not only talented players but players who complement each other. In activities that require complex levels of interaction such as basketball and rugby, **cooperation** between team members is essential in order that intricate tactical manoeuvres can be carried out effectively. It is also essential that team members can rely on each other to do their own job and not interfere with someone else's efforts. Very often in hockey and soccer, skilful forwards will feel isolated and possibly starved of chances because the midfield are not doing their job in getting the ball 'up front' quickly enough. They therefore decide to go back and 'help' to do the job of the midfield players. The midfield players may well now win the ball but are unable to release it forward as there are no forwards in position to give the ball to.

## Group size

The size of the group is also thought to be a problem affecting 'productivity' that has to be addressed in terms of both coordination and motivation. In developing a successful team the teacher or coach needs to harness the talents of many individuals, but how many is always a problem. If we follow Steiner's equation, as much of the supporting research in this area has, we can see that as the traditional sayings go 'more is not always better' and 'too many cooks can spoil the broth'. In other words, there comes a point in a team's development when all the resources for potential success are in place and adding further so-called talented players may actually be unproductive. Duplication of roles and effort is not necessary as it very often leads to confusion and lack of effort. An interesting aspect of research has shown that group size has a direct correlation with group effectiveness. As group size increases there is a decline in individual effort and eventual productivity. This phenomenon was first noted over 100 years ago by a Frenchman called Ringlemann.

## The Ringlemann effect

Research has generally shown that in larger groups each individual does not always give their best effort. In observing a 'tug-of-war' competition during the nineteenth century, Ringlemann noted in various events two, three, and up to eight competitors. As the groups got bigger, the individual effort within the group deteriorated. Instead of the eight-man team pulling eight times as hard as one man, they actually only pulled approximately four times as hard, thus showing a positive decline. Ringlemann showed this decline as follows: One person 100%, two persons 93%, three persons 85%, four persons 77%, five persons 70%, six persons 65%, seven persons 58% and eight persons 49% of potential. In other words he noted that there was an inverse relationship between the number of people performing a task and the amount of effort expended by each of them.

In following up this very early and potentially worrying research Ingham and colleagues (1974) concluded that this effect first noted by Ringlemann and originally attributed to poor coordination (eg, a lack of simultaneous maximal tension) was actually more related to decreased motivation.

## Social loafing

The conclusions of Ingham et al. that differences or losses in actual group productivity (performance) were more likely as a result of reduced motivation has been termed **social loafing**.

Research directed towards explaining social loafing has grown. Latane, Harkins and Williams (1979) proposed that performers demonstrated both **allocation strategies** and **minimising strategies**. This suggests that performers *are* motivated to work hard in groups, but save their best performances for when they are performing alone or under close scrutiny, when it personally benefits them more (allocation strategies). The minimising strategy proposes that performers are motivated to give as much or as little (minimum) effort in order to 'get by' and achieve the task.

Group activities and team games provide plenty of opportunity for performers to 'loaf' and take it easy, as their individual performance is not necessarily being scrutinised or assessed. They may also feel that their performance is not bringing them the recognition it deserves, eg, they feel 'lost' in the crowd or anonymous. Their individual performance/role is not easily identifiable. Performers within a team situation have also been shown to reduce effort as they don't wish to make it easy for less accomplished or less productive individuals to get a 'free ride'. They themselves don't wish to be seen as the 'sucker' doing other people's jobs.

## Strategies for reducing social loafing

1. Identify situations that allow social loafing to occur.

2. Identify individual contributions and not just group outcomes.

3. Ensure that individuals understand the importance of their contribution and role within the team.

4. All players' contributions should be identified and evaluated individually and sometimes publicly (statistics should be kept).

5. Regular feedback on individual's contributions and effort should be given.

6. Although extrinsic rewards/reinforcements can be used to motivate individuals, eg, players of the week, tackle of the week, most assists of the season, intrinsic motivation should mainly be used.

7. Ensure that players know what others' roles and contributions should be.

8. Games can be videoed to carry out observation checklists.

9. Ensure that fitness is at a high level thus ensuring that players don't feel the need to take strategic rests (loaf) at crucial times.

10. Develop variety in practice and training to ensure that players stay interested and maintain levels of attention.

11. Develop a good knowledge of each player to ensure that personal or non-game issues are not having a detrimental effect on the performance.

12. Develop team cohesion.

# Cohesion

When considering why some teams are more or less successful than others it is often stated that the successful team was more **cohesive** and vice versa. Thus the concept of group cohesion has become a widely researched area in group dynamics. There has been much argumentative debate about whether group cohesion helps to create a successful team, or whether the fact that a team is initially successful in turn creates cohesion. Certainly there is considerable evidence to support the belief that there is a positive correlation between success and cohesion. Success, particularly early on, leads to greater feelings of self and group satisfaction and thus higher cohesion; however, the individual's perceptions of cohesion have also been shown to lead to greater satisfaction with group structure and organisation, although the supporting research is less convincing.

Cohesion is now generally defined as 'a *continuously changing* (dynamic) *process which is shown by the*

Fig 26.6. In order to win a team needs all its players working together as a cohesive unit during competitions

*tendency of a group to stay together in order to achieve certain instrumental objectives, targets or goals or for the satisfaction of its members*' (Carron et al., 1998). An earlier general definition by Festinger, Shacter and Back (1950) had defined cohesion as 'the total field of forces which act on members to remain in a group'. Thus individuals are seen as being motivated to stay together as a group by *either*:

1. the attractiveness of the group, ie, the person wants to be involved in the group and values membership; or

2. the benefits they can gain from it (increased recognition).

In this early research the effects of cohesion were also assessed in terms of both interactive and coactive groups. In 'interactive' teams such as basketball, soccer, netball and hockey (where there is a high division of labour and specialised skills are brought together for the good of the whole) perceived cohesion was thought to be important for success. In contrast, team cohesion was seen as less vital for coactive teams such as rowing, swimming and relay, where members rely less on each other and just have to complete their own task successfully.

Later research developed these two basic assessments of cohesion into two further categories, referred to as **task cohesion** and **social cohesion**.

**Task cohesion** relates to how well the team works together to achieve common targets or goals, ie, win the league. The level of a team's 'desire to win' and be the best is directly linked to their level of group effort and teamwork.

**Social cohesion** relates to how much the members of the team like each other and integrate socially (interpersonal attractions among members).

Research in this area has raised many questions along the following lines.

1. In order to be successful do teams need to have both task *and* social cohesion?

2. Is one more effective than the other in developing success?

In order to try to answer these questions Albert Carron (1982) proposed a conceptual model in order to highlight the many pre-existing variables (antecedents) that could influence the development of group cohesion. Carron's framework highlighted four major categories of antecedents (factors) that contribute to group cohesion:

- **situational/environmental elements** (usually consistent), eg, group size; age; contracts; geography; distinctive kit

- **personal elements** (not always consistent), eg, similar/dissimilar; member satisfaction; gender; motivational reasons, ie, task, affiliation, self, attitudes, aspirations, expectations

- **team elements**, eg, desire for success; shared team experiences (winning and losing can both create cohesion)

- **leadership elements**, eg, decision-making style adopted; participative style helps create cohesion, communication, compatability with performers (see leadership).

These four categories of antecedents were seen as affecting both 'task' and 'social' cohesion in relation to either the group or the individual. Thus while the team's objectives may be the same for all, the individual motives for joining and maintaining the group may well be different.

Taking this view, later research by Carron (1988), Widmeyer et al. (1985, 1990) began to look in more detail at this apparent circular relationship between success and cohesion, suggesting that both group members' perceptions of the total group (group integration) and the individual's attractions to the group needed to be looked at in detail. Thus both individual and group attributions could be measured and analysed in relation to whether they were either task or socially orientated.

Questionnaires such as the Group Environment Questionnaire GEQ (Widmeyer, 1985) appear to be the most effective for measuring and evaluating levels of cohesion.

**Sociograms** have also been used to give an even greater insight into how individuals relate to each other within teams.

In order to understand the levels of interpersonal relationships team members are asked to nominate three people who may relate to specific posed questions. Confidentiality is paramount.

For example:

- choose three people who you get on best with
- choose your three best friends
- choose three people who you would be prepared to room with
- choose three people who you like best to train with.

Sociograms can be used to identify

- friendship patterns/choices
- possibility of cliques
- members' perceptions
- social isolates
- level of group attraction.

What this research has shown is that performance success leads to increased cohesion which in turn leads to increased performance and also that there

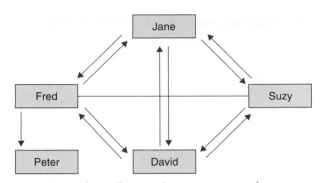

Fig 26.7. Example to illustrate the construction of a sociogram

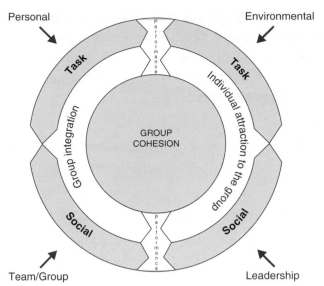

Fig 26.8. An illustration of both the reciprocal and circular relationship between group and individual perceptions on group cohesion and the influencing variables

appears to be a more positive relationship between task cohesion and performance than between social cohesion and performance. Thus, groups performing at the highest professional levels are very often able to put aside their negative personal feelings for one another (poor social cohesion) and work incredibly hard to promote the team effort and performance in order to win (high task cohesion). Questions have been raised, however, as to whether this is because individuals perceive coordination and interdependence on one another as being essential for success and thus work hard to ensure it happens, particularly in interactive team sports rather than coactive sports.

## Strategies for developing team cohesion

Carron and Spinks (1997) suggested that both the leader and the individual team members had a part to play.

1. Distinctiveness: group name, T-shirts, clothing (collective identity).
2. Good coach/team communication.
3. Honest/open discussions.
4. Role clarity (understanding role).
5. Role acceptance (satisfied with and accept role).
6. Team conformity (social and task norms adhered to).
7. Togetherness (team meet regularly or travel together, etc).
8. Sacrifices (if high status players make sacrifices for the team).

9. Goals and objectives (clear, challenging group performance goals).
10. Cooperation (ensure group cooperation rather than individualistic).
11. Avoid formation of social cliques.
12. Avoid too many team changes (rapid turnover).
13. Know and understand individuals within and outside the team.
14. Players to give 100% effort at all times (set good example).
15. Social support amongst team mates (positive reinforcement).

# Leadership

The study of leaders and leadership has always been based on the assumption that the leadership of a group, eg, team captain, teacher or coach, is a crucial element affecting overall group performance. Thus leadership is seen as any behaviour that moves a group closer to attaining its goals.

> Leadership is: *'the behavioural process of influencing individuals and groups towards set goals.'*
>
> (J.L. Barrow, 1977)

This view probably includes all or most people's ideas of what constitutes the role of leadership in all areas of society, not just sport. We all feel that a leader is good at making decisions and has good interpersonal qualities such as a high level of communication skills. They can motivate by giving appropriate feedback and are generally tactful and diplomatic. They are confident, show initiative in being able to organise and direct the group, giving good instructions and advice.

The leader must know what the goals and objectives of the group are (have vision) and be able to organise and structure the situation in order to achieve them. In order to achieve targets a leader should be seen as part of the group. The leader should have all the qualities, skills and beliefs of the group but to a greater degree; they will, therefore, tend to serve as a model for the group in some way. It is important, however, that a leader does not appear too remote or excessively advanced compared to the group, as its other members may feel that they can never achieve the standards being set.

Very often the role of leader becomes entwined with that of manager. Martens (1987) warns that these two roles, while very often being carried out by the same person, are actively different. He views leaders in a sporting situation as having a significant impact on both the sports performers' actual performance and their psychological well-being. A manager, on the other hand, is seen as someone who keeps things running smoothly, being generally concerned with planning, organising, budgeting and staffing, etc.

Fig 26.9. A good leader is able to articulate and exemplify the goals and values of the group, represent the group and give rewards impartially

## Theories related to leadership: nature or nurture?

Three general groups of theories have emerged relating to the effectiveness of a leader: the **trait**, **situational** and **interactionist** perspectives. As in most of the topics we have discussed, the traditional early research into what makes an effective leader was carried out from either a trait or behaviouristic perspective.

Effective leadership was believed to be as a result of specific innate personality characteristics. Thus the theory of the '**great man**' emerged (Carlyle, 1841) which fostered a belief that great leaders, more often than not men, were born not made. These 'great men' were thought to have universal/common traits. Trait theory suggested that certain personality and physical attributes such as height, weight, physical attractiveness, self confidence, intelligence and sensitivity might be associated with leader success. If this view were true, then we would assume that the same leaders would be effective in all situations. Do you think this is true for all sport?

It may be true that the particular traits identified are all useful or necessary, to some degree, for leadership to be effective. Penman, Hastad and Cords (1974) identified a positive correlation between successful coaches and behaviour tending towards an authoritarian style of leadership. However, a person possessing these particular skills or abilities is not necessarily guaranteed to be a good leader. Research has generally proved inconclusive in identifying consistent personality characteristics, ie, leaders are not consistently found to be particular kinds of people who differ in predictable ways from non-leaders.

Disillusioned with the shortcomings of the trait approach psychologists began to adopt a more situational approach to their research. The situational approach recognises that the leaders and group members are involved in a variety of roles according to the demands of the situation. Different kinds of leader may be needed for dangerous and technically demanding situations, particularly if large numbers are involved. Developing out of this view the interactional approach proposed that the effectiveness of leadership is as a result of both situational and individual factors.

While not ignoring the leader's personal characteristics, the interactional approach stresses their appropriateness to the group in a given situation. Thus what the group's goal or task is will be highly influential in the selection of the right type of leader – someone who can fulfil the specific demands of the situation. It also acknowledges that there is more than one way of becoming a leader. Two ways in which leaders develop or are validated have been suggested.

1. **Prescribed leaders** – in a more formal situation the leader is assigned by a higher authority and imposed on a team or a group. The captain of the English cricket team is appointed by the T.C.C.B.

2. **Emergent leaders** – a leader who achieves their status or authority by having the support of the group usually emerges from the group as a result of having the appropriate skills, knowledge or expertise that the group members need or value.

Whether a leader **emerges** from the 'pack' or is **prescribed** from above they will still exert their influence among the team or group by virtue of their personal qualities which we highlighted earlier. Leadership is generally seen as very complex social interaction.

## Fiedler's contingency theory of leadership

Although coming more from the interactional perspective it is still tentatively linked to the original trait theory. Fiedler's contingency model

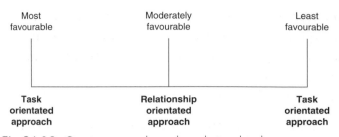

Fig 26.10. Continuum to show the relationship between situation and leadership approach

(1967) tried to analyse and explain the apparent link between a leader's personal qualities or leadership style and the situational requirements of the task, in other words, what do leaders do in order to be effective? He emphasised that the effectiveness of a leadership style is contingent (dependent) on the overall situation and can't just be determined by assessing the leader's traits or behaviour. He identified and used two types of leadership style to highlight his findings, relationship motivated or task motivated.

1. **Task centred leader** – a leader who focuses on setting goals; getting the task done; meeting the objectives; concentrating on performance and productivity.

2. **Relationship centred leader** – a leader who focuses on developing and maintaining good interpersonal relationships, is considerate and permissive.

According to Fiedler, how effective each of these styles of leadership was depended on the 'favourableness' of the situation, ie, certain situations suit certain styles of leadership. The 'favourableness' of the situation depends on three factors.

1. The quality of the leader's relationship with the rest of the team or group (reciprocal trust and confidence).

2. The leader's position of power and authority and resources available for them to use to carry out the task.

3. The structure of the task itself (clear or poorly defined).

Although Fiedler's contingency theory was not directly a sport specific model, the variety of situations in which it was tested included a basketball team. What the theory demonstrated was that in order to be effective teachers and coaches must be able to adapt their style of leadership according to the favourableness of the situation.

For a teacher or coach a highly favourable situation would be one in which:

- the teacher or coach has good/positive/warm relationships with their students or community
- there are clear discipline structures
- the teacher is highly respected and has power and authority
- the parents/community are very supportive
- the institution has excellent all round facilities
- the calibre of the students is high
- the students have good levels of motivation to achieve the task/skills
- the task is clear/unambiguous.

A moderately favourable situation would be one in which:

- the teacher or coach has friendly relationships with students
- the venue is an urban school or club
- limited facilities are available
- good parental support is offered.

The least favourable situation would be one in which:

- there are poor relationships with group or community
- the task is unstructured
- the leader's position is weak
- there is no community support
- there is a poor discipline structure
- there are only poor facilities.

**ACTIVITY 9**

Discuss what type of approach a coach/teacher might emphasise with the following groups?
a) highly professional already task orientated players
b) beginners or low skilled players.
Why do you think this is? Give some practical examples of how this might happen in real life?

As can be seen in fig 26.10 above a task orientated approach adopted by a teacher or coach will be more effective in either highly favourable or least favourable situations, ie, the extremes of the continuum. A relationship orientated style is thought to be more effective in a moderately favourable situation. By adopting or emphasising a certain style of leadership, a teacher or coach does not necessarily exclude any other ways of dealing with the players or group members.

Although this model and findings are intuitively attractive and give us an insight into the idea of different styles of leadership being effective in different situations, what teachers and coaches must keep in mind is that leadership, particularly in a sporting environment, is a highly dynamic process. More recent research has suggested that there are many more variable factors to consider when deciding on which style to adopt, eg, gender, motives, abilities, previous experience, level of learning of both individuals and the group as a whole, as well as the demands of the situation.

## Other contingency models in brief

In considering the maturity of the group Hersey and Blanchard's **Life Cycle theory** (1976/82) also supported the idea that leaders should be able to adapt both task or person orientated qualities to fit the demands of the group in various situations. The demands of the group were seen as changing in relation to their 'life cycle' experiences, ie, with inexperienced groups the leader must be directive and provide emotional support, but when they are experienced the leader must allow the team members more control over decisions made (autonomy).

House's (1971) **Path-Goal theory** again states that a leader's role is to help the group achieve its goals. In order to 'facilitate' this the leader can adopt one of several styles according to the demands of the situation and the needs of the group. These styles are:

- directive
- achievement orientated
- supportive
- participative (whole group included).

For instance, if a group of experienced professionals were being required to carry out boring routine tasks then they would benefit from the coach being supportive (praising, reinforcing), or the coach joining in to show that the skills were not beneath them, ie, participative rather than directive leadership. Vroom and Yetton's **decision making model** (1973) suggests that in order to encourage greater participation and performance output decision making in a group can be adapted between three styles:

- autocratic (teacher/coach makes decisions)
- consultative (considers group's views and coach makes decision)
- delegative (delegates decisions to others).

It was suggested that by analysing the specific demands/goals/targets of the situation a leader would be able to adopt the right style for dealing with and completing the task effectively.

Chelladurai and Haggerty (1978) adopted Vroom and Yetton's model to form their '**normative model**' for decision styles in coaching (fig 26.11).

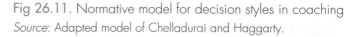

| Autocratic | Consultative | Participative | Delegative |

Fig 26.11. Normative model for decision styles in coaching
*Source*: Adapted model of Chelladurai and Haggarty.

Out of this they developed a decision or leadership-style questionnaire to test the styles of leadership generally adopted by certain groups in specific studies. They suggested that newly formed groups or beginners needed a more task orientated approach in order to initiate them to the requirements of the task. As experience of the task and thus levels of skills developed (development of 'life cycle') a more person orientated approach could be adopted. Finally the group might not need any leader at all. This simplistic view related to sport has to be treated with caution, however, as research has often shown that beginners need more support and may be put off by a demanding task orientated leadership style. Equally so, experienced athletes may need specific technical help and supportive leadership from their coach.

What this type of research highlights, however, is that the maturity (both physical/psychological) and experience levels of the group/team constitute continually changing dimensions of the situation that have to be taken into account when adopting a style of leadership.

# Styles of leadership

We have already identified several leadership styles, two of the more popular being task orientated (focus on task production) and personal relationship orientated (concern for people). Also refer back to the section on teaching styles (Mosston and Ashworth, 1986).

Different styles of leadership were identified as early as 1939 by Lewin et al. In their investigations of adult leadership styles on 10-year-old boys attending after-school clubs Lewin used three basic styles. Different groups of boys experienced different styles of leadership.

## Autocratic leaders

This type of leader adopts a very authoritarian style generally based on strong rule structures. They tend to be very inflexible, make all the decisions and

rarely get involved on a personal level with the group or team members (remote). They are usually very task orientated.

- Leader centred.
- Task orientated associated with performance of specific tasks/elements of play/meeting specific goals.
- Personal authority of leader stressed.
- More likely to be effective in team sports/with greater number of performers.
- Effective when decisions have to be made quickly.
- Better with clear/impersonal goals.
- Better in **most** favourable and **least** favourable situations.

## Democratic leaders

This type of leader only makes decisions after consulting the group. They are usually more informal, relaxed and active within the group than the autocratic leader. In addition, they show a keen interest in the various people within the group. They are prepared to help, explain and give appropriate feedback and encouragement.

- Performer centred.
- Cooperative approach allows performer input into decision making.
- Leader set in the context of whole team effort.
- More likely to be successful in individual sports/individual coaching situations.
- Better in moderately favourable conditions.
- Better when decisions don't have to be made quickly.

## Laissez-faire

This type of leader leaves the group to 'get on' by themselves and generally plays a passive role. They do not interfere, either by directing or coordinating. Being generally unsure of the task they tend not to make or give any positive or negative evaluations.

- Makes no decisions.
- Group determines the work to be done and the pace of it.
- Acts as a consultant.

The results put forward by Lewin et al. were specifically related to patterns of aggression and cooperation. Those boys in the group with the autocratic leader tended to become aggressive with each other, working independently and in competition with each other. They also worked hard when the leader was present and were generally submissive to the leader.

Those boys with the democratic leader were more consistent in their approach to work – although less work was completed it was of a similar quality. They related better to one another. They were generally more interested, cheerful and cooperative, altogether more amenable and continued to work when left alone.

The boys in the *laissez-faire*-led group were also generally aggressive towards each other, being restless and easily discouraged. They also produced very little work.

Lewin et al.'s study indicates that leadership style is a more important factor than personality, ie, that democratic leaders are apparently more effective. Further research and critics (eg, Smith and Peterson, 1988) have argued that the 'effectiveness' of leadership style depends on what the targets or set criteria are. If measured in terms of productivity then the autocratic leader would have been the more effective as that group produced the most work, but only when directly supervised. The implications of this may be that performers used to an autocratic style of leadership/coaching/teaching do not take responsibility for themselves when the leader is not present. In addition an authoritarian leadership style may lead to hostility. Alternatively, if the effectiveness of a leadership style was judged in developing good group mood, cooperative behaviour and steady work then the democratic style was best. The fact that the third group hardly did any work at all indicates, however, that leadership of some sort is important. This is definitely the case in sport where the *laissez-faire* approach is generally not recommended.

## Chelladurai's multi-dimensional model of leadership related to sport

There has been a great deal of research to try to apply the many non-sporting contingency models and theories to the sporting setting. The so-called 'unique' characteristics of sporting teams/groups, however, together with a lack of specific support and application success, suggested that a more sports specific model of leadership was required By bringing together the many positive aspects of different research and contingency models Chelladurai put forward his sport specific multi-dimensional model in 1980. Through this model he argued that the style adopted by a leader in sport, and its relative effectiveness, depended not only on the demands and constraints of the situation together with the characteristics of the leader, but also on the characteristics and demands of the *group*. Thus more detail was added to the effectiveness 'melting pot'.

His model suggests therefore, that in order to achieve

- high performance levels and
- good group team satisfaction

(both Chelladurai's measures of effective leadership), a leader has to be even more dynamic and changeable in relation to the characteristics of the situation, leader and group. Three types of interdependent behaviour will help to produce the required outcomes.

1. **Required behaviour** – the type of behaviour appropriate to or required by the situation or task, eg, teachers are expected to conform to certain norms and express certain accepted values.
2. **Preferred behaviour** – the type of behaviour preferred by the group or performer. Different

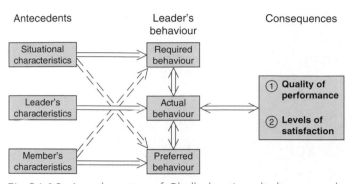

Fig 26.12. An adaptation of Chelladurai's multi-dimensional model (1980)

groups will demand different things from the leader, ie, achievement of performance levels (task orientated) by some or fun and enjoyment for others, eg, professional sports team and an over 60s keep fit class.

3. **Actual leader behaviour** – the behaviour shown by the teacher or coach in a specific situation. This is usually as a result of group preferences and situational demands.

The more that the actual behaviour of the teacher or coach matches that of the behaviour preferred by the group and is demanded by the situation (high congruence) then the greater the probability that the desired outcomes will be achieved, ie, the performance will be of a high quality and the group will experience enhanced levels of satisfaction and enjoyment. Thus leadership will have been effective, but only in that specific situation.

## Leadership scales

Chelladurai highlighted five main but general types (dimensions) of leadership behaviour that could be adopted, developed and indeed measured. He called this a *leadership scale for sports* (LSS) and leaders, coaches and teachers can score either high or low.

1. **Training and instruction** (levels of instructional behaviour)

   High ⟵――――――⟶ Low

   A coach who has a high level of orientation in this area adopts a rather structured approach where the main aim is to improve the level and/or quality of the performance. They will emphasise hard and demanding training and give plenty of instructions with regard to technique. They will also endeavour to control, coordinate and manipulate the activities of team/group members by structuring and coordinating the activities of the members.

2. **Democratic behaviour** (level of decision-making style)

   High ⟵――――――⟶ Low

   A coach adopting a very democratic style (high) will allow the performer to take part in decision making as far as it relates to training, tactics and goal setting. They will also tend to join in with training where appropriate.

3. **Autocratic behaviour** (level of decision-making style)

   High ⟵――――――⟶ Low

   A coach adopting a very autocratic style (high) will try to remain aloof from his team members. They will rely heavily on their personal authority and generally make decisions concerning training, tactics, goals, etc.

4. **Social support behaviour** (level of motivational tendencies)

   High ⟵――――――⟶ Low

   A coach who is genuinely concerned for the all-round social and psychological well-being of a performer or team and not just their sporting performance would be said to be highly socially supportive. They attempt to develop warm and sociable relationships and a positive group atmosphere.

5. **Positive feedback** (level of motivational tendencies)

   High ⟵――――――⟶ Low

   A coach who continually gives praise and encouragement but only in recognition of good performance or behaviour would score high on the positive feedback scale.

The many and various factors (antecedents) which can influence the three dimensions of effective

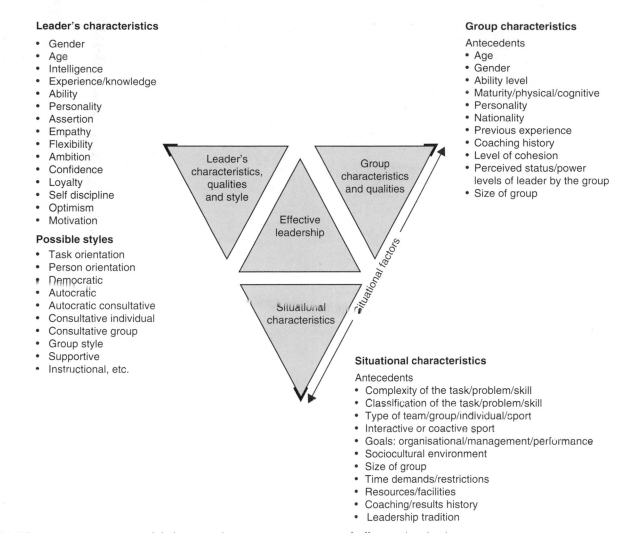

**Leader's characteristics**

- Gender
- Age
- Intelligence
- Experience/knowledge
- Ability
- Personality
- Assertion
- Empathy
- Flexibility
- Ambition
- Confidence
- Loyalty
- Self discipline
- Optimism
- Motivation

**Possible styles**

- Task orientation
- Person orientation
- Democratic
- Autocratic
- Autocratic consultative
- Consultative individual
- Consultative group
- Group style
- Supportive
- Instructional, etc.

**Group characteristics**

Antecedents
- Age
- Gender
- Ability level
- Maturity/physical/cognitive
- Personality
- Nationality
- Previous experience
- Coaching history
- Level of cohesion
- Perceived status/power levels of leader by the group
- Size of group

Leader's characteristics, qualities and style

Group characteristics and qualities

Effective leadership

Situational characteristics

Situational factors

**Situational characteristics**

Antecedents
- Complexity of the task/problem/skill
- Classification of the task/problem/skill
- Type of team/group/individual/sport
- Interactive or coactive sport
- Goals: organisational/management/performance
- Sociocultural environment
- Size of group
- Time demands/restrictions
- Resources/facilities
- Coaching/results history
- Leadership tradition

Fig 26.13. An interactionist model showing the many components of effective leadership

leadership can be seen in fig 26.13, which highlights the main finding of leadership research that there is no ideal or perfect type of style that is guaranteed effective in all situations. A leader must adopt and adapt the style according to the group and the situation. In this complex and demanding situation no one can be ignored in order to ensure the smooth interaction between coach, performer and the situation. All may have their own individual, independent and possibly conflicting needs. This should help to ensure that potential develops into successful performance.

Research into performers' preferred styles of leadership have been rather inconclusive and open to cross interpretations and criticism. The research has however helped to give the sports profession

and sports psychologists in particular certain insights into preferred notional styles.

## Preferred leadership styles

In any situation be it competition/training/practice a coach/leader is continually having to decide what is best for performers and to balance this with their own ideas and preferences.

In general all performers prefer training, instruction and rewards thus the coaching/training environment should emphasise:

- skill development
- positive feedback
- concern for self esteem
- concern for personal development.

1. **Young players** below mid teens tend to prefer a relationship orientated approach with low level task orientated behaviours. Positive feedback alongside lots of tactical and technical input was also required.

2. **Slightly older performers** with well-developed (mature) physical skills tend to prefer a more autocratic style of coaching. Equally, as performers get older, they tend to prefer or require a more socially supportive coach.

3. **Elite athletes** tend to prefer a coach to take over control and responsibility for their training. They feel this helps them to achieve their goals more effectively (high task motivation). They have also been shown to prefer high levels of social support in a more democratic atmosphere.

4. **Beginner/novice performers** generally prefer a low level of heavy instruction and training.

5. **Male sports performers** prefer coaches or teachers to demonstrate high levels of autocratic behaviour together with high levels of instructional and training behaviour. They also prefer their coach to be more socially supportive than do female performers.

6. **Female sports performers** tend to prefer teachers or coaches to be more democratic enabling the performers to participate more in the decision-making process. Male and female athletes tend to be much more alike than different. Their preferences are more dependent upon the nature of the individual performer than gender.

7. **Team sports performers**, particularly those who take part in interactive activities like basketball, football and netball rather than coactive activities like rowing, prefer a more autocratic style with high levels of demanding training and instruction, but they also require regular rewards and praise.

8. **Coactive sports performers** have been shown to prefer a more democratic style of leadership with higher levels of social support. These findings are similar to those suggested by the path-goal contingency model.

---

**ACTIVITY 10**

You will have now realised that choosing the correct style of leadership according to the demands and constraints of the situation, type of group and the leader's personal characteristics is crucial for leadership to be effective. Look at the following scenarios and try to assess and explain which style of leadership you would adopt in each situation as the teacher or coach.

a) One of your better players is having a bad game and you need to substitute him/her.

b) You have been appointed as the new team manager of a top football team who have previously had the same manager for ten years. You are meeting them for the first time.

c) You are the coach of a top international athlete.

d) One of your team members is not playing well and is obviously distracted from the task.

e) Your team are top of the league but keep letting in silly goals.

f) One of your team is unhappy about being continually on the substitute's bench.

Fig 26.14. Decisions about substitutions and initial selection don't always suit everybody

# Summary

## Social facilitation

- Social facilitation is the arousal effects that the presence of others, either audience or coactors, has on a person's level of performance.

- The presence of others will increase the probability that the dominant response occurs by increasing levels of arousal – this observation is based on the drive theory. For beginners or those with poorly learned skills the dominant response will generally serve to inhibit performance. For experts or those performing well-learned tasks the effect will generally be to enhance the quality of the performance level.

- Cottrell argued that the effects of social facilitation were enhanced by evaluation apprehension.

- A supportive audience can give home teams an advantage. However, they can also potentially have a negative effect through high expectations.

## Group dynamics

- Group dynamics are inter-group processes such as cohesion, communication, power roles, leadership and social facilitation.

- A group in sport has a collective identity and a sense of shared purpose and objectives. It involves interpersonal attraction, person and task interdependence and very often structured levels and modes of communication.

- Groups are characterised by the six Is.

- Effective groups/teams are formed in four stages: forming, storming, norming and performing.

- Teachers and coaches are continually striving to enhance the performance of groups/teams by bringing together the best individuals.

- Group productivity = potential productivity – losses due to faulty group processes. Therefore, although the best individuals do usually make good teams, good performance is not always guaranteed.

- The Ringlemann and social loafing effects have been used to explain the effects of increase of group size and reduced motivation on group effectiveness.

- Social loafing often occurs when within a team, a player loses their sense of identity and individuality. Social loafing can be reduced by increasing personal responsibility, identifiability and social incentives.

## Cohesion

- Debate over the effects and results of cohesion is still going on but generally success is more likely to result in cohesion than derive from it.

- Team cohesion is a dynamic process whereby the members of the team are motivated to stay together as a group.

- Groups are motivated to stay together and work together for either task and/or social orientated reasons.

- Cohesion can therefore take the form of task cohesion or social cohesion.

## Leadership

- Leadership is any behaviour that enables a group to attain its goals.

- Emergent or prescribed leaders possess a variety of characteristics which are both innate and learned, but there are no specific traits that guarantee a good leader.

- Effective leaders learn to be both task orientated and person orientated according to their own characteristics/qualities and the demands of the situation, together with the demands and expectations of the group.

- There are several models and theories of leadership including Fiedler's contingency model, which links the choice of effective styles to the favourableness of specific situations.

- Chelladurai's multi-dimensional model is specific to sporting situations and states that optimum performance and enhanced satisfaction are more likely to occur when a leader's required, preferred and actual behaviours are consistent.

# Review Questions

1. What is the phenomenon known as social facilitation?

2. Explain evaluation apprehension.

3. Explain the six Is related to groups.

4. Explain how groups develop through various stages.

5. What factors influence a group's productivity?

6. Why is role clarity and acceptance important?

7. How might a performer experience role conflict?

8. Explain by using a sporting example what the Ringlemann effect is.

9. What is social loafing?

10. Using an example from sport, show how a teacher or coach could try to limit the effects of social loafing.

11. Explain the trait approach to leadership.

12. Explain the behavioural approach to leadership.

13. Within a sporting context, how can a person become a leader? Give examples.

14. What advantages does the interactionist approach to leadership have?

15. Explain the three types of 'leader behaviour' suggested by Chelladurai's model.

16. What did Fiedler mean by favourableness?

17. How did Fiedler see favourableness affecting the style of leadership?

18. Using examples from sport explain the positive and negative effects of autocratic style of leadership.

19. What is a person orientated leader?

20. Explain, using examples, why leadership styles for a novice and an elite performer might differ.

# 27. Optimising Performance

Within competitive sport and physical education in general performers are continually in situations which affect their emotional state. Certain emotional states can strengthen a person's motivation and enhance their performance. However, being in an energised state, creating drive and experiencing increased arousal as a result of stress can lead to anxiety, which may in turn have a negative effect on performance.

Before you read this chapter it may be beneficial to remind yourself of what is meant by arousal and its associated affects. Originally drive theory dominated 1960s research as a way of explaining arousal and social facilitation. It saw arousal developing as a result of a performer's drives which developed from a performer's basic needs, for instance in competitive sport a performer 'needs to win', therefore they train and play hard or may even cheat, if they are frustrated, in order to achieve their objective. The relationship between arousal and performance was seen as a linear one. There is little support for this view in present day sports psychology. For the past 20 years or so the inverted 'U' hypothesis has been found a more convincing explanation for predicting the relationship between arousal and performance. Below par performance is seen as a result of either too high or too low levels of arousal. However, don't forget that not all performers or sports have or need the same levels of optimum arousal.

We also considered some of the newer research in this area, for instance catastrophe theory, which suggests that the relationship between anxiety and performance does not follow the symmetrical shaped inverted 'U'.

Owing to the multi-dimensional nature of arousal and anxiety many people within sport use the terms arousal, stress and anxiety synonomously and continually interchange the terms. It is important, however, that we have clear definitions of these three terms in order to appreciate that although they are very closely related they are also distinct concepts. Within this chapter we will consider the nature of the relationship between stress and arousal and anxiety together with the causes and effects. In addition we will consider what effective measures can be taken to control a performer's levels of stress, arousal and anxiety.

Once you have read this chapter you should have a better understanding of:

- anxiety
- stress
- stress management
- goal setting.

Here is a list of the terms to be covered in this chapter. It is important that you understand them.

- Anxiety
- Cognitive anxiety
- Somatic anxiety
- State anxiety
- Trait anxiety
- Competitive anxiety

- Control
- Coping strategies
- Imagery
- Visualisation
- Self directed relaxation
- Progressive relaxation techniques

- A-trait
- A-state
- Competitive A-trait
- SCAT
- Stress
- Eustress
- Stressors
- General adaptation syndrome
- Stress process

- Biofeedback
- Self talk
- De-sensitising procedures
- Outcome goals
- Performance goals
- Long-term goals
- Short-term goals
- Goal specificity
- Realistic goals

# KEY WORDS

**Arousal** is seen as a general internal state of physiological and psychological activity and alertness varying from deep sleep to intense excitement (highly energised) and is linked to the intensity dimension of motivation.

**Anxiety** is seen as being a negative emotional state usually associated with feelings of apprehension and worry, caused by over arousal due to a person being stressed.

**Stress** is seen as being the result of the performer perceiving an imbalance between what is being demanded of them (stressors can be physiological or psychological) and whether they think they are capable of meeting that demand, particularly if failure has serious consequences.

# Anxiety

Although arousal is a neutral physiological state, the concept of anxiety is linked to the negative emotional feelings a person experiences as a result of the cognitive and physiological effects of arousal and stress (see stress). Anxiety is usually therefore associated with feelings such as nervousness, worry and apprehension. These feelings are particularly prevalent in sporting situations when winning or not losing are very important for various reasons.

Related to sports psychology anxiety is usually seen as having two different components, **cognitive** anxiety and **somatic** anxiety.

# Cognitive anxiety

The vague unpleasant thoughts a sportsperson may develop which are usually associated with concerns about under achieving and negative expectations are said to be the results of cognitive anxiety brought on by stress. A sportsperson experiencing cognitive anxiety would have problems with concentration as levels of attention are interfered with, influenced by images of failure.

Cognitive anxiety is usually experienced earlier than somatic anxiety and will be greatly influenced by the performer's expectations of success.

# Somatic anxiety

This type of anxiety is usually as a result of a performer's negative perception of the body's physiological reactions to stress. A performer worries more because they perceive that a queasy stomach, increased sweating, clammy hands and so on – all the body's naturally occurring responses to increased arousal – are going to have a negative effect on performance.

For some performers the prospect of facing an 'extreme' climb, playing in their first big final or facing their first vault in a gymnastic lesson holds no real threat and creates only a slightly increased level of nervousness. They are rarely seriously unnerved by the prospect of new experiences and accept the slight apprehension as natural.

For others, however, the mere thought of being asked to demonstrate in front of a class or audience always triggers extreme arousal and serious levels of anxiety. In their research psychologists have therefore differentiated between anxiety that results from a changing 'mood state' and is usually short lived and anxiety that is more associated with a person's general characteristics or personality traits (see Speilberger's 1966 self report test: State, trait anxiety inventory – STAI).

## State anxiety

In certain situations sports performers do not feel anxious at all yet in others they feel highly anxious. State anxiety is a temporary emotional state and refers to subjective but consciously perceived feelings of nervousness and worry as a result of increased arousal when faced with certain situations. A player's levels of state anxiety can vary in intensity from situation to situation and also at various times within the situation. For instance, defending a corner in the last minute of a game you are winning 1–0 will obviously increase your level of state anxiety. State anxiety can be either cognitive or somatic and research has shown it can even be

- What might sports performers find threatening in general sporting situations?
- Why do you find situations in sport threatening?
- Discuss your findings with the rest of the group.

**ACTIVITY**

a learned response, ie, certain situations create or cause it more than others. More up-to-date research has suggested that:

- somatic state anxiety is related to the performer's *perceptions* of their level of physiological arousal not arousal per se

- cognitive state anxiety is related to the mental appraisal of arousal – it can be both negative (telic) or positive (paratelic).

## Trait anxiety

The general acquired behavioural tendency of a person to become worried or anxious, ie, a stable characteristic, is referred to as 'trait anxiety'. A person with a high level of trait anxiety is generally

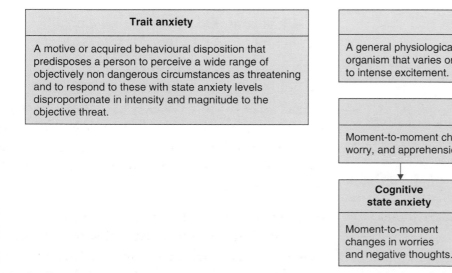

**TRAIT**

| Trait anxiety |
|---|
| A motive or acquired behavioural disposition that predisposes a person to perceive a wide range of objectively non dangerous circumstances as threatening and to respond to these with state anxiety levels disproportionate in intensity and magnitude to the objective threat. |

**STATES**

| Arousal |
|---|
| A general physiological and psychological activation of the organism that varies on a continuum from deep sleep to intense excitement. |

| State anxiety |
|---|
| Moment-to-moment changes in feelings of nervouseness, worry, and apprehension associated with arousal of the body. |

| Cognitive state anxiety | Somatic state anxiety |
|---|---|
| Moment-to-moment changes in worries and negative thoughts. | Moment-to-moment changes in perceived physiological arousal. |

Fig 27.1. Trait anxiety and state anxiety
Source: Weinberg and Gould, 1995.

predisposed to develop high levels of arousal quickly and easily. They generally react to situations with a very high and often disproportionate level of state anxiety. They have a tendency to over react in situations that the vast majority of people would view objectively as non threatening. This has been referred to by some as a possible innate response. More up-to-date research has suggested that it exerts a great deal of influence on a performer's cognitive interpretation of arousal and this can further affect actual physiological arousal.

# Anxiety within sport (competitive anxiety)

Performing well in difficult, challenging or highly emotional circumstances, ie, competitive situations, is a problem to the vast majority of sports performers, in particular those at the most elite of professional levels. Anxiety states can negatively affect a performer's concentratin, attention and level of information processing in competitie situations. It is important that coaches are aware of these effects, can measure and predict them in relation to specific circumstances, and then possibly control them. Important points to note from research into this area are that both elite and average performers experience intense anxiety both prior to, and during, performance. The difference being that elite performers are able to control their anxiety at crucial times within their performance. In addition the performer's perception of the anxiety is also crucial.

Research in this area has shown that both state and trait anxiety can usually be measured through self report tests (eg, Speilberger's STAI). State anxiety can be measured in relation to specific situations and circumstances. The general predisposition of a person to worry more, ie, trait anxiety, can also be measured. The application of these general research measures to sport has shown that people in sport who are measured as having high levels of trait anxiety (high A-trait) will perceive certain situations, particularly competitive situations, as highly threatening (stressful). Their response will be

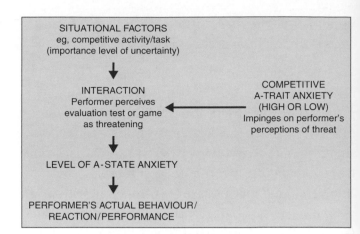

Fig 27.2. Interactionist relationship between a competitive situation and personality factors

a disproportionate one, resulting in severe state anxiety (high A-state) together with a possible inhibited performance.

## Factors affecting competitive anxiety

### Pre-competition

*A-state anxiety can be affected by the performer's perception of:*

- fear of failure/making mistakes/performing badly

- fear of evaluation

- fear of competition/importance of event

- fear of injury/danger

- lack of control/good opposition/unfamiliar pitch/biased refereeing.

### During competition

*Factors which can affect anxiety levels during competition:*

- Evaluation of others **during** competition – crowd/opposition/coach/coactors

- Interaction with others – friendly/aggressive opposition/enjoyment factors/decisions of officials

- Injury during competition/fatigue

- Influence of the environment – weather pitch conditions

- Success/failure **during** competition – time left/ score line.

- Type of task – contact or other.

## Martens: sport competition anxiety test (SCAT)

In developing a more specific sports related test of trait anxiety in sporting situations, Martens (1977) proposed his sport competition anxiety text (SCAT). He felt that although this was seen as a global measure, due to the links between trait and state, this would be a more effective measure of trait, thus a more helpful predictor of possible state anxiety in sport. It is a generally accepted view that competitive situations in sport create anxiety at varying levels in the vast majority of performers. Martens identified that certain performers suffered from this global competitive trait anxiety: a performer's tendency specifically to perceive competitive sporting situations as potentially threatening and to respond to these situations with heightened feelings of apprehension and/or tension. The SCAT test developed over five years was a simple, straightforward 15 item scale self report test (don't forget that self report tests in general have been questioned because of bias). However, it proved generally very reliable in measuring levels of trait anxiety in competitive situations and thus in helping coaches to predict a performer's probable specific anxiety state.

Martens went on to develop his SCAT further in recognition of the more up-to-date multi-dimensional view of the nature of anxiety: The competitive state anxiety inventory (CSAI2) had separate measures for both cognitive and somatic anxiety and has been the most commonly used within sports psychology.

The use of such tests as Martens' indicated two general patterns:

- **Cognitive anxiety** increases in the days leading up to the competition, remains high, but

does not increase just prior to the start of the competition. During the competition it is found to fluctuate normally as a result of the performer's perceptions of success or failure.

- **Somatic anxiety** tends to remain low until rising quite dramatically a few hours prior to the event and decreasing during the competition.

Validity of SCAT:

- easy to administrate

- can be used with large groups

- can be open bias/respondents can reply how they think they **should** not how they actually feel

- responses are open to misunderstanding by non-experts

- the questionnaire is not sensitive to small changes in anxiety levels

- the questionnaire system is inconvenient in a real sport situation/can actually interfere with anxiety response

- high scores on the intensity of anxiety do not necessarily mean this state is detrimental.

As research into this area of anxiety developed, the reliability of basic pre-competitive tests as predictors of actual state anxiety and ultimately behaviour and performance is being called into question. Anxiety states, as we have already said, are changing mood states, and these have been shown to alter considerably in relation to arousal once games or competitions have started. Although many performers measure high levels of competitive A-trait this may not directly affect their anxiety state and thus actual performance. They may have learnt through experience to cope with it, or through specific psychological coaching how to reduce their own levels of anxiety.

The skill of the coach/teacher is in knowing and being able to identify, both in the build-up to competition and during, those performers who

| | HARDLY EVER | SOMETIMES | OFTEN |
|---|---|---|---|
| 1. Before I compete I worry about not performing well. | a ☐ | b ☐ | c ☐ |
| 2. When I compete I worry about making mistakes. | a ☐ | b ☐ | c ☐ |
| 3. Before I compete I am calm. | a ☐ | b ☐ | c ☐ |
| 4. I get nervous waiting to start a game. | a ☐ | b ☐ | c ☐ |

Fig 27.3. Examples of sport competition anxiety test (SCAT) questions – a performer is asked to complete a number of questions of which the following are selected examples. Dummy questions are also included to disguise what is being asked

(Adapted from Martens)

| | NOT AT ALL | A LITTLE BIT | MODERATELY SO | VERY HIGHLY SO |
|---|---|---|---|---|
| 1. I am nervous about the competition. | 1 | 2 | 3 | 4 |
| 2. My body feels tense. | 1 | 2 | 3 | 4 |
| 3. I feel uncomfortable. | 1 | 2 | 3 | 4 |
| 4. I don't feel relaxed. | 1 | 2 | 3 | 4 |
| 5. I am confident. | 1 | 2 | 3 | 4 |
| 6. I don't think I will perform as well as I can. | 1 | 2 | 3 | 4 |

Fig 27.4. Examples of questions to measure state anxiety (CSAI2) – these are related to feelings expressed by sporting performers prior to a specific competition (up to one hour before). Performers are advised that these feelings are natural and to fill in the questions quickly, not worrying over the questions themselves

are feeling just right, those who are too anxious and equally those who may need motivating. Sports psychologists are suggesting that the effects of the interrelated anxiety and arousal concepts also need to be considered in relation to some of the newer interactionist theories, eg,

catastrophe theory (see arousal). Fazey and Hardy (1988) argue that physiological arousal has a 'normal' impact, however cognitive anxiety has the 'potential' for a major effect on performance, ie, catastrophe.

# Stress

As we have already stated, the term stress is very often used in conjunction with or instead of anxiety and vice versa. It is generally seen as a state of psychological tension produced by certain perceived physiological and/or psychological pressures or forces acting on a performer within a certain environment or situation.

Research in this area has suggested that in analysing stress as a sequential process it is important to differentiate between the performer's perceptions of stress and actual potential environmental stressors. The effects of these two aspects have been shown to be different. Additional research (Selye, 1974) has also shown, if the performer's perceptions of the situation are taken into account, that although stress is usually viewed as having a negative or damaging effect on performance and behaviour, it can also have positive effects.

Many top class performers have stated that they need to feel under pressure in order to perform well.

Fig 27.5. Many individuals seek out potentially stressful situations

# Eustress (good stress)

Many sports performers such as rock climbers, hang-gliders, etc. positively seek out so-called stressful situations in order to test their capabilities to the limit. Others claim that being in a relatively stressful situation helps them focus, pay attention and generally develop skills and enjoyment within the context of sport. The positive benefits in terms of self satisfaction and enhanced intrinsic motivation gained from having coped with a stressful situation are seen as being greater than the negative effects of the stress. It is, however, the potentially harmful distress or bad stress that has generally generated most of the research.

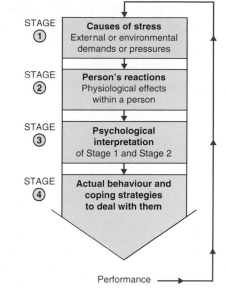

Fig 27.6 The four stages of stress

**ACTIVITY 2**

- Make a list of all the activities in sport that you feel may create eustress.
- Compare your list with the rest of the group.
- Is your list the same? If not, why not?
- Try to explain the sorts of feelings that are developed when taking part in these activities.
- Do you think these experiences happen more during or after the activity (retrospectively)? Why?

# The stress process

Various sequential models (eg, McGrath, 1970; Cox, 1975) have been put forward to illustrate the multivariate nature and the stages involved in the stress process. In general *four* basic stages of stress have been identified (fig 27.6).

A performer is said to experience stress when they perceive that they are not capable of carrying out a particular task. Faced with a particular situation, game or task that may have been set by the teacher or coach, a performer will make a quick cognitive evaluation of what is required, comparing this with what they think are their own abilities, skill levels and experience. The demands of the situation/task are then perceived as threatening or not depending on whether an imbalance between task and capabilities is detected.

Fig 27.7. Children experience greater levels of state anxiety after losing or winning

Research has shown that problems occur because the performer's subjective perceptions of the situational demands and their own capabilities are used to evaluate the situation, not the objective or actual demands and capabilities. Different performers and athletes will not perceive demands always in the same way and, obviously, they will therefore respond and ultimately perform in different ways. Viewing stress as a sequential process has certain advantages. It has been suggested that it is a cyclic process: the performer's actual behaviour feeds back and affects their future evaluations and perceptions.

> In discussion with your group make a list of all the things that you find stressful. Do you all find the same things stressful or are there differences of opinion? Why do you think this is the case?
>
> ACTIVITY 3

## Causes of stress

Events, constant irritations or demanding situations that confront us in daily life that lead to stress are called **stressors**. However, people's perceptions of what constitutes a stressor are different. In a tennis competition a performer who is there for the first time may perceive the experience as highly stressful. A well-established performer may not.

Within life in general there are said to be three basic categories of stressors:

- environmental
- occupational
- life events.

The general stressors a performer may have to face up to in sport are said to fall into two categories: intrinsic within the performer themselves or to do with the situation. Personal or intrinsic sources of stress are generally related to high trait anxiety, low self esteem and social physique anxiety. These in turn will have an effect on a performer's interpretation of situational sources of stress in terms of the importance of the event or contest and the uncertainty that surrounds the outcome (Martens 1987). Examples of more sports specific stressors are given below.

# Sports specific stressors

## Competition

Competitive situations have been shown to be potentially very stressful particularly if the event is important. A cup final or a last game of the season with relegation looming are obviously potentially more stress producing than a mid season game. Even within the context of a game there are certain periods which are more critical than others and thus potentially more stressful (see anxiety). Uncertainty within players/performers with regard to the outcome or over evaluation by others has also proved to be a serious source of stress.

## Frustration

Frustration occurs when a performer is prevented from reaching their goal and can be a common source of stress (see aggression). It may be that a performer feels generally inadequate or specifically inadequate, for instance they want to be a good basketball player but are too small or they keep continually losing out to an opposition attacking player. A performer can become frustrated by external factors over which they have no control (see attributions). Frustration can lead to possible aggression and potentially even more stress.

## Conflict

The very nature of physically demanding sport can lead to stress through physical contact. However, conflict in this sense usually refers to a performer experiencing two or more contradictory motives or goals. A player may have to make a decision between playing for their club or playing for a representative team or within the context of a particular game between playing safe or taking a chance and possibly risk losing the game. External influences or domestic difficulties, eg, family social pressures, may also conflict with a demanding training schedule.

## Personal

Many performers will put undue pressure on themselves thus heightening state anxiety and therefore stress. As already discussed, performers with high levels of trait anxiety (high A-trait) are predisposed to seeing sporting situations as more threatening than people with a low A-trait. In addition when we discussed personality earlier we described Type A and Type B personalities. People with the Type A personalities who are excessively competitive, tense, constantly work to deadlines, become easily frustrated, hostile and continually need their self esteem bolstered are susceptible to greater levels of stress. However, many psychologists will argue that Type A behaviour is not really a specific characteristic in itself but is a series of sub characteristics. It does highlight, however, that certain personal characteristics or ways of dealing with life can lead to heightened levels of stress. Eysenck (1963) also linked arousal to individual differences (see personality).

## Physiological and climatic

Placing the body under severe physical, physiological or climatic strain has also been shown to create stress. Intense or unusual levels of training or playing in very hot, humid conditions can create enormous amounts of physiological stress on a performer. The perceived pressure and necessity to train at extreme levels can also lead to stress. Over using injuries can develop stress both physically and psychologically.

## Audience

While some may find performing in front of an audience an exhilarating experience, others may find it extremely stressful.

## Further examples of sporting stressors

- Rewards/incentives/prizes
- Prestigious events
- Representative honours/games
- Social evaluation
- 'Win at all costs' attitude
- Pre-match pep talks
- Parental pressure
- Inconsistent coaching/training

- Excessive time demands
- Repetitive practices
- Excessive expectations
- Emotional blackmail
- Concerns about self image, eg, overweight.

# Responding to stress

Having perceived an imbalance between the general or specific demands of the task and their own capabilities a performer's stress response can either be psychological (cognitive) or physiological (somatic). Their response will vary according to the degree of perceived threat. Anger, apathy and anxiety are the most common psychological (cognitive) responses to stress. When faced with an immediately threatening situation the body reacts in the short term by increasing psychological arousal.

In describing the general adaptation syndrome (GAS) Selye (1956) explained his generally accepted view of how a person's body responds to prolonged stress. Selye identified three stages of the GAS.

## Alarm reaction stage

This involves physiological changes associated with the emotions of 'fight or flight' reactions. The sympathetic systems of the ANS (autonomic nervous system) are therefore activated. Levels of adrenaline, blood sugar, heart rate, blood pressure all increase. Sympathetic arousal can continue for some time after the level of stress or perceived threat has reduced or disappeared.

## Resistance stage

If the stress continues the body will try to revert to normal levels of functioning thus coping with the increased adrenaline levels. Usually the level of sympathetic nervous activity decreases.

## Exhaustion/collapse stage

In trying to deal with the continued stress and coping with the various hormonal changes the body has gradually depleted its own resource. The adrenal cortex fails to function correctly resulting in physiological problems like ulcers, heart disease and high blood pressure. The body is unable to fight infection and in extreme cases death can occur.

# Reducing stress

In competitive sport the great majority of performers will be under some form or degree of stress. Audiences will always be present. Teams and individuals of equal ability repeatedly compete against each other. Indeed, the whole learning process is one in which the teacher or coach continually sets new and challenging (stressful) tasks for the learner/performer.

Stress to a certain degree can be good for a performer or even actively sought (eustress). It is important though that the negative aspects of stress and anxiety states, eg, worrying about not performing to our capabilities, etc., are not allowed to inhibit performance – very often performers get caught up in a downward stress cycle. Therefore, in order to optimise performance they need to be able to manage or cope with stress in order that the optimal combination of arousal related to emotions is achieved.

- As the effects of stress and anxiety are almost unique to each sports performer it is important that the coach has an in-depth knowledge of the performer's psychological and physiological makeup.

- In addition, the coach/performer must be aware of the various effects and responses associated with stress and heightened state anxiety, eg, both somatic and cognitive anxiety, before they can learn to control them.

- The coach/performer also needs to be aware of the sources of stress.

- Both coaches and performers need to be able to *recognise* the various signs and realise that some of these are the body's natural ways of preparing. Being aware of these effects can help to reduce cognitive anxiety at experiencing them.

Having got to grips with these points a coach can then ensure that they individualise their coaching programmes in order to boost confidence and ensure optimum performance.

## Measuring and recognising stress

The following are aids to assessing stress levels in performers.

1. Self report tests, State Trait Anxiety Inventory (STAI), SCAT, CSAI2.

2. Observation.

3. Measuring physiological responses.

| SYMPTOMS OF HEIGHTENED STATE ANXIETY | | |
|---|---|---|
| **Physiological** | **Psychological** | **Behavioural** |
| • Increased heart rate<br>• Increased blood pressure<br>• Increased sweating<br>• Increased pupil dilation<br>• Increased respiration<br>• Increased muscle tension<br>• Increased blood sugar<br>• Increased adrenaline<br>• Cold, clammy hands<br>• Constant need to urinate<br>• Butterflies in stomach<br>• Constantly feeling sick<br>• Cotton mouth<br>• Headaches | • Worry<br>• Apprehension<br>• Inability to make decisions<br>• Narrowing of attention<br>• Limited direction of attention<br>• Feeling of lack of control<br>• Feeling overwhelmed<br>• Negative self talk | • Nail biting<br>• Rapid talking<br>• Muscle twitching<br>• Scowling<br>• Pacing<br>• Yawning<br>• Trembling<br>• Broken voice<br>• Dazed look in eyes<br>• Sleeping difficulties<br>• Perform better in non evaluative situations<br>• Irritability/aggression |

Fig 27.8. Symptoms of stress, arousal and heightened state anxiety

A teacher or coach must be able to differentiate between long- and short-term stress.

Often stress is inadvertently placed on a performer, particularly young performers. It is most important that teaching and coaching should be appropriate to the individual or team.

More up-to-date research has tended to focus on controlling levels of arousal which can affect either somatic or cognitive anxiety. Arousal is generally seen as the central influence on stress and anxiety. As we have seen when an imbalance between demand and capability is perceived stress occurs and manifests itself in increased arousal which in turn affects both the physiological and psychological balance of the body.

> Choose a practical activity and, working through the four-stage model, write down the practical situation demands, cognitive appraisal, perceived level of threat, somatic and physiological reactions and actual behavioural performance responses under the headings Stage 1 through to Stage 4.

**ACTIVITY 4**

# Managing stress

A simplistic way of viewing the management of stress is that teachers and coaches should try to:

• reduce the problem

• reduce the stress

• control arousal

This can be achieved through either cognitive or somatic techniques. The techniques can be classed as mainly somatic (relating to physiological aspects, ie, the body) or cognitive (related to psychological aspects, ie, thinking). However, as performers can experience both kinds of anxiety at the same time, some of the techniques may also combine elements

of each. Top class performers are experts at using either or both in order to maintain psychological control during top level competition.

# Reducing the problem

Direct action can be taken to alleviate the stress, for instance:

• don't enter competitions

• don't ask novices or people with high A-trait to demonstrate in front of a class

• don't set targets too high

• reduce stressors to match the appropriate levels of the performer's perceived ability, eg, lower box/vault height

• reduce teacher/coach/parental unrealistic expectations and pressure

• don't ask performers to do dangerous activities or activities they may perceive as frightening

• devalue the importance of the competition.

**Control** is a key issue here. If a performer feels in control of a situation then stress can be reduced considerably, in particular cognitive anxiety. This will also help to alleviate learned helplessness (see attributions).

## Cognitive reappraisal

Possible redefinition or modification are also important, that is encouraging a performer to reduce the effects of irrational beliefs, eg, that they always have to play well. Cognitive redefinition/modification of the situation can help a performer (noting that things could be worse), eg, the performance was worse in training. Or it could be getting them to accept that even if they lose it does not make them a bad person or a poor, incompetent performer.

Attribution retraining already mentioned can also be helpful in these situations by encouraging a performer to attribute control internally. Being in control of the situation will help a performer develop both general confidence and self efficacy.

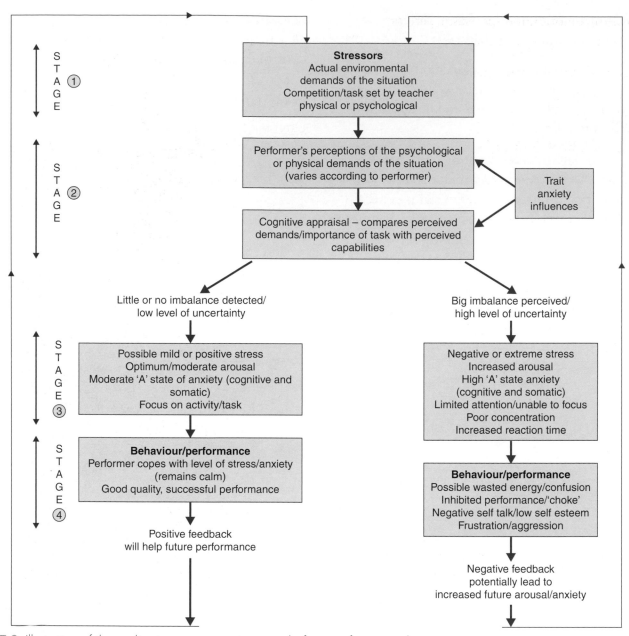

Fig 27.9. Illustration of the cyclic stress process: stress results from performer and situation interaction

By persuading a performer to take responsibility for themselves and cope with the situation a teacher/coach can help a performer deal with any problems they may have to face. A performer can be helped to take responsibility by getting them involved in setting their own goals. Realistic short-term and long-term performance goals should be negotiated. Again this should help a performer's self efficacy together with their ability to cope. Giving a performer as much information as possible about the competitive situation (their progress,

goals, etc) can help to reduce a performer's level of uncertainty.

## Reducing or coping with stress

### Imagery

The intervention technique of imagery has become very popular with sports psychologists. However, imagery has been used for many different purposes. As well as the control or regulation of arousal, improving concentration, building confidence and controlling emotional responses, ie, stress management, it has been used for:

- skill and strategy acquisition (mental rehearsal)
- skill maintenance
- self imagery manipulation
- attention/pain control.

Although imagery and mental rehearsal are often closely associated some psychologists argue that there is a distinction between them.

Imagery is a basic cognitive function and is associated with long-term changes in a performer's behaviour. By recalling appropriate stored information from the memory a player is able to generate images of movement experiences. In many cases this has been shown to be almost as good and effective as actual movement experience.

Imagery can be used to:

- create a mental picture of new experiences in the mind; or
- recreate a mental picture of a previous experience.

Although it is usually associated with visualisation imagery can be:

- **visual** – picture yourself being successful, eg, hitting a winning smash at Wimbledon
- **auditory** – you hear the sound of the ball hitting the racket
- **kinaesthetic** – tactile, eg, feel the power and muscular control associated with the smash
- **emotional** – imagine feelings of success, self satisfaction from the victory, confidence, etc.

Ideally, imagery should involve as many of the senses as possible in order to develop or recreate a more distinct image. Achieving a relaxed state of attention will facilitate the use of all the senses during imagery.

By attaching emotions and feelings to the image performers can help themselves recall situations or behavioural responses more effectively. This can help in the control of current emotions and anxieties and

Fig 27.10. Golfers are avid proponents of imagery. They visualise themselves carrying out each shot successfully before attempting to hit the ball

by developing self confidence in the control of potential emotions and anxieties. Research to support the fact that imagery works explains that it is only really effective when a performer can link psychological and symbolic coding of movement patterns to psycho/neuro muscular actions.

*Factors which a performer should concentrate on to successfully use mental rehearsal:*

- the exact details of the movement in question
- the exact details of a successful outcome

- the 'feel' of the movement
- visualising the exact equipment used
- visualising the environment as it would be for physical practice
- recapturing the emotions of being involved in a competitive situation
- mental rehearsal should be practised frequently as it is a skill in its own right
- mental rehearsal should be practised alongside (alternatively with) physical practice
- the use of an appropriate relaxation technique prior to the use of mental rehearsal could help the quality of mental rehearsal eg, Jacobsen's PMR.

# The use of imagery to control arousal

Imagery can be used either to decrease or increase arousal. Research has suggested that imagery can help to:

- improve concentration
- reduce anxiety
- develop confidence
- control emotions.

In order to reduce arousal, images of previous situations when certain responses have had a negative effect on performance are imagined by the performer. They then try to imagine themselves dealing with and controlling the stress in different circumstances, for instance dealing with the bad call in tennis in a more positive manner, possibly linking an appropriate phrase to remind them to take a deep breath and 'stay cool' in the future. They then imagine themselves carrying out this more positive behaviour. In a more relaxed state they are then able to concentrate more on the task and not allow their overall arousal levels to get the better of them in the actual situation when and if it arises. Arousal, and thus state anxiety, can also be reduced by a performer picturing a place where they feel emotionally at ease with themselves and totally unstressed, perhaps on a beach in the sunshine or by

the pool, 'the sun on your back, the sensation of sand beneath your feet, your body glowing with health and strength'. This process has obvious links with relaxation techniques. The cognitive coping strategy of focusing on emotional images particularly related and relevant to the impending activity has been shown to be very effective in creating positive attitudes, developing confidence and achieving objectives. This has been termed **preparatory arousal**, and is commonly known as 'psyching up'.

There are two basic types of imagery: **internal** and **external**.

## Internal imagery

You only see what you would see if you were actually executing the skill yourself. As a hockey player taking a penalty flick you would see the goal, goalkeeper, the ball going in the net and the kinaesthetic feelings associated with your grip on the stick and stance and so on.

## External imagery

You see yourself as others would see you, as though you were watching yourself perform on video. Although techniques in relation to others would be seen, as it is external there would be little kinaesthesis attached to the image.

There is evidence to suggest that internal imagery is slightly more effective than external due to the fact that it helps to develop kinaesthetic awareness. The general view, however, is that most performers tend to choose a style which suits them and often continually interchange between both types in order to develop the necessary clear and effective image.

# Effective imagery

In order to develop effective imagery a performer and coach should ensure that:

- performers' present image skills levels are evaluated
- imagery is practised regularly and built into the daily routine of the performer

- the performer tries to use as many senses as possible to develop a **vivid** image
- image is **controllable** by the performer
- imagery is carried out in an appropriate setting (initially this may mean no distractions)
- the performer believes it can work
- the performer does not have unrealistic expectations
- the performer builds up the levels and use of imagery over a period of time
- the performer imagines both carrying out the movement and the end result
- images should not be overly long; usually the same length of time as the actual movement
- the performer practises using the image in realistic situations.

After practising and developing imagery skills an experienced performer will be able to use imagery even under potentially distracting circumstances.

# Relaxation

Psychologists have suggested and researched many forms of relaxation to reduce stress. Meditation, breathing control, self hypnosis and biofeedback techniques are all ways that have been used to reduce arousal, and thus reduce stress and anxiety. What has been realised is that just telling someone to relax before or during a game is not enough. The performer needs to know *how* to relax in order that they can have self control and be able to direct relaxation when and where necessary. Relaxation skills involve both somatic relaxation learned through various progressive muscle relaxation training and cognitive relaxation through Benson's (1975) meditation techniques. Many sports performers actively use and extol the virtues of self-induced relaxation to reduce arousal levels to the optimum. Relaxation helps to inhibit panic and self doubt enabling the performer to stay calm. By helping people to sleep it also helps reduce the effects of fatigue.

## Self direction relaxation

This purpose of this technique is to reduce specific and general muscle tension in order to relax fully prior to competitive or stressful situations. With help, a performer is able to identify areas of tension and fully relax. Eventually through practice a performer is able to sit quietly and free the tension from muscles in a very short period of time. The progressive technique below is a process for helping performers learn how to relax.

## Progressive relaxation technique

This technique has been regularly developed and modified by sports psychologists, although the central theme of it was first developed by Edmund Jacobson in 1938. This is generally a lengthy process whose main purpose is to reduce somatic stress by teaching performers to recognise and feel tension and then to be able to progressively reduce it by 'letting go'. Performers are asked to tense specific muscles. By learning what tension feels like they are then taught to experience relaxing specific muscles. By progressively relaxing and tensing a performer is able to develop an awareness of what tension feels like, as the two feelings are mutually exclusive. Thus, when in a performance situation, they can recognise tension and carry out the relevant relaxation of not only specific muscles but general groups of muscles in order that total relaxation can be experienced. Eventually with practice this can be a relatively quick process which can be carried out before, after or during time breaks within games. It is felt that learning to reduce body tension will serve to decrease mental pressure (stress) by allowing the player to worry less. In a relaxed state they can maintain sufficient levels of attention on the necessary techniques of the game and not on muscle tension. Ideally conditions should be appropriate to allowing relaxation to happen, eg, quiet, subdued surroundings, lying down, loose clothing, etc. More experienced athletes, however, are able to focus and, by using 'trigger' controls, can relax almost at will.

## Mental relaxation (cognitive control)

The technique of relaxation response was developed by Herbert Benson (1975). It is a form of meditation, but linked directly to sport. Again this is a lengthy process. Performers are asked to find a quiet place conducive to relaxing. Although it is difficult, they try to focus the mind on one key point, a thought or a word, eg, 'chill', 'calm', 'relax'. By slowly repeating this over and over every time they exhale, a performer eventually learns to induce a feeling of calm and can reduce and control the attentional wandering of the mind. Eventually a person will be able to relax and concentrate or focus on one particular thing. A performer must be aware though that for many events total relaxation immediately prior to an event is not necessarily a good thing.

## Breathing control

There are many general techniques for controlling breathing. Offering a means of controlling breathing has been shown to be an effective method of helping a performer to reduce muscle tension and relax. This again initially reduces the somatic effects of stress and anxiety. However, breathing control can be practised before, after or during the event in order to produce relaxation which can help with imagery, thus helping to enhance technique and performance. Practice is again necessary in order to develop the correct techniques. By consciously controlling the depth and rate of breathing immediately prior, for instance, to an important shot performers can reduce distractions. It will help to maintain their level of control and composure and thus reduce the effects of both somatic and cognitive anxiety.

## Biofeedback

This technique is again linked to controlling muscular tension and helps a performer deal with long-term stress. Performers are taught to control physiological or autonomic responses, ie, heart rate, respiration rates and muscle tension, by being attached to a machine which measures and

Fig 27.11. Biofeedback techniques have been used to train elite marksmen to fire between heart beats in order to improve accuracy (Landers 1985)

amplifies specific internal muscular nervous action. Through practice the performer learns to relax the specific muscles that the machine is attached to by using a method that suits them; the performer is able to assess the level of tension in the muscles by the noise levels of the machine and learns to reduce it by relaxing. The machine provides objective biological feedback, either visual or auditory, with regard to their success rate at reducing tension, thus helping motivation. The main point of developing this awareness is so that eventually the performer can transfer this relaxation technique to the competitive or game situation. They no longer have to rely on the machine to inform them of muscle tension, but can recognise the tension via natural physiological changes occurring. Relaxation techniques can then be applied. Biofeedback has also been developed further by some to include the voluntary control of other bodily functions such as heart rate and blood pressure.

## Self talk

Self talk is linked to controlling cognitive anxiety. Interpretations and perceptions of performance during and after an activity can also have a considerable effect on either the present performance or future performance. Different interpretations and reactions can also affect our emotions and feelings. How a performer interprets their actual performance can therefore lead to stress, anxiety, frustration and anger. A performer can interpret both their good and bad performance in either a negative or positive way: this can lead to what is known as **positive** or **negative self talk**. Comments or thoughts can be directed either against the performance or against their emotions. It is a cognitive modification.

## Positive self talk

This is used to maintain attention levels and focus positively on the task. Remaining optimistic helps a performer's level of motivation and self esteem; it can also reduce cognitive state anxiety. They are able to focus on the task and what to do better and not on worrying. Positive self talk is therefore crucial for concentration. A performer should always try to avoid the negatives can't, never and not. Mood words are particularly useful: 'stay, tough, fast, hard, I can do it!' etc.

## Negative self talk

In using negative self talk the performer is usually self critical and undermines confidence. It serves to increase worry and doubt about future performance, eg, the next serve. It can lead to frustration, anger and increased muscle tension. For instance, having just double-faulted in tennis the resulting negative self talk would be:

- 'What a totally stupid shot that was'
- 'What a time to double fault'
- 'I've no chance of getting back into the game now!'

This could result in smashing the racket into the ground. This performer is not concentrating on what can be done or what should be done to improve the situation. In this situation the positive self talk would be:

- 'I need to watch the ball more when I throw up the ball higher'
- 'This next one goes in'

- 'There's still plenty of time left to turn this match around.'

Thus, while being aware of the difficulties, this positive performer is motivated to carry on and persists. Positive self talk therefore emphasises the importance of developing and maintaining both a constructive mood and approach. It is important that a performer does not allow negative thoughts to become the focus of attention even though, because of stress, they are usually the ones that come into a player's head or mouth first, because self-fulfilling prophecy may be the result.

---

**ACTIVITY 6**

Suggest two positive and two negative comments to go with each of the following situations in relation to both technique and emotions.
- A missed tennis forehand.
- A missed penalty in football, hockey, or free shot in netball or basketball.
- A missed putt in golf.
- A player returning from injury has a setback in training.

---

**ACTIVITY 7**

In future practical situations, try to substitute a positive thought or comment for a negative one! Under stress you will find this quite difficult as usually your first thought is a negative one. Try to stop negative thoughts. Breathe in hard and as you breathe out in a strong but controlled manner try to relax, focus and repeat the positive statement to yourself. Keep repeating this until it becomes a trigger.

---

Very often experienced performers use cue words to trigger off positive thoughts either to reduce anxiety or increase levels of attention and concentration on specific details. Examples are as follows.

1. A basketball player when learning a new skill such as a set shot may use simple cue words

like: 'flex' (knees), 'sight' (basket), 'extend' (knees), 'push' (ball forwards basket), 'flick' (wrist).

2. Tennis players or cricketers who repeatedly fail to watch the ball onto the racket or bat may use self instructional cues of 'watch!' or 'ball' in order to try to break the habit.

3. A skier hitting a mogul may shout 'bend!', 'extend!' or 'down!' and 'up!' in order to remind themselves of the technique.

4. A performer can also motivate themselves, eg, a 400 m runner coming off the last bend can shout to themselves, 'fast! fast! fast!' or 'attack! attack!' in order to help them kick for the line and keep pushing hard!

# Systematic de-sensitising procedures (SD)

SD is generally seen as a procedure for learning and practising relaxation as an active coping skill for self control of anxiety. Although there has been some debate, this technique has been shown to be effective in a wide range of situations including sport. As a form of 'counter conditioning' it was mainly developed by Joseph Wolpe (1958). The main principles of the procedures are that a sportsperson highlights specific situations (10 to 15) that they either fear or that produce levels of anxiety associated with a specific problem. These scenarios are then placed in a hierarchical list with the least intensity of anxiety at the bottom and the greatest intensity of anxiety at the top. Relaxation techniques such as those already described are then used to deal with the least threatening but still anxiety-producing situation. When in a totally relaxed state the performer is clearly able to visualise themselves, through internal imagery, dealing successfully with this anxiety-producing situation. They then move on to dealing with the next level of threatening situation. With help and by pairing potentially stress-provoking situations with relaxation they are gradually able to work through the hierarchical list of anxiety-producing situations in their mind.

Ultimately they are able to deal confidently with situations that they previously found very stressful. Once they can do this visually without feeling anxious, the chances are they will be able to cope with the real-life situations. The SD technique has been shown to work in as few as eight one-hour sessions. However, the technique does require the performer to be able to carry out relaxation and interrelated visualisation techniques which obviously require more long-term psychological training.

In order for these various stress controlling or anxiety reducing techniques to be effective the performer needs to be trained to use them. This psychological skills training needs to be carried out over a prolonged period and is not just something that can be quickly taught or developed. It needs to be practised regularly as an integrated part of training and development. Mental preparation

| Greatest intensity of anxiety | 1. Playing a full game |
| 2. Coming up to the 18th hole |
| 3. Bunker shots |
| 4. Putting |
| 5. Teeing off |
| 6. Walking to the first tee |
| 7. Waiting to start in the club house |
| 8. Practice putting green |
| 9. Practice hole |
| 10. Changing rooms/meeting other players |
| 11. Meeting caddy |
| 12. Parking at the course |
| 13. Morning of the match/preparing to travel to the course |
| 14. Lying in bed the night before a big competition |
| Least intensity of anxiety | 15. A few days before the competition |

Fig 27.12. Example of a hierarchical list of stress-provoking scenarios or stimuli experienced by a golfer returning after a poor season/tour causing loss of form and confidence

and control is now seen by many as the essential difference between successful top level performers and those who 'can't cope' and are generally unsuccessful. Many coaches have been quoted as saying that sport at the very top levels is up to 80 per cent mental! It is now clearly realised that just getting a performer to practise and practise their movement skills in order to correct poor performance is often not the answer. There can be many underlying root causes of a performer's inability to carry out skills under pressure.

# Goal setting

*'A goal is what an individual is trying to accomplish. It is the object or aim of an action.'*

(Lock, 1981)

Goal setting is generally seen as an extremely powerful technique for enhancing performance. However, it must be carried out correctly. When used effectively, goal setting can help focus a performer's attention, help self confidence, enhance both the intensity and persistence dimensions of motivation and ultimately have a positive effect on performance. As can be understood from the previous section, goal setting can be used to help performers feel in control of relatively stress-provoking situations and thus help them to cope with their anxieties. However, if you refer back to intrinsic and extrinsic motivation, you will understand that when used improperly the setting of goals, particularly the wrong or unrealistic goals, not only has a negative effect on motivation but can also be a significant source of stress and anxiety in the immediate performance situation. This can lead in turn to impairment, not enhancement, of performance in the long term. Goal setting should be used with caution by coaches and teachers.

According to research based around the findings of industrial research carried out by Lock et al. (1985) goals are seen as direct motivational strategies setting standards a performer is psychologically motivated to try to achieve, usually within a specific time.

In these discrete terms goal setting is generally thought to affect performance in the following way.

1. **Attention** – goal setting helps to direct a performer's attention (focus) to the important aspects of the task.
2. **Effort** – goal setting helps to mobilise or increase the appropriate degree of effort a performer needs to make in relation to specific task.
3. **Persistence** – goal setting helps a performer maintain their efforts over time.
4. **New strategies** – goal setting helps a performer to develop new and various strategies in order to achieve their goals, eg, learning (problem solving).

## Goal orientation

In considering all the factors that can affect the effectiveness of goal setting, the personality of the performer is important. The level or style of the performer's goal orientation has a differential influence (Lambert Moore Dixon 1999). High achievers (see achievement motivation) with high n.Ach and low n.Af motivational levels prefer challenging but realistic goals. In comparison, low achievers (low n.Ach/high n.Af) avoid challenging goals and usually adopt either very easy or incredibly hard goals. In addition children in the 'social comparison' stage usually focus on competitive and outcome goals. Task orientated performers prefer performance and process goals.

Goal orientation could be:

- performance orientated
- success orientated (outcome)
- failure orientated.

Most coaches and performers in sport, and people throughout their lives in general, set goals for themselves: the secret is to set the right goals and use them in the right context. Generally, in order to

Fig 27.13. When goal attainment is unrealistic or unattainable it only serves to confirm failure, resulting in anxiety and inhibition of performance

| | |
|---|---|
| **S** – Specific | |
| **M** – Measurable | |
| **A** – Accepted | |
| **R** – Realistic | |
| **T** – Time phased | |
| **E** – Exciting | |
| **R** – Recorded | |

Fig 27.14. Performance goals should be S.M.A.R.T.E.R. *Source*: N.C.F Principles.

be effective, goals need to provide direction and enhance motivation. Goals are also seen as playing an important role in stress management. They are the standards against which perceived success or failure are measured and thus link to present attributions of success or failure.

## Types of goals

The types of goals a performer either adopts or is set by the coach (goal orientation) can have a significant effect on both the performer and ultimately the performance. In addition to subjective goals, eg, having fun and enjoyment, and objective goals, eg, reaching a particular standard, two further goals have been identified: **outcome** goals and **performance** goals.

## Outcome goals

Outcome goals generally focus on the end product. Successful competitive results, that is winning a match or gaining some tangible reward, are usually the standard or goal set. Performers who continually make social comparisons of themselves against other performers are said to be outcome goal orientated. Winning and being successful enables this type of performer to maintain a positive self image as they perceive themselves as having high personal ability (see intrinsic and extrinsic motivation and attribution.) However, a performer may produce the best game or time in their lives and still lose, as their level of achievement depends on the performance of others. They play better, you do not achieve your outcome goal, ie, failure.

## Performance and process goals

These generally focus on a performer's present standard of performance compared with their own previous performance, that is they are self referent. Levels of success are judged in terms of mastering new skills or beating a personal best. Developing a performance goal orientation has been shown to reduce anxiety in competitive situations as the performers are not worrying about social comparisons and demonstrating their competence. They can concentrate on the process of developing their performance further, ie, process goals. Process goals focus on what can be done in order to achieve the improvement in performance required. For example, keeping your head down and following through more in order to improve your effective strike rate off the tee in golf. Performance orientated individuals tend to attribute success to internal and controllable factors, eg, effort, and therefore are able to experience and maintain higher levels of pride and self satisfaction. A performer adopting performance goals (goal orientated approach) is able to maintain motivation for longer and more consistently as competition for social comparisons is not the be all and end all of their lives. What matters for them is raising their levels of perceived ability by learning new skills.

Sports psychologists have suggested that performers who adopt different goal setting styles (outcome or performance) set different types of practice and competitive goals that will affect future cognitions and ultimately performance.

Although it is difficult for performers in modern sport not to consider winning and losing, by continually emphasising and focusing on performance goals the coach should ensure that ultimately outcome goals are achieved. For every outcome goal that is set there should be several performance and process goals.

## Goal specificity

Very often when teachers or coaches set goals for performers they are far too general. Telling a performer to 'try hard' or 'do your best' have been shown to be less effective than more specific objective goals. It is important that goals are specific, clear and unambiguous. This helps when evaluating goals as improvements can be assessed more easily.

Imagine you are the coach of a swimmer. Rather than just saying 'You need to improve', make a list of what specific goals you think would be effective to develop their performance.

ACTIVITY 8

## Goal difficulty

In general, psychological research supports the view that difficult but realistic goals are the most effective type of goals to set. Setting easy goals has been shown to be of little value as this can result in lack of real effort and therefore motivation. Goals that are very difficult have not been shown to significantly impair performance in the long run, particularly for performance orientated athletes.

However, unrealistic goals have been shown to be stressful leading to heightened arousal, high A-state anxiety, possibly frustration, reduced future confidence and ultimately poor performance. It is obviously important, therefore, that teachers and coaches have a good understanding of the performer's or group's level of experience, ability and skill in order that appropriate goals can be set. For example, a performer with a high need to avoid failure (n.A.f) may set inappropriate goals which ensure either easy success or definite failure.

## Additional factors affecting goals

### Long- and short-term goals

Individual research into whether short- or long-term goals are best is somewhat equivocal. It has generally supported the view that both need to be set. A performer needs to have an overview of where they are heading. At the same time they need to have sub-goals to enhance and reinforce development towards the main long-term goal. Short-term goals can be used to give the performer levels of progress and achievement. Interim success can serve to develop confidence, reduce anxiety, and maintain levels of motivation. Developing psychological training goals in order to reduce aspects of anxiety such as learning relaxation techniques can be seen as short-term goals within the context of overall performance, so set both short- and long-term goals.

### Goal acceptance and commitment

It is important that the performer is involved in the goal setting process rather than having them set from some external source. The performer is more able to perceive the targets as fair and achievable and therefore more likely to accept them. They are also far more likely to be prepared to work towards them if they have been responsible for setting the goals in the first place. By understanding the needs and personality of the performer a coach is more aware of how much time is available for training, etc, and through negotiation they can endeavour to foster goal acceptance and commitment.

## Goal evaluation

In setting short- and long-term goals in order to chart progression, it is important that the goals can be measured in order that evaluation can take place. Setting goals without evaluation is generally a waste of time – evaluation should be accurate and happen on a regular basis. However, if evaluation becomes excessive it could possibly lead to an outcome orientated approach rather than a performance process approach.

It may be that, in the light of progress, new short-term goals can be negotiated and set. A performer may be finding the training too easy or may have achieved certain levels of success earlier than expected. New variables not thought of at first may also need to be taken into account. However, goals should not be continually changed as this may lead to a performer's uncertainty. It may also prove difficult to lower goals as performers may perceive this as some form of failure. It is important to emphasise their temporary nature and inform the performer of possible setbacks.

This point links closely with the fact that a coach must take on the following responsibilities.

1. **Develop goal achievement strategies** – there is no point in goals being set if a performer is not given strategies for reaching those goals. These strategies can actually also be the short-term goals. This is where the teachers or coaches sporting specific knowledge comes into play. Running, training or skills schedules can be put into operation, eg, a performer may have to cover so many miles per week or train for longer than 20 minutes, three times per week, etc.

2. **Log the goals** – by committing the goals to paper there is no chance of their being forgotten or misinterpreted. It can be seen as a kind of unofficial contract between performer and coach/teacher.

3. **Provide goal support** – in order to achieve certain goals the performer will need to make a certain commitment in terms of time and possibly even financially. This may need the regular support and understanding of their families. Facilities will be needed along with possible physiotherapy and rehabilitation support. Financial backing, motivation or an occasional shoulder to cry on may be needed.

*Simple principles of goal setting*

1. Set specific goals
2. Set difficult but realistic goals
3. Set long- and short-term goals
4. Set performance and process goals as well as outcome goals
5. Set practice and competition goals
6. Write down goals
7. Develop goal achievement strategies
8. Consider participant personality
9. Foster individual goal commitment
10. Provide goal support
11. Provide for goal evaluation
12. Provide feedback

# Summary

## Anxiety

- The concepts of stress, arousal and anxiety are closely associated terms and are often used interchangeably.
- Anxiety is a negative emotional state associated with feelings of apprehension and worry caused by over arousal as a result of being stressed.
- There are two distinguishable types of anxiety. Trait anxiety is a predisposition to perceive situations as potentially more threatening than they are. State anxiety is the changing emotional state experienced in specific situations.
- A person with high levels of A-trait anxiety is likely to respond with potentially higher levels of A-state anxiety.
- State anxiety responses can be somatic or cognitive.

## Anxiety within sport

- Competitive A-trait has been found to be a general characteristic to perceive competitive situations as highly threatening and to respond disproportionately with higher levels of state anxiety.
- Competitive A-trait can be measured via SCATs.

## Stress

- Stress can be either positive (eustress) or negative.
- The causes of stress are referred to as stressors.
- Stressors can be very specific or general. The level of their effect depends on a person's perceptions of them in relation to their own perceived capabilities (cognitive appraisal).
- Specific examples of sporting stressors are competition, frustration, conflict, environmental factors.
- The general adaptation syndrome has been used as a way of explaining the body's actual stress response.
- The GAS is seen as developing through three stages: alarm/reaction, resistance and exhaustion.
- The overall psychological and physiological stress process is seen as being a cyclic one.

## Managing stress

- Stress management helps reduce both somatic and cognitive anxiety.
- Personal control is seen as a key issue in reducing stressful situations. Cognitive modification, attribution retraining and coping strategies have all been developed to help.
- Somatic techniques deal with mainly the physiological aspects of stress and involve various types of 'relaxation' such as progressive relaxation.
- Imagery, goal setting and cognitive modification techniques can help to improve concentration; improve attention; control emotional states. This is generally known as cognitive stress management.
- Imagery can be internal or external.
- All psychological skills training techniques require regular practice and integration into the normal preparation routines of performers.

## Goal setting

- Goals will not be effective unless they are linked to specific and realistic strategies for achieving them.
- The effectiveness of goals is dependent on the interaction between individuals, ie, coach/performer and the situation.
- Goals can be subjective or objective and can be focused on performance process or outcome.
- Performance goals should adhere to the 'smarter' principles.

# Review Questions

1. Give a definition of arousal.

2. Give a brief explanation of how both drive theory and the inverted 'U' hypothesis have been used to link arousal to performance.

3. Using examples from sport explain the difference between **trait anxiety** and **state anxiety**.

4. Using examples from sport distinguish between somatic and cognitive anxiety.

5. What do sports psychologists mean by competitive trait anxiety?

6. Explain how psychologists have tried to measure competitive trait anxiety.

7. Explain and give sporting examples of the effect a high competitive A-trait can potentially have on performance.

8. Make a list of at least four cognitive and four somatic symptoms of increased levels of state anxiety.

9. Give a definition of stress and eustress.

10. What are the four stages of stress development?

11. What are stressors?

12. Give two specific sporting examples for each of the following types of stressors: competition; frustration; conflict; physiological; climatic; personal.

13. How can parental pressure cause stress?

14. Explain the three stages of the GAS.

15. Why is stress management in sport so important?

16. What are the main ways we can measure and recognise stress?

17. Describe the main physiological signs associated with increased levels of stress.

18. Describe the main psychological/cognitive and behavioural signs associated with increased levels of stress.

19. Choose an example from sport other than the one in the chapter and work through the stress process model (fig 27.9) giving practical examples all the way through from environmental demands to behaviour/performance and feedback.

20. Explain what the technique of imagery involves and how it can help stress management.
21. What are the two types of imagery? Explain the difference.
22. How can a coach and performer ensure that imagery is effective?
23. How does relaxation help to reduce somatic stress?
24. What is the intervention technique of progressive relaxation?
25. What is the biofeedback technique?
26. Give examples of positive self talk and explain why it is important.
27. What is the systematic de-sensitising procedure?
28. What are the main effects of goal setting?
29. Explain outcome goals and performance goals.
30. Why are social comparisons important for outcome goal orientated athletes?
31. Explain the many important factors that have to be taken into account when setting goals.
32. What are goal achievement strategies?
33. Is goal support important?

## Further reading and references

A.A.H.P.H.E.R.D., *Psychological Aspects of PE* (1981)

J A Adams, 'A Closed-loop theory of motor learning', *Journal of Motor Behaviour*, 3, pp 111–50

G W Allport, *Attitudes* (Clark University Press, 1935)

— *The Nature of Prejudice* (Addison-Wesley, 1954)

R Arnot & C Gaines, *Sports Talent* (Penguin, 1986)

R Atkinson & R Shiffrin, 'Human Memory: A proposed system of its control processes', in K Spence & J Spence (eds), *The Psychology of Learning and Motivation* vol 2 (London Academic Press, 1968)

— 'The Control of Short Term Memory', *Scientific American*, 224, pp 82–90 (1971)

A Bandura, *Aggression – Social Learning Analysis* (Prentice-Hall, 1973)

R A Baron, *Human Aggression* (Plenum, 1977)

H Benson, *The Relaxation Response* (Morrow, 1975)

Billing, 'An Overview of Task Complexity – Motor Skills', *Theory into Practice*, 1980, 4, pp 18–23

E Bilodeau & I Bilodeau, 'Motor Skills and Learning' in P Farnsworth (ed) *Annual Reviews of Psychology* (CA Annual Review, 1961)

— 'Variable frequency of knowledge of results and the learning of a simple skill', *Journal of Experimental Psychology*, 55, pp 379–83

D Broadbent, *Perception and Communication* (Pergamon, 1958)

J Bruner, 'The nature and uses of immaturity', *American Psychologist*, 27, pp 687–708

R B Cattell, *The Scientific Analysis of Personality* (Penguin, 1965)

P Chelladurai, 'Leadership in Sport Organisations', *Canadian Journal of Sport Psychology*, 5, p 226

B J Cratty, *Teaching Motor Skills* (Prentice-Hall, 1973)

D Coon, *Introduction to Psychology* (West Publishing Co, 1983)

M Czikszentmitialyi, *Beyond Boredom and Anxiety* (Jossey-Bass, 1975)

E Deci, *Intrinsic Motivation and Self Determination in Human Behaviour* (Plenum, 1985)

H Eysenck, 'Biological Basis of Personality' *Nature*, 199, pp 1031–4 (1963)

L Festinger, *A Theory of Cognitive Dissonance* (Harper Row, 1957)

P Fitts, 'Perpetual Motor Skills Learning', in A W Melton (ed), *Categories of Human Learning* (Academic Press, 1964)

P Fitts & M Posner, *Human Performance* (Brooks Cove, 1967)

E Fleishmann, *The Structure and Measurement of Physical Fitness* (Prentice-Hall, 1964)

R Gagne, *The Conditions of Learning* (Holt, Rinehart & Winston, 1977)

A M Gentile, *A Working Model of Skill Acquisition with application to teaching* (Quest, 1972)

D Gill, *Psychological Dynamics of Sport* (Human Kinetics, 1986)

D A Girdano, G S Eversley & D E Dusek, *Controlling Stress and Tension. A Holistic Approach* 3rd edition (Prentice-Hall, 1990)

R Gross, *Psychology: The Science of Mind and Behaviour* (Hodder & Stoughton, 1996)

E R Guthrie, *The Psychology of Learning* (Harper & Row, 1952)

C L Hull, *Principles of Behaviour* (Appleton-Century Crofts, 1943)

E Jacobson, *Progressive Relaxation* (University of Chicago Press, 1938)

F S Keller, 'The Phantom Plateau', *Journal of Experimental Analysis of Behaviour*, 1, pp 1–13

J Kelso, *Human Motor Behaviour and Introduction* (Hillsdale, 1982)

B Knapp, *Skill in Sport* (Routledge, 1972)

R Lazarus & A Monat, *Personality* (Prentice-Hall, 1979)

E Lock & G Latham, 'The Application of Goal Setting to Sport', *Journal of Sport Psychology*, 7, pp 205–22 (1985)

R A Magill, *Motor Learning: Concepts and Applications* (Wm C Brown, 1989)

A Maslow, *Towards a Psychology of Being* (Van Nostrand-Reinhold 1968)

R Martens, *Competitive Anxiety in Sport* (Human Kinetics, 1990)

E McBride & A Rothstein, 'Mental and physical practice and the learning and retention of open and closed skills,' *Perceptual and Motor Skills*, 49 (1979)

J McGrath (ed) *Social and Psychological Factors in Stress* (Holt, Rinehart & Winston, 1970)

E D McKinney, *Motor Learning: Concepts and Applications* (Wm C Brown, 1989)

G P Meredith, *Information and Skill* (BBC, 1958)

W Mischel, *Personality and Assessment* (Wiley, 1968)

M Moston & S Ashworth, *Teaching Physical Education* (Merril, 1986)

National Coaching Foundation, *Motivation and Mental Toughness*, 1996

B Ogilvy & T Tutko, *Problem Athletes and How to Handle them* (Palham Books, 1966)

C Osgood & Tannenbaum 'The principle of congruity in the prediction of attitude change', *Psychology Review*, 62, pp 42–55 (1955)

Y B Oxendine, *Psychology of Motor Learning* (Prentice-Hall, 1984)

M Robb, *The Dynamics of Motor Skill Association* (Prentice-Hall, 1972)

Z Ruben & E McNeil, *The Psychology of Being* (Harper & Row, 1983)

G H Sage, *Sport and American Society* (Addison Wesley, 1974)

R A Schmidt, *Motor Learning and Performance* (Human Kinetics, 1991)

R A Schmidt, *Motor Control and Learning. A Behavioural Emphasis* (Human Kinetics, 1988)

— *Instructor's Guide* (Human Kinetics, 1991)

— *Motor Learning and Performance* (Human Kinetics, 1991)

P Secord & C Backman, *Social Psychology* (McGraw-Hill, 1964)

H Selye, *Stress without Distress* (New American Library, 1974)

R Singer, *The Learning of Motor Skills* (Macmillan, 1982)

B F Skinner, *Science and Human Behaviour* (Macmillan, 1953)

L Stallings, *Motor Learning from Theory to Practice* (C V Mosby Co, 1982)

E L Thorndike, *Human Learning* (Appleton-Century Crofts, 1931)

N Triplett, 'The dynamogenic factors in pace making and competition, *American Journal of Psychology*, 9, pp 507–33 (1989)

R Weinberg & D Gould, *Foundations of Sport and Exercise Psychology* (Human Kinetics, 1995)

B Weiner, *Theories of Motivation from Mechanism to Cognition* (Rand McNally, 1972)

— *Achievement Motivation and Attribution Theory* (General Learning Press, 1974)

— *An Attribution Theory of Motivation and Emotion* (Springer-Verlag, 1986)

A T Welford, *Fundamentals of Skill* (Methuen, 1968)

— *Skilled Performance: Perceptual and Motor Skills* (Scott Foresman & Co, 1976)

H T A Whiting, Acquiring Ball Skill (Bell & Sons, 1969)

W Widmeyer, L Brawley, A Carron, 'The effects of group size in sport', *Journal of Sport and Exercise Psychology*, 12, pp 177–90 (1990)

J Wolpe, *Psychotherapy by Reciprocal Inhibition* (Stanford University Press, 1958)

R Zajonc, 'Attitudinal Effects of Mere Exposure', *Journal of Personality and Social Psychology – Monograph Supplement*, 9, part 2, pp 1–27

# COURSEWORK AND RESEARCH

4

# 28. Practical Coursework

Each of the examination boards has particular criteria which differ in nature. Some of the advice in this chapter will be applicable to all of them while some may need to be modified in some way. The first key piece of advice is to obtain a copy of the relevant specification criteria as soon as possible either directly from the teacher or downloaded from the examination board website. Ensure the restrictions concerning the selection of activities are fully understood.

The chapter is subdivided into sections offering generic advice for some aspects of assessment and examination board specific advice for other sections. Due to the diverse nature of each specification it is not possible to cover all requirements in detail. However, some of the information can be adapted to suit the specific needs of particular criteria.

Within the chapter there are sections on:

- Practical performance and preparation for assessment
- Analysis of skills and performance
- Synthesis of theory and practical

- Personal Exercise Programme (AQA)
- Personal Performance Portfolio (OCR)
- Individual Performance Portfolio (Edexcel)

A brief outline of each examination board requirements is shown in the table below.

| Exam board | AS level | A2 level |
|---|---|---|
| AQA | • One practical activity selected from choice of groups<br>• Personal Exercise Programme | • One practical activity which may be the same as that offered at AS level or different<br>• Written/verbal observation and analysis of performance compared to an elite performer<br>• Synoptic assignment |
| Edexcel | • Two practical activities selected from choice of three groups<br>• Written coursework<br>  1. Analysis of performance<br>  2. Study of local and national provision for selected activity<br>• Development of Individual Performance Portfolio (IPP) | • Factors affecting performance<br>• Personal Exercise Plan (PEP)<br>• One practical activity which may be the same as that offered at AS level or different<br>• Continued development of IPP |

*(Continued)*

| OCR | • Two practical activities selected from choice of ten groups<br>• Personal Performance Portfolio (PPP)<br>  1. Anatomical and physiological knowledge<br>  2. Acquiring and performing movement skills<br>  3. Contemporary studies<br>  4. Evaluation of chosen activity<br>  5. Action planning<br>  6. Review | • Two practical activities selected from choice of ten groups<br>• Verbal evaluation and appreciation of performance<br>• Personal Performance Portfolio (PPP) |
| --- | --- | --- |

As you can see there are many common elements but each course is very different in its exact requirements. As such the advice offered in this chapter must be adapted to suit the particular needs of each one.

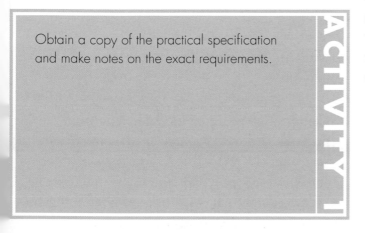

Obtain a copy of the practical specification and make notes on the exact requirements.

ACTIVITY 1

The aim of the practical coursework component is to assess not only the physical skills and application of strategies and tactics, but to bring together all the various theoretical components allowing the optimisation of performance. The task facing students is to use their knowledge and understanding of the theoretical aspects of the course to identify weaknesses in their performance, possible causes and use the acquired knowledge to eradicate the faults.

This element of the course aims to develop many skills and prepare students to fulfil a number of roles. Fig 28.1 outlines such roles.

In order to complete each of these roles successfully, time must be devoted to practise and development of knowledge about the rules, scoring systems, tactics, strategies, technical skills, specific terminology, physical preparation, psychological requirements and any other areas that may hinder or promote performance.

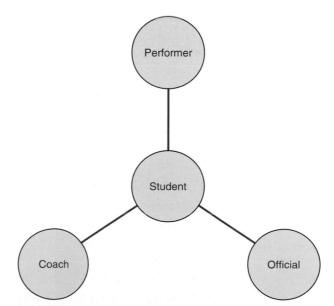

Fig 28.1. A student will fulfil a number of roles

It may be easier to view this section of the course as progressive, with the foundation skills and knowledge being laid during the AS year and the refining and optimising of performance occurring during the A2 year. Many of the skills developed via practices at AS level will be examined in more detail during full competitive situations at A2 level.

Many students may often neglect the practical element of the course and tend to focus on the theoretical aspects. However, a large percentage of the final marks are allocated to this section, up to 30%. Therefore time should be devoted to developing the skills required from the onset of the course and not left until close to the final assessment or moderation. A common error is to concentrate on the development of the stronger activity and ignore the weaker activity until later in the course. This is often too late to actually develop the consistency and quality of skills required to achieve the highest marks.

To fully understand the nature of performance and how to facilitate improvement, links should be made with the theoretical components as frequently as possible. Individual strengths and weaknesses should be identified and as the course progresses possible causes and corrective measures can be implemented.

# Practical performance and preparation for assessment

The selection of activities must be carefully considered as there may be restrictions, for example, the combination of two invasion games is not usually permitted. In addition to your own experience, other factors may include the time available to complete extra training, the opportunity for extra-curricular activities, the accessibility of facilities and resources plus the expertise of teachers and coaches.

The nature of assessment is broadly similar for all examination boards, requiring the demonstration of named core skills related to a specific activity, the difficulty of which gradually increase due to the requirement of executing effectively in more pressurised or demanding situations.

**ACTIVITY 2**

- List possible activities that may be selected based on your experience and strengths.
- Outline the opportunities which will allow skills and performance to develop outside normal lesson time.
- Select the required number of activities and highlight the core skills to be assessed.

The marking of the practical activities is conducted by continual assessment. This allows for ongoing development of performance and caters for students who may have an 'off day' during a moderator's visit. There are several key terms that need to be outlined in order to fully understand the assessment procedure:

- *Skills in isolation* – the demonstration of specific core skills which will be compared to a correct technical model (see later for full explanation).

- *Conditioned practice* (**AQA**)/*structured practice* (**Edexcel**)/*conditioned competitive situation* (**OCR**) – the demonstration of core skills and some tactical awareness in a more pressured practice situation, but not a full game or equivalent competitive situation.

- *Competitive situation* – demonstration of core skills; strategies and tactics; the application of the psychological and physiological qualities needed within a fully competitive environment or appropriate alternative.

To facilitate development, the various skills need to be analysed to identify personal strengths and personal weaknesses. More detailed advice to complete this process is outlined in the next section.

Each activity is different in terms of core skills and examples from different categories are shown in fig 28.2 which illustrate the diverse nature of each activity.

Once this process has been completed for all the core skills time should be devoted to rectify faults. The assessment is based on competence of performance when compared to a correct technical

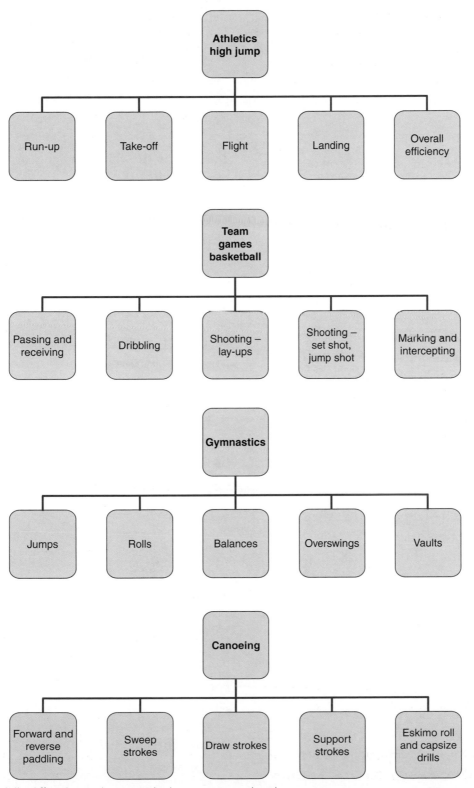

Fig 28.2. The core skills differ depending on which activity is undertaken

- Identify the core skills and their subroutines for each of your chosen activities.
- List your strongest and weakest skills.
- Outline any specific requirements for your conditioned practices.

model (see next section for further details) and marks are awarded to sub-routines of the skill as well as end result. For example, the sub-routines for a squash stroke may be: the grip, footwork and preparation, shot positioning and timing, follow-through and recovery and, finally, effectiveness.

To develop the necessary skills and tactical awareness required time must be given to practice. It is of no use simply reading books or watching videos informing you how to complete the skills correctly. They may be useful as a reference resource but there is no substitute for actually performing the skills.

Training sessions are always easier with others, not just because it is more sociable but they can actually help to improve your performance by observing and coaching. If the practice takes place with another student who has limited knowledge of the activity, outline the identified weaknesses of the skills and prepare a sheet of the correct techniques and coaching points required.

However, if time can be spent with a teacher or another student who is experienced and is able to identify your weaknesses this may be of greater benefit. Allocated time for development may be available either during lessons or extra-curricular activities.

Further time for development may take place at a local club and the expertise of their coaches may be utilised. If this is the case it may be advisable to inform them of the specification criteria, so that they are aware of your aims and the specific skills that need to be developed.

When possible, video record any practice sessions and analyse your development. Evaluate any progress and restructure your training schedule as required.

To develop the effective application of your skills in a competitive situation, set targets for each game or event and ask someone to evaluate your performance. Do not set too many each time, possibly two or three, but try to concentrate on these and don't get over-concerned with other areas of weakness – they can be targets next time.

When developing skills don't try to change everything at once or expect a huge improvement in performance overnight. The process may take months or years to complete. Many elite performers strive to make minor modifications to their technique in order to achieve the optimum performance. The aim of the AS/A2 course is not to make you compete at this level but to be competent performers. Try to remember that when developing your practical performance.

## Assessment procedures

Whichever specification is followed the assessment of the practical is broadly similar. The school/college will be assigned an external moderator to ensure the marking criteria are applied correctly by the teachers when compared to recommended national standards. The moderation may involve either:

- one school/college
- a group of schools/colleges
- video evidence.

The moderator may not see all the activities being offered by the school/college due to time restrictions, availability of facilities or numbers involved. However, the assumption must be made that they will observe any possible combination of activities and as a consequence you should be fully prepared. This may involve not only the actual practical performance but any analysis of performance requirements. The best way to prepare for the moderation is to start practising the core skills as early in the course as possible and give yourself the opportunity to experience as many conditioned situations as possible to develop your skills.

The moderation usually involves both AS and A2 students. Consequently it may be easy to lose focus and concentration. Many students assume the moderator is not watching them because they are at the other end of the sports hall or far side of the playing field. They may be assessing you at any time.

A common error during the moderation visit involves a lack of concentration during the demonstrations of the core skills. Many students appear to not apply themselves fully and produce weaker demonstrations compared to their actual ability. This may be due to the misconception that they are easy, do not require much attention and are less intense compared to the conditioned practice or competitive situation.

It also helps to make the effort to dress appropriately and 'look the part'. This will at least give the moderator the impression that some preparation and thought has been given to the assessment rather than simply turning up on the day.

The nature of physical activity inevitably involves mistakes being made during performance; it is almost unavoidable. Even performers at the highest level make errors of judgement or are influenced by the environment, occasion and opponents. If mistakes are made do not worry about them, redirect your attention and concentrate on the task ahead. The moderator will look at the overall performance not just one small part.

If the selected activity is a team game or one that involves other performers, do not try to be the centre of attention all the time. The assessment is based on your ability to fulfil a role within a specific position. Marks may be lost because of the inability to implement certain tactics, strategies and systems of play.

The moderator may require the analysis of your own performance and a comparison with another student. If this does happen further advice is outlined in the next section covering all aspects of preparation for this assessment.

# Analysis of skills and performance

As the course progresses there will be a requirement to analyse your own performance and the performance of others in greater detail. In order to successfully achieve this, a coaching cycle should be used to ensure a consistent approach; an example is shown in fig 28.3.

Understanding each element is crucial if the coaching process is to be effective and actually develop skills and their application.

- *Performance* – the actions of the performer either in isolation, practice or competitive situation.
- *Observation* – the actions of the performer are watched either by another person or video recorded.
- *Analysis* – the actions of the performer are assessed. Notes should be taken when possible to highlight key strengths and weaknesses.
- *Evaluation* – the actions of the performer are compared to a correct technical model, competent performer or past performances.
- *Planning* – possible causes of weaknesses are identified and corrective measures devised to eradicate the problems. These may be in the

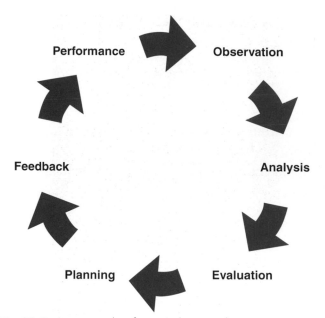

Fig 28.3. An example of a coaching cycle

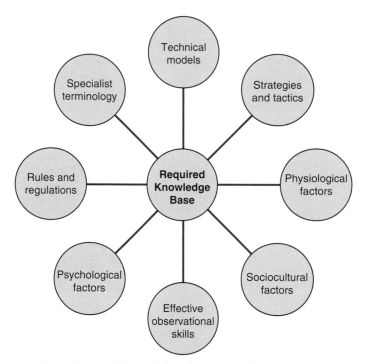

Fig 28.4. Required knowledge for successful completion of the coaching cycle

form of physical practices, physiological adaptations or psychological preparation. It is also important at this stage not to neglect the strengths of the performer, but to maintain a level of training to ensure they do not decline at the expense of improving the weaknesses.

• *Feedback* – the identified training adaptations are discussed with the performer and implemented during the forthcoming performances.

When the coaching and analysis process occurs there are many factors that may need to be considered and knowledge of each must be established if the outcome is to be successful. Many students can identify basic faults in technique and performance but not expand their responses with the use of detailed technical information or appropriate terminology. Fig 28.4 highlights some of the knowledge that may be required to successfully complete the coaching cycle.

As you can see the knowledge base required to be an effective coach, who is able to observe and analyse performance, is wide-ranging and varied. During the course of your studies you should aim to improve each of them.

For your selected activities place in rank order the types of knowledge outlined in fig 28.4 and assess your own strengths and weaknesses as a coach.

**ACTIVITY 4**

## Technical models

Often reference will be made to your performance compared to a 'correct technical model'. This term refers to the performance of a skill which is considered to be of a very high standard. There may actually be several variations of a skill and different performers may have their own individual peculiarities but still be highly successful. Similarly, as many activities become exposed to scientific and technological support, alterations in techniques are becoming more common as actions and techniques are refined.

As a consequence it is advisable to base your comparisons on the most recent information or a performer who is generally accepted as being close to the norm. The technique of many international competitors may be considered unique and inadvisable to coach to developing athletes. For example, the technique of the South African bowler Paul Adams and the running style of 400 metre sprinter Michael Johnson are unlikely to be actively encouraged amongst younger performers, but are highly effective for them personally.

There are many resources for appropriate technical models, often published by the national governing bodies. Suitable sources any include:

- Coaching manuals
- Photographs
- Instructional videos
- CD-ROMs
- Internet
- Television recorded performances with expert commentary
- Live events.

When studying and developing an awareness of each skill, refer back to the specific sub-routines identified previously. A thorough knowledge and understanding of each phase of the skill is vital if the observation and analysis process is to be effective.

For each skill make diagrams and notes of the key points for each sub-routine. Initially concentrate on the major technical points, including the correct terminology, but later, once these are well learnt and easily recognised, develop an awareness of the more advanced technical points.

Fig 28.5. A unique technique may only work well for a particular individual

A useful aid to developing this understanding is a chart containing all the basic information for each

> **ACTIVITY 5**
>
> Research and find relevant resources to identify the key technical points for each of the core skills.

sub-routine of the specific skill. Often an A3 piece of paper, divided as shown in table 28.1, can be easily constructed and contain all the information required.

When questioned about your own or someone else's performance, give the moderator a structured answer and discuss each sub-routine fully before moving on to the next. Learn the order of them as one of your first tasks.

Table 28.1. Sub-routine information chart

| | Sub-routine 1 | Sub-routine 2 | Sub-routine 3 | Sub-routine 4 |
|---|---|---|---|---|
| Diagram or photographs of this phase | | | | |
| Correct technique (*Include 2 or 3 points*) | | | | |
| Common faults (*Include 2 or 3 points*) | | | | |
| Corrective practices (*Include one per fault*) | | | | |

## Observation advice

When observing any performance, the various viewing angles may provide different information about the effectiveness of performance. Imagine when watching a sporting event on television the numerous camera angles employed by the editor and the different impression and information that is produced by each. It is now common practice in many high level sporting events to use such technology to aid referees in their final decision. This approach should be employed to aid your observation and analysis.

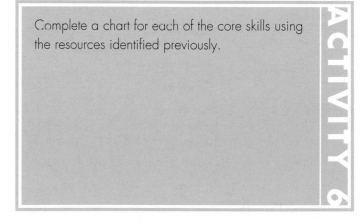

Complete a chart for each of the core skills using the resources identified previously.

ACTIVITY 6

Different views give very different perspectives and the aim of the observation should be identified clearly. The actual execution of skills may require a position close to the action if possible from the side,

front and rear, while the observation of tactical awareness and effective implementation may require a location further away. However, a view from behind the field of play may provide different information compared to one from the side or elevated in a stand. It may be advisable to vary your position to maximise the information upon which to base your judgements.

When observing, either live or from video evidence, make notes to remind you of specific instances or actions. Divide the observation sheet into sections covering the areas required. For example, when observing a game, the sheet may consist of sections for attacking skills, defensive skills, tactics and set plays.

## Analysis of personal performance

Before any personal development of skill and technique can occur, your own performance must be analysed and evaluated. This can be achieved in a number of ways:

- Teacher/coach observing performance and providing feedback
- Another student observing performance and providing feedback
- Video recording of performance and personal analysis.

The latter is in many ways the most useful, as you can see the faults (via visual guidance) and develop a better understanding of the exact modifications needed. Video footage is also useful as a means of stopping the action and making specific comparisons to the technical model, which may be more difficult during live or full speed actions.

Once the actual skill has been analysed the next stage in the process involves the evaluation of the effectiveness of its application, either during conditioned practices or competitive situations.

For game activities these are often split into the following sections:

- Effectiveness of attacking skills
- Effectiveness of defensive skills
- Effective implementation of strategies and tactics
- Effective implementation of physiological and psychological factors which affect performance.

Other activities have alternative categories which are more appropriate, for example, swimming and athletics may require the comments to be based on two events and gymnastic events on agilities and twists. Detailed requirements need to be obtained from the specification criteria.

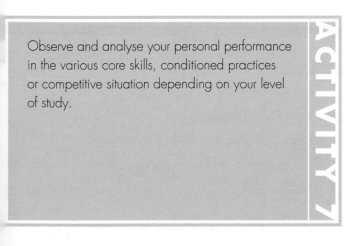

Observe and analyse your personal performance in the various core skills, conditioned practices or competitive situation depending on your level of study.

ACTIVITY 7

Once this process has been completed a structured training programme should be followed to develop the identified weaknesses in the skills. Frequently assess your development either via a teacher/coach or by video recording again. Don't just assume

because practice is taking place an improvement will occur – you may be practising the wrong technique!

## Assessment of observation and analysis of performance

As with all the other areas, each examination board has its own assessment structure for this aspect of the course and it may differ between AS and A2 level. Assessment may be completed in a written format, orally (with or without the use of prepared notes), by direct questioning from the assessor or it may be student-led with supplementary questions as required.

Whatever the method of assessment, preparation is the key to success. A common failing is to assume the technical knowledge is easy and describing the strengths and weaknesses is straightforward. The answers of many students lack specific terminology and are rushed and confused.

If questioned on the various corrective practices to eradicate weaknesses, try to be precise and explain in detail their structure and possible variations. Avoid using the similar practices for all areas, develop a range of ideas.

Often this part of the assessment will develop into a discussion or explanation of the theoretical aspects which may be responsible for weaknesses and methods to overcome them. Detailed advice regarding this aspect is offered in the next section.

### Key points to remember

- Develop notes and observations of performances
- Be logical and use correct technical terminology
- Break the skill down into phases or sub-routines
- Make reference to the correct technical model or elite performers
- Understand appropriate strategies and tactics
- Develop an awareness of rules
- Develop a range of corrective practices with progressions.

For each skill or aspect of performance to be analysed and discussed answer the following questions:
- What is the major identified weakness in the performance?
- Outline a corrective practice or drill to improve the performance.

# Synthesis of theory and practical

The purpose of this section is to assess your knowledge of the theoretical components and your ability to apply it, causing an improvement in performance to occur. Factors which may be potential causes of weakness can be drawn from any aspect of the specification. If possible this should be the case as it illustrates your appreciation and understanding of the whole specification, not just components within it. Many students tend to concentrate their answers on the psychological and physiological components and make limited reference to the sociocultural factors.

Use of the term 'corrective measures' or 'corrective practices' expects a student to make reference to a variety of theoretical information and not simply outline physical drills or practices.

The question could be posed for any skill or aspect of performance:

*'What factors may have caused my weaknesses, what can I do to improve and why might this help?'*

The reasons identified may not actually have contributed to any weaknesses in performance but the process of identifying them must still take place. Try not to use the same possible cause for each skill, identify different factors. A common fault is to repeat the same cause for several skills, for example,

'lack of practice', or 'not enough flexibility', etc. If you repeat yourself you may not be credited with the marks.

Based on the analysis of performance, each weakness identified should have a possible theoretical cause explained in detail with an appropriate corrective measure. This demonstrates an understanding of the application of the theoretical components and should allow you to appreciate how many factors can actually affect the performance of an individual.

Outlined below are topics which may have affected the development and performance of your chosen activities. The lists are not complete and other factors may be included. If there are areas which may have influenced your development, explain the reasons why and outline how this knowledge can be used to rectify the situation.

## Physiological factors

- Inefficient use of levers and bones
- Lack of specific fitness components
- Physiological composition of the individual
- Dietary considerations
- Inappropriate training methods
- Poor application of training principles
- Lack of structured training programme.

## Psychological factors

- Personality type
- Personal abilities
- Plateaus and associated causes
- Theories of learning experienced
- Types of practice
- Methods of teaching
- Forms of guidance
- Types of motivation
- Transfer of learning
- Effectiveness of Information Processing system
- Aggression

- Attitude
- Group dynamics and leadership
- Arousal levels
- Achievement motivation
- Stress, anxiety and poor stress management techniques
- Self efficacy and learned helplessness.

## Sociocultural factors

- Physical education experiences
- National Curriculum
- Experiences of play, sport and physical recreation
- Historical factors and traditions
- Equal opportunities – gender, race, social class, disability, socio-economic group
- Provision of facilities – public, private and voluntary

- National Lottery
- Government initiatives
- Funding
- Role models
- Effectiveness of national and local organisations.

As you can see from the list above there are many theoretical aspects that may be linked to your development, you just have to think about which have had the greatest impact on you personally.

When completing this section think logically and arrange your notes in an organised manner. This makes revision and discussion more effective and thorough.

An example of this structured procedure is outlined below in note form, with a possible cause for each of the identified weaknesses taken from a different theoretical area.

---

Course – A2
Activity – Basketball
Area of assessment – Attacking

| Weakness #1 | *Passing and receiving*<br>When playing against a zone defence sometimes too slow to give the pass to a player cutting to the basket.<br>Passing lacks variety around the key – too often give similar type of pass which can be intercepted. |
|---|---|
| Possible cause (psychological factor) | Lack of anticipation and focus during the game. As a result vital cues missed which delay the reaction time and therefore slows the information processing system. |
| Corrective practice | Improve selective attention – develop ability to focus on cues and block out irrelevant information. Concentrate on key points of technique or planned moves and ignore the actions of the defenders.<br>Operant conditioning will help to develop ability to cope in similar situations and recognise specific stimuli and their correct responses. Reinforcement from a coach or other players will help this process.<br>Example: in training play against a zone defence with players cutting to the basket and attempt to use a variety of passes to break down the defence.<br>When move breaks down stop, analyse fault and repeat drill. |

*(Continued)*

*(Continued)*

| | |
|---|---|
| **Weakness #2** | *Dribbling*<br>When making a fast break from defence, although the dribbling skill is fine there is a lack of speed to get away from the opponents quickly. They are often able to get back into a defensive position and stop the fast break. |
| Possible cause (physiological factor) | Lack of explosive leg power and speed to drive away quickly over a short distance. Specifically in the hamstrings, quadriceps, gastrocnemius and soleus muscles. |
| Corrective practice | Structured training programme to include weight training and plyometric exercises.<br>Weight training would involve exercises such as squats, power cleans and hamstring curls, working at high intensity, for example 90% maximum lift, completing four sets of five repetitions.<br>Plyometrics would involve hopping and bounding exercises and depth jumps. The number of sets and repetitions would vary, but possibly be three sets of ten contacts per exercise. |
| **Weakness #3** | *Shooting*<br>When under pressure both the jump shot and lay-up technique falter against players of equal or higher standard. |
| Possible cause (sociocultural factor) | Limited playing experience within a structured competitive environment containing players of good standard. Mostly played within school either during National Curriculum Physical Education lessons or examination preparation lessons. Very few inter-school fixtures and lack of suitable local provision. |
| Corrective practice | School could arrange more extra-curricular activities and develop more club-links with visits from better qualified coaches.<br>Highlight the issue of lack of club provision to the local sports development officer, who may initiate a suitable programme if there is sufficient interest.<br>Research provision in a wider area and enquire about membership. |

*Notes on the comments above*

- Technical terminology used is specific to the activity of basketball.

- Although all three theoretical areas used as possible causes in this example, it is possible to use one area several times. For example, the possible causes for two weaknesses may both be psychologically based.

- No repetitive answers – search the specification and use different reasons, show the moderator you have an understanding of many areas from both AS and A2 modules.

Completing the analysis in this way should allow for the development of a logical and structured understanding of each area. This particular example is based on a student studying the A2 course and as such the analysis is based around the application of various skills when attacking in the game situation. At AS level the analysis may be more specific to the technical competence of the skill in isolation. For example, rather than discuss the effectiveness of passing when attacking a zone defence, the comments may focus on the correct hand placement on the ball, the weight transference, the execution of the pass and the recovery. As mentioned before check the exact requirements of the specification being studied to understanding what is required and modify the advice offered.

For the identified weaknesses highlighted in activity 8 complete the following tasks:
- What is a possible theoretical cause of each weakness?
- Outline a practical method which could be implemented based on this knowledge.
- Repeat the procedure for two other identified weaknesses.
- Repeat for all aspects of performance which need to be analysed.

**ACTIVITY 9**

It may be the case that the teacher or moderator may direct the questions which may be taken from any part of the specification. If this does occur, take your time and prepare your response logically before starting your answer.

## A Personal Exercise Programme (AQA AS level)

The advice outlined below is directed primarily at the AQA specification, but elements of it may be adapted for use with other specifications. As mentioned previously it is essential to obtain a copy of the relevant criteria from your member of staff or by downloading it from the examination board website.

The Personal Exercise Programme (PEP) is divided into three main sections, and further subdivided as shown on fig 28.6.

The aim of the Personal Exercise Programme is not, as many students assume, to change your level of fitness dramatically within a limited space of time.

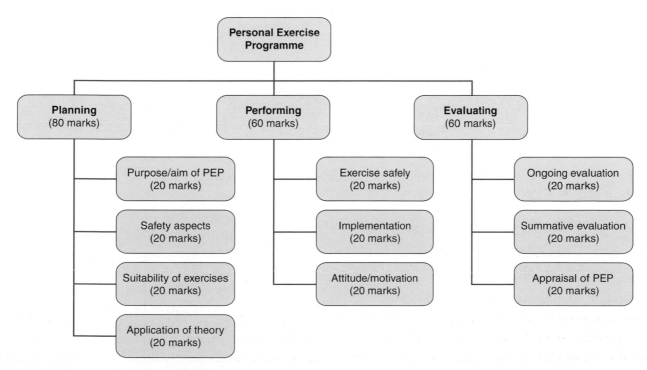

g 28.6. How the score on the Personal Exercise Programme is made up

A large number of students will already be competing at high levels and any improvement expected will be minimal. As a result there are no marks for improvement.

Its purpose is to allow you to demonstrate your ability to apply various theoretical aspects of the course and construct a structured training regime for a specific activity. A major difference to similar coursework at GCSE level is the requirement to justify the reasons for implementing the programme and evaluating the sessions completed in more depth. If you train regularly and your training regime is set by your coach, the PEP may be incorporated into the existing schedule. It should not be seen to interfere with any form of ongoing training or periodised programme, but complement it.

However, if your programme is set and modified by a coach you must still complete all the relevant sections fully and justify why different theoretical aspects have been applied. While many students follow a schedule set by their coach they cannot access the marks available in the planning and evaluation sections if they do not clearly justify the reasons for their actions.

The specification criteria require you to use only one training method or exercise activity. If you already train seriously for a specific activity you may well incorporate several methods into your regime. This information is useful to record in a diary but there is no need to explain in detail each method of training – limit the planning section to one method only. There are no additional marks for outlining more than one type of exercise activity.

There are four training methods from which to select, as shown in fig 28.7.

The length of time to follow the PEP may vary, but it should last ideally a minimum of six weeks, completing at least two sessions per week. Although many may complete more than this number, this is the amount that should be written up and evaluated in detail.

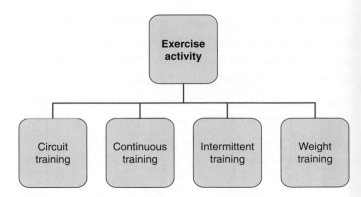

Fig 28.7. Training methods

The PEP is marked against set criteria and within each section certain elements must be fully explained, discussed and justified. Outlined below is a series of suggested questions that need to be answered within each section and an explanation of what may be included for each one.

# Planning the Programme

## Section 1

*Purpose/aim of the programme in relation to prior fitness and performance levels*

- What sport/activity is the PEP designed for?
- What is your current level of performance?
- Are there any health or injury problems which need to be considered?

### Advice

Limit your training to one sport/activity.

Outline the activity and any particular position, event, etc., in which you may specialise.

Give a brief summary of how often you participate, current standard of performance, club involvement, representative honours, etc.

Discuss possible factors that may hinder the training programme or which may be influential considerations when devising the schedule.

- What are the fitness/ability requirements of the activity and why?

- Are there specific requirements for your specialist position and/or event?

## Advice

Outline both the health and skill related components of fitness required. Expand your explanation to include specific examples of when they are needed during performance.

Discuss any particularly relevant factors, for example, reaction time for a sprinter or explosive leg power for a basketball player.

Comments about your strengths and weaknesses during performance would be useful to include, both general and skill related.

- What fitness tests were completed and why?
- Were the tests valid and reliable?
- How do the fitness results compare to national averages?

## Advice

The criteria only require the outlining of tests actually linked to your specific aims. However, it may be useful to include the results from all tests completed as it helps to illustrate how the aims have been constructed.

Explain in detail the procedures for the tests linked to the aims and discuss their validity, reliability and suitability with reference to the chosen activity.

Most of the completed tests will be standard tests as outlined in the textbook, but it is possible to include others if they are deemed suitable. You may wish to devise and include your own skill specific tests.

If possible use data from national averages as a basis for the construction of your aims. If these are unavailable try to use data from school/college students.

- What are the overall aims of the PEP?
- What are the specific aims of the PEP?

- Have specific targets been set which are measurable?

## Advice

Explain how you intend to complete the PEP in terms of number of sessions per week, facilities used, etc.

Clearly state the aims for both fitness and skill development. Do not give vague targets, such as 'improve stamina' or 'better passing'. Remember the targets have to be evaluated at the end of the PEP.

## Section 2

*Awareness of safety aspects/equipment/physical/physiological*

- What does the warm-up involve and why?
- Are there any sport specific related stretches?
- What does the cool-down involve and why?

## Advice

Explain the structure of the warm-up and the benefits gained from its completion.

Outline the exercises, the muscles involved and the type of stretching. Diagrams may be useful to aid your explanation.

Discuss the benefits specific exercises may have on your sporting performance.

Explain the structure of the cool-down and the benefits gained from its completion.

- What safety issues need to be considered to ensure the selected training method is completed without injury?
- How are the specific techniques/exercise completed correctly?
- What safety considerations need to be considered regarding the facilities and equipment?

## Advice

Discuss general safety consideration for the training method, such as exercise selection and order; dehydration; recovery periods; etc.

Explain clearly how exercises are completed correctly. Again diagrams may aid clarity.

Outline checks that need to be performed on equipment and facilities, such as slippery surfaces, weights collars, benches, etc.

- Are there any personal factors which need to be considered?

## Advice

Discuss issues such as age, gender, illness, physical condition, recovery from injury and anything else you feel may be of concern during training sessions.

## Section 3

*Suitability/purpose of exercise/techniques used to improve fitness and skills*

- What methods of training are suitable to develop the specified aims and why?
- What do these forms of training involve?
- Which method of training is most suitable to the needs of the PEP?

## Advice

Outline all the methods of training and discuss their merits and shortfalls.

Select the most appropriate method and justify the reasons for doing so.

Make reference to the stated aims of the PEP.

Explain the potential benefits not only in terms of fitness but skill and performance development.

- What specific exercises/sessions are included using the selected training method?
- What is the purpose of each with reference to muscle and skill development?

## Advice

Outline each of the exercises involved and/or the type of session to be completed.

Justify the reason for inclusion by outlining the potential benefits to be gained both in terms of muscle development and actual skilled performance within the selected sport/activity.

## Section 4

*Appropriate application of activities within the programme in relation to theoretical areas*

- What principles of training need to be considered and how do they relate to the selected training method?
- Has the F.I.T.T. principle been discussed?
- Do the planned sessions show 'progression' and 'overload'?

## Advice

Outline briefly all the relevant principles of training and explain how they can be applied to your training method and schedule. Don't just copy sections of the textbook – apply the knowledge to your situation.

Explain how they are intended to be utilised during the PEP. Don't worry if this has to change, it's part of the ongoing evaluation and modification process.

- What are the workload intensities to be used and how have they been calculated?
- Why are the intensities at this level?
- How and when might they alter during the course of the PEP?

## Advice

Outline the workload intensity. This may include for example the weight lifted, the intended training zone for heart rate, the exercise time, recovery periods, number of repetitions and sets, etc.

Explain how these have been calculated and justify the reasons for doing so. Don't worry if they are actually wrong when you start training, they can be evaluated and adjusted accordingly.

- Are there any other factors that need to be considered?

## Advice

This section may include information about age, gender, overtraining, seasonal factors, cycles within a periodised programme and any other theoretical aspects which may be relevant.

There is no requirement to include nutritional or dietary considerations.

There is also no requirement to complete detailed information regarding the physiological adaptations of training.

# Performing the programme

## Section 5

*Completion of exercise/technique in safe/efficient manner*

- Has a warm-up and cool-down been completed for each session as outlined in the 'planning' section?
- Have all safety checks been completed to ensure the facilities and equipment are fit for use?
- Has the selected training method and selected exercises been completed correctly as outlined in the 'planning' section?

## Advice

The member of staff will assess your ability to complete all the safety aspects correctly as outlined in the 'planning' section. To achieve the highest marks they will need to observe you completing the training sessions correctly independently.

If you complete the warm-up, cool-down and training method correctly but do not explain each fully in the first section you cannot access all the marks.

## Section 6

*Implementation of planned programme*

- Have the training sessions been completed as planned?
- Have the details of exercises and workload intensities been included?
- Have clear outlines of each session been kept with relevant modifications?

## Advice

Keep clear and accurate records of all the sessions completed.

For each, outline the intended aims including any changes made based on previous evaluation.

Include details of workloads, repetitions, sets, target zones, etc.

Ensure you complete at least two sessions per week for the duration of the PEP.

## Section 7

*Attitude/motivation towards improving personal training/fitness/skill level*

- Have all the sessions been completed as planned?
- Have other training sessions and competitive performances been completed?
- Have you gained a good understanding of training methodology and are you able to explain why the PEP has been structured in a particular way and justify those reasons?

## Advice

Complete as many training sessions as possible and provide evidence of additional activities that have been undertaken. Extra sessions do not have to be evaluated.

To gain the higher marks, if questioned you must demonstrate a good level of theoretical understanding of all aspects of your PEP.

# Evaluating the programme

## Section 8

*Ongoing and personal evaluation of level of training/fitness and of improvement in level of skill*

- Has an evaluation been completed for each training session?
- Is the evaluation logical and structured?
- Was the session completed as planned and did it meet its stated aims?
- Were the workload intensities correct?
- What was the recovery period (if applicable)?

### Advice

Complete a detailed evaluation after each session and include reference to the aims.

Discuss the appropriateness of workload intensities and comment on the need to make alterations based on the principles of training.

- Were the exercises completed safely including the warm-up and cool-down?
- What modifications are needed for the next session?
- Has the fitness training to date made any impact on performance levels and skills?

### Advice

Comment on the appropriateness of the exercises and outline any alterations that may be needed. For example, more emphasis may need to be placed on the upper body during the warm-up or certain exercises in a circuit may need to be made easier/harder.

Reference could also be made to the effect the training may be having on your sporting performance, either in a positive or negative manner. There may well not be a noticeable difference.

## Section 9

*Summative evaluation of programme in terms of aims, performance, the improvement of skill and outcomes*

- Did the PEP meet its stated aims?
- Did the PEP affect your fitness, skills and performance level?

### Advice

Discuss the overall effectiveness of the PEP with clear reference to the fitness and skill targets.

Comment on any changes that may/may not have taken place.

If there has been no improvement outline possible reasons for the lack of development.

- What were the results of the retests?
- Were the fitness tests appropriate – if not, how would they change in the future?

### Advice

Analyse any changes in the various components of fitness. Remember only the tests for the specific aspects of fitness targeted need to be completed.

Discuss the effectiveness of the tests and modifications for future use. Outline the reasons why some tests may have been of limited use.

- Was the selected training activity suitable to achieve the stated aims?
- Were the selected exercises suitable?
- What changes would be made if the PEP were to be repeated or used as a basis for further training?

### Advice

Discuss the effectiveness of the training method and exercises used. Explain either why they were appropriate or the limitations their selection caused. For example, the stated aim may have been to develop stamina and circuit training used. Could any gains have been increased by used continuous training?

Outline specific alterations in the training activity or exercises; try not to give vague descriptions.

# Section 10

*Appraisal of programme in terms of a discussion/ explanation/justification through synthesis of theory*

- Were the principles of training applied correctly?
- Were the workload intensities suitable for achieving the stated aims?
- What changes would be made if the PEP were to be repeated or used as a basis for further training?

## Advice

Using specific examples from the 'performance' section discuss whether or not the principles of training were used effectively.

Explain in detail each principle and how, if appropriate, it may be applied differently during future training. For example, the overload may have been too quick or the exercises not sufficiently specific to the activity or stated aim.

## Key points to remember

- No marks for improvement.
- Don't set unrealistic targets.
- Only method of training needs to be used.
- Don't just copy theory from the textbook – it must be applied to you as a performer.
- Justify the reasons for applying theoretical aspects in a particular manner.

## E Individual Performance Portfolio (Edexcel AS/A2 level)

The Individual Performance Portfolio (IPP) is a key piece of evidence which needs to be collated from the start of the course. It should be a record of the ongoing development of performance and contain information which has influenced your programme of study.

The IPP does not need to follow a set format, but the information contained within it should be easily

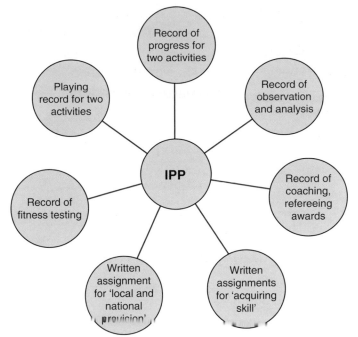

Fig 28.8. Required elements of IPP

assessable and illustrate contributory factors linked to your progress. The folder must contain certain elements, which are shown in fig 28.8.

The knowledge gained during the AS course should be used as a foundation for the A2 course and the optimising of performance. Therefore the IPP must be viewed as an ongoing piece of coursework and as a valuable aid to support your development.

The AS course requires the IPP to include two areas related specifically to one of the chosen practical activities:

- ***An analysis of performance***
  Much of the advice offered in the previous section, Analysis of skills and performance, can be used to complete this aspect.

- ***A study of local and national provision for that activity***
  A 600–800-word project must be completed outlining the provision of the selected activity from grass roots to elite level. Information about the various organisations, progression routes, facilities, funding, initiatives, schemes and resources should be included.

Within the IPP, during the A2 section of the course, similar information regarding performance of the selected activity must continue. A major aim of the course is to develop a 'reflective performer', who has the ability to analyse their performance, evaluate contributory factors and implement suitable modifications allowing improvement to occur. As such the IPP must be regarded as a working document constantly being updated.

Additionally there must also be the inclusion of a Personal Exercise Plan related to your particular activity. Weaknesses in your fitness components must be highlighted with reference to your actual performance. A specific training regime then needs to be designed to improve these aspects and subsequently lead to an improved performance in the competitive situation.

The PEP should last a minimum of 6 weeks, but ideally be completed over an 8–12 week period to allow physiological adaptations to occur. Much of the advice offered in the previous section relating to the AQA Personal Exercise Programme can be adapted to include the relevant information for each section.

There are four areas of assessment as outlined in fig 28.9.

The successful completion of the PEP should allow you to develop a greater appreciation of the theoretical aspects of the course and create an understanding of their application to a practical situation. This in turn should facilitate an improvement in written responses on the examination papers.

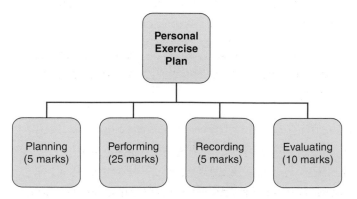

Fig 28.9. Personal Exercise Plan assessment

## Personal Performance Portfolio (OCR AS/A2 level)

The Personal Performance Portfolio (PPP) is an ongoing record of your practical performance and the various theoretical components which influence future development. It should be viewed as an integral aspect of the course and work upon it should start immediately. Each PPP will be characterised by being personal to the student and reflect the relative strengths and weaknesses each possesses with reference to one of the two chosen activities.

As the various theoretical topics are covered in the classroom-based lessons, complete the relevant section required in the PPP. A structured approach such as this will reduce the burden of completing the entire piece of coursework near the final deadline.

The PPP is subdivided into three main sections which are outlined in fig 28.10.

Advice for the completion of each section is outlined below. However, it may be advisable to refer back to previous sections of the chapter to refresh your memory and gain more detailed advice for the analysis of performance and synthesis of theory aspects required to complete the PPP.

## Introduction

Within this section all student details need to be outlined, including name; candidate number; centre number; chosen activity; signed declaration of independent work and a table of contents including respective page numbers.

## Section A: Theory

For each of the three theoretical aspects to be covered there are specific topics which need to be outlined. There are no marks for the inclusion of other areas which are not listed in the specification criteria.

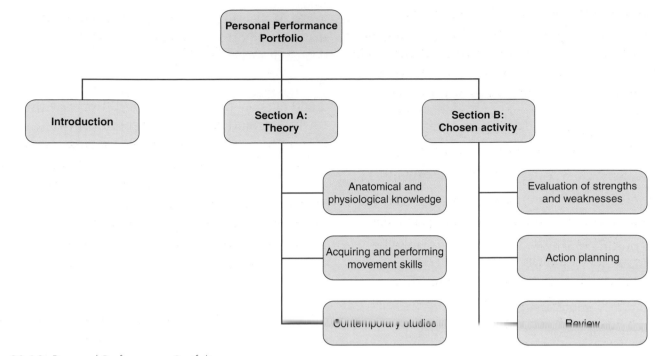

Fig 28.10. Personal Performance Portfolio

## Anatomical and physiological knowledge

- For the chosen activity, the various components of fitness should be identified and reasons given to justify their importance to effective performance.

- The benefits of a structured warm-up and cool-down should be discussed, including the effect on the vascular system, the speed and force of muscular contraction and a suitable series of exercises outlined in detail.

## Acquiring and performing movement skills

- Outline the major coaching points for one skill from the selected activity (see previous guidance)

- Outline a series of progressive practices suitable to develop the named skill.

## Contemporary studies

- The relevant national governing body should be identified and the following information provided:
  a) Name, address and contact information
  b) Promotional and grass root schemes
  c) Regional structure
  d) Regional and national competitions
  e) Coaching awards
  f) Doping control and testing.

- Outline your individual progress within the participation pyramid and discuss the influence of the named national governing body on your development.

# Section B: Chosen Activity

## Evaluation of strengths and weaknesses

In order to complete these sections fully, refer to the advice offered earlier in the chapter (see section on analysis of skills and performance). Initially outline major strengths of the performance and then move on to the weaknesses.

The evaluation may be based on three areas; skills, strategies and tactics, and fitness for the chosen activity.

## Action planning

Once the performance has been evaluated, identified areas of weakness may be used as a basis for development and clear goals must be set. Each of the goals set must be realistic and achievable linking to either skill, strategies and tactics or fitness development. For example, a rugby player may set a goal of increasing the number of successful tackles made during a game, but not one that would expect every tackle attempted to be successful.

Several key points should be included in the action plan:

- A realistic time scale, based on the difficulty of the identified goals.

- An outline of how the goals are to be reached.

- An outline of the evaluation method used to assess if the goal has been reached. Ideally an objective measurement is preferable, rather than one that is subjective.

- An ongoing record of training diary and implementation of the action plan.

- An ongoing record of evaluation of the action plan.

## Review

On completion of the development plan/training programme an evaluation must be completed to assess its overall effectiveness. Reference should be made to the original stated aims and the relative degree of success.

If there has been little or no improvement, comments need to be made suggesting why this may be the case and an outline of possible modifications for future use.

## Bibliography

A complete bibliography must be included, referencing any sources of information used to construct the PPP.

When progressing to the A2 level of the course, the PPP must still be completed but it is not directly marked. However, it should be viewed as an integral aspect of the course and regarded as a working document outlining the development of skills and performance. Reference should be made to the various theoretical components and how they influence performance. These notes can subsequently form the basis for the verbal evaluation and appreciation assessment aspect of the coursework module.

# Summary

## The key points for preparation for the practical coursework

The following points can be applied to any of the different specifications:

- Check the requirements and choose the activities carefully. Don't just assume any combination of activity can be taken.

- Start preparation for the final assessment at the beginning of the course – don't leave it until the last few weeks.

- Learn the correct techniques for the chosen activities.

- Take time to analyse your strengths and weaknesses.

- Set realistic targets for performance development.

- Evaluate progress regularly and revise targets.

- Look for the links between the theoretical aspects of the course and personal practical performance.

- Keep notes updated regularly and use them as a revision resource.

- Enjoy it – the practical aspect of the course is supposed to be fun!

# 29. Requirements and Assessment of the Written Investigation at AS and the Project at A2

## Chapter introduction

The following chapters give details about the optional written components of the Assessment and Qualifications Alliance (AQA) Sport and Physical Education course and Edexcel's Physical Education course. The principles applied could be adopted for a variety of extended pieces of work where similar criteria are required. For example, any project coursework components.

This chapter gives a brief overview of the requirements for the written coursework at AS and A2 and information about the method of assessment. The remaining chapters deal in more general terms with aspects of good practice regarding development of an extended piece of research. Guidance is also given for addressing the assessment criteria effectively.

After reading this chapter you should:

- Have an understanding of your coursework requirements
- Know how to produce a timetable or plan to outline your coursework completion
- Know how to record a bibliography.

## A A general overview (AQA)

If you choose this coursework option from the AQA specification, you will be given the opportunity to complete a sport-related project investigation linked to any area of the Sport and Physical Education specification. You will be expected to observe a sports performer of your choice and analyse their strengths and weaknesses. Based on your observations and evaluation at A2 you will be expected to devise a method to improve the performance for one of the activities you observed and implement this method, assessing whether or not it was successful in terms of improving performance. Provided you are motivated and work within the guidelines given this coursework should go a long way to helping you achieve a good overall grade as it is 'worth' 18% at AS and 10% at A2, giving you some confidence before taking the final two papers. It is not therefore, something which you

should attempt to 'rush off' in a week (especially as your staff will be marking your planning!).

## E A general overview (Edexcel)

If you choose the research project from the Edexcel specification you will be given the opportunity to research, analyse and evaluate an area related to practical performance. You would be expected to choose a topic relevant to contemporary sport and use a variety of research materials to analyse the area of study. At A2 you would also be expected to include some independent research as well as collecting material from secondary sources.

## A E AS written coursework requirements

The project should be approximately 1,500 words in length (8–12 sides of A4). AQA and Edexcel have

## KEY TERMS

An **empirical** study involves the collection of data. This data could arise naturally, for example by recording the quantity of newspaper coverage of women's sport in the popular press. Data can also be obtained from an experiment that you have set up, for example, the times achieved by middle distance runners in front of and then without an audience.

specified a format which should be adopted. This is dealt with in the following chapters, but the headings are given in figs 29.1 and 29.2. Make sure you know which board you are studying!

**A E** A2 project requirements

The A2 project should be an empirical study. It should be a minimum of 2,000 words in length (13–15 sides of A4). AQA and Edexcel have specified a format which should be adopted. This is dealt with in detail in subsequent chapters, but the headings are given in figs 29.3 and 29.4.

Your completed work is assessed by your teachers. A representative sample of the work carried out in your school or college is then sent to an external moderator, who compares this work from other centres and hopefully confirms the marks awarded by your teachers.

Your teachers will base their assessment on specific criteria laid down by AQA and Edexcel. You should ask them for an up-to-date version of these criteria.

It would be a good idea to become familiar with the assessment criteria for your coursework so that

```
Contents AQA (AS)

Acknowledgements       Pg.1
Planning               Pg.
Observation            Pg.
Analysis               Pg.
Evaluation             Pg.
Bibliography           Pg.
Appendices (optional)
```

Fig 29.2. Specified format for AQA Written Investigation at AS Level

```
Contents Edexcel (A2)

Abstract                   Pg.1
Acknowledgements           Pg.
Planning                   Pg.
Literature review          Pg.
Research method            Pg.
Results                    Pg.
Discussions/Conclusions    Pg.
Appraisal
```

Fig 29.3. Specified format for Edexcel Research Project at A2 Level

```
Contents Edexcel (AS)

Acknowledgements        Pg.1
Planning                Pg.
Literature review       Pg.
Discussions/Conclusions Pg.
Appraisal               Pg.
```

Fig 29.1. Specified format for Edexcel Research Project at AS Level

```
Contents AQA (A2)

Abstract                   Pg.1
Acknowledgements           Pg.
Planning                   Pg.
Observation and analysis   Pg.
Evaluation                 Pg.
Support from relevant
   literature              Pg.
Method                     Pg.
Results                    Pg.
Discussions and
   conclusion              Pg.
Appraisal                  Pg.
Bibliography               Pg.
Appendices (optional)
```

Fig 29.4. Specified format for AQA project at A2 level

you gain an overall impression of what you have to do before you start so that you can check your work matches the requirements as you progress. Failure to match the requirements will result in a low mark regardless of the quality of your project.

The remainder of this chapter explains the criteria group headings for AQA and Edexcel in more detail. Owing to the differences in the criteria, they are recorded separately.

# A  AQA AS criteria

## Planning

You will be awarded marks for evidence of your planning throughout the development of the written investigation, so this needs to be demonstrated. This may be achieved in part through discussion with your tutor, but something more tangible will be required. This means you will have to plan a timetable to complete all written investigation tasks (see fig 29.5).

## Observation

Once you have decided who to observe and planned the session to ensure you get a clear indication of the performer's strengths and weaknesses across the five core skills, you run or organise the session. In

this section marks are awarded for using appropriate data collection sheets and for making accurate qualitative and quantitative observations of each of the five core skills.

## Analysis

Your analysis of performance in the five core skills should be based on the evidence recorded on your data collection sheets. You are expected to identify, with justification, the performer's major strengths and/or weaknesses for each core skill.

## Evaluation

This is based on your analysis. You are expected to identify the greatest area of weakness and explain how improvement in this area will bring about the greatest improvement in performance.

## Bibliography

This section should contain a record of the publications used. There are several recognised ways in which to record sources used:

For a textbook:
Author/s (Year) *Title*, where published: publisher.
Coolican, H. (1990) *Research Methods and Statistics in Psychology*, London: Hodder & Stoughton.

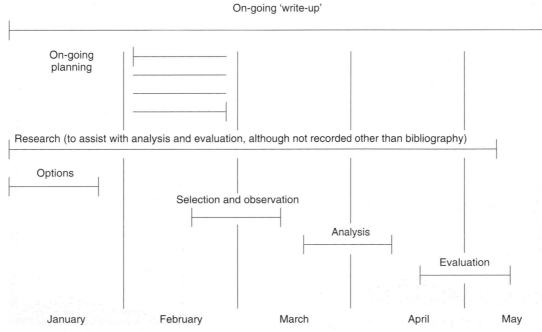

Fig 29.5. AQA project development plan (AS)

For a journal:
Author/s (Year) Title of article. *Journal*, Volume No, Pages.
Biddle, S. Mitchell, J. Armstrong, N. (1991) The assessment of physical activity in children. *British Journal of Physical Education, Research Supplement*, 10, 4–8.

Before adopting an approach check with your tutor in case a specific method is required.

The important point about this section is that:

- it should be accurate, ie, you have actually used the articles/books that you list
- it should be possible to obtain the referenced material from the information given
- it should be in alphabetical order (on author's name).

## Communication

To score highly on this section you will need to ensure that your project:

- is well written
- is clearly presented
- uses a variety of clearly labelled graphics.

## A AQA A2 criteria

### Abstract

An abstract is a summary. It is included so that individuals looking for specific information (possibly to complete a project of their own) can read the abstract and establish whether it is worth considering further; ie, does it cover the area that they are researching? An abstract should include information on the aims of the investigation, the method, your findings and conclusion. It should be fairly short – no more than 200 words.

### Planning

You will be awarded marks for evidence of your planning throughout the development of your project, so this needs to be demonstrated. This may be achieved in part through discussion with your tutor, but something more tangible will be required. This means you will have to plan a timetable to complete all of the project tasks (see fig 29.6).

### Observation and analysis

Once you have decided who to observe and planned the session to ensure you get a clear indication of the performer's weaknesses, you run or organise the session. In this section marks are awarded for using appropriate data collection sheets, for accurately recording your observations and for making an appropriate analysis of the performer's major faults, in demonstration and competitive situations.

### Evaluation

You need to evaluate the quality of the performance you observed and give a brief discussion of some of the factors that may be responsible for the level of performance. You also need to select an area of weakness to improve and justify its selection.

### Support from relevant literature

Here you must demonstrate that you can access information relevant to your topic from a variety of sources. Having gathered this information, you must demonstrate understanding of it, by using it to develop your ideas and to establish a clear link between the review material and the resultant method for optimising performance.

### Reporting of method

For this part of the assessment at A2 you must state your research and null hypotheses (see below). For A2 you must write up your experimental design: you need to explain in detail how the data was gathered. You should take care to give a precise account of the method employed, so that someone else could replicate the procedure if they wished.

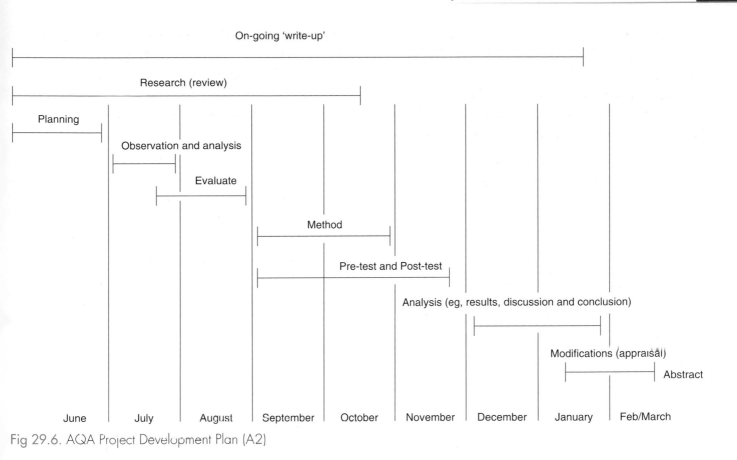

Fig 29.6. AQA Project Development Plan (A2)

Where possible you should give evidence of carrying out the method successfully.

## Results

The results section should be a presentation of the data gained from the experimental design.

## Discussion/Conclusion

The discussion should explain what the results mean. This is your opportunity to show your understanding by:

- commenting on the validity of your results (see below)
- analysing the findings and linking them to the review section.

At this point the research hypothesis can be accepted or rejected. You should then state a conclusion based on this, which links in with your initial hypothesis/ses and review section.

## Validity

The validity of a test ensures that it measures what it is supposed to measure; ie, in retrospect you might decide that the design you set up for your experiment did not really test what you wanted to test, or at least could be improved to make it more valid. For example, you might be measuring the effects of verbal feedback on performance of a

---

**KEY WORD**

**Hypothesis/ses** A statement/prediction about the outcome of the experiment you have devised; ie, what you expect to happen. For example, if you are investigating the effects of extrinsic motivation on performance you might predict that: Extrinsic motivation will have a positive effect on performance. This would be your experimental hypothesis.

basketball lay-up shot. It would therefore be important that the performer only received the 'correct' type of feedback. If others were using the gym at the same time to practise lay-up shots the performer could still receive visual feedback, in the form of the others' attempts. Thus the test would not be totally valid.

## Appraisal

This is an appraisal of your method. You should make suggestions for modifications to your method to further optimise performance. These modifications should reflect any limitations in your methodology already established in your discussion.

## References/Bibliography

This section should contain a record of the publications used. There are several recognised ways in which to record sources used:

For a textbook:
Author/s (Year) *Title*, where published: publisher.
Coolican, H. (1990) *Research Methods and Statistics in Psychology*, London: Hodder & Stoughton.

For a journal:
Author/s (Year) Title of article. *Journal*, Volume No, Pages.
Biddle, S. Mitchell, J. Armstrong, N. (1991) The assessment of physical activity in children. *British Journal of Physical Education, Research Supplement*, 10, 4–8.

Before adopting an approach check with your tutor in case a specific method is required.

The important point about this section is that:

- it should be accurate, ie, you have actually used the articles/books that you list

- it should be possible to obtain the referenced material from the information given

- it should be in alphabetical order (on author's name).

## Communication

To score highly on this section you will need to ensure that your project:

- is well written

- is clearly presented – neatly written or word processed

- uses a variety of clearly labelled graphics.

If word processed, the text should:

- be well spaced (1.5 line spacing)

- have a reasonable sized font (point 12, Times New Roman)

- be spell-checked and proofread.

In addition the report will need to be well organised. If you follow the guidelines contained in this section, including the headings given, this should satisfy the criteria. Examiners/moderators also normally appreciate the inclusion of appropriate diagrams, sketches, graphs, charts, tables, etc; but they must enhance and support the report, rather than merely adding bulk.

In addition you will be expected to demonstrate orally your understanding of the work you have undertaken. At various points through the completion of your project, you will probably be involved in individual interviews with your tutor. During these sessions, it is important that you convince your tutor that you are knowledgeable about the work you are undertaking, have been actively researching information and understand the concepts involved.

Further detail on each of the groupings may be found in the following chapters.

## E Edexcel AS criteria
### Introduction and planning

You will be awarded marks for evidence of your planning so this needs to be demonstrated. This means you will have to plan a timetable to complete all of the project tasks (see table 29.1). In addition

Table 29.1. Edexcel Project Development Plan

| Project | Time |
|---|---|
| Introduction | |
| Purpose | |
| Method of research | |
| Research 'search' | |
| Literature review | |
| Discussion | |
| Conclusion | |
| Appraisal | |

you need to introduce your area of study and the purpose of the investigation. If your project is different from the rest of your group you may also access some originality marks.

## Literature review

Here you must demonstrate that you can access information relevant to your topic from a variety of sources. Having gathered this information, you must demonstrate understanding of it, by using it to develop your ideas and to establish a clear link between the review material and the issue being investigated.

## Discussion/Conclusion

The discussion/conclusion should explain what the reviewed material means (using more than one source). It is your opportunity to show your understanding. You will also be assessed on your written style so try to make it clear and make sure there are no spelling errors.

## Appraisal

You should make suggestions for further investigation and research. You should also identify limitations of your study, explaining how it could be improved.

## E Edexcel A2 criteria

The study route for Edexcel provides the opportunity to research a related aspect in Unit 2 and to develop this into an empirical investigation in Unit 5. Your findings from Unit 2 can be used as a basis for your hypothesis in Unit 5. Thus the assessment criteria develop from AS to A2.

The AS requirements of:

- Introduction and Planning
- Literature Review

are repeated, but lead to a research method.

## Research method

You should take care to give a full and clear account of the methods used and justify why you used them.

## Results

The results section should be a presentation of the data gained from the research method and an analysis of that data.

## Discussion/Conclusion

The discussion should explain what the results mean. This is your opportunity to show your understanding by:

- commenting on the validity of your results
- analysing the findings and linking them to the review section

At this point the research hypothesis can be accepted or rejected. You should then state a conclusion based on this which links in with your initial hypothesis/ses and review section.

## Appraisal

You should make suggestions for further investigation and research. You should also identify limitations of your study, explaining how it could be improved.

# References/Bibliography

This section should contain a record of the publications used. There are several recognised ways in which to record sources used:

For a textbook:
Author/s (Year) *Title*, where published: publisher.
Coolican, H. (1990) *Research Methods and Statistics in Psychology*, London: Hodder & Stoughton.

For a journal:
Author/s (Year) Title of article. *Journal*, Volume No, Pages.
Biddle, S. Mitchell, J. Armstrong, N. (1991) The assessment of physical activity in children. *British Journal of Physical Education, Research Supplement*, 10, 4–8.

Before adopting an approach check with your tutor in case a specific method is required.

The important point about this section is that:

- it should be accurate, ie, you have actually used the articles/books that you list

- it should be possible to obtain the referenced material from the information given

- it should be in alphabetical order (on author's name).

# 30. Observation, Analysis and Evaluation

## Chapter introduction

This chapter discusses how to select your performer/s and activity for observation. Possible methods of analysis are given, before considering the evaluation.

After reading this chapter you should:

- Have thought about the activity and performer/s you wish to base your coursework on
- Know what you should consider for inclusion on your data collection sheets
- Know how to analyse and evaluate performance.

## **A E** Observation and analysis

Lesson plans and observation sheets as mentioned in the planning section, should be prepared before attempting this aspect of the project.

As previously mentioned your first problem is to decide who to observe. It might be helpful to consider the following points before making this decision:

- **What activities from the list in the specification am I interested in?**
  *Choose an activity that is of interest to you. You might be very knowledgeable about squash, for example, but no longer be interested in playing it, therefore you would probably be better off selecting another activity that you enjoy more.*

- **Are there any restrictions an my choice of activity?**

- **What activities do I coach, play, or do I know anything about?**
  *You will need to analyse a performer's strengths and weaknesses. This is obviously much easier if you are*

already familiar with the required techniques/tactics of a particular activity. If you are not already involved in coaching, volunteer, your powers of observation and analysis will improve with practice.

- **What performers could I get access to?**
  *Do you play in a club? Do any of your friends/family play a sport you could observe? It is better to use someone other than classmates as they will have their own studies to complete and may not have the time available to help you.*

- **What link am I hoping to make with the specification?**
  *You might have already decided that you want to investigate effects of fitness on performance, therefore to make the project more feasible you should really select a subject who you know lacks fitness (from earlier observations).*

Use your responses to these points to complete Table 30.1

Once you have established their willingness to help and explained the possible commitment required from them, you should prepare for the session/s you wish to observe. Initially you should observe

Table 30.1. Your potential subjects

| | |
|---|---|
| What sports/activities am I interested in? | |
| Delete any activity from this list if it is not on the specification | |
| Which of the remaining activities do you coach/feel confident you could coach? | |
| Who do you know who plays these sports/activities? | |
| Who from this list would be a reliable subject? | |
| Which of these performers are you most likely to be able to help? | |

You now have your subjects!

a match/training session to establish the performers' strengths and weaknesses. It is vital that you have some way of objectively measuring **performance**. This will help in your evaluation.

At AQA AS you must observe the five core skills for your selected activity. At A2 you must observe performance in demonstration and competitive situations.

It is essential to record qualitative and quantitative aspects of performance. At A2 you will need to use these to demonstrate the effectiveness of your method.

There are many different ways of conducting an analysis of performance. Think about the activities shown, how are they are analysed by 'experts' on television? Hopefully you will have identified typical match statistics as:

- number of aces
- points won on first serve
- unforced errors and so on for tennis
- percentage of possession
- number of corners, etc, in football
- fouls
- free throws
- offensive and defensive moves, etc, in basketball.

**TENNIS**

Aspects used for analysis:

**FOOTBALL**

Aspects used for analysis:

Your analysis is likely to focus on one performer, and be more in-depth than the examples given above. You might decide to use a video so that you can repeatedly review the performance. This is a

# BASKETBALL

Aspects used for analysis:

---

good idea if you are only focusing on one skill, but might be time consuming if the performance is extended. Whether live or recorded you are trying to establish:

- what the performer can do
- what the performer has difficulty in doing
- what the performer omits
- what effects the above have on performance.

Example match analysis sheets can be found in appendix 2B.

In addition to completing your analysis of the technical/tactical aspects of the performance, it is also a good idea to consider some of the physiological, psychological and sociological factors which may affect the quality of the performance so that you can record your observations on these areas as well. For example, a tennis player may not play the most appropriate shot for any of the following reasons:

- they are technically unable to do so
- they lack the necessary confidence
- they lack the fitness to get into position to play the shot
- they lack the necessary motivation to make the effort, etc.

By making brief notes on these aspects at the time of the observation you can refer to them, if appropriate, during your evaluation. (They may also

be useful to you in your synoptic assignment (AQA, A2)).

It is important that you justify why you have said an aspect of performance is a strength or a weakness. For example, in badminton a strength may be the depth of an overhead clear. Justification? It puts the opponent at the back of the court and gives the performer time to take up a commanding position. At AS strengths and/or weaknesses for each core skill should be identified, while at A2 (AQA) only weaknesses need analysing. Once the performance has been analysed it can be evaluated.

# A Evaluation

Having completed the observation and analysis, the performance needs to be evaluated. This involves two tasks at AS and six tasks at A2:

1. placing the performance in the context of other performers (A2)

2. discussing the variety of factors which may account for the quality of the performance (A2)

3. rank ordering the faults of the performance (AS and A2)

4. justifying why certain aspects of the performance should be worked on before others (AS and A2)

----------------------------------------------------------

5. research appropriate sources of information to assist with devising a method to improve performance (A2)

6. devise a method to improve performance (A2).

## 1 Placing the performance in the context of other performers (A2)

This aspect of the project serves two purposes. It provides the examiners and moderators who will look at your work with the opportunity to assess the relevance of your fault correction. In addition, by discussing the quality of other performances you can lead into a discussion of your performer. For example, by discussing the technical/tactical ability of a performer who has achieved a better standard than your performer you can use this to outline your performer's weaknesses and conversely you can discuss your performer's strengths by comparing higher performance to a weaker performer.

To achieve this you should give some background information about the performer, for example, a paragraph about:

- the level they play at, recreational, club, county
- how often they play
- their 'history' of representation.

Thus you are attempting to give an idea of where your performer will 'fit' in the broader picture.

Once you have identified where you think they will fit, a brief explanation of why you have placed them in this position should complete the requirements for this aspect of the assessment.

## 2 Discussing the variety of factors which may account for the quality of the performance (A2)

This is where you demonstrate your ability to apply the theory work you have been covering to a practical situation. You should take each section of the specification and look for possible reasons to explain the quality of the performance. Some examples are given in Table 30.2. Read through these and then try to extend the table for each of the areas in relation to the performer you are observing. Access to a copy of the specification would be helpful to complete this task.

As mentioned previously it is a good idea to broaden your observation to look out for some of these additional factors that may affect performance. You should identify as many as possible from across the specification, but you do not need to discuss them in any great depth at this stage. The information you gain from this exercise can also be used as preparation for your synoptic assignment. (A2)

## 3 Rank ordering the faults of the performance (AS and A2)

You need to consider all the weaknesses you recorded during your observation and place them in order of importance, ie, the faults causing the most problem should be at the top of the list, whereas those factors having little or no effect on performance should appear last.

## 4 Justifying why certain aspects of the performance should be worked on before others (AS and A2)

Once you have rank ordered the recorded faults from the observation you need to explain why you have placed them in the order you have. For example, you may have observed a squash player. She may have many faults with her technique and be lacking in motivation and fitness. You might feel that if you could improve the technique so she was more successful that this would help with motivation. Once motivated you might feel that the player would then engage in some appropriate training. Thus you would consider the technical side of the performance first, and work on that before addressing issues of motivation and fitness levels. You would then consider the technical faults and establish which were having the greatest effect. For example, you may have noticed that the player fails to play a straight forehand drive due to poor body position and that, although effective, her drop shot is technically poor. Rather than work on the drop shot, which is effective, your priority would be to work on the body position for the drive.

Remember at A2 you need to implement a method to improve the areas you decide to focus on, therefore choose something which can be implemented!

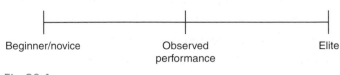

Beginner/novice | Observed performance | Elite

Fig 30.1.

Table 30.2. Factors affecting performance

| Module area | Possible factors affecting performance | Possible factors affecting performance: based on observed performer |
|---|---|---|
| 1. Physiological and psychological factors which improve performance | • lack of fitness (this can be broken down to the appropriate components of fitness)<br>• learning plateau<br>• stage of learning<br>• inappropriate structure of training sessions | |
| 2. Sociocultural and historical effects on participation in physical activity and their influence on performance | • type of school<br>• PE curriculum<br>• socio-economic group<br>• race<br>• gender | |
| 3. Analysis and evaluation of the factors which improve performance | • type of training<br>• amount of training<br>• methods of training | |
| 4. Physiological, biomechanical and psychological factors which optimise performance | • gender<br>• arousal levels<br>• anxiety<br>• self efficacy<br>• learned helplessness<br>• poor biomechanical technique<br>• attitudes | |
| 5. Factors affecting the nature and development of elite performance | • financial pressure<br>• cultural influences<br>• levels of aggression<br>• sponsorship<br>• organisation of sport<br>• country | |

## 5 Research appropriate sources of information to assist with devising a method to improve performance (A2)

t is very important that you base your method o improve performance on relevant theory.

In other words through completing the project you are demonstrating your in-depth understanding of an area of the specification. To acquire this in-depth knowledge you will need to consult appropriate texts, journals, the internet and so on.

## 6 Devise a method to improve performance (A2)

Once you have carried out some research you should be able to put together a plan to improve the quality of the performance you observed. You will be marked on the appropriateness of your method.

Once the evaluation is completed if you are following the AS with AQA your final task is to compile a bibliography of sources consulted and to 'put the project together'.

Table 30.3. Progress report

| Task | Completed ✓ | Still to do ✗ |
|---|---|---|
| Selected performer | | |
| Planned session for analysis | | |
| Prepared analysis sheets | | |
| Considered factors which may affect performance (A2) | | |
| Evaluated performance | | |
| Research associated with identified faults/weaknesses | | |
| Devised method to enhance performance (A2) | | |

ACTIVITY 1

# 31. Planning

This chapter discusses the planning aspects of developing a research project. Regardless of the examination board, planning is obviously vital at the start of any activity, but it should be remembered that the whole of the project development should be considered, and plans modified when necessary.

There are many approved methods of carrying out research, and while they are not all identical, there appears to be a common consensus about the overall stages that should be employed. Before planning can really begin, an understanding of the task ahead is essential so that it can be broken down into manageable stages. The basic steps that should be followed are outlined in fig 31.1.

After reading this chapter you should have:

- A clear idea about how to start your coursework
- Selected your areas of interest from the specification
- Decided on the scope of your coursework
- Formulated a draft hypothesis.

Those completing the AS written coursework need only consider the first two stages of the model, while those at A2 should work through the complete process.

## A E Identifying the research problem

The first stage as indicated in fig 31.1 is to identify the research problem. In other words you know that you have to carry out some research, but on what? What do you want to do the project on? One of the most difficult aspects regarding the project is deciding what to study; what at first seems to be a straightforward task, becomes complex. Faced with the problem of becoming committed to a specific idea, it is easy to put off the inevitable in the hope that inspiration will come, but unfortunately you could have a long wait! While it is good that you are not restricted in your choice of study (other than to the specification), this does present you with a vast choice and makes your decision harder.

In an attempt to get started, it is often helpful to break this first stage down into smaller tasks as shown in fig 31.2. A good starting point for those following the Edexcel specification and AQA at A2 would be to identify the areas of the course that are of specific interest to you. In order to do this:

- read through the specification and your notes to date and 'grade' each of the sections and subsections (don't forget the areas of the specification still to be covered)

- extend table 31.1, listing your 'top ten' in rank order in terms of areas of interest from the specification.

The area of study is obviously important, as you should be working on your project over an extended period. You should choose something that you will be interested in, and not something that someone else thinks will be a good idea.

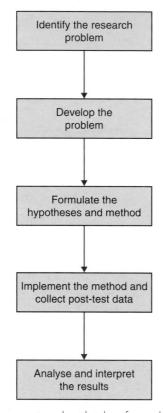

Fig 31.1. Tasks associated with identifying the research problem

# A E Developing the research problem

Having established some areas of the specification of interest, you need to consider each in turn in order to determine whether they can be applied to the research problem; in other words would this topic allow you to address the assessment criteria? Reconsider table 31.1, would any of the three topics be appropriate? If at A2, hopefully you will have discounted topics 1 and 2 due to the difficulty of implementing a method based on them. For example, under topic 1 you might decide to observe a year 9 shot putter. Your observation of his or her performance might reveal that their poor distance is due to their ectomorphic

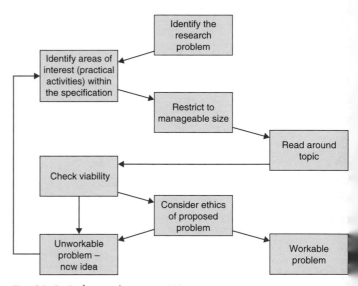

Fig 31.2. Refining the topic (1)

Table 31.1. Syllabus 'top ten'

| Specification area | Topic | Rank order | Taught by |
|---|---|---|---|
| (AQA) eg, Module 1 Physiological factors affecting performance | Body types, physique and involvement in sport | 1 | JS |
| (AQA) Module 1 Psychological factors affecting performance | Personality and relationship to performance in sport | 2 | SH |
| (Edexcel) Unit 2 Acquiring skill | Styles of teaching | 3 | JS |

somatotype. A method to alter their body type and thus improve performance is likely to be impossible, and unethical, therefore this topic is clearly unmanageable. Similarly with topic 2 you might decide that someone needs a complete change of personality to be successful and, however desirable this might be, it presents the same problems as the previous topic!

Topic 3, however, would be manageable if you felt the performance was poor due to an inappropriate teaching style. Methods of teaching could be researched and a series of coaching sessions developed based on the most appropriate teaching style.

Re-examine your areas of interest and check that they could be applied correctly to the coursework problem. You should also bear in mind that at AS there is no need to create or implement a method, but at A2 there is.

Don't be afraid to start – write down your general ideas as they arise: however vague or confused these are, they can be refined or discarded later on. If you try to create the perfect sentence to describe your ideas, you are unlikely to write anything at all. Once you have something written down, it can be shown to staff or discussed with other students. In this way your initial ideas can be sorted and refined.

When you have established the area of the specification to work within, it will need refinement. Although the project must ultimately be your own work, the more discussion you have with others at this stage the better. Therefore try to address the following questions with someone else

> **KEY WORD**
>
> **Scale** refers to the size of the problem to be addressed. You should try to limit your investigation to a specific question. For example, rather than the effects of fatigue on performance in tennis, this can be scaled down to the effects of fatigue on accuracy of the tennis serve.

as you will benefit from hearing their ideas and points of view.

**Is the scale of the project appropriate?** (If the scale or scope is too broad the study will be too large to research in depth.) Look at table 31.2. **Which research areas are appropriate or inappropriate in terms of scale?**

Although all of the examples given in table 31.2 could be used as the basis of a study, none could be used as they stand at the moment; some obviously need more work than others in order to arrive at a manageable area to research.

Refining the initial topic can be difficult; you could try to create levels and increase the focus of the topic at each level for the topics shown in table 31.2 (the first is done for you in fig 31.3). Apply this method to refine the topic you ranked at number 1 in your version of table 31.1 so that the final level focuses on a particular question or issue that reflects what you would like to investigate. Record your final topics in table 31.3.

Table 31.2. Scale of topics

| | |
|---|---|
| • Factors affecting performance in a gymnastic routine | (Appropriate/inappropriate) |
| • Organisation of training sessions to improve performance | (Appropriate/inappropriate) |
| • Use of extrinsic motivation in football to improve performance | (Appropriate/inappropriate) |
| • Use of training programmes to improve all-round performance | (Appropriate/inappropriate) |

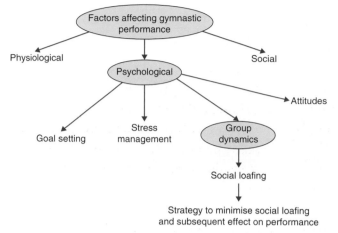

Fig 31.3. Refining the topic (2)

Table 31.3. Development of specification area of interest

| Rank order from table 31.1 | Application |
| --- | --- |
|  |  |

## A AQA AS written investigation

The written investigation requirements at AS for AQA are somewhat different in nature than the project at A2 or Edexcel's Research Project's. If you are an AQA AS student you should consider the following:

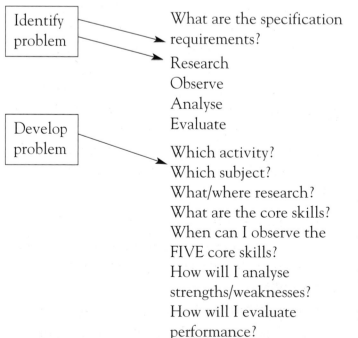

## KEY TERM

**Experimental design** is the method you devise to test your hypothesis; ie, the situation you set up so that you can collect data to support your initial prediction.

The specification requirement in terms of planning is to produce a timetable to show how/when you will complete these aspects. AQA AS students should now move on to chapter 32.

Once you have established the research problem you should plan a realistic and detailed timetable to indicate how you will complete each phase of the written coursework.

## Formulating the hypothesis

Your next step is to establish whether your idea is viable. To help you check this you need to form a draft hypothesis and experimental design. These are dealt with in more detail in the Relevant Literature Section; all you need at present is an idea of the question you want to ask (the research problem), your predicted outcome to the question (hypothesis) and the experimental design you will use to test your prediction. An example is given in table 31.4. Extend this table with the information relating to your topic.

Although you will probably alter your hypothesis and design in the light of further research, this is an important part of the process. Failure to establish that your idea asks a valid question and is measurable at this stage could result in a waste of your time.

Although you obviously do not want to decide exactly what you are going to work on to improve a performance before you have even seen it, you will at least have some ideas about what might affect performance, and whether it is within your scope to investigate further. Information of this kind at your

Table 31.4. Research question, hypothesis and design

| Research problem | Predicted outcome (Draft hypothesis) | Design outline |
|---|---|---|
| Effects of extrinsic motivation on optimising performance | A series of rewards from a significant other will have a positive effect on performance | Devise 'measure' of performance; devise graded programme of rewards with performer, reward desired performance behaviour over time; re-evaluate performance |

finger tips will be invaluable to you, and not wasted effort, as it can be put to good use in the synoptic coursework (AQA, A2) where you have to apply a number of the specification areas to a performance.

You should consider the following before progressing further:

- **Is there available literature on the topic?** Your staff, school/college or local library staff might know where to look. You could browse through references and recommended reading books.

- **Are there likely to be any organisations you could approach for information?** You will need to be careful here though as many organisations (especially the Football Association) receive so many requests for information that they are usually unable to respond.

- **Can you get the information you need from media sources** (eg, newspapers, radio, television)?

- **Who do you know who can help?** If you are involved with a good standard sports club, are there people with the expertise you require (especially in terms of 'volunteers' for any experiment you may wish to conduct)?

To summarise:

1. What data/information do you need to collect?

2. Can it be collected?

3. How will you collect it?

If your response to these questions relies solely on someone else, or you cannot answer some of the questions, you should probably reconsider your topic and select another option from table 31.3. If, however, you feel your idea is still viable, the final task relating to this first stage is to ensure your project does not pose an ethical problem.

## Ethical considerations

When conducting research, you need to be aware of a variety of ethical issues. The most relevant ethical areas for you to avoid are:

- plagiarism
- fabrication and falsification of data and information
- selective use of data
- inappropriate use of subjects.

The first three areas will be dealt with in turn at a later stage. At this point of the development process, however, the fourth area should be considered in more detail. Most projects will involve the use of volunteers, who will place a large amount of trust in you to treat them fairly, psychologically as well as physically. The following titles are all related to the specification, but would be rejected on the grounds that they are potentially unethical. Why do you think they are considered unethical?

- Use of alcohol to reduce pre-match tension
- Use of an intensive weight training programme to increase leg strength of 11-year-old male sprinters
- Use of caffeine tablets to enhance performance
- Use of creatine to aid strength development

- Use of maximum heart rate to calculate training intensity for 0–50s squash team
- Use of an abusive audience in training to prepare for playing 'away'
- Sole use of negative feedback to improve performance.

See table 31.5 for reasons for rejection. In addition to the points emphasised from the above examples, you should also ensure:

- that you comply with any guidelines given by your school/college
- that where a physical session is taking place, there is a properly qualified coach taking the session or close at hand
- that any practice is safe, especially when in a potentially dangerous situation or if using potentially dangerous equipment: eg, diving or martial arts sessions, cycling road races, use of gymnastic apparatus, use of trampolines, use of javelin, etc.
- that the title does not imply racial or sexual discrimination.

Once satisfied that your project is ethical you should be in a position to begin your work on developing the research problem (stage 2, fig 31.1). If you are still experiencing difficulty in choosing a project, some suggested titles from the specification areas are given in Appendix 2a.

You should now have some idea of:

- what interests you
- what is feasible in terms of the coursework problem.

You now need to find an appropriate performance to work with! Ideally you would observe any performance, establish the weaknesses of that performer and then set about devising a means to strengthen their performance. In reality, however, you might be more successful if you decide on your areas of strength (in terms of the specification theory) and then match this with the appropriate subject!

Table 31.5. Ethical problems posed by titles

| | |
|---|---|
| Use of alcohol to reduce pre-match tension | involves administration of drugs |
| Use of an intensive weight training programme to increase leg strength of 11-year-old male sprinters | subject/s still physically developing, therefore strength training should be avoided as it could lead to physical damage/injury |
| Use of caffeine tablets to enhance performance | involves administering drugs |
| Use of creatine to aid strength development | involves administering drugs |
| Use of maximum heart rate to calculate training intensity for the 0–50s squash team | not appropriate to inflict high intensity exercise on 'older' groups from a safety point of view |
| Use of an abusive audience in training to prepare for playing 'away' | could be psychologically damaging for subject/s |
| Sole use of negative feedback to improve performance | very discouraging for the subject/s – may totally demotivate them |

# 32. Developing the Research Problem and Using Relevant Literature

## Chapter introduction

This chapter discusses ways to complete the second phase of the project as shown in fig 31.1 – how to develop the research problem and begin to formulate the experimental hypothesis. In order to develop the research problem, you will need to gain a greater understanding of it. This is achieved by completing a **review** of the available literature on the topic. This chapter gives a general overview of the requirements of a review section, and then gives a more detailed account of how to construct the review.

After reading this chapter you should:

- Understand the purpose of a literature review
- Know how to structure a literature review
- Know the difference between a research, null and experimental hypothesis
- Understand the importance of variables.

## A E The purposes of a review

The general purpose of the review is:

- to give an introduction to the research area related to your investigation
- to give you an opportunity to demonstrate your knowledge and understanding of the research relating to your investigation
- to give you sufficient knowledge to make informed decisions about the content and format of your hypothesis and design.

To complete a good review you will need to access the appropriate (and hopefully recent) research and literature available for your topic; analyse and evaluate it; and include conflicting research where it exists. It should be your evaluation of the available research, not just a repeat of it. Great care must be taken while writing the review not to plagiarise other people's work. Note-taking rather than copying from the text should help you avoid this potential pitfall.

Your first task is to locate literature related to your area of investigation. You need to provide evidence of your research by referencing a number and variety of sources of information. Some towns and counties have specialist libraries which you could visit or contact to ask for specific information. It is worth asking your school/college librarians if they know of any such specialist centres that you could access. There is no short cut to this part of the process; it will be time consuming, but it lays the foundations for the rest of your project.

### KEY WORD

**Plagiarism** means the copying of other people's work and reporting it as your own. There is no problem with using other people's work, provided that you acknowledge whose work it is.

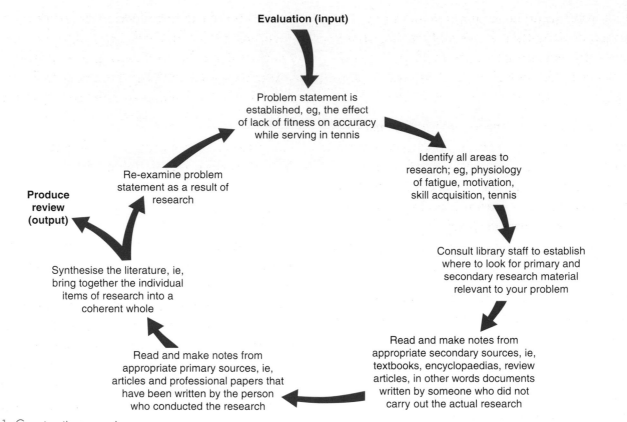

**Evaluation (input)**

Problem statement is established, eg, the effect of lack of fitness on accuracy while serving in tennis

Identify all areas to research; eg, physiology of fatigue, motivation, skill acquisition, tennis

Consult library staff to establish where to look for primary and secondary research material relevant to your problem

Read and make notes from appropriate secondary sources, ie, textbooks, encyclopaedias, review articles, in other words documents written by someone who did not carry out the actual research

Read and make notes from appropriate primary sources, ie, articles and professional papers that have been written by the person who conducted the research

Synthesise the literature, ie, bring together the individual items of research into a coherent whole

Re-examine problem statement as a result of research

**Produce review (output)**

Fig 32.1. Constructing a review

Fig 32.1 summarises the process of developing the literature review. Firstly it shows the work conducted during the evaluation stage as necessary input in order to determine an appropriate problem for investigation. Once this is established you need to identify all related topics within the area of investigation, and find information relating to these areas. (Libraries will have a variety of indexes to different bodies of knowledge. You should use these indexes to establish what publications will be of use to you, and where they can be found.) Having located relevant sources of information you will need to read and make notes from them (remember to record the sources used for the bibliography).

Secondary sources of information may also provide references to primary sources, which you could obtain if you needed more detail on a particular study. Next follows the processing of this information which will hopefully lead to the output of the components of the review. If you are unable to construct a suitable review at this stage it might

be necessary to re-examine your problem statement and modify it in some way, starting the 'cycle' again.

## **A E** The structure of the review

The final review should cover three distinct areas (*although presented under one heading*):

1. an introduction to the research area
2. evidence of research relating to your evaluation
3. discussion of your proposed method for improving performance, based on the research presented in the review.

## Introduction

Although it is probable that the reader of your project will be knowledgeable about the topic you are investigating, you still need to 'set the scene' for them

### First part

Firstly you should give a general introduction by restating the aspects of performance you wish to work on to bring about an improvement in performance, ie, rather than simply stating that your project is investigating the effects of anxiety on performance, you should try to place the investigation into context. For example:

*Coaches are always striving to find ways to enhance the performance of their athletes. As the gap between first and second place becomes even smaller, it is essential that the coach examines all possible areas for improvement. In recent years this has led to an increase in studies concerned with the psychology of sports performance, and in particular the relationship between arousal, anxiety and performance.*

The reader should be given a clear idea of your choice of topic and its relevance to the course you are studying.

## Second part

Secondly you should give some *brief* background information to the topic; for example:

*Theories relating to the relationship originated with the Drive Theory and have continued to be developed as greater knowledge and understanding has been acquired. In more recent years Hanin presented his theory called Zones of Optimal Functioning. He established that …*

In this way the reader is being provided with the necessary background information so that they may understand the direction of your project and its connection to existing theory.

## Third part

Thirdly you should give a brief introduction to the nature of the problem you will be researching; for example:

*It would appear therefore that athletes have an optimal state anxiety which will vary from individual to individual. Knowledge of the athlete's own specific optimal zone of state anxiety would presumably be of great interest to the coach. This study attempts to examine whether it is possible to identify an individual's optimal zone of state anxiety and keep them in this zone, thereby improving their performance.*

Can you identify the problem statement?)

By the end of the introduction the reader should have a clear idea about the area of theory being dealt with and the purpose of the project. It should lead them gently into the remainder of the review section which examines existing theory in more depth.

The introduction should not be lengthy – a side of A4 (or less) is normally sufficient.

## Evidence of research

Depending on the research problem you may need to give operational definitions at this point; ie, explain the terms or concepts you are using. For example, if discussing the effects of fatigue, an explanation of the types and causes of fatigue may be given in the review section (although a clear explanation of your working definition of the subject's fatigued state must also be given in the method section). It might be appropriate to give more than one definition where different interpretations of the term exist; for example, if discussing fitness you might give examples of the different types before establishing which particular aspect you were concerned with.

## KEY TERM

An **operational definition** is an explanation of the meaning of a specific term in the context of your experiment. For example, your study might be investigating the effects of different motivational techniques on delaying fatigue. Although we all have an idea of the meaning of the term fatigue, this isn't concrete enough. We need to know how you will establish at what point the performer becomes fatigued. You might decide that for this experiment a subject is fatigued once they are unable to stay with the 'bleep' in the Bleep Test, or when the performer achieves 80% of their maximum heart rate. Either explanation would be your operational definition of fatigue.

Once these terms have been explained the main analysis and synthesis of the research material should be recorded. The process of gathering and recording the research material is dealt with in fig 32.1, but the processing of this information and final output needs further explanation.

## Analysis

As mentioned above, repeating other people's work will not meet the review requirements. Once you have gathered and made notes on all sources of information you require, you need to analyse it so that you understand the concepts involved. Armed with a greater understanding of the topic, you then synthesise the information; ie, you bring together the individual items of research into a coherent whole, looking for similarities and differences amongst the information you have gathered. This is not an easy task; you need to find a way to break the research up into manageable chunks, and group the information you have found.

## Synthesis

One approach is to look for concepts within your investigation. For example, if looking into the effects of massed versus distributed practice, it would be simpler to deal with one type of practice first; begin with a definition of its meaning, based on the ideas of the majority of the research references, but comment where there appears to be disagreement or inconsistencies. Next you could establish the situations where its use appears to be most and least successful, looking for consensus and differences of opinion among researchers.

Once you have pursued all aspects of that form of practice, repeat the process for the other type of practice. You could also look out for any overlap between the types of practice. In this way you can bring together the work of different people rather than keeping it separate, and demonstrate your understanding. You must, however, remember to make specific references to the original authors when making a point, so that the reader knows that your comments are substantiated by acknowledged experts in the field, and are not simply your thoughts and feelings on the subject.

## Conclusions

If the synthesis is thorough, an overall picture of the available research should emerge, making conclusions a fairly straightforward process. Once this is completed you should be in a position to write a structured and logical review (output).

# Linking research to proposed method (A2 only)

You need to make sure that you can relate the theory to your intended work so that a link develops between the review and your resultant hypothesis and design. For example, if you are trying to improve a basketball player's success rate at set shots you may research others' work on the effectiveness of massed versus distributed practice. If your research reveals that for the standard of your performer massed practice is thought to be most beneficial, then this type of practice should be used in your method.

Although it is not a requirement at AS (Edexcel) to formulate a method, you do need to discuss your findings in your review and formulate hypotheses about the relevance of your research to practical performance, thus this would still be a useful exercise for you.

# A E Reporting of method (A2)

This section looks at the style that should be employed when writing the method section and its content; thus it covers the third and fourth phases of the project development in fig 31.1 – formulating the method and explaining its relevance (AS); formulating the methods and hypotheses; implementing the method and collecting post-test data (A2).

# Hypothesis (A2 only)

At the end of the review section, or beginning of the method section, you should specify the research problem in a concise manner. This is achieved through formulating and then recording hypotheses, which are statements about the relationship between at least two variables.

For example, if the problem being investigated was:

*'an investigation into the effects of a local muscular endurance training programme on accuracy of service'*

then the hypotheses associated with this problem might be as follows:

*A – Service accuracy would improve as a result of a local muscular endurance training programme.*

*B – There will be no significant difference in service accuracy after a period of local muscular endurance training.*

---

## KEY WORD

A **variable** in an experiment is something which can be changed or altered while other aspects of the experiment remain constant. For example, the method of providing feedback to a performer could be varied during an experiment, as could their level of performance, while the task they were completing (a specific move) remained the same.

---

The variables in these statements are service accuracy and the training programme.

Both of these hypotheses should be included, although apparently conflicting. They represent two of the types that can be used in project work, a summary of which is given below:

## Research hypothesis

All hypotheses are research hypotheses, thus any statement about the predicted outcome of an investigation could be called the research hypothesis. For example, a study looking into sports participation by school children and school leavers might have the following hypothesis:

*Year 12 pupils will spend a greater amount of time participating in sporting activities than their 16-year-old counterparts who have left school.*

The variables here are amount of time spent participating in physical activity and age.

## Experimental hypothesis

This is the name given to hypotheses when they refer to the predicted outcome of an experiment. Therefore projects containing an experiment will have experimental hypotheses. (Projects without an experimental design, for example those using surveys or interviews as a means to collect data, are not classified as experimental, thus they have research hypotheses rather than experimental.)

## Directional/one-tailed hypothesis

These predict the direction of the outcome of the investigation, for example:

*The use of verbal feedback in the learning of a basic netball skill will result in an increase in performance.*

## Two-tailed hypothesis

The direction of the outcome of the investigation is not predicted. The hypothesis simply states that there will be an effect, thus the example above would now read:

*The use of verbal feedback in the learning of a basic netball skill will have an effect on the subject's performance.*

## Null hypothesis

This is the prediction that the variables will have no effect, ie, that any changes in results are due to

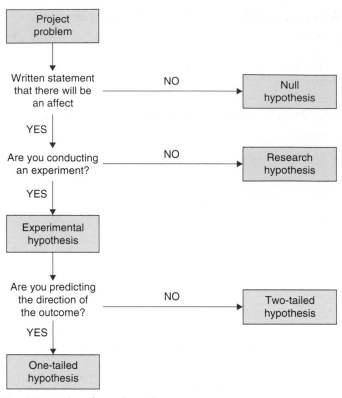

Fig 32.2. Classifying hypotheses

chance. Using the above example, this would become:

*The use of verbal feedback in the learning of a basic netball skill will have no effect on performance.*

See fig 32.2: to test your understanding categorise hypotheses A and B on p 793 and the examples given in table 32.1. (You will need to decide from the statement the way the data is likely to be collected). Answers are given in table 32.2.

Table 32.1. Classifying hypotheses

| Hypothesis | Type |
|---|---|
| A | |
| B | |
| 1. women's sports events receive a different amount of newspaper coverage to men's; | |
| 2. the number of women's football clubs in my area is unaffected by the local development plan; | |
| 3. reaction time of 100 m sprinters will improve as a result of sound stimuli training; | |
| 4. fatigue will affect the quality of a backhand drop shot in the game of squash; | |
| 5. economic factors have led to the majority of first division rugby clubs using shared grounds; | |
| 6. the use of verbal feedback in the learning of a basic basketball skill will affect performance; | |
| 7. more fouls will be committed by Premiership standard football players during tournament matches than league games; | |
| 8. a greater number of year 7 pupils (age 11) will participate in extra-curricular sport sessions than those in years 9 and 11 (age 13 and 15); | |
| 9. there will be no significant difference in the $\dot{V}O_2$ max of race walkers and middle distance runners; | |
| 10. socio-economic grouping will have an affect on the types of sports participated in. | |

Table 32.2. Classifying hypotheses – answers

| |
|---|
| A  EXPERIMENTAL hypothesis (one-tailed) |
| B  NULL hypothesis |
|   1.  RESEARCH hypothesis (two-tailed) |
|   2.  NULL hypothesis |
|   3.  EXPERIMENTAL hypothesis (one-tailed) |
|   4.  EXPERIMENTAL hypothesis (two-tailed) |
|   5.  RESEARCH hypothesis (one-tailed) |
|   6.  EXPERIMENTAL hypothesis (two-tailed) |
|   7.  RESEARCH hypothesis (one-tailed) |
|   8.  RESEARCH hypothesis (one-tailed) |
|   9.  NULL hypothesis |
|  10.  RESEARCH hypothesis (two-tailed) |

When recording your hypotheses, you need only state whether they are research, experimental or null. You need to know whether they are one-tailed or two-tailed if you are going to carry out statistical tests, but this information is not recorded at this stage.

As mentioned above, a hypothesis is a statement about the relationship between at least two different variables: the **dependent** variable or **independent** variable. See table 32.3.

When drawing up your research hypothesis ensure that it:

- leads naturally from your review
- is concise
- contains an independent and dependent variable
- is testable.

## KEY TERM

The **independent variable** is used to see if it is related to the dependent variable, eg, a specific method of providing feedback. You can control this variable.

### ACTIVITY 1

You observed and analysed a club basketball player. They were very skilful in practice, but made a significant number of errors during important matches. Your evaluation was that they needed to learn to control their level of arousal and so you devised a stress management programme for them.

- State your likely hypothesis.
- State the corresponding null hypothesis.
- What would the dependent variable be?
- What would the independent variable be?
- Is the hypothesis likely to be an experimental or research hypothesis?

Table 32.3. Dependent and independent variables

| Hypothesis | Dependent variable | Independent variable |
|---|---|---|
| 1. the number of women's football clubs in my area is unaffected by the local development plan; | No of women's football clubs | Local development plan |
| 2. reaction time of 100 m sprinters will improve as a result of sound stimuli training; | Reaction time | Sound stimuli training |
| 3. fatigue will affect the quality of a backhand drop shot in the game of squash; | Quality of backhand drop | Level of fatigue |

*(Continued)*

Table 32.3. (*Continued*)

| Hypothesis | Dependent variable | Independent variable |
|---|---|---|
| 4. economic factors have led to the majority of first division rugby clubs using shared grounds; | No of clubs using shared grounds | Economic factors |
| 5. the use of verbal feedback in the learning of a basic basketball skill will affect performance; | Performance level | Verbal feedback |
| 6. more fouls will be committed by Premiership standard football players during tournament matches than league games; | No of fouls committed | Type of match |
| 7. a greater number of year 7 pupils (age 11) will participate in extracurricular sport sessions than those in years 9 and 11 (age 13 and 15); | No of pupils participating | Age |
| 8. there will be no significant difference in the $\dot{V}O_2$ max of race walkers and middle distance runners; | $\dot{V}O_2$ levels | Type of athlete |
| 9. socio-economic grouping will have an affect on the types of sports participated in; | Types of sports participated in | Socio-economic group |
| 10. women's sports events receive a different amount of newspaper coverage to men's. | Amount of newspaper coverage | Gender of participant |

Table 32.4. Progress report

| Task | Completed ✓ | Still to do ✗ |
|---|---|---|
| Extensive and relevant notes from texts | | |
| Extensive and relevant notes from newspapers/magazines/journals | | |
| Extensive and relevant notes from the internet or other sources | | |
| Record of sources used for reference/bibliography | | |

**ACTIVITY 2**

# 33. Method

## Chapter introduction

At A2 the method is implemented in order to establish whether there has been any improvement in performance. To demonstrate this you must ensure that you have devised some way of measuring it before implementing your method. The results from this pre-test can then be compared to the post-test results, once you have completed your investigation.

It is likely therefore that you will need to adopt a repeated measures design.

After reading this chapter you should know:

- The difference between a related and unrelated experimental design
- Which type of design you should use for your coursework
- How to write up a method.

## **A** **E** Experimental designs

These may be categorised into related or unrelated designs, which refer to the subjects used:

- **Related designs** – when the same subjects are used for the whole of the experiment (repeated measures); when this isn't appropriate, 'doubles' are used. Subjects are matched with another using relevant criteria – one completing one part of the experiment while their double completes the other (matched pairs).

- **Unrelated designs** – when no attempt is made to match subjects. They might involve just one subject (single subject design), or groups who have not been matched (independent samples).

Each design type has its own advantages and disadvantages. You need to select the most appropriate for your experiment to ensure you obtain data relevant to your hypothesis.

## Repeated measures

In this type of design the experimental group are tested before and after the experimental treatment

(see fig 33.1). For example, if investigating the possible effect of a stress management programme on performance of set shots during match situations, performance will be tested before starting the programme and then again once the programme has

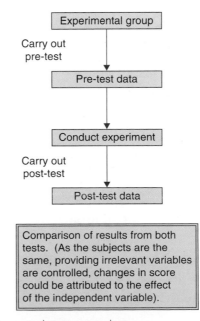

Fig 33.1. Repeated measures design

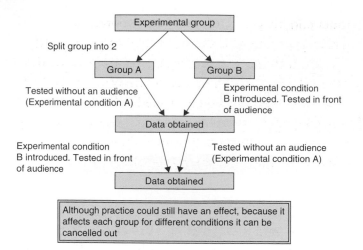

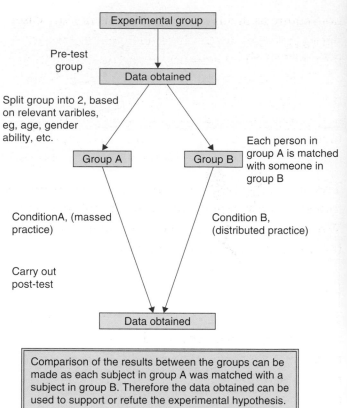

Fig 33.2. Repeated measures design using counter-balancing. Although practice could still have an effect, it can be cancelled out because it affects each group for different conditions

been completed. Data is collected from the same group twice in the form of a pre- and post-test.

The main disadvantage of this test is that the subjects may improve their performance due to practice. This is potentially overcome by counterbalancing: one of the possible ways of achieving this is shown in fig 33.2. (Although in the example given counterbalancing would not be an option.)

## Matched pairs

This method has the advantage that different subjects are used in each condition, therefore the data obtained will not be affected by practice. It does present other problems though: you must ensure that each member of group A is matched with a subject in group B. Careful selection of subjects is therefore required, plus an understanding of the important variables for the experiment.

An example of the design is shown in fig 33.3. A possible experimental hypothesis for this type of design would be that distributive practice will be more effective than massed practice in improving the success rate of basketball lay-ups. In other words, it provides the opportunity to measure the effects of more than one condition.

Fig 33.3. Matched pairs. Comparison of the results between the groups can be made as each subject in group A was matched with a subject in group B. Therefore the data obtained can be used to support or refute the experimental hypothesis

## Independent samples

This design involves the use of two different groups of subjects who have not been specifically matched. The advantages here are that it saves time trying to find 'like pairs' of subjects, and means there will be no practice or order effect. The obvious disadvantage is that the data obtained may be due to the independent variable or due to the differences in the individuals between the groups. One way of attempting to overcome this problem would be to allocate subjects at random to each of the groups, although this might still be ineffective.

## A E Writing up the method section

At first this might appear to be a less significant part of the project, and consequently one which does not require as much attention. This is not the case! Writing up your method provides the reader with information about your design and an explanation of the design decisions that you have made. Thus not only will you be gathering marks for your write-up in this section, but also for your choice of method, ie, the means by which you attempted to gain the necessary data to support your hypothesis.

The method section can be presented in continuous format, or broken down into separate sub-headings. Whichever format you prefer you should ensure that it contains the following information:

# Operational definitions

These are not always necessary, but it is a good idea to look at the dependent variable in your research/experiment hypothesis and decide if it requires defining in this way. Which of the dependent variables listed in table 32.4 would you give operational definitions? For example, do you know exactly what is meant in the following hypotheses:

- number 3: What exactly is a quality shot?
- number 5: How is performance being measured?
- number 6: What constitutes a foul?

The independent variable does not normally require an operational definition as a greater explanation of it is automatically given when writing up the method section. For example, the independent variable for hypothesis number 3 is level of fatigue. During the course of the write-up, you would probably explain how to induce the different levels of fatigue required, thus giving a working definition.

## An outline of the design adopted

You need to state the nature of the experimental design. Why did you select this particular research method and what were the conditions that the research was carried out under? What are the independent and dependent variables? What irrelevant variables have you managed to control? If you want to measure the effect of the

independent variable, remove the potential irrelevant variables; you need therefore to identify them and then control their effects by keeping them out of the project where possible.) What irrelevant variables could not be controlled? (There will be some beyond your control. If you are aware of them, their possible effects can be examined in the discussion section of the project.)

## Irrelevant variable

These are variables which are irrelevant to the investigation, but which might have an effect. For example, the weather would be irrelevant to a study concerned with the effectiveness of types of practice and distance thrown in the discus. However, although irrelevant it could affect the results of the study if the pre-test session was held on a calm day, and the post-test session on a very windy day. This irrelevant variable would need to be controlled, possibly by carrying out the tests at the same time, or by moving the tests inside.

Try to remember that this section should not give details about how the data was collected, but why it was collected in the manner it was. It should outline the design decisions that you made so that you could collect data appropriate to your hypothesis.

# Outlining equipment, materials and resources

You need to include sufficient detail so that the investigation could be replicated; leave out unnecessary detail which states the obvious. For example, detail regarding the number of basketballs required would be useful, but information about the pencil the researcher uses to record the scores would not! Specifications of specific equipment should be given and if commercial items are used the source of such items should be listed (eg, Multi-Stage Fitness Test, Loughborough University). If conducting an experiment, a diagram or photograph of the lay-out might also be useful. If you have designed a data collection sheet or questionnaire a copy of this should also be included.

# A precise and full account of the procedure adopted

The procedure should be described with sufficient clarity that the experiment could be duplicated accurately by the reader. Try to describe exactly what happened from the start of the experiment to the finish. The most common problem here is lack of relevant detail. Include any standardised instructions, ie, any instructions given to each participant, or those participants within a specific group. For example, if teaching a lay-up shot in basketball using massed and distributed practice, what were the common coaching points given to the performers? Exactly what format did the practice sessions take? Were all performers present at the same time? If not, where were they? You must ensure the reader is left in no doubt about the procedure that was adopted.

The bulk of the information for this part of the project should already be available to you from the planning stages. It might be necessary, however, to alter some of your initial plans in the light of research you carried out while compiling the literature review. For example, you might have decided to investigate the effects of an audience on an accuracy task, believing that your subject would perform better if trained in front of a large audience. Further research as a result of compiling the review may have thrown some doubts on your original beliefs. As a consequence you may decide to alter your design, selecting a small supportive audience to begin with before progressing onto a larger, unknown audience, now that you have a greater awareness of the variables that can influence your results. This is to be expected so don't worry if your design has changed since the planning stage.

The experimental design and procedure should be written in standard academic prose – in the third person and past tense. For example, rather than writing:

*I instructed the player to hit the twenty golf balls to get the ball to stop as close to the marker as possible. Then I measured the distance of each ball from the marker.*

a more acceptable format would be:

*The subject was instructed to hit twenty golf balls using his normal swing, so that the ball came to rest as close to the marker as possible. The distance of each ball from the marker was then measured.*

Once you are satisfied that you have recorded all the necessary information you should move on to analyse your results. This is dealt with in the next chapter.

---

Check your progress by filling in table 33.1
Table 33.1. Progress report

| Task | Completed ✓ | Still to do ✗ |
|---|---|---|
| Stated research hypothesis arising from research | | |
| Stated null hypothesis | | |
| Considered irrelevant variables | | |
| Recorded main items of equipment/resources required | | |
| Written up the procedure to improve performance IN DETAIL | | |
| Explained why the method would bring about the desired outcome | | |

ACTIVITY 1

# 34. The Results (A2)

## Chapter introduction

This chapter discusses ways to address the final phase of the project (see fig 31.1) – how to analyse the results. The chapter begins by giving a general overview of some of the methods that could be employed to analyse your data, and then discusses ways in which your data could be organised and presented. Examples are also given of students' work to illustrate some of the points made.

After reading this chapter you should:

- Know the difference between raw data, descriptive statistics and inferential statistics
- Understand that different types of data need to be 'treated' differently
- Know the difference between nominal, ordinal and interval data
- Know how to present data.

## A E Data analysis

Once you have gathered your data, it needs to be analysed in order to support or refute your hypotheses. In other words it is not sufficient to leave it in its 'raw' form. The purpose of data analysis is to organise your data in such a way that it can be summarised and easily interpreted by the reader. Analysis can be through the use of descriptive or inferential statistics.

### Raw data

This means data collected from the research experiment which has not undergone any refinement. For example, if you use a written questionnaire to collect data from a group of 30 people, each person's written response would form part of the raw data. If conducting a match analysis of several badminton matches, the data sheets from each match would be the raw data. Raw data is all the data that you collect.

### Descriptive statistics

These allow you to organise your raw data into a more easily readable and understandable form. For example, rather than merely listing 20 subjects, raw scores the scores could be presented in graphical form or frequency distribution tables. Descriptive statistics also allow you to summarise your data, commonly using the mean, median and the mode depending on the type of data you have acquired.

### Inferential statistics

Given the probable nature of your investigation, it is unlikely that you would use inferential statistics, check the assessment criteria for your subject before pursuing further. They are included here for completeness.

Inferential statistics are used to infer or imply that the results gained from an experiment using a relatively small sample of subjects would be the same even if a larger group were used. For example if you found that distributive practice resulted in greater improvements in performance of say, the forehand drive in squash, and this was supported by the use of inferential statistics, then you could assume that this would be the case for all groups with the same characteristics as the subjects in your sample.

Unfortunately you cannot choose any statistical method for your results. The nature of your research question and the data you collect will affect your choice. For example, someone researching a possible relationship between ethnic grouping and sports participated in would be unlikely to use the same method to analyse their results as someone measuring the effects of a training schedule on performance. The reason for this is that the data, although numerical in both cases, is actually of different types; so that there are different mathematical rules governing what can be done to it. Table 34.1 contains different types of data that might be recorded while carrying out a research project.

While the data gained from table 34.1 is written as numbers, the numbers cannot all be mathematically manipulated in the same way. For example, it is possible to subtract the losing team's score shown in '3' from the winning team's score to establish their winning margin. The resulting figure would make sense in the context of the statement, ie, the winning team won by a margin of 13 points. This makes sense, but the same mathematical manipulation of the figures shown in '1' would not: if you subtracted the '1' representing playing every day from the '3' representing once a week, the answer would be '2'. This number would be meaningless in terms of the initial question asked. Thus different types of numbers have different allowable manipulations that can be performed on them if a meaningful result is to be obtained. The allowable types of manipulation are based on whether the numbers are categorised as nominal, ordinal or interval. These categories are explained below. You must ensure that you know the type or level of data you are collecting so that you choose an appropriate statistical method to summarise your data.

Table 34.1. Different types of data

| 1. | Write 1 if you play every day, 2 for every other day, 3 for once a week |
|----|----|
| 2. | 45% of the audience agreed that this was a better match than last week |
| 3. | The home team won 28–15 |
| 4. | 50 people said that while they preferred hockey to football they still liked badminton the best |
| 5. | There was a total of $12 \text{ cm}^2$ of women's sports coverage in local papers that week |
| 6. | The fastest time was 10.25 seconds |
| 7. | The furthest distance was 15.50 metres |

# Nominal data

These are numbers which are used as a convenient means of categorising data. Nominal data often occurs in questionnaires. For example:

### Question 1

*State the number that represents the type of school you attended:*

1. Comprehensive   2. Grammar   3. Technical
4. Church          5. Private    6. Boarding
7. Other

### Question 2

*State the number/s that represent the different types of sport you have participated in during school physical education lessons:*

1. Netball      2. Football     3. Rugby
4. Hockey       5. Basketball   6. Badminton
7. Squash       8. Tennis       9. Swimming
10. Athletics   11. Other

The responses to the questions are really only shorthand labels, used to represent the different categories. Nominal scales do not therefore have size or order. Results using this scale cannot be mathematically manipulated (ie, use of addition, division etc.). For example, the '9' representing swimming above cannot be compared to the '7' representing squash in the way we would normally compare numbers – the '9' does not mean that swimming is bigger, better, or worth more than squash! Despite this, nominal data is still useful in those projects where categories of answers need to be recorded. If your data is nominal, tables 34.2 and 34.3 show some of the allowable types of manipulation on this data.

Table 34.2. Example of descriptive statistics allowable on this nominal data

| Type | Comments |
|------|----------|
| Mode | Allowable as it does not change the categories, but simply states the most frequently occurring one |

Table 34.3. Example of inferential statistical test allowable on nominal data

| Type | Comments |
|------|----------|
| Sign test | Experiment must have a related design so that pairs of scores may be used |
| Chi-squared | The data must be unrelated |

# Ordinal

Unlike nominal data, ordinal data does have an implied order. For example, the numbers assigned to athletes to represent their placing after a race are ordinal, as it is possible to tell from the data the order that the athletes crossed the line. Data obtained from the following question would also be ordinal:

**Question 3**

*Place the following sports in order of preference:*
*Badminton*
*Squash*
*Cricket*
*Volleyball*

Ordinal data still does not contain size: although we know which activity subjects prefer, we cannot tell from the data how much they prefer one activity over another.

Ordinal data can result from questionnaires; eg, where subjects are asked to rank activities, their attitudes and so on; or in more traditional experimental projects where the researcher 'invents' a scale to measure a subject's performance. For example, a researcher might divide a football goal into sections as in fig 34.1. The subject would be allocated points depending in which section they managed to strike the ball. In this way the pre-test scores of the subject could be compared with their post-test scores.

This type of data is still classified as ordinal as it is not possible to measure the exact difference between scores. Look at fig 34.2: three subjects' shots at goal are recorded, in which subject X scores 59, subject Z scores 58 and subject Y scores 70. From these scores we can place the players in order:

1. Subject Y: 70 points
2. Subject X: 59 points
3. Subject Z: 58 points

We cannot, however, say exactly how much better one player was than another, as the scale used is not precise enough. It could be argued from the raw data

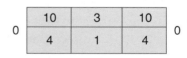

Fig 34.1. Points allocation based on researchers' divisions of football goal area

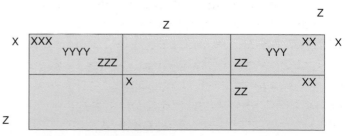

Fig 34.2. Areas hit by subjects

shown in fig 34.2 that subject X and subject Y were much closer in terms of performance (the discrepancy between scores was 11), than they were to subject Z, despite the apparent closeness of X's and Z's scores. As a result of this, the statistics that can be applied to this type of data are still restricted.

## Interval

This type of data allows an additional level of measurement to be carried out. It is allowable because this type of data not only gives an implied

order to results obtained, but also uses a scale where the intervals between each value along the scale are identical in size. For example, suppose a researcher is measuring the effects of different types of feedback on accuracy of a golf putt. If the researcher measures the exact distance the ball rests from the pin (rather than banding as in the football example above) under different experimental conditions, any arithmetic operation can be carried out because the data recorded is interval – the scale used when measuring distance uses equal intervals (the distance between 1.4 m and 2.4 m will be the same as the distance between 4.4 m and 5.4 m).

To check your understanding of the different categories of data, complete activity 1.

Table 34.4. Example of descriptive statistics allowable on ordinal data

| Type | Comments |
|------|----------|
| Mode | Allowable as it does not change the categories, but simply states the most frequently occurring one |
| Median | States the middle number of the resultant ordered list (in the above example the median would have been 59) |

Table 34.5. Example of inferential statistical test allowable on ordinal data, in addition to that stated above for nominal data

| Type | Comments |
|------|----------|
| Wilcoxon (T) signed ranks test | Experiment must have related design |
| Mann-Whitney (U) Test | Experiment must have an unrelated design |
| Wilcoxon rank sum test | Experiment must have an unrelated design |
| Spearman's p correlation coefficient | Used to establish a correlation between variables. Data is in the form of related pairs |

**ACTIVITY 1**

Classify the following types of data:

- Answer to a questionnaire about preferred sports:
  7 badminton
  12 soccer
  3 squash
  10 hockey
- 1st, 2nd and 3rd place in an athletics event.
- Number of points scored in a basketball match.
- Numbers used to represent playing positions in a rugby team.
- Time taken to complete a task.
- Rank order of players in terms of ability.
- Actual distance thrown in an athletic competition.
- Measures of 'quality': Marks out of 5 for the 'nearness' to the basket – 5 points if the basket is scored, 3 if it hits the rim, 1 if it hits the backboard.
- Survey of local newspapers to establish media coverage of 6 different sports activities, using the following classification:
  1. men's football 2. women's football
  3. men's hockey 4. women's hockey
  5. men's tennis 6. women's tennis
- Lane numbers used to represent lanes on an athletics track.

Table 34.6. Example of descriptive statistics allowable on this interval data

| Type | Comments |
|------|----------|
| Mode | Allowable as it does not change the categories, but simply states the most frequently occurring one |
| Median | States the middle number of the resultant ordered list (in the above example the median would have been 59) |
| Mean | States the mathematical average of a set of scores |
| Standard deviation | Gives an estimate of the difference of the scores of a particular group from the mean |

Table 34.7. Example of inferential statistical tests allowable on interval data, in addition to those given for nominal and ordinal data

| Type | Comments |
|------|----------|
| T-test for related sample | Experiment must have related design |
| T-test for unrelated designs | Experiment must have an unrelated design |
| Pearson's r correlation coefficient | Used to establish a correlation between variables |
| | Data is in the form of related pairs |

## Organisation and presentation of data

Once you have established the type of data you have collected and analysed it, you need to consider how to organise and present it so that it is easy to understand. There are many ways of doing this, and

Table 34.8a and b. Number of points scored by each subject (in subject order), experimental condition: (a) reaction test scores when single response was required (b) reaction test scores when a choice of responses was required

(a)

| 28 | 15 | 28 |
|----|----|----|
| 25 | 23 | 28 |
| 40 | 34 | 40 |
| 19 | 18 | 28 |
| 40 | 45 | 25 |

(b)

| 14 | 10 | 15 |
|----|----|----|
| 13 | 13 | 13 |
| 28 | 15 | 13 |
| 8 | 10 | 15 |
| 26 | 26 | 13 |

part of your task will be to select an appropriate method.

## Raw data

This can be included in the results section if it is not too bulky. (For example, you would not include all 100 of your questionnaire returns, or 50 match analysis sheets! But you should not discard this material; keep it in case it needs to be viewed by the person assessing your project.)

Non-bulky raw data can be represented in the results section in tabular form; tables 34.8a and 34.8b show scores gained by subjects during an experiment.

Although 'complete', data presented in this manner is not easy to interpret at a glance. The following are not immediately obvious: the range of scores, the most common scores or which experimental condition resulted in lower scores. Therefore organisation of data does not stop here. Data could be rearranged in one of several more meaningful forms, depending on what the experimenter is using it for. For example, frequency tables could be used.

# Frequency distribution of data

The presentation of data in table 34.9 has shown some progression. In other words it is easier for the reader to make sense of the results. This is because the data has been rearranged into numerical order and the number of times a particular score has been recorded is indicated in brackets. Therefore the

reader can see at a glance the range of scores, the most frequently occurring one and the condition when the lowest scores were achieved.

If there was a large range of scores it is also possible to produce grouped frequency distribution tables; for example, see tables 34.10 and 34.11.

Obviously you need not restrict yourself to the use of tables, a variety of graphs may be used equally effectively to organise your data, or a mixture of the two.

Project example 1 (see p 814) was produced by a student investigating whether 14 strides was the optimum run-up length (in terms of distance achieved) for 14-year-old novice long jumpers. Notice how they have displayed the raw data (table A1.1) and then developed this (tables A1.2 and A1.3) to highlight the critical aspect of the results in relation to their experimental hypothesis, ie, the length of run up which produced the furthest distance jumped and then a comparison with the distance achieved when using 14 strides. The table containing the raw data includes this information, but it is much easier to see in the subsequent tables. The student has then represented this data graphically (fig A.1) to reinforce the information. In project example 2, the student was investigating changes in aerobic fitness of race walkers as a result of an endurance training programme. Again they have included their raw data (pre-test and post-test levels achieved by each subject for the multi-stage

Table 34.9. Frequency distribution of data – number of times of occurrence indicated in bracket

| Single response | Choice of response |
|---|---|
| 15 (1) | 8 (1) |
| 18 (1) | 10 (2) |
| 19 (1) | 13 (5) |
| 23 (1) | 14 (1) |
| 25 (2) | 15 (3) |
| 28 (4) | 26 (2) |
| 34 (1) | 28 (1) |
| 40 (3) | |
| 45 (1) | |
| n 5 15 | n 5 15 |

Table 34.10. Single response scores

| Number of points | 1→10 | 11→20 | 21→30 | 31→40 | 41→50 |
|---|---|---|---|---|---|
| Number of subjects | 0 | 3 | 7 | 4 | 1 |

Table 34.11. Choice response scores

| Number of points | 1→10 | 11→20 | 21→30 | 31→40 | 41→50 |
|---|---|---|---|---|---|
| Number of subjects | 3 | 9 | 3 | 0 | 0 |

fitness test – tables A1.4 and A1.5) and from this they have used standard tables to predict the subjects' $\dot{V}O_2$ max. This information is also represented in table form – tables A1.6 and A1.7. They then condense this information by establishing the average $\dot{V}O_2$ max of each group of athletes (table A1.8), again supporting this table graphically (fig A1.2). They have then placed the subjects' performances in rank order and conducted an inferential statistical test on this data to see if there is a significant difference in the values achieved (table A1.9).

Whether you use descriptive or inferential statistics to analyse your data, it is important to complete each of the following steps:

1. Organise data into a form which is easy to read (remember to show progression).

2. Use descriptive statistics to summarise the important features of the data (by using an appropriate method for the type of data you have collected, as outlined above).

3. If necessary or desirable, carry out an appropriate statistical test using inferential statistics (as outlined above), to establish whether the results gained support your initial experimental hypothesis.

4. Make a simple statement of results at the end of the results section. The data collected from the experiment should have related to the project hypothesis/ses. If the results are inconsistent with your initial hypothesis, then that hypothesis should be refuted. If, however, the results are consistent, then the hypothesis should be accepted and the initial theory which you were examining, supported.

The value of recording quantitative data as well as qualitative data becomes apparent when trying to represent your results graphically. It is much easier to present a trend of figures rather than statements about performance (unless a questionnaire design has been used). If you have collected data throughout your method (for example, over a six-week period) this can also be shown graphically. The more data you have collected and can present the more you will have to discuss and base your conclusions on.

# 35. The Final Stages

## Chapter introduction

This chapter covers the remaining items you need to complete in order to finish your project. The discussion, conclusion and appraisal are all important aspects of the project and you will need time in order to complete them thoroughly. They provide you with the opportunity to demonstrate to the reader that you have understood the work you have undertaken and the implications of your results. To illustrate the points made, examples of students' work have been included.

After reading this chapter you should know:

- What to include in your discussion
- How to state your conclusion
- What to include in an appraisal.

## A E Discussion

At the end of the results section, you should have clearly stated the outcome of your experiment in relation to your original hypotheses. The discussion section should be used to justify to the reader why you rejected or accepted the hypotheses; you need to *interpret* your results. This means that you will have to examine and critically evaluate the findings of your study. You can achieve this by:

- commenting on the validity of your results (ie, did your method ensure that only the independent variable had any effect on your results, or were some other, previously unaccounted for, variables responsible?)

- explaining in words what your results mean (to supplement the graphical representation of data used in the results section)

- stating how the results relate to your original hypothesis

- commenting on the similarities/differences of your findings to accepted theories or results from similar experiments

- mentioning any inconsistencies or contradictions in the results and possible reasons for these. Remember, this should be a discussion; if possible try to present more than one potential explanation.

Try not to forget that the purpose of conducting the investigation was to establish the effect of one variable on another, eg, the effect of the independent variable on the dependent variable, such as the effect of distributed practice (independent variable) on achieving a 'length' forehand drive in squash (dependent variable). Your discussion should therefore reflect this, and you should comment on whether your results have shown a relationship between the variables under investigation, or whether some other variable is responsible for the results you obtained. For example, your investigation may have been based on using a particular type of feedback to optimise performance and unknown to you until later, at the same time your subject was receiving additional relevant training, which they had not been taking part in prior to your investigation. It would be difficult to establish, therefore, whether the improvement in performance was due to the type of feedback, or the additional training. See project example 4 (Appendix 1).

## A E Conclusion

This follows on from the discussion. It should be a brief summary of the outcome of the study confirming the findings stated at the end of the results section. It should be used to reiterate the relationship of the outcome to the hypotheses. See project examples 2 and 3 in Appendix 1.

## A E Appraisal

This is your opportunity to make further suggestions for modifications to the current method to further optimise performance. In other words during your discussion and conclusion you will have established whether there was any improvement in performance as a result of your method. You are now required to take this a step further forward, and indicate what you would do next to help the performer even more. This could be by making slight adjustments to the current method, or it could mean returning to your list of faults from your initial observation and tackling a new area. Whatever you choose, you must ensure that it is a logical progression based on the post-test results.

## A Bibliography

This should be recorded after your appraisal. Details regarding the format of the bibliography are given on p 776.

## A E Project completion

Before handing in the final version of your work make a couple of final checks. Make sure:

- It is neat – even if it is word processed this does not necessarily mean the work is neat. Check you have used the same font size and spacing throughout, and that you have not added any handwritten labels where you could have used a computer package.

- It is well written – flowing text, and no typing or spelling errors.

- It is well organised – a good idea is to follow the order of the assessment criteria, or the order given in this book.

- It has a variety of appropriate illustrations throughout – for example, you might include photographs of aspects of the observation of performance, diagrams or photographs of the method being implemented, tables and graphs of results, diagrams or photographs in the discussion section to illustrate a point of technique.

Once you are satisfied, it is time to hand the work in (and probably start your revision!).

## Further reading

H Coolican, *Research Methods and Statistics in Psychology* (Hodder & Stoughton, 1990)

MD Gall, WR Borg, JP Gall, *Educational Research, An Introduction* 6th edition (Longman, 1996)

J Green, M D'Oliveira, *Learning to Use Statistical Tests in Psychology* (Open University Press, 1982)

S Heyes, M Hardy, P Humphreys, P Rookes, *Starting Statistics in Psychology and Education: a Student Handbook* (Weidenfeld & Nicolson, 1986)

JR Morrow Jr, AW Jackson, JG Disch, DP Mood, *Measurement and Evaluation in Human Performance* (Human Kinetics, 1995)

JR Thomas, JC Nelson, *Research Methods in Physical Activity* 3rd edition (Human Kinetics, 1996)

WJ Vincent, *Statistics in Kinesiology* (Human Kinetics, 1995)

# 36. Synoptic Assessment

## Chapter introduction

This chapter gives an overview of synoptic assessment. Why it is required, what it is and how to approach it.

After reading this chapter you should:

- Understand the nature of synoptic assessment
- Know how to 'link' different aspects of your course to performance
- Understand the requirements of the AQA Synoptic Assignment.

## A E  Synoptic assessment

Now that A level Physical Education is modular, in theory it would be possible to study an aspect of your course, say anatomy and physiology, be examined in this during the first four months of study, and then never look at this area of work again. Some would argue that this made the qualification easier, so synoptic assessment was introduced.

Synoptic assessment forces you to revisit areas of the specification prior to your final examination. Synoptic assessment could be in one of two forms:

- part/all of a written paper completed as part of your final examination

- coursework.

Different boards will require different types of synoptic assessment, but they will all aim to test you in some way on all aspects of the specification. In addition to visiting all areas of work, the assessment should 'mix' content areas. For example, you might be taught the different components of the course by different teachers, and might be used to treating each subject area separately. You may have a folder

for physiology, a folder for social cultural issues and a folder for sports psychology. The synoptic assessment will require that you:

- know the content of all of these folders

- can link the content from all of these folders and apply them to practical activity.

For example, a question in the examination might ask you to discuss possible factors affecting a player's free throw ability in basketball. Your answer could include any/all of the following topics:

- Anatomy and Physiology:
  a) Biomechanical problems with the technique
  b) Application of forces
  c) Level of fitness
  d) Energy pathways.

- Social, Cultural:
  a) Opportunity to participate/train
  b) Implication of local sport organisation.

- Sports Psychology:
  a) Arousal
  b) Motivation
  c) Learned helplessness
  d) Personality.

It is important, therefore, that when you revise you try to link all elements of work:

- back to sport
- to each other.

One way of achieving this is to write a paragraph linking the topic you have just revised to a sport of your choice.

For example, if you have just completed work on Newton's laws you might apply this topic to a sprinter:

---

**First law** – sprinter has to overcome inertia in order to move off the blocks at the start of the race.

**Second law** – as the sprinter's mass will remain constant throughout the race, the only way to affect his/her momentum is through the application of force. The more force applied, the faster the sprinter will travel.

**Third law** – the sprinter applies a force backwards against the ground, which applies an equal and opposite ground reaction force onto the sprinter, propelling him/her forwards.

**Gravity** – gravity is forcing the performer down throughout the race.

---

This can then be developed by looking at summaries from other areas of the specification. Try answering the following questions; if you can, you have already got a good synoptic grasp of the specification!

---

- How does the performer's body type, physique, build affect his/her performance?
- What examples of antagonistic muscle action are there?
- Explain how one of the techniques involves the use of levers.
- What effects would training have on the performance?
- How would you classify the skills demonstrated?
- How does the concept of reaction time fit in?
- What sort of feedback would be appropriate to develop performance?
- How might negative and positive reinforcement affect performance?
- How could a training session be organised?
- Would guidance be useful?
- What effect has the National Curriculum had on this activity?
- How has this activity developed?
- How are athletes with disabilities catered for in this event?
- What energy sources are being used?
- What sort of attitude does the performer have and why?
- How might the performer attribute their success/failure?

---

Synoptic assessment could also be through coursework. In the case of AQA you are required to complete a synoptic assignment. This involves writing a 1,000–3,000 word essay which links six different topic areas of the specification to a performance that you have observed (again it could be based on the observation you made for your practical/project coursework).

# A Synoptic assignment

To gain high marks for this assignment you have to make sure that the areas you decide to discuss are relevant to the performance that you have observed.

For example, if you observed a beginner at trampolining it is unlikely you would discuss group dynamics and social loafing as factors affecting the performance as these are more related to team sports.

It is also important that you keep relating back to the observed performance so that the examiner can assess your level of understanding. There is little point in simply reproducing the theory from books,

it must be applied. For example, application of force is very important in trampolining, but rather than restating Newton's laws and work on forces, it should be repeated and applied.

Where appropriate you could use illustrations to help your explanation. The six topics you consider should be from across the specification, ie, they can not all be based on the physiological aspects of the course. Therefore you need to include work from modules one, two, four and five. The other two topic areas can be from any other area. For example, in the case of the trampolinist you might consider fig 36.1.

---

One of the observed faults was that the performer did not achieve sufficient height when completing the basic moves. Considering Newton's third law of motion which states that for every action there is an equal and opposite reaction the performer may not be applying sufficient force into the bed, thus the force generated from the bed is insufficient to gain the required height. Lack of height may also be due to …

---

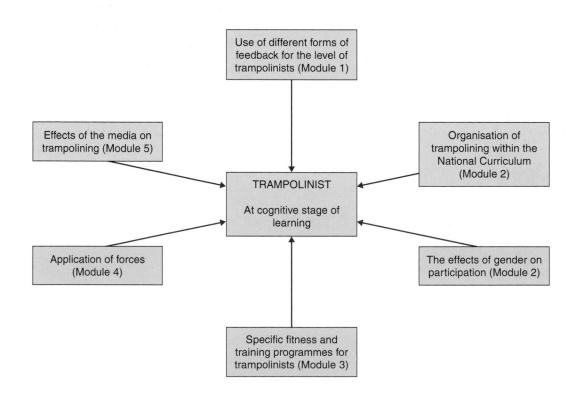

Fig 36.1.

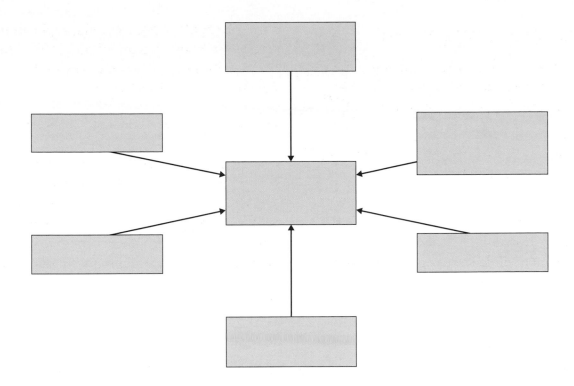

Fig 36.2.

Complete fig 36.2 with appropriate topics for your observation.

Remember you only have to write between 1,000 to 3,000 words, and that this includes your introduction, in which you need to give a brief description of the performance. This means that you only need to write between 150 and 500 words per topic.

Work for the synoptic assignment can be prepared in the same way as your revision for the synoptic question paper as explained above.

Finally, as with all coursework, you should ensure that it is well organised and neatly presented. As it is coursework, don't forget you can show your assignment to your teachers and they can suggest improvements before sending your work off for marking. If you are going to take advantage of this you must ensure you start your assignment early to allow time for feedback.

# Appendix 1  Project examples
## Contributions from Kevin Middleton and Stuart Monk

## Project example 1

Table A1.1. Raw data

| Subject no. | Sex | Age | Height (m) | Weight (Kg) | Take off foot | Length of inside leg (cm) | Length of stride (cm) | 6 Strides (m) | 10 Strides (m) | 14 Strides (m) | 18 Strides (m) | 22 Strides (m) |
|---|---|---|---|---|---|---|---|---|---|---|---|---|
| 1 | m | 14 | 1.60 | 44 | Right | 81 | 90 | 4.50 | 4.90 | 5.05 | 5.08 | 4.72 |
| 2 | m | 14 | 1.67 | 44 | Left | 78 | 85 | 3.20 | 4.00 | 4.40 | 4.45 | 3.95 |
| 3 | m | 14 | 1.60 | 51 | Left | 84 | 95 | 3.30 | 3.53 | 3.60 | 3.90 | 3.70 |
| 4 | f | 14 | 1.49 | 51 | Left | 71 | 109 | 3.56 | 3.61 | 3.80 | 3.94 | 3.45 |
| 5 | f | 14 | 1.47 | 38 | Left | 67 | 90 | 3.03 | 3.70 | 3.95 | 3.96 | 3.20 |
| 6 | f | 14 | 1.52 | 57.5 | Left | 68 | 102 | 3.35 | 3.75 | 3.80 | 3.80 | 3.70 |

Table A1.2. Further distance jumped

| Subject no. | Best distance jumped (m) | Stride length |
|---|---|---|
| 1 | 5.08 | 18 |
| 2 | 4.45 | 18 |
| 3 | 3.90 | 18 |
| 4 | 3.94 | 18 |
| 5 | 3.96 | 18 |
| 6 | 3.80 | 18 |

Table A1.3. Distance achieved at 14 strides compared with furthest distance achieved

| Subject no. | 14 strides (m) | Furthest distance achieved at | Best distance jumped (m) | Difference (cm) |
|---|---|---|---|---|
| 1 | 5.05 | 18 strides | 5.08 | +.03 |
| 2 | 4.40 | 18 strides | 4.45 | +.05 |
| 3 | 3.60 | 18 strides | 3.90 | +30 |
| 4 | 3.80 | 18 strides | 3.94 | +14 |
| 5 | 3.95 | 18 strides | 3.96 | +.01 |
| 6 | 3.80 | 18 strides | 3.80 | – |

The data clearly shows that for these novices, 18 strides would appear to be the optimum with an overall average improvement of 8.8 cm (44.09 cm/6).

# Project example 2

## Investigation results

Tables A1.4 and A1.5 display the results obtained by all of the athletes taking part in the MSFT on both days, in terms of levels achieved alongside resting pulse rates.

The results are given, where bpm is equivalent to beats per minute, and the MSFT score is shown with the level first followed by the shuttle; ie, 10.7 where 10 is the level and 7 is the shuttle.

These results now require **transformation**, from the level/shuttle format that they are currently in to show the true level of $\dot{V}O_2$ max achieved by each athlete, to see if the experimental hypothesis stays true.

The transformation from the current form to the $\dot{V}O_2$ max format, is achieved using a booklet included with the MSFT package, which shows all the level/shuttles with the appropriate level

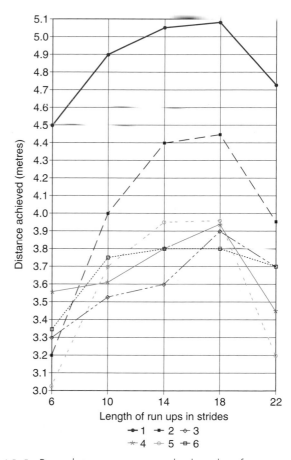

Fig A1.1. Raw data outcomes on the lengths of run ups

of $\dot{V}O_2$ max. This can be shown by two similar tables.

Again, $\dot{V}O_2$ max is measured as millilitres of oxygen per kilogram of body weight per minute. A statement of results can be expressed thus:

Table A1.4. Walkers' MSFT levels

| Subject no. | Resting pulse (bpm) | MSFT level |
|---|---|---|
| 1 | 72 | 9.8 |
| 2 | 72 | 14.3 |
| 3 | 80 | 10.7 |
| 4 | 70 | 14.4 |
| 5 | 76 | 9.0 |
| 6 | 76 | 10.7 |
| 7 | 72 | 12.6 |
| 8 | 68 | 15.1 |
| 9 | 76 | 11.0 |

Table A1.6. Walkers' $\dot{V}O_2$ max levels

| Subject no. | Predicted $\dot{V}O_2$ max |
|---|---|
| 1 | 45.8 |
| 2 | 61.1 |
| 3 | 48.7 |
| 4 | 61.7 |
| 5 | 43.3 |
| 6 | 48.7 |
| 7 | 55.4 |
| 8 | 64.0 |
| 9 | 50.2 |

Table A1.5. Walkers' MSFT levels (Post-test scores)

| Subject no. | Resting pulse | MSFT level |
|---|---|---|
| 1 | 68 bpm | 15.3 |
| 2 | 76 bpm | 13.2 |
| 3 | 78 bpm | 12.0 |
| 4 | 76 bpm | 12.0 |
| 5 | 80 bpm | 13.3 |
| 6 | 80 bpm | 12.0 |
| 7 | 72 bpm | 10.8 |
| 8 | 72 bpm | 10.8 |
| 9 | 70 bpm | 11.6 |

Table A1.7. Walkers' $\dot{V}O_2$ max levels

| Subject no. | Predicted $\dot{V}O_2$ max |
|---|---|
| 1 | 64.6 |
| 2 | 57.6 |
| 3 | 53.7 |
| 4 | 53.7 |
| 5 | 57.6 |
| 6 | 53.7 |
| 7 | 49.3 |
| 8 | 62.7 |
| 9 | 51.9 |

*Note:* The above results for the corresponding $\dot{V}O_2$ max levels to the MSFT levels, are in this instance given as $\dot{V}O_2$ max in: millilitres of oxygen per kilogram of body weight per minute, and are as calculated by Loughborough University.

The race walkers scored higher in the MSFT after the period of training. Therefore the experimental hypothesis:

*'A race walker will achieve a higher level on the MSFT after a period of endurance training.'*

is highlighted as being accepted prior to statistical analysis and average working, the next step to strengthen the validity of the experimental hypothesis.

## Statistical analysis of results

The validity of the results *may* become a lot clearer following the undergoing of some sort of statistical analysis. It must be remembered that inferential statistical tests do not 'prove' anything; they only indicate which of the two hypotheses is preferable

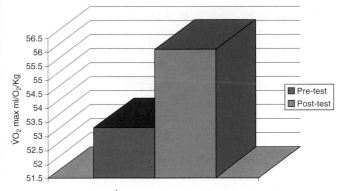

Fig A1.2. Average $\dot{V}O_2$ max values for race walkers

Table A1.8. Average $\dot{V}O_2$ max values for race walkers before and after training, measured in $ml/O_3/kg$ body weight

| Stage of experiment | Ave. $\dot{V}O_2$ |
|---|---|
| Pre-test results | 53.22 |
| Post-test results | 56.09 |
| Difference | $-2.87\,ml/O_2/Kg$ |

on the basis of the given data and are not the 'be-all and end-all' of the investigation conclusion. The hypotheses being analysed are:

*Null (H0): There will be no difference between the $\dot{V}O_2$ max scores of the race walkers after the period of training, as tested by the MSFT.*

*Experimental (H1): A race walker will reach a higher level of the MSFT after a period of training, thus having a higher $\dot{V}O_2$ max level.*

There are various statistical tests that are to mathematicians and biologists alike, which are suitable for this type of data analysis.

The test used in this instance will be the Mann-Whitney U-Test, a test for comparing two sets of data with null and experimental hypotheses linking them. The method used in the Mann-Whitney U-Test is set out using ranks and set formulae to link the sums of the ranks:

$Ua = Ra - \frac{1}{2}na(n + 1)$, & $Ub = Rb - \frac{1}{2}snb(n + 1)$, where 'a' and 'b' are the two sets of data, 'n' is the number of athletes in each group and 'R' is the sum of the ranks for that particular set of athletes.

The given answers or 'U' a and b, will then be compared and the smallest taken to be compared with a critical value from the Mann-Whitney U-Test table of critical values.

The test will commence thus:

Treating *all* of the data as a whole, rank the data from 1–18:

(*Note*: A signifies the walkers' pre-test data, B the walkers' post-test data.)

The results are given in the transformed $\dot{V}O_2$ max forms, where:

**Res** = result
**Ran** = rank
**Gro** = group

The ranks for A and B will now be summed thus:

$R(a) = 2 + 4 + 5 + 8 + 13 + 15.5 + 15.5 + 17 + 18\{ql\}$

{text} $R(a) = 98$

$R(b) = 1 + 3 + 6.5 + 6.5 + 10 + 10 + 10 + 12 + 14\{ql\}$

$R(b) = 73\{ql\}$

Now the values of Ua and Ub will be calculated using the formulae already given previously:

$Ua = Ra - \frac{1}{2}n(n + 1)$, where n is the number of terms
$Ua = 98 - \frac{1}{2} \times 9(9 + 1)$
$Ua = 98 - \frac{1}{2} \times 90$
$Ua = 98 - 45$
$Ua = 53$

$Ub = Rb - \frac{1}{2}n(n + 1)$, where n is the number of terms
$Ub = 73 - \frac{1}{2} \times 9(9 + 1)$
$Ub = 73 - \frac{1}{2} \times 90$
$Ub = 73 - 45$
$Ub = 28$

Table A1.9. Mann-Whitney U-test

| res | 64.6 | 64 | 62.7 | 61.7 | 61.1 | 57.6 | 57.6 | 55.4 | 53.7 | 53.7 | 51.9 | 50.2 | 49.3 | 48.7 | 48.7 | 45.8 | 43.3 | |
|-----|------|----|------|------|------|------|------|------|------|------|------|------|------|------|------|------|------|----|
| **ran** | 1 | 2 | 3 | 4 | 5 | 6.5 | 6.5 | 8 | 10 | 10 | 10 | 12 | 13 | 14 | 15.5 | 15.5 | 17 | 18 |
| **gro** | B | A | B | A | A | B | B | A | B | B | B | B | B | A | A | A | A | A |

The smallest value out of Ua and Ub is now selected from the two. This value (in this case it equals 28) is now compared to the **critical value** for the appropriate values of 'n' for both sets of athletes, in this instance 9.

From the Mann-Whitney Table of critical values, this value for 9 sets of data in both groups is equivalent to **17** degrees of freedom.

Mann-Whitney says that:

*'When the smallest value of U (28) is compared to the critical value for N a and b, if the U value is less than or equal to this critical value then the Null Hypothesis is rejected.'*

So:

$17 < 28$, so in this case the hypothesis:

*Null (H0): 'There will be no difference between the $\dot{V}O_2$ max scores of the race walkers after the period of training, as tested by the MSFT'*

is rejected, throwing further backing behind the experimental hypothesis to be true.

# Project example 3

## Discussion

The graphs clearly show an increase in the distance jumped as the length of the run up increased up to 18 strides. They also show a decrease in distance as the run up is increased further. The reason for the decrease after 18 strides could be that the run up may have been too long. This idea was put forward by Geoffrey Dyson, ie, that the length of run up is determined by the athlete's ability to accelerate at top speed at the board, without being tired out before take-off.

There were no anomalies in the raw data apart from subject 6 who achieved the same distance for both 14 and 18 strides. The reason for this could be that the subject had a long running stride which meant they would have a longer run up, in terms of metres covered compared to the other subjects. This may have made the run up too long for them.

Although the average improvement is shown as 8.8 cm, this could be misleading as this is due mainly to subjects 3 and 4; ie, their improvements were 30 cm and 14 cm. The other subjects' improvements were only marginal. Subjects 3 and 4 may have made such drastic improvements because they needed a longer run-up in order to reach their optimum speed off the board.

Closer inspection shows that subjects 1, 2 and 5 have achieved very similar distances and that they have only improved by a few centimetres unlike subjects 3 and 4. Thus although they did improve they must have had around their optimum run-up length.

Refer to tables A1.2–1.3 to review the theory that Roy Hawkey stated, ie, that a greater speed can be achieved through increasing the length of the run up, this would appear to be the case for subjects 1, 2, 3, 4 and 5 up to the 18 strides.

In conclusion these results clearly show that distance achieved is affected by run-up length. In all but one case the subjects showed improvement (although small in some instances, competitions could be won or lost on these types of differences). Therefore the experimental hypothesis:

$H_1$ = *The long jump distance achieved by 14-year-olds will be reduced when using a run-up less than 14 strides*

is accepted and $N_1$ rejected.

$H_2$ = *The long jump distance achieved by 14-year-olds will be reduced when using a run-up greater than 14 strides*

is rejected and therefore $N_2$ accepted.

# Project example 4
## Validity of the investigation

Before entering the mainstream discussion of the investigation, it is important to note that the experiment as a whole ran very smoothly and was an enjoyable task to have to carry out.

- The pattern that it followed was as easy to perform as the results were to interpret. Luck was obtained in that the weather conditions were near enough the same (give or take a slight change in the wind speed on one occasion), and that all of the athletes taking part were *fit* and *enthusiastic*, a vital factor in the successful running of an experiment of this particular nature.

- The investigation in general gave the required results that could undergo worthwhile comparison, possibly because of the factors mentioned above.

- The pre-test (basic 'training session' that the athletes were put through before the start of the MSFT) were well organised and ran smoothly on both occasions, while the MSFT was staged at the same time of day in both instances to avoid any correctable differences between the running of the two tests.

- The equipment used for the investigation is naturally very simplistic in design, and so was easy to set up and administer. The tape recording of the MSFT was heard amicably at *all* points of the shuttle in both directions by *all* of the athletes on *both* occasions that the test was run.

- The width of the track meant that competitors had to settle for less than one lane (6 lanes, 9 competitors), a small problem in design and procedure, but one that was easily dealt with by allocating each athlete their own 'space'.

- Of course it must be remembered that as each athlete dropped out more room was available so it was not that significant a design flaw.

As the investigation developed, the major design flaw encountered was in the way that the athletes' **final** MSFT level was collected. Athletes were requested to remember exactly what shuttle they were on, while the recording would indicate what level they had reached.

Fatigue as the test progressed may have meant that the athletes in both instances almost forgot what shuttle they were up to, until the recording indicated that a new level had begun.

None of the competitors indicated that this was an actual flaw in the investigation, but if the investigation were to be modified, a person would be assigned the job of counting every competitor's shuttles using a sheet like this running example (using numbers on each competitor's t-shirt).

Table A1.10 is shown as a worked example, where the athletes are numbered 1–9 as with the experiment in this instance.

The top row displays the levels of the MSFT, while the left-hand column shows the shuttles completed of that particular level. Thus, while the MSFT is running the grid reads downwards from the top left-hand corner. The / symbol indicates that no athletes dropped out on that particular shuttle, while the numbers in the boxes show the numbered athletes that *did* drop out on that shuttle: eg, athletes 4 and 6 dropped out on level 10, shuttle 7.

This would make the whole administration of the MSFT easier for both the invigilators and the athletes themselves, giving even less opportunity for experimental error in the results.

Other modifications to the general experimental design could include:

- Holding the test *indoors* instead of outdoors to eliminate weather conditions appearing as a variable.

Table A1.10. Worked example

|  | 7 | 8 | 9 | 10 | 11 | 12 | 13 | 14 | 15 | 16 |
|---|---|---|---|---|---|---|---|---|---|---|
| 1 | / | / | / | / | / | / | 1 |  |  |  |
| 2 | / | / | 3 | 7 | / | / | / |  |  |  |
| 3 | / | / | / | 2 | / | / | / |  |  |  |
| 4 | / | / | / | / | / | / | / |  |  |  |
| 5 | / | / | / | / | / | / | / | 8 |  |  |
| 6 | / | / | 5 | / | / | / | / | / |  |  |
| 7 | / | / | / | 4 6 | / | / | 9 | / |  |  |
| 8 | / | / | / | / | / | / | / | / |  |  |
| 9 | / | / | / | / | / | / | / | / |  |  |
| 10 | / | / | / | / | / | / | / | / |  |  |

- Holding the test along a slightly wider shuttle to give each athlete more room in which to run.

- Having athletes of exactly the same age, sex and ability in each group thus giving the best possible comparison of results.

# Appendix 2a and b Suggested Project Titles

## Appendix 2A

### Psychology/Skill acquisition

- Use of feedback to improve performance of a complex skill
- Use of visual and verbal guidance to improve technique
- Use of distributed practice to teach the high serve to a novice player
- Use of massed practice to optimise performance
- Consideration of changing the organisation of training sessions to improve performance
- Increasing confidence to optimise performance
- Transfer of skills between diving and trampolining
- Teaching styles and effect on performance.

### Social/cultural

- Opportunity to participate and its effect on performance
- Positive discrimination and its effect on performance
- Provision and its effects on performance.

### Physiological/fitness and training

- Planning an exercise programme to improve performance
- Use of interval training to improve speed
- Use of circuit training to improve games play
- Use of mobility training to improve performance in gymnastics

- The effects of plyometric training on the performance of a line out in rugby
- Use of plyometric training to improve jumping ability of volleyball players
- Reduction in unforced errors in a game of badminton due to training
- Use of aerobic training to increase $VO_2$ max in cyclists
- Improvement in mid-field play due to increased aerobic fitness.

## Appendix 2B

### Example match analysis sheets for squash

#### 1. Analysis of basic shots

Every shot played by the performer is recorded during each rally: $+$equals a good shot, $-$equals a poor shot.

| Basic shot | Forehand | Backhand |
|---|---|---|
| Service | | |
| Straight drive | | |
| Cross-court drive | | |
| Boast | | |
| Volley | | |
| Drop shot | | |

This type of analysis gives information on the 'quality' of the shots played, and the frequency of their use, thus you can establish whether the performer is avoiding playing a particular shot, or overuses a shot.

## 2. Analysis of winning shots

In addition to recording the score the winning shot is also recorded.

Player 2 wins a lot of the initial rallies on the forehand side of the court. If this were to continue throughout the game Player 1 would be advised to keep the ball on his/her opponent's backhand side, thus playing on their opponent's weaker side. If you were coaching Player 2, although pleased at their victory, you might use this information to suggest a weakness on their backhand side and work on this in subsequent sessions.

This type of analysis can be extended by recording the shots of the player being analysed, whether they win the rally or not. If analysing Player 1, for example, the table would record his/her final losing shot, rather than Player 2's winning shot (see p 823).

| Player 1 | Player 2 | Explanation |
| --- | --- | --- |
| OR | (FH) | Player 1 starts the game and serves from the right-hand side of the court |
| | | Player 2 wins the rally |
| | OR (FHB) | Player 2 wins the rally with a forehand boast |
| | IL (FHX) | Player 2 wins the rally with a forehand cross-court drive |
| (BHD) | 2R | Player 1 wins the rally with a backhand drive |
| OR | (FHB) | Player 2 wins the rally with a forehand boast |
| | 2R (FHV) | Player 1 wins the rally with a forehand volley |
| | 3L (FHV) | Player 1 wins the rally with a forehand volley |
| | 4R | … |

## 3. Style of play

You could record whether the player plays in an attacking or defensive manner. Attacking play in squash can be measured by recording the number of attacking shots played from the front of the court, (winning kills, dropshots or angled shots), whereas defensive play can be measured by recording shots played at the back of the court (lengths, widths, boasts and lobs). This can easily be applied to other activities once you have identified the appropriate attacking and defensive plays.

| Player 1 | Player 2 | Explanation |
|----------|----------|-------------|
| OR (−FHD) | | Player 1 starts the game and serves from the right-hand side of the court. |
| | | Player 1 plays a loose forehand drop, allowing Player 2 to play a winning shot |
| (−FH) | OR | Player 2 serves, Player 1 plays a poor length forehand drive, allowing Player 2 to play a winning shot |
| (−BHX) | IL | Player 2 serves, Player 1 plays a poor width backhand cross-court drive, allowing Player 2 to play a winning shot |
| (+BHX) | 2R | Player 2 serves, Player 1 plays a good length backhand drive to win the rally |
| OR (−BHX) | | Player 1 serves, Player 1 plays a poor length backhand cross-court drive, allowing Player 2 to play a winning shot |
| (−FHD) | 2R | Player 2 serves, Player 1 plays a loose forehand drop, allowing player 2 to play a winning shot |
| (−BHX) | 3L | Player 2 serves, Player 2 plays a poor width backhand cross-court drive, allowing Player 2 to play a winning shot |
| | 4R | Player 2 serves, … |

*Note*: The explanation given above is there to explain the example, it would not be necessary to record this information during the game.

# Appendix 3 Fitness Test Ratings

The following tables give test ratings for fitness tests described in chapter 6.

Table A3.1. Grip strength norms

| Classification | Non-dominant (Kg) | Dominant (Kg) |
|---|---|---|
| **Women** | | |
| Excellent | >37 | >41 |
| Good | 34–36 | 38–40 |
| Average | 22–33 | 25–37 |
| Poor | 18–21 | 22–24 |
| Very poor | <18 | <22 |
| **Men** | | |
| Excellent | >68 | >70 |
| Good | 56–67 | 62–69 |
| Average | 43–55 | 48–61 |
| Poor | 39–42 | 41–47 |
| Very Poor | <39 | <41 |

For persons over 50 yrs of age, reduce scores by 10%.
*Source*: Data from Corbin, Lindsay and Tolson (1978) Concepts in Physical Education.

Table A3.2. 30 m sprint test

| Time (secs) | | Rating |
|---|---|---|
| Male | Female | |
| <4.0 | <4.5 | Excellent |
| 4.2–4.0 | 4.6–4.5 | Good |
| 4.4–4.3 | 4.8–4.7 | Average |
| 4.6–4.5 | 5.0–4.9 | Fair |
| >4.6 | >5.0 | Poor |

Table A3.3. Classification of aerobic fitness ($Vo_2$ max in ml $Kg^1$ $MCN^1$)

| Age (yrs) | Low | Fair | Average | Good | High |
|---|---|---|---|---|---|
| **Women** | | | | | |
| 20–29 | <24 | 24–30 | 31–37 | 38–48 | 49+ |
| 30–39 | <20 | 20–27 | 28–33 | 34–44 | 45+ |
| 40–49 | <17 | 17–23 | 24–30 | 31–41 | 42+ |
| 50–59 | <15 | 15–20 | 21–27 | 28–37 | 38+ |
| 60–69 | <13 | 13–17 | 18–23 | 24–34 | 35+ |
| **Men** | | | | | |
| 20–29 | <25 | 25–33 | 34–42 | 43–52 | 53+ |
| 30–39 | <23 | 23–30 | 31–38 | 39–48 | 49+ |
| 40–49 | <20 | 20–26 | 27–35 | 36–44 | 45+ |
| 50–59 | <18 | 18–24 | 25–33 | 34–42 | 43+ |
| 60–69 | <16 | 16–22 | 23–30 | 31–40 | 41+ |

*Source*: Data from American Heart Association (1972).

Table A3.4. Normative scores for the abdominal curl conditioning test

| Stage | Number of sit-ups | Standard | |
|---|---|---|---|
| | Cumulative | Male | Female |
| 1. | 20 | Poor | Poor |
| 2. | 42 | Poor | Fair |
| 3. | 64 | Fair | Fair |
| 4. | 89 | Fair | Good |
| 5. | 116 | Good | Good |
| 6. | 146 | Good | Very good |
| 7. | 180 | Excellent | Excellent |
| 8. | 217 | Excellent | Excellent |

Table A3.5. Sit and reach test ratings

| Male | Female | Rating |
|---|---|---|
| >35 | >39 | Excellent |
| 31–34 | 33–38 | Good |
| 27–30 | 29–32 | Fair |
| <27 | <29 | Poor |

Table A3.6. Illinois agility run test

| Time (secs) | | Rating |
|---|---|---|
| Male | Female | |
| <15.2 | <17.0 | Excellent |
| 16.1–15.2 | 17.9–17.0 | Good |
| 18.1–16.2 | 21.7–18.0 | Average |
| 18.3–18.2 | 23.0–21.8 | Fair |
| >18.3 | >23 | Poor |

Table A3.7. Stick drop test

| Reaction time | Rating |
|---|---|
| >42.5 | Excellent |
| 37.1–42.5 | Good |
| 29.6–37.0 | Average |
| 22.0–29.5 | Fair |
| <22 | Poor |

Table A3.8. Vertical jump test scores

| Distance (cm) | | Rating |
|---|---|---|
| Male | Female | |
| >60 | >47 | Excellent |
| 51–59 | 36–46 | Good |
| 41–50 | 29–35 | Average |
| 27–40 | 25–34 | Poor |
| <26 | <24 | Very poor |

# Exam Board Tables

This chapter contains all the modules you will follow as part of your course and where to find the relevant sections in the book.

Table (*Continued*)

(Continued)

Table (*Continued*)

| Key specification topic | Chapter | Page number |
|---|---|---|
| OBLA and sporting performance | 6 | 129 |
| Sources of energy in the body | 4 | 93 |
| Glycogen depletion and loading | 5, 4 | 112, 107 |
| Types of muscle fibre | 1 | 24 |
| Motor unit innervation | 1 | 22 |
| The control of movement – muscle spindle apparatus | 1 | 24 |

| **AQA** | Module No: 4 (PED4) Physiological, Biomechanical and Psychological Factors which Optimise Performance | | |
|---|---|---|---|
| | Achievement motivation | 25 | 676 |
| | Aggression (types, causes, effects and theories) | 24 | 651 |
| | Anxiety | 27 | 718 |
| | Arousal (causes, effects and theories) | 25 | 669 |
| | Assertive behaviour | 24 | 653 |
| | Attentional narrowing | 21, 25 | 589, 674 |
| | Attitudes | 24 | 640 |
| | Attribution retraining | 25 | 686 |
| | Attribution theory | 25 | 681 |
| | Catastrophe theory | 25 | 675 |
| | Chelladurai's multi-dimensional model of leadership | 26 | 711 |
| | Cognitive dissonance | 24 | 646 |
| | Cohesion | 26 | 703 |
| | Controlling aggression | 24 | 658 |
| | Drive theory | 25 | 671 |
| | Evaluation apprehension | 26 | 695 |
| | Fiedler's contingency model of leadership styles | 26 | 707 |
| | Frustration aggression hypothesis | 24 | 656 |
| | Goal setting | 27 | 735 |
| | Group dynamics | 26 | 696 |

*(Continued)*

Table (*Continued*)

| | Key specification topic | Chapter | Page number |
|---|---|---|---|
| | Group productivity | 26 | 700 |
| | Iceberg profile | 24 | 638 |
| | Interactionist theory | 24 | 634 |
| | Inverted 'u' hypothesis | 25 | 672 |
| | Leadership (types and styles) | 26 | 705 |
| | Learned helplessness | 25 | 684 |
| | Personality (structure and theories) | 24 | 623 |
| | Personality (assessment and testing) | 24 | 623 |
| | Persuasive communication | 24 | 644 |
| | Profile of mood states | 24 | 638 |
| | Ringleman effect | 26 | 702 |
| | Self efficacy | 25 | 686 |
| | Social facilitation | 26 | 693 |
| | Social learning | 24 | 633, 657 |
| | Social loafing | 26 | 702 |
| | Stress | 27 | 722 |
| | Stress management | 27 | 727 |
| | Trait theories | 24 | 627 |
| **AQA** | Module No: PED5 | | |
| | UK sport | 11 | 259 |
| | Sport coach UK | 11 | 261 |
| | Department for culture, media and sport (DCMS) | 11 | 253 |
| | Governing bodies of sport | 11 | 272 |
| | BOA – British Olympic Association | 11 | 262 |
| | National lottery | 11 | 280 |
| | International organisations | 11 | 264 |
| | Sports aid | 11 | 279 |

| Key specification topic | Chapter | Page number |
|---|---|---|
| Law and order | 13 | 354 |
| Excellence | 12 | 330 |
| Talent identification | 12 | 332 |
| Issue of participation – participation pyramid | 12 | 296 |
| World games | 14 | 358 |
| Modern Olympics | 14 | 361 |
| Olympic ideal | 14 | 363 |
| So – who controls sports? | 13 | 344 |
| Sportsmanship | 13 | 345 |
| Sport – the law | 13 | 354 |
| Drugs | 13 | 351 |
| Hooliganism | 13 | 348 |
| Talent identification | 12 | 332 |
| Commercialisation | 13 | 334 |
| Media | 13 | 341 |
| Sponsorship | 13 | 337 |
| USA | 15 | 404 |
| Participation pyramid | 12 | 327 |
| DCMS | 11 | 253 |
| Sport England | 11 | 259 |
| UK Sport | 11 | 259 |
| UK sports institute (UKSI) | 11 | 260 |
| Sport coach UK | 11 | 261 |
| British Olympic Association (BOA) | 11 | 262 |
| NGB | 11 | 272 |
| National lottery | 11 | 280 |
| Sports aid | 11 | 279 |
| France | 15 | 429 |

*(Continued)*

Table (*Continued*)

| | Key specification topic | Chapter | Page number |
|---|---|---|---|
| | Respiratory volumes and capacities (at rest) | 3 | 84 |
| | Gaseous exchange and tissue respiration | 3 | 83 |
| | Respiratory response to exercise | 3 | 85 |

| **OCR** | Module No: 1 (Unit 2562) The Application of Physiological and Physiological Knowledge to Improve Performance – Section B | | |
|---|---|---|---|
| | Ability | 18 | 536 |
| | Arousal theories (and links to motivation) | 25 | 669 |
| | Classification of movement skills | 18 | 540 |
| | Conditioning theories of learning | 20 | 562 |
| | Drive theory | 25 | 671 |
| | Feedback | 21 | 589 |
| | Guidance | 23 | 606 |
| | Information processing | 21 | 577 |
| | Memory systems | 21 | 581 |
| | Motivation | 25 | 663 |
| | Motor programmes | 22 | 595 |
| | Motor control | 22 | 595 |
| | Observational learning | 20 | 571 |
| | Practice (types) | 23 | 610 |
| | Reaction time | 21 | 583 |
| | Reinforcement | 20 | 565 |
| | Schema theory | 22 | 597 |
| | Selective attention | 21 | 580 |
| | Skill and performance | 18 | 531 |
| | Stages of learning | 19 | 552 |
| | Styles of teaching | 23 | 616 |
| | Task analysis | 18 | 545 |
| | Transfer of learning | 23 | 603 |

*(Continued)*

Table (*Continued*)

| OCR | Module No: 2 – 2563 Contemporary Studies in PE | | |
|---|---|---|---|
| | Key specification topic | Chapter | Page number |
| | Play | 10 | 212 |
| | Physical recreation | 10 | 216 |
| | Physical education | 10 | 222 |
| | National curriculum | 10 | 226 |
| | Outdoor education | 10 | 233 |
| | Outdoor recreation | 10 | 233 |
| | Sport | 10 | 237 |
| | Sport England | 11 | 259 |
| | UK Sport | 11 | 259 |
| | Participation pyramid | 12 | 296 |
| | Sportscoach UK | 11 | 261 |
| | UK sports institute (UKSI) | 11 | 260 |
| | Women's sports foundation | 12 | 313 |
| | Sporting policies | 12 | 249, 254 |

| OCR | Module No: 2 – 2563 | | |
|---|---|---|---|
| | Disability sport England | 12 | 321 |
| | Governing bodies | 11 | 272 |
| | National lottery | 11 | 280 |
| | Emergent society | 15 | 394 |
| | Organisation of sport in UK | 11 | 250 |
| | Media | 13 | 341 |
| | Sponsorship | 13 | 337 |
| | Ethics of sport/deviance | 13 | 346 |
| | Violence | 13 | 347 |
| | Doping | 13 | 351 |
| | Socio-economic | 12 | 329 |

| Key specification topic | Chapter | Page number |
|---|---|---|
| Race/ethnic minorities | 12 | 303 |
| Gender | 12 | 309 |
| Tribal societies | 15 | 388 |
| Disability | 12 | 317 |
| Young people | 12 | 327 |
| Elderly people 50+ | 12 | 326 |
| Sport in schools | 11 | 254 |
| Mass media | 13, 14 | 342, 371 |
| Ethics/deviancy | 13 | 334 |
| Doping | 13 | 351 |
| Olympic pressures | 14 | 361 |
| Violence | 13 | 355 |
| Sponsorship | 13 | 337 |
| American dream | 15 | 407 |
| Sport and politics | 11 | 246 |

| **OCR** | **Module No: 2565: Option A1 – Historical Studies in PE** | | |
|---|---|---|---|
| | Popular recreation | 16 | 490 |
| | Cultural factors – victorian Britain | 16 | 471 |
| | River towns – aquatic sports | 16 | 492 |
| | Sports festivals | 16 | 490 |
| | Games – real tennis | 16 | 495 |
| | Games – football | 16 | 498 |
| | Games – cricket | 16 | 499 |
| | Public schools | 17 | 506 |
| | Technical and social development – stage 1 | 17 | 507 |
| | Liberal headmasters – stage 2 | 17 | 510 |
| | Athleticism – stage 3 | 17 | 509, 512 |

*(Continued)*

Table (*Continued*)

**OCR**    Module No: 2566 – Exercise and Sport Physiology

*(Continued)*

Table (*Continued*)

| Key specification topic | Chapter | Page number |
|---|---|---|
| Sport England | 11 | 259 |
| UK sport | 11 | 259 |
| British sports trust | 11 | 268 |
| TOPS (NJSP) – sports policies | 11 | 287 |
| Active Sports – sports policies | 11 | 282 |
| Organisation of sport | 11 | 250 |
| Outdoor recreation/wilderness sports | 15 | 422 |
| INSEP | 15 | 436 |
| Commercialisation of sport | 13 | 334 |
| Deviance in the olympics | 13 | 345 |
| Medieval England | 16 | 468 |
| Victorian Britain | 16 | 471 |
| Public schools | 17 | 506 |
| Levels of sport performance | 12 | 296 |
| Race | 12 | 303 |
| Socio-economic | 12 | 329 |
| Gender | 12 | 309 |
| Age | 12 | 326 |
| Disability | 12 | 317 |
| Commercialisation of sport/media/sponsorship | 13 | 334, 341, 337 |
| European Charter (European sport) | 11 | 266 |
| Modern olympic games | 14 | 361 |
| Commercial pressure in olympics | 14 | 366 |
| Women and olympism | 14 | 372 |
| Drugs and olympics | 14 | 374 |
| Political pressures | 14 | 364 |
| City bids | 14 | 366 |
| Paralympic games | 14 | 380 |

*(Continued)*

Table (Continued)

| Edexcel | Module No: 2 Enhancing Performance (Section A – Acquiring Skill) | | |
|---------|------------------------------------------------------------------|---------|-------------|
| | Key specification topic | Chapter | Page number |
| | Ability | 18 | 536 |
| | Classification of movement skills | 18 | 540 |
| | Conditioning theories of learning | 20 | 562 |
| | Feedback | 21 | 589 |
| | Guidance | 23 | 606 |
| | Information processing | 21 | 577 |
| | Memory systems | 21 | 581 |
| | Motivation | 25 | 663 |
| | Motor memory programmes | 22 | 595 |
| | Phases of learning | 19 | 552 |
| | Practice (types and factors affecting) | 23 | 610 |
| | Reaction time | 21 | 583 |
| | Reinforcement | 20 | 565 |
| | Schema theory | 22 | 597 |
| | Selective attention | 21 | 580 |
| | Skill and performance | 18 | 531 |
| | Styles of teaching | 23 | 616 |
| | Transfer of learning | 23 | 603 |
| **Edexcel** | **Module No: Unit 2: Section B: Research Project** | | |
| | Project overview | 29 | 769, 774 |
| | Planning | 31 | 783 |
| | Literature review | 32 | 789 |
| | Discussion/conclusion | 35 | 808 |
| | Appraisal | 35 | 809 |
| **Edexcel** | **Module No: 3 Exercise and Training** | | |
| | Warm-up and cooling down | 7 | 149 |

| Key specification topic | Chapter | Page number |
|---|---|---|
| Immediate effects of exercise | 7 | 163 |
| Musculo-skeletal structures in action: types of muscle fibre | 1 | 24 |
| Long-term musculo-skeletal adaptations | 1, 7 | 19, 164 |
| Musculo-skeletal locations – muscle contraction | 1 | 30, 29 |
| Musculo-skeletal locations – movement analysis | 1 | 41 |
| The cardiac cycle | 2 | 52 |
| Cardiac dynamics and blood pressure | 2 | 58, 64 |
| Neural and hormonal influences on H.R. | 2 | 55 |
| Vaso motor control | 2 | 66 |
| Blood and oxygen transport | 2 | 60 |
| The mechanics of breathing | 3 | 77 |
| Definition of respiratory volumes | 3 | 84 |
| Gaseous exchange at the tissues | 3 | 83 |
| Effects of asthma on athletic performance | 3, 7 | 84, 174 |
| Factors affecting $VO_2$ max | 6 | 129 |
| Long-term adaptive responses | 7 | 164 |
| Effect of altitude training/blood doping/EPO | 7 | 167 |
| The components of fitness | 6 | 123 |
| Measurement of fitness – a battery of tests | 6 | 133 |
| Issues in testing | 6 | 138 |
| Principles of training | 7 | 145 |
| Methods of training | 7 | 151 |
| Individual differences | 7, 6 | 146, 139 |
| Specialised training – periodisation | 7 | 170 |

| **Edexcel** | Module No: Unit 4 – Global Trends in International Sport | | |
|---|---|---|---|
| | USA | 15 | 404 |
| | Australia | 15 | 441 |

(Continued)

Table (*Continued*)

| Edexcel | Module No: 6 – Section B Option A – Sports Mechanics | | |
|---|---|---|---|
| | Key specification topic | Chapter | Page number |
| | Fundamental qualities of motion | 9 | 186 |
| | Analysis of linear motion – speed, velocity, accel. | 9 | 186 |
| | Force and force/time graphs | 9 | 184, 191 |
| | Planes and axes of rotation | Intro | 3 |
| | Centre of gravity | 9 | 197 |
| | Momentum | 9 | 189 |
| | Fluid friction – air-resistance/drag | 9 | 193 |
| | The Bernoulli effect | 9 | 195 |
| | Angular motion and the moment of inertia | 9 | 203 |

| Edexcel | Module No: 6 Scientific Principles of Exercise and Performance Section B – Sports Physchology Option | | |
|---|---|---|---|
| | Achievement motivation | 25 | 676 |
| | Aggression | 24 | 651 |
| | Anxiety | 27 | 718 |
| | Arousal | 25 | 669 |
| | Assertion | 24 | 653 |
| | Attitudes | 24 | 640 |
| | Attribution theory | 25 | 681 |
| | Chelladurai's multi-dimensional model of leadership | 26 | 711 |
| | Cohesion | 26 | 703 |
| | Controlling aggression | 24 | 658 |
| | Cue-utilisation theory | 25 | 674 |
| | Drive theory | 25 | 671 |
| | Evaluation apprehension | 26 | 695 |
| | Fiedler's contingency model of leadership styles | 26 | 707 |
| | Frustration aggression hypothesis | 24 | 656 |
| | Group dynamics | 26 | 696 |

(Continued)

Table (*Continued*)

# Index

Page numbers in italics refer to figures and tables

one repetition maximum test 127, 158
onset of blood lactate accumulation (OBLA) 118–19,
129–31, 141, 165
open loop control 595–6
operant conditioning theory 564, 642
ossification 11
osteocytes 9
outcome goals 736
outdoor pursuits
in Australia 443–4
availability of 235
Countryside Commission 263–4
cross-curricular implications of 236
danger and 234–5
English Tourist Board 264
environmental effects 236–7
Forestry Commission 264
in France 437–8
growth of 234
national parks 237, 263
National Playing Fields Association 264
National Rivers Authorities 264
outdoor education 233
outdoor recreation 233–4
Outward Bound Movement 237, 443
risk and 234, 236
and school curriculum 235–6
Union Nationale des Centres de Plein Air (UCPA) 437–8
in USA 422–4
Outward Bound Movement 237, 443
over-conformity 347
overtraining 173–4
oxygen
arterial-venous oxygen difference (a-$\dot{V}O_2$ diff) 83
debt 115–16
deficit 115
maximal oxygen uptake ($\dot{V}O_2$ max) 128–31, 139, 142, 165
*see also* respiratory system
oxymyoglobin link 120

Paralympic Games 323, 380, 382
parasympathetic nervous system 55–6, 57
participation
constraint factors 301–2
development continuum 296–8
discrimination 298
evaluating public sector programmes 302–3
girls in physical education 315
national strategy for 331–2
older people 326–7
social exclusion 299–302
socio-economic group differences 329–30
stratification of society 298–301
trends in (DCMS) 297–8
young people 327–9
*see also* disability sport; gender; race; women

pedestrianism 483
perceptual narrowing 589, 674
perceptual trace 597–8
performance enhancing substances *see* ergogenic aids
performance goals 736–7
performance plateau effect 557–9
perimeter advertising 338
periosteum 9
Personal Exercise Programme
AQA AS level 759–65
in Individual Performance Portfolio 766
Personal Performance Portfolio 766–8
personality
and achievement motivation 676–7, 735
Cattell's trait theory 629–32
cognitive approach 625
criticism of research into 629, 632–3, 637
definitions of 626
extroversion 628–9
Eysenck's type theory 627–9
humanistic approach 625, 633
idiographic approach 624
interactionist approach 625, 633–5
introversion 629
mood states 638
nature vs. nurture 626
nomothetic approach 624
psychoanalytic approach 625, 626–7
psychological core 636
role related behaviour 636
situational approach 625, 633–5
social learning approach 625
and sporting behaviour 623–4, 637–8
testing 634, 637
trait approach 625, 627–33
Type A 636, 725
Type B 636, 725
type theory 625, 627–9
typical response 636
persuasive communication 644–6
phosphocreatine 112, 116
Physical Activity Readiness Questionnaire (PAR-Q) 174–6
physical education
Active Sports Programme 283–4
Activemark award scheme 282–3
administration of 230–1
aims of 222–4
assessment in 229–30
in Australia 443–6
balance of activities in 225
benefits of 227, 229
centralised system 225
as competitive sport 231–3
and concept of play 215
definition of 222
in France 429–32, 434